# More Than Just a T

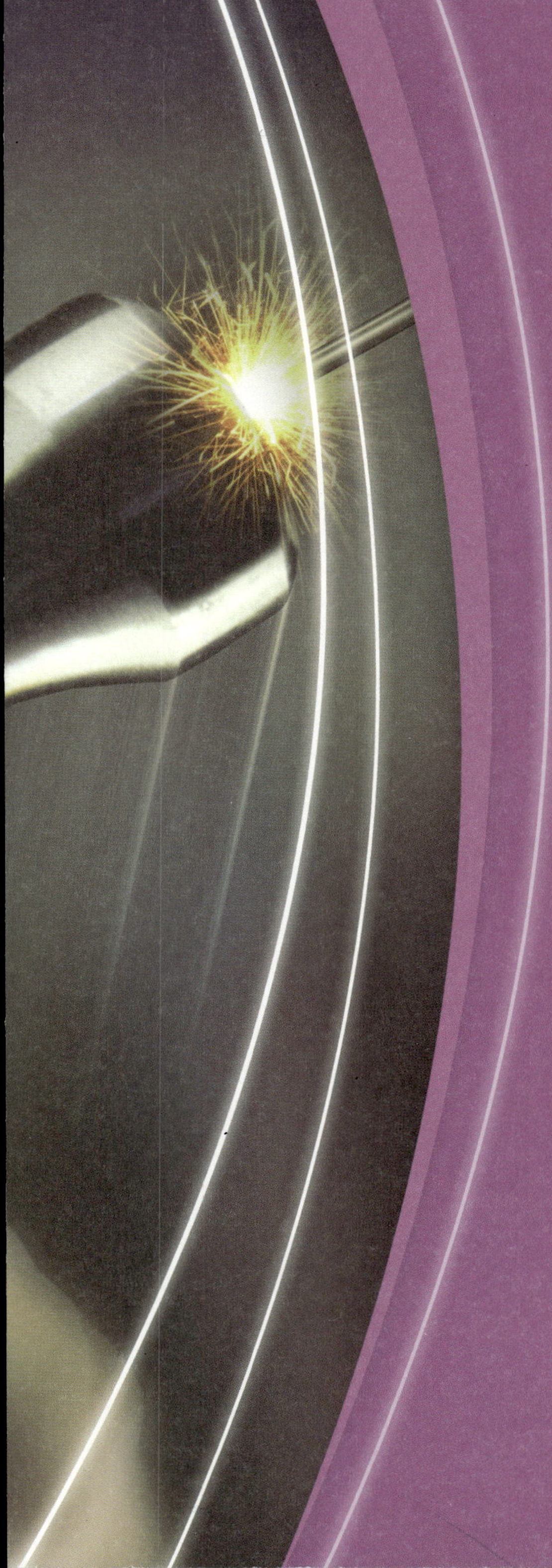

## Internet Resources

**Step 1** Connect to Math Online glencoe.com

**Step 2** Connect to online resources by using QuickPass codes. You can connect directly to the chapter you want.

IM7048c1

Enter this code with the appropriate chapter number.

### For Students

Connect to ***StudentWorks Plus Online*** which contains all of the following online assets. You don't need to take your textbook home every night.

- Personal Tutor
- Chapter Readiness Quizzes
- Multilingual eGlossary
- Concepts in Motion
- Chapter Test Practice
- Test Practice

### For Teachers

Connect to professional development content at glencoe.com and ***eBook Advance Tracker*** at AdvanceTracker.com

### For Parents

Connect to glencoe.com for access to ***StudentWorks Plus Online*** and all the resources for students and teachers that are listed above.

Glencoe McGraw-Hill

# IMPACT Mathematics

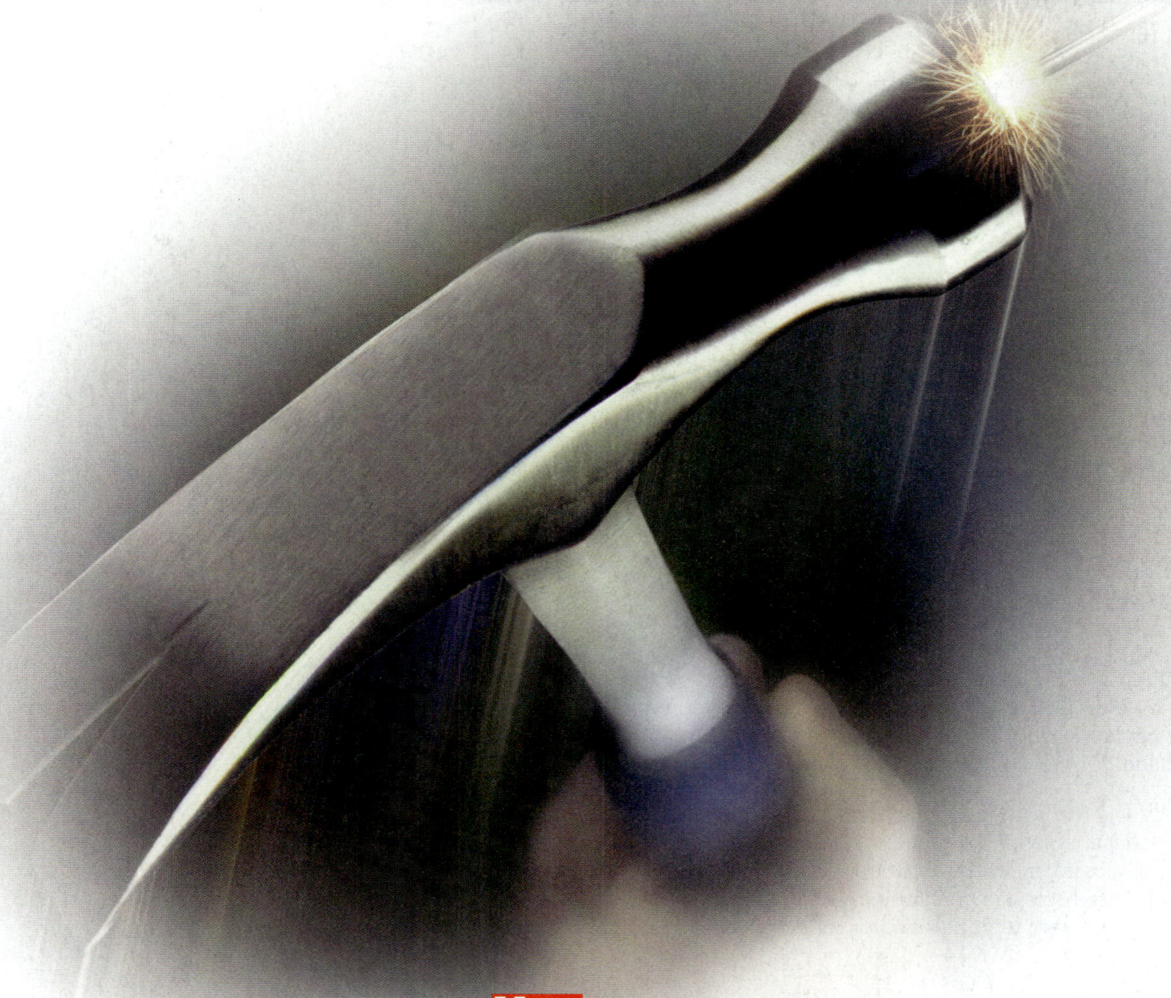

McGraw Hill Glencoe

New York, New York   Columbus, Ohio   Chicago, Illinois   Woodland Hills, California

COURSE 2

Teacher Guide

## About the Cover

Hammers can be used to drive nails. They can also be used to shape metal that is struck against an anvil.

In ancient times, the renowned Greek mathematician Pythagoras noticed the exceptional sounds of hammers striking anvils. He determined that the weights of different-sized hammers were proportional, with weights of 12, 9, 8, and 6 pounds. Upon further examination, he determined that the harmonious sounds were a result of the numerical relationships among the hammers' weights and discovered a connection among numbers, ratios, and music.

These materials include work supported in part by the National Science Foundation under Grant No. ESI-9726403 to MARS (Mathematics Assessment Resource Service). Any opinions, findings, and conclusions or recommendations expressed in this material are those of the authors and do not necessarily reflect the views of the funding agencies. For more information on MARS, visit http://www.nottingham.ac.uk/education/MARS.

The McGraw-Hill Companies

**Macmillan/McGraw-Hill**
**Glencoe**

The algebra content for *IMPACT Mathematics* was adapted from the series *Access to Algebra,* by Neville Grace, Jayne Johnston, Barry Kissane, Ian Lowe, and Sue Willis. Permission to adapt this material was obtained from the publisher, Curriculum Corporation of Level 5, 2 Lonsdale Street, Melbourne, Australia.



Send all inquiries to:
Glencoe/McGraw-Hill
8787 Orion Place
Columbus, OH 43240-4027

ISBN: 978-0-07-888707-9
MHID: 0-07-888707-0

Printed in the United States of America.

3 4 5 6 7 8 9 10 WDQ 17 16 15 14 13 12 11 10

COURSE 2

# Contents in Brief

**Focal Points and Connections**
See pages vi and vii for key.

# Principal Investigator

**Faye Nisonoff Ruopp**
Brandeis University
Waltham, Massachusetts

# Consultants and Developers

## Consultants

**Frances Basich Whitney**
Project Director, Mathematics K–12
Santa Cruz County Office of Education
Santa Cruz, California

**Robyn Silbey**
Mathematics Content Coach
Montgomery County Public Schools
Gaithersburg, Maryland

**Dr. Selina Vásquez Mireles**
Associate Professor of Mathematics
Texas State University—San Marcos
San Marcos, Texas

**Teri Willard**
Assistant Professor
Central Washington University
Ellensburg, Washington

## Special thanks to:

**Peter Braunfeld**
Professor of Mathematics Emeritus
University of Illinois

**Sherry L. Meier**
Assistant Professor of Mathematics
Illinois State University

**Judith Roitman**
Professor of Mathematics
University of Kansas

## Developers

**Senior Project Director**
Cynthia J. Orrell

**Senior Curriculum Developers**
Michele Manes, Sydney Foster, Daniel Lynn Watt, Ricky Carter, Joan Lukas, Kristen Herbert

**Curriculum Developers**
Haim Eshach, Phil Lewis, Melanie Palma, Peter Braunfeld, Amy Gluckman, Paula Pace

**Special Contributors**
Elizabeth D. Bjork, E. Paul Goldenberg

# Project Reviewers

Glencoe and Education Development Center would like to thank the curriculum specialists, teachers, and schools who participated in the review and testing of the first edition of *IMPACT Mathematics*. The results of their efforts were the foundation for this second edition. In addition, we appreciate all of the feedback from the curriculum specialists and teachers who participated in review and testing of this edition.

**Debra Allred**
Math Teacher
Wiley Middle School
Leander, Texas

**Tricia S. Biesmann**
Retired Teacher
Sisters Middle School
Sisters, Oregon

**Kathryn Blizzard Ballin**
Secondary Math Supervisor
Newark Public Schools
Newark, New Jersey

**Linda A. Bohny**
District Supervisor of Mathematics
Mahwah Township School District
Mahwah, New Jersey

**Julia A. Butler**
Teacher of Mathematics
Richfield Public School Academy
Flint, Michigan

**April Chauvette**
Secondary Mathematics Facilitator
Leander ISD
Leander, Texas

**Amy L. Chazaretta**
Math Teacher/Math Department Chair
Wayside Middle School, EM-S ISD
Fort Worth, Texas

**Franco A. DiPasqua**
Director of K–12 Mathematics
West Seneca Central
West Seneca, New York

**Mark J. Forzley**
Junior High School Math Teacher
Westmont Junior High School
Westmont, Illinois

**Virginia G. Harrell**
Education Consultant
Brandon, Florida

**Lynn Hurt**
Director
Wayne County Schools
Wayne, West Virginia

**Andrea D. Kent**
7th Grade Math & Pre-Algebra
Dodge Middle School, TUSD
Tucson, Arizona

**Russ Lush**
6th Grade Teacher & Math Dept. Chair
New Augusta–North
Indianapolis, Indiana

**Katherine V. Martinez De Marchena**
Director of Education 7–12
Bloomfield Public Schools
Bloomfield, New Jersey

**Marcy Myers**
Math Facilitator
Southwest Middle School
Charlotte, North Carolina

**Joyce B. McClain**
Middle School Mathematics Consultant
Hillsborough County Schools
Tampa, Florida

**Suzanne D. Obuchowski**
Math Teacher
Proctor School
Topsfield, Massachusetts

**Michele K. Older**
Mathematics Instructor
Edward A. Fulton Jr. High
O'Fallon, Illinois

**Jill Plattner**
Math Program Developer (Retired)
Bend La Pine School District
Bend, Oregon

**E. Elaine Rafferty**
Retired Math Coordinator
Summerville, South Carolina

**Karen L. Reed**
Math Teacher—Pre-AP
Chisholm Trail Intermediate
Fort Worth, Texas

**Robyn L. Rice**
Math Department Chair
Maricopa Wells Middle School
Maricopa, Arizona

**Brian Stiles**
Math Teacher
Glen Crest Middle School
Glen Ellyn, Illinois

**Nimisha Tejani, M.Ed.**
Mathematics Teacher
Kino Jr. High
Mesa, Arizona

**Stefanie Turnage**
Middle School Mathematics
Grand Blanc Academy
Grand Blanc, Michigan

**Kimberly Walters**
Math Teacher
Collinsville Middle School
Collinsville, Illinois

**Susan Wesson**
Math Teacher/Consultant
Pilot Butte Middle School
Bend, Oregon

**Tonya Lynnae Williams**
Teacher
Edison Preparatory School
Tulsa, Oklahoma

**Kim C. Wrightenberry**
Math Teacher
Cane Creek Middle School
Asheville, North Carolina

# Focal Points

**The Curriculum Focal Points identify key mathematical ideas for this grade. They are not discrete topics or a checklist to be mastered; rather, they provide a framework for the majority of instruction at a particular grade level and the foundation for future mathematics study. The complete document may be viewed at www.nctm.org/focalpoints.**

**KEY**

**G7-FP1** Grade 7 Focal Point 1
**G7-FP2** Grade 7 Focal Point 2
**G7-FP3** Grade 7 Focal Point 3
**G7-FP4C** Grade 7 Focal Point 4 Connection
**G7-FP5C** Grade 7 Focal Point 5 Connection
**G7-FP6C** Grade 7 Focal Point 6 Connection
**G7-FP7C** Grade 7 Focal Point 7 Connection

**G7-FP1** **Number and Operations and Algebra and Geometry: Developing an understanding of and applying proportionality, including similarity**
Students extend their work with ratios to develop an understanding of proportionality that they apply to solve single and multistep problems in numerous contexts. They use ratio and proportionality to solve a wide variety of percent problems, including problems involving discounts, interest, taxes, tips, and percent increase or decrease. They also solve problems about similar objects (including figures) by using scale factors that relate corresponding lengths of the objects or by using the fact that relationships of lengths within an object are preserved in similar objects. Students graph proportional relationships and identify the unit rate as the slope of the related line. They distinguish proportional relationships ($\frac{y}{x} = k$, or $y = kx$) from other relationships, including inverse proportionality ($xy = k$, or $y = \frac{k}{x}$).

**G7-FP2** **Measurement and Geometry and Algebra: Developing an understanding of and using formulas to determine surface areas and volumes of three-dimensional shapes**
By decomposing two- and three-dimensional shapes into smaller, component shapes, students find surface areas and develop and justify formulas for the surface areas and volumes of prisms and cylinders. As students decompose prisms and cylinders by slicing them, they develop and understand formulas for their volumes (*Volume* = *Area of base* × *Height*). They apply these formulas in problem solving to determine volumes of prisms and cylinders. Students see that the formula for the area of a circle is plausible by decomposing a circle into a number of wedges and rearranging them into a shape that approximates a parallelogram. They select appropriate two- and three dimensional shapes to model real-world situations and solve a variety of problems (including multistep problems) involving surface areas, areas and circumferences of circles, and volumes of prisms and cylinders.

**G7-FP3** **Number and Operations and Algebra: Developing an understanding of operations on all rational numbers and solving linear equations**
Students extend understandings of addition, subtraction, multiplication, and division, together with their properties, to all rational numbers, including negative integers. By applying properties of arithmetic and considering negative numbers in everyday contexts (e.g., situations of owing money or measuring elevations above and below sea level), students explain why the rules for adding, subtracting, multiplying, and dividing with negative numbers make sense. They use the arithmetic of rational numbers as they formulate and solve linear equations in one variable and use these equations to solve problems. Students make strategic choices of procedures to solve linear equations in one variable and implement them efficiently, understanding that when they use the properties of equality to express an equation in a new way, solutions that they obtain for the new equation also solve the original equation.

# Connections to the Focal Points

**G7-FP4C** **Measurement and Geometry:** Students connect their work on proportionality with their work on area and volume by investigating similar objects. They understand that if a scale factor describes how corresponding lengths in two similar objects are related, then the square of the scale factor describes how corresponding areas are related, and the cube of the scale factor describes how corresponding volumes are related. Students apply their work on proportionality to measurement in different contexts, including converting among different units of measurement to solve problems involving rates such as motion at a constant speed. They also apply proportionality when they work with the circumference, radius, and diameter of a circle; when they find the area of a sector of a circle; and when they make scale drawings.

**G7-FP5C** **Number and Operations:** In grade 4, students used equivalent fractions to determine the decimal representations of fractions that they could represent with terminating decimals. Students now use division to express any fraction as a decimal, including fractions that they must represent with infinite decimals. They find this method useful when working with proportions, especially those involving percents. Students connect their work with dividing fractions to solving equations of the form $ax = b$, where $a$ and $b$ are fractions. Students continue to develop their understanding of multiplication and division and the structure of numbers by determining if a counting number greater than 1 is a prime, and if it is not, by factoring it into a product of primes.

**G7-FP6C** **Data Analysis:** Students use proportions to make estimates relating to a population on the basis of a sample. They apply percentages to make and interpret histograms and circle graphs.

**G7-FP7C** **Probability:** Students understand that when all outcomes of an experiment are equally likely, the theoretical probability of an event is the fraction of outcomes in which the event occurs. Students use theoretical probability and proportions to make approximate predictions.

# Program Philosophy

In developing *IMPACT Mathematics* we have relied on our collective experiences as teachers, parents, and former students. Our main goal is to offer a curriculum that respects the background and knowledge of middle school teachers, recognizes the competence and energy of middle school students, and addresses the need for intellectually challenging and inclusive mathematics materials. With *IMPACT Mathematics,* we have combined the best of what is known as "reform" curricula with the best of "traditional" curricula, incorporating more active involvement on the part of students in making sense of important mathematical ideas.

With middle grades teachers and students in mind, we have created a comprehensive curriculum for Grades 6 through 8 that completes a full year of algebra by the end of Grade 8. While the number and operations, geometry, and data and probability strands were created especially for this program, the algebra strand is based on the highly successful Australian program, *Access to Algebra,* developed by Curriculum Corporation.

The rewarding and interesting introduction to algebra offered by this program can help develop and maintain students' ongoing interest in all areas of mathematics. The materials created for *IMPACT Mathematics* follow the *Access to Algebra* material in style: use of narrative and realistic contexts, personalization in the form of cartoons in which middle grades students explain how they approach problems, and opportunities for students to choose or create their own problems.

## Conceptual Understanding and Basic Skills

Discussions regarding mathematics learning in both professional circles and the popular media might lead you to believe that teaching for conceptual understanding and teaching basic skills are mutually exclusive. But, in fact, the opposite is true. Conceptual understanding and basic skills are not opposing interests; they go hand in hand and support each other.

*IMPACT Mathematics* makes the big ideas as well as the important skills of mathematics accessible to middle school students. It presents mathematical ideas intact, not broken down into bite-sized bits that lack the big idea. *IMPACT Mathematics* helps students both build new mathematical ideas and see how these new ideas relate to ideas they have already developed. In this way, *IMPACT Mathematics* takes a conceptual approach.

At the same time, *IMPACT Mathematics* recognizes that for students to be able to use the new ideas and procedures effectively, they need practice. Practice need not be the enemy of learning; the enemy of learning is mindless drill. Instead, practice can encourage students to stay interested in the mathematical concepts. *IMPACT Mathematics* provides plenty of opportunity for practice, but with variety and contrast to keep students' attention focused.

## Algebraic Focus in a Comprehensive Program

*IMPACT Mathematics* is a comprehensive program including number and operations, proportional reasoning, geometry, probability, and data, with a focus on the development of algebraic thinking. The program takes a developmental approach to algebra. Student understanding of the algebra strand–interwoven with and related to the other mathematical strands–evolves over a three-year period, allowing the ideas and skills to develop and become familiar over time.

Most students develop strong algebraic ideas in the early years of elementary school, but they do not acquire ways of expressing and manipulating them in algebraic terms until later, when algebra is formally taught. For example, young children know how to share \$36 among three people by first distributing the ten dollar bills and then distributing the ones. Later, if children learn a standard method for dividing $3\overline{)36}$ they may see again that the process is like dividing $3\overline{)30}$, then dividing $3\overline{)6}$, and finally adding the results. If this process is written out as $\frac{36}{3} = \frac{30}{3} + \frac{6}{3}$, that concise statement contains an important idea about adding fractions and an even more general algebraic idea. Students who understand *why* $\frac{36}{3} = \frac{30}{3} + \frac{6}{3}$ know that the sum of $\frac{30}{3}$ and $\frac{6}{3}$ must be $\frac{36}{3}$, and not $\frac{36}{6}$. The idea, expressed more generally, is $\frac{a}{3} + \frac{b}{3} = \frac{a+b}{3}$, and even more generally, is $\frac{a}{c} + \frac{b}{c} = \frac{a+b}{c}$, and so leads to the distributive law of division over addition.

Our approach in *IMPACT Mathematics* is to start with algebra as a notation for "generic" arithmetic, a description of processes that students understand. Later, algebra also becomes a handy language for "unlocking secrets" (equation solving) and building mathematical models. By the end of Course 3, students will have learned both to express functions using variables and to graph these functions. They will have also learned how to use variables to set up and solve equations, as well as how to factor some familiar polynomials, and to understand the origin and use of the quadratic formula.

## Use of Manipulatives and Calculators

Manipulatives and calculators can be powerful tools for teaching and learning mathematics. There is, however, much discussion and controversy about the appropriateness of their use. As the authors of *IMPACT Mathematics*, we believe that when manipulatives and calculators are used, they must be used to support the content learning. More specifically, we consider the important mathematical ideas first and then determine whether manipulatives or calculators can be used in learning those ideas more completely.

We believe it is critical that students develop good number sense and calculation skills before they work extensively with calculators. For example, we incorporate graphing calculators in Course 3 to explore families of functions, but only *after* students have a firm idea of how to graph "parent" functions by hand. Graphing technology can then be used to allow students to graph more complex functions, analyze their behavior, and compare representations. Similar to our philosophy of integrating skills with understanding, we believe that students need experiences with pencil and paper along with graphing technology.

## Organization by Content

*IMPACT Mathematics* often uses applications to help develop a particular mathematical concept or place it in context. However, *IMPACT Mathematics* remains organized by mathematical content, not by contexts. This organization helps both teacher and student keep the mathematical ideas at the fore, easily recognizable and never buried or lost in the settings. While the mathematical focus shifts with each chapter, the *IMPACT Mathematics* approach offers opportunities to connect topics to one another so that earlier learning is not abandoned as new ideas are introduced.

## Developing Concepts in Varied Contexts

The contexts used for developing concepts and practicing skills include real-world applications, as well as mathematical settings such as number puzzles, and-the world of the imagination such as a factory that uniformly resizes objects using stretching machines. Sometimes, *IMPACT Mathematics* provides exercises that are *not* set in contexts or integrated into word problems precisely so that students can focus on the mathematical ideas, undistracted by surrounding material.

## A Final Note

The unique power of mathematics stems from the world of the imagination in which one envisions triangles with perfectly straight sides, or two-dimensional objects embedded in perfectly smooth planes. In the real world, all objects are three dimensional (even a line drawn on paper has thickness, or it wouldn't be visible!), all lines are irregular, and all surfaces are pitted. Likewise, all measurements are only approximations, and no physical object can have an irrational length. Our minds reason well precisely because we can ignore irregularities and focus instead on the essential features. We can reason about quantities that no physical ruler can measure but that we can "measure" with our mental rulers. In sum, we reason well because we can abstract reality.

We, the authors of *IMPACT Mathematics*, recognize that all people, from early childhood on, do reason abstractly, and that what grows over time is both their ability to recognize the abstractions, and the formality with which they are able to express abstractions. We also recognize that mathematics, while not simply common sense, is rooted in common sense. Mathematics is a human product that has developed as an extension and a codification of ways of thinking that are natural to us all. Students must not think of mathematics as a departure from natural, logical thinking. To that aim *IMPACT Mathematics* is written to help students use and sharpen their own logical thinking, learn to be comfortable with the abstractions that give mathematics its power, develop their ideas and mathematical imagination, and acquire the skills that support all that good thinking and the ability to express it clearly to others.

We hope you will enjoy teaching and learning with these materials.

# Expectations

## Entrance Expectations for Course 2

*What students should know as they finish Course 1;*
*What students should know as they begin Course 2*

### Algebra

- Understand the concept of a variable
- Solve simple one- and two-step equations with the variable on one side only

### Geometry

- Understand area and perimeter and have committed important formulas to memory
- Calculate volume of a rectangular prism and understand capacity
- Give reasonable estimates for angle measures and measure angles with a protractor
- Plot points in the first quadrant

### Number and Operation

- Are proficient with fraction and decimal operations
- Move efficiently among fraction, decimal, and percent representations

### Data and Probability

- Conduct simple experiments to determine experimental probabilities
- Calculate theoretical probabilities in simple situations with a small number of equally likely outcomes
- Calculate measures of central tendency
- Interpret bar graphs, line graphs, Venn Diagrams, line plots, and stem-and-leaf plots

# Exit Expectations for Course 2

## Entrance Expectations for Course 3

*What students should know as they finish Course 2;*
*What students should know as they begin Course 3*

### Algebra

- Write algebraic expressions to represent situations and patterns
- Apply the distributive property to expand expressions and to factor out a common monomial factor (includes combining like terms)
- Solve single-variable linear equations in which the variable appears on both sides (by doing the same thing to both sides)
- Recognize a linear relationship from a written description, a table, a graph, or an equation
- Have a thorough understanding of slope (rise/run, rate of change, constant change, and so on)

### Geometry

- Understand volume and surface and have important formulas committed to memory
- Understand and apply ideas about similarity and scale factor including map scales
- Understand and apply the relationship between scale factor, area, and volume
- Plot points in all four quadrants
- Apply the distance formulas

### Number and Operation

- Are proficient with operations with signed numbers
- Are proficient in working with positive and negative integer exponents
- Are proficient with percent operations, including calculating percent increase and percent decrease
- Understand ratios, rates, and proportions and solve problems that require comparing ratio or solving proportions and find unit rates
- Understand the distinction between rational and irrational numbers and use the Pythagorean Theorem

### Data and Probability

- Calculate probabilities in situations involving multipart outcomes (tossing four coins, spinning two spinners, and so on)
- Conduct simple simulations to find probabilities
- Interpret circle graphs, stem-and-leaf plots, and identify misleading graphs
- Understand the purpose of sampling and the importance of selecting a random sample

# The Instructional Cycle

*IMPACT Mathematics* is designed to actively engage students in their own learning. To facilitate the learning and teaching process, *IMPACT Mathematics* is designed around a three-step instructional cycle.

## Introduce

Each multiday lesson begins with a class discussion, activity, or problem designed to introduce the mathematics and help set a context for learning. To help guide the introduction, **Explore** activities and **Think & Discuss** questions are provided in the student materials.

## Develop

Each lesson in *IMPACT Mathematics* is composed of in-class **Investigations** that provide a mix of worked-out examples, direct modeling through cartoons, and interactive problem sets. During Investigations, the mathematics, not an artificial format, determines the approach and the day's activity. Most Investigations are designed to last about 45 minutes or one class period.

The **Share & Summarize** questions signal the end of each Investigation. These questions offer students an opportunity to share what they did and what was learned. For teachers they offer an important assessment opportunity.

## Assign & Assess

Independent assignments and opportunities to assess what students have learned are a regular part of the curriculum. The **On Your Own Exercises** at the end of each lesson are an integral part of program instruction and are intended for individual work done primarily outside of class. You will find three types of problems in each set of On Your Own Exercises.

- *Practice & Apply* problems provide opportunities for students to reinforce and directly apply the skills and concepts they have learned in each of the Investigations.
- *Connect & Extend* problems relate student learning in the lesson to other mathematical topics and strands, and sometimes require students to stretch their thinking.
- *Mixed Review* problems are an important part of the instructional and assignment structure. Frequent review of previously learned skills helps students maintain mastery and replaces the need to reteach topics.

### Steps in the Instructional Cycle

**INTRODUCE**

The multiday lesson begins with a full-class discussion, activity, or problem. The teacher poses questions, orchestrates an activity, or monitors strategies students use to solve problems. **Explore** activities and **Think & Discuss** questions can be used to guide discussion.

**DEVELOP**

In-class **Investigations** provide a mix of worked out examples, direct modeling through cartoons, and interactive problem sets. Students may work independently or in small, collaborative groups. Most investigations can be completed in one class period. The mathematical

# Assessment

The assessment tools in *IMPACT Mathematics* are broader than those in traditional mathematics programs. They encompass the processes of problem solving, reasoning, communication, connections, concepts, applications, representational strategies, and procedures.

## In the Student Edition

- **Share & Summarize** questions provide a forum for students to summarize and share their learning with the class.
- **On Your Own Exercises,** an integral part of daily instruction, are independent assignments intended for individual work outside of class.
- **Review & Self-Assessment** provides students with an opportunity to reflect on the important topics within the chapter and to prepare for formal assessment.

## In the Teacher's Guide

- **Problem Set Wrap-Ups** ensure students are making appropriate progress through an Investigation.
- **Troubleshooting** notes provide remedial work students might need in order to move on to the next Investigation successfully.
- **Additional Examples** can be used as on-the-run assessment tools.
- **Quick Checks** provide checklists of what students should be able to do at the end of each lesson.
- **Quick Quizzes** provide brief end-of-lesson assessment opportunities.

## In the Chapter Resource Masters

- A **Pretest** determines whether students have the prerequisite skills for the course.
- **Chapter Tests** provide a comprehensive evaluation of chapter content.
- **Performance Assessments** provide open-ended opportunities to measure student achievement. They can be used to supplement or replace items on chapter and semester tests, as take-home assignments, as group assessments, or as challenge or extra-credit problems.
- **Semester Tests** provide cumulative midyear and end-of-year evaluations.

content of the Investigations determines the approach and the day's activity. Homework or assignment guides are available for each Investigation, and each Investigation wraps up with **Share & Summarize** questions.

## ASSIGN & ASSESS

Independent assignments and assessment opportunities provide rich opportunities for students to demonstrate their learning. Each lesson concludes with **On Your Own Exercises**. The types of problems included in each set of On Your Own Exercises are

- **Practice & Apply,** which are similar to the Investigations.
- **Connect & Extend,** which relate the lesson topics to other mathematical topics and strands.
- **Mixed Review,** which provides review of previously learned skills to maintain mastery.

# About MARS

## Mathematics Assessment Resource Service

**MARS, the Mathematics Assessment Resource Service,** is a U.S.-based international team that created the performance-based assessments in the ***IMPACT Mathematics*** program. MARS is under the direction of a Mathematics Board that includes teachers and recognized United States and international experts in the mathematics education and assessment fields.

## Background

An NSF grant (National Science Foundation grant #ESI-9726403) has supported the many years of research, development, and evaluation that form the basis of the high-quality, performance-based assessments that comprise the assessment section of ***IMPACT Mathematics***.

## Development Process

Each assessment task is carefully constructed to assess the broad domain of mathematical performance that national and local standards specify. Tasks go through a development and review process to ensure validity and usability for student evaluation and continued improvement in instruction.

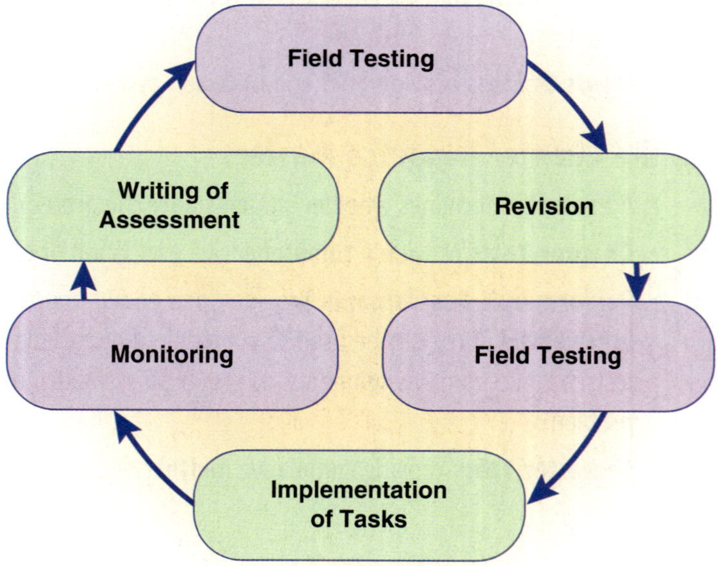


During the writing and revision process, the scoring rubric is refined and student work is collected. Rubrics, along with scored student work, accompany the MARS assessments, allowing teachers to evaluate student knowledge and progress and better inform instruction.

## Evaluative Evidence

Over the years, MARS performance-based assessments have been used both throughout the United States and internationally. Evidence shows that the MARS assessments test a broader range of skills and knowledge than many state tests and are comparably challenging overall.

**Figure 1.** In one particular study, teachers used MARS assessments as part of a formative-assessment piece prior to taking the SAT-9 standardized test. The data show that students in classrooms receiving the MARS treatment outperformed control classrooms without MARS.

**Figure 1**
**Average Gain in Math Percentile Rank Between 1999 SAT-9 and 2000 SAT-9**

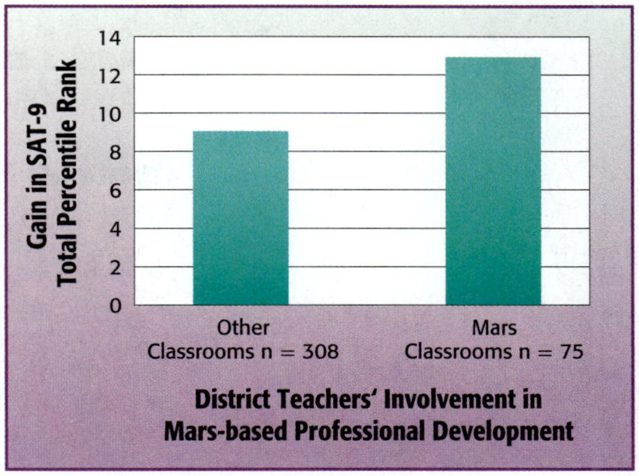


**Source:** Noyce Foundation Annual Report 2000

**Figure 2**
**Student Achievement By Performance Levels on Mars Exam Comparison Between First Year and 2005**

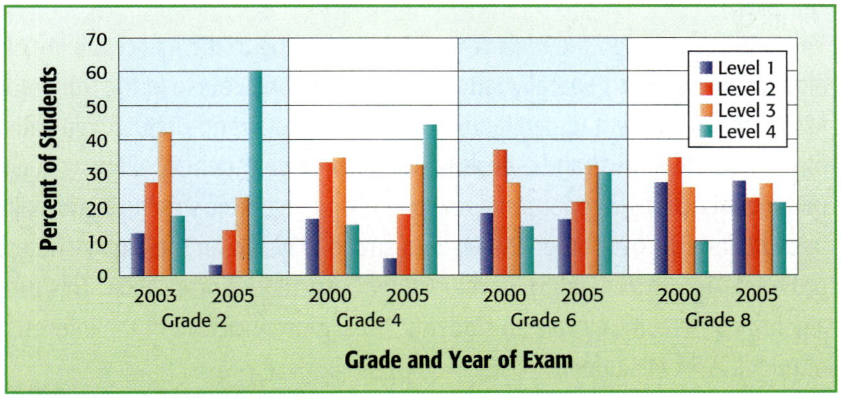


**Source:** Noyce Foundation Annual Report 2005

**Figure 2.** Over time, the evidence for MARS follows similar trends. The number of students performing at the highest levels (Level 4) of the MARS assessments climbs each year and at every grade level, while the number performing at the lower levels (Level 1) declines.

# Research Support

## The Research Used to Develop IMPACT Mathematics

To attain excellence in mathematics learning, there is a need for high-quality curricula that allow students to think deeply about mathematics, require them to explain their ideas, and connect their understanding to other contexts both within and outside of mathematics. *IMPACT Mathematics* relied heavily on key research about mathematics education during its development. Some of these are discussed below.

***Principles and Standards for School Mathematics*** (National Council of Teachers of Mathematics, 1989)

***Curriculum Focal Points for Prekindergarten through Grade 8 Mathematics*** (NCTM, 2006)

The National Council of Teachers of Mathematics produced a set of national math standards in 1989 and reshaped those standards in 2006 with the intent of improving mathematics education on a national level. These publications emphasize the belief that all students can and should learn and understand important mathematical ideas. *IMPACT Mathematics* is both a comprehensive program, including the strands of number and operations, proportional reasoning, geometry, probability, and data, as well as a program focused on the development of algebraic thinking.

***Algebra for Everyone*** (NCTM, 1990)

*Algebra for Everyone* put forth the view of algebra as the gateway course, a course that must be part of the basic knowledge of all. Therefore, algebra must be taught on a broadened scale, where students come into it with the appropriate mathematical background and disposition.

***Algebra in the K–12 curriculum: Dilemmas and possibilities*** (NCTM Algebra Working Group, 1995)

This report examined the research evidence pointing to the inaccessibility of the traditional algebra curriculum, generally taught as a stand-alone course in the 9th grade. In *IMPACT Mathematics*, student understanding of the algebra strand—interwoven with and related to the other mathematical strands—evolves over a three-year period, allowing such important ideas as patterns, functions, proportional reasoning, and algebraic structure and skills to develop and become familiar over time. The algebra strand is based on the highly successful Australian program, *Access to Algebra*, developed by Curriculum Corporation. This program provided an algebra curriculum relevant to students' lives, more inclusive of the interests and experiences of middle school students.

**The National Forum to Accelerate Middle-Grades Reform**

The Forum identified three components of academically excellent curricula: academic rigor, equity, and developmental appropriateness. The main goal of *IMPACT Mathematics* is to offer a curriculum that respects the background and knowledge of middle school teachers, recognizes the competence and energy of middle school students, and addresses the need for intellectually challenging and inclusive materials.

*IMPACT Mathematics* has combined the best of research on "reform" curricula with the best of "traditional" curricula, incorporating more active involvement on the part of students in making sense of important mathematical ideas.

## Evidence of Effectiveness:
### New York City Mathematics Results

Since the adoption of *IMPACT Mathematics* in grades 6–8, New York City students have seen their test scores improve dramatically. When compared against other students in the state, the positive trend is immediately apparent.

The graph in Figure 1 shows the performance on New York mathematics tests of students who used *IMPACT Mathematics*.

- In **Grade 6** in 2007, **10.5% more** students performed at Levels 3 and 4 on the state test than in the previous year.
- In **Grade 7**, **11.6% more** students performed at the highest levels.
- In **Grade 8**, **6.7% more** students performed at higher levels than their 2006 peers.

**Figure 1**
**Students' Performance in Levels 3 and 4**
**Percent Increase in Grades 6–8**

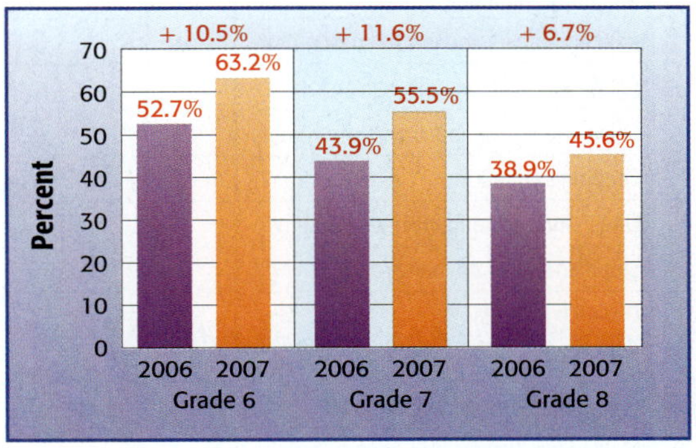


**Figure 2**
**New York State Mathematics Achievement Comparisons (Grades 3–8 at Levels 3 and 4)**

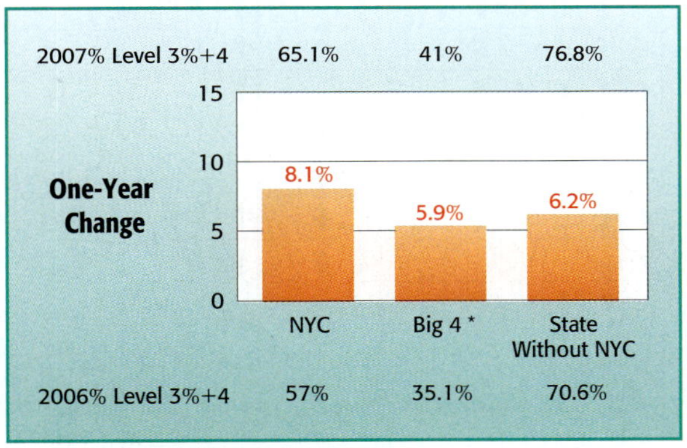


*Buffalo, Rochester, Syracuse, and Yonkers

The graph in Figure 2 shows the comparison of students in New York City (where *IMPACT Mathematics* is the core mathematics curriculum) to their peers in other large cities within the state of New York and to New York State on the whole.

In 2007, the number of students using *IMPACT Mathematics* in New York City who performed at the top levels on state tests increased by 8.1% from 2006. The rest of the state (where other math programs are used) did not see such gains.

# Scope & Sequence

## Algebra

| | TOPICS | Course 1 | | | | | | | | | | Course 2 | | | | | | | | | | Course 3 | | | | | | | | | | | |
|---|---|---|---|---|---|---|---|---|---|---|---|---|---|---|---|---|---|---|---|---|---|---|---|---|---|---|---|---|---|---|---|---|---|
| | | 1 | 2 | 3 | 4 | 5 | 6 | 7 | 8 | 9 | 10 | 1 | 2 | 3 | 4 | 5 | 6 | 7 | 8 | 9 | 10 | 1 | 2 | 3 | 4 | 5 | 6 | 7 | 8 | 9 | 10 | 11 | 12 |
| | **Algebraic Representations** | Develop | | | | | | | | | | Develop | | | | | | | | | | Develop | | | | | | | | | | | |
| Coordinate Graphs | Plotting and reading points | | | | | | | | F | | F | | | | | | C | | C | | | C | C | | | | C | C | C | | C | | |
| Coordinate Graphs | Make predictions | | | | | | | | F | | F | | C | | | | | | F | | | F | F | | | | | C | C | | C | | |
| Coordinate Graphs | Modeling situations | | | | | F | | | F | | C | | C | | | | | | F | | C | F | F | | | | | F | F | | F | | |
| Coordinate Graphs | Relate to tables and written descriptions | | | | | F | | C | F | C | | | | | | | | | F | | | F | F | | | | | F | F | | F | | |
| Coordinate Graphs | Relate to equations and expressions | | | | | | | C | C | | C | | | | | | | | F | | | F | F | | | | | F | F | | F | | |
| Coordinate Graphs | Solve equations, approximate solutions | | | | | | | | C | F | | | | | | | | | F | | | F | F | | | | | F | F | | F | | |
| Coordinate Graphs | Graphing equations | | | | | | | | C | C | | | | | | | | | F | | | F | F | | | | | F | F | | F | | |
| Coordinate Graphs | Direct, indirect, and inverse variation | | | | | | | | | | | | | | | | | | F | | C | F | C | | | | | C | | | | | |
| Coordinate Graphs | Slope and rates of change | | | | | | | | C | | | | | | | | | | F | | C | F | F | | | | | C | | | C | | |
| Coordinate Graphs | Distance formula | | | | | | | | | | | | | | | | | F | | | | | | | | | | | | | | | |
| Coordinate Graphs | Coordinate models of transformations | | | | | | | | | | | | | | | | | | | | | C | | | | | F | | | | F | | |
| Tables and Graphs | Analyze change vs. time data | | | | | | | | F | | F | | | | | | C | | F | | | F | C | | | | | | C | | F | | |
| Tables and Graphs | Making predictions and generalizations | F | C | | | C | | | F | | F | C | C | C | C | C | F | | F | F | | F | F | | | | | C | F | | C | | |
| Tables and Graphs | Modeling data patterns | | C | C | | F | | | F | C | F | F | C | | C | C | F | | F | C | | C | F | | | | | C | C | | | | |
| Tables and Graphs | Relate to written descriptions | | | F | | F | | | F | | F | F | | | | | | | F | F | | C | F | | | | | F | C | | | | |
| Tables and Graphs | Relate to equations and expressions | | | | | | | | C | C | C | F | | C | | C | | | F | F | | F | | | | C | | F | F | C | F | | |
| Tables and Graphs | Solve equations, approximate solutions | | | C | | | | | | F | | F | | | | | | | F | F | | F | F | | | | | F | C | C | F | | |
| Tables and Graphs | "What's My Rule?" | | C | F | | | | | | C | | F | | | | | | | F | F | | | | | | | | | | | | | |
| | **Algebraic Reasoning** | Develop | | | | | | | | | | Develop | | | | | | | | | | Develop | | | | | | | | | | | |
| Patterns and Numeric Forms | Find and describe patterns | | F | F | | | C | F | C | | C | C | F | C | C | F | F | | F | | C | F | F | | C | | | | F | | F | | C |
| Patterns and Numeric Forms | Extend and generalize patterns | | F | F | | | C | F | C | | | C | F | C | C | F | F | | F | | C | F | F | | C | | | | F | | F | | C |
| Patterns and Numeric Forms | Create and verify patterns | F | F | F | | | C | F | | | | C | F | C | C | F | F | | F | | | F | | | C | | | | F | | | | |
| Patterns and Numeric Forms | Express patterns as algebraic rules | | C | C | | | | | | | C | F | F | | | F | | | F | F | | F | | | | | | | F | | C | | |
| Patterns and Numeric Forms | "What's My Rule?" | | | F | | | | | | C | | F | | | | | | | F | F | | | | | | | | | | | | | |
| Patterns and Numeric Forms | Equivalent expressions | | | F | | C | | | | C | | F | C | C | C | C | | | C | F | | F | F | | F | F | | C | | C | C | | C |
| Patterns and Numeric Forms | Factoring, expanding, simplifying | | | | | | | | | | | F | | | | | | | C | F | | F | F | | C | F | | C | C | F | | | |
| Patterns and Numeric Forms | Signed numbers and operations | | | | | | | | | | | | | F | | | | | | | | | | | F | | | | | | | | |
| Patterns and Numeric Forms | Absolute value and opposites | | | | | | | | F | | | | | F | | | | | | | | | | | | | | C | | | | | |
| Patterns and Numeric Forms | Exponents, roots, and radicals | | | F | | | | C | | | | | C | | F | C | | | | | | | | | F | | | | | C | | | |
| Patterns and Numeric Forms | Scientific notation | | | C | | | | | | | | | | | F | | | | | | | | | | F | | | | | | | | |
| Patterns and Numeric Forms | Evaluating expressions | | | C | | | | | | C | | F | F | C | C | | | | F | F | | C | | | C | F | | C | C | C | | | F |
| Patterns and Numeric Forms | Flowcharts and backtracking | | | | | | | | | F | | F | | | | | | | | F | | C | | | | | | C | | F | | | |
| Patterns and Numeric Forms | Verify solutions by substitution | | | | | | | | | F | | F | | | | | | | | F | | F | F | | F | C | | F | F | | | | |

**KEY**

**F** = This topic is a Focus of Instruction in this chapter.

**C** = This topic is Connected to the content of the chapter and is either reviewed in this chapter or informally introduced.

**Expose:** Ideas are introduced at an informal concrete level and will be fully developed later in the program.

**Develop:** Ideas are formalized and fully developed.

**Apply:** Ideas are reviewed and used to extend understanding of related ideas.

| | TOPICS | Course 1 | | | | | | | | | | Course 2 | | | | | | | | | | Course 3 | | | | | | | | | | | |
|---|---|---|---|---|---|---|---|---|---|---|---|---|---|---|---|---|---|---|---|---|---|---|---|---|---|---|---|---|---|---|---|---|---|
| | | 1 | 2 | 3 | 4 | 5 | 6 | 7 | 8 | 9 | 10 | 1 | 2 | 3 | 4 | 5 | 6 | 7 | 8 | 9 | 10 | 1 | 2 | 3 | 4 | 5 | 6 | 7 | 8 | 9 | 10 | 11 | 12 |
| | **Algebraic Reasoning** | Develop | | | | | | | | | | Develop | | | | | | | | | | Develop | | | | | | | | | | | |
| Properties and Rules | Order of operations | C | | F | | | | | | C | C | F | C | | C | | | | | | | | | | | | | | | | | | C |
| | Combining like terms | | | F | | | | | | F | C | F | | | | | | | C | C | | C | C | | | C | | | C | | | | C |
| | Formulas | F | | F | | | | C | | C | C | F | C | | | | | F | | | | | | | | | | | | C | | | |
| | Distributive property | | | F | | | | | | | | F | | | | | | | | F | | C | C | | C | F | | | | F | | | C |
| | Laws of exponents | | | F | | | | | | | | | F | | F | | | | | | | | | | F | C | | | | C | | | |
| | Additive and multiplicative inverse | | | F | C | | | | | | C | C | | | | | | | | C | | | | | | C | | C | | | | | |
| | Additive and multiplicative identities | | | | C | | | | | | C | C | | | | | | | | | | | | | | C | | C | | | | | |
| | Zero product rule | | | | | | | | | | C | | | | | | | | | | | | | | | | | | C | F | C | | |
| | Pythagorean Theorem | | | | | | | | | | | | | | | | | F | | | | | | | | | | | | | | | |
| | Operations with radicals | | | | | | | | | | | | | | | | | | | | | | | | F | | | | | C | | | |
| | **Functions and Relations** | Develop | | | | | | | | | | Develop | | | | | | | | | | Develop | | | | | | | | | | | |
| Linear Expressions/Equations | Recognize as equations, graphs, tables | | | C | | | | | | C | | | | | | | | | F | F | | F | F | | | | | F | | | C | | |
| | Relate equations, graphs, and tables | | | | | | | | C | C | C | C | | | | | | | F | F | | F | F | | | | | F | | | C | | |
| | Modeling situations | | | | | | | | C | C | C | | | | | | | | F | C | | F | F | | | | | F | | | C | | |
| | Direct and indirect variation | | | | | | | | | | | | | | | | | | F | C | C | F | F | | | | | C | | | | | |
| | Slope and rates of change | | | | | | | | | | | | | | | | | | F | C | C | F | F | | | | | C | | | C | | |
| | Slopes of parallel and perpendicular lines | | | | | | | | | | | | | | | | | | C | | | F | F | | | | | | | | | | |
| | Intercepts | | | C | | | | | C | C | C | | | | | | | | F | | | F | F | | | | | C | | | | | |
| | Symbolic forms and effects of parameters | | | | | | | | | C | | | | | | | | | F | | | F | F | | | | | C | | | C | | |
| | Solve equations using backtracking | | | | | | | | | F | | F | | | | | | | | C | | C | | | | | | C | | | | | |
| | Solve using guess-check-improve | | | | | | | | | F | | C | | | | | | | | F | | C | | | | | | C | | | | | |
| | Solve equations symbolically | | | | | | | | | F | | | | | | | | | | F | | C | F | | | | | F | | F | | | |
| | Solve, approximate graphically | | | | | | | | | F | | | | | | | | | | | | F | F | | | | | | | | | | |
| | Solve inequalities | | | | | | | | | | | | | | | | | | | | | C | C | | | | | F | | | | | |
| | Solve systems of equations/inequalities | | | | | | | | | | | | | | | | | | | F | | | | | | | | F | | | | | |
| Quadratic Expressions/Equations | Recognize as equations, graphs, tables | | | | | | | | | | | | | | | | | | | | | | | | F | | | | F | F | | | |
| | Relate equations, graphs, and tables | | | | | | | | | | | C | | | | | | | | | | | | | F | | | | F | F | | | |
| | Modeling situations | | | | | | | | | | | | | | | | | | | | | | | | F | | | | F | F | C | | |
| | Intercepts | | | | | | | | | | | | | | | | | | | | | | | | F | | | | F | F | F | | |
| | Symbolic forms and effects of parameters | | | | | | | | | | | | | | | | | | | | | | | | F | | | | F | F | F | | |
| | Zero product rule | | | | | | | | | | | | | | | | | | | | | | | | | | | | F | F | C | | |
| | Solve equations using backtracking | | | | | | | | | F | | | | | | | | | | | | | | | C | | | | C | F | | | |
| | Solve using guess-check-improve | | | | | | | | | F | | | | | | | | | | | | | | | C | | | | C | C | | | |
| | Solve, approximate graphically | | | | | | | | | | | | | | | | | | | | | | | | C | | | | C | C | C | | |
| | Solve factored equations | | | | | | | | | | | | | | | | | | | | | | | | | | | | | F | C | | |
| | Solve by factoring | | | | | | | | | | | | | | | | | | | | | | | | | | | | | F | C | | |
| | Solve by completing the square | | | | | | | | | | | | | | | | | | | | | | | | | | | | | F | | | |
| | Solve using the quadratic formula | | | | | | | | | | | | | | | | | | | | | | | | | | | | | F | | | |
| | Number of solutions | | | | | | | | | | | | | | | | | | | | | | | | | | | | C | F | F | | |
| Exponential Expressions/Equations | Recognize as equations, graphs, tables | | | | | | | | | | | | | | | | | | | | | | | | | | | | | | C | | |
| | Relate equations, graphs, and tables | | | | | | | | | | | | | | | | | | | | | | | | | | | | | | C | | |
| | Modeling situations | | | | | | | | | | | | | | | | | | | | | | | | | | | | | | C | | |
| | Rates of change and asymptotes | | | | | | | | | | | | | | | | | | | | | | | | | | | | | | C | | |
| | Symbolic forms and effects of parameters | | | | | | | | | | | | | | | | | | | | | | | | | | | | | | C | | |
| | Solve, approximate graphically | | | | | | | | | | | | | | | | | | | | | | | | | | | | | | F | | |
| Rational Expressions/Equations | Symbolic forms and effects of parameters | | | | | | | | | | C | | | | | | | | | | | | | | | | | | F | | F | | F |
| | Graphs, intercepts, and asymptotes | | | | | | | | | | | | | | | | | | | | | | | | | | | | F | | F | | C |
| | Modeling situations | | | | | | | | | | C | | | | | | | | | | F | | | | | | | | F | | C | | F |
| | Solving equations | | | | | | | | | | C | | | | | | | | | | F | | | | | | | | C | | C | | F |

# Geometry

| | TOPICS | Course 1 | | | | | | | | | | Course 2 | | | | | | | | | | Course 3 | | | | | | | | | | | |
|---|---|---|---|---|---|---|---|---|---|---|---|---|---|---|---|---|---|---|---|---|---|---|---|---|---|---|---|---|---|---|---|---|---|
| | | 1 | 2 | 3 | 4 | 5 | 6 | 7 | 8 | 9 | 10 | 1 | 2 | 3 | 4 | 5 | 6 | 7 | 8 | 9 | 10 | 1 | 2 | 3 | 4 | 5 | 6 | 7 | 8 | 9 | 10 | 11 | 12 |
| | **Two-Dimensional Shapes** | Develop | | | | | | | | | | Apply | | | | | | | | | | Apply | | | | | | | | | | | |
| Polygons | Definitions and properties | F | | | | C | | C | | | | | | | | C | | | | | | | C | | | | C | | | | | | |
| Polygons | Classification and naming | F | | | | C | | C | | | | | | | | C | | | | | | | | | | | | | | | | | |
| Polygons | Reflectional symmetry | C | | | | | | | | | | | | | | | | | | | | | | | | | F | | | | | | |
| Polygons | Rotational symmetry | | | | | | | | | | | | | | | | | | | | | | | | | | F | | | | | | |
| Polygons | Angle sums of polygons | F | | | | | | | | | | | | | | | | | | | | | | | | | | | | | | | |
| Polygons | Area and perimeter | F | C | C | | | | C | | | | | | | | C | | C | | | C | | | | | | C | | | | | | |
| Polygons | On the coordinate plane | | | | | | | | C | | | | | | | | | | | | | | | | | | C | | | | | | |
| Quadrilaterals | Definitions and properties | F | | | | C | | | | | | | | | | C | | | | | | | | | | | C | | | | | | |
| Quadrilaterals | Determining uniqueness | C | | | | F | | | | | | | | | | | | | | | | | | | | | | | | | | | |
| Quadrilaterals | Interior angle sum | F | | | | | | | | | | C | | | | | | | | | | | C | | | | | | | | | | |
| Triangles | Acute, right, obtuse | F | | | | | | | | | | | | | | | | | | | | | | | | | C | | | | | | |
| Triangles | Equilateral, isosceles, scalene | F | | | | | | | | | | | | | | C | | | | | | | | | | | C | | | | | | |
| Triangles | Properties of special triangles | F | | | | | | | | | | | | | | C | | | | | | | | | | | | | | | | | |
| Triangles | Triangle inequality | F | | | | | | | | | | | | | | | | | | | | | | | | | | | | | | | |
| Triangles | Triangle Sum Theorem | C | | | | | | | | | | | | | | | | | | | | | | | | C | | | | | | | |
| Triangles | Pythagorean Theorem | | | | | | | | | | | | | | | | | F | | | | | | | | | | | | | | | |
| Angles | Estimate and measure | F | | | | | C | C | | | | | | | | | | | | | | | | | | | | | | | | | |
| Angles | Classify acute, right, obtuse | F | | | | | | | | | | | | | | | | | | | | | | | | | C | | | | | | |
| | **Geometric Relationships** | Expose | | | | | | | | | | Develop | | | | | | | | | | Apply | | | | | | | | | | | |
| Congruence | Definition and properties | | | | | F | | C | | | | | | | | | | | | | | | C | | | | C | | | | | | |
| Congruence | Identifies, determines congruence | | | | | F | | | | | | | | | | | | | | | C | | F | | | | C | | | | | | |
| Congruence | Identify corresponding parts | | | | | F | | | | | | | | | | | | | | | C | | F | | | | C | | | | | | |
| Congruence | As special case of similarity | | | | | | | | | | | | | | | | | | | | C | | | | | | C | | | | | | |
| Congruence | Represented by transformation | | | | | | | C | | | | | | | | | | | | | | | F | | | | F | | | | | | |
| Similarity | Definition and properties | | | | | F | | | | | | | | | | | | | | | C | | C | | | | C | | | | | | |
| Similarity | Identifies, determines similarity | | | | | F | | | | | | | | | | | | | | | C | | | | | | C | | | | | | |
| Similarity | Properties of similar figures | | | | | F | | | | | | | | | | | | | | | C | | | | | | C | | | | | | |
| Similarity | Scale factors | | | | | F | | | | | | | | | | | | | | | F | C | | | | | F | | | | C | | |
| Similarity | Congruence as scale factor of 1 | | | | | F | | | | | | | | | | | | | | | | | | | | | C | | | | | | |
| Similarity | Relation to area and perimeter | | | | | C | | C | | | | | | | | | | | | | C | | | | | | C | | | | | | |
| Similarity | Relation to surface area and volume | | | | | | | C | | | | | | | | C | | | | | C | | | | | | | | | | | | |
| Similarity | Relation to ratio and rates | | | | | F | | | | | | | | | | | | | | | F | | C | | | | C | | | | | | |
| Similarity | Proportional reasoning | | C | | | C | C | | | | C | | | | | | | | | | F | C | | | | | F | | | | | | |
| Similarity | AA Similarity Property | | | | | F | | | | | | | | | | | | | | | | | | | | | C | | | | | | |
| Similarity | Indirect measurement | | | | | C | | | | | | | | | | | | | | | | | | | | | | | | | | | |
| Similarity | Scale drawings and maps | | | | | C | | | | | | | | | | | | | C | | C | | | | | | F | | | | | | |

| | TOPICS | Course 1 | | | | | | | | | | Course 2 | | | | | | | | | | Course 3 | | | | | | | | | | | |
|---|---|---|---|---|---|---|---|---|---|---|---|---|---|---|---|---|---|---|---|---|---|---|---|---|---|---|---|---|---|---|---|---|---|
| | | 1 | 2 | 3 | 4 | 5 | 6 | 7 | 8 | 9 | 10 | 1 | 2 | 3 | 4 | 5 | 6 | 7 | 8 | 9 | 10 | 1 | 2 | 3 | 4 | 5 | 6 | 7 | 8 | 9 | 10 | 11 | 12 |
| | **Three-Dimensional Figures** | Develop | | | | | | | | | | Develop | | | | | | | | | | Apply | | | | | | | | | | | |
| Spatial Visualization | Visualizing structures | | | | | | | F | | | | | | | | F | | | | | | | | | | | C | | | | | | |
| Spatial Visualization | Creating and drawing structures | | | | | | | C | | | | | | | | F | | | | | | | | | | | C | | | | | | |
| Spatial Visualization | Types of 3-D drawings | | | | | | | | | | | | | | | C | | | | | | | | | | | | | | | | | |
| Spatial Visualization | Determining unique structures | | | | | | | | | | | | | | | F | | | | | | | | | | | | | | | | | |
| 3-D Solids | Definitions and properties | | | | | | | C | | | | | | | | F | | | | | | | | | | | | | | | | | |
| 3-D Solids | Prisms and pyramids | | | | | | | F | | | | | | | | F | | | | | | | | | | | | | | | | | |
| 3-D Solids | Cones and cylinders | | | | | | | | | | | | | | | F | | | | | | | | | | | | | | | | | |
| 3-D Solids | Nets | | | | | | | C | | | | | | | | F | | | | | | | | | | | | | | | | | |
| 3-D Solids | Volume and surface area | | | | | | | F | | | | | | | | F | | | | | | | | | | | | | | | | | |
| | **Measurement** | Develop | | | | | | | | | | Develop | | | | | | | | | | Apply | | | | | | | | | | | |
| Perimeter and Area | Approximation and estimation | F | C | C | | | | F | | | | | | | | | | C | | | C | | | | | | | | | | | | |
| Perimeter and Area | Formulas for squares and rectangles | F | | | | | | F | | | | | | | | C | | | | | | | | | | | | | | | | | |
| Perimeter and Area | Areas of parallelograms | | | | | | | F | | | | | | | | C | | | | | | | | | | | | | | | | | |
| Perimeter and Area | Areas of triangles | | | | | | | F | | | | | | | | C | | | | | | | | | | | | | | | | | |
| Perimeter and Area | Areas of circles and circumference | F | | | | | | F | | | | | | | | C | | | | | | | | | | | | | | | | | |
| Perimeter and Area | Relating perimeter and area | F | | | | | | C | | | | | | | | | | | | | | | | | | | | | | | | | |
| Perimeter and Area | Changes due to scale factor | | | | | C | | | | | | | | | | | | | | | F | | | | | | C | | | | | | |
| Perimeter and Area | Maximizing and minimizing | F | | | | | | | | | | | | | | | | | | | | | | | | | | | | | | | |
| Perimeter and Area | Pythagorean Theorem | | | | | | | | | | | | | | | | | F | | | | | | | | | | | | | | | |
| Surface Area and Volume | Approximation and estimation | | | | | | | F | | | | | | | | | | | | | | | | | | | | | | | | | |
| Surface Area and Volume | Formulas for prisms and cylinders | | | | | | | F | | | | | | | | F | | | | | | | | | | | | | | | | | |
| Surface Area and Volume | Formulas for pyramids and cones | | | | | | | | | | | | | | | F | | | | | | | | | | | | | | | | | |
| Surface Area and Volume | Relating surface area and volume | | | | | | | F | | | | | | | | F | | | | | | | | | | | | | | | | | |
| Surface Area and Volume | Changes due to scale factor | | | | | | | | | | | | | | | F | | | | | | | | | | | | | | | | | |
| Surface Area and Volume | Maximizing and minimizing | | | | | | | | | | | | | | | F | | | | | | | | | | | | | | | | | |
| Surface Area and Volume | Capacity | | | | | | | F | | | | | | | | F | | | | | | | | | | | | | | | | | |
| | **Coordinate Geometry** | Develop | | | | | | | | | | Develop | | | | | | | | | | Develop | | | | | | | | | | | |
| Coordinate Representations | Plotting and reading points | | | | | | | | F | | | | | | | | C | | C | | | C | | | C | C | | C | C | | C | | |
| Coordinate Representations | Graphing equations | | | | | | | | C | | | C | | | | | | | F | | | F | | | F | | | F | F | | F | | |
| Coordinate Representations | Relating graphs, tables, equations | | | | | | | | C | C | | C | | | | | | | F | | | F | | | F | | | F | F | | F | | |
| Coordinate Representations | Written descriptions of graphs | | | | | | | | F | | | | | | | | | | C | | | F | | | F | | | C | F | | | | |
| Coordinate Representations | Approximating and finding solutions | | | | | | | | C | | | C | | | | | | | | | | C | | | F | | | F | F | | F | | |
| Coordinate Representations | Direct and indirect variation | | | | | | | | | | | | | | | | | | F | | C | F | | | | | | C | | | | | |
| Coordinate Representations | Slope of a line and rates of change | | | | | | | | C | | | | | | | | | | F | | C | F | | | | | | C | | | C | | |
| Coordinate Representations | Equations of lines | | | | | | | | C | | | | | | | | | | F | | C | F | | | | | | C | | | F | | |
| Coordinate Representations | Slopes of parallel lines | | | | | | | | | | | | | | | | | | C | | | F | | | | | | | | | F | | |
| Coordinate Representations | Slopes of perpendicular lines | | | | | | | | | | | | | | | | | | C | | | F | | | | | | | | | | | |
| Coordinate Representations | Distance formula | | | | | | | | | | | | | | | | | F | | | | | | | | | | | | | | | |
| Transformations | Reflectional symmetry | | | | | | | | | | | | | | | | | | | | | | | | | | F | | | | | | |
| Transformations | Rotational symmetry | | | | | | | | | | | | | | | | | | | | | | | | | | F | | | | | | |
| Transformations | Translations | | | | | | | | | | | | | | | | | | | | | C | C | | | | F | | | | C | | |
| Transformations | Changes of magnitude (dilations) | | | | | | | | | | | | | | | | | | | | | | | | | | F | | | | C | | |
| Transformations | Rotations | | | | | | | | | | | | | | | | | | | | | | | | | | F | | | | | | |
| Transformations | Compound transformations | | | | | | | | | | | | | | | | | | | | | | | | | | F | | | | C | | |
| Transformations | Congruence and similarity | | | | | | | | | | | | | | | | | | | | | | | | | | F | | | | | | |
| Transformations | Relating to equations | | | | | | | | | | | | | | | | | | | | | F | | | | | C | | | | F | | |

# Number and Operations

| | TOPICS | Course 1 | | | | | | | | | | Course 2 | | | | | | | | | | Course 3 | | | | | | | | | | | |
|---|---|---|---|---|---|---|---|---|---|---|---|---|---|---|---|---|---|---|---|---|---|---|---|---|---|---|---|---|---|---|---|---|---|
| | | 1 | 2 | 3 | 4 | 5 | 6 | 7 | 8 | 9 | 10 | 1 | 2 | 3 | 4 | 5 | 6 | 7 | 8 | 9 | 10 | 1 | 2 | 3 | 4 | 5 | 6 | 7 | 8 | 9 | 10 | 11 | 12 |
| | **Numbers and Number Sense** | Develop | | | | | | | | | | Develop | | | | | | | | | | Apply | | | | | | | | | | | |
| Whole Numbers | Magnitude of large, small numbers | | | F | | | | | | | | | C | | F | | | | | | | | | | C | | | | | | | | |
| Whole Numbers | Operations on odd and even numbers | | | | | | | | | | | C | C | | | | | | | | | | | | | | | | | | | | |
| Whole Numbers | Factors and multiples | C | | F | C | | | | | | | | F | | | | | | | | C | | | C | | | C | | | | | | C |
| Whole Numbers | Common factors and multiples | | | | C | | | | | | | | F | | | | | | | | C | | | C | | | | | | | | | C |
| Whole Numbers | Factor pairs and area models | | | | C | | | | | | | C | F | | | | | | | | | | | | | C | | | | | | | C |
| Whole Numbers | Greatest common factor | | | | C | | | | | | | | F | | | | | | | | | | | | | C | | | | | | | C |
| Whole Numbers | Least common multiple | | | | C | | | | | | | | F | | | | | | | | C | | | | | C | | | | | | | C |
| Whole Numbers | Prime and composite | | | | | | | | | | | | F | | | | | | | | | | | | | | | | | | | | |
| Whole Numbers | Relatively prime | | | | | | | | | | | | F | | | | | | | | | | | | | C | | | | | | | |
| Whole Numbers | Prime factorization | | | | | | | | | | | | F | | | | | | | | | | | | | | | | | | | | |
| Whole Numbers | Fundamental Theorem of Arithmetic | | | | | | | | | | | | F | | | | | | | | | | | | | | | | | | | | |
| Whole Numbers | Factor trees | | | | | | | | | | | | F | | | | | | | | | | | | | | | | | | | | |
| Signed Numbers | Meaning and basic concepts | | | | | | | | C | | | | | F | C | | | | | | | | | | | | | | | | | | |
| Signed Numbers | Concrete and number line models | | | | | | | | F | | | | | F | | | | F | C | | | | | | | | | C | | | | | |
| Signed Numbers | Four quadrant coordinate model | | | | | | | | F | | | | | C | | | | | | | | | | | | | | | | | | | |
| Signed Numbers | Comparison | | | | | | | | F | | | | | F | C | | | | | | | | | | | | | | | | | | |
| Signed Numbers | Order | | | | | | | | F | | | | | F | | | | | | | | | | | | | | | | | | | |
| Signed Numbers | Absolute value and opposites | | | | | | | | F | | | | | F | | | | | | | | | | | | | | | | | | | |
| Signed Numbers | Addition and subtraction | | | | | | | | | | | | | F | | | | | | | | | | | | | | | | | | | |
| Signed Numbers | Multiplication and division | | | | | | | | | | | | | F | | | | | C | | | | | | | | | | | | | | |
| Signed Numbers | Meaning in exponential notation | | | | | | | | | | | | | | F | | | | | | | | | | F | | | | | | | | |
| Signed Numbers | Negative slope | | | | | | | | | | | | | | | | | | F | | | F | C | | | | | | | | | | |
| Exponents and Roots | Meaning and basic concepts | | | F | | | | | | | | | F | | | | | | | | | | | | C | | | | | | | | |
| Exponents and Roots | Positive and negative exponents | | | F | | | | | | | | | F | | F | | | | | | | | | | F | | | | | | | | |
| Exponents and Roots | Scientific notation | | | F | | | | | | | | | | | F | | | | | | | | | | F | | | | | | | | |
| Exponents and Roots | Laws of exponents | | | F | | | | | | | | | F | | F | | | | | | | | | | F | | | | | | | | |
| Exponents and Roots | Used in expressions and equations | | | F | | | | | | | | | F | | F | | | | | | | | | | F | C | | | C | C | | | |
| Exponents and Roots | Geometric interpretation of square | | | F | | | | | | | | | | | | | | | | | | | | | | | | | | | | | |
| Exponents and Roots | Geometric interpretation of cube | | | F | | | | | | | | | | | | | | | | | | | | | | | | | | | | | |
| | **Rationals and Irrationals** | Develop | | | | | | | | | | Apply | | | | | | | | | | Apply | | | | | | | | | | | |
| Fraction and Decimal Concepts | Rational and irrational numbers | | F | | | | | | | | | | | | | | | F | | | | | | | F | | | | | | | | C |
| Fraction and Decimal Concepts | Geometric and number line models | | F | | C | | C | | | | | | | F | | | | F | | | | | | | | | | | | | | | |
| Fraction and Decimal Concepts | Fractional relationships to a whole | | F | | F | C | F | | | | | | | | | | | | | | C | | | | | C | | | | | | | C |
| Fraction and Decimal Concepts | Comparison | | F | | F | | F | | C | | | | | | C | | | F | | | C | | | C | | | | | | | | | |
| Fraction and Decimal Concepts | Benchmarks for comparison | | F | | F | | F | | | | | | | | | | | F | | | | | | | | | | | | | | | |
| Fraction and Decimal Concepts | Order | | F | | F | | F | | C | | | | | C | C | | | F | | | | | | | | | | | | | | | |
| Fraction and Decimal Concepts | Naming equivalent fractions | | F | | C | C | C | | | | C | | | | | | C | F | | | C | | | C | | | | | | | | C | F |
| Fraction and Decimal Concepts | Naming equivalent decimals | | F | | F | | F | | | | | | | | | | | F | | | | | | | | | | | | | | | |
| Fraction and Decimal Concepts | Fraction and decimal equivalencies | | F | | C | | C | | | | | | | | | | | C | | | C | | | C | | | | | | | | | |
| Fraction and Decimal Concepts | Fraction and decimal approximations | | F | | C | | C | | | | | | | C | | | | C | | | C | | | | | | | | | | | | |
| Fraction and Decimal Concepts | Fractions as indicated division | | F | | C | | C | | | | | | | | | | | | | | F | | | C | | | | | | | | | C |
| Fraction and Decimal Concepts | Repeating decimals | | F | | C | | C | | | | | | | | | | | | | | | | | | F | | | | | | | | |
| Fraction and Decimal Concepts | Relating fractions and decimals | | F | | C | | C | | | | | | | | | | | | | | F | | | C | C | | | | | | | | |
| Fraction and Decimal Concepts | Converting fractions to decimals | | F | | C | | C | | | | | | | | | | | | | | C | | | C | C | | | | | | | | |
| Fraction and Decimal Concepts | Converting decimals to fractions | | F | | C | | C | | | | | | | | | | | | | | C | | | C | C | | | | | | | | |

| | TOPICS | Course 1 | | | | | | | | | | Course 2 | | | | | | | | | | Course 3 | | | | | | | | | | | |
|---|---|---|---|---|---|---|---|---|---|---|---|---|---|---|---|---|---|---|---|---|---|---|---|---|---|---|---|---|---|---|---|---|---|
| | | 1 | 2 | 3 | 4 | 5 | 6 | 7 | 8 | 9 | 10 | 1 | 2 | 3 | 4 | 5 | 6 | 7 | 8 | 9 | 10 | 1 | 2 | 3 | 4 | 5 | 6 | 7 | 8 | 9 | 10 | 11 | 12 |
| | **Percents** | Develop | | | | | | | | | | Develop | | | | | | | | | | Apply | | | | | | | | | | | |
| Meaning and Representations | Definition and basic concepts | | | | | | F | | | | | | | | | | | | | | C | | | F | | | | | | | | | |
| Meaning and Representations | Greater than 100 or less than 1 | | | | | | F | | | | | | | | | | | | | | C | | | F | | | | | | | | | |
| Meaning and Representations | Common scale comparisons | | | | | | F | | | | | | | | | | | | | | F | | | | | | | | | | | | |
| Meaning and Representations | Relating to fractions and decimals | | | | | | F | | | | | | | | | | | | | | C | | | F | | | | | | | | | |
| Meaning and Representations | Relating to ratios and proportions | | | | | | C | | | | | | | | | | | | | | F | | | F | | | | | | | | | |
| Meaning and Representations | Converting to a decimal | | | | | | F | | | | | | | | | | | | | | C | | | | | | | | | | | | |
| Meaning and Representations | Converting to a fraction | | | | | | F | | | | | | | | | | | | | | C | | | | | | | | | | | | |
| Meaning and Representations | Estimate percent using benchmarks | | | | | | F | | | | | | | | | | | | | | C | | | C | | | | | | | | | |
| Meaning and Representations | Calculate percent | | | | | | F | | | | | | | | | | | | | | F | | | F | | | | | | | | | |
| Meaning and Representations | Solve percent problems (all cases) | | | | | | C | | | | | | | | | | | | | | F | | | F | | | | | | | | | |
| Meaning and Representations | Relating to proportional reasoning | | | | | | F | | | | | | | | | | | | | | F | | | F | | | | | | | | | |
| Meaning and Representations | Percent increase and decrease | | | | | | F | | | | | | | | | | | | | | F | | | F | C | | | | | | | | |
| | **Ratios and Rates** | Expose | | | | | | | | | | Develop | | | | | | | | | | Apply | | | | | | | | | | | |
| Meaning and Representations | Basic concepts | | C | | C | F | C | | | | C | | | | | | | | F | | F | | | | | | | | | | | | |
| Meaning and Representations | Comparison statements | | | | | F | C | | | | | | | | | | | | | | F | | | | | | | | | | | | |
| Meaning and Representations | Part-to-part comparisons | | | | | F | | | | | | | | | | | | | | | F | | | | | | C | | | | | | |
| Meaning and Representations | Part-to-whole comparisons | | C | | | F | F | | | | | | | | | | C | | | | F | | | | | | C | | | | | C | |
| Meaning and Representations | Relating unlike quantities or units | | | | | F | C | | | | | | | | | | | | F | | F | | | | | | | | | | | | |
| Meaning and Representations | Types and uses of ratio notation | | | | | F | | | | | | | | | | | | | | | F | | | | | | | | | | | | |
| Meaning and Representations | Equivalent ratios and ratio tables | | | | | F | | | | | | | | | | | | | F | | F | | | | | | | | | | | | |
| Meaning and Representations | Comparing ratios | | C | | C | F | C | | | | | | | | | | C | | F | | F | | | | | | | | | | | | |
| Meaning and Representations | Equivalent rates | | | | | F | | | | | | | | | | | | | F | | F | F | | | | | | | | | | | |
| Meaning and Representations | Rate tables and rate graphs | | | | | F | | | | | | | | | | | | | F | F | F | F | | | | | | | | | | | |
| Meaning and Representations | Slope and rates of change | | | | | | | | | | | | | | | | | | F | F | C | F | | | | | | | | | | | |
| Proportions | Definition and basic concepts | | | | | | C | | | | | | | | | | | | C | | F | F | | | | | C | | | | | | |
| Proportions | Proportions as equations | | | | | | | | | C | | | | | | | | | | | F | F | | F | | | | | | | | | C |
| Proportions | Checking if a proportion exists | | | | | | | | | | | | | | | | | | F | | F | C | | F | | | | | | | | | |
| Proportions | Methods of solving proportions | | | | | | | | | | | | | | | | | | | | F | | | F | | | | | | | | | C |
| Proportions | Proportional relationships | | | | | | | | | | | | | | | | | | F | | F | F | | F | | | C | | | | | | |
| Proportions | Proportional reasoning | | C | | | | C | | | | C | | | | | | | | C | | F | | | F | C | | C | | C | | | C | |
| | **Algorithms and Operations** | Develop | | | | | | | | | | Apply | | | | | | | | | | Apply | | | | | | | | | | | |
| Fractions | Generating equivalent fractions | | F | C | C | | C | | | | | | | | | | | | | | C | | | C | | | | | | | | | C |
| Fractions | Fraction, mixed number conversions | | F | | C | | | | | | | | | | | | | | | | | | | | | | | | | | | | C |
| Fractions | Percent, decimal conversion | | F | | C | | F | | | | | | | | | | | | | | | | | F | | | | | | | | | |
| Fractions | Addition and subtraction | | | | F | | | C | | | | | | C | | | | | | | | | | | | | | | | | | | C |
| Fractions | Multiplication and division | | | | F | | | C | | | | | | C | | | | | | | | | | | | | | | | | | | C |
| Decimals | Fraction, percent conversions | | F | | F | | F | | | | | | | | | | | | | | | | | F | | | | | | | | | |
| Decimals | Addition and subtraction | | | | C | | | C | | | | C | | C | | | | | | | | | | | | | | | | | | | |
| Decimals | Multiplication and division | | | | C | | | C | | | | C | | C | | | | | | | | | | | | | | | | | | | |
| Signed Numbers | Addition and subtraction | | | | | | | | | | | | | F | | | | | | | | | | | | | | | | | | | |
| Signed Numbers | Multiplication and division | | | | | | | | | | | | | F | | | | | | | | | | | | | | | | | | | |

# Probability and Statistics

| | TOPICS | Course 1 | | | | | | | | | | Course 2 | | | | | | | | | | Course 3 | | | | | | | | | | | |
|---|---|---|---|---|---|---|---|---|---|---|---|---|---|---|---|---|---|---|---|---|---|---|---|---|---|---|---|---|---|---|---|---|---|
| | | 1 | 2 | 3 | 4 | 5 | 6 | 7 | 8 | 9 | 10 | 1 | 2 | 3 | 4 | 5 | 6 | 7 | 8 | 9 | 10 | 1 | 2 | 3 | 4 | 5 | 6 | 7 | 8 | 9 | 10 | 11 | 12 |
| | **Data Analysis** | Develop | | | | | | | | | | Develop | | | | | | | | | | Develop | | | | | | | | | | | |
| Graphs and Displays | Line plots | | | | F | | C | | | | F | | | | | | F | | | | | | | | | | | | | | | | |
| Graphs and Displays | Stem-and-leaf plots | | | | | | | | | | F | | | | | | F | | | | | | | | | | | | | | | | |
| Graphs and Displays | Box plots | | | | | | | | | | | | | | | | | | | | | | | | | | | | | | | F | |
| Graphs and Displays | Venn Diagrams | C | | | | | | | | | F | | | | | | | C | | | | | | | | | | | | | | | |
| Graphs and Displays | Circle graphs | | | | | | C | | | | C | | | | | | F | | | | | | | | | | | | | | | | |
| Graphs and Displays | Frequency tables | | | | | | C | | | | F | | | | | | C | | | | | | | | | | | | | | | | |
| Graphs and Displays | Histograms | | | | | | | | | | F | | | | | | | | | | | | | | | | | | | | | | |
| Graphs and Displays | Scatter plots | | | | | | | | C | | F | | | | | | | | | | | | | | | | | | | | | | |
| Graphs and Displays | Choose appropriate displays | | | | | | | | | | F | | | | | | F | | | | | | | | | | | | | | | | |
| Graphs and Displays | Skewness and symmetry | | | | | | | | | | F | | | | | | | | | | | | | | | | | | | | | | |
| Modeling and Analysis | Identify patterns and trends | | C | F | | | | | C | | F | | | | | | F | | C | | | C | C | | C | | | | C | | | | |
| Modeling and Analysis | Identify clusters, gaps, and outliers | | | | | | | | | | F | | | | | | | | | | | | | | | | | | | | | | |
| Modeling and Analysis | Describe shape and scatter | | | | | | | | | | F | | | | | | | | C | | | | F | | C | | | | C | | | | |
| Modeling and Analysis | Compare data sets | | | | | | | | | | F | | | | | | F | | | | | | C | | | | | | | | | | |
| Modeling and Analysis | Fit a line by "eyeballing" | | | | | | | | | | C | | | | | | | | C | | | | F | | | | | | | | | | |
| Modeling and Analysis | Make predictions and generalizations | | C | C | | | | | | | F | | | | | | F | | C | | | | C | | C | | | | C | | | | |
| Modeling and Analysis | Misleading graphs | | | | | | | | | | C | | | | | | F | | | | | C | | | | | | | | | | | |
| Modeling and Analysis | Law of large numbers | | | | | | | | | | F | | | | | | | | | | | | | | | | | | | | | C | |
| Modeling and Analysis | Outlier affect on measurers of center | | | | | | | | | | | | | | | | | | | | | | C | | | | | | | | | | |
| Modeling and Analysis | Compare measures of center | | | | | | | | | | | | | | | | F | | | | | | | | | | | | | | | | |
| Modeling and Analysis | Choose appropriate measure of center | | | | | | | | | | | | | | | | C | | | | | | | | | | | | | | | | |
| Statistical Measures | Frequency | | | | F | | | | | | C | | | | | | | | | | | | | | | | | | | | | | |
| Statistical Measures | Range | | | | F | | | | | | | | | | | | | | | | | | | | | | | | | | | | |
| Statistical Measures | Mode | | | | F | | | | | | | | | | | | | | | | | | | | | | | | | | | | |
| Statistical Measures | Median | | | | F | | | | | | | | | | | | | | | | | | | | | | | | | | | | |
| Statistical Measures | Mean | | | | F | | | | | | | | | | | | | | | | | | | | | | | | | | | | |
| Statistical Measures | Quartiles | | | | | | | | | | | | | | | | | | | | | | | | | | | | | | | F | |
| Surveys and Sampling | Sample survey vs. census | | | | | | | | | | | | | | | | F | | | | | | | | | | | | | | | | |
| Surveys and Sampling | Randomization | | | | | | | | | | C | | | | | | F | | | | | | | | | | | | | | | | |
| Surveys and Sampling | Simple random sample | | | | | | | | | | | | | | | | F | | | | | | | | | | | | | | | | |
| Surveys and Sampling | Sample size | | | | | | | | | | C | | | | | | F | | | | | | | | | | | | | | | | |
| Surveys and Sampling | Law of large numbers | | | | | | | | | | F | | | | | | C | | | | | | | | | | | | | | | | |
| Surveys and Sampling | Bias in survey methods | | | | | | | | | | C | | | | | | C | | | | | | | | | | | | | | | | |
| Surveys and Sampling | Population and sample identification | | | | | | | | | | | | | | | | F | | | | | | | | | | | | | | | | |

| | TOPICS | Course 1 | | | | | | | | | | Course 2 | | | | | | | | | | Course 3 | | | | | | | | | | | |
|---|---|---|---|---|---|---|---|---|---|---|---|---|---|---|---|---|---|---|---|---|---|---|---|---|---|---|---|---|---|---|---|---|---|
| | | 1 | 2 | 3 | 4 | 5 | 6 | 7 | 8 | 9 | 10 | 1 | 2 | 3 | 4 | 5 | 6 | 7 | 8 | 9 | 10 | 1 | 2 | 3 | 4 | 5 | 6 | 7 | 8 | 9 | 10 | 11 | 12 |
| | **Probability** | Develop | | | | | | | | | | Develop | | | | | | | | | | Develop | | | | | | | | | | | |
| Basic Concepts and Rules | Measure between 0 and 1 | | | | | | | | | | F | | | | | | F | | | | | | | | | | | | | | | F | |
| Basic Concepts and Rules | Empirical and theoretical probabilities | | | | | | | | | | F | | | | | | F | | | | | | | | | | | | | | | F | |
| Basic Concepts and Rules | Equally likely | | | | | | | | | | F | | | | | | C | | | | | | | | | | | | | | | F | |
| Basic Concepts and Rules | Compound events | | | | | | | | | | C | | | | | | | | | | | | | | | | | | | | | F | |
| Basic Concepts and Rules | Mutually exclusive events | | | | | | | | | | C | | | | | | | | | | | | | | | | | | | | | F | |
| Basic Concepts and Rules | Independent events | | | | | | | | | | F | | | | | | F | | | | | | | | | | | | | | | C | |
| Basic Concepts and Rules | Dependent events | | | | | | | | | | F | | | | | | F | | | | | | | | | | | | | | | C | |
| Basic Concepts and Rules | Confidence | | | | | | | | | | C | | | | | | | | | | | | | | | | | | | | | | |
| Basic Concepts and Rules | Expected value | | | | | | | | | | C | | | | | | | | | | | | | | | | | | | | | | |
| Counting Methods | Counting trees | | | | | | | | | | F | | | | | | F | | | | | | | | | | | | | | | F | |
| Counting Methods | Combinations | | | | | | | | | | | | | | | | F | | | | | | | | | | | | | | | F | |
| Counting Methods | Permutations | | | | | | | | | | | | | | | | | | | | | | | | | | | | | | | F | |
| Experiments and Simulations | Estimate likelihood | | | | | | | | | | C | | | | | | C | | | | | | | | | | | | | | | C | |
| Experiments and Simulations | Relate to theoretical probabilities | | | | | | | | | | F | | | | | | | | | | | | | | | | | | | | | C | |
| Experiments and Simulations | Analyze fairness | | | | | | | | | | C | | | | | | F | | | | | | | | | | | | | | | C | |

# Pacing

*IMPACT Mathematics* and the accompanying support materials allow you to create a mathematics course that meets the needs of your students. The chart shown on these two pages offers general suggestions for pacing your students through the book.

| Chapter | Lesson (Investigation) | Day(s) |
|---|---|---|
| 1 | Lesson 1.1(1) | 1–2 |
| | Lesson 1.1(2) | 3–4 |
| | Lesson 1.1(3) | 5–6 |
| | Lesson 1.1(4) | 7 |
| | Lesson 1.2(1) | 8–9 |
| | Lesson 1.2(2) | 10 |
| | Lesson 1.2(3) Inquiry<br>Quiz, Lessons 1.1–1.2 | 11 |
| | Lesson 1.3(1) | 12–13 |
| | Lesson 1.3(2) | 14 |
| | Lesson 1.3(3) | 15 |
| | Lesson 1.3(4) | 16 |
| | Quiz, Lesson 1.3 | 17 |
| | Chapter 1 Review | 18 |
| | Chapter 1 Test | 19 |
| 2 | Lesson 2.1(1) | 20–21 |
| | Lesson 2.1(2) | 22 |
| | Lesson 2.1(3) | 23 |
| | Lesson 2.1(4) | 24 |
| | Lesson 2.2(1) | 25–26 |
| | Lesson 2.2(2) | 27 |
| | Lesson 2.2(3) | 28 |
| | Quick Quiz, Lessons 2.1–2.2 | 29 |
| | Lesson 2.3(1) | 30–31 |
| | Lesson 2.3(2) | 32 |
| | Lesson 2.3(3) | 33 |
| | Lesson 2.3(4) Inquiry<br>Quiz, Lesson 2.3 | 34 |
| | Chapter 2 Review | 35 |
| | Chapter 2 Test | 36 |

| Chapter | Lesson (Investigation) | Day(s) |
|---|---|---|
| 3 | Lesson 3.1(1) | 37–38 |
| | Lesson 3.1(2) Inquiry | 39 |
| | Lesson 3.1(3) | 40 |
| | Lesson 3.1(4) | 41 |
| | Lesson 3.1(5) | 42 |
| | Lesson 3.1(6) | 43 |
| | Lesson 3.2(1) | 44–45 |
| | Lesson 3.2(2) | 46 |
| | Lesson 3.2(3) | 47 |
| | Lesson 3.2(4) | 48 |
| | Quiz, Lesson 3.1–3.2 | 49 |
| | Chapter 3 Review | 50 |
| | Chapter 3 Test | 51 |
| 4 | Lesson 4.1(1) | 52–53 |
| | Lesson 4.1(2) | 54 |
| | Lesson 4.1(3) | 55 |
| | Lesson 4.1(4) Inquiry | 56 |
| | Lesson 4.2(1) | 57–58 |
| | Lesson 4.2(2) | 59 |
| | Lesson 4.2(3) | 60 |
| | Quiz, Lessons 4.1–4.2 | 61 |
| | Chapter 4 Review | 62 |
| | Chapter 4 Test | 63 |

| Chapter | Lesson (Investigation) | Day(s) |
|---|---|---|
| 5 | Lesson 5.1(1) | 64–65 |
| | Lesson 5.1(2) | 66 |
| | Lesson 5.1(3) Inquiry | 67 |
| | Lesson 5.2(1) | 68–69 |
| | Lesson 5.2(2) | 70 |
| | Lesson 5.2(3) | 71 |
| | Quiz, Lessons 5.1–5.2 | 72 |
| | Lesson 5.3(1) | 73–74 |
| | Lesson 5.3(2) | 75 |
| | Lesson 5.3(3) | 76 |
| | Quiz, Lesson 5.3 | 77 |
| | Chapter 5 Review | 78 |
| | Chapter 5 Test | 79 |
| 6 | Lesson 6.1(1) | 80–81 |
| | Lesson 6.1(2) | 82 |
| | Lesson 6.1(3) | 83 |
| | Lesson 6.1(4) Inquiry | 84 |
| | Lesson 6.2(1) | 85–86 |
| | Lesson 6.2(2) | 87 |
| | Lesson 6.2(3) | 88 |
| | Quiz, Lessons 6.1–6.2 | 89 |
| | Lesson 6.3(1) | 90–91 |
| | Lesson 6.3(2) | 92 |
| | Lesson 6.3(3) | 93 |
| | Lesson 6.3(4) | 94 |
| | Quiz, Lesson 6.3 | 95 |
| | Chapter 6 Review | 96 |
| | Chapter 6 Test | 97 |
| 7 | Lesson 7.1(1) | 98–99 |
| | Lesson 7.1(2) | 100 |
| | Lesson 7.2(1) | 101–102 |
| | Lesson 7.2(2) | 103 |
| | Quiz, Lesson 7.1–7.2 | 104 |
| | Lesson 7.3(1) | 105–106 |
| | Lesson 7.3(2) | 107 |
| | Lesson 7.3(3) Inquiry<br>Quiz, Lesson 7.3 | 108 |
| | Chapter 7 Review | 109 |
| | Chapter 7 Test | 110 |

| Chapter | Lesson (Investigation) | Day(s) |
|---|---|---|
| 8 | Lesson 8.1(1) | 111–112 |
| | Lesson 8.1(2) | 113 |
| | Lesson 8.1(3) | 114 |
| | Lesson 8.1(4) Inquiry | 115 |
| | Lesson 8.2(1) | 116–117 |
| | Lesson 8.2(2) | 118 |
| | Lesson 8.2(3) | 119 |
| | Lesson 8.2(4) | 120 |
| | Quiz, Lessons 8.1–8.2 | 121 |
| | Lesson 8.3(1) | 122–123 |
| | Lesson 8.3(2) | 124 |
| | Lesson 8.3(3) | 125 |
| | Lesson 8.3(4) | 126 |
| | Quiz, Lesson 8.3 | 127 |
| | Chapter 8 Review | 128 |
| | Chapter 8 Test | 129 |
| 9 | Lesson 9.1(1) | 130–131 |
| | Lesson 9.1(2) Inquiry | 132 |
| | Lesson 9.2(1) | 133–134 |
| | Lesson 9.2(2) | 135 |
| | Lesson 9.2(3) | 136 |
| | Quiz, Lessons 9.1–9.2 | 137 |
| | Lesson 9.3(1) | 138–139 |
| | Lesson 9.3(2) | 140 |
| | Lesson 9.3(3) | 141 |
| | Lesson 9.3(4) | 142 |
| | Lesson 9.4(1) | 143–144 |
| | Lesson 9.4(2) | 145 |
| | Lesson 9.4(3) | 146 |
| | Quiz, Lessons 9.3–9.4 | 147 |
| | Chapter 9 Review | 148 |
| | Chapter 9 Test | 149 |
| 10 | Lesson 10.1(1) | 150–151 |
| | Lesson 10.1(2) | 152 |
| | Lesson 10.2(1) | 153–154 |
| | Lesson 10.2(2) | 155 |
| | Lesson 10.2(3) | 156 |
| | Lesson 10.2(4) | 157 |
| | Lesson 10.2(5) | 158 |
| | Lesson 10.2(6) Inquiry<br>Quiz, Lessons 10.1–10.2 | 159 |
| | Lesson 10.3(1) | 160–161 |
| | Lesson 10.3(2) | 162 |
| | Lesson 10.4(1) | 163–164 |
| | Lesson 10.4(2) | 165 |
| | Quiz, Lessons 10.3–10.4 | 166 |
| | Chapter 10 Review | 167 |
| | Chapter 10 Test | 168 |

COURSE 2

# Table of Contents



**Focal Points and Connections**
See pages vi and vii for key.

G7-FP3

**Focal Points and Connections**
See pages vi and vii for key.

G7-FP3

# 3 Signed Numbers



**Focal Points and Connections**
See pages vi and vii for key.

G7-FP3

**Focal Points and Connections**
See pages vi and vii for key.

G7-FP3

**Focal Points and Connections**
See pages vi and vii for key.

G7-FP2

G7-FP4C

**Focal Points and Connections**
See pages vi and vii for key.

**G7-FP6C**

**G7-FP7C**

# 7 Real Numbers .......... 318



**Focal Points and Connections**
See pages vi and vii for key.

G7-FP3

G7-FP5C

**Focal Points and Connections**
See pages vi and vii for key.

G7-FP1
G7-FP3
G7-FP5C

# 9 Equations ........ 434



**Focal Points and Connections**
See pages vi and vii for key.

G7-FP3

G7-FP5C

**Focal Points and Connections**
See pages vi and vii for key.

G7-FP1

G7-FP4C

CHAPTER 1

# Expressions

## *Chapter Overview*

In this chapter, students will manipulate expressions beginning at the concrete level by creating sequences of shapes and then writing a rule to describe each sequence. After becoming familiar with writing simple rules, students will investigate writing algebraic expressions and formulas that relate to specific situations.

Then students are introduced to the distributive property at the concrete level using bags and blocks. As they become familiar with the models, they are introduced to symbolic representations using flowcharts and tables.

Links to past and future content found in **The Big Picture** illustrate vertical alignment throughout the program.

## The Big Picture

| Links to the Past | Chapter 1 | Links to the Future |
|---|---|---|
| **Course 1: Chapter 3** (pp. 108–195) Patterns, Numbers, and Rules | **Lesson 1.1** (p. 4) Variables and Expressions | **Course 3, Chapter 5** (pp. 204–257) Algebraic Expressions |
| **Course 1: Chapter 3** (pp. 108–195) Patterns, Numbers, and Rules | **Lesson 1.2** (p. 30) Expressions and Formulas | **Course 3, Chapter 1** (pp. 2–63) Linear Relationships |
| **Course 1: Chapter 3** (pp. 108–195) Patterns, Numbers, and Rules | **Lesson 1.3** (p. 49) The Distributive Property | **Course 3, Chapter 5** (pp. 204–257) Algebraic Expressions |

# Mathematical Background

An important part of algebra is developing facility in manipulating expressions, regardless of the real quantities they represent. In this chapter, students take first steps in that direction. The Theory of Multiple Intelligences states that students have varied learning styles and various ways of cognitively processing ideas. The investigations in this chapter deliberately activate kinesthetic, concrete, and visual styles of learning, particularly in the bags-and-blocks model.

**Operations with Expressions** Students will learn some ways in which expressions can be manipulated, especially those related to the distributive property of multiplication over addition and over subtraction. This important property of the real number system underpins the simplification and factoring of expressions, which in turn provide powerful means of gaining algebraic insight into the nature of a particular expression.

Chapter 1 also introduces some of the major algebraic conventions used in forming expressions, especially those with multiplication, division, and exponents. Two meanings of variable are introduced (a quantity that can vary and an unknown).

For a further discussion of the many meanings of variable, see Chapter 2, NCTM 1988 Yearbook, "The Ideas of Algebra, K–12."

**Mathematical Background** *gives additional information on mathematics content and research, and suggestions for further reading.*

**Flowcharts** Students use flowcharts to build expressions and reinforce the concepts of order of operations. Backtracking formalizes the intuitive process that many students use to solve equations; it is also a powerful strategy for solving a particular class of equations.

## Additional Reading

According to Sutherland and Rojano in A Spreadsheet Approach to Solving Algebra Problems, which appeared in *Journal of Mathematical Behavior,* spreadsheets help students understand the meaning of variables and algebraic expressions. In the Spreadsheet investigation on page 40, students use a spreadsheet to explore how much a business should charge for orders.

CHAPTER 1

# Planning Guide

## Lesson Resources

The **Planning Guide** presents important planning information for the entire chapter, including lesson objectives, suggested pacing, materials, and extra resources.

| | Lesson 1.1 (Pacing: 7 days) | Lesson 1.2 (Pacing: 4 days) | Lesson 1.3 (Pacing: 5 days) |
|---|---|---|---|
| **Lesson Title** | **Variables and Expressions** (p. 4) | **Expressions and Formulas** (p. 30) | **The Distributive Property** (p. 49) |
| **Lesson Objectives** | • To write a rule to describe a sequence or relate two quantities<br>• To use variables to write expressions<br>• To evaluate expressions<br>• To use flowcharts to build expressions and solve equations | • To practice using variables to write expressions<br>• To use expressions to solve problems<br>• To develop and use formulas to find specific quantities<br>• To use a spreadsheet to calculate quantities using formulas | • To understand and apply the distributive property<br>• To use parentheses in expanding or factoring<br>• To combine like terms |
| **Materials** | Chapter 1 Master 1, Chapter 1 Master 2, Lesson 1.1 Master 1 | computer, spreadsheet software, Lesson 1.2 Master 1 | Chapter 1 Master 2, bags, blocks |
| ***Quick Review Math Handbook*** | **Lesson 5.1** Writing Expressions and Equations<br>**Lesson 5.2** Simplifying Expressions<br>**Lesson 5.3** Evaluating Expressions and Formulas | **Lesson 5.3** Evaluating Expressions and Formulas | **Lesson 5.2** Simplifying Expressions<br>**Lesson 5.4** Solving Linear Equations |
| **Print Resources** | CRM Refresher Worksheets (pp. 7–23)<br>CRM Study Guide and Intervention (p. 25)<br>CRM Skills Practice (p. 26)<br>CRM Problem-Solving Practice (p. 27)<br>CRM Enrichment (p. 28)<br>• Investigation Notebook and Reflection Journal<br>• Differentiation Handbook | CRM Study Guide and Intervention (p. 31)<br>CRM Skills Practice (p. 32)<br>CRM Problem-Solving Practice (p. 33)<br>CRM Enrichment (p. 34)<br>• Investigation Notebook and Reflection Journal<br>• Differentiation Handbook | CRM Study Guide and Intervention (p. 37)<br>CRM Skills Practice (p. 38)<br>CRM Problem-Solving Practice (p. 39)<br>CRM Enrichment (p. 40)<br>• Investigation Notebook and Reflection Journal<br>• Differentiation Handbook |
| **Technology Resources** | TeacherWorks Plus<br>Classroom Presentation Toolkit<br>ExamView Assessment Suite<br>StudentWorks Plus<br>Math Online Brain Pops • Concepts in Motion | TeacherWorks Plus<br>Classroom Presentation Toolkit<br>ExamView Assessment Suite<br>StudentWorks Plus<br>Math Online Brain Pops • Concepts in Motion | TeacherWorks Plus<br>Classroom Presentation Toolkit<br>ExamView Assessment Suite<br>StudentWorks Plus<br>Math Online Brain Pops • Concepts in Motion |

*Included in the Impact Mathematics Manipulative Kit

# Assessment Resources

## MARS Assessment: Teaching with Purpose

### Differences

In *Differences,* students work with number chains and make generalizations about their work. Students also complete number machines, find the differences between the branches, and explain their answers algebraically.

### Targeting the Task

- **Diagnostic**—Use Exercises 1–3 in the *Differences* assessment to determine students' understanding of how to work with number chains, make generalizations, and be able to explain their work algebraically. For those students who do not have this understanding, completing this unit is needed.
- **Formative**—Exercises 1–3 can be administered individually according to the lessons.

**MARS Performance-Based Assessment** asks students to perform tasks or solve problems that appear in authentic (real-world) contexts.

CRM **Chapter 1 MARS Assessment** (pp. 58–62)

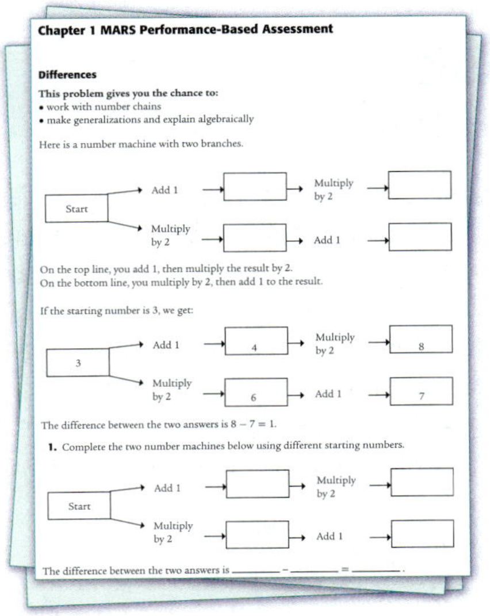
**Chapter 1 MARS Performance-Based Assessment**

**Differences**

**This problem gives you the chance to:**
- work with number chains
- make generalizations and explain algebraically

Here is a number machine with two branches.



On the top line, you add 1, then multiply the result by 2.
On the bottom line, you multiply by 2, then add 1 to the result.

If the starting number is 3, we get:



The difference between the two answers is 8 − 7 = 1.

1. Complete the two number machines below using different starting numbers.



The difference between the two answers is ______ − ______ = ______.

## Assessment Planning Guide

Assessments are available for investigations, lessons, and chapters.

**ExamView** Assessment Suite — Customize and create multiple versions of tests and quizzes.

| | Student Edition | Teacher Edition | Other Resources |
|---|---|---|---|
| **Diagnostic** | | | CRM Course Pretest (pp. 3–6)<br>Math Online Online Chapter Quiz |
| **Formative** | Share & Summarize (pp. 8, 12, 17, 20, 34, 39, 52, 55, 59, 62) | Troubleshooting (pp. 8, 10, 12, 14, 15, 19, 20, 32, 34, 37, 39, 51, 57, 59)<br>On the Spot Assessment (pp. 30, 55)<br>Quick Check (pp. 29, 48, 68)<br>Quick Quiz (pp. 29, 48, 68) | CRM Quick Quiz (pp. 29, 35, 41) |
| **Summative** | Review & Self-Assessment (pp. 69–71) | | CRM Chapter 1 Test: Forms A and B (pp. 46–53)<br>CRM Standardized Test Practice (pp. 58–59) |
| **Performance-Based** | In Your Own Words (pp. 29, 48, 68) | | CRM MARS Performance-Based Assessment (pp. 56–57)<br>CRM Chapter Performance Assessment (pp. 54–55) |

The **Assessment Resources** displays the array of assessment opportunities including materials in the Student Edition, Teacher Guide, and CRMs.

# Differentiated Instruction

## *Reaching* All Learners

Below are suggestions on differentiating the materials presented in this chapter. Additional modifications should be considered.

For remediation or enrichment, the activities and modifications found on the **Differentiated Instruction** provide additional instruction options.

### Approaching Level AL

**Mathematical Rules** In order to write rules mathematically, students must understand their literal meaning in English. This may be especially difficult for poor readers. If students are having trouble understanding the literal meaning of a problem or a pattern, you can help them develop strategies for making the problems meaningful. Such strategies might include working with a partner to read the problem and extract the important information, or trying to connect the problem with their own life experiences.

### Beyond Level BL

**Application** Have students create a real world problem that fits the expression $3t + 7$. Once the students have completed their problem, have them share with the class. Discuss how the many different problems all are interpreted the same way.

### On Level OL

**Interpretation** Have students break into two groups. Give each group a different geometric design, not letting the other group see the design. Ask students to write clear directions explaining how to make the design. Then pair one student from each group and have students take turns reading the directions for their design while the partner draws it. Stress that the students must not say anything about the design other than the directions. Then compare the drawings to the originals.

### English Language Learners ELL

**Distinguishing Expressions** Some students have difficulty distinguishing expressions such as $4m^2$ and $(4m)^2$ since both expressions may be read as *four m squared*. Distinguishing between these two expressions is vital. Students may benefit from reading the two expressions aloud differently. Many people use the term *quantity* to designate the amount in parentheses, so $(4m)^2$ may be read as *four m the quantity squared.*

**KEY**

AL Approaching Level   OL On Level   BL Beyond Level   ELL English Language Learners

## *Intervention Planning Guide*

CRM Assess students' prerequisite skills and knowledge using the **Chapter Pretest** found in the Chapter 1 Resource Masters, pp. 38–41.

| **Intensive Intervention** two or more years below grade level | **Strategic Intervention** below grade level | **On Level** | **Beyond Level** |
|---|---|---|---|
| **If** students miss 75% of the exercises: | **If** students miss 50% of the exercises: | **If** students miss 25% of the exercises: | **If** students miss 0%–10% of the exercises: |
| **Then** use *Math Triumphs,* an intensive intervention | **Then** choose a resource: | **Then** choose a resource: | **Then** choose a resource: |
| *Math Triumphs,* Grade 7<br>• Chapter 9: Variables and Expressions | CRM Study Guide and Intervention (pp. 25, 31, 37)<br>• Investigation Notebook and Reflection Journal<br>• Differentiation Handbook<br>Math Online Brain Pops • Concepts in Motion | CRM Skills Practice (pp. 26, 32, 38)<br>CRM Problem-Solving Practice (pp. 27, 33, 39)<br>• Investigation Notebook and Reflection Journal | CRM Enrichment (pp. 28, 34, 40)<br>• Differentiation Handbook |

The **Intervention Planning Guide** prescribes both enrichment and remediation resources, including *Math Triumphs.*

### *Literature Connections*

**Recommended Outside Reading for Students**

**Nonfiction**

Great Source Education Group Staff. *Algebra to Go: A Mathematics Handbook.* Great Source Education Group, 2000.

This book is designed as a reference for students in grades 8 and higher. In addition to explanations of topics in algebra, the book contains tips for solving problems, writing, taking tests, and using computers.

**Fiction**

Connell, David D. *The Case of the Mystery Weekend.* Scientific American Books for Young Readers, 1994.

Written in the style of the old Dragnet series, this novel relates what happens when two young math detectives, heading for a mystery weekend, get lost and must use problem-solving and other math skills to solve a real mystery.

The fiction and non-fiction books in **Literature Connections** offer opportunities for students to explore math concepts in contexts outside of the math classroom.

### Mc Graw Hill Professional Development

Targeted professional development has been articulated throughout the *IMPACT Mathematics* series. The **McGraw-Hill Professional Development Video Library** provides short videos that support the mathematics standards. Log on to www.glencoe.com.

Model Lessons

Instructional Strategies

## CHAPTER 1 Expressions

### Real-Life Math

**Algebra in the Strangest Places** To encourage students to think about algebra in the everyday world, suggest the path of a football kick. Ask a volunteer to draw the path on the board. Explain that a path of this type is a parabola, and can be represented by an algebraic equation. Ask students to think of other specific contexts in which algebraic equations might be used.

**Think About It** Answers may vary. The average speed of an ant is about 2.5 to 3.5 centimeters per second.

# CHAPTER 1 Expressions

## Real-Life Math

**Algebra in the Strangest Places** You might think that algebra is a topic found only in textbooks. But you can find algebra all around you, in some of the strangest places.

Did you know there is a relationship between the speed at which ants crawl and the air temperature? If you were to find some ants outside and time them as they crawled, you could actually estimate the temperature. Here is the algebraic equation that describes this relationship.

Celsius temperature → $t$

$$t = 15s + 3$$

ant speed in centimeters per second → $s$

There are many ordinary and extraordinary places where you will encounter algebra.

**Think About It** What do you think is the speed of a typical ant?

### *Contents in Brief*



**Math Online** Take the **Chapter Readiness Quiz** at glencoe.com.

Each chapter has a separate **Chapter Resource Masters** booklet that contains lesson worksheets, chapter and lesson assessments, and chapter and lesson black-line masters.

### Chapter Resources

- CRM Chapter 1 Resource Masters
- CRM English/Spanish Family Letter (pp. 1–2)
- CRM Course 2 Refresher Worksheets (pp. 3–19)
- CRM Lesson Masters (pp. 24, 30, 36)
- CRM Chapter 1 Pretest (pp. 3–6)
- CRM Chapter 1 Tests (pp. 46–53)

**Math Online** Online Readiness Quiz • eGlossary

# Dear Family,

The class is about to begin an exciting year of *IMPACT Mathematics.* Some of the topics that will be studied include exponents, three-dimensional geometry, ratios, probability, and data analysis. Throughout the year, your student will also develop and refine skills in algebra.

The class will begin by looking at algebraic expressions and variables. Once the students are familiar with variables and expressions, they will create flowcharts to represent equations and to solve equations. The class will also explore the use of formulas in real-world situations, including computer spreadsheets.

### Key Concept–Algebraic Expressions and Variables

Algebraic expressions are combinations of numbers, letters, and mathematical symbols.

$b + 2 \qquad 5m^2 - 4 \qquad 10(9y - 2) \qquad \frac{3x + 2}{4}$

**Variables** are letters or symbols that can change or that represent unknown quantities. In the expression $b + 2$, the variable is $b$. The value of an expression depends on the number substituted for its variable(s). The following are examples.

When $b = 0$, $b + 2$ equals $0 + 2$, or 2.
When $b = 1$, $b + 2$ equals $1 + 2$, or 3.
When $b = 100$, $b + 2$ equals $100 + 2$, or 102.

### Chapter Vocabulary

| | | |
|---|---|---|
| algebraic expression | backtracking | flowchart |
| distributive property | formula | equivalent expressions |
| like terms | exponent | polynomial |
| variable | | |

### Home Activities

- Identify the variable in each Key Concept algebraic expression.
- Use the thermometer illustration in Investigation 1 to convert daily temperature readings. Use the formula $F = \frac{9}{5}C + 32$ to check your conversions.
- Look for examples of expressions and formulas in everyday situations.
- Create a spreadsheet of expenses for a family outing, such as a trip to the movies.

3

## Family Letter

Another version of the Family Letter, available in English and Spanish, is found in the Chapter 1 Resource Masters. You may want to send a copy of this letter home with your students.

**Key Concept–Algebraic Expressions and Variables** Students can be very apprehensive about variables because they are unfamiliar. Use everyday materials, such as bags, boxes, or bowls to represent variables. Fill the item with slips of paper with random letters on them and pick one out to illustrate a value of the variable.

**Home Activities**

- Ask students to go through a newspaper with their family and identify any unknowns that they find. Use the situations to define variables.
- Search through magazines to find examples of tables that appear. Discuss what type of information is being displayed in the table.

Mathematical **Vocabulary** is highlighted and defined in context within each lesson. Key Vocabulary is listed before each chapter.

## Key Vocabulary

**English (Spanish)** *Introduce the most important terms from Chapter 1.*

**exponent (exponente)** A symbol written above and to the right of a quantity that tells how many times the quantity is multiplied by itself. For example: $t \cdot t \cdot t$ is written $t^3$. (p. 12)

**flowchart (flujograma)** A visual diagram that shows each step in evaluating an algebraic expression. (p. 18)

**like terms (términos semejantes)** In an algebraic expression, terms with the same variables raised to the same powers. (p. 62)

**formula (fórmula)** An algebraic "recipe" that shows how to calculate a particular quantity. (p. 35)

**distributive property (propiedad distributive)** The distributive property of multiplication over addition states that for any numbers $n$, $a$, and $b$, $n(a + b) = na + nb$. The distributive property of multiplication over subtraction states that for any numbers $n$, $a$, and $b$, $n(a - b) = na - nb$. (p. 49)

**equivalent expressions (expresiones equivalentes)** Expressions that always give the same result when the same values are substituted for the variables. For example, $2K + 6$ is equivalent to $2(K + 3)$. (p. 54)

**polynomial (polinomio)** A monomial or the sum or difference of two or more monomials. (p. 61)

LESSON 1.1

# Variables and Expressions

### Objectives

- To use variables to write expressions
- To understand the order of operations
- To practice using expressions to represent specific situations
- To use flowcharts to build expressions
- To solve equations using backtracking

## *Overview*

Change is all around us. Sometimes we can use mathematics to help us make sense of the changing world. In this lesson, students begin to understand how expressions develop by learning how sequences can be expressed as a rule. Next, students learn how algebraic expressions can be used to describe these kinds of situations. Then they use variables to show unknown quantities and practice using expressions to represent situations. In the last investigation, students use flowcharts to build expressions and to solve equations by backtracking.

The **Overview** provides a synopsis of the investigations in the lesson and makes connections to content presented before or after the lesson.

## *Advance Preparation*

You may want to use Chapter 1 Master 1, Chapter 1 Master 2, and Lesson 1.1 Master 1 to assist students in recording their answers.

| | Summary | Materials | On Your Own Exercises (pp. 21–29) | Assessment Opportunities |
|---|---|---|---|---|
| **Investigation 1** (p. 5) Pacing: 2 days | Students create sequences that correspond to a rule and write rules that correspond to a sequence | Chapter 1 Master 1 | Practice & Apply: 1–6<br>Connect & Extend: 31, 32<br>Mixed Review: 39 | • Share & Summarize (p. 8)<br>• Troubleshooting (p. 8) |
| **Investigation 2** (p. 9) Pacing: 2 days | Students write algebraic expressions to represent situations in context. | Lesson 1.1 Master 1 | Practice & Apply: 7–11<br>Connect & Extend: 33, 34<br>Mixed Review: 39 | • Share & Summarize (p. 12)<br>• Troubleshooting (p. 10) |
| **Investigation 3** (p. 12) Pacing: 2 days | Students learn conventions for representing operations and exponents in expressions and practice evaluating expressions. | | Practice & Apply: 12–21<br>Connect & Extend: 35, 36<br>Mixed Review: 39 | • Share & Summarize (p. 17)<br>• Troubleshooting (pp. 12, 14, 15) |
| **Investigation 4** (p. 17) Pacing: 1 day | Students use flowcharts to build expressions and to solve equations by backtracking. | Chapter 1 Master 2 | Practice & Apply: 22–30<br>Connect & Extend: 37<br>Mixed Review: 39 | • Share & Summarize (p. 20)<br>• Troubleshooting (pp. 19, 20) |

The concise table in the **Lesson Planner** includes a summary of the content, materials needed, and assessment opportunities for each investigation.

# Leveled Lesson Resources

CRM *Available in:* **Chapter 1 Resource Masters**

The page reductions on the **Leveled Lesson Resources** show the corresponding lesson worksheets, lesson masters, and the Quick Quiz from the Chapter Resource Masters (CRMs).

Also on TeacherWorks™ Lesson 1.1

## Study Guide and Intervention (p. 21) AL

**Lesson 1.1 Study Guide and Intervention**
***Variables and Expressions***

An algebraic expression contains variables, numbers, and at least one operation. To rewrite an algebraic expression, you can combine terms and use exponents. To evaluate an algebraic expression, replace each variable with its numeral value and then use the order of operations to simplify.

**Example 1** Rewrite the expression $y + y + y + 7$.

$y + y + y + 7 = 3y + 7$ Combine $y + y + y$ as $3y$.

**Example 2** Rewrite the expression $4 \cdot x \cdot x \cdot x$.

$4 \cdot x \cdot x \cdot x = 4 \cdot x^3$ Use an exponent to write $x \cdot x \cdot x$ as $x^3$.
$= 4x^3$ Combine $4 \cdot x^3$ as $4x^3$.

**Example 3** Evaluate $6x - 7$ for $x = 8$

$6x - 7 = 6(8) - 7$ Replace $x$ with 8.
$= 48 - 7$ Use the order of operations.
$= 41$ Subtract 7 from 48.

**Example 4** Evaluate $x^3 + 4$ for $x = 3$.

$x^3 + 4 = 3^3 + 4$ Replace $x$ with 3.
$= 27 + 4$ Use the order of operations.
$= 31$ Add 27 and 4.

**Exercises**

Rewrite each expression.

1. $c + c$ 2. $d \cdot d$ 3. $12 + u \cdot u \cdot u \cdot u$
4. $a + a + a + a - b \cdot b \cdot b$ 5. $6w + w + w$ 6. $9s \cdot s \cdot s \cdot s \cdot s$

Evaluate each expression for $a = 4$, $b = 2$, and $c = 7$.

7. $5b^3$ 8. $5 + 6c$ 9. $\frac{b^4}{4}$
10. $6a^2$ 11. $7c$ 12. $2b^5 + 6$

## Skills Practice (p. 22) AL OL

**Lesson 1.1 Skills Practice**
***Variables and Expressions***

Evaluate each expression for $w = 2$, $x = 3$, $y = 5$, and $z = 6$.

1. $2w$ 2. $y + 5$ 3. $9 - z$
4. $\frac{z}{3}$ 5. $3 + 4z$ 6. $6y - 5$
7. $y^2$ 8. $2x^3$ 9. $\frac{z}{2}$

Evaluate each expression for $m = 3$, $n = 7$, and $p = 9$.

10. $2m + 7$ 11. $12 - 3m$ 12. $5p$
13. $3.3p$ 14. $3.3p + 2$ 15. $2p + 3.3$
16. $20 + 2n$ 17. $20 - 2n$ 18. $\frac{n}{7}$
19. $n^2$ 20. $6m^2$ 21. $\frac{p^2}{3}$
22. $1.1 + n$ 23. $p - 8.1$ 24. $3.6m$
25. $3n^2 - 2$ 26. $3 + m^3$ 27. $2.1 + p^2$
28. $\frac{m^2}{9}$ 29. $\frac{2.5m + 2.5}{5}$ 30. $\frac{(n+2)^2}{3}$

## Problem-Solving Practice (p. 23) AL OL

**Lesson 1.1 Problem-Solving Practice**
***Variables and Expressions***

Solve.

1. **Field Trip** The seventh grade math classes are going on a field trip. The field trip will cost $7 per student. Write an expression to find the cost of the field trip for $s$ students. What is the total cost if 26 students go on the trip?
2. **Soccer** Jason earns $20 per game as a referee in youth soccer games. Write an expression to find how much money Jason will earn for refereeing any number of games. Let $n$ represent the number of games Jason has refereed. How much will he earn for refereeing 6 games?
3. **Profit** The city basketball league pays $150 to rent the arena for a basketball game. The league makes a profit by selling tickets to the game. Write an expression to show how much the basketball league makes at a game for any amount of money collected from ticket sales. Let $t$ represent the money collected. How much will the league earn if it collects $500?
4. **Savings** Kata has a savings account that contains $230. She decides to deposit $5 each month from her monthly earnings for baby-sitting. Write an expression to find how much money Kata will have in her savings account after $x$ months. Let $x$ represent the number of months. Then find out how much she will have in her account after 1 year.
5. **Money** Mr. Wilson has $2,500 in his savings account and $m$ dollars in his checking account. Write an expression that describes the total amount that he has in both accounts.
6. **Animals** There are 6 chickens and $h$ horses on Ruidoso Farm on any given day. Write an expression to represent the total number of legs on the animals. How many legs are there if 5 horses are on the farm?
7. **T-shirts** The band wants to order t-shirts. The t-shirts cost $15 each plus a shipping fee of $10. Write an expression to find the total cost of $c$ t-shirts.
8. **Temperature** The expression $\frac{9}{5}C + 32$, where C stands for temperature in degrees Celsius, is used to convert Celsius to Fahrenheit. If the temperature is 20 degrees Celsius, find the temperature in degrees Fahrenheit.

## Enrichment (p. 24) BL

**Lesson 1.1 Enrichment**
***Variables and Expressions***

**Albert Einstein's Famous Theory**

When you have solved the puzzle below, the letters in the heavy black boxes will spell the name of an important scientific theory proposed by Albert Einstein. His theory relates mass and energy.

**Use these clues to complete the puzzle below.**

1. A language of symbols.
2. To evaluate an expression, you ________ the variable with a number.
3. To find a specific numerical value for an algebraic expression.
4. An expression must contain at ________ one operation as well as variables or numbers.
5. The order of ________ helps you to know which operation to do first when evaluating an expression.
6. A symbol that stands for an unknown quantity.
7. The worth of something.
8. You call $2a + 3b$ an algebraic ________.
9. The process of finding the product of two numbers is called ________.
10. In an algebraic expression, you should ________ or divide before you add or subtract.

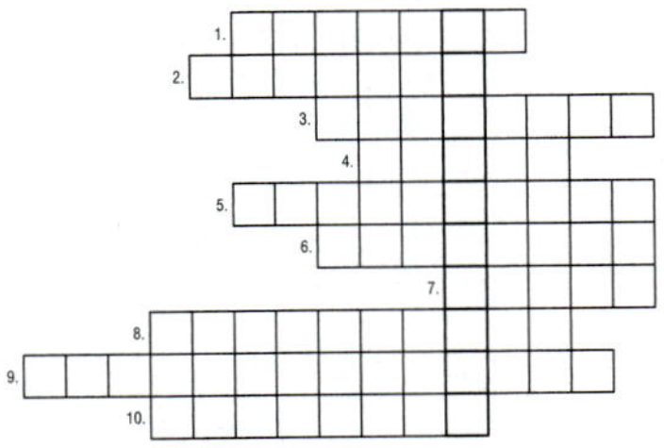

## Lesson Quick Quiz (p. 25) AL OL BL

**Lesson 1.1 Quick Quiz**

1. An arcade charges $1 for a rechargeable game card that you need to play each game. Each game costs $2.50. How many games will Eric play for $20?
2. Complete the flowchart. Then write the equation the flowchart represents.
3. Make a flowchart to represent $3(n + 1) - 4 = 65$. Use backtracking to find $n$.
4. Evaluate each of the following if $g = 4$.
   a. $2\frac{g}{5}$
   b. $\frac{2}{5}g$
   c. $3g^2$
   d. $\frac{g+2}{12}$

## Lesson Master 1 (p. 26)

**Lesson 1.1 Master 1**
***Variables and Expressions***

**Investigation 2 , Develop & Understand A**

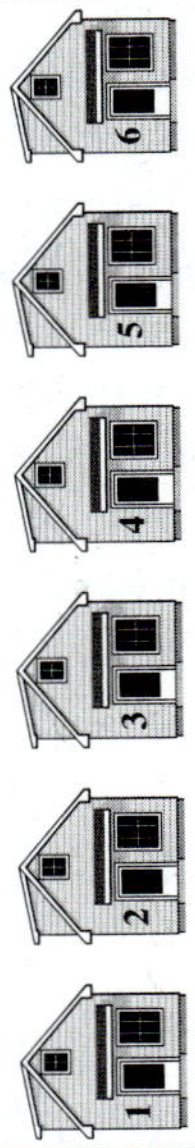

# Additional Lesson Resources

### Teacher Tech Tools
- TeacherWorks
- ExamView Assessment Suite
- Classroom Presentation Toolkit
- Advance Tracker

### Student Tech Tools
- StudentWorks Plus

Math Online eGlossary • Concepts in Motion

### Other Print Products
- Investigation Notebook and Reflection Journal
- Quick Review Math Handbook

## LESSON 1.1 Variables and Expressions

### Introduce

**Patterns** This lesson focuses on rules describing patterns in a variety of situations. Students write rules and then incorporate variables to express their rules using the language of algebra.

One way to lead into the Think & Discuss is to have students use Jing's rule to draw a sequence of shapes. You may want to have students use graph paper, or Chapter 1 Master 1, to draw a 2-unit-by-3-unit rectangle. Then write the rule, "Draw a rectangle twice the size of the preceding rectangle" on the board.

Ask students to make a sequence of rectangles that they believe fits this rule. If students are confused by the ambiguous rule, encourage them to do what seems to make the most sense.

Have them share their completed sequences and compare their response with Caroline's and Jahmal's sequences in the student text.

**Think & Discuss**

*Suggested Grouping: Individuals*

It is important that students recognize that a rule should clearly define only one sequence. You may want to discuss why a rule that defines more than one sequence could cause confusion. For example, if a person carpeting a floor was told to double the size of a rectangular piece of carpet, doubling it in "the wrong way" would produce a carpet that wouldn't fit the floor.

# LESSON 1.1 Variables and Expressions



Have you ever been given directions, only to find yourself lost? Most people would agree that being clear and precise is important in giving directions, as well as in other situations in and outside of mathematics. Consider this situation. Jing drew a rectangle. She then wrote a rule for generating a sequence of shapes starting with this rectangle.

*Rule:* Draw a rectangle twice the size of the preceding rectangle.

By following Jing's rule, Caroline drew this sequence.

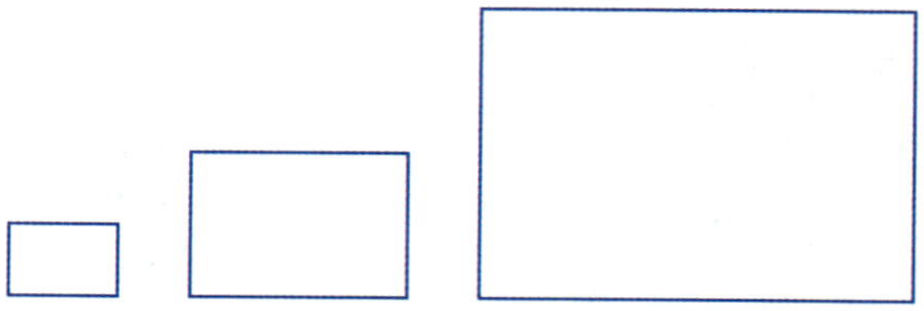

Jahmal followed Jing's rule and drew this sequence.

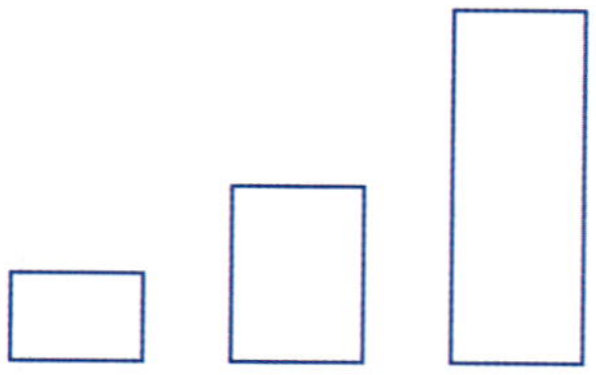

① Both could be correct. It depends on how you interpret "twice the size." Caroline doubled the dimensions of the rectangle at each stage. Jahmal doubled the area by doubling only the height.

③ Possible rule: Draw a rectangle with base and height twice the length of those of the preceding rectangle.

**Think & Discuss**

Could both sequences above be correct? Explain your answer. See ①.

Rosita also followed Jing's rule. The sequence she drew was different from both Caroline's and Jahmal's. What might Rosita's sequence look like? See ②.

Rewrite the rule so that Caroline's sequence is correct but Jahmal's is not. Try to make your rule clear enough that anyone following it would get the sequence Caroline did. See ③.

②

# Investigation 1 Sequences an

Each lesson is composed of **Investigations** that provide a mix of worked out examples, direct modeling through cartoons, and interactive exercise sets.

You have just seen how three studen
draw three different sequences. This
It can be interpreted in more than o
everyday life, it is often important to state rules in such a way that everyone will get the same result.

## Develop & Understand: A

1. Create a sequence of shapes in which each shape can be made by applying a rule to the preceding shape. On a blank sheet of paper, draw the first shape of your sequence and write the rule. Try to make your rule clear enough that anyone following it will get the sequence that you have in mind. Answers will vary.
2. Exchange starting shapes and rules with your partner. Follow your partner's rule to draw at least the next three shapes in the sequence. Answers will vary.
3. Compare the sequence you drew in Exercise 2 with your partner's original sequence. Are they the same? If not, describe how they are different and why. If either your rule or your partner's rule is ambiguous, work together to rewrite it to make it clear. Answers will vary.

Rules are often used to describe how two quantities are related. For example, a rule might tell you how to calculate one quantity from another.

### Example

For a school play, adult tickets cost \$10 and student tickets cost \$5. The rule for finding the revenues for the school play can be calculated using the following rule.

*Multiply the number of adults in attendance by 10. Multiply the number of students in attendance by 5. Add the two products.*

Suppose 210 adults and 103 students attend the play. You can apply the rule to calculate the play's revenues.

$$\begin{aligned} \text{Revenues} &= 210 \cdot 10 + 103 \cdot 5 \\ &= 2{,}100 + 515 \\ &= 2{,}615 \end{aligned}$$

So, the play revenues would be \$2,615.



# Investigation 1

***On Your Own Exercises***
Pages 21–29
Exercises 1–6, 31, 32

**Creating Rules** In the first part of the investigation, students create their own rules. The goal is for students to recognize the need for clarity and precision in a rule so that they can better write and apply rules in other situations.

In the second part of the investigation, students apply some rules taken from common situations. They also look at ways to approximate rules.

Before starting the investigation, introduce the term *ambiguous*. Some students may already know what this word means, but be sure that they understand its meaning as it relates to rules. One explanation you could give is that a rule is ambiguous if it can be interpreted in two or more different ways.

## Develop & Understand: A

*Suggested Grouping: Pairs*

▶ **Exercise 1** You may want students to use graph paper, or Chapter 1 Master 1, to help them draw shapes with the correct dimensions for their rules.

### Example

Point out that when a rule tells how two quantities are related, the rule can be used to find one quantity when given the other quantity. Also point out that it is often helpful to state a verbal rule in your own words.

## Reaching All Learners

**AL Approaching Level** If some students are having difficulty thinking of a sequence for Exercise 1, suggest they rewrite Jing's rule so that it is unambiguous and then apply it to a different shape. You might also have pairs that have successfully created a sequence and written an unambiguous rule share their patterns and strategies with students having difficulty.

Worked out **Examples** provide direct instruction when appropriate for the content.

## Develop & Understand: B

*Suggested Grouping: Individuals*

▶ **Exercise 5** Some students may not be familiar with bulk, or loose, tea. Make sure students understand that no matter how many people are having tea, Hannah's grandmother always includes one extra spoonful in the teapot.

▶ **Exercise 6** Encourage students to list or reorganize the relevant information in the exercise to help them distinguish between the various times, temperatures, and weights that are mentioned.

Students apply the mathematics concepts and skills in the interactive exercise sets found in each **Develop and Understand.**

5a. Five spoonfuls
5b. Possible answer: Use one spoonful for each person.
5c. For the answer given in Part b, four spoonfuls are needed.

**Real-World Link**
It is believed that people first began drinking hot tea more than 5,000 years ago in China. Iced tea was not introduced until 1904 at the St. Louis World's Fair. An Englishman named Richard Blechynden added ice to the drink because no one was buying his hot tea.

5d. Possible answer: Use one and a half spoonfuls for each person and two extra. This would give eight spoonfuls of tea for four people.

In Exercises 4–6, you will look at some common rules for finding one quantity from another.

## Develop & Understand: B

**4.** You can use the following rule to estimate how many miles away a bolt of lightning struck.

*Count the seconds between seeing the lightning flash and hearing the thunder. Then divide by 5.*

Use the rule to estimate how far away a bolt of lightning struck if you counted 15 seconds between the flash and the thunder. 3 mi

**5.** Hannah's grandmother uses the following rule to figure out how many spoonfuls of tea to put in her teapot.

*Use one spoonful for each person and then add one extra spoonful.*

**a.** How much tea would Hannah's grandmother use for four people?

**b.** Hannah's grandfather thinks this rule makes the tea too strong. Make up a rule that he might like better.

**c.** Using your rule from Part b, how many spoonfuls of tea are needed for four people?

**d.** Hannah's cousin, Amy, likes her tea much stronger than Hannah's grandmother does. Create a rule Amy might like. Use it to figure out how many spoonfuls of tea would be needed for four people.

**6.** A cookbook gives the following rule for roasting beef.

*Cook for 20 minutes at 475°F. Then lower the heat to 375°F and cook for 15 minutes per pound. If you like rare beef, remove the roast from the oven. If you like it medium, cook it an additional 7 minutes. If you like it well done, cook it an additional 14 minutes.*

What is the total cooking time for a four-pound beef roast if you like it medium? 87 min, or 1 h 27 min

The rules in Exercises 4–6 are fairly simple. Many rules involve more complicated calculations. If you do not need to find an exact value, you can sometimes use a simpler rule to find an approximation.



## Reaching All Learners

**BL** **Beyond Level** Challenge students to use the rules in the opposite direction. For example, in Exercise 4, determine how many seconds would elapse between the lightning flash and the thunder if a storm is 10 miles away. 50 seconds

**Reaching All Learners** strategies suggest adjustments for lessons and tailor instruction to encompass a wide variety of learning styles and modalities.

## Develop & Understand: C

**7.** You can convert temperatures from degrees Celsius (°C) to degrees Fahrenheit (°F) using this rule.

*Multiply the degrees Celsius by 1.8 and add 32.*

Copy and complete the table to show some Celsius temperatures and their Fahrenheit equivalents.

| Degrees Celsius | Degrees Fahrenheit |
|---|---|
| 0 | 32 |
| 10 | 50 |
| 20 | 68 |
| 30 | 86 |
| 40 | 104 |
| 50 | 122 |

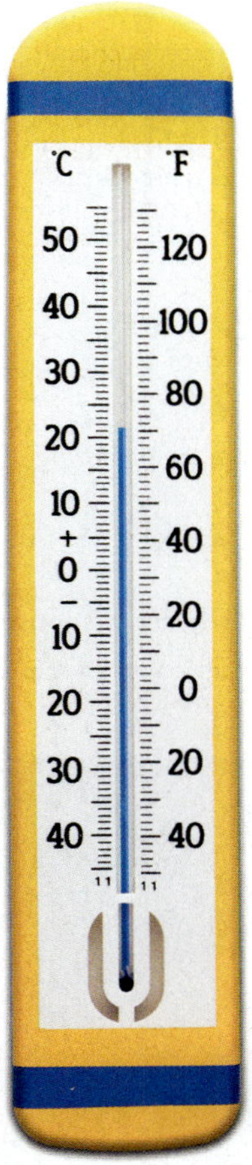


**8.** The Lopez family spent its summer vacation in Canada. Canadians use degrees Celsius to report temperatures. Ms. Lopez used the following rule to convert Celsius temperatures to Fahrenheit temperatures.

*Multiply the degrees Celsius by 2 and add 30.*

This rule makes it easy to do mental calculations, but it gives only an *approximation* of the actual Fahrenheit temperature.

**a.** Complete this table to show the approximate Fahrenheit temperatures this rule gives for the listed Celsius temperatures.

| Degrees Celsius | Approximate Degrees Fahrenheit |
|---|---|
| 0 | 30 |
| 10 | 50 |
| 20 | 70 |
| 30 | 90 |
| 40 | 110 |
| 50 | 130 |

**b.** For which Celsius temperature do the two rules above give the same result? 10°C

**c.** For which Celsius temperatures in the table does Ms. Lopez's rule give a Fahrenheit temperature that is too high?
20°C, 30°C, 40°C, and 50°C



## Develop & Understand: C

*Suggested Grouping: Individuals*

▶ **Exercise 8** Introduce the estimation strategy of approximate rules. As with all approximations, the purpose of an approximate rule is to have an efficient way of getting a good idea of the result. However, what makes an efficient and good approximation depends on the individual and the situation, so there may be many different valid approximations to a rule.

## *Reaching All Learners*

**BL** **Beyond Level** Ask students to write a rule that could be used to find an approximation of the Celsius temperature when given a temperature in degrees Fahrenheit using the guess-check-and-improve problem-solving strategy. Have them use the Fahrenheit temperatures they found in Exercise 7 to test their rules. Then have them evaluate how well their rules approximate the Celsius temperatures and revise the rules if needed. Possible rule: Subtract 30 and divide by 2.

▶ **Exercise 10** Discuss advantages and disadvantages of approximate rules.

## Share & Summarize

In **Question 1**, students need to be familiar with a number line. You may want to review with students what the positive number line looks like and how you move along it. You also may want to have students share the different rules they wrote and have the class decide whether the new rules are truly unambiguous.

**Question 2** asks students to write a rule for a common situation. You may also want to have them write an approximate rule for finding the cost of any weight (in pounds) of bananas. Have them explain why they chose this approximation. Possible rules: Multiply the weight, in pounds, by 50 cents to find the cost in cents. Divide the weight, in pounds, by 2 to find the cost in dollars. Or, count $1 for every 2 pounds of bananas.

The **Share & Summarize** questions signal the end of each Investigation and are designed to bring closure to the day's activity.

**9.** One day, the Lopez family flew from Toronto, where the temperature was 37°C, to Winnipeg, where the temperature was 23°C.

**a.** Use the rule from Exercise 7 to find the exact Fahrenheit temperatures for the two cities. 98.6°F, 73.4°F

**b.** Use Ms. Lopez's rule from Exercise 8 to find the approximate Fahrenheit temperatures for the two cities. 104°F, 76°F

**c.** For which city did Ms. Lopez's rule give the more accurate temperature? Winnipeg

**10.** Look back at your answers to Exercises 8 and 9. What happens to the Fahrenheit approximation as the Celsius temperature increases? The approximation becomes less accurate.

## Share & Summarize

**1.** Below are the first term and a rule for a sequence.

*First term:* 20

*Rule:* Write the number that is two units from the preceding number on the number line.

**a.** Give the first few terms of two different sequences that fit the rule.

**b.** Rewrite the rule so that only one of your sequences is correct.

**2.** At the corner market, bananas cost 49¢ a pound. Write a rule for calculating the cost of a bunch of bananas. Multiply 49¢ by the number of pounds.

1a. Possible sequences: 20, 22, 24, 26, 28, ... 20, 18, 16, 14, 12, ... 20, 22, 20, 22, 20, 22, ...

1b. Possible rule: Add 2 to the preceding number. Only the first sequence fits this rule.

### Real-World Link

About fifty percent of Toronto's two-and-a-half million population was born outside of Canada, making the city one of the most multicultural cities in the world. Toronto is the capital of the province of Ontario.

## Troubleshooting

Some students may still have difficulty seeing the different ways that a rule can be interpreted. The following activity is fun and can help emphasize the point.

Divide the class in half. Give each group a different geometric design, not letting the other group see the design. Ask students to write clear directions explaining how to make the design. Then pair one student from each group and have students take turns reading the directions for their design while the partner draws it. Stress that they must not say anything about the design other than the directions. Then compare the drawings to the originals.

**Troubleshooting** includes common misconceptions or procedural errors students might make and solutions to overcome those errors.

## Investigation 2 Write Expressions

**Vocabulary**

algebraic expression

variable

You have seen that algebraic expressions can be used to represent situations in which a quantity changes, or *varies.* In this investigation, you will write algebraic expressions to describe many other situations.

### Develop & Understand: A

Jay, Lamar, Davina, Bart, Tara, and Freda live in a row of houses that are numbered 1 to 6. Use the clues below to help you solve Exercises 1–3.

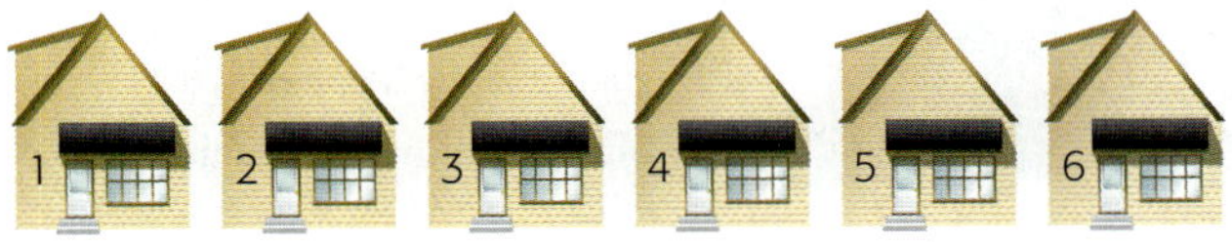

- Jay owns some DVDs.
- Lamar lives next to Jay and three houses from Freda. Lamar has 2 fewer DVDs than Jay.
- Davina lives on the other side of Jay and has three times as many DVDs as Lamar.
- Bart lives in house 2 and has 4 more DVDs than Jay.
- If Tara had 13 more DVDs, she would have four times as many as Jay.
- Jay acquired all of his DVDs from Freda, who lives in house 6. Freda had 17 DVDs before she gave $p$ of them to Jay.
- The person in house 5 owns the most DVDs.

1. Determine who lives in each house. (Hint: Focus on where the people live. Ignore the other information.)

2. Let $p$ stand for the number of DVDs that Jay has. Write an expression containing the variable $p$ for the number of DVDs that each person has.

3. Use your expressions to help determine how many DVDs that Jay has. (Hint: Experiment with different values of $p$. Only one value of $p$ gives the person in house 5 the most DVDs.) 6

1. 1: Tara; 2: Bart; 3: Lamar; 4: Jay; 5: Davina; 6: Freda
2. Jay: $p$; Lamar: $p - 2$; Davina: $3(p - 2)$; Bart: $p + 4$; Tara: $4p - 13$; Freda: $17 - p$



## Investigation 2

***On Your Own Exercises***
Pages 21–29
Exercises 7–11, 33, 34

**Modeling Expressions** In this investigation, students model algebraic expressions. They begin to explore situations with unknown quantities as well as those with quantities that can change. Students are immersed in situations where they must write expressions and then find values for the expressions that fit the parameters of the problem. Students are asked to think of situations that can be described by a given algebraic expression.

### Develop & Understand: A

*Suggested Grouping: Small Groups*

▶ **Exercise 1** Students will not need to use their algebra skills to determine which person lives in each house. They can use logical reasoning to solve the problem. Most will start by placing Bart in house number 2 and Freda in house number 6 because that information is given in the clues. Students may then place Lamar, Jay, Davina, and Tara respectively. You may wish to use Lesson 1.1 Master 1, Row of Houses, to help students record their answers in a logical manner.

▶ **Exercises 1 and 2** You may want to suggest that students plan how they will organize their data before they start to solve the problem. Some students may use a table to organize their data.

▶ **Exercise 3** Students evaluate expressions for different values of $p$ to find what value of $p$ will result in Davina having the most CDs. Students may find it helpful to organize their data in a table.

### Reaching All Learners

**OL On Level** Read aloud important information and hints so that students have a chance to use both auditory and visual skills in understanding the problem. For example, read aloud and emphasize the hint in Exercise 1 that suggests students ignore any information not needed to solve the problem, such as how many CDs are owned by each person.

## Develop & Understand: B

*Suggested Grouping: Pairs*

▶ **Exercise 4** Note that the variable refers to the number of pounds, rather than merely to the weight, emphasizing that it is the *number* that is represented by a variable.

**Real-World Link**

Ask questions such as the following:

- About how many feet long is a newborn? A little less than 2 feet
- About how many feet long is the person after 4 years? A little more than 3 feet
- How old is a person who is three times his or her birth length? 12 years old

**Real World Links** engage students with interesting facts and add to the problem-solving context with examples from real life.

In Exercises 1–3, the variable $p$ could have only one value. The variable was used to represent the unknown quantity: Jay's number of DVDs. As you saw, it is helpful to be able to use a variable to represent an unknown quantity. Now you have two ways to think about variables. A **variable** is a quantity that can change or an unknown quantity. An **algebraic expression** contains at least one variable and may contain operations.

## Develop & Understand: B

**For these situations, the variables represent unknown quantities rather than quantities that change.**

**4.** Esteban bought $N$ apples.

**a.** Granny Smith bought four times as many apples as Esteban. Write an expression to show how many apples she bought. $4N$

**b.** Esteban used 11 apples in a pie. How many does he have left? $N - 11$

**5.** Suppose a bag of potatoes weighs $t$ pounds. In Parts a–d, write an expression for the number of pounds in each bag of vegetables below. Each expression should include the variable $t$.

**a.** a bag of carrots weighing 3 pounds more than a bag of potatoes $t + 3$

**b.** a bag of corn weighing 2 pounds less than a bag of potatoes $t - 2$

**c.** a bag of broccoli weighing 5 pounds less than a bag of corn $(t - 2) - 5$, or $t - 7$

**d.** a bag of beans weighing 3 pounds more than a bag of broccoli $(t - 7) + 3$, or $t - 4$

**e.** Order the five bags from lightest to heaviest. Broccoli, beans, corn, potatoes, carrots

**Real-World Link**

The average newborn is about 20 inches long. It takes people about 4 years to double their length at birth and 8 more years to grow to three times their birth length. A person "only about 3.5 times the height of a newborn" is quite tall.

**6.** Baby Leanne is $L$ inches tall. Write expressions, in terms of the variable $L$, to represent the heights in inches of the members of Leanne's family.

**a.** her 4-year-old brother Tim, who is twice as tall as Leanne $2L$

**b.** her 6-year-old sister Kerry, who is 5 inches taller than Tim $2L + 5$

**c.** her mother, who is 15 inches shorter than four times Leanne's height $4L - 15$

**d.** her father, who is 15 inches shorter than twice Kerry's height $2(2L + 5) - 15$, or $4L - 5$

**e.** Baby Leanne is about 20 inches long. Check the expressions you wrote in Parts a–d by substituting this value and determining whether the heights are reasonable. Tim is 40 in., or 3 ft 4 in.; Kerry is 45 in., or 3 ft 9 in.; her mother is 65 in., or 5 ft 5 in.; her father is 75 in., or 6 ft 3 in.; The heights seem reasonable.



## Troubleshooting

Watch for students who use the number of pounds of a bag of potatoes as the basis for writing the expression in Exercises 5c and 5d. For example, some students may not read the problem carefully and decide that a bag of broccoli is 5 lb lighter than a bag of potatoes, when it is actually lighter than a bag of corn. These students would write the expression as $t - 5$ instead of $(t - 2) - 5$, or $t - 7$. Encourage students to make a list of the vegetables and the expression showing how many pounds each bag weighs for a quick reference.

7. Sasha has $k$ nickels in her pocket.

a. Write an expression for the value of Sasha's nickels in cents. Find the value of the expression for $k = 4$. $5k$, 20¢

b. Sasha also has 60¢ in other coins. Write an expression for the total value, in cents, of all her change. $5k + 60$

c. Find the total value for $k = 5$ and $k = 12$. 85¢, \$1.20

d. Yesterday, Sasha had $k$ nickels in her pocket and no other money. She spent 70¢ on pencils. What was the total value of her coins after she bought the pencils? Could $k$ be *any* whole number? Why? $5k - 70$; No; since 70¢ is 14 nickels, $k$ must be 14 or greater.

8. Malik rides the city bus to school and back each weekday. The bus fare is $F$ cents each way. He starts each week with \$5 for bus fare. Write an expression for each of the following.

a. the amount, in cents, Malik spends on bus fare in one day $2F$

b. the amount he has left when he gets home on Monday $500 - 2F$

c. the total bus fare he has spent by lunch time on Thursday $7F$

d. the amount of bus fare he spends each week $10F$

e. the amount he has left at the end of the week $500 - 10F$

f. What would happen if $F$ was 60? Possible answers: \$5 would not be enough for a week's bus fare.

9. You can sometimes make sense of an expression by inventing a meaning for its symbols. For example, for the expression $k - 4$, you can let $k$ represent the number of kittens in a pet shop. Then $k - 4$ could stand for the number of kittens in the shop after four have been sold.

Interpret each expression below by creating a meaning for the symbols.

a. $d + 10$

b. $3a$

c. $f - 4$

9a. Possible answer: If I have $d$ dollars, $d + 10$ is the number of dollars I have after my brother gives me 10 more dollars.

9b. Possible answer: If $a$ is the number of apples picked by each student, $3a$ is the number picked by 3 students.

9c. Possible answer: If a leaky rediator starts with $f$ quarts of fluid, $f - 4$ is the amount of fluid left after 4 quarts have escaped.

▶ **Exercises 7 and 8** Students are asked to consider possible restrictions on given variables. This may be a student's first exposure to the concept of domain. Encourage students to talk about these limitations. After discussing these exercises, you may want to have students identify any limitations on other expressions they have written for bags-and-blocks situations in prior investigations.

▶ **Exercise 7** Students need to realize that Sasha must have at least 70¢, or 14 nickels, in order to purchase the pencil. It follows that when $k$ is less than 14, the problem doesn't make sense.

▶ **Exercise 8** Students are exposed to an upper limitation. If the fare is greater than 50¢, then the \$5 that Neeraj has will not be enough money to ride the bus 10 times in one week.

▶ **Exercise 9** Students may wish to share their scenarios with the class. This would provide a forum to check for the reasonableness of the situations. The variety of situations may help students realize how they can use expressions in their lives.

## Share & Summarize

Have students discuss their answers to Share & Summarize in pairs. You may want to have students decide whether there are any values of $h$ that do not make sense. Some students may note that while $h$ must be greater than or equal to 0, its value does not have to be a whole number since someone may study for part of an hour.

## Investigation 3

***On Your Own Exercises***
Pages 21–29
Exercises 12–21, 35, 36

**Exponents** This investigation introduces the conventions used to write and evaluate expressions. Students will study ways to write repeated multiplication as $a \cdot a \cdot a \cdot a$ or as $a^4$. Students then use the order of operations to evaluate expressions.

Discuss the use of an *exponent.* Be sure students understand that an exponent tells how many times a number or a variable is multiplied by itself.

You may wish to write the following two expressions on the board and discuss with students the standard notation for writing expressions:

- $d \cdot d \cdot d$ is written $d^3$. Students should know that this can be read as *d cubed* or as *d to the third power.*
- $a \cdot 4 \cdot a$ is written $4a^2$, **not** as $a^2 4$ or $4aa$ or $a4a$. Students should be aware of the two conventions illustrated in this expression: using exponents and writing the number factor before the variable factor.

**Math Link**
An expression with base $t$ and exponent 2 is read as *t squared.*

Math Links remind students about information they should already know.

## Share & Summarize

Let $h$ represent the number of hours Ella spent on homework last week.

1. Jack spent half as much time on his homework as Ella had on hers. Write an expression for the number of hours he spent.
2. Describe a situation that the expression $2h + 1$ might represent.
3. Write another algebraic expression containing the variable $h$. Describe a situation that your expression might represent.
Possible answer: $\frac{1}{7}h$ is the average number of hours Ella spent doing homework each day last week.

1. $\frac{1}{2}h$
2. Possible answer: Leslie spent twice as much time as Ella did on her homework, plus 1 hour.

## Investigation 3 Evaluate Expressions

**Vocabulary**
exponent

When you study mathematics, it is important to know the shortcuts that are used for writing expressions. You already know that when you want to show a number times a variable, you can leave out the multiplication sign. Instead of $6 \times t$ or $6 \cdot t$, you can write $6t$. Note that the number is normally placed before the variable.

What if you want to show that the variable $t$ is multiplied by itself? You could write $t \times t$, $t \cdot t$, or $tt$. However, an **exponent** is usually used to tell how many times a quantity is multiplied by itself. So, $t \cdot t$ is written $t^2$, and $t \cdot t \cdot t$ is written $t^3$.

**Math Link**
In the expression $t^2$, $t$ is called the base and the $^2$ is the exponent.

Here are some other examples.

- The expression $2 \cdot s \cdot s \cdot s$ is written $2s^3$.
- The expression $m \cdot 5 \cdot m$ is written $5m^2$.
- The expression $2p \cdot p \cdot p$ is written $2p^3$.
- The expression $x \cdot x \cdot y \cdot 7$ is written $7x^2y$ or $7yx^2$.

It is also important to understand the rules for *evaluating,* or finding the value of, expressions. You learned some of these rules when you studied arithmetic.



## Troubleshooting

If students are having difficulty writing expressions, suggest that they first assign a value for the variable and then write a numerical expression. They can use the numerical expressions to help find any patterns or rules.

① 47, 4 (Note: Some students may not use the correct order of operations.)

② Answers will vary. (Note: Most calculators will use the correct order of operations, but some will not.)

## Think & Discuss

Evaluate each expression without using a calculator. See ①.

$$7 + 8 \cdot 5 \qquad 7 - 6 \div 2$$

Now use your calculator to evaluate each expression. Did you get the same answers with the calculator as you did without? See ②.

Most calculators will multiply and divide before they add or subtract. This *order of operations* is a convention that everyone uses to avoid confusion. If you want to indicate that the operations should be done in a different order, you need to use parentheses.

Look at how the use of parentheses affects the value of the expressions below.

$$2 + 3 \cdot 5 = 2 + 15 = 17 \qquad 7 - 6 \div 2 = 7 - 3 = 4$$

$$(2 + 3) \cdot 5 = 5 \cdot 5 = 25 \qquad (7 - 6) \div 2 = 1 \div 2 = \frac{1}{2}$$

Which expression below means "add 4 and 6 and then multiply by $n$"? Which means "multiply 6 by $n$ and then add 4"? $(4 + 6)n$, $4 + 6n$

$$4 + 6n \qquad (4 + 6)n$$

There are also rules for evaluating expressions involving exponents.

**Cartoons** provide direct modeling of mathematical reasoning and problem-solving strategies in accessible and inviting formats for middle grades students.

## Think & Discuss

*Suggested Grouping: Whole Class*

As part of a whole-class discussion, have students evaluate the first two expressions in this section. Record volunteers' answers on the board. Then have students use their calculators to evaluate the expression and compare their answers to those on the board.

Discuss the *order of operations* with students, explaining that it is a convention that was devised so that everyone calculates expressions in the same way.

Students need to know whether or not their calculators compute using the order of operations. For calculators that don't follow this convention, students will have to learn to insert parentheses when entering expressions in the calculators in order to get the correct answer. For example, on a calculator that does not automatically multiply first, $2 + 8 \cdot 9$ would have to be entered as $2 + (8 \cdot 9)$ or as $8 \cdot 9 + 2$.

Write $2 + 3 \cdot 5$ on the board. Ask students questions such as these:

- In the expression $2 + 3 \cdot 5$, which operation do you perform first? Second? Why? Multiply 3 and 5 first. Add 2 and 15 second. This follows the order of operations.

Challenge students to find a way to rewrite the expression $2 + 3 \cdot 5$ so that everyone would add 2 and 3 before they multiply. Lead the discussion so that students suggest putting parentheses around $2 + 3$, so, $(2 + 3) \cdot 5 = 25$.

Then ask students:

- Which expression means add 4 and 6 and then multiply by $n$: $4 + 6n$ or $(4 + 6)n$? $(4 + 6)n$

## Think & Discuss

*Suggested Grouping: Pairs*

Have students think about whether Zach or Malik has made the right calculation.

If students think the expressions are the same, have them substitute a number for *m,* such as 2, and evaluate the expression Zach's way, $4 \cdot (2)^2 = 16$, and then Malik's way, $(4 \cdot 2)^2 = 64$.

Explain that in order to keep expressions like $4m^2$ unambiguous, we agree to the convention that exponents are evaluated before multiplication. In this expression, we square *m* before we multiply by 4.

Students should recognize that once parentheses are inserted around 4*m* in $4m^2$, the expression $(4m)^2$ means *take 4m and square it.*

Think & Discuss questions help introduce the lesson by sparking ideas and promoting discussion.

## Develop & Understand: A

*Suggested Grouping: Individuals*

- **Exercises 1–8** Students simplify addition and multiplication expressions. They need to use the order of operations to correctly place parentheses.
- **Exercises 9–12** Students evaluate expressions containing exponents.
- **Exercise 13** In this exercise, various misinterpretations of the expression $3t^2$ are dealt with explicitly. Have students report their thinking to the whole class. It is especially important that students analyze the errors in the other four calculations so that they see where mistakes are often made in evaluating expressions.

① No; for $m = 2$, the first statement gives $2^2 \cdot 4 = 16$, and the second gives $(4 \cdot 2)^2 = 64$.

## Think & Discuss

Who is correct, Malik or Zach? Malik

Does "find $m^2$ and multiply it by 4" give the same result as "find $4m$ and square it?" Try it for $m = 2$ to see. See ①.

Think again about who is correct, Malik or Zach. Then add parentheses to the expression $4m^2$ so it will give the other boy's calculation. $(4m)^2$

## Develop & Understand: A

**Rewrite each expression without using multiplication or addition signs.**

| | | |
|---|---|---|
| **1.** $r + r$   $2r$ | **2.** $r \cdot r$   $r^2$ | **3.** $t + t + t$   $3t$ |
| **4.** $5 \cdot g \cdot g \cdot g$   $5g^3$ | **5.** $5s + s$   $6s$ | **6.** $2.5m \cdot m$   $2.5m^2$ |

**7.** Copy the expression $6 + 3 \cdot 4$.

**a.** Insert parentheses, if necessary, so the resulting expression equals 18. Parentheses are not necessary.

**b.** Insert parentheses, if necessary, so the resulting expression equals 36. $(6 + 3) \cdot 4$

**8.** Write an expression that means "take a number, multiply it by 6, and cube the result." $(6m)^3$

**Evaluate each expression for $r = 3$.**

| | |
|---|---|
| **9.** $5r^2$   45 | **10.** $(5r)^2$   225 |
| **11.** $2r^4$   162 | **12.** $(2r)^4$   1,296 |

**13.** When Kate, Jin Lee, Darnell, Zach, and Maya tried to find the value of $3t^2$ for $t = 7$, they came up with five different answers. Only one of their answers is correct.

Kate: $t^2 = 49$, so $3t^2 = 349$

Jin Lee: $3t^2 = 3 \cdot 7^2 = 42$

Darnell: $3t^2 = 3 \cdot 7^2 = 3 \cdot 49 = 147$

Zach: $3t^2 = 37^2 = 1{,}369$

Maya: $3t^2 = 3 \cdot 7^2 = 21^2 = 441$

**a.** Which student evaluated the expression correctly? Darnell

**b.** What mistake did each of the other students make in thinking about the expression?

13b. Kate found that $t^2$ was 49, but then she put 3 in front of 49 instead of multiplying 49 by 3. Jin Lee interpreted $7^2$ as $7 \cdot 2$, rather than as $7 \cdot 7$. When Zach substituted 7 for *t*, he wrote $37^2$ instead of $3(7^2)$. Maya evaluated 3*t* and then squared the result, rather than finding $t^2$ and multiplying the result by 3.



## Troubleshooting

Watch for students who confuse addition and multiplication of variables. Suggest that they substitute numbers for variables in Exercises 1 and 2 to see whether the expressions are equal.

You have explored ways of expressing multiplication and repeated multiplication, like $3t$ and $t^2$. Now you will look at some ways to express division.

### Example

Three friends won a prize of $P$ dollars in the community talent show. They want to share the prize money equally. There are several ways to express the number of dollars each student should receive.

All three expressions in the example above are correct, but the forms $\frac{1}{3}P$ and $\frac{P}{3}$ are used more commonly in algebra than $P \div 3$.

## Develop & Understand: B

**14.** In the prize-money example, $P$ stands for the dollar amount of the prize, and $\frac{P}{3}$ shows each friend's share.

**a.** If the prize is \$30, how much will each friend get? \$10

**b.** Suppose $\frac{P}{3} = \$25$. How much total prize money is there? \$75

**Find the value of each expression for $k = 5$.**

**15.** $k^3 - 2$ 123

**16.** $12 - k$ 7

**17.** $\frac{k^2 - 1}{12}$ 2

**18.** $\frac{7k}{5}$ 7

**19.** $\frac{7}{5}k$ 7



### Example

Have students read the example in the student text showing different ways to express division. The cartoon presents conventions for representing division in expressions. Students need to understand that although the expressions all look different, the expressions are equivalent in terms of their meaning.

Some students may have difficulty with the idea that $\frac{P}{3}$, $P \div 3$, and $\frac{1}{3}P$ represent the same quantity because they have difficulty with the arithmetic equivalents, like $\frac{5}{3}$, $5 \div 3$, and $\frac{1}{3} \cdot 5$. Some may need to substitute numbers for $P$ to be convinced.

## Develop & Understand: B

*Suggested Grouping: Individuals*

▶ **Exercise 17** You may wish to discuss this exercise as a class. Some students may have difficulty evaluating the expression. These students may square and divide before they subtract, thinking

$$(5 \cdot 5) \div 12 - 1 = \frac{25}{12} - 1 = \frac{13}{12}.$$

Remind them that the numerator and the denominator of a fraction each represent one value and should be evaluated separately. Only after evaluating the numerator can the fraction be evaluated.

## Troubleshooting

In Exercises 18 and 19, watch for students who do not realize that $\frac{7k}{5}$ is the same as $\frac{7}{5}k$.

In the first case, 7 is multiplied by $k$ and then the result is divided by 5. In the second case, 7 is divided by 5, and the result is multiplied by $k$.

If students don't see this, ask them to substitute a value for $k$ in each expression. This will bring up some conversation about the fact that the order in which multiplication and division are performed in these expressions doesn't make a difference.

## Develop & Understand: C

*Suggested Grouping: Pairs*

▶ **Exercise 21a** Some students might be uncomfortable that the answer is an algebraic expression, rather than a single number. Reassure these students that although each person's earnings will be a specific amount, that amount will vary based on the number of cards sold. Since we don't know the number of cards sold, the earnings are best expressed using a variable.

▶ **Exercises 22–24** Students begin to work with multi-variable expressions, where the number of friends, cards, and price per card may vary. It is important for students to realize that there are several quantities in these problems that can vary.

**Wrap-Up** The *What if?* format is useful in illustrating this variance as students build on a given situation. For example, after writing the expression for **Exercise 22a**, students might ask themselves, what if the number of friends in the business changes? How would the expression change? This may help them solve **Exercise 22b**.

Likewise, to solve **Exercise 22c**, they may ask, what if the number of cards sold changes? How would the expression change? Asking these questions can help them see exactly what is changing in each problem situation.

You might mention to students that they should be asking *What if?* questions in other situations as well in order to develop this questioning technique as a habit of mind.

## Develop & Understand: C

Kate, Zach, Maya, and Darnell earn money by selling greeting cards that they create on a computer.

**20.** In their first week in business, they sold 19 cards for $B$ dollars each. They equally shared the money that they collected.

**a.** Write an expression that describes each friend's share. $\frac{19B}{4}$

**b.** What is the value of your expression if $B$ is \$2.00? If $B$ is \$2.60? If $B$ is \$3.00? \$9.50, \$12.35, \$14.25

**c.** The friends wrote the equation $\frac{19B}{4} = 7.60$ to describe what happened their first week in business. What does the equation indicate about the money that each friend made? Each friend earned \$7.60.

**d.** Starting with the equation in Part c, find how much the friends charged for each card. \$1.60

**21.** This week, the friends received orders for 16 greeting cards.

**a.** If they sell the cards for $B$ dollars each, how much will each friend earn? $\frac{16B}{4}$

**b.** The friends would like to earn \$12 apiece for selling the 16 cards. How much will they have to charge for each card? \$3

**22.** In Exercises 20 and 21, the price of a greeting card was the only variable. Kate wants to be able to vary three amounts, the number of friends working on the cards, the number of cards, and the charge per card, and still be able to calculate how much each person would make.

Write an expression for how much each friend would earn in each situation.

**a.** Three friends sell 19 greeting cards for $B$ dollars each $\frac{19B}{3}$

**b.** $F$ friends sell 19 cards for $B$ dollars each $\frac{19B}{F}$

**c.** Four friends sell $P$ cards for $B$ dollars each $\frac{PB}{4}$

**d.** $F$ friends sell $P$ cards for $B$ dollars each $\frac{PB}{F}$

**23.** Suppose the price per card increases by \$2, from $B$ to $(B + 2)$. Write an expression for how much $F$ friends would each make after selling $P$ cards at this new price. $\frac{P(B+2)}{F}$

**24.** Suppose the price per card increases by $K$ dollars, from $B$ to $(B + K)$. Write an expression for how much $F$ friends would each make after selling $P$ cards at this new price. $\frac{P(B+K)}{F}$



## *Reaching* All Learners

**BL Beyond Level** Have students explain why the trick in Question 1 works. Students may note that some operations are undone. For example, the multiplication, or squaring, done in step 1 is undone in step 3. The division in step 3 undoes the multiplication of $n$ and 2. At this point, the expression is some number plus two, or $n + 2$. When the number, $n$, is subtracted in step 4, the result is 2.

## Share & Summarize

1. Write an algebraic expression that describes this set of calculations.

   Step 1. Take some number and square it. $\frac{n^2 + 2n}{n} - n$

   Step 2. Add 2 times the starting number.

   Step 3. Divide that result by your starting number.

   Step 4. Subtract your starting number.

2. Write an expression that describes this set of calculations.

   Step 1. Take some number and triple it. $10 - \frac{n - 3n}{n^2}$

   Step 2. Subtract your result from your starting number.

   Step 3. Divide that result by the square of your starting number.

   Step 4. Subtract the result from 10.

3. Find the value of $\frac{5 + 15x^2}{13}$ when $x = 2$. 5

**Math Link**

If you follow the steps in Question 1 carefully, your answer will be 2 when $n$ is any positive number. Try it with your expression.

## Investigation 4 Flowcharts

**Vocabulary**

backtracking

flowchart

In this investigation, you will use a tool that can help you evaluate expressions and solve equations.

In preparing for a party, Maya bought five bags of bagels and four extra bagels.

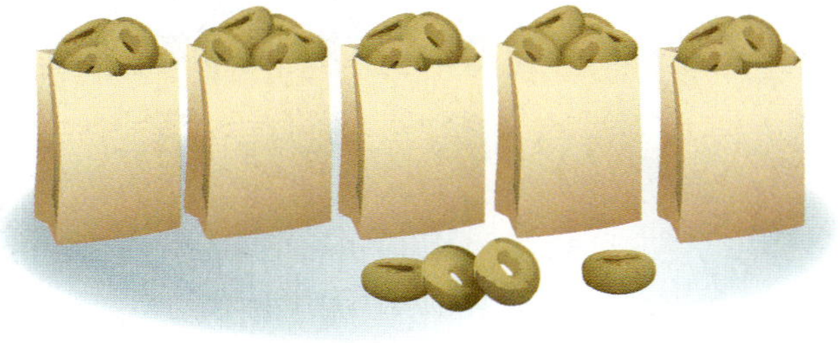



## Share & Summarize

Ask students to complete all four steps in Question 1 and share their results before writing the equation. They should all get 2. Students may have seen these number tricks before. Although writing the expression is the focus of the lesson, some students may be interested in pursuing why the trick works. This can be motivating for students who want an additional challenge. Other students may be satisfied with verifying that the pattern holds for several different values of $n$.

## Investigation 4

***On Your Own Exercises***

Pages 21–29

Exercises 22–30, 37

**Flowcharts** In this investigation, students will be working with flowcharts to build expressions. Then they use the flowcharts to work backward and to solve some equations. The method of *backtracking,* or working backward from the output of an equation, allows students to formalize the thinking they did in Investigation 1 where they had to follow a rule.

Flowcharts allow students to record their thinking in building and then "undoing" their equations. Some students may remember this method from a previous course. If so, have them review the method quickly or work immediately on the exercise sets in the investigation.

You may wish to use Chapter 1 Master 2, Flowcharts, to provide a method for students to record answers.

Ask students to tell the expression that gives the total number of bagels, when $n$ is the number of bagels in each bag. They should come up with $5n + 4$.

**Flowcharts** Tell students that they could use a diagram, or *flowchart,* to find the total number of bagels.

Explain that each arrow represents a *mathematical action* and each oval represents the result of an action. The *input* and the *output* are always ovals. Be sure students know that there are *n* bagels in each bag. Walk students through the flowchart by asking questions such as:

- What is shown by the input? The number of bagels in each bag
- What mathematical action is shown by the first arrow? Multiply by 5.
- What result is shown by the middle oval? The number of bagels in 5 bags
- What mathematical action is shown by the second arrow? Add 4.
- What output is shown by the last oval? The number of bagels in 5 bags plus 4 more bagels

Be sure students understand that the sequence of the mathematical actions should follow the order of operations.

## Develop & Understand: A

*Suggested Grouping: Pairs*

▶ **Exercises 4 and 5** Students will need to consider carefully what mathematical action or operation comes first.

▶ **Exercise 5** Students may have difficulty figuring out what mathematical action, or operation, to put on the first arrow. If they find it difficult, ask them to think about telling a story about *n*. They can ask themselves, what happened to *n* first? Then what happened? What happened after that? Often telling the story of the number helps students understand the order in which the operations are performed.

Every effort is made to show answers on the reduced student page, or in the TG margin. **Additional Answers** can be found in the chapter Answer Appendix.



If *n* represents the number of bagels in each bag, the total number of bagels Maya purchased is $5n + 4$. To find the total number of bagels, you multiply the number in each bag by 5 and then add 4. You can make a diagram, called a **flowchart**, to show these steps.

$$n \xrightarrow{\times 5} 5n \xrightarrow{+4} 5n + 4$$

Input (n) — Output (5n + 4)

The oval at the left side of the flowchart represents the *input.* In this case, input is the number of bagels in each bag. Each arrow represents a *mathematical action.* The oval to the right of an arrow shows the result of a mathematical action. The oval at the far right represents the *output.* In this case, output is the total number of bagels.

To evaluate $5n + 4$ for a particular value of *n,* substitute that value for the input and follow the steps until you reach the output. Here is the same flowchart with an input, the value of *n,* of 3.

$$3 \xrightarrow{\times 5} 15 \xrightarrow{+4} 19$$

In Exercises 1–5, you will use flowcharts to find outputs for given inputs. You will also create flowcharts to match algebraic expressions.

## Develop & Understand: A

**Copy and complete each flowchart by filling the empty ovals.**

**1.** $8 \xrightarrow{\times 4} 32 \xrightarrow{-5} 27$

**2.** $n \xrightarrow{\times 6} 6n \xrightarrow{-1} 6n - 1$

**3.** $5 \xrightarrow{\times 3} 15 \xrightarrow{-1} 14 \xrightarrow{\div 3} \frac{14}{3}$

**4.** Consider the expressions $6y + 1$ and $6(y + 1)$. See margin.

**a.** Make a flowchart for the expression $6y + 1$.

**b.** Make a flowchart for the expression $6(y + 1)$. How is this flowchart different from the flowchart in Part a?

**5.** Consider the expressions $\frac{n+2}{3}$ and $n + \frac{2}{3}$. See margin.

**a.** Make a flowchart for each expression.

**b.** Use your flowcharts to find outputs for three or four *n* values. Do both flowcharts give the same outputs? Explain why or why not.



### Additional Answers

4a. $y \xrightarrow{\times 6} 6y \xrightarrow{+1} 6y + 1$

4b. $y \xrightarrow{+1} y + 1 \xrightarrow{\times 6} 6(y+1)$

In this flowchart, addition comes before multiplication. In Part a, multiplication comes before addition.

5a. $n \xrightarrow{+2} n + 2 \xrightarrow{\div 3} \frac{n+2}{3}$;

$n \xrightarrow{+\frac{2}{3}} n + \frac{2}{3}$

5b. They give different outputs; in the first, $n + 2$ is divided by 3, and in the second, $\frac{2}{3}$ is added to *n*.

Maya had $5n + 4$ bagels, where $n$ is the number of bagels in each bag. Suppose she had a total of 79 bagels. How could you find the number of bagels in each bag? That is, how could you find the value of $n$ for which $5n + 4 = 79$?

Leon used a flowchart to find this number by **backtracking**, or working backward. This is how he did it.

*Since 79 is the output, I'll put it in the last oval.*

*I add 4 to get 79, so the number in the second oval must be 75.*

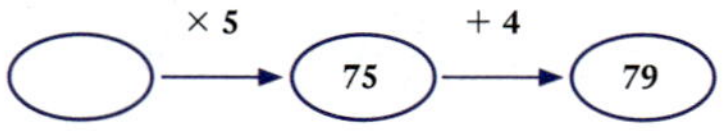


*Since 5 times a number is 75, the number of bagels in each bag must be 15.*

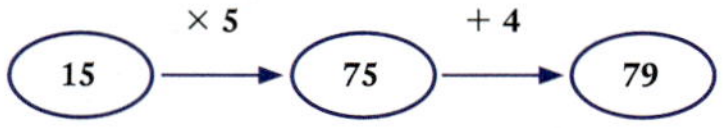


The input Leon found, 15, is the solution of the equation $5n + 4 = 79$. Now you will practice solving equations using the backtracking method.

## Develop & Understand: B

**6.** Libby put an input into this flowchart and got the output 53. Use backtracking to find Libby's input. 12

Leon solved some equations by backtracking. Exercises 7–9 show the flowcharts he used. Do Parts a and b for each flowchart.

**a.** Write the equation that Leon was trying to solve.

**b.** Backtrack to find the solution.

**7.**

7a. $3n - 7 = 26$
7b. 11

**8.**

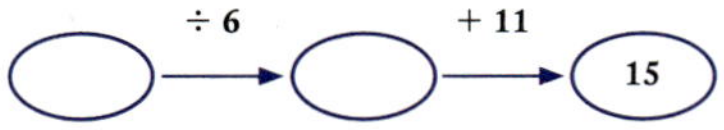


8a. $\frac{n}{6} + 11 = 15$
8b. 24

**9.**

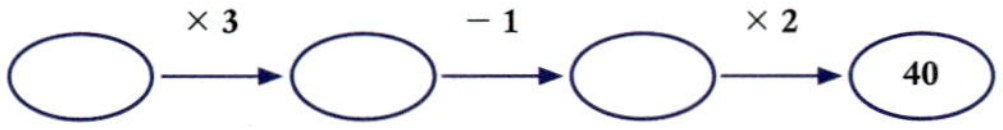


9a. $2(3n - 1) = 40$
9b. 7



## Troubleshooting

Watch for students who forget that they should think about what must have happened to the number and who simply apply the operation on the arrows. For example, a common error in **Exercise 7** would be to take 26 and simply subtract 7 to get the second oval.

Encourage students to articulate what they are doing. At some point they will begin to automate the process by doing the inverse operation of each action.

**Backtracking** To introduce how flowcharts can be used to backtrack, draw the flowchart for Maya's bagels on the board.

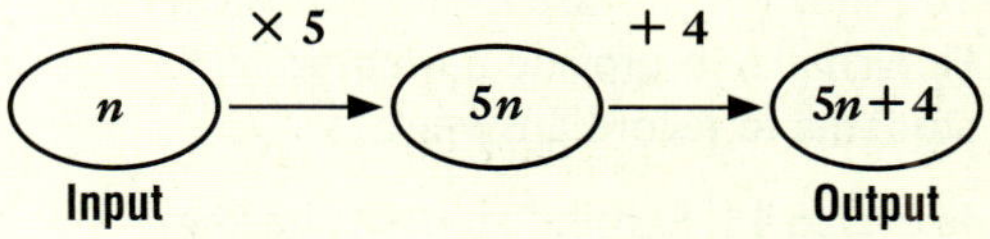


Walk through Leon's thinking on how to complete the flowchart. When discussing how to use the flowchart, some students may refer to "undoing" steps, for example, subtraction undoes addition, so the middle oval can be computed by finding $79 - 4 = 75$. Then since division undoes multiplication, the first oval can be computed by finding $75 \div 5 = 15$.

## Develop & Understand: B

*Suggested Grouping: Individuals*

▶ **Exercise 9** Some students may notice when backtracking that whenever the operation is addition, they subtract; likewise, when the operation is multiplication, they divide to undo the mathematical action. They may use this observation to write clues beneath the original flowchart. For example, in **Exercise 9**, they may write underneath the arrows, from right to left, $\div 2$, $+1$, and $\div 3$.

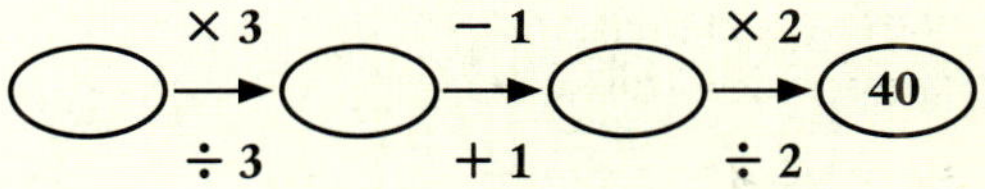


Then given the output number, they can use the clues to work from right to left to find the input number.

Other students may solve by finding missing numbers. For example, in **Exercise 9**, they will think what number times 2 equals 40. 20

Next they will think what number minus 1 is 20. 21 Finally they will think what number times 3 equals 21. 7

## Develop & Understand: C

*Suggested Grouping: Pairs*

You may wish to use Chapter 1 Master 2, Flowcharts, to provide a method for students to record answers.

▶ **Exercise 11** Remind students having difficulty drawing the flowchart to think about the mathematical actions in the equation. Have them think about which operation happens first to the variable *n*. Encourage them to continue this process for each step. Students should realize that 1 was added to the number and then that sum was multiplied by 2. The product was divided by 3, and finally 1 was subtracted from the quotient.

### Share & Summarize

Ask students to work on their descriptions in small groups. If you have each group read their descriptions aloud to the class, students may develop vocabulary for describing the "undoing" of the mathematical actions. If students are interested and have sufficient understanding of backtracking, you may wish to introduce the term *inverse operations.* Explain that addition and subtraction are inverse operations, as are multiplication and division.

Now that you have some experience using backtracking to solve equations, you can use backtracking to solve more challenging equations.

## Develop & Understand: C

**10.** Lakeisha and Mateo were playing a game called *Think of a Number.*

Lakeisha must use Mateo's output to figure out his starting number.

**a.** Draw a flowchart to represent this game. See below.

**b.** What equation does your flowchart represent? See below.

**c.** Use backtracking to solve your equation from Part b. Check your solution by following Lakeisha's steps. 9

**11.** Consider this expression.

$$\frac{2(n+1)}{3} - 1$$

**a.** Draw a flowchart for the expression. See below.

**b.** Use backtracking to find the solution of $\frac{2(n+1)}{3} - 1 = 5$. 8

### Share & Summarize

Create an equation that can be solved by backtracking. Write a paragraph explaining to someone who is not in your class how to use backtracking to solve your equation. See ①.

① Possible answer: To solve the equation $3(2n + 1) = 15$, think, "Something times 3 is 15, so $(2n + 1)$ must be 5. And since $2n$ plus 1 is 5, $2n$ must be 4, which means $n$ is 2."

10a. ( ) $\xrightarrow{\cdot 2}$ ( ) $\xrightarrow{+3}$ ( ) $\xrightarrow{\cdot 10}$ (210)

10b. $10(2n + 3) = 210$

11a. ($n$) $\xrightarrow{+1}$ ($n + 1$) $\xrightarrow{\cdot 2}$ ($2(n + 1)$) $\xrightarrow{\div 3}$ ($\frac{2(n+1)}{3}$) $\xrightarrow{-1}$ ($\frac{2(n+1)}{3} - 1$)



### Reaching All Learners

**OL On Level** If you have time, let students make up some of their own ***Think of a Number*** games and play them with a partner.

### Troubleshooting

If students are having difficulty with backtracking, encourage them to write a simple equation, choose an input number, and draw their own flowcharts. Then have them think about what would happen if they started with the output and needed to figure out the input. This skill will be revisited in future lessons, so students will have opportunities for additional practice.

## Practice & Apply

**Use the first term or stage and the rule given to create a sequence. Tell whether your sequence is the only one possible. If it is not, give another sequence that fits the rule.**

**1.** *First term*: 40
*Rule*: Divide the preceding term by 2. 40, 20, 10, 5, $\frac{5}{2}$, ... ; This is the only sequence possible.

**2.** *First stage*:  See below.
*Rule*: Draw a shape with one more side than the preceding shape.

**3.** Starting with a closed geometric figure with straight sides of equal lengths, you can use the rule below to create a design.

*Find the midpoint, or middle point, of each side of the figure. Connect the midpoints in order to make a new shape. It will be the same shape as the original but smaller.*

**a.** Copy this square. Follow the rule three times, each time starting with the figure you drew the previous time.

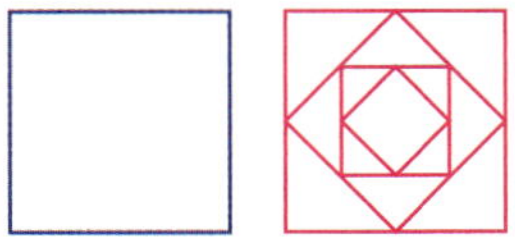

**b.** Copy this triangle. Follow the rule three times, each time starting with the figure you drew the previous time.

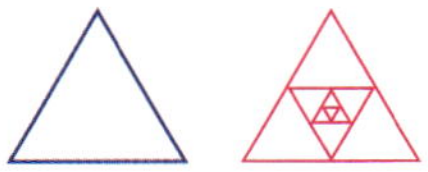

**c.** Draw your own shape. Follow the rule three times to make a design. Designs will vary.

**4.** **Measurement** Sergio is making a dessert that requires three eggs for each cup of flour.

**a.** How many eggs does he need for three cups of flour? 9

**b.** For a party, Sergio made a large batch of his dessert using a dozen eggs. How much flour did he use? 4 cups

2. 

This is not the only possible sequence. Any sequence of shapes with 3 sides, 4 sides, 5 sides, and so on will work.



ce & Apply exercises
e opportunities for
ents to reinforce and directly
the skills and concepts they
in each Investigation.

**On Your Own Exercises**
**Lesson 1.1**

**Investigation 1**
Pages 5–8
Practice & Apply: 1–6
Connect & Extend: 31, 32

**Investigation 2**
Pages 9–12
Practice & Apply: 7–11
Connect & Extend: 33, 34

**Investigation 3**
Pages 12–17
Practice & Apply: 12–21
Connect & Extend: 35, 36

**Investigation 4**
Pages 17–20
Practice & Apply: 22–30
Connect & Extend: 37

**Assign Anytime**
Mixed Review: 39

▶ **Exercise 2** You may want to have students share some different possibilities for the sequence to demonstrate that it is ambiguous.

▶ **Exercise 3** Some students may need an explanation of the term *midpoint*. Others may not understand how to apply the rule. If either is the case, work through **Part a** as a class, and ask students to work through **Part b** independently. Be sure that students draw regular polygons.

On Your Own Exercises at the end of each lesson offer daily opportunities for independent assignments and homework, and opportunities for teachers to assess student learning.

**Lesson 1.1** Variables and Expressions **21**

▶ **Exercise 5** Some students may solve this exercise by calculating the charge for each child ($5.00 per hour for one, plus $2.00 per hour for the next, and so on). Others may use a fixed family rate: $7.00 per hour for the Newsomes and $9.00 per hour for the Fosters

▶ **Exercise 6** Watch for errors in multiplication or misplaced decimal points. You may want to discuss why Mr. Lopez's approximate rule works by comparing it to the actual rule. Point out that 0.62 is a little more than 0.50, or half.

5a. $21; Possible explanations: Since there are 2 children, she earned $7 per hour for 3 hours, or $21 total. *Or,* she earned $15 for the first child, plus $6 for the additional child, for a total of $21.

5d. Possible answer: She could watch 2 children for 4 hours. She could watch 3 children for 3 hours.

**5. Economics** Kendra uses this rule to figure out how much to charge for babysitting.

*Charge $5 per hour for one child, plus $2 per hour for each additional child.*

**a.** Last Saturday, Kendra watched the Newsome twins for 3 hours. How much money did she earn? Explain how you found your answer.

**b.** Mr. Foster hires Kendra to watch his three children for 2 hours. How much will she charge? $18

**c.** Does Kendra earn more for watching two children for 3 hours or three children for 2 hours? 2 children for 3 hours

**d.** Kendra hopes to earn $25 next weekend to buy her sister a birthday present. Describe two ways she could earn at least $25 babysitting.

**6. Measurement** You can convert speeds from kilometers per hour to miles per hour by using this rule.

*Multiply the number of kilometers per hour by 0.62.*

**a.** Convert each kilometers-per-hour value in the table below to a miles-per-hour value.

| Kilometers per Hour | Miles per Hour | Approximate Miles per Hour |
|---|---|---|
| 50 | 31 | 35 |
| 60 | 37.2 | 40 |
| 70 | 43.4 | 45 |
| 80 | 49.6 | 50 |
| 90 | 55.8 | 55 |
| 100 | 62 | 60 |
| 110 | 68.2 | 65 |
| 120 | 74.4 | 70 |

**b.** As part of his job, Mr. Lopez does a lot of driving in Canada. He uses the following rule to approximate the speed in miles per hour from a given speed in kilometers per hour.

*Divide the number of kilometers per hour by 2 and add 10.*

Use Mr. Lopez's rule to convert each kilometers-per-hour value in the table to an approximate miles-per-hour value.
See the table in Part a.

**c.** For which kilometers-per-hour values from the tables are the results for the two rules closest? 80 kph

**d.** For which kilometers-per-hour values in the table does Mr. Lopez's rule give a value that is too high? 80 kph, 70 kph, 60 kph, and 50 kph

**7.** Here are clues for a logic puzzle.

- Five friends, Alano, Bob, Carl, Dina, and Bonita, live in a row of houses numbered 1 to 5.
- They all keep tropical fish for pets.
- Dina got her fish from Bonita's next-door neighbor Alano. Alano had 21 fish before he gave *f* of them to Dina.
- Carl has twice as many fish as Dina, who lives in house 2. Carl does not live next to Dina.
- Bonita lives in house 4 and has 3 fewer fish than Carl.
- Bob has 4 more fish than Dina.

**a.** Who lives in which house?

**b.** Write expressions to describe the number of fish each person has.

**c.** If the five neighbors have a total of 57 fish, how many fish does Dina have? 7

7a. 1: Bob; 2: Dina; 3: Alano; 4: Bonita; 5: Carl

7b. Alano: $21 - f$; Bob: $f + 4$; Carl: $2f$; Dina: $f$; Bonita: $2f - 3$

**8.** Keshon has *s* stamps in his collection.

**a.** Keshon's older sister, Jamila, has three times as many stamps as Keshon. Write an expression for the number of stamps she has. $3s$

**b.** Jamila decides to give Keshon 13 of her stamps. How many stamps will she have left? How many stamps will Keshon have? $3s - 13$, $s + 13$

**9.** Franklin, a golden retriever, weighs *p* pounds. In Parts a–c, write an expression for the weight of the dog in pounds. Each expression should include the variable *p*.

**a.** Tatu, a pug, weighs 49 pounds less than Franklin. $p - 49$

**b.** Mia, a Chihuahua, weighs $\frac{1}{17}$ as much as Franklin. $\frac{1}{17}p$

**c.** Lucy, a Great Dane, weighs twice as much as Franklin, minus 15 pounds. $2p - 15$

**d.** Franklin weighs 68 pounds. How much do Tatu, Mia, and Lucy weigh? Tatu: 19 lb; Mia: 4 lb; Lucy: 121 lb



On Your Own Exercises

▶ **Exercise 7** Help students who are having trouble getting started to set up a table for organizing the information. Encourage them to record the known facts first and then to work through the rest of the clues. You may wish to distribute Lesson 1.1 Master 1, Row of Houses, to help students record their thinking in a logical manner.

▶ **Exercise 9b** Look for different ways students may write their answers: $\frac{1}{17}p$, $\frac{p}{17}$, and so on.

**Lesson 1.1** Variables and Expressions 23

On Your Own Exercises

**10.** Mr. Karnowski has a stack of 125 sheets of graph paper. He is passing out $g$ sheets to each of his students.

**a.** Write an expression for the number of sheets he will pass out to the first 5 students. $5g$

**b.** Write an expression for the number of sheets he will have left after he has given sheets to all 25 students in his class. $125 - 25g$

**c.** What would happen if $g$ was 6? He would not have enough graph paper for the class.

**11.** The Marble Emporium sells individual marbles and bags of marbles. Each bag contains the same number of marbles.

**a.** Rita bought a bag of marbles, plus one extra marble. Is it possible that she bought an even number of marbles? Explain.

**b.** Lorena bought two bags of marbles, plus one extra marble. Is it possible that Lorena has an even number of marbles? Explain.

11a. Yes; if the bag contains an odd number of marbles, Rita must have bought an even number.

11b. No; if $n$ is the number of marbles in each bag, the number in 2 bags is $2n$, which must be even. So the number in 2 bags plus 1 marble is $2n + 1$, which must be odd.

**c. Challenge** Let $n$ stand for *any whole number.* Use what you have discovered in Parts a and b to write an algebraic expression containing $n$ that means *any odd number.* Write another expression that means *any even number.* Possible answer: any odd number: $2n + 1$; any even number: $2n$



24 CHAPTER 1 Expressions

**Rewrite each expression without using multiplication or addition signs.**

**12.** $t + t + t + t$ $4t$

**13.** $4 \cdot xy \cdot xy$ $4(xy)^2$, or $4x^2y^2$

**14.** $6g + g + g$ $8g$

**15.** $8 \cdot c \cdot c \cdot d \cdot d$ $8c^2d^2$

**16.** Find the value of $9 - 3D^2$ for $D = 1.1$. 5.37

**17.** Without using a calculator, find the value of $9 - 3D^2$ for $D = \frac{1}{2}$. $8\frac{1}{4}$

**Evaluate each expression for $h = 4$.**

**18.** $\frac{h^2 - 3}{13}$ 1

**19.** $\frac{3h}{4}$ 3

**20.** $9h \div 2$ 18

**21.** Luna, Mason, and Gabriel make and sell hand-painted t-shirts. They make a profit of $D$ dollars for each shirt they sell.

**a.** If they sell 13 t-shirts, how much total profit will they make? $13D$

**b.** If the three friends equally divide the profit from selling the 13 shirts, how much will each receive? $\frac{13D}{3}$

**c.** Suppose each friend received $39 from selling the 13 shirts. How much profit did the students earn for each shirt? $9

**d.** Suppose $F$ more friends join the business. If the group sells 20 t-shirts and divides the profit equally, how much will each friend receive? $\frac{20D}{F+3}$

**e.** If the new, larger group of friends sells $X$ shirts, how much profit will each friend receive? $\frac{XD}{F+3}$

**Copy and complete each flowchart.**

**22.** (12) —$\times 2$→ (24) —$+ 12$→ (36)

**23.** ($n$) —$- 6$→ ($n - 6$) —$\times 3$→ ($3(n - 6)$)

**24.** (7) —$\times 2$→ (14) —$+ 3$→ (17) —$\div 2$→ (8.5)

**25.** (9) —$\times 5$→ (45) —$- 4$→ (41)



On Your Own Exercises

▶ **Exercises 16 and 17** Students may be challenged by having to square a decimal or a fraction. Point out that both values for $D$ are simple enough for them to square mentally. If students are confused about which operation to perform first, remind them that finding the value of a number raised to an exponent always occurs before other operations.

▶ **Exercise 19** Students may notice that if $h = 4$, the expression simplifies to 3 because they are multiplying by 4 and then dividing by 4, which is the same as multiplying 3 by 1. Point out to them that they should be looking for these shortcuts in evaluating expressions.

▶ **Exercises 22–25** You may wish to have students use Chapter 1 Master 2, Flowcharts, as a way of recording their answers.

**Lesson 1.1** Variables and Expressions 25

▶ **Exercise 26** Students are asked to create a flowchart from an equation. Remind them to interpret $3a$ as 3 times $a$ in their flowcharts.

▶ **Exercise 29b** Encourage students to think carefully about which operations are performed first to yield 46. It may be useful to emphasize that the first step in undoing this equation, or in backtracking to find the solution, is to think about what number added to 1 gives 46 (or subtracting 1 from 46). This realization will help students later as they solve other kinds of equations.

*On Your Own Exercises*

**26.** Consider the expression $3a \div 4$.

**a.** Draw a flowchart to represent the expression. See below.

**b.** Use your flowchart to find the value of the expression for $a = 8$. 6

**c.** Use your flowchart to solve $3a \div 4 = 6$. Explain each step in your solution. 8; Multiply 6 by 4 and divide the result, 24, by 3.

**27.** Lara drew this flowchart.

**a.** What equation was Lara trying to solve? $16n - 4 = 28$

**b.** Copy and complete the flowchart.

**28.** In a game of *Think of a Number,* Jin Lee told the following to Darnell.

- *Think of a number.*
- *Subtract 1 from your number.*
- *Multiply the result by 2.*
- *Add 6.*

**a.** Draw a flowchart to represent this game. See below.

**b.** Darnell said he came up with 10. Write an equation that you could solve to find Darnell's number. $2(n - 1) + 6 = 10$

**c.** Use backtracking to solve your equation. Check your solution by following Jin Lee's steps. 3

**29.** Luis wrote the expression $9(2x + 1) + 1$.

**a.** Draw a flowchart for Luis' expression. See margin.

**b.** Use your flowchart to solve the equation $9(2x + 1) + 1 = 46$. 2

**30.** Consider this equation.

$$\frac{3m \cdot 2}{6} = 1$$

**a.** Draw a flowchart to represent the equation. See below.

**b.** Use backtracking to find the solution. 1

26a.

28a.
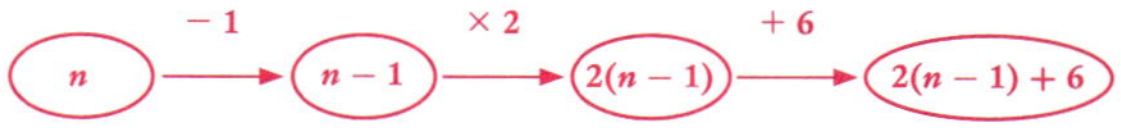


30a.
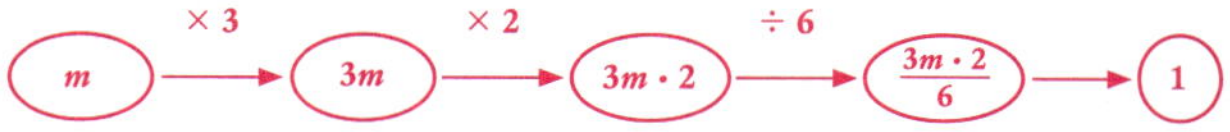




**Additional Answer**

29a.
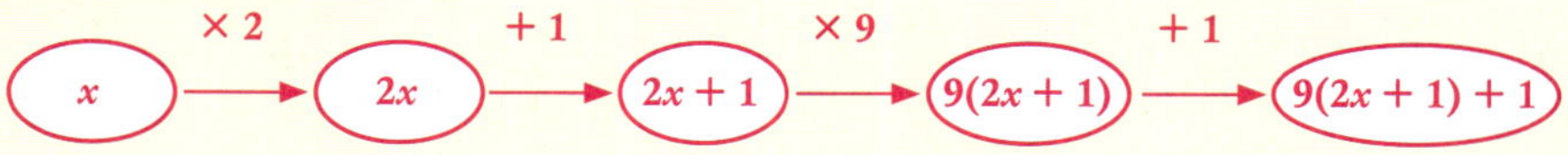

On Your Own Exercises

The exercises in **Connect & Extend** relate student learning to other mathematical topics and strands.

## Connect & Extend

31a. 1, 4, 2, 1, 4, 2, 1, ... ; The number 4, 2, 1 repeat.

31b. 8, 4, 2, 1, 4, 2, 1, ... ; After the first 4 terms, the numbers 4, 2, 1 repeat.

31c. Possible answer: 7, 22, 11, 34, 17, 52, 26, 13, 40, 20, 10, 5, 16, 8, 4, 2, 1, 4, 2, 1, ... ; 3, 10, 5, 16, 8, 4, 2, 1, 4, 2, 1, ... ; After the first several terms, the numbers 4, 2, 1 repeat.

31d. The sequence is 331, 994, 497, 1,492, 746, 373, 1,120, 560, 280, 140, 70, 35, 106, 53, 160, 80, 40, 20, 10, 5, 16, 8, 4, 2, 1, 4, 2, 1, ... ; The sequence eventually becomes the repeating pattern 4, 2, 1.

31e. Whatever number you start with, the sequence eventually starts repeating 4, 2, 1, 4, 2, 1, ...

**31.** You can produce a sequence of numbers by applying the following rule to each term.

*If the number is even, get the next number by dividing by 2. If the number is odd, get the next number by multiplying by 3 and adding 1.*

**a.** Use this rule to produce a sequence with 1 as the first term. Describe the pattern in the sequence.

**b.** Now use the rule to produce a sequence with 8 as the first term. Keep finding new terms until you see a pattern in the sequence. Describe what happens.

**c.** Use the rule to generate two more sequences. Keep finding new terms until you see a pattern.

**d.** Using your calculator and the rule, generate a sequence with 331 as its first term. Again, keep finding new terms until you see a pattern.

**e.** Describe what you discovered in Parts a–d.

**32. Measurement** One mile is about 1.6 kilometers.

**a.** Which is the greater distance, 1 mile or 1 kilometer? 1 mi

**b.** Los Angeles and New York City are about 2,460 miles apart. How many kilometers apart are the two cities? About 3,936 km

**c.** If the speed limit on a road in Canada is 50 kilometers per hour, what is the speed limit in miles per hour? 31.25 mph

**d.** Jin and Franklin traveled with their families by car to visit relatives during the summer. Jin traveled about 500 miles and Franklin traveled about 700 kilometers. Who traveled the greater distance? Explain your reasoning. Jin; Possible explanation: 500 mi equal 800 km.

**e.** In Investigation 1, you learned that lightning is 1 mile away for every 5 seconds you count between the lightning and the following clap of thunder. About how many seconds would it take you to hear the thunder if the lightning was 1 kilometer away? About 3 s

▶ **Exercise 31** Students should decide that the rule given eventually ends up in the same repeating pattern (1, 4, 2, 1, 4, 2, and so on) regardless of the value of the first term. Note that while students will probably convince themselves this is always true, no one has ever proven so. If students enjoy this exercise, there are more such "looping" rules in Marilyn Burns' *Math for Smarty Pants.*

▶ **Exercise 32** Students apply a rule for converting from miles to kilometers. You may want to have students compare this rule to the one they used for Exercise 6.



**Lesson 1.1** Variables and Expressions 27

▶ **Exercise 35** This exercise previews the distributive property which students will learn in Lesson 3 of this chapter. At this point, it is important only that they have an intuition that these expressions are equivalent. They will be able to prove this in Lesson 3.

On Your Own Exercises

**33.** Tito's Taxi charges \$3.20 for the first mile plus \$2.40 for each additional mile.

**a.** Which expression gives the fare, in dollars, for a trip of $d$ miles? Assume that the trip is at least one mile.

$d + 3.20 + 2.40$ $\quad$ $3.20(d + 2.40)$

$2.40(d - 1) + 3.20$ (circled) $\quad$ $d(2.40 + 3.20)$

**b.** How much would it cost to travel one mile? Three miles? \$3.20, \$8

**c.** Tito thought he might make more money if his drivers charged for every sixth of a mile, not every mile. The new rate is \$1.60 for the first $\frac{2}{6}$ mile, plus 40¢ for each additional $\frac{1}{6}$ mile.

If a person travels $n$ sixths of a mile, which expression gives the correct fare? Assume that the person travels at least $\frac{2}{6}$ mile.

$1.60 + 40n$ $\quad$ $1.60 + 0.40n$

$1.60 + 40(n - 2)$ $\quad$ $1.60 + 0.40(n - 2)$ (circled)

**d.** Use the formula you chose in Part c to calculate trip fares for one mile and three miles. Compare the results to those for Part b. Does Tito's Taxi make more money with this new rate plan? \$3.20, \$8; The results are the same as for Part b; no

**Real-World Link**

Profit is the amount of money a business earns. It is calculated by subtracting expenses, or what was spent, from income, or what was earned.

**34. Challenge** The members of a music club are raising money to pay for a trip to the state jazz festival. They are selling CDs and t-shirts.

**a.** Each CD costs the club \$2.40. The club is selling the CDs for \$12.00 apiece. Write an expression to represent how much profit the club will make for selling $c$ CDs. $12c - 2.4c$, or $9.6c$

**b.** Each t-shirt costs the club \$3.50. The club is selling the t-shirts for \$14.50. Write an expression to represent how much profit the club will make for selling $s$ t-shirts. $14.5s - 3.5s$, or $11s$

**c.** Now write an expression that gives the profit for selling $c$ CDs and $s$ t-shirts. $12c - 2.4c + 14.5s - 3.5s$, or $9.6c + 11s$

**d.** Ludwig sold 10 of each item. Johann sold 7 CDs and 12 t-shirts. Use your expression from Part c to calculate how much money each club member raised. \$206, \$199.20

**35. Preview** Consider the expressions $x(x - 1)$ and $x^2 - x$.

**a.** Choose five values for $x$. Evaluate both expressions for those values. Organize your results in a table. See margin.

**b.** What appears to be the relationship between the two expressions? Possible answer: The expressions seem to be the same.



## Additional Answer

35a. Possible table:

| $x$ | $x(x-1)$ | $x^2 - x$ |
|---|---|---|
| 0 | 0 | 0 |
| 1 | 0 | 0 |
| 2 | 2 | 2 |
| 5 | 20 | 20 |
| 10 | 90 | 90 |

36a. Answers will vary. Any number less than 0 or greater than 1 will work.
36b. Answers will vary. Any number between 0 and 1 will work.
38. Answers will vary. Possible answer: A band charges $25n + 100$ to play at a school dance; $n$ represents the number of hours the band plays, 25 represents the band's hourly charge, 100 represents the set-up fee.
39a. False; the graph on the right indicates that *Alien Trek* is more exciting. The graph on the left indicates that it is more expensive.

**Mixed Review**

39b. True; the graph on the left indicates that *Robo Race* is more difficult. The graph on the right indicates that it has lower-quality graphics.
39c. True; the graph on the left indicates that *Alien Trek* is less difficult. The graph on the right indicates that it is more exciting.
39d. False; the graph on the left indicates that *Robo Race* is less expensive. The graph on the right indicates that it has lower-quality graphics.

**36. Challenge** In this exercise, you will compare $x^2$ and $x$ for different values of $x$.

**a.** Find three values for $x$ such that $x^2 > x$.

**b.** Find three values for $x$ such that $x^2 < x$.

**c.** Find a value for $x$ such that $x^2 = x$. Can you find more than one? 0, 1

**37. Number Sense** In a game of *Think of a Number;* the input was 3 and the output was 2. Tell whether each of the following could have been the game's rule.

**a.** Think of a number. Double it. Add 3 to the result. Then divide by 5. No

**b.** Think of a number. Subtract 2 from it. Multiply the result by 4. Then divide by 2. Yes

**c.** Think of a number. Divide it by 3. Add 5 to the result. Then divide by 3 again. Yes

**38. In Your Own Words** Describe a situation that can be represented by the expression $25n + 100$. Explain what the 25, the 100, and the $n$ represent in your situation.

**39.** The graphs give information about two video games. Use the graphs to determine whether each statement is true or false. Explain how you decided.

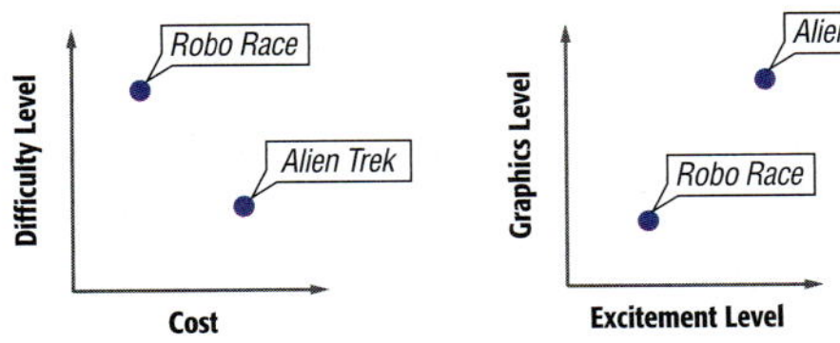


**a.** The more exciting game is less expensive.

**b.** The more difficult game has lower-quality graphics.

**c.** The less difficult game is more exciting.

**d.** The less expensive game has better graphics.



**Mixed Review** is an important part of the instructional and assignment structure, helping students to maintain mastery.

On Your Own Exercises

**Exercise 36** Students have an opportunity to explore some of the properties of fractions and whole numbers in this exercise. If students have difficulty in answering Part b, they may not realize at first that they need to investigate numbers less than 1.

**Exercise 37** Challenge students to think of another *Think of a Number* game that would work for an input of 3 and an output of 2.

## Quick Check

**Informal Assessment** Students should be able to:

- ✔ develop strategies for identifying and describing patterns
- ✔ describe observed patterns using an informal rule
- ✔ understand the order of operations
- ✔ use conventions for representing operations and exponents in expressions
- ✔ create flowcharts to represent input/output equations
- ✔ solve equations by backtracking

## Quick Quiz

**1.** A game arcade charges $1 for a rechargeable game card that you need to play each game. Each game costs $2.50. How many games will Eric play for $20? 7 games

**2.** Complete the flowchart.

(4) —× 4→ (16) —+ 5→ (21)

Write the equation the flowchart represents. $4n + 5 = 21$

**3.** Make a flowchart to represent $3(n + 1) - 4 = 65$. Use backtracking to find $n$.

(22) —+ 1→ (23) —× 3→ (69) —− 4→ (65)

**4.** Evaluate each of the following if $g = 4$.

a. $\frac{2g}{5}$ $\frac{8}{5}$ or $1\frac{3}{5}$

b. $\frac{2}{5}g$ $\frac{8}{5}$ or $1\frac{3}{5}$

c. $3g^2$ 48

d. $\frac{g + 2}{12}$ $\frac{6}{12}$ or $\frac{1}{2}$

LESSON 1.2

# Expressions and Formulas

## Objectives

- To practice using variables to write expressions
- To use expressions to solve problems
- To develop and use formulas to find specific quantities
- To identify restrictions on variables
- To use a spreadsheet to make a chart

The **Objectives** list summarizes the main mathematical concepts presented in the lesson.

## *Overview*

Students will discover how they might actually use algebra. They will write algebraic expressions to represent a variety of situations and describe situations that can be shown by a given expression. They use formulas and backtracking to find answers. In the last problem set, students use a table and graphs as representations for expressions to organize data and help them find who won a race. Finally, they use all these skills to make a spreadsheet for a business - one of the most common uses of algebra.

## *Advance Preparation*

You may want to use Lesson 1.2 Master 1, Tortoise Table and Grid, as a way for students to record answers and a blank grid for making a graph.

The suggestions found in **Advance Preparation** give tips in preparing for the lesson that might not be apparent from reading the materials list.

| | Summary | Materials | On Your Own Exercises (pp. 43–48) | Assessment Opportunities |
|---|---|---|---|---|
| **Investigation 1** (p. 32) Pacing: 2 days | Students use expressions to describe situations and solve problems. They also determine restrictions on variables. | | Practice & Apply: 1–9<br>Connect & Extend: 14–15<br>Mixed Review: 20–32 | • Share & Summarize (p. 34)<br>• Troubleshooting (pp. 32, 34) |
| **Investigation 2** (p. 35) Pacing: 1 day | Students use and develop formulas for additional practice in finding the value of expressions. | Lesson 1.2 Master 1 | Practice & Apply: 10–13<br>Connect & Extend: 16–18<br>Mixed Review: 20–32 | • Share & Summarize (p. 39)<br>• Troubleshooting (pp. 37, 39) |
| **Inquiry Investigation 3** (p. 40) Pacing: 1 day | Students identify what is varying in given situations. They also invent situations from given expressions. | computer, spreadsheet software | | |

# Leveled Lesson Resources

CRM *Available in:* **Chapter 1 Resource Masters**

Also on TeacherWorks™ Lesson 1.2

## Study Guide and Intervention (p. 27) AL

**Lesson 1.2 Study Guide and Intervention**
***Expressions and Formulas***

The formula $d = rt$ relates distance $d$, rate $r$, and time $t$, traveled.

**Example 1** **Find the distance traveled if you drive 40 miles per hour for 3 hours.**

$d = rt$

$d = 40 \cdot 3$ Replace $r$ with 40 and $t$ with 3.

$d = 120$ The distance traveled is 120 miles.

The formula $P = 2(\ell + w)$ relates perimeter $P$, length $\ell$, and width $w$ for a rectangle. The formula $A = \ell w$ relates area $A$, length $\ell$, and width $w$ for a rectangle.

**Example 2** **Find the perimeter and area of a rectangle with length 7 feet and width 2 feet.**

$P = 2(\ell + w)$ $A = \ell w$

$P = 2(7 + 2)$ $A = 7 \cdot 2$

$P = 2(9)$ $A = 14$

$P = 18$

The perimeter is 18 feet. The area is 14 square feet.

**Exercises**

**Solve.**

1. **Train Travel** How far does a train travel in 12 hours at 48 miles per hour?
2. **Travel** How long does it take a car traveling 40 miles per hour to go 200 miles?

**Find the perimeter and area of each rectangle.**

3. 3 in. by 7 in.
4. 6 m by 9 m
5. 3 ft by 12 ft
6. 3 cm by 5 cm

## Skills Practice (p. 28) AL OL

**Lesson 1.2 Skills Practice**
***Expressions and Formulas***

**Solve.**

1. **Air Travel** A plane is traveling 9 miles per minute. How much time is needed to travel 216 miles?
2. **Jogging** What is the rate, in feet per second, of a girl who jogs 315 feet in 45 seconds?

**Find the perimeter and area of each rectangle.**

3. 2 mm by 6 mm
4. 5 ft by 4 ft
5. 45 m by 75 m
6. 84 mi by 126 mi
7. a rectangle that is 21 inches long and 13 inches wide
8. a square that is 25 centimeters on each side

**Find the missing dimension of each rectangle.**

9. 20 in.; Perimeter = 208 in.
10. Area = 210 m²; 10 m
11. 625 mi; Perimeter = 2,402 mi
12. 8 ft; Area = 216 ft²
13. The perimeter of a rectangle is 100 centimeters. Its width is 9 centimeters. Find its length.
14. The area of a rectangle is 319 square kilometers. Its width is 11 kilometers. Find its length.

## Problem-Solving Practice (p. 29) AL OL

**Lesson 1.2 Problem-Solving Practice**
***Expressions and Formulas***

1. **Distance** Cara will move from her hometown of Seattle, Washington, to Portland, Oregon, which is 175 miles away. Cara wants to make the drive in 3 hours or less. Use the distance formula, $d = rt$, where $d$ is the total distance, $r$ is the speed of travel, and $t$ is the length of time, to determine the minimum average speed Cara must drive to arrive in Portland in 3 hours.
2. **Interest** For Adam's tenth birthday, his grandparents opened a savings account in his name. They made an initial deposit of $750. During the year, Adam made no additional deposits and no withdrawals. At the end of the first year, Adam's money had earned $26.25 in interest. Use the formula $I = Prt$, where $I$ is the amount of interest earned, $P$ is the original amount deposited, $r$ is the interest rate, and $t$ is the time, in years, that the money is invested, to determine what the interest rate is on his savings account. Write your answer as a percent.
3. **Temperature** Lisa looks at her outdoor thermometer and finds it is 12°C. Her brother asks her what 12°C is in degrees Fahrenheit. Use the formula $F = \frac{9}{5}C + 32$, where $F$ is degree Fahrenheit and $C$ is degrees Celsius, to find the equivalent temperature in degrees Fahrenheit. Round to the nearest whole number.
4. **Farming** A farmer has plans to leave part of his cornfield as grass for erosion control. The grass section will be a 12-foot square. The dimensions of the cornfield are 60 feet long by 40 feet wide. What is the actual square footage planted in corn?

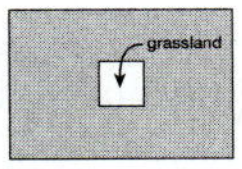


5. **Construction** The City of Detroit wants to put a fence around part of the city park to make a playground. The city has 120 feet of fencing for the playground.
   a. What dimensions of the playground will give the maximum area?
   b. What is the area of the playground with the dimension found in part a?
   c. The City of Detroit will add 1 foot of new top soil to the entire fence area. Use the formula $V = \ell \cdot w \cdot h$ to find how many cubic feet of top soil will need to be purchased.

## Enrichment (p. 30) BL

**Lesson 1.2 Enrichment**
***Expressions and Formulas***

**Mathematics and Social Studies**

Since the discovery that Earth is round, people have been fascinated with the prospect of making ever faster trips around the world. Ferdinand Magellan's ship *Victoria* set sail on September 20, 1519, and completed the first voyage around the world about three years later on September 6, 1522. With more consistent modes of transportation came new records in circling Earth.

**Solve each problem by finding the average speed it took to circle Earth. Use 24,900 miles to approximate the distance around Earth.**

1. **Dirigible** In 1929, Graf Zeppelin made the first round-the-world dirigible flight in 21 days, 8 hours on the *LZ127*. What was Zeppelin's average speed in miles per hour?
2. **Airplane** Air Force bomber *Lucky Lady II* made the first nonstop flight around the world in 1949. The flight took 94 hours. What was the average speed of the *Lucky Lady II* on that trip?
3. **Spaceship** In 1961, Yuri Gagarin and Bherman Titov of Russia each circled Earth in a little over an hour and 45 minutes. At what speed must one travel to circle Earth at its surface in an hour and 45 minutes?

**In Exercises 4–6, assume that each aircraft travels at a constant rate. Use 24,900 miles as the distance traveled. How long would it take each aircraft to circle Earth?**

4. a commercial plane of the 1930s traveling at 168 mph
5. a Boeing 707 cruising at 640 mph
6. a Concorde flying at 1,450 mph
7. **Ballooning** Jules Verne wrote about circling Earth in a hot air balloon in his novel *Around the World in Eighty Days* (1873). Suppose it were possible for a hot air balloon to circle Earth in 80 days. What would be the average speed in miles per hour?

34 Chapter 1

## Lesson Quick Quiz (p. 31) AL OL BL

**Lesson 1.2 Quick Quiz**

1. Write an expression that shows the number of inches in $w$ feet, eight inches.
2. Noah has $y$ lacrosse balls.
   a. Write an expression for the number of balls Christina has if she has 3 less than twice the number of balls Noah has.
   b. Are there any restrictions on $y$?
3. Make up a story for the expression $12b + 7$.

## Lesson Master 1 (p. 32)

**Lesson 1.2 Master 1**
***Expressions and Formulas***

**Investigation 2, Develop & Understand B**

**The Tortoise Race**

| Time (min) | Distance from Start (m): Tortoise 1 | Tortoise 2 | Tortoise 3 | Comments |
|---|---|---|---|---|
| 0 | 3.1 | 0 | 0 | They 're off! |
| 1 | 4.0 | 1.3 | 0.17 | Tortoise 1 is well in font |
| 2 | 4.9 | 2.6 | 0.66 | Tortoise 3 looks hopeless |
| 3 | | | | |
| | | | | |
| | | | | |
| | | | | |
| | | | | |

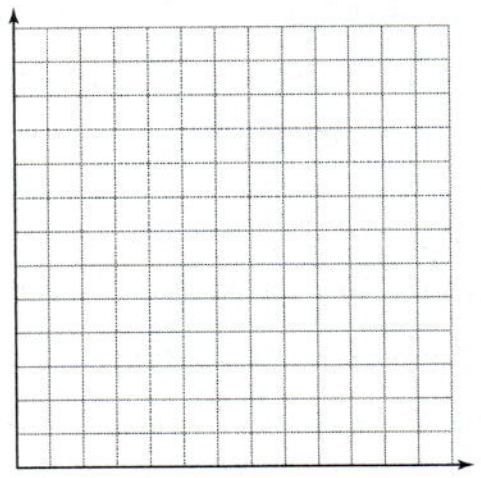

# Additional Lesson Resources

### Teacher Tech Tools
- TeacherWorks
- ExamView Assessment Suite
- Classroom Presentation Toolkit
- Advance Tracker

### Student Tech Tools
- StudentWorks Plus
- Math Online eGlossary • Concepts in Motion

### Other Print Products
- Investigation Notebook and Reflection Journal
- Quick Review Math Handbook

LESSON 1.2

# Expressions and Formulas

## Introduce

**Algebraic Expressions** Introduce the lesson by telling students that they will learn how to use algebraic expressions to help them solve problems.

Emphasize to students that the situation represented by an algebraic expression represents both information you know and what information you want to find out. The variable represents what is *not* known about a situation in terms of what *is* known about the situation.

### Think & Discuss

*Suggested Grouping: Small Groups*

Have students read the first three paragraphs and the cartoon preceding the Think & Discuss section. Then have them answer the questions in the text. Be sure students understand the relationship between the number of calendars sold and the amount of money raised. Some students may write the expression as $12c + 2$. This is also correct because of the commutative property of addition.

You may wish to take some time to review some of the properties of rational numbers. Knowing how to use and apply these properties can help students compute mentally and evaluate equations.

- Commutative property of addition: the order in which two or more numbers is added does not affect the sum: $a + b = b + a$
- Commutative property of multiplication: the order in which two or more numbers is multiplied does not affect the product: $a \cdot b = b \cdot a$
- Associative property of addition: how two or more addends are grouped does not affect the sum: $(a + b) + c = a + (b + c)$
- Associative property of multiplication: how two or more factors are grouped does not affect the product: $(a \cdot b) \cdot c = a \cdot (b \cdot c)$

LESSON 1.2

# Expressions and Formulas



Before you write an expression to describe a situation, you need to figure out what is varying.

Zoe, Darnell, Maya, and Zach are members of a community group that raises money for various charities. Every year, the community group holds a calendar sale.

Last year's calendars pictured different animals. All the profits from the sale were given to a wildlife preservation fund. The students agreed to each donate $2 of their own money to the fund in addition to the money that they collected from the calendar sale. They sold the calendars for $12 each.

### Think & Discuss

How much money did each student collect for the fund? Consider both the money they earned for selling the calendars and the money they donated themselves. Zoe: 26; Darnell: 86; Maya: 302; Zach: 1,202

What is varying in this situation? The number of calendars sold and the amount of money raised

Write an expression for the total amount of money given to the fund by each student. Tell what your variable represents. $2 + 12c$, where $c$ is the number of calendars sold



## On the Spot Assessment

You may want to have students identify the property shown in each of the first four equations given below.

$6.5 + 2.9 = 2.9 + 6.5$
Commutative property of addition

$(3 \cdot 5) \cdot 8.2 = 3 \cdot (5 \cdot 8.2)$
Associative property of multiplication

$6.4 + (2.7 + 2.3) = (6.4 + 2.7) + 2.3$
Associative property of addition

$1.8 \cdot 4 = 4 \cdot 1.8$
Commutative property of multiplication

**On the Spot Assessment** points out common errors and gives ideas for remediation. Teachers can quickly correct student errors before problems become persistent.

For its summer project, the community group hosted a walkathon to raise money for cancer research. A successful radio campaign prompted people to request more information. The community group responded by sending informational packets.

Zoe, Darnell, Maya, and Zach each spent time one weekend preparing packets, including addressing them. It takes about an hour for one student to prepare 80 packets. On Monday, after school, they each completed another 50 packets.

Zoe, Darnell, and Maya discussed how much time they spent on the project.

### Think & Discuss

About how many packets did each of the three students prepare? Consider both the packets prepared over the weekend and those completed on Monday. Zoe: 370; Darnell: 610; Maya: 1,010

When you calculated how many packets each student prepared, what was varying? The number of hours spent preparing packets over the weekend

Write an expression for the total number of packets prepared by a volunteer working for $t$ hours. $80t + 50$, where $t$ is the number of hours spent preparing packets over the weekend

Zach prepared 690 packets. How long did he spend preparing packets over the weekend? 8 hours



**Teacher Tips** Students should realize that the number of hours each person works preparing packets varies. As a result, the number of packets prepared by each person will also vary.

You may want to review how to complete a flowchart, as you or a volunteer draws one on the board.

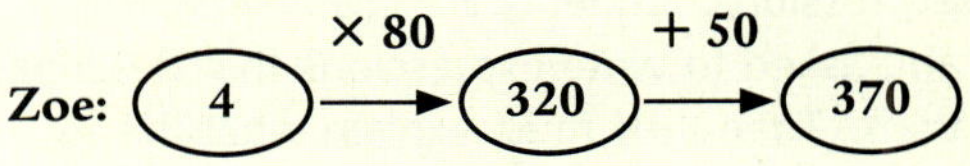


Some students may prefer to use number sense to find the number of hours that Zach worked. They know that Darnell worked 7 hours to make 610 packets. Since Zach made 80 more packets than Darnell, he must have worked one hour longer, or 8 hours.

Other students may use guess-check-and-improve to find the answer. Encourage these students to find other ways to solve the problem.

*Teacher Tips give practical suggestions for teaching lessons, organizing materials, managing collaborative group work, and more.*

# Investigation 1

***On Your Own Exercises***
Pages 43–48
Exercises 1–9, 14–15

**Write Algebraic Expressions** Students continue their work with algebraic expressions. Students are given situations and asked to write expressions that describe them. Then they must explain what the variable in their expressions represents. In the second problem set, students explore how a single expression can describe a multitude of situations.

## *Develop & Understand: A*

*Suggested Grouping: Pairs*

▶ **Exercise 1** This exercise helps students understand how two expressions can contain a variable as well as the same numbers and operations, yet have different values and represent different situations. Have students test their expressions using different inputs to make sure that the expressions make sense.

▶ **Exercise 2** Some students may think that every time Mr. Gordon adds the quantity of flour asked for in the recipe, he adds one additional cup. For example, they may think that if he doubles the recipe, he will add two additional cups of flour.

▶ **Exercise 3** Students backtrack to find the value of the variable. Some students may have the variable represent the number of yards in one round trip. This will change their expression in 3a to $2d + 600$. To find the answer to 3b, students will need to solve the equation, then divide the value of $d$ by 2.

▶ **Exercise 4** Students are encouraged to use the formula to find the area of a square. Students who approach the problem in this way will use exponents when writing the expression. This previews the use of formulas studied in the next investigation.

# Investigation 1 What's the Variable?

In this investigation, you will write algebraic expressions to match situations. You will figure out which of several situations match a given expression. You will also make up your own situations based on an expression and a given meaning for the variable.

## *Develop & Understand: A*

1. A movie ticket costs \$6, and a box of popcorn costs \$2.

   a. Owen was meeting friends at the theater to see a movie. He arrived first and bought one ticket. He decided to buy a box of popcorn for each of his friends. Write an expression for the total amount Owen spent. Choose a letter for the variable in your expression, and tell what the variable represents.

   1a. $6 + 2B$, where $B$ is the number of friends or the number of boxes of popcorn

   b. Another group of friends was meeting to see a movie. They planned to share one box of popcorn among them. Write an expression for the total amount the group spent, and tell what the variable represents. $6t + 2$, where $t$ is the number of friends or the number of tickets

2. A pancake recipe calls for flour. To make thicker pancakes, Mr. Gordon measures out an extra cup of flour. He then divides the flour into three equal portions so that he can make blueberry pancakes, banana pancakes, and plain pancakes. Write an expression for how much flour is in each portion, and tell what your variable represents. $\frac{w + 1}{3}$, where $w$ is the number of cups of flour in the recipe

3. Pablo made two round trips to the beach and then traveled another 600 yards to the market.

   a. Write an expression to represent the total distance Pablo traveled. Be sure to say what your variable represents. $2(2d) + 600$, or $4d + 600$, where $d$ is the distance to the beach

   b. If Pablo walked a total of 1,584 yards, how far is it to the beach? 246 yd

4. Ms. Franklin wants to till the ground to add new sections to her garden. She wants three square sections with the same side length and another section with an area of 7 square meters.

   a. Write an expression to represent the total area of the sections Ms. Franklin needs to till. $3r^2 + 7\ m^2$, where $r$ is the side length of a square section

   b. Ms. Franklin's son, Justice, offers to help her. If they share the work equally, how many square meters will each have to till? $\frac{3r^2 + 7}{2}\ m^2$



### *Troubleshooting*

Watch for students who let the variable in **Exercise 4a** stand for data other than the side of the squares. Some students may let the variable represent either the area of each square section or the total area of the three square sections, and they may write expressions for the situation as $3a + 7$ and $a + 7$, respectively. While these are acceptable responses for the information given, encourage students to look at other alternatives. If necessary, review how to find the area of a square. Then ask students to write an expression based on that information.

5. Holden received \$60 for his birthday. Each week, for $x$ weeks, he spent \$4 of the money to go ice skating. $60 - 4x$

a. How much money, in dollars, did Holden have left after $x$ weeks?

b. Does *any* number make sense for the value of $x$? If not, describe the values that do not make sense.

5b. Since $4 \cdot 15 = 60$, Holden will spend all his money after 15 weeks. So, $x$ values greater than 15 do not make sense. Since $x$ is the number of weeks, it must be a whole number greater than 0.

A single expression can represent numerous situations, depending on what the variable represents.

### Example

Consider the expression $c + 10$.

- If $c$ is the number of cents in Koto's piggy bank, $c + 10$ could represent the number of cents in the bank after she drops in another dime.
- If $c$ is the number of gallons of gas left in Ms. Flores' gas tank, $c + 10$ could represent the number of gallons after she adds 10 gallons.
- If there are $c$ members in the science club, $c + 10$ could represent the number of members after 10 new students join.

Think of some other situations $c + 10$ could represent.

## Develop & Understand: B

**In Exercises 6–11, decide whether the expression $2d + 5$ can represent the answer to the question. If it can, explain what $d$ stands for in that situation.**

6. Lucy bought two tickets to a symphony concert and five tickets to a movie. How much did she pay? No, unless each movie ticket is \$1

7. Sam bought several pens for \$2 each and a notebook for \$5. How much did he spend altogether? Yes; $d$ stands for the number of pens.

8. A herd of zebras walked a certain distance to a watering hole. On the return trip, a detour added an extra 5 km. How many kilometers did the herd walk altogether? Yes; $d$ stands for the distance to the water.



▶ **Exercise 5b** Discuss the restrictions. Most students will recognize that Holden will not have any money left after 15 weeks. They may be less likely to note that the variable must be a positive whole number.

### Example

Write the expression $c + 10$ on the board and tell students that this expression describes a situation. Have a volunteer read the first situation in the text. Discuss how the situation fits the expression. You may wish to use numbers to illustrate why this situation can be shown by the expression. Repeat for the other two situations. Then have students tell about other situations that could be described by the expression.

## Develop & Understand: B

*Suggested Grouping: Pairs*

▶ **Exercises 6–11** Be sure students understand that there can be two parts to each answer. They first decide whether the expression describes the situation. Then when the expression does describe the situation, students must explain what the variable stands for in the situation.

## Reaching All Learners

**OL On Level** Have students explain why the expression $2d + 5$ cannot be used to describe the situation in **Exercises 6, 9, and 11**. Students can use their reasoning and language arts skills to write their explanations. Knowing why a situation is not described by a given expression can help students recognize when and why an expression does describe a situation.

▶ **Exercises 12–15** These exercises show students how the same expression can describe different situations depending on what the variable represents.

▶ **Exercise 16** Students are asked to describe a situation shown by an expression that contains an exponent. Most students will remember using a number squared in a previous exercise set and use area as part of their descriptions.

**Wrap-Up** Have students compare the expressions and variables in **Exercises 12–15**. Students will see that the expressions are the same in all four problems. Then have students share their situations for each problem. Most students will supply the same situation, but students may find that the situation can vary even when parameters are given.

***Share & Summarize***

This kind of exercise will be familiar to students by now. Students can exchange situations with a partner and check that their partner's situation is reasonable.

**9.** There are two dogs in the house and five more in the yard. How many dogs are there altogether? No

**10.** Because their parents were sick, Neva and Dario spent twice as many hours as usual doing housework during the week plus an extra 5 hours on the weekend. How many hours of housework did they do? Yes; $d$ stands for the usual number of hours they spend doing housework.

**11.** Blake gets paid \$5 for every hour he babysits plus a \$2 bonus on weekends. How much money does he earn if he babysits on Saturday? No

**Describe a situation that can be represented by each expression.**
12–16. See below.

**12.** $4m - 3$, if $m$ stands for the number of pages in a book

**13.** $4m - 3$, if $m$ stands for the distance in kilometers from home to school

**14.** $4m - 3$, if $m$ stands for the number of eggs in a waffle recipe

**15.** $4m - 3$, if $m$ stands for the number of milliliters of water in a beaker of water

**16.** Describe two situations that can be represented by the expression $10 - x^2$. Discuss with your partner how your situations match the expression.

***Share & Summarize***

Describe two situations that can be represented by this expression.

$$3t + 7$$

Explain how your situations match the expression. Check by trying some values for the variable $t$ and seeing whether the solutions make sense. See ①.

① Possible situation: 7 more than the number of tea bags in 3 boxes of tea. $t$ represents the number of tea bags in a box, so 3 boxes contain $3t$ tea bags; 7 more than the number of tea bags in 3 boxes is $3t + 7$.

12. Possible answer: 3 fewer than the number of pages in 4 copies of a book
13. Possible answer: 3 fewer than the number of kilometers in 2 round trips to school
14. Possible answer: 3 fewer than the number of eggs in 4 waffle recipes
15. Possible answer: 3 fewer than the number of milliliters of water in 4 beakers of water
16. Possible answer: The unplanted portion of a 10 $m^2$ garden with an $x$-by-$x$ square area planted; the front surface area of a picture frame that covers a 10 $ft^2$ area with an $x$-by-$x$ square area reserved for the picture



## Troubleshooting

Watch for students who confuse the variable ***d*** with an abbreviation for dogs in **Exercise 9.** This is a common confusion when using a variable as an abbreviation for a word. For example, looking at the expression $2d + 5$, students often think of $2d$ as 2 dogs. They might then think that two dogs in the house can be abbreviated as $2d$. If they make this error, ask them what $d$ stands for. They should respond the *number* of dogs. Therefore, $2d$ stands for 2 times the number of dogs, not 2 dogs. For example, if $d = 3$ dogs, then $2d = 2 \cdot (3 \text{ dogs}) = 6$ dogs.

# Investigation 2 Formulas

**Vocabulary**

formula

**Materials**

- graph paper

Weather reports in most countries give temperatures in degrees Celsius. If you are like most Americans, however, a temperature of 20°C is something you have heard, but you may not know whether it is very hot, pleasantly warm, or fairly chilly.

### Think & Discuss

Test your sense of how warm these Celsius temperatures are.

- Which outdoor attire do you think is most appropriate when the temperature is 33°C? Is it a winter coat, jeans and a sweatshirt, or shorts and a t-shirt? Shorts and a t-shirt
- Which outdoor activity do you think is most appropriate in 10°C weather? Is it swimming, soccer, or skiing? Soccer

In the previous lesson, you used a rule to convert Celsius degrees to Fahrenheit. You multiplied the degrees in Celsius by 1.8 and added 32.

We often refer to this kind of rule as a **formula**, an algebraic "recipe."

The Celsius-Fahrenheit conversion formula is sometimes written as shown below.

What we want to know

How we calculate it

$$F = \frac{9}{5}C + 32$$

In the formula, the variable $C$ represents the temperature in degrees Celsius. The variable $F$ represents the temperature in degrees Fahrenheit.

This formula can also be written as shown below.

$$F = \frac{9C}{5} + 32$$



## Investigation 2

***On Your Own Exercises***
Pages 43–48
Exercises 10–13, 16–18

**Using Formulas** In this investigation, students learn that formulas are algebraic "recipes" used to represent relationships between variables that describe situations in contexts.

Begin the investigation by asking students what units are used to measure temperature. Most students will be familiar with both Fahrenheit and Celsius units of measurement from prior mathematics courses.

### Think & Discuss

*Suggested Grouping: Whole Class*

Discuss the two questions as part of a whole-class discussion. You may want to have students tell how they came up with their answers. Some students will know the Celsius scale. Others may use benchmarks to compare the Celsius temperature to a Fahrenheit temperature before answering. Tell these students that they can use a *formula* to convert temperatures from degrees Celsius to degrees Fahrenheit.

Explain to students that formulas represent relationships. Formulas are usually written as algebraic equations, with what you want to know by itself on the left-hand side, and the rule for calculating it on the right-hand side.

Direct students' attention to the formulas in the text. Point out what each variable represents and how the equation can be used. Ask questions such as:

How can you find the temperature in degrees Fahrenheit if you know the temperature in degrees Celsius? Substitute the Celsius temperature for $C$ in the equation and solve for $F$.

Why can the formula be written in two ways? Possible answer: $\frac{9}{5}C$ and $\frac{9C}{5}$ are two ways to write the same amount.

Some students may need to substitute values into the two formulas to be reassured that they name the same amount.

## Example

Walk students through how to use the formula to convert temperatures from degrees Celsius to degrees Fahrenheit. Remind them to follow the order of operations. If you have students use the formula to check their answers to the Think & Discuss questions on the previous page, they should calculate 33°C = 91.4°F and 15°C = 59°F.

## Develop & Understand: A

*Suggested Grouping: Pairs*

- **Exercises 1 and 2** Students substitute values in a given formula to find quantities of flour. In **Exercise 1b**, they need to backtrack to find the quantity of flour.
- **Exercise 3** Students compare two formulas to determine which formula uses more shortening per quantity of flour. They verify their answers by substituting values in each formula, and testing that the expected results are obtained.

### Example

Use the formula to find the Fahrenheit equivalent of 20°C.

| | |
|---|---|
| $F = \frac{9}{5}C + 32$ | Start with the formula. |
| $F = \frac{9}{5} \cdot 20 + 32$ | Substitute 20 for C. |
| $F = 68$ | Simplify. |

So, 20°C is the same as 68°F.

Following the example above, find the Fahrenheit equivalents of 33°C and 10°C. Were your answers to the Think & Discuss questions on page 35 reasonable?

### Real-World Link

Worldwide, wheat flour has a greater consumption than any other cereal grain. Fortification of wheat flour is an effective means for supplying vitamins and minerals to the world population. The percentage of wheat flour fortification increased from 18% to 27% from 2004 to 2007.

### Develop & Understand: A

1. Most pastry is made from flour, shortening, and water. There are different types of pastry. In *short pastry,* the relationship between the amount of flour $F$ and the amount of shortening $S$ is given by the following formula.

$$S = \frac{1}{2}F \qquad \text{or} \qquad S = \frac{F}{2}$$

   a. Alice wants to make lemon tarts with short pastry using exactly 800 grams of flour. How much shortening should she use? 400 g
   b. Daryl wants to make short pastry for cheese sticks, but he has only 250 grams of shortening. What is the maximum amount of flour he can use? 500 g

2. The relationship between flour and shortening in *flaky pastry* is given by the following formula.

$$S = \frac{3}{4}F \qquad \text{or} \qquad S = \frac{3F}{4}$$

   How much shortening would you need to add to 200 grams of flour to make flaky pastry? 150 g

3. Which type of pastry, short or flaky, needs more shortening for a given amount of flour? Check your answer by testing the amount of shortening for two amounts of flour. Flaky pastry

4. You saw that the relationship between temperature in degrees Celsius and degrees Fahrenheit is given by this formula.

$$F = \frac{9}{5}C + 32$$

a. Convert 38°C to degrees Fahrenheit. 100.4°F

b. Water freezes at 0°C. How many degrees Fahrenheit is this? 32°F

c. Water boils at 100°C. How many degrees Fahrenheit is this? 212°F

d. Convert 50°F to degrees Celsius. 10°C

**Math Link**

The diameter is the longest measurement across a circle. It equals twice the radius.

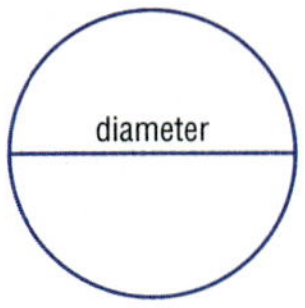


5. The formula for the area of a circle is $A = \pi r^2$, where $r$ is the radius. The Greek letter $\pi$ is not a variable. It is a number equal to the circumference of any circle divided by its diameter.

a. Your calculator probably has a button that automatically gives a good approximation for $\pi$. Do you recall some approximations that you have previously used?

b. What is the value of $\pi r^2$ for $r = 5.6$? About 98.5

c. Why is the standard order of operations important when finding the area of a circle?

d. Tetromino's Pizza makes a pizza with a diameter of 12 inches. Use the formula to find the area of a 12-inch pizza. About 113.1 $in^2$

e. Tetromino's 12-inch pizza costs $7.50. They also make a pizza with a diameter of 24 inches, which sells for $25. Which size is the better buy? Explain your answer.

f. Tetromino's smallest round pizza has an area of 78.5 $in^2$. Write the equation that you would need to solve to find the radius of the pizza. Solve your equation. $78.5 = \pi r^2$; $r$ is about 5.0 in.

5a. Answers will vary; some students may recall $\frac{22}{7}$ or 3.14.

5c. The order of operations indicates that you need to square $r$ before multiplying by $\pi$.

5e. The 24-inch pizza; the 12-inch pizza costs about 6.6¢ per $in^2$ and the 24-inch pizza costs about 5.5¢ per $in^2$.

6. In Course 1, you found the measures of the interior angles of several polygons.

a. What is the sum of the measures of the interior angles of a square? Of a rectangle? Of any quadrilateral? 360°, 360°, 360°

b. Write an expression for the sum of the measures of the interior angles of quadrilateral $ABCD$. $48° + 157° + 55° + x°$

c. What is the measure of angle $A$? 100°

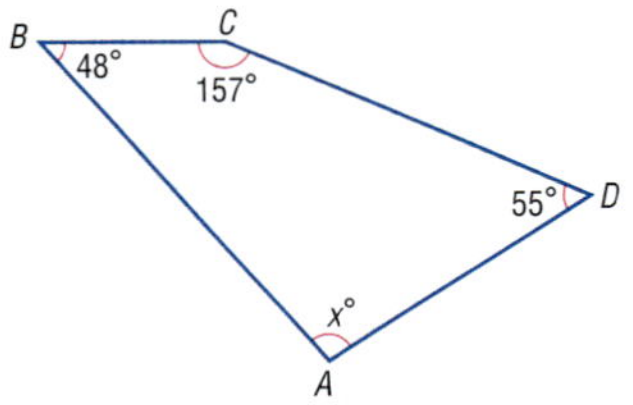




▶ **Exercise 4d** Students are asked to backtrack to convert from degrees Fahrenheit to degrees Celsius.

▶ **Exercise 5** Students review the value of $\pi$ and recall that it is not a variable. Students use $\pi$ in area formulas.

▶ **Exercise 6** Some students may add the three known angle measures and subtract the sum from 360°. Others may subtract each known angle measure from 360° one at a time. Either way, their answers should match.

**Wrap-Up** In **Exercise 5e**, students may use one of these strategies to find the answer.

- Students may find the area of each pizza and then divide the price by the area to find the cost per square inch. Then they can compare the cost per square inch for each pizza to choose the more economical buy.
- Students may find the area of each pizza. They can compare the two areas to find that the area of the 24-inch pizza is four times as great as the area of the 12-inch pizza. If the costs were proportional, the cost of the larger pizza would be 4 times as great as the cost of the smaller pizza, or 4 × $7.50, or $30. Since the larger pizza costs less than $30, it is the better buy.

**Math Link**

Discuss with students whether pizza is usually advertised using the diameter or the radius of the pizza. What items, if any, can students think of that are advertised using the radius rather than the diameter? Sample answer: 2-way radios

## Troubleshooting

In **Exercises 5d and 5e**, watch for students who use the diameter instead of the radius to find the area of the pizza. This is a good opportunity to point out the helpful notes in the side margins of the student page. Remind students that in the area formula for a circle, it is the radius, not the diameter, that is squared.

## Develop & Understand: B

*Suggested Grouping: Small Groups*

▶ **Exercise 7** Students are asked to choose equations to describe the motion of each tortoise.

**Teacher Tips** Have students look at the illustration and read the information about the tortoises. You may want students to predict which tortoise will win the race. Accept any reasonable answer that students can support.

### Real-World Link

Ask students what they know about tortoises and turtles. Encourage interested students to research the typical speed of tortoises. Students may also be intrigued by the longevity of tortoises.

Now you will use formulas to help you analyze a race.

## Develop & Understand: B

Three tortoises entered a ten-meter race.

### Real-World Link

Tortoises live on land while their aquatic cousins, turtles, live in and around water. The limbs of tortoises and freshwater turtles have fingers and toes. Marine turtles have flat flippers.

Tortoise 1 was especially slow. He moved at only 0.9 meter per minute, so he was given a 3.1-meter head start.

Tortoise 2 roared along at 1.3 meters per minute and received no head start.

Tortoise 3 also received no head start. Her distance was equal to the square of the time, in minutes, since the race began, multiplied by 0.165.

**7.** It would be useful to have a formula that tells each tortoise's distance from the starting line at any time after the race began. For each tortoise, choose the formula below that describes its distance $D$ from the starting point $m$ minutes after the race began.

| | | |
|---|---|---|
| $D = 3.1m + 0.9$ | $D = 1.3m$ | $D = 0.165 + m^2$ |
| $D = 3.1 + 0.9m$ | $D = 0.165m^2$ | $D = 10 - 1.3m$ |

Tortoise 1: $D = 3.1 + 0.9m$; Tortoise 2: $D = 1.3m$; Tortoise 3: $D = 0.165m^2$

You can use the formulas that you found in Exercise 6 to figure out the tortoises' positions at any time during the race. A table or a graph showing the positions of the tortoises at various times can help you understand how the race progressed.

**8.** Make a table like the one below that shows the tortoises' positions at various times during the race. To find a tortoise's distance at a given time, substitute the time value into the tortoise's formula. In your table, include whole-number minutes and any other time values that help you understand what happens during the race.

**The Tortoise Race**

| Time (min) | Distance from Start (m) | | | Comments |
|---|---|---|---|---|
| | Tortoise 1 | Tortoise 2 | Tortoise 3 | |
| 0 | 3.1 | 0 | 0 | They're off! |
| 1 | 4.0 | 1.3 | 0.17 | Tortoise 1 is well in front. |
| 2 | 4.9 | 2.6 | 0.66 | Tortoise 3 looks hopeless! |
| 3 | 5.8 | 3.9 | 1.49 | |
| 4 | 6.7 | 5.2 | 2.64 | |
| 5 | 7.6 | 6.5 | 4.13 | |
| 6 | 8.5 | 7.8 | 5.94 | |
| 7 | 9.4 | 9.1 | 8.09 | |
| 8 | 10.3 | 10.4 | 10.56 | |

**9.** On a single set of axes, make graphs that show the position of each tortoise at the times in your table. Use a different color or symbol for each tortoise.

**10.** Use your table and graph to determine which tortoise won the race. You may need to add values to your table or extend your graph to find the winner.

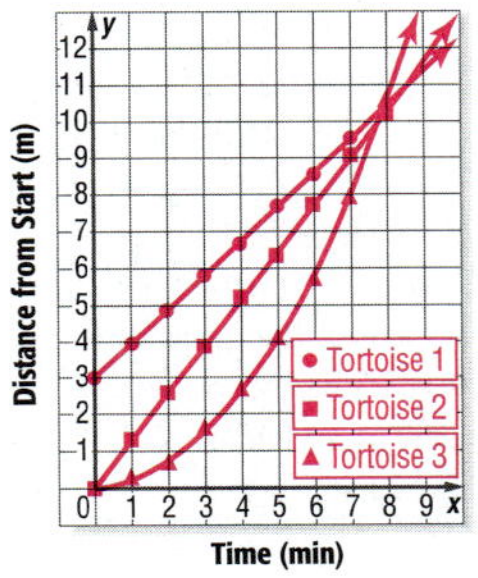


### *Share & Summarize*

A *cube* is a block with six identical square faces.

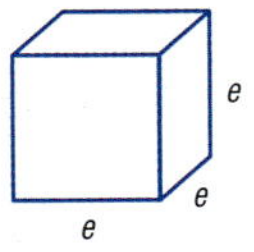


**1.** The *surface area* of a cube is the total area of all six faces. Write a formula for the surface area $S$ of a cube with edge length $e$. Explain why your formula is correct.

**2.** Use your formula to find the surface area of a cube with edges of length 8 cm. 384 $cm^2$

9 Note: Students may or may not connect the points on the graphs.

10. Tortoise 1 won. Tortoise 1 reached the finish line in 7.67 min, Tortoise 2 in 7.69 min, and Tortoise 3 in 7.78 min.

1. $S = 6e^2$; Each face has area $e^2$, and there are 6 faces, so the total area is $6e^2$.



▶ **Exercise 8** Students are asked to make a table to show the positions of the tortoises at various times during the race. Remind students that when they choose a value of $m$, they must substitute it into each of the three equations, evaluate the equations, and record the answers in a table. You may wish to use Lesson 1.2 Master 1.

▶ **Exercise 9** Students graph points from the table they constructed in the prior problem. This method of representing data is especially effective for visual learners.

**Wrap-Up** Some students may find the correct times but choose the tortoise with the greatest time as the winner. Remind them that the winner of a race is the one with the least time. Encourage them to discuss their problem-solving strategies. Students who have had experience in solving equations may prefer to solve the three equations for $D = 10$ and choose the fastest time.

### *Share & Summarize*

Students are asked to write a formula for finding the surface area of a cube. Most students will find the area of each side, $e^2$, then multiply the area by the number of sides. So the formula to find the surface area is $A = 6e^2$.

## *Troubleshooting*

Watch for students who want to graph all the equations in **Exercise 9** as linear equations. Remind them that not all graphs are straight lines. You may want to show them examples of nonlinear graphs.

In **Inquiry Investigations**, which appear once per chapter, students explore and reinforce concepts through application of the scientific method.

## Inquiry Investigation 3

*Suggested Grouping: Small Groups*

### Materials and Preparation

Students will need access to a computer and to spreadsheet software to complete this investigation. It would be preferable to have all students perform the investigation at the same time in a computer lab.

Introduce the lesson and exercise setting before allowing students to work with the spreadsheet software. Have students read the first three paragraphs. Be sure that students understand that Jo sells her cards in packs of 10 for $15 each. She charges a flat $7 fee to ship the cards, regardless of the size of the order.

Direct students' attention to the first spreadsheet. Discuss the labels in the spreadsheet. Students need to know spreadsheet terminology in order to follow the directions in this investigation. Review the terminology by asking questions such as:

- How are the rows in a spreadsheet labeled? They are in numerical order.
- How are the columns in a spreadsheet labeled? They are in alphabetical order.
- What is a cell? The box at the intersection of a column and a row.
- A cell is labeled by the column and the row. Which comes first? The column
- What is in cell B1 on the spreadsheet? The label Price
- What cell contains the label Price with Shipping? Cell C1



## Inquiry Investigation 3 Formulas and Spreadsheets

**Materials**

- computer with spreadsheet software (one per group)

Jo has started her own business selling hand-painted note cards. She designs and paints the front of the cards. Then she bundles the finished cards with envelopes in packs of ten.

Using her Web site, Jo has started to get orders from specialty shops. She charges $15 for each pack of cards. By charging $7 for shipping regardless of the order size, she hopes to encourage large orders.

To help her calculate how much to charge for orders, Jo set up a computer spreadsheet. She entered headings in the first three columns.

**Math Link**
Each box is called a *cell*. This is Cell A2.

| | A | B | C |
|---|---|---|---|
| 1 | Number of Packs | Price | Price with Shipping |
| 2 | | | |
| 3 | | | |
| 4 | | | |

When she gets a new order, Jo enters the number of packs ordered into Column A, Row 2. This is Cell A2.

To have the spreadsheet do the calculations automatically, Jo entered formulas into Cells B2 and C2. She used the name of Cell A2 as the variable. This commands the spreadsheet to use the value in Cell A2 for its calculations.

**Math Link**
Notice the expressions in Cells B2 and C2. The equals signs tell the spreadsheet that the entry uses a formula to evaluate.

| | A | B | C |
|---|---|---|---|
| 1 | Number of Packs | Price | Price with Shipping |
| 2 | | = A2 * 15 | = A2 * 15 + 7 |
| 3 | | | |
| 4 | | | |

Look at the formula in Cell B2. It commands the spreadsheet to calculate the price of the number of packs entered in Cell A2.

"Multiply the value in A2 by 15."

The formula in Cell C2 calculates the price with shipping.

"Multiply the value in A2 by 15 and then add 7."

## Try It Out

Set up a spreadsheet just like Jo's.

1. Answers will vary. When no value is given in A2, most spreadsheets will evaluate the formula using an input of 0.

**1.** Without highlighting the cells, look at Cells B2 and C2. What do they display? Why do you think this may have happened?

**2.** Jo received an order from Conrad's Cards and Gifts for 5 packs of cards. Use your spreadsheet to find how much Jo charges for 5 packs, both with and without shipping. To do this, select Cell A2. Then type "5" and press the return key or an arrow key. Without shipping: $75; with shipping: $82

**3.** Suppose Jo gets three more orders of 8 packs, 10 packs, and 30 packs. Find the charges with shipping for these orders. 8 packs: $127; 10 packs: $157; 30 packs: $457

## Try It Again

Jo realized that most orders were in multiples of 5. She wanted to avoid changing her spreadsheet for every order. A friend suggested that she make a chart listing the charges for various orders. She could print the chart and would not have to turn to her computer so often.

To make her chart, Jo used the Fill Down command. To do this, she selected all the cells in Columns B and C, from Row 2 to Row 21.

The Fill Down command took the formulas in the top cells, B2 and C2, and copied them into Cells B3–B21 and C3–C21.

The formulas in Column B all looked like the formula in Cell B2. The formulas in Column C all looked like the one in Cell C2.

| | A | B | C |
|---|---|---|---|
| 1 | Number of Packs | Price | Price with Shipping |
| 2 | | 0 | 7 |
| 3 | | | |
| 4 | | | |
| 5 | | | |
| 6 | | | |
| 7 | | | |
| 8 | | | |
| 9 | | | |
| 10 | | | |
| 11 | | | |
| 12 | | | |
| 13 | | | |
| 14 | | | |
| 15 | | | |
| 16 | | | |
| 17 | | | |
| 18 | | | |
| 19 | | | |
| 20 | | | |
| 21 | | | |
| 22 | | | |

4. The cell name, A2, changed to A14. Possible explanation: The spreadsheet changed the input cell so that the formula uses the value of the cell in Column A from that row.

**4.** Copy the formulas in your spreadsheet just like Jo did. Then look at the formulas in Cells B14 and C14. They do not look *exactly* like the formulas in Cells B2 and C2. For example, the formula in Cell B14 should be A14*15. What changed? Why do you think this happened?

Go on



Inquiry

Tell students that one of the benefits of a spreadsheet is that it does mathematical calculations. Formulas are used to tell the computer what calculations to perform.

Discuss how to write a formula, stressing that the equal sign in front of the formula allows the computer to recognize that it is to perform a calculation. Ask students questions such as:

- Look at Cell B2. What is this formula telling the spreadsheet to do? Calculate the price of the number of packs entered in Cell A2.
- Look at Cell C2. What is the formula doing? It is calculating the price with shipping, using the value entered in Cell A2.

## Try It Out

Students set up spreadsheets to show Jo's business transactions. If any of your students are not familiar with computers or the very basic spreadsheet mechanics, you may need to supplement the directions in the text.

▶ **Exercise 3** Students enter data for three more orders and calculate the total charge for each. Be sure that they understand that they are to replace the data in Cell A2 for each order.

## Try It Again

If possible, demonstrate how to use the Fill Down command. Be sure that students realize why the cells in the spreadsheet on page 41 are highlighted and that they understand how they can highlight the cells in their spreadsheet.

▶ **Exercise 11** The groups make a spreadsheet for the situation of their choosing. Some students may need help in labeling the columns as well as with writing and entering formulas. You may want to have groups either share their spreadsheets with the class or display their printouts.

## What Did You Learn?

The two questions in this section help students look back on what they have learned from this activity. If time permits, have students answer the questions in class.

Students should be able to identify the variables in formulas entered in a spreadsheet, describe how a formula is changed when it is copied to another cell, and tell how a spreadsheet can be helpful.

Inquiry

To finish her chart, Jo needed to enter the order amounts into Column A, the numbers from 5 to 100 by fives. However, she did not want to take the time to type each number into its cell. She thought of an easier way to do it.

Jo entered the first number, 5, into Cell A2. Then she typed the formula A2+5 into Cell A3.

**5.** What number would the spreadsheet calculate for Cell A3? 10

Jo used the Fill Down command to fill the cells in Column A, from Row 4 to Row 21, with her formula for Cell A3.

**6.** Do you think the formula in Cell A4 is *exactly* the same as the formula in Cell A3? If not, what do you think the formula is? No, A3 + 5

**7.** What value would be calculated for Cell A4? 15

**8.** Try it with your spreadsheet. What happened? What does Column A look like now?

**9.** What numbers are given in Row 14 of your spreadsheet? What do these numbers mean?

**10.** Look at your spreadsheet to find what Jo should charge, with shipping, for an order of 45 packs of cards. $682

**11.** Design a spreadsheet of your own for a formula or equation. Show a reasonable range of values, using an increment in the inputs to give about 20 to 30 rows of calculations. Label the columns clearly. Spreadsheets will vary.

8. The formula was copied into the cells, each using the cell in the previous row as its input. Column A now has the values 5, 10, 15, ... , 100.
9. 65, 975, 982; For 65 packs of cards, the price without shipping is $975 and with shipping is $982.

### What Did You Learn?

**12.** A spreadsheet cell contains the formula D3*4–1.

**a.** What is the variable in this formula? D3

**b.** The formula in this cell is copied to the cell below it. What is the formula in the new cell? D4*4–1

**13.** Name at least one way in which spreadsheets can be helpful.
Possible answer: You can use them to make a lot of calculations quickly. You can make several calculations using different inputs without typing each calculation yourself.

42 CHAPTER 1 Expressions

## Practice & Apply

2b. $\frac{40p + 500}{p}$ or $40 + \frac{500}{p}$

**1.** A ticket to the symphony costs \$27 for adults and \$10.50 for children.

**a.** Write an expression for the total ticket cost in dollars if *A* adults and three children attend the symphony. $27A + 31.5$

**b.** Write an expression for the total ticket cost if two adults and *C* children go to the symphony. $54 + 10.5C$

**2.** Anica and her friends are organizing a trip to the state skateboarding championships. The bus they will rent to take them there and back will cost \$500. Anica estimates that each person will spend \$40 for meals and souvenirs.

**a.** If *p* people go on the trip, what will be the total cost for travel, meals, and souvenirs? $40p + 500$

**b.** What will be the cost per person if *p* people go on the trip?

**c.** What will be the total cost per person if 25 people go on the trip? \$60

**3.** A full storage tank contains 2,160 gallons of water. Every 24 hours, 4.5 gallons leak out of the tank.

**a.** How many gallons of water will be in the tank *H* hours after it is filled? $2{,}160 - \frac{4.5H}{24}$

**b.** How many gallons of water will be in the tank after *D* days? $2{,}160 - 4.5D$

**c.** How many gallons of water will be in the tank after *W* weeks? $2{,}160 - 31.5W$

In Exercises 4–6, determine whether the expression $9m - 4$ can be used to represent the answer to the question. If it can, explain what *m* represents.

**4.** The ski club bought nine lift tickets and received a \$4 discount on the total price. What was the total cost for the tickets? Yes; *m* is the price of a ticket.

**5.** Of the nine people on a baseball field, four are girls. How many are boys? No

**6.** Last Saturday, Kenya listened to her new CD nine times. But the ninth time she played it, she skipped a 4-minute song she did not like. How much time did Kenya spend listening to her CD last Saturday? Yes; *m* is the number of minutes it takes to play the CD once.



On Your Own Exercises
Lesson 1.2

**Investigation 1**
Pages 32–34
Practice & Apply: 1–9
Connect & Extend: 14, 15

**Investigation 2**
Pages 35–39
Practice & Apply: 10–13
Connect & Extend: 16–18

**Assign Anytime**
Mixed Review: 20–32

▶ **Exercise 2b** Most students will simply divide the answer to ***2a*** by ***p***. If no student comes up with the expression $40 + \frac{500}{p}$, challenge students to explain why it also is correct.

▶ **Exercise 10** You may wish to read aloud the hint for Part c. Some students may use the guess-check-and-improve strategy to solve.

On Your Own Exercises

7. Possible answer: The total cost for having 3 pizzas delivered if the delivery fee is $2
8. Possible answer: The number of ounces left in 2 pitchers of lemonade after filling an 8-oz glass

**In Exercises 7–9, describe a situation that the expression can represent.**

**7.** $3p + 2$, if $p$ is the price of a pepperoni pizza in dollars

**8.** $2x - 8$, if $x$ is the number of ounces in a pitcher of lemonade

**9.** $\frac{L^2}{2}$, if $L$ is the length of a square piece of paper Possible answer: The area of half the piece of paper

**10.** Three friends, Aisha, Mika, and Caitlin, have electronic robot toys that move at different speeds. They decide to have a ten-meter race. 10a–c. See margin.

- Aisha's robot travels 1 meter per second.
- Mika's robot moves 0.9 meter per second.
- Caitlin's robot's speed is 1.3 meters per second.

**a.** If they all start together, whose robot will win? How long will each robot take to reach the finish line?

**b.** To make the next race more interesting, the friends agree to give Mika's and Aisha's robots a head start.

- Mika's robot has a three-meter head start, so it has to travel only seven meters.
- Aisha's robot has a two-meter head start, so it has to travel only eight meters.

Whose robot wins this race? Whose comes in second? Whose comes in last?

**c.** The girls decide they would like the robots to finish as close to *exactly* together as possible. How much of a head start should Mika's and Aisha's robots have for this to happen?

Hint: Use your calculator. Caitlin's robot takes $10 \div 1.3 = 7.6923077$ seconds to travel ten meters. How can you position the other two robots so that they take this same amount of time?

## Additional Answers

10a. Caitlin's wins; Caitlin's: 7.7 s, Aisha's: 10 s, Mika's: 11.1 s

10b. Caitlin's (7.7 s) just wins, with Mika's (7.8 s) second and Aisha's (8 s) last.

10c. Aisha's needs a 2.3076923 m head start, and Mika's needs a 3.07692308 m head start.

On Your Own Exercises

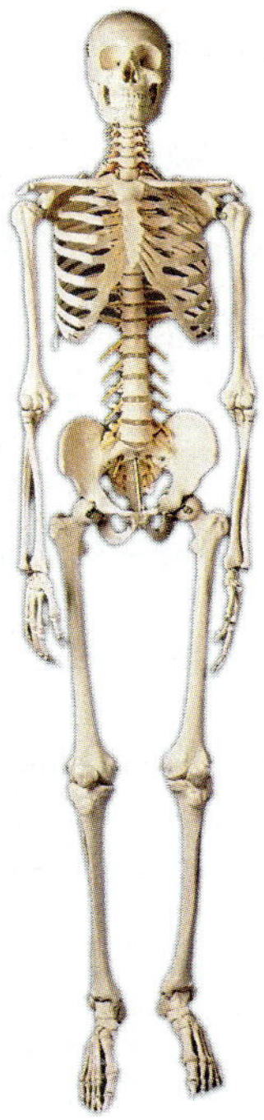

**11. Measurement** By measuring certain bones, forensic scientists can estimate a person's height. These formulas show the approximate relationship between the length of the tibia, or shin bone, $t$ and height $h$ for males and females. The measurements are in centimeters.

$$\text{males: } h = 81.688 + 2.392t$$

$$\text{females: } h = 72.572 + 2.533t$$

**a.** How tall is a male if his tibia is 38 cm long? Give your answer in centimeters. Use the facts that 2.54 centimeters are about one inch and 12 inches equals one foot to find the height in feet. 172.584 cm or about 5.66 ft

**b.** How tall is a female if her tibia is 38 centimeters long? Give your answer in centimeters and in feet. 168.826 cm, or about 5.54 ft

**c.** If a woman is 160 centimeters tall, or about 5.25 feet, how long is her tibia? About 34.5 cm

**12. Physics** The distance in meters an object falls in $T$ seconds after it is dropped, not taking into account air resistance, is given by the formula below.

$$D = 4.9T^2$$

**a.** A stone is dropped from a high cliff. How far will it have fallen after three seconds? 44.1 m

**b.** After dropping from a plane, a parachutist counts slowly to ten before pulling the ripcord to unfold her parachute. How far does she fall while she is counting? Answers will vary. If the counting takes 10 s, she will fall 490 m.

**c.** Shelley dropped a pebble from a cliff and timed it as it fell. The pebble hit the water 3.7 seconds after she dropped it. How high is the cliff above the water? About 67 m

**d.** The watch Shelley used was accurate only to the nearest 0.1 second. This means that the actual time it took the pebble to fall may have been 0.1 second less or 0.1 second more than what Shelley timed.

Find a range of heights for the cliff to allow for this error in timing the pebble's fall. Answers will vary. Using 3.6 and 3.8 for $T$, the cliff is between 63.5 m and 70.8 m high.


**Lesson 1.2** Expressions and Formulas 45

▶ **Exercise 15c** Students are asked whether there are any restrictions placed on *s*. If students believe there are no restrictions, have them make a table of values for *s* using 1 to 5. Then ask whether there are any values that are too small.



On Your Own Exercises

**13. Geology** Geologists estimate that Earth's temperature rises about 10°C for every kilometer *k* below Earth's surface.

**a.** Suppose it is 50°C on the surface of Earth. What is the formula for the temperature *T* in degrees Celsius at a depth of *k* km? $T = 50 + 10k$

**b.** If it is 50°C on the surface, what is the temperature at a depth of 15 km? 200°C

**Connect & Extend**

**14.** A rental car costs $35 per day plus $0.10 per mile.

**a.** What is the cost, in dollars, to rent the car for five days if you drive a total of *M* miles? $5(35) + 0.1M$, or $175 + 0.1M$

**b.** What is the cost to rent the car for five days if you drive *M* miles each day? $5(35 + 0.1M)$, or $175 + 0.5M$

**c.** What is the cost to rent the car for *D* days if you drive a total of 85 miles? $8.5 + 35D$

**d.** What is the cost to rent the car for *D* days if you drive 85 miles each day? $D(0.1 \cdot 85 + 35)$, or $43.5D$

**e.** What would be the cost per person if three people share the cost of renting the car in Part d? $\frac{43.5D}{3}$, or $14.5D$

**15. Geometry** The diagram shows the square floor of a store. A square display case with sides of length three feet stands in a corner of the store. The manager wants the floor area painted. Assume the display case cannot be moved.

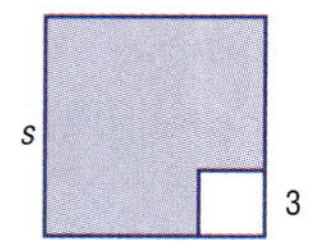


**a.** How many square feet need to be painted? $s^2 - 9$

**b.** The manager hires two people to paint the floor. How many square feet would each person have to paint if they share the job equally? $\frac{s^2 - 9}{2}$

**c.** Are there any restrictions on the value of *s*? If so, explain why and tell what the restrictions are. If not, explain why not.

15c. The value of *s* must be greater than 3 because the sides of the store's floor must be longer than the sides of the display case.

**16.** The formula below helps scuba divers figure out how long they can stay under water.

$$T = \frac{120V}{d}$$

*T*: approximate maximum time, in minutes, a diver can stay under water

*V*: volume of air in the diver's tank, in cubic meters, before compression

*d*: depth of the water, in meters

**a.** Antonio has one cubic meter of air compressed in his tank. He is 4 meters under water. How long can he stay down? 30 min

**b.** How long can Antonio stay eight meters under water with one cubic meter of air in his tank? 15 min

**c.** If Antonio wanted to stay four meters under water for one hour, how much air would he need? 2 $m^3$

### Real-World Link

A *single* hit enables the batter to reach first base; a *double,* to reach second base; a *triple,* to reach third base; and a *home run,* to make a complete circuit of the bases and score a run.

A batting average and a slugging percentage are different. A *batting average* is a measure of the number of hits a player makes for every time at bat. A *slugging percentage* figures in how many bases the batter ran for every time at bat.

**17. Geometry** The formula for the area of a trapezoid is $A = \frac{h(B + b)}{2}$, where *B* and *b* are the lengths of the two parallel sides and *h* is the height.

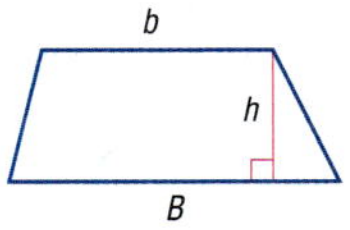


**a.** Find the area of a trapezoid with parallel sides of length 6 cm and 7 cm and height 5 cm. 32.5 $cm^2$

**b.** The area of a trapezoid is 6 $cm^2$. What might be the values of *h*, *B*, and *b*? Possible answer: $B = 4$ cm, $b = 2$ cm, $h = 2$ cm

**18.** A baseball player's slugging percentage *P* can be computed with the following formula.

$$P = \frac{S + 2D + 3T + 4H}{A}$$

*S* is the number of singles, *D* is the number of doubles, *T* is the number of triples, *H* is the number of home runs, and *A* is the number of official at bats.

**a.** Suppose a professional baseball player hit 112 singles, 20 doubles, 0 triples, and 66 home runs in 643 at bats. What was his slugging percentage? 0.647

**b.** What if the player hit 61 singles, 21 doubles, 0 triples, and 70 home runs in 509 at bats? What was his slugging percentage? 0.752



On Your Own Exercises

▶ **Exercise 16** Students use a formula with three variables to find the value of *T*, *V*, or *d*, depending upon the given information. Students can practice solving several different equations.

▶ **Exercise 17b** Encourage students to work backward to solve the problem.

### Real-World Link

You may wish to have a student read this aloud. Then discuss the meaning of batting average and slugging percentage.

▶ **Exercises 20–29** With comparison problems involving inequalities, students may have a tough time remembering which symbol to use. Remind students that the open end of the symbol always faces the number of greater value.

▶ **Exercise 31** Students may need to be reminded that in a quadrilateral, the interior angle measures must sum to 360 degrees.

**Quick Check** and **Quick Quiz** provide informal end-of-lesson opportunities for assessing students' understanding and progress.

## Quick Check

**Informal Assessment** Students should be able to:

- ✔ practice using variables to write expressions
- ✔ use expressions to solve problems
- ✔ develop and use formulas to find specific quantities
- ✔ use a spreadsheet to make a chart

## Quick Quiz

1. Write an expression that shows the number of inches in $w$ feet, eight inches. $12w + 8$
2. Noah has $y$ lacrosse balls.
   a. Write an expression for the number of balls Christina has if she has 3 less than twice the number of balls Noah has. $2y - 3$
   b. Are there any restrictions on $y$? Yes, Noah must have more than one ball.
3. Make up a story for the expression $12b + 7$. Possible answer: Jeremy has 7 more than 12 times the number of model airplanes that Elmore has.





**19. In Your Own Words** Knowing that five pennies equal one nickel, Rob wrote the equation $5P = N$, where $P$ is the number of pennies and $N$ is the number of nickels. Explain why this equation does or does not represent this situation.

19. Possible answer: If Rob wants to compare the monetary values, his equation is correct. If Rob wants to compare the number of coins, his equation is incorrect.

## Mixed Review

**Number Sense** Fill in each ◯ with >, <, or =.

| | |
|---|---|
| **20.** $33\frac{1}{3}\% = \frac{1}{3}$ | **21.** $\frac{7}{8} > 85\%$ |
| **22.** $0.398 < \frac{2}{5}$ | **23.** $-5 < -1$ |
| **24.** $0.\overline{5} = \frac{5}{9}$ | **25.** $\frac{31}{40} > 75\%$ |
| **26.** $\frac{347}{899} > \frac{347}{900}$ | **27.** $\frac{6}{7} < \frac{7}{8}$ |
| **28.** $80\% > \frac{45}{60}$ | **29.** $0.01 < 0.1$ |

**Geometry** Find each missing angle measure.

**30.**

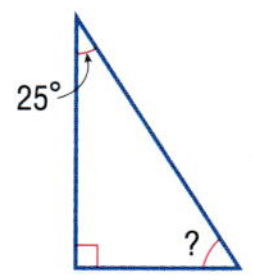


65°

**31.**

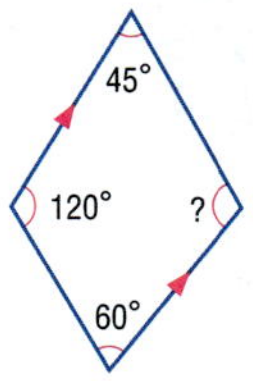


135°

**32.** There are twenty-five students in Ms. Johnson's seventh grade class. Fifteen of the students are girls.

a. Write a ratio that represents the number of girls to the number of boys. $\frac{15}{10}$ or $\frac{3}{2}$

b. Write three equivalent ratios.

c. What percent of the class is boys? 40%

32b. Answers will vary. Possible answers: $\frac{3}{2}$, $\frac{30}{20}$, $\frac{150}{100}$

LESSON 1.3

# The Distributive Property

## Overview

In this lesson, students learn about the distributive property of multiplication over addition and subtraction. They learn about different ways to group blocks and then move on to rearranging symbolic expressions. It is important that students understand the distributive property since it is a key element in elementary symbolic manipulation. It provides the backbone of the processes of collecting like terms and of factoring and expanding expressions.

### Objectives

- To understand and apply the distributive property
- To remove parentheses by multiplying
- To insert parentheses by factoring expressions
- To perform numerical calculations using the distributive property
- To combine like terms to simplify solutions

## Advance Preparation

You will need 3 bags and 6 blocks to demonstrate the Think and Discuss preceding Investigation 2. Copies of Chapter 1 Master 2, Flowcharts, can be used to help students record their answers.

| | Summary | Materials | On Your Own Exercises (pp. 63–68) | Assessment Opportunities |
|---|---|---|---|---|
| **Investigation 1** (p. 51) Pacing: 2 days | Students learn that two forms of an expression can represent the same concrete situation. | Chapter 1 Master 2, bags and blocks | Practice & Apply: 1–3<br>Connect & Extend: 27, 28<br>Mixed Review: 46–53 | • Share & Summarize (p. 52)<br>• Troubleshooting (p. 51) |
| **Investigation 2** (p. 53) Pacing: 1 day | Students see that there are two different ways to write an expression. | | Practice & Apply: 4–9<br>Connect & Extend: 29<br>Mixed Review: 46–53 | • On the Spot Assessment (p. 55)<br>• Share & Summarize (p. 55) |
| **Investigation 3** (p. 56) Pacing: 1 day | Students rewrite expressions inserting and removing parentheses. | | Practice & Apply: 10–15<br>Connect & Extend: 30–33<br>Mixed Review: 46–53 | • Share & Summarize (p. 59)<br>• Troubleshooting (pp. 57, 59) |
| **Investigation 4** (p. 60) Pacing: 1 day | Students learn to simplify expressions by combining like terms. | | Practice & Apply: 16–26<br>Connect & Extend: 34–44<br>Mixed Review: 46–53 | • Share & Summarize (p. 62) |

# Leveled Lesson Resources

CRM *Available in:* **Chapter 1 Resource Masters**

Also on TeacherWorks™ Lesson 1.3

## Study Guide and Intervention (p. 33) AL

**Lesson 1.3 Study Guide and Intervention**
***The Distributive Property***

The expressions $2(1 + 5)$ and $2 \cdot 1 + 2 \cdot 5$ are equivalent expressions because they have the same value of 12. The **distributive property** combines addition and multiplication.

**Symbols**

$a(b + c) = ab + ac$

$(b + c)a = ba + ca$

**Model**

The distributive property also combines subtraction and multiplication.

**Example 1** **Use the distributive property to expand each expression. Then evaluate the expression if possible.**

a. $2(6 + 3)$

$2(6 + 3) = 2 \cdot 6 + 2 \cdot 3$
$= 12 + 6$
$= 18$

b. $7(m + 5)$

$7(m + 5) = 7m + 7 \cdot 5$
$= 7m + 35$

**Example 2** **Use the distributive property to factor each expression.**

a. $12y + 36$

$12y + 36 = 12(y + 3)$

b. $18z^2 + 63z$

$18z^2 + 63z = 9(2z^2 + 7z)$
$= 9z(2z + 7)$

**Exercises**

**Use the distributive property to expand or factor each expression. Then evaluate the expression, if possible.**

1. $3(8 + 2)$
2. $2(9 + 11)$
3. $5(19 - 6)$
4. $3(d + 4)$
5. $(w - 5)4$
6. $2(c + 7)$
7. $15a - 60$
8. $22b^2 + 42b$
9. $42n^3 - 56n^6$

## Skills Practice (p. 34) AL OL

**Lesson 1.3 Skills Practice**
***The Distributive Property***

**Use the distributive property to expand each expression. Then evaluate the expression.**

1. $8(50 + 4)$
2. $(20 + 9)5$
3. $2(60 + 4)$
4. $7(40 - 2)$
5. $4(400 - 2)$
6. $4(16 + 5)$
7. $8(4 + 1)$
8. $9(24 - 19)$
9. $3(7 + 11)$
10. $10(12 - 4)$
11. $(21 + 9)5$
12. $7(1 + 10)$
13. $2(1 + 6)$
14. $4(15 + 25)$
15. $15(100 + 6)$
16. $12(22 + 52)$

**Use the distributive property to expand each expression.**

17. $4(d + 2)$
18. $1(u - 3)$
19. $6(f + 5)$
20. $2(g - 3)$
21. $3(x - 7)$
22. $8(b + 4)$
23. $(9 - b)5$
24. $4(c + 1)$
25. $12(2 - y)$
26. $7(a + 1)$
27. $11(k - 20)$
28. $9(r - 1)$

**Use the distributive property to factor each expression.**

29. $3x + 27$
30. $15 - 35y$
31. $42q - 21$
32. $36 - 60m^2$
33. $48b^2 + 64$
34. $24r - 32r^2$
35. $18w^2 + 30w$
36. $40a + 60a^2$
37. $66d^2 - 11d$
38. $28g + 42g^2$
39. $54b^2 - 18b$
40. $24s + 96s^2$

## Problem-Solving Practice (p. 35) AL OL

**Lesson 1.3 Problem-Solving Practice**
***The Distributive Property***

1. **Farming** Mr. Johannsen has the same number of ducks and rabbits on his farm. Write an expression to represent the number of animal legs on the farm. If he has 40 of each animal, how many legs are there?

2. **Stamps** Amy buys retired stamps from the U. S. Postal Service catalog. Last month, she bought the same number of \$0.37 Candy Heart stamps, \$0.48 Niagara Falls stamps, and \$0.80 Special Olympics stamps. Write an expression to find how much Amy spent on stamps. If she bought 8 of each stamp, how much did she spend?

3. **Fundraising** The table shows the cookie sales for Tina's scout troop. Each kind of cookie costs the same amount. Write an expression to find the troop's total cookie sales. If each box costs \$3.50, how much money did the troop make?

| Kind of Cookie | Number of Boxes |
|---|---|
| Mint | 60 boxes |
| Vanilla sandwich | 42 boxes |
| Peanut butter | 56 boxes |

4. **Geometry** Jonah drew two identical squares, each with side length $s$. Write an expression to show the total area of the two squares. What is the total area of the two squares if the side length is 8 cm?

5. **Savings** Daniel wants to buy a bicycle that costs \$200. He saves the same amount each month from the money he earns mowing lawns. He also saves \$15 of his monthly allowance.

a. If $x$ represents the amount he earns mowing lawns each month, write an expression to show Daniel's total savings after 8 months.

b. If Daniel earns \$25 each month mowing lawns, how long will it take him to save enough money to buy his bicycle?

## Enrichment (p. 36) BL

**Lesson 1.3 Enrichment**
***The Distributive Property***

What Day Was It?

To find the day of the week on which a date occurred, follow these steps.

- Use the formula $s = d + 2m + \left[\frac{3(m + 1)}{5}\right] + y + \left[\frac{y}{4}\right] - \left[\frac{y}{100}\right] + \left[\frac{y}{400}\right] + 2$

  where $s$ = sum
  $d$ = day of the month, using whole numbers from 1 to 31
  $m$ = month, where March = 3, April = 4, and so on, up to December = 12; then January = 13 and February = 14
  $y$ = year (For dates in January or February use the previous year)

- Evaluate expressions inside the special brackets [ ] by dividing and then discarding the remainder, using only the whole number part of the quotient.

- After finding the value of $s$, divide $s$ by 7 and note the remainder. The remainder 0 represents Saturday, 1 represents Sunday, 2 represents Monday, and so on to 6 represents Friday.

**Example** **On December 7, 1941, Pearl Harbor was bombed. What day of the week was it?**

Let $d = 7$, $m = 12$, and $y = 1941$.

$s = d + 2m + \left[\frac{3(m + 1)}{5}\right] + y + \left[\frac{y}{4}\right] - \left[\frac{y}{100}\right] + \left[\frac{y}{400}\right] + 2$

$s = 7 + 2(12) + \left[\frac{3(12 + 1)}{5}\right] + 1941 + \left[\frac{1941}{4}\right] - \left[\frac{1941}{100}\right] + \left[\frac{1941}{400}\right] + 2$

$s = 7 + 24 + \left[\frac{39}{5}\right] + 1941 + \left[\frac{1941}{4}\right] - \left[\frac{1941}{100}\right] + \left[\frac{1941}{400}\right] + 2$

$s = 7 + 24 + 7 + 1941 + 485 - 19 + 4 + 2$

$s = 2{,}451$

Now divide $s$ by 7. $2{,}451 \div 7 = 305$ R1

Since the remainder is 1, December 7, 1941, was a Sunday.

**Exercises** **Use the formula to solve each problem.**

1. Verify today's date.
2. What will be the day of the week for April 13, 2012?
3. On what day of the week was the Declaration of Independence signed, July 4, 1776?
4. On what day of the week were you born?

## Lesson Quick Quiz (p. 37) AL OL BL

**Lesson 1.3 Quick Quiz**

1. Combine like terms to simplify this polynomial: $6x - 6y + 5x$.

2. Rewrite this expression by removing the parentheses: $1.5(2c + 10)$.

3. Use the distributive property to rewrite this expression: $24y + 8y^2$.

4. Find two different ways of writing a rule that produces the table below:

| Input | 0 | 1 | 2 | 3 |
|---|---|---|---|---|
| Output | 2 | 6 | 10 | 14 |

# Additional Lesson Resources

### Teacher Tech Tools

- TeacherWorks
- ExamView Assessment Suite
- Classroom Presentation Toolkit
- Advance Tracker

### Student Tech Tools

- StudentWorks Plus
- Math Online eGlossary • Concepts in Motion

### Other Print Products

- Investigation Notebook and Reflection Journal
- Quick Review Math Handbook

LESSON 1.3

# The Distributive Property



## Vocabulary

distributive property

If you have ever solved a multiplication problem like $4 \cdot 24$ by thinking, "It's $4 \cdot 20$ plus $4 \cdot 4$" or "It's 4 less than $4 \cdot 25$," you were using a mathematical property called the **distributive property**. Using this property, you can change the way you think about how numbers are grouped.

For example, rather than think about 4 groups of 24, you can think about 4 groups of 20 added to 4 groups of 4. As you will see, this property is helpful for more than just mental arithmetic.

You can use bags and blocks to help you think about algebraic expressions. Bags and blocks can help you look more closely at the distributive property, too.

### Think & Discuss

Shaunda, Kate, and Malik are each holding one bag and two extra blocks.

Find the total number if each bag contains the following number of blocks.

- 5 blocks 21
- 20 blocks 66
- 100 blocks 306
- $b$ blocks $3b + 6$

How did you find your answers? Explanations will vary.



## The Distributive Property

LESSON 1.3

## Introduce

**Shortcuts** Ask students whether they have ever used shortcuts to do a multiplication problem, such as $4 \cdot 24$. Some may break apart the problem to find $4 \cdot 20 = 80$ and $4 \cdot 4 = 16$, then add those products to find $4 \cdot 24 = 96$. Explain that this strategy has a name. It is called the *distributive property of multiplication over addition.*

### Think & Discuss

*Suggested Grouping: Small Groups*

Have 3 bags and 6 blocks in the front of the room, arranged in 3 groups of 1 bag and 2 blocks each. This mirrors the arrangement in the illustration in the text.

**Teacher Tips** Have students look at page 50 to see how Sona and Omar found the total number of blocks. Ask students to compare their strategies for finding the number of blocks with those given by Omar and Sona.

Students should see that Sona first found the number of blocks in each group and then multiplied the number of blocks in each group by the number of groups.

Omar found the number of blocks in all the bags and the total number of loose blocks and then added the answers together to find the total number of blocks.

Each method of grouping shows that there are 66 blocks altogether.

Have students tell whose method they prefer and explain why.

Write the expressions showing Sona's and Omar's methods on the board. Have students tell how you would rewrite the expressions if there were $b$ blocks, then have students write their answers under the original expressions.

| Sona | Omar |
|---|---|
| $3(20 + 2)$ | $(3 \cdot 20) + (3 \cdot 2)$ |
| $3(b + 2)$ | $(3 \cdot b) + (3 \cdot 2)$ |
| | $3b + 6$ |

Students need to realize that these two expressions are different ways to think about, and to represent, the same situation. When the same value is substituted for the variable in each expression, the answer to both is the same.



Here is how Sona and Omar found the total number of blocks when there were 20 in each bag.

Sona's method: "Each person has 22 blocks, so I multiplied 22 by 3 and got 66."

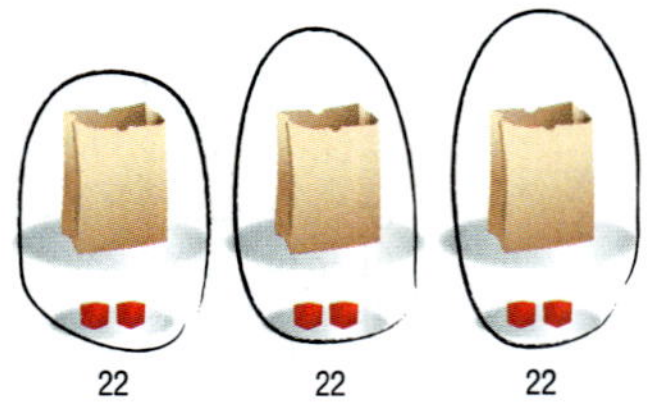


$$3(20 + 2) = 3 \cdot 22 = 66$$

Omar's method: "There are 3 bags, that's 60 blocks, and 3 sets of 2 leftover blocks, that's 6 more. So, there are 66 blocks."

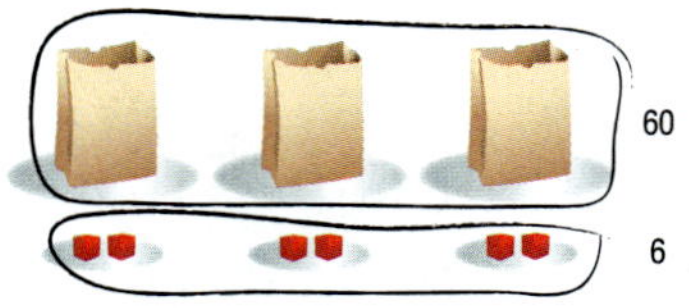


$$3 \cdot 20 + 3 \cdot 2 = 60 + 6 = 66$$

**Math Link**
The following are four different ways to say the same thing.

| | |
|---|---|
| $3 \times 22$ | $3(22)$ |
| $3 \cdot 22$ | $3 * 22$ |

Sona's and Omar's methods both work no matter how many blocks are in each bag. You can express their methods in symbols for $b$ blocks in each bag.

| Sona's method | Omar's method |
|---|---|
| $3(b + 2)$ | $3b + 3 \cdot 2 = 3b + 6$ |

Which way do *you* like to think about this situation? Or do you have another way?

Regardless of which method you prefer, the important thing to understand is that these two ways of looking at the situation give the same answer.

$$3(b + 2) = 3b + 6$$

# Investigation 1 Bags and Blocks

One way to see how different expressions can describe the same situation is to consider different groupings of a given number of bags and blocks. Each grouping will have the same total number of blocks, so the expressions you create must represent the same quantity.

## Develop & Understand: A

**1.** Brigitte placed three blocks in front of each of four bags. For each situation, show two ways of finding the total number of blocks that she has. If you need help, look back at Sona's and Omar's methods.

**a.** 6 blocks in each bag

**b.** 15 blocks in each bag

**c.** 100 blocks in each bag

**d.** $b$ blocks in each bag

1a. $4(6 + 3)$, $(4 \cdot 6) + (4 \cdot 3)$
1b. $4(15 + 3)$, $(4 \cdot 15) + (4 \cdot 3)$
1c. $4(100 + 3)$, $(4 \cdot 100) + (4 \cdot 3)$
1d. $4(b + 3)$, $4b + (4 \cdot 3)$

**2.** Keenan set four blocks in front of three sets of two bags. For each situation, show two ways of finding the total number of blocks that he has. 2a–d. See margin.

**a.** 7 blocks in each bag

**b.** 11 blocks in each bag

**c.** 100 blocks in each bag

**d.** $b$ blocks in each bag

**3.** Flowcharts can also help you see different ways to express a quantity.

**a.** Think about how you might create a flowchart to calculate the total number of blocks in the situation from Exercise 2. Draw and label a flowchart that has four ovals. See below.

**b.** Use an input of $b$ for your flowchart. Find the output expression. Possible answer: $3(2b + 4)$

**c.** Draw another flowchart to find the number of blocks in this situation. But this time, use only three ovals. Use an input of $b$ and find the output expression.

3a. Possible flowchart:

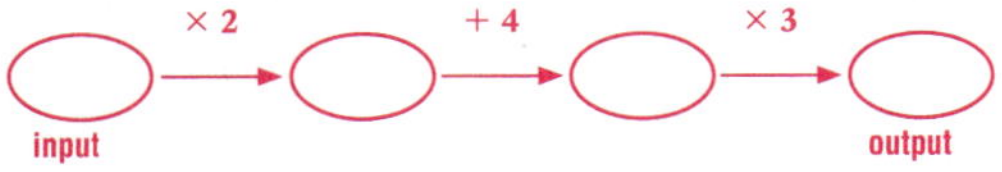


3c. Possible flowchart:

# Investigation 1

***On Your Own Exercises***
Pages 63–68
Exercises 1–3, 27, 28

**Grouping** In this investigation, students are introduced to the distributive property using bags-and-blocks models. They use the distributive property to write an expression in two ways. Then they move to flowcharts and tables to show that the two ways of showing an expression have the same result.

## Develop & Understand: A

*Suggested Grouping: Pairs*

▶ **Exercises 1 and 2** Students use drawings of the bag-and-blocks models to show two ways to find the total number of blocks.

▶ **Exercise 3** Students are asked to draw a flowchart showing the two ways used to find the total number of blocks in the previous problem. You may wish to have students record their work on Chapter 1 Master 2, Flowcharts.

**Additional Answers**

Possible answers:

2a. $3(14 + 4)$, $(3 \cdot 14) + (3 \cdot 4)$

2b. $3(22 + 4)$, $(3 \cdot 22) + (3 \cdot 4)$

2c. $3(200 + 4)$, $(3 \cdot 200) + (3 \cdot 4)$

2d. $3(2b + 4) = 6b + 12$, $(3 \cdot 2b) + (3 \cdot 4) = 6b + (3 \cdot 4)$

## Troubleshooting

Watch for students who do not use the order of operations to complete their flowcharts in Exercise 3. Have them use the values in Exercises 2a and 2c as input values in their flowcharts. They can check to see whether their respective output values are the same as those calculated in Exercise 2.

**Wrap-Up** In **Exercise 5**, students encounter a subtraction situation for the first time in this lesson. Discuss the subtraction situation. Have students present their answers for this problem and share their strategies. Emphasize that regardless of which calculation method is used, the total number of blocks is the same.

### Share & Summarize

Students move from using words to describe a specific situation to using symbols to describe a general situation. They should realize that the two ways to find the total number of blocks result in the same answer. Some students may need to write an expression for **Exercise 1** before making the generalization in **Exercise 2**.

If students have difficulty understanding the different ways to find a total, you can still continue to the next investigation. Students will look at the distributive property again using a different context in future investigations.

**4.** Solana placed one block in front of each of four bags. Find two expressions for the total number of blocks that she has.
Possible expressions: $4(b + 1)$, $4b + 4$

**5.** Simon and Zoe's teacher held up three bags and told the class that each contained the same number of blocks. She removed two blocks from each bag. How can you express the number of blocks still in the bags?

To answer this question, Simon and Zoe decided to experiment by starting with seven blocks in each bag.

**a.** If $b$ blocks are in each bag, Zoe's reasoning can be expressed in symbols as $3b - 6$. Write an expression that fits Simon's reasoning. $3(b - 2)$

**b.** Copy and complete the table to show the results of using Zoe's and Simon's methods for various numbers of blocks.

| Number of Blocks | $b$ | 2 | 4 | 7 | 10 | 18 | 22 |
|---|---|---|---|---|---|---|---|
| Zoe's Method | $3b - 6$ | 0 | 6 | 15 | 24 | 48 | 60 |
| Simon's Method | $3(b - 2)$ | 0 | 6 | 15 | 24 | 48 | 60 |

### Share & Summarize

Devon put five blocks in front of each of two bags.

**1.** Describe, in words, two ways of finding the total number of blocks if you know the number of blocks in each bag.

1. Multiply the number of blocks in each bag by 2 and then add 10. Add 5 to the number of blocks in a bag and multiply the result by 2.

**2.** Write two rules, in symbols, for finding the total number of blocks if there are $s$ blocks in each bag.
Possible rules: $2s + 10$, $2(s + 5)$

# Investigation 2 The Same and Different

**Vocabulary**

equivalent expressions

In the last investigation, you discovered more than one way to find the total number of blocks in a bags-and-blocks situation. You can also use tables and flowcharts to help figure out why two expressions can *look* different but produce the same outputs.

Kaya, Maria, and Luis played the *What's My Rule?* game. Luis made up a rule for finding the output for any input. Next, Kaya and Maria gave Luis several inputs. Then, he told them the outputs his rule would produce. The girls organized the input/output values in a table.

| Input | 1 | 3 | 6 | 4 | 5 |
|---|---|---|---|---|---|
| Output | 8 | 12 | 18 | 14 | 16 |

Kaya and Maria used their data to guess Luis' rule. When they gave their rules, Luis had a dilemma.

Kaya and Maria described two rules that fit the table. If the input is represented by $K$, Kaya's rule is written in symbols as $2K + 6$. Maria's rule is written as $2(K + 3)$.

It is reasonable to believe that the calculation $2K + 6$ will always give the same result as the calculation $2(K + 3)$. To help you see *why* this works and why it *must* work no matter what $K$ is, insert the missing multiplication signs.



# Investigation 2

***On Your Own Exercises***
Pages 63–68
Exercises 4–9, 29

**Equivalent Expressions Game** The best way to introduce the game is to play a round with the class. Here are the steps:

- Think of a rule and let students know that your rule can use one or more of the operations of addition, multiplication, and subtraction. Try, on the first round, to think of a rule that has a clear connection to the distributive property, such as $3x + 12$, or $3(x + 4)$.
- Tell students it is their job to figure out your rule by giving you inputs, one by one. Call on different students to supply inputs. You, in turn, will tell them the outputs for each input.
- Write their inputs in a table, with the corresponding outputs, and ask students to guess the rule at any point in the game.

As you play *What's My Rule?* with the class, you can help them observe patterns that can help them discover the rule, such as:

- Ask for inputs in an order that gives you information, such as, 0, 1, 2, ... .
- The output for 0 tells you what is added.
- If all outputs are even, the number multiplying the input is an even number.

If students guess the rule $3x + 12$, and your rule was $3(x + 4)$, you can say that you had a different rule, but it gives the same result. Allow them to keep guessing until they find your rule.

Likewise, $x + x + x + 12$ is also a different rule that gives the same result.

The game motivates students to think of different ways to express rules. Play a few rounds with them, and if you have time, ask a student to come to the front of the room and think of a rule. Then have the student play the game with the class.

## Example

This example shows why two expressions are *equivalent*. This explanation gives students experiences in unpacking an expression. Make sure that students understand why these expressions give the same result.

Walk students through the example as you write the expressions on the board. If students are having difficulty following the logic, draw parentheses around each $K + 3$ in the second step to help them see the two groups of $K + 3$. Other students may need to replace $K$ with a number to clarify their thinking.

## Develop & Understand: A

*Suggested Grouping: Pairs*

▶ **Exercise 1** Students draw flowcharts for two equivalent expressions. This gives students more practice in thinking about how the order of operations applies to expressions.

▶ **Exercise 2** Students write expressions from statements. Then they show that their expressions are equivalent to $2K + 6$.

**Wrap-Up** Ask students to share their rules from **Exercise 3** with the class. Have them explain why each rule is equivalent to $2K + 6$.

### Example

Start with $2(K + 3)$, and insert the missing multiplication sign.

$$2 \cdot (K + 3)$$

This is two groups of $(K + 3)$, which can be written as follows.

$$K + 3 + K + 3$$

This is the same as $K + K + 3 + 3$, or

$$2K + 6.$$

So, $2K + 6$ and $2(K + 3)$ are **equivalent expressions**. That means they must give the same result for every value of $K$.

## Develop & Understand: A

**1.** Look more closely at the expressions $2K + 6$ and $2(K + 3)$.

**a.** Draw a flowchart for each expression. See below.

**b.** For one of the expressions, you multiply first and then add. For the other, you add first and then multiply. Which expression is which? In $2K + 6$, you multiply first; in $2(K + 3)$, you add first.

**2.** You have seen that $2K + 6$ and $2(K + 3)$ are two ways of writing the same thing. And remember, Luis was thinking of a rule that was different from both of these but gave the same outputs.

The rules below are also equivalent to $2K + 6$ and $2(K + 3)$. Using $K$ for the input, write an expression for each rule. Show that your expression is equivalent to $2K + 6$. See margin.

**a.** Add the input to 6 more than the input.

**b.** Add 2 more than the input to 4 more than the input.

**c.** Add 2 to the input, and double the sum. Add 2 to the result.

**d.** Add 5 to the input, and double the sum. Subtract 4 from the result.

**3.** Write another rule, in words, that is equivalent to $2K + 6$.
Possible rule: Add 2 less than the input to 8 more than the input.

You have seen that in the *What's My Rule?* game, the rule can often be written in more than one way. You will now look at input/output tables from the game and express each rule in two ways.

1a.

### Additional Answers

2a. $K + (K + 6) = K + K + 6 = 2K + 6$

2b. $(K + 2) + (K + 4) = K + 2 + K + 4$
$= K + K + 2 + 4 = 2K + 6$

2c. $2(K + 2) + 2 = K + 2 + K + 2 + 2 =$
$K + K + 2 + 2 + 2 = 2K + 6$

2d. $2(K + 5) - 4 = K + 5 + K + 5 - 4 =$
$K + K + 5 + 5 - 4 = 2K + 6$

## Develop & Understand: B

4. Here is an input/output table for a game of *What's My Rule.*

| Input | 0 | 1 | 2 | 3 | 4 |
|---|---|---|---|---|---|
| Output | 6 | 8 | 10 | 12 | 14 |

a. Use symbols to write two rules for this game. One rule should involve multiplying first and then adding. The other should involve adding first and then multiplying. Substitute some other inputs to check that the two rules give the same output. Possible rules: $2n + 6$, $2(n + 3)$

b. Why do the two rules give the same output for a given input?

4b. Possible answer: Both rules are equal to $n + n + 6$. (Note: Students may use bags and blocks to explain their thinking.)

Use symbols to write two rules for the data in each table. One rule should involve multiplying first and then adding or subtracting. The other should involve adding or subtracting first and then multiplying.

5.

| Input | 2 | 3 | 4 | 5 | 6 |
|---|---|---|---|---|---|
| Output | 0 | 5 | 10 | 15 | 20 |

Possible rules: $5(n - 2)$, $5n - 10$

6.

| Input | 0 | 1 | 2 | 3 | 4 |
|---|---|---|---|---|---|
| Output | 4 | 4.5 | 5 | 5.5 | 6 |

Possible rules: $0.5(n + 8)$, $0.5n + 4$

Copy and complete each table. Then write another expression that gives the same outputs as the given expression. Check your expressions by substituting input values from your tables.

7.

| $j$ | 0 | 1 | 3 | 8 | 17 | 20 |
|---|---|---|---|---|---|---|
| $4(j + 2)$ | 8 | 12 | 20 | 40 | 76 | 88 |

Possible expression: $4j + 8$

8.

| $x$ | 2 | 3 | 4 | 5 | 6 | 18 | 42 | 82 |
|---|---|---|---|---|---|---|---|---|
| $5x + 5$ | 15 | 20 | 25 | 30 | 35 | 95 | 215 | 415 |

Possible expression: $5(x + 1)$

### Share & Summarize

1. Write three expressions that are equivalent to $3P + 12$.

1. Possible expressions: $2P + 6 + P + 6$, $P + P + P + 12$, $3(P + 4)$

2. Use symbols to write two rules for the data in the table. One rule should involve multiplying first and then adding or subtracting. The other should involve adding or subtracting first and then multiplying. Possible rules: $4(k - 3)$, $4k - 12$

| Input, $k$ | 3 | 4 | 13 | 24 | 42 | 50 |
|---|---|---|---|---|---|---|
| Output | 0 | 4 | 40 | 84 | 156 | 188 |



## On the Spot Assessment

Before moving on, be sure that students understand that for each input value, equivalent expressions must give the same result. If students are having trouble with this concept, you may want to use bags and blocks to illustrate the example on page 54.

## Develop & Understand: B

*Suggested Grouping: Pairs*

▶ **Exercises 4–6** Students are asked to write two rules for each table. You may want to point out that the two rules use the same operations but in a different sequence.

**Analyze the Table** Students may use one of these strategies to find a rule for the table in Exercise 4 that involves adding first and then multiplying:

- Students may look at the output numbers to find a pattern. Since all the numbers are even, they are multiples of 2. So the output value is the sum of an input number and another number multiplied by 2. For example, when the sum of 0 and some number is multiplied by 2, the product is 6. So the number is 3. Students then try this rule to verify that it works for all values.
- Some may look at the patterns in output values. The difference between these output numbers is 2, indicating that the inputs are multiplied by 2. Students proceed from this step in the same way as in the first strategy.
- Others may concentrate on one pair and try to find a rule to get from the input number to the output number.

▶ **Exercises 7 and 8** Students are asked to write another expression that gives the output value.

### Share & Summarize

**Exercise 1** asks students to write equivalent expressions. Students should be able to explain why the expressions are equivalent.

**Exercise 2** asks students to write rules for a table of values. Be sure students' rules include two operations—multiplication and either addition or subtraction.

## Investigation 3

***On Your Own Exercises***
Pages 63–68
Exercises 10–15, 30–33

**Using Parentheses** Begin the investigation by writing the equation $4(n + 2) = 4 \cdot n + 4 \cdot 2 = 4n + 8$ on the chalkboard. Remind students that they have already performed computations like this.

Tell them that when you remove parentheses, it is called *expanding*. Ask students how the expanded form compares to the form using parentheses. Students should note that there is a change in the *form* of an expression without a change in the *value* that it gives.

### Develop & Understand: A

*Suggested Grouping: Pairs*

▶ **Exercise 1a** Students need to realize that checking whether the two expressions for $n = 2$ are true does not prove that the two expressions are equal for all values of $n$.

**Teacher Tips** Students may use one of these strategies to prove that the equation in **Exercise 1b** is true:

- Some students may think of $4(n + 2)$ as 4 groups of $(n + 2)$ or $(n + 2) + (n + 2) + (n + 2) + (n + 2) = 4n + 8$.
- Other students may use a bags-and-blocks model to demonstrate their equivalency: 4 bags and 8 extra blocks has the same number of blocks as 4 groups, each containing 1 bag and 2 extra blocks.
- Others may rely on the distributive property to show that the equation is true.

## Investigation 3 Use Parentheses

**Vocabulary**
expand
factor

The distributive property explains how you can write expressions in different ways. Using the distributive property to remove parentheses is called **expanding**. Using the distributive property to insert parentheses is called **factoring**.

*removing parentheses (expanding)*

$$4(n + 2) = 4 \cdot n + 4 \cdot 2 = 4n + 8$$

*inserting parentheses (factoring)*

Expanding and factoring allow you to change the *form* of an expression, or what it looks like, without changing the output values it gives.

You have seen that rewriting an expression in a different form can be useful for simplifying calculations and comparing expressions. Later, you will see that rewriting expressions can help you solve equations.

In this investigation, you will practice using the distributive property to rewrite expressions. First, you will focus on expanding expressions, or removing parentheses.

### Develop & Understand: A

**1.** Consider the equation $4(n + 2) = 4n + 8$.

**a.** Is the equation true for $n = 2$? Yes

**b.** It is impossible to check that $4(n + 2) = 4n + 8$ for every value of $n$. How do you know that this equation is true for any value of $n$?
The distributive property tells us that $4(n + 2) = 4n + 8$.

**Decide whether each equation is true for all values of $n$. Explain how you decided.**

**2.** $5(n + 6) = 5n + 30$
True, distributive property

**3.** $7(n + 3) = 7n + 3$
Not true, $7(n + 3) = 7n + 21$

**4.** $(n + 12) \cdot 9 = 9n + 108$
True, distributive property

**5.** $1.5(n + 2.5) = 1.5n + 3.75$
True, distributive property

**6.** $2(n + 4) = 2n + 4$
Not true, $2(n + 4) = 2n + 8$

**7.** $(n + 9) \cdot 8 = n \cdot 8 + 72$
True, distributive property

Expand each expression. That is, rewrite it to remove the parentheses. Check the resulting expression by making sure it gives the same values as the original expression for at least three values of $x$.

**8.** $4(2x + 3)$ $8x + 12$

**9.** $4(3x + 7)$ $12x + 28$

**10.** $0.5(2x + 8)$ $x + 4$

**Expand each expression.**

**11.** $3(n - 4)$ $3n - 12$ **12.** $4(2n + 7)$ $8n + 28$ **13.** $8(3n - 3)$ $24n - 24$

**14.** $1(4n - 7)$ $4n - 7$ **15.** $2(2n - 3.5)$ $4n - 7$ **16.** $10(n + 10)$ $10n + 100$

**17.** $1(n + 1)$ $n + 1$ **18.** $0(n + 9{,}999)$ $0$ **19.** $2(n + 0)$ $2n$

The expressions below look a bit different from those in Exercises 11–19, but the distributive property still works. Expand each expression. If you are uncertain about a result, test it by substituting values for the variables.

**20.** $r(n + 1)$ $rn + r$ **21.** $n(2 + 7)$ $2n + 7n$, or $9n$ **22.** $x(4 - 3n)$ $4x - 3nx$

**23.** $2(n + 9n)$ $2n + 18n$, or $20n$ **24.** $n(2 + 18)$ $2n + 18n$, or $20n$ **25.** $2(1.5n + 2.5n)$ $3n + 5n$, or $8n$

Now you will use the distributive property to insert parentheses.

### Example

To rewrite $3d + 21$ by inserting parentheses, think about how the distributive property could have been used to produce the expression.

Both parts of the expression, $3d$ and 21, can be rewritten as three times something.

$$3d + 21 = 3 \cdot d + 3 \cdot 7$$
$$= 3(d + 7)$$

You can check this result by using the distributive property to expand $3(d + 7)$.

$$3(d + 7) = 3 \cdot d + 3 \cdot 7$$
$$= 3d + 21$$

### Math Link

In mathematics, sometimes you use more than just standard parentheses. Here are a few grouping symbols you might encounter.

| | |
|---|---|
| Parentheses: | ( ) |
| Brackets: | [ ] |
| Braces: | { } |



▶ **Exercises 8–19** Students practice expanding expressions. Note that the manipulation is now quite decontextualized and that students are dealing with symbols irrespective of their contexts.

▶ **Exercises 20–25** Students work with expressions containing two variables. Students should be aware that the process of expanding is the same regardless of the number of variables.

**Wrap-Up** Before moving on, make sure that students understand that expanding an expression changes the form but not the value. Students will have the opportunity for additional practice in later problem sets.

### Example

Explain to students that in the previous examples, they used the distributive property to remove parentheses. Sometimes it is useful to take an expression and insert parentheses, or *factor* the expression.

Write $3d + 21$ on the board. Tell students that this is an expanded expression. Ask students how they think the expression looked before it was expanded. Walk students through the explanation in the Example on page 57.

## Troubleshooting

In **Exercises 8–19**, watch for students who do not multiply each part when expanding an expression. These students only use expanding for the first part of the expression. For example, in **Exercise 11**, students might show $3(n - 4) = 3n - 4$. Remind them to expand the entire expression. Encourage students to substitute values for $n$ to make sure that the expressions name the same value.

Rewriting an expression by inserting parentheses is called *factoring* because the resulting expression is the product of factors.

You could factor $3d + 21$ in other ways. For example, you could write $\frac{1}{2}(6d + 42)$ or $0.1(30d + 210)$. However, working with these expressions is more complicated. Unless the expression you are factoring contains fractions or decimals, use only whole numbers in your factors.

The examples below show how some other expressions can be factored.

$$7 + 7x = 7 \cdot 1 + 7 \cdot x = 7(1 + x)$$

$$7t - 3t = 7 \cdot t - 3 \cdot t = (7 - 3)t = (4)t = 4t$$

$$6m + 3m^2 = 3m \cdot 2 + 3m \cdot m = 3m(2 + m)$$

$$s + ms + nms = s + m \cdot s + n \cdot m \cdot s = s(1 + m + nm)$$

After you factor, look carefully at the expression inside the parentheses. You may find that more factoring can be done.

### Example

Factor the expression $27p^2 + 18p$.

Since 9 divides both parts of the expression, it can be rewritten as follows.

$$27p^2 + 18p = 9(3p^2 + 2p)$$

Now look at the expression inside the parentheses. Since $p$ divides both $3p^2$ and $2p$, the expression can be factored further.

$$9(3p^2 + 2p) = 9p(3p + 2)$$

So, $27p^2 + 18p = 9p(3p + 2)$.

Not all expressions can be easily factored. For example, no whole number or variable evenly divides both parts of $5x + 7$.



**Teacher Tips** Students may have given other ways to write the expression $3d + 21$. Some possibilities include $0.5(6d + 42)$, or $1.5(2d + 14)$. In most cases the last two expressions are not considered very useful. We are really interested in the simplest product: one with whole numbers and variables.

Tell students that when they factor a number, they should express it as the product of whole number factors (not including 1) unless there are fractions or decimals in the expression being factored. For example, the factored form of 35 is $5 \cdot 7$, not $0.5 \cdot 70$.

As you walk students through the examples of factoring, you may wish to ask students questions such as:

- Both parts of this expression can be rewritten as something times what number?
- What number should I write outside the parentheses when I factor this expression?
- What should I write inside the parentheses when I factor this expression?

If students don't give their answers in simplest form, you will need to preview the Example by asking whether the expression inside the parentheses can be factored.

### Example

Tell students that they should factor an expression until it cannot be factored any further.

Walk students through the Example. Students should understand that if the expression inside the parentheses can be factored, then the expression can be factored further.

Be sure students understand that some expressions cannot be factored.

## Mathematical Background

When mathematicians speak of factoring an integer like 35, they mean producing a set of integer factors whose product is 35. We cannot precisely describe what it means to factor an expression, but the general idea can be explained through examples. For example, the expression $\frac{1}{2}x + \frac{1}{2}$ is properly factored as $\frac{1}{2}(x + 1)$ even though the factor outside the parentheses is not an integer; and, similarly, $\frac{1}{2}\pi + \frac{1}{3}\pi x$ is properly factored as $\pi\left(\frac{1}{2} + \frac{1}{3}x\right)$ even though neither of the factors are integers.

The notion of getting the simplest product is probably the least misleading, even though it doesn't say precisely what's meant by simplest. In this lesson, the term ***whole number*** is used in place of ***integer***.

## Develop & Understand: B

Determine whether there is a whole number or variable that divides both parts of each expression. If there is, use the distributive property to rewrite the expression using parentheses. Check the resulting expression by expanding it.

**26.** $4a + 8$ $4(a + 2)$ **27.** $4b + 12$ $4(b + 3)$ **28.** $4c + 17$ No

**29.** $3g - 15$ $3(g - 5)$ **30.** $5f + 13$ No **31.** $8h - 24$ $8(h - 3)$

**Factor each expression. Check the resulting expression by expanding it.**

**32.** $22s + 33$ $11(2s + 3)$ **33.** $34t - 4$ $2(17t - 2)$

**34.** $45m + 25k$ $5(9m + 5k)$ **35.** $7j^2 + 3j$ $j(7j + 3)$

**36.** $4t + 9t$ $t(4 + 9) = 13t$ **37.** $8g^2 + 12g$ $4g(2g + 3)$

**38.** $10m + 15t + 25$ $5(2m + 3t + 5)$ **39.** $8 - 16h^2 + 20h$ $4(2 - 4h^2 + 5h)$

**40.** Every morning, Tonisha and her dog, Rex, run to the local park, around the park, and back home. It is 400 meters to the park and $x$ meters around the park. Write two expressions for the total distance, in meters, they run in a week. One of your expressions should involve parentheses. Possible answer: $7(800 + x)$; $5{,}600 + 7x$

**41.** Explain why $4t + 9t$ and $6k + 9m$ can be factored. Explain why $4k + 9m$ cannot be factored.

41. $4t$ and $9t$ have $t$ as a common factor, $6k$ and $9m$ have 3 as a common factor, but nothing evenly divides both $4k$ and $9m$.

**42. Prove It!** Show that $2k + 3k = 5k$ by first factoring $2k + 3k$. Then check that $2k + 3k = 5k$ for $k = 7$ and $k = 12$.

### Share & Summarize

1. Create an expression in factored form. Give it to your partner to expand. Expressions will vary.
2. Create an expression that can be factored. Give it to your partner to factor. Expressions will vary.
3. Explain how expanding and factoring are related. Both involve the distributive property and parentheses. When you expand, you get rid of parentheses; when you factor, you add parentheses.

42. $2k + 3k = k(2 + 3) = 5k$

Check: $2k + 3k = 5k$ | $2k + 3k = 5k$

$2(7) + 3(7) = 5(7)$ | $2(12) + 3(12) = 5(12)$

$14 + 21 = 35$ ✓ | $24 + 36 = 60$ ✓



## Troubleshooting

If students are having difficulty with expanding and factoring, they probably need more practice. There are many additional exercises in the On Your Own Exercises section, and you can use these to help them.

## Develop & Understand: B

*Suggested Grouping: Individuals*

▶ **Exercises 26–31** Students determine whether an expression can be factored, and if so, factor it.

▶ **Exercises 32–37** Students factor expressions with two parts.

▶ **Exercises 38 and 39** Students factor an expression with three parts.

▶ **Exercise 40** Students use data in a context. They write two expressions to describe the data. Depending on the first expression students write, they may use either factoring or expanding to write the second expression.

▶ **Exercise 42** Students use factoring as a preview to adding terms in an expression. Students factor one side of an equation and show that it has the same value as the other side of the equation.

**Wrap-Up** Discuss **Exercises 41 and 42** as a class. Students' explanations for Exercise 41 should have a reference to the fact that both terms in the first two expressions can be evenly divided by the same number. The terms in $4k + 9m$ do not have any common factors.

You may wish to discuss Exercise 42 further because it is a preview to adding like terms. If students understand the reasoning presented here, they will have a stronger basis when the skill is formally presented.

### Share & Summarize

Encourage students to invent challenging expressions for their partners to factor and expand. The act of creating these problems gives students insight into the workings of the distributive property. Some students may come up with expressions that in fact cannot be factored. If they do, ask them to tell their partners why they can't be factored.

When explaining how expanding and factoring are related, students may use language such as, *one undoes the other.* In fact, this is a good way for them to think about these processes.

# Investigation 4

***On Your Own Exercises***
Pages 63–68
Exercises 16–26, 34–44

**Combining Like Terms** Begin the Investigation by writing the expression $3s + 5p + w + 4s + 4p + 2w$ on the board. Ask the students what you can do to make the expression appear simpler. The students should want to group the terms that contain $s$, $p$, and $w$ together.

It may be helpful to reinforce that $5p$ is the same as $p + p + p + p + p$. It may also be helpful to remind students about the use of parentheses and factoring so that you work from the above expression to $3s + 4s + 5p + 4p + w + 2w$ and then to $(1 + 4)s + (5 + 4)p + (1 + 2)w$. This shows students how the previous lessons tie in to what they are currently learning.

Remind students that they are not changing the value of the expression, only the way the expression looks. By combining like terms, you are simplifying the expression and making it easier to read.

### Develop & Understand: A

▶ **Exercise 3** Make sure students understand that the rows represent people and the columns represent the items of clothing.

# Investigation 4 Combine Like Terms

**Vocabulary**
- like terms
- monomial
- polynomial

***Real-World Link***
In a recent year, 4,051,990 tax returns claimed clothing donations with a value of $5,836,108,000.

Zach, Simon, and Maria collected clothes to donate to a local clothing drive. Each student brought the following items.

| | Shirts | Pairs of Pants | Sweaters |
|---|---|---|---|
| Zach | 3 | 5 | 1 |
| Simon | 4 | 4 | 2 |
| Maria | 5 | 2 | 3 |

Simon wrote a list of all of the clothes the three friends donated.

3 shirts + 4 shirts + 5 shirts + 5 pants + 4 pants + 2 pants + 1 sweater + 2 sweaters + 3 sweaters

Maria put all of the shirts in one bag. She put all of the pants in another bag and all of the sweaters in a third bag. She wrote a list of what was in each bag. Maria's list was used to label the bags.

### Develop & Understand: A

1. Zach wondered how Simon's and Maria's lists could look so different. Explain how you could use Simon's list to create Maria's list.
2. Can you use Maria's list to create Simon's list? Why or why not?
3. At the shelter, the clothing was distributed among five people. Fill in the table to show what each person might have received.

| | Shirts | Pairs of Pants | Sweaters |
|---|---|---|---|
| Jose | 2 | 3 | 1 |
| Lola | 2 | 2 | 0 |
| Morris | 3 | 1 | 2 |
| Cheyenne | 3 | 4 | 1 |
| Ethan | 2 | 1 | 2 |

1. Combine the three groups of shirts on Simon's list, the three groups of pants, and the three groups of sweaters. $(3 + 4 + 5)$ shirts $+ (5 + 4 + 2)$ pants $+ (1 + 2 + 3)$ sweaters $= 12$ shirts $+ 11$ pants $+ 6$ sweaters.
2. No, because you cannot tell from Maria's list how to split up the clothing; there are lots of different ways to divide it.
3. Many other solutions are possible. The totals must stay the same: 12 shirts, 11 pants, 6 sweaters.

5. When a bag has just one type of clothing in it, you can use one number to label it, 3 sweaters. If there are several kinds of clothing in the bag, you have to say how many of each, 2 shirts, 3 pants, and 1 sweater. The only way to use a single number for a bag with multiple kinds of clothing in it would be to say something like "6 pieces of clothing." But you do not know what kinds of clothing are in the bag or how many of each there are.

**4.** Maria put each person's clothing into a separate bag. She wrote a list of what was in each bag. For example, Maria's list for Jose's clothing was 2 shirts, 3 pants, and 1 sweater. Use your table entries to write a list like Maria's for Cheyenne's clothing. Sample answer: 3 shirts + 4 pants + 1 sweater

**5.** Zach thought Maria's new list was too long. He thought she should label each bag with just one number, like she did in her first list. Explain whether or not it is possible to label the bags that way.

**6.** Think about the bags and blocks scenarios you used to explore the distributive property in Investigation 1. How do the bags and blocks apply to the donated clothing situations? See margin.

In this investigation, you will work with algebraic expressions called *polynomials.*

A **monomial** is a number or the product of a number and variables. The expressions $x$, $2y$, $\frac{1}{2}xy$, 7, and $45x^3$ are all examples of monomials.

A **polynomial** is an algebraic expression containing one or more terms. Each term must be a *monomial,* and the terms can be combined using only *addition* or *subtraction.*

### Example

$x^2 + 3y$ is an example of a polynomial. It contains two terms: $x^2$ and $3y$. $x^2$ is a monomial because it is the product of a number, 1, and two variables, $x$, and $x$ again. $3y$ is the product of 3 and $y$, so it is also a monomial.

$\frac{y}{8}$ is a monomial because it can be rewritten as $\frac{1}{8} \cdot y$, the product of a number and a variable.

### Think & Discuss

Molly and Alonso each thought of an algebraic expression.

Molly wrote $3x \cdot x + 2$ on the board.

Alonso wrote $x^2y + 5$.

What makes each expression a polynomial?

$x^2y + 5$; $3x \cdot x + 2$ can be rewritten as a polynomial.

$x^2y + 5$ is the sum of two monomials; each term is a number or the product of a number and variable(s). In the case of $x^2y$, the number is 1; in the case of 5, there are 0 variables. $3x \cdot x + 2$ can be rewritten as a $3x^2 + 2$, which is the sum of two monomials.

### Math Link

Some words use "mono" (meaning "one") and "poly" (meaning "more than one" or "extra"). A *polynomial* is an expression with several terms, and a *monomial* is a polynomial with only one term. A *monorail* has one of what item? A *polygon* has several of what mathematical figure?



### Example

Discuss the meanings of *polynomial* and *monomial*. As a class make a list of words that contain the prefix *poly-* or *mono-* such as *monocle* or *polygon*. Allow the students to refer to a dictionary if needed.

Use these words to create an understanding of the mathematical term. Stress to the students that the *terms* or pieces of a polynomial are always separated by an addition or a subtraction symbol. Reassure students that they work with monomials all the time when they are adding or subtracting numbers.

### Additional Answer

6. Bags and blocks represented different numbers just as shirts, pants, and sweaters are different items of clothing.

## *Reaching* All Learners

**ELL English Language Learners** English Language Learners may have a better understanding of the terms monomial and polynomial if you spend time discussing words in their native languages that have *mono-* or *poly-* as prefixes. Then assist them in making the connection to monomial and polynomial through their native language. Not all languages use the prefix concept, but most languages do have words for things like a unicycle.

## Develop & Understand: B

*Suggested Grouping: Pairs*

▶ **Exercises 8–15** Remind students that they are changing the polynomial to what it would look like if you were using the distributive property.

▶ **Exercise 16** Stress to the students that in order for monomials to be like terms, the monomials must have the exact same variables raised to the same power.

### Share & Summarize

When creating their pictures ask students if they can use a different object to represent $3x$ than they use to represent $5x$. Do the pictures for 3 and 10 need to relate to $3x$ and $5x$ at all? These questions can spark a great discussion and will assist in clarifying the major misconceptions of combining like terms.

7. Three of the terms are $b$ times some other number. The distributive property states that you can add up the other numbers first and then multiply the sum by $b$, and the result will be the same as if you multiplied each number by $b$ and then added them. So, $5b + 20b - b = b(5 + 20 - 1) = 24b$.
8. $6x + 4x + 2x = x(6 + 4 + 2) = x(12) = 12x$
9. $20y - 8y + 4y = y(20 - 8 + 4) = y(16) = 16y$
10. $7x - 3y + 8x = x(7 + 8) - 3y = 15x - 3y$
11. $3x + 2y + 5x + 18y + 1 = x(3 + 5) + y(2 + 18) + 1 = 8x + 20y + 1$
12. $x + x^2 + 3x + 2x^2 = x(1 + 3) + x^2(1 + 2) = 4x + 3x^2$
13. This polynomial cannot be simplified. You could rewrite it in standard order as $14x^2 - 3x + 4y^3 + 2y - 5$
14. $5x + 8xy + 10x + 3xy = x(5 + 10) + xy(8 + 3) = 15x + 11xy$

Terms in an algebraic expression that have exactly the same variables and exponents are called **like terms**.

### Example

$3x$ and $2x$ are like terms. $4y^2$ and $0.5y^2$ are like terms.

$y^2$ and $2x^2$ are not like terms because their variables are different. $3xy$, $5x$, and $x^3$ are not like terms either. Although they all have $x$ *as a variable*, all of their variables and exponents do not match exactly.

When Maria put all of the shirts in one bag and added for a total, she was *combining like terms*. She found the total of each set of things that were all the same. You can do the same in a polynomial. Just as you factored expressions in Investigation 3, you can use the distributive property to combine like terms in a polynomial.

$$3x + 4x + 6 = x(3 + 4) + 6 = 7x + 6$$

## Develop & Understand: B

7. Use the distributive property to explain why $5b + 20b - b = 24b$.

**In each exercise, combine like terms to simplify the polynomial as much possible.**

8. $6x + 4x + 2x$
9. $20y - 8y + 4y$
10. $7x - 3y + 8x$
11. $3x + 2y + 5x + 18y + 1$
12. $x + x^2 + 3x + 2x^2$
13. $14x^2 + 4y^3 - 3x - 5 + 2y$
14. $5x + 8xy + 10x + 3xy$
15. $3x + 12xy + 6x + 7y^2 - 10xy$ See margin.
16. Can you simplify the polynomial $x + x^2$ by combining like terms? Explain why or why not. See margin.

### Share & Summarize

Draw a picture to represent the polynomial $3x + 5x + 3 + 10$. Draw a second picture to show how to simplify the polynomial by combining like terms. See margin.



### Additional Answers

15. $3x + 12xy + 6x + 7y^2 - 10xy = x(3 + 6) + xy(12 - 10) + 7y^2 = 9x + 2xy + 7y^2$
16. No; since $x$ is the same as $x^1$, it has a different exponent from $x^2$. Like terms must have exactly the same variables and exponents.

### Share & Summarize

## Practice & Apply

**1.** Suppose there are five bags with $n$ blocks in each bag and three extra blocks beside each bag.

**a.** Write one factored expression and one expanded expression for the total number of blocks as you did in Exercises 1–5 on pages 51 and 52. Possible answer: $5(n + 3)$, $5n + 15$

**b.** Check that your two expressions give the same total for $n = 8$, $n = 12$, and $n = 25$. Both expressions should give 55 for $n = 8$, 75 for $n = 12$, and 140 for $n = 25$.

**c.** Explain, using a picture if you like, why your two expressions must give the same total number of blocks for any value of $n$.

1c. Because 5 groups of 1 bag and 3 blocks is the same as 5 bags and $3 \cdot 5$, or 15, blocks

**2.** Suppose there are four sets of three bags with three blocks in front of each set. For each situation, show two ways to find the total number of blocks.

**a.** 5 blocks in each bag Possible answer: $4(15 + 3)$, $4 \cdot 15 + 4 \cdot 3$

**b.** 100 blocks in each bag Possible answer: $4(300 + 3)$, $4 \cdot 300 + 4 \cdot 3$

**c.** $b$ blocks in each bag Possible answer: $4(3b + 3)$, $4 \cdot 3b + 4 \cdot 3$

**3.** Brandi has five bags with the same number of blocks in each. She removes two blocks from each bag. For each situation below, show two ways of finding the total number of blocks in the bags.

**a.** The bags start with 7 blocks in each. $5(7 - 2)$, $5 \cdot 7 - 5 \cdot 2$

**b.** The bags start with 50 blocks in each. $5(50 - 2)$, $5 \cdot 50 - 5 \cdot 2$

**c.** The bags start with $p$ blocks in each. $5(p - 2)$, $5 \cdot p - 5 \cdot 2$

**4.** Consider the expressions $3(T - 1)$ and $3T - 3$.

**a.** Copy the table, and complete the first four columns. In the last four columns, choose your own input values and calculate the output for both rules. Use fractions for at least two input values.

| $T$ | 4 | 11 | 100 | 30 | | | | |
|---|---|---|---|---|---|---|---|---|
| $3T - 3$ | 9 | 30 | 297 | 87 | | | | |
| $3(T - 1)$ | 9 | 30 | 297 | 87 | | | | |

The last four columns will vary.

**b.** Show that $3(T - 1)$ and $3T - 3$ are equivalent expressions.
Possible answer: $3(T - 1) = T - 1 + T - 1 + T - 1 = 3T - 3$

**c.** Find two more expressions that are equivalent to $3(T - 1)$ and $3T - 3$. Possible answer: $2(T - 1) + (T - 1)$, $T + T + T - 3$



**On Your Own Exercises**
**Lesson 1.3**

**Investigation 1**
Pages 51–52
Practice & Apply: 1–3
Connect & Extend: 27, 28

**Investigation 2**
Pages 53–55
Practice & Apply: 4–9
Connect & Extend: 29

**Investigation 3**
Pages 56–59
Practice & Apply: 10–15
Connect & Extend: 30–33

**Investigation 4**
Pages 60–62
Practice & Apply: 16–26
Connect & Extend: 34–44

**Assign Anytime**
Mixed Review: 46–53

▶ **Exercise 1** This exercise is similar to the concrete models that students completed at the beginning of the chapter and should be relatively familiar to students.

**Lesson 1.3** The Distributive Property **63**

▶ **Exercises 5–7** These exercises give students more practice in using a table to generate different expressions that have the same value. Students can then check whether or not the new expression has the same value.

▶ **Exercises 10–15** These exercises involve expanding expressions and checking each new expression to make sure that it has the same value as the given expression.

On Your Own Exercises

Copy and complete each table. Then, for each table, write another expression that gives the same outputs. Check your new expression to make sure it generates the same values.

**5.**

| $h$ | 0 | 1 | 2 | 7 | 42 | 47 |
|---|---|---|---|---|---|---|
| $2(h + 3)$ | 6 | 8 | 10 | 20 | 90 | 100 |

Possible expression: $2h + 6$

**6.**

| $r$ | 3 | 5 | 10 | 11 | 22 | 23 |
|---|---|---|---|---|---|---|
| $5(r - 2)$ | 5 | 15 | 40 | 45 | 100 | 105 |

Possible expression: $5r - 10$

**7.**

| $n$ | 4 | 5 | 6 | 8 | 44 | 100 |
|---|---|---|---|---|---|---|
| $\frac{n-4}{4}$ | 0 | 0.25 | 0.5 | 1 | 10 | 24 |

Possible expression: $\frac{n}{4} - 1$

**For each *What's My Rule?* table, find two ways to write the rule in symbols. Choose your own variable.**

**8.**

| Input | 0 | 1 | 2 | 3 | 4 |
|---|---|---|---|---|---|
| Output | 8 | 10 | 12 | 14 | 16 |

Possible rules: $2(x + 4)$, $2x + 8$

**9.**

| Input | 0 | 1 | 2 | 3 | 4 |
|---|---|---|---|---|---|
| Output | 6 | 6.5 | 7 | 7.5 | 8 |

Possible rules: $\frac{1}{2}(x + 12)$, $\frac{1}{2}x + 6$

**Math Link**
Expanding an expression means rewriting it to remove the parentheses.

For Exercises 10–15, expand each expression. Check the resulting expression by making sure it gives the same values as the original expression for several values of the variable.

**10.** $5(3j + 4)$ $15j + 20$
**11.** $0.2(4k + 9)$ $0.8k + 1.8$
**12.** $2(n - 7)$ $2n - 14$
**13.** $n(n - 6)$ $n^2 - 6n$
**14.** $3(3n + 3)$ $9n + 9$
**15.** $0(n + 875)$ $0$

**Factor each expression, if possible.**

**16.** $4a + 8$ $4(a + 2)$
**17.** $18 + 5b$
**18.** $3g - 15$ $3(g - 5)$
**19.** $18 - 2A$ $2(9 - A)$
**20.** $11v + 3v$
**21.** $5z^2 + 2z$ $z(5z + 2)$

17. not possible
20. $v(11 + 3) = 14v$

In each exercise, combine like terms to simplify the polynomial as much as possible.

**22.** $14x^2 + 5y - 6x + 23 + 7x - 3y$ $14x^2 + x + 2y + 23$
**23.** $\frac{1}{3}xy + 13x + \frac{5}{6}xy - 4x$ $\frac{7}{6}xy + 9x$
**24.** $2y - 4x^2 + 2y^2 - 4x^2 + 14y - 3xy$ $16y - 8x^2 + 2y^2 - 3xy$



64 CHAPTER 1 Expressions

**25.** Thomas and Courtney are sorting footballs, basketballs, and tennis balls into different storage containers for gym classes. Here is how Thomas sorted the balls.

| Container 1 | Container 2 | Container 3 |
|---|---|---|
| 9 footballs | 12 basketballs | 24 tennis balls |

Courtney suggests sorting instead by gym class, A, B, and C. She puts some of each type of ball in each container.

**a.** Write a polynomial that represents the sorting that Thomas did. $9f + 12b + 24t$

**b.** Write one polynomial that represents how Courtney sorted the balls.

**c.** Which expression tells you more about the balls? Which tells you more about the gym classes?

**d.** If the gym classes need the same number of each type of ball, what polynomial would represent each container? $3 \cdot (3f + 4b + 8t)$

**26.** Logan's karate class is having a bake sale. In total, the class brought 96 cookies. Complete a table to show how many each person might have brought. Possible answer given.

| | Chocolate Chip | Sugar Cookies | Oatmeal Raisin | Peanut Butter |
|---|---|---|---|---|
| Aiden | 20 | 0 | 6 | 6 |
| Hailey | 0 | 12 | 9 | 9 |
| Logan | 0 | 6 | 10 | 10 |
| Monica | 0 | 4 | 0 | 4 |

**a.** What is the shortest polynomial you could write to represent your table's values? How many terms does it have?

**b.** Suppose Hailey's mom takes all the cookies home to package them to sell. She makes six bags of equal numbers of cookies. Write a polynomial that could represent the packaged cookies. See margin.

25b. Possible answer: $(3f + 4b + 10t) + (2f + 6b + 8t) + (4f + 2b + 6t)$

25c. The first tells you more about the balls. You can easily see how many there are. The second tells you what each gym class will have available.

26a. Polynomial with 4 terms; $20c + 22s + 25r + 29p$



On Your Own Exercises

▶ **Exercises 25 and 26** Remind students to identify each variable used.

**Additional Answer**

26b. Possible answer:

$(10c + 6s) + (10c + 6p) + (10s + 6r) + (6s + 4r + 6p) + (6r + 10p) + (9r + 7p)$

**Lesson 1.3** The Distributive Property 65

▶ **Exercise 29** Many students enjoy working on exercises such as this in which they must use logical reasoning to find the answer. The basis for the logical reasoning in this exercise involves familiarity with the distributive property.



On Your Own Exercises

## Connect & Extend

27b. 4 bags with 3 blocks removed from each is the same as 4 bags with 12 blocks removed.

28a. Possible expressions: $5(n - 20)$, or $5n - 100$

28b. Possible expressions: $15(5n - 100)$; or $75n - 1{,}500$

**27.** Joshua has 4 bags of blocks. He removes 3 blocks from each bag.

**a.** Write two expressions for the total number of blocks in Joshua's bags now. Possible expressions: $4(n - 3)$, $4n - 12$

**b.** Explain, using a picture if you like, why your two expressions must give the same total number of blocks for any value of the variable.

**28.** The rock band "The Accidents" brought five boxes of its new CD, *Waiting to Happen,* on its tour. Each box holds the same number of CDs. The band hoped to sell all of the CDs, but it sold only 20 CDs from each box.

**a.** Write an expression that describes the total number of unsold CDs.

**b.** Write an expression that describes how much the band will earn, in dollars, by selling the remaining CDs for $15 each.

**29.** In this pattern of toothpicks, the width of the figure increases from one figure to the next. Using symbols, write two rules for finding the number of toothpicks in a figure. Use parentheses in only one of your rules. Use $w$ to represent the width of a figure.
Possible answer: $4 + 2w$, $2(2 + w)$

Figure 1 Figure 2 Figure 3 Figure 4

**Expand each expression. Check your answer by substituting 1, 2, and 10 for the variable.**

**30.** $7Q(Q + 8)$ $7Q^2 + 56Q$

**31.** $9L(M + 3L)$ $9LM + 27L^2$

**32.** $8R(\frac{1}{2} - R)$ $4R - 8R^2$

**33.** $3(D^2 - \frac{D}{2})$ $3D^2 - \frac{3D}{2}$

**Factor each expression.**

**34.** $3m^2 + 6m$ $3m(m + 2)$

**35.** $2t + 4t^2$ $2t(1 + 2t)$

**36.** $4L + 3L^2$ $L(4 + 3L)$

**37.** $3P + mP$ $P(3 + m)$

**38.** **Challenge** When you take any whole number, add $\frac{1}{2}$, and then multiply the sum by 2, the result is an odd number. Explain why.
$2(n + \frac{1}{2}) = 2n + 1$, and $2n$ must be even, so $2n + 1$ must be odd.

On Your Own Exercises

**39. Challenge** This fraction contains variables.

$$\frac{8x + 4z + 2}{2}$$

To simplify this fraction, you might first think of it as

$$\frac{1}{2}(8x + 4z + 2).$$

Then you can apply the distributive property.

$$\frac{1}{2}(8x + 4z + 2) = \frac{1}{2}(8x) + \frac{1}{2}(4z) + \frac{1}{2}(2)$$
$$= 4x + 2z + 1$$

Use this method to simplify each fraction.

**a.** $\frac{12x + 6z + 3}{3}$ $4x + 2z + 1$ **b.** $\frac{10x^2 + 5x}{5}$ $2x^2 + x$

**40. World Cultures** In some countries, long multiplication is taught to students using a grid. Here is how to multiply 15 and 31 using a grid.

| • | 10 | 5 |
|---|---|---|
| 30 | 300 | 150 |
| 1 | 10 | 5 |

The product of 15 and 31 is 465, the total of the four numbers inside the grid. Use the grid method to find each product.

**a.** 14 • 56 **b.** 23 • 23 **c.** 45 • 21

40a. 784

| • | 10 | 4 |
|---|---|---|
| 50 | 500 | 200 |
| 6 | 60 | 24 |

40b. 529

| • | 20 | 3 |
|---|---|---|
| 20 | 400 | 60 |
| 3 | 60 | 9 |

40c. 945

| • | 40 | 5 |
|---|---|---|
| 20 | 800 | 100 |
| 1 | 40 | 5 |

**41. Challenge** You can use factoring to prove some interesting facts about numbers.

**a.** If you start with a whole number greater than 1 and add it to its square, the result will never be a prime number. Explain why not. (Hint: Use $x$ to stand for the whole number. Then $x^2$ is its square, and $x^2 + x$ is the whole number added to its square.)

**b.** If you start with a whole number greater than 2 and subtract it from its square, the result can never be a prime number. Explain.

41a. Possible answer: $x^2 + x = x(x + 1)$, which is the product of two whole numbers greater than 1 and therefore cannot be prime.

41b. Possible answer: $x^2 - x = x(x - 1)$, which is the product of two whole numbers greater than 1 and therefore cannot be prime.



**Lesson 1.3** The Distributive Property 67

▶ **Exercises 47–52** When students solve percent equations it may be helpful to look if the student is setting up the proper proportion. In general, the percent proportion is percent/100 = "equal"/"of", or an equivalent form. This proportion will allow you and the students an opportunity to determine if an error has been made in solving the problem.

## Quick Check

**Informal Assessment** Students should be able to:

✔ use the distributive property to write two forms of the same expression

✔ rewrite expressions by inserting and removing parentheses

✔ combine like terms to simplify polynomials

## Quick Quiz

1. Combine like terms to simplify this polynomial: $6x - 6y + 5x$. $11x - 6y$
2. Rewrite this expression by removing the parentheses: $1.5(2c + 10)$. $3c + 15$
3. Use the distributive property to rewrite this expression: $24y + 8y^2$. $8y(3 + y)$
4. Find two different ways of writing a rule that produces the table below:

| Input | 0 | 1 | 2 | 3 |
|---|---|---|---|---|
| Output | 2 | 6 | 10 | 14 |

$4n + 2$ or $2(2n + 1)$



**In each exercise, expand and combine like terms. Show that the original expression is equivalent to your final combined expression by substituting 2 for $x$ and 3 for $y$.**

**42.** $3x(4x + 6y^2) + y(y + 5x)$ $12x^2 + 18x^2y + y^2 + 5xy$

**43.** $x(2y + 4) + 6y^2(2 + 3x) + 8x(y + y^2)$ $12y^2 + 26xy^2 + 10xy + 4x$

**44.** Are the following expressions equivalent? Explain.

$$5xy(2x^2 + 3y + 4x) + x^2y(5 + 6y) + 3(x^2y + 4xy^2) \text{ and}$$

$$10x^3y + 27xy^2 + 28x^2y + 6x^2y^2$$

44. Yes, if you expand the first expression and collect like terms, it is equivalent to the second.

**45. In Your Own Words** Suppose you are talking to a student two years younger than you are. Explain why $3(b + 4) = 3b + 12$, not $3b + 4$. You might want to draw a picture to help explain the idea.

45. Possible explanation: The expression $3(b + 4)$ means you have three groups of $b + 4$, or $(b + 4) + (b + 4) + (b + 4)$. The three 4s can be added together for a sum of 12.

**46. Probability** On a scale from 0 (impossible) to 100 (certain to happen), rate the chances of each event happening today.

a. You do homework. Answers will vary.

b. Someone in the world has a baby. 100

c. Someone in your city has a baby.

d. You learn to drive. Answers will vary.

e. It snows somewhere in your country. Answers will vary.

46c. Answerswill depend on the size of the city.

## Mixed Review

**Fill in the blanks.**

**47.** 75 % of 152 = 114

**48.** 0.5% of 200 = 1

**49.** $33\frac{1}{3}$% of 45 = 15

**50.** 300 % of 20 = 60

**51.** 45% of 45 = 20.25

**52.** 80% of 400 = 320

**53.** In April 2008, you could have received about 40.125 Indian rupees for 1 U.S. dollar.

a. About how many U.S. dollars could you have received in exchange for 100 Indian rupees? About 2.5

b. How many Indian rupees could you have received in exchange for 100 U.S. dollars? About 4,013

CHAPTER 1

# Review & Self-Assessment

## Chapter Summary

In this chapter, you followed common rules and rules for creating sequences, and you wrote rules for others to follow. You learned that many situations can be described using algebraic expressions and *variables*. You evaluated expressions and used *flowcharts* to *backtrack* to solve equations.

By using different values for a variable, you explored what happens in a situation as a variable changes. You also worked with mathematical *formulas*.

You found that the same situation can often be described with several *equivalent expressions* and that sometimes one expression is more useful than another. You saw that you could change expressions into equivalent expressions by using the *distributive property* to *expand* and *factor* them.

**Vocabulary**

- backtracking
- distributive property
- equivalent expressions
- expand
- exponent
- factor
- flowchart
- formula
- like terms
- monomial
- polynomial
- variable

## Strategies and Applications

The questions in this section will help you review and apply the important ideas and strategies developed in this chapter.

### Using formulas and evaluating expressions

**1.** The formula for the circumference of a circle is $C = 2\pi r$, where $r$ is the radius. If the radius of a circle is 4.3 cm, what is its circumference? About 27 cm

**Evaluate each expression for $r = 2$.**

**2.** $\frac{r}{2}$ 1 **3.** $\frac{3}{2}r$ 3 **4.** $3r^2$ 12

### Solving equations by backtracking

**5.** Consider the expression $4(2n - 1) + 5$.

**a.** Draw a flowchart to represent the expression. See margin.

**b.** Use backtracking to solve the equation $4(2n - 1) + 5 = 21$. 2.5

**6.** Find the length of a rectangle with width 4.2 cm and area 98 $cm^2$. About 23.3 cm

### Using the distributive property

**Use the distributive property to rewrite each expression.**

**7.** $3(0.5r + 7)$ $1.5r + 21$ **8.** $\frac{10x - 6}{2}$ $5x - 3$

**9.** $3g + 9g^2$ $3g(1 + 3g)$ **10.** $49s - 14s$ $7s(7 - 2)$, or $35s$



CHAPTER 1

# Review & Self-Assessment

## Chapter Summary

This summary helps students recall the major topics of the chapter

## Vocabulary

Students should be able to explain each of the terms listed in the vocabulary section.

**Review & Self-Assessment** allows students an opportunity to reflect on the important topics within the chapters and to prepare for formal assessment.

▶ **Exercise 1** Some students may need to be reminded to use 3.14 to represent $\pi$. You may also wish to ask students to round their answer to the nearest whole number.

▶ **Exercise 6** Ask students to round their answers to the nearest tenth. Watch for students who label the length as $cm^2$.

Several formative assessment opportunities are found in the Chapter Resources Masters, including two equivalent **Chapter Test** forms as well as a **Performance Assessment** for each chapter and each semester.

**Additional Answer**

5a.

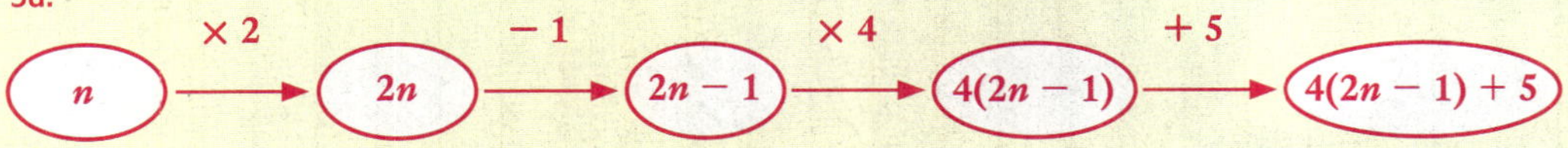

▶ **Exercise 14** Watch for students who write the answer as $g(7 + 3)$ or $g(10)$. While both represent the same amount, $10g$ is the most common way to represent this quantity.

▶ **Exercise 15** Watch for students whose answer is 576. Remind them that exponents are evaluated before executing other operations.

▶ **Exercises 16 and 17** Some students may need to review the order of operation before answering these exercises.



**Review & Self-Assessment**
**Chapter 1**

**11.** Find two rules, using symbols, that could produce this table.
Possible rules: $4x + 4$, $4(x + 1)$

| **Input** | 0 | 1 | 2 | 3 | 4 |
|---|---|---|---|---|---|
| **Output** | 4 | 8 | 12 | 16 | 20 |

## Demonstrating Skills

**Rewrite each expression without using multiplication or addition signs.**

**12.** $s + s + s + s$ $4s$ **13.** $7 \cdot b \cdot b \cdot b$ $7b^3$ **14.** $7g + 3g$ $10g$

**15.** Find the value of $6y^2$ for $y = 4$. 96

**Insert parentheses to make each equation true.**

**16.** $3 \cdot 5 - 2 = 9$ $3 \cdot (5 - 2) = 9$ **17.** $4 + 7 \cdot 3 = 33$ $(4 + 7) \cdot 3 = 33$

**Use the distributive property to expand each expression.**

**18.** $5(x + 4)$ $5x + 20$ **19.** $3(a + 2b + 3c)$ $3a + 6b + 9c$ **20.** $3y(y - \frac{1}{3})$ $3y^2 - y$

**Factor each expression. Check the resulting expression by expanding it.**

**21.** $25r - 50$ $25(r - 2)$ **22.** $16h - 4h^2$ $4h(4 - h)$ **23.** $9x - 81y + 27z$ $9(x - 9y + 3z)$

**24.** Julian's mother uses the following rule when making mashed potatoes.

*Use two potatoes per person and add one for the pot.*

**a.** How many potatoes would Julian's mother use for eight people? 17 potatoes

**b.** Julian's mother used 23 potatoes to make her last batch of mashed potatoes. How many people did she serve? 11 people

**c.** Julian feels that his mother's rule makes too many mashed potatoes. Make up a rule that he might like better.

**d.** Using your rule from part c, how many potatoes are needed for five people?

24c. Students' answers will vary. Sample answer: One potato per person and one for the pot.

24d. Students' answer will vary. Sample answer based upon the rule from part c: 6 potatoes.

**25.** Backpacks Unlimited has determined that students can safely carry up to 25 pounds in their backpacks without harming themselves. However, for children under ten years old, the weight allowance can be calculated by using the following rule.

*Divide the child's age by 10 and multiple the result by 25.*

**a.** How much does Backpacks Unlimited believe an eight-year-old child can safely carry? 20 pounds

**b.** According to this rule, how much can a 15-year-old safely carry? 25 pounds

**c.** A backpack weighs $12\frac{1}{2}$ pounds. What is the youngest age that can safely carry this backpack? Age five

**70** **CHAPTER 1** Expressions

26. $3(7+4)=3(11)=33$
27. $6(5+3)+(2\cdot 8)=6(8)+16=48+16=64$
28. $x(7-4+3)=x(6)=6x$
29. $x(2+8)=x(10)=10x$
30. $y(21-18)+5x=3y+5x$
31. This polynomial cannot be simplified.
32. $4x^2+x(3+12)=4x^2+15x$
33. $y^2(16+9)+x(5+16)+7=25y^2+21x+7$
34. $a(7+13)+b(11-5)=20a+6b$
35. This polynomial cannot be simplified.
36. $y^3(18-4+6)-7y=20y^3-7y$
37. $13x^2+x(2+11)+(5+8)=13x^2+13x+13$

*Show your work:* (a) First, write an expression to represent the total cost. 5 notebooks can be represented by $5n$, 1 package of pencils by $p$, and 4 folders by $4n$, so the expression representing the cost is $C=5n+p+4f$. (b) Substitute the cost of each item in the expression to find the total cost. $C=5n+p+4f=5\cong 4.85+2.35+4\cong 0.55=24.25+2.35+2.20=28.80$ The total cost of the items is \$28.80.



**In each exercise, combine like terms and simplify the polynomial as much as possible.**

**26.** $(7\cdot 3)+(4\cdot 3)$

**27.** $(6\cdot 5)+(2\cdot 8)+(6\cdot 3)$

**28.** $7x-4x+3x$

**29.** $2x+8x$

**30.** $21y-18y+5x$

**31.** $15x-15y$

**32.** $4x^2+3x+12x$

**33.** $16y^2+5x+16x+9y^2+7$

**34.** $7a+11b+13a-5b$

**35.** $7x^2+11y^2-9x+2$

**36.** $18y^3-4y^3+6y^3-7y$

**37.** $13x^2+2x+5+11x+8$

**38.** $21a^2+15b-20a^2+b$
$a^2(21-20)+b(15+1)=a^2+16b$

**39.** $11x+12y^2+13x-4y^2+15x$
$x(11+13+15)+y^2(12-4)=39x+8y^2$

## Test-Taking Practice

**SHORT RESPONSE**

**1** Let $n$ represent the cost of a notebook, $p$ represent the cost of a package of pencils, and $f$ represent the cost of a folder.

**A** Write an algebraic expression to represent the total cost $C$ of 5 notebooks, 1 package of pencils, and 4 folders.

**B** A notebook costs \$4.85, a package of pencils costs \$2.35, and a folder costs \$0.55. Find the total cost of 5 notebooks, 1 package of pencils, and 4 folders.

***Show your work.***

***Answer*** ________________ $C=5n+p+4f$; \$28.80

**MULTIPLE CHOICE**

**2** What is the value of $3m+2n$ if $m=5$ and $n=3$?

**A** 8
**B** 16
**C** 19
**(D)** 21

**3** Which one correctly combines like terms in $8+5x-2x+4$?

**F** $19x$
**G** $12+7x$
**(H)** $12+3x$
**J** $4+3x$

**4** Find the width of a rectangle with length 6.4 mm and area 20.48 mm$^2$.

**(A)** 3.2 mm
**B** 3.84 mm
**C** 6.4 mm
**D** 14.08 mm

**5** Which expression has the same value as $3(x+4)-(y+2)$?

**F** $2x+10$
**G** $3x-y+14$
**(H)** $3x-y+10$
**J** $3x-4y+10$

CHAPTER 2

# Exponents

## Chapter Overview

In this chapter, students use stretching and shrinking machines to learn about factors and multiples. Later, the machines model helps students understand the product, quotient, and power laws of exponents.

## The Big Picture

| Links to the Past | Chapter 2 | Links to the Future |
|---|---|---|
| **Course 1, Chapter 3** (pp. 108–195) Patterns, Numbers, and Rules | **Lesson 2.1** (p. 74) Factors and Multiples | **Course 2, Chapter 7** (pp. 318–365) Real Numbers |
| **Course 1, Chapter 3** (pp. 108–195) Patterns, Numbers, and Rules | **Lesson 2.2** (p. 92) Exponent Machines | **Course 2, Chapter 7** (pp. 172–209) Magnitude of Numbers |
| **Course 1, Chapter 3** (pp. 108–195) Patterns, Numbers, and Rules | **Lesson 2.3** (p. 107) More Exponent Machines | **Course 3, Chapter 4** (pp. 144–203) Exponents and Exponential Variation |

# Mathematical Background

Stretching and shrinking machines will be used in this chapter. Using the "stretching machine" as a model for multiplication, with repeated applications of the machine related to repeated multiplication, is a natural lead-in to the laws of exponents.

A nice connection to make in this chapter is the analogy between exponentiation and integer multiplication. This analogy is often encapsulated by saying: "Just as multiplying by a positive integer indicates repeated addition, so raising to a positive integer power indicates repeated multiplication."

So $na = a + a + \ldots + a$ ($a$ is an addend $n$ times),
and $a^n = a \cdot a \cdot \ldots \cdot a$ ($a$ is a factor $n$ times).

**Analogy between Exponentiation and Integer Multiplication** Each of the three basic laws of exponents, all of which students will encounter in this chapter, have an exact counterpart in multiplication.

| Laws of Exponents | Laws of Multiplication |
|---|---|
| $a^m a^n = a^{m+n}$ | $ma + na = (m + n)a$ |
| $(a^m)^n = a^{m \cdot n}$ | $n(ma) = (nm)a$ |
| $(ab)^n = a^n b^n$ | $n(a + b) = na + nb$ |

Students will be expected to understand and at times construct informal proofs of these laws, similar to this one:

To see that $a^m \cdot a^n = a^{m+n}$, we need to count the number of $a$'s in the expression $a^m \cdot a^n$ and to observe that there will be $m + n$ of them.

**Laws of Exponents** Perhaps the most difficult thing for students to remember is that exactly the same idea (repeating an operation) is expressed in very different notations for addition ($na$) and for multiplication ($a^n$).
In this chapter, we focus on the laws of exponents:

**Product Laws**

| | |
|---|---|
| $a^m \cdot a^n = a^{m+n}$ | $(a \cdot b)^m = a^m \cdot b^m$ |

**Quotient Laws**

| | |
|---|---|
| $a^m \div a^n = a^{m-n}$ | $(a \div b)^m = a^m \div b^m$ |

**Power of a Power Law**

| |
|---|
| $(a^m)^n = a^{m \cdot n}$ |

## Additional Reading

**What the Research Says ...**

According to a recent review by the National Reading Panel, repetition and multiple exposures to vocabulary words are effective in increasing student comprehension. In Lessons 2.1 through 2.3, students will see vocabulary words highlighted, and in the Chapter Review, they will see the chapter vocabulary words listed.

CHAPTER 2

# Planning Guide

## *Lesson Resources*

| | Lesson 2.1 (Pacing: 5 days) | Lesson 2.2 (Pacing: 4 days) | Lesson 2.3 (Pacing: 5 days) |
|---|---|---|---|
| **Lesson Title** | **Factors and Multiples** (p. 74) | **Exponent Machines** (p. 92) | **More Exponent Machines** (p. 107) |
| **Lesson Objectives** | • To identify all the factors of a given number<br>• To understand and distinguish prime and composite numbers<br>• To find prime factorizations<br>• To identify multiples<br>• To find common and GCFs, and common and LCMs<br>• To see how factors and multiples are related | • To model the behavior of exponents using stretching and shrinking machines<br>• To understand and apply the product laws of exponents | • To model the behavior of exponents using stretching and shrinking machines<br>• To understand and apply the quotient laws of exponents<br>• To understand and apply the power of a power law of exponents |
| **Materials** | Chapter 2 Master 1, Chapter 2 Master 2, Lesson 2.1 Master 1, Lesson 2.1 Master 2, Lesson 2.1 Master 3 | Chapter 2 Master 2 | Chapter 2 Master 1 |
| ***Quick Review Math Handbook*** | **Lesson 1.3** Factors and Multiples | **Lesson 3.1** Powers and Exponents | **Lesson 3.1** Powers and Exponents |
| **Print Resources** | CRM Study Guide and Intervention (p. 3)<br>CRM Skills Practice (p. 4)<br>CRM Problem-Solving Practice (p. 5)<br>CRM Enrichment (p. 6)<br>• Investigation Notebook and Reflection Journal<br>• Differentiation Handbook | CRM Study Guide and Intervention (p. 13)<br>CRM Skills Practice (p. 14)<br>CRM Problem-Solving Practice (p. 15)<br>CRM Enrichment (p. 16)<br>• Investigation Notebook and Reflection Journal<br>• Differentiation Handbook | CRM Study Guide and Intervention (p. 18)<br>CRM Skills Practice (p. 19)<br>CRM Problem-Solving Practice (p. 20)<br>CRM Enrichment (p. 21)<br>• Investigation Notebook and Reflection Journal<br>• Differentiation Handbook |
| **Technology Resources** | TeacherWorks Plus<br>Classroom Presentation Toolkit<br>ExamView Assessment Suite<br>StudentWorks Plus<br>Math Online Brain Pops • Concepts in Motion | TeacherWorks Plus<br>Classroom Presentation Toolkit<br>ExamView Assessment Suite<br>StudentWorks Plus<br>Math Online Brain Pops • Concepts in Motion | TeacherWorks Plus<br>Classroom Presentation Toolkit<br>ExamView Assessment Suite<br>StudentWorks Plus<br>Math Online Brain Pops • Concepts in Motion |

*Included in the Impact Mathematics Manipulative Kit

# Assessment Resources

## MARS Assessment: Teaching with Purpose

### Aunt Mabel

In *Aunt Mabel,* students make trials and choose the best plan. In the exercise, Aunt Mabel decides to share her lottery winnings with her nephew, and gives him a choice of three payment options. Students must decide which option gives Bill the most money.

### Targeting the Task

- **Diagnostic**—Use Exercises 1–3 in the *Aunt Mabel* assessment to determine students' understanding of how to make trials, choose the best plan and use reason to support their answer. For those students who do not have this understanding, completing this unit is needed.
- **Formative**—Exercises 1–3 can be administered individually according to the lessons.
- **Summative**—Administer the complete *Aunt Mabel* performance-based assessment.

CRM **Chapter 2 MARS Assessment** (pp. 37–39)

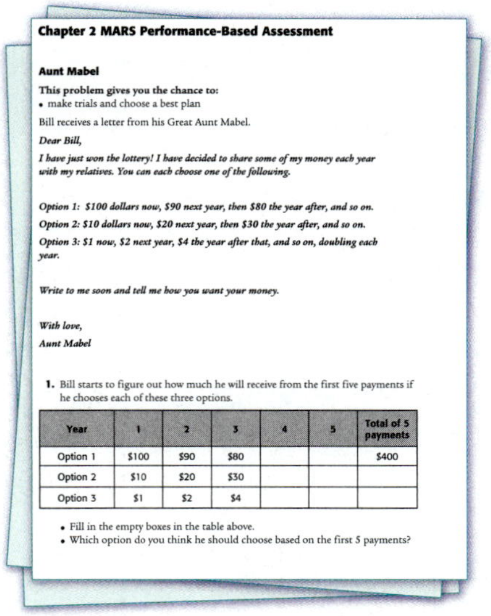

**Chapter 2 MARS Performance-Based Assessment**

**Aunt Mabel**

**This problem gives you the chance to:**
- make trials and choose a best plan

Bill receives a letter from his Great Aunt Mabel.

***Dear Bill,***

***I have just won the lottery! I have decided to share some of my money each year with my relatives. You can each choose one of the following.***

***Option 1: $100 dollars now, $90 next year, then $80 the year after, and so on.***
***Option 2: $10 dollars now, $20 next year, then $30 the year after, and so on.***
***Option 3: $1 now, $2 next year, $4 the year after that, and so on, doubling each year.***

***Write to me soon and tell me how you want your money.***

***With love,***
***Aunt Mabel***

**1.** Bill starts to figure out how much he will receive from the first five payments if he chooses each of these three options.

| Year | 1 | 2 | 3 | 4 | 5 | Total of 5 payments |
|---|---|---|---|---|---|---|
| Option 1 | $100 | $90 | $80 | | | $400 |
| Option 2 | $10 | $20 | $30 | | | |
| Option 3 | $1 | $2 | $4 | | | |

- Fill in the empty boxes in the table above.
- Which option do you think he should choose based on the first 5 payments?

## Assessment Planning Guide

Assessments are available for investigations, lessons, and chapters.

**ExamView** Assessment Suite — Customize and create multiple versions of tests and quizzes.

| | Student Edition | Teacher Edition | Other Resources |
|---|---|---|---|
| **Diagnostic** | | | CRM Chapter 2 Pretest (pp. 23–26)<br>Math Online Online Chapter Quiz |
| **Formative** | Share & Summarize (pp. 77, 79, 82, 85, 96, 100, 103, 108, 110, 113) | Troubleshooting (pp. 75, 82, 85, 94, 96, 103, 108, 109, 113)<br>On the Spot Assessment (p. 80)<br>Quick Check (pp. 90, 106, 119)<br>Quick Quiz (pp. 91, 106, 119) | CRM Quick Quiz (pp. 7, 17, 22) |
| **Summative** | Review & Self-Assessment (pp. 120–123) | | CRM Chapter 2 Test: Forms A and B (pp. 27–34)<br>CRM Standardized Test Practice (pp. 39–40) |
| **Performance-Based** | In Your Own Words (pp. 91, 106, 119) | | CRM MARS Performance-Based Assessment (pp. 37–38)<br>CRM Chapter Performance Assessment (pp. 35–36) |

# Differentiated Instruction

## *Reaching* All Learners

Below are suggestions on differentiating the materials presented in this chapter. Additional modifications should be considered.

### Approaching Level AL

**Reinforcement** Have students work in pairs and practice using exponents. On a sheet of paper, each student should write out an exponent problem that they are comfortable solving. The students should then trade papers and answer the question. If help is necessary, they can consult each other. Continue this until the allotted time is completed.

### Beyond Level BL

**Review Game** Have students create a review game for students who are having a difficult time with the concept of exponents. The game needs to have rules and some form of strategy, but having one winner is not necessary. The games can then be played by the entire class to review.

### On Level OL

**Divisibility Game** Have the students create a large 5 by 5 square on a piece of paper to play a game similar to "BINGO". Have the students randomly fill in the divisibility rules and numbers from 10 to 100. Alternate selecting a rule and choosing a number and call out numbers. In order to cross something off on their sheet, the number must fit one of the divisibility rules called, or the divisibility rule called must work on the number crossed off. The first person to get "BINGO" becomes the next caller.

### English Language Learners ELL

**Word Web** Have students create a web of words in their first language. Words in the web should correspond to English words that represent exponents, powers, multiplication and additional terms that will assist the students in understanding the concepts in English.

**KEY**

AL Approaching Level   OL On Level   BL Beyond Level   ELL English Language Learners

# Intervention Planning Guide

CRM Assess students' prerequisite skills and knowledge using the **Chapter Pretest** found in the Chapter 2 Resource Masters, pp. 23–26.

| **Intensive Intervention** two or more years below grade level | **Strategic Intervention** below grade level | **On Level** | **Beyond Level** |
|---|---|---|---|
| **If** students miss 75% of the exercises:<br>**Then** use *Math Triumphs,* an intensive intervention | **If** students miss 50% of the exercises:<br>**Then** choose a resource: | **If** students miss 25% of the exercises:<br>**Then** choose a resource: | **If** students miss 0%–10% of the exercises:<br>**Then** choose a resource: |
| *Math Triumphs,* Grade 7<br>• Chapter 8: Integer Operations | CRM Study Guide and Intervention (pp. 3, 13, 18)<br>• Investigation Notebook and Reflection Journal<br>• Differentiation Handbook<br>Math Online Brain Pops • Concepts in Motion | CRM Skills Practice (pp. 4, 14, 19)<br>CRM Problem-Solving Practice (pp. 5, 16, 20)<br>• Investigation Notebook and Reflection Journal | CRM Enrichment (pp. 6, 16, 21)<br>• Differentiation Handbook |

## Literature Connections

### Recommended Outside Reading for Students

**Nonfiction**

Huff, Darrell. *How to Lie with Statistics.* W. W. Norton & Company, 1954, 1993.

This classic book, illustrated by Irving Geis, warns readers of methods used to persuade an audience with statistics. Many techniques of manipulating statistics are explained, including the use of scale, presentation, and sample bias.

**Fiction**

Scieszka, Jon and Smith, Lane. *Math Curse.* Viking, 1995.

This book tells the funny story of a student who begins to see everything she encounters throughout the day as a math problem. Many questions arise which are related to different topics in mathematics, including the topic of *average*.

## Mc Graw Hill Professional Development

Targeted professional development has been articulated throughout the *IMPACT Mathematics* series. The **McGraw-Hill Professional Development Video Library** provides short videos that support the mathematics standards. Log on to www.glencoe.com.

Model Lessons

Instructional Strategies

CHAPTER 2

## Introduce

**Astronomical Figures** The "Astronomical Figures" feature describes distances in space and provides a bit of background regarding a recent mission to the planet Mars, along with the cost of the mission. Explain to students that in this chapter they will learn alternative ways to express large numbers. Ask students how they might represent very large numbers if they didn't want to write out all the digits. Finally, ask students to think of other contexts besides space and astronomy in which they might have to deal with very large numbers.

**Think About It** Have students look for a pattern in the numbers in the "Astronomical Figures" feature. Use scientific notation to write \$150,000,000 as $1.5 \times 10^8$ dollars.

CHAPTER 2

# Exponents

### Contents in Brief



## Real-Life Math

**Astronomical Figures** The distances from the Sun to each of the planets in our solar system varies from about 35,980,000 miles to 2,796,000,000 miles. These distances are easier to write in shorthand, $3.598 \times 10^7$ miles and $2.796 \times 10^9$ miles. The distance from the Sun to the star nearest to it, Proxima Centauri, is about 25,000,000,000,000 miles. It would be much easier for an astronomer to write this distance as $2.5 \times 10^{13}$ miles.

Mars, the fourth planet in the solar system, is $1.41 \times 10^8$ miles from the Sun. On July 4, 1997, the *Mars Pathfinder* from the National Aeronautics and Space Administration landed on Mars. The spacecraft put the surface rover *Sojourner* on the planet. *Sojourner* sent detailed photos back to Earth, giving us our first up-close views of our sister planet.

**Think About It** The Mars Pathfinder Mission was part of a NASA program with a spending limit of \$150,000,000. Can you write this dollar amount without listing all of the zeros?

**Math Online** Take the **Chapter Readiness Quiz** at glencoe.com.

72

### Chapter Resources

- CRM Chapter 2 Resource Masters
- CRM English/Spanish Family Letter (pp. 1–2)
- CRM Lesson Masters (pp. 8–12)
- CRM Chapter 2 Pretest (pp. 23–26)
- CRM Chapter 2 Test (pp. 27–34)
- **Math Online** Online Readiness Quiz • eGlossary

# Dear Family,

The class is about to begin Chapter 2 about exponents, factors, multiples, and prime numbers. Exponents can be thought of as a shortcut method of expressing repeated multiplication. For example, $4 \cdot 4 \cdot 4$ is the same as $4^3$. The base is 4, which is the number to be multiplied. The exponent is 3, which is the number of 4s that are multiplied together.

### Key Concept–Exponents

Students will use a machine model to help learn about exponents. *Stretching machines* are a model of multiplication. They stretch any input by the number on the machine. This machine will stretch something 4 times. Suppose you put a one-inch piece of gum into the machine. How long will it be when it comes out the machine?

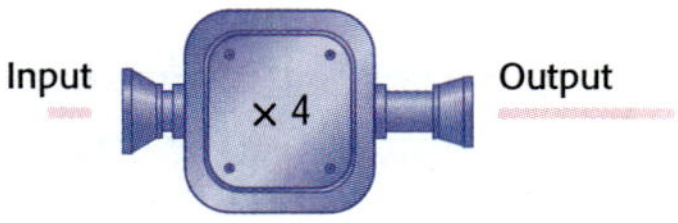


A *repeater machine* is a special type of stretching machine that models exponents. Look at the repeater machine at the right. It will stretch an input 4 times, then 4 times again, and then 4 times again. A one-inch piece of gum goes through the ×4 machine 3 times, for a total of 64 stretches, and comes out 64 inches long.

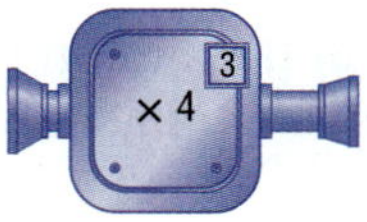


### Chapter Vocabulary

| | |
|---|---|
| base | least common multiple |
| common factor | multiple |
| common multiple | order of operations |
| composite number | power |
| exponent | prime factorization |
| factor | prime number |
| factor pair | product law of exponents |
| greatest common factor | relatively prime |

### Home Activities

Have your student think about common uses of exponents. Challenge them to use exponents to represent large numbers, such as the U.S. national debt.

73

## Family Letter

Another version of the Family Letter, available in English and Spanish, is found in the Chapter 2 Resource Masters. You may want to send a copy of this letter home with your students.

**Key Concept–Exponents** To enable students to grasp the concept of exponents, it may be helpful to have the students discuss exponents at home. After a class discussion, ask the students to go home and quiz their family members on exponents. The students may be surprised by what their family members remember or they may be able to assist their family members in understanding the concept of repeated multiplication.

### Home Activities

- To assist students in preparing to work on exponents at home, have a class discussion regarding some uses of exponents, such as finance, loans.

## Key Vocabulary

**English (Spanish)** *Introduce the most important terms from Chapter 2.*

**base (base)** The number in an exponential expression that is multiplied by itself. For example, in $t^3$, $t$ is the base; in $10^4$, 10 is the base. (p. 93)

**exponent (exponente)** A symbol written above and to the right of a quantity that tells how many times the quantity is multiplied by itself. For example: $t \cdot t \cdot t$ is written $t^3$. (p. 79)

**power (potencia)** A number that is written using an exponent. (p. 93)

**factor (factor)** To use the distributive property to insert parentheses. (p. 76)

**factor pair (par de factores)** A factor pair for a number is two factors whose product equals that number. For example, the factor pairs for 24 are 1 and 24, 2 and 12, 3 and 8, and 4 and 6. (p. 76)

**composite number (número compuesto)** A whole number greater than 1 with more than two factors. (p. 78)

**prime number (número primo)** A whole number greater than 1 with only two factors: itself and 1. (p. 78)

**common factor (factor común)** A common factor of two or more numbers is a number that is a factor of all the numbers. For example, 5 is a common factor of 15, 25, and 40. (p. 80)

**least common multiple (mínimo común múltiplo)** The least common multiple of two or more numbers is the smallest of their common multiples. For example, the LCM of 6 and 15 is 30. (p. 83)

LESSON 2.1

# Factors and Multiples

### Objectives

- To identify all the factors of a given number
- To understand and distinguish prime and composite numbers
- To find prime factorizations
- To identify multiples
- To find common and GCFs, and common and LCMs
- To see how factors and multiples are related

## Overview

This lesson reviews and extends what students know about factors and multiples. They will apply these topics in this chapters and the next as they work with equivalent fractions and convert among fractions, decimals, and percents. The lesson uses stretching machine models to teach factors. Stretching machines increase an input by a given factor. When an object such as a strand of spaghetti or a rope is the input, the output of the stretching machine is a longer version of the input. The stretching-machine model is used in this lesson to develop ideas about factors, multiples, prime and composite numbers, and relative primes.

## Advance Preparation

You may want to make transparencies of the Lesson 2.1 Masters to facilitate class discussion while presenting new topics.

| | Summary | Materials | On Your Own Exercises (pp. 86–91) | Assessment Opportunities |
|---|---|---|---|---|
| **Investigation 1** (p. 75) Pacing: 2 days | Students use stretching machines to review general concepts of factors. | Lesson 2.1 Master 1 | Practice & Apply: 1–4<br>Connect & Extend: 26–30<br>Mixed Review: 41–45 | • Share & Summarize (p. 77)<br>• Troubleshooting (p. 75) |
| **Investigation 2** (p. 77) Pacing: 1 day | Students are introduced to prime and composite numbers. | Chapter 2 Master 1 | Practice & Apply: 5–10<br>Connect & Extend: 31–34<br>Mixed Review: 41–45 | • Share & Summarize (p. 79) |
| **Investigation 3** (p. 80) Pacing: 1 day | Students find greatest common factors and relatively prime numbers. | Lesson 2.1 Master 2 | Practice & Apply: 11–16<br>Connect & Extend: 35–36<br>Mixed Review: 41–45 | • On the Spot Assessment (p. 80)<br>• Share & Summarize (p. 82)<br>• Troubleshooting (p. 82) |
| **Investigation 4** (p. 83) Pacing: 1 day | Students learn about multiples and find least common multiples. | Lesson 2.1 Master 3 | Practice & Apply: 17–25<br>Connect & Extend: 37–40<br>Mixed Review: 41–45 | • Share & Summarize (p. 85)<br>• Troubleshooting (p. 85) |

# Leveled Lesson Resources

CRM *Available in:* **Chapter 2 Resource Masters**

Also on TeacherWorks™ Lesson 2.1

## Study Guide and Intervention (p. 3) AL

**Lesson 2.1 Study Guide and Intervention**
***Factors and Multiples***

The **greatest common factor (GCF)** of two or more numbers is the largest number that is a factor of each number. The GCF of prime numbers is 1. The least nonzero multiple of two or more numbers is the **least common multiple (LCM)** of the numbers.

*Example 1* Find the GCF of 42 and 60 using prime factors.

Method 1 Write the prime factorization. Circle the common prime factors.

$60 = 2 \times 2 \times 3 \times 5$
$42 = 2 \times 3 \times 7$

Method 2 Divide by common prime factors. Divide both 42 and 60 by 2. Then divide the quotients by 3.

7 10
3)21 30
2)42 60 ← Start here.

The common prime factors are 2 and 3. Multiply the common prime factors to get the GCF. The GCF of 42 and 60 is 2 × 3, or 6.

*Example 2* Find the LCM of 8 and 12 using prime factors.

Method 1 Write the prime factorization.

$8 = 2 \times 2 \times 2 = 2^3$
$12 = 2 \times 2 \times 3 = 2^2 \times 3$

The prime factors of 8 and 12 are 2 and 3. Multiply the greatest power of both 2 and 3.

Method 2 Divide by common prime factors.

2 3
2)4 6
2)8 12 ← Start here.

Start dividing by common prime factors until both numbers cannot be divided by the same divisor. Then multiply the divisors and final quotients to get the LCM.

The LCM of 8 and 12 is $2^3 \times 3$, or 24.

*Exercises*

Find the GCF of each set of numbers.

**1.** 18, 30 **2.** 60, 45 **3.** 24, 72

Find the LCM of each set of numbers.

**4.** 4, 6 **5.** 6, 9 **6.** 5, 9

## Skills Practice (p. 4) AL OL

**Lesson 2.1 Skills Practice**
***Factors and Multiples***

Find the GCF of each set of numbers.

**1.** 14, 20 **2.** 16, 42
**3.** 8, 18 **4.** 24, 36
**5.** 72, 22 **6.** 77, 15
**7.** 32, 80 **8.** 90, 120
**9.** 45, 30 **10.** 12, 62
**11.** 15, 27 **12.** 21, 28

Find the LCM of each set of numbers.

**13.** 2, 8 **14.** 6, 10
**15.** 10, 11 **16.** 10, 12
**17.** 9, 18 **18.** 4, 22
**19.** 12, 30 **20.** 4, 13
**21.** 25, 30 **22.** 250, 30
**23.** 200, 18 **24.** 70, 90

## Problem-Solving Practice (p. 5) AL OL

**Lesson 2.1 Problem-Solving Practice**
***Factors and Multiples***

**1. Table Tennis** Rebecca has 20 table tennis balls and 16 table tennis paddles. She wants to sell packages of balls and paddles bundled together. What is the greatest number of packages she can sell with no leftover balls or paddles?

**2. Work** Alano and Abey both work at night. Alano has every fourth night off, and Abey has every sixth night off. If they are both off tonight, how long will it be before they are both off again?

**3. Bake Sale** Volunteers at a bake sale want to sell slices of banana nut bread and raisin bread packaged together. They have 63 slices of banana nut bread and 45 slices of raisin bread, and they plan to use all the bread. What is the greatest number of packages they can put together? How many slices of each type of bread are in a package?

**4. Movies** Faith spent the same amount of money on video cassettes as she did on DVDs. If cassettes cost $12 and DVDs cost $16, what is the least amount of money she could have spent on each?

**5. Fruit Trees** Mr. Farber has 84 pear trees and 180 apple trees. He wants to plant the trees in rows of equal width. Find the most trees that can be planted in a row if each row has only one type of tree.

**6. Paper Goods** At a party store, paper cups come in packages of 15, paper plates come in packages of 30, and napkins come in packages of 20. In order to have the same number of cups, plates, and napkins, what is the least number of each that must be purchased?

## Enrichment (p. 6) BL

**Lesson 2.1 Enrichment**
***Factors and Multiples***

**Sundaram's Sieve**

This arrangement of numbers is called Sundaram's Sieve. Like the Sieve of Eratosthenes, Sundaram's arrangement can be used to find prime numbers.

| | | | | | | | | | |
|---|---|---|---|---|---|---|---|---|---|
| 4 | 7 | 10 | 13 | 16 | 19 | 22 | 25 | 28 | 31 |
| 7 | 12 | 17 | 22 | 27 | 32 | 37 | 42 | 47 | 52 |
| 10 | 17 | 24 | 31 | 38 | 45 | 52 | 59 | 66 | 73 |
| 13 | 22 | 31 | 40 | 49 | 58 | 67 | 76 | 85 | 94 |
| 16 | 27 | 38 | 49 | 60 | 71 | 82 | 93 | 104 | 115 |

Here's how to use Sundaram's Sieve to find prime numbers. If a number, $n$, is not in the Sieve, then $2n + 1$ is a prime number. If a number, $n$, is in the Sieve, then $2n + 1$ is not a prime number.

32 is in the sieve. $2 \times 32 + 1 = 65$ 65 is not prime.
35 is not in the sieve. $2 \times 35 + 1 = 71$ 71 is prime.

**1.** Does the sieve give all the primes up to 99? all the composites?

**2.** Sundaram's Sieve is constructed from arithmetic sequences. Describe the pattern used to make the first row.

**3.** How is the first column constructed?

**4.** How are the second through fifth rows constructed?

**5.** How would you add a sixth row to the sieve?

**6.** Use Sundaram's Sieve to find 5 four-digit prime numbers. You will need to add more numbers to the sieve to do this.

## Lesson Quick Quiz (p. 7) AL OL BL

**Lesson 2.1 Quick Quiz**

For each machine in Exercises 1–3, name at least three different connections that will give the same output. You may not use the ×1 machine or change the order of the machines to describe a new connection.

**1.** ×36

**2.** ×24

**3.** ×100

**4.** Which of the following numbers are not factors of 18? How do you know? 8, 9, 2, 4, 12, 36, 3

**5.** For each number pair, list any common factors other than 1, and then find the greatest common factor. If the numbers are relatively prime, say so.
**a.** 24 and 56
**b.** 15 and 23
**c.** 8 and 15

**6.** Write the first five multiples of 7.

## Lesson Masters 1–5 (pp. 8–12)

**Lesson 2.1 Master 1**
***Factors and Multiples***

**Lesson 2.1 Introduction**

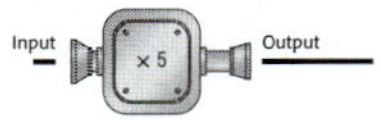


**Investigation 1 Introduction**

# Additional Lesson Resources

### Teacher Tech Tools
- TeacherWorks
- ExamView Assessment Suite
- Classroom Presentation Toolkit
- Advance Tracker

### Student Tech Tools
- StudentWorks Plus
- Math Online eGlossary • Concepts in Motion

### Other Print Products
- Investigation Notebook and Reflection Journal
- Quick Review Math Handbook

# LESSON 2.1 Factors and Multiples

## Introduce

**Stretching-machine Model** You can use a transparency of Lesson 2.1 Master 1 to introduce students to the stretching-machine model and to explain how it works. Cover the picture of the connection at the bottom of the master to show only the top three machines.

Work through some examples with the class. Encourage volunteers to think of inputs and to have their classmates tell what the output would be. When students are comfortable working with the machines, proceed to the Think & Discuss.

### Think & Discuss

Discuss students' answers to the questions in this activity. You may want to have them work through the questions independently, to see how well they understand how stretching machines work, before discussing the answers as a class.

To choose the correct machines, some students may think *Input times what number equals output?* Others may divide the output by the input. Encourage students to check their answers by finding the output given the input and the machine they selected.

The last question asks students to think about different lengths that can be made from a $\times 2$ and a $\times 3$ machine. Be sure they understand that they can use either or both machines, and that they can use the machines more than once; that is, they can take the output and run it through the same machine again. If someone brings up the idea of connecting the two machines together and running an input first through one and then the other, lead right into Investigation 1.

# LESSON 2.1 Factors and Multiples



Imagine that you work at a stretching factory. The factory has an incredible set of machines that will stretch almost anything.

To double the length of a stick of gum, for example, you can put it through a $\times 2$ machine.

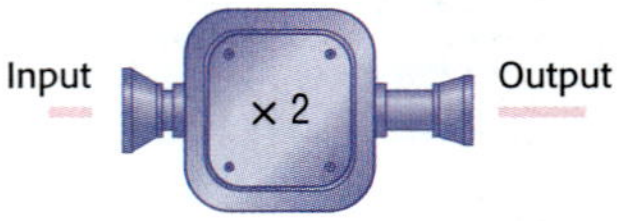


To stretch modeling clay to five times its length, you can use a $\times 5$ machine.

The factory has machines for every whole-number stretch up to 200. This means there is a $\times 1$ machine, a $\times 2$ machine, a $\times 3$ machine, and so on, up to $\times 200$.

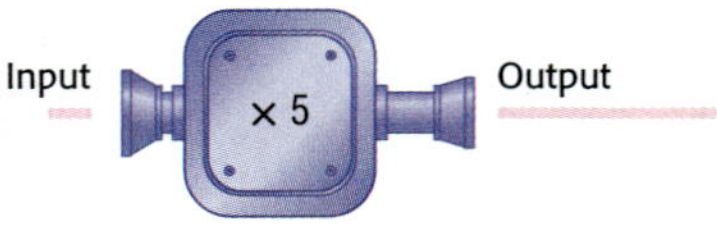

**Real-World Link**
Licorice candy is flavored with juice from the licorice herb. The herb is native to southern Europe and is often used to mask the taste of bitter medicines.

### Think & Discuss

- Your supervisor has asked you to fill the following orders. Tell which machine you would use to perform each stretch.

  Order 1: Stretch a 1-foot chain into a 5-foot chain. $\times 5$ machine
  Order 2: Stretch a 2-inch pencil into a 16-inch pencil. $\times 8$ machine
  Order 3: Stretch a 3-inch wire into a 21-inch wire. $\times 7$ machine
- Your co-worker, Winnie, sends a 1-foot piece of licorice through the $\times 2$ machine five times. How does this change the length of the licorice? See ① below.
- Another co-worker, Bill, puts a 1-foot piece of licorice through the $\times 1$ machine five times. How does this change the length of the licorice? It does not; a $\times 1$ machine does nothing to the length.
- This afternoon, you will be using the $\times 2$ machine and the $\times 3$ machine to stretch 1-foot strands of spaghetti. Give ten different output lengths you can make using one or both of these machines. Answers will vary. Correct lengths will have only 2s and 3s for prime factors.

① It doubles the length five times. The length changes from 1 ft to 2 ft to 4 ft to 8 ft to 16 ft to 32 ft.

# Investigation 1 Factors

**Vocabulary**

factor

factor pair

Machines in the stretching factory can be hooked together. When machines are hooked together, the output of one machine becomes the input for the next. For example, when a 1-foot piece of licorice passes through the connection below, the ×2 machine stretches it into a 2-foot piece. Then the ×3 machine stretches the 2-foot piece into a 6-foot piece.

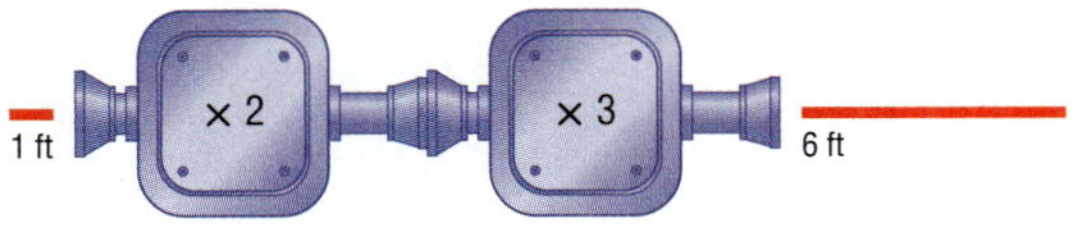


## Develop & Understand: A

**1.** Winnie is using this connection to stretch rope.

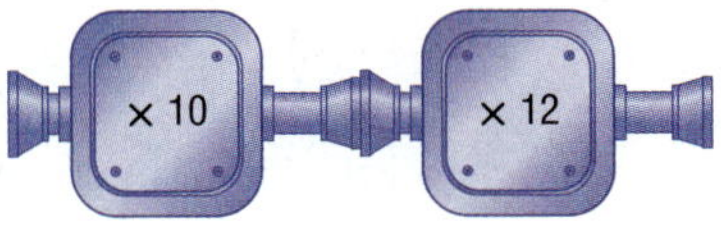


**a.** What happens to a 1-foot length of rope put through this connection? It is stretched to 10 ft and then to 120 ft.

**b.** What single machine would do the same stretch as Winnie's connection? ×120

**c.** Would Winnie get the same result if she used this connection? Explain.

1c. Yes; the first connection multiplies the length by 10 • 12, and the second multiplies it by 12 • 10. Order does not matter in multiplication.

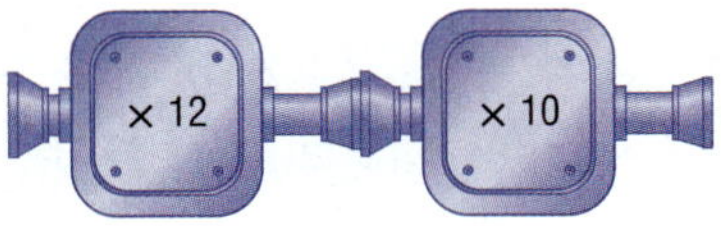


**2.** Bill wants to use a connection of five ×1 machines to stretch a rope to five times its length. Winnie says this will not work. Who is right? Why? Winnie; the ×1 machine does not change the length of an input.

**3.** What happens when a 1-foot piece of rope is sent through a connection of two ×5 machines? It is stretched to 25 times its length, or to 25 ft.



# Investigation 1

***On Your Own Exercises***
Pages 86–91
Exercises 1–4, 26–30

**Factors** In this investigation, students will be using the stretching-machine model to make connections between whole numbers and their factors. Students informally review the *multiplication identity* and the *commutative property of multiplication* as they work with factor pairs.

Show students how a connection works. You can use a transparency of Lesson 2.1 Master 1 to model this. Provide students with different inputs and have them find the related outputs. Be sure they understand that the output of one machine is the input of the next machine in the connection.

## Develop & Understand: A

*Suggested Grouping: Whole Class*

This problem set has students find the output of connections. Students should see that many machines can be replaced by connections: you can get the same output from a ×12 machine as from a ×6 and ×2 connection or from a ×3 and ×4 connection.

▶ **Exercise 1c** Students verify the commutative property of multiplication, although they are not expected to use its formal name.

## Troubleshooting

In Exercise 2, it is common for students to think at first that five ×1 machines are equivalent to one ×5 machine. You might ask them to work through the connection one machine at a time, giving the output after each machine. They should see by this that five ×1 machines multiply the input by 1 each time, leaving the length unchanged.

## Develop & Understand: B

*Suggested Grouping: Pairs or Small Groups*

▶ **Exercises 4–7** Students may list the machines in any order. However, you may want to tell them to consider the same machines connected in a different order to be the same. For example, you might tell them to consider a ×2 and ×6 connection to be the same as a ×6 and ×2. In the same exercises, except for Exercise 6, they also may add any number of ×1 machines as part of their solutions.

▶ **Exercise 8** This exercise previews the idea of prime numbers. Students will probably take some time to determine that the ×101 machine cannot be replaced.

**Wrap-Up** Introduce the terms *factor* and *factor pair,* making sure students understand the relationship and the differences between the two terms. You may want to relate factor pairs to connections: the number on one machine is one factor; the number on the other machine is the other factor.

## Develop & Understand: C

*Suggested Grouping: Pairs*

Students move away from the stretching-machine model as they find factors and factor pairs for numbers. Working in pairs can make it is easier for students to find all the factor pairs.

▶ **Exercises 9–14** Students may need help developing a systematic approach to problem solving or organizing their work. Suggest the following:

- Write 1 on the left side of your paper and the number to be factored on the right side. (Some students may prefer to draw a line and place the numbers at either end of the line.)
- Then test for factors, beginning with 2. If 2 is a factor, place it to the right of the 1 and write the other number in that factor pair to the left of the end number. (Spacing is not important.)
- Test the next number, and the next, until you reach a number you have already written on the line.
- The numbers you wrote are the factors. List them in pairs.

6a. ×8 and ×8, ×4 and ×16, ×2 and ×32
6b. Two ×2 and a ×16; three ×4; a ×2, a ×8, and a ×4; any connection from Part a with one ×1
6c. Three ×2 and a ×8; two ×4 and two ×2; any connection from Part a with two ×1; any connection from Part b with one ×1
7. Two ×9; a ×3 and a ×27; two ×3 and a ×9; four ×3; any of the previous connections with any number of ×1

When a stretching machine breaks down, you can use your knowledge of connections to replace it.

## Develop & Understand: B

**4.** If a ×12 machine breaks down, what machines can you connect to replace it? ×2 and ×6, ×3 and ×4

**5.** If a ×51 machine breaks down, what machines can you connect to replace it? ×3 and ×17

**6.** Suppose a ×64 machine breaks down.
 **a.** What two-machine connections will replace it?
 **b.** What three-machine connections will replace it?
 **c.** What four-machine connections will replace it?

**7.** If a ×81 machine breaks down, what connections will replace it?

**8.** If a ×101 machine breaks down, what connections will replace it? There are none.

When you figure out what connections will replace a particular machine, you are thinking about *factors* of the machine's number. A **factor** of a whole number is another whole number that divides into it without a remainder. For example, 1, 2, 3, 4, 6, 8, 12, and 24 are factors of 24.

When you found two-machine connections, you were finding *factor pairs.* A **factor pair** for a number is two factors whose product equals that number. Here are the factor pairs for 24.

1 and 24  2 and 12  3 and 8  4 and 6

Order does not matter in a factor pair. In fact, 2 and 12 is the same pair as 12 and 2.

### Math Link

A number is divisible by:

- 2 if the ones digit is divisible by 2.
- 3 if the sum of the digits is divisible by 3.
- 4 if the number formed by the last two digits is divisible by 4.
- 5 if the ones digit is 0 or 5.
- 6 if the number is divisible by both 2 and 3.
- 8 if the number formed by the last three digits is divisible by 8.
- 9 if the sum of the digits is divisible by 9.
- 10 if the ones digit is 0.

## Develop & Understand: C

**List the factors of each number.** 9–13. See margin.

**9.** 21  **10.** 36

**11.** 37  **12.** 63

**13.** List all the factors of 150. Then list all the factor pairs for 150.

**14.** List all the factors of 93. Then list all the factor pairs for 93. 1, 3, 31, 93; 1 and 93, 3 and 31



### Additional Answers

9. 1, 3, 7, 21
10. 1, 2, 3, 4, 6, 9, 12, 18, 36
11. 1, 37
12. 1, 3, 7, 9, 21, 63
13. 1, 2, 3, 5, 6, 10, 15, 25, 30, 50, 75, 150; 1 and 150, 2 and 75, 3 and 50, 5 and 30, 6 and 25, 10 and 15

**Share & Summarize** 1–2. See margin.

1. Explain how finding a connection to replace a broken machine involves finding factors.
2. Describe some methods you use for finding factors of a number.

# Investigation 2 Prime Numbers

**Vocabulary**

- composite number
- prime factorization
- prime number

**Materials**

- copy of the stretching-machine table

You, Winnie, and Bill plan to open your own stretching factory. Since stretching machines are expensive, you decide to buy only machines with stretches up to ×50. You also decide not to purchase any machine that can be replaced by connecting other machines together or by using the same machine more than once.

## Develop & Understand: A

1. The table lists stretching machines from ×1 to×50. On a copy of the table, cross out all the machines that can be replaced by other machines. Circle the machines that cannot be replaced. When you finish, compare your table with your partner's.

| | | | | | | | | | |
|---|---|---|---|---|---|---|---|---|---|
| ×1 | ×2 | ×3 | ~~×4~~ | ×5 | ~~×6~~ | ×7 | ~~×8~~ | ~~×9~~ | ~~×10~~ |
| ×11 | ~~×12~~ | ×13 | ~~×14~~ | ~~×15~~ | ~~×16~~ | ×17 | ~~×18~~ | ×19 | ~~×20~~ |
| ~~×21~~ | ~~×22~~ | ×23 | ~~×24~~ | ~~×25~~ | ~~×26~~ | ~~×27~~ | ~~×28~~ | ×29 | ~~×30~~ |
| ×31 | ~~×32~~ | ~~×33~~ | ~~×34~~ | ~~×35~~ | ~~×36~~ | ×37 | ~~×38~~ | ~~×39~~ | ~~×40~~ |
| ×41 | ~~×42~~ | ×43 | ~~×44~~ | ~~×45~~ | ~~×46~~ | ×47 | ~~×48~~ | ~~×49~~ | ~~×50~~ |

2. The machines that you crossed out can be replaced by using the machines that you circled.
   a. Explain how the ×24 machine can be replaced.
   By using the ×2 machine three times and the ×3 machine once
   b. Explain how the ×49 machine can be replaced.
   By using the ×7 machine twice
   c. Choose three more crossed-out machines. Explain how each can be replaced by using the machines that you circled.
   Answers will vary.



**Additional Answers**

**Share & Summarize**

1. Possible answer: To replace a machine, you must find combinations of machines that stretch the same number of times as the original machine. This means finding machines with numbers that multiply to give the number of the original machine. These numbers are the factors of the original machine's number.
2. Possible answers:
   - I know that 1 and the number itself are factors.
   - If the number is even, I know that 2 and half of the number are factors.
   - If the number is odd, I only need to check odd numbers.
   - If a number is a factor, I know its factors are also factors of the original number.
   - I check numbers in order from least to greatest. If a number is a factor, I list both it and the other number in the factor pair. When I get a factor that is a repeat of a number I already have, I am done.

**Share & Summarize**

Have students share their answers for Exercise 2. You may want to suggest any method given in the sample answer that students do not supply themselves.

In particular, you may need to help them find the relationship showing that an odd number has only odd factors. This may be intuitive for students who reason that because odd numbers are not evenly divisible by 2 and all even numbers are evenly divisible by 2, an odd number cannot have an even factor; if it did, it would be evenly divisible by 2. Other students may need to review some of the factors they listed in the problems for Exercises 9-14 to discover this fact.

## Investigation 2

**On Your Own Exercises**

Pages 86–91

Exercises 5–10, 31–34

**Prime Numbers** Use the opening scenario to set up the situation in Develop & Understand. To check that students understand the situation, you may want to ask them if they would need both a ×2 machine and a ×4 machine in the factory. They should suggest that an object could go through the ×2 machine twice and the output would be the same as if it went though the ×4 machine, so the ×4 machine is not needed. Then ask if they would need both a ×2 and a ×3 machine. They would need both, since there are no combinations that would have the same output as a ×2 machine or a ×3 machine.

## Develop & Understand: A

*Suggested Grouping: Pairs*

You may want to provide each student with a table from a copy of Chapter 2 Master 1 to save time copying the table in Exercise 1; they should keep their copies for future reference.

▶ **Exercise 1** You may want to ask students to explain their choices so you can assess their understanding. Note that the ×1 machine will be crossed out in Exercise 5.

▶ **Exercise 3** This is a good assessment of how students are thinking about factors. The ideas may be a bit difficult for some students to articulate, so be sure to give them some time to express themselves.

**Teacher Tips** Read the definitions of *prime* and *composite* numbers. Point out that the numbers on the irreplaceable machines are prime numbers. Some students may find it helpful to use word associations to remember that *composite* numbers are *composed* of other numbers. Be sure students realize that 1 is neither a prime number nor a composite number.

***Example***

Model how to find the prime factorization of 20, showing students how to draw a factor tree. Point out that it does not matter which two factors are chosen first. By writing the factors in order of increasing value, it is easy to see that the resulting prime factorizations are the same.

**Additional Answers**

3. Possible answer: The number on a circled machine has only two factors—1 and the number itself. Since the number cannot be written as a product of smaller factors, there is no combination of machines that can replace the machine.

4. Possible answer: To do an odd stretch, you don't need the $\times 2$ machine at all. To do an even stretch, you can put the object through the $\times 2$ machine until you have completed the stretch or until there is only an odd-numbered stretch left to do.

5. No; Possible explanation: The $\times 1$ machine does not change the length of an input, so it is not needed.

**3.** Use the idea of factors to explain why the circled machines cannot be replaced. See margin.

**4.** Why is $\times 2$ the only even-numbered machine that you need? See margin.

**5.** Winnie points out that you can save more money by not purchasing a $\times 1$ machine. Bill says, "There is no connection that can replace the $\times 1$ machine. We must buy it!"

What do *you* think? Does your factory need the $\times 1$ machine? Explain. If you think it is not needed, cross it out in your table.

The numbers on the machines that cannot be replaced, excluding the $\times 1$ machine, are *prime numbers.* A **prime number** is a whole number greater than 1 with only two factors, itself and 1.

The numbers on the machines that can be replaced are *composite numbers.* A whole number greater than 1 with more than two factors is a **composite number**. The number 1 is neither prime nor composite.

Any composite number can be written as a product of prime numbers. Here are some examples.

$10 = 5 \cdot 2 \qquad 117 = 3 \cdot 3 \cdot 13 \qquad 693 = 3 \cdot 3 \cdot 7 \cdot 11$

When you write a composite number as a product of prime numbers, you are finding its **prime factorization**. You can use a *factor tree* to find the prime factorization of any number.

***Example***

Below are the steps for making a factor tree for the number 20. Two possible factor trees are shown.

- Find any factor pair for 20. Draw a "branch" leading to each factor.
- If a factor is prime, circle it. If a factor is not prime, find a factor pair for it.
- Continue until you cannot factor any further.

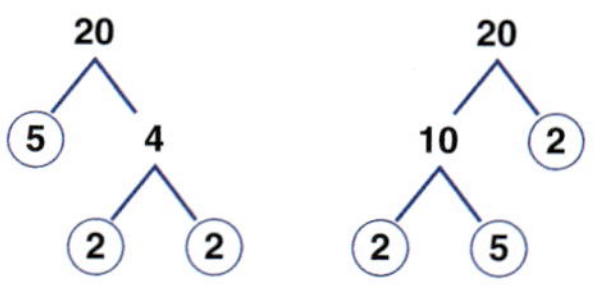


Both of these factor trees show that the prime factorization of 20 is $2 \cdot 2 \cdot 5$. Remember, when you multiply numbers, order does not matter.



## *Reaching All Learners*

**ELL English Language Learners** A few students may be confused by the use of the word *product* in the definition of *prime factorization.* They may not be able to think of a *product* as anything but a single number: 24 is the product of 6 and 4, for example. If any express confusion, direct them to look at the examples shown in the text. You also might want to point out that a product requires at least two numbers to be multiplied, so writing a number *as a product* means writing it using at least two numbers multiplied together.

**Real-World Link**
The greatest prime number discovered so far has 4,053,946 digits. This number can be written in a shorthand that uses an exponent.

$2^{13,466,917} - 1$

When a factor occurs more than once in a prime factorization, you can use *exponents* to write the factorization in a shorter form. Since $20 = 2 \cdot 2 \cdot 5$, the prime factorization of 20, using exponents, is $2^2 \cdot 5$.

## Develop & Understand: B

**6.** Use a factor tree or another method to find the prime factorization of 24. $2 \cdot 2 \cdot 2 \cdot 3$ or $2^3 \cdot 3$

**7.** Use a factor tree or another method to find the prime factorization of 49. $7 \cdot 7$ or $7^2$

**8.** Explain how your answers to Exercises 6 and 7 are related to the machines needed to replace a ×24 machine and a ×49 machine in your stretching factory.

Use a factor tree to find the prime factorization of each number. Write the prime factorization using exponents when appropriate.

**9.** 100 $2^2 \cdot 5^2$

**10.** 99 $11 \cdot 3^2$

**11.** 5,050 $2 \cdot 5^2 \cdot 101$

**12.** 111,111 $3 \cdot 7 \cdot 13 \cdot 11 \cdot 37$

## Share & Summarize

**1.** Describe the difference between a prime number and a composite number. Give three examples of each.

**2.** Find the prime factorization of each composite number you listed in Question 1. Answers will vary.

8. The prime factorization for 24 includes three 2s and one 3. To replace a ×24 machine, use the ×2 machine three times and the ×3 machine once. The prime factorization for 49 includes two 7s. To replace the ×49 machine, use the ×7 machine twice.

1. A prime number has only two factors, 1 and itself. A composite number has more than two factors. Examples of primes are 2, 29, and 41. Examples of composites are 25, 34, and 56.



## Develop & Understand: B

*Suggested Grouping: Individuals*

▶ **Exercises 9–12** Help students think about organizing their work on the page, making sure they are leaving plenty of room to draw the trees for each problem, so the factors will be easily read and understood.

## Share & Summarize

Students may find prime factorizations useful, particularly when thinking about least common multiples and greatest common factors in the next two investigations. If students are having difficulties finding factors because of weak multiplication skills, you might have them create a multiplication table to practice their skills and for future reference.

If students are having difficulty identifying prime and composite numbers and finding prime factorizations, review the definitions. Also, have them work through the Additional Examples below.

**Additional Examples** Have students state whether each number is prime or composite. If the number is composite, have them make a factor tree to show its prime factorization.

- 12 Composite: $2 \cdot 2 \cdot 3$ or $2^2 \cdot 3$
- 17 Prime
- 65 Composite: $5 \cdot 13$
- 21 Composite: $3 \cdot 7$
- 23 Prime
- 39 Composite: $3 \cdot 13$
- 774 Composite: $2 \cdot 3 \cdot 3 \cdot 43$ or $2 \cdot 3^2 \cdot 43$

## Reaching All Learners

**AL Approaching Level** If students do not know how to begin making their factor trees, suggest that they start by using a systematic approach to see if the number can be evenly divided by 2, 3, and so on. They can continue this strategy for each factor that is not prime.

## Investigation 3

***On Your Own Exercises***
Pages 86–91
Exercises 11–16, 35–36

**Scheduling** Introduce the investigation by describing the context for the Explore activity: the scheduling problems resulting from many users needing the same stretching machines at the same time.

### Explore

*Suggested Grouping: Small Groups*

- **Play** Have students work in small groups to make a schedule. There are many different schedules that avoid conflicts with the common machines.
- **Report** Then have groups compare their schedules.
- **Score** If students are engaged, you might challenge them to find as many different schedules as they can for the eight orders. Give each group one point for each order they find.

**Teacher Tips** Discuss the definition of common factor. You may want to make the distinction that factors are found for one number while common factors are found for two or more numbers.

**Additional Answer**
② Possible answer:

| Time | My Orders | Winnie's Orders |
|---|---|---|
| 10:00 | stretch ×32 | stretch ×21 |
| 10:30 | stretch ×15 | stretch ×14 |
| 11:00 | stretch ×99 | stretch ×16 |
| 11:30 | stretch ×49 | stretch ×6 |

## Investigation 3 Common Factors

**Vocabulary**
- common factor
- greatest common factor, GCF
- relatively prime

Business has been good at your factory. You have earned enough to buy one machine for every prime-number stretch from 2 to 101. However, there still do not seem to be enough machines to go around. You find that you and your co-workers often need to use the same machine at the same time.

### Explore

Here are the orders that you and Winnie are scheduled to fill this morning.

| Time | Your Orders | Winnie's Orders |
|---|---|---|
| 10:00 | stretch ×32 | stretch ×16 |
| 10:30 | stretch ×15 | stretch ×21 |
| 11:00 | stretch ×99 | stretch ×6 |
| 11:30 | stretch ×49 | stretch ×14 |

Which machines do you and Winnie need to use at the same time? See ①.

Rearrange the schedule so both you and Winnie can fill your orders. See ② in margin.

① At 10:00, we both need the ×2 machine. At 10:30, we both need the ×3 machine. At 11:00, we both need the ×3 machine. At 11:30, we both need the ×7 machine.

The scheduling exercises in Explore occurred when the stretch numbers had a *common factor.* A **common factor** of two or more numbers is a number that is a factor of all of the numbers.

### On the Spot Assessment

To make sure students understand the new term, you might discuss how to find the common factors for at least one of the number pairs below.
Find the common factors for each pair of numbers.

- 6 and 18 1, 2, 3, 6
- 6 and 27 1, 3
- 18 and 27 1, 3, 9
- 6, 18, and 27 1, 3

## Develop & Understand: A

**In Exercises 1–3, list the factors of each number. Then find the common factors of the numbers.**

1. Factors of 100: 1, 2, 4, 5, 10, 20, 25, 50, 100; factors of 75: 1, 3, 5, 15, 25, 75; common factors: 1, 5, 25
2. Factors of 33: 1, 3, 11, 33; factors of 132: 1, 2, 3, 4, 6, 11, 12, 22, 33, 44, 66, 132; common factors: 1, 3, 11, 33
3. Factors of 36: 1, 2, 3, 4, 6, 9, 12, 18, 36; factors of 84: 1, 2, 3, 4, 6, 7, 12, 14, 21, 28, 42, 84; factors of 112: 1, 2, 4, 7, 8, 14, 16, 28, 56, 112; common factors: 1, 2, 4
4. No; 2 is a factor of 8, so if 8 is a factor of both numbers, 2 must also be a factor of both numbers.

**1.** 100 and 75

**2.** 33 and 132

**3.** 36, 84, and 112

**4.** Is it possible for two numbers to have 8 as a common factor but not 2? If so, give an example. If not, explain why not.

**5.** Is it possible for two numbers to have no common factors? If so, give an example. If not, explain why not. No; 1 is a common factor for every pair of numbers.

**6.** Is it possible for two numbers to have only one common factor? If so, give an example. If not, explain why not. Yes; the only common factor of 5 and 7 is 1.

The **greatest common factor** of two or more numbers is the greatest of their common factors. The abbreviation **GCF** is often used for greatest common factor. Two or more numbers are **relatively prime** if their only common factor is 1.

### Example

Look at the common factors of 12 and 16.

Factors of 12: **1**, **2**, 3, **4**, 6, 12 Factors of 16: **1**, **2**, **4**, 8, 16

The common factors of 12 and 16 are 1, 2, and 4. Therefore, 12 and 16 are *not* relatively prime. The GCF of 12 and 16 is 4.

Now consider the common factors of 8 and 15.

Factors of 8: **1**, 2, 4, 8 Factors of 15: **1**, 3, 5, 15

The only common factor of 8 and 15 is 1. Therefore, 8 and 15 are relatively prime. The GCF of 8 and 15 is 1.



## Mathematical Background

The sense in which the primeness of two numbers is relative can be difficult to articulate. Consider the prime numbers to be building blocks for composite numbers. Then, for two numbers, find the building blocks of each—their prime factorizations. If the numbers have no factors in common, they are *relatively prime.*

In terms of necessary stretching machines, a prime number is one that cannot be replaced. If a machine in one connection breaks down, there is no chance of replacing it with a machine from the other connection.

## Develop & Understand: A

*Suggested Grouping: Pairs*

If students are comfortable with finding factors, identifying common factors will not be difficult. However, having students work in pairs is helpful because each student can factor one number in the pair and check his or her partner's work before circling the common factors.

▶ **Exercises 1–3** If students forget to list 1 as a factor, have them find a factor pair for each of two prime numbers. If necessary, remind them that 1 is always a factor.

**Teacher Tips** Introduce the terms greatest common factor, or GCF, and relatively prime.

Point out that relatively prime and prime are different ideas. A prime number is one number with only two factors. Relatively prime numbers are two or more numbers that have only the number 1 as a common factor. Relatively prime numbers can be composites while prime numbers cannot.

### Example

Discuss how to find the GCF and how to determine if two numbers are relatively prime. When you finish the first example, ask:

Why are 12 and 16 not relatively prime? They have common factors other than 1: 2 and 4.

After finding the GCF of 8 and 15, have students generalize the results:

Will 1 always be the greatest common factor of two or more relatively prime numbers? Explain. Yes; because 1 is their only common factor, it is also the greatest common factor.

You might also challenge students to explain why, if one number is a factor of another, that number will be the greatest common factor of those two numbers.

## Develop & Understand: B

*Suggested Grouping: Pairs*

You may wish to make a transparency of Lesson 2.1 Master 2, which reproduces the game board, to use to model the game. The master also includes four blank grids that students can use to play the game, so you may also want to provide each pair of students with a copy.

Read the directions for the game with the class. Point out that the greatest common factor does not need to be on the game board. Also stress the importance of crossing out each pair of numbers after the score is determined. As the board fills, this will help students focus on which two numbers are being used in the current round, since the numbers will be the only numbers on the board that are circled but not crossed out.

Using the game board shown, a game might begin as follows:

- Player A circles the number 14.
- Player B circles the number 16 and finds the greatest common factor of 14 and 16. The GCF is 2, so that is Player B's score.
- The circled numbers are crossed out.
- Player B circles the number 13.
- Player A circles the number 26 and finds the greatest common factor of 13 and 26. The GCF is 13, so that is Player A's score. After two rounds, the score is 13 to 2. The game board is shown below.

### Share & Summarize

You might conduct these questions as a class activity, or have students complete them on their own, perhaps as a journal entry. Discuss possible moves with the class.

**Additional Answers**
**Share & Summarize**

1. Possible answer: 12, 18, 21, 24, or 27. The factors of 15 are 1, 3, 5, and 15. I cannot get 15 points or 5 points because they are not factors of any available number. 3 is a factor of 12, 18, 21, 24, and 27, so any of these will give a GCF of 3.
2. Possible answer: 10 gives my opponent only 2 points. I figured out the most points my opponent could get for each possibility, and 2 is the least.

2. Possible answer: For a round in which I circled the first number, I tried to find a number that shared small GCFs with the other numbers available on the board. Whenever possible, I chose a prime number that was not a factor of the other available numbers because it would be relatively prime with any number my partner might pick. When this was not possible, I tried to find any number that was relatively prime with the other numbers. For a round in which I circled the second number, I tried to find the number that had the greatest possible common factor with the first. I found that writing out the factors for the numbers is a helpful technique.

## Develop & Understand: B

The *GCF Game* will give you practice finding greatest common factors and determining whether numbers are relatively prime.

**GCF Game Rules**

For the game board, create a 4 × 4 grid of consecutive numbers. One possible board is shown here.

| | | | |
|---|---|---|---|
| 12 | 13 | 14 | 15 |
| 16 | 17 | 18 | 19 |
| 20 | 21 | 22 | 23 |
| 24 | 25 | 26 | 27 |

Then follow this procedure.

- Player A circles a number.
- Player B circles a second number.
  Player B's score for this turn is the GCF of the two circled numbers. Cross out the circled numbers.
- Any number that is not crossed out is circled by Player B.
- Another number that has not been crossed out is circled by Player A. Player A's score for the turn is the GCF of the two numbers. Cross out the circled numbers.
- Until all numbers have been crossed out, continue to take turns. The player with the higher score at the end of the game wins.

1. Play *GCF Game* four times with your partner. As you play, think about strategies that you can use to score the most points.
2. Describe the strategies that you used when playing *GCF Game.* Use the terms *relatively prime* and *greatest common factor* in your explanation.

### Share & Summarize 1, 2. See margin

1. Here is the board for a round of *GCF Game.* Your partner has just circled 15. Which number would you circle? Why?

| | | | |
|---|---|---|---|
| 12 | 13 | 14 | 15 |
| 16 | 17 | 18 | 19 |
| 20 | 21 | 22 | 23 |
| 24 | 25 | 26 | 27 |

2. You make the first move in this round of *GCF Game.* Which number would you circle? Why?

| | | | |
|---|---|---|---|
| 6 | 7 | 8 | 9 |
| 10 | 11 | 12 | 13 |
| 14 | 15 | 16 | 17 |
| 18 | 19 | 20 | 21 |



## Troubleshooting

If students are still struggling with finding factors and greatest common factors, you can have them play the GCF game with a partner in a group of four. As they play, the partners can discuss why certain moves are better than others. You might also provide students with copies of Lesson 2.1 Master 2 to take home and play with family members. Have them copy the directions for the game on the back of the sheet before they leave school if they won't be taking their books home.

| | | | |
|---|---|---|---|
| 12 | 13 | 14 | 15 |
| 16 | 17 | 18 | 19 |
| 20 | 21 | 22 | 23 |
| 24 | 25 | 26 | 27 |

# Investigation 4 Multiples

**Vocabulary**

- **common multiple**
- **multiple**
- **least common multiple (LCM)**

**Materials**

- 3 strips of paper labeled 1–40

In the previous investigations, you found factors of a given number. Now you will find numbers that have a given number as a factor.

For example, think about numbers that have 20 as a factor. You can easily generate such numbers by multiplying 20 by whole numbers.

$$20 \cdot 1 = 20$$
$$20 \cdot 2 = 40$$
$$20 \cdot 3 = 60$$
$$20 \cdot 4 = 80$$

The products 20, 40, 60, and 80 are *multiples* of 20. A **multiple** of a whole number is the product of that number and another whole number.

2. No; Possible explanation: To find a multiple of a number, you multiply it by another whole number, and there is no limit to the number of whole numbers by which you can multiply.

4. Yes; yes; A number equals itself times 1, so it is both a factor and a multiple of itself.

## Develop & Understand: A

1. List four multiples of 20 that are greater than 1,000. Possible answer: 1,020; 1,040; 1,060; 1,080
2. Is there a limit to how many multiples a whole number greater than 0 can have? Explain.
3. Is there a limit to how many factors a whole number greater than 0 can have? Explain. Yes; Explanations will vary.
4. Is a number its own factor? Is a number its own multiple? Explain.
5. How can you determine whether 1,234 is a multiple of 7? See whether 1,234 ÷ 7 has a remainder.

A **common multiple** of a set of numbers is a multiple of all the numbers. The **least common multiple** is the smallest of the non-zero multiples. The abbreviation **LCM** is often used for least common multiple.

### Example

Consider the multiples of 6 and 9.

Multiples of 6: 6, 12, **18**, 24, 30, **36**, 42, 48, **54**, 60, 66, **72**, ...

Multiples of 9: 9, **18**, 27, **36**, 45, **54**, 63, **72**, 81, ...

The numbers 18, 36, 54, and 72 are common multiples of 6 and 9. The LCM is 18.



## Reaching All Learners

**OL On Level** Many students confuse factors and multiples at this point. It is helpful for some students to think of multiples as "the opposite" of factors. Others may benefit from having a poster or other reference posted in the classroom. On one half, the poster can describe multiples and show examples of multiples. On the other half, the poster can describe factors and show examples of factors.

# Investigation 4

***On Your Own Exercises***
Pages 86–91
Exercises 17–25, 37–40

**Word Web** To help students differentiate between factors and multiples, you may want to introduce this investigation by having students brainstorm about what they just learned about factors. You might create a *word web* to show their responses. Write *Factor* in the middle of the board and circle it. Have students suggest related words or ideas that the word *factor* suggests to them and explain each suggestion. Write the suggestions around the word *factor,* noting the conceptual connection on the line connecting the words when possible.

**Teacher Tips** Introduce the term multiple, stressing that the numbers multiplied are whole numbers other than 0. You might ask questions like these to have students think about factors and multiples of the same number as a way to reinforce the concepts:

- What are the factors of 12? 1, 2, 3, 4, 6, 12
- What are the first five multiples of 12? 12, 24, 36, 48, 60
- What are the factors of 14? 1, 2, 7, 14
- What are the first five multiples of 14? 14, 28, 42, 56, 70

## Develop & Understand: A

*Suggested Grouping: Pairs*

▶ **Exercise 3** One explanation students might give is that a factor of a number has to be less than the number but greater than 1. So, there can't be more factors than the value of the number to be factored. (In fact, 2 is the only number whose value is the same as the number of factors it has. All other numbers have fewer factors.)

## Develop & Understand: B

*Suggested Grouping: Individuals*

You can either distribute copies of Lesson 2.1 Master 3 for students to cut and tape together to form number lines, or have them write out their own on strips of paper. Some students will be able to see their findings more easily if they use two different-colored pens or pencils in this problem set.

▶ **Exercises 6b and 7b** Encourage students to explain mathematically what the numbers have in common. While the literal interpretation that they both have a circle and a square around them is correct, students should look for why they are all marked in this way while other numbers are not.

## Develop & Understand: C

*Suggested Grouping: Pairs*

This problem set puts the ideas of common multiple and least common multiple into a realistic context. Students might not immediately recognize the connection between these puzzle-like problems and common and least common multiples. Let students make this connection themselves or hear it from their classmates either while working the exercises or when discussing the Share & Summarize that follows.

### Additional Answers

6a. Students should have circled 2, 4, 6, 8, 10, 12, 14, 16, 18, 20, 22, 24, 26, 28, 30, 32, 34, 36, 38, and 40. They should have drawn a square around 3, 6, 9, 12, 15, 18, 21, 24, 27, 30, 33, 36, and 39.

7a. Students should have circled 4, 8, 12, 16, 20, 24, 28, 32, 36, and 40. They should have drawn a square around 6, 12, 18, 24, 30, and 36.

8c. Possible answer: 2, 3, and 4, in that order, have the most multiples on the strip. The common multiples of 2 and 3 occur every sixth number (6 times on the strip) while the common multiples of 2 and 4 occur every fourth number (10 times on the strip).

## Develop & Understand: B

**6.** Use a strip of paper labeled with the whole numbers from 1 to 40.

1 2 3 4 5 6 7 8 9 10 11 12 13 14 15 16 17 18 19 20 21 22 23 24 25 26 27 28 29 30 31 32 33 34 35 36 37 38 39 40

**a.** Circle all the multiples of 2 between 1 and 40. Draw a square around all the multiples of 3. See margin.

**b.** List the common multiples of 2 and 3 between 1 and 40. What do these numbers have in common? 6, 12, 18, 24, 30, 36; They are multiples of 6.

**c.** What are the next three common multiples of 2 and 3? 42, 48, 54

**d.** What is the LCM of 2 and 3? 6

**7.** Use a new strip of paper labeled from 1 to 40.

1 2 3 4 5 6 7 8 9 10 11 12 13 14 15 16 17 18 19 20 21 22 23 24 25 26 27 28 29 30 31 32 33 34 35 36 37 38 39 40

**a.** Circle all the multiples of 4 between 1 and 40. Draw a square around all the multiples of 6. See margin.

**b.** List the common multiples of 4 and 6 between 1 and 40. What do these numbers have in common? 12, 24, 36; They are multiples of 12.

**c.** What are the next three common multiples of 4 and 6? 48, 60, 72

**d.** What is the LCM of 4 and 6? 12

**8.** Look at your third numbered strip.

1 2 3 4 5 6 7 8 9 10 11 12 13 14 15 16 17 18 19 20 21 22 23 24 25 26 27 28 29 30 31 32 33 34 35 36 37 38 39 40

**a.** Which two numbers greater than 1 have the most common multiples between 1 and 40? 2 and 4

**b.** What is the LCM of these two numbers? 2

**c.** How do you know these two numbers have the most common multiples of all the pairs you could choose? See margin.

Use the idea of LCMs to help solve the next set of exercises.

## Develop & Understand: C

Jada often attends family reunions in the summer.

- Her mother's family, the Coles, has a reunion every third summer.
- Her father's family, the Brooks, has a reunion every fourth summer.
- Her stepfather's family, the Turners, has a reunion every sixth summer.

This summer, Jada attended all three reunions.



## *Reaching* All Learners

**ELL English Language Learners** Students may need to have the word *reunion* defined. Depending upon your students' command of English, you may wish to provide a basic definition as "a festive gathering of people with shared interests." In this situation, it is the gathering of family members.

The word itself consists of *re,* which means again, and *union,* which means a joining or meeting. So, *reunion* means "to meet again."

9a. 12; Possible explanation: I found the LCM of 3 and 4.

9c. Yes; no; 48 is a multiple of 12. 70 is not a multiple of 12.

**9.** Think about the Cole and Brooks reunions.

**a.** How many years will it be until the Cole and Brooks reunions occur in the same summer again? Explain how you found your answer.

**b.** How many years will it be until the second time both reunions happen again? 24

**c.** Will both reunions be held 48 years from now? Will both be held 70 years from now? How do you know?

**10.** Now think about the Cole and Turner reunions.

**a.** How many years will it be until the Cole and Turner reunions occur in the same summer again? Explain how you found your answer. 6; Possible explanation: I found the LCM of 3 and 6.

**b.** How many years will it be until the second time both reunions happen again? 12

**c.** Will both reunions be held 40 years from now? How do you know? No; 40 is not a multiple of 6.

① For any two families, the number of years between summers when both have reunions is the LCM of the numbers of years between each family's reunions. The number of years between summers when all three reunions occur is the LCM of 3, 4, and 6, the number of years between Cole, Brooks, and Turner reunions, respectively.

**11.** Now consider the Turner and Brooks reunions.

**a.** How many years will it be until the Turner and Brooks reunions are held in the same summer again? Explain how you found your answer. 12; Possible explanation: I found the LCM of 4 and 6.

**b.** How many years will it be until the second time both reunions happen again? 24

**c.** Will both reunions be held 72 years from now? How do you know? Yes; 72 is a multiple of 12.

**12.** How many years will it be until all three reunions occur in the same summer again? 12

### Share & Summarize

Explain how your answers to the Exercises 9–12 are related to the ideas of common multiples and least common multiples. See ①.



▶ **Exercises 9–12** Watch for students who have difficulty determining the relevant information needed to solve each problem. Suggest that they list the data from the opening paragraph in the form of *Name: Years until next reunion.*

The Cole family data would be *Cole: 3 years.* Have students refer to their lists as they solve each problem.

### Share & Summarize

Have students write their responses, either in their journals or on a sheet of paper. Then have them share their explanations with the class.

**Teacher Tips** Suggest that students who have difficulty remembering what a multiple is to use word-association clues, such as multiply to find a multiple.

## Troubleshooting

Students should understand the difference between factors and multiples since this is the last time these topics will be discussed independent of other topics. In later investigations, students will be applying the concepts to solve other situations. If necessary, give them additional examples like these:

List the factors and the first six multiples for both 12 and 18, and then find the GCF and LCM. Factors of 12: 1, 2, 3, 4, 6, 12; Factors of 18: 1, 2, 3, 6, 9, 18; Multiples of 12: 12, 24, 36, 48, 60, 72; Multiples of 18: 18, 36, 54, 72, 90, 108; GCF: 6; LCM: 72

**Investigation 1**
Pages 75–77
Practice & Apply: 1–4
Connect & Extend: 26–30

**Investigation 2**
Pages 77–79
Practice & Apply: 5–10
Connect & Extend: 31–34

**Investigation 3**
Pages 80–82
Practice & Apply: 11–16
Connect & Extend: 35, 36

**Investigation 4**
Pages 83–85
Practice & Apply: 17–25
Connect & Extend: 37–40

**Assign Anytime**
Mixed Review: 41–45

▶ **Exercise 1** If students list any number of ×1 machines and one ×18 machine, point out that while this connection would produce the desired result, the ×18 machine is broken.

▶ **Exercise 2** Students should see that no machine can replace the ×37 machine because 37 has no factors other than 1 and itself.

▶ **Exercise 4** You might have students explain how to use the factors for 28 from Exercise 3 to find the factors for 56. Students should note that all of the factors for 28 are factors for 56, but the factor pairs are different; they should also see that 56 has more factors since it is twice 28.

## On Your Own Exercises
**Lesson 2.1**

### Practice & Apply

**1.** The ×18 machine at the stretching factory breaks down one day.

**a.** What two-machine connections could you use to replace this machine? ×2 and ×9, ×3 and ×6

**b.** What three-machine connections could you use? ×1, ×2, and ×9; ×1, ×3, and ×6; ×2 and two ×3

**c.** What four-machine connections could you use?

1c. Two ×1, a ×2, and a ×9; two ×1, a ×3, and a ×6; one ×1, a ×2, and two ×3

**2.** What connections can be used to replace a ×37 machine? There are none.

**3.** List all the factors of 28. Then list all the factor pairs for 28. 1, 2, 4, 7, 14, 28; 1 and 28, 2 and 14, 4 and 7

**4.** List all the factors of 56. Then list all the factor pairs for 56. 1, 2, 4, 7, 8, 14, 28, 56; 1 and 56, 2 and 28, 4 and 14, 7 and 8

**Describe how you could fill the order using only prime number stretching machines.**

**5.** Stretch a piece of rope to 12 times its original length.

5. Put it through the ×2 twice and the ×3 once.

**6.** Stretch a piece of twine to 21 times its original length.

6. Put it through the ×3 and the ×7.

**7.** Stretch a crayon to 72 times its original length. Put it through the ×2 three times and the ×3 twice.

**Use a factor tree or another method to find the prime factorization of the given number. Use exponents in your answer when appropriate.**

**8.** 84 $2^2 \cdot 3 \cdot 7$  **9.** 64 $2^6$  **10.** 1,272 $2^3 \cdot 3 \cdot 53$

**What are the common factors of the two numbers? What is the GCF of the two numbers? Are the two numbers relatively prime?**

**11.** 13 and 24 1; 1; yes

**12.** 50 and 75 1, 5, 25; 25; no

**13.** 144 and 54 1, 2, 3, 6, 9, 18; 18; no

**14.** 24 and 35 1; 1; yes

86 **CHAPTER 2** Exponents

15. Possible answer: 16; The factors of 24 are 1, 2, 3, 4, 6, 8, 12, and 24. 12 and 24 are not factors of any number remaining on the board, so I cannot get 12 or 24 points. 8 is a factor of 16, so choosing 16 gives me the most possible points.

16. Possible answer: 25; The factors of 25 are 1, 5, and 25. 5 and 25 are not factors of any other number on the board, so my opponent can score only 1 point.

**15.** Suppose you are playing the *GCF Game* with your partner. Below is the board so far. Your partner has just circled 24. Which number would you circle? Why?

| | | | |
|---|---|---|---|
| 12 | 13 | 14 | 15 |
| 16 | 17 | 18 | 19 |
| 20 | 21 | 22 | 23 |
| 24 | 25 | 26 | 27 |

**16.** Suppose you are playing the *GCF Game* with your partner. Below is the board so far. You circle the first number in this round. Which number should you circle? Why?

| | | | |
|---|---|---|---|
| 16 | 17 | 18 | 19 |
| 20 | 21 | 22 | 23 |
| 24 | 25 | 26 | 27 |
| 28 | 29 | 30 | 31 |

**List five multiples of each number.**

**17.** 14 Possible answer: 14, 28, 42, 56, 70

**18.** 66 Possible answer: 66, 132, 198, 264, 330

**19.** 25 Possible answer: 25, 50, 75, 100, 125

**20.** Is 3,269,283 a multiple of 3? How do you know?
Yes; Possible explanation: $3 \cdot 1{,}089{,}761 = 3{,}269{,}283$

**21.** Is 1,000 a multiple of 3? How do you know?
No; Possible explanation: 1,000 divided by 3 leaves a remainder of 1.

**22.** List all the common multiples of 3 and 5 that are less than 60.
15, 30, 45

**23.** List all the common multiples of 7 and 14 that are less than 60.
14, 28, 42, 56

**24.** List all the common multiples of 2, 3, and 15 that are less than 100.
30, 60, 90

**25.** Adriana earns money by walking dogs after school and on weekends. She walks Madeline every other day, Buddy every fourth day, and Ernie every fifth day. Today, she walked all three dogs.

**a.** How many days will it be before Adriana walks Madeline and Buddy on the same day again? 4

**b.** How many days will it be before she walks Buddy and Ernie on the same day again? 20

**c.** How many days will it be before she walks Madeline and Ernie on the same day again? 10

**d.** How many days will it be before she walks all three dogs on the same day again? 20

**e.** Which dogs will Adriana walk 62 days from today? Madeline



On Your Own Exercises

▶ **Exercises 22–24** Students who have worked with negative numbers might be tempted to list some in their answers. If so, remind them that multiples are products of whole numbers, which are always positive.

▶ **Exercises 27–29** Remind students to consider that the factors of an odd number are also odd numbers. Encourage them to keep a good record of any guesses if they use the guess-check-and-improve strategy.

▶ **Exercise 31** Point out that in this exercise, students must add primes instead of multiplying them as they do when writing prime factorizations.

On Your Own Exercises

## Connect & Extend

**26. Geometry** Simone wants to form a rectangle from 12 square tiles.

26a.

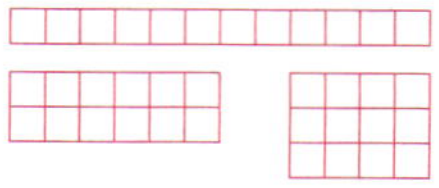

**a.** Sketch every possible rectangle Simone could make.

**b.** What are the factor pairs of 12? How are the factor pairs related to the rectangles you sketched in Part a? See margin.

**c.** Simone wants to form a rectangle from 20 square tiles. Give the dimensions of each possible rectangle she could make. Tell how you know you have found all the possibilities. See margin.

**27.** Daryll said, "I am thinking of a number. The number is less than 50, and 2 and 4 are two of its nine factors. What is my number?" 36

**28.** Emma said, "I am thinking of a number. The number is less than 100, 19 is one of its four factors, and the sum of its digits is 12. What is my number?" 57

**Math Link**

The next greatest perfect number is 496. As of 1999, there were only 38 known perfect numbers, all of which are even. No one knows how many perfect numbers there are or whether there are any odd perfect numbers.

**29.** Jacinta said, "One of the factors of my number is 24. What other numbers must also be factors of my number?" 1, 2, 3, 4, 6, 8, 12

**30.** The *proper factors* of a number are all of its factors except the number itself. For example, the proper factors of 6 are 1, 2, and 3. A *perfect number* is a number whose proper factors add to that number. For example, 6 is a perfect number because $1 + 2 + 3 = 6$.

There is one perfect number between 20 and 30. What is it? 28

**31.** *Goldbach's conjecture* states that every even number except 2 can be written as the sum of two prime numbers. For example, $10 = 3 + 7$ and $24 = 19 + 5$. Although the conjecture appears to be true, no one has ever been able to prove it.

**a.** Write each of the numbers 4, 36, and 100 as the sum of two prime numbers. See margin.

**b.** Choose two even numbers of your own. Write each as the sum of two prime numbers. Answers will vary.



### Additional Answers

26b. 1 and 12, 2 and 6, 3 and 4; The factor pairs are the dimensions of the rectangles.

26c. $1 \times 20$, $2 \times 10$, $4 \times 5$; Possible answer: I listed a rectangle for each factor pair.

31a. Possible answer: $4 = 2 + 2$, $36 = 19 + 17$, $100 = 17 + 83$

**32.** A *reversible prime* is a prime number whose digits can be reversed to form another prime number. For example, 13 is a reversible prime because reversing its digits gives 31, another prime number. There are nine reversible primes between 10 and 100. List them all.
11, 13, 17, 31, 37, 71, 73, 79, 97

**33.** *Twin primes* are prime numbers that differ by 2. For example, 11 and 13 are twin primes. Find three more pairs of twin primes.
Possible answer: 3 and 5, 17 and 19, 29 and 31

**34. History** The Greek mathematician and astronomer Eratosthenes created a technique for finding prime numbers. The technique is known as the *Sieve of Eratosthenes* because nonprime numbers are sifted out, like sand through a sieve, leaving the prime numbers.

**a.** To create the Sieve of Eratosthenes, start with a grid of numbers from 1 to 100 and follow these steps.

| | | | | | | | | | |
|---|---|---|---|---|---|---|---|---|---|
| ~~1~~ | 2 | 3 | ~~4~~ | 5 | ~~6~~ | 7 | ~~8~~ | ~~9~~ | ~~10~~ |
| 11 | ~~12~~ | 13 | ~~14~~ | ~~15~~ | ~~16~~ | 17 | ~~18~~ | 19 | ~~20~~ |
| ~~21~~ | ~~22~~ | 23 | ~~24~~ | ~~25~~ | ~~26~~ | ~~27~~ | ~~28~~ | 29 | ~~30~~ |
| 31 | ~~32~~ | ~~33~~ | ~~34~~ | ~~35~~ | ~~36~~ | 37 | ~~38~~ | ~~39~~ | ~~40~~ |
| 41 | ~~42~~ | 43 | ~~44~~ | ~~45~~ | ~~46~~ | 47 | ~~48~~ | ~~49~~ | ~~50~~ |
| ~~51~~ | ~~52~~ | 53 | ~~54~~ | ~~55~~ | ~~56~~ | ~~57~~ | ~~58~~ | 59 | ~~60~~ |
| 61 | ~~62~~ | ~~63~~ | ~~64~~ | ~~65~~ | ~~66~~ | 67 | ~~68~~ | ~~69~~ | ~~70~~ |
| 71 | ~~72~~ | 73 | ~~74~~ | ~~75~~ | ~~76~~ | ~~77~~ | ~~78~~ | 79 | ~~80~~ |
| ~~81~~ | ~~82~~ | 83 | ~~84~~ | ~~85~~ | ~~86~~ | ~~87~~ | ~~88~~ | 89 | ~~90~~ |
| ~~91~~ | ~~92~~ | ~~93~~ | ~~94~~ | ~~95~~ | ~~96~~ | 97 | ~~98~~ | ~~99~~ | ~~100~~ |

**Step 1.** Cross out 1.

**Step 2.** Circle 2. Then cross out every multiple of 2 after 2, that is, 4, 6, 8, 10, and so on.

**Step 3.** Circle 3. Cross out every multiple of 3, that is, 6, 9, 12, 15, and so on, after 3 that has not already been crossed out.

**Step 4.** Circle 5, the next number that is not crossed out. Cross out every multiple of 5, that is, 10, 15, 20, 25, and so on, after 5 that has not already been crossed out.

Continue in this manner, circling the next available number and crossing out its multiples, until every number is either crossed out or circled. When you are finished, all the prime numbers between 1 and 100 will be circled.

**b.** Explain why this technique guarantees that only the prime numbers will be circled. The number circled at each step cannot have any smaller numbers as a factor. It would already be crossed out if it did.

**Real-World Link**
Using only a primitive tool and shadows to measure the angle of the Sun's rays, Eratosthenes, who lived more than 2,200 years ago, was able to accurately calculate the circumference of Earth.



On Your Own Exercises

▶ **Exercise 34** You may want to provide students with a copy of Chapter 2 Master 2.

**Lesson 2.1** Factors and Multiples **89**

▶ **Exercise 37c** Students must subtract the LCM of two numbers to find an earlier date. This is a variation of how they used LCMs in Investigation 4 Exercises 9–12.

## Quick Check

**Informal Assessment** Students should be able to:

✔ identify all the factors of a given number

✔ understand and distinguish prime and composite numbers

✔ find prime factorizations

✔ identify multiples

✔ find common and greatest common factors, and common and least common multiples

✔ see how factors and multiples are related



**35.** A kindergarten teacher passed out 30 large stickers and 90 small stickers to his students. Each child received the same number of large stickers and the same number of small stickers. No stickers were left.

**a.** How many children could have been in the class? List all of the possibilities. 1, 2, 3, 5, 6, 10, 15, 30

**b.** How is the greatest number of children that could have been in the class related to the GCF of 30 and 90? It is 30, which is the GCF of these numbers.

### Math Link

Two whole numbers are consecutive if their difference is 1.

**36.** In Parts a–d, determine whether each pair of consecutive numbers is relatively prime.

**a.** 7 and 8 Yes **b.** 14 and 15 Yes **c.** 20 and 21 Yes **d.** 55 and 56 Yes

**e.** Choose two more pairs of consecutive numbers. Determine whether they are relatively prime. Number pairs will vary. Any pair of consecutive numbers is relatively prime.

**f.** Use evidence from Parts a–e to make a *conjecture*, an educated guess, about any pair of consecutive numbers. Any pair of consecutive numbers is relatively prime.

### Real-World Link

The Constitution states that a senator must be at least 30 years old, have been a U.S. citizen for nine years, and, when elected, be a resident of the state from which he or she is chosen.

**37. Social Studies** In the United States, senators are elected for six-year terms and presidents are elected for four-year terms. One of the Senate seats in Nebraska was up for election in the year 2000, the same year a president was elected.

**a.** What is the next year the same Senate seat will be up for election and a presidential election will take place? Assume the seat is not vacated early. 2012

**b.** List three other years when this will happen. What do these years have in common? Possible answer: 2024, 2036, 2048; They all are 2000 plus a multiple of 12.

**c.** When was the last year *before* 2000 that this Senate seat was up for election in the same year as a presidential election? 1988

**38.** Tai found that the LCM of 3 and 5 is 15 and that the LCM of 2 and 3 is 6. He concluded that he could find the LCM of any two numbers by multiplying them.

**a.** Copy and complete this table to show the product and the LCM of each pair of numbers.

**b.** Is the LCM of two numbers always equal to their product? If not, use the table to predict when the LCM of a pair of numbers is the product.

| Numbers | Product | LCM |
|---|---|---|
| 2 and 3 | 6 | 6 |
| 2 and 4 | 8 | 4 |
| 2 and 5 | 10 | 10 |
| 3 and 4 | 12 | 12 |
| 3 and 6 | 18 | 6 |
| 6 and 9 | 54 | 18 |
| 4 and 10 | 40 | 20 |

38b. Possible answer: If the only common factor of the numbers is 1, the LCM is the product.

39. To find the LCM of two numbers, Ivan first writes their prime factorizations. He then decides where each prime number appears the most. For example, 3 appears twice for 252, so he writes down 3 two times. If the most a prime appears is once, then he writes that number only once. For example, he wrote the prime factorizations of 210 and 252.

$210 = 2 \cdot 3 \cdot 5 \cdot 7 \qquad 252 = 2 \cdot 2 \cdot 3 \cdot 3 \cdot 7$

2 appears twice for 252, 3 appears twice for 252, 5 appears once for 210, 7 appears once for both 210 and 252. So, the LCM is $2 \cdot 2 \cdot 3 \cdot 3 \cdot 5 \cdot 7$, or 1,260.

Try Ivan's method on at least two more pairs of numbers. Answers will vary.

40. **In Your Own Words** Choose a composite number between 20 and 100. Use the ideas from the lesson to write a short report about your number. Your report should include a discussion about the factors and multiples of your number and give your number's prime factorization. Reports will vary.

## Mixed Review

41. **Probability** Sophia bought two dozen superballs to give out at her birthday party. She put them in a bag. A third of the superballs were blue, 25% were striped, an eighth were hot pink, and the rest were made to glow in the dark.

**a.** Rohan arrived first. Sophia asked him to reach into the bag without looking and take a ball. What is the probability that Rohan's ball will glow in the dark? $\frac{7}{24}$

**b.** Rohan picked a blue ball. Lucita arrived next and said she hoped to pick hot pink. What is the probability she will get her wish? $\frac{3}{23}$

**c.** Lucita did not get what she wanted. But Emilio, who picked next, did get hot pink. What was the probability of this happening? $\frac{3}{22}$

**d.** Emilio traded with Lucita for her striped superball. Tadi picked next, hoping for a glow-in-the-dark ball. What is the probability of him choosing one? $\frac{7}{21}$, or $\frac{1}{3}$

**Use the distributive property to rewrite each expression with parentheses.**

42. $18 - 4f$ $2(9 - 2f)$

43. $13 - 26m$ $13(1 - 2m)$

44. $45x + 15$ $15(3x + 1)$

45. $16x^2 + 48x$ $16x(x + 3)$



On Your Own Exercises

## Quick Quiz

For each machine in Exercises 1–3, name at least three different connections that will give the same output. You may not use the $\times 1$ machine or change the order of the machines to describe a new connection.

1. $\times 36$ Possible answer: $\times 2$ and $\times 18$, $\times 3$ and $\times 12$, $\times 4$ and $\times 9$, $\times 6$ and $\times 6$

2. $\times 24$ Possible answer: $\times 2$ and $\times 12$, $\times 3$ and $\times 8$, $\times 4$ and $\times 6$

3. $\times 100$ Possible answer: $\times 2$ and $\times 50$, $\times 4$ and $\times 25$, $\times 5$ and $\times 20$, $\times 10$ and $\times 10$

4. Which of the following numbers are not factors of 18? How do you know?
8, 9, 2, 4, 12, 36, 3 8, 4, 12, 36; there are no whole numbers that you can multiply any of these numbers by and get 18.

5. For each number pair, list any common factors other than 1, and then find the greatest common factor. If the numbers are relatively prime, say so.
   a. 24 and 56 Common factors: 2, 4, 8; GCF: 8
   b. 15 and 23 Relatively prime
   c. 8 and 15 Relatively prime

6. Write the first five multiples of 7. 7, 14, 21, 28, 35

LESSON 2.2

# Exponent Machines

**Objectives**

- ▶ To model the behavior of exponents using stretching and shrinking machines
- ▶ To understand and apply the product laws of exponents

## Overview

In this lesson, students learn exponents through a concrete model of stretching and shrinking machines. The model we use was developed by Peter Braunfeld and Max Beberman in 1963, at the University of Illinois. By hooking up stretching and shrinking machines, students can work with a model that demonstrates the laws of exponents.

If students have worked with this model before, you may want to move more quickly through Investigation 1.

## Advance Preparation

You may want to make an overhead transparency of Chapter 2 Master 2 to use as you discuss exponent machines.

| | Summary | Materials | On Your Own Exercises (pp. 104–106) | Assessment Opportunities |
|---|---|---|---|---|
| **Investigation 1** (p. 93) Pacing: 2 days | Students work with stretching machines to model repeated multiplication and to begin work with exponents. | Chapter 2 Master 2 | Practice & Apply: 1–17<br>Connect & Extend: 43–44<br>Mixed Review: 47–51 | • Share & Summarize (p. 96)<br>• Troubleshooting (p. 94) |
| **Investigation 2** (p. 96) Pacing: 1 day | Students use hookups of stretching machines to model the law of exponents, $a^b \cdot a^c = a^{b+c}$ | | Practice & Apply: 18–35<br>Connect & Extend: TK<br>Mixed Review: 47–51 | • Share & Summarize (p. 100)<br>• Troubleshooting (pp. 96, 103) |
| **Investigation 3** (p. 100) Pacing: 1 day | Students use hookups of stretching machines to model the law of exponents, $a^c \cdot b^c = (a \cdot b)^c$. Students also explore erroneous "sum laws" to see why they do not work. | | Practice & Apply: 36–41<br>Connect & Extend: 42, 45<br>Mixed Review: 47–51 | • Share & Summarize (p. 103) |

# Leveled Lesson Resources

CRM *Available in:* **Chapter 2 Resource Masters**

Also on TeacherWorks™
Lesson 2.2

## Study Guide and Intervention (p. 13) AL

**Lesson 2.2 Study Guide and Intervention**
***Exponent Machines***

A number that is expressed using an exponent is called a **power**. The **base** is the number that is multiplied. The **exponent** tells how many times the base is used as a factor. So, $4^3$ has a base of 4 and an exponent of 3, and $4^3 = 4 \cdot 4 \cdot 4 = 64$.

***Example 1*** **Evaluate each expression.**

**a.** $5^2$ — 5 is a factor 2 times.
$5 \cdot 5 = 25$ — Multiply.

**b.** $\left(\frac{1}{4}\right)^3$ — $\frac{1}{4}$ is a factor 3 times.
$\frac{1}{4} \cdot \frac{1}{4} \cdot \frac{1}{4} = \frac{1}{64}$ — Multiply.

The **product laws of exponents** state that when multiplying exponential expressions with the same base, $a^b \cdot a^c = a^{b+c}$. When multiplying exponential expressions with the same exponent, $a^c \cdot b^c = (a \cdot b)^c$.

***Example 2*** **Rewrite each expression using the product laws of exponents.**

**a.** $3^7 \cdot 8^7$
$(3 \cdot 8)^7$ — $a^c \cdot b^c = (a \cdot b)^c$
$24^7$ — Multiply the bases.

**b.** $12^9 \cdot 12^5$
$12^{9+5}$ — $a^b \cdot a^c = a^{b+c}$
$12^{14}$ — Add the exponents.

***Exercises***

**Evaluate each expression without using a calculator.**

**1.** $2^5$ **2.** $3^4$ **3.** $\left(\frac{1}{2}\right)^6$

**4.** $12^2$ **5.** $\left(\frac{2}{5}\right)^2$ **6.** $50^1$

**Rewrite each expression using the product laws of exponents.**

**7.** $4^3 \cdot 5^3$ **8.** $7^{15} \cdot 7^{22}$ **9.** $15^{13} \cdot 15^{10}$

**10.** $32^{26} \cdot 32^{43}$ **11.** $12^3 \cdot 5^3$ **12.** $6^{14} \cdot 15^{14}$

## Skills Practice (p. 14) AL OL

**Lesson 2.2 Skills Practice**
***Exponent Machines***

**Rewrite each expression using a single base.**

**1.** $2^3 \cdot 2^5$ **2.** $10^2 \cdot 10^7$

**3.** $1^4 \cdot 1$ **4.** $6^3 \cdot 6^3$

**5.** $4^2 \cdot 4^3$ **6.** $9^8 \cdot 9^6$

**7.** $7^4 \cdot 7^2$ **8.** $13^2 \cdot 13^4$

**9.** $(3^2)(3^3)$ **10.** $(9^2)(9^2)$

**11.** $a^2 \cdot a^3$ **12.** $n^8 \cdot n^3$

**13.** $(p^4)(p^4)$ **14.** $(z^6)(z^7)$

**15.** $(6b^3)(3b^4)$ **16.** $(v^3)(v^7)$

**17.** $11a^2 \cdot 3a^6$ **18.** $10t^2 \cdot 4t^{10}$

**19.** $(8c^2)(9c)$ **20.** $(4f^8)(5f^6)$

**21.** $(8^5)(8^3)$ **22.** $(21^9)(21^5)$

**23.** $t^9 \cdot t^3$ **24.** $b^4 \cdot b^{13}$

**25.** $(m^6)(m^6)$ **26.** $(u^{11})(u^{10})$

**27.** $(r^7)(r^{20})$ **28.** $(w)(w^9)$

**29.** $4d^5 \cdot 8d^6$ **30.** $7j^{50} \cdot 6j^{50}$

**31.** $(5b^9) \cdot (6b^2)$ **32.** $12^1 \cdot 12^2$

## Problem-Solving Practice (p. 15) AL OL

**Lesson 2.2 Problem-Solving Practice**
***Exponent Machines***

1. **Biology** Ms. Masse's biology class is conducting an experiment to record the growth of a certain kind of bacteria. Each student has a lab dish containing 2 bacteria which are able to double every day. How many bacteria will be present in a student's lab dish after two weeks?

2. **Computers** In 1995, the average home computer had a speed of about $10^6$ cycles per second. In 2004, the average home computer had a speed that was $10^3$ times as fast as the speed of a computer in 1995. What was the approximate speed of the average home computer in 2004 in cycles per second? Write your answer as a power of 10.

3. **Catering** A gourmet meal catering company is planning an event for $2^7$ people. One week before the event, they find out that the number of people has doubled. Will there be $2^8$ or $2^{14}$ people at the event? Explain.

4. **Homework** Vance and Ko are trying to simplify the expression $3^8 \cdot 3^7$. Their answers are different:

   Ko's work: $3^8 \cdot 3^7 = (3 \cdot 3)^{(8+7)} = 9^{15}$

   Vance's work: $3^8 \cdot 3^7 = 3^{(8+7)} = 3^{15}$

   Which student is correct? Identify the mistake made by the other student.

5. **Farming** A chicken farmer has $4^5$ chickens in each barn. He has $2^5$ barns. Write a multiplication expression to find the total number of chickens on the farm. Then rewrite the expression using a single base.

6. **Science** In her lab, Julie has $2^7$ samples of sand from different beaches around the world. She estimates that in each sample there are about $10^7$ grains of sand. Approximately how many grains of sand does she have in all? Write your answer as a power.

7. **Elections** For the county election there are $3^4$ polling locations. Each polling location needs $8^4$ ballots. A ballot distributor uses the expression $3^4 \cdot 8^4$ to find the total number of ballots needed for the election. Rewrite this expression using a single base.

## Enrichment (p. 16) BL

**Lesson 2.2 Enrichment**
***Exponent Machines***

**Exponents**

Numbers can be expressed in several ways. Some numbers are expressed as sums. Some numbers are expressed as products of factors, while other numbers are expressed as powers.

Two ways to express 27 are $3 \cdot 3 \cdot 3$ and $3^3$.

The number 1 million can be expressed in the following ways.

| | | | |
|---|---|---|---|
| 1,000,000 | $1{,}000 \cdot 1{,}000$ | $100 \cdot 100 \cdot 100$ | $10^2 \cdot 10^2 \cdot 10^2$ |
| $1{,}000{,}000^1$ | $1{,}000^2$ | $100^3$ | $10^6$ |

**Express the numbers below as powers using the given exponents.**

**1.** 16; exponents: 2 and 4 **2.** 81; exponents: 2 and 4

**3.** 64; exponents: 2 and 6 **4.** 256; exponents: 2 and 8

**5.** 625; exponents: 2 and 4 **6.** 729; exponents: 2 and 6

**7.** 2,401; exponents: 2 and 4 **8.** 4,096; exponents: 2 and 12

**9.** 6,561; exponents: 2 and 8 **10.** 390,625; exponents: 2 and 8

Numbers that can be named as powers with like bases can be multiplied by adding the exponents.

$$8 \cdot 8 = 2^3 \cdot 2^3 = 2^{3+3} = 2^6$$

**Rewrite each pair of factors as powers with like bases. Then multiply by adding the exponents.**

**11.** $9 \cdot 9$ **12.** $4 \cdot 4$

**13.** $16 \cdot 8$ **14.** $125 \cdot 25$

**15.** $27 \cdot 9$ **16.** $81 \cdot 27$

**17.** $49 \cdot 49$ **18.** $121 \cdot 121$

## Lesson Quick Quiz (p. 17) AL OL BL

**Lesson 2.2 Quick Quiz**

**Fill in the missing input, machine, or output in each situation.**

**1.**

**2.**

**3.**
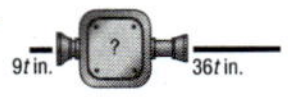


**Rewrite each of the following as simply as you can using laws of exponents.**

**4.** $2^n \cdot 2$

**5.** $25^n \cdot 4^n$

**6.** $b^n \cdot b^0$

**7.** $12^5 \cdot \left(\frac{1}{3}\right)^5$

**8.** $3x^2 \cdot 4x^3$

# Additional Lesson Resources

### Teacher Tech Tools
- TeacherWorks
- ExamView Assessment Suite
- Classroom Presentation Toolkit
- Advance Tracker

### Student Tech Tools
- StudentWorks Plus
- Math Online eGlossary • Concepts in Motion

### Other Print Products
- Investigation Notebook and Reflection Journal
- Quick Review Math Handbook

## LESSON 2.2 Exponent Machines

### *Introduce*

**Stretching** As a class, discuss what types of industry would benefit from having a stretching machine. A fabric making company, a sheet metal manufacturer, or a yarn company could use this type of machine. Discuss how these types of companies would use a stretching machine. Now connect these concepts for the students to see how exponents relate to their ideas.

**Think & Discuss**

Suggested Grouping: Pairs

Have the students determine the effects of using a ×4 machine and a ×5 machine on a 1-inch piece of taffy. What happens if you use a 2-inch piece of taffy?

# LESSON 2.2 Exponent Machines



① The ×1 machine would stretch the taffy to 1 inch long. The ×2 machine would stretch it to 16 inches. We already know that using the ×3 machine twice stretches the taffy to 27 inches, 3 • 27 is surely more than 30 inches. Any other machine would make it even longer. So, Winnie must have used the ×1 machine or the ×2 machine.

Business is good at your stretching factory. In fact, you have received more orders than you can handle. Winnie has noticed that many of the orders that you receive can be filled by using just one machine.

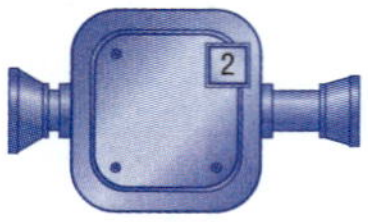


Winnie thinks that this new machine can be used instead of connecting two of the same machines together. If you specialize in single-machine orders, you can save time. No one will have to run from one machine to another, and you will never have to worry about two people needing the same machine at the same time. You decide to give Winnie's plan a try.

**Think & Discuss**

If you start with a one-inch piece of taffy, what lengths between 1 and 30 inches can you make by using a single machine twice? 1, 4, 9, 16, 25

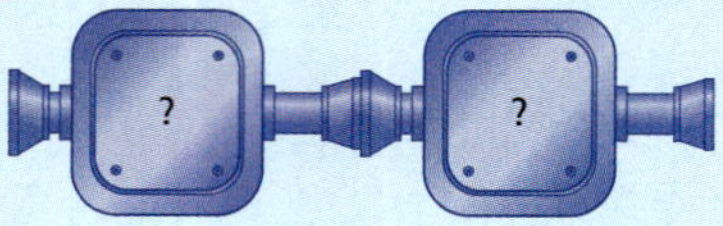


What lengths can you make by using a single machine three times? 1, 8, 27

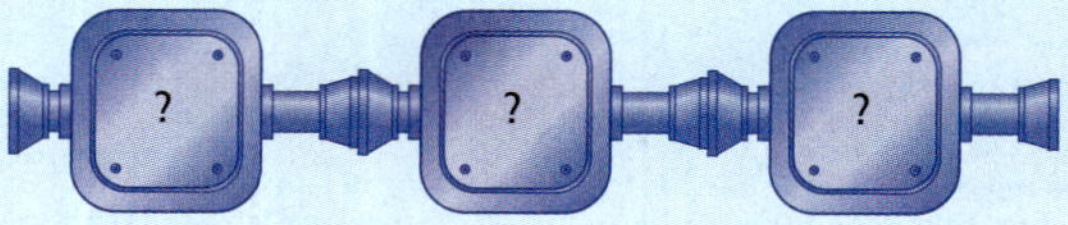


Winnie filled an order that stretched a one-inch piece of taffy to a length less than 30 inches, using a single machine four times. What machine might she have used? See ①.

Will your new plan of using one machine per order mean that there are lengths that your factory cannot produce? Yes, any number that has two different factors, like 6 (2 • 3).



**Reaching** *All Learners*

**ELL English Language Learners**
Ask students to tell you the word in their native language that is used to describe stretching an object. Then ask the students for the word in their first language that is used for exponent. As a group discuss similarities in their meanings.

# Investigation 1 Model Exponents

**Vocabulary**

- base
- power

The stretching machines occasionally break down at your factory. Your employees usually find a way to work around this problem.

## Develop & Understand: A

1. One of the ×10 machines broke down. Annie connected two machines together to do the same work as a ×10 machine. The output from the first machine becomes the input for the second.

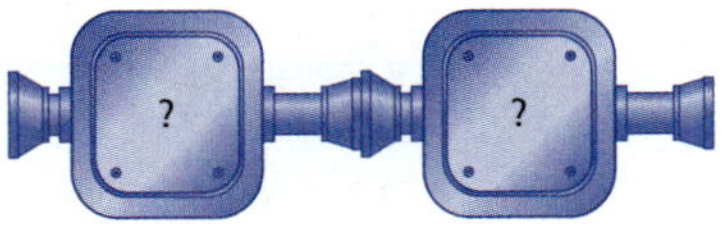


What two machines connected together do the same work as a ×10 machine? Is there more than one arrangement that will work?
A ×5 and a ×2, in either order

2. What stretching machine does the same work as two ×2 machines connected together? A ×4 machine

exponent
$2^4$
base

If you send a 1-inch piece of taffy through a ×2 machine four times, its length becomes $1 \cdot 2 \cdot 2 \cdot 2 \cdot 2 = 16$ inches. You learned that $2 \cdot 2 \cdot 2 \cdot 2$ can be written $2^4$. The expression $2^4$ is read "two to the fourth **power**." The 2 is called the **base**, and the raised 4 is called the exponent.

Suppose some of the machines automatically feed a piece of taffy through several times. You write an exponent to indicate the number of times each machine is applied. For example, sending taffy through a $\times 2^4$ machine is the same as putting it through a ×2 machine four times.

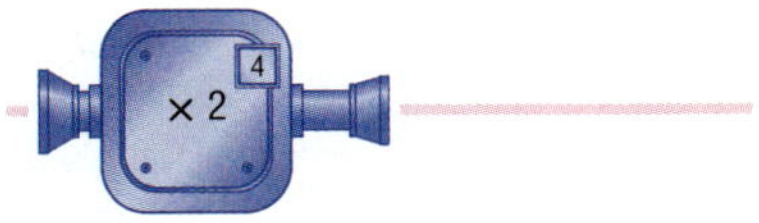


These adjusted machines are *repeater* machines because they repeatedly stretch the input by the same factor. The original machine, or *base* machine, is a ×2 machine.



# Investigation 1

***On Your Own Exercises***
Pages 104–106
Exercises 1–17, 43–46

**Model Exponents** Students should be comfortable with the machine model before beginning the exercises in Investigation 1.

In this investigation, students practice using the model of stretching machines and connecting machines together so that the output of one becomes the input of the next.

## Develop & Understand: A

*Suggested Grouping: Pairs*

You may want to provide students with copies of Chapter 2 Master 2, Connection Table, to record their answers to Exercise 3. You could also use a transparency of this master to discuss the exercise.

▶ **Exercise 2** Watch for students who think that the machines add rather than multiply. Despite the ×2 on the machines, students can still be confused if they think of as ×2 as "2 longer than" rather than "2 times as long." Take advantage of each opportunity to have students say aloud the proper names of the machines, such as "times 2."

**Teacher Tips** Introduce "repeater machines"—machines with exponents to signify the number of times the machine is to be applied.

## Mathematical Background

It is more accurate to say that "any nonzero number to the 0 power is 1," since $0^0$ is usually considered undefined. If we look at the function $f(x) = x^0$ and plug in 0 for $x$, we should expect to get $f(0) = 1$, since $f(x)$ is 1 for every other number. However, if we look at the function $g(x) = 0^x$ and plug in 0 for $x$, we might expect to get $g(0) = 0$, since $g(x)$ is 0 for every other number. There is no right way to reconcile this dilemma, so $0^0$ is left undefined. This subtlety should not be problematic for students, since we do not have an $x^0$ machine and never ask them to find $0^0$.

For further discussion, you may want to ask students to find $0^0$ on their calculators and discuss the result.

## Develop & Understand: B

*Suggested Grouping: Pairs*

▶ **Exercises 3–5** Be sure students understand that they need to calculate the total stretch. In addition, they need to tell the number of times a machine is to be applied and to say how much the machine stretches an item each time it is applied.

▶ **Exercise 7** Students consider what an exponent of 0 might mean. Discuss the machine metaphor here. Usually it is difficult to explain why a number to the 0 power is 1. In this case, the exponent tells you how many times to use the machine. Zero means "don't use the machine at all," so it leaves the stick unchanged. We've seen that the $\times 1$ machine also leaves the stick unchanged. Then for any number $n$, $\times n^0$ has the same effect as $\times 1$ and $n^0 = 1$.

**Teacher Tips** Discuss the $\times\frac{1}{2}$ machine. Make sure students understand that this machine multiplies the length of a segment by $\frac{1}{2}$, shrinking it to half its length.

You might ask students to give examples of other shrinking machines—machines with fractional multipliers—and to explain how these machines would change the length of an input.

## Develop & Understand: B

**For each repeater machine, tell how many times the base machine is applied and how much the total stretch is.**

3. Applied 2 times; stretched 10,000 times
4. Applied 5 times; stretched 16,807 times
5. Applied 7 times; stretched 78,125 times

**3.**

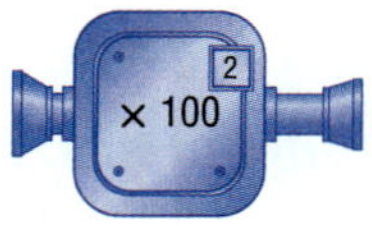


**4.**

**5.**

**6.** Find three repeater machines that will do the same work as a $\times 64$ machine. Draw or describe them using exponents.
Possible answer: $\times 8^2$, $\times 4^3$, $\times 2^6$

**7.** In a repeater machine with 0 as an exponent, the base machine is applied 0 times.

**a.** What do these machines do to a piece of chalk? Nothing; the chalk comes out the same length it went in.

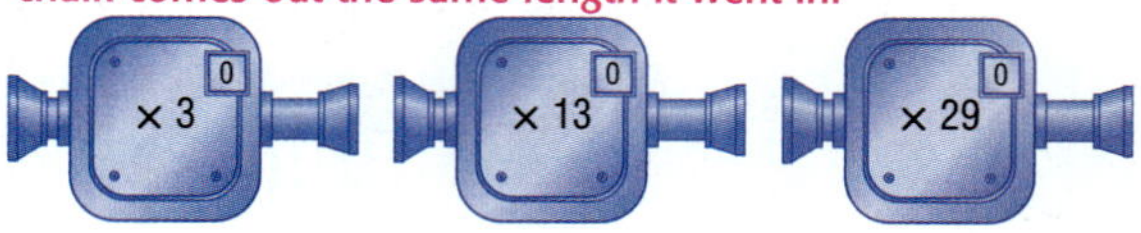


**b.** What do you think the value of $6^0$ is? 1

**Evaluate each expression without using a calculator.**

**8.** $7^0$ 1

**9.** $2^5$ 32

**10.** $4^2$ 16

**11.** $3^3$ 27

Peter found a $\times\frac{1}{2}$ machine in a corner of the factory. He was not sure what it would do, so he experimented with some licorice. This is what he found.

Each piece of licorice was compressed to half its original length. Peter decided this was a *shrinking* machine.



## Troubleshooting

Watch for students who confuse the notation of a repeater machine with a multiplication expression. For example, they may think of the repeater machine $\times 7^5$ in Exercise 4 as repeating $7 \cdot 5$. Review with them the idea of connections of the same base, pointing out that the exponent is a shortcut notation for strings of machine connections. You might write several expressions involving exponents on the board and have students explain their meaning.

## Develop & Understand: C

**Try a shrinking machine for yourself.**

13a. They stay the same length.

13b. They shrink to $\frac{1}{8}$ in.

15. About 5 in.; A $\times\left(\frac{1}{2}\right)^2$ machine shrinks a stick to $\frac{1}{4}$ its length, so the original stick must have been 4 times the length of this stick, which is about 1.25 in.

**12.** If a foot-long sandwich is put into the machine to the right, how many inches long will it be when it emerges? 4 in.

Like stretching machines, shrinking machines can be used in connections and repeater machines.

**13.** What happens when one-inch gum is sent through these connections?

**a.**

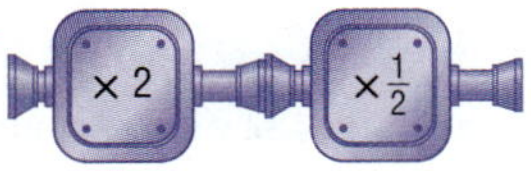


**b.**

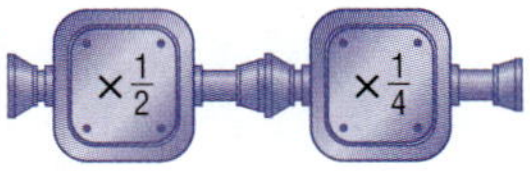


**14.** Evan put a one-inch stick of gum through a $\times\left(\frac{1}{3}\right)^2$ machine. How long was the stick when it came out the machine? $\frac{1}{9}$ in.

**15.** This stick of gum came out of a $\times\left(\frac{1}{2}\right)^2$ machine. Estimate the length of the input stick in inches. Explain how you found your answer.

**16.** Armando put a one-inch piece of gum through a $\times\frac{1}{10}$ repeater machine. It came out $\frac{1}{100{,}000}$ in. long. What is the missing exponent? 5

**Find a single machine that will do the same job as the connection given below.**

**17.** a $\times 2^3$ machine followed by a $\times\left(\frac{1}{2}\right)^2$ machine $\times 2$

**18.** a $\times 5^{99}$ machine followed by a $\times\left(\frac{1}{5}\right)^{100}$ machine $\times\frac{1}{5}$

**Evaluate each expression without using a calculator.**

**19.** $\left(\frac{1}{2}\right)^5$ $\frac{1}{32}$

**20.** $\left(\frac{1}{4}\right)^2$ $\frac{1}{16}$

**21.** $\left(\frac{1}{3}\right)^3$ $\frac{1}{27}$

**22.** $\left(\frac{1}{7}\right)^0$ 1

**Real-World Link**
For centuries, Native Americans chewed the sap, called *chicle*, of the sapodilla tree. Settlers took up the habit. In the late 1800s, chewing gum began to be made commercially from chicle, sugar, and flavorings.



## Develop & Understand: C

*Suggested Grouping: Individuals*

This exercise set gives students practice working with machines with fractional multipliers, which actually shrink the input items. The shrinking model is introduced here so that students can think about rational numbers raised to powers. This is an area that is traditionally difficult for students; but with the model of a machine, the effect of $\left(\frac{1}{3}\right)^2$ as in **Exercise 14** should be more easily understood.

▶ **Exercises 14–16** Ask students to think about raising a fraction to a power. If students are having difficulty, ask them to think of the intermediate stages in the process: After the first $\times\frac{1}{3}$ machine, a 1-inch stick is a $\frac{1}{3}$-inch stick; after the second $\times\frac{1}{3}$ machine, the $\frac{1}{3}$-inch stick is $\frac{1}{3}$ as long as when it went in, that is, $\frac{1}{3}\cdot\frac{1}{3}$, or $\frac{1}{9}$, inch long.

▶ **Exercise 17** Students may think of the connections of fractions with the same factor repeated several times in the numerator and the denominator. So, in Exercise 16, $(2)^3\cdot\left(\frac{1}{2}\right)^2$ can be thought of as a fraction with two factors of 2 in the denominator and three factors of 2 in the numerator.

## *Reaching All Learners*

**OL On Level** Some students may benefit from a physical model of raising a fraction to an exponent. Start with a whole piece of paper, tear it in half, throw one half away. Connect tearing paper in half to putting a stick through the $\times\frac{1}{2}$ machine. Tear the half sheet into two quarter sheets and connect this to putting a stick through the $\times\frac{1}{2}$ machine twice.

## Share & Summarize

These questions ask students to work with some of the main ideas of this investigation: 0 as an exponent, a fraction repeater machine, and a connection of a fraction machine and a whole-number machine.

It is important for students to have a thorough understanding of repeater machines and connections. Investigations 3 and 4 and Lesson 2.3 develop laws of exponents based on these models.

**Analyze the Table** The concept of a number to the 0 power will be explored again later, but if you want to present an alternative way to think about this idea here, you might consider showing a table of powers.

| | |
|---|---|
| $10^4$ | 10,000 |
| $10^3$ | 1,000 |
| $10^2$ | 100 |
| $10^1$ | 10 |
| $10^0$ | 1 |

If we look at the table beginning with $10^4$, we see that the value in the right column is $\frac{1}{10}$ the output above it. The last item on the left in the table would be $10^0$ and on the right would be $\frac{1}{10}$ of 10, or 1. You can continue this argument to include negative exponents as well.

## Investigation 2

***On Your Own Exercises***
Pages 104–106
Exercises 18–35, TK

**Product Law of Exponents** In this investigation, students develop a product law of exponents: $a^b \cdot a^c = a^{b+c}$. They gain an understanding of this law by creating connections of repeater machines and then considering a single machine that will do the same work.

**Teacher Tips** Have students read about Evan's mistake of sending a 1-inch noodle through the $\times 2^3$ machine instead of through the $\times 2^5$ machine. Discuss the options presented by coworkers in the cartoon.

## Share & Summarize

1. If you put a two-inch toothpick through this machine, how long will it be when it comes out the machine? 2 in.

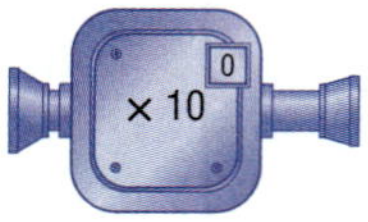


2. A one-inch-long beetle crawled into a repeater machine and emerged $\frac{1}{16}$ in. long. Through what repeater machine did it go? Is there more than one possibility?

   2. There are two possibilities: $\times\left(\frac{1}{4}\right)^2$ and $\times\left(\frac{1}{2}\right)^4$

3. What single repeater machine does the same work as a $\times 3^5$ machine followed by a $\times\left(\frac{1}{3}\right)^3$ machine? $\times 3^2$

## Investigation 2 Multiply Expressions with the Same Base

**Vocabulary**

- order of operations
- product law of exponents

Evan's supervisor asked him to stretch a one-inch noodle into a 32-inch noodle. Evan intended to send the noodle through a $\times 2^5$ machine, but he accidentally put it through a $\times 2^3$ machine. His co-workers had several suggestions for how he could fix his mistake.

### Think & Discuss

Will all of the suggestions work? Why or why not? They will all work. See the teaching notes for possible explanations.

Evan's mistake was not so terrible after all. He figured out how to find single repeater machines that do the same work as some connections.



## Troubleshooting

If students are having trouble with the concepts presented in this investigation or if you feel they need additional examples, provide a simple connection of two $\times 3$ machines and two $\times\frac{1}{3}$ machines and ask students to put a stick through each machine, one at a time. Then rearrange the machines so that each $\times 3$ machine is followed by a $\times\frac{1}{3}$ machine; students will be able to see the "canceling-out" effect immediately.

### Example

Evan found a single machine for this connection.

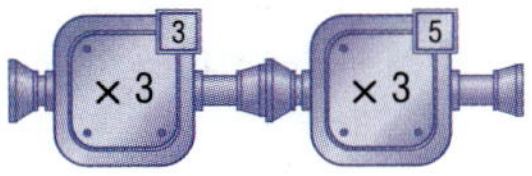


He reasoned, "The first machine tripled the noodle's length three times. The second machine took that output and tripled *its* length five times. The original noodle's length was tripled 3 + 5 times, or eight times in all. That means a $\times 3^8$ machine would do the same thing."

## Develop & Understand: A

**Follow Evan's reasoning to find a single repeater machine that will do the same work as each connection.**

**1.**

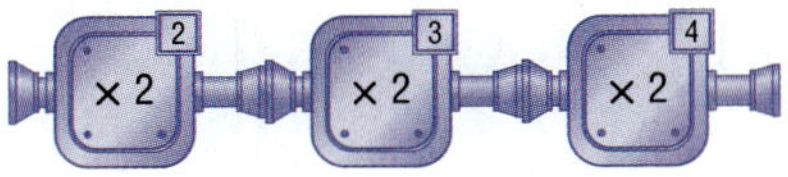


$\times 2^9$

**2.**

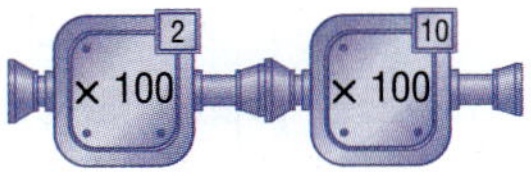


$\times 100^{12}$

**3.**

$\times 7^{61}$

**4.**

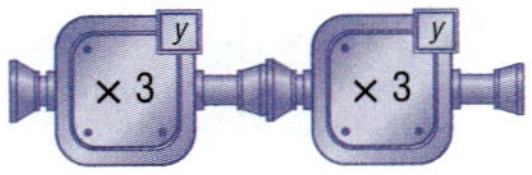


$\times 3^{y+y}$, or $\times 3^{2y}$



### Think & Discuss

*Suggested Grouping: Whole Class*

Some may not readily see that Everett's solution—sending it through a $\times\left(\frac{1}{2}\right)^3$ machine and then a $\times 2^5$ machine—will work. It is important that this method is understood by the whole class, since it reviews the material they learned earlier. Jon's solution—sending the noodle through the $\times 2^3$ machine and then through a $\times\frac{1}{2}$ machine—also reviews earlier material.

After students are convinced that Everett's and Jon's suggestions work, focus the discussion on Ana's solution. Ask students whether it's true that $2^3 \cdot 2^2 = 2^5$, and to explain how to prove this using machines.

Sample proof: Students might compute $2^5 = 32$ and $2^3 = 8$ and then determine that a $\times 4$ machine is needed to complete the task. So a $\times 4$ machine does the same work as a $\times 2^2$ machine,

**Example** Read through the Example with the class. Ask students whether they agree with Evan's logic. Then ask,

What single machine will do the same thing as a connection of two $\times 3^2$ machines?
a $\times 3^4$ machine or a $\times 81$ machine

### Develop & Understand: A

*Suggested Grouping: Individuals*

▶ **Exercise 4** Students may struggle with this exercise because it involves variable exponents. You might suggest that they think of *y* as a certain number in this situation, so they see that they will be doubling the exponent as a result of the connection. If students understand the rule of "adding exponents," then they should be able to apply it even in this situation.

**Teacher Tips** Exercise 4 is worth discussing with the whole class, since it brings up a exercise that students often stumble over: What does it mean to have a variable in the exponent?

**Example** Refer students to the cartoon explaining one way to think about $2^{20} \cdot 2^5$. They should notice that these numeric expressions behave in the same way as the repeater machines.

Explain to students that Malik's "discovery" is one of the product laws of exponents. Write the law on the board, or refer students to it in their books.

$$a^b \cdot a^c = a^{b+c}$$

Make sure students understand that to apply the law, the bases—represented by the letter a in the law's statement—must be the same in all the expressions being multiplied.

You have seen that a connection of repeater machines with the same base can be replaced by a single repeater machine. When you multiply exponential expressions with the same base, you can replace them with a single expression.

## Example

Malik thought about how he could rewrite the expression $2^{20} \cdot 2^5$.

Malik's idea is one of the **product laws of exponents**, which can be expressed like the following.

| Multiplying Expressions with the Same Base |
|---|
| $a^b \cdot a^c = a^{b+c}$ |

Actually, this law can be used with more than two expressions. As long as the bases are the same, to find the product you can add the exponents and use the same base.

$$3^2 \cdot 3^3 \cdot 3^{10} = 3^{2+3+10}$$
$$= 3^{15}$$

## Develop & Understand: B

**Rewrite each expression as a power of 2. It may help to think of the expressions as connections of ×2 machines.**

**5.** $2 \cdot 2$ $2^2$ **6.** $2^5 \cdot 2^4$ $2^9$ **7.** $2^{10} \cdot 2$ $2^{11}$

**8.** $2^{10} \cdot 2^{10}$ $2^{20}$ **9.** $2^0 \cdot 2^3$ $2^3$ **10.** $2^m \cdot 2^n$ $2^{m+n}$

**For each connection, determine whether there is a single repeater machine that will do the same work. If so, describe or draw it.**

**11.**

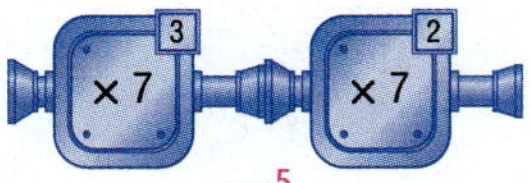


$\times 7^5$

**12.**

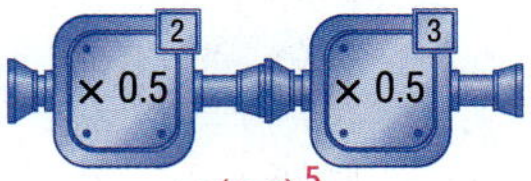


$\times (0.5)^5$

**13.**

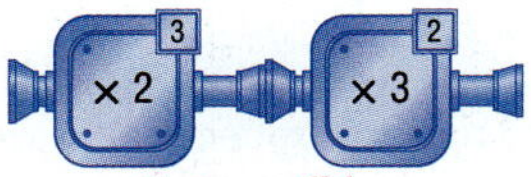


Not possible

**14.**

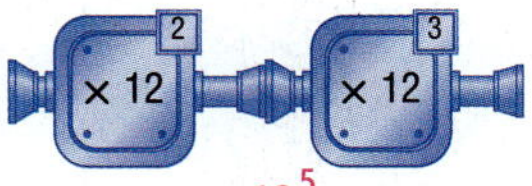


$\times 12^5$

**15.**

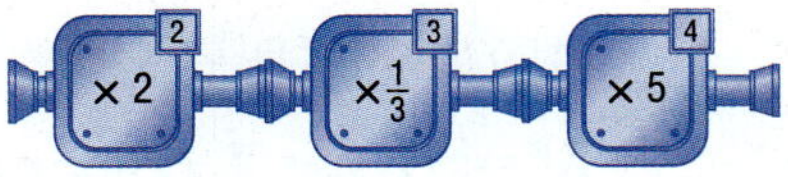


Not possible

**Tell what number should replace the question mark to make each statement true.**

**16.** $5 \cdot 5 \cdot 5 = ?^3$ 5 **17.** $2.7^{10} \cdot 2.7^? = 2.7^{12}$ 2

**18.** $\left(\frac{1}{5}\right)^4 \cdot \left(\frac{1}{5}\right)^6 = \left(\frac{1}{5}\right)^?$ 10 **19.** $1.2^? \cdot 1.2^2 = 1.2^2$ 0

**20.** $\frac{2}{3} \cdot ? = \left(\frac{2}{3}\right)^2$ $\frac{2}{3}$ **21.** $a^{20} \cdot a^5 = a^?$ 25

**If possible, rewrite each expression using a single base. For example, $6^2 \cdot 6^3$ can be rewritten $6^5$.**

**22.** $3^3 \cdot 3^3 \cdot 3^4$ $3^{10}$ **23.** $2^5 \cdot 5^2$ Not possible **24.** $4 \cdot 4 \cdot 4$ $4^3$

**25.** $4x^3 \cdot y^2$ Not possible **26.** $4^4 \cdot 2^2$ $4^5$, or $2^{10}$ **27.** $a^n \cdot a^m$ $a^{n+m}$

When you simplify algebraic expressions involving exponents, it is important to keep the **order of the operations** in mind.

**Math Link**

By the order of operations, $2b^3$ means $2 \cdot b^3$, not $(2 \cdot b)^3$.

### Example

$$2b^3 \cdot 5b^2 = 2 \cdot b^3 \cdot 5 \cdot b^2$$
$$= 2 \cdot 5 \cdot b^3 \cdot b^2$$
$$= 10b^5$$



## Develop & Understand: B

*Suggested Grouping: Individuals or Pairs*

Students now move from the machine model to numbers with exponents. Also, the exercises require students to decide whether the product law they have learned applies or not. Not all of the expressions they are given can be rewritten.

▶ **Exercises 5–10** Watch for students who think that the bases should be multiplied. For example, some students may think that in Exercise 6, $2^5 \cdot 2^4 = 4^9$. This confusion is easily addressed if students return to thinking about machines. Lead them step-by-step through the process of putting a 1-inch stick through each ×2 machine. They should see that these machines would never become ×4 machines.

▶ **Exercise 9** This exercise includes $2^0$. Students may approach this in one of two ways.

- They may remember that any nonzero number raised to the 0 power is simply 1, so the answer must be $1 \cdot 2^3$, or $2^3$.
- Alternatively, they may simply apply the product law to find $2^0 \cdot 2^3 = 2^{0+3} = 2^3$.

▶ **Exercises 17, 19** These include numbers whose base is a decimal. If students seem puzzled by this, ask them to think of this as a fraction machine, the same way they thought of a $\times\frac{1}{2}$ machine.

**Example** Review the Example after the exercise set with the class, so students see how to multiply expressions with coefficients. Although this exercise could be constructed using the machine analogy, it may be more obvious to students in the numerical form. You may need to review the commutative and associative properties of multiplication.

**Math Link**

To assist students in understanding the difference between the notation, have the students work through $2b^3$ and $(2b)^3$ when $b = 3$. The students will see that $2b^3 = 54$ and $(2 \cdot b)^3 = 216$. Have the students use a variety of values for $b$ and every time they perform the calculation, the answers will not match.

## Develop & Understand: C

*Suggested Grouping: Pairs*

▶ **Exercises 28–31** The best strategy for solving these exercises is the one presented in the Example: Rearrange the factors so that the coefficients are together and the variables are together. Then combine the coefficients using multiplication. Finally, combine the variables using the product law of exponents.

### Share & Summarize

For Exercise 2, it is fine if students continue to use the machine model to explain their thinking. Other students may want to use the shortcut technique presented in the Example.

## Investigation 3

**On Your Own Exercises**
Pages 104–106
Exercises 36–41, 42, 45

**Multiplying Expressions with the Same Exponent** In this investigation, students develop a second product law of exponents, $a^c \cdot b^c = (a \cdot b)^c$.

## Develop & Understand: A

*Suggested Grouping: Pairs*

Students explore connections of stretching machines with the same exponents and different bases.

## Develop & Understand: C

**Simplify each expression.**

**28.** $2b \cdot 2b$ $4b^2$, or $(2b)^2$

**29.** $5z^2 \cdot 6z^2$ $30z^4$

**30.** $5a^2 \cdot 3a^4$ $15a^6$

**31.** $z^2 \cdot 2z^3 \cdot 6z^2$ $12z^7$

### Share & Summarize

**1.** Find a single repeater machine to do the same work as this connection. $\times 5^9$

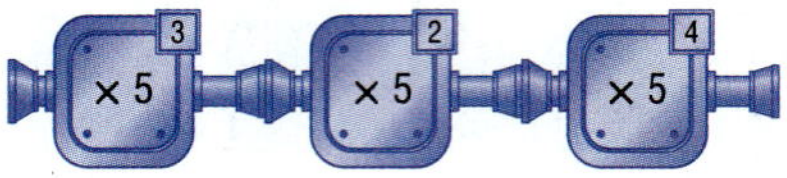


**2.** In your own words, write the rule that lets you figure out the missing exponent in equations like $3^3 \cdot 3^{16} = 3^?$ and $r^{15} \cdot r^? = r^{23}$. Possible answer: When you multiply a number raised to a power by the same number raised to a power, the result is the same number raised to the sum of the two powers.

## Investigation 3 Multiply Expressions with the Same Exponent

Combining expressions that have the same base can make products much easier to understand. Do you think you can simplify products that do not have the same base?

## Develop & Understand: A

**1.** Maxine has an order from a golf course designer to put palm trees through a $\times 2^3$ machine and then through a $\times 3^3$ machine. She thinks she can do the job with a single repeater machine. What single repeater machine should she use? $\times 6^3$

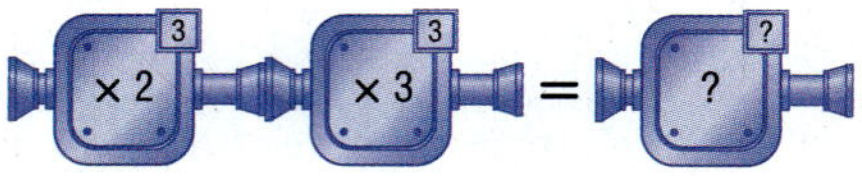




## *Reaching* All Learners

**AL** **Approaching Level** If students have trouble with the Share & Summarize questions, have them think about or rephrase the questions in terms of machines. If you have two repeater machines with the same base number but with different exponents (different number of repetitions), how can you replace them with a single machine? When students can answer the general questions in terms of the machines, explain again the connection between the machines and exponential notation.

**2.** Maxine also needs to stretch some pine trees to $10^2$ times their original lengths. Her ×10 machine is still broken, and someone is using the $\times 10^2$ machine. Find a connection of two repeater machines that will do the same work as a $\times 10^2$ machine. To get started, think about the connection that you could use to replace the ×10 machine.

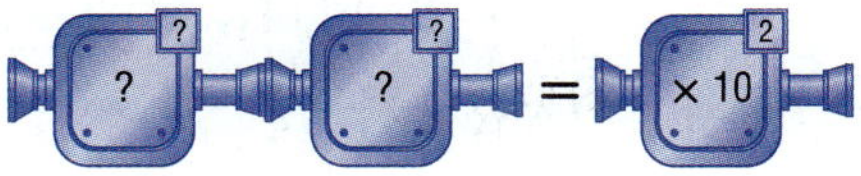


$\times 2^2 \times 5^2$

**For each connection, find a single repeater machine to do the same work.**

**3.**

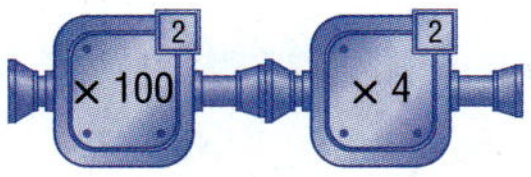


$\times 400^2$

**4.**

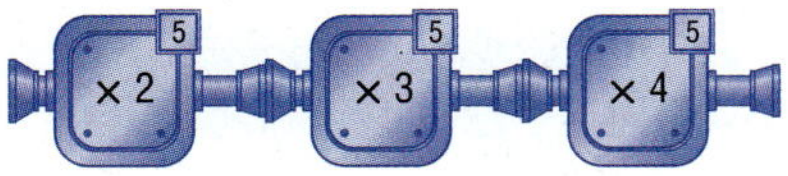


$\times 24^5$

**5.**

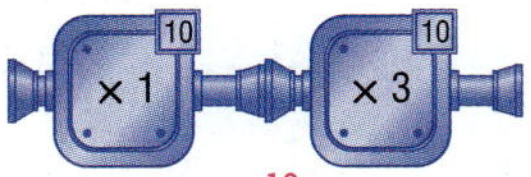


$\times 3^{10}$

**6.**

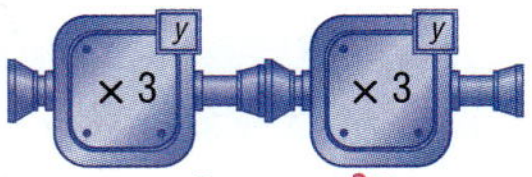


$\times 9^y$, or $\times 3^{2y}$

You can use the same kind of thinking that you used in the above exercises to multiply expressions with the same exponent.

## *Example*

Maya multiplied $4^2 \cdot 3^2$ by thinking about stretching machines.

▶ **Exercise 2** It may be difficult for students to know how to approach Exercise 2. Encourage them to think about a machine connection that will do the same thing as a ×10 machine. They may use the fact that the connection of the ×2 machine and the ×5 machine will do the work of a ×10 machine and see that they can they could combine these two machines and then connect them up again.

A series of machines like this ×2 ×5 ×2 ×5 is the equivalent of a $\times 10^2$ machine, but it is not a connection of 2 repeater machines. Of course, when you multiply, the order of factors doesn't matter. So 2 × 5 × 2 × 5 is the same as 2 × 2 × 5 × 5.

In machines, we have, ×2 ×2 ×5 ×5.

The two ×2 machines side by side can be replaced by a $\times 2^2$ machine, and the two ×5 machines can be replaced by a $\times 5^2$ machine.

As with the numerical expression, order doesn't matter; so $\times 5^2$ and $\times 2^2$ works just as well.

**Example** With the whole class, discuss Maya's strategy for combining machines and the corresponding product law of exponents on the top of the next page. Ask,

How is Maya's strategy different from Malik's rule—the previous product law of exponents?

Students should understand that in Malik's rule, the bases have to be the same but the exponents can be different. Maya's strategy involves combining machines in which the bases are different and the exponents are the same.

## *Reaching All Learners*

**BL Beyond Level** Ask students to look again at Exercise 4 on page 97, where they determined that the answer is $3^{2y}$. In Exercise 6 on page 101, students will probably say that the answer is $9^y$. Ask students whether the two answers are the same and to justify their responses. This relates to the power of a power law students will learn later. In fact, $3^{2y} = (3^2)^y = 9^y$.

## Develop & Understand: B

*Suggested Grouping: Pairs*

▶ **Exercises 7–17** Ask students to think about whether the new product law applies before they solve each exercise. Not all of the expressions in this exercise set can be rewritten.

▶ **Exercises 18–21** These provide an excellent test of whether students are properly applying the law of exponents $a^c \cdot b^c = (a \cdot b)^c$. As you circulate around the room, you might ask students to explain their thinking for solving these exercises.

Use Maya's idea to multiply $5^3 \cdot 2^3$. Use your calculator to check your answer. $10^3$

Maya's idea is another *product law of exponents.*

| Multiplying Expressions with the Same Exponents |
|---|
| $a^c \cdot b^c = (a \cdot b)^c$ |

You can use this law with more than two expressions. If the exponents are the same, multiply the expressions by multiplying the bases and using the same exponent. For example, $2^8 \cdot 3^8 \cdot 7^8 = (2 \cdot 3 \cdot 7)^8 = 42^8$.

## Develop & Understand: B

**Rewrite each expression using a single exponent. For example, $2^3 \cdot 3^3$ can be rewritten $6^3$.**

**7.** $100^2 \cdot 3^2$ $300^2$

**8.** $10^{20} \cdot 25^{20}$ $250^{20}$

**9.** $5^{100} \cdot 5^{100} \cdot 2^{100}$ $50^{100}$

**10.** $\left(\frac{1}{3}\right)^a \cdot \left(\frac{1}{5}\right)^a$ $\left(\frac{1}{15}\right)^a$

**11.** $1{,}000^5 \cdot 3^5$ $3{,}000^5$

**12.** $x^2 \cdot y^2$ $(xy)^2$

**For each connection, determine whether there is a single repeater machine that will do the same work. If so, describe it.**

**13.**
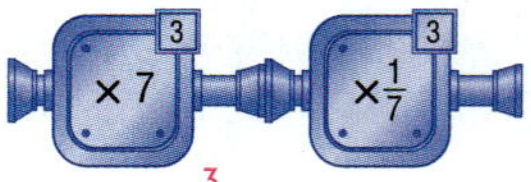

$\times 1^3$, or $\times 1$

**14.**
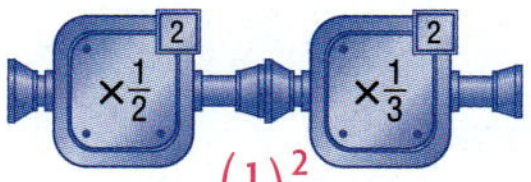

$\times\left(\frac{1}{6}\right)^2$

**15.**
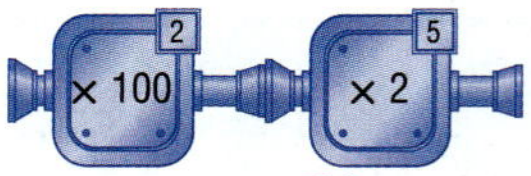

Not possible

**16.**
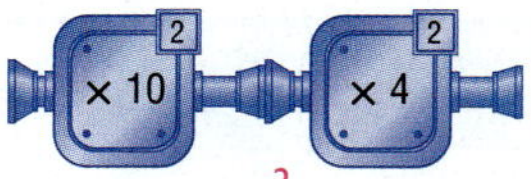

$40^2$

**17.**
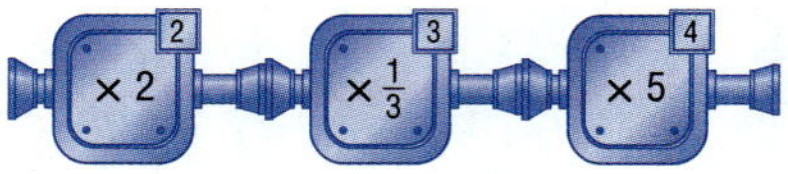

Not possible

**Tell what number should replace the question mark to make each statement true.**

**18.** $100^? \cdot 3^2 = 300^2$ 2

**19.** $4^{20} \cdot 25^{20} = ?^{20}$ 100

**20.** $5^{100} \cdot \left(\frac{1}{2}\right)^{100} = ?^{100}$ $\frac{5}{2}$

**21.** $\left(\frac{1}{3}\right)^3 \cdot \left(\frac{1}{5}\right)^3 = \left(\frac{1}{15}\right)^?$ 3

You have worked with the product laws of exponents. Do you think there are similar laws for sums of exponential expressions? You will explore this question in the next exercise set.

## Develop & Understand: C

**Determine whether each statement is true or false. Explain how you decided.**

**22.** $2^3 + 2^4 = 2^7$

**23.** $3^2 + 5^2 = 8^2$

**24.** From your answers to Exercises 22 and 23, do you think $2^a + 2^b = 2^{a+b}$ for any numbers $a$ and $b$? No

**25.** From your answers to Exercises 22 and 23, do you think $a^2 + b^2 = (a + b)^2$ for any numbers $a$ and $b$? No

22. False; $2^3 + 2^4 = 8 + 16 = 24$, and $2^7 = 128$
23. False; $3^2 + 5^2 = 9 + 25 = 34$, and $8^2 = 64$

### Share & Summarize

**1.** In your own words, write the rule that lets you find the missing base in equations like $3^{30} \cdot 2^{30} = ?^{30}$ and $5^{15} \cdot ?^{15} = 100^{15}$.

**Find the missing numbers.**

**2.** $15^3 \cdot 4^3 = ?^3$ 60

**3.** $3^7 \cdot 3^? = 3^{12}$ 5

**4.** $\left(\frac{2}{5}\right)^{12} \cdot \left(\frac{2}{5}\right)^3 = \left(\frac{2}{5}\right)^?$ 15

**5.** $2^2 \cdot ?^2 = 18^2$ 9

**6.** You have seen two product laws for working with exponents. Explain how you know when to use each rule.

**Product Laws**

$a^b \cdot a^c = a^{b+c}$

$a^c \cdot b^c = (a \cdot b)^c$

1. Possible answer: When one base raised to a power is multiplied by another base raised to the same power, the product is equal to the product of the two original bases raised to that power.

6. When multiplying powers with the same base, use the first law. When multiplying powers with the same exponent, use the second law.



## Troubleshooting

If students have trouble with the Share & Summarize questions, have them rephrase the questions in terms of machines. If you have two repeater machines with different base numbers but with the same exponents (number of repetitions), how can you replace them with a single machine? When students can answer the general questions in terms of the machines, explain again the connection between the machines and exponential notation.

## Develop & Understand: C

*Suggested Grouping: Small Groups*

These exercises are important because they address common confusions. Because of the close relationship between the laws of exponents and analogous laws for repeated addition, students often think they can simplify sums of numbers written with exponents.

▶ **Exercises 22–23** Students can calculate the right side and the left side and see whether the two results are equal. For example, $2^3 = 8$, $2^4 = 16$. The sum is 24. But $2^7 = 128$, which is not equal to 24.

If students answer Exercises 22 and 23 correctly, they should have little trouble determining that the statements in Exercises 24 and 25 are not true. In fact, counterexamples are given in Exercises 22 and 23, respectively.

▶ **Exercises 24–25** Ask students for their answers. Most students will correctly answer "no" to both of these questions. You might then challenge them by presenting an example for which the statement is true.

> If I let both $a$ and $b$ be 1, then I get $2^1 + 2^1 = 4$, which is $2^2$.
> How can this be?
> You told me $2^a + 2^b$ is not equal to $2^{a+b}$.

Help students realize that this is only a special instance. Unless the statement is true for all values of $a$ and $b$, the statement cannot be considered a rule.

For **Exercise 25**, ask students whether there is a special instance for which $a^2 + b^2 = (a + b)^2$. This statement is true when $a = 0$ or $b = 0$. But again, unless the statement is true for all values of $a$ and $b$, the statement is not a rule.

### Share & Summarize

For these questions, it is fine if students continue to use the machine model to explain their thinking. Hopefully, other students will want to use the shortcut techniques available in the product laws of exponents.

**Investigation 1**
Pages 93–96
Practice & Apply: 1–17
Connect & Extend: 43–44

**Investigation 2**
Pages 96–100
Practice & Apply: 18–35

**Investigation 3**
Pages 100–103
Practice & Apply: 36–41
Connect & Extend: 42, 45

**Assign Anytime**
Mixed Review: 47–51

▶ **Exercise 5 Extension** Ask students to list on the board all possible connections for a $\times 100$ machine. Remind them that changing the order of a set of machines or factors does not constitute a new connection.

▶ **Exercises 12–20** Make sure students do not use a calculator to evaluate these expressions; the goal is to have students become familiar with exponents.

▶ **Exercise 15** Students may incorrectly multiply $3 \cdot 2$ first and then raise the product to the third power. You may want to go over this exercise in class and review order of operations. Students also need to be reminded that although the exponent of 3 is not indicated, the exponent is 1; 3 is the same as $3^1$.



**Practice & Apply**

**Supply the missing information for each diagram.**

1.
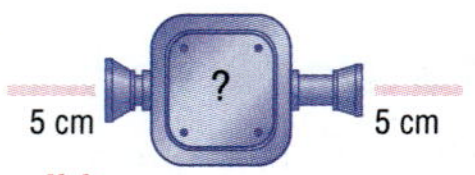

Possible answers: $\times 1$, or $\times 3^0$

2.
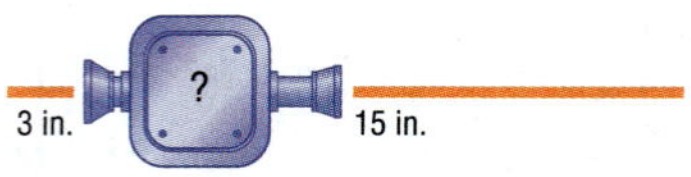

$\times 5$

3.
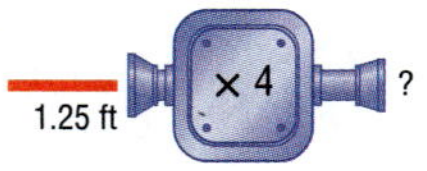

5-ft output

4.
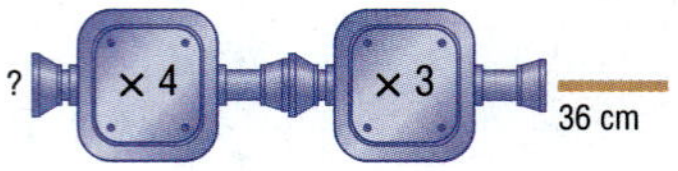

3-cm input

**If possible, find a connection that will do the same work as the given stretching machine. Do not use ×1 machines.**

5.
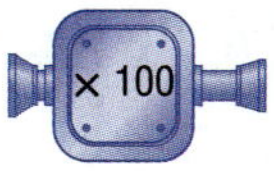


6.

7.
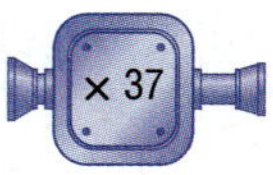


8.
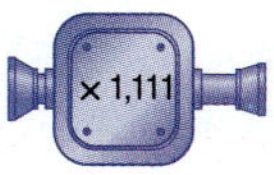


5. Possible answer: $\times 25 \times 4$
6. Possible answer: $\times 3 \times 33$
7. Not possible
8. Possible answer: $\times 11 \times 101$

9. Find two repeater machines that will do the same work as a $\times 81$ machine. $\times 9^2$, $\times 3^4$

10. Find a repeater machine that will do the same work as a $\times\frac{1}{8}$ machine.

10. $\times\left(\frac{1}{2}\right)^3$

11. This stick of gum exited a $\times 3^2$ machine. Without measuring, estimate the length of the input stick in centimeters. Explain how you found your answer.

11. About 1 cm; a $\times 3^2$ machine stretches a stick to 9 times its length, so the original stick must have been $\frac{1}{9}$ this length, which is about 9 cm.

**Evaluate each expression without using your calculator.**

12. $6^2$ 36
13. $9^2$ 81
14. $\left(\frac{1}{3}\right)^3$ $\frac{1}{27}$
15. $3 \cdot 2^3$ 24
16. $8^1$ 8
17. $x^1$ $x$

**Do each calculation in your head. (Hint: Think about stretching and shrinking machines.)**

18. $\left(\frac{1}{3}\right)^5(3)^5$ 1
19. $(4)^6\left(\frac{1}{4}\right)^6$ 1
20. $\left(\frac{1}{10}\right)^7(10)^8$ 10

If possible, find a repeater machine to do the same work as each connection.

21.
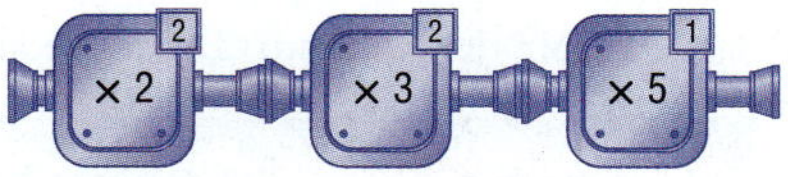

Not possible

22.
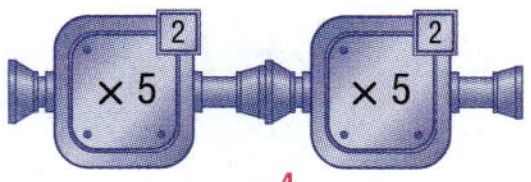

$\times 5^4$

If possible, rewrite each expression using a single base.

**23.** $6^4 \cdot 6^2$ $6^6$

**24.** $4^{10} \cdot 5^3$ Not possible

**25.** $1.1^{100} \cdot 1.2^{101}$ Not possible

**26.** $7^{10} \cdot 7^k$ $7^{10+k}$

**27.** $4^n \cdot 4^m$ $4^{n+m}$

**28.** $a^{20} \cdot a^5$ $a^{25}$

Simplify each expression.

**29.** $3c \cdot 5c$ $15c^2$

**30.** $10z^2 \cdot z^2$ $10z^4$

**31.** $2a^3 \cdot 10a$ $20a^4$

If possible, find a repeater machine to do the same work as each connection.

32.
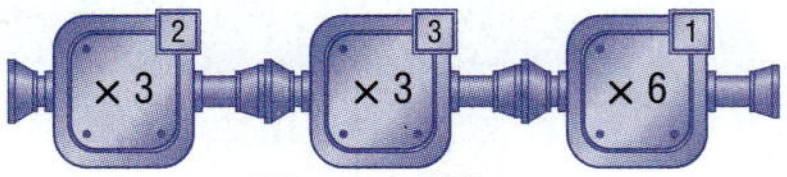

Not possible

33.
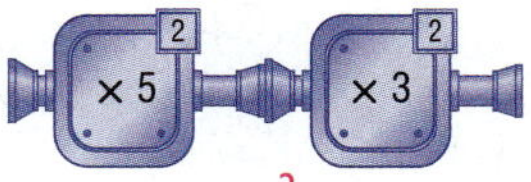

$\times 15^2$

34.
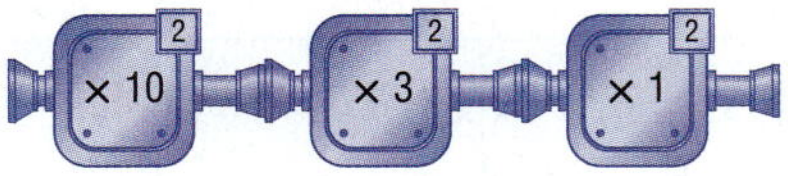

$\times 30^2$

35.
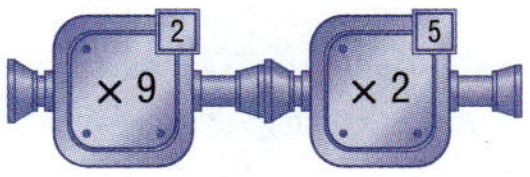

Not possible

If possible, rewrite each expression using a single base and a single exponent.

**36.** $2^3 \cdot \left(\frac{1}{3}\right)^3$ $\left(\frac{2}{3}\right)^3$

**37.** $4^0 \cdot 5^2$ $5^2$

**38.** $1^{100} \cdot 5^2$ $5^2$

**39.** $3^9 \cdot \left(\frac{1}{3}\right)^7$ $3^2$

**40.** $\left(\frac{1}{2}\right)^2 \cdot \left(\frac{1}{5}\right)^2$ $\left(\frac{1}{10}\right)^2$

**41.** $6^4 \cdot 2^4$ $12^4$

**Connect & Extend**

**42.** Patrick has a one-inch sewing needle. He says that putting the needle through a ×3 machine five times will have the same effect as putting it through a ×5 machine three times. Jane says the needles will turn out different lengths.

**a.** Who is correct? Explain how you know.

**b.** In Part a you compared $3^5$ and $5^3$. Are there *any* two different numbers, $a$ and $b$, for which $a^b = b^a$? Your calculator may help you. $a = 2, b = 4$

42a. Jane; $1 \cdot 3 \cdot 3 \cdot 3 \cdot 3 \cdot 3 = 243$ and $1 \cdot 5 \cdot 5 \cdot 5 = 125$





▶ **Exercises 23–31 and 36–41** Many students will benefit from creating and referring to a brief summary that lists all the key rules for simplifying expressions with exponents, along with a numerical example of each rule. Be sure students' lists include ×0, ×1, the two product laws of exponents, and an example with coefficients. This kind of list is also a great study aid.

▶ **Exercises 23–28** Students use the law $a^b \cdot a^c = a^{b+c}$. You may want to go over one of these in class to be sure students are applying this law correctly. Watch for students who find a way to simplify the expressions that don't have the same base.

▶ **Exercises 29–31** Students use the law $a^b \cdot a^c = a^{b+c}$, but remind them to multiply the coefficients independently of the variables.

▶ **Exercise 42b** Students may see this as a difficult exercise at first. But, in fact, they have seen the example that works ($2^4 = 4^2$).

## Quick Check

**Informal Assessment** Students should be able to:

- ✔ model the behavior of exponents using stretching and shrinking machines
- ✔ understand and apply the product laws of exponents

## Quick Quiz

Fill in the missing input, machine, or output in each situation.

**1.** 30 in.

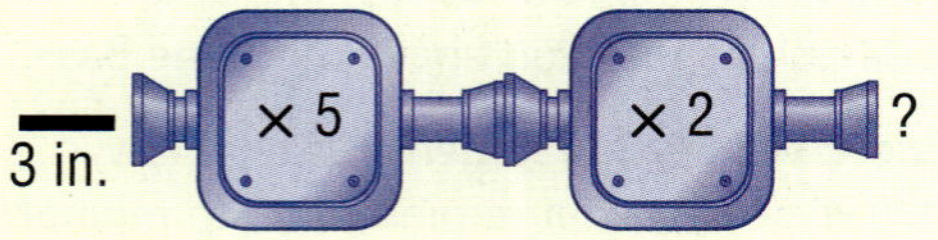


**2.** 2 cm

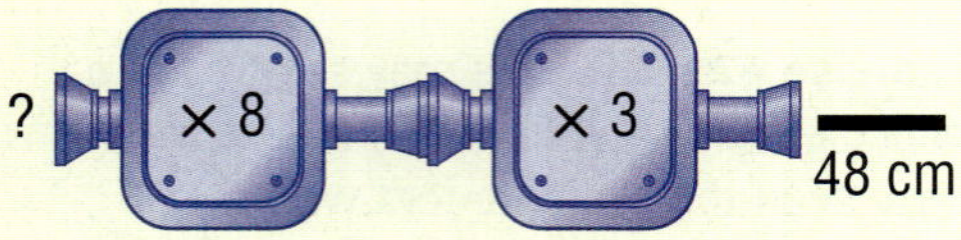


**3.** ×4 machine

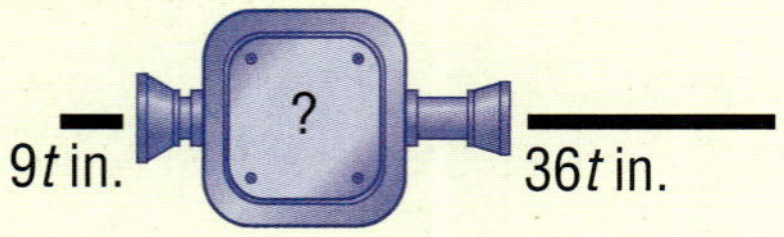


Rewrite each of the following as simply as you can using laws of exponents.

**4.** $2^n \cdot 2$ $2^{n+1}$

**5.** $25^n \cdot 4^n$ $100^n$

**6.** $b^n \cdot b^0$ $b^n$

**7.** $12^5 \cdot \left(\frac{1}{3}\right)^5$ $4^5$

**8.** $3x^2 \cdot 4x^3$ $12x^5$





★ indicates multi-step problem

**43.** The left column of the chart lists the lengths of input pieces of ribbon. Stretching machines are listed across the top. The other entries are the outputs for sending the input ribbon from that row through the machine from that column. Copy and complete the chart.

×10 ×1 ×5

| Input Length | Machine | | | |
|---|---|---|---|---|
| | ×2 | ? | ? | ? |
| $\frac{1}{2}$ | 1 | 5 | $\frac{1}{2}$ | $\frac{5}{2}$ |
| 3 | 6 | 30 | 3 | 15 |
| 7 | 14 | 70 | 7 | 35 |

★**44.** The left column of the chart lists the lengths of input chains of gold. Repeater machines are listed across the top. The other entries are the outputs you get when you send the input chain from that row through the repeater machine from that column. Copy and complete the chart.

$\times 2^6$ $\times 2^7$ $\times 2^8$

| Input Length | Repeater Machine | | | |
|---|---|---|---|---|
| | $\times 2^3$ | ? | ? | ? |
| 5 | 40 | 160 | 640 | 1,280 |
| 2 | 16 | 64 | 256 | 512 |
| 3 | 24 | 96 | 384 | 768 |

**45.** Write the prime factorization of each number using exponents.

**a.** 27 $3^3$ **b.** 12 $2^2 \cdot 3$ **c.** 100 $2^2 \cdot 5^2$ **d.** 999 $3^3 \cdot 37$

**46.** **In Your Own Words** Choose one of the product laws of exponents and explain it so a fifth grader could understand. Use stretching and shrinking machines in your explanation if you wish.
Explanations will vary.

**Fill in the blanks to make each a true statement.**

**47.** $\frac{1}{8} + \frac{1}{3} + \_\_\_\_ = 1$ $\frac{13}{24}$ **48.** $\frac{2}{7} + \frac{3}{10} + \_\_\_\_ = 1$ $\frac{29}{70}$

**Sketch a graph to match each story.**

**49.** Paul charted his height from when he was age 3 until he turned age 12.

**50.** The space shuttle was launched on Monday, orbited the planet for ten days, and then returned to Earth.

**51.** Darius threw the ball into the air and watched as it rose, fell, and then hit the ground.

49.

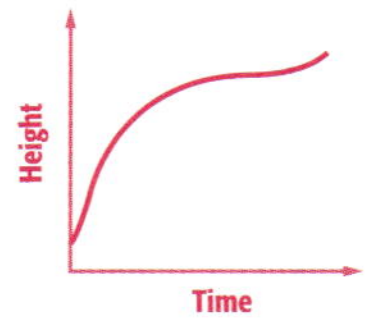


### Math Link

The only factors of a prime number are the number itself and 1. The *prime factorization* of a number expresses the number as a product of prime numbers, 12 = 2 • 2 • 3.

### Mixed Review

50.

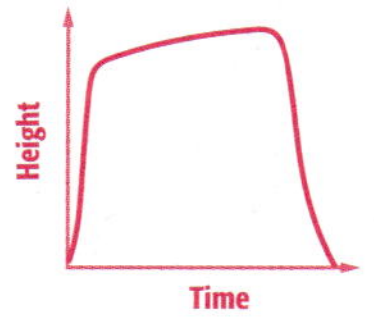


51.

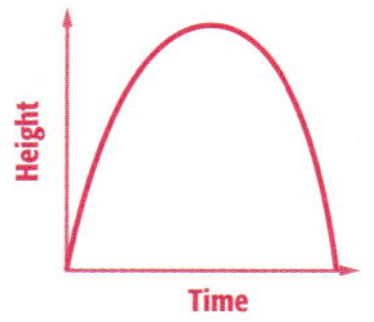

LESSON 2.3

# More Exponent Machines

### Objectives

- To model the behavior of exponents using stretching and shrinking machines
- To understand and apply the quotient laws of exponents
- To understand and apply the power of a power law of exponents

## Overview

In this lesson, we continue using the stretching and shrinking model to think about division of numbers with exponents. In addition to learning about the quotient laws of exponents, students explore the power of a power law of exponents.

The problems and activities throughout this lesson involve only nonnegative exponents. In later chapters, students explore negative numbers and negative exponents in depth.

## Advance Preparation

You may want to make an overhead transparency of Chapter 2 Master 1, to use in class. You might also want to provide copies of the blank master to students to use for their work.

| | Summary | Materials | On Your Own Exercises (pp. 117–119) | Assessment Opportunities |
|---|---|---|---|---|
| **Investigation 1** (p. 107) Pacing: 2 days | Students are introduced to the new division machines as machines that "undo" the multiplication machines with the same base. | Chapter 2 Master 1 | Practice & Apply: 1–5<br>Mixed Review: 57–59 | • Share & Summarize (p. 108)<br>• Troubleshooting (p. 108) |
| **Investigation 2** (p. 109) Pacing: 1 day | Students use shrinking machines to model the law of exponents $\frac{a^b}{a^c} = a^{b-c}$. | | Practice & Apply: 6–11<br>Mixed Review: 57–59 | • Share & Summarize (p. 110)<br>• Troubleshooting (p. 109) |
| **Investigation 3** (p. 111) Pacing: 1 day | Students use super machines to model and work with the power of a power law of exponents $(a^b)^c = a^{b \times c}$ | | Practice & Apply: 12–28<br>Connect & Extend: 29–56<br>Mixed Review: 57–59 | • Share & Summarize (p. 113)<br>• Troubleshooting (p. 113) |
| **Inquiry Investigation 4** (p. 114) Pacing: 1 day | Students use blocks to simulate the Tower of Hanoi puzzle. | paper, 5 blocks | | |

# Leveled Lesson Resources

CRM *Available in:* **Chapter 2 Resource Masters**

Also on TeacherWorks™ Lesson 2.3

## Study Guide and Intervention (p. 18) AL

**Lesson 2.3 Study Guide and Intervention**
***More Exponent Machines***

The **quotient laws of exponents** state that when dividing expressions with the same base, $a^b \div a^c = a^{b-c}$. When dividing expressions with the same exponent, $a^c \div b^c = (a \div b)^c$.

**Example 1** **Rewrite each expression using the quotient laws of exponents.**

**a.** $12^9 \div 12^5$

$12^{9-5}$ — $a^b \div a^c = a^{b-c}$

$12^4$ — Subtract the exponents.

**b.** $\frac{21^4}{7^4}$

$\left(\frac{21}{7}\right)^4$ — $a^c \div b^c = (a \div b)^c$

$3^4$ — Divide the bases.

The **power of a power law of exponents** states that when raising a power to a power, $(ab)^c = a^{b \cdot c}$.

**Example 2** **Rewrite each expression using the power of a power law of exponents.**

**a.** $(4^3)^6$

$4^{3 \cdot 6}$ — $(a^b)^c = a^{b \cdot c}$

$4^{18}$ — Multiply the exponents.

**b.** $(5^6)^6$

$5^{6 \cdot 6}$ — $(a^b)^c = a^{b \cdot c}$

$5^{36}$ — Multiply the exponents.

**Exercises**

**Rewrite each expression using the quotient laws of exponents.**

**1.** $7^{11} \div 7^4$ **2.** $\frac{15^{22}}{15^{18}}$

**3.** $\frac{48^5}{8^5}$ **4.** $56^{13} \div 8^{13}$

**5.** $\frac{23^{19}}{23^{13}}$ **6.** $96^{32} \div 12^{32}$

**7.** $\frac{45^{18}}{45^{17}}$ **8.** $102^8 \div 51^8$

**Rewrite each expression using the power of a power law of exponents.**

**9.** $(7^3)^4$ **10.** $(8^2)^2$

**11.** $(3^8)^9$ **12.** $(15^{12})^3$

**13.** $(23^1)^{46}$ **14.** $(52^{16})^4$

**15.** $(256^6)^{15}$ **16.** $(132^{10})^0$

## Skills Practice (p. 19) AL OL

**Lesson 2.3 Skills Practice**
***More Exponent Machines***

**Rewrite each expression using a single base.**

**1.** $5^{10} \div 5^2$ **2.** $\frac{10^6}{10^2}$

**3.** $\frac{7^9}{7^6}$ **4.** $12^8 \div 12^3$

**5.** $\frac{100^9}{100^8}$ **6.** $\frac{2^3}{2}$

**7.** $r^8 \div r^7$ **8.** $z^{10} \div z^8$

**9.** $\frac{q^8}{q^4}$ **10.** $\frac{g^{12}}{g^8}$

**11.** $y^7 \div y^2$ **12.** $\frac{z^{12}}{z^5}$

**13.** $\frac{6^{11}}{6^3}$ **14.** $\frac{15^3}{15^2}$

**15.** $\frac{9^9}{9^7}$ **16.** $\frac{18^4}{18^4}$

**17.** $\frac{7^6}{7^5}$ **18.** $\frac{95^{21}}{95^{18}}$

**19.** $\frac{v^{30}}{v^{20}}$ **20.** $\frac{n^{19}}{n^{11}}$

**21.** $(2^4)^5$ **22.** $(5^{18})^1$

**23.** $(7^8)^8$ **24.** $(4^9)^{11}$

**25.** $(10^{10})^{10}$ **26.** $(12^{15})^0$

**27.** $(x^{15})^3$ **28.** $(s^5)^{14}$

**29.** $(a^8)^{12}$ **30.** $(9^x)^y$

**31.** $(z^2)^r$ **32.** $(b^y)^7$

## Problem-Solving Practice (p. 20) AL OL

**Lesson 2.3 Problem-Solving Practice**
***More Exponent Machines***

**1. Sports** There are $2^{12}$ people signed up to run in a marathon. Half of the people are from out of town. Are there $2^{11}$ or $2^6$ people from out of town? Explain.

**2. Computers** A computer has a total memory of $10^9$ bytes divided equally among 10 computer chips. How many bytes of memory are on each computer chip? Write your answer as a power of 10.

**3. Biology** A biologist has about $10^{12}$ bacteria cells growing in her lab. If the cells are spread out evenly among $10^3$ colonies, about how many bacteria cells are in each colony? Write your answer as a power of 10.

**4. Geometry** A square has a side length of $3^{12}$ mm. Linette and Mitiku are trying to find the area of the square. Their answers are different:

Linette's work: $(3^{12})^2 = 3^{(12 \cdot 2)} = 3^{10}$

Mitiku's work: $(3^{12})^2 = 3^{(12 \div 2)} = 3^6$

Which student is correct? Identify the mistake made by the other student.

**5. Capacity** Suppose $7^5$ grains of sand fit along the edge of a cube. Juan writes $(7^5)^3$ to find out how many grains of sand it will take to fill the entire cube. Will it take $7^8$ or $7^{15}$ grains of sand to fill the cube? Explain.

**6. Geometry** The area of a circle is found by using the equation $A = \pi r^2$, where $A$ is the area and $r$ is the radius of the circle. Write the equation you would use to find the area of a circle that has a radius of $8^6$ mm.

## Enrichment (p. 21) BL

**Lesson 2.3 Enrichment**
***More Exponent Machines***

**Dividing Powers with Different Bases**

Some powers with different bases can be divided. First, you must be able to write both as powers of the same base. An example is shown below.

$$\frac{8^2}{2^5} = \frac{(2^3)^2}{2^5}$$ To find the power of a power, multiply the exponents.

$$= \frac{2^6}{2^5}$$

$$= 2^1 \text{ or } 2$$

This method could not have been used to divide $\frac{9^2}{2^5}$, since 9 cannot be written as a power of 2 using integers.

**Simplify each fraction using the method shown above. Express the solution without exponents.**

**1.** $\frac{8^2}{2^2}$ **2.** $\frac{16^4}{8^3}$ **3.** $\frac{9^3}{3^3}$

**4.** $\frac{81^4}{3^4}$ **5.** $\frac{3^9}{81^2}$ **6.** $\frac{32^4}{16^4}$

**7.** $\frac{125^2}{25^3}$ **8.** $\frac{6^6}{216^2}$ **9.** $\frac{1000^3}{10^6}$

**10.** $\frac{64^3}{8^5}$ **11.** $\frac{27^5}{9^4}$ **12.** $\frac{343^3}{7^5}$

## Lesson Quick Quiz (p. 22) AL OL BL

**Lesson 2.3 Quick Quiz**

**Fill in the missing input, machine, or output in each situation.**

**1.**

**2.**
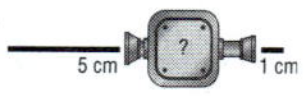


**3.**
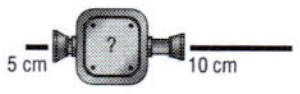


**4.**

**Rewrite these as simply as you can using rules of exponents.**

**5.** $2^4 \div 2^1$

**6.** $7^n \div 2$

**7.** $25^n \cdot 4^n$

**8.** $(4^3)^n$

**9.** $24^{10} \cdot \left(\frac{1}{3}\right)^{10}$

# Additional Lesson Resources

### Teacher Tech Tools

- TeacherWorks
- ExamView Assessment Suite
- Classroom Presentation Toolkit
- Advance Tracker

### Student Tech Tools

- StudentWorks Plus
- Math Online eGlossary • Concepts in Motion

### Other Print Products

- Investigation Notebook and Reflection Journal
- Quick Review Math Handbook

LESSON 2.3

# More Exponent Machines

Peter arrived at the resizing factory one day to find a whole new set of machines. Instead of × symbols, the machines had ÷ symbols. Peter's supervisor explained that the factory was getting more orders for shrinking things. The factory purchased a new type of shrinking machine that uses whole numbers instead of fractions. For example, a ÷2 machine divides the length of whatever enters the machine by 2.



### Think & Discuss

How long will a meterstick be after traveling through each machine?

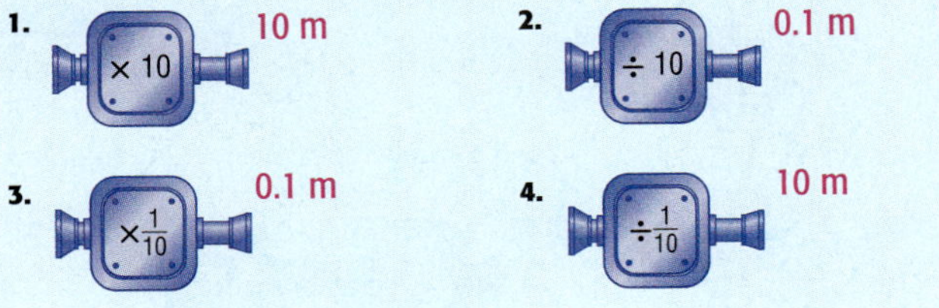


## Investigation 1 Division Machines with Exponents

The new shrinking machines can be connected to other shrinking machines and to stretching machines.

### Develop & Understand: A

If a yardstick is put into each machine, how many inches long will it be when it comes out of the machine?

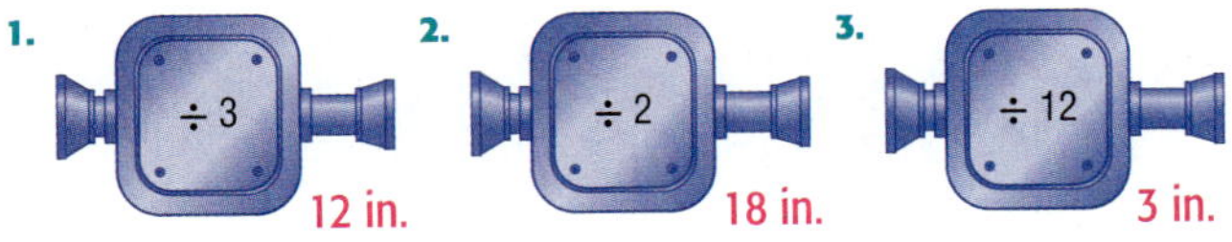




## *Reaching* All Learners

**AL Approaching Level** When students experience difficulty with the concept of dividing by a fraction less than 1, I have them refer to an inch ruler and determine, for instance, how many half inches are in 3 inches, how many fourth inches are in 2 inches, and so on. This exercise helps to reinforce the notion that dividing a whole number by a fraction less than 1 results in a quotient greater than the whole number.

More Exponent Machines LESSON 2.3

## Introduce

**Division** Introduce students to the new division machines. Suggest to students that they can think about a $\div m$ machine as a machine that undoes the work of a $\times m$ machine. For example, a ×3 machine triples the length of a stick, and a ÷3 machine returns the stick to its original length. A $\times\frac{1}{3}$ machine also undoes the work of a ×3 machine; but in this lesson, we want to concentrate on the division machines.

Ask students to imagine that the resizing factory has other machines that add to or subtract from the length of an item. For example, a +7 machine would need to follow a −7 machine in order to restore the input item to its original length.

Any two operations that undo each other are called *inverse* operations. The idea of inverses is important throughout mathematics, and students get a good taste of inverses in the early part of this lesson.

### Think & Discuss

Students are already familiar with the four × machines, and the ÷10 and ÷machines should not cause much confusion. However, the $\div\frac{1}{10}$ machine may cause a bit of discussion. Early student reaction may be that the stick that comes out is $\frac{1}{10}$ as long. Tell students to remember, though, that the $\div\frac{1}{10}$ machine must undo the $\times\frac{1}{10}$ machine.

## Investigation 1

***On Your Own Exercises***
Pages 117–119
Exercises 1–5

**Division Machines** You may wish to use Chapter 2 Master 1 to help students record their answers.

### Develop & Understand: A

*Suggested Grouping: Pairs*

▶ **Exercises 1–5** Be sure students note that these exercises ask for answers in inches.

▶ **Exercise 5** This exercise is more difficult than Exercises 1–4; it might help students to think of this machine as one that undoes a $\times 0.1$ machine.

▶ **Exercises 6–8** Students work for the first time with repeater machines that perform division. They may need to go back to basics, thinking about what a repeater machine does. They may need to think of the $\div 2^3$ machine, for example, as one that divides by 2, then divides by 2 again, and then divides by 2 a third time.

▶ **Exercises 9–12** Students look at connections of repeater $\times 3$ machines and $\div 3$ machines. If students struggle, encourage them to break up the machines and pair up machines that undo one another. Some students may prefer to think of a $\div 3$ machine as a $\times \frac{1}{3}$ machine and solve some of the exercises using a product law of exponents learned earlier. This sets the stage nicely for the quotient laws in the next investigation.

**Wrap-Up** If students seem to be having trouble with the division machines, you may want to bring the class together to share solutions before moving on to the Share & Summarize questions.

### *Share & Summarize*

It is certainly possible to solve **Exercise 1** without using division machines. The goal is for students to find both fraction-multiplication and division machines that work. Have students work on the question independently and then share their answers so that students who focused on the division machines, for example, are reminded of the similarities to the multiplication machines.

**Exercise 2** asks students to find a repeater machine to "cancel" the $\div 5^4$ and leave an additional $\times 25$. Students must recognize that $25 = 5^2$ in order to answer the question.



**4.** 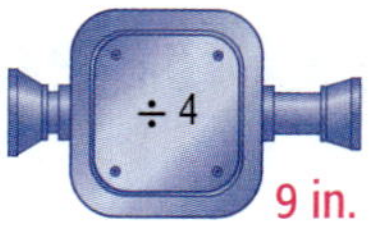

9 in.

**5.** 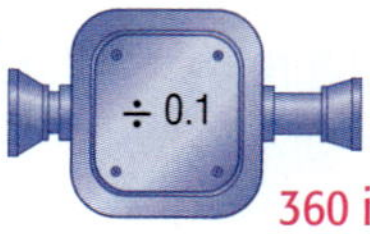

360 in.

Some of the new shrinking machines are designed to make repeater machines. If a yardstick is put into each repeater machine, how many inches long will it be when it exits?

**6.** 

4 in.

**7.** 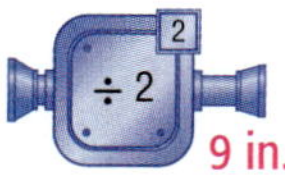

9 in.

**8.** 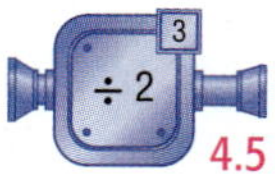

4.5 in.

**9.** If a one-inch paper clip is put through this connection, what will be its final length? 9 in.

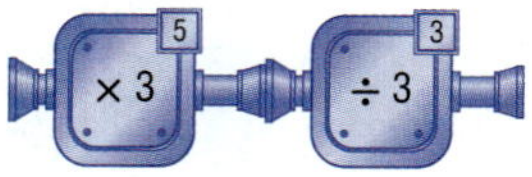


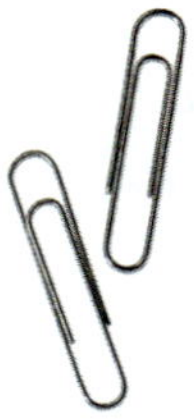

Find a single repeater machine to do the same work as each connection.

**10.** 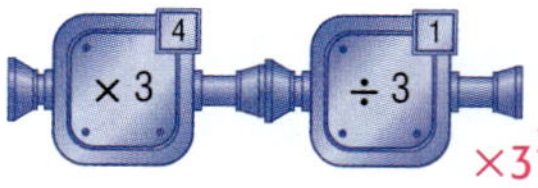

$\times 3^3$

**11.** 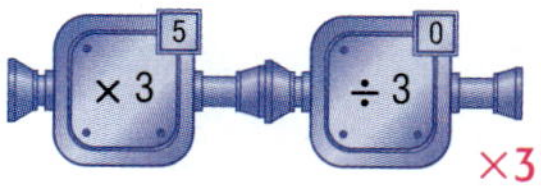

$\times 3^5$

**12.** 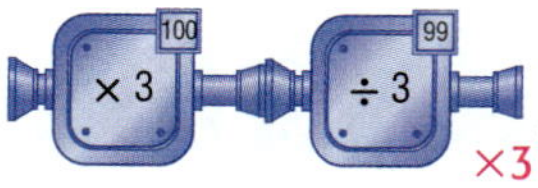

$\times 3^1$

### *Share & Summarize*

1. Find two repeater machines that will shrink a one-inch gummy worm to $\frac{1}{16}$ of an inch.

1. Possible answers: $\div 2^4$, $\div 4^2$, $\times \left(\frac{1}{2}\right)^4$, $\times \left(\frac{1}{4}\right)^2$

2. A one-inch gummy worm was sent through this connection and emerged 25 inches long. What is the first machine in the connection? $\times 5^6$

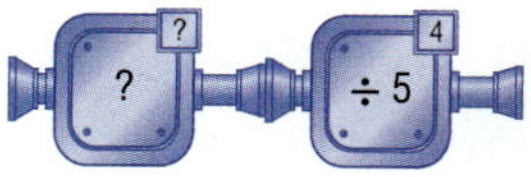




## Troubleshooting

If students come up with only multiplication machines for the first question, you may want to ask them to find division machines that work.

## Investigation 2 Divide Expressions with Exponents

The machine model can help you divide exponential expressions.

### Example

Here is how Shaunda thought about $3^5 \div 3^3$ connection.

Shaunda had discovered one of the *quotient laws of exponents.*

| Dividing Expressions with the Same Base | |
|---|---|
| $a^b \div a^c = a^{b-c}$ | $\frac{a^b}{a^c} = a^{b-c}$ |

### Develop & Understand: A

3. $2.9^1$, or 2.9

12. Not possible
14. Not possible
16. $a^{n-m}$
17. Not possible

**Write each expression as a power of 2.9.**

**1.** $2.9^5 \div 2.9^3$ $2.9^2$ **2.** $2.9^{10} \div 2.9^6$ $2.9^4$ **3.** $2.9^{13} \div 2.9^{12}$

**4.** $2.9^{13} \div 2.9^{11}$ $2.9^2$ **5.** $2.9^{25} \div 2.9^{25}$ $2.9^0$, or 1 **6.** $2.9^8 \div 2.9^3$ $2.9^5$

**Evaluate each expression without using your calculator.**

**7.** $2^3 \div 2^3$ 1 **8.** $2^{10} \div 2^{10}$ 1 **9.** $2^{15} \div 2^{15}$ 1

**If possible, rewrite each expression using a single base.**

**10.** $5^5 \div 5^2$ $5^3$ **11.** $3^4 \div 3^2$ $3^2$ **12.** $2^5 \div 3^4$ **13.** $3^2 \div 3^0$ $3^2$

**14.** $2^8 \div 3^2$ **15.** $a^{10} \div a$ $a^9$ **16.** $a^n \div a^m$ **17.** $a^n \div b^m$



## Investigation 2

**On Your Own Exercises**
Pages 117–119
Exercises 6–11

**Quotient Laws** In this investigation, students use division machines to develop two quotient laws of exponents.

These laws are counterparts to the product laws from Lesson 2.2, and that connection should be made clear to students.

Remind students that division by zero is undefined. So, in the quotient law given after the cartoon, $a \neq 0$.

### Example

Begin by walking students through the example in which Shaunda thinks about connections of 3 and 4 machines that have the same base. If students have worked with multiplying and dividing numbers written as fractions, you may want to write something like this on the board:

$$\frac{3^5}{3^3} = \frac{\cancel{3} \cdot \cancel{3} \cdot \cancel{3} \cdot 3 \cdot 3}{\cancel{3} \cdot \cancel{3} \cdot \cancel{3}}$$

Three of the 3s in the numerator "cancel" the 3s in the denominator. We are left with just $3 \cdot 3$, or $3^2$, in the numerator. Be sure to relate the canceling to the "undoing" of the machines: each ÷3 machine undoes a ×3 machine, so each pair has the same effect as a ×1 machine.

### Develop & Understand: A

*Suggested Grouping: Pairs*

▶ **Exercises 10–17** Ask students to share their answers. In particular, ask whether anyone found a way to simplify **Exercise 12, 14, or 17**. If so, take some time to find out what those students did, and have the class discuss it.

### Troubleshooting

Look for students who do division exercises such as $\frac{2^a}{2^b}$ by "canceling out" the bases to get $\frac{1^a}{1^b}$. Students will be less likely to do this if they think of translating these exercises into machine language.

## Example

Discuss the Example with the whole class. Ask students whether they prefer writing the expression as $\left(\frac{2}{3}\right)^2$ or as $\frac{4}{9}$. Both forms are useful.

Explain that the form $\left(\frac{a}{b}\right)^c$ is useful because it is much easier to simplify a fraction—divide both numerator and denominator by any common factors before the fraction is raised to a power.

For example, $\left(\frac{6}{8}\right)^3 = \left(\frac{3}{4}\right)^3 = \frac{27}{64}$.

We know $\left(\frac{6}{8}\right)^3 = \frac{216}{512}$, but it is not obvious that $\frac{216}{512} = \frac{27}{64}$.

Review the quotient law of exponents given after the cartoon. This law applies to expressions with the same exponent. It is parallel to the second product law of exponents. In this law, $b \neq 0$.

## Develop & Understand: B

*Suggested Grouping: Individuals*

▶ **Exercises 24 and 25** Students justify why it is possible to divide the bases when the exponents are the same. If a student questions why they should assume that $b \neq 0$, you might ask what would happen if $b = 0$. They should know that division by 0 is undefined.

**Teacher Tips** If students are having difficulty with the general argument for Exercises 24 and 25, encourage them to substitute numbers for the variables. For example, in Exercise 25, substitute 2 for *a*, 5 for *b*, and 3 for *c*.

Then $\frac{2^3}{5^3} = \frac{2 \cdot 2 \cdot 2}{5 \cdot 5 \cdot 5} = \left(\frac{2}{5}\right)\left(\frac{2}{5}\right)\left(\frac{2}{5}\right) = \left(\frac{2}{5}\right)^3$

Then replace 2, 5, and 3 by *a, b,* and *c*. The final step is to assure students that there is nothing special about the numbers chosen. Any exponent will work as long as it is the same for the two bases.

## Share & Summarize

This question asks students to articulate the first quotient law. The second law is not covered, since the most recent exercise was a general proof of the second quotient law. It is essential that students are able to explain that the difference between the two exponents on the left must be the same as the exponent on the right.

---

Though you may not be able to rewrite an expression using a single base, there may still be a way to simplify the expression.

### Example

Kate wondered if it would be possible to simplify an expression like $2^2 \div 3^2$. Simon and Jin Lee tried to help her decide.

This led the class to discuss another quotient law of exponents.

| Dividing Expressions with the Same Exponent |
|---|
| $a^c \div b^c = (a \div b)^c$ |
| $\frac{a^c}{b^c} = \left(\frac{a}{b}\right)^c$ |

## Develop & Understand: B

**Write each expression in the form $c^m$. The variable *c* can be a fraction or a whole number.**

**18.** $2^2 \div 5^2$ $\left(\frac{2}{5}\right)^2$ **19.** $5^6 \div 5^2$ $5^4$ **20.** $a^2 \div 2^2$ $\left(\frac{a}{2}\right)^2$

**21.** $a^9 \div b^9$ $\left(\frac{a}{b}\right)^9$ **22.** $3^7 \div 3^4$ $3^3$ **23.** $x^n \div y^n$ $\left(\frac{x}{y}\right)^n$

**24. Prove It!** Show that $\frac{a^3}{b^3} = \left(\frac{a}{b}\right)^3$, for $b \neq 0$. (Hint: Write $a^3$ and $b^3$ as products of *a*'s and *b*'s. Regroup the quotient into a string of $\left(\frac{a}{b}\right)$'s.)

**25.** Do you think $\frac{a^c}{b^c} = \left(\frac{a}{b}\right)^c$ for $b \neq 0$ and any value of *c* greater than or equal to 0? Explain.

24. $\frac{a^3}{b^3} = \frac{a \cdot a \cdot a}{b \cdot b \cdot b} = \frac{a}{b} \cdot \frac{a}{b} \cdot \frac{a}{b} = \left(\frac{a}{b}\right)^3$

25. Yes; Possible explanation: If $c > 0$, you can always rewrite and regroup like I did for Exercise 24; you get $\frac{a}{b}$ multiplied by itself *c* times. If $c = 0$, you get $\frac{a^0}{b^0} = \frac{1}{1} = 1 = \left(\frac{a}{b}\right)^0$.

### Share & Summarize

In your own words, write the rule that lets you find the missing exponent in equations like $5^{16} \div 5^8 = 5^?$ and $r^? \div r^{10} = r^5$. See ①.

① When you divide a base raised to a power by the same base raised to a power, the result is the base raised to the difference of the powers.



## Reaching All Learners

**BL Beyond Level** To provide students more practice with general arguments and the laws of exponents, ask them to "prove" any of the four laws below. Students have seen arguments for the first three laws listed here but not general arguments with variables.

$a^b \cdot a^c = a^{b+c}$

$a^c \cdot b^c = (ab)^c$

$a^b \div a^c = a^{b-c}$

$a^c \div b^c = (a \div b)^c$

# Investigation 3 Power Law of Exponents

Your resizing factory is a success. You decide to order a shipment of *super machines.* Here is one of the new machines.

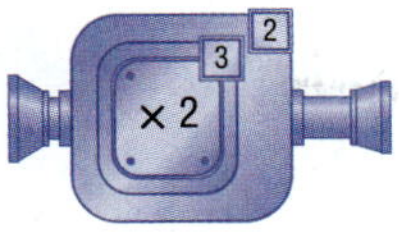


Peter was excited to try the machine, but he was not sure what it would do. He found this diagram in the manufacturer's instructions.

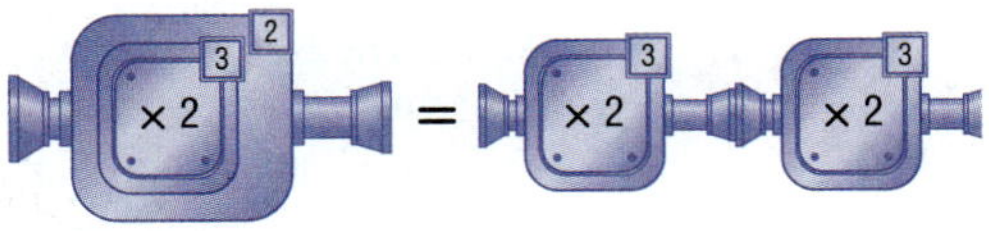

### Real-World Link

Improperly discarded chewing gum can be a litter nightmare. Schools and businesses spend thousands of dollars every year cleaning chewing gum from floors, carpets, and furniture.

### Think & Discuss

If Peter puts a one-inch stick of gum through the above super machine, how long will it be when it comes out the machine? 64 in.

How many times would Peter need to apply a ×2 machine to do the same work as this new super machine? 6

Peter used the shorthand notation $\times(2^3)^2$ to describe this super machine. Why is this shorthand better than $\times 2^{3\,2}$? See ①.

Describe or draw a connection of three repeater machines that will do the same work as a $\times(4^2)^3$ machine. See ②.

① $\times 2^{3\,2}$ could be confused with $\times 2^{32}$.

② Possible answer: $\times 4^2 \times 4^2 \times 4^2$

### Develop & Understand: A

Careta has an order from a kite maker who wants to stretch different types of string. If a one-inch piece of kite string is sent through each super machine, how long will it be when it exits?

1. 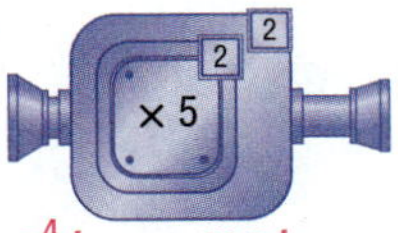

$5^4$ in., or 625 in.

2. 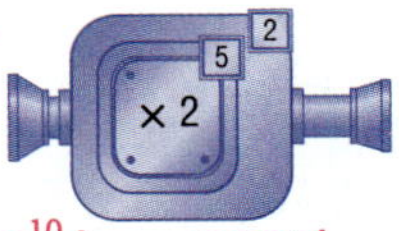

$2^{10}$ in., or 1,024 in.

3. 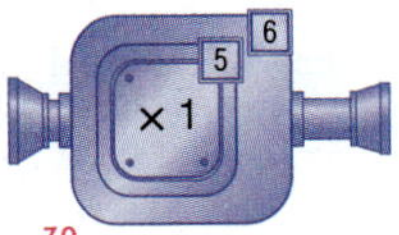

$1^{30}$ in., or 1 in.

4. 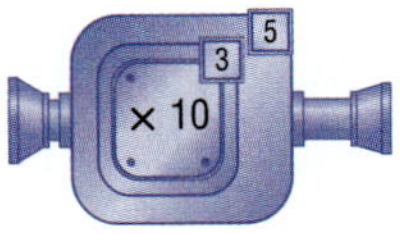

4. $10^{15}$ in., or 1,000,000,000,000,000 in.



# Investigation 3

**On Your Own Exercises**
Pages 117–119
Exercises 12–28, 29–56

**Power of a Power** This investigation takes the machine metaphor to a new level: repeaters of repeater machines. This is simply to make a point about, and to give students a visual image of, the power of a power law: $(a^b)^c = a^{b \cdot c}$

Have the students read the text. Then ask them to describe what a super machine really does, given the manufacturer's instructions. One good explanation is: "It's a repeater machine of repeater machines!"

### Think & Discuss

*Suggested Grouping: Pairs*

Students should be able to calculate what happens to the 1-inch stick in stages. After the first time through a $\times 2^3$ machine, the stick is 8 inches long. After feeding the 8-inch stick through a $\times 2^3$ machine, we get a stick that is $8 \cdot 2 \cdot 2 \cdot 2$, or 64, inches long.

**Teacher Tips** It is important for students to understand the need for parentheses in writing "powers of powers" in order for them to communicate clearly in their mathematical writing. Ask,

- In what ways might $2^{3\,2}$ be confusing?
- How do parentheses clarify?

### Develop & Understand: A

*Suggested Grouping: Pairs*

▶ **Exercises 1–4** Ask students to think about outputs of super machines. **Exercise 5** asks them to show the connections that the super machines represent. Some students might find it helpful to think about the connections of repeater machines first. For example, they may, for the first machine in **Exercise 1**, think about connecting two $5^2$ machines together to come up with a final answer of $5^2 \cdot 5^2 = 625$.

▶ **Exercise 3** Ask students to think about the simplest machine that could replace the machine given in order to help them recognize the "easy" exercises and use shortcuts.

▶ **Exercise 6** Students may need to work backward by thinking first of equal factors of 81: $81 = 9 \cdot 9$, and $9 = 3^2$. Therefore, one super machine is $\times(3^2)^2$.

***Example***

Refer students to the Example, which explains how Maya thought about $\times(4^3)^2$. Describe the power of a power law and how it relates to the super machine and to repeated multiplication.

For $\times(4^3)^2$, you can remind them that the outer exponent 2 indicates "multiply what's in the parentheses by itself." So we have $4^3 \cdot 4^3$.

We can break this down even further, as Maya did: each $4^3$ is really $4 \cdot 4 \cdot 4$, and

$(4 \cdot 4 \cdot 4) \cdot (4 \cdot 4 \cdot 4) =$
$4 \cdot 4 \cdot 4 \cdot 4 \cdot 4 \cdot 4$.



**5.** For each super machine in Exercises 1–4, describe or draw a connection of two or more repeater machines that would do the same work.

5. Possible answers: $\times5^2\times5^2$, $\times2^5\times2^5$, $\times1^5\times1^5\times1^5\times1^5\times1^5\times1^5$, $\times10^3\times10^3\times10^3\times10^3\times10^3$

**6.** Describe a super machine that will stretch a one-inch strand of kite string to 81 inches. Do not use 1 for either exponent.

Possible answer: $\times(3^2)^2$

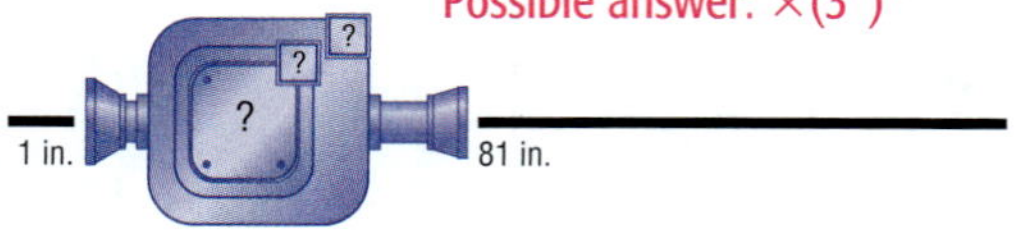


**7.** Consider the expression $(4^3)^2$.

**a.** Draw a super machine that represents this expression.

7a.

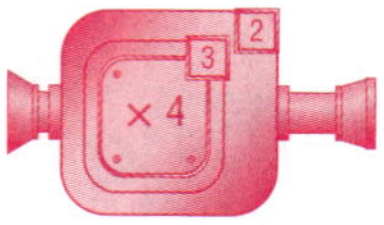


**b.** How many times would you need to apply a $\times4^3$ machine to do the same work as your super machine? 2

**c.** How many times would you need to apply a $\times4$ machine to do the same work as your super machine? 6

The expressions represented by the super machines can be simplified.

***Example***

In Exercise 7, Zoe added the exponents and decided it would take five $\times4$ machines to do the same work as the $\times(4^3)^2$ super machine. Maya thought the answer was six. She drew a diagram to explain her thinking to Zoe.

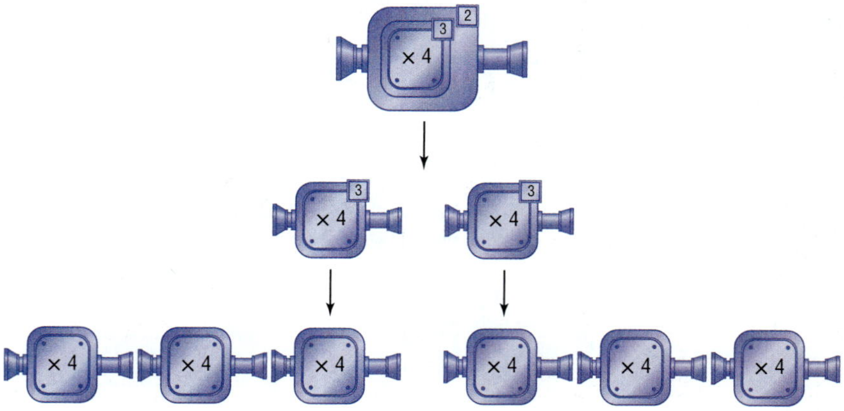


Maya's diagram convinced Zoe that she should have multiplied the exponents rather than adding them. The diagram shows that $(4^3)^2 = 4^{3 \cdot 2} = 4^6$.

The diagram Maya used demonstrates an example of the *power of a power law of exponents.*

**Raising a Power to a Power**

$(a^b)^c = a^{b \cdot c}$

## Develop & Understand: B

**Write each expression as a power of 2.**

**8.** $(2^4)^2$ $2^8$

**9.** $(2^2)^3$ $2^6$

**10.** $(2^4)^3$ $2^{12}$

**11.** $(2^2)^2$ $2^4$

**12.** $(2^1)^7$ $2^7$

**13.** $(2^0)^5$ $2^0$

**Tell what number should replace the question mark to make each statement true.**

**14.** $4 = 2^?$ 2

**15.** $4^? = (2^2)^3$ 3

**16.** $4^4 = (?^2)^4$ 2

**17.** $2^3 \cdot 4^? = 2^{13}$ 5

**18.** $2^7 \div 4^3 = 2^?$ 1

**19.** $?^3 \div 2^3 = 2^3$ 4

**20.** $8^2 = 2^?$ 6

**21.** $2^7 + 2^7 = 2^?$ 8

**22.** Use a calculator to check your answers for Exercises 8–21. To evaluate an expression like $(2^4)^2$, push the exponent key twice. To find $(2^4)^2$, you could use the following keystrokes.

See students' work.

2 [^] 4 [^] 2

or

2 [$y^x$] 4 [$y^x$] 2

### Share & Summarize

Tell whether each equation is true or false. If an equation is false, rewrite the expression to the right of the equal sign to make it true.

**1.** $3^5 \cdot 3^3 = 3^{15}$ False, $3^8$

**2.** $(2^5)^0 = 1$ True

**3.** $(a^3)^4 = a^7$ False, $a^{12}$

**4.** $a^{30} \div a^2 = a^{15}$ False, $a^{28}$

**5.** $(a^5)^3 = a^{15}$ True

**6.** $a^4 \cdot a^3 = a^7$ True

**7.** Explain the difference between $(a^b)^c$ and $a^b \cdot a^c$. Refer to stretching and shrinking machines if they help you explain.

Possible answer: $(a^b)^c$ means "do $\times a^b$ $c$ times." $a^b \cdot a^c$ means "do $\times a$ $b$ times and then do $\times a$ $c$ times."



## Troubleshooting

In Exercise 18, watch for students who are tempted to treat the bases as the fraction $\frac{2}{4}$ and change the exercise to $\frac{1^7}{2^3}$. Explain that to change $\frac{2}{4}$ to $\frac{1}{2}$, the exponents of 2 and 4 must match. For example, $\frac{4^5}{6^5} = \left(\frac{4}{6}\right)^5 = \left(\frac{2}{3}\right)^5$, according to the quotient law of exponents.

Discuss the power of a power law of exponents, which is given in the box at the top of page 113. It might be helpful for students to work through Maya's strategy a few times with other super machines, for example, $(3^4)^2$, $(5^3)^2$, $(7^2)^3$.

## Develop & Understand: B

*Suggested Grouping: Individuals*

▶ **Exercise 13** Zero is an exponent. Students should note right away that the number in parentheses, $2^0$, is 1, since it is a number raised to the 0 power, and, therefore, give the answer as $1^5$, or 1. Other students might choose to apply the law and just multiply the exponents.

▶ **Exercise 18** If students have trouble, ask them to think about the numerator and the denominator in terms of machines. Ask whether there is a way to think about the $4^3$ machine in terms of $\times 2$ machines. Students might work backward from the law of exponents and respond that $4^3 = (2^2)^3 = 2^6$.

▶ **Exercise 21** Some students may be tempted to add bases or exponents and get $2^7 + 2^7 = 4^7$ or $2^7 + 2^7 = 2^{14}$. Ask those students to try to verify their answers with calculators. They will not get the results they expected, so students should start thinking about proper use of the appropriate exponent law. If we think of $2^7$ as "some number," then we have two of that number or $2 \cdot 2^7$. By one of the product laws of exponents, this is $2^8$.

### Share & Summarize

Have students work on Exercises 1–6 individually as you circulate around the room to see whether students understand the questions. At this point, students should feel confident answering these questions.

Ask students to work individually to write their answers to Exercise 7 and then share their answers with a partner. Encourage students to draw machines or to use symbolic notation to describe the differences.

Inquiry

# Investigation 4

*Suggested Grouping: Small Groups*

## Materials and Preparation

Each group will need 6 blocks labeled 1, 2, 3, 4, 5, and 6.

This very rich puzzle has many layers of opportunity for the teacher. In this investigation, students first solve an intriguing puzzle: How do you move all the disks from one spike to another, following the rules laid out in the description of the exercise?

From there, students find how the number of moves depends on the number of disks they must move. Each time a disk is added, the number of moves is twice the previous number of moves plus 1. This is a slightly more complicated form of exponential growth than what they saw in Lesson 2.3.

The general formula, which students will need help discovering, represents the number of moves needed to move d disks from one spike to another: $2^d - 1$. The support will have to come in at least two places: helping students find the most efficient algorithm for moving the disks and then expressing the numerical pattern they find in the table they create.

**Make a Prediction** Students will probably not have a good sense for this pattern; it is not a simple exponential function. Remind students not to draw conclusions about the pattern too soon. Once students solve the first three exercises and see that moving 2 disks requires 2 moves more than moving 1 disk and that moving 3 disks requires 4 moves more than moving 2 disks, students may begin thinking in terms of 2s or powers of 2.

Encourage students to move somewhat quickly through these exercises in order to get some initial ideas but not to puzzle about them too long. At some point, be sure students have figured out that they may move a disk back onto Spike A.



Inquiry

# Investigation 4 The Tower of Hanoi

### Materials

- 6 blocks, labeled 1, 2, 3, 4, 5, and 6

The Tower of Hanoi is a famous puzzle invented in 1883 by French mathematician Edouard Lucas. Lucas based the puzzle on the following legend.

*At the beginning of time, the priests in a temple were given three golden spikes. On one of the spikes, 64 golden disks were stacked, each one slightly smaller than the one below it.*

*The priests were assigned the task of moving all the disks to one of the other spikes while being careful to follow these rules.*

- *Move only one disk at a time.*
- *Never put a larger disk on top of a smaller disk.*

*When they completed the task, the temple would crumble and the world would vanish.*

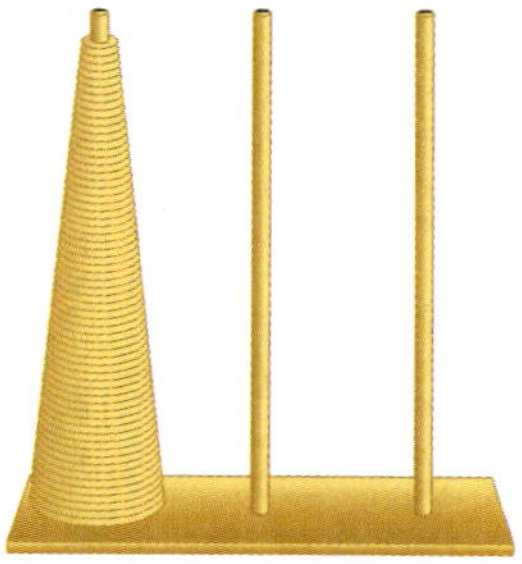

In this investigation, you will figure out how long it would take to move all the disks from one spike to another. We will start by assuming the disks are so large and heavy that the priests can move only one disk per minute.

## Make a Prediction

Imagine that the spikes are labeled A, B, and C and that the disks start out on spike A. Since it can be overwhelming to think about moving all 64 disks, it may help to first consider a much simpler puzzle. Remember, a larger disk cannot be placed on top of a smaller disk.

1. Suppose the puzzle started with only one disk on spike A. How long would it take to move the disk to spike B? 1 min
2. Suppose the puzzle started with two disks on spike A. How long would it take to move both disks to spike B? What would be the moves? See margin.
3. Try again with three disks. How long would it take? What would be the moves? See margin.



**Additional Answers**

2. 3 min; Move the top disk to C, then move the second disk to B, and then move the disk on C to B.

3. 7 min; Move the top disk to C, then move the second disk to B, and then move the disk on C to B. Now move the third disk to C. Move the top disk on B to A, move the second disk to C, and finally move the disk on A to C.

4. Predictions will vary. Each time a disk is added, the time is double the previous time plus 1 min.
5. Predictions will vary. The correct answer is $2^{64} - 1$ min, or about $1.84 \cdot 10^{19}$ min.

**4.** Predict how the total time required to solve the puzzle will change each time you increase the number of disks by one.

**5.** Predict how long it would take to move all 64 disks. Write down your prediction so you can refer to it later.

## Try It Out

Luckily, you do not need 64 golden disks to try the Tower of Hanoi puzzle. You can model it with some simple equipment. Your puzzle will have five "disks," rather than 64. You will need a blank sheet of paper and five blocks, labeled 1, 2, 3, 4, and 5.

Label your paper with the letters A, B, and C as shown. Stack the blocks in numerical order with 5 on the bottom, next to the A.

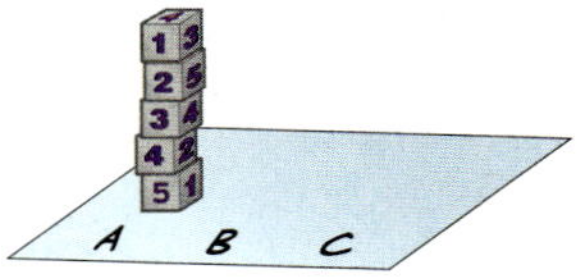


To solve the puzzle, you need to move all the blocks to another position, either B or C, following these rules.

- Move only one block at a time.
- Never put a larger number on a smaller number.

This is not an easy puzzle. To solve it, you might want to start with a puzzle using only two or three blocks. As you explore, look for a *systematic* way to move all the blocks to a new position.

7. Possible answers: The number of moves for a tower is twice the number for the previous tower, the tower with one less disk plus 1. Or the number of moves required to solve a puzzle of height $n + 1$ is the number required for height $n$ plus $2^n$. Or the number of moves required for a tower of height $n$ is $2^n - 1$.

## Try It Again

**6.** Solve the puzzle again for towers of 1, 2, 3, 4, and 5 blocks. This time, count the number of moves it takes you to solve each puzzle. Record your data in a table.

| **Tower Height** | 1 | 2 | 3 | 4 | 5 |
|---|---|---|---|---|---|
| **Number of Moves** | 1 | 3 | 7 | 15 | 31 |

**7.** Describe any patterns you see that might help you make predictions about how many moves it would take for larger towers.

**8.** Use your pattern to fill in a table like the one below. Then use a sixth cube to test your prediction for a tower of height 6.

| **Tower Height** | 6 | 7 | 8 | 9 | 10 |
|---|---|---|---|---|---|
| **Number of Moves** | 63 | 127 | 255 | 511 | 1,023 |

Go on



Inquiry

## Try It Out

One way to move the disks is try to solve a simpler exercise. Suppose we want to move two disks to Spike B. Move disk 1 to Spike C, disk 2 to Spike B, and then disk 1 on top of disk 2.

1.
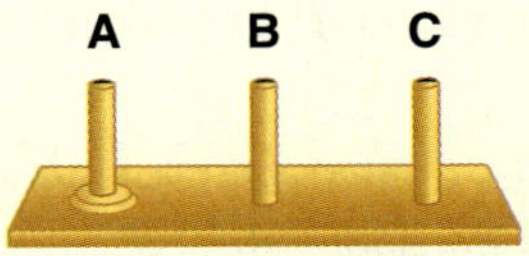


2.
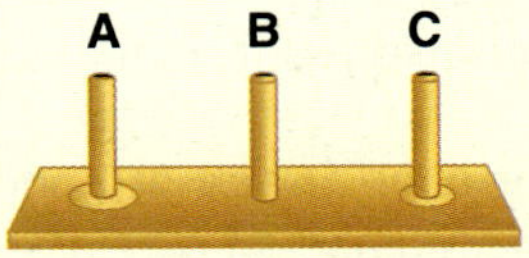


3.
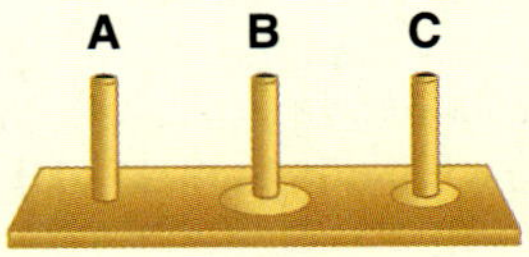


4.
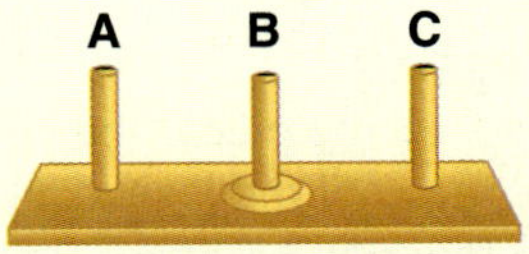


To move three disks to Spike B, move disks 1 and 2 to Spike C following the strategy above; then move disk 3 to Spike B. Finally, move disk 1 back to Spike A, disk 2 to Spike B, and then disk 1 to Spike B.

The reasoning can continue to any number of disks: Move $(d - 1)$ disks to Spike B, move the bottom disk to Spike C, and then move the $(d - 1)$ disks to Spike C.

Before moving on to counting the number of moves, it's important that all of the groups see how to move the disks and can articulate how the number of moves grows.

## Try It Again

▶ **Exercise 9** Students write an algebraic expression relating the number of disks and the number of moves. Some students may recognize that all the numbers are odd. If no one notices that they are all 1 less than a power of 2, you may need to lead them down that road.

**Analyze the Table** Copy the table below onto an overhead transparency or a blackboard, and add a third row for powers of 2. Have students help you fill in the powers of 2, and ask whether they see a relationship between the powers of 2 and the numbers in the "number of moves" row. They should notice that the number of moves is always 1 less than the corresponding power of 2. If the class can articulate that much, then help them write the expression $2^d - 1$.

## Back to the Legend

Students finally have all the pieces they need to solve the puzzle of the legend: How long will it take to move all 64 disks? The answer is $2^{64} - 1$ minutes, which they must convert to years to get a sense of what that means.

Certainly once they have the expression or rule, students can plug that into their calculators to find the solution. A scientific calculator will give a result of $1.844674407 \times 10^{19}$ when $2^{64}$ is entered.

Dividing this number by 60, by 24, and by 365 gives $3.509654504 \times 10^{13}$ years or about 35,096,500,000,000 years.

## What Did You Learn?

Exercises 13–15 are intended as homework for students to process and then to share what they have learned. Exercise 14 asks students to put the length of time into context. Some students may realize that since the puzzle supposedly started at the beginning of time, they need to take the time from then to now into account.

Inquiry

**9.** Write an expression for the number of moves it would take to solve the puzzle for a tower of height $t$. Add 1 to each entry in the second row of your table for Question 6 and then look at the pattern again. $2^t - 1$

### Back to the Legend

**10.** Assume that one disk is moved per minute. Figure out how long it would take to solve the puzzle for the heights shown in the table below. Report the times in appropriate units. After a while, minutes are not very useful.

| Tower Height | 1 | 2 | 3 | 4 | 5 | 6 | 7 | 8 | 9 | 10 |
|---|---|---|---|---|---|---|---|---|---|---|
| Number of Moves | 1 | 3 | 7 | 15 | 31 | 63 | 127 | 255 | 511 | 1,023 |
| Time | | | | | | | | | | |

10. Chart: Time row (left to right)
1 min.
3 min.
15 min.
31 min.
1 hr 3 min
2 hr 7 min
4 hr 15 min
8 hr 31 min
17 hr 3 min

**11.** How long would it take to move all 64 disks? Give your answer in years. How does your answer compare to your prediction in Question 5? $2^{64} - 1$ min $\approx 1.845 \times 10^{19}$ min $\approx 3.510 \times 10^{13}$ yr

**12.** You are able to move blocks at a much faster pace than one per minute. What if the disks the priests used were smaller and lighter, so they could also work faster?

**a.** If one disk is moved per second, how long would it take to finish the puzzle? About $5.850 \times 10^{11}$ yr

**b.** If ten disks are moved per second, how long would it take to finish? About $5.850 \times 10^{10}$ yr

### What Did You Learn?

**13.** When you move a piece in the Tower of Hanoi puzzle, you often have two choices of where to place it. Explain how you decide which move to make. See margin.

**14.** Suppose the legend is true and the priests can move pieces at the incredible rate of ten per second. Do you think they are likely to finish the puzzle in your lifetime? Explain. See margin.

**15.** Write a newspaper article about the Tower of Hanoi puzzle. You might mention the legend and the time it takes to move the disks for towers of different heights. Articles will vary.

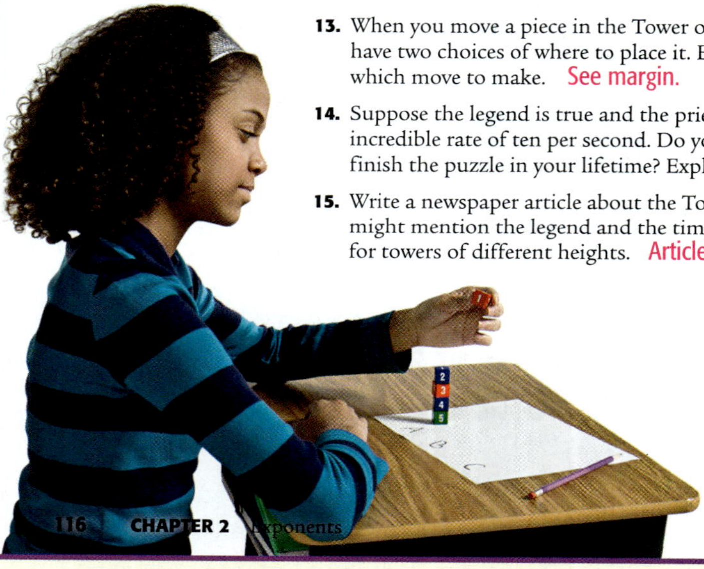



| Tower Height | 1 | 2 | 3 | 4 | 5 |
|---|---|---|---|---|---|
| Number of Moves | 1 | 3 | 7 | 15 | 31 |
| $2^d$ | $2\ (2^1)$ | $4\ (2^2)$ | $8\ (2^3)$ | $16\ (2^4)$ | $32\ (2^5)$ |

### Additional Answers

13. Possible answer: If one of the piles has a smaller disk on top, there is no choice. If the disk I am moving is smallest and the number of pieces in the pile I am moving from is odd, I move the top disk to the pile I want it to end on. If the number of disks in the pile I am moving from is even, I move the top disk to the pile I do not want it to end on.

14. Possible answer: No; even at this fast rate, it will be a very long time before they finish.

**Practice & Apply**

**A 12-inch ruler is put through each machine. Find its exit length.**

**1.** 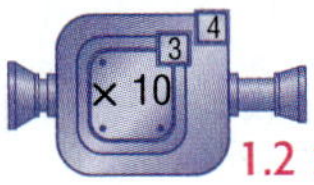

$1.2 \times 10^{13}$

**2.** 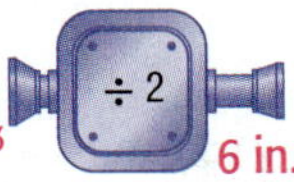

6 in.

**3.** 

120 in.

**4.** 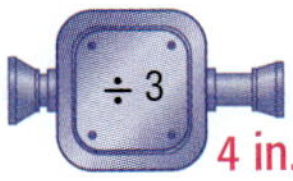

4 in.

**5.** 

3 in.

**Write each expression using a single base.**

**6.** $2.7^{10} \div 2.7$ $2.7^9$

**7.** $0.2^{10} \div 0.2^{10}$ $0.2^0$

**8.** $a^{20} \div a^5$ $a^{15}$

**9.** $\frac{s^{100}}{s}$ $s^{99}$

**10.** $\frac{a^n}{a^m}$ $a^{n-m}$

**11.** $5^4 \div 5^2$ $5^2$

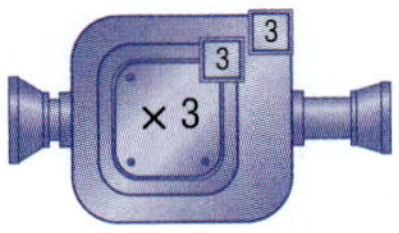


**12.** Ana was working with this super machine.

**a.** How many times would Ana need to apply a $\times 3^3$ machine to do the same work as this super machine? 3

**b.** How many times would she need to apply a $\times 3$ machine to do the same work as this machine? 9

**c.** If Ana puts a one-inch bar of silver through this machine, how long will it be when it exits? 19,683 in.

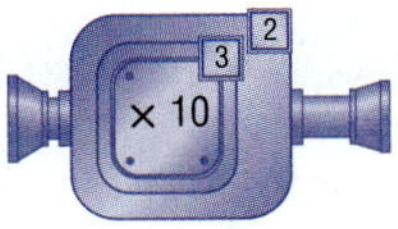


**13.** Here is Evan's favorite super machine.

**a.** How many times would Evan need to apply a $\times 10^3$ machine to do the same work as this super machine? 2

**b.** How many times would he need to apply a $\times 10$ machine to do the same work? 6

**c.** If Evan puts a one-inch bar of gold in this machine, how long will it be when it comes out the machine? 1,000,000 in.

**Write each expression as a power of 2.**

**14.** $(4^2)^3$ $2^{12}$

**15.** $2^4 \div 4^2$ $2^0$

**16.** $2^3 \div 2^3$ $2^0$

**Write each expression using a single base and a single exponent.**

**17.** $(0.5^2)^2$ $0.5^4$

**18.** $(2.5^9)^0$ $2.5^0$

**19.** $(1.9^5)^3$ $1.9^{15}$

**20.** $(p^{25})^4$ $p^{100}$

**21.** $(p^4)^{25}$ $p^{100}$

**22.** $(5^n)^2$ $5^{2n}$

**23.** $(5^2)^n$ $5^{2n}$

**24.** $(4n)^3$

**25.** $(3^2)^3$ $3^6$

**26.** $(5^2)^2$ $5^4$

**27.** $(99^1)^5$ $99^5$

**28.** $(100^0)^5$ $100^0$

24. Correct as is



**On Your Own Exercises**
Lesson 2.3

**Investigation 1**
Pages 107–108
Practice & Apply: 1–5

**Investigation 2**
Pages 109–110
Practice & Apply: 6–11

**Investigation 3**
Pages 111–113
Practice & Apply: 12–28
Connect & Extend: 29–56

**Assign Anytime**
Mixed Review: 57–59

▶ **Exercises 13c and 29** These are worth going over in class, since they require students to think about numbers that multiply to one million. This previews their study of powers of 10 later in the chapter. If students are having trouble thinking about the exercise, ask them what two equal numbers multiply to one million. They should respond, 1,000 · 1,000. Then ask them whether they can write 1,000 as a power of 10. This should help them with the solution $(10^3)^2$. You can then ask them whether this is the same as $(10^2)^3$.

▶ **Exercises 35–49** These exercises ask students to pull together all of the laws of exponents they have learned and practice them, deciding for each expression which is the appropriate law to use.

## Additional Answers

35. $\left(\frac{7}{3}\right)^5$

36. Not possible

37. $s^{101}$

38. $500^{14}$

39. $6^3$

40. Not possible

41. $2^0$

42. $5^2$

43. $36^b$ or $6^{2b}$

44. $x^{2x}$

45. $d^2$

46. $2^p$

47. $a^{n+m}$

48. $4^2$

49. $10^4$





## Connect & Extend

**29. Preview** Describe two super machines that would stretch a bar of gold to one million times its original length. Possible answer: $(10^2)^3$, $(10^3)^2$

**Math Link**
5,280 feet = 1 mile

**Preview** A one-inch bar of titanium is put through each super machine. How long will it be when it comes out of the machine? Give your answers in inches, feet, and miles.

**30.**
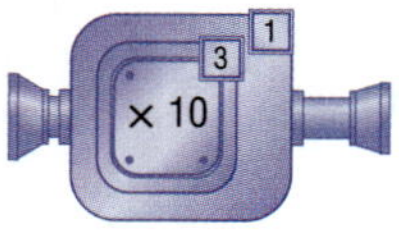


30. 1,000 in.; 83.3 ft; 0.016 mi

**31.**
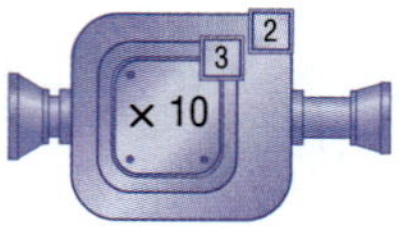


31. 1,000,000 in.; 83,333.3 ft; 15.8 mi

**32.**
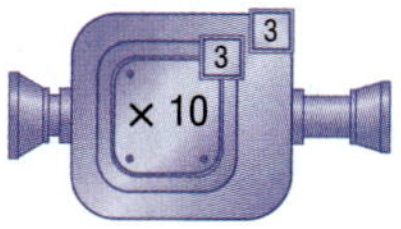


32. 1,000,000,000 in.; 83,333,333.3 ft; 15,782.8 mi

**33.**
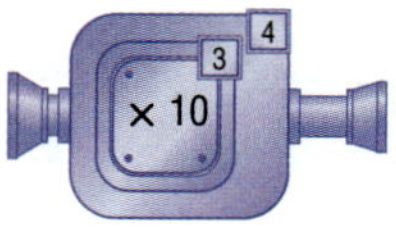


33. 1,000,000,000,000 in.; 83,333,333,333.3 ft; 15,782,828.3 mi

**34.** How long will the bar of copper be when it exits this connection? 300 in.

For Exercises 35–49, rewrite each expression using a single base or a single exponent, if possible. For example, $3^7 \div 5^7$ can be rewritten $\left(\frac{3}{5}\right)^7$. You will have to decide which exponent laws to apply. Here are the laws you have seen so far.

| Product Laws | Quotient Laws | Power of a Power Law |
|---|---|---|
| $a^b \cdot a^c = a^{b+c}$ | $a^b \div a^c = a^{b-c}$ | $(a^b)^c = a^{b \cdot c}$ |
| $a^c \cdot b^c = (a \cdot b)^c$ | $a^c \div b^c = (a \div b)^c$ | |

35–49. See margin.

**35.** $7^5 \div 3^5$ **36.** $7^5 \cdot 5^7$ **37.** $s^{100} \cdot s$

**38.** $1{,}000^{14} \div 2^{14}$ **39.** $6^5 \div 6^2$ **40.** $100^{100} \div 25^{25}$

**41.** $(2^0)^3$ **42.** $10^2 \cdot \left(\frac{1}{2}\right)^2$ **43.** $6^b \cdot 6^b$

**44.** $(x^2)^x$ **45.** $d^2 \cdot d^0$ **46.** $10^p \div 5^p$

**47.** $a^n \cdot a^m$ **48.** $(4x)^2 \div x^2$ **49.** $(10^2)^3 \div 10^2$

**50. In Your Own Words** Choose one of the quotient laws of exponents and explain the law so a fifth grader could understand it. You can refer to stretching and shrinking machines if they help you explain. Explanations will vary.

**Challenge** **Use what you know about exponents to write each expression in a simpler form.** 51–56. See margin.

**51.** $m^3n^5 \cdot m^5n^2$

**52.** $a^3b^4c \cdot 2ab^3c^2$

**53.** $14^p \div 7^{2p}$

**54.** $2y^3z \cdot (6yz^4)^2$

**55.** $\dfrac{x^2yz^3}{x^3y^2z}$

**56.** $\dfrac{15m^3n^2}{60k^3m^4n^2}$

## Mixed Review

**57. Geometry** A rectangle has a perimeter of 12 feet. Its length is 4 feet. Find the width. 2 feet

**58.** The circumference of a circle is 35 centimeters. Find the diameter. State your answers in terms of $\pi$. $\frac{35}{\pi}$ cm

**59. Statistics** Karina kept a record in minutes of the length of each phone call she made last week. Here are the results.

| | | | | | | | | |
|---|---|---|---|---|---|---|---|---|
| 7 | 37 | 3 | 24 | 29 | 54 | 12 | 18 | 25 |
| 15 | 19 | 22 | 32 | 35 | 18 | 21 | 15 | 22 |

**a.** Make a histogram of the phone call times. Use ten-minute intervals on the horizontal axis.

**b.** Describe the distribution of phone call times. Possible answer: There was one call between 50 and 60 min, but the rest were less than 40 min long. The majority, 12 of the 18, were between 10 and 30 min long.

59a. **Phone Call Lengths**

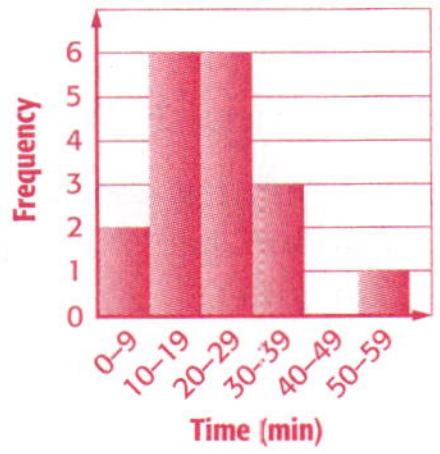




## Additional Answers

51. $m^8n^7$

52. $2a^4b^7c^3$

53. $\left(\frac{2}{7}\right)^p$

54. $72y^5z^9$

55. $\dfrac{z^2}{xy}$

56. $\dfrac{1}{4k^3m}$

On Your Own Exercises

▶ **Exercises 51–56** Review these exercises in class. If students have difficulty, ask them to regroup the expressions to make computation easier. For example, in Exercise 51, students can rewrite the expression as $m^3m^5 \cdot n^5n^2$.

## Quick Check

**Informal Assessment** Students should be able to:

✔ model the behavior of exponents using stretching and shrinking machines

✔ understand and apply the quotient laws of exponents

✔ understand and apply the power of a power law of exponents

## Quick Quiz

Fill in the missing input, machine, or output in each situation.

**1.** 3 cm

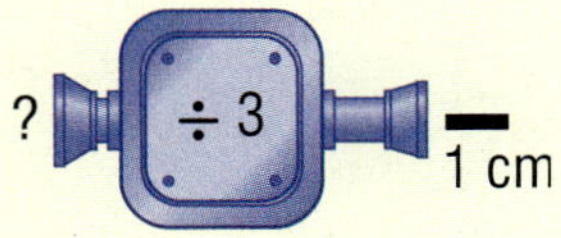


**2.** ÷ 5

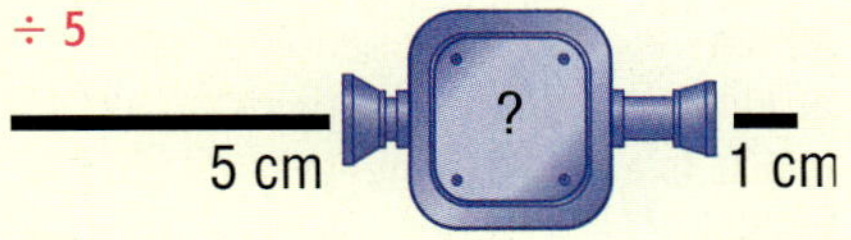


**3.** × 2

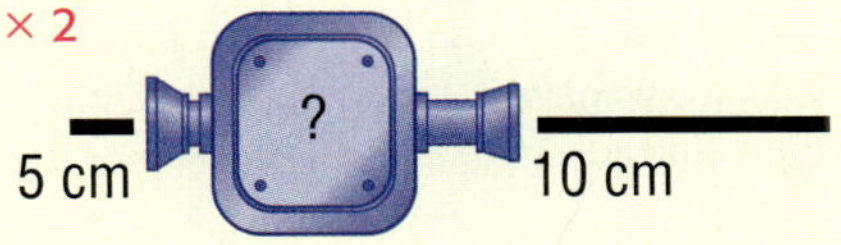


**4.** 10,000 cm

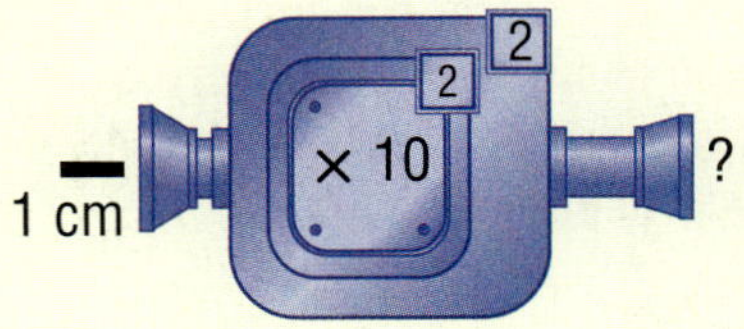


Rewrite these as simply as you can using rules of exponents.

**5.** $2^4 \div 2^1$ $2^3$

**6.** $7^n \div 2$ $7^n \div 2$

**7.** $25^n \cdot 4^n$ $100^n$

**8.** $(4^3)^n$ $4^{3n}$

**9.** $24^{10} \cdot \left(\frac{1}{3}\right)^{10}$ $8^{10}$

CHAPTER 2

# Review & Self-Assessment

## Chapter Summary

This summary helps students recall the major topics of the chapter.

## Vocabulary

Students should be able to explain each of the terms listed in the vocabulary section.

**Additional Answers**

2. Possible answer: Find any factor pair for the number, and draw branches from the number to each factor. If a factor is prime, circle it. If a factor is not prime, find a factor pair for it. Continue until you cannot factor any further. When you are done, the product of the circled numbers is the prime factorization. Here is a factor tree for 30. The prime factorization of 30 is 5 • 3 • 2.

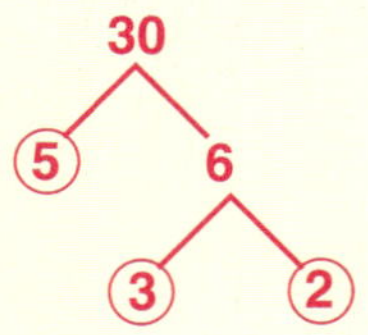


3. Sample answer: You can determine if a number is a multiple of another number by dividing that number by the other and if it results in a whole number than it is a multiple.
4. Sample answer: Lisa is correct. Two numbers will always have a common multiple. By multiplying the two numbers together, you will always be able to find a number that is a multiple of both.
5. Sample answer: No, it is not possible for a number to have fewer multiples than factors because every number has an infinite amount of multiples.

CHAPTER 2

# Review & Self-Assessment

## Chapter Summary

In this chapter, you used the idea of stretching machines to help think about *factors, multiples,* and *prime* and *composite numbers.* You learned to find the prime factorization of a number and to find the *greatest common factor* or *least common multiple* of a group of numbers.

Stretching and shrinking machines also helped you understand the laws of exponents.

| Product Laws | Quotient Laws | Power of a Power Law |
|---|---|---|
| $a^b \cdot a^c = a^{b+c}$ | $a^b \div a^c = a^{b-c}$ | $(a^b)^c = a^{b \cdot c}$ |
| $a^c \cdot b^c = (a \cdot b)^c$ | $a^c \div b^c = (a \div b)^c$ | |

### Vocabulary

- base
- common factor
- common multiple
- composite number
- exponent
- factor
- factor pair
- greatest common factor, GCF
- least common multiple, LCM
- multiple
- order of operations
- power
- prime number
- product law of exponents
- relatively prime

1. Possible answer: A prime number has only two factors, 1 and the number itself. A composite number has more than two factors. Possible examples: 7 and 13 are prime; 6 and 9 are composite.

2–5. See margin.

## Strategies and Applications

The questions in this section will help you review and apply the important ideas and strategies developed in this chapter.

**Understanding and applying concepts related to factors and multiples**

**1.** Describe the difference between a prime number and a composite number. Give two examples of each.

**2.** Explain how to use a factor tree to find the prime factorization of a number. Illustrate your explanation with an example.

**3.** How can you determine if a number is a multiple of another number? Explain.

**4.** Lisa and Claudio are discussing whether or not two numbers will always have a common multiple. Lisa says that two numbers always have a common multiple while Claudio says that it is possible for two numbers not to have a common multiple. Who is correct? Explain your reasoning.

**5.** Is it possible for a number to have fewer multiples than factors? Discuss.

**6.** Kamilah set her computer's clock to ding every 20 minutes, quack every 30 minutes, and chime every 45 minutes. At noon, her computer dinged, quacked, and chimed at the same time.

**a.** In how many minutes will Kamilah's computer ding and quack at the same time? 60

**b.** In how many minutes will her computer quack and chime at the same time? 90



120 CHAPTER 2 Exponents

**c.** In how many minutes will her computer ding, chime, and quack at the same time? 180

**d.** What sounds will the computer make at 4:30 P.M.? Quack and chime

**e.** How many times per hour will Kamilah's computer clock ding? Quack? Chime? 3 times, twice, once

## Strategies and Applications

The questions in this section will help you review and apply the important ideas and strategies developed in this chapter.

### Working with stretching and shrinking machines

**If a 1-cm stick of gum is sent through each super machine, how long will it be when it exits?**

**7.**

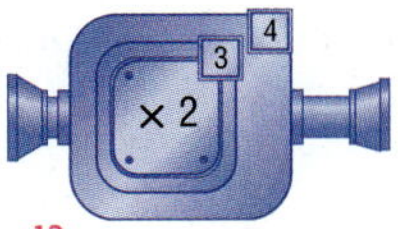


$2^{12}$ cm, or 4,096 cm

**8.**

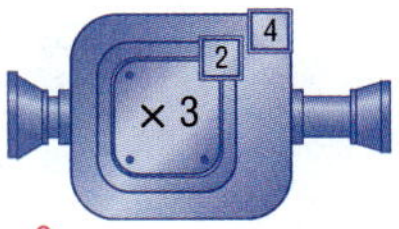


$3^8$ cm, or 6,561 cm

**Find a single repeater machine to do the same work as each connection.**

**9.**

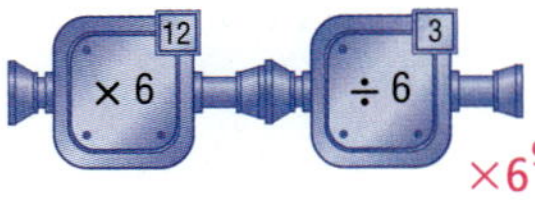


$\times 6^9$

**10.**

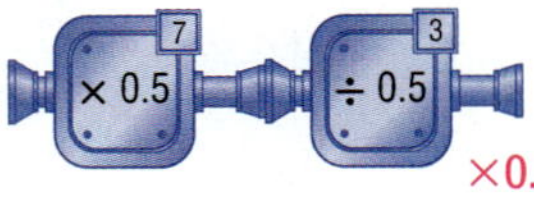


$\times 0.5^4$

### Understanding the laws of exponents

**11.** Explain why $a^b \div a^c = a^{b-c}$. You can refer to stretching and shrinking machines if they help you explain.

**12.** Explain why $2^0 = 1$. You can refer to stretching and shrinking machines if they help you explain.

**13.** Explain why $(5^2)^2$ and $5^2 \cdot 5^2$ both equal $5^4$ when they each follow a different law of exponents.

## Demonstrating Skills

**Simplify each expression.**

**14.** $2^3 \cdot 2^4$ $2^7$ **15.** $(7^6)^2$ $7^{12}$ **16.** $4^2 \cdot 4^2$ $4^4$ **17.** $11^7 \div 11^4$ $11^3$ **18.** $\frac{x^{12}}{x^9}$ $x^3$

11. Possible answer: If you put a stick through a $\times a^b$ machine and then through a $\div a^c$ machine, each $\div a$ shrink cancels a $\cdot a$ stretch, leaving $(b - c)$ stretches.

12. Possible answers: A $\times 2^0$ machine doubles the length of a stick 0 times. In other words, it does not change the length. This is the same as putting the stick through a $\times 1$ machine.

13. Possible answer: Both $(5^2)^2$ and $5^2 \cdot 5^2$ produce the same result of $5^4$ because $2 \cdot 2$ and $2 + 2$ both equal 4.



***Review & Self-Assessment***
**Chapter 2**

▶ **Exercises 9 and 10** As students complete these exercises they may be confused as to what the question is really asking. Rephrase the question so that students realize they need to simplify the work done by the repeater machines into the task of one machine. This can be accomplished by using their rules for exponents.

▶ **Exercise 17** Students may be confused because the operation in this exercise is addition and none of their laws of exponents had anything to do with the bases being added. This is the entire point of the question—to make sure that students realize that the only time the laws apply is when the bases are multiplied or divided.

▶ **Exercises 30–34** As students work through these questions, they may not see how they can rewrite the expression since the bases are not the same. Tell the students to write the question out the long way using repeated multiplication. At this point, the students will see that since the powers are the same, the bases can be multiplied together.

▶ **Exercises 60–64** Review the difference between greatest common factor and least common multiple with the students prior to them beginning work on these questions.



21. False; $5^{16}$
24. False; $3^{10}$
35. $a^3b^5c^5$
36. $2^{2+xy}x^2y^6$
37. $3lm^6n^2$
45. 1, 2, 3, 6, 9, 18
46. 1, 2, 4, 8, 16, 32, 64
47. 1, 43
48. 1, 2, 4, 8, 16, 32
49. 1, 11, 121
50. Sample answers: 14, 21, 28
51. Sample answers: 22, 44, 66
52. Sample answers: 84, 126, 168
53. Sample answers: 160, 240, 320
54. Sample answers: 208, 312, 416
60. GCF: 3; LCM: 36
61. GCF: 1; LCM: 253
62. GCF: 14; LCM: 28
63. GCF: 6; LCM: 54
64. GCF: 4; LCM: 40
65. Yes, 1,392 is a multiple of 8. Sample answer: 1,392 is evenly divisible by 8 174 times.
66. No, 7 is not a factor of 227. Sample answer: 227 is not evenly divisible by 7. So, 7 cannot be a factor of 227.

**Tell whether each equation is true or false. If an equation is false, rewrite the expression to the right of the equal sign to make it true.**

**19.** $2^4 \cdot 2^3 = 2^7$ True **20.** $(3^3)^3 = 3^6$ False; $3^9$ **21.** $5^{20} \div 5^4 = 5^{24}$

**22.** $(7^3)^0 = 7$ False; 1 **23.** $a^{10} \div a^5 = a^5$ True **24.** $3^4 \cdot 3^2 \cdot 3^4 = 3^{32}$

**Tell what number should replace each question mark to make each statement true.**

**25.** $4^2 \cdot ?^7 = 4^9$ 4 **26.** $(7^3)^? = 1$ 0 **27.** $\frac{10^5}{10^2} = 10^?$ 3

**28.** $\left(\frac{1}{4}\right)^2 \cdot ? = \left(\frac{1}{4}\right)^3$ $\frac{1}{4}$ **29.** $(1.2^7)^? = 1.2^{21}$ 3

**Rewrite each expression using a single exponent.**

**30.** $15^5 \times 10^5$ $150^5$ **31.** $2^8 \cdot 9^8$ $18^8$ **32.** $\left(\frac{1}{5}\right)^7 \cdot \left(\frac{1}{3}\right)^7$ $\left(\frac{1}{15}\right)^7$

**33.** $2{,}000^2 \cdot 4^2$ $8{,}000^2$ **34.** $\left(\frac{2}{3}\right)^9 \cdot \left(\frac{2}{5}\right)^9$ $\left(\frac{4}{15}\right)^9$

**Use what you know about exponents to write each expression in simplest form.**

**35.** $a^2bc^3 \cdot ab^4c^2$ **36.** $(2xy^3)^2 \cdot \frac{2}{y^2}$ **37.** $3mn \cdot lm^5n$

**38.** $\frac{6a^4b^8}{2ab^3}$ $3a^3b^5$ **39.** $\frac{7m^4n^4}{21l^2m^3n}$ $\frac{1mn^3}{3l^2}$

**Determine whether each pair of numbers is relatively prime. For those that are not, give one common factor of the pair.**

**40.** 37 and 42 Yes **41.** 8 and 9 Yes **42.** 51 and 119 No; 17

**43.** 18 and 21 No; 3 **44.** 100 and 101 Yes

**List the factors of each number.**

**45.** 18 **46.** 64 **47.** 43 **48.** 32 **49.** 121

**List three multiples of each number.**

**50.** 7 **51.** 11 **52.** 42 **53.** 80 **54.** 104

**Give the prime factorization of each number. Use exponents when appropriate.**

**55.** 246 $2 \cdot 3 \cdot 41$ **56.** 56 $2^3 \cdot 7$ **57.** 81 $3^4$ **58.** 150 $2 \cdot 3 \cdot 5^2$ **59.** 71 $1 \cdot 71$

**Find the greatest common factor and the least common multiple of each pair of numbers.**

**60.** 9 and 12 **61.** 11 and 23 **62.** 14 and 28

**63.** 6 and 54 **64.** 8 and 20

**65.** Is 1,392 a multiple of 8? Explain how you know.

**66.** Is 7 a factor of 227? Explain how you know.

70. Student answers may vary. Sample answer: Computerized robots could move the pieces at a faster rate following a logical pattern making the work go faster.
71. No, there are more moves to make than there are minutes in which the average person lives.
72. Sample answer: It is a logical thinking exercise which involves looking for patterns and developing formulas to solve the puzzle.

*Show your work.* To find when both busses will be in the station, find the LCM of 12 and 10. Multiples of 12: 12, 24, 36, 48, 60, 72, … Multiples of 10: 10, 20, 30, 40, 50, 60, … The LCM is 60, so both busses will be in the station in 60 minutes.

*Answer:* 60 minutes

**67.** List all the common multiples of 3 and 5 which are less than 50. 15, 30, 45

**68.** Dalton said, "One of the factors of my number is 18. What other numbers must also be factors of my number? 2, 3, 6, 9

**69.** Diana said, "I am thinking of a number. It is less than 50. 9 is one of its 9 factors and the sum of its digits is nine. What is my number? 36

## Tower of Hanoi

**70.** How might the use of technology make the moving of the tower of disks from one rod to the next become easier to complete?

**71.** Would the Tower of Hanoi puzzle be possible for you to solve in your lifetime if you moved one disk per minute? Explain your reasoning.

**72.** Why is the Tower of Hanoi puzzle considered a mathematical exercise?

## Test-Taking Practice

*SHORT RESPONSE*

**1** A large tour group is waiting at a bus station for two buses to visit New York City. One bus comes every 12 minutes and a second bus comes every 10 minutes. Suppose both buses have just left the station. At the earliest, how many minutes will the group have to wait for both buses to return to the station?

***Show your work.***

***Answer*** ____________________

*MULTIPLE CHOICE*

**2** Find the GCF of 18 and 24.
**A** 2
**B** 3
**C** 4
**(D)** 6

**3** Find the LCM of 4, 8, and 16.
**F** 24
**(G)** 16
**H** 48
**J** 64

**4** Which list contains only prime numbers?
**A** 5, 21, 33
**B** 7, 13, 15
**(C)** 11, 37, 79
**D** 27, 31, 63

**5** Find the prime factorization of 45.
**F** $2 \cdot 3 \cdot 5$
**G** $2 \cdot 2 \cdot 5$
**(H)** $3 \cdot 3 \cdot 5$
**J** $5 \cdot 5 \cdot 3 \cdot 3$

**6** Which factorization is a prime factorization?
**A** $2 \cdot 42 \cdot 5$
**(B)** $2 \cdot 3 \cdot 5$
**C** $3 \cdot 5 \cdot 6$
**D** $3 \cdot 3 \cdot 9$

**7** Find the GCF of 2, 3, and 6.
**(F)** 1
**G** 2
**H** 3
**J** 6



Review & Self-Assessment
Chapter 2

▶ **Exercise 1** Remind students that this question is really asking for the least common multiple of 12 and 10.

CHAPTER 3

# Signed Numbers

## Chapter Overview

The chapter begins with an Inquiry Investigation to introduce addition and subtraction with signed numbers. Students play a game that is a prelude to the "walking the number line" model. As students develop their understanding of signed numbers, they move from the concrete model to a more abstract level of thinking.

Students build on this understanding as they learn how to multiply and divide with signed numbers. Finally, students learn to find range, mean, median, and mode of a set of data that includes positive and negative numbers.

## The Big Picture

| Links to the Past | Chapter 3 | Links to the Future |
|---|---|---|
| **Course 1, Chapter 4** (pp. 196–287) Fraction and Decimal Operations | **Lesson 3.1** (p. 126) Add and Subtract with Negative Numbers | **Course 3, Chapter 5** (pp. 204–257) Algebraic Expressions |
| **Course 1, Chapter 4** (pp. 196–287) Fraction and Decimal Operations | **Lesson 3.2** (p. 154) Multiply and Divide with Negative Numbers | **Course 3, Chapter 5** (pp. 204–257) Algebraic Expressions |

# Mathematical Background

For many people, signed-number arithmetic is a problem area. Though the rules of signed-number arithmetic are sometimes hard to state in words, the patterns make sense once the concept of signed numbers is clear.

Until we encounter signed numbers for the first time, we have a sense of numbers meaning "how much" there is of something: how much money, how much weight, how much time. Negative numbers can also be thought of that way—how much debt, for example. The idea that a debt is "negative money" can sometimes help students think about signed-number arithmetic, but it may be a subtle idea.

Here's the subtlety. We say that $-5$ is less than $-2$, because negative 5 is to the left of negative 2 on the number line. But if we are relating negative numbers to debts, we also say (correctly) that $-5$ represents a greater debt. How can $-5$ be both less than and greater than $-2$?

**Magnitude** Sometimes we need to think about the magnitude of a number (also called the absolute value of the number, or how far the number is from zero) independently from the "direction" of that distance. We encounter this distinction in real life. Distance from the surface of the Earth (in the air or down a mine shaft) is positive, but altitude or elevation includes direction and can be positive or negative. In fact, distance, including the "distance" a number is from 0, is always positive. Speed is independent of direction; velocity includes direction.

When we think of greater and lesser debts, we are looking only at the magnitude of the debt and ignoring the fact that it is all debt (all "negative"). When we think of bank balances, we must keep track of sign as well as magnitude, in order to know whether the balance is positive or negative.

**Order** When we say that $-5 < -2$ or that $5 > -20$, we are talking about order on a number line. The set of all real numbers (numbers like $-\frac{3}{8}$, $2\pi$, $4\frac{2}{3}$, 43.618, $-0.00001$, $1.27 \times 10^{-23}$, 0, $-12$, and so on) has a property called *order* that makes such comparisons possible. All numbers on the number line are real numbers; all real numbers are points on the number line.

As students progress into more advanced mathematics and physics in high school, they will encounter other numbers (complex numbers, for example, and vectors) that cannot be ordered the way the real numbers can. But the ideas of magnitude and direction that students are learning right now will hold for these new numbers as well; in fact, arithmetic with these new numbers will be very similar to arithmetic with signed numbers in that it takes into account both magnitude and direction.

## Additional Reading

According to Lampert and Cobb in "Communication and Language," talking helps students move from concrete objects to related mathematics concepts. The process of coming to see concrete situations in mathematical terms is called *mathematizing.* In Lesson 3.1, two students are shown communicating their different ways of thinking about negative numbers. Throughout this chapter, students discuss different models of negative numbers until they are comfortable performing operations without the models.

CHAPTER 3

# Planning Guide

## Lesson Resources

| | Lesson 3.1 (Pacing: 7 days) | Lesson 3.2 (Pacing: 5 days) |
|---|---|---|
| **Lesson Title** | **Add and Subtract with Negative Numbers** (p. 126) | **Multiply and Divide with Negative Numbers** (p. 154) |
| **Lesson Objectives** | • To add and subtract signed numbers<br>• To use number sense when working with signed numbers<br>• To predict the sign of a sum or difference involving negative and positive numbers | • To multiply and divide with signed numbers<br>• To predict the sign of a product or quotient involving signed numbers<br>• To develop number sense with signed numbers<br>• To find mean, median, and mode for a set of data |
| **Materials** | two-color counters* (or dry beans), mat, blank sheets of paper, paper arrow, direction cube, walking cube, Lesson 3.1 Masters 1, 2, 3, 4, 5, 6, 7, 8 | |
| ***Quick Review Math Handbook*** | **Lesson 1.4** Integer Operations | **Lesson 1.4** Integer Operations |
| **Print Resources** | CRM Study Guide and Intervention (p. 6)<br>CRM Skills Practice (p. 7)<br>CRM Problem-Solving Practice (p. 8)<br>CRM Enrichment (p. 9)<br>• Investigation Notebook and Reflection Journal<br>• Differentiation Handbook | CRM Study Guide and Intervention (p. 16)<br>CRM Skills Practice (p. 17)<br>CRM Problem-Solving Practice (p. 18)<br>CRM Enrichment (p. 19)<br>• Investigation Notebook and Reflection Journal<br>• Differentiation Handbook |
| **Technology Resources** | TeacherWorks Plus<br>Classroom Presentation Toolkit<br>ExamView Assessment Suite<br>StudentWorks Plus<br>Math Online Brain Pops • Concepts in Motion | TeacherWorks Plus<br>Classroom Presentation Toolkit<br>ExamView Assessment Suite<br>StudentWorks Plus<br>Math Online Brain Pops • Concepts in Motion |

*Included in the Impact Mathematics Manipulative Kit

# Assessment Resources

## MARS Assessment: Teaching with Purpose

### Integers

In *Integers,* students find pairs of positive and negative integers with a sum of zero. Students also perform simple addition and subtraction with positive integers, negative integers, and zero.

### Targeting the Task

- **Diagnostic**—Use Exercise 1 in the *Integers* assessment to determine students' understanding of how to add simple positive and negative integers. For those students who do not have this understanding, completing this unit is needed.
- **Formative**—Exercise 4 can be administered individually according to the lessons.
- **Summative**—Administer the complete *Integers* performance-based assessment.

CRM **Chapter 3 MARS Assessment** (pp. 35–38)

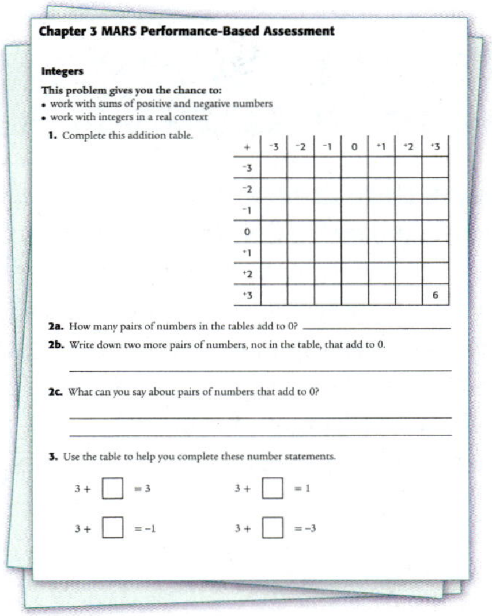

**Chapter 3 MARS Performance-Based Assessment**

**Integers**

**This problem gives you the chance to:**
- work with sums of positive and negative numbers
- work with integers in a real context

**1.** Complete this addition table.

| + | ⁻3 | ⁻2 | ⁻1 | 0 | ⁺1 | ⁺2 | ⁺3 |
|---|---|---|---|---|---|---|---|
| ⁻3 | | | | | | | |
| ⁻2 | | | | | | | |
| ⁻1 | | | | | | | |
| 0 | | | | | | | |
| ⁺1 | | | | | | | |
| ⁺2 | | | | | | | |
| ⁺3 | | | | | | | 6 |

**2a.** How many pairs of numbers in the tables add to 0? ______

**2b.** Write down two more pairs of numbers, not in the table, that add to 0.

______

**2c.** What can you say about pairs of numbers that add to 0?

______

______

**3.** Use the table to help you complete these number statements.

3 + ☐ = 3 　　 3 + ☐ = 1

3 + ☐ = −1 　　 3 + ☐ = −3

## Assessment Planning Guide

Assessments are available for investigations, lessons, and chapters.

**ExamView® Assessment Suite** Customize and create multiple versions of tests and quizzes.

| | Student Edition | Teacher Edition | Other Resources |
|---|---|---|---|
| **Diagnostic** | | | CRM Chapter 3 Pretest (pp. 21–24)<br>Math Online Online Chapter Quiz |
| **Formative** | Share & Summarize (pp. 130, 139, 142, 145, 147, 156, 159, 161, 164) | Troubleshooting (pp. 130, 132, 138, 156, 159, 162, 164)<br>On the Spot Assessment (pp. 147, 164)<br>Quick Check (pp. 153, 168)<br>Quick Quiz (pp. 153, 168) | CRM Quick Quiz (pp. 153, 168) |
| **Summative** | Review & Self-Assessment (pp. 169–171) | | CRM Chapter 3 Test: Forms A and B (pp. 25–32)<br>CRM Standardized Test Practice (pp. 39–40) |
| **Performance-Based** | In Your Own Words (pp. 155, 168) | | CRM MARS Performance-Based Assessment (pp. 35–38)<br>CRM Chapter Performance Assessment (pp. 33–34) |

# Differentiated Instruction

## *Reaching* All Learners

Below are suggestions on differentiating the materials presented in this chapter. Additional modifications should be considered.

### Approaching Level AL

**Temperature Change** During Lesson 3.1 look up the temperature for the day. Ask students to record, for the next ten days, how the temperature is changing based on today's temperature using signed numbers. It may be helpful to bring in a newspaper clipping of the weather or have a computer with a weather website available for the students to check the temperatures. Once the ten days have past, ask the students to determine the total amount of change that occurred – find the sum of the change.

### Beyond Level BL

**Review Game** Have students work together to create a game involving signed numbers. It should not mimic the game used in Lesson 3.1 Investigation 2. The game can use any skills they have learned so far, but must focus on skills from Chapter 3, especially signed numbers. Once the games are complete, allow the students time to share their games with the class. It will be a great opportunity for the students to review for tests or quizzes.

### On Level OL

**Measures of Central Tendency** Have students take their quiz and/or test scores for the term and compute the mean, mode, median, and range. Then ask the students to decide which measure best represents how they are doing in the course to this point. Also, ask the students if they think that the mean represents the grade that shows how much they understand the content of the course. This is an excellent way to end the chapter following Lesson 3.2.

### English Language Learners ELL

**Language Day** Have students spend time in class allowing them to share their first language with the class. Set aside one day for each different language. Ask students to share with the rest of the class the terminology of their first language related to the day's lesson. This will allow students to use their native language and relate to what you are discussing in English. The English Language Learner students will benefit from conversing in English and making the connection of their first language to the content of the day.

**KEY**

AL Approaching Level OL On Level BL Beyond Level ELL English Language Learners

## *Intervention Planning Guide*

CRM Assess students' prerequisite skills and knowledge using the **Chapter Pretest** found in the Chapter 3 Resource Masters, pp. 21–24.

| Intensive Intervention<br>two or more years below grade level | Strategic Intervention<br>below grade level | On Level | Beyond Level |
|---|---|---|---|
| **If** students miss 75% of the exercises:<br>**Then** use *Math Triumphs,* an intensive intervention | **If** students miss 50% of the exercises:<br>**Then** choose a resource: | **If** students miss 25% of the exercises:<br>**Then** choose a resource: | **If** students miss 0%–10% of the exercises:<br>**Then** choose a resource: |
| *Math Triumphs,* Grade 7<br>• Chapter 8: Integer Operations | CRM Study Guide and Intervention (pp. 6, 16)<br>• Investigation Notebook and Reflection Journal<br>• Differentiation Handbook<br>Math Online Brain Pops • Concepts in Motion | CRM Skills Practice (pp. 7, 17)<br>CRM Problem-Solving Practice (pp. 8, 18)<br>• Investigation Notebook and Reflection Journal | CRM Enrichment (pp. 9, 19)<br>• Differentiation Handbook |

## *Literature Connections*

### Recommended Outside Reading for Students

**Nonfiction**

Reimer, Luetta. *Mathematicians Are People, Too: Stories from the Lives of Great Mathematicians.* Pearson Learning, 1990.

This book relates stories of mathematical discovery through the ages and includes biographies of great mathematicians. The historical approach to math provides an enjoyable tool for interdisciplinary study.

**Fiction**

Tahan, Malba. *The Man Who Counted: A Collection of Mathematical Adventures.* W. W. Norton & Co., 1993.

This set of stories and puzzles follows the adventures of a mathematically talented man who solves conflicts and gives advice in old Arabia.

### McGraw-Hill Professional Development

Targeted professional development has been articulated throughout the *IMPACT Mathematics* series. The **McGraw-Hill Professional Development Video Library** provides short videos that support the mathematics standards. Log on to www.glencoe.com.

Model Lessons

Instructional Strategies

CHAPTER 3

# Signed Numbers

## Introduce

**Soaring to New Heights** Before having students read the chapter opener, you might engage the students in a discussion about how they would measure elevation. How would you compare the elevation of Mt. Rainier and Mt. Everest? Clearly, there is a need for some kind of elevation scale. Once the need for a scale is established, you and your students can discuss where to set the 0 mark on the scale. Then it will make sense to measure the elevation of other points from that point.

The level of the ocean intuitively makes sense for the 0 mark since it is the breakpoint between land and water. So, a place with an elevation lower than the ocean level would have an elevation less than 0. Thus, an elevation scale must involve negative numbers.

**Think About It** Since 30,323 is greater than 29,028, the Dead Sea must be below sea level.

CHAPTER 3

# Signed Numbers

## Real-Life Math

**Soaring to New Heights** How high is the highest mountain? How deep is the deepest part of the ocean? How are height and depth measured?

We call height and depth *elevation.* We measure elevation from sea level, the average level of the ocean. Parts of the world that are at sea level have an elevation of 0. Denver, the "mile-high" city, is approximately one mile above sea level. Its elevation is approximately one mile. Death Valley is 282 feet below sea level. We say that its elevation is −282 feet.

**Think About It** If the Dead Sea is 30,324 feet less than Mt. Everest's elevation, is it below sea level?

### Contents in Brief



**Math Online** Take the **Chapter Readiness Quiz** at glencoe.com.

### Chapter Resources

- CRM Chapter 3 Resource Masters
- CRM English/Spanish Family Letter (pp. 1–2)
- CRM Lesson Masters (pp. 11–15)
- CRM Chapter 3 Pretest (pp. 21–24)
- CRM Chapter 3 Test (pp. 25–32)
- Math Online Online Readiness Quiz • eGlossary

# Dear Family,

In Chapter 3, the class will be working with negative numbers. Students will use numbers that have negative signs in sums, differences, products, quotients, exponents, and graphs.

### Key Concept–Addition of Signed Numbers

The class will use a variety of models to represent the addition of signed numbers. Two models are shown below for finding the sum of 3 and −2.

**Two-Color Chip Model**

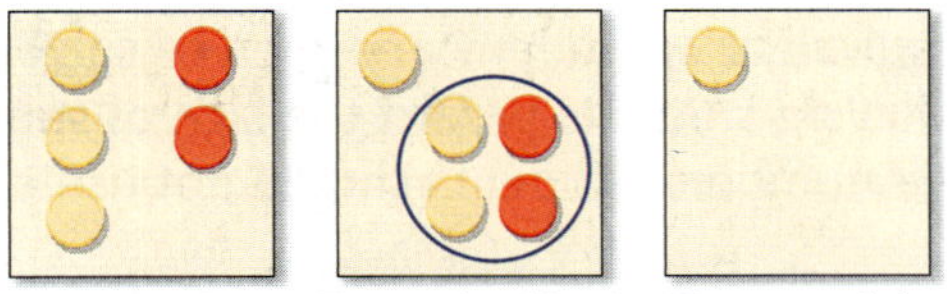

The numbers 3 and −2 are modeled. | The grouping of 2 and −2 forms a zero pair. | The sum equals 1.

**Number-Line Model**

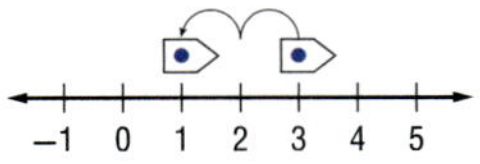


Your student will also use models to simplify expressions involving subtraction, multiplication, and division. In the final investigation, the class will apply these skills to analyze data sets involving signed numbers.

### Home Activities

Look for occurrences of negative numbers in real-world situations.

- Elevations below sea level
- The national debt
- Temperatures below zero
- Sports-related situations, such as below par golf scores and football carries resulting in loss of yardage
- Balances of overdrawn bank accounts

## Family Letter

Another version of the Family Letter, available in English and Spanish, is found in the Chapter 3 Resource Masters. You may want to send a copy of this letter home with your students.

**Key Concept–Addition of Signed Numbers** Students may feel overwhelmed by the variety of methods that are available to solve signed number problems. Assure them that mastering all of the methods are not necessary. They represent a variety of ways to solve the same problem. The students can select the method that they relate with the best.

### Home Activities

- Signed numbers are all around. It will be helpful to students to understand that any decrease can be expressed as a negative number.
- Ask students to talk with their families and discuss where they use negative numbers in their daily lives.

LESSON 3.1

# Add and Subtract with Negative Numbers

### Objectives

- To add and subtract signed numbers
- To use number sense when working with signed numbers
- To predict the sign of a sum or difference involving negative and positive numbers

## *Overview*

Students model how to add and subtract signed numbers. The students then learn to "walk the number line" to learn how to compute sums of signed numbers. The lesson then goes on to identify several equivalent operations and then to solve simple inequalities. The lesson closes by having students predict the sign of sums and differences of positive and negative numbers. Students should not use calculators.

## *Advance Preparation*

You will need a cube with three faces labeled *Ship* and three faces labeled *Shark,* a cube with faces labeled *F1, F2, F3, B1, B2,* and *B3*, and several sheets of blank paper.

| | Summary | Materials | On Your Own Exercises (pp. 148–153) | Assessment Opportunities |
|---|---|---|---|---|
| **Investigation 1** (p. 128) Pacing: 2 days | Students will learn to add and subtract negative numbers using the Two-Color Chip model. | two-color counters (or dry beans), mat | Practice & Apply: 1–6<br>Mixed Review: 70–79 | • Share & Summarize (p. 130)<br>• Troubleshooting (p. 130) |
| **Inquiry Investigation 2** (p. 131) Pacing: 1 day | Students will use a game to familiarize themselves with signed number operations in an informal way. | Lesson 3.1 Master 1, Lesson 3.1 Master 2, blank sheets of paper, paper arrow, direction cube, walking cube | | • Troubleshooting (p. 132) |
| **Investigation 3** (p. 134) Pacing: 1 day | Students are introduced to the "walking the number line" model for adding and subtracting with signed numbers. | Lesson 3.1 Master 3, Lesson 3.1 Master 4, Lesson 3.1 Master 5 | Practice & Apply: 7–27<br>Connect & Extend: 44–45<br>Mixed Review: 70–79 | • Share & Summarize (p. 139)<br>• Troubleshooting (p. 138) |
| **Investigation 4** (p. 140) Pacing: 1 day | Students use the number line pictures to discover two sets of equivalent operations. | | Practice & Apply: 28–38<br>Connect & Extend: 46–47<br>Mixed Review: 70–79 | • Share & Summarize (p. 142) |
| **Investigation 5** (p. 143) Pacing: 1 day | Students solve inequalities with signed numbers. | | Practice & Apply: 39–40<br>Connect & Extend: 48–61<br>Mixed Review: 70–79 | • Share & Summarize (p. 145) |
| **Investigation 6** (p. 146) Pacing: 1 day | Students predict the sign of sums and differences involving signed numbers. | | Practice & Apply: 41–43<br>Connect & Extend: 62–68<br>Mixed Review: 70–79 | • On the Spot Assessment (p. 147)<br>• Share & Summarize (p. 147) |

# Leveled Lesson Resources

CRM *Available in:* **Chapter 3 Resource Masters**

Also on TeacherWorks™ Lesson 3.1

## Study Guide and Intervention (p. 6) AL

**Lesson 3.1 Study Guide and Intervention**
***Add and Subtract with Negative Numbers***

To add or subtract integers, it is helpful to use counters or a number line.

**Example 1** Use a chip model to find 4 + (−6).

- Use a chip model.
- Combine a set of 4 positive counters and a set of 6 negative counters on a mat.
- Make zero pairs with one positive chip and one negative chip.
- Remove the zero pairs from the mat.
- The chips that are left represent the answer.

4 + (−6)   4 + (−6) = −2

**Example 2** Use a number line to find 4 + (−6).

- Walk the number line.
- Start at 4.
- The operation is addition, so face the pointer to the right.
- You are adding a negative number, −6. Move backward six spaces.

End: −2 Start: 4

**Exercises**
Draw chip models to show how to find each sum or difference.

**1.** −5 + (−2) **2.** 8 − 1 **3.** −7 − 10

Walk the number line to compute the sum or difference.

**4.** 16 + (−11) **5.** −8 − (−6) **6.** −10 + 4

**7.** −3.75 + 4.5 **8.** $\frac{25}{4} - (-\frac{14}{4})$ **9.** $-6\frac{2}{5} - \frac{4}{5}$

## Skills Practice (p. 7) AL OL

**Lesson 3.1 Skills Practice**
***Add and Subtract with Negative Numbers***

Draw chip models to show how to find each sum or difference.

**1.** 5 + (−8) **2.** −3 − 3

Walk the number line to find each sum or difference.

**3.** −3 − (−8) **4.** −7 + (−7)

**5.** −8.5 − 10.25 **6.** $7\frac{1}{3} - 9\frac{2}{3}$

**7.** −2.5 − 2.5 **8.** −11 + (−12)

Write the addition or subtraction equation represented by the drawing.

**9.** End: −7 Start: 5

**10.** Start: −2 End: 6

Compute the sum or difference. Then write an equivalent expression.

**11.** 14 + (−27) **12.** −2.8 − 1.6

**13.** $-2 + 3\frac{1}{2}$ **14.** $\frac{21}{4} - (-\frac{7}{4})$

In Exercises 15 and 16, find three positive and three negative values that make the inequality true. Describe all the values of *y* that make the inequality true.

**15.** $4 - y > 0$ **16.** $y - 6 < 0$

## Problem-Solving Practice (p. 8) OL AL

**Lesson 3.1 Problem-Solving Practice**
***Add and Subtract with Negative Numbers***

Solve.

**1. Football** A team gained 5 yards on their first play of the game. Then they lost 6 yards. Draw a chip model to find the total change in yardage.

**2. Money** Roger owes his mom $10.50. He borrows another $5.25 from her. Walk the number line to find the amount Roger owes his mom. Record your steps by making a number-line drawing. Write the addition equation next to your drawing.

**3. Golf** Juanita's score was 5 over par on the first 9 holes. Her score was 4 under par on the second 9 holes.
**a.** Write a subtraction equation to find Juanita's score over or under par. Then solve it.
**b.** What addition equation could you use to find Juanita's score over or under par?

**4. Roller Coaster** A roller coaster begins at $90\frac{3}{4}$ feet above ground level. Then it ascends $15\frac{1}{8}$ feet.
**a.** Write an addition equation to find the height of the coaster after its first ascent. Then solve it.
**b.** What subtraction equation could you use to find the height of the coaster after its first ascent?

**5. Temperature** The average temperature in Calgary, Canada, is 22°C in July and −11°C in January. Find the range of these two temperatures.

**6. Airplane** The inequality $37{,}000 - x > 0$ represents a plane's height, in feet, above 0 altitude. Describe all possible values of *x* that would make the inequality true.

## Enrichment (p. 9) BL

**Lesson 3.1 Enrichment**
***Add and Subtract with Negative Numbers***

**Distance on the Number Line**

To find the distance between two points on a number line, subtract their coordinates. Then, take the absolute value of the difference.

−4 − 3 = −7
|−7| = 7

You can also find the distance by finding the absolute value of the difference of the coordinates.

|−4 − 3| = 7

Graph each pair of points. Then write an expression using absolute value to find the distance between the points.

**1.** *A* at −5 and *B* at 2

**2.** *C* at −7 and *D* at −1

**3.** *E* at −5 and *F* at 5

**4.** *W* at 0 and *X* at 6

**5.** *Y* at −4 and *Z* at 0

## Lesson Quick Quiz (p. 10) AL OL BL

**Lesson 3.1 Quick Quiz**

**1.** Find the average of these seven numbers: −2, −1, 0, 15, −3, 1, −4.

**2.** Use the "walking the number line" model to explain why adding a negative number is equivalent to subtracting the positive of that number.

**3.** Will the following sums and differences be A) always negative, B) always positive, or C) sometimes negative, sometimes positive, and sometimes zero?
**a.** Negative number minus positive number
**b.** Negative number plus positive number
**c.** Negative number plus negative number

## Lesson Masters 1–5 (pp. 11–15)

**Lesson 3.1 Master 1**

**Captain's Game Plank**

You can use this plank to play *The Captain's Game.* Choose a game piece of your choice to move along the plank, but be sure that the game piece has two distinct sides. One side of the game piece will always represent the front of your body and the other side will always represent the back of your body. For example, the writing on one side of an eraser could always stand for your front while the blank side could always stand for your back.

# Additional Lesson Resources

### Teacher Tech Tools
- TeacherWorks
- ExamView Assessment Suite
- Classroom Presentation Toolkit
- Advance Tracker

### Student Tech Tools
- StudentWorks Plus
- Math Online eGlossary • Concepts in Motion

### Other Print Products
- Investigation Notebook and Reflection Journal
- Quick Review Math Handbook

LESSON 3.1

# Add and Subtract with Negative Numbers

## Introduce

**Using Negative Numbers** Discuss negative numbers with students to assess their knowledge and experience with this topic. Have students give examples of how they might use negative numbers in their daily lives. Students may mention low elevations, cold temperatures, debt, and percent change.

Have students read the top cartoon. You may want to have students use Zoe's reasoning to tell how to locate other negative numbers on a number line.

Then have students read the bottom cartoon. Some students may need to review the definition of opposite. Bring out the idea that opposites are on opposite sides of zero. They are the same distance from zero on a number line. Encourage these students to give examples of other opposite numbers.

Review the definition of *absolute value*. Students should remember that absolute value is the distance from zero on a number line. Ask students why we use the term opposite to describe pairs of positive and negative numbers with the same absolute value.

LESSON 3.1

# Add and Subtract with Negative Numbers



### Vocabulary

**absolute value**

You have probably seen negative numbers used in many situations. Below par golf scores, elevations below sea level, temperatures below 0°, and balances of overdrawn bank accounts can all be described with negative numbers.

Zoe and Darnell have different ways of thinking about negative numbers.

Zoe and Darnell both used positive numbers when they thought about negative numbers. Zoe actually used the **absolute value** of −4. Since −4 and 4 are both four units from 0, both have absolute value 4.

To show the absolute value of a number, draw a vertical line on each side of the number.

$$|4| = 4$$

$$|-4| = 4$$

**Math Link**

The *absolute value* of a number is its distance from 0 on the number line.

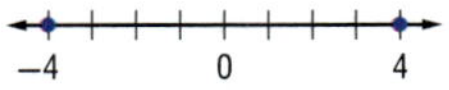


## Think & Discuss

These questions will help you review some important ideas about negative numbers.

- Order these numbers from least to greatest.
  **−5, −3.5, −0.25, 0, 1.75, 4, 4.2**
  4 −5 0 −3.5 4.2 −0.25 1.75
- Express each number using the fewest negative signs possible.

  $-(-2)$ **2**

  $-(-(-(-(7))))$ **7**

  $-(-(-5.5))$ **−5.5**
- How can you tell whether a number is positive or negative by counting how many negative signs it has? **See ①.**
- How can you tell whether $-x$ is positive or negative? **See ②.**
- Explain why the following is true. **See ③.**

  If $x$ is positive, then $|x| = x$.
- Tell for what numbers the following is true. **For $x \leq 0$**

  $|x| = -x$

① If the number of negative signs is even, the number is positive. If the number of negative signs is odd, the number is negative.

② You have to know whether $x$ is negative or positive; $-x$ has the opposite sign. If $x$ is zero, it is neither positive nor negative.

③ Possible answer: $|x|$ is the distance of $x$ from 0 on the number line. If $x$ is positive, this is just $x$ units.

In this lesson, you will expand your understanding of negative numbers by learning how to add and subtract negative and positive numbers.

Throughout the lesson, do your calculations without a calculator. This will help you better understand why the operations work the way they do.



### Think & Discuss

*Suggested Grouping: Whole Class*

Pose the Think & Discuss questions to the whole class. Students will use these concepts as they work with negative numbers in this lesson.

If students are having difficulty answering the second question—writing numbers with the fewest number of negative signs—you might suggest that they use Darnell's thinking to help them understand and remember these concepts.

In the third question, students must make a general statement about the relationship between the number of negative signs in front of a numeral and the associated number's sign.

If students have difficulty understanding how to determine whether $-x$ is positive or negative, ask them to test a few cases. Be sure they test positive and negative numbers. You might want to encourage students to read $-x$ as *the opposite of x* instead of as *negative x* to reinforce the idea that $-x$ is not always negative.

In the last two questions, students relate the value of $x$ to the absolute value of $x$. Discuss students' explanations for why each statement is true. Some students may think that the last statement is false since the absolute value of any number is a positive number. Have them think about a specific number, such as −5, then think $-(-5) = 5$. After listening to students' explanations, encourage them to provide examples to show that the explanations are true.


**Lesson 3.1** Add and Subtract with Negative Numbers **127**

# Investigation 1

***On Your Own Exercises***
Pages 148–153
Exercises 1–6

**Two-Color Chip Model** Students will use algebra tiles, two-color chips or two types of distinguishable items—one to represent positive numbers and one to represent negative numbers. Students may have difficulty using the chips because they do not concretely resemble positive or negative numbers. If students prefer, they can label small sheets of paper as +$10 and −$10 instead of the two-color chips. Once the value is determined, the students make zero pairs. This is an important connection for students to make.

### Think & Discuss

*Suggested Grouping: Pairs*

Once students have discussed a situation in pairs, it may be helpful to meet with another pair and share their situations. Then as a class, create categories that fit the majority of the situations. Ask the students why they think that many of the situations revolve around money.

### Develop & Understand: A

*Suggested Grouping: Individuals*

▶ **Exercise 1** Students may get confused because some choices do not have any pairs that form zeros. Reinforce to students that this is a way to represent change and not every problem must show change.



# Investigation 1 The Two-Color Chip Model

### Materials

- two-color counters (or dry beans)
- mat

### Math Link

Integers are natural numbers, their opposites, and zero.

{..., −3, −2, −1, 0, 1, 2, 3, ...}

Learning the "rules" for adding and subtracting integers is easier when you have a model for what is happening. The model in this investigation involves chips, or counters, that represent the numbers.

Think carefully about how you are using the chips to model each situation. Later, you will not use the chips, but the chip model can become a mental model for helping you think about integers.

### Think & Discuss

In any situation, if you add an amount to an existing quantity and then subtract the same amount, you end up with the original quantity. Also, if you subtract an amount and then add the same amount, you end up with the original quantity.

Suppose you have $20. You earn $10 doing yard work. You spend $10 at the movies. How much money do you have? Explain how you know. See ①.

Discuss with a partner a situation that involves subtracting an amount and then adding the same amount. See ②.

① 20; Adding 10 and subtracting 10 results in the original amount.

② Answers will vary. Possible answer: Withdrawing $25 from depositing $25 to a savings account would result in the original balance.

### Develop & Understand: A

It is important to be able to make zero when using the chip model to add and subtract positive and negative numbers. One positive chip (yellow) and one negative chip (red) combine to make zero.

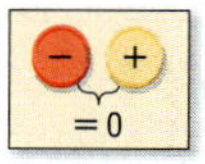


For Exercises 1–6, use a–f below.

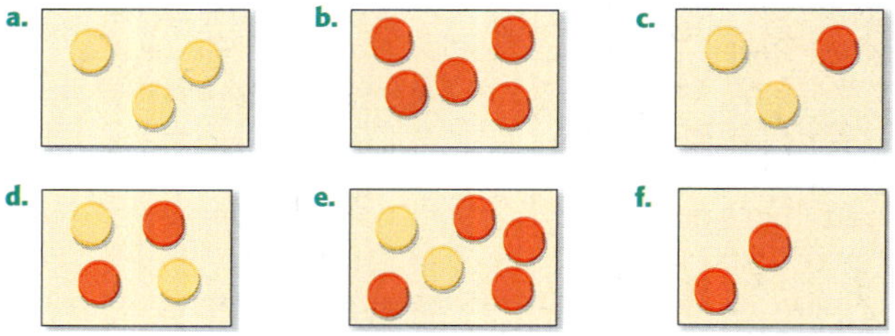


1. Draw each set on your paper. Circle chip pairs that form zeros. Count the remaining chips to find the value of the set.

2. What chips would you add to each set to make the set equal to zero?

1a. 3
1b. −5
1c. 1
1d. 0
1e. −2
1f. −2

2a. 3 red
2b. 5 yellow
2c. 1 red
2d. None
2e. 2 yellow
2f. 2 yellow

3a. 1 red; $3 + (-1)$
3b. 7 yellow; $-5 + 7$
3c. 1 yellow; $3 + (-1)$
3d. 2 yellow; $4 + (-2)$
3e. 4 yellow; $-4 + 6$
3f. 4 yellow; $-2 + 4$
4a. 4 red chips (3 red chips and 3 yellow chips will make zero, leaving 1 red chip)
4b. 4 yellow chips (combine with 4 red chips to make zero, leaving 1 original red chip)
4c. 2 red chips (combine with 2 yellow chips to make zero, leaving original red chip)
4d. 1 red chip (original chips equal to zero)

**Real-World Link**
With a bank account, a deposit into the account is a positive transaction (credit) while taking money from a bank machine is a withdrawal, or negative transaction (debit).

**3.** What chips would you add to each set to write an expression that is equal to 2? For example, for A, $3 + (-1) = 2$. Write an expression for each set.

**4.** What chips would you add to make each set equal to $-1$? Explain how you know. 4e–f. See below.

**5.** What chips would you add to each set to write an expression that is equal to $-2$? Write a related equation for each set. See below.

**6.** If possible, what chips would you *remove* from each set to make it equal to 1? Draw each set and draw an X through each chip that you would remove. See margin.

You can use the chip models to solve addition exercises.

### *Example*

In this example, chip models are used to add $-6$ and 2.

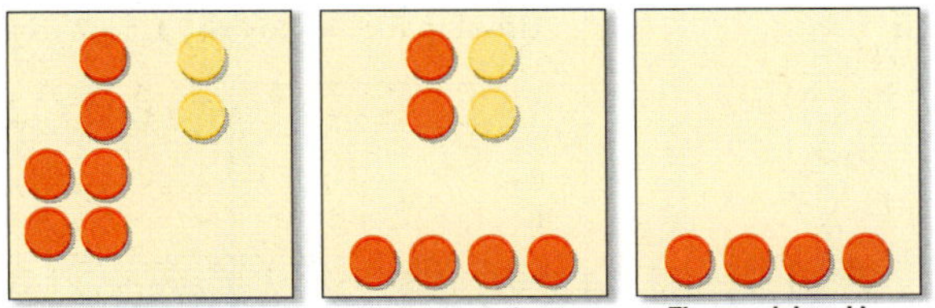

Show original numbers. | Represent $-6$ as $-4$ plus $-2$. Make a zero pair. | The remaining chips represent the sum.

| | | |
|---|---|---|
| **Step 1.** | $-6 + 2$ | Write the original numbers. |
| **Step 2.** | $[-4 + (-2)] + 2$ | Rewrite $-6$ as $-4$ plus $-2$. |
| **Step 3.** | $-4 + (-2 + 2)$ | Group $-2$ and 2. |
| **Step 4.** | $-4 + 0$ | Add $-2$ and 2 to get 0. |
| **Step 5.** | $-4$ | Add $-4$ and 0. |

4e. 1 yellow chip (3 yellow chips and 3 red chips will make zero, leaving 1 red chip)
4f. 1 yellow chip (1 red chip and 1 yellow chip will make zero, leaving 1 red chip)

5a. 5 red; $3 + -5 = -2$
5b. 3 yellow; $-5 + 3 = -2$
5c. 3 red; $2 + -4 = -2$
5d. 2 red; $2 + -4 = -2$
5e. None; Set already equals $-2$; $2 + -4$
5f. None; Set already equals $-2$



▶ **Exercise 3** Students will be writing signed number expressions to represent their work. This may make some students apprehensive. Assure students that the habit of writing a sign for each number will come with practice.

▶ **Exercise 6** In order to determine how well students understand this question, ask students how to tell if a set can be equal to 1.

**Example**

This example extends what the students worked on in the Develop & Understand section. Students will add signed numbers using the two-color chip pairs. If students have difficulty making the connection, walk through an example from the Develop & Understand exercises.

**Real-World Link**
Ask students to give examples of other places where positive and negative numbers are used.

## Additional Answers

6a.

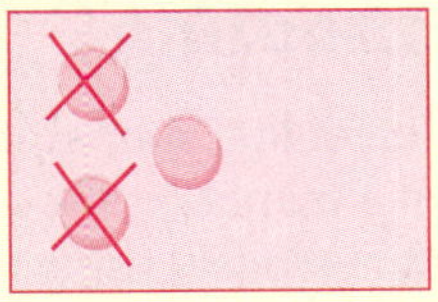

6b. Cannot remove to make 1

6c. Set already equals 1.

6d.

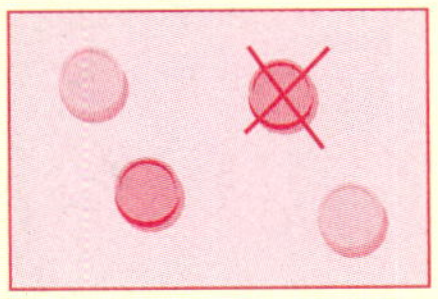

6e.

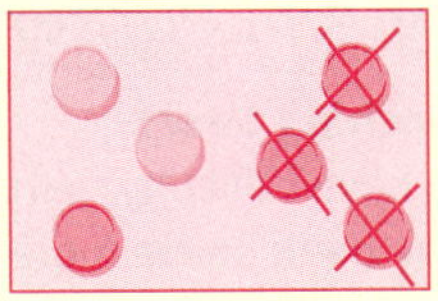

6f. Cannot remove to make 1

## Develop & Understand: B

*Suggested Grouping: Individuals*

▶ **Exercise 7** Ask the students to make a sketch of their model so that you can assist when questions arise.

▶ **Exercise 8** Remind students that in these examples the red chips represent negative numbers and the yellow chips represent the positive numbers.

**Example**

The question subtracts −2 from 5. This will cause students to become confused. The expression becomes 5 − (−2) but students will want to simplify −2 − 5. Go over the wording making sure that the students recognize the word form in the statement.

## Develop & Understand: C

*Suggested Grouping: Pairs*

▶ **Exercise 9** Have the students complete this Exercise by taking turns -- one person simplifying the expression, and one person checking the model. Have the students discuss any discrepancies they have with you or with another pair.

**Share & Summarize**

Ask a volunteer to demonstrate using colored chips on the overhead. If no one volunteers to simplify the expression, create a simpler expression for the students to simplify and then come back to the original expression as the students are more comfortable with the concept.

---

7a. $7 + (-3) \rightarrow 4 + (3 + (-3)) \rightarrow 4 + 0 \rightarrow 4$
7b. $-5 + 4 \rightarrow -1 + (-4 + 4) \rightarrow -1 + 0 \rightarrow -1$
7c. $4 + (-10) \rightarrow (4 + (-4)) + (-6) \rightarrow 0 + -6 \rightarrow -6$
7d. $[-1 + (-8) \rightarrow -9]$
7e. $-6 + (-2) \rightarrow -8$
7f. $2 + 9 \rightarrow 11$

## Develop & Understand: B

**7.** Use chip models to find each sum. Record each step using an expression.

**a.** $7 + (-3)$ **b.** $-5 + 4$ **c.** $4 + (-10)$
**d.** $-1 + (-8)$ **e.** $-6 + (-2)$ **f.** $2 + 9$

**8.** Write an addition equation for each chip mat.

**a.** **b.** **c.**

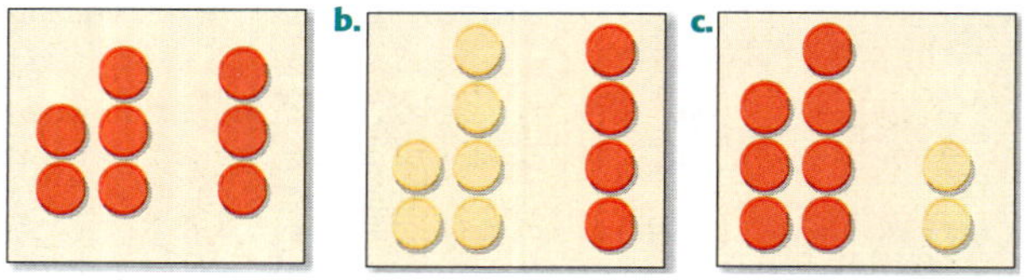

$-5 + (-3) = -8$ $6 + (-4) = 2$ $-7 + 2 = -5$

You can also use chip models to solve subtraction exercises. Sometimes it is necessary to add zero pairs.

**Example**

Use chip models to subtract −2 from 5, or $5 - (-2)$.

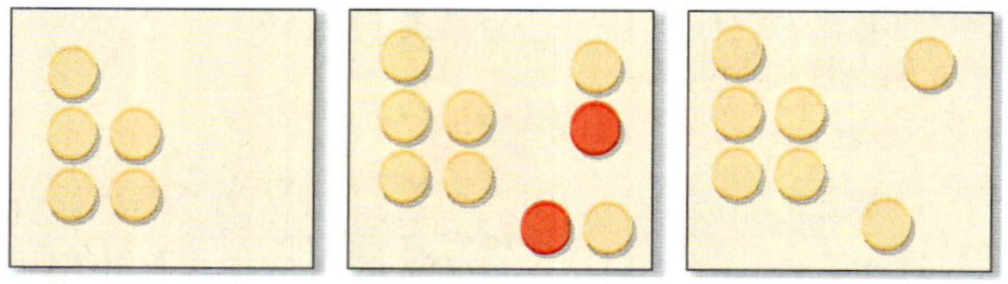

Represent the first number. Add zero pairs. Remove the second number.

**Step 1.** 5 Write the first number.
**Step 2.** $5 + [2 + (-2)]$ Add 0 in the form of 2 and −2.
**Step 3.** $5 + 2 + (-2)$ Subtract −2.
**Step 4.** 7 Add 5 and 2.

## Develop & Understand: C

9a. $-5 - (-3) \rightarrow -2$
9b. $2 - 8 \rightarrow 2 + (6 + (-6)) - 8 \rightarrow -6$
9c. $-5 - 4 \rightarrow -5 + (4 + (-4)) - 4 \rightarrow -9$

**9.** Use chip models to model each expression. Then solve.

**a.** $-5 - (-3)$ **b.** $2 - 8$ **c.** $-5 - 4$

**10.** How many zero pairs can you add to any number and not change its value? An unlimited number

**Share & Summarize**

Explain how you can you use a two-color chip model to subtract $3 - (-5)$. Start with 3 yellow chips. Add 5 zero pairs of chips. Remove 5 red chips. Eight yellow chips remain.



---

**Reaching All Learners**

**AL Approaching Level**
Students who have difficulty with this lesson may need some more time working with the two-color chips. Give these students additional problems to simplify. It may be helpful to pair these students with Beyond Level students for some extra support.

**Troubleshooting**

Students will forget that subtracting the opposite of a number is the same as addition. Model *t* using the two-color chip model. Reinforce with some additional problems.

Inquiry

# Investigation 2 A Number Line Model

**Materials**

- a copy of the plank
- several blank sheets of paper
- a paper arrow

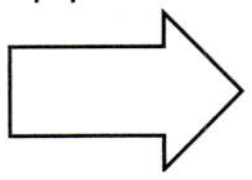

- a direction cube with 3 faces labeled *Ship* and 3 labeled *Shark*
- a walking cube with faces labeled *F1, F2, F3, B1, B2,* and *B3*

Imagine that you are on the crew of a pirate ship commanded by a very generous captain. He has decided to give victims who must walk the plank a chance to survive. He has formulated a game that he can play with his victims, but he has asked your help in testing and revising the game.

## The Captain's Game

The captain has set up an eight-foot plank that extends from the ship toward the water. He has drawn lines on the plank at one-foot intervals.

The victim starts by standing in the center of the plank, with four feet in front of him or her and four feet behind him or her. To decide where the victim should move, the captain rolls two cubes, a *direction* cube and a *walking* cube.

**Direction Cube** If the captain rolls *Ship,* the victim faces the ship. If he rolls *Shark,* the victim faces the sharks in the water.

**Walking Cube** If the captain rolls *F1, F2,* or *F3,* the victim must walk forward 1, 2, or 3 steps. If he rolls *B1, B2,* or *B3,* the victim must walk backward 1, 2, or 3 steps.

Go on



Inquiry

Inquiry

## Investigation 2

*Suggested Grouping: Pairs*

### Materials and Preparation

Each pair of students should have the following materials:

- one direction cube with three faces labeled Ship and three faces labeled Sharks
- one walking cube with sides labeled F1, F2, F3, B1, B2, B3
- several sheets of blank paper
- a paper arrow
- a plank, as described below

You can make planks with masking tape or chalk, but all planks must have lines at 1-foot intervals. If you lack space, each pair can play the game using Lesson 3.1 Master 1, Plank gameboard. As students play the game, they can use Lesson 3.1 Master 2, Plank Table, to record their results.

The game was designed to encourage some of the thinking that students will need as they begin adding and subtracting signed numbers. For example, if students see that facing the sharks and moving backward has the same result as facing the ship and moving forward, they have made an important connection. Both movements put them in a more advantageous position—farther away from the shark-infested waters. This is introduced more formally in Investigation 2 as students discover that subtracting a negative number is equivalent to adding the opposite of the negative number.

In addition to giving students an informal look at adding and subtracting with signed numbers, this activity has students think about probability concepts and data collection. Students can observe and explain that as the length of the plank increases, so does the average number of moves necessary to complete one game. There are also ample opportunities to discuss data collection.

## Try It Out

Students work in pairs as they play the game. Each person should be the captain and the victim at least once.

## Make a Prediction

Students' answers to Exercise 3 will vary because the ideal number of moves is entirely subjective. However, it is important that students are clear about what they consider to be an ideal number of moves, because their answers to Exercises 4 and 6 will depend on this number. Once students have set their ideal number of moves, they must reason mathematically to determine the length of the plank that will generate that ideal number of moves.

You may wish to highlight that there is an element of industrial design involved in designing games. All designers need to experiment with elements of their games to make the game as enjoyable as possible. Often mathematics assists designers in making choices about these elements.

## Check Your Prediction

Before students begin this part of the investigation, you might want to have a class discussion about data collection. Ask students how many games they needed to play to get a sense of the average number of moves in a game. Emphasize the idea that the more games that are played, the more accurate the estimate of the average number of moves will be.

Explain that you could use technology to help you generate a large number of cases: you may be able to program the results of the rolls into a graphing calculator or a computer and create a simulation of the activity.

Inquiry

The captain continues to roll the cubes until the victim walks off the edge of the plank, either into the shark-infested water or onto the safety of the ship's deck.

## Try It Out Answers will vary.

Play the game with a partner using a drawing of the plank and a paper arrow. Take turns playing the roles of the captain and the victim. For each game, keep track of the number of times the cubes are rolled before the victim falls to the sharks or reaches safety. Then answer the questions.

**1.** Did the victim in each game make it to the ship, or was he or she forced to jump into the water?

**2.** How many moves did it take to complete each game?

## Make a Prediction Answers will vary.

The captain is thinking about changing the length of the plank. If the plank is too short, games will not last long enough to entertain him. If the plank is too long, he will become bored with the game. Your challenge is to determine a plank length that results in an interesting game that is neither too short nor too long.

**3.** To keep the game interesting, what do you think the ideal number of moves should be?

**4.** How long do you think the plank should be so that the *average* number of moves is about the right number?

## Check Your Prediction Answers will vary.

**Math Link**
To find the average, add up the total number of moves in all trial games. Then divide by the number of trial games.

One way to check your prediction is to collect data. Play at least three games with the plank length that you specified. Record the number of moves for each game. Then find the average number of moves for all the games that you played.

**5.** Is the average number of moves close to the number you specified in Question 3?

**6.** If the plank length that you predicted is too long or too short, adjust it. Play the game at least three times with the new length. Continue adjusting the plank length until the average number of moves for a particular length is about what you recommended in Question 3.



## Troubleshooting

Watch for students who count each roll of the two number cubes as two moves instead of one move. Make sure students understand that when the text asks them to keep track of the number of times the cubes are rolled, it means the number of times the pair of cubes are rolled. They should also understand that when the book refers to the number of moves, it is referring to the number of times the victim moves. For each move, the captain rolls two number cubes. Students will need this information as they work on Exercises 1–7.

You might put the results of your games in a table.

| Plank Length | Number of Moves | | | Average Number of Moves |
|---|---|---|---|---|
| | Game 1 | Game 2 | Game 3 | |
| | | | | |
| | | | | |
| | | | | |
| | | | | |
| | | | | |
| | | | | |

## What Did You Learn?

**7.** In one round of the game, the victim moved two steps in the direction of the ship. What might the captain have rolled when he rolled the two cubes? List as many possibilities as you can.
Ship, F2 or Shark, B2

**8.** Write a letter to the captain giving him your recommendation. Include the following information in your letter. Letters will vary.

- the number of moves you think is ideal
- how long the plank should be
- how you know that this plank length will give your ideal number of moves

Inquiry

Encourage students to complete the table in Exercise 6 as they test their games. If students are satisfied with their first version of the game, they will only complete the top row of the table. You may wish to have students record their moves on Lesson 3.1 Master 2, Plank Table.

## What Did You Learn?

▶ **Exercise 7** Students are given a move and determine what was rolled by the number cubes.

▶ **Exercise 8** Most students will report that a good game needs a 10- to 14-foot-long plank. However the focus should be on students' justifications for their recommendations, not on the recommended length of the plank. Look to see that students use the data collected in the investigation to justify their recommendation.

## Investigation 3

***On Your Own Exercises***
Pages 148–153
Exercises 7–27, 44–45

**Walking the Number Line** In this investigation, students are introduced to the "walking the number line" model. This model helps students learn how to add and subtract signed numbers. After familiarizing themselves with the model, students make drawings of their number-line walks. They also begin to solve more challenging exercises requiring the addition and subtraction of signed numbers.

The student text suggests that students "walk the number line" with a pointer and a small number line. The model is introduced with this assumption. If you have the space and resources, you might want to have students physically walk the number line before using the paper models. You can create number lines using masking tape or sidewalk chalk on the floor in an open space in your school or outside. Then students can actually "walk the number line" themselves. You will need to adapt the opening materials accordingly.

If you choose to have students make smaller number lines and pointers, you can have them draw and cut out the materials. If you select this option, encourage students to make their number lines and pointers as large as possible. You may want to give each student a copy of Lesson 3.1 Master 3, Number Line and Pointer. This Lesson Master has a number line that extends from −9 to 9 and a pointer that students can cut out. You can enlarge the Lesson Master to make it easier for students to work with.

Review with students how to show the addition and subtraction of two positive numbers on a number line. Tell them that they can use a similar method to add and subtract negative numbers.

## Investigation 3 Add and Subtract on the Number Line

**Materials**

- number line and pointer

In earlier grades, you may have learned to add and subtract positive numbers on the number line. For example, to find $2 + 3$, you start at 2 and move three spaces to the right. The number on which you end, 5, is the sum.

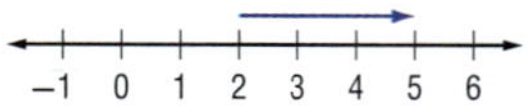


To find $6 - 4$, start at 6 and move four spaces to the left.

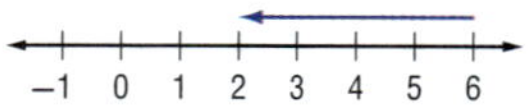


In a similar way, you can "walk the number line" to calculate sums and differences involving negative numbers.

Before you walk the number line, create a large number line that goes from −9 to 9 and a pointer that looks like the one below.

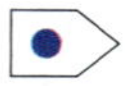

Once you have created your number line and pointer, you are ready to walk the number line.

134 CHAPTER 3 Signed Numbers

Here is how to find the solution to $3 + (-2)$ by using your number line.

- Place your pointer, point up, on 3.

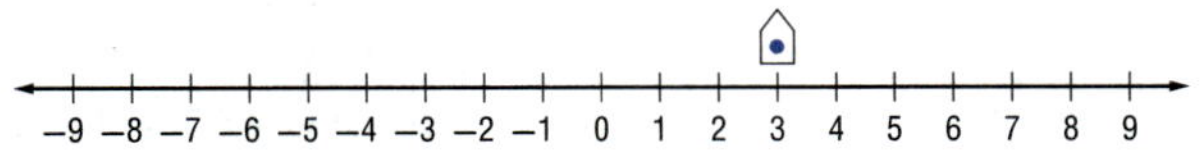


- Look at the operation. Since it is *addition,* face your pointer in the *positive direction,* to the right.

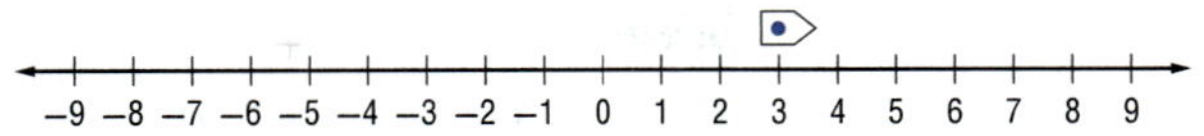


- Look at the number being added, $-2$. Since it is *negative,* move the pointer *backward,* opposite the direction the pointer is facing, two spaces. The pointer ends on 1, which means the answer is 1. The complete addition equation for this sum is $3 + (-2) = 1$.

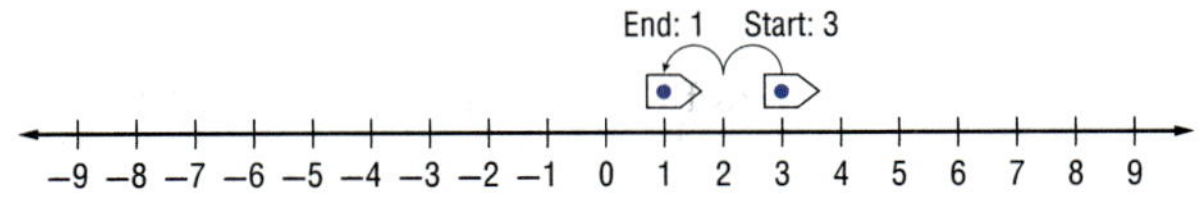


Next, you will consider a subtraction example, $-2 - 6$.

- Place your pointer, point up, on $-2$.

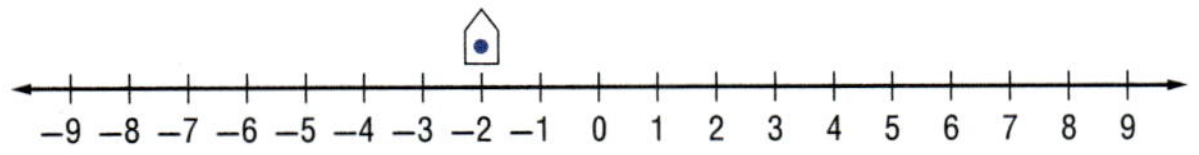


- Look at the operation. Since it is *subtraction,* face your pointer in the *negative direction,* to the left.

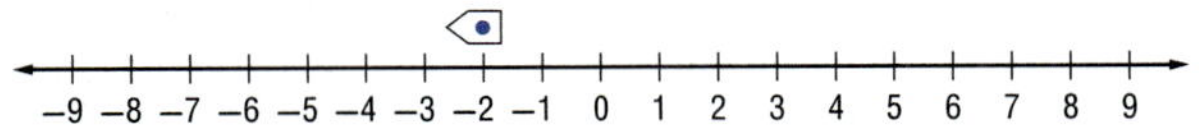


- Look at the number being subtracted, 6. Since it is *positive,* move the pointer *forward,* in the direction the pointer is facing, six spaces. The answer is $-8$. The complete subtraction equation for this difference is $-2 - 6 = -8$.

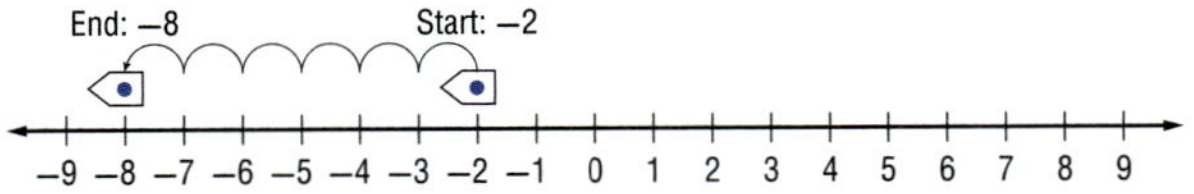




**Teacher Tips** Read through with your students the directions for using the model to find sums. Go over the use of the number line to find $3 + (-2)$. If you are using human-size number lines, adapt the directions accordingly. In this case, the student's body becomes the pointer, so he or she faces the way the pointer would point on the paper model.

Use your version of the model to walk students through the steps for subtracting signed numbers. You may want to have students show each step on their models as you discuss each step.

**Additional Examples** You may wish to use the model to show how to find the sum or difference of two positive numbers. This will encourage students to build on their experience with subtraction and number lines and may help them reinforce what is being shown by the model. Then have the class practice using the model to find these sums and differences.

$4 + (-1)$ 3
$-2 + 3$ 1
$-2 + (-3)$ $-5$
$4 - (-1)$ 5
$-2 - 3$ $-5$
$-2 - (-3)$ 1

**Lesson 3.1** Add and Subtract with Negative Numbers **135**

Review the rules for walking the number line given at the top of page 136. Be sure students know that the operation determines which direction the pointer will face and that the sign determines whether the pointer moves forward or backward.

You may want to write these rules in a chart. You can display the chart to reinforce students' learning and to help them as they use the model to solve exercises. This will give students a handy reference as they learn to use the model.

### *Think & Discuss*

Students are asked to explain how to use a number line to find $5 + (-3)$. Each picture represents one step. You may want to guide their answers by asking questions such as these:

- Why is the pointer at 5 in the first picture? 5 is the first addend.
- Why does the pointer face right in the second picture? The operation is addition, so the pointer faces in the positive direction.
- Why did the pointer move backward in the third picture? The number being added is negative, so the arrow moves backward.



When you walk the number line, the operation determines the direction the pointer faces.

- If the operation is addition, face the pointer to the right in the positive direction. 
- If the operation is subtraction, face the pointer to the left in the negative direction. 

The sign of the number being added or subtracted determines the direction to move the pointer.

- If the number is positive, move the pointer forward, in the direction it is pointing.

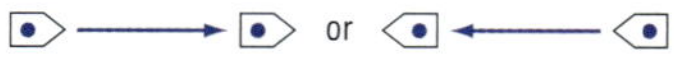


- If the number is negative, move the pointer backward, opposite the direction it is pointing.

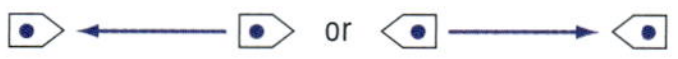


### *Think & Discuss*

The number lines below show the steps for finding $5 + (-3)$. Explain each step.

Start pointer at 5.

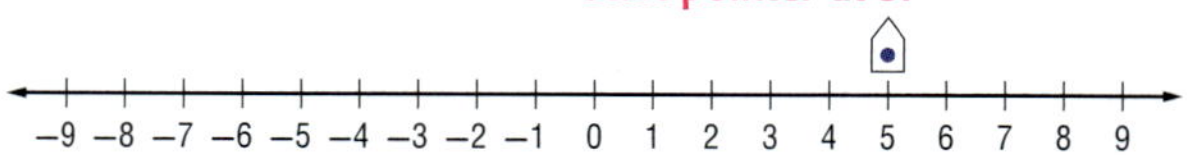


The operation is addition, so face the point to the right.

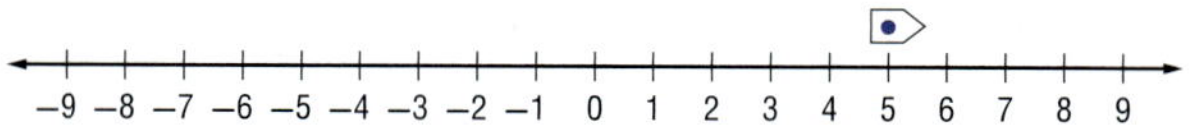


You are adding a negative number, −3. Move backward 3 spaces.

Now you will have an opportunity to compute some sums and differences with the number line.

## Develop & Understand: A

For Exercises 1–4, walk the number line to find each sum or difference. Describe your steps in words. Be sure to include the following in your descriptions. 1–4. See margin.

- your starting position on the number line
- the direction the pointer is facing
- whether you move forward or backward and how far you move
- your ending position on the number line, which is the answer
- the complete equation that represents your moves on the number line

1. $5 + (-2)$
2. $-4 + (-3)$
3. $3 - (-2)$
4. $-8 - (-2)$

**Estimate each sum or difference. Then, find each sum or difference by walking the number line.**

5. $3 + (-5.25)$ Possible estimate: $-2$; $-2.25$
6. $5 - 6\frac{1}{3}$ Possible estimate: $-1$; $-1\frac{1}{3}$
7. $-6 - 2.23$ Possible estimate: $-8$; $-8.23$
8. $-\frac{2}{3} - \left(-1\frac{1}{3}\right)$ Possible estimate: 0; $\frac{2}{3}$
9. When Bret woke up one morning, the temperature was $-15$°F. By noon, the temperature had risen 7°F. What was the temperature at noon? $-8$°F
10. Colleen was hiking in Death Valley, parts of which are at elevations below sea level. She began her hike at an elevation of 300 feet and hiked down 450 feet. At what elevation did she end her hike? $-150$ ft, or 150 ft below sea level

### Additional Answers

1. Start at 5, face right, move backward 2, end at 3; $5 + (-2) = 3$
2. Start at $-4$, face right, move backward 3, end at $-7$; $-4 + (-3) = -7$
3. Start at 3, face left, move backward 2, end at 5; $3 - (-2) = 5$
4. Start at $-8$, face left, move backward 2, end at $-6$; $-8 - (-2) = -6$

## Develop & Understand: A

*Suggested Grouping: Pairs*

In this exercise set, students use the "walking the number line" model to find sums and differences. After they practice the model using whole numbers, students experience adding and subtracting with nonintegers. Since it is difficult to precisely locate nonintegers on the number line, students are forced to begin forming a more abstract notion of movement on the number line. Instead of counting a whole number of steps to move from one integer to another, students must be more aware of where they are on the number line at all times and must think about what is going on. After practicing with the model, students apply their skills to solve exercises relating to situations.

▶ **Exercises 5–8** Have students struggling with finding fractions and decimals on the number line break down the number-line movement into steps. Have them place their pointer on the first number in the exercise and then move the whole number of steps. Ask them to look at the whole-number part of the decimal or fraction and move that number of spaces. Then have them look at the fractional part of the decimal or fraction and move that number of spaces. You can make this process more detailed by having students move one space at a time.

▶ **Exercise 9** The limits were purposefully extended so that students would have experience using the number-line model to show subtraction of integers that are more than 9 units from zero. Students will need to use a number line that extends at least from $-15$ to $-8$. Some students won't need to create a physical number line but will be able to imagine a number line with a larger range. For students who want to use a number line, you can use Lesson 3.1 Master 4, Blank Number Lines and Pointer, which contains several copies of number lines with no number labels.

Some students may use the "walking the number line" model. Other students may draw a picture of a thermometer or a vertical number line and then count the 7 spaces from $-15$ to $-8$ to find the change in temperature.

**Teacher Tips** You may want to have students who are having difficulty following the steps in the Example below to first show each step on their number line models. They can compare how their model looks with the drawing in the text, on the board, or on an overhead.

**Example**

Walk students through the steps on how to make a drawing to show −3 − (−7). You may want to draw a number line on the board as you ask questions such as these:

- Where will you first draw the pointer? −3 since it is the number being subtracted from
- Which direction will the pointer face? Why? The operation is subtraction, so the pointer faces in the negative direction.
- Will the pointer move forward or backward? Explain. Backward because the number being subtracted is negative
- How many spaces did the pointer move? 7
- Why do we use the arrow? Where does it start and end? The arrow shows the direction of the movement. It starts on −3, the number being subtracted from, and ends 7 marks to the right on 4.

Label the number line with *Start: −3* and *End: 4*. Then ask students to give the difference of −3 − (−7). 4

Emphasize that labeling the starting and ending points is important for two reasons. First, it helps to make number-line pictures even clearer. While it does not seem difficult to read the number line when the starting and ending points are integers, it is almost impossible to identify numbers exactly on the number line that are not integers. Second, it foreshadows work with number-line pictures that students will do in Investigation 4.

Be sure students understand that the drawing shows exactly what would happen if students were to use the physical "walk the number line" model.

You can make drawings to record your moves on the number line. Once you get comfortable walking the number line, you may be able to add and subtract just by making a drawing. Your drawings can show very easily the steps you take to find a sum or a difference.

**Example**

Make a drawing to record the steps for finding −3 − (−7).

First, draw a pointer over −3. Since you are subtracting, draw the pointer so that it faces left. Make sure the dot on the pointer is directly over −3.

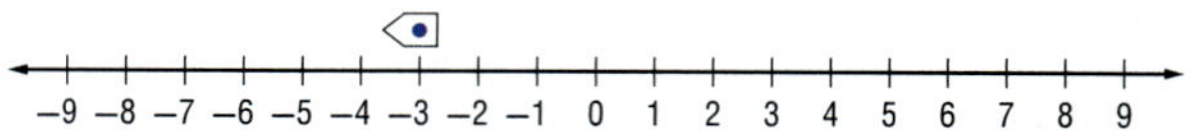


Since the number you are subtracting is −7, move backward seven spaces. Draw an arrow from the pointer to the ending number.

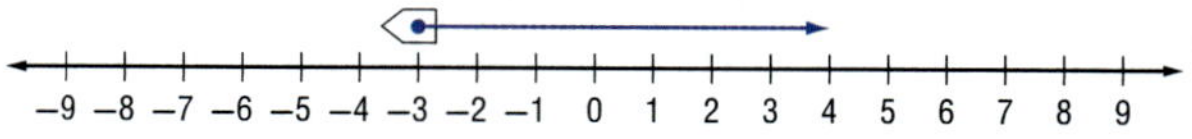


Finish your drawing by adding some labels. Write *Start* and the number where you started above the pointer. Write *End* and the number where you ended above the arrowhead.

Adding labels is especially important when you find sums and differences involving fractions and decimals because it is hard to show the numbers precisely on the number line.

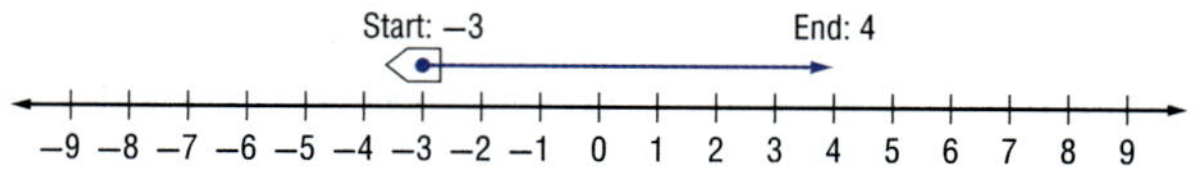


Notice that the final number-line drawing captures all your moves. It shows the number at which you began, the direction of your pointer, whether you moved forward or backward, how far you moved, and your ending number.



## Troubleshooting

Watch for students who mix up the rules for "walking the number line." Some students will think that the operation dictates whether you move forward or backward instead of determining the direction of the pointer. Similarly, they will think that the sign determines the direction the pointer points, not whether you move forward or backward.

This can be hard to spot because students who mix up the rules can still get the correct answer because they are acting out an equivalent operation.

## Develop & Understand: B

Walk the number line to compute each sum or difference in Exercises 11–16. Record your steps by making a number-line drawing. Write the complete addition or subtraction equation next to each drawing.

**11.** $-3 + (-2)$

**12.** $5 - 8$

**13.** $-5 - (-2)$

**14.** $-5 + 7$

**15.** $2 + (-7.2)$

**16.** $2\frac{2}{3} - \left(-6\frac{1}{3}\right)$

11. $-3 + -2 = -5$

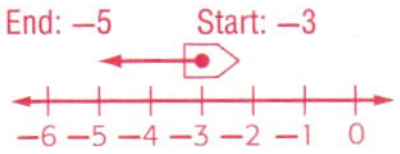


12. $5 - 8 = -3$

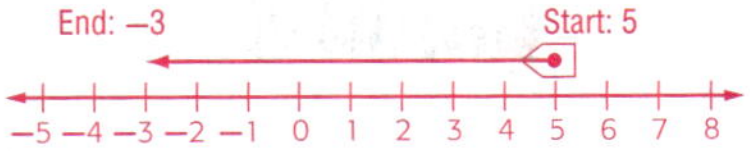


13, 14. See below.

15, 16. See margin.

**Write an addition or subtraction equation for each drawing.**

17. $-2 + (-5) = -7$

18. $8 + (-8) = 0$

19. $-5\frac{1}{3} - \left(-12\frac{2}{3}\right) = 7\frac{1}{3}$

**17.**

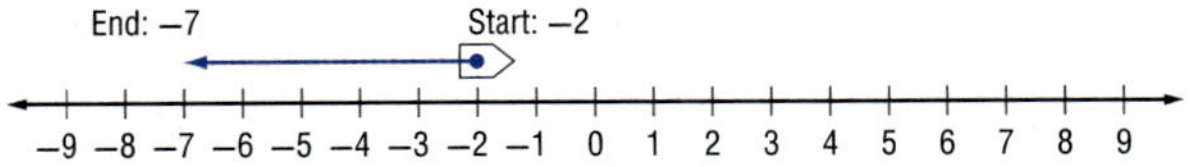


**18.**

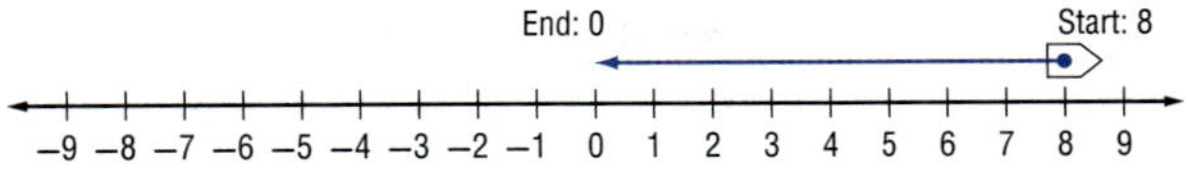


**19.**

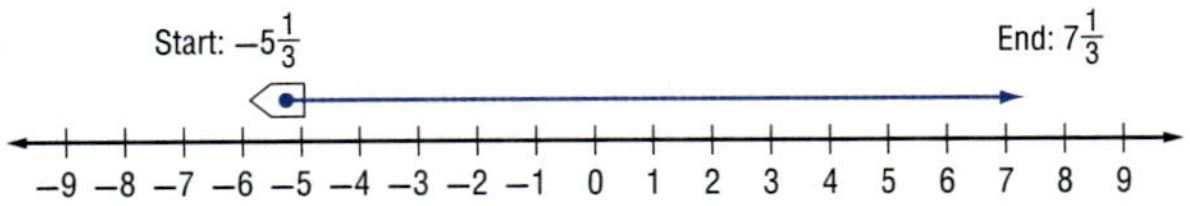


### Share & Summarize

Write one addition equation and one subtraction equation. On a separate sheet of paper, make a number-line drawing for each.

Trade drawings with your partner. Write equations that match your partner's drawings. Check with your partner to make sure the equations match the drawings. Answers will vary.

13. $-5 - (-2) = -3$

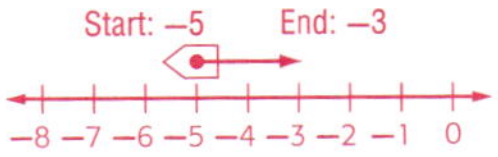


14. $-5 + 7 = 2$

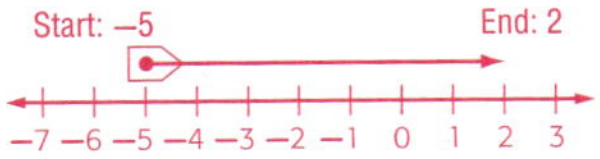




### Additional Answers

15. $2 + -7.2 = -5.2$

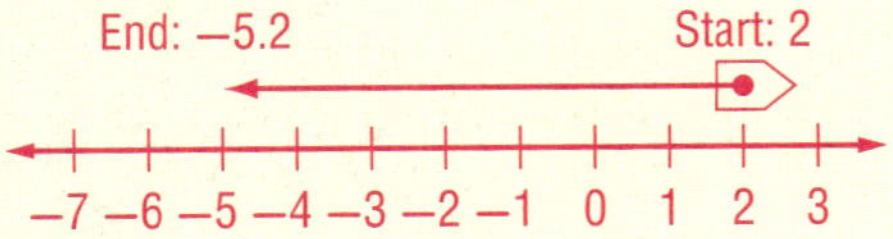


16. $2\frac{2}{3} - -6\frac{1}{3} = 9$

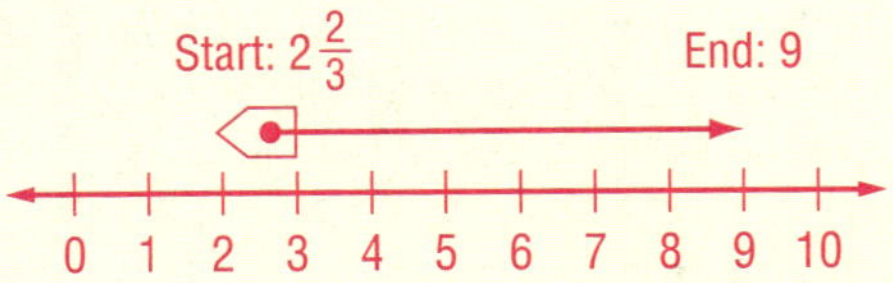


## Develop & Understand: B

*Suggested Grouping: Individuals*

To save time when students are creating number-line pictures, you can use copies of Lesson 3.1 Master 5, Number Lines, which has blank number lines with numbers extending from −9 to 9.

▶ **Exercises 11–16** Students draw number-line pictures to compute sums and differences. These are all variations of the Example.

Watch for students who create a number-line picture where one endpoint is the first number in the sum or difference while the other endpoint is the second number in the sum or difference. For example, for Exercise 11, some students may be tempted to draw a number-line picture with endpoints −3 and −2. Students who make this error are confused by the model and are not thinking through the walking process as they create their picture. To help them, you might suggest they get out their pointer and act out the sum or difference using rules laid out in Investigation 3 before drawing a number-line picture.

▶ **Exercises 17–19** Students reverse the process of creating a number-line picture. They must analyze a number-line picture and decide what equation is shown by the drawing.

### Share & Summarize

In this Share & Summarize, students practice creating and interpreting number-line pictures. You might ask students to think about what all of the addition number-line pictures have in common and what all of the subtraction number-line pictures have in common.

## Investigation 4

**On Your Own Exercises**
Pages 148–153
Exercises 28–38, 46–47

**Equivalent Operations** In this investigation, students continue to use a number line as they formalize what they might have already observed: adding a negative is equivalent to subtracting the opposite of the negative (or a positive), and subtracting a negative is equivalent to adding the opposite of the negative (or a positive).

**Think & Discuss**

You may want to use an overhead and draw the two number lines or have students draw the number lines on the board as you discuss the exercise.

### Develop & Understand: A

*Suggested Grouping: Pairs*

You may wish to have students use copies of Lesson 3.1 Masters 6, 7, 8, Number Lines I, Number Lines II, and Number Lines III, to record their answers to this exercise set. The Lesson Master pages have two number lines with the starting and ending points labeled for each exercise. Students draw in the picture of the pointer and the arrow and write the corresponding addition and subtraction equation for each number line.

**Teacher Tips** Watch for students who think that they should add or subtract the two endpoint numbers to find the sum or difference. For example, some students might think that Exercise 1 represents the equation $5 - 2 = 3$ or $2 - 5 = (-3)$. Students who are doing this are not thinking through the model correctly. You might suggest that these students do one or more of these things.

1. Review the rules for "walking the number line" set out in Investigation 3.
2. Draw the pointer and the arrow before writing the equation represented by the picture. Sometimes it is easier to create equations that represent pictures than it is to create pictures that represent equations.
3. Physically act out the model.



## Investigation 4 Equivalent Operations

You have practiced writing addition and subtraction equations to match number-line drawings. For each complete number-line drawing, there is only one equation that matches.

What if a number-line drawing shows only the starting and ending values and not the pointer or the arrow?

**Think & Discuss** See margin.

What number-line drawings start at $-3$ and end at 2?

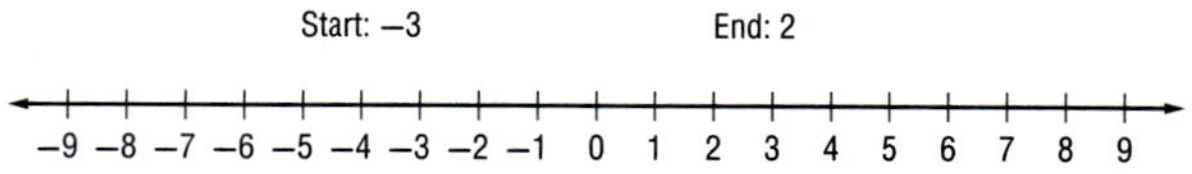


What equation does each number-line drawing represent?

In Exercises 1–6, you will use number-line drawings to explore the relationship between addition and subtraction.

### Develop & Understand: A

In Exercises 1–6, make two copies of each number line. Complete one to represent an addition equation and the other to represent a subtraction equation. Write the equations your drawings represent.

1\. $5 + (-3) = 2$

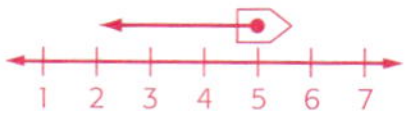


$5 - 3 = 2$

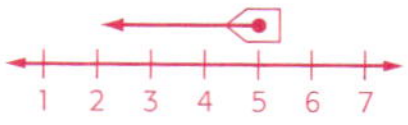


**1.**

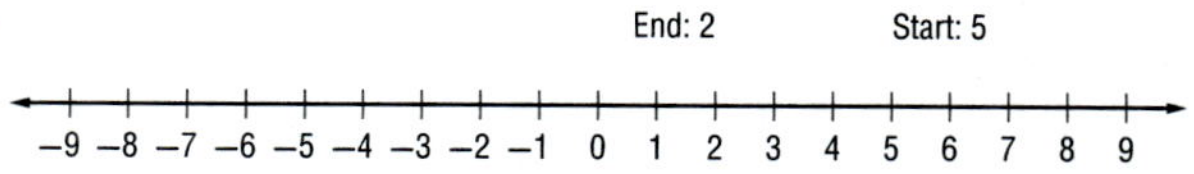


**2.**

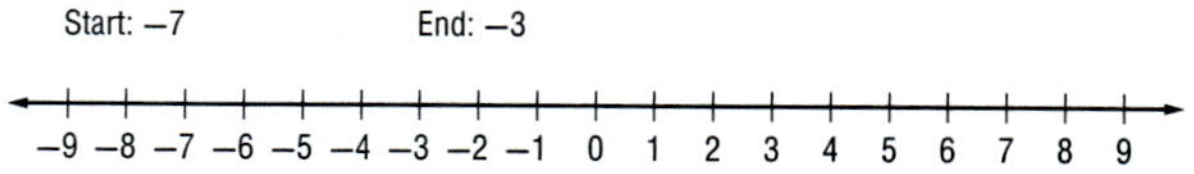


$-7 + 4 = -3$

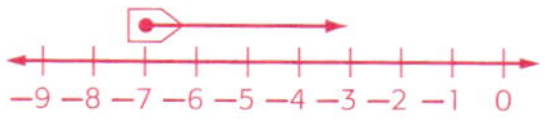


$-7 - (-4) = -3$

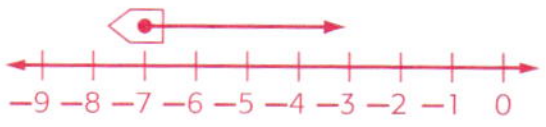




**Additional Answers**
**Think & Discuss**

If the pointer faces the positive direction, the drawing looks like this and the equation is $-3 + 5 = 2$:

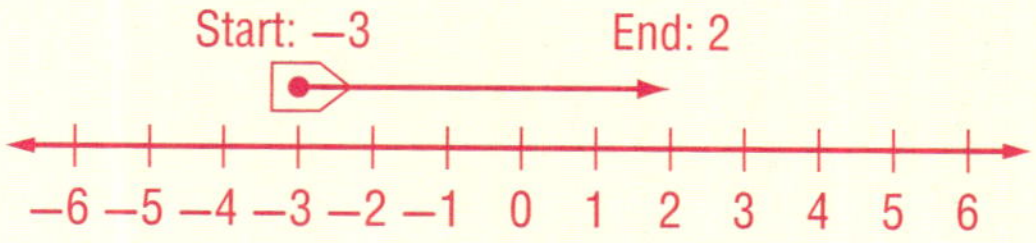


If the pointer faces the negative direction, the drawing looks like this and the equation is $-3 - (-5) = 2$:

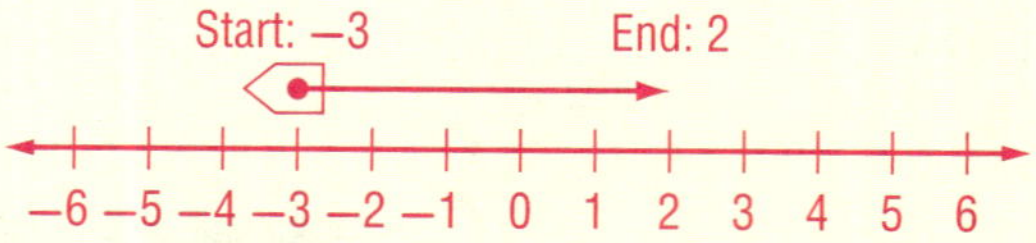

3. $3 + (-4) = -1$

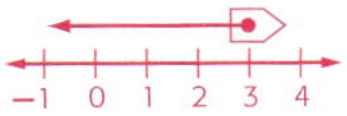


$3 - 4 = -1$

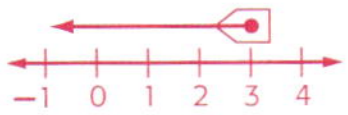


4–6. See below.

**3.** End: −1 Start: 3

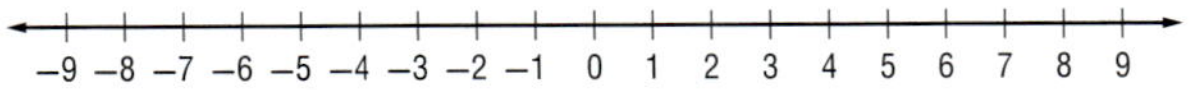


**4.** End: −9 Start: −6

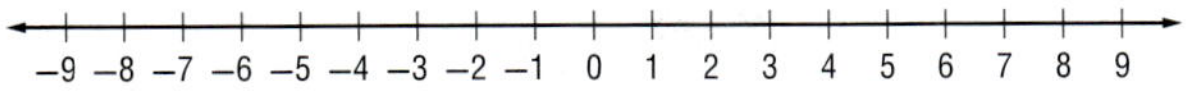


**5.** Start: 5.25 End: 7.75

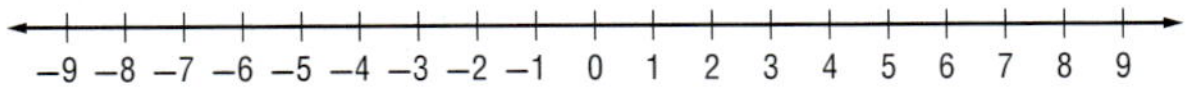


**6.** Start: $-3\frac{1}{3}$ End: $2\frac{1}{3}$

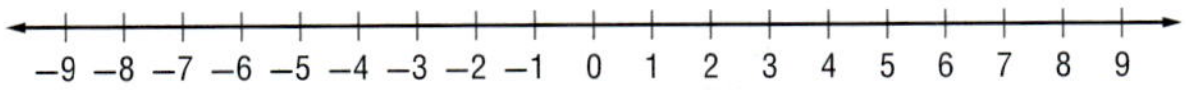


## Think & Discuss

Describe the two ways that you can move from a start point to an end point when you walk the number line. See ①.

What other move on the number line accomplishes the same thing as facing the negative direction and moving forward? See ②.

What other move accomplishes the same thing as facing the positive direction and moving forward? See ③.

① You can point the pointer toward the end point and move forward, or you can point it away from the end point and move backward.

② Facing the positive direction and moving backward

③ Facing the negative direction and moving backward

In Exercises 1–6, you wrote two equations that started and ended at the same place on the number line.

Since you started with the same number and found the same result after adding or subtracting, you were really doing *equivalent* operations.

4. $-6 + (-3) = -9$

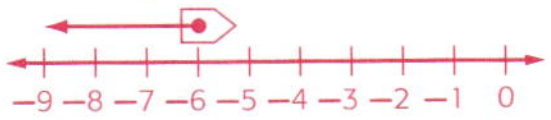


$-6 - 3 = -9$

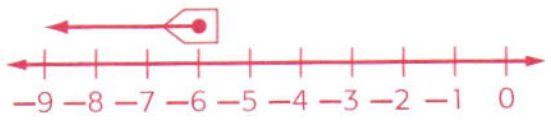


5. $5.25 + 2.5 = 7.75$

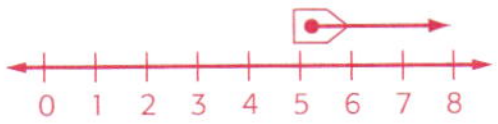


$5.25 - (-2.5) = 7.75$

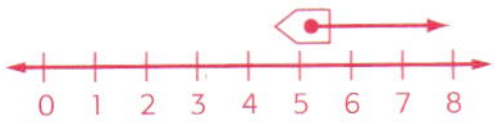


6. $-3\frac{1}{3} + -5\frac{2}{3} = 2\frac{1}{3}$

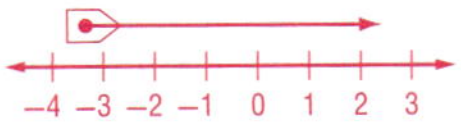


$-3\frac{1}{3} - \left(-5\frac{2}{3}\right) = 2\frac{1}{3}$

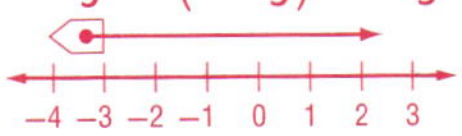




**Wrap-Up** Have volunteers share the equations they wrote for Exercises 1–6. If any students had difficulty drawing the number lines, you may want volunteers to reproduce their drawings on the board or an overhead projector. Students should understand that when "walking the number line," there are two ways to move from a start number to an end number. They should be able to describe these moves for any two pairs of numbers before progressing to the Think & Discuss questions in the next section.

## Think & Discuss

The Wrap-Up provided a natural transition into this section. Ideally, as students describe their thoughts about the movements in Exercises 1–6, they make informal conjectures about the equivalency of adding a positive and subtracting a negative and subtracting a positive and adding a negative. The questions in this section should help them make their conjectures more explicit and formalize their understanding of the pairs of equivalent operations.

Once students understand the two sets of equivalent moves, you can discuss the implications for sums and differences of signed numbers.

Guide the discussion of the two ways to move on the number line into a discussion of the operations used in the two equations. Have students compare the two equations they wrote for Exercise 3. They should note that in one case they added −4 and in the other they subtracted 4. When the inverse operation is used, the sign of the number added or subtracted changes. Tell students that since you started with the same number and found the same answer after adding or subtracting, the operations are *equivalent*.

After students have translated the equivalent moves, you might ask them some questions like the following one which asks them to use equivalent operations:

How can I use operations to describe how to move from 3 to −8? Add −11 or subtract 11.

Students should have a sufficient understanding of equivalent operations to answer Exercises 7–12.

## Develop & Understand: B

*Suggested Grouping: Pairs*

This exercise set asks students to write equivalent equations and solve exercises. You may want to have Lesson 3.1 Masters 6, 7, 8 available for students who want to use a number line to write and solve exercises. Students will need to think about scale when solving Exercises 5 and 6.

▶ **Exercises 7–10** Students find the sum or difference, write their answer as an equation, and then write an equivalent equation

▶ **Exercises 11–12** Students make sense of equivalent equations in a exercise-solving context.

▶ **Exercise 12** Some students subtract the starting elevation, −600 feet, from the ending elevation, 92 feet. These students would use this equation to solve the exercise: $92 - (-600) = 692$. Other students will use reasoning to break apart the exercise. They will add the change in elevation from −600 feet to sea level, or 600 feet, and the change in elevation from sea level to 92 feet, or 92 feet. These students would use this equation to solve the exercise: $600 + 92 = 692$.

**Wrap-Up** You might want to have students share their thinking about Exercises 11 and 12. Discussing strategies and seeing the equivalent operations in context can help students understand them better.

### Share & Summarize

Students might fill in the blanks for Questions 2–4 in a variety of ways. In Question 1, the completed sentence is "Adding a negative is equivalent to subtracting a positive." A more precise sentence is "Adding a negative is equivalent to subtracting the opposite of the negative." Regardless of how they frame the rule, all students should have a clear understanding of the two equivalent sets of operations.

You might want to have a whole-class discussion of students' answers to Question 5. This will give the whole class an opportunity to see several approaches to understanding these equivalencies.



## Develop & Understand: B

**Compute each difference. Write your answer in the form of a subtraction equation. Then write an addition equation that is equivalent to the subtraction equation.**

7. $2 - 5$ — $2 - 5 = -3$, $2 + (-5) = -3$

8. $-2 - (-3.2)$ — $-2 - (-3.2) = 1.2$, $-2 + 3.2 = 1.2$

**Compute each sum. Write your answer in the form of an addition equation. Then write an equivalent subtraction equation.**

9. $-6 + (-5)$ — $-6 + (-5) = -11$, $-6 - 5 = -11$

10. $-1 + 7\frac{1}{4}$ — $-1 + 7\frac{1}{4} = 6\frac{1}{4}$, $-1 - \left(-7\frac{1}{4}\right) = 6\frac{1}{4}$

In Exercises 11 and 12, write an addition and a subtraction equation that gives the answer to the question.

11. When Sawyer went to sleep, the temperature outside was −2°F. The temperature dropped 12°F overnight. What was the temperature when Sawyer awoke?

12. **Challenge** Rosa was hiking near the Dead Sea. She began her hike at an elevation of −600 feet and ended the hike at 92 feet. What was the change in her elevation?

11. Possible answers: $-2 + (-12) = -14$°F, $-2 - 12 = -14$°F

12. Possible answers: $92 - (-600) = 692$ ft, $600 + 92 = 692$ ft

### Share & Summarize

Complete each sentence. The first is done for you.

1. Adding a negative is equivalent to subtracting a positive.
2. Subtracting a negative is equivalent to adding a positive.
3. Adding a positive is equivalent to subtracting a negative.
4. Subtracting a positive is equivalent to adding a negative.
5. Using the number line or anything else you would like, explain why the statements above are true. See margin.



**Additional Answer**
**Share & Summarize**

5. Possible answer: When you add a negative on the number line, you direct the pointer in the positive direction and move backward. This is a move to the left. When you subtract a positive, you direct the pointer in the negative direction and move forward. This is also a move to the left.

When you add a positive, you direct the pointer in the positive direction and move forward. This is a move to the right. When you subtract a negative number, you direct the pointer in the negative direction and move backward. This is also a move to the right.

# Investigation 5 Inequalities and Negative Numbers

Just as with equations, signed numbers can be used with inequalities.

In the next two exercise sets, you will add and subtract with negative numbers as you solve inequalities.

**Math Link**

An *inequality* is a mathematical statement that one quantity is greater than or less than another. Inequalities use the following symbols.

$>$ greater than

$<$ less than

These symbols indicate that quantities may be equal.

$\geq$ greater than or equal to

$\leq$ less than or equal to

## Develop & Understand: A

**Tell what number you could put in each blank to make a sum of 0.**

**1.** $3 +$ ___ $-3$

**2.** $-7.2 +$ ___ $7.2$

**3.** Look at your answers to Exercises 1 and 2.

**a.** If you have a positive number, what number could you add to it to get a sum of 0? The opposite of the number

**b.** If you have a negative number, what number could you add to it to get a sum of 0? The opposite of the number

**Give one number in each blank to make a sum less than 0.**

**4.** $-6 +$ ___ Answer must be less than 6.

**5.** $-4.3 +$ ___ Answer must be less than 4.3.

**6.** $\frac{1}{2} +$ ___ Answer must be less than $-\frac{1}{2}$.

**7.** $3 +$ ___ Answer must be less than $-3$.

**8.** In Exercises 4–7, how did you figure out what number to put in the blank?

8. Possible answer: I found the number that was 1 less than the number that would make the sum 0, the opposite of the number.

**9.** In Exercise 1, you found a number that gives a sum of 0 when it is added to 3. This is the same as solving the *equation* $3 + x = 0$. In Exercise 7, you found a number that gives a sum less than 0 when it is added to 3. To solve the *inequality* $3 + x < 0$, though, it is not enough to find a single number.

**a.** Find three more solutions of the inequality $3 + x < 0$. Draw a number-line picture for each sum. Answers will vary.

**b.** Describe *all* the $x$ values that are solutions of $3 + x < 0$. It may help to think about walking the number line.

Any number less than $-3$



### *Reaching* All Learners

**AL Approaching Level** For students who seem to be struggling with inequalities, suggest that they use a number line to help them determine the results.

### On the Spot Assessment

Give the students a Rapid Fire Quiz. Have the students take out a small sheet of paper and give them two questions, one for greater than and one for less than. Once the questions are complete, have students switch papers for a quick check.

## Investigation 5

***On Your Own Exercises***
Pages 148–153
Exercises 39–40, 48–61

**Inequalities and Negative Numbers**
Students will learn how negative numbers can affect the inequality symbol when solving.

### Develop & Understand: A

*Suggested Grouping: Pairs*

▶ **Exercise 10** Students generalize what they did for Exercises 4–7. This helps prepare students for predicting signs of sums and differences in the Investigation 6.

**Teacher Tips** In Exercise 9b, students may visualize the expression as $x + 3$ on the number line. These students will imagine the pointer and arrow as a single entity, or unit, representing $+ 3$.

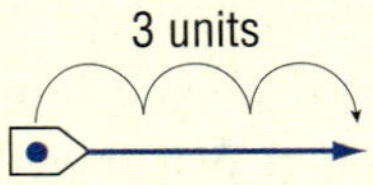


Students should realize that the only values of $x$ that make $x + 3 < 0$ true are the values for which the arrow is on a point less than zero. As students visualize moving the unit on the number line, it soon becomes obvious that the arrow is on points less than zero only when the pointer is on points that are less than $-3$.

Some students will visualize the expression as $3 + x$ on a number line. This picture will have the pointer based at 3, moving in the direction the pointer is pointing. Because the sign of $x$ is not known, we do not know which direction the pointer should point or how far the pointer should move. The two possible number-line pictures that describe $3 + x$ are the following:

Negative $x$:

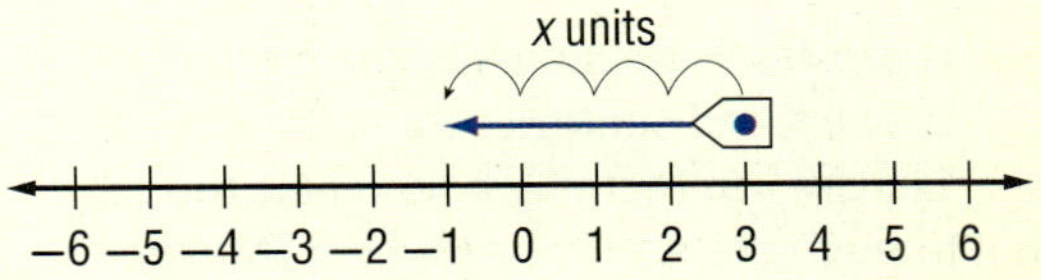


Positive $x$:

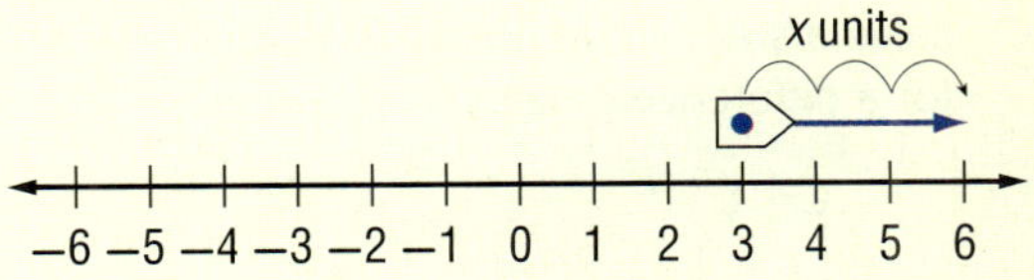

**Teacher Tips** It is immediately clear that $x$ cannot be positive since no matter how small $x$ is, the second number-line picture always lands on a positive number. Once that is clear, students must figure out how to use the first number-line picture to come up with an answer. Since we are looking for a sum less than zero, the arrow must land on a value less than zero. The length of the arrow must be more than 3, so $x$ must be less than $-3$.

## Develop & Understand: B

*Suggested Grouping: Pairs*

In this exercise set, students extend their thinking to include subtraction of signed numbers. They use inequalities and number lines in their explorations. The exercises in the exercise set mirror those in Exercises 1–10, so the difficulties your students faced while solving those exercises may reoccur as they work though these exercises. It is not important for students to master solving simple inequalities at this time.

▶ **Exercises 11–13** Students use number sense to determine that any number, positive or negative, subtracted from itself is zero. This should be intuitive for most students.

▶ **Exercises 14–17** Students continue their exploration of inequalities by finding a number that can be subtracted from a given number to have a difference that is greater than zero.

Watch for students who solve for a difference less than zero. Most students who make this error will not have read the directions carefully. Similar exercises in Exercises 1–10 ask students to find sums less than zero, so some students may assume that since the exercises are similar they should find a difference less than zero here. Other students may not be clear on the meaning of greater than and less than. Review these concepts with these students.

**Wrap-Up** Have students share their answers and strategies for solving Exercise 19. Learning how others thought through the exercise may help students solidify their understanding of inequalities. It may also promote a discussion on how to solve a subtraction inequality when looking for a difference greater than zero.



**10.** Now think about what you might do if you wanted to solve an inequality related to each of Exercises 4–7.

**a.** What number could you add to a given positive number to get a sum less than 0? Any number less than its opposite

**b.** What number could you add to a given negative number to get a sum less than 0? Any number less than its opposite

## Develop & Understand: B

**Tell what number you could put in each blank to make a difference of 0.**

**11.** $\frac{2}{3}$ − _____ $\frac{2}{3}$ **12.** −3 − _____ −3

**13.** Look at your answers to Exercises 11 and 12.

**a.** If you have a positive number, what number could you subtract from it to get a difference of 0? The number itself

**b.** If you have a negative number, what number could you subtract from it to get a difference of 0? The number itself

**Give one number in each blank to make a difference greater than 0.**

**14.** 7 − _____ **15.** −2.4 − _____

**16.** $\frac{3}{4}$ − _____ **17.** 5 − _____

**18.** In Exercises 14–17, how did you figure out what number to put in the blank?

**19.** In Exercise 17, you found a number that, when subtracted from 5, gives a difference greater than 0. That is, you found one solution of the inequality $5 - x > 0$.

**a.** Find three more solutions of the inequality $5 - x > 0$. Draw a number-line picture for each difference. Answers will vary.

**b.** Describe all the solutions of the inequality $5 - x > 0$. It might help to use a number-line picture. Any number less than 5

**20.** Now think about what you might do if you wanted to solve an inequality related to each of Exercises 14–17.

**a.** What number could you subtract from a given positive number to get a difference greater than 0? Any number less than the original number

**b.** What number could you subtract from a given negative number to get a difference greater than 0? Any number less than the original number

14. Answer must be less than 7.
15. Answer must be less than −2.4.
16. Answer must be less than $\frac{3}{4}$.
17. Answer must be less than 5.
18. Possible answer: I found the number that was 1 less than the number that would make the difference 0, the opposite of the number.

## Think & Discuss

Consider the following expressions.

Expression 1: $\boxed{n}$ Expression 2: $\boxed{5n + 8}$

For what value of $n$ does Expression 1 equal Expression 2?
For $n = -2$

For what value(s) of $n$ is Expression 1 greater than Expression 2?
For values less than $-2$

For what value(s) of $n$ is Expression 1 less than Expression 2?
For values greater than $-2$

## Develop & Understand: C

21. For each pair of expressions, determine the values that make the following statements true.
    a. Expression 1 is greater than Expression 2.
    b. Expression 1 is equal to Expression 2.
    c. Expression 1 is less than Expression 2.

| Expression 1 | Expression 2 |
|---|---|
| $3a + 6$ | 15 |
| $2y$ | $y + 7$ |
| $3k + 8$ | $-13$ |
| $5m + 1$ | $3m + 9$ |

21. $3a + 6$ and 15:
a. For values greater than 3
b. For $a = 3$
c. For values less than 3

$2y$ and $y + 7$:
a. For values greater than 7
b. For $y = 7$
c. For values less than 7

$3k + 8$ and $-13$:
a. For values greater than $-7$
b. For $k = -7$
c. For values less than $-7$

$5m + 1$ and $3m + 9$:
a. For values greater than 4
b. For $m = 4$
c. For values less than 4

## Share & Summarize

1–5. See margin.

Without doing the calculation, tell whether each sum or difference is positive or negative. Explain how you know.

1. $-25 + 36$
2. $-53 - (-14)$
3. $45 - 87$
4. $123 - (-220)$
5. Choose two of the previous expressions. Find the sum or difference. Explain your steps so that someone who is not in your class could understand them. You may refer to the number-line model or another method that makes sense to you.



### Think & Discuss

*Suggested Grouping: Pairs*

Students may not know where to begin working on these questions. Suggest that each person pick an expression and then choose a number to start with. Once the students begin plugging numbers into their expression, the comparison will begin.

### Develop & Understand: C

*Suggested Grouping: Three Students*

▶ **Exercise 21** For each row of the table, have each student take a part *a*, *b*, or *c*. Then have the students switch parts for the next row and continue until they have completed the table.

**Math Link**

One way to assist students in remembering which direction the inequality symbol goes, is to tell them that it is the mouth of a crocodile and that the crocodile only swallows up the larger value.

### Share & Summarize

Students use what they have learned to tell whether a sum or a difference is positive or negative. Although students have not been asked similar questions, they should be able to answer these questions. Encourage students to share their answers to Question 5 with the class. Some students will use number lines or inequalities to support their answers. Others may use number sense.

**Additional Answers**
**Share & Summarize**

1. Positive; starting at $-25$ and moving to the right more than 25 units gives a sum greater than 0.
2. Negative; starting at $-53$ and moving to the right less than 53 units gives a sum less than 0.
3. Negative; starting at 45 and moving to the left more than 45 units gives a sum less than 0.
4. Positive; starting at 123 and moving to the right moves me even farther from 0 in the positive direction.
5. Possible answer: For $45 - 87 = -42$, think about starting at 45 on the number line. Subtracting 87 means you move to the left 87 units. After 45 units, you're at 0, and you still have to move another 42 units to the left, so you end at $-42$.

# Investigation 6

**On Your Own Exercises**
Pages 148–153
Exercises 41–43, 62–68

**Predicting** This investigation reinforces students' understanding of how to add and subtract signed numbers.

Discuss the opening paragraph with students. Tell students that they will be able to develop and test their strategies during this investigation.

## Develop & Understand: A

*Suggested Grouping: Individuals*

These three exercises set up the investigation by getting students to begin thinking about what signs are possible when working with particular sums and differences involving signed numbers. While it is possible to make up a sum and a difference for the first two exercises, it is impossible for the third exercise. This impossibility motivates the need to determine the sign of various combinations of positive and negative numbers in sums and differences. This is the focus of the remainder of the investigation.

**Wrap-Up** Have individuals share their answers in small groups and reach a consensus about the details that should be included in their explanations. They can share their final solutions with the class.

Discuss the eight ways positive and negative numbers can be combined to add and subtract. Tell them that in the next exercise set they will classify these combinations by looking at the sign of the answer.

## Develop & Understand: B

*Suggested Grouping: Pairs*

Students classify the sums and differences of combinations of negative and/or positive numbers as always positive, always negative, or sometimes positive, sometimes negative, and sometimes zero. At this point, the students have done enough work with "walking the number line" to be able to use the model to justify their answers, a first step toward proof.

# Investigation 6 Predict Signs of Sums and Differences

Look over your answers to the Share & Summarize on the previous page. Can you always use your strategy to predict whether a sum will be positive or negative? If you can, you have a way to check that sums and differences have the correct sign.

## Develop & Understand: A

1. If possible, give an example in which the sum of a positive number and a negative number is negative. If it is not possible, explain why.
2. If possible, give an example in which the difference between two negative numbers is positive. If it is not possible, explain why.
3. If possible, give an example in which the sum of two negative numbers is positive. If it is not possible, explain why.

1. Answers will vary. The positive number must be less than the absolute value of the negative number.
2. Answers will vary. Using the form $a - b = c$, if $a > b$, then $c$ is positive.
3. Not possible; Possible explanation: When you add two negative numbers on the number line, you start to the left of 0, direct the pointer in the positive direction (to the right), and then move backward (to the left). This will always result in another number to the left of 0, which must be negative.

Positive and negative numbers can be combined in sums and differences in eight ways.

- positive + positive
- positive + negative
- negative + negative
- negative + positive
- positive − positive
- positive − negative
- negative − negative
- negative − positive

You will now explore each of these combinations.

## Develop & Understand: B

Figure out whether the sums or differences in each category are *always negative; always positive;* or *sometimes positive, sometimes negative, and sometimes 0.* Explain how you know you are correct.

4–11. See margin.

4. positive + positive
5. positive + negative
6. negative + negative
7. negative + positive
8. positive − positive
9. negative − positive
10. positive − negative
11. negative − negative



**Additional Answers**

4. Always positive; Possible explanation: On the number line, you start to the right of 0 and move farther to the right, so the answer will be to the right of 0.
5. Sometimes positive, sometimes negative, and sometimes 0; Possible explanation: These three examples show the three possibilities:
$3 + (-2) = 1, 3 + (-5) = -2,$
$3 + (-3) = 0$
6. Always negative; Possible explanation: On the number line, you start to the left of 0 and move farther to the left, so the answer will be to the left of 0.

**See page 171A for Additional Answers to Exercises 7 to 11.**

**12.** Look at your work from Exercises 4–11. See below.

**a.** Which combinations produce sums or differences that are sometimes negative, sometimes positive, and sometimes 0?

**b.** Choose one of the combinations from Part a. Without doing the calculation, figure out how you can tell whether a given sum or difference involving that combination will produce a negative number, a positive number, or 0.

## *Share & Summarize*

**1.** Suppose the sum of two numbers is less than 0.

**a.** Could both numbers be negative? If so, give an example. If not, explain why not. Yes; Possible example: $-1 + (-1) = -2$

**b.** Could both numbers be positive? If so, give an example. If not, explain why not. No; the sum of two positives is always positive.

**c.** Could one number be negative and one positive? If so, give an example. If not, explain why not. Yes; Possible example: $-3 + 1 = -2$

**2.** Suppose the difference between two numbers is greater than 0.

**a.** Could both numbers be positive? If so, give an example. If not, explain why not. Yes; Possible example: $9 - 3 = 6$

**b.** Could both numbers be negative? If so, give an example. If not, explain why not. Yes; Possible example: $-8 - (-12) = 4$

**c.** Could one number be negative and one positive? If so, give an example. If not, explain why not. Yes; Possible example: $6 - (-4) = 10$

12a. positive + negative, negative + positive, positive − positive, negative − negative

12b. Possible answers:
positive + negative and negative + positive: If the positive number is greater than the absolute value of the negative number, the sum will be positive. If the absolute value of the negative number is greater than the positive number, the sum will be negative. If the absolute value of the negative number equals the positive number, the sum will be 0.
positive − positive and negative − negative: If the first number is greater, the difference will be positive. If the second number is greater, the difference will be negative. If the numbers are equal, the difference will be 0.



▶ **Exercise 12** Students use their answers to Exercises 4–11 to look at the combinations that are sometimes negative, sometimes positive, and sometimes zero. In Part b, students choose one of these combinations and find the conditions that produce a positive answer, a negative answer, and a zero answer. You may want to ask different pairs of students to choose different combinations of numbers and report their findings to the class. This way you can be sure that all possibilities are investigated.

**Wrap-Up** Have a pair of students relate their finding from Exercise 12b. This will allow all students to learn how to determine if a sum or difference will be positive, negative, or zero.

## *Share & Summarize*

These questions require that students process some of the relationships in the investigation in reverse order. They are given the sign of a sum or difference and asked to determine the sign of the two numbers being added or subtracted. After completing the questions individually, have students share answers as a whole class.

## On the Spot Assessment

This investigation provides the only opportunity for students to focus on classifying signs of sums and differences of signed numbers. It is not crucial that rules developed be memorized, but it is important that students understand why the rules work. If students are having difficulty understanding the rules, you might act out the eight cases on the number line.

**Investigation 1**
Pages 128–130
Practice & Apply: 1–6

**Investigation 3**
Pages 134–139
Practice & Apply: 7–27
Connect & Extend: 44–45

**Investigation 4**
Pages 140–142
Practice & Apply: 28–38
Connect & Extend: 46–47

**Investigation 5**
Pages 143–145
Practice & Apply: 39–40
Connect & Extend: 48–61

**Investigation 6**
Pages 146–147
Practice & Apply: 41–43
Connect & Extend: 62–68

**Assign Anytime**
Mixed Review: 70–79

▶ **Exercises 7–9** Make sure that students explain how to find the answers, and that they do not just write the equations.

**On Your Own Exercises**
**Lesson 3.1**

## Practice & Apply

In Exercises 1–5, draw chip models to show how to find each sum or difference.

1. $-2 + 7$
2. $3 - 11$
3. $8 - (-3)$
4. $9 + (-4)$
5. $-5 - 6$

6. Use the chip board below for Exercises a–c.

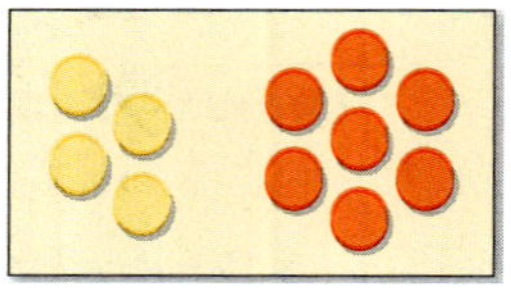

a. What is the value of the board? $-3$

b. Explain two ways to change the numbers of chips on the board without changing the value shown on the board.

c. Describe a real-life problem this board could represent. Answers will vary.

6b. Pair yellow with red chips and remove the four pairs, leaving only 3 red chips; add any number of pairs of yellow and red chips

In Exercises 7–9, walk the number line to find each sum or difference. Describe your steps in words. Include the following in your descriptions. See below.

- where on the number line you start
- the direction the pointer is facing
- whether you move forward or backward and how far you move
- the point on the number line at which you end, which is the answer
- the complete addition or subtraction equation

7. $-8 + 5$
8. $8 + (-4)$
9. $3 - (-5)$

**Walk the number line to compute each sum or difference.**

10. $-6 - 3$ $-9$
11. $-2 + (-4)$ $-6$
12. $2 + (-11)$ $-9$
13. $-9 - (-5)$ $-4$
14. $4 - 9$ $-5$
15. $-6 + 14$ 8
16. $-5 - (-11)$ 6
17. $12 - (-10)$ 22

**Estimate each sum or difference. Then, walk the number line to compute each sum or difference.**

18. $2\frac{1}{5} - \left(-3\frac{2}{5}\right)$
19. $-8.25 + 1.75$
20. $-\frac{13}{2} - \left(-\frac{13}{4}\right)$
21. $4.9 - (-3.2)$

Answers:

1. 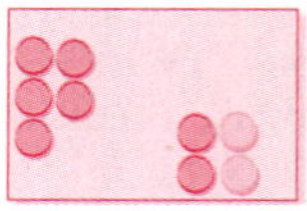
5

2. 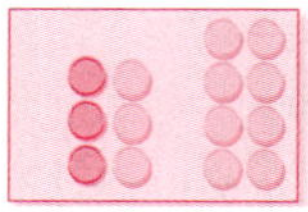
$3 + (-11) = -8$

3. 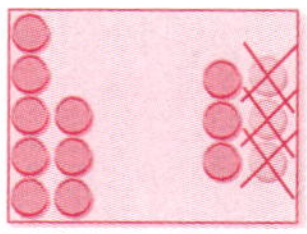
11

4. 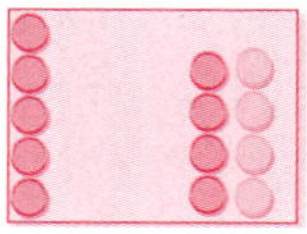
5

5. 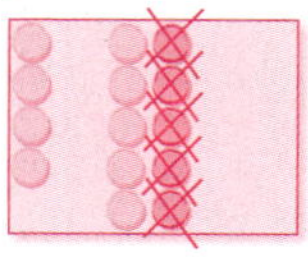
$-11$

7. Start at $-8$, point right, move forward 5, end at $-3$; $-8 + 5 = -3$
8. Start at 8, point right, move backward 4, end at 4; $8 + (-4) = 4$
9. Start at 3, point left, move backward 5, end at 8; $3 - (-5) = 8$

18. Possible estimate: 5; $5\frac{3}{5}$
19. Possible estimate: $-6$; $-6.5$
20. Possible estimate: $-3\frac{1}{2}$; $-\frac{13}{4}$
21. Possible estimate: 8; 8.1

Walk the number line to compute each sum or difference. Record your steps by making a number-line drawing. Write the complete addition or subtraction equation next to the drawing. 22–27. See margin.

**22.** $-2 + (-7)$

**23.** $6 - (-2)$

**24.** $5 - 7$

**25.** $-3 + 11$

**26.** $2.2 - 1.4$

**27.** $-5\frac{1}{3} + 2\frac{5}{6}$

In Exercises 28–31, write the addition or subtraction equation represented by the drawing.

**28.** $-3 + (-3) = -6$

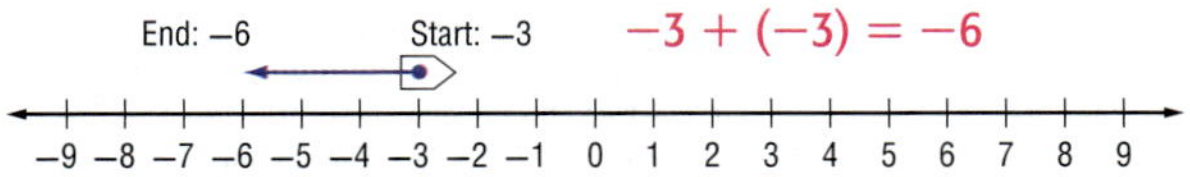


**29.** $-5 + 12 = 7$

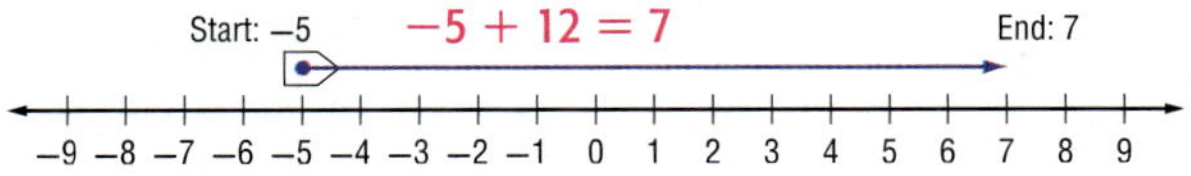


**30.** $-5 - (-9) = 4$

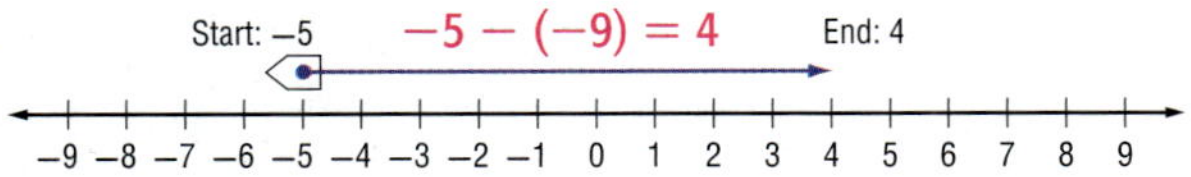


**31.** $2 - 11 = -9$

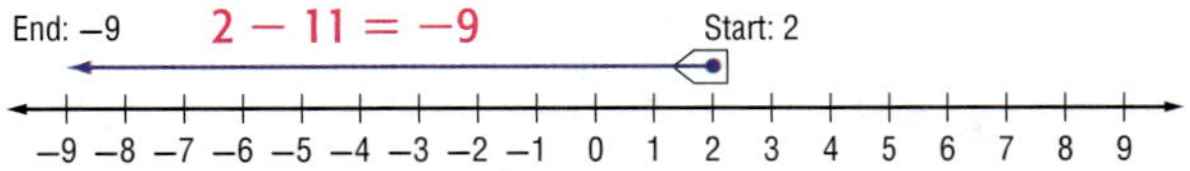


**32.** The sum of two numbers is $-8$. What could the numbers be? Give three possibilities. Possible answer: $-3$ and $-5$, 1 and $-9$, $-11$ and 3

Write an addition equation and a subtraction equation for each situation. You might want to make a drawing.

**33.** Start value: $-7$

End value: 9 $-7 + 16 = 9, -7 - (-16) = 9$

**34.** Start value: $2\frac{1}{7}$

End value: $-3\frac{3}{7}$ $2\frac{1}{7} + \left(-5\frac{4}{7}\right) = -3\frac{3}{7}, 2\frac{1}{7} - 5\frac{4}{7} = -3\frac{3}{7}$



On Your Own Exercises

## Additional Answers

22. $-2 + (-7) = -9$

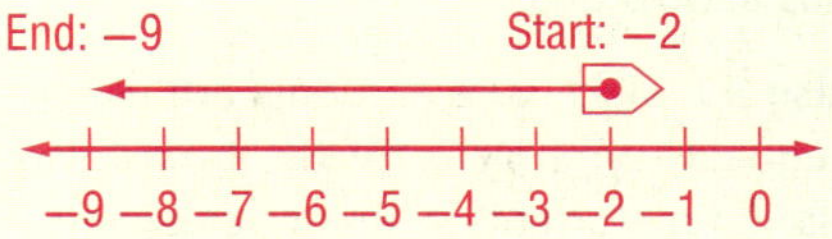


23. $6 - (-2) = 8$

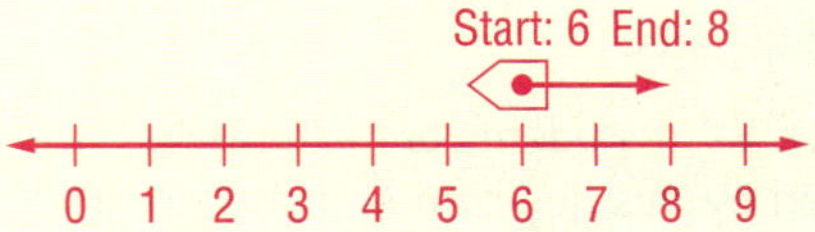


24. $5 - 7 = -2$

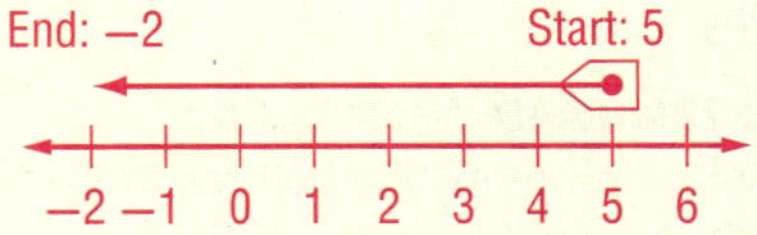


25. $-3 + 11 = 8$

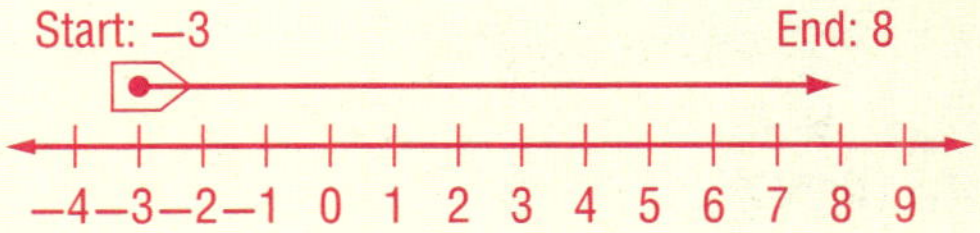


26. $2.2 - 1.4 = 0.8$

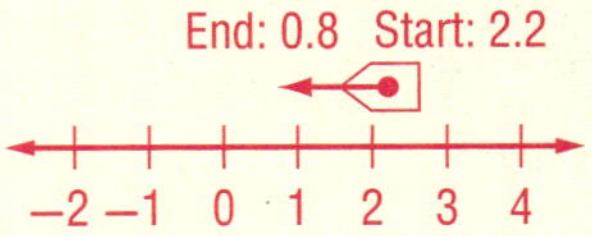


27. $-5\frac{1}{3} + 2\frac{5}{6} = -2\frac{1}{2}$

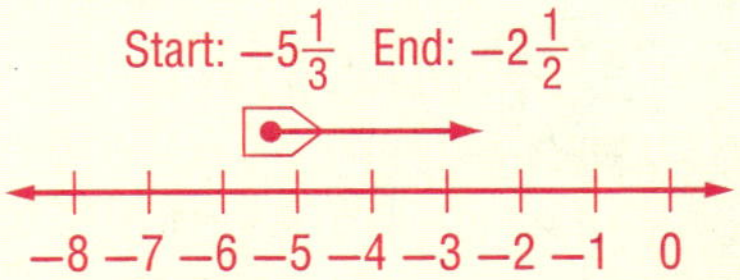

▶ **Exercises 35–38** Students may need reminding that adding the opposite is the same as subtracting.

▶ **Exercise 39** Make sure students are using the inequality symbols correctly. It may also be helpful for students who are struggling to do the questions out of order. Begin with the two expressions equal and then do the inequality parts.

▶ **Exercise 41** If students are extremely bothered by this question and choose to give up, instruct the students that the situation is not possible, but have them explain why.

▶ **Exercises 42 and 43** Watch out for students who do not justify their responses. These students may be having difficulty and do not want to seek out help.



Compute each difference. Write your answer in the form of a subtraction equation. Then write an equivalent addition equation.

**35.** $25.2 - (-3.4)$ $25.2 - (-3.4) = 28.6, 25.2 + 3.4 = 28.6$

**36.** $-43 - 18$ $-43 - 18 = -61, -43 + (-18) = -61$

Compute each sum. Write your answer in the form of an addition equation. Then write an equivalent subtraction equation.

**37.** $-6 + (-9)$ $-6 + (-9) = -15, -6 - 9 = -15$

**38.** $-21.8 + 17.4$ $-21.8 + 17.4 = -4.4, -21.8 - (-17.4) = -4.4$

**39.** Expression 1 equals $5x$. Expression 2 equals $3x + 8$. Find values for $x$ such that:

- Expression 1 is greater than Expression 2 Values greater than 4
- Expression 1 equals Expression 2 4
- Expression 1 is less than Expression 2 Values less than 4

**40. Algebra** In this exercise, solve the inequality $-5 - y < 0$.

**a.** Find three positive values of $y$ that make the inequality true.

**b.** Find three negative values of $y$ that make the inequality true.

**c.** Describe *all* the values of $y$ that make the inequality true.

40a. Answers will vary.
40b. Answers will vary. Must be a number between $-5$ and 0.
40c. All values greater than $-5$

**41.** If possible, give an example in which a negative number is subtracted from a positive number and the result is negative. If it is not possible, explain why.

41. Not possible; Possible explanation: Subtracting a negative number is the same as adding a positive number; the sum of two positive numbers cannot be negative.

**42. Number Sense** The sum of two numbers is greater than 0.

**a.** Could both numbers be negative? If so, give an example. If not, explain why not.

42a. No; Possible explanation: The sum of two negative numbers is always negative.

**b.** Could both numbers be positive? If so, give an example. If not, explain why not. Yes; Possible example: $2 + 2 = 4$

**c.** Could one number be negative and one positive? If so, give an example. If not, explain why not. Yes; Possible example: $-3 + 5 = 2$

**43.** The difference between two numbers is less than 0.

**a.** Could both numbers be positive? If so, give an example. If not, explain why not. Yes; Possible example: $2 - 5 = -3$

**b.** Could both numbers be negative? If so, give an example. If not, explain why not. Yes; Possible example: $-5 - (-2) = -3$

**c.** Could one number be negative and one positive? If so, give an example. If not, explain why not. Yes; Possible example: $-5 - 3 = -8$

## Connect & Extend

**Complete each computation by walking the number line. Explain each step you take.**

44. −8; Put the pointer at 3, facing right. Move backward 4 spaces. Move backward 2 spaces. Face pointer left. Move forward 5 spaces.

45. 2; Put the pointer at −2, facing left. Move forward 9 spaces. Face pointer to the right. Move forward 2 spaces. Face pointer to the left. Move forward 4 spaces. Move backward 15 spaces.

**44.** $3 + (-4) + (-2) - 5$ **45.** $-2 - 9 + 2 - 4 - (-15)$

**46. Statistics** The chart shows the high temperature, in degrees Fahrenheit, for the first ten days of the year in a small Alaskan town. What is the average of these temperatures? 1.1°F

| Date | 1/1 | 1/2 | 1/3 | 1/4 | 1/5 | 1/6 | 1/7 | 1/8 | 1/9 | 1/10 |
|---|---|---|---|---|---|---|---|---|---|---|
| Temp (°F) | 3 | 1 | 13 | 5 | 2 | 2 | −4 | −7 | −2 | −2 |

**47.** Lazaro said, "If you add −3 to my sister's age, you will get my age." Lazaro is 12. How old is his sister? 15

**Without calculating each sum or difference, figure out whether it is less than 0, greater than 0, or equal to 0.**

**48.** $-8 - 9$ Less than 0 **49.** $-3 - (-\pi)$ Greater than 0 **50.** $-78 + 2^6$ Less than 0

**51.** Copy and complete the flowchart.

9 —(· 3)→ 27 —(− 20)→ 7

52a. −1 and −5, −2 and −4, −3 and −3

**52.** *Integers* are counting numbers, their opposites, and zero ..., −3, −2, −1, 0, 1, 2, 3, ... . The sum of two negative integers is −6.

**a.** What could the integers be? List all the possibilities.

**b.** Find two more pairs of negative numbers (not integers) whose sum is −6. Possible answer: $-4.2 + (-1.8)$, $-\frac{2}{7} + \left(-5\frac{5}{7}\right)$

**Algebra** Use the distributive property to rewrite each expression as simply as you can.

**53.** $6x - (-2x)$ $8x$ **54.** $3z - 5z$ $-2z$ **55.** $7x + (-2x)$ $5x$

### Math Link

The *absolute value* of a number, its distance from 0, is represented with vertical lines. $|5| = 5$ because 5 is 5 units from 0. $|-7| = 7$ because −7 is 7 units from 0.

**56. Prove It!** Marta thinks that for all values of $x$ and $y$, the following equation is true.

$$|x + y| = |x| + |y|$$

If $x$ is −5 and $y$ is −6, the two sides of the equation become

$$|x + y| = |-5 + -6| = |-11| = 11 \text{ and}$$
$$|x| + |y| = |-5| + |-6| = 5 + 6 = 11.$$

Is Marta correct? If so, explain why. If not, give an example of values for $x$ and $y$ such that $|x + y| \neq |x| + |y|$. No; Possible example: $|-1 + 2| \neq |-1| + |2|$





▶ **Exercises 44–45** Make sure that students explain how they know their answers are correct. Otherwise, they might solve the exercises by evaluating the expressions and that would defeat the purpose of the exercises.

▶ **Exercise 46** Ask students to look at the table and describe what they would do to find the average.

▶ **Exercise 52b Extension** There are several extension questions you could ask that are algebraic in nature, such as, How many pairs of negative integers have a sum of −7? −8? −9?

▶ **Exercise 56 Extension** Once students have determined that $|x + y| \neq |x| + |y|$, the obvious question is this: "If $|x + y| \neq |x| + |y|$, what is the relationship between $|x + y|$ and $|x| + |y|$? Is one greater than the other? Is one greater than or equal to the other? Is there no relationship?"

It turns out that $|x + y| \leq |x| + |y|$. You can prove this by thinking about cases: How do you show the inequality holds if $x$ and $y$ are negative? What if $x$ is positive and $y$ is negative? What if $x$ is negative and $y$ is positive? What if $x$ and $y$ are both positive? The inequality $|x + y| \leq |x| + |y|$ is known as the Triangle Inequality.

▶ **Exercise 62** You may wish to have students who are having difficulty thinking and computing with fractions first determine the integer between $-\frac{1}{2}$ and $-1\frac{1}{2}$ (−1) and work from that number. Then the students can use mental math or draw number lines to find the missing numbers.



**57.** Choose a number. Write down both the number and its opposite.

**a.** What happens when you add the two numbers? Their sum is 0.

**b.** Will the same thing happen when you add *any* number to its opposite? Explain why or why not.

57b. Yes; Possible explanation: Adding a number and its opposite is equivalent to subtracting the number from itself, which always has a result of 0.

**Algebra** Solve each equation by using backtracking or another method.

**58.** $x + (-9) = 1.5$ 10.5 **59.** $y - 3 = -0.5$ 2.5 **60.** $3 - x = 8.4$ −5.4

**61.** What values of y make each inequality true?

**a.** $2 + y < 0$ Any value less than −2

**b.** $-10 < 2 + y$ Any value greater than −12

**c.** $-10 < 2 + y$ and $2 + y < 0$ Any value between −2 and −12

**62.** Copy each exercise. Fill in the blank with a number that gives a sum between $-1\frac{1}{2}$ and $-\frac{1}{2}$. See margin.

**a.** 10 + ____ **b.** −1.2 + ____

**c.** −2 + ____ **d.** − 84 + ____

**e.** In Parts a–d, what did you need to do to make the answer between $-1\frac{1}{2}$ and $-\frac{1}{2}$?

**Algebra** Without solving each equation, determine whether the value of $x$ is less than 0, equal to 0, or greater than 0.

**63.** $x - 3 = -5$ Less than 0 **64.** $-x + 3 = 5$ Less than 0

**65.** $4 - x = 9$ Less than 0 **66.** $x - 3 = 12$ Greater than 0

**67.** In this exercise, you will investigate the possible results for the sum of two positive numbers and a negative number.

**a.** Choose two positive numbers and one negative number. Is their sum positive, negative, or 0? Answers will vary.

**b.** Suppose you repeat Part a with different numbers. Will the sum be always positive; always negative; or sometimes positive, sometimes negative, and sometimes 0? How do you know?

67b. Sometimes positive, sometimes negative, and sometimes 0; Possible explanation: The sum of two positive numbers is another positive. If you add that positive sum to a negative number, the sum may be positive, negative, or 0.



## Additional Answers

62a. Answers will vary; any number between $-10\frac{1}{2}$ and $-11\frac{1}{2}$ will work.

62b. Answers will vary; any number between −0.3 and 0.7 will work.

62c. Answers will vary; any number between 0.5 and 1.5 will work.

62d. Answers will vary; any number between 82.5 and 83.5 will work.

62e. Possible answer: I know that −1 is between $-1\frac{1}{2}$ and $-\frac{1}{2}$, so I found a number that made each sum equal to −1.

68. **In Your Own Words** Write a letter to a student a year younger than you. Explain how to subtract a negative number from another negative number. Include examples. Answers will vary. Check students' work.

69. **Preview** In the next investigation, you will explore the multiplication and division of signed numbers.

a. Complete the equation: $(-2) + (-2) + (-2) =$ ____. $-6$

b. Write a multiplication expression that represents the sum in Part a. $3(-2)$ or $(-2)3$

c. What is the sign of the first factor in the multiplication expression? Of the second factor? Of the product?

69c. Answer depends on expression; answer depends on expression; negative

## Mixed Review

70. Evaluate $\frac{1}{2}k^2$ for each value of $k$.

a. 0 $0$ b. $\frac{1}{2}$ $\frac{1}{8}$ c. 1.2 $0.72$ d. 4 $8$

71. Evaluate $10m^2$ for each value of $m$.

a. 0 $0$ b. $\frac{1}{2}$ $2\frac{1}{2}$ c. 1.2 $14.4$ d. 4 $160$

72. Evaluate $3p^2 + 10$ for each value of $p$.

a. 0 $10$ b. $\frac{1}{2}$ $10\frac{3}{4}$ c. 1.2 $14.32$ d. 4 $58$

**Find each sum. Simplify your answers as much as possible.**

73. $\frac{1}{25} + \frac{4}{25}$ $\frac{5}{25}$, or $\frac{1}{5}$

74. $\frac{1}{10} + \frac{6}{10}$ $\frac{7}{10}$

75. $\frac{2}{5} + \frac{1}{5} + 3$

76. $\frac{1}{2} + \frac{1}{3}$ $\frac{5}{6}$

77. $\frac{4}{9} + \frac{5}{6}$

78. $1\frac{1}{5} + 2\frac{3}{4}$

75. $3\frac{3}{5}$, or $\frac{18}{5}$

77. $\frac{23}{18}$ or $1\frac{5}{18}$

78. $\frac{79}{20}$ or $3\frac{19}{20}$

79. **Statistics** The table shows the approximate distribution of blood types in the U.S. population. "Positive" and "negative" indicate whether a person's blood has a particular component called the *Rh factor*.

a. What percentage of people in the United States have Rh-negative blood? 16%

b. The projected U.S. population in 2050 is 391,000,000 people. If the distribution of blood types remains fairly constant, how many people in 2050 will have AB-negative blood? 3,910,000

**Blood Types in the U.S.**

| Blood Type | Percent |
|---|---|
| O positive | 38 |
| O negative | 7 |
| A positive | 34 |
| A negative | 6 |
| B positive | 9 |
| B negative | 2 |
| AB positive | 3 |
| AB negative | 1 |



On Your Own Exercises

## Quick Check

**Informal Assessment** Students should be able to:

- ✔ add and subtract signed numbers
- ✔ use number sense when working with signed numbers
- ✔ predict the sign of a sum or difference involving negative and positive numbers

## Quick Quiz

1. Find the average of these seven numbers: −2, −1, 0, 15, −3, 1, −4. $\frac{6}{7}$ or about 0.86

2. Use the "walking the number line" model to explain why adding a negative number is equivalent to subtracting the positive of that number. Possible answer: In both cases you move the same number of units to the left. When you add a negative number on the number line, you direct the pointer in the positive direction and move backward. This is a move to the left. When you subtract a positive of that number, you direct the pointer in the negative direction and move forward. This is also a move to the left.

3. Will the following sums and differences be A) always negative, B) always positive, or C) sometimes negative, sometimes positive, and sometimes zero?
   a. Negative number minus positive number A
   b. Negative number plus positive number C
   c. Negative number plus negative number A

LESSON 3.2

# Multiply and Divide with Negative Numbers

### Objectives

- ▶ To multiply and divide with signed numbers
- ▶ To predict the sign of a product or quotient involving signed numbers
- ▶ To develop number sense with signed numbers

## Overview

In this lesson, students learn how to multiply and divide with negative numbers. Students build on their understanding of addition and subtraction of signed numbers and study patterns in computation to learn rules for multiplying and dividing with signed numbers. Students should not use calculators in this lesson unless otherwise indicated.

## Advance Preparation

No advance preparation is needed for this lesson.

| | Summary | Materials | On Your Own Exercises (pp. 165–168) | Assessment Opportunities |
|---|---|---|---|---|
| **Investigation 1** (p. 155) Pacing: 2 days | Students learn rules for multiplying negative and positive numbers by thinking of multiplication as repeated addition. | | Practice & Apply: 1–6<br>Connect & Extend: 34–36<br>Mixed Review: 61–65 | • Share & Summarize (p. 156)<br>• Troubleshooting (p. 156) |
| **Investigation 2** (p. 157) Pacing: 1 day | Students learn rules for multiplying two negative numbers by examining patterns in products involving positive and negative numbers. | | Practice & Apply: 7–20<br>Connect & Extend: 37–46<br>Mixed Review: 61–65 | • Share & Summarize (p. 159)<br>• Troubleshooting (p. 159) |
| **Investigation 3** (p. 160) Pacing: 1 day | Students derive rules for dividing with signed numbers from their rules for multiplying with signed numbers. | | Practice & Apply: 21–28<br>Connect & Extend: 47–55<br>Mixed Review: 61–65 | • Share & Summarize (p. 161) |
| **Investigation 4** (p. 162) Pacing: 1 day | Students will compute the measures of central tendency: range, mode, median, and mean for data that involves signed numbers. | | Practice & Apply: 29–33<br>Connect & Extend: 56–59<br>Mixed Review: 61–65 | • On the Spot Assessment (p. 164)<br>• Share & Summarize (p. 164)<br>• Troubleshooting (pp. 162, 164) |

# Leveled Lesson Resources

CRM *Available in:* **Chapter 3 Resource Masters**

Also on TeacherWorks™
Lesson 3.2

## Study Guide and Intervention (p. 19) AL

**Lesson 3.2 Study Guide and Intervention**
***Multiply and Divide with Negative Numbers***

**Multiplying and Dividing with Negative Numbers**
If both numbers are negative, the answer is *positive*. If one number is negative and the other is positive, the answer is *negative*.

**Negative Numbers and Exponents**
If a negative number has an even exponent, the result is *positive*. If a negative number has an odd exponent, the result is *negative*.

**Example 1** **Multiply $5(-2)$.**
$5(-2) = -10$ The integers have different signs. The product is negative.

**Example 2** **Multiply $-6(-9.2)$.**
$-6(-9.2) = 55.2$ The integers have the same sign. The product is positive.

**Example 3** **Multiply $(-7)^2$.**
$(-7)^2 = (-7)(-7) = 49$ The exponent is an even number. The product is positive.

**Example 4** **Divide $\frac{30}{-5}$.**
$\frac{30}{-5}$ The integers have different signs.
$\frac{30}{-5} = -6$ The quotient is negative.

**Example 5** **Divide $-100 \div (-5)$.**
$-100 \div (-5)$ The integers have the same sign.
$-100 \div (-5) = 20$ The quotient is positive.

**Exercises**

Multiply.

**1.** $-5(8)$ **2.** $-3\left(-\frac{7}{4}\right)$ **3.** $10(-8.2)$

**4.** $-8\left(1\frac{2}{7}\right)$ **5.** $-12(-12)$ **6.** $(-8)^2$

Divide.

**7.** $-12 \div 4$ **8.** $-34.5 \div (-15)$ **9.** $\frac{18}{-2}$

**10.** $-36 \div (-3)^2$ **11.** $-10\frac{2}{5} \div 10$ **12.** $\frac{-80}{-20}$

**13.** $350 \div (-25)$ **14.** $-440 \div (-2)^3$ **15.** $\frac{-256}{4^2}$

## Skills Practice (p. 20) AL OL

**Lesson 3.2 Skills Practice**
***Multiply and Divide with Negative Numbers***

**Compute each product.**

**1.** $-4(\frac{2}{3})$ **2.** $-2(-8)$

**3.** $12\frac{3}{4}(-4)$ **4.** $-6(5.125)$

**5.** $-10(-9)$ **6.** $-(5)^2$

**7.** $(-5)^2$ **8.** $-3.2(5)$

**9.** $8.4(-6)$ **10.** $(-6)^3$

**Find each quotient.**

**11.** $-15 \div 3$ **12.** $-24 \div (-8)$

**13.** $22.48 \div (-2)$ **14.** $\frac{-49}{-0.7}$

**15.** $-8 \div (-8)$ **16.** $\frac{36}{-4}$

**17.** $2.25 \div (-1.5)$ **18.** $\frac{0}{-9}$

**19.** $-36 \div 2.4$ **20.** $\frac{-8^2}{4}$

**Without calculating each product, predict whether it is less than 0 or greater than 0.**

**21.** $5 \cdot (-4)$ **22.** $-5 \cdot (-9)$

**23.** $(-5)^2$ **24.** $(-5)^3 \cdot (-9)^3$

**25.** $(-3)^4 \cdot (-7)^9$ **26.** $(-6)^3 \cdot (-1)^8$

## Problem-Solving Practice (p. 21) OL AL

**Lesson 3.2 Problem-Solving Practice**
***Multiply and Divide with Negative Numbers***

Solve.

**1. Weather** Over the past seven days, Mrs. Cho found that the temperature outside had dropped a total of 35 degrees. Find the average drop in temperature each day.

**2. Diving** A deep-sea diver descends below the surface of the water at a rate of 60 feet each minute. What is the depth of the diver after 10 minutes?

**3. Stock** A computer stock lost 2 points each hour. How long does it take before the stock loses 10 points?

**4. Drought** A drought can cause the level of the local water supply to drop by a few inches each week. Suppose the level of the water supply drops a $\frac{1}{4}$ inch each day. How many days have passed if the water supply has dropped a foot, 12 inches?

**5. Hot Air Balloon** Paul and Karen went on a hot air balloon ride. The table shows the relationship between the change in altitude and the change in air temperature for 45 minutes of their flight. What is the range of the temperature during their flight?

| Change in Altitude (Feet) | Change in Air Temperature (°F) |
|---|---|
| 0 | 0° |
| 500 | −1.75° |
| 1,000 | −3.5° |
| 2,000 | −7° |
| 3,000 | −10.5° |
| −500 | 1.75° |
| −1,000 | 3.5° |

**6. Hot Air Balloon** Look at the table in Exercise 5. What was the mean temperature change during Paul and Karen's flight? What was the median temperature change?

## Enrichment (p. 22) BL

**Lesson 3.2 Enrichment**
***Multiply and Divide with Negative Numbers***

**Division by Zero?**

Some interesting things happen when you try to divide by zero. For example, look at these two equations.

$$\frac{5}{0} = x \qquad \frac{0}{0} = y$$

If you can write the equations above, you can also write the two equations below.

$$0 \cdot x = 5 \qquad 0 \cdot y = 0$$

However, there is no number that will make the left equation true. This equation has no solution. For the right equation, *every* number will make it true. The solutions for this equation are "all numbers."

Because division by zero leads to impossible situations, it is not a "legal" step in solving a problem. People say that division by zero is undefined, or not possible, or simply not allowed.

**Describe the solution set for each equation.**

**1.** $\frac{-2}{3}x = 0$ **2.** $x \cdot 0 = 0$

**3.** $x \cdot 0 + 7 = x$ **4.** $\frac{0}{x} = 0$

**5.** $\frac{x}{-4} = 0$ **6.** $\frac{0}{x} = -5$

**What values for $x$ must be excluded to prevent division by 0?**

**7.** $\frac{1}{-6x^2}$ **8.** $\frac{1}{x-1}$

**9.** $\frac{1}{-0.25x + 1}$ **10.** $\frac{0}{(-2\frac{1}{2})x}$

**11.** $\frac{1}{-2x - 2}$ **12.** $\frac{1}{3x + 6}$

**13.** $\frac{1}{-2x + 3}$ **14.** $\frac{1}{-\frac{x}{5} - 4}$

## Lesson Quick Quiz (p. 23) AL OL BL

**Lesson 3.2 Quick Quiz**

**1.** Explain how to divide two negative numbers. How do you know your rule works?

**2.** Will $-3 \cdot (-6) + 2 \cdot 5 - 25 \cdot (-62)$ be greater than zero, equal to zero, or less than zero? Explain how you know.

# Additional Lesson Resources

### Teacher Tech Tools
- TeacherWorks
- ExamView Assessment Suite
- Classroom Presentation Toolkit
- Advance Tracker

### Student Tech Tools
- StudentWorks Plus
- Math Online eGlossary • Concepts in Motion

### Other Print Products
- Investigation Notebook and Reflection Journal
- Quick Review Math Handbook

# LESSON 3.2 Multiply and Divide with Integers

## Introduce

**Brainstorm** You might want to introduce multiplication and division of negative numbers by brainstorming with your class situations when it would be helpful to be able to multiply or divide signed numbers.

Ask students to describe instances when they might want to multiply 4 and 2. Students' examples may include counting-type situations, such as finding the number of pens in 4 packages of 2 pens each or measurement situations such as finding the total length of four 2-foot boards.

Repeat for 5 · −3. Students may suggest situations such as the total yardage of 5 football plays with a 3-yard loss in each play or 5 hours with the temperature decreasing 3 degrees in each.

### Explore

Have students read the Explore and work the exercise. You may want to have students work in pairs. When they have completed their work, discuss their answers and the strategies that students used to solve the exercise. Students may use one of these strategies:

- Some students will approach the exercise mechanically and compute the sum of the thirty numbers before dividing by 30.
- Some will multiply the number of days for each positive temperature by the positive temperature, then add these totals to the daily negative lows for all days with negative temperatures, and divide the sum by 30.
- Others will compute the sum of the positive temperatures separately from the negative temperatures, then add the two sums and divide the result by 30.

Regardless of the approach, students should recognize that knowing how to multiply signed numbers would make finding the average low temperature immensely easier. This may increase both students' understanding of why it is important to learn how to multiply signed numbers and their desire to learn this skill.



# LESSON 3.2 Multiply and Divide with Negative Numbers

In this lesson, you will use what you have learned about addition and subtraction of signed numbers to help you understand how to multiply and divide them.

### Explore

The table lists the lowest temperatures in degrees Celsius for each day during the month of November at a weather station in Alaska.

The first row lists the different low temperatures. The second row tells the number of days in November with each daily low temperature. For example, the first column indicates that the low temperature was −4°C two days during the month.

**November Temperatures in Alaska**

| Daily Low Temperature (°C) | −4 | −3 | −2 | −1 | 0 | 1 | 2 | 3 | 4 |
|---|---|---|---|---|---|---|---|---|---|
| Days at This Temperature | 2 | 1 | 2 | 4 | 2 | 3 | 6 | 6 | 4 |

Use what you learned in Lesson 3.1 to find the mean, or average, low temperature during the month of November. 1°C

How did you compute the mean? See ① below.

If you calculated the total of the temperatures by using only addition, you probably found the process to be rather tedious. In this lesson, you will learn how to multiply and divide with negative numbers so you can perform calculations like this one quickly and efficiently.

Again, try to do the calculations without a calculator. This will help you understand why the operations work the way that they do.

① Possible answer: I added all the daily low temperatures (−4 + −4 + −3 + −2 + −2 + ...) and divided by the number of days (30). See teaching notes for other strategies.

## Investigation 1 Multiply a Positive and a Negative

When you first learned to multiply positive numbers, you thought of multiplication as repeated addition. For example, the product of 3 and 5 can be thought of as three 5s, or $5 + 5 + 5$. It can also be thought of as five 3s, or $3 + 3 + 3 + 3 + 3$.

### Develop & Understand: A

**Use the way of thinking described above to calculate each product.**

1. $2 \cdot (-8)$ $-16$
2. $-3 \cdot 2$ $-6$
3. $-5 \cdot 4$ $-20$
4. $3 \cdot (-7.5)$ $-22.5$
5. $-5\frac{1}{3} \cdot 3$ $-16$
6. $-1 \cdot 6$ $-6$

#### Think & Discuss

Look for patterns in your computations in Exercises 1–6.

Can you see a shortcut that you could use to compute the product of a positive and a negative number? See ①.

Use your shortcut to find the following products.

$2 \cdot (-45)$ $-90$ $\qquad$ $-32 \cdot 11$ $-352$

① Possible answer: Multiply the numbers as if they were both positive, and put a negative sign in front of the result.

### Develop & Understand: B

Now you will investigate products in which the positive number is a fraction or a decimal.

7. $\frac{1}{2} \cdot (-10)$ $-5$
8. $\frac{1}{3} \cdot (-9)$ $-3$
9. $\frac{2}{3} \cdot (-9)$ $-6$
10. $\frac{4}{5} \cdot (-15)$ $-12$
11. $-12 \cdot 0.25$ $-3$
12. $1\frac{1}{2} \cdot (-20)$ $-30$
13. $-5 \cdot 1.2$ $-6$
14. $3.2 \cdot (-1.1)$ $-3.52$
15. $-\frac{2}{3} \cdot \frac{3}{8}$ $-\frac{6}{24}$, or $-\frac{1}{4}$
16. $\frac{1}{7} \cdot \left(-\frac{14}{3}\right)$ $-\frac{14}{21}$, or $-\frac{2}{3}$

Multiplying with negative numbers can help you explore some interesting situations. Use what you learned in Exercises 1–16 to complete Exercises 17–24.



### Mathematical Background

The formal proof that the rules for multiplying signed numbers rely on are the definition of opposite and the distributive property. It states that if $a$ and $b$ are real numbers, then we want to show that $a \cdot (-b)$ and $-a \cdot b$ are equal to $-(a \cdot b)$. We examine the first case, $a \cdot (-b)$. The proof for the second case is similar. Start by adding $a \cdot b$ to $a \cdot (-b)$. We can see that $a \cdot b + a \cdot (-b) = a \cdot (b + (-b)) = a \cdot 0 = 0$. If the sum of $a \cdot b$ and $a \cdot (-b)$ is equal to zero, they must be opposites. So, $a \cdot (-b) = -(a \cdot b)$, as we wanted to prove.

This proof is included only to help you understand the underpinnings of the rules for multiplying with signed numbers. You probably should *not* share the proof with the class.

## Investigation 1

***On Your Own Exercises***
Pages 165–168
Exercises 1–6, 34–36

**Multiplication** In this investigation, students first calculate the product of two integers. Then they find products where at least one factor is a fraction or a decimal before using their new skill to solve exercises in context.

### Develop & Understand: A

*Suggested Grouping: Pairs*

Students use repeated addition to multiply a negative and a positive number. You may want to have students write the expressions to show a positive number times a negative number so this strategy makes more sense. For example, in Exercise 2, students rewrite $-3 \cdot 2$ as $2 \cdot (-3)$. Then they can think of 2 groups of $-3$, or $-3 + (-3)$. "Walking the number line" can be a helpful way to reinforce the concept of multiplication as groupings of numbers.

**Wrap-Up** Be sure that all students have recorded the correct answers to these six computations. They will look for patterns in these products in the next section.

#### Think & Discuss

*Suggested Grouping: Pairs*

Most students will notice that the product of a positive number and a negative number is always negative. Encourage them to use this pattern to find a shortcut for performing the multiplication. Although they may use a less precise vocabulary, students should determine that they can find the product of a positive number and a negative number by multiplying their absolute values and placing a negative sign in front of the product.

### Develop & Understand: B

*Suggested Grouping: Pairs*

Students use multiplication rules to find the product of a negative number and a positive number, including fractions and decimals. These exercises help students develop number sense.

**Lesson 3.2** Multiply and Divide with Negative Numbers 155

## Develop & Understand: C

*Suggested Grouping: Pairs*

This exercise set provides students with opportunities to use their rule for multiplying positive and negative numbers in mathematical and situational contexts.

▶ **Exercise 17b** Some students will find the distance the diver has descended and then convert that measurement to an elevation. They will multiply the distance the diver descends per minute by the number of minutes she has been diving. After five minutes, Cora will have dived $50 \cdot 5$, or 250 feet. Since she is 250 feet deeper than when she began at 0 elevation, she must be at an elevation of $-250$ feet.

- Others will approach the exercise more algorithmically and consider the change in elevation. These students will think that for every minute, Cora's elevation changes by $-50$ feet. After 5 minutes, her elevation is at $-50 \cdot 5$, or $-250$ feet.

▶ **Exercise 19** Students make sense of the rules for multiplying signed numbers. If students can think of a situational context in which it makes sense that $3 \cdot -8 = -24$, they will have a better understanding of the rule for multiplying signed numbers.

▶ **Exercise 20a** Students are given the product of two numbers and asked to find the two numbers. This exercise requires combinatoric thinking as students find all possible combinations of integers that have a product of $-14$.

▶ **Exercise 20b** Some students will derive their factor pairs from other factor pairs. Other students may think about patterns when multiplying decimals. They will use these patterns to find other factor pairs. Other students may use guess-check-and-improve.

**Wrap-Up** Students may increase their number sense by listening to classmates' strategies for solving **Exercise 20b**.

### Share & Summarize

The Share & Summarize asks students to formalize a rule they have most likely internalized throughout the investigation. Students will revisit this rule in Lesson 3, when they create a visual representation of rules for predicting signs of products and quotients involving signed numbers.

### Real-Word Link

The maximum depth recommended for recreational scuba diving is generally 130 feet. Beyond that depth, divers need special training and equipment to keep themselves safe from the effects of pressure.

## Develop & Understand: C

You might want to use a calculator to help you answer Exercises 17 and 18.

**17.** Cora jumps into the ocean from a boat. She starts at an elevation of 0 feet, and her elevation decreases 50 feet every minute.

  **a.** What is her elevation after one minute? $-50$ ft

  **b.** What is her elevation after five minutes? $-250$ ft

  **c.** What is her elevation after $n$ minutes? $-50n$ ft

You know that you can convert Celsius temperatures to Fahrenheit temperatures with the formula $F = \frac{9}{5}C + 32$, where $C$ is the temperature in degrees Celsius and $F$ is the temperature in degrees Fahrenheit.

**18.** Temperatures on Mercury, the planet closest to our sun, range from $-173°C$ to $427°C$. Convert these temperatures to find the range of temperatures on Mercury in degrees Fahrenheit. $-279.4°F$ to $800.6°F$

**19.** Create a word-problem exercise that requires calculating $3 \cdot (-8)$.

19. Possible problem: The low temperature Monday was 0°C. The low temperature decreased by 8°C each day for the next three days. What was the low temperature on Thursday?

**20.** The product of two integers is $-14$. (Remember: The *integers* are the whole numbers and their opposites, ... , $-3, -2, -1, 0, 1, 2, 3, ...$ .)

  **a.** What could the integers be? List all the possibilities. 1 and $-14$, $-1$ and 14, 2 and $-7$, $-2$ and 7

  **b.** Find three more pairs of numbers, not necessarily integers, that have a product of $-14$. Possible answer: 0.1 and $-140$, $-\frac{1}{2}$ and 28, 5 and $-2.8$

**Use guess-check-and-improve to solve each equation.**

**21.** $3x = -6$ $-2$

**22.** $-2y = -12$ 6

**23.** $4x + 15 = 3$ $-3$

### Share & Summarize

Is the product of a positive number and a negative number:

- always negative?
- always positive?
- sometimes positive, sometimes negative, and sometimes 0?

Always negative



### Troubleshooting

In **Exercise 20a**, watch for students who forget that the expressions $-1 \cdot 14$ and $1 \cdot (-14)$ have a product of $-14$. Some students may need to be reminded that both 1 and $-1$ are integers.

### Reaching All Learners

OL **On Level** Post chart paper in the classroom where the class keeps track of the rules for multiplying and dividing signed numbers. Each time they learn a new rule, they add it to the list. They keep track of rules for how to multiply and divide with signed numbers and how to predict the sign of products and quotients of signed numbers.

# Investigation 2 Multiply Two Negatives

In Investigation 1, you used addition to figure out how to multiply a negative number by a positive number. You cannot use that strategy with two negative numbers because you cannot add a negative number of times. However, the pattern in products of a positive number and a negative number can help you figure out how to multiply two negative numbers.

## Develop & Understand: A

1. Find each product.
   a. $-3 \cdot 4$ −12
   b. $-3 \cdot 3$ −9
   c. $-3 \cdot 2$ −6
   d. $-3 \cdot 1$ −3
   e. $-3 \cdot 0$ 0

2. In Exercise 1, what happens to the product from one expression to the next? Why?

   2. The product increases by 3 because each time the number being multiplied by −3 decreases by 1; the product includes one fewer "group" of −3.

3. Now use your calculator to compute these products.
   a. $-3 \cdot (-1)$ 3
   b. $-3 \cdot (-2)$ 6
   c. $-3 \cdot (-3)$ 9
   d. $-3 \cdot (-4)$ 12
   e. $-3 \cdot (-5)$ 15

4. Did the pattern you observed in Exercise 2 continue? Yes

### Think & Discuss

Look for patterns in your computations in Exercises 1–4. What do you think the rule is for finding the product of *any* two negative numbers? Possible answer: The product is equal to the product of the opposites of the negative numbers.

Use your rule to find each product. Check your results with your calculator.

| $-5 \cdot (-7)$ | $-10 \cdot (-90)$ | $-2 \cdot (-4.4)$ | $-1.2 \cdot (-7)$ |
|---|---|---|---|
| 35 | 900 | 8.8 | 8.4 |



## Reaching All Learners

**AL Approaching Level**
Remind students of the "walking the number line" model they used earlier. Facing a negative direction and walking backwards produces a positive movement.

## Investigation 2

***On Your Own Exercises***
Pages 165–168
Exercises 7–20, 37–46

**Patterns** Students learn how to multiply two negative numbers.

### Develop & Understand: A

*Suggested Grouping: Individuals*

Students observe patterns in the products of a positive and a negative number. They continue the pattern to multiply two negative numbers. Students then use a calculator to check the multiplication and verify that the pattern is correct.

▶ **Exercise 2** Students see that as the positive factor decreases by 1, the product increases by 3. Students may explain this pattern by thinking that each decrease in the positive factor is taking away −3, so each product will increase by 3. Understanding this connection helps students make sense of the rule for multiplying two negative numbers.

▶ **Exercise 4** It might be easier for some students to discover the pattern if they write all 10 products in order in one column, beginning with Exercise 1a and ending with Exercise 3e.

**Wrap-Up** Have students share their observations about the patterns formed by the exercises in this exercise set. Be sure that all students are aware of the pattern in the products before continuing.

### Think & Discuss

In Exercises 1–4, students observed the effects of multiplying two negative numbers. They are now asked to use that observation to make a conjecture about what the rule states. They also make sense of the rule.

Most students will say that the product of two negative numbers is equal to the product of the opposites of the negative numbers, although they may use a different vocabulary. Once students have identified the correct rule, have the class test the rule by finding the products of $-5 \cdot -7$ 35, $-10 \cdot -90$ 900, $-2 \cdot -4.4$ 8.8, and $-1.2 \cdot -7$ 8.4.

You may want to review the four ways to combine positive and negative numbers and the sign of their products before students complete Exercises 5–9.

| | |
|---|---|
| positive · positive | answer: positive |
| positive · negative | answer: negative |
| negative · positive | answer: negative |
| negative · negative | answer: positive |

## Develop & Understand: B

*Suggested Grouping: Pairs*

▶ **Exercises 5–6** Watch for students who forget to count negative numbers or 1 and −1 as integers.

▶ **Exercises 8–9** Students solve equations with two operations. Remind students to keep in mind the order of operations as they solve for *x*.

**Wrap-Up** You may wish to have students discuss how they solve the equations in Exercises 7–9. Some students may look for missing factors in Exercise 7. They may ask −4 times what number equals 12. Others students may use backtracking or draw a flowchart.

**Example**

Discuss the convention for notation of exponents and negative numbers. Students already know that the placement of parentheses can change the value of an expression. Explain how the placement of the parentheses can affect the value of a negative number and an exponent.

Walk students through the Example, stressing how the order of operations can be used to evaluate the expression. To help students differentiate between $(-2)^4$ and $-2^4$, encourage students to read $-2^4$ as the opposite of $2^4$, not as negative $2^4$.

There are four ways to combine positive and negative numbers in products.

- positive · positive
- positive · negative
- negative · positive
- negative · negative

You now know how to multiply each combination and what kind of results to expect.

## Develop & Understand: B

**If you know the result of a multiplication, can you figure out what the factors might have been? Try these exercises.**

**5.** Suppose the product of two integers is 12. What could the integers be? List all the possibilities. 1 and 12, −1 and −12, 2 and 6, −2 and −6, 3 and 4, −3 and −4

**6.** Suppose the product of *three* integers is 12. What could the integers be? List all the possibilities.

6. 1, 1, and 12; 1, −1, and −12; −1, −1, and 12; 1, 2, and 6; 1, −2, and −6; −1, 2, and −6; −1, −2, and 6; 1, 3, and 4; 1, −3, and −4; −1, 3, and −4; −1, −3, and 4; 2, 2, and 3; 2, −2, and −3; −2, −2, and 3

**Use your understanding of signed numbers and the guess-check-and-improve method to solve each equation.**

**7.** $-4x = 12$ −3

**8.** $-3x + 5 = 11$ −2

**9.** $3 - 4x = -17$ 5

When you use exponents to indicate repeated multiplication of a negative number, you need to be careful about notation. Put the negative number *inside* the parentheses, and put the exponent *outside* the parentheses.

**Example**

Calculate $(-2)^4$ and $-2^4$.

| Notation | Meaning | Calculation |
|---|---|---|
| $(-2)^4$ | −2 to the fourth power | $(-2) \cdot (-2) \cdot (-2) \cdot (-2) = 16$ |
| $-2^4$ | the opposite of $2^4$ | $-(2 \cdot 2 \cdot 2 \cdot 2) = -16$ |



## Reaching All Learners

**BL Beyond Level** If your class is interested in exercises like Exercises 5 and 6, there are a number of extension questions that they could examine. Every number has a certain number of factor pairs that produce that number. In Exercise 5, students found that 12 has 6 factor pairs. Have students examine the relationship between a product and how many factor pairs have that product. Some relationships students may find are that prime numbers always have 2 pairs, squares of prime numbers always have 3 pairs, and square numbers in general have an odd number of factor pairs.

## Develop & Understand: C

**Evaluate each expression.**

**10.** $(-3)^2$ 9

**11.** $-3^2$ $-9$

**12.** $-4^2$ $-16$

**13.** $(-4)^2$ 16

**14.** $(-2)^1$ $-2$

**15.** $(-2)^2$ 4

**16.** $(-2)^3$ $-8$

**17.** $(-2)^4$ 16

**18.** $(-2)^5$ $-32$

**19.** $(-2)^6$ 64

**20.** Look for patterns in your answers to Exercises 14–19.

**a.** For what values of $n$ is $(-2)^n$ positive? Even values

**b.** For what values of $n$ is $(-2)^n$ negative? Odd values

**21.** Dylan said the solution of $x^2 = 16$ is 4. Felipe stated that there is another solution. Is Felipe correct? If so, find the other solution. Felipe is correct. The other solution is $-4$.

**Solve each equation. (Hint: Each equation has two solutions.)**

**22.** $x^2 = 36$ 6 or $-6$

**23.** $x^2 = \frac{1}{36}$ $\frac{1}{6}$ or $-\frac{1}{6}$

### Share & Summarize

**1.** Is the product of two negative numbers: Always positive

- always negative?
- always positive?
- sometimes positive, sometimes negative, and sometimes 0?

**2.** Consider the expression $(-3)^m$.

**a.** If $m$ is an even number, is $(-3)^m$ positive or negative? How can you tell?

2a. Positive; Possible explanation: An even exponent means the base will be used as a factor an even number of times. That means there will be pairs of factors whose product is positive, so the entire product will be positive.

**b.** If $m$ is an odd number, is $(-3)^m$ positive or negative? How can you tell? Negative; Possible explanation: An odd exponent means the base will be used as a factor an odd number of times. Grouping in pairs will leave one factor by itself. The pairs will each multiply to give a positive number, and then multiplying by the extra factor makes the entire product negative.



## Develop & Understand: C

*Suggested Grouping: Pairs*

Students practice computing with signed numbers and exponents. They are required to think algebraically as they come up with a rule for determining whether any given power of $-2$ will be positive or negative. Then they solve equations with two answers.

▶ **Exercise 20** It may be hard for some students to articulate their thinking. Many students will say that every other number in the pattern is positive. Push these students to pinpoint a concise description of the pattern. You can check their understanding by asking questions such as:

- Is $(-2)^{2{,}421}$ positive or negative? Negative

▶ **Exercise 21** This is the first time students have had to think about more than one solution to an equation. These equations have both positive and negative solutions. You might want to point out to the class that now that they can operate with signed numbers, they should look for solutions to equations that are negative, positive, and zero.

### Share & Summarize

In Question 1, the reason a negative number times a negative number is equal to a positive number is very difficult to understand, even for most adults. As long as students know the rule well and can see how this definition might have grown out of the pattern developed in multiplying negatives and positives, you should not be concerned if students do not completely understand why this rule works.

Question 2 asks students to make a generalization about taking signed numbers to positive integer powers. They should be able to use thinking similar to that used in Exercise 13, but at a more general level here.

## Troubleshooting

In Exercises 10–13, watch for students who confuse the meanings of parentheses in negative numbers with exponents. The similarity of Exercises 10 and 11 and of Exercises 12 and 13 can help catch this error early. Have students write out the calculation for each exercise. For example, in Exercise 10, $(-3)^2 = -3 \cdot -3 = 9$.

## Investigation 3

**On Your Own Exercises**
Pages 165–168
Exercises 21–28, 47–55

**Rational Numbers** Tell students that the numbers they have used in this lesson are *rational numbers.* That is, each number can be written as a quotient of two integers, with a divisor not equal to 0. All other numbers are *irrational numbers.*

*Terminating* and *repeating decimals* are rational numbers. Students should remember that a terminating decimal ends, and that they can easily convert a terminating decimal to a fraction by using place values. For example, $0.75 = \frac{75}{100}$. They can then divide the numerator and denominator by the same number, 25, to write the fraction in lowest terms: $\frac{3}{4}$.

A repeating decimal repeats a pattern of digits, such as the 6 in $0.\overline{6}$ and 21 in $0.\overline{21}$. The repeating digits are designated by drawing a bar over the digits.

After students read the cartoon, walk students through a few examples of how to divide with negative numbers.

### Develop & Understand: A

*Suggested Grouping: Pairs*

Students divide with signed numbers by transforming division exercises into multiplication exercises.

**Wrap-Up** Be sure that students have the correct answers for all exercises so that they can look for patterns in the following Think & Discuss section.

### Think & Discuss

Students use patterns they observe to conjecture about the rule for dividing signed numbers. Some students may want to circle exercises with one negative number or write like exercises in one column on their paper. Students should find:

1. When one number is negative, divide the absolute value of the numbers and place a negative sign in front of the quotient.
2. When both numbers are negative, divide the absolute values of the numbers. The result is a positive number.

# Investigation 3 Divide with Negative Numbers

You can solve any division exercise by thinking about a corresponding multiplication exercise. Look at how Kate solves $30 \div 5$.

### Develop & Understand: A

**Use Kate's method to solve each division exercise.**

1. $21 \div (-3)$ $-7$
2. $-64 \div (-2)$ $32$
3. $-24 \div 48$ $-0.5$, or $-\frac{1}{2}$
4. $-2 \div (-32)$ $\frac{1}{16}$, or $0.0625$
5. $-\frac{6}{5}$ $-1.2$, or $-1\frac{1}{5}$
6. $\frac{9}{-27}$ $-\frac{1}{3}$, or $-0.\overline{3}$
7. $-2.16 \div (-54)$ $0.04$
8. $\frac{-3}{-0.3}$ $10$

### Think & Discuss

Look for patterns in your computations in Exercises 1–8.

- Can you see a shortcut for computing a quotient when exactly one of the numbers is negative? See ①.
- Can you see a shortcut for computing the quotient of two negative numbers? Possible answer: Divide the absolute values of the numbers.

Use your shortcut to find each quotient.

$44 \div (-2.2)$ $-20$ $-\frac{7}{3}$ $-2.\overline{3}$ or $-2\frac{1}{3}$ $-56 \div (-2)$ $28$

① Possible answer: Divide the absolute values of the numbers, and put a negative sign in front of the result.



## Reaching All Learners

**AL Approaching Level** In this exercise set, some students may have difficulty using Kate's method to find the quotients that are fractions or decimals. Since the point of solving these exercises is to understand division and to find patterns in the quotients, allow these students to use Kate's methods to solve these exercises with whole-number quotients. They show the same patterns as the exercises in the text.

1. $-42 \div 6$ $-7$
2. $-15 \div (-5)$ $3$
3. $21 \div (-3)$ $-7$
4. $\frac{-8}{-4}$ $2$
5. $\frac{-16}{4}$ $-4$
6. $\frac{12}{-2}$ $-6$
7. $-35 \div -7$ $5$
8. $\frac{-9}{-9}$ $1$

## Develop & Understand: B

9. Suppose a scuba diver begins his dive at an elevation of 0 feet. During the dive, his elevation changes at a constant rate of $-2$ feet per second. How long will it take for him to reach an elevation of $-300$ feet? 150 s, or 2.5 min

10. The Marianas Trench, south of Guam, contains the deepest known spot in the world. This spot, called Challenger Deep, has an elevation of $-36{,}198$ feet.

    Suppose Jamie entered the ocean above this spot. He started at an elevation of 0 feet and moved at a constant rate of $-50$ feet per minute.

    If Jamie was able to go deep in the ocean without being affected by the pressure and his tank contained enough air, how long would it take him to reach the bottom of Challenger Deep? 723.96 min, or slightly more than 12 hours

11. Write four division expressions with a quotient of $-4$. Possible answer: $20 \div -5$, $-16 \div 4$, $12 \div -3$, $24 \div -6$

### Real-World Link

Water exerts pressure on a scuba diver. The deeper the diver, the greater the pressure. Divers are trained to make the pressure in the body's air spaces, the lungs, sinuses, and ears, equal to the outside water pressure.

**Solve each equation.**

12. $\frac{30}{x} = -15$ $-2$

13. $\frac{x}{-4} = 20$ $-80$

### Share & Summarize

Which of the following statements is true for each situation? Explain how you know. See margin.

- The result is always negative.
- The result is always positive.
- The result is sometimes negative, sometimes positive, and sometimes zero.

1. Dividing a positive number by a negative number
2. Dividing a negative number by a positive number
3. Dividing a negative number by a negative number



## Develop & Understand: B

*Suggested Grouping: Pairs*

Students practice dividing signed numbers in situational contexts. They also backtrack to solve equations.

▶ **Exercises 9–10** Students can consider the distance of the dive and solve the exercises without using negative numbers. They could consider the elevations and use negative numbers to solve the exercise. You can help students make sense of the rules for dividing with signed numbers by comparing the two sets of strategies for each exercise.

▶ **Exercise 11** Students may use one of these strategies to solve this exercise:

- Some students will come up with one pair of numbers whose quotient is $-4$ and then derive the other pairs from the first pair. For example, students might see that $-4$ divided by 1 is equal to $-4$. They might then multiply each factor by the same number and find these number pairs: $-8$ divided by 2; 12 divided by $-3$, and so on.
- Other students may think of basic facts with a quotient of 4 and use rules to place the negative sign in the dividend or divisor to find a negative quotient.

▶ **Exercises 12 and 13** Students backtrack to solve equations. You may want to remind students that they can substitute their answer for $x$ in the equations and simplify their expression to check their answers.

### Share & Summarize

You might want to have several members of the class explain to the whole group their thinking for these questions.

Students should feel comfortable dividing with signed numbers. Although they will have plenty of opportunities in subsequent investigations to practice what they have learned in various mathematical contexts, this is their main opportunity to focus on the operation and try to make sense of it. If students are having difficulty understanding how division works, you might try to explain the rules by having them think of division exercises of the form $n \div m$ as $n \cdot \frac{1}{m}$.

### Additional Answers
### Share & Summarize

1. Always negative; Possible explanation: The result is the number you need to multiply the negative number by to get the positive number. This cannot be positive, because a positive times a negative is negative. It cannot be 0, because 0 times a negative number is 0.
2. Always negative; Possible explanation: The result is the number you need to multiply the positive number by to get the negative number. This cannot be positive, because a positive times a positive is positive. It cannot be 0, because the product of 0 and a positive number is 0.
3. Always positive; Possible explanation: The result is the number you need to multiply one of the negative numbers by to get the other. This cannot be negative, because a negative times a negative is positive. It cannot be 0, because the product of 0 and a negative number is 0.

**Lesson 3.2** Multiply and Divide with Negative Numbers 161

# Investigation 4

**On Your Own Exercises**
Pages 165–168
Exercises 29–33, 56–59

**Signed Numbers and Data** Students will be using signed numbers as data and will find the mean, median, range, and mode for this data.

### Think & Discuss

*Suggested Grouping: Pairs* If possible have one member of each pair familiar with golf scoring.

Students will be adding signed numbers regarding how a person did on a golf course relative to par. It may be tough for students to grasp that −2 is a better score than +2 for golf. To help them understand, explain that −2 means that they did better than the average by 2 strokes.

### Develop & Understand: A

*Suggested Grouping: Individuals*

▶ **Exercise 1** Remind students that over par is a positive value and under par is a negative value.

▶ **Exercises 2 and 3** Students may need reinforcing that a negative score is better than a positive one in golf. Also the larger the absolute value of a negative number, the smaller the number is. It may help students if they look at a number line when answering these questions.

▶ **Exercises 4–7** In these exercises, students will be computing the range, mode, median, and mean of Sondra's golf score. If students are having difficulty remembering what to do, refer them to the Math Link for assistance.

**Math Link**
This Link defines the range, mode, median, and mean for students. It is an excellent resource for assisting students in their computations. Students may need further explanation of the mean. You may want to tell the students that the mean is most often what people refer to when they use the word *average*.

# Investigation 4 Signed Numbers and Data

You have been learning how to add, subtract, multiply, and divide with integers. In this investigation, you will analyze data by finding range, mean, median, and mode for the data.

### Think & Discuss

In golf, "par" is a number assigned to an individual hole or to a course of holes. The par tells the number of strokes, or hits, it should take a golfer to get a golf ball in the hole. A golfer's score is reported as the number of strokes above or below par that it took to finish the course. If par for a course is 72, then a golfer who finishes with 75 strokes is *3 over par.* A golfer who finishes with 69 strokes is *3 under par.*

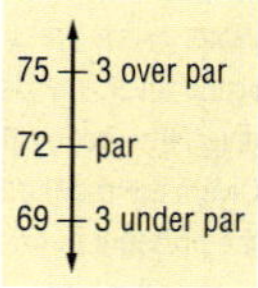


Suppose you relate golf scores to integers.

What number would you use to represent par? 0

What number would you use to represent *3 under par?* −3

What number would you use to represent *3 over par?* 3

Is a negative or positive score better? Why? Negative; Negative scores indicate fewer strokes.

**Math Link**
The *range* of a data set is the difference between the minimum and maximum values.

The *mode* is the value that occurs most often.

The *median* is the middle value when all values are listed from least to greatest.

The *mean* is the distribution of the total of the values in a data set among the members of the data set.

### Develop & Understand: A

Sondra plays for her school's golf team. Last spring, she played on the school's home golf course 8 times.

Her scores are shown below.

| | | | |
|---|---|---|---|
| 2 over par | par | 3 over par | 5 under par |
| 1 over par | 2 under par | par | 1 over par |

1. Rewrite Sondra's scores using positive and negative integers with par being zero. 2, 0, 3, −5, 1, −2, 0, 1
2. What was Sondra's minimum, or best, score? −5; 5 strokes under par
3. What was Sondra's maximum, or worst, score? 3; 3 strokes over par
4. What is the range of Sondra's scores? Show your work. $3 - (-5) = 8$; the range is 8 strokes
5. What is the mode of Sondra's scores? 0 and 1
6. What is the median of Sondra's scores? Show your work.
7. What is the mean of Sondra's scores? Show your work. 0; $-5 + (-2) + 0 + 0 + 1 + 1 + 2 + 3 = 0$; $0 \div 8 = 0$

6. $\frac{1}{2}$; $0 + 1 = 1$; $1 \div 2 = \frac{1}{2}$



**Reaching All Learners**

**ELL English Language Learners**
Students may need assistance with understanding the terms range, mode, median, and mean. Show the students how to make each computation and then ask the students to tell you how they would describe the work in their first language. Allow them to make notes of this and if necessary, use it when they are completing their assignments.

**Troubleshooting**

When finding the median, it is quite common for students to forget to put the data in order from least to greatest.

14. You will have to realize that, when listed in order, the data will include two −6's, three −3's, three 8's, and so on. Or, you will have to realize there are 31 temperatures. The median is the 16th temperature from the top or the bottom; median is 12°F.

**8.** Find the mean score for four other players. Their scores are listed below. Which players score below par on the average? Victoria and Lynn

**a.** Lakita 4, −2, 6, −1, −2, 0, −1, 2 $\frac{6}{8}$ or $\frac{3}{4}$ stroke above par

**b.** Dana −1, 0, 8, −2, 2, 3 $\frac{10}{6}$ or $1\frac{2}{3}$ strokes above par

**c.** Victoria −3, −1, 0, −1, 1, −2 1 stroke below par

**d.** Lynn 5, −3, 2, −5, −2, −1 $\frac{4}{6}$ or $\frac{2}{3}$ stroke below par

**9.** Lakita played another round of golf. What must have been her score to have a mean score of par for all nine rounds? −6

**10.** Padma played seven rounds of golf. The mean, median, and mode of all seven scores were par, or 72 strokes. What could have been her scores? 67, 68, 72, 72, 72, 73, 80

## Develop & Understand: B

One January, a science class from a Maine high school recorded the town's overnight low temperatures. The low temperatures are listed in the following *frequency table.*

| Temperature (°F) | −8 | −6 | −5 | −3 | −2 | 0 | 3 | 8 | 9 | 12 | 14 | 15 | 17 | 20 | 23 |
|---|---|---|---|---|---|---|---|---|---|---|---|---|---|---|---|
| Frequency | 1 | 2 | 1 | 3 | 1 | 1 | 1 | 3 | 1 | 3 | 4 | 1 | 3 | 5 | 1 |

**Real-World Link**

The record low temperature ever recorded in the United States was −79.8°F (rounded off to −80°F) at Prospect Creek Camp in the Endicott Mountains of northern Alaska on January 23, 1971.

**11.** What is the mode temperature reading? 20°F

**12.** For how many days was the temperature recorded? 31 days

**13.** What is the range of temperatures? 23 − (−8) = 31°F

**14.** Since the data is in a frequency table, what will you need to do to find the median temperature? What is the median temperature? See above.

**15.** Since the data set is in a frequency table, what do you need to do to find the mean temperature? What is the mean temperature? See margin.

**16.** The minimum value of a set of 6 numbers is −10, and the maximum value is 20. If mean is 5, what are the 4 numbers? Use 4 different values. Answers will vary. Possible answers: 1, 2, 8, 9; The sum of the 4 numbers must equal 20.

### Think & Discuss

If you were visiting Maine during January, which statistics about the night lows would be most helpful? See ① in margin.

What does each number tell you about the data? See ② in margin.

Suppose the minimum temperature dropped to −20°F instead of −8°F. Which measure of center (mean, median, or mode) is affected? By how much? The mean will decrease by 0.39 degrees.



▶ **Exercise 8** This exercise is looking for the mean score. Use this language in discussion so that students make the connection.

▶ **Exercise 9** It may be useful to ask students what score is par to assist them in answering this question.

**Wrap-Up** Once students have completed their exercises, it may be useful for the students to meet in pairs or small groups to discuss their results and the processes they used to attain their results.

## Develop & Understand: B

*Suggested Grouping: Pairs*

▶ **Exercises 12 and 15** Students may need assistance in interpreting the results represented in the frequency table. Remind the class the frequency means that the temperature that is given was recorded *the frequency* number of times. For example, the temperature reached a low of −6 on two separate occurrences.

▶ **Exercise 14** When finding the median, students need to make sure that they list temperatures for which *the frequency* is greater than one, *the frequency* number of times.

▶ **Exercise 15** If students are having difficulty determining what value to divide by, have them refer to their results from Exercise 12.

### Think & Discuss

*Suggested Grouping: Small Groups*

As the students are meeting in their small groups, ask one person to take notes, which can be shared in a class discussion. Stress to the students the importance of being able to justify their answers with data.

**Additional Answers**

15. You can either add in the repeated temperatures or multiply the frequency by the temperature and add up the products. Then divide by the total number of days, 31. $\frac{281}{31} = 9.06$°F is the mean.

**Think & Discuss**

① Answers will vary. Possible answers: The mean would be an indicator of a typical reading. The range would indicate the fluctuations throughout the month.

② The mode tells which temperature reading occurs most often. The median tells the temperature reading is in the middle when data are listed from least to greatest. The mean quotient obtained from dividing the sum of the numbers by the number of addends.

▶ **Exercises 19–24** If the students are having a difficult time remembering what to do to find the range, mode, median, and/or mean, refer them to the Math Link on p. 162.

**Share & Summarize**

Question 1 is an excellent problem to determine how well the students understand the measures of central tendency.

Students may have difficulty finding the words to describe what they know for Questions 2 and 3. It may be easier for the students to explain using a concrete example.

**Real-World Link**

In 1980, Earl Campbell, of the Houston Oilers, averaged 5.2 yards per carry.

21. From least to greatest the yards are −3, −1, −1, 1, 2, 2, 2, 5, 6, 6, 11, 12; since the middle two numbers are both 2, the middle of the data is 2 so the median is 2 yards.

23. The sum of the yards is $-3 + (-1) + (-1) + 1 + 2 + 2 + 2 + 5 + 6 + 6 + 11 + 12 = 42$; $42 \div 12$ is $3\frac{1}{2}$, so the mean is $3\frac{1}{2}$ yards.

1. Mean is the distribution of the average of the data set. Median is the middle value when values are ordered from least to greatest. Mode is the value that appears most often.

3. Answers will vary. Possible answer: The mean may be smaller since adding positive numbers to negative numbers will decrease the sum of the data values.

## Develop & Understand: C

In football, a running back carries the ball in hopes of gaining yards. He loses yards when he is tackled behind the line where the play began, or the *line of scrimmage.*

During Friday night's football game, Kanye carried the ball 12 times during the second half of the game. In the numbers below, a positive number indicates a gain and a negative number indicates a loss.

2 1 6 −1 12 2 −3 11 5 2 −1 6

**17.** What was Kanye's worst carry (minimum)? −3; 3 yards lost

**18.** What was Kanye's best carry (maximum)? 12; 12 yards gained

**19.** What is the range of yardage of Kanye's carries? Show your work. $12 - (-3) = 15$; the range is 15 yards

**20.** What is the mode? 2 yards; he carried for 2 yards three times

**21.** What is the median yardage of the 12 carries? Show your work.

**22.** Add two additional carries so that the median is 3. Students must add 4 and one other number greater than or equal to 4.

**23.** What is the mean yardage of the 12 carries? Show your work.

**24.** Add another carry that makes the mean 3 yards. A carry of −3, or 3 yards lost

**Share & Summarize**

**1.** Explain the difference between mean, median, and mode.

**2.** How does including both positive and negative integers in a set of data affect finding the range of the data? Answers will vary. Possible answer: The range may be greater than the maximum.

**3.** How does including both positive and negative integers in a set of data affect finding the mean of the data?

**4.** Is there ever a time that you would find the mean of a set of data by dividing by a negative number? Why or why not? No, the divisor is the number of entries in the data set.



**On the Spot Assessment**

Place 5 quiz or test scores on the board and ask the students to compute the mean, mode, median, and range. This is a quick check to see if the students are understanding.

**Troubleshooting**

If the students answer yes to the Share & Summarize Question 4, it will be obvious that they need more practice in understanding what the mean measures.

**Practice & Apply**

5b. Possible answer: $-45$ and $\frac{1}{3}$, 1.5 and $-10$, $-\frac{3}{5}$ and 25

**Compute each product.**

1. $-3 \cdot 52$ $-156$
2. $6.2 \cdot (-5)$ $-31$
3. $-36 \cdot \frac{1}{2}$ $-18$
4. $-2 \cdot 4 + 3 \cdot \left(-\frac{1}{3}\right)$ $-9$
5. The product of two integers is $-15$.
   a. What could the integers be? List all the possibilities. 1 and $-15$, $-1$ and 15, 3 and $-5$, $-3$ and 5
   b. Find three more pairs of numbers, not necessarily integers, with a product of $-15$.
6. Solve $-3x + 4 = -5$. 3

**Compute each product.**

7. $-3 \cdot (-32)$ 96
8. $-\frac{1}{2} \cdot (-35)$ 17.5
9. $-5 \cdot (-0.7)$ 3.5
10. $-2.5 \cdot (-7)$ 17.5
11. $-2^5 \cdot (-3)$ 96
12. $-3 \cdot (-5^3)$ 375
13. $-3 \cdot (-5)^3$ 375
14. $-3^2 \cdot (-3)^2$ $-81$

**Without calculating each product, determine whether it is less than 0 or greater than 0.**

15. $3 \cdot (-2)$ Less than 0
16. $3 \cdot 2$ Greater than 0
17. $-3 \cdot 2$ Less than 0
18. $-3 \cdot (-2)$ Greater than 0
19. The product of two integers is 9. What could the integers be? List all the possibilities. 3 and 3, $-3$ and $-3$, $-1$ and $-9$, 1 and 9
20. Solve $-5y + 13 = 3$. 2

**Find each quotient.**

21. $-3 \div 2.5$ $-1.2$
22. $-3 \div (-25)$ 0.12
23. $45 \div (-360)$ $-0.125$
24. $\frac{-45}{-90}$ 0.5, or $\frac{1}{2}$
25. One number divided by a *negative* number is 0.467. What could the two numbers be? Think of three possibilities. Write them as division equations. Possible answer: $-467 \div -1{,}000$; $-46.7 \div -100$; $-4.67 \div -10$

**Solve each equation.**

26. $5x = -20$ $-4$
27. $3y = -\frac{6}{5}$ $-\frac{2}{5}$
28. $\frac{w}{9} = -5$ $-45$



**On Your Own Exercises**
Lesson 3.2

**Investigation 1**
Pages 155–156
Practice & Apply: 1–6
Connect & Extend: 34–36

**Investigation 2**
Pages 157–159
Practice & Apply: 7–20
Connect & Extend: 37–46

**Investigation 3**
Pages 160–161
Practice & Apply: 21–28
Connect & Extend: 47–55

**Investigation 4**
Pages 162–164
Practice & Apply: 29–33
Connect & Extend: 56–59

**Assign Anytime**
Mixed Review: 61–65

▶ **Exercise 4** Students need to use the order of operations to evaluate the expression.

▶ **Exercise 25** Extension You may want to share the three possible answers given to show that three equations that are multiples of one another are equivalent, even when the multiple is $-1$.

▶ **Exercise 35** Although the calculation of windchill is messy and involved, students should be able to do it with the help of a calculator.



On Your Own Exercises

31. $\frac{-7}{11}$ or $-0.\overline{63}$ degrees; in other words, on average the temperature was barely below zero degrees

33. The median would become 1.5 degrees and the mean would become $\frac{5}{12}$ or less than half a degree above zero.

For Exercises 29–33, use the following data list collected from Fahrenheit temperatures in Alaska. Show your work to support each answer.

$$-12, 8, 11, -6, -3, -15, 8, 5, -2, -9, 8$$

**29.** What is the range of the data? From −15 to 11, which is a range of 26 degrees

**30.** What is the median temperature? −2 degrees

**31.** What is the mean temperature? What does the mean tell about the temperature for these eleven days?

**32.** What is the mode temperature? 8 degrees

**33.** How would the median change if another temperature, 12°, is added to the data? How would the mean change?

## Connect & Extend

**34.** As a parachutist descends into Death Valley, her elevation decreases 15 feet every second. Five seconds before she lands, she is at an elevation of −127 feet. What is the elevation of her landing place? −202 ft

**35.** **Physical Science** When it is cold outside and the wind is blowing, it feels colder than it would at the same temperature without any wind. Scientists call this outside temperature the *windchill*.

For example, if the temperature outside is 15°F and the wind speed is 20 mph, the equivalent windchill temperature is about −2°F. That means that even though the thermometer reads 15°F, it *feels* as cold as it would if you were in no wind at −2°F.

Meteorologists use the following formula to calculate windchill. The variable $s$ represents wind speed in mph, and $t$ represents actual temperature in °F.

$$\text{windchill} = 35.74 + 0.6215t - 35.75\left(s^{0.16}\right) + 0.4275t\left(s^{0.16}\right)$$

This formula works for wind speeds between 5 mph and 60 mph.

**a.** If the wind blows at 20 mph and the temperature is −5°F, what is the windchill? −29°F

**b.** If the wind blows at 30 mph and the temperature is −10°F, what is the windchill? −39°F

**c.** **Challenge** If the wind blows at 25 mph and the windchill is −51°F, what is the actual temperature? −20°F

**36.** Pedro said, "I'm thinking of a number. When I multiply my number by −2 and subtract 4, I get −16." What is Pedro's number? 6

### Real-World Link

In November 2001, the National Weather Service implemented a new windchill temperature formula using the latest advances in computer modeling. The previous formula was based on the 1945 Siple and Passel Index.

On Your Own Exercises

37. Less than 0
38. Greater than 0
39. Less than 0
40. Greater than 0
41. Greater than 0
42. Greater than 0

44. Not possible; no real number multiplied by itself yields a negative number.

47. Less than −1
48. Between 0 and 1
49. Less than −1
50. Answers will vary. The sum of the temperatures must be −210°F.
51. Answers will vary. The average of the third and fourth numbers must be −21.

**Without calculating, predict whether each product is less than 0, equal to 0, or greater than 0.**

**37.** $(-4)^3 \cdot (-2)^2$ **38.** $(-3)^5 \cdot (-6)^3$ **39.** $(-1)^5 \cdot 5^2$

**40.** $(-2)^2 \cdot (-972)^{90}$ **41.** $-45^2 \cdot (-35)^5$ **42.** $(-2)^8 \cdot (-5)^8$

**Challenge** If possible, solve each equation. If it is not possible, explain why.

**43.** $y^3 = -8$ $-2$ **44.** $x^2 = -9$

**Describe the values of *b* that make each inequality true.**

**45.** $3b < 0$ *b* must be less than 0. **46.** $3(b - 2) < 0$ *b* must be less than 2.

Without calculating, determine whether the quotient in Exercises 47–49 is less than −1, between −1 and 0, between 0 and 1, or greater than 1.

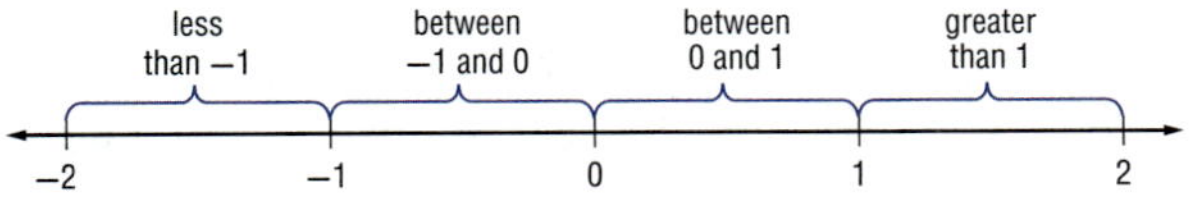


**47.** $1 \div \left(-\frac{3}{5}\right)$ **48.** $\frac{-555.233}{-5{,}552}$ **49.** $78.3636 \div (-25.33)$

**50.** The mean of 10 temperatures is −21°F. Assuming that the temperatures are not all the same, what could the temperatures be?

**51.** The median of 6 temperatures is −21°F. Assuming that the temperatures are not all the same, what could the temperatures be?

**Use guess-check-and-improve to solve each equation. Be careful, some equations have two solutions.**

**52.** $\left(\frac{1}{y}\right)^2 = \frac{1}{9}$ 3 or −3 **53.** $y^2 = \frac{1}{9}$ $\frac{1}{3}$ or $-\frac{1}{3}$

**Challenge** Solve each equation.

**54.** $\left(\frac{1}{z}\right)^2 = 16$ $\frac{1}{4}$ or $-\frac{1}{4}$ **55.** $-\frac{5}{x} + 4 = 2$ $\frac{5}{2}$

For Exercises 56–59, use the data below that compares actual rainfall to the normal rainfall for each month. The amount of rainfall is reported as "inches above or below normal rainfall."

| Jan | Feb | Mar | Apr | May | June | July | Aug | Sep | Oct | Nov | Dec |
|---|---|---|---|---|---|---|---|---|---|---|---|
| +1.0 | −0.5 | −0.2 | +0.7 | +1.1 | +0.3 | −1.6 | −2.0 | −0.3 | +0.5 | 0.0 | −1.2 |

**56.** What does the November entry of 0.0 suggest about November's rainfall? November's rainfall was normal, not below or above the average amount.



▶ **Exercises 37–42** Make sure that students explain how they figured out their answers for this question. Otherwise, students might compute the products to get their answers, and that would defeat the purpose of the exercise.

▶ **Exercises 50 and 51** Watch for students who divide −21 by 10 in Exercise 50 and by 6 in Exercise 51. Review the meaning of *average* with these students.

## Quick Check

**Informal Assessment** Students should be able to:

- ✔ multiply and divide with signed numbers
- ✔ predict the sign of a product or quotient involving signed numbers
- ✔ demonstrate number sense with signed numbers
- ✔ find mean, median, and mode for a set of data

## Quick Quiz

1. Explain how to divide two negative numbers. How do you know your rule works? Possible answer: Divide the absolute values of the numbers. I can multiply to check the rule. The result is the number you need to multiply one of the negative numbers by to get the other. This cannot be negative, because a negative number times a negative number is a positive number. It cannot be 0, because the product of 0 and a negative number is 0.

2. Will $-3 \cdot (-6) + 2 \cdot 5 - 25 \cdot (-62)$ be greater than zero, equal to zero, or less than zero? Explain how you know. It will be greater than zero.

   Possible explanation: Find the product of each part of the expression.

   The product of two negative numbers is a positive number.

   The product of two positive numbers is a positive number.

   The product of a positive number and a negative number is a negative number.

   However, when you subtract a negative number, it is like adding its opposite, or a positive number. The sum of three positive numbers is a positive number.



On Your Own Exercises

57. Two inches below normal in August was the biggest difference from normal since normal would be reported as zero change.

58. For the year, the rainfall was −2.2″ or 2.2 inches below normal. This is the sum of all the comparisons.

59. On the average, the rainfall was really close to normal because $-\frac{2.2}{12}$ is −0.1833 ... , or not quite two-tenths of an inch below normal per month.

**57.** Was the biggest change from normal rainfall an amount below normal or an amount above normal? Explain.

**58.** For the year, was the rainfall above or below normal rainfall? How did you determine this?

**59.** On average, how did the actual rainfall compare to the normal rainfall per month for this year?

**60.** **In Your Own Words** Write a letter to a student a year younger than you. Explain how to divide a negative number by another negative number. Include examples. Answers will vary. Check students' work.

### Mixed Review

**61.** Which of the following expressions are equal to each other? a and c, e and h

| | |
|---|---|
| **a.** $m + m + m + m + m$ | **b.** $(5m)^5$ |
| **c.** $5m$ | **d.** $m^5$ |
| **e.** $3 \cdot 3 \cdot 3 \cdot 3$ | **f.** $4 \cdot 3$ |
| **g.** $4^3$ | **h.** $3^4$ |

**62.** Match each point on the graph to the coordinates given.

**a.** (2, 1)
**b.** (3, 4)
**c.** (1, −3)
**d.** (−2, −4)
**e.** (−2, 0)
**f.** (−2, 3)

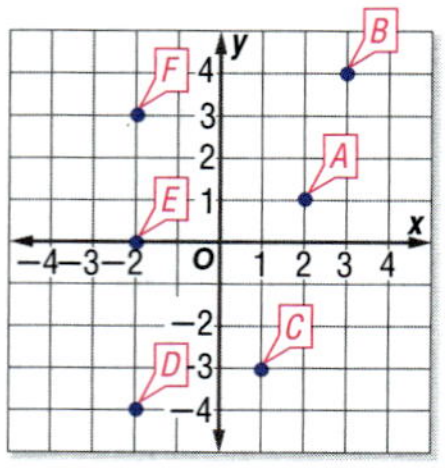


**Write each expression in exponential form.**

**63.** $t \cdot t \cdot t$ $t^3$

**64.** $n \cdot n \cdot n \cdot n$ $n^4$

**65.** $\pi \cdot r \cdot r$ $\pi r^2$

**66.** $\pi \cdot r \cdot r \cdot r$ $\pi r^3$

**67.** $y \cdot y \cdot y \cdot y \cdot y$ $y^5$

**68.** $z \cdot z \cdot z \cdot z \cdot z \cdot z \cdot z$ $z^7$

168 CHAPTER 3 Signed Numbers

CHAPTER 3

# Review & Self-Assessment

## Chapter Summary

You began this chapter learning about operations with signed numbers. Using the number-line model, you thought about addition and subtraction as facing a particular direction on a number line and moving forward or backward. You discovered some rules for these calculations and then used them to develop rules for multiplication and division. In addition, you used signed numbers when finding the mean, median, and mode of data sets.

**Vocabulary**

absolute value

## Strategies and Applications

The questions in this section will help you review and apply the important ideas and strategies developed in this chapter.

### Add and subtract with negative numbers

Using the "walk the number line" model or any other strategy you know, describe how to compute each sum or difference.

**1.** $2-(-9)$ **2.** $-9+3$

**3.** Describe a real-world situation that can be solved in two ways using signed numbers, one involving subtraction and one involving addition. Then write an equation to represent each solution. Answers will vary.

### Multiply and divide with negative numbers

Describe how to compute each product or quotient.

**4.** $-3.5 \cdot 4$ Strategies will vary; the product is $-14$. **5.** $-9 \div (-4.5)$ Strategies will vary; the quotient is 2.

Without computing, determine whether each expression is greater than 0, less than 0, or equal to 0. Explain how you know.

**6.** $(-33)^5 \cdot (-27)^2$ **7.** $\dfrac{-5^{58} \cdot (-12)^{23}}{-5^3}$

## Demonstrating Skills

Compute each sum, difference, product, or quotient.

**8.** $3 \cdot (-3)$ $-9$ **9.** $-2.3 - 7.9$ $-10.2$

**10.** $5.2 \div (-2.6)$ $-2$ **11.** $3.4 + (-5)$ $-1.6$

**12.** $-3.2 - (-0.9)$ $-2.3$ **13.** $-0.2 + 9.1$ $8.9$

**14.** $-7 \cdot (-8.3)$ $58.1$ **15.** $(-2)^4 \cdot (-5)$ $-80$

1. Possible answer: To walk the number line, start at 2, point to the left, and move backward 9 units to 11.
2. Possible answer: To walk the number line, start at $-9$, point to the right, and move forward 3 units to $-6$
6. Less than 0; The exponent on the first factor is odd, so the first factor is negative; the exponent on the second factor is even, so the second factor is positive; negative • positive = negative.
7. Less than 0; The numerator is greater than 0 because the first factor is negative, no parentheses, and the second factor is negative, odd exponent; and negative • negative = positive; denominator is less than 0; positive ÷ negative = negative.



CHAPTER 3

# Review & Self-Assessment

## Chapter Summary

This summary helps students recall the major topics of the chapter

## Vocabulary

Students should be able to explain each of the terms listed in the vocabulary section.

▶ **Exercise 15** Remind students that they need to use their rules for order of operation and work the exponent before they multiply by $-5$.

▶ **Exercises 27 and 28** Remind students that subtraction is the same as adding the opposite of a number.

Amiri kept track of his weight over a year's time. In the chart below, a positive number indicates a weight gain. A negative number indicates a weight loss.

| Jan. | Feb. | Mar. | Apr. | May | June | July | Aug. | Sept. | Oct. | Nov. | Dec. |
|---|---|---|---|---|---|---|---|---|---|---|---|
| −3 | 2 | 0 | −5 | −4 | −2 | 0 | 0 | −2 | −2 | 1 | 3 |

16. $3 - (-5) = 8$; The range is 8 pounds.
17. $-3 + 2 + 0 (-5) + (-4) + (-2) + 0 + 0 (-2) + (-2) + 1 + 3 = -12 \div 12 = -1$; So the mean is −1 pounds.
21. $4 + (-2)$
$= 2 + 2 + (-2)$
$= 2 + (2+(-2))$
$= 2 + 0$
$= 2$
22.
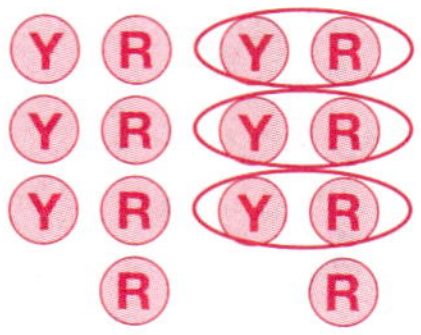

So, $3 + -4 = -1$
23. $-1 + (-4) = -5$;
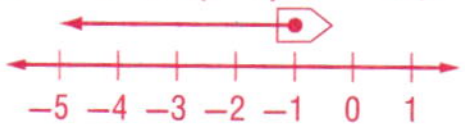

24. $6 - (-3) = 9$;
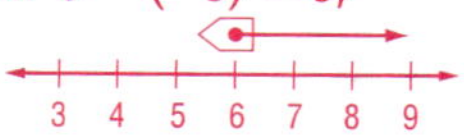


**16.** What is the range of Amiri's weight loss and gain?

**17.** What is Amiri's mean weight change?

**18.** Over the whole year did Amiri gain or lose weight? By how much? Amiri lost weight by 12 pounds.

**19.** What is the mode? 0 and −2

**20.** What is the median? −1

**21.** **Models** Write an expression to show the sum of 4 and −2. Simplify your expression.

**22.** **Models** Create a two-color chip model to show the sum of 3 and −4. Yellow represents positive values. Red represents negative values.

Walk the number line to compute each sum or difference. Record your steps by making a number-line drawing.

**23.** $-1 + (-4)$ **24.** $6 - (-3)$

Compute each difference. Then write an addition equation that is equal to the subtraction equation.

**25.** $17 - 21$ $-4$; $17 + (-21)$ **26.** $-2 - 12$ $-14$; $-2 + (-12)$

Compute each sum. Then write an equivalent subtraction equation.

**27.** $-15 + 11$ $-4$; $-15 - (-11)$ **28.** $6 + (-7)$ $-1$; $6 - 7$

For Exercises 29 and 30, write an addition and a subtraction equation can be used to find the answer to each question.

**29.** The Tiger football team started with the ball on the 23-yard line and lost 5 yards on its first play. On what yard line did the team start its next play? $23 + (-5) = 18$; $23 - 5 = 18$

**30.** The temperature yesterday was −4°F. There is a 15°F increase in temperature today. What is today's temperature? $-4 + 15 = 11$; $-4 - (-15) = 11$; 11°F

Consider the following expressions.

Expression 1: $\boxed{2x}$ Expression 2: $\boxed{x + 7}$

**31.** For what value(s) of $x$ is Expression 1 equal to Expression 2?
For $x = 7$

**32.** For what value(s) of $x$ is Expression 1 greater than Expression 2?
For values greater than 7

**33.** For what value(s) of $x$ is Expression 1 less than Expression 2?
For values less than 7

## Test-Taking Practice

*SHORT RESPONSE*

**1** Evaluate the following expression. Use the order of operations. Show all of your steps.

$$3 + (-2) + (-4)(2) - (-9) \div (-3)(4 - 5)$$

*Show your work.*

*Answer* ______________

*Show your work.*
$3 + (-2) + (-4)(2) - (-9) \div (-3)(4 - 5) = 3 + (-2) + (-8) + (-9) \div (-3)(-1) = 3 + (-2) + (8) - (3)(-1) = 3 + (-2) + (-8) + 3 = -4$

*Answer:* $-4$

*MULTIPLE CHOICE*

**2** Find the difference.

$$27 - (-5)$$

A $-32$
B 12
C 22
(D) 32

**3** Evaluate the expression. Use correct order of operations.

$$(5 + 6) - (7 - 3)^2 + 2 \cdot 4$$

(F) 3
G 11
H 13
J 35

**4** Find the value of the expression.

$$\frac{8(-3)(7)}{(-4)(-6)}$$

A $-\frac{6}{5}$
(B) $-7$
C $\frac{35}{24}$
D 7

**5** Find the quotient.

$$72 \div (-2) \div 4 \div (-3)$$

F $-3$
G $\frac{8}{3}$
(H) 3
J 9



Review & Self-Assessment
Chapter 3

▶ **Exercises 31–33** Once the students arrive at the solution to Exercise 33, they will be able to do a comparison with their classmates regarding the relative values of expressions. This activity is a great starting point for discussing the intricacies of inequalities.

**Lesson 3.1, Develop & Understand: B** (p. 146)

7. Sometimes positive, sometimes negative, and sometimes 0; Possible explanation: These three examples show the three possibilities: $-2 + 3 = 1$, $-5 + 2 = -3$, $-3 + 3 = 0$

8. Sometimes positive, sometimes negative, and sometimes 0; Possible explanation: These three examples show the three possibilities: $3 - 2 = 1$, $3 - 5 = -2$, $3 - 3 = 0$

9. Always negative; Possible explanation: A negative minus a positive is the same as a negative plus a negative. The answer to Exercise 6 shows that the result is always negative.

10. Always positive; Possible explanation: A positive minus a negative is the same as a positive plus a positive. The answer to Exercise 4 shows that the result is always positive.

11. Sometimes positive, sometimes negative, and sometimes 0; Possible explanation: A negative minus a negative is the same as a negative plus a positive. The answer to Exercise 7 shows that the result may be positive, negative, or 0.

Notes

CHAPTER 4

# Magnitude of Numbers

## Chapter Overview

In this chapter, students work with powers of 10 and learn how to express large numbers in scientific notation. Students also investigate scientific notation on their calculators. Students then revisit the laws of exponents and build on their understanding to evaluate expressions with negative exponents.

## The Big Picture

| Links to the Past | Chapter 4 | Links to the Future |
|---|---|---|
| **Course 1, Chapter 3** (pp. 108–195) Patterns, Numbers, and Rules<br>**Course 2, Chapter 2** (pp. 72–123) Exponents | **Lesson 4.1** (p. 174) Scientific Notation | **Course 3, Chapter 4** (pp. 144–203) Exponents and Exponential Variation |
| **Course 1, Chapter 3** (pp. 108–195) Patterns, Numbers, and Rules<br>**Course 2, Chapter 2** (pp. 72–123) Exponents | **Lesson 4.2** (p. 194) Negative Exponents | **Course 2, Chapter 7** (pp. 318–365) Real Numbers<br>**Course 3, Chapter 4** (pp. 144–203) Exponents and Exponential Variation |

# Mathematical Background

How do scientists who routinely work with extremely large or extremely minute numbers handle them? Astronomers dealing with distances in the universe, biologists mapping the nucleotides in the DNA of a single chromosome, physicists measuring the size of an atom—all employ numbers that are generally expressed using exponents. In this chapter, students study exponents and the procedures for computing with them in greater depth, building on their work with positive exponents.

**Patterns of Exponents** Already familiar with positive exponents as a way of expressing repeated multiplication, students will now learn the meanings of a wider range of exponent expressions:

- A negative integer raised to a positive integer exponent
- Any integer raised to a negative integer exponent

Students explore the patterns that characterize each of these kinds of expressions, some of which are different from the early concept many students will have that exponents produce a sequence of values that always "get bigger and bigger." Though the patterns are now more varied, you will want to help students see how their basic understanding of the meaning of exponents still applies. For example, students should recognize that

$$a^n \cdot a = a^{n+1}$$

whether $n$ is negative, positive, or 0.

**Negative Integer Bases** Note that a common point of confusion arises around the notation of negative integer bases. Students often forget that $(-5)^2$ is not the same as $-5^2$. In $(-5)^2$, $-5$ is being multiplied by itself; the result is 25. In $-5^2$, there are really two operations. First, 5 is being raised to the second power: 25. Then, 25 is being multiplied by $-1$, with the final result of $-25$. (In the latter case, following the order of operations, the exponent must be computed before the multiplication.)

## Additional Reading

According to Grouws and Cebulla in *Improving Student Achievement in Mathematics,* students who develop conceptual understanding early perform best on procedural knowledge later. In Lessons 4.1 and 4.2, stretching, shrinking, and repeater machine models are used to help students understand the concepts of positive and negative exponents.

CHAPTER 4

# Planning Guide

## *Lesson Resources*

| | Lesson 4.1 (Pacing: 5 days) | Lesson 4.2 (Pacing: 4 days) |
|---|---|---|
| **Lesson Title** | **Scientific Notation** (p. 174) | **Negative Exponents** (p. 194) |
| **Lesson Objectives** | • To multiply and divide numbers by powers of 10<br>• To write numbers using scientific notation<br>• To use a calculator to work with numbers in scientific notation | • To relate negative exponents to both multiplication by fractions and repeated division<br>• To evaluate simple expressions with negative exponents<br>• To apply laws of exponents to expressions with negative exponents<br>• To write numbers in scientific notation with negative exponents |
| **Materials** | calculator | |
| ***Quick Review Math Handbook*** | **Lesson 1.4** Integer Operations | **Lesson 1.4** Integer Operations |
| **Print Resources** | CRM Study Guide and Intervention (p. 3)<br>CRM Skills Practice (p. 4)<br>CRM Problem-Solving Practice (p. 5)<br>CRM Enrichment (p. 6)<br>• Investigation Notebook and Reflection Journal<br>• Differentiation Handbook | CRM Study Guide and Intervention (p. 8)<br>CRM Skills Practice (p. 9)<br>CRM Problem-Solving Practice (p. 10)<br>CRM Enrichment (p. 11)<br>• Investigation Notebook and Reflection Journal<br>• Differentiation Handbook |
| **Technology Resources** | TeacherWorks Plus<br>Classroom Presentation Toolkit<br>ExamView Assessment Suite<br>StudentWorks Plus<br>Math Online Brain Pops • Concepts in Motion | TeacherWorks Plus<br>Classroom Presentation Toolkit<br>ExamView Assessment Suite<br>StudentWorks Plus<br>Math Online Brain Pops • Concepts in Motion |

*Included in the Impact Mathematics Manipulative Kit

# Assessment Resources

## MARS Assessment: Teaching with Purpose

**Land and Water**

In *Land and Water,* students work with large numbers in both standard form and scientific notation to calculate the percentages of Earth's surface covered by land and by water. Students also use proportion.

**Targeting the Task**

- **Diagnostic**—Use Exercises 1–2 in the *Land and Water* assessment to determine students' understanding of proportion and how to work with large numbers in both scientific notation and standard form. For those students who do not have this understanding, completing this unit is needed.
- **Formative**—Exercises 1–2 can be administered individually according to the lessons.
- **Summative**—Administer the complete *Land and Water* performance-based assessment.

**CRM Chapter 4 MARS Assessment** (pp. 24–27)

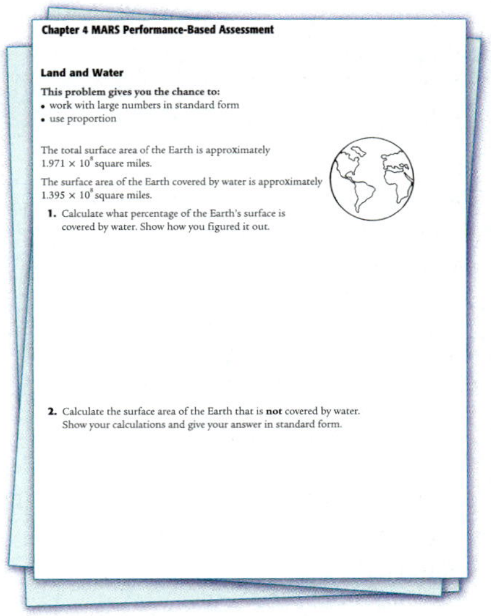
Chapter 4 MARS Performance-Based Assessment

**Land and Water**

**This problem gives you the chance to:**
- work with large numbers in standard form
- use proportion

The total surface area of the Earth is approximately $1.971 \times 10^8$ square miles.

The surface area of the Earth covered by water is approximately $1.395 \times 10^8$ square miles.

1. Calculate what percentage of the Earth's surface is covered by water. Show how you figured it out.

2. Calculate the surface area of the Earth that is **not** covered by water. Show your calculations and give your answer in standard form.

## Assessment Planning Guide

Assessments are available for investigations, lessons, and chapters.

ExamView Assessment Suite — Customize and create multiple versions of tests and quizzes.

| | Student Edition | Teacher Edition | Other Resources |
|---|---|---|---|
| **Diagnostic** | | | CRM Chapter 4 Pretest (pp. 13–16)<br>Math Online Online Chapter Quiz |
| **Formative** | Share & Summarize (pp. 177, 181, 184, 199, 201) | Troubleshooting (pp. 175, 176, 180, 182, 184, 195, 197, 198, 201)<br>On the Spot Assessment (pp. 175, 181, 196)<br>Quick Check (pp. 193, 206)<br>Quick Quiz (pp. 193, 206) | CRM Quick Quiz (pp. 7, 12) |
| **Summative** | Review & Self-Assessment (pp. 207–209) | | CRM Chapter 4 Test: Forms A and B (pp. 17–22)<br>CRM Standardized Test Practice (pp. 28–29) |
| **Performance-Based** | In Your Own Words (pp. 193, 205) | | CRM Chapter Performance Assessment (p. 23)<br>CRM MARS Performance-Based Assessment (pp. 24–27) |

# Differentiated Instruction

## *Reaching* All Learners

Below are suggestions on differentiating the materials presented in this chapter. Additional modifications should be considered.

### Approaching Level AL

**Exponent Review** Have students work in pairs and create 10 problems that involve the rules for exponents. On a note card have them write a problem and then on another note card have them write the solution. When they are finished, each pair should have 20 note cards. Have the pairs exchange note card packs with another pair. Now have the students play a game of memory. Mix the cards up and place them face down on the desks. The idea is to match problems with correct solutions. Each person takes turns flipping 2 cards over, if they form a match, the person removes both cards from the desk. Play continues until all matches are found.

### Beyond Level BL

**Very Small Numbers** Have students work in pairs to determine at least 4 different areas that use scientific notation for recording information that involves very small numbers. Once the pairs have found their topics, ask them to create a visual that can be hung in the classroom and displayed for other students to see how small numbers are used in the real-world. You may even ask the pairs to provide a small presentation in front of the class to share this information.

### On Level OL

**Scientific Notation Matching** Have students work in pairs to write 5 large numbers and 5 very small numbers. On a note card have the students write the number in scientific notation and another note card, have the students write the number in standard notation. When they are finished, each pair should have 20 note cards. Have the pairs exchange note card packs with another pair. Now have the students play a game of memory. Mix the cards up and place them face down on the desks. The idea is to match problems with correct solutions. Each person takes turns flipping 2 cards over, if they form a match, the person removes both cards from the desk. Play continues until all matches are found.

### English Language Learners ELL

**Technology** Have students work in teams to look on the internet and find 3 examples of places where scientific notation is used. The internet is useful because students can view articles in their first language. Once the students have found examples, have them write a paragraph in their first language describing what they found. Next have each team practice presenting this information in English. Once the students are comfortable, have them share what they found with the class.

**KEY**

AL Approaching Level OL On Level BL Beyond Level ELL English Language Learners

## *Intervention Planning Guide*

CRM Assess students' prerequisite skills and knowledge using the **Chapter Pretest** found in the Chapter 4 Resource Masters, pp. 13–16.

| **Intensive Intervention** two or more years below grade level | **Strategic Intervention** below grade level | **On Level** | **Beyond Level** |
|---|---|---|---|
| **If** students miss 75% of the exercises: **Then** use *Math Triumphs,* an intensive intervention | **If** students miss 50% of the exercises: **Then** choose a resource: | **If** students miss 25% of the exercises: **Then** choose a resource: | **If** students miss 0%–10% of the exercises: **Then** choose a resource: |
| *Math Triumphs,* Grade 7<br>• Chapter 7: Whole Numbers and Integers<br>• Chapter 8: Integer Operations | CRM Study Guide and Intervention (pp. 3, 8)<br>• Investigation Notebook and Reflection Journal<br>• Differentiation Handbook<br>Math Online Brain Pops • Concepts in Motion | CRM Skills Practice (pp. 4, 9)<br>CRM Problem-Solving Practice (pp. 5, 10)<br>• Investigation Notebook and Reflection Journal | CRM Enrichment (pp. 6, 11)<br>• Differentiation Handbook |

### *Literature Connections*

**Recommended Outside Reading for Students**

**Nonfiction**

Woods, Michael, and Woods, Mary. *Ancient Computing.* Runestone Press, 2000.

This book describes the clever calculation techniques used in early civilizations. Students will read about the origins of the base-10 number system and scientific notation. In addition, they learn that an Egyptian scribe wrote an algebra textbook more than 3,500 years ago.

**Fiction**

Pappas, Theoni. *Fractals, Googles, and Other Mathematical Tales.* Wide World Publishing/Tetra, 1999, 1993.

This collection of math stories and facts centers around Penrose the cat and his view of the history of mathematics. Sidebars supplement the tales. Topics include decimals, multiple dimensions, base-10 and base-12 number systems.

### Professional Development

Targeted professional development has been articulated throughout the *IMPACT Mathematics* series. The **McGraw-Hill Professional Development Video Library** provides short videos that support the mathematics standards. Log on to www.glencoe.com.

CHAPTER 4

# Magnitude of Numbers

## Introduce

**Astronomical Information** In this chapter, students will be studying ways of expressing really large and really small numbers. One example of really large numbers is given as the distances of the planets in our solar system from the sun. Ask students to tell you other places where really large numbers can be found. Ask the students how they would use the values written in the second column. This is an excellent springboard into discussions about the form of scientific notation and its function in everyday life.

**Think About It** Have students compare the two values for Earth's distance. Use this as a transition from standard notation to scientific notation.

CHAPTER 4

# Magnitude of Numbers

### Contents in Brief



## Real-Life Math

**The Solar System** The center of the solar system is the Sun, and planet distances are given in terms of each planet's distance from the Sun. Astronomical information, such as planets' distances, can be found in reference books and on Internet sites. Planet distances, in miles, are shown below.

| | | | |
|---|---|---|---|
| Mercury: | 36,000,000 | Venus: | $6.7 \times 10^7$ |
| Earth: | 93,000,000 | Earth: | $9.3 \times 10^7$ |
| Jupiter: | 484,000,000 | Mars: | $1.42 \times 10^8$ |
| Saturn: | 887,000,000 | Uranus: | $1.78 \times 10^9$ |
| Neptune: | 2,794,000,000 | | |

**Think About It** Suppose you want to list the planets in order according to their distances from the Sun. How can you use the data to order the distances from least to greatest?

**Math Online** Take the **Chapter Readiness Quiz** at glencoe.com.

### Chapter Resources

- CRM Chapter 4 Resource Masters
- CRM English/Spanish Family Letter (pp. 1–2)
- CRM Lesson Masters (pp. 1–2)
- CRM Chapter 4 Pretest (pp. 13–16)
- CRM Chapter 4 Tests (pp. 17–22)

**Math Online** Online Readiness Quiz • eGlossary

# Dear Family,

Chapter 2 used repeater machines to model expressions such as $2^4$. The class learned that the 2 is called the *base,* and the raised 4 is called the *exponent.*

$$2^4 = 2 \cdot 2 \cdot 2 \cdot 2 = 16$$

In this chapter, your student will study **scientific notation**. This notation is a mathematical shorthand that is often used to represent the magnitude of very large and very small numbers, like the distance between planets and the size of an atom.

### Key Concept–Scientific Notation

In scientific notation, a number between 0 and 10 is multiplied by a power of 10. The following repeater machines model changing the scientific notation expressions $1.5 \times 10^3$ and $2.1 \times 10^{-2}$ to standard form.

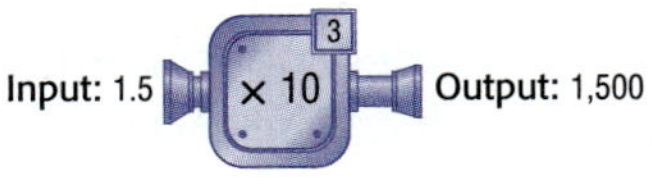


$1.5 \times 10^3 = 1{,}500$

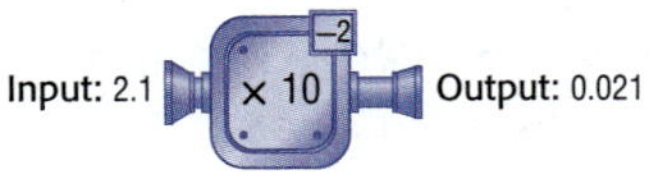


$2.1 \times 10^{-2} = 0.021$

In the expression $2.1 \times 10^{-2}$, the exponent is negative. The class will explore negative exponents in Lesson 4.2.

### Chapter Vocabulary

**relative error** **scientific notation**

### Home Activities

- Discuss real-world situations that involve very large and very small, or greater and lesser numbers.
- Use scientific notation to express numbers found in newspapers, magazines, and print advertisements.

173

## Family Letter

Another version of the Family Letter, available in English and Spanish, is found in the Chapter 4 Resource Masters. You may want to send a copy of this letter home with your students.

**Key Concept–Scientific Notation** This topic uses the repeater machines that the students first encountered in Chapter 2. In this chapter, the students will use the machines for each product of ten they need to represent a number using scientific notation. Ask students to describe how the repeater machines work. Use this as a starting point for the lesson.

**Home Activities**

- Have students ask their families where they use very large or very small numbers.
- Have students write a large number for their families and ask them to write the number in a different way. Hopefully the family members will recall scientific notation. If not, have the student show how the number can be written using scientific notation.

## Key Vocabulary

**English (Spanish)** *Introduce the most important terms from Chapter 4.*

**scientific notation (notación científica)** A number that is expressed as the product of a number greater than or equal to 1 but less than 10, and a power of 10. For example, 5,000,000 written in scientific notation is $5 \times 10^6$. (p. 178)

**relative error (error relativo)** The ratio of the difference between the predicted amount and the actual amount to the actual amount. (p. 185)

LESSON 4.1

# Scientific Notation

## Objectives

- To multiply and divide numbers by powers of 10
- To write numbers using scientific notation
- To use a calculator to work with numbers in scientific notation

## Overview

This lesson presents students with some useful ways of dealing with large numbers. First, they learn ways to represent large numbers by using powers of 10 and scientific notation. They practice using scientific notation correctly, sometimes with the help of a calculator. A second emphasis is on the importance of the precision of large numbers. When someone says "3 million years old," students should know this is not an exact age but a good approximation. Similarly, they should understand why it makes little sense to add two numbers like $3.2 \times 10^{25}$ and $6.8 \times 10^{10}$. The second is so much smaller than the first that the "sum" would not be a significant increase over the first number.

## Advance Preparation

You may want to familiarize yourself with the calculators that the students have so that you can assist them with understanding how to use scientific notation.

| | Summary | Materials | On Your Own Exercises (pp. 189–193) | Assessment Opportunities |
|---|---|---|---|---|
| **Investigation 1** (p. 175) Pacing: 2 days | Students use powers of 10 to represent numbers. Students multiply and divide numbers by powers of 10. | | Practice & Apply: 1–20<br>Connect & Extend: 41–55<br>Mixed Review: 62–77 | • On the Spot Assessment (p. 175)<br>• Share & Summarize (p. 177)<br>• Troubleshooting (pp. 175, 176) |
| **Investigation 2** (p. 178) Pacing: 1 day | Students convert between numbers in scientific notation and standard notation. Students rewrite numbers using scientific notation. | | Practice & Apply: 21–35<br>Connect & Extend: 56–57<br>Mixed Review: 62–77 | • On the Spot Assessment (p. 181)<br>• Share & Summarize (p. 181)<br>• Troubleshooting (p. 180) |
| **Investigation 3** (p. 182) Pacing: 1 day | Students use their calculators to explore contexts in which they use numbers expressed in scientific notation. | calculator | Practice & Apply: 36–40<br>Connect & Extend: 58–60<br>Mixed Review: 62–77 | • Share & Summarize (p. 184)<br>• Troubleshooting (pp. 182, 184) |
| **Inquiry Investigation 4** (p. 185) Pacing: 1 day | Students will compute the relative error associated with various real-life situations. | calculator | | |

# Leveled Lesson Resources

CRM *Available in:* **Chapter 4 Resource Masters**

Also on TeacherWorks™ Lesson 4.1

## Study Guide and Intervention (p. 3) AL

**Lesson 4.1 Study Guide and Intervention**
***Scientific Notation***

A number is in scientific notation when it is written as the product of a number and a power of ten. The number must be greater than or equal to 1 and less than 10.

- To write a number in standard notation, you apply the order of operations. First evaluate the power of ten and then multiply.
- To write a number in scientific notation, move the decimal point to the right of the first nonzero number. Then, find the power of ten by counting the number of places moved.

**Example 1** **Write $6.1 \times 10^3$ in standard notation.**

$6.1 \times 10^3 = 6.1 \times 1{,}000$ — $10^3 = 1{,}000$

$= 6.100$ — Move the decimal point 3 places to the right.

$= 6{,}100$

**Example 2** **Write 62,500 in scientific notation.**

$62{,}500 = 6.250 \times 10{,}000$ — Move the decimal point 4 places to get a number between 1 and 10.

$= 6.25 \times 10^4$

**Exercises**

**Write each number in standard notation.**

1. $7.25 \times 10^2$
2. $2.5 \times 10^3$
3. $9.95 \times 10^5$
4. $8.80 \times 10^4$
5. $3.18 \times 10^6$
6. $6.12 \times 10^3$

**Write each number in scientific notation.**

7. 325
8. 9,210
9. 200
10. 5,120
11. 561
12. 1,230
13. 6 million
14. 53 thousand
15. 8 hundred

## Skills Practice (p. 4) AL OL

**Lesson 4.1 Skills Practice**
***Scientific Notation***

**Write each number in standard notation.**

1. $3.1 \times 10^2$
2. $2.3 \times 10^3$
3. $6.10 \times 10^5$
4. $7.87 \times 10^4$
5. $1.06 \times 10^7$
6. $2.11 \times 10^{10}$

**Find the value of *N* in each equation.**

7. $11 \times 10^N = 11{,}000$
8. $N \times 10^9 = 6{,}787{,}000$
9. $1.6 \times 10^4 = N$
10. $0.0921 \times 10^N = 9.21$
11. $4.05 \times 10^3 = N$
12. $N \times 10^2 = 0.098$

**Write each number in scientific notation.**

13. 230
14. 3 hundred
15. 720
16. 2,790
17. 5 million
18. 8,800

**Estimate the value of each expression. Then use your calculator to evaluate it. Give your answers in scientific notation.**

19. $5 \times 10^2 + 42 \times 10^2$
20. $6.2 \times 10^{16} - 1.1 \times 10^{12}$
21. $(1.05 \times 10^8) \div 2$
22. $(2.1 \times 10^4) \cdot 4$
23. $25 \cdot (5.68 \times 10^8)$
24. $18 \times 10^8 - 6.8 \times 10^6$
25. $2.7 \times 10^3 + 9.8 \times 10^4$
26. $(24 \times 10^8) \div 50$

## Problem-Solving Practice (p. 5) AL OL

**Lesson 4.1 Problem-Solving Practice**
***Scientific Notation***

**Solve.**

1. **Iceberg** The biggest iceberg ever seen split off the Ross Ice Shelf in Antarctica during the spring of 2000. It was estimated to weigh about 4,000,000,000,000 tons. Write its weight in scientific notation.
2. **Planets** The average distance between Earth and the Sun is 92,960,000 miles. Write this distance in scientific notation.
3. **Wealth** In 2007, the wealthiest man in the world's assets were estimated at about $58,500,000,000. Write this value in scientific notation.
4. **Baseball** Willie Mays hit $6.6 \times 10^2$ career home runs. Write $6.6 \times 10^2$ in standard notation.
5. **Earth** The mass of Earth is about 6,580,000,000,000,000,000,000 tons. There are 2,000 pounds in one ton. Write the mass of Earth in pounds in scientific notation.
6. **Light** The speed of light is about $2.998 \times 10^8$ meters per second or about $1.86 \times 10^5$ miles per second. Write these values in standard notation.
7. **Population** The population of Texas was 23,507,783 according to a 2006 U.S. Census estimate.
   a. Round this estimate to the nearest hundred thousand.
   b. Write the estimate in scientific notation.
   c. What is the relative error if the number from Part b was used to represent the population of Texas?
8. **Population** The projected population of the world for the year 2025 is about 7,900,000,000.
   a. Suppose the population in 2025 is 7,500,000,000. Find the difference between the projected population in 2025 and the actual population.
   b. Divide the difference from Part a by the actual population in 2025. Express this relative error to four decimal places, in scientific notation, and as a percent error to the nearest percent.

## Enrichment (p. 6) BL

**Lesson 4.1 Enrichment**
***Scientific Notation***

**The Speed of Light**

Light travels at approximately 186,000 miles per second. You can use the formula below to find how long it takes light to travel from one place to another.

$$\frac{\text{distance}}{\text{speed of light}} = \text{time}$$

For example, the Sun is about $9.3 \times 10^7$ miles from Earth. If a gigantic explosion were to occur on the sun, how long would it take to see it from Earth?

$$\frac{93{,}000{,}000}{186{,}000} = 500 \leftarrow \text{Write } 9.3 \times 10^7 \text{ as } 93{,}000{,}000.$$

It would take about 500 seconds to see the explosion.

Now you need to change seconds to minutes, since minutes is a more sensible unit for time in this case. To change seconds to minutes, divide.

$$\frac{500}{60} \rightarrow 60\overline{)500} = 8, \quad 480, \quad 20$$

It would take about 8 minutes to see the explosion from Earth.

**Compute each amount of time it takes for light to travel to Earth from each place. When appropriate, change seconds to a sensible unit.**

| | Location | Closest Distance to Earth | Time (in seconds) | Time (in a sensible unit) |
|---|---|---|---|---|
| 1. | Moon | $2.2 \times 10^5$ mi | | |
| 2. | Halley's Comet | $3.11 \times 10^6$ mi | | |
| 3. | Mars | $3.46 \times 10^7$ mi | | |
| 4. | Venus | $2.57 \times 10^7$ mi | | |
| 5. | Jupiter | $3.67 \times 10^8$ mi | | |
| 6. | Pluto | $2.67 \times 10^9$ mi | | |
| 7. | nearest star | $2.48 \times 10^{13}$ mi | | |

## Lesson Quick Quiz (p. 7) AL OL BL

**Lesson 4.1 Quick Quiz**
***Scientific Notation***

**Rewrite each number in standard notation.**

1. $438 \times 10^6$
2. $\left(\frac{6}{10}\right)^2$

**Write each number in scientific notation.**

3. 45,000,000
4. 239.4

**Suppose you save $100 each month beginning now, but stuff it in your mattress so that it doesn't earn interest.**

5. How many years would it take to save 1 million dollars?
6. How many years would it take to save 1 billion dollars?
7. Would one billion dollar bills fit in your mattress? Explain any assumptions you make and show your work.

# Additional Lesson Resources

### Teacher Tech Tools

- TeacherWorks
- ExamView Assessment Suite
- Classroom Presentation Toolkit
- Advance Tracker

### Student Tech Tools

- StudentWorks Plus
- Math Online eGlossary • Concepts in Motion

### Other Print Products

- Investigation Notebook and Reflection Journal
- Quick Review Math Handbook

# LESSON 4.1 Scientific Notation

## Introduce

**Distances in Space** Start a discussion about distances between planets and stars with students.

### Think & Discuss

*Suggested Grouping: Whole Class*

Allow students a few minutes to read and enjoy the cartoons before discussing what makes them funny.

For the first cartoon, students will see that a billion is already real money and that it is the scale of federal spending that makes the quote funny.

For the second, the fact that a student is relieved that the destruction is a billion years away (which, indeed, is a lot more than a million years) is funny because a million years is already an extremely long time compared to a human's lifetime. Over the lifetime of a planet, however, a million years is not such a long period of time.

The third cartoon shows the lack of number sense of many people in the world—even doctors! "99% safe" and "1 in a million chance something will go wrong" provide very different statistics. The first is 10,000 times as likely as the second.

Finally, the last cartoon addresses the precision of large numbers. "A million" rarely means exactly a million, but rather "close to a million." You might ask students to give a reasonable age range for a rock that is labeled "1 million years old."

# LESSON 4.1 Scientific Notation



How far is it from your house to your school? You may be close enough to walk to school. Or, you may travel a farther distance, perhaps a few miles, by bus. Think about how far the Apollo astronauts traveled to go to the moon and how far the *Mars Pathfinder* traveled to Mars.

In this lesson, you will learn a new way of writing and working with very large numbers.

### Think & Discuss

What is funny about each of these cartoons? See teaching notes.

### Reaching All Learners

**ELL English Language Learners** Students may have a difficult time spotting the humor in the cartoons. Discuss humor, what makes something humorous, and how words in the English language can take on alternate meanings. Ask students to tell a story that is humorous in their first language. Discuss what makes the story humorous. When the story is told in English is the story still funny? Discuss why it is or is not.

# Investigation 1 Powers of 10

Previously, you have worked with 1 million, 1 billion, and 1 trillion. These numbers can be expressed as powers of 10.

$$1 \text{ million} = 1{,}000{,}000 = 10^6$$

$$1 \text{ billion} = 1{,}000{,}000{,}000 = 10^9$$

$$1 \text{ trillion} = 1{,}000{,}000{,}000{,}000 = 10^{12}$$

It is often useful to talk about large numbers in terms of powers of 10. Imagine ×10 repeater machines when working with such powers.

**Math Link**

Here are some other big numbers.

| | |
|---|---|
| $10^{15}$ | quadrillion |
| $10^{18}$ | quintillion |
| $10^{21}$ | sextillion |
| $10^{24}$ | septillion |
| $10^{27}$ | octillion |
| $10^{30}$ | nonillion |

① Possible answer: If the input length is a whole number, add a number of zeros equal to the exponent. If the input length is a decimal number, move the decimal point to the right the number of places equal to the exponent.

### Think & Discuss

Your factory is so successful, you plan a celebration. To make decorations, you send streamers through stretching machines.

Find the length of the streamer that exits each machine. Give your answers in centimeters.

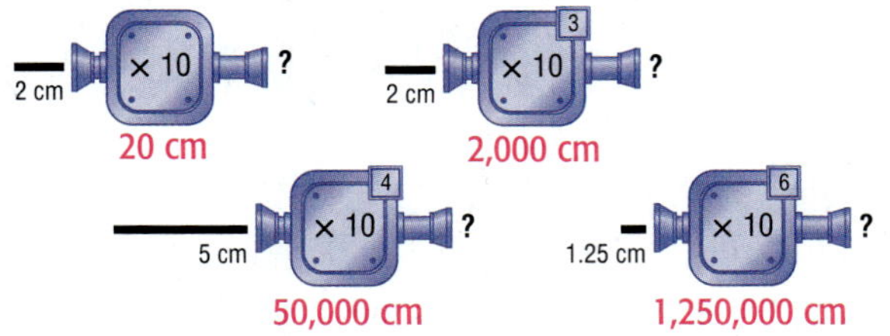


If you know the length of the input streamer and the exponent on the ×10 repeater machine, how can you find the length of the output streamer? See ①.

Find the exponent of each repeater machine. (Note: The output streamer is not drawn to scale.)

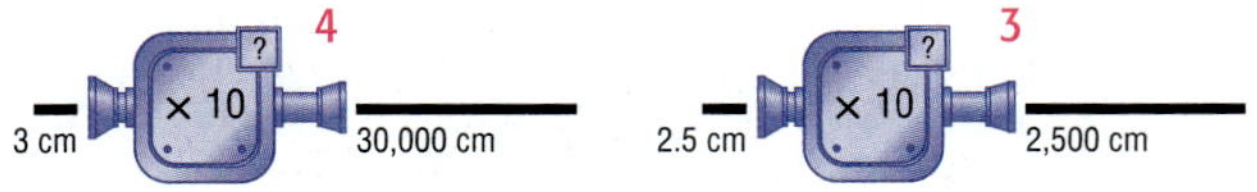


If you know the length of the input and output streamers, how can you find the exponent of the ×10 repeater machine? Possible answer: If the input length is a whole number, count the number of zeros added to the input length to get the output length. The number of added zeros is the exponent. If the input length is a decimal, then count the places the decimal moved to the right to get from the input length to the output length. That number is the exponent.



### On the Spot Assessment

Ask the students to tell you what number $4.6 \times 10^4$ is when you use the repeater machine. What exponent would you need to write 85,000,000 in scientific notation? 460,000; 7

### Troubleshooting

If students are struggling with the repeater machines, ask the students to add as many zeros as the exponent in the first set of questions. In the second set of questions, ask the students to count the number of positions past the decimal point there are from what goes in the machine versus what comes out.

## Investigation 1

***On Your Own Exercises***
Pages 189–193
Exercises 1–20, 41–55

**Powers of 10** In this investigation, students use stretching and shrinking machines to work with powers of 10. You may want to start with a short discussion about why so many things are described in powers of 10. For example, in talking about money, we often give amounts in terms of how many billion: "The deficit is around 5.4 billion dollars" or "The number of people in the world is around 6.3 billion."

### Think & Discuss

Since students should be familiar with the stretching machines, this material can be discussed rather quickly.

When discussing the first group of machines, ask students to explain how to use the exponent to predict the length of the streamer. They may refer to the relationship between the exponent and the number of zeros or the number of decimal places moved in the length of the output streamer. For example, in the second machine, the output streamer must have 3 zeros because the exponent is 3 ($2 \times 10^3 = 2{,}000$). In the fourth machine, the decimal place had to be moved 6 places because the exponent is 6 ($1.25 \times 10^6 = 1{,}250{,}000$).

Have students try to generalize a rule for determining the length of an output streamer, given the input length and the exponent. They may suggest the "counting zeros" technique but have trouble stating the relationship for situations involving decimals, such as that in the fourth machine. If so, review how to multiply decimals by powers of 10. Since the exercises include whole numbers and decimals, you may wish to provide several more examples that have decimal input numbers such as 2.35 inches.

For the second group of machines, students will need to work backward. Again, have students try to generalize a rule for determining the exponent, given the input and output lengths.

**Lesson 4.1** Scientific Notation 175

## Develop & Understand: A

*Suggested Grouping: Pairs*

Because our number system is a base-10 system, students should recognize how convenient it is to multiply with powers of 10. Multiplying by powers of 10 changes the position, or place value, of the digits, but does not change the digits or their order. Students may be familiar with these ideas but may need practice using them in the context of the stretching machines.

▶ **Exercise 1** This exercise is particularly interesting because it illustrates the true magnitude of change caused by repeated applications of a ×10 machine. Help students to realize that the input straw was only $\frac{1}{100}$ the length of the output straw.

▶ **Exercises 3–11** Students should be able to apply the generalizations they discussed in Think & Discuss. Be sure that they can state why these generalizations work. That is, "adding zeros" (with whole numbers) and "moving the decimal point" (with decimals) really means "multiplying by a power of 10." Have students note that these exercises cover all three types of situations—finding output lengths, finding exponents, and finding input lengths.

▶ **Exercise 6** Call attention to the fact that this exercise involves different units of measure. You might ask:

- How can you determine the repeater number when the input is in meters and the output is in kilometers? Change the meters to kilometers or the kilometers to meters first.

1. About 0.12 cm; A $\times 10^2$ machine stretches a straw to 100 times its original size. This straw is about 12 cm, and the input straw must have been $\frac{1}{100}$ of this length.

## Develop & Understand: A

**1.** The beverage straw below exited a $\times 10^2$ machine. Without measuring, estimate the length of the input straw in centimeters. It may be helpful if you copy the straw onto your paper. Explain how you found your answer.

**2.** The straw to the right went into a $\times 10$ machine. Without measuring, estimate the length of the output straw in centimeters. About 15 cm

**Find the length of each output straw.**

**3.**

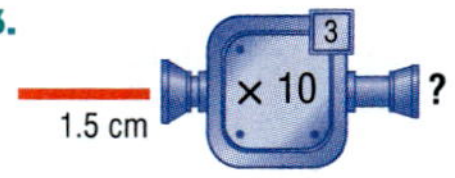


1,500 cm, 15 m

**4.**

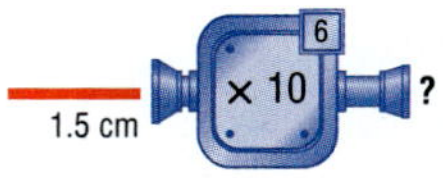


1,500,000 cm, or 15,000 m, or 15 km

**5.**

4,300 cm, or 43 m

**Find each exponent.**

**6.**

3

**7.**

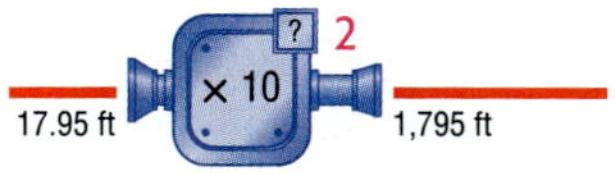


2

**8.**

5

**Find the length of each input straw.**

**9.**

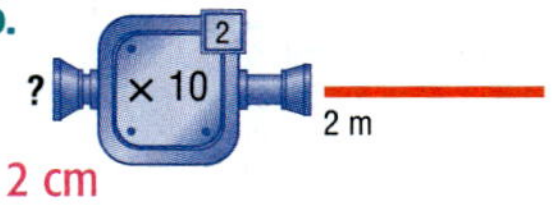


2 cm

**10.**

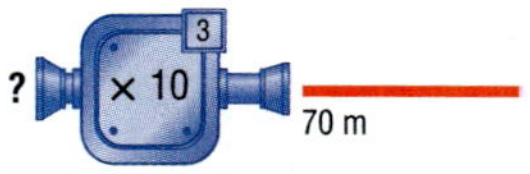


0.07 m, or 7 cm

**11.**

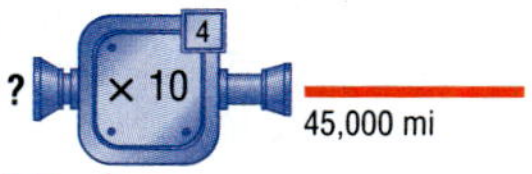


4.5 mi



### Troubleshooting

Students may forget that the ×10 machine not only adds a zero to the end of a number, but it also moves the decimal place to the right for each power of 10.

In Exercises 12–31, you will work with expressions involving powers of 10. As you work, it may help to think of repeater machines. For example, you could use the machine below to think about $5 \times 10^3$.

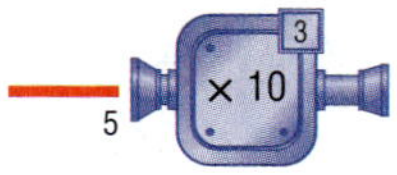


**Real-World Link**

The human eye blinks an average of 4,200,000, or $4.2 \times 10^6$, times a year.

## Develop & Understand: B

**Find each product.**

**12.** $8 \times 10^5$ 800,000

**13.** $18.6 \times 10^8$ 1,860,000,000

**14.** $9{,}258 \times 10^4$ 92,580,000

**15.** $1{,}620 \times 10^5$ 162,000,000

**16.** $4 \times 10^{12}$ 4,000,000,000,000

**17.** $14.9 \times 10^{11}$ 1,490,000,000,000

**Find the value of *N* in each equation.**

**18.** $6 \times 10^N = 600$ 2

**19.** $8.6 \times 10^N = 86{,}000$ 4

**20.** $54 \times 10^N = 5{,}400{,}000$ 5

**21.** $2{,}854 \times 10^N = 285{,}400$ 2

**22.** $N \times 10^2 = 800$ 8

**23.** $N \times 10^3 = 47{,}000$ 47

**24.** $N \times 10^6 = 54{,}800{,}000$ 54.8

**25.** $N \times 10^4 = 3{,}958$ 0.3958

**26.** $85 \times 10^4 = N$ 850,000

**27.** $9.8 \times N = 9{,}800{,}000$ 1,000,000, or $10^6$

**28.** $0.00427 \times 10^N = 42.7$ 4

**29.** $N \times 10^{11} = 24{,}985{,}000{,}000$ 0.24985

**30.** $5 \times 10^N = 5{,}000{,}000{,}000{,}000$ 12

**31.** $N \times 10^{11} = 3{,}568{,}000{,}000{,}000$ 35.68

### Share & Summarize

1. What repeater machine would stretch a 6-inch straw to 6 million inches? $\times 10^6$
2. What repeater machine would stretch a 3-inch straw to 3 billion inches? $\times 10^9$
3. What repeater machine would stretch a 2.3-million-inch straw to 2.3 billion inches? $\times 10^3$



## Reaching All Learners

**AL Approaching Level** If students have difficulty with Exercises 18–29 you may want to encourage them to create "machine stories" for them. That is, they should translate the numerical expressions into machine situations, which they then describe to their partner. For instance, "$6 \times 10^N = 600$" can be translated into "I took a 6-inch stick and put it through a 10 repeater machine. It came out 600 inches long, so the exponent (or exponents) on the machine must have been . . . ."

As preparation for Exercises 12–31, you may want to show the example that follows Exercise 11 and have students write numerical expressions corresponding to several of the Exercises 1–11.

## Develop & Understand: B

*Suggested Grouping: Pairs*

This exercise set provides a few numerical practice exercises for students. The idea of a number times a power of 10 is a nice lead-in to the next investigation, which focuses on scientific notation.

### Share & Summarize

Questions 1–3 ask students to connect numbers with a machine model. If students have difficulty, you may want to return to Exercises 1–11 and have students practice translating the machine exercises into numerical expressions or words. You might also have students practice translating the numerical expressions in Exercises 12–29 into machine exercises or words. The key idea is that each expression represents a machine stretch.

If students do not answer Question 3 correctly, you may want to spend some time reviewing different ways to compare a million and a billion. To get from a million to a billion, you must multiply by 1,000. This means sending the stick through a 31,000 machine. Ask,

- What power of 10 is 1,000? 3rd

Alternately, students might prefer using laws of exponents. If you consider turning a 1-million-inch stick into a 1-billion-inch stick, the following reasoning works:

1 million is $10^6$ and 1 billion is $10^9$. So we want to know what repeater machine will give an output of $10^9$ for an input of $10^6$. By one of the product laws of exponents, we see that the machine must be a $\times 10^3$ machine, since $10^6 \times 10^3 = 10^{6+3} = 10^9$.

## Investigation 2

***On Your Own Exercises***
Pages 189–193
Exercises 21–35, 56–57

**Scientific Notation** Scientific notation is a convention that makes it easy to communicate the values of numbers. For convenience and because of limited display space, calculators use scientific notation to display very large and very small numbers. In this investigation, we concentrate on very large numbers.

**Example**

Be sure that students understand that the three expressions do indeed equal 5,878,000,000,000. You might ask them to think about why a large number might be written in a more compact form.

After discussing the Example, use the third expression to present the concept of scientific notation. Explain that the first factor of the product is a number that has exactly one nonzero digit to the left of its decimal place. This explanation may make more sense than explaining that the first factor must be at least 1 but less than 10. The second factor is a power of 10.

**Additional Examples** When you introduce how to write numbers in scientific notation, you may want to show several examples, such as:

- $52.67 \times 10^3$ Incorrect; $5.267 \times 10^4$
- $0.349 \times 10^8$ Incorrect; $3.49 \times 10^7$
- $8 \times 10^2$ Correct
- $5.1 \times 10^3$ Correct
- $8{,}304 \times 10$ Incorrect; $8.304 \times 10^4$

Ask students to identify which are in scientific notation and which are not. These exercises occur in the text, but it is helpful to students to process the definition before tackling exercises on their own. This is truly a case where students must learn something—how numbers are represented in scientific notation—rather than where they must figure out something.

## Investigation 2 Work with Scientific Notation

**Vocabulary**
- **greater**
- **lesser**
- **scientific notation**

Powers of 10 give us an easy way to express very large and very small, or **greater** and **lesser** numbers, without writing a lot of zeros. This is useful in many fields, such as economics, engineering, computer science, and other areas of science.

For example, astronomers need to describe great distances, like the distances between planets, stars, and galaxies. Chemists often need to describe small measurements, like the sizes of molecules, atoms, and quarks.

In this investigation, you will focus on a method for expressing large numbers. In Lesson 4.2, you will see how this method can be used to express small numbers, as well.

**Real-World Link**
The Centaurus system includes Alpha Centauri, the star, other than our own Sun, that is closest to Earth.

### Example

Astronomical distances are often expressed in lightyears. For example, the Centaurus star system is 4.3 lightyears from Earth. A *lightyear* is the distance light travels in one year. One lightyear is approximately 5,878,000,000,000 miles.

There are many ways to express the number of miles in a lightyear as the product of a number and a power of 10. Here are three.

$$5{,}878 \times 10^9 \qquad 58.78 \times 10^{11} \qquad 5.878 \times 10^{12}$$

Can you explain why each of these three expressions equals 5,878,000,000,000? In each case, multiplying the first factor by the indicated power of 10 results in a product of 5,878,000,000,000.

The third expression above is written in scientific notation. A number is in **scientific notation** when it is expressed as the product of a number greater than or equal to 1 but less than 10, and a power of 10.

at least 1 but less than 10 — a power of 10

$$\mathbf{5.878 \times 10^{12}}$$



### Reaching All Learners

**OL On Level** Ask students to compile a list of all of the places where they think that scientific notation can be used to make understanding of large numbers easier. Have the students do this independently, then in pairs, and in small groups. Finalize the activity with a whole class discussion. If students are having trouble coming up with ideas, allow the students to look in books, or on the internet for ideas.

The chart lists the outputs in scientific and standard notation of some repeater machines.

| Machine | Scientific Notation | Standard Notation | Example of Number |
|---|---|---|---|
| 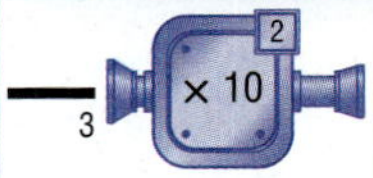  | $3 \times 10^2$ | 300 | length of a football field in feet |
| 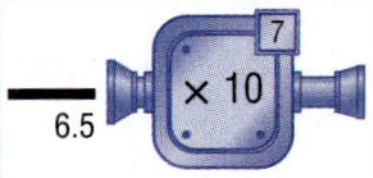  | $6.5 \times 10^7$ | 65,000,000 | years since dinosaurs became extinct |
| 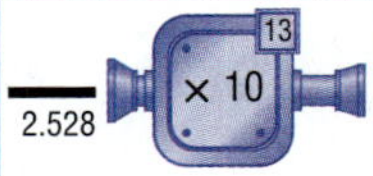  | $2.528 \times 10^{13}$ | 25,280,000,000,000 | distance from Earth to Centaurus star system in miles |

Scientific notation can help you compare the sizes of numbers.

**Math Link**

When writing expressions in scientific notation, × is used instead of • to indicate multiplication.

### Think & Discuss

Here are three numbers written in standard notation.

74,580,000,000,000,000,000

8,395,000,000,000,000,000

242,000,000,000,000,000,000

- Which number is greatest? How do you know? See ①.
- Which number is least? How do you know? See ②.

Here are three numbers written in scientific notation.

$3.723 \times 10^{15}$ $9.259 \times 10^{25}$ $4.2 \times 10^{19}$

- Which number is greatest? How do you know? See ③.
- Which number is least? How do you know? $3.723 \times 10^{15}$; The number with the least exponent is least.

① 242,000,000,000,000,000,000; Since all the numbers are whole numbers, the number with the most digits is greatest.

② 8,395,000,000,000,000,000; Since all the numbers are whole numbers, the number with the fewest digits is least.

③ $9.259 \times 10^{25}$; The number with the greatest exponent is greatest.



## Mathematical Background

There are many different ways to express multiplication of numbers ·, ×, and the use of parentheses. Students may not understand why there are so many ways to express the same operation. Or, students may not be comfortable using the symbol ×. Discuss with students the importance of consistency so that people all over the world are able to understand that what they are stating means scientific notation.

**Analyze the Table** Discuss the examples shown in the chart. This chart helps students make the connection between the machine model, scientific notation, and standard notation.

At this point, you may want to ask students why they think the scientific-notation convention exists.

### Think & Discuss

*Suggested Grouping: Pairs*

Because the numbers written in standard notation are not aligned, students will need to count the digits, or places, in order to compare the numbers. You may want to review with students how to compare whole numbers with the same number of digits and whole numbers with a different number of digits. For numbers that have the same number of digits, if the first digits are the same, compare the second digits; if the second digits are the same, compare the third digits; and so on. If the numbers have a different number of digits, the one with more digits is greater.

Students should recognize that numbers written in scientific notation are much easier to compare.

**Additional Examples** You may want to write three numbers in scientific notation, such as these, on the board: $5.1398 \times 10^3$, $1.72 \times 10^5$, and $1.72 \times 10^3$. Have students write the numbers in standard form and compare them to verify that the number with the greatest exponent is the greatest and that they need compare digits only when the powers of 10 are the same. Have students generalize this rule and explain why it works.

In order from least to greatest:

- $1.72 \times 10^3$ (1,720)
- $5.1398 \times 10^3$ (5,139.8)
- $1.72 \times 10^5$ (172,000)

You may need to review several times that a number in scientific notation is a product of two factors: one factor is a number at least 1 but less than 10, and the other factor is a power of 10.

## Develop & Understand: A

*Suggested Grouping: Small Groups*

Because students often find scientific notation tricky at first, encourage them to work in small groups to solve these exercises.

Students practice recognizing numbers written in scientific notation and translating between standard notation and scientific notation. The last exercise uses a context for which scientific notation is truly necessary: comparing distances from the different planets to the sun.

Students will get more practice changing numbers from standard notation into scientific notation in the next exercise set. For now, they will probably think about how many places to the left they have to move the decimal point to get a single digit before it and then making the exponent of the 10 equal to that number. In a sense, they undo the strategy for translating a number into standard notation.

**Wrap-Up** Have students share the methods they used for Exercises 9–14. You can direct the discussion by asking,

- How do you take a number written in standard notation and rewrite it in scientific notation?

If someone describes the "moving the decimal point" strategy, take advantage of that moment to talk about what moving the decimal point to the left does to a number. Then ask,

- How does 6.2 compare to 62? It is $\frac{1}{10}$ as much.
- How does 0.05 compare to 5? It is $\frac{1}{100}$ as much.
- What computation are you really doing when you move the decimal point one place to the left? Dividing by 10 Two places to the left? Dividing by 100 Three places to the left? Dividing by 1,000
- How can you get back to the original value of a number if you divide it by 10? Multiply by 10 Divide it by 100? Multiply by 100 Divide it by 1,000? Multiply by 1,000

Then have students try to generalize a strategy for writing a number in scientific notation. Their rules should include the idea that the number of 10s by which you multiply, that is, the exponent of 10, is equal to the number of places you moved the decimal point.

## Develop & Understand: A

**Tell whether each number is written correctly in scientific notation. For those that are not written correctly, describe what is incorrect.**

1. $6.4535 \times 10^{52}$ Correct
2. $41 \times 10^{3}$ 41 is not between 1 and 10
3. $0.4 \times 10^{6}$ 0.4 is not between 1 and 10
4. $1 \times 10^{1}$ Correct

**Write each number in standard notation.**

5. $1.28 \times 10^{6}$ 1,280,000
6. $9.03 \times 10^{5}$ 903,000
7. $6.02 \times 10^{23}$ 602,000,000,000,000,000,000,000
8. $5.7 \times 10^{8}$ 570,000,000

**Write each number in scientific notation.**

9. 850 $8.5 \times 10^{2}$
10. 7 thousand $7 \times 10^{3}$
11. 10,400,000 $1.04 \times 10^{7}$
12. 659,000 $6.59 \times 10^{5}$
13. 83 million $8.3 \times 10^{7}$
14. 27 billion $2.7 \times 10^{10}$
15. The table shows the average distance from each planet in the solar system to the Sun.

| Planet | Distance from Sun (km) Standard Notation | Distance from Sun (km) Scientific Notation |
|---|---|---|
| Earth | 149,600,000 | $1.496 \times 10^{8}$ |
| Jupiter | 778,300,000 | $7.783 \times 10^{8}$ |
| Mars | 227,900,000 | $2.279 \times 10^{8}$ |
| Mercury | 57,900,000 | $5.79 \times 10^{7}$ |
| Neptune | 4,497,000,000 | $4.497 \times 10^{9}$ |
| Saturn | 1,427,000,000 | $1.427 \times 10^{9}$ |
| Uranus | 2,870,000,000 | $2.87 \times 10^{9}$ |
| Venus | 108,200,000 | $1.082 \times 10^{8}$ |

a. Complete the table by expressing the distance from each planet to the Sun in scientific notation.

b. Order the planets from closest to the Sun to farthest from the Sun. Mercury, Venus, Earth, Mars, Jupiter, Saturn, Uranus, Neptune



### Reaching All Learners

**BL Beyond Level** One example of space travel that continues is that of spacecrafts Voyager 1 and 2. Assign students the task of identifying the current distance of each spacecraft from Earth. By using the data in the table, and some research, the students will get hands on practice dealing with very large numbers.

### Troubleshooting

Remind students that proper scientific notation only has one digit in front of the decimal point. Students may also forget that standard notation for large numbers has no decimal points.

Scientific notation is useful for ordering numbers only if the convention is followed properly, that is, the first part of the number is between 1 and 10. Otherwise, the power of 10 may not tell you which number is the greatest.

**Math Link**

Here are some really big numbers.

| | |
|---|---|
| $10^{45}$ | quattuordecillion |
| $10^{57}$ | octadecillion |
| $10^{60}$ | novemdecillion |
| $10^{63}$ | vigintillion |
| $10^{100}$ | googol |

The expressions below show the same number written in four ways as the product of a number and a power of 10. However, none of these expressions is in scientific notation. If you compare these numbers by looking at the powers of 10, you might not realize that they are all equal.

$0.0357 \times 10^8$ $35.7 \times 10^5$ $3{,}570 \times 10^3$ $357{,}000 \times 10^1$

You can change numbers like these into scientific notation without changing them into standard form first.

### Example

Write $357 \times 10^4$ in scientific notation.

The first step is to change 357 to a number between 1 and 10. To do this, divide by 100, or $10^2$. To compensate, you need to multiply by 100, or $10^2$.

The last step is to simplify $10^2 \times 10^4$ by applying the product law of exponents.

$$\begin{aligned} 357 \times 10^4 &= \frac{357}{100} \times 100 \times 10^4 \\ &= 3.57 \times 10^2 \times 10^4 \\ &= 3.57 \times 10^6 \end{aligned}$$

### Develop & Understand: B

**Write each number in scientific notation.**

**16.** $13 \times 10^2$ $1.3 \times 10^3$

**17.** $0.932 \times 10^3$ $9.32 \times 10^2$

**18.** $461 \times 10^4$ $4.61 \times 10^6$

**19.** $59 \times 10^5$ $5.9 \times 10^6$

**20.** $98.6 \times 10^9$ $9.86 \times 10^{10}$

**21.** $197 \times 10^6$ $1.97 \times 10^8$

### Share & Summarize

How can you tell whether a number greater than 1 is written in scientific notation? Possible answer: If it is written as a number, greater than or equal to 1 but less than 10, times a power of 10, it is in scientific notation.



**Teacher Tips** Scientific notation is useful for ordering numbers only if the convention is followed properly, that is, if the first part of the number is between 1 and 10. Otherwise, the power of 10 may not tell you which number is greatest.

### Example

Walk students through the Example of how to rewrite $357 \times 10^4$ in scientific notation. Then have students rewrite the four expressions above the Example in scientific notation. Review with them how moving the decimal point relates to dividing or multiplying by powers of 10.

### Develop & Understand: B

*Suggested Grouping: Pairs*

Students practice rewriting a few numbers in scientific notation. If your students seem to have a good handle on the ideas, you may want to use these exercises as an assessment of how individual students are doing. Do students understand how to convert a number given as a number times a power of 10 into scientific notation?

### Share & Summarize

Ask for volunteers to share their answers. Students will have more practice working with numbers in scientific notation and rewriting numbers that are not written correctly. The main goal of this investigation is that students can recognize whether or not a number is written correctly in scientific notation.

If students do not correctly describe a number written in scientific notation, it is not necessary at this point to drill the definition and ask students to identify examples and nonexamples of it. Rather, keep it in mind as you move on. Periodically ask students,

- Is the answer written in scientific notation? How do you know?

## Reaching All Learners

**AL Approaching Level** If your students are struggling with scientific notation, allowing them to work in pairs will help them solidify their understanding. Encourage pairs to take different roles for each exercise. The first person may rewrite the number in scientific notation; the second person may check it against the example to see that the steps make sense. For the next exercise, have them swap roles.

## On the Spot Assessment

Have the students write 1,437,000,000,000 in scientific notation. Then have students determine what the number $1.44 \times 10^{11}$ is in standard notation. Ask students to tell you which number is larger and why.

## Investigation 3

***On Your Own Exercises***
Pages 189–193
Exercises 36–40, 58–60

**Interpreting the Display** Students learn how to use calculators to work with numbers in scientific notation. This involves both entering the numbers correctly and interpreting the display when an answer is given in scientific notation.

### *Think & Discuss*

*Suggested Grouping: Whole Class*

Have students find $2^{40}$ on their calculators and tell what the result is. Lead students to realize that since the second square had 2 grains and the amount was doubled at each stage, 1.099511628 cannot be correct.

Tell students that your calculator display for $2^{33}$ is 8,589,934,592, and write this number on the board. Next ask them to find $2^{34}$ by hand by doubling your calculator display for $2^{33}$. Write the answer, 17,179,869,184, on the board. Finally, tell them that your calculator display for $2^{34}$ is $1.7179869183^{10}$, and write this number on the board. Ask:

- Do you see any relationship between the last two numbers I wrote? What do you think the 10 means in the last number?

Suggest that students think of the last number, $1.7179869183^{10}$, as a number in scientific notation, with the decimal as the number factor and the 10 as the exponent. Have them write this number in standard notation and compare it with the second number, which they calculated by hand. The two numbers are identical, except for the last digit. This should help to convince them of the validity of the calculator display.

For further verification, students can use their own calculators to find successive powers of 2 until their calculators switch from standard notation to scientific notation, and then they can follow the steps outlined above.

At this point, discuss with students that calculators vary in the way they display exponents. With some calculators, "E 19" replaces "$\times 10^{19}$." The 19 still represents the power of 10. Students may need to mentally reinsert "× 10."



## Investigation 3 Scientific Notation on a Calculator

There is a well-known story about a ruler who placed rice on the squares of a chessboard as a reward for one of his subjects. The first square had two grains of rice, and every square after that had twice as many as the previous square.

The table describes the number of grains of rice on each square.

| Square | Number of Grains (as a product) | Number of Grains (as a power of 2) |
|---|---|---|
| 1 | 1 • 2 | $2^1$ |
| 2 | 1 • 2 • 2 | $2^2$ |
| 3 | 1 • 2 • 2 • 2 | $2^3$ |
| 4 | 1 • 2 • 2 • 2 • 2 | $2^4$ |
| 5 | 1 • 2 • 2 • 2 • 2 • 2 | $2^5$ |
| 6 | 1 • 2 • 2 • 2 • 2 • 2 • 2 | $2^6$ |
| 7 | 1 • 2 • 2 • 2 • 2 • 2 • 2 • 2 | $2^7$ |

### *Think & Discuss*

There are $2^{40}$ grains of rice on square 40. Evaluate this number on your calculator. What does the calculator display? What do you think this means? See ①.

① $1.099511628 \times 10^{12}$; Explanations will vary. (Note: Calculator displays will vary in the number of decimal places displayed and the notation used to indicate the power of 10.)

Numbers too large to fit in a calculator's display are expressed in scientific notation. Different calculators show scientific notation in different ways. When you entered $2^{40}$, you may have seen one of these displays.

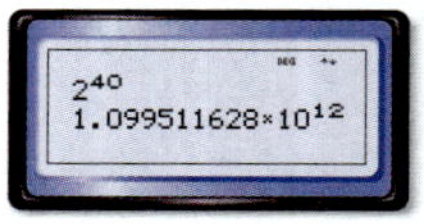

Both of these represent $1.099511628 \times 10^{12}$. When you read the display, you may need to mentally insert the "× 10."

If you continued the table, what power of 2 would represent the number of grains of rice on square 64, the last square on the chessboard? $2^{64}$

Use your calculator to find the number of rice grains on square 64. Give your answer in scientific notation. $1.844674407 \times 10^{19}$



### *Troubleshooting*

When reading a calculator, students whose output uses E may not understand that the E represents the × 10 part of scientific notation. Stress to the students that writing E on their work shows that they are not truly understanding the output from the calculator.

## Develop & Understand: A

**Use your calculator to evaluate each expression. Give your answers in scientific notation.**

**1.** $3^{28}$ **2.** $4.05^{21}$ **3.** $7.95^{12}$ **4.** $12^{12}$

**5.** It would be difficult to order the numbers in Exercises 1–4 as they are given. It should be much easier now that you have written them in scientific notation. List the four numbers from least to greatest.

**6.** Light travels at a speed of about 186,000 miles per second.

**a.** How many miles does light travel in a day? $1.60704 \times 10^{10}$

**b.** How many miles does light travel in a year? $5.865696 \times 10^{12}$

When the result of a calculation is a very large number, your calculator automatically displays it in scientific notation. You can also enter numbers into your calculator in scientific notation. Different calculators use different keys, but a common one is [EE].

For example, to enter $2.4 \times 10^{12}$, press

2.4 [EE] 12 [ENTER].

### Real-World Link

A *day* is the time it takes for one rotation of a planet. A *year* is the time it takes for a planet to make one revolution around the sun. On Jupiter, a day is about 10 Earth hours long, and a year is about 12 Earth years.

1. $2.2877 \times 10^{13}$
2. $5.7089 \times 10^{12}$
3. $6.3739 \times 10^{10}$
4. $8.9161 \times 10^{12}$
5. $7.95^{12}, 4.05^{21}, 12^{12}, 3^{28}$

## Develop & Understand: B

**Estimate the value of each expression. Then use your calculator to evaluate it. Give your answers in scientific notation.**

**7.** $5.2 \times 10^{15} + 3.5 \times 10^{15}$ $8.7 \times 10^{15}$

**8.** $(6.5 \times 10^{18}) \cdot (1.8 \times 10^{15})$ $1.17 \times 10^{34}$

**9.** $(8.443 \times 10^{18}) \div 2$ $4.2215 \times 10^{18}$

**10.** Estimate the value of each expression. Then use your calculator to evaluate it. Give your answers in scientific notation.

**a.** $6 \times 10^{12} + 4 \times 10^{2}$ $6 \times 10^{12}$

**b.** $8.5 \times 10^{20} + 1.43 \times 10^{45}$ $1.43 \times 10^{45}$

**c.** $4.92 \times 10^{22} - 9.3 \times 10^{5}$ $4.92 \times 10^{22}$

**d.** How do your results in Parts a–c compare to the numbers that were added or subtracted?

**e.** Write the numbers in Part a in standard notation. Then add them. How does your result compare to the result you found in Part a? If the answers are different, try to explain why.

6,000,000,000,400; The answers are different. One of the numbers being added or subtracted is so small relative to the other number that it affects only decimal places that are not shown on the display.

10d. In each case, the result is equal to one of the original numbers.



## Reaching All Learners

**BL Beyond Level** Have the students work on determining the amount of time a day and a year is for each planet of the solar system in terms of an Earth day and year. Ask the students to make a chart or table to show this data in scientific and standard notation. Post the results in the classroom.

## Develop & Understand: A

*Suggested Grouping: Individuals*

On most calculators, a number with more than 10 digits will automatically be displayed in scientific notation. After students complete Exercise 5, check their understanding by asking them to explain why numbers are easier to compare when all are written in scientific notation.

▶ **Exercise 6** Watch for students who are not sure that they need to multiply. Ask questions such as, Will light travel farther in a day than in a second?

Also watch for students who miss intermediate steps. Students may not think to multiply by 60 to find the distance in a minute and by 60 again to find the distance in an hour but may simply multiply by only 24.

**Wrap-Up** If students had trouble with the unit equivalences or intermediate steps in Exercise 6, you may want to walk through the exercise with the whole class.

To lead into the next exercise set, walk students through the steps of entering numbers in scientific notation using the example in the text of $2.4 \times 10^{12}$.

## Develop & Understand: B

*Suggested Grouping: Pairs*

Students should work individually on Exercises 7–9 and then pair up for Exercise 10.

**Wrap-Up** Ask the class, How can it be that the sum of two numbers is one of those numbers?

The point to make is that these numbers are very large and that there is a notion of relative difference. That is, if you have a billion of something and take 1 away, most people would still say you have a billion rather than saying you have 999,999,999. In fact, it was unlikely you had exactly 1 billion to begin with, but rather you had something close to 1 billion. So subtracting a very small number essentially has no effect.

## Develop & Understand: C

*Suggested Grouping: Pairs*

If you wish to have students find the assumptions on their own, you might turn this exercise set into a class mini-project and have groups of students gather various parts of the data. Ask students to:

1. Go to a small local library and estimate the number of books in the library by determining the number of bookshelves, the number of individual shelves per bookshelf, and the number of books per shelf.
2. Randomly select several books from several different sections of the library and find the total number of pages. Make a good estimate for the average number of pages in a book in the library.
3. Survey each of the books in Part 2 to find how many lines are on a page of text. Make a good estimate for the average number of lines per page in a book.
4. Count the characters in a single line of text in each book. Be sure to include spaces and punctuation marks. Make a good estimate for the average number of characters in a line of text in a book.
5. Use these estimates to find the approximate number of gigabytes necessary to hold all the information in all of the books in the library.

### Share & Summarize

Students should realize that calculators cannot have an "infinite display"; there is some limit to the number of digits that can be shown. The calculator display does not have to show all the places because it shows the number of places. On some calculators, the number that follows an E or a space is the number of places, the exponent of 10.

Question 2 is key: When you deal with very large and very small numbers it is important to think about relative size.

**Real-World Link**

In 2007, the U.S. Library of Congress held over 20 million books. Its collections also include audio materials, maps, microforms, and visual materials.

## Develop & Understand: C

In 1945, a librarian at Harvard University estimated that there were ten million books of "worthwhile" printed material. Suppose you wanted to enter all of this printed material into a computer for storage.

Use your calculator to solve the following exercises. When appropriate, record your answers in scientific notation. Make these assumptions as you work.

- The average book is 500 pages long.
- The average page holds 40 lines of text.
- The average line holds 80 characters.

**11.** How many characters are on one page of an average book? 3,200

**12.** How many characters are in the average book?

**13.** How many characters were in all the "worthwhile" books in 1945?

**14.** One *byte* of computer disk space stores about one character of text. A *gigabyte* of computer disk space is $1 \times 10^9$ bytes, so a gigabyte can store about $1 \times 10^9$ characters. How many gigabytes are needed to store all the "worthwhile" books from 1945? 16,000

12. 1,600,000, or $1.6 \times 10^6$
13. $1.6 \times 10^{13}$

### Share & Summarize

**1.** Explain, in a way that a fifth grader could understand, why a calculator sometimes displays numbers in scientific notation.

**2.** Explain why sometimes when you add two numbers in scientific notation on your calculator, the result is just the greater of the two numbers. One of the numbers being added is so small relative to the other number that it affects only decimal places that are not shown on the display.

1. Some numbers have too many digits to display on a calculator screen. Calculators use this special notation as a way to write big numbers so they take less space.

## Troubleshooting

If students have difficulty with the Share & Summarize questions, spend some time going back over the basic ideas. Emphasize:

- Scientific notation is a convention that makes it easier for scientists to talk to each other about quantities represented by big numbers.
- There are only two rules about how the number is written: the number factor is between 1 and 10 and the other factor is a power of 10.
- Calculators display numbers in scientific notation for your convenience and because the display space is limited.

Inquiry

# Investigation 4 Relative Error

**Vocabulary**

**relative error**

**Materials**

- scientific or graphing calculator

4. As the population of a situation increases, the relative error becomes smaller if the absolute error remains the same.

***Math Link***

The absolute value of a number is its distance from 0 on the number line. The absolute value of both 2 and −2 is 2.

Most things in life are not perfect. Errors occur all around us everyday. If you open a carton of eggs at the grocery store, you may find a broken one. If you take a test at school, you may miss a question. Mail is sometimes delivered to the wrong address. Errors do occur. The magnitude of the error depends on the *relative size* of the error to the overall situation.

## Make a Prediction

If you miss three points on a test, what might you be able to tell about your performance?

1. Suppose you missed three points out of a total ten points. What percent of points did you miss? 30%
2. What percent of points did you miss if the test had 100 total points? 3%
3. If you have 1,000 points on tests throughout the semester and miss three points, what percent of points did you miss? 0.3%

Missing three points on the 100-point test is a small error relative to the size of the test. Missing three points on the ten-point test is a large error relative to the size of the test. To analyze the "seriousness" of an error, you have to think about it relative to the size of the object or population being measured.

4. In general, what can you say about the relative size of an error as compared to the overall population?

## Try It Out

Before the presidential election of 2004, forecasters predicted that $1.18 \times 10^8$ people would vote. When the election was over, 62,040,610 votes had been cast for President Bush, and 59,028,111 votes had been cast for Senator Kerry.

5. What was the total number of people who voted in the election? 121,068,721
6. What was the difference, in absolute value, between the prediction and the actual voter turnout? $121{,}068{,}721 - 118{,}000{,}000 = 3{,}068{,}721$
7. Divide the difference from Question 6 by the total number of actual voters from Question 5. This number is the **relative error**. Express this value to four decimal places, in scientific notation, and as a percent error to the nearest percent.
   $\frac{3{,}068{,}721}{121{,}068{,}721} = 0.0253 = 2.53 \times 10^{-2}$ which is just under 3%

**Go on**



Inquiry

Inquiry

## Investigation 4

*Suggested Grouping: Pairs*

### Materials and Preparation

It will be helpful for the students if they are able to use a calculator to assist them in their computations for relative error. In addition, you may wish to research additional situations where relative error can be computed such as data from a recent election or actual data from a classroom assessment.

### Make a Prediction

If students are having difficulty understanding how to compute the percentages, remind them that they take the part and divide it by the whole.

### Try It Out

In order to answer these questions, students will need to read carefully to make sure they are using the data that is requested. It will also help students in their calculations if they are allowed to use a calculator.

▶ **Exercise 5** If students are struggling with determining the answer, remind them that in order to compute a total, you need to find the entire number of people participating. This means that you need to find the sum of the people who voted for either candidate.

▶ **Exercise 7** Students may benefit from having the process of computing relative error spelled out more explicitly, as though it were a formula to use. This will allow students to see exactly what information is needed for future computations.

▶ **Exercise 8** Students may not understand how there can be a relative error of 1. Ask students to tell you what percentage 1.00 represents. As students move the decimal place, they will see that it is equal to 100%. Now if students revisit the question, it may be more clear than before.

▶ **Exercise 10** If students are having trouble understanding how to compare the relative errors, give the students a hint and tell them to look at the numbers as percentages.



**Real-World Link**
Presidential elections are held every four years.

9b. $\frac{3,068,721}{2,931,279} = 1.0469 = 1.05 \times 10^0$, which is about 105%

10. $2.53 \times 10^{-2}$ is a much smaller number than $1.05 \times 10^0$, so the error in the national election was less than the error in the state election. This is even easier to see when you think about a 3% error compared to over 100% error.

**8.** Suppose the relative error is 1. What does this tell you about the percent of error? It would be 100%.

**9.** Suppose a state election predicted a voter turnout of six million, but only 2,931,279 actually voted.

**a.** What is the difference, in absolute value, between the prediction and actual voter turnout? 3,068,721

**b.** Divide the difference from Part a by the number of people who actually voted. Express this relative error to four decimal places, in scientific notation, and as a percent error to the nearest percent.

**10.** In Question 7, you found the relative error for predicting voter turnout in the presidential election was $2.53 \times 10^{-2}$ compared to a relative error in the state election of $1.05 \times 10^0$. In which scenario was the relative error smaller? That is, which estimate for voter turnout was better? Explain.

What might appear to be a really large error, such as an estimation that is off by more than three million, may be *relatively* small when compared to the population being estimated. However, there are times when an error appears to be quite small but becomes a large *actual* error when magnified over a long period of time or in several situations.

13. The error for a population in the thousands will be ±5, the error for a population in the ten thousands will be ±50, the error for a population in the hundred thousands will be ±500, and so on

## Try It Again

Each town in Baxter County reported its population in scientific notation to the county seat. This sparked a debate about how much of an error would be created between the actual population and the reported population in the county.

**11.** Complete the table. Use your calculator to do the calculations.

| Town | Actual Population | Population in Scientific Notation | Actual Error in Report \|actual population – population in scientific notation\| | Relative Error in Report [actual error/ actual population] |
|---|---|---|---|---|
| Springfield | 1,414,999 | $1.41 \times 10^6$ | 4,999 | 0.0035 |
| Cedarville | 806,499 | $8.06 \times 10^5$ | 499 | 0.0006 |
| Hillsboro | 545,489 | $5.45 \times 10^5$ | 489 | 0.0009 |
| Plainview | 17,848 | $1.78 \times 10^4$ | 48 | 0.003 |
| Charleston | 48,543 | $4.85 \times 10^4$ | 43 | 0.0009 |
| Lewis City | 6,024 | $6.02 \times 10^3$ | 4 | 0.0007 |

14. Yes; Possible answer: The actual population numbers have been rounded in scientific notation form. Suppose the actual population for Springfield was 1,415,000, which would have been reported as $1.42 \times 10^6$. The actual population would have been less than the scientific notation value.

15. County population: 2,839,402 population; 6,082 actual errors in report; this is only two-tenths of a percent of error, but it would be a loss of over 6 million dollars to the county.

**12.** Is the relative error for any town greater than 1%? No, all are 0.0035 or less, which is less than half a percent.

**13.** Because of rounding, the scientific notation population numbers for all of these towns are less than the actual populations. Can you predict the possible maximum error, above or below, that is possible for a town's population if the population is expressed in scientific notation?

**14.** Is it possible for a town's actual population to be less than the population expressed in scientific notation? Explain.

**15.** Find the actual population in the entire county by adding the entries in the "actual population" column. Find the actual error in the report for the entire county by adding the entries in the "actual error in report" column. The error is the amount by which the county underestimated its population.

In your opinion, is it a small error or a large error? What if the county gets $1,000 per person in state tax money? How much would the county stand to lose by underestimating its population in this way?

## What Did You Learn?

**16.** Suppose you hear that a person on your street will receive an annual raise of $5,000 today. What else would you need to know to decide how substantial this raise is? Use the term *relative* in your answer.
I would need to know the person's total income. If he or she makes $50,000 per year, this is a substantial raise relative to his or her current salary. If he or she makes $150,000 per year, it is not as substantial of a relative raise.





## Try It Again

In these exercises, students again compute relative error. The table for Exercise 11 spells out exactly what steps the students need to take to answer all of the questions.

▶ **Exercise 11** As students are completing the table, tell them to pay particular attention to the number of digits that they are not using when they write the population in scientific notation. This is a quick way for students to check their actual error numbers.

## What Did You Learn?

Students may not understand what the question is asking because of the vocabulary that is used. It may be helpful to students, especially English Language Learners, for you to rephrase the question.

**Investigation 1**
Pages 175–177
Practice & Apply: 1–20
Connect & Extend: 41–55

**Investigation 2**
Pages 178–181
Practice & Apply: 21–35
Connect & Extend: 56–57

**Investigation 3**
Pages 182–184
Practice & Apply: 36–40
Connect & Extend: 58–60

**Assign Anytime**
Mixed Review: 62–77

▶ **Exercises 3 and 4** Make sure that the students carefully read the directions. The answers should be in kilometers, but the problem is given in centimeters or millimeters. Remind students that to convert from centimeters to kilometers, you would divide by 10,000 and for millimeters to kilometers, you would divide by 100,000.

▶ **Exercises 10–13** Explain to students that the question is really asking them to do the same thing that they did in Exercises 8 and 9. The only difference is that the repeater machine is not given.

On Your Own Exercises
Lesson 4.1

## Practice & Apply

**Math Link**

1 cm = $\frac{1}{100}$ m

1 mm = $\frac{1}{1,000}$ m

1 km = 1,000 m

Supply each missing value. For Exercises 3 and 4, give the answer in kilometers.

**1.**
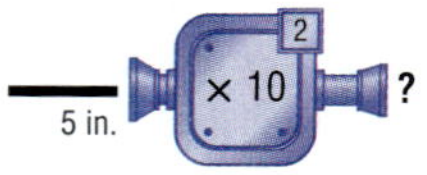

500 in.

**2.**
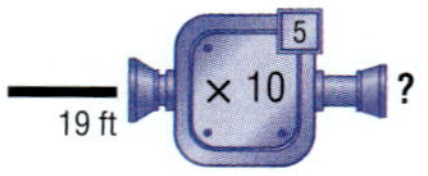

1,900,000 ft

**3.**
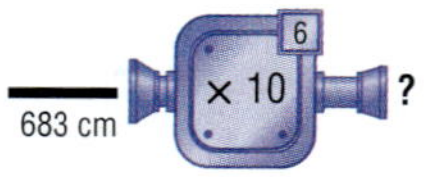

683,000,000 cm; 6,830 km

**4.**
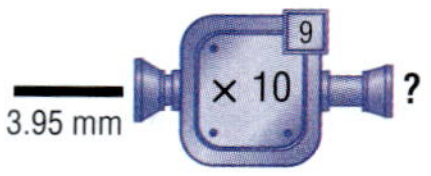

3,950,000,000 mm; 3,950 km

Find each product.

**5.** $4 \times 10^3$ 4,000 **6.** $62 \times 10^4$ 620,000 **7.** $15.8 \times 10^2$ 1,580

Find each exponent.

**8.** 2

**9.** 4
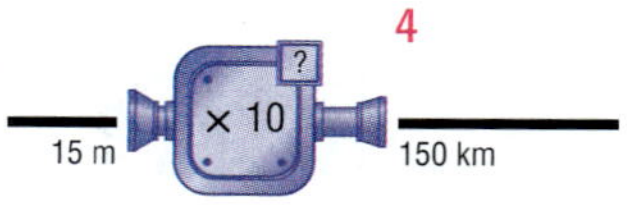


Find the value of *N* in each equation.

**10.** $8 \times 10^N = 80$ 1

**11.** $53 \times 10^N = 5,300$ 2

**12.** $9.9 \times 10^N = 99,000$ 4

**13.** $6.13 \times 10^N = 6,130$ 3

**Find the length of each input.**

**14.**

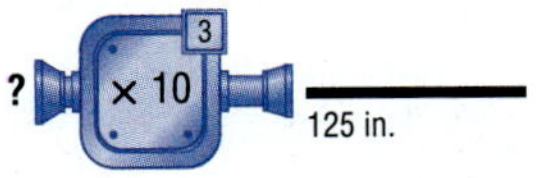


0.125 in.

**15.**

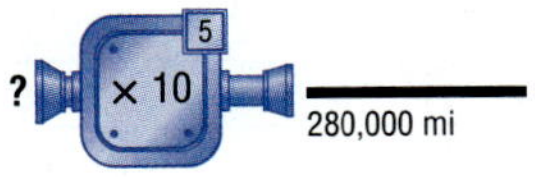


2.8 mi

**16.**

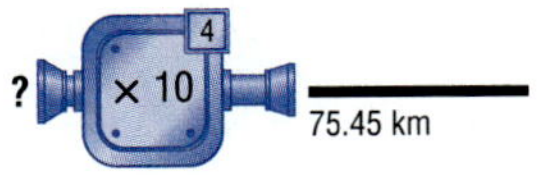


0.007545 km

**Find the value of *N* in each equation.**

**17.** $N \times 10^2 = 900$ 9

**18.** $523 \times N = 52{,}300$ $10^2$

**19.** $0.0614 \times N = 6.14$ $10^2$

**20.** $N \times 10^6 = 39{,}650{,}000$ 39.65

**Write each number in standard notation.**

**21.** $8 \times 10^1$ 80

**22.** $5 \times 10^3$ 5,000

**23.** $7.5 \times 10^2$ 750

**24.** $3.54 \times 10^8$ 354,000,000

**25.** $3.4 \times 10^5$ 340,000

**26.** $6.19 \times 10^7$ 61,900,000

**Write each number in scientific notation.**

**27.** 300 $3 \times 10^2$

**28.** ten thousand $1 \times 10^4$

**29.** 158,000 $1.58 \times 10^5$

**30.** 8,350,000,000 $8.35 \times 10^9$

**31.** 183 billion $1.83 \times 10^{11}$

**32.** 421,938,000,000,000 $4.21938 \times 10^{14}$

**33.** four trillion six billion $4.006 \times 10^{12}$

**34.** 192,850,000,000 $1.9285 \times 10^{11}$





▶ **Exercises 21–24** Students may need to be reminded that when writing a number in standard notation you do not just add zeros to the number, the decimal place must be moved as well.

▶ **Exercises 28 and 33** It may be helpful for students to write the number out before trying to turn it into scientific notation.

▶ **Exercise 35a** Students may be confused by this question. It is the work to complete the last column in the table, it is not a new calculation.

▶ **Exercises 38–40** You may want to go over these exercises with the whole class. Consider discussing a shortcut using the laws of exponents to solve Exercise 39. In Exercise 40, some students may multiply 6.02 by 15 to get $90.30 \times 10^{23}$ and then rewrite the answer in proper scientific notation.



On Your Own Exercises

★ indicates multi-step problem

**Real-World Link**
Venus is the brightest planet in the solar system. It can often be seen in the morning and at night. Venus is sometimes called the Morning Star or the Evening Star.

**35.** **Astronomy** The table shows the mass of the planets in the solar system, the Sun, and Earth's moon.

| Celestial Body | Mass (kg) Standard Notation | Mass (kg) Scientific Notation |
|---|---|---|
| Sun | 1,990,000,000,000,000,000,000,000,000,000 | $1.99 \times 10^{30}$ |
| Mercury | 330,000,000,000,000,000,000,000 | $3.30 \times 10^{23}$ |
| Venus | 4,870,000,000,000,000,000,000,000 | $4.87 \times 10^{24}$ |
| Earth | 5,970,000,000,000,000,000,000,000 | $5.97 \times 10^{24}$ |
| Mars | 642,000,000,000,000,000,000,000 | $6.42 \times 10^{23}$ |
| Jupiter | 1,900,000,000,000,000,000,000,000,000 | $1.90 \times 10^{27}$ |
| Saturn | 568,000,000,000,000,000,000,000,000 | $5.68 \times 10^{26}$ |
| Uranus | 86,800,000,000,000,000,000,000,000 | $8.68 \times 10^{25}$ |
| Neptune | 102,000,000,000,000,000,000,000,000 | $1.02 \times 10^{26}$ |
| Moon | 73,500,000,000,000,000,000,000 | $7.35 \times 10^{22}$ |

a. Write the mass of each planet and the moon in scientific notation. See table.

b. Order the planets and the moon by mass, from least to greatest.

c. Which planet has about the same mass as Earth? Venus

35b. The moon, Mercury, Mars, Venus, Earth, Uranus, Neptune, Saturn, Jupiter

**36.** Refer to the table of masses in Exercise 35. Find how many times greater the mass of Earth is than the mass of each body.

a. Mercury 18 times  b. Venus 1.23 times  c. The moon 81.2 times

**37.** Refer to the table of masses in Exercise 35. Find how many times greater the mass of each body is than the mass of Earth.

a. The Sun  b. Jupiter 318 times  c. Saturn 95.1 times

d. Uranus 14.5 times  e. Neptune 17.1 times

37a. $3.33 \times 10^5$ times

**Estimate the value of each expression. Then use your calculator to evaluate it. Give your answers in scientific notation.**

**38.** $7.35 \times 10^{22} - 1.33 \times 10^{21}$  $7.217 \times 10^{22}$

**39.** $6.42 \times 10^{45} + 4.55 \times 10^{45}$  $1.097 \times 10^{46}$

**40.** $6.02 \times 10^{23} \times 15$  $9.03 \times 10^{24}$

## Connect & Extend

**41.** A dollar bill is approximately 15.7 cm long.

**a.** How long would one thousand dollar bills laid end-to-end be? 157 m

**b.** How long would one million dollar bills laid end-to-end be? 157 km

**c.** The distance from Earth to the Sun is about $1.5 \times 10^8$ km. How many dollar bills, taped together end-to-end, would it take to reach the Sun? About $9.55 \times 10^{11}$

**Math Link**

12 inches = 1 foot

5,280 feet = 1 mile

**Find the length of each output.**

**42.**

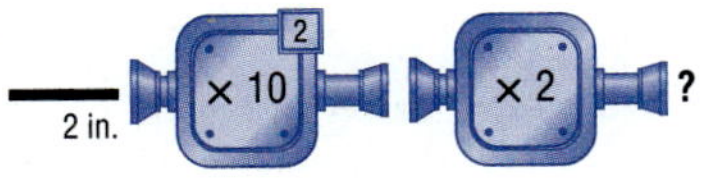


400 in.

**43.**

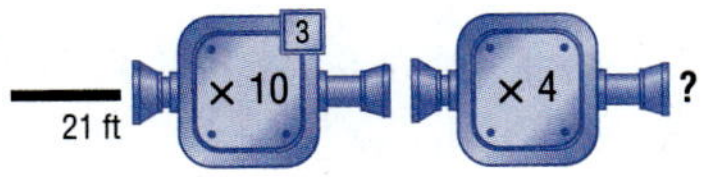


84,000 ft

**44.**

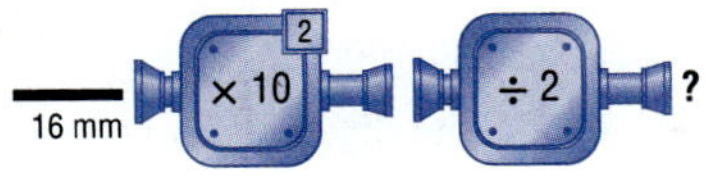


800 mm

**45.**

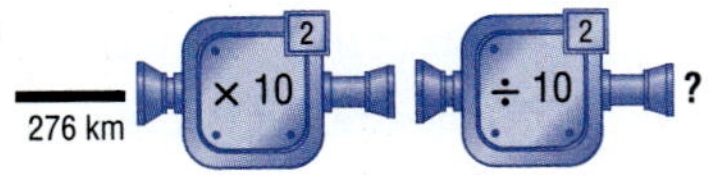


276 km

**Find the length of each output.**

**46.**

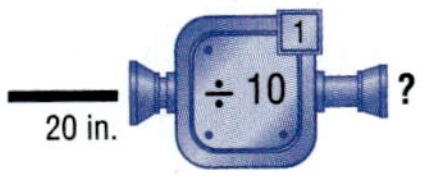


2 in.

**47.**

0.5 in.

**48.**

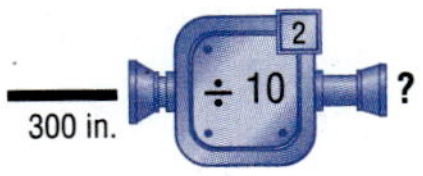


3 in.

**49.**

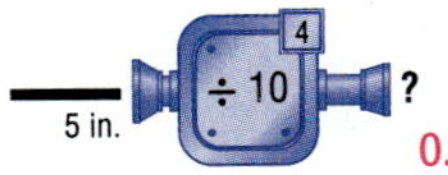


0.0005 in.





▶ **Exercise 45** Hopefully students will recognize that the first machine is a $\times 10^2$ machine and the second machine is a $\div 10^2$ machine. Since the machines are opposite operations for the exact same value, nothing with the original number changes. The machines and therefore the operations cancel each other out.

▶ **Exercises 46–49** These exercises are a great introduction to Lesson 4.2. It may be helpful to recall them when you begin the next lesson.

▶ **Exercise 56** For this question, it may be helpful for the students to write each value in the same form, either standard notation or scientific notation. This way the students can make a comparison based on numbers that all look the same.

▶ **Exercise 58** Students may need to be reminded that there are 100 centimeters in a meter.

On Your Own Exercises

**Find the value of $N$ in each equation.**

**50.** $N \times \frac{1}{10^2} = 8$ 800 **51.** $N \times \frac{1}{10^4} = 12$ 120,000 **52.** $N \times \frac{1}{10^6} = 4.927$ 4,927,000

**53.** $17 \div 10^1 = N$ 1.7 **54.** $128.4 \div 10^3 = N$ 0.1284 **55.** $714 \div 10^8 = N$ 0.00000714

56. $10^5$, half a million, $2.5 \times 10^7$, a quarter of a billion, $10^9$, two thousand million

**56.** List these six numbers from least to greatest.

| | | |
|---|---|---|
| a quarter of a billion | $2.5 \times 10^7$ | two thousand million |
| $10^9$ | half a million | $10^5$ |

**57. Geometry** Carson arranged $10^3$ one-centimeter cubes into a large cube.

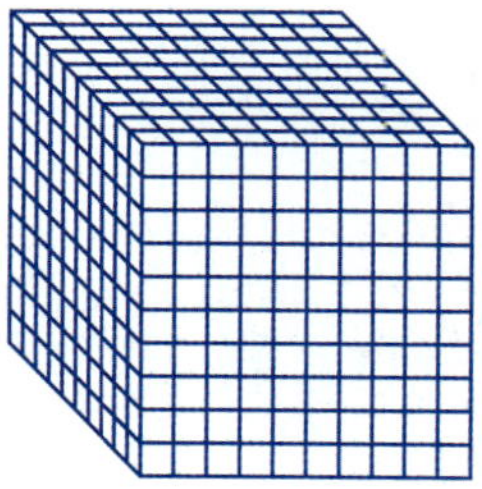

**a.** What is the length of an edge of the cube, in centimeters? 10

**b.** What is the volume of the cube, in cubic centimeters? 1,000, or $10^3$

Sophie arranged $10^6$ one-centimeter cubes into a large cube.

**c.** What is the edge length of the new cube, in centimeters? What is the volume of the new cube, in cubic centimeters? 100, $10^6$

**d.** What is the volume of the new cube, in cubic meters? What is the volume of the first large cube, in cubic meters? 1, 0.001

**e.** What is the area of a face of the new cube, in square centimeters? 10,000

**58. Geometry** Irena stacked $10^6$ two-centimeter cubes into a tower. Part of the tower is shown here. What would be the height of the tower in meters? $2 \times 10^4$

**59. Preview** Fill in the exponents below. (Hint: Fill in the exponents you know first. Then fill in the others by continuing the pattern.)

$5{,}000 = 5 \times 10^?$ 3

$500 = 5 \times 10^?$ 2

$50 = 5 \times 10^?$ 1

$5 = 5 \times 10^?$ 0

$0.5 = 5 \times 10^?$ −1

$0.05 = 5 \times 10^?$ −2

60b. About \$139,000,000 in \$1 bills will fill one freight car, so about 65,468 freight cars will be needed. \$13.9 billion in \$100 bills will fill a freight car, so about 655 freight cars would be needed.

**60. Economics** In October 2007, the U.S. national debt was \$9.1 trillion, or $\$9.1 \times 10^{12}$.

**a.** If the government could pay back \$1 million each year and the debt did not increase, how long would it take to pay off the entire debt? 9.1 million years

**b.** A typical railway freight car measures 3 meters by 4 meters by 12 meters. A dollar bill is approximately 15.7 cm long and 6.6 cm wide. A stack of 100 dollar bills is one centimeter high.

How many freight cars would it take to carry the 2007 U.S. federal deficit in \$1 bills? In \$100 bills? (Hint: a \$100 bill is the same size as a \$1 bill.)

**c.** In 2007, the estimated population of the United States was 301,000,000. Suppose that every person in the country gave the government \$1 each minute. How long would it take to pay off the deficit? About 21 days

**d.** Invent another example to illustrate the size of the federal deficit. Examples will vary.

**61. In Your Own Words** Explain why scientific notation is a useful way to write greater and lesser numbers. See ①.

### Mixed Review

① Possible answer: Scientific notation provides an efficient way to write greater and lesser numbers without writing as many digits.

**62.** Find 33% of 140. 46.2

**63.** Find 14% of 31. 4.34

**64.** What percent of 250 is 15? 6%

**65.** What percent of 12 is 0.12? 1%

**Write each expression in the form $c^m$.**

**66.** $5^3 \cdot 5^2$ $5^5$

**67.** $2^7 \cdot 2^2$ $2^9$

**68.** $a^2 \cdot a^3$ $a^5$

**69.** Use the expression given to complete the table. Then write another expression that gives the same values. Check your expression with the values in the table. $2(m-1) = 2m - 2$

| $m$ | 1 | 2 | 3 | 4 | 5 | 100 |
|---|---|---|---|---|---|---|
| $2(m-1)$ | 0 | 2 | 4 | 6 | 8 | 198 |

**Find each product.**

**70.** $-4 \cdot 12$ $-48$

**71.** $8 \cdot (-2.5)$ $-20$

**72.** $-2 \cdot 4 \cdot (-8)$ $64$

**73.** $3 \cdot \left(-\frac{1}{6}\right)$ $-\frac{1}{2}$

**Find each quotient.**

**74.** $-50 \div 4$ $-\frac{25}{2}$, or $-12.5$

**75.** $-4 \div 48$ $-\frac{1}{12}$, or $-0.08\overline{3}$

**76.** $-8 \div (-64)$ $\frac{1}{8}$, or $0.125$

**77.** $144 \div (-10)$ $-\frac{72}{5}$, or $-14.4$



On Your Own Exercises

▶ **Exercise 60** You may want to spend some time discussing this exercise in class. These kinds of comparisons are common in the media, and it would be interesting to discuss which ones are most powerful to the students and why. What did students choose as their models? Which ones give you a better sense for the magnitude of the debt—ones in which you think about your share of the debt or geometric ones in which you think about the number of dollar bills?

▶ **Exercise 60d** If students are struggling with another example, ask them to think of other ways of comparing sizes of things. This will be a great starting point for a discussion.

### Quick Check

**Informal Assessment** Students should be able to:

✓ multiply and divide numbers by powers of 10

✓ write numbers using scientific notation

✓ use a calculator to work with numbers in scientific notation

### Quick Quiz

Rewrite each number in standard notation.

**1.** $438 \times 10^6$ 438,000,000

**2.** $\left(\frac{6}{10}\right)^2$ 0.36

Write each number in scientific notation.

**3.** 45,000,000 $4.5 \times 10^7$

**4.** 239.4 $2.394 \times 10^2$

Suppose you save \$100 each month beginning now, but stuff it in your mattress so that it doesn't earn interest.

**5.** How many years would it take to save 1 million dollars? Answers will vary, but should be more than 800 years.

**6.** How many years would it take to save 1 billion dollars? Answers will vary, but should be more than 800,000 years.

**7.** Would one billion dollar bills fit in your mattress? Explain any assumptions you make and show your work. Answers will vary, but students will probably say no.

**Lesson 4.1** Scientific Notation 193

LESSON 4.2

# Negative Exponents

### Objectives

- To relate negative exponents to both multiplication by fractions and repeated division
- To evaluate simple expressions with negative exponents
- To apply laws of exponents to expressions with negative exponents
- To write numbers in scientific notation with negative exponents

## Overview

This lesson introduces the use of negative numbers as exponents. Students use shrinking machines to think about how negative exponents behave and learn to relate negative exponent notation to the model. They then revisit the laws of exponents and scientific notation, using negative exponents.

## Advance Preparation

You may want to revisit some of the things you used in Chapter 2 to explain exponent rules to students.

| | Summary | Materials | On Your Own Exercises (pp. 202–205) | Assessment Opportunities |
|---|---|---|---|---|
| **Investigation 1** (p. 194) Pacing: 2 days | Students revisit the stretching and shrinking machine model to apply negative numbers as exponents in repeater machines. They look for patterns to explore the notation of negative exponents. | | Practice & Apply: 1–3<br>Connect & Extend: 57–62<br>Mixed Review: 75–93 | • On the Spot Assessment (p. 196)<br>• Share & Summarize (p. 198)<br>• Troubleshooting (pp. 195, 197) |
| **Investigation 2** (p. 198) Pacing: 1 day | This brief investigation provides practice evaluating a variety of expressions that use exponents and negative numbers. | | Practice & Apply: 4–24<br>Connect & Extend: 63–71<br>Mixed Review: 75–93 | • Share & Summarize (p. 199)<br>• Troubleshooting (p. 198) |
| **Investigation 3** (p. 200) Pacing: 1 day | Students revisit the laws of exponents and scientific notation, now with negative exponents in the mix. | | Practice & Apply: 25–56<br>Connect & Extend: 72–73<br>Mixed Review: 75–93 | • Share & Summarize (p. 201)<br>• Troubleshooting (p. 201) |

# Leveled Lesson Resources

CRM *Available in:* **Chapter 4 Resource Masters**

Also on TeacherWorks™ Lesson 4.2

## Study Guide and Intervention (p. 8) AL

**Lesson 4.2 Study Guide and Intervention**

***Negative Exponents***

Extending the pattern below shows that $4^{-1} = \frac{1}{4}$ or $\frac{1}{4^1}$.

$4^2 = 16$ ) $\div 4$
$4^1 = 4$ ) $\div 4$
$4^0 = 1$ ) $\div 4$
$4^{-1} = \frac{1}{4}$

This suggests the following definition.
$a^{-n} = \frac{1}{a^n}$, for $a \neq 0$ and any integer $n$.

**Laws of Exponents**

Product Laws
$a^b \times a^c = a^{b+c}$
$a^c \times b^c = (a \times b)^c$

Quotient Laws
$a^b \div a^c = a^{b-c}$
$a^c \div b^c = (a \div b)^c$

Power of a Power Law
$(a^b)^c = a^{b \times c}$

***Example 1*** **Evaluate each expression.**

**a.** $5^{-2}$
$5^{-2} = \frac{1}{5^2}$
$= \frac{1}{25}$

**b.** $4 \cdot 2^{-1}$
$4 \cdot 2^{-1} = 4 \cdot \frac{1}{2}$
$= \frac{4}{2}$
$= 2$

***Example 2*** **Write each expression using only positive exponents.**

**a.** $3^{-4}$
$3^{-4} = \frac{1}{3^4}$

**b.** $(y^{-2})^4$
$y^{-2 \cdot 4} = y^{-8} = \frac{1}{y^8}$

**c.** $6^7 \cdot 6^{-4}$
$6^7 \cdot 6^{-4} = 6^{7+(-4)} = 6^3$

***Exercises***

**Evaluate each expression.**

**1.** $-2 \cdot 6^{-2}$ **2.** $-3^{-1}$ **3.** $7 \cdot 6^{-3}$ **4.** $3^3 \cdot 4^3$
**5.** $50 \cdot 5^{-2}$ **6.** $(-4)^{-3}$ **7.** $125 \div 5^4$ **8.** $8^2 \div 4^2$

**Rewrite each expression using a single base or exponent.**

**9.** $7^2 \cdot 7^{-4}$ **10.** $10^{-2} \div 10^4$ **11.** $n^4 \div n^{-8}$ **12.** $c^{12} \cdot c^{-3}$

**Write each expression using only positive exponents.**

**13.** $6^{-4}$ **14.** $(-7)^{-3}$ **15.** $b^{-6} \cdot b^{-4}$ **16.** $9^7 \div 9^{-5}$

## Skills Practice (p. 9) AL OL

**Lesson 4.2 Skills Practice**

***Negative Exponents***

**Find the length of the output if a 24-inch input is sent through each connection.**

**1.**
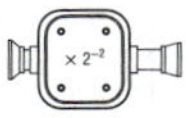


**2.**
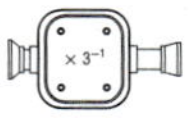


**3.**
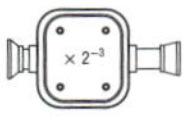


**Evaluate each expression.**

**4.** $3^5 \cdot 2^{-5}$ **5.** $72 \cdot (-2)^3$ **6.** $a^{-7} \div b^{-7}$

**7.** $6^{-3}$ **8.** $(-5)^{-4}$ **9.** $-10^5$

**10.** $(10^3)^{-4}$ **11.** $9^3 \cdot 9^{-2}$ **12.** $\left(\frac{1}{2}\right) \cdot 4^{-1}$

**13.** $-64 \cdot 8^{-2}$ **14.** $5^2 \div 5^{-3}$ **15.** $x^{-4} \cdot x^5$

**Write each expression using only positive exponents.**

**16.** $3^{-4} \div 3^{-6}$ **17.** $8^{-7}$ **18.** $(10^{-4})^2$

**19.** $(-2)^{-6}$ **20.** $(-40)^{-3} \times (-40)^4$ **21.** $18^{-5} \div 6^{-5}$

**22.** $(n^{-10})^{-3}$ **23.** $(b^{-8})^{-2}$ **24.** $q^{-5} \cdot q^7$

**25.** $(-7)^{-2}$ **26.** $11^2 \times 11^{-10}$ **27.** $27^9 \div 27^{12}$

## Problem-Solving Practice (p. 10) AL OL

**Lesson 4.2 Problem-Solving Practice**

***Negative Exponents***

Solve.

**1. Solar System** The distance between Earth and the Sun is about $10^{-5}$ the diameter of the solar system. Write this number using a positive exponent.

**2. Paper** The paper used by the students at Hopkins Middle School is approximately $6^{-3}$ inch thick. How thick are 50 sheets of paper? Write your answer without using exponents.

**3. Time** A microsecond is a measure of time that is equal to one millionth of a second. Express this number as a power of 10 with a negative exponent.

**4. Measurement** There are $10^{-2}$ meters in 1 centimeter. At the site of an automobile accident, a state trooper uses a measuring tape to determine that the width of a tire track is 20 centimeters. Express this number as a fraction of a meter in simplest form.

**5. Homework** As Libby was working on her math homework, she computed $2^{-3}$ by writing the following equation.

$$2^{-3} = -8$$

What was Libby's error? Explain. Then give the correct answer.

**For Exercises 6–9, refer to the following information.**

Kevin's father is an entomologist. He studies insects. The table to the right shows the mass of four common insects.

| Insect | Mass (g) |
|---|---|
| Honeybee | $8^{-2}$ |
| Ant | $16^{-2}$ |
| Housefly | $9^{-2}$ |
| Moth | $4.5^{-2}$ |

**6. Honeybees** A small honeybee hive contains about 20,000 bees. What is the mass, in grams, of a hiveful of honeybees?

**7. Insects** How many times heavier is the heaviest insect than the lightest insect? Round your answer to the nearest tenth.

**8. Mosquitoes** A mosquito's mass is about $\frac{2}{25}$ the mass of a housefly. What is the mass of a mosquito?

**9. Ants** It is estimated that an ant can lift approximately 20 times its own body mass. How many grams can the average ant lift?

## Enrichment (p. 11) BL

**Lesson 4.2 Enrichment**

***Negative Exponents***

**Proving Definitions of Exponents**

Recall the rules for multiplying and dividing powers with the same base. Use these rules, along with other properties you have learned, to justify each definition. Abbreviations for some properties you may wish to use are listed below.

Associative Property of Multiplication (APM)
Additive Identity Property (AIP)
Multiplicative Identity Property (MIP)
Inverse Property of Addition (IPA)
Inverse Property of Multiplication (IPM)

**Write the reason for each statement.**

**1.** Prove: $a^0 = 1$

| Statement | Reason |
|---|---|
| Let $m$ be an integer, and let $a$ be any nonzero number. | **a.** Given |
| $a^m \cdot a^0 = a^{m+0}$ | **b.** ________ |
| $a^m \cdot a^0 = a^m$ | **c.** ________ |
| $\frac{1}{a^m} \cdot (a^m \cdot a^0) = \frac{1}{a^m} \cdot a^m$ | **d.** ________ |
| $\left(\frac{1}{a^m} \cdot a^m\right) \cdot a^0 = \frac{1}{a^m} \cdot a^m$ | **e.** ________ |
| $1 \cdot a^0 = 1$ | **f.** ________ |
| $a^0 = 1$ | **g.** ________ |

**2.** Prove: $a^{-n} = \frac{1}{a^n}$

| Statement | Reason |
|---|---|
| Let $n$ be an integer, and let $a$ be any nonzero number. | **a.** Given |
| $a^{-n} \cdot a^n = a^{-n+n}$ | **b.** ________ |
| $a^{-n} \cdot a^n = a^0$ | **c.** ________ |
| $a^{-n} \cdot a^n = 1$ | **d.** ________ |
| $(a^{-n} \cdot a^n) \cdot \frac{1}{a^n} = 1 \cdot \frac{1}{a^n}$ | **e.** ________ |
| $a^{-n} \cdot \left(a^n \cdot \frac{1}{a^n}\right) = 1 \cdot \frac{1}{a^n}$ | **f.** ________ |
| $a^{-n} \cdot 1 = 1 \cdot \frac{1}{a^n}$ | **g.** ________ |
| $a^{-n} = \frac{1}{a^n}$ | **h.** ________ |

## Lesson Quick Quiz (p. 12) AL OL BL

**Lesson 4.2 Quick Quiz**

**1.** $5.4 \div (10 \cdot 10 \cdot 10)$

**a.** Rewrite this expression as a multiplication expression.

**b.** Rewrite this expression using negative exponents.

**c.** Write the answer in scientific notation.

**2.** Fill in the missing values.

**a.** $3.9 \times 10^{?} = 0.00039$

**b.** $? \times 10^{-2} = 0.01$

**c.** $5.61 \times 10^{-1} = ?$

**3.** Without actually calculating it, will $2^{-3} \cdot 2^{-2} \cdot 2^7$ be greater or less than zero? How do you know?

**4.** Find the value of ? in each equation.

**a.** $3^{-2} \cdot 3^7 = ?$

**b.** $\frac{1}{4} \cdot 4^{-2} = ?$

**c.** $6^{-2} \cdot ? \cdot 6^{-1} = \frac{1}{6}$

**d.** $2 \cdot 2^{?} = \frac{1}{8}$

# Additional Lesson Resources

### Teacher Tech Tools

- TeacherWorks
- ExamView Assessment Suite
- Classroom Presentation Toolkit
- Advance Tracker

### Student Tech Tools

- StudentWorks Plus
- Math Online eGlossary •
  Concepts in Motion

### Other Print Products

- Investigation Notebook and Reflection Journal
- Quick Review Math Handbook

LESSON 4.2

# Negative Exponents

## Introduce

**Negative Exponents** This lesson revisits the stretching and shrinking machine model to apply negative numbers as exponents in repeater machines. You may want to briefly review with students what a stretching machine and a shrinking machine each do.

### *Think & Discuss*

As you discuss the hookup, focus on students' solving strategies. Collect the different ways that students thought about the exercise and record them on the board. To help students understand which ways are equivalent, you might ask questions such as these:

- How is your way like this other way I wrote down?
- Why do both/all of these different ways work?
- Why isn't there just one way to do it?

Most students will think in terms of first stretching the 1-inch stick by $3^5$ and then shrinking it by $3^3$. They may multiply 1 by 3, then multiply again by 3, and so on. Then they divide the final product by 3, then divide again by 3, and then divide again by 3.

Some students may recall the laws of exponents right away and may combine the machines into one step that stretches the 1-inch stick by $3^2$.

**Investigation 1**

***On Your Own Exercises***
Pages 202–205
Exercises 1–3, 57–62

**Review** Students review connections of stretching and shrinking machines to remember how shrinking can undo stretching. The context of the machines provides a visual model for students to later make sense of methods for simplifying expressions with negative exponents. The lesson then uses patterns to introduce the notation of negative exponents.

LESSON 4.2

# Negative Exponents

You have seen that negative numbers can be used to show amounts that are less than 0, such as low temperatures, debts, and elevations below sea level. Negative numbers can also be used as exponents.



You have learned that positive exponents mean repeated multiplication. For example, $3^4$ means $3 \cdot 3 \cdot 3 \cdot 3$. But what does $3^{-4}$ mean?

In this lesson, you will see that you can extend what you know about positive exponents to help you understand and work with expressions involving negative exponents.

### *Think & Discuss*

In Chapter 2, you used stretching and shrinking machines as a way to think about exponents.

Take a look at this connection.

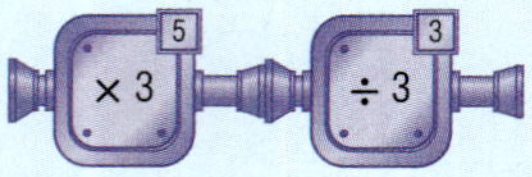


If you put a one-inch stick of modeling clay through this connection, how long will it be when it exits? Describe at least two ways that you could figure this out. See ①.

① 9 in.; Possible strategies: Multiply the length by 3 five times, then divide by 3 three times. Or, stretching 5 times and shrinking 3 times is a net stretch of 2 times, so multiply by 3 twice. Or, one of the quotient laws of exponents says $3^5 \div 3^3 = 3^2$, so putting the gum through this connection is equivalent to putting it through a $\times 3^2$ machine.

## Investigation 1 Model Negative Exponents

You will soon use shrinking machines to help you think about negative exponents. First, though, you will review connections of machines with positive exponents.



### *Mathematical Background*

Because the stretching and shrinking machine model uses lengths of concrete objects such as gum or sticks, it does not make sense to have a negative length. Thus, the model excludes raising negative numbers to a power. These kinds of exercises will be addressed later in the lesson, separate from the model.

194 CHAPTER 4 Magnitude of Numbers

## Develop & Understand: A

**If possible, find a single repeater machine that will do the same work as the given connection.**

**1.** 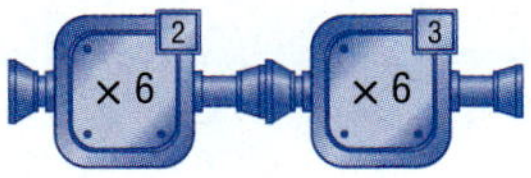


$\times 6^5$

**2.** 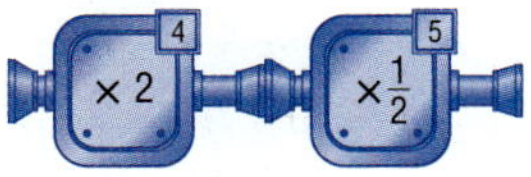


$\times \frac{1}{2}$

**3.** 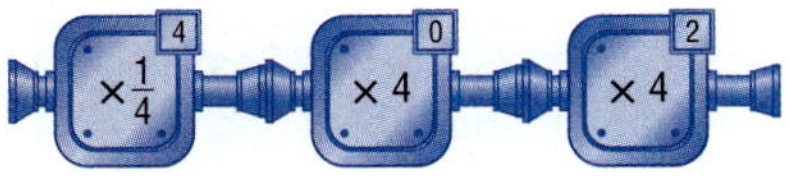


$\times \left(\frac{1}{4}\right)^2$

Jordan is a new employee at the resizing factory. He is assigned to all the machines with base 3. A clown troupe has asked him to stretch some ribbons for its balloons. To become familiar with the machines, Jordan sends one-centimeter pieces of ribbon through them and records the lengths of the outputs.

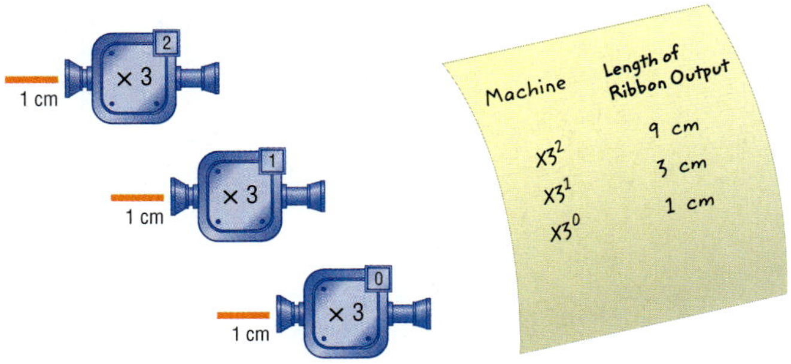


### Think & Discuss

Jordan noticed a pattern in the outputs. Each time the number of repeats is reduced by 1, the resulting length is $\frac{1}{3}$ the previous length. Why? He is reducing the amount of stretch by a factor of 3.

Some of Jordan's base 3 machines have negative exponents. When he puts one-centimeter ribbons through a $\times 3^{-1}$ machine, a $\times 3^{-2}$ machine, and a $\times 3^{-3}$ machine, the pattern in the output length continues.



## Troubleshooting

In Exercise 3, watch for students who think that $4^0$ is zero. Remind students that they can think of the 0 exponent as meaning "don't apply the machine at all" to help them remember why $n^0$ is 1.

## Develop & Understand: A

*Suggested Grouping: Pairs or Individuals*

Students review how stretching and shrinking machines work as they simplify expressions through the context of the machines.

▶ **Exercise 1** Students look at stretching machines. Some students may recall that they can add the exponents to find the value of a single machine if the bases are the same.

▶ **Exercises 2 and 3** Students revisit fractions raised to a power. Some students may look at the exponents to find the number of times the fraction and its reciprocal are multiplied. Since a fraction and its reciprocal can be combined to make a repeater value of 1, students may match as many pairs as possible and then evaluate what remains.

**Wrap-Up** You might want to have students explain how they found each answer. This can help all students review the earlier concepts and ensure that they understand and can use the repeater model.

Discuss Jordan's employment at the resizing factory and his test cases with base 3 machines.

### Think & Discuss

Students review concepts from the earlier chapter. They should easily explain why each output in the pattern is $\frac{1}{3}$ less than the output for the previous machine.

Tell students that some machines have negative exponents and that they can continue the pattern to find the output for the $\times 3^{-1}$ machine, the $\times 3^{-2}$ machine, and the $\times 3^{-3}$ machine.

## Develop & Understand: B

*Suggested Grouping: Whole Class and Individuals*

This exercise set focuses on familiarizing students with negative-exponent notation and helping them relate it to the familiar machine model.

Discuss Exercises 4–6 as a whole class. Then have students work Exercises 7–10 individually, immediately followed by a whole-class review of the answers.

▶ **Exercise 5** Be sure students understand that they can substitute any of these machines for each other. If students have difficulty seeing that the machines do the same thing, you may want to have them use each machine to find outputs using the same input. Then have them compare the outputs.

## Develop & Understand: B

**4.** Continue Jordan's pattern in the chart below.

| What Went In | Machine | What Came Out |
|---|---|---|
| 1-cm ribbon |   | 9-cm ribbon |
| 1-cm ribbon |   | 3-cm ribbon |
| 1-cm ribbon |   | 1-cm ribbon |
| 1-cm ribbon | 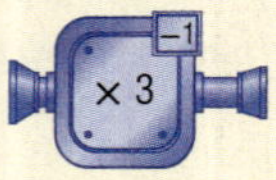  | $\frac{1}{3}$-cm ribbon |
| 1-cm ribbon | 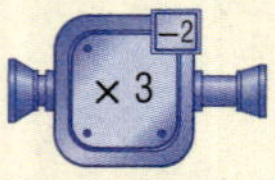  | $\frac{1}{9}$-cm ribbon |
| 1-cm ribbon | 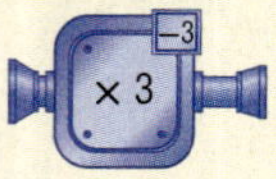  | $\frac{1}{27}$-cm ribbon |

**5.** After conducting several experiments, Jordan concluded that these three machines do the same thing.

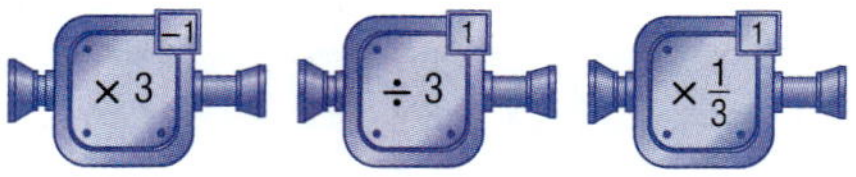


**a.** Suppose you put an 18-inch length of rope into a $\times 3^{-1}$ machine. Describe two ways that you could figure out how long the resulting piece would be. Multiply by $\frac{1}{3}$ or divide by 3

**b.** Describe two other repeater machines, one using multiplication and one using division, that do the same thing as a $\times 3^{-2}$ machine.

5b. $\times\left(\frac{1}{3}\right)^2$ and $\div 3^2$

**c.** Describe two other repeater machines, one using multiplication and one using division, that do the same thing as a $\times 3^{-3}$ machine. $\times\left(\frac{1}{3}\right)^3$ and $\div 3^3$



### Reaching All Learners

**AL Approaching Level** If students are struggling, put the students into small groups with a mix of skill levels. Assign each group four questions and have them create machines to perform the given task. This will act as a review for students who are on or beyond level, and will enable to the students who are approaching the level to have a confident foundation for their work.

### On the Spot Assessment

Ask the students to describe what would happen if you put a 1 mm piece of ribbon into a $\times 4^{-2}$ machine, a $\div 4^2$ machine, and then ask the students if there is another machine that would do the same work.

**6.** Jordan repeated the pattern shown in Exercise 4 with two other bases.

**a.** With base 2, Jordan found that each time the exponent was reduced by 1, the output length was half the previous output length. Complete the chart on the left below to show what happened to one-centimeter ribbons.

**b.** A similar pattern appeared when Jordan put one-centimeter ribbons through base 4 machines. Complete the chart on the right below.

| Machine | What Came Out |
|---|---|
| $\times 2^{2}$ | 4-cm ribbon |
| $\times 2^{1}$ | 2-cm ribbon |
| $\times 2^{0}$ | 1-cm ribbon |
| $\times 2^{-1}$ | $\frac{1}{2}$-cm ribbon |
| $\times 2^{-2}$ | $\frac{1}{4}$-cm ribbon |
| $\times 2^{-3}$ | $\frac{1}{8}$-cm ribbon |

| Machine | What Came Out |
|---|---|
| $\times 4^{2}$ | 16-cm ribbon |
| $\times 4^{1}$ | 4-cm ribbon |
| $\times 4^{0}$ | 1-cm ribbon |
| $\times 4^{-1}$ | $\frac{1}{4}$-cm ribbon |
| $\times 4^{-2}$ | $\frac{1}{16}$-cm ribbon |
| $\times 4^{-3}$ | $\frac{1}{64}$-cm ribbon |

**Machines with other bases also follow the pattern. If you put a 72-inch pole through each machine, how long would each output be?**

**7.** $\times 2^{-1}$ 36 in.

**8.** $\times 3^{-2}$ 8 in.

**9.** $\times 8^{-1}$ 9 in.

**10.** $\times 2^{-3}$ 9 in.



▶ **Exercise 6** Students may want to use one of the methods they found in Exercise 5 to calculate the output values. If they do so, have them verify that the pattern of the answers matches the pattern described in the directions.

▶ **Exercises 7–10** Students practice applying the negative exponent notation. They may use either multiplication of fractions or repeated division to find the output.

**Wrap-Up** Be sure students can explain the patterns in Exercises 3, 4, and 6. These exercises provide them with a reference point for seeing how negative exponents work.

## *Troubleshooting*

Watch for students who are confused by the negative exponent notation in Exercises 7–10. For instance, students may think that a $2^{-3}$ machine means to subtract 8 from the 72-inch pole rather than to divide the length by 8, or they may think it means a negative number, −8. Have these students rewrite each negative exponent machine as a division machine to do the exercises.

**Lesson 4.2** Negative Exponents 197

## Share & Summarize

After discussing the generalization, students should understand that:

1. A negative exponent in a repeater machine does the same thing as a shrinking machine. A shrinking machine can involve dividing by a number greater than 1 or multiplying by a fraction between 0 and 1.
2. The base is the number being multiplied and the exponent is the number of times the number is multiplied. Students may state this fact in terms of the shrinking machine. Their answer might be that the "shrink factor" (the number in the circle on the machine) tells the factor by which you shrink and the repeater number (in the box, as the exponent) tells how many times to shrink.

You may wish to expand the discussion by having either pairs of students or the whole class generate a list of equivalent representations for $\times 2^{-4}$ such as $\times\frac{1}{16}$, $\div 2^4$, or $\left(\frac{1}{2}\right)^4$. Have students describe in their own words why these representations are equivalent.

## Investigation 2

***On Your Own Exercises***

Pages 202–205

Exercises 4–24, 63–71

**Expressions** This investigation is a brief one that provides practice evaluating a variety of expressions that use exponents and negative numbers.

### *Example*

Walk students through the Example on how to evaluate expressions with negative exponents. Students may have little difficulty evaluating the first expression ($4^{-3}$) if they think about the shrinking machines used in the first investigation. However, this is their first exposure to a connection that has one machine with a negative exponent. After discussing why the machine works, you may want to ask:

- What single machine will do the same thing as the connection of these machines? A $\times\frac{1}{2}$ or a $\times 2^{-1}$ machine



## Share & Summarize

In general, when you put something in a multiplication machine with a negative exponent, like $\times 2^{-4}$, how can you find the output length? See ①.

① Possible answers: Find the base to the exponent as if the exponent were positive, and divide the input length by the result. *Or,* change the base to a fraction by putting 1 over the base, and do the exercise with the new base and the absolute value of the exponent.

## Investigation 2 Evaluate Expressions with Negative Exponents

Thinking about shrinking machines can help you evaluate expressions with negative exponents.

### *Example*

Evaluate $4^{-3}$.

Think about a $\times 4^{-3}$ machine. Putting something through a $\times 4^{-3}$ machine is equivalent to putting it through a $\times\left(\frac{1}{4}\right)^3$ machine, so $\times 4^{-3} = \left(\frac{1}{4}\right)^3$, or $\frac{1}{64}$.

Evaluate $2^{-3} \cdot 2^2$.

Think about this connection.

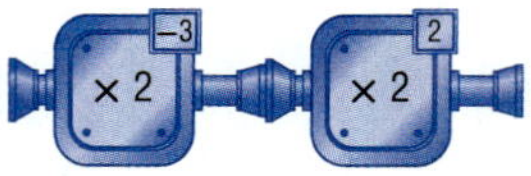


The $\times 2^{-3}$ machine halves the length of an input three times.

The $\times 2^2$ machine doubles the length twice.

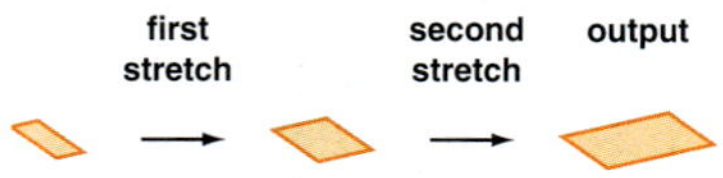


The output is half the length of the original input. The connection is the same as a $\times\frac{1}{2}$ or a $\times 2^{-1}$ machine. So, $2^{-3} \cdot 2^2 = \frac{1}{2}$, or $2^{-1}$.



## *Troubleshooting*

It is important that students understand how to put any length through a shrinking machine with a negative repeater number. If students are still struggling with this, give them some additional practice rewriting each machine as a series of repeated division steps or repeated multiplication of fractions.

Now you will practice evaluating expressions with negative exponents. Pay attention to how you evaluate the expressions. Be ready to share your approach with your class.

## Develop & Understand: A

**Evaluate each expression.**

**1.** $3^{-4}$ $\frac{1}{81}$
**2.** $2^{-1}$ $\frac{1}{2}$
**3.** $3^{-3} \cdot 3^{5}$ 9
**4.** $7^{5} \cdot 7^{-7}$ $\frac{1}{49}$
**5.** $3^{9} \cdot 3^{-6}$ 27
**6.** $-49 \cdot 7^{-2}$ $-1$
**7.** $256 \cdot 4^{-3}$ 4
**8.** $32 \cdot 1^{-5}$ 32
**9.** $-60 \cdot 6^{-1}$ $-10$
**10.** $2^{-2} \cdot 3^{-1}$ $\frac{1}{12}$
**11.** $2^{-1} \cdot 3^{-1} \cdot 5^{-2}$ $\frac{1}{150}$
**12.** $2^{-2} \cdot 4^{2} \cdot 2^{-1}$ 2
**13.** Which is greater, $5^{-1}$ or $5^{-2}$? Why? $5^{-1}$ is greater because $\frac{1}{5} > \frac{1}{25}$.
**14.** Describe a connection of two repeater machines, one with a negative exponent, that does the same work as a $\times 5^{0}$ machine.
**15.** Is it possible to shrink something to a length of 0 by using shrinking machines? Why or why not? See margin.

14. Answers will vary. The exponents must be opposites, as in $\times 5^{2} \times 5^{-2}$.

## Develop & Understand: B

You sometimes need to take extra care to be sure you understand a mathematical expression. For example, in expressions such as $-3^{-2}$ and $(-3)^{-2}$, the two negative symbols give two different kinds of information.

**16.** Why is $-3^{-2} = -\frac{1}{9}$? $-3^{-2} = -(3^{-2}) = -\frac{1}{9}$
**17.** Why is $(-3)^{-2} = \frac{1}{9}$? $(-3)^{-2} = \frac{1}{(-3)^{2}} = \frac{1}{9}$
**18.** What does $-4^{-2}$ equal? $-\frac{1}{16}$
**19.** Write an expression that has a negative exponent and equals $-\frac{1}{27}$. Possible answer: $-3^{-3}$

**Evaluate each expression.**

**20.** $-5^{-2}$ $-\frac{1}{25}$
**21.** $(-3)^{3}$ $-27$
**22.** $-1^{-5}$ $-1$
**23.** $(-1)^{-5}$ $-1$
**24.** $(-5)^{-3}$ $-\frac{1}{125}$
**25.** $-2^{4}$ $-16$

### Share & Summarize

1. Give two values of $n$ for which $(-2)^{n}$ is positive.
2. Give two values of $n$ for which $(-2)^{n}$ is negative.
3. Give two values of $n$ for which $(-2)^{n}$ is not an integer.
4. Write an expression with a negative exponent that equals $-\frac{1}{64}$.

1. Any even values will work.
2. Any odd values will work.
3. Any negative values will work.
4. Possible answers: $-8^{-2}$ or $(-4)^{-3}$



## Mathematical Background

Negative numbers raised to powers are often initially confusing to students. Earlier, students learned that $-3^2$ meant the opposite of $3^2$. This can be written as $-(3^2)$ or $-9$. They learned that $(-3)^2$ meant $(-3) \cdot (-3)$, or 9. The same thing holds true with negative numbers raised to negative exponents. Help students remember that, assuming $b > 0$, $-a^{-b}$ is the opposite of $a^{-b}$, or $-(a^{-b})$, while $(-a)^{-b}$ means $1/[(-a) \cdot (-a) \cdot (-a)...]$ $b$ times.

## Develop & Understand: A

*Suggested Grouping: Pairs or Individuals*

▶ **Exercise 12** Students may find changing $4^2$ to a base of 2 simplifies their work.

▶ **Exercise 13** Watch for students who think that $5^{-2}$ is greater than $5^{-1}$ because 2 is greater than 1. Have these students write each of these terms using division. Then have them calculate each term to see what they get.

▶ **Exercise 14** Students are asked to come up with two repeater connections that might give $5^0$. The exponents for this pair of machines should be opposites, such as $5^3$ and $5^{-3}$.

## Develop & Understand: B

*Suggested Grouping: Pairs or Individuals*

▶ **Exercises 16–17** These exercises may take time and further explanation since they often cause confusion for students.

**Wrap-Up** You might want to tell students not to assume that all negative numbers raised to a power will have a negative answer. Nor are all numbers raised to negative powers negative.

### Share & Summarize

List the class's responses to Questions 1–3 and compare them. Help students see that there are many correct responses. You may want to ask students what all the correct values have in common to help them generalize their work.

### Additional Answers

15. Technically, no. You can get smaller and smaller lengths by repeatedly sending the input through standard shrinking machines, machines that multiply the length by fractions, or machines with negative exponents, but the length will never be 0. The result of $1 \div 10 \div 10 \div 10 \div 10 \div 10 \div 10 \div ...$, for instance, gets smaller each time you divide by 10, but it never reaches 0. In reality, with real materials such as ribbon you would eventually get such a small piece you would no longer call it a length of ribbon.

## Investigation 3

***On Your Own Exercises***
Pages 202–205
Exercises 25–56, 72–73

**Scientific Notation** Students revisit familiar content on laws of exponents and scientific notation, now with negative exponents in the mix. You may want to review the laws of exponents. Some students may want to clarify how each law works by substituting numbers for the variables.

Remind students that division by zero is undefined, so implied in the quotient law is that the denominator is not equal to zero.

### *Develop & Understand: A*

*Suggested Grouping: Pairs or Individuals*

▶ **Exercises 16 and 17** These exercises involve creating and evaluating complex fractions. For example, $\left(\frac{2}{3}\right)^{-1}$ can be written as $\frac{1}{\frac{2}{3}}$.

If students are stuck, you may want to help them realize that this is really a division exercise that they can rewrite as $1 \div \frac{2}{3}$.

**Wrap-Up** You may want students to explain how they simplified the expressions in Exercises 19–21. Some students may benefit from an explanation of why there is not a variable in the answer to Exercise 21.

## Investigation 3 Laws of Exponents and Scientific Notation

In Chapter 2, you learned about the laws of exponents, which describe how to simplify expressions with exponents.

| Product Laws | Quotient Laws | Power of a Power Law |
|---|---|---|
| $a^b \cdot a^c = a^{b+c}$<br>$a^c \cdot b^c = (a \cdot b)^c$ | $a^b \div a^c = a^{b-c}$<br>$a^c \div b^c = (a \div b)^c$ | $(a^b)^c = a^{b \cdot c}$ |

Now you will apply these laws to expressions with negative exponents.

### Develop & Understand: A

The product laws work for negative exponents as well as for positive exponents. In Exercises 1–6, use the product laws to rewrite each expression using a single base. Use a calculator to check your answers.

1. $50^{-6} \cdot 50^{12}$ $50^6$
2. $2^5 \cdot 2^{-6} \cdot 2^3$ $2^2$
3. $0.5^{-10} \cdot 0.5^{-10}$ $0.5^{-20}$
4. $3^{-1} \cdot 9$ $3^1$, or 3
5. $-3^{-3} \cdot 2^{-3} \cdot 4^{-3}$ $-24^{-3}$
6. $10^{-23} \cdot 10^{23}$ $10^0$, or 1

The quotient laws and the power of a power law also work for negative exponents. In Exercises 7–12, use the appropriate law to rewrite each expression using a single base. Use a calculator to check your answers.

7. $7^3 \div 7^5$ $7^{-2}$
8. $12^{-4} \div 4^{-4}$ $3^{-4}$
9. $10^{-5} \div 10^3$ $10^{-8}$
10. $(3^{-3})^2$ $3^{-6}$
11. $2.3^2 \div 2.3^{-6}$ $2.3^8$
12. $(2^{-5})^{-5}$ $2^{25}$

**Rewrite each expression using a single base or exponent.**

13. $m^{23} \cdot m^{-17}$ $m^6$
14. $7^{-x} \cdot 7^x$ $7^0$, or 1
15. $a^{-3} \div b^{-3}$ $\left(\frac{a}{b}\right)^{-3}$

**Rewrite each expression using only positive exponents.**

16. $\left(\frac{2}{3}\right)^{-1}$ $\left(\frac{3}{2}\right)^1$, or $\frac{3}{2}$
17. $\left(\frac{1}{2}\right)^{-3}$ $2^3$
18. $10^{-7}$ $\left(\frac{1}{10}\right)^7$, or $\frac{1}{10^7}$

**Simplify each expression as much as you can.**

19. $-3n \cdot -3n$ $9n^2$
20. $5n \div 2n^{-2}$ $\frac{5}{2}n^3$
21. $4y^2 \cdot 3y^{-2}$ 12



### *Reaching* All Learners

**AL Approaching Level** Watch for students who do not understand how to apply the laws of exponents to Exercises 1–12. Instead, they may methodically try to calculate each exercise to come up with a numerical answer. Encourage them to think about using a stretching or shrinking machine to find the value. Have them practice writing verbal descriptions for what each machine would do and use those descriptions to think about what will happen to the input length.

In Lesson 4.1, you used scientific notation to represent very large numbers. You can also use scientific notation to represent very small numbers. For small numbers, scientific notation involves negative powers of 10.

**Math Link**

In scientific notation, a number is expressed as a power of 10 and as the product of a number greater than or equal to 1 but less than 10. For example, 5,400 is written $5.4 \times 10^3$.

## Develop & Understand: B

A 5.3-cm drinking straw is sent through each machine. Give the length of the straw that emerges from each machine. Write your answers as decimals.

**22.**

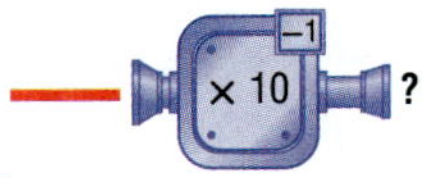


0.53 cm

**23.**

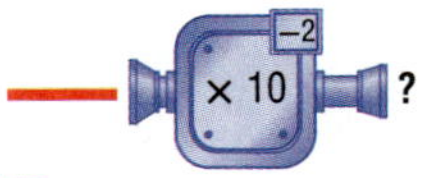


0.053 cm

**24.**

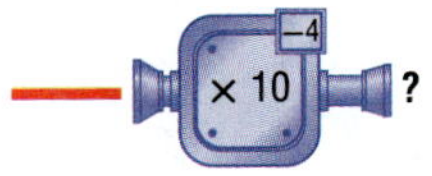


0.00053 cm

**25.**

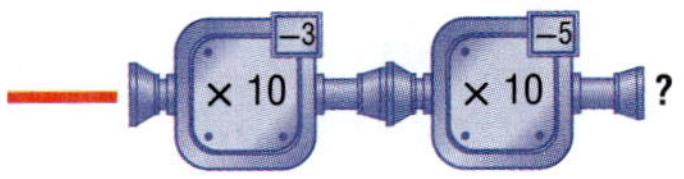


0.000000053 cm

**26.** Write your answers for Exercises 22–25 in scientific notation.
$5.3 \times 10^{-1}$, $5.3 \times 10^{-2}$, $5.3 \times 10^{-4}$, $5.3 \times 10^{-8}$

**27.** List your answers for Exercises 26 from greatest to least.
$5.3 \times 10^{-1}$, $5.3 \times 10^{-2}$, $5.3 \times 10^{-4}$, $5.3 \times 10^{-8}$

**Find each missing value.**

**28.** $3 \cdot 10^{?} = 0.03$ $-2$

**29.** $4.5 \cdot 10^{?} = 0.00045$ $-4$

**30.** $? \cdot 10^{-3} = 0.0065$ 6.5

**31.** $1 \cdot ? = 0.00000001$ $10^{-8}$

**32.** There are 86,400 seconds in a day. How many days long is a second? Express your answer in scientific notation.
About $1.157 \times 10^{-5}$

### Share & Summarize

**1.** Without calculating the product, how can you tell whether $2^{-4} \cdot 2^3$ is greater than 0 or less than 0?

1. It is greater than 0 because both factors are greater than 0.

**2.** Which is smaller, $1 \times 10^{-6}$ or $1 \times 10^{-7}$? How do you know?
$1 \times 10^{-7}$ because it has a smaller power of 10.



## Troubleshooting

Watch for students who multiply rather than divide to find the number of days in one second in Exercise 32. These students will find $1 \cdot 86{,}400 = 86{,}400$. Encourage them to think about the context of the exercise to check the reasonableness of their answer. They might ask themselves whether there will be more or less than one day in one second.

You may want to begin with a brief reminder of how to write numbers in scientific notation. Remind students that one factor is a number greater than 1 and less than 10 and the other factor is a power of 10. Then give students one or two examples of large numbers, such as 540,000 and 20,000,000, to write in scientific notation. $540{,}000 = 5.4 \times 10^5$ and $20{,}000{,}000 = 2 \times 10^7$

## Develop & Understand: B

*Suggested Grouping: Whole Class*

Students write numbers less than zero in scientific notation. They write a number in standard form and in scientific notation.

▶ **Exercises 22–24** Students practice applying negative exponents to small numbers written in scientific notation. Ask students to describe in words what each of the machines does, before they actually calculate the answer.

**Wrap-Up** Revisit Exercise 27. Be sure that students understand that since 5.3 is the same for all numbers in scientific notation, they can order the numbers by looking at the power of 10. They should understand that the greater the power of 10, the greater the number.

### Share & Summarize

Students can work with a partner to discuss each question and come up with a shared response before you discuss these questions with the whole class. Encourage students to justify their responses.

If students are struggling with using negative exponents in scientific notation, have them create a chart as shown below and use it to record different numbers. Have them focus on patterns they see in the results and work with them to generate their own descriptions of the relationship between the $10^{-n}$ term and how the decimal point moves.

| Number | What does it equal? | Exponent | How does decimal point move? |
|---|---|---|---|
| $3.4 \times 10^{-4}$ | 0.00034 | −4 | 4 places left |

## On Your Own Exercises
**Lesson 4.2**

### Investigation 1
Pages 194–197
Practice & Apply: 1–3
Connect & Extend: 57–62

### Investigation 2
Pages 198–199
Practice & Apply: 4–24
Connect & Extend: 63–71

### Investigation 3
Pages 200–201
Practice & Apply: 25–56
Connect & Extend: 72–73

### Assign Anytime
Mixed Review: 75–93

▶ **Exercises 1–7** If students are having difficulty solving these exercises, review the machine model.

▶ **Exercises 8–13** This set of exercises focuses on the use of negative exponents and gives students practice linking it to the machine model.

## On Your Own Exercises
**Lesson 4.2**

### Practice & Apply

Find the length of the output if an 144-inch input is sent through each machine.

**1.**
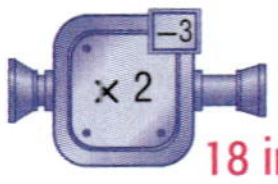

18 in.

**2.**
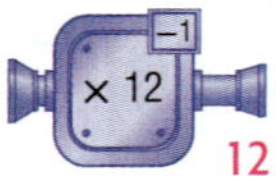

12 in.

**3.**

16 in.

If possible, find a single repeater machine that will do the same work as the given connection.

**4.**

$\div 2^5$, or $\times 2^{-5}$

**5.**
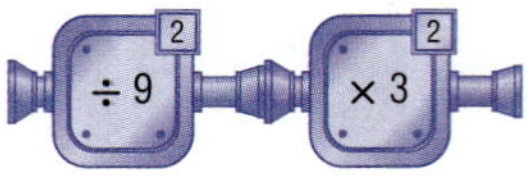

$\div 3^2$, or $\times 3^{-2}$

**6.**

$\times 2^4$

**7.**
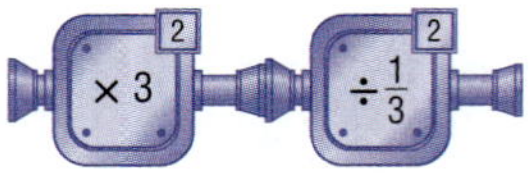

$\times 3^4$

Describe a machine with a negative exponent that does the same work as the given machine.

**8.**
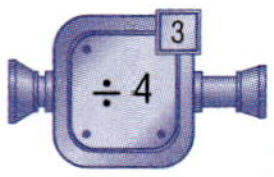

$\times 4^{-3}$

**9.**

$\times 6^{-2}$

**10.**
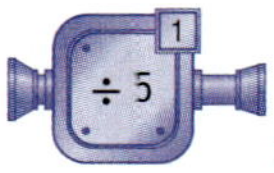

$\times 5^{-1}$

**11.**

$\times 3^{-5}$

**12.**
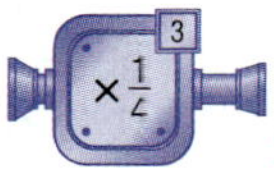

$\times 4^{-3}$

**13.**
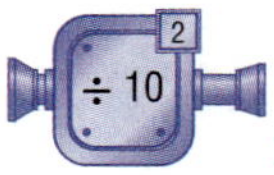

$\times 10^{-2}$

202 CHAPTER 4 Magnitude of Numbers

On Your Own Exercises

**14.** Without calculating, figure out whether $4^{-3}$ or $4^{-4}$ is greater. Explain how you decided. $4^{-3}$ because $\frac{1}{4^3}$ is greater than $\frac{1}{4^4}$.

**Evaluate each expression.**

**15.** $-343 \cdot 7^{-2}$ $-7$ **16.** $-1{,}375 \cdot 5^{-3}$ $-11$ **17.** $128 \cdot 2^{-5}$ $4$

**18.** $-72 \cdot 9^{-1}$ $-8$ **19.** $48 \cdot 6^{-1}$ $8$ **20.** $243 \cdot 3^{-4}$ $3$

**21.** $-9 \cdot 1^{-3}$ $-9$ **22.** $4{,}096 \cdot 8^{-2}$ $64$ **23.** $-11 \cdot 11^{-1}$ $-1$

**24.** How could you rewrite Exercise 22 in division? In multiplication using a positive exponent? $4{,}096 \div 8^2$; $4{,}096 \times \frac{1}{8^2}$

**Decide whether each statement is true. If the statement is false, explain why.**

**25.** $2^{-2} \cdot 2^{-1} = 2^{-3}$ True **26.** $5^{-3} \cdot 5^{-1} \cdot 5^2 = 5^{-2}$ True

**27.** $3^{-1} \cdot 4^{-3} = 12^{-4}$ **28.** $3^{-2} \cdot 3^{-3} = 9^{-5}$

**29.** $x^{-5} \div x^7 = x^{-12}$ True **30.** $k^{-2} \div k^{-5} = k^3$ True

**31.** $w^{-2} \div w^{-5} = w^{-7}$ **32.** $b^{-8} \div g^{-4} = bg^{-2}$

27. False; you cannot add exponents of numbers with different bases.

28. False; when you multiply expressions with the same base, you do not multiply the bases: $3^{-2} \times 3^{-3} = 3^{-5}$.

31. False; when dividing, you subtract rather than add exponents: $w^{-2} \div w^{-5} = w^3$.

32. False; there are two different bases with different exponents, so you cannot use either quotient law.

**Without evaluating, tell whether each expression is greater or less than 1.**

**33.** $3^{-4} \cdot 3^5$ Greater than 1 **34.** $2^{-1} \cdot 2^{-3}$ Less than 1

**35.** $1^{-3} \div 2^{-3}$ Greater than 1 **36.** $10^{-5} \div 10^3$ Less than 1

**Evaluate each expression.**

**37.** $-4^{-2}$ $-\frac{1}{16}$ **38.** $(-5)^{-1}$ $-\frac{1}{5}$

**39.** $-2^3$ $-8$ **40.** $(-10)^4$ $10{,}000$

**Rewrite each expression using a single base and a single exponent.**

**41.** $\frac{1}{2^{-2}} \cdot 4^{-2}$ $2^{-2}$ **42.** $100^{-20} \div -25^{-20}$ $-4^{-20}$

**43.** $-3^{100} \cdot -\frac{5}{6^{100}} \cdot 10^{100}$ $5^{101}$ **44.** $\left(\frac{1}{3}\right)^{-a} \cdot \left(\frac{1}{5}\right)^{-a}$ $\left(\frac{1}{15}\right)^{-a}$, or $15^a$

**45.** $-1{,}000^0 \div 3^0$ $-1^1$ **46.** $15^{-5} \cdot \left(\frac{1}{5}\right)^{-5}$ $3^{-5}$

▶ **Exercises 25–32** If students are struggling with these exercises, remind them of their rules for dealing with exponents from Chapter 2.

▶ **Exercises 29–32** Remind students that the statements are true only if each denominator is not zero.

▶ **Exercises 41–46** Students may struggle with these exercises if they are not comfortable with powers of bases. For a hint, tell students to look at the other bases in the problem. If at least one of the other bases is prime, try to see if they can rewrite one of the other numbers using this base.

▶ **Exercises 53–56** Watch out for students who apply the exponent to the coefficient.

53. $-\frac{6}{4}a^2$ or $-\frac{3}{2}a^2$

On Your Own Exercises

**Find the value of *n* in each equation.**

**47.** $7.24 \times 10^n = 0.00724$ $-3$

**48.** $5 \times 10^n = 0.5$ $-1$

**49.** $n \times 10^{-4} = 0.000104$ 1.04

**50.** $9.2 \cdot n = 0.0092$ $10^{-3}$

**51.** A mile is $1.609 \times 10^5$ centimeters. How many miles is a centimeter? Express your answer in scientific notation. About $6.215 \times 10^{-6}$ mi

**52.** There is $7.8125 \times 10^{-3}$ gallon in an ounce. How many ounces are in a gallon? Express your answer in scientific notation. $1.28 \times 10^2$ oz

**Challenge** Simplify each expression.

**53.** $-6a^{-2} \div (4a^{-4})$

**54.** $-\frac{1}{2}x^{-3} \cdot x^4$ $-\frac{1}{2}x$

**55.** $z^2 \cdot 2z^{-3} \div (-6z^{-2})$ $-\frac{z}{3}$

**56.** $9b^4 \cdot 9b^{-8}$ $81b^{-4}$

**Connect & Extend** **Find the length of the output if a meterstick is sent through each connection.**

**57.** 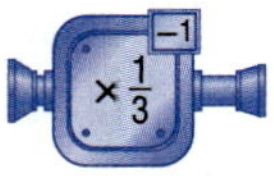

3 m

**58.** 

16 m

**59.** 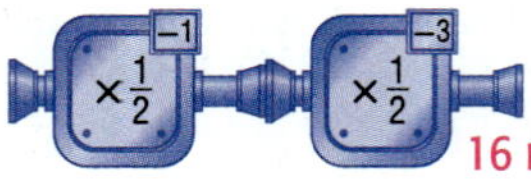

16 m

**60.** 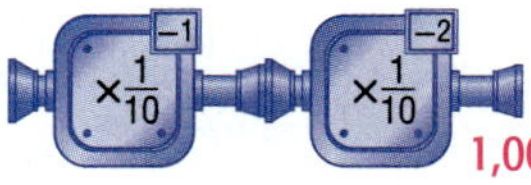

1,000 m

**61.** A 1-inch length of modeling clay went into each machine. Complete the charts.

| Machine | What Came Out |
|---|---|
| 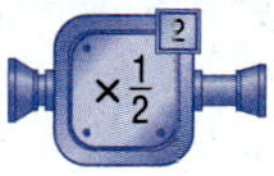  | $\frac{1}{4}$-in. stick |
|   | $\frac{1}{2}$-in. stick |
| 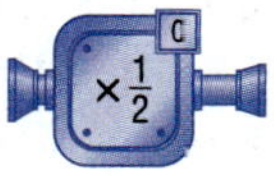  | 1-in. stick |

| Machine | What Came Out |
|---|---|
|   | 2-in. stick |
| 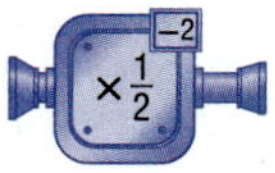  | 4-in. stick |
| 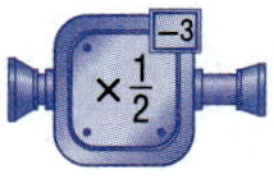  | 8-in. stick |

204 CHAPTER 4 Magnitude of Numbers

62. **Challenge** Describe a machine that has a negative exponent and that does the same work as the machine shown below. $\times\left(\frac{1}{4}\right)^{-3}$

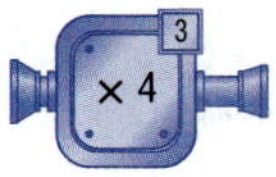


63. **Challenge** A strand of wire is sent through this connection. It emerges 2 inches long. What was the starting length? 5,760 in.

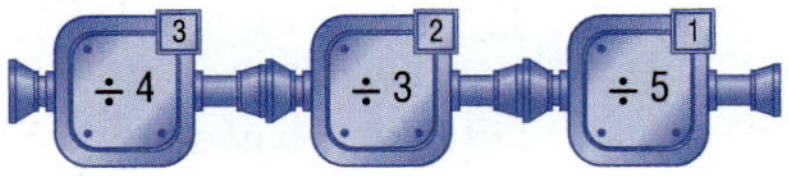


**Without calculating, figure out whether each expression is positive or negative. Explain how you decided.** See margin.

64. $(-4)^{-1}$
65. $(-4)^{-2}$
66. $(-4)^{-3}$
67. $(-4)^{-4}$
68. $(-2)^{-3}$
69. $(-2)^{-2}$
70. $(-5)^{-1}$
71. $(-10)^{-6}$

72. **Prove It!** It is true that $\left(\frac{1}{2}\right)^{-1} = (2^{-1})^{-1} = 2^1 = 2$. In Parts a–c, you will explain each step in this calculation.
   a. Why does $\left(\frac{1}{2}\right)^{-1} = (2^{-1})^{-1}$? Because $\frac{1}{2} = 2^{-1}$
   b. Why does $(2^{-1})^{-1} = 2^1$?
   c. Why does $2^1 = 2$?

73. **Physics** Protons, neutrons, and electrons are *stable* particles. They can exist for a very long time. But many other particles exist for only very short periods of time. A *muon,* for example, has an average life of 0.000002197 second.
   a. Write this length of time in scientific notation. $2.197 \times 10^{-6}$ s
   b. A particular muon existed for half the average life of this type of particle. How long did it exist? About $1.099 \times 10^{-6}$ s
   c. Another muon existed for three times the average life of this type of particle. How long did it exist? $6.591 \times 10^{-6}$ s

74. **In Your Own Words** Write a letter to someone in your family who does not know what negative exponents are. In your letter, describe why $3^{-1}$ is equal to $\frac{1}{3}$. Answers will vary.

72b. Because of the power of a power law, $(2^{-1})^{-1} = 2^{-1 \cdot -1} = 2^1$

72c. Because any number to the first power equals that number



On Your Own Exercises

▶ **Exercise 63** If students are having difficulty with this question, ask the students to go back through their work and look for a multi-machine problem for which they had the starting size. Have them retrace their steps now to complete this question.

**Additional Answers**

64. Negative; $\frac{1}{-4}$ is negative
65. Positive; $(-4)^2$ is positive, so $\frac{1}{(-4)^2}$ is positive.
66. Negative; $(-4)^3$ is negative, so $\frac{1}{(-4)^3}$ is negative.
67. Positive; $(-4)^4$ is positive, so $\frac{1}{(-4)^4}$ is positive.
68. Negative; $(-2)^3$ is negative, so $\frac{1}{(-2)^3}$ is negative.
69. Positive; $(-2)^{-2}$ is positive, so $\frac{1}{(-2)^2}$ is positive.
70. Negative; $\frac{1}{-5}$ is negative.
71. Positive; $(-10)^6$ is positive, so $\frac{1}{(-10)^6}$ is positive.

## Quick Check

**Informal Assessment** Students should be able to:

- ✔ relate negative exponents to both multiplication by fractions and repeated division
- ✔ evaluate simple expressions with negative exponents
- ✔ apply the law of exponents to expressions with negative exponents
- ✔ write numbers in scientific notation with negative exponents

## Quick Quiz

1. $5.4 \div (10 \cdot 10 \cdot 10)$
   a. Rewrite this expression as a multiplication expression. $5.4 \cdot \frac{1}{10} \cdot \frac{1}{10} \cdot \frac{1}{10}$
   b. Rewrite this expression using negative exponents. $5.4 \times 10^{-3}$
   c. Write the answer in scientific notation. $5.4 \times 10^{-3}$
2. Fill in the missing values.
   a. $3.9 \times 10^{?} = 0.00039$ $-4$
   b. $? \times 10^{-2} = 0.01$ 1
   c. $5.61 \times 10^{-1} = ?$ 0.561
3. Without actually calculating it, will $2^{-3} \cdot 2^{-2} \cdot 2^{7}$ be greater or less than zero? How do you know? Greater than zero because all the factors are greater than zero.
4. Find the value of ? in each equation.
   a. $3^{-2} \cdot 3^{7} = ?$ 243
   b. $\frac{1}{4} \cdot 4^{-2} = ?$ $\frac{1}{64}$
   c. $6^{-2} \cdot ? \cdot 6^{-1} = \frac{1}{6}$ 36
   d. $2 \cdot 2^{?} = \frac{1}{8}$ $-4$





## Mixed Review

**Order each group of numbers from least to greatest.**

**75.** $\frac{6}{5}, 0.2, \frac{3}{5}, 0.4, \frac{5}{3}$ $0.2, 0.4, \frac{3}{5}, \frac{6}{5}, \frac{5}{3}$

**76.** 0.75, 0.18, 0.25, 0.025, 0.7 0.025, 0.18, 0.25, 0.7, 0.75

**Find each product. Express your answers in scientific notation.**

**77.** $(5 \times 10^{14}) \times (11 \times 10^{13})$ $5.5 \times 10^{28}$

**78.** $(8 \times 10^{9}) \times (6 \times 10^{6})$ $4.8 \times 10^{16}$

**Fill in the blanks to make true statements.**

**79.** $0.5 + \_\_\_\_ = 1$ 0.5

**80.** $0.5 + 0.25 + \_\_\_\_ = 1$ 0.25

**81.** $\frac{1}{8} + \_\_\_\_ = 1$ $\frac{7}{8}$

**82.** $\frac{8}{5} - \_\_\_\_ = 1$ $\frac{3}{5}$

**83.** $\frac{9}{12} + \frac{3}{12} - \_\_\_\_ = 1$ 0

**84.** $\frac{3}{5} + \frac{7}{10} - \_\_\_\_ = 1$ $\frac{3}{10}$

**Find the product or quotient.**

**85.** $12(-25)$ $-300$

**86.** $-352 \div 11$ $-32$

**87.** $\frac{2}{3} \cdot \left(-\frac{4}{5}\right)$ $-\frac{8}{15}$

**88.** $\frac{2}{3} \div \left(-\frac{4}{5}\right)$ $-\frac{5}{6}$

**89.** **Hobbies** Clara wants to display her collection of 30 first-class stamps in groups of equal size. What group sizes are possible? Groups of 1, 2, 3, 5, 6, 10, 15, and 30

**Find each product.**

**90.** $4 \cdot \frac{1}{10^2}$ 0.04

**91.** $61 \cdot \frac{1}{10^2}$ 0.61

**92.** $842 \cdot 10^{-3}$ 0.842

**93.** $750 \times 10^{-4}$ 0.075

CHAPTER 4

# Review & Self-Assessment

## Chapter Summary

In this chapter, you learned about powers of 10. In addition, you found that sometimes it is useful to express large numbers in scientific notation.

You discovered what negative numbers mean as exponents. You learned that the laws of exponents apply when the exponents are negative. You also practiced writing very small numbers in scientific notation.

### Vocabulary

- greater
- lesser
- relative error
- scientific notation

1. Possible answer: Imagine there is a decimal point at the right end of the number. Move the decimal to the left until you have a number between 1 and 10. Multiply this number by 10 raised to the number of decimal places you moved. For the number 336,000,000, you move the decimal 8 places to get 3.36, so the number in scientific notation is $3.36 \times 10^8$.
2. Possible answer: Divide 1,234 by 1,000 to get 1.234. To compensate, multiply $10^9$ by 1,000, or $10^3$, to get $10^{12}$. The number in scientific notation is $1.234 \times 10^{12}$.

4. As the exponent is reduced by 1, the value is divided by 2:1 $\div 2 = \frac{1}{2}$.

## Strategies and Applications

### Expressing large numbers in scientific notation

1. Explain how to write a large number in scientific notation. Use an example to demonstrate your method.
2. Explain how to write $1{,}234 \times 10^9$ in scientific notation.

### Evaluating expressions involving negative exponents

3. What are two ways to find the value of $\left(\frac{1}{2}\right)^{-1} \cdot \left(\frac{1}{2}\right)^{-1}$? See margin.
4. Use the facts that $2^2 = 4$, $2^1 = 2$, and $2^0 = 1$ to explain why $2^{-1} = \frac{1}{2}$.
5. How can you use the laws of exponents to tell whether $3^4 \cdot 3^{-6}$ is greater than 1 or less than 1? Since the bases are the same, you can add the exponents. $4 + -6$ is $-2$. $3^{-2}$ is a fraction less than 1.

## Demonstrating Skills

**Write each number in scientific notation.**

6. 123,000 $1.23 \times 10^5$
7. 57,700,000 $5.77 \times 10^7$
8. $45 \times 10^6$ $4.5 \times 10^7$
9. $321 \times 10^3$ $3.21 \times 10^5$
10. $684 \times 10^5$ $6.84 \times 10^7$
11. $92 \times 10^7$ $9.2 \times 10^8$
12. Earth is approximately 93,000,000 miles from the Sun. Express this number in scientific notation. $9.3 \times 10^7$
13. Mars is approximately $1.42 \times 10^8$ miles from the Sun. Express this number in standard notation. 142,000,000 miles



3. Possible answers: $\left(\frac{1}{2}\right)^{-1} = \frac{1}{\frac{1}{2}} = 2$, and $2 \cdot 2 = 4$; or

$$\left(\frac{1}{2}\right)^{-1} \cdot \left(\frac{1}{2}\right)^{-1} = \left(\frac{1}{2}\right)^{-1+-1} = \left(\frac{1}{2}\right)^{-2} = \left(\frac{1}{4}\right)^{-1} = \frac{1}{\frac{1}{4}} = 4;$$

$$\text{or } \left(\frac{1}{2}\right)^{-1} \cdot \left(\frac{1}{2}\right)^{-1} = \left(\frac{1}{2} \cdot \frac{1}{2}\right)^{-1} = \left(\frac{1}{4}\right)^{-1} = \frac{1}{\frac{1}{4}} = 4$$

# Review & Self-Assessment

CHAPTER 4

## Chapter Summary

This summary helps students recall the major topics of the chapter.

## Vocabulary

Students should be able to explain each of the terms listed in the vocabulary section.

▶ **Exercises 6–9** Students may not remember how to write numbers in scientific notation. Remind the students that a number written in scientific notation has only one digit in front of the decimal place. To write a number in scientific notation, move the decimal point so that one digit is in front of the decimal place. Count the number of times that you move the decimal point — this is the value of the exponent. The exponent is positive if you are taking a number greater than one and writing it in scientific notation. The exponent is negative if you are taking a number less than one and turning it into scientific notation.

▶ **Exercises 23–30** As students work to simplify expressions involving exponents ask the students to refresh your memory about the rules for simplifying exponents. Hopefully, the students will give you the appropriate rules, if not, assist them in using the appropriate rules to simplify the expressions. In addition, remind students that an exponential expression is not fully simplified until no exponents remain.

▶ **Exercise 32** For many students, it may be helpful to convert all of the numbers into standard form before determining the order. For other students it may be more beneficial to write all of the numbers in scientific notation. Stress to the students that this is a prime example of how their learning styles and comfort level plays into how they approach solving the problem.

Review & Self-Assessment
Chapter 4

14b. $5 \times 10^{-1} \times 10^{-1} \times 10^{-1}$

32a. $1.03 \times 10^{-4}$, $1.1 \times 10^{-3}$, $0.13 \times 10^{-2}$, $10.03 \times 10^{-1}$, $1.1 \times 10^{3}$, $1.03 \times 10^{4}$

32b. $1.03 \times 10^{-4}$, $1.1 \times 10^{-3}$, $1.1 \times 10^{3}$, $1.03 \times 10^{4}$

**14.** Imagine putting a 5-foot fishing rod into this connection of shrinking machines.

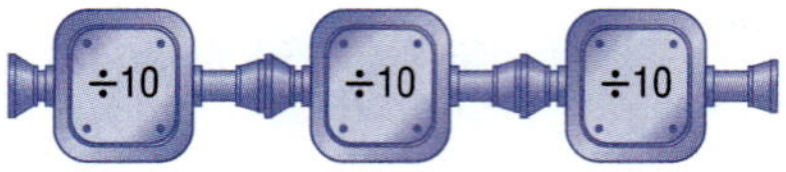


**a.** Write this situation using multiplication. $5 \cdot \frac{1}{10} \cdot \frac{1}{10} \cdot \frac{1}{10}$

**b.** Write this situation using negative exponents.

**c.** What is the length of the exiting fishing rod? 0.005 ft

**Find each missing value.**

**15.** $8.3 \times 10^{?} = 0.0083$ $-3$

**16.** $3.7 \times ? = 0.00037$ $10^{-4}$

**17.** $1.9 \times 10^{?} = 0.19$ $-1$

**18.** $3.2 \times ? = 0.00000032$ $10^{-7}$

**Write each number in standard notation.**

**19.** $1.4 \times 10^{-2}$ 0.014

**20.** $6.21 \times 10^{-5}$ 0.0000621

**21.** $7.52 \times 10^{-3}$ 0.00752

**22.** $8.119 \times 10^{-6}$ 0.000008119

**Simplify each expression as much as possible.**

**23.** $256 \cdot 2^{-5}$ 8

**24.** $3y^{2} \cdot y^{-3}$ $3y^{-1}$, or $\frac{3}{y}$

**25.** $4^{-1} \cdot 4^{-3}$ $\frac{1}{256}$

**26.** $-1^{-3}$ $-1$

**27.** $(-5)^{-2}$ $\frac{1}{25}$

**28.** $-4^{3}$ $-64$

**29.** $-5^{-2}$ $-\frac{1}{25}$ or $-0.04$

**30.** $-4^{-3}$ $-\frac{1}{64}$ or $-0.015625$

**31.** A typical flu virus has a diameter of $2 \times 10^{-7}$ meter. Write the diameter in standard notation. 0.0000002 m

**32.** Consider the following numbers.

| | | |
|---|---|---|
| $1.03 \times 10^{4}$ | $1.1 \times 10^{-3}$ | $1.03 \times 10^{-4}$ |
| $0.13 \times 10^{-2}$ | $1.1 \times 10^{3}$ | $10.03 \times 10^{-1}$ |

**a.** Order the numbers from least to greatest.

**b.** Which numbers are written in scientific notation?

Review & Self-Assessment
Chapter 4

## Test-Taking Practice

***SHORT RESPONSE***

**1** Simplify the expression shown below. Write your answer in standard form.

$$\frac{(5.1 \times 10^3)(2 \times 10^4)}{3 \times 10^9}$$

***Show your work.***

***Answer*** ____________________

*Show your work:*
$\frac{10.2 \times 10^7}{3 \times 10^9} =$
$3.4 \times 10^{-2} = 0.034$

***MULTIPLE CHOICE***

**2** What is $8.2 \times 10^4$ written in standard form?
**A** 0.00082
**B** 8,200
**C** 0.82
**D** 82,000

**3** Write $45.78 \times 10^{-4}$ in scientific notation.
**F** $4.578 \times 10^{-3}$
**G** $4.578 \times 10^{-4}$
**H** $4.578 \times 10^{-5}$
**J** $4.6 \times 10^{-3}$

**4** What is 0.00068 written in scientific notation?
**A** $6.8 \times 10^{-4}$
**B** $6.8 \times 10^{-5}$
**C** $68 \times 10^{-5}$
**D** $0.68 \times 10^{-3}$

**5** Simplify the expression $(6^4 \div 6^{-3}) \times 6^{-5}$.
**F** $6^{-4}$
**G** $6^{-2}$
**H** $6^2$
**J** $6^6$

**6** Which expression is equivalent to $7 \times 3^{-2}$?
**A** $\frac{1}{9^2}$
**B** $\frac{7}{9}$
**C** $10^{-2}$
**D** $21^{-1}$

**7** Simplify the expression $10^{-2} \times 1^{-2} \times 10$.
**F** 0.01
**G** 0.1
**H** 10
**J** 100



**Chapter 4** Review & Self-Assessment **209**

CHAPTER 5

# Geometry in Three Dimensions

## *Chapter Overview*

Students learn to describe a three-dimensional structure by looking at different flat views. They explore the relationship between surface area and volume, and then they use this knowledge as they explore more deeply those relationships while learning about nets that fold into a solid.

Students will then learn how to measure weight and mass of solids in both metric and customary systems of measurements. This will include converting measurements within each system.

## The Big Picture

| Links to the Past | Chapter 5 | Links to the Future |
| --- | --- | --- |
| **Course 1, Chapter 1** (pp. 2–55) Polygons, Angles, and Circles<br>**Course 1, Chapter 7** (pp. 396–465) Area, Volume, and Capacity<br>**Course 2, Chapter 2** (pp. 72–123) Exponents | **Lesson 5.1** (p. 212) Surface Area and Volume | **Course 2, Chapter 7** (pp. 318–365) Real Numbers |
| **Course 1, Chapter 1** (pp. 2–55) Polygons, Angles, and Circles<br>**Course 1, Chapter 7** (pp. 396–465) Area, Volume, and Capacity | **Lesson 5.2** (p. 228) Nets and Solids | **Course 2, Chapter 7** (pp. 318–365) Real Numbers |
| **Courses 1, Chapter 1** (pp. 2–55) Polygons, Angles, and Circles.<br>**Course 1, Chapter 7** (pp. 396–465) Area, Volume, and Capacity. | **Lesson 5.3** (p. 240) Mass and Weight | |

# Mathematical Background

An important part of our geometry strand is developing and improving students' visualization skills. Future mathematical study requires students to picture in their minds things they cannot see with their eyes. For example, in calculus, they must picture two-dimensional shapes rotating to create three-dimensional solids. In fields outside of mathematics, visualization is just as important. Architects must "see" a building from the plans, and surgeons must "see" their way through surgery without really seeing everything.

We work on developing these skills throughout the chapter, in part by introducing nets. Students create their own nets for given solids and analyze whether given nets will, in fact, fold into a closed solid.

**Platonic Solids** Students explore nets and the connection to surface area. Two of the questions students explore relate to making nets from just one shape, primarily just squares or just triangles. This could lead to an exploration of Platonic solids. A Platonic solid is a three-dimensional solid in which all faces are the same regular polygon and the same number of faces meet at each vertex. Within a given Platonic solid, all faces must be equilateral triangles, squares, or other regular polygons. With some guidance, middle school students can create the proof that there are only five possible solids meeting these requirements.

If you want to conduct this exploration of Platonic solids, you should have lots of equilateral triangles, squares, regular pentagons, regular hexagons, and regular heptagons on paper for students to cut out. They will need at least 35 triangles, 10 squares, 15 pentagons, and 3 each of the other shapes.

The idea is to pick a shape and make all the possible Platonic solids with that shape as a face. One question to answer is, What is the minimum number of faces meeting at a vertex? With a little experimenting, students will see that if only two faces meet at a vertex, you can never form a closed solid. So at least three faces must meet at a vertex. Students can then try to create solids by placing 3, 4, 5, and 6 of each shape at a vertex and continuing until the solid closes.

## Additional Reading

According to Lehrer in "Developing Understanding of Measurement," one conceptual foundation of measurement is the following: The sum of the measures of two parts that make up the whole equals the measure of the whole (additivity). In Lesson 5.2, students find the surface area of figures by subdividing them using nets.

CHAPTER 5

# Planning Guide

## *Lesson Resources*

| | Lesson 5.1 (Pacing: 4 days) | Lesson 5.2 (Pacing: 4 days) | Lesson 5.3 (Pacing: 4 days) |
|---|---|---|---|
| **Lesson Title** | **Surface Area and Volume** (p. 212) | **Nets and Solids** (p. 228) | **Mass and Weight** (p. 240) |
| **Lesson Objectives** | • To measure surface area and volume of prisms<br>• To understand that for a given volume, the cube is the rectangular prism with the minimum surface area<br>• To articulate some applications of surface area and volume | • To decide if a given net will fold into a closed three-dimensional solid<br>• To create nets that will fold into given shapes<br>• To use information about the nets of an object to find surface area and volume | • To identify the difference between weight and mass<br>• To measure the mass of an item<br>• To determine the volume of mass an object can hold<br>• To identify and use appropriate units for measuring mass and weight<br>• To convert between units of mass and weight<br>• To use an object's mass or weight as a benchmark for discussing the mass and weight of other items |
| **Materials** | grid paper, colored paper, scissors, tape, rulers, compasses or circle templates | grid paper, scissors, metric ruler, 12-oz. beverage can, tape, Lesson 5.2 Masters 1-11 | kitchen or mail scale in grams, cup measure, flour, water, ruler, scissors, kitchen or postal scale in ounces, bathroom scale in pounds |
| ***Quick Review Math Handbook*** | **Lesson 6.6** Surface Area<br>**Lesson 6.7** Volume | **Lesson 6.6** Surface Area | **Lesson 7.4** Mass and Weight |
| **Print Resources** | CRM Study Guide and Intervention (p. 3)<br>CRM Skills Practice (p. 4)<br>CRM Problem-Solving Practice (p. 5)<br>CRM Enrichment (p. 6)<br>• Investigation Notebook and Reflection Journal<br>• Differentiation Handbook | CRM Study Guide and Intervention (p. 8)<br>CRM Skills Practice (p. 9)<br>CRM Problem-Solving Practice (p. 10)<br>CRM Enrichment (p. 11)<br>• Investigation Notebook and Reflection Journal<br>• Differentiation Handbook | CRM Study Guide and Intervention (p. 24)<br>CRM Skills Practice (p. 25)<br>CRM Problem-Solving Practice (p. 26)<br>CRM Enrichment (p. 27)<br>• Investigation Notebook and Reflection Journal<br>• Differentiation Handbook |
| **Technology Resources** | TeacherWorks Plus<br>Classroom Presentation Toolkit<br>ExamView Assessment Suite<br>StudentWorks Plus<br>Math Online Brain Pops • Concepts in Motion | TeacherWorks Plus<br>Classroom Presentation Toolkit<br>ExamView Assessment Suite<br>StudentWorks Plus<br>Math Online Brain Pops • Concepts in Motion | TeacherWorks Plus<br>Classroom Presentation Toolkit<br>ExamView Assessment Suite<br>StudentWorks Plus<br>Math Online Brain Pops • Concepts in Motion |

*Included in the Impact Mathematics Manipulative Kit

# Assessment Resources

## MARS Assessment: Teaching with Purpose

**Toothpaste**

In *Toothpaste,* students solve problems about the volume of a cylinder. Students calculate the diameter of a cylinder of toothpaste; the volume used per application; and how long the toothpaste cylinder will last.

**Targeting the Task**

- **Diagnostic**—Use Exercises 1–3 in the *Toothpaste* assessment to determine students' understanding of how to work with problems about the volume and diameter of a cylinder. For those students who do not have this understanding, completing this unit is needed.
- **Formative**—Exercises 1–3 can be administered individually according to the lessons.
- **Summative**—Administer the complete *Toothpaste* performance-based assessment.

CRM **Chapter 5 MARS Assessment** (pp. 44–46)

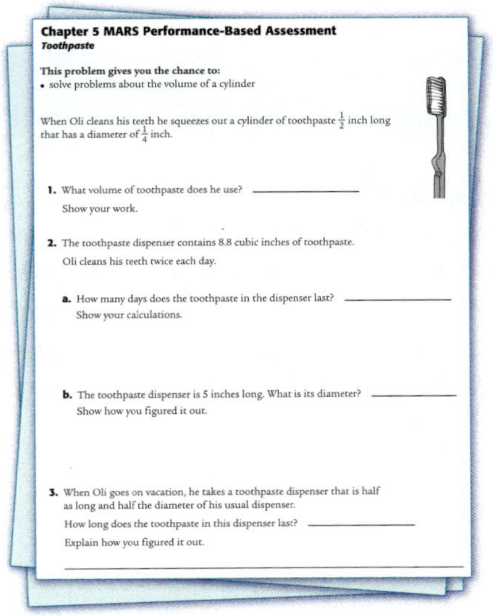
**Chapter 5 MARS Performance-Based Assessment**
***Toothpaste***

**This problem gives you the chance to:**
- solve problems about the volume of a cylinder

When Oli cleans his teeth he squeezes out a cylinder of toothpaste $\frac{1}{2}$ inch long that has a diameter of $\frac{1}{4}$ inch.

1. What volume of toothpaste does he use? ________
   Show your work.
2. The toothpaste dispenser contains 8.8 cubic inches of toothpaste.
   Oli cleans his teeth twice each day.
   a. How many days does the toothpaste in the dispenser last? ________
      Show your calculations.
   b. The toothpaste dispenser is 5 inches long. What is its diameter? ________
      Show how you figured it out.
3. When Oli goes on vacation, he takes a toothpaste dispenser that is half as long and half the diameter of his usual dispenser.
   How long does the toothpaste in this dispenser last? ________
   Explain how you figured it out.

## Assessment Planning Guide

Assessments are available for investigations, lessons, and chapters.

ExamView Assessment Suite — Customize and create multiple versions of tests and quizzes.

| | Student Edition | Teacher Edition | Other Resources |
|---|---|---|---|
| Diagnostic | | | CRM Chapter 5 Pretest (p. 29)<br>Math Online Online Chapter Quiz |
| Formative | Share & Summarize (pp. 215, 219, 230, 233, 234, 244, 247, 250) | Troubleshooting (pp. 229, 230, 233, 242, 245, 250)<br>On the Spot Assessment (pp. 212, 213, 217, 231, 241, 244, 245, 246, 248)<br>Quick Check (pp. 227, 239, 255)<br>Quick Quiz (pp. 227, 239, 255) | |
| Summative | Review & Self-Assessment (pp. 256–259) | | CRM Chapter 5 Test: Forms A and B (pp. 33–40)<br>CRM Standardized Test Practice (p. 42) |
| Performance-Based | In Your Own Words (pp. 226, 238, 254) | | CRM Chapter Performance Assessment (p. 41)<br>CRM MARS Performance-Based Assessment (p. 44)<br>CRM Semester Performance Assessment (p. 57) |

# Differentiated Instruction

## *Reaching* All Learners

Below are suggestions on differentiating the materials presented in this chapter. Additional modifications should be considered.

### Approaching Level AL

**Solids to Nets** After completing Lesson 5.2, ask each student to bring in an example of a solid, such as a soup can. Encourage the students to be creative with their objects. Once the students bring the object to class, have the students create a sketch of the object and a net of the object. Remind the students to include measurements in their sketch and labels on their nets.

### Beyond Level BL

**Prime Factorization and Volume** After completing Lesson 5.3, place the students in small groups and give each group a number that has a considerable list of prime factors. Have the students write out the prime factorization of the number, and determine at least 3 possible dimensions of a rectangular prism that has that assigned volume. Ask the students to create a net for each of the possible prisms. Then ask the students to determine the surface area that corresponds to each net.

### On Level OL

**Nets to Solids** After completing Lesson 5.2, have students take a complicated solid three-dimensional picture (such as a sand castle or an ornate building) and turn it into a net. Include enough dimensions so that the students can then determine the volume of the object and its surface area.

### English Language Learners ELL

**Solid Flash Cards** After completing Lesson 5.2, ask students to make a list of all the words that represent solid shapes in their first language. Once the list is completed, have the students write each word on one side of a note card with a picture of the solid. Then assist the students in determining the proper English word that matches the solid, and write that word on the other side of the note card. The students now have a set of flash cards to assist them in understanding the proper name for the solid in English and their first language.

**KEY**

AL Approaching Level OL On Level BL Beyond Level ELL English Language Learners

## Intervention Planning Guide

CRM Assess students' prerequisite skills and knowledge using the **Chapter Pretest** found in the Chapter 5 Resource Masters, p. 29.

| Intensive Intervention<br>two or more years below grade level | Strategic Intervention<br>below grade level | On Level | Beyond Level |
|---|---|---|---|
| **If** students miss 75% of the exercises:<br>**Then** use *Math Triumphs*, an intensive intervention | **If** students miss 50% of the exercises:<br>**Then** choose a resource: | **If** students miss 25% of the exercises:<br>**Then** choose a resource: | **If** students miss 0%–10% of the exercises:<br>**Then** choose a resource: |
| *Math Triumphs*, Grade 7<br>• Chapter 6: Three-Dimensional Figures | CRM Study Guide and Intervention (pp. 3, 8, 24)<br>• Investigation Notebook and Reflection Journal<br>• Differentiation Handbook<br>Math Online Brain Pops • Concepts in Motion | CRM Skills Practice (pp. 4, 9, 25)<br>CRM Problem-Solving Practice (pp. 5, 10, 26)<br>• Investigation Notebook and Reflection Journal | CRM Enrichment (pp. 6, 11, 27)<br>• Differentiation Handbook |

### Literature Connections

**Recommended Outside Reading for Students**

**Nonfiction**

Swetz, F. *Learning Activities from the History of Mathematics.* J Weston Walch, 1993.

Biographies of 23 mathematicians from many centuries and cultures are features in this book, along with study questions. The book investigates a variety of historical problems, including the geometry concepts studied in this chapter—perimeter, area, and circumference.

**Fiction**

Neuschwander, Cindy. *Sir Cumference and the Dragon of Pi.* Charlesbridge Publishing, 1999.

This book takes readers on an adventure as young boy, Radius, gives his father, Sir Cumference, the wrong potion to cure a bellyache. Radius must solve the riddle of the ratio of a circle's circumference to its diameter to get the dosage to cure his father. Written as a fantasy, with a dragon as a main character, the book introduces the concept of pi.

### Professional Development

Targeted professional development has been articulated throughout the *IMPACT Mathematics* series. The **McGraw-Hill Professional Development Video Library** provides short videos that support the mathematics standards. Log on to www.glencoe.com.

Model Lessons

Instructional Strategies

CHAPTER 5

# Geometry in Three Dimensions

## Introduce

**Patterns and Plans** Have a volunteer read aloud to the class the first paragraph. Discuss the meaning of two-dimensional drawings and three-dimensional drawings. When students are comfortable with the meaning of these two terms, ask another volunteer to read aloud the last two paragraphs. Discuss the meaning of elevations and blueprints. Encourage students to think of places where they might use a blueprint.

If possible, bring a blueprint to class. Blueprints of houses, office buildings, cars, and even television show spaceships are available on the Internet for you to print before class.

**Think About It** Discuss ideas with students. You may wish to give some hints if students are having difficulty. Some examples include: fashion designers, automobile manufacturers, landscape designers, and set designers for theatrical productions.

CHAPTER 5

# Geometry in Three Dimensions

### Contents in Brief



## Real-Life Math

**Patterns and Plans** Some of the most powerful examples of using two-dimensional drawings to represent three-dimensional objects can be found in different types of designing. Architects must be very skilled at drawing three-dimensional objects so there is no confusion about what the drawings represent.

Before a house is built, an architect creates drawings of what the house will look like. The drawings include elevations that show how the house will look from two sides.

In addition, the plans for a house include blueprints, which show how the interior will be divided into rooms. Blueprints show details such as where doors are and which way they open as well as where to place items like sinks, the stove, and the bathtub. Construction workers and contractors refer to blueprints when they work on projects.

**Think About It** Can you think of other careers or companies that use two-dimensional drawings to represent three-dimensional objects?

**Math Online** Take the **Chapter Readiness Quiz** at glencoe.com.

210

### Chapter Resources

- CRM Chapter 5 Resource Masters
- CRM English/Spanish Family Letter (pp. 1–2)
- CRM Lesson Masters (pp. 13–23)
- CRM Chapter 5 Pretest (pp. 29–32)
- CRM Chapter 5 Tests (pp. 33–40)
- **Math Online** Online Readiness Quiz • eGlossary

# Dear Family,

In Chapter 5, the class will begin studying three-dimensional geometry, focusing on prisms and cylinders. Students will learn how to use two-dimensional nets to represent three-dimensional solids. They will also learn the relationship between measures of mass and weight.

### Key Concept–Nets

A **net** is a flat figure that can be folded to form a closed, three-dimensional object. This type of object is called a geometric **solid**.

Nets made of squares and rectangles can be used to represent cubes and **prisms**. Nets that include circles can be used to represent **cylinders**.

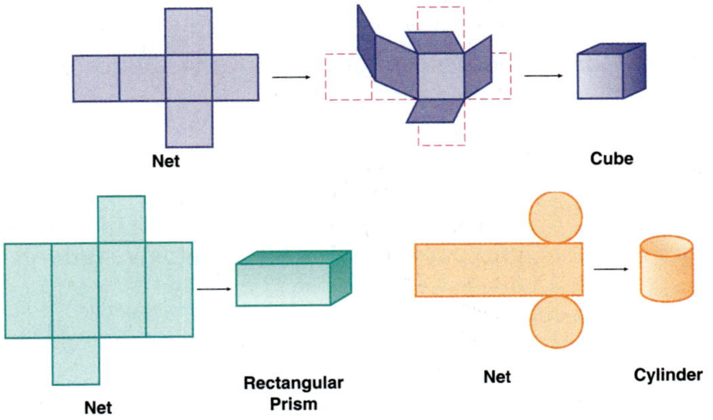


Students will use nets and models to find the surface area and volume of geometric solids. Finally, your student will explore weight and mass.

### Chapter Vocabulary

| | |
|---|---|
| **mass** | **volume** |
| **surface area** | **weight** |

### Home Activities

- Look at common household objects, such as tissue boxes and canned goods, from different perspectives.
- Make nets from food containers by deconstructing objects, such as empty cereal boxes and movie theater popcorn tubs.
- Estimate the mass and weight of objects, like pencils, books, dinner plates, chairs, and tables. Discuss the appropriate unit of measure for each, such as milligrams, grams, kilograms, ounces, or pounds.

## Family Letter

Another version of the Family Letter, available in English and Spanish, is found in the Chapter 5 Resource Masters. You may want to send a copy of this letter home with your students.

**Key Concept–Nets** A net is a pattern in two-dimensions that can be cut and folded to represent a three-dimensional object or solid. Often students struggle with visualizing a solid and a net can be made to act as a model and will be a valuable tool to these students. The students will also use nets to assist in determining surface area, and volume.

### Home Activities

- Many household objects can be represented with a net. Have students ask their families to describe the shape of an object and to sketch a net. If the object is complicated, it may be best to deconstruct the object to create the net.
- Many items for household consumption have a mass listed on the package. Have students and their families compare the units for mass that are listed on various items. What are the most common units seen? What are the least common units seen?

## Key Vocabulary

**English (Spanish)** *Introduce the most important terms from Chapter 5.*

**mass (masa)** A measurement of the amount of matter in an object. (p. 240)

**weight (peso)** The pull of gravity on an amount of matter. (p. 240)

**surface area (área de superficie)** The area of the exterior surface of an object, measured in square units. (p. 213)

**volume (volumen)** The space inside a three-dimensional object, measured in cubic units. (p. 213)

LESSON

# 5.1 Surface Area and Volume

## Objectives

- ▶ To calculate the surface area and volume of a prism
- ▶ To use prime factorization to determine possible dimensions of a prism if given the volume
- ▶ To understand that for a given volume, the cube is the rectangular prism with the minimum surface area
- ▶ To articulate some applications of surface area and volume

## *Overview*

In this lesson, students explore surface area and volume relationships in geometric solids as well as some applications of these ideas to science. The notion of counting cubes to find volume is used as a way to create a formula for the volume of any prism: area of base times height, or perhaps better, area of one base times the distance between the bases. Students explore some ideas about minimizing surface area for a given volume.

## *Advance Preparation*

You may want to have models of solids available for students to use to help visualize the objects. If models are not available, grid paper may assist in helping students to create their own models.

| | Summary | Materials | On Your Own Exercises (pp. 223–227) | Assessment Opportunities |
|---|---|---|---|---|
| **Investigation 1** (p. 213) Pacing: 2 days | Students will use what they know about area of two-dimensional objects to determine surface area and volume of prisms. | (optional) grid paper, rulers, scissors, tape | Practice & Apply: 1–5<br>Connect & Extend: 11–13<br>Mixed Review: 18–34 | • On the Spot Assessment (pp. 212, 213)<br>• Share & Summarize (p. 215) |
| **Investigation 2** (p. 216) Pacing: 1 day | Students generalize the volume formula to include other prisms and cylinders. | (optional) grid paper, rulers, scissors, tape | Practice & Apply: 6–10<br>Connect & Extend: 14–17<br>Mixed Review: 18–34 | • On the Spot Assessment (p. 217)<br>• Share & Summarize (p. 219) |
| **Inquiry Investigation 3** (p. 220) Pacing: 1 day | Students use their knowledge of surface area and volume to build a better beverage can. | colored paper, scissors, tape, rulers, compasses or circle templates | | |

# Leveled Lesson Resources

CRM *Available in:* **Chapter 5 Resource Masters**

Also on TeacherWorks™
Lesson 5.1

## Study Guide and Intervention (p. 3) AL

**Lesson 5.1 Study Guide and Intervention**
***Surface Area and Volume***

The volume $V$ of a prism, a cylinder, or any three dimensional object is the area of the base $B$ times the height $h$, or $V = Bh$.

The surface area of a prism is equal to the sum of the areas of its faces. For a rectangular prism with length $l$, width $w$, and height $h$, the surface area is $S = 2lw + 2lh + 2wh$. Remember that the area of a circle is equal to $\pi r^2$.

**Example 1** Find the volume of the prism to the right.

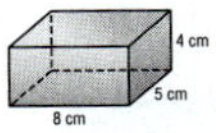

$V = Bh$ — Volume of a prism
$V = (l \cdot w)h$ — The base is a rectangle, so $B = l \cdot w$.
$V = (8 \cdot 5)4$ — $l = 8, w = 5, h = 4$
$V = 160$ — Simplify.

The volume is 160 cubic centimeters.

**Example 2** Find the surface area of the prism above.

$SA = 2lw + 2lh + 2wh$ — Surface area of a prism
$SA = 2(8)(5) + 2(8)(4) + 2(5)(4)$ — $l = 8, w = 5, h = 4$
$SA = 184$ — Simplify.

The surface area is 184 square centimeters.

**Exercises**

**Find the volume of each solid. Round to the nearest tenth if necessary.**

1. 2. 3.

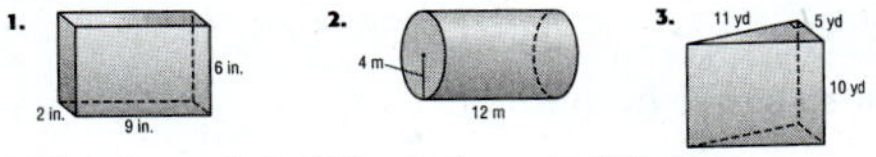

**Find the surface area of each solid. Round to the nearest tenth if necessary.**

4. rectangular prism: length, 2.3 in.; width, 7 in.; height, 8 in.
5. cylinder: radius, 4 cm; height, 8.2 cm
6. Find the area of the parallelogram below. If you built a structure 3 inches high with this parallelogram as its base, what would be its volume? What would be its surface area?

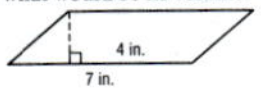

## Skills Practice (p. 4) AL OL

**Lesson 5.1 Skills Practice**
***Surface Area and Volume***

**Solve.**

1. How much wood will be needed to make a toy box that is 3 feet by 1 foot by 1.5 feet?
2. Consider the triangle shown at the right.
   a. What is the area of the triangle?
   b. If you built a prism 15 cm high using this triangle as a base, what would be its volume?

**Find the volume and surface area of each solid. Round to the nearest tenth if necessary.**

3. 4. 5.

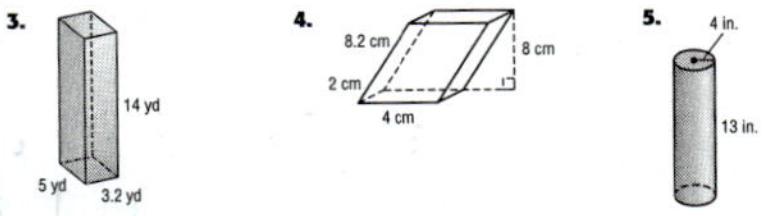

6. Consider the triangle shown at the right.
   a. What is the area of the triangle?
   b. If you built a prism 7 centimeters high using this triangle as a base, what would be its volume?

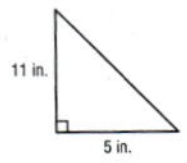

7. Consider the pentagon shown at the right.
   a. What is the area of the pentagon?
   b. If you built a prism 3 inches high using this pentagon as a base, what would be its volume?

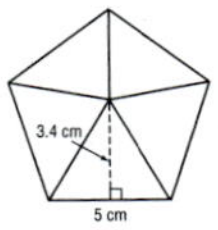

## Problem-Solving Practice (p. 5) AL OL

**Lesson 5.1 Problem-Solving Practice**
***Surface Area and Volume***

**Solve.**

1. **Donations** Lawrence is donating some outgrown clothes to charity. The dimensions of the box he is using are shown at the right. How many cubic feet of clothes will fit in the box?

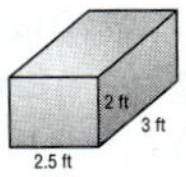

2. **Camping** The entrance to a tent used for camping is shown at the right. Find the area of the entrance of the tent. If the tent is 8 feet long, what is the volume of the tent?

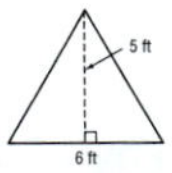

3. **Farm Life** A trough used for watering horses is shown in the figure at the right. The trough is half of a cylinder. How manycubic feet of water will the trough hold? Round to the nearesttenth.

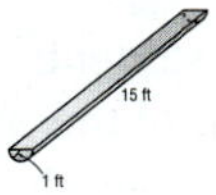

4. **Banking** The top and sides of the cake shown at the right are to be covered with frosting. Calculate the area that will be covered with frosting.

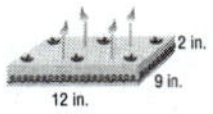

5. **Gifts** A birthday gift is placed inside the box shown at the right. What is the minimum amount of wrapping paper needed to wrap this gift?

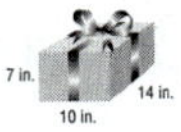

6. **Soup** Consider the design for a can of soup shown at the right. What is the area of the base of the can? If the can were 4 inches tall, how much soup would it hold? Round to the nearest tenth.

## Enrichment (p. 6) BL

**Lesson 5.1 Enrichment**
***Surface Area and Volume***

**Sliced Solids**

In the diagrams on this page, a plane slices through a solid figure. The intersection of the plane with the solid is called a *cross section*. The drawings for each problem show a sliced solid and the dimensions of the resulting cross section.

**Find the surface areas of the two solids that result from the slice. Round to the nearest tenth.**

1. One-fourth of the cube is sliced off the top.

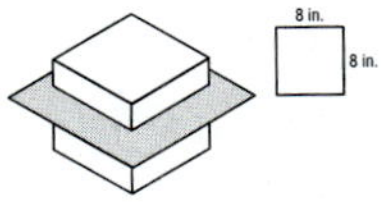

2. One-third of the prism is sliced off the back.

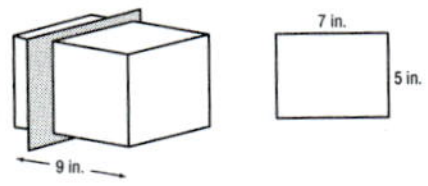

**Find the volume of the two solids that result from the slice. Round to the nearest tenth.**

3. The cube is sliced in half.

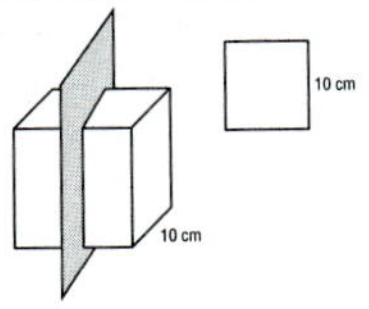

4. The cylinder is sliced in half.

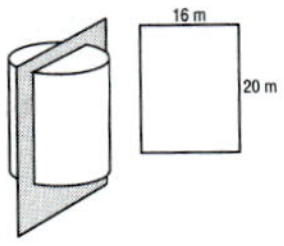

5. The cylinder is sliced in half.

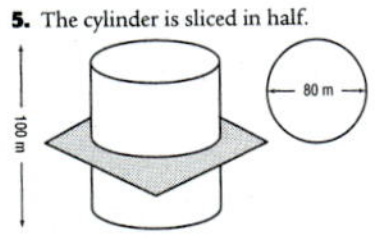

6. The prism is sliced in half.

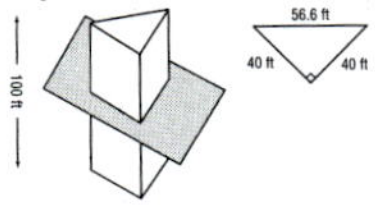

## Lesson Quick Quiz (p. 7) AL OL BL

**Lesson 5.1 Quick Quiz**

1. A block prism has a volume of 36 cubic units.
   a. What is the least surface area it could have?
   b. What is the greatest surface area it could have?
2. Find a cylinder and a rectangular prism that have the same volume. Describe the dimensions of each object. (Hint: It may be easier to start with the cylinder.)

# Additional Lesson Resources

### Teacher Tech Tools
- TeacherWorks
- ExamView Assessment Suite
- Classroom Presentation Toolkit
- Advance Tracker

### Student Tech Tools
- StudentWorks Plus
- Math Online eGlossary
- Concepts in Motion

### Other Print Products
- Investigation Notebook and Reflection Journal
- Quick Review Math Handbook

## LESSON 5.1 Surface Area and Volume

### Introduce

**Surface Area and Volume** Students may need some refreshing when it comes to the meanings and computations involved in determining the surface area and volume of solids. It may be advantageous to review how to compute the area and perimeter of rectangles and squares prior to beginning this lesson.

#### Think & Discuss

Direct students' attention to the figures at the top of the page. As you discuss the two questions in the Think & Discuss section, compile a list of what the prisms have in common:

- two identical faces (same size and shape)
- the identical two faces are opposite and parallel
- the other faces are parallelograms

You can use this list to lead into the definition of a prism.

Students may divide the prisms into two types: those with parallelogram faces and those with rectangular faces. This is because many students do not see rectangles as a special kind of parallelogram, one with all right angles, but rather see them as two different kinds of shapes. If you notice this, you may want to take a moment to clarify the ideas. First ask students to define a parallelogram. A good definition would be something like "a quadrilateral with opposite sides parallel." Ask them whether a rectangle fits that definition. Is it a quadrilateral? Are opposite sides parallel? So, is every rectangle a parallelogram? Yes! Is every parallelogram a rectangle? No! These ideas are not essential for moving on in this lesson, but it is nice to clarify these issues when they come up.

# LESSON 5.1 Surface Area and Volume



### Vocabulary

**prism**

① They all have two faces that are the same size and shape and parallel to each other; their other faces are parallelograms.

② All the prisms have faces, and all their faces have straight sides. Some of the nonprisms have circular faces; the sphere does not have faces. Some of the nonprisms have a flat face on one end and come to a point on the opposite end; none of the prisms are like this. The sides of some of the nonprisms are triangles; all the sides of the prisms are parallelograms.

These figures are *prisms.*

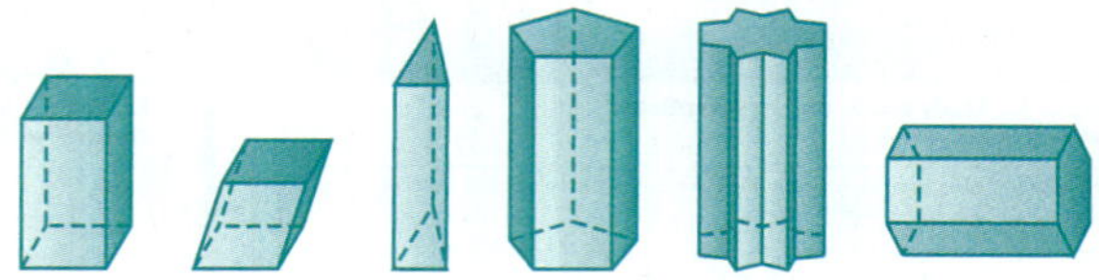

These figures are not prisms.

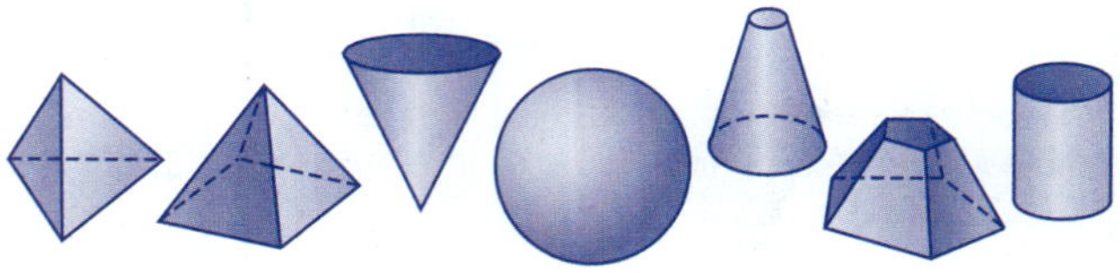

#### Think & Discuss

What do all the prisms have in common? See ①.

How are the nonprisms different from the prisms? See ②.

All **prisms** have two identical, parallel faces. These two faces are always polygons. A prism's other faces are always parallelograms.

A prism is sometimes referred to by the shape of the two identical faces on its ends. For example, a *triangular prism* has triangular faces on its ends, and a *rectangular prism* has rectangular faces on its ends.

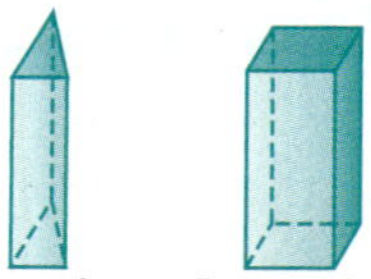

Triangular Prism    Rectangular Prism



#### On the Spot Assessment

What are the defining characteristics of a prism? A prism has two identical parallel faces that are polygons while the other faces are all parallelograms.

# Investigation 1 Measure Prisms

**Vocabulary**

surface area

volume

You encounter prisms in many everyday situations. Your bedroom is a prism. A cereal box is a prism. The box you receive in the mail with a new book is also a prism. Each prism has different characteristics.

In this investigation, you will explore two specific characteristics of prisms: **surface area** and **volume**.

### Think & Discuss

Look around your classroom and choose a prism.

What are the dimensions of your prism? You can estimate the dimensions if it is difficult to measure them. Answers will vary depending on object.

What does it mean to measure the volume of your prism? Estimate its volume and include units in your answer. See ①.

What does it mean to measure the surface area of your prism? Estimate its surface area and include units in your answer. See ② in margin.

① Answers should refer to students' prior experiences in Course 1. Volume tells the amount of space an object takes up, which can often be measured by determining how much the object will hold (in terms of capacity). Volume is measured in cubic units and takes into account the area of the base and the height of the three-dimensional object.

### Develop & Understand: A

**1.** Consider a box with a bottom that is 16 centimeters by 6 centimeters and a height of 8 centimeters.

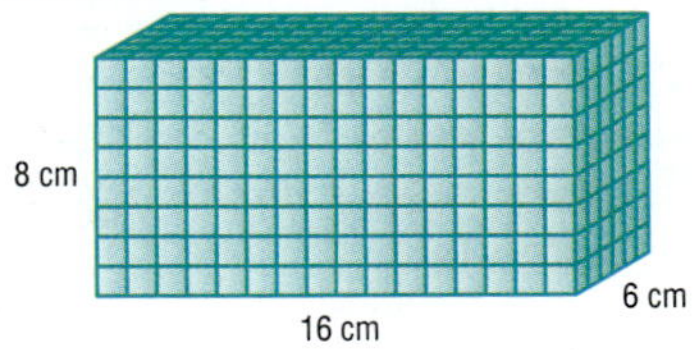


**a.** How many centimeter cubes would be needed to cover the bottom of the box? It will take 96 cubes to cover the bottom; $16 \cdot 6 = 96$.

**b.** How many layers like the one covering the bottom could be stacked in the box? The height allows for 8 layers.

**c.** How many total cubes would be needed to fill the box? It will take 768 cubes to fill the box.

**d.** What calculation can you use to show the number of cubes needed? How is this related to the dimensions of the box? $16 \cdot 6 \cdot 8 = 768$ cubes. The formula is each side measure multiplied together.

**2.** Mrs. White needs to purchase a briefcase. She found two briefcases that she can afford, but she is not sure which will give her room to pack the most belongings. Determine the volume of each briefcase to find out which will hold more. See margin.

Briefcase A: 17 inches long, 12 inches wide, 6 inches deep

Briefcase B: 18 inches long, 10 inches wide, 6.5 inches deep



# Investigation 1

***On Your Own Exercises***
Pages 223–227
Exercises 1–5, 11–13

**Prisms** You may want to review some of the terms used to describe prisms. Show students a rectangular prism and discuss the properties. Point out the relationship between the planes of the figure, noting pairs of parallel lines, perpendicular lines, and skew lines. Be sure students are comfortable with the terms.

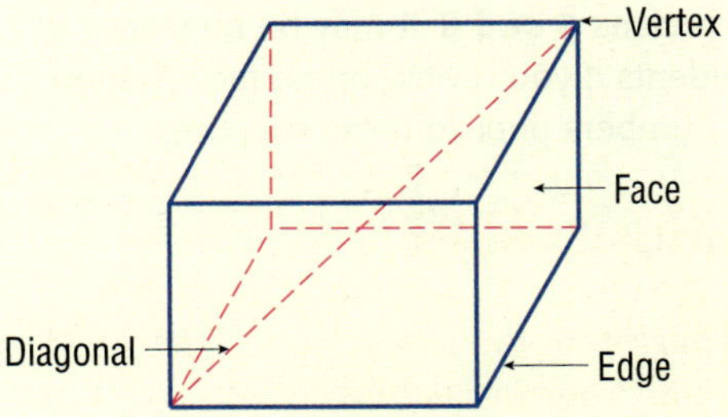


### Think & Discuss

*Suggested Grouping: Pairs*

After students select their item, have each student discuss the questions with their partner. Have volunteers share their responses as a class discussion to make sure that students are on the right path.

### Develop & Understand: A

*Suggested Grouping: Pairs*

▶ **Exercise 1** It may be useful for students to have a model of the prism for this question. The model can be made of cubes, or a paper model made from grid paper.

▶ **Exercise 2** Remind students of what shape the briefcases represent. They may not realize that the briefcase is an example of a rectangular prism.

### On the Spot Assessment

What is the volume of a rectangular prism that measures 4 inches long, 6 inches tall, and 3 inches deep? 72 cubic inches

### Additional Answers

② Answers should refer to students' prior experiences in Course 1. Surface area includes the area of each face of a three-dimensional object. Area tells what is needed to cover a flat surface, so surface area tells what is needed to cover all the flat surfaces of a three-dimensional object. Surface area is measured by finding the dimensions of each face, calculating its area, and adding those areas together for the object.

2. Briefcase A has a volume (capacity) of $17 \cdot 12 \cdot 6 = 1{,}224$ cubic inches; Briefcase B has a volume (capacity) of $18 \cdot 10 \cdot 6.5 = 1{,}170$ cubic inches; Briefcase A will hold more of Mrs. White's belongings.

▶ **Exercise 3** Remind students that the surface area of an object is the sum of the areas of all of the exterior surfaces.

## Develop & Understand: B

*Suggested Grouping: Individuals*

▶ **Exercise 4** Students may become discouraged and think that they are doing something incorrect when they find the volume of each prism to be the same. They may become even more discouraged when they compute the surface area and find all of these values different. Make sure to discuss why this occurs.

▶ **Exercises 5 and 6** It may be beneficial to students if you review prime factorization of numbers prior to these exercises.

**Additional Answers**

5. $72 = 2 \cdot 2 \cdot 2 \cdot 3 \cdot 3$; For example, by multiplying two factors together you could have a box with dimensions of 4 by 3 by 6 or 4 by 2 by 9.

5a.

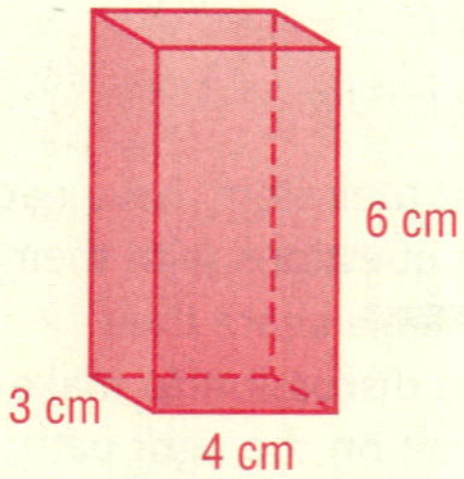


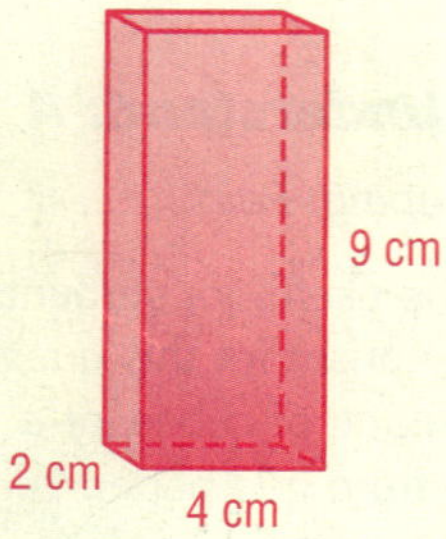


**See Additional Answers on page 259A for Exercise 6.**

3. Nancy plans to store flour in a plastic container in her pantry. Three rectangular prism containers each hold the same amount of flour. Nancy wants to make an environmentally friendly decision by choosing the container that is made from the smallest amount of plastic. Find the surface area of each container to determine which is produced using the least material.

   Container 1: 6 inches by 3 inches by 8 inches

   Container 2: 4 inches by 6 inches by 6 inches

   Container 3: 4 inches by 2 inches by 18 inches

## Develop & Understand: B

4. Compare the volumes and surface areas of boxes A, B, and C.

   Box A:

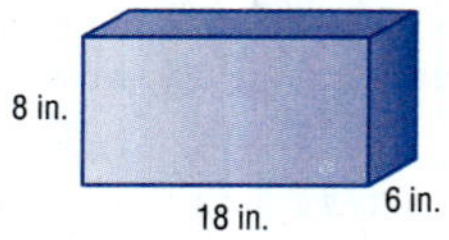


   Box B:

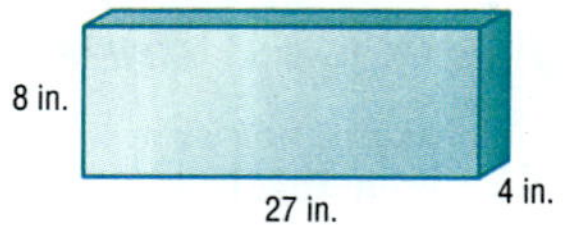


   Box C:

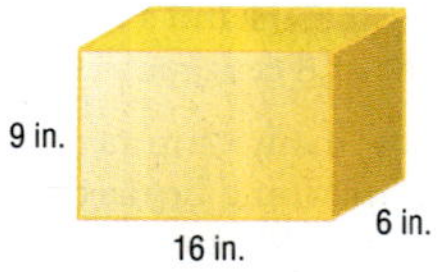


5. Determine the prime factorization of 72. See margin.
   a. Use this information to sketch and label two different rectangular prisms with a volume of 72 cubic centimeters. See margin.
   b. Which of your prisms has the greatest surface area? See below.
6. Determine the prime factorization of 600. See margin.
   a. Use this information to sketch and label two different rectangular prisms with a volume of 600 cubic centimeters. See margin.
   b. Which of your prisms has the least surface area?
   Answers will vary. A prism with dimensions 10 cm by 10 cm by 6 cm has the least surface area.

3. All the containers hold 144 cubic inches; Container 1 has a surface area of $2(6 \cdot 3) + 2(3 \cdot 8) + 2(6 \cdot 8) = 36 + 48 + 96 = 180$ square inches; Container 2 has a surface area of $4(4 \cdot 6) + 2(6 \cdot 6) = 96 + 72 = 168$ square inches; Container 3 has a surface area of $2(4 \cdot 2) + 2(2 \cdot 18) + 2(4 \cdot 18) = 16 + 72 + 144 = 232$ square inches; Nancy should buy Container 2.
4. All three boxes have a volume of 864 cubic inches. Box A has a surface area of 600 square inches. Box B has a surface area of 712 square inches. Box C has a surface area of 588 square inches. Boxes can have the same volume but different surface areas.

5b. Answers will vary. A prism with dimensions 1 cm by 1 cm by 72 cm has the greatest surface area.



## Mathematical Background

Prime factorization is a unique way of looking at a number, and then translating the information into possible measurements for computing the volume of a prism. The measurements are found by multiplying values from the prime factors so that you end up with 3 values. You want only three values, because the volume of a prism is found by taking the product of the length, width, and height of the prism.

**Real-World Link**
One feature of a vehicle given in cubic units is the *cargo room.* This is the space available in the trunk of the vehicle. If an employer provides a car to an employee, there may be a minimum amount of cargo room required to carry materials.

9. Greatest surface area: a prism with dimensions 1 yd by 1 yd by 8 yd; Least surface area: a prism with dimensions 2 yd by 2 yd by 2 yd

10a. Yes, there is a pattern. For each inch the length increases, the surface area increases by 22 square inches. The volume increases by 30 cubic inches.

## Think & Discuss

Consider your answers to Exercises 5 and 6. Work with a partner to state a formula to find the volume of a rectangular prism.

Can you think of another way to write the formula? Volume = length × width × height; Volume = area of the base × height

## Develop & Understand: C

**Use your calculator for the following exercises.**

**7.** Find the volume of a rectangular prism with dimensions 6.5 cm by 4 cm by 10.2 cm. 265.2 cubic centimeters

**8.** A rectangular prism has a volume of 48 cubic feet and a surface area of 88 square feet. What are its dimensions? 6 feet × 4 feet × 2 feet

**9.** A rectangular prism has a volume of 8 cubic yards. Assume the dimensions are whole numbers. What dimensions yield a prism with the greatest surface area? The least surface area?

You have looked at the surface area and volume of many different rectangular prisms. Now you will explore what happens when you change a dimension of the prism by a unit.

**10.** Complete the following table about a rectangular prism.

| Length (inches) | Width (inches) | Height (inches) | Surface Area ($in^2$) | Volume ($in^3$) |
|---|---|---|---|---|
| 4 | 5 | 6 | 148 $in^2$ | 120 $in^3$ |
| 5 | 5 | 6 | 170 $in^2$ | 150 $in^3$ |
| 6 | 5 | 6 | 192 $in^2$ | 180 $in^3$ |
| 7 | 5 | 6 | 214 $in^2$ | 210 $in^3$ |

**a.** Is there a pattern to the increase in surface area? In volume?

**b.** Explain why a pattern does or does not exist. See margin.

**c.** What happens if you keep the length as 4 inches, keep the height as 6 inches, and increase the width of the prism by 1-inch increments? See margin.

## Share & Summarize 1–4. See margin.

**1.** How do you calculate the volume of a rectangular prism?

**2.** How do you calculate the surface area of a rectangular prism?

**3.** If you know the volume of a rectangular prism, can you always determine its surface area? Why or why not?

**4.** How can prime factorization help you design a rectangular prism with a given volume?



## Think & Discuss

*Suggested Grouping: Pairs*

This asks the students to look at their work and write a formula for volume in two different ways. The students may need a hint with the second way. Tell them to think about area and how area relates to volume.

## Develop & Understand: C

*Suggested Grouping: Individuals*

▶ **Exercises 8 and 9** These exercises may be difficult for the students. Tell students that the dimensions will be whole numbers. If they are still having difficulty, encourage students to use prime factorization to find the volume and then check to see if the surface area is correct.

▶ **Exercise 10a** If students are not able to see a pattern, encourage them to look at the differences between the values in each column.

**Wrap-Up** Once the students have completed the exercises, have them form pairs and discuss their results. Once the pairs have had time to talk, ask the pairs to form small groups. To review what students have learned ask each small group to share a solution to the exercises.

## Share & Summarize

These questions would make an excellent check for understanding. Put students in groups of four. Ask each person to take out a sheet of paper and to fold it twice, once the long way, and once the short way. In each box they will answer a question. All students begin with the first question. Once everyone has finished, pass the sheet to the left, check the solution to the first question, and answer the second question. Repeat until all questions are answered and the paper is back with the person who wrote the answer to the first question.

**Additional Answers**

10b. The pattern exists because you are multiplying 5 and 6 by one more. For surface area, you have an increase of 5 on two sides and an increase of 6 on 2 sides, 5 · 2 + 6 · 2 = 22. For volume, you have an increase of 1 · 5 · 6.

10c. The pattern would stay the same. The surface area and volume will also stay the same, but the size of the increments will change. It does not matter which side is a specific measurement. Because of the associative law of multiplication, the order in which numbers are multiplied does not change the product.

**See Additional Answers on page 259A for Share & Summarize Exercises 1–4.**

## Investigation 2

***On Your Own Exercises***
Pages 223–227
Exercises 6–10, 14–17

**Volume** In Course 1, students explored the concept of volume using unit blocks, with an edge length of 1 unit. The same unit blocks are used here. In this investigation, students examine prisms that are not block structures and continue their exploration of volume. Students are introduced to prisms with triangles and parallelograms as bases, as well as to cylinders, prism-like figures. Students use the same fundamental principle of building up from the base with layers of blocks in the shapes of the bases.

### Develop & Understand: A

*Suggested Grouping: Pairs*

If possible, borrow modeling clay from an art teacher and model the solids described in Exercises 1b, 1c, 2b, and 2c. Foam blocks from the floral department of a crafts store can also be used.

▶ **Exercise 1** Students are asked to think about a triangular base in terms of a square and should realize that the area of the base is half the area of the square. They are then asked to imagine having blocks the "right shape" that would fit this triangular base with height of one unit, the same height as the blocks they've been using.

▶ **Exercise 2** Students should notice that the block base has the same area as the parallelogram, and thus the area is 1 square unit.

**Math Link**
If time permits, assist the students in constructing their own one unit block using grid paper.

## Investigation 2 Volume of Prisms and Cylinders

**Vocabulary**
**base**
**cylinder**

Will your method for finding the volume of a rectangular prism work for other prisms? The exercises that follow will help you draw a conclusion.

Remember that a prism has two identical, parallel faces that can be any type of polygon. These faces are called the **bases** of the prism.

**Math Link**
Your block has an edge length of 1 unit and a volume of 1 cubic unit. Each face has an area of 1 square unit.

### Develop & Understand: A

**1.** This triangle is half of the face of a square block that has an edge length of one unit.

**a.** What is the area of this triangle? $\frac{1}{2}$ square unit

**b.** If you cut one of your blocks in half as shown here, you could build a structure 1 unit high with the triangle as its base. What would be the volume of this structure? $\frac{1}{2}$ cubic unit

**c.** If you built a structure 10 units high that had the triangle as its base, what would be its volume? 5 cubic units

**2.** The dashed lines on the parallelogram below show the relationship between the parallelogram and a face of one of your blocks.

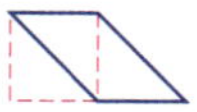

**a.** What is the area of the parallelogram? 1 square unit

**b.** If you had blocks like the one shown here, you could build a structure 2 units high that had the parallelogram as its base. What would be its volume? 2 cubic units

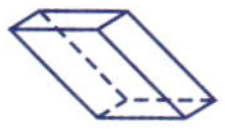

**c.** If you could build a structure $h$ units high with this parallelogram as its base, what would be its volume? $h$ cubic units



### *Reaching All Learners*

**AL Approaching Level** Students who are having difficulty visualizing the solids will benefit by having manipulatives on hand that they can use to construct the solids. If manipulatives are not available, the students can create their own manipulatives using grid paper and nets. Have students construct several different rectangular, square, and triangular prisms in addition to a cylinder.

A **cylinder** is a three-dimensional object with two parallel, identical circular bases. The following are cylinders.

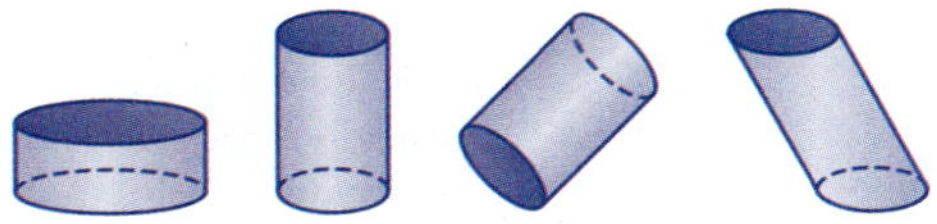

3. The segments in the figure below show the relationship between the circle and a face of one of your blocks.

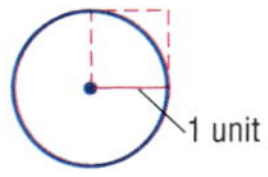


a. What is the area of the circle?

b. If you had blocks like this one, you could build a structure 3 units high with the circle as its base. What would be its volume?
3$\pi$ cubic units, or about 9.42 cubic units

c. If you could build a structure 1,000 units high with this base, what would be its volume? 1,000$\pi$ cubic units, or about 3,142 cubic units

4. Felix drew a rectangular floor plan for a playroom.

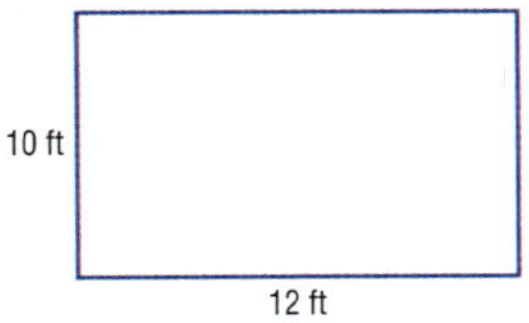


a. What is the area of the floor? 120 ft$^2$

b. If the playroom has 8-foot ceilings, what is its volume? 960 ft$^3$

c. If the playroom has 10-foot ceilings, what is its volume? 1,200 ft$^3$

5. Here is a design for a large oil tank.

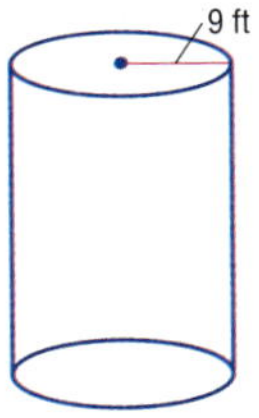


a. What is the area of the base of the tank?

b. If the tank is 50 feet high, how much water will it hold (in cubic feet)?

c. If the tank is $h$ feet high, how much water will it hold? 81$\pi h$ ft$^3$, or about 254.5$h$ ft$^3$

**Math Link**

The area of a circle is $\pi r^2$, where $r$ is the radius and $\pi$ is about 3.14.

3a. $\pi$ square units, or about 3.14 square units

5a. 81$\pi$ ft$^2$, or about 254.5 ft$^2$

5b. 4,050$\pi$ ft$^3$, or about 12,723 ft$^3$



▶ **Exercise 3** Students are given the area formula of a circle. The important realization is that the radius is 1 unit (the same as a side of the square), so the total area is $\pi$ square units.

▶ **Exercises 3 and 5** Students are asked to calculate with $\pi$. You might remind them that $\pi$ represents a non-repeating, infinite decimal. The pi key on the calculator gives a better approximation of the value than 3.14 does, but it is still an approximation.

▶ **Exercises 4 and 5** Students are given measurements for the base rather than a view of the number of units. The strategy for finding the volume should still be the same: find the area of the base and multiply by the height.

**On the Spot Assessment**

What is the area of a circle with diameter 6 centimeters?
9$\pi$ cm$^2$ $\approx$ 28.3 cm$^2$

If the circle represents the base of a cylinder with a height of 10 centimeters, what is the volume of the cylinder? 90$\pi$ cm$^3$ $\approx$ 282.6 cm$^3$

**Wrap-Up** Before moving on to the next problem set, ask students to share their answers for Exercises 4 and 5. Make sure that they report the volumes in cubic feet. You may need to again discuss the differences between units, square units, and cubic units.

### Think & Discuss

*Suggested Grouping: Pairs*

Have students describe and test their strategies for finding the volume of a prism. Then have them explain why the same strategy will work to find the volume of a cylinder.

## Develop & Understand: B

*Suggested Grouping: Small Groups*

This exercise set is designed to give students a visual, intuitive idea of why the volume formula they have discovered (area of base times height) will work even for an oblique prism.

First, have students look at the prisms on the left side of the page. Then ask them to explain the difference between right and oblique prisms. There are different ways to state this: "In right prisms, the polygonal faces are lined up." Or, "In right prisms, the connecting faces are rectangles." Students might also notice that in a right rectangular prism, any pair of opposite faces may be used as the bases.

If you have decks of cards available, use them to demonstrate these ideas. Either give two decks to each group, or do Exercise 6 as a demonstration. Stack up one deck as a right prism. With the other deck, start with it stacked as a right prism and then push the cards so that they form an oblique prism. Ask students to answer Exercises 6a–6d on their papers first, and then to share their answers with the group or the whole class. (Stacks of coasters would also work quite well.)

The notion that the two decks have the same volume because they contain the same cards (this is the "amount of stuff inside") is important for understanding volume relationships.

### Think & Discuss

- Describe a single strategy that you think will work for finding the volume of *any* prism. Test your strategy with the prisms in Investigations 1 and 2. Multiply the area of the base by the height.
- Will the same strategy work for the volume of any *cylinder?* If not, can you modify the strategy so that it *will* work? Yes

## Develop & Understand: B

In the previous exercises, you have been finding the volumes of *right prisms,* where the sides are perpendicular to the base. Some prisms, called *oblique prisms,* are slanted.

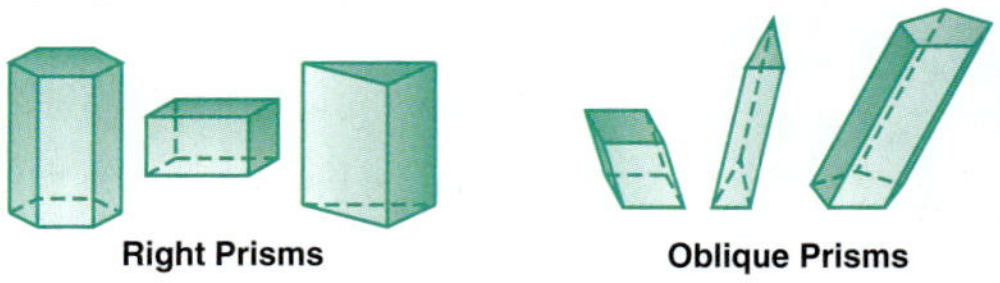


6. This right prism has been sliced into very thin pieces, like a deck of cards. These "cards" have then been pushed into an oblique prism, but the cards themselves have not changed. See margin.

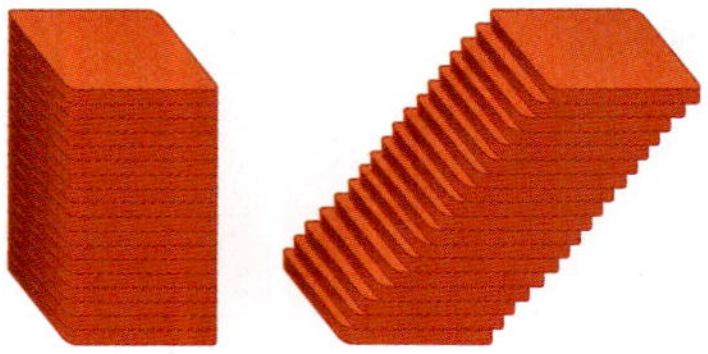

a. If each card is 5 centimeters wide and 8 centimeters long and the stack is 15 centimeters high, what is the volume of the first "deck"?

b. Is the volume of the second deck *the same as, greater than,* or *less than* the volume of the first deck? Explain your answer.

c. Is the base of the second deck *the same as, greater than,* or *less than* the base of the first deck? Explain.

d. The diagram at the right shows how to measure the height of an oblique prism. Is the height of the second deck *the same as, greater than,* or *less than* the height of the first deck? Explain.

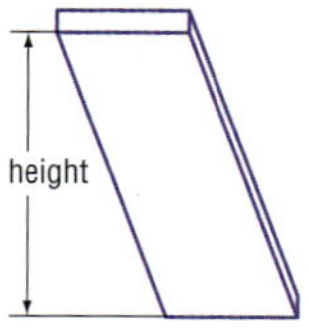




### Additional Answers

6a. 600 $cm^3$

6b. The same; they contain the same number of cards and the cards are the same size.

6c. The same; for both decks, the base is a single card, and the cards are the same size.

6d. The same; the decks have the same number of cards and the cards are the same thickness.

**7.** Now think about a deck of circular cards.

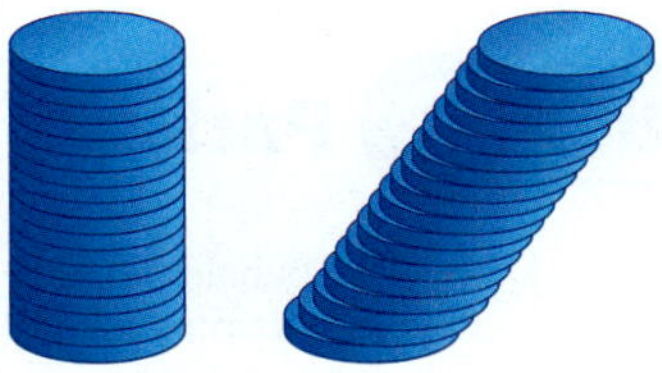

**a.** If the cards each have radius 4 cm and the stack is 9 cm high, what is the volume of the first deck? $144\pi\ \text{cm}^3$, or about $452.4\ \text{cm}^3$

**b.** Is the volume of the second deck *the same as, greater than,* or *less than* the volume of the first deck? Explain.

**c.** Is the base of the second deck *the same as, greater than,* or *less than* the base of the first deck? Explain.

**d.** Is the height of the second deck *the same as, greater than,* or *less than* the height of the first deck? Explain. The same; the decks have the same number of cards and the cards are the same thickness.

**8.** Will the formula *area of base* × *height* give you the volume of an oblique prism? Explain. See margin.

7b. The same; they have the same number of cards and the cards are the same size.

7c. The same; for both decks, the base is a single card, and the cards are the same size.

## Share & Summarize

**1.** Write a formula for the volume of a prism based on the area of the base $A$ and the height $h$. Explain why your formula works.

**2.** Write a formula for the volume of a rectangular prism, using $l$, $w$, and $h$. Write another formula for the volume of a cylinder, using $r$ and $h$. $V = lwh$, $V = \pi r^2 h$

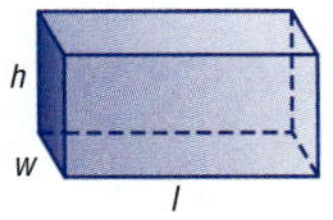


Rectangular Prism

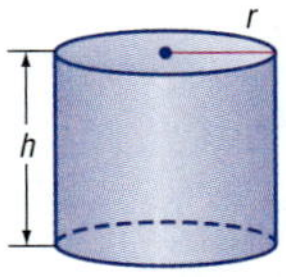


Cylinder

1. $V = Ah$; Volume is the amount of space in a 3D figure. Using the card prisms as an example, the amount of space is the area of a card (the base) times the height of the stack. For an actual prism, use the area of the base times the height.



The fact that the heights of the two decks are the same may be a little harder to see. Ask students to explain why they think the heights are the same or why they think the heights are different. If no one can express a good reason, ask some prompting questions like:

- Do they have the same number of cards? Yes
- In both decks, are the cards stacked right on top of each other, or are they arranged differently? In both decks, they are stacked.
- Are the cards thicker in one deck than the other? No
- If you stack cards that have the same thickness but stack them a little off center, will the stack be taller than if the cards were lined up perfectly? No

This type of thinking should lead students to see that the stacks are, in fact, the same height. Students can go on to Exercises 7 and 8 on their own or in small groups.

**Wrap-Up** Ask several students to share their answers for Exercise 8, including their explanations.

## Share & Summarize

These two problems ask students to write the volume formulas for prisms based on the work they have been doing. The first asks students to generalize $V = Ah$; the second asks students to write formulas in terms of the dimensions for a rectangular solid and a cylinder. As a follow-up, you may want to ask students to find the formula for the volume of a cube as a special case of the rectangular solid. You may want to put these formulas on a poster or in some other way make them a permanent, visible part of the room for later reference.

### Additional Answer

8. Yes; if a right prism has been pushed into an oblique prism and no parts have been added or removed from it, it will still occupy the same amount of space, that is, it will still have the same volume.

## Inquiry Investigation 3

*Suggested Grouping: Pairs*

### Materials and Preparation

Students may need scratch paper they can bend into cylinders to help them think about the activity.

This investigation can be done anytime after Investigation 2. The creativity shown by students will increase if the scenario of "being slightly outrageous" for a convention is accepted by them, so extra energy expended in promoting the scenario is well spent.

### Make a Prediction

Based on earlier work, students should have a good sense for how things change in this situation. Without making exact calculations, they should be able to say that for a tall container, the base and hence the radius would get smaller if the volume remained the same. For a very short container, the radius of the base would have to get bigger if the container were to maintain the same volume.



## Inquiry Investigation 3 Package Design

### Materials

- materials for making models of beverage containers

Bursting Bubbles beverage company wants to attract attention to its products at an upcoming convention. The company normally packages its carbonated water in 350-milliliter cylindrical cans that are 15 centimeters high.

Bursting Bubbles wants to show creativity at the convention by packaging its carbonated water in new containers of different shapes. The company has commissioned you, a mathematician, to investigate some other sizes and shapes and to make a recommendation.

Company representatives tell you that the new containers can be any height at all, but they must have a volume of 350 milliliters. It is now up to you to create some attention-getting containers.

The company gave the required volume in milliliters (mL). You probably already know that there are 1,000 mL in 1 liter (L). To do this investigation, you also need to know that 1 milliliter has the same volume as 1 cubic centimeter.

### Make a Prediction

You decide to design some cylindrical containers first. As the height of the can changes, the base area must also change to keep the volume fixed at 350 milliliters.

**1.** You could design a really tall container, even as tall as 1 meter (100 cm). To keep the volume 350 milliliters, would the radius of the base circle have to increase or decrease as the height of the can increased? Decrease

**2.** Suppose you designed a very short can, even as short as 2 centimeters. To keep the volume 350 milliliters, would the radius of the base circle have to increase or decrease as the height decreased? Increase

**Math Link**

The number $\pi$, pronounced "pie" and spelled pi, is about 3.14. Your calculator probably has a $\pi$ key to make these calculations easier.

## Try It Out

**3.** Bursting Bubble's standard cans are 15 centimeters high. What is the radius of the circular base of these cans?

To find the radius, you can use a strategy of systematic trial and error. The table shows the volume for a base radius of 3 centimeters and of 2.5 centimeters. Use a calculator to find the radius that would give a volume of 350 milliliters. Keep searching until you get within 1 milliliter of 350 milliliters.
Answers should be between 2.72 cm and 2.73 cm.

| Base Radius (cm) | Base Area ($cm^2$) ($A = \pi \times r \times r$) | Volume (mL, want 350) (base area × height) |
|---|---|---|
| 3 | 28.27 | 424.05 mL (too large) |
| 2.5 | 19.635 | 294.525 mL (too small) |

**4.** Choose five heights from the table below and make your own table. Complete your table with radius values that give a volume within 1 milliliter of 350 milliliters. See possible table entries below.

| Height (cm) | Radius of Base Circle (cm) | Volume ($cm^3$) |
|---|---|---|
| 1 | 10.56 | 350.33 |
| 2 | 7.46 | 349.67 |
| 3 | 6.09 | 349.55 |
| 5 | 4.72 | 349.95 |
| 10 | 3.34 | 350.46 |
| 20 | 2.36 | 349.95 |

| Height (cm) | Radius of Base Circle (cm) | Volume ($cm^3$) |
|---|---|---|
| 30 | 1.928 | 350.34 |
| 50 | 1.493 | 350.14 |
| 75 | 1.22 | 350.70 |
| 90 | 1.113 | 350.25 |
| 100 | 1.056 | 350.33 |
| 150 | 0.862 | 350.15 |

**5.** Were your predictions from Questions 1 and 2 correct? Yes

## Try It Again

The committee wants you to consider other shapes, not just cylinders, that might get attention at the convention. You can think about cones, spheres, other prisms, anything you want.



Inquiry

## Try It Out

The guess-check-and-improve problem-solving strategy, using a calculator for tracking down the volume, is used deliberately. Teachers report this method keeps the focus on the concept of volume and generates visual images of the shapes they are considering.

## Try It Again

In this section, students explore two other shapes for containers: spheres and cones. You might want to talk about the appeal of each. Which would be nice to drink out of? Which would grab more attention? How would the containers look on the shelves? Would the spheres keep rolling off? How would a company logo look on the container?

▶ **Exercise 6** Just as they did for cylinders, students can use trial and error to find different cones with a volume of 350 mL. Consider having students summarize their results by creating a graph of height versus radius.

Some students may think to use the cylinders they found in Try It Out as a starting point for finding the size of cone-shaped containers in Exercise 6. For each cylinder with volume 350 mL, students can make a cone with the same radius and the height three times as big, canceling the factor of $\frac{1}{3}$ in the volume equation. However, watch out for students who try to make the radius three times as big as well. Since the value of the radius is squared in the equation for volume, this would give them a container nine times bigger than the starting cylinder.

▶ **Exercise 7** When students begin working on the sphere, they should use trial and error to find the radius that works. The problem is stated in such a way ("find as many spheres as you can") that students will have to figure out for themselves that only one sphere has the appropriate volume. Since the volume depends on only the radius, a sphere with a longer radius will have more volume; a sphere with a shorter radius will have less volume. Unlike the cylinder and cone, there is no second dimension (height) to alter, compensating for a change in the radius.

## What Did You Learn?

This section could be done for homework with students presenting their models the next day. Encourage creativity in the designs, and ask students to prove that their models have a volume of 350 mL. If you have access to a science lab and if the models can hold water or popcorn, you could actually test out the capacity of some models.

Inquiry

Here are two shapes, with formulas for their volumes. Use this information to answer the next set of questions.

**Cone**

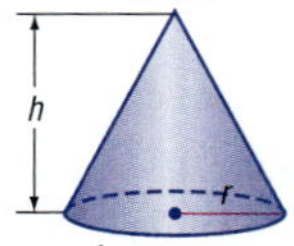


Volume = $\frac{1}{3}$ base area × height, or $\frac{1}{3}\pi r^2 h$

**Sphere**

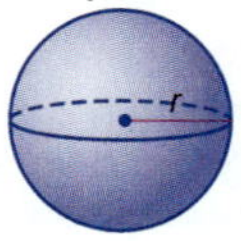


Volume = $\frac{4}{3}\pi r^3$

6. Try the cone shape first. Choose at least three heights for the cone. For each height, find the radius needed to give a cone a volume of 350 mL. Get within 1 mL of 350 mL.

6. Possible answer:

| Height (cm) | Radius (cm) |
|---|---|
| 10 | 5.78 |
| 100 | 1.83 |
| 1 | 18.28 |

7. Using the formula for the volume of a sphere, find as many spheres as you can with a volume of 350 mL.

7. Only one sphere has this volume: the sphere with a radius of about 4.37 cm.

8. Find at least two other shapes for containers with a volume of 350 mL. Answers will vary.

### What Did You Learn?

Choose one design to present to the company.

9. Describe your design to the company, including its dimensions. Answers will vary.
10. Explain why your design might be successful at the convention. Explanations will vary.
11. Make a model of your design to show the company. Models will vary.

## *Practice & Apply*

4. $2(30 \cdot 8) + 2(25 \cdot 8) = 480 + 400 = 880$ square feet; will not paint the floor and ceiling

### *Math Link*

The formula for the area of a parallelogram is $bh$, where $b$ is the base and $h$ is the height. The formula for the area of a triangle is $\frac{1}{2}bh$, where $b$ is the base and $h$ is the height.

6c. Possible answers: a 4 cm by 8 cm rectangle, a triangle with base 16 cm and height 4 cm, a 32 cm by 1 cm rectangle

7a. Each triangle has area $\frac{1}{2}(6)(5.2)$ cm$^2$, or 15.6 cm$^2$; six triangles are 93.6 cm$^2$.

In Exercises 1–4, show your work.

1. What volume of sand will be needed to fill a sandbox that is 3 feet by 4 feet by 1.5 feet? $3 \cdot 4 \cdot 1.5 = 18$ cubic feet
2. How much material will Sara use to make a cardboard jewelry box that is 6 cm by 6 cm by 3 cm? $4(6 \cdot 3) + 2(6 \cdot 6) = 72 + 72 = 144$ square cm
3. How much space does a bed take up if it is 30 inches high, 75 inches long, and 50 inches wide? $75 \cdot 30 \cdot 50 = 112{,}500$ cubic inches
4. How much space will be covered by paint if you paint the walls of a room that is 30 feet long, 25 feet wide, and 8 feet high?
5. A refrigerator advertises a capacity of 24 cubic feet. Which is more likely to be the dimensions of the refrigerator? Explain. Choice b is more likely. A refrigerator will not be 12 feet tall.
   a. 12 feet by 2 feet by 1 foot
   b. 6 feet by 2 feet by 2 feet
6. Here is a parallelogram.

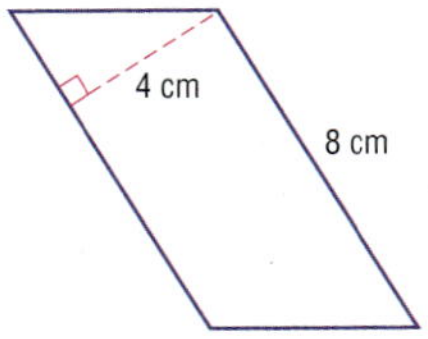


   a. What is the area of the parallelogram? 32 cm$^2$
   b. If you build a prism 1 cm high using this parallelogram as a base, what will be its volume? 32 cm$^3$
   c. Draw two other bases for containers that would have the same volume for a 1 cm height.
7. Six equilateral triangles are joined to form a hexagon.

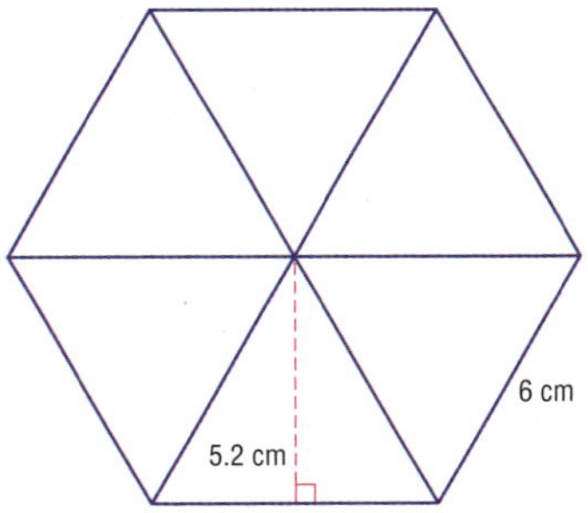


   a. What is the area of the hexagon? Explain how you found your answer.
   b. If you built a prism on this base with a height of $h$ cm, what would be its volume? $93.6h$ cm$^3$



*On Your Own Exercises*
**Lesson 5.1**

**Investigation 1**
Pages 213–215
Practice & Apply: 1–5
Connect & Extend: 11–13

**Investigation 2**
Pages 216–219
Practice & Apply: 6–10
Connect & Extend: 14–17

**Assign Anytime**
Mixed Review: 18–34

▶ **Exercises 3 and 4** In these exercises, students move from generic "units" (the blocks) to structures with specific measurements. Watch to be sure students report their answers in appropriate units (square units for area and cubic units for volume).

▶ **Exercise 5** Students may not make the connection that the capacity of the refrigerator refers to the volume. The students then need to use prime factorization to determine possible measures for the volume.

▶ **Exercise 7b** Tell students that since the height of the prism is $h$, there will be an $h$ left in their answer.

▶ **Exercise 8** Just like Exercise 7, the answers will have variables in them since the radius of the base of the cylinder is unknown.

▶ **Exercise 11** This exercise is asking the students to use $A$ to represent the area of the base which is presented in the explanation of the exercise. Students may miss that and have difficulty writing the formula for volume in a different way. Stress that a different way does not mean rearrange the letters; since the only operations performed are multiplication, and multiplication is commutative, the order in which you write the equation does not change.

On Your Own Exercises

8b. $\pi r^2$ m$^3$

9c. Answers will vary. For a rectangular room, the volume should be length times width times height.

10. Possible answer: a 6 by 6 by 10 and a 36 by 1 by 10 rectangular prism, a cylinder with radius about 3.4 cm and height about 10 cm, and any triangular prism so that $\frac{1}{2}bh$ for the triangle is 6 cm$^2$ and the height is 60 cm

**Connect & Extend**

11a. $V = A \cdot l$; the area of the triangle base would be found using the base and height of the triangle, which are the same base and height in the formula for the volume.

**8.** The base of a cylinder has radius $r$ meters. Write your answers in terms of $\pi$.

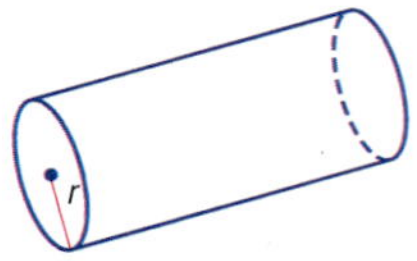


a. What is the area of the cylinder's base? $\pi r^2$ m$^2$

b. If the height of the cylinder is 1 m, what is its volume (in m$^3$)?

c. If the height is 10 m, what is the volume? $10\pi r^2$ m$^3$

d. What is the cylinder's volume if its height is $h$ meters? $\pi r^2 h$ m$^3$

**9.** You can find, or at least make a good estimate of, the volume of a room in your home.

a. Draw the base (floor) of the room. Show the measurements in feet or meters. Indicate if you measured exactly. If you estimated, describe how you made your estimates. Answers will vary.

b. What is the height of the room? Do you know exactly or did you approximate it? Answers will vary.

c. What is the volume of the room?

**10.** Give the dimensions of four different containers that each have a volume of 360 cubic centimeters. They should not all be rectangular prisms.

**11.** Let $l$ represent length, $w$ represent width, and $h$ represent height. You know that a formula for finding the volume of a rectangular prism is $V = l \cdot w \cdot h$. You have also learned that this formula can be expressed as $V = A \cdot h$, where $A$ represents the area of the rectangular base of the prism.

a. As you probably remember, the formula for finding the area of a triangle is $A = \frac{1}{2} b \cdot h$. The formula for finding the volume of a triangular prism is $V = \frac{1}{2} b \cdot h \cdot l$, where $l$ is the height of the triangular prism. How else could the formula be written? Why?

b. If you have a prism with a base shaped like a parallelogram, what would be the formula for the volume? Write the formula two different ways.

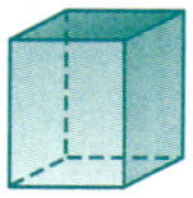

$V = b \cdot h \cdot H$, where $b$ is the base, $h$ is the height of the parallelogram, and $H$ is the height of the prism. $V = A \cdot H$, where $A$ = area of the base and $H$ is the height of the prism.



224 CHAPTER 5 Geometry in Three Dimensions

**12.** Tom is working at a manufacturing facility and has been asked to prepare a presentation regarding the packaging used to ship products to customers. The current shipping box holds five DVDs. On average, the manufacturer sends two or more boxes to each customer.

To reduce the charges for shipping, Tom thinks that the size of the box should be doubled to hold more DVDs. Currently, the shipping box is 6 inches by 10 inches by 8 inches. Tom thinks that the length of each side should be doubled in order to double the volume to ship ten DVDs instead of five.

Help Tom evaluate the situation. Create a table like the following to record your results. What if the manufacturer doubles the box size again?

| Length (inches) | Width (inches) | Height (inches) | Surface Area (in$^2$) | Volume (in$^3$) |
|---|---|---|---|---|
| 6 | 10 | 8 | 376 | 480 |
| 12 | 20 | 16 | 1,504 | 3,840 |
| 24 | 40 | 32 | 6,016 | 30,720 |

**a.** What happens to the surface area and volume as the box dimensions are doubled?

**b.** Suppose Tom only doubles one dimension instead of all dimensions. What happens to the surface area and volume? Try doubling different sides.

| Length (inches) | Width (inches) | Height (inches) | Surface Area (in$^2$) | Volume (in$^3$) |
|---|---|---|---|---|
| 12 | 10 | 8 | 592 | 960 |
| 24 | 10 | 8 | 1,024 | 1,920 |
| 48 | 10 | 8 | 1,888 | 3,840 |
| 6 | 20 | 8 | 656 | 960 |
| 6 | 10 | 16 | 632 | 960 |

12a. Surface area increases by a factor of 4, volume by a factor of 8.

12b. Doubling any one side gives the same volume. However, the surface area is different. Each time one side is doubled, the volume also doubles. This seems right because the original volume is $l \cdot w \cdot h$ and the increased volume is $(2 \cdot l) \cdot w \cdot h$ or $2 \cdot l \cdot w \cdot h$.



On Your Own Exercises

▶ **Exercise 12a** Once the students complete the table, they should have enough information to answer this question. If students are struggling, tell them to look at the change in the surface area and volume as they go down the column of the table.

**Lesson 5.1** Surface Area and Volume 225

▶ **Exercise 15** The result that the middle container holds more water may seem counter-intuitive, but if students believe their development of volume formulas, they must believe this as well.



15. The middle container holds the most water, 471 mL. The others both hold about 452 mL.

***Real-World Link***

Young children do not understand that glasses of different shapes can hold the same amount of water. If given a choice of several glasses, they might always want the tallest glass or the widest glass because they think it holds the most.

16. Possible answer:

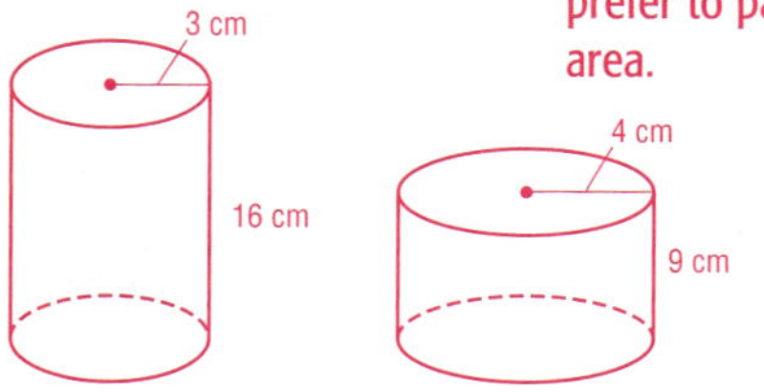


**13.** Many cereal boxes have dimensions of about 6 cm by 20 cm for the base and are about 27 cm high.

**a.** What volume of cereal could this shape box hold? 3,240 $cm^3$

**b.** Give the dimensions (in cm) of four other rectangular boxes that have this same volume. See margin.

**c.** Give the dimensions of two other containers that have this same volume. They do not have to be rectangular boxes. See margin.

**14.** Here are three cylinders that you probably have in your house. Choose one and find its volume. See margin.

- a penny (It is hard to measure the height of a single penny, but it is not hard to measure the height of 10 pennies and then divide that measurement by ten.)
- a soup can
- a strand of spaghetti

**15.** Which of these containers holds the most water?

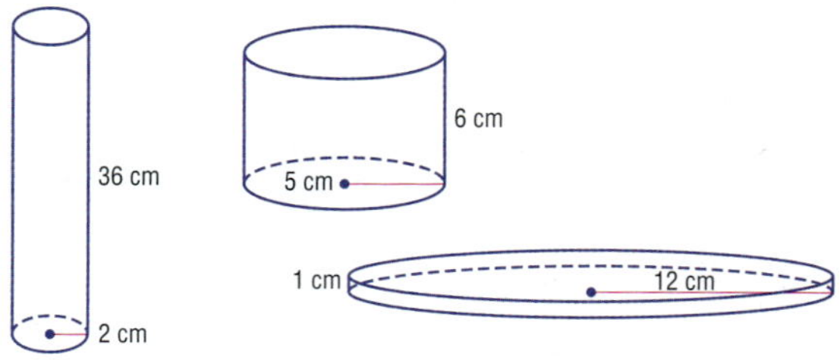


**16.** Draw two glasses that look different but hold the same amount of water. Show their dimensions. See below.

**17. In Your Own Words** Give two examples of structures with the same volume and different surface areas. Suppose you are making one of these structures for art class, and you want to paint them. Which one will need less paint? Explain. Answers will vary. Check students' work. Possible answers: Rectangular prisms with dimensions 12 ft by 3 ft by 2 ft and 18 ft by 4 ft by 2 ft; I would prefer to paint the 12 by 3 by 2 prism because it has less surface area.



**Additional Answers**

13b. Possible answer: 18 by 20 by 9, 9 by 9 by 40, 10 by 18 by 18, 3,240 by 1 by 1

13c. Possible answer: a triangular prism with base area 324 $cm^2$ (say, a triangle with height 18 cm and base 36 cm) and height 10 cm, and a cylinder with base area 324 $cm^2$ (a circle with radius about 10.16 cm) and height 10 cm

14. Possible answers: A penny has a diameter of about 2 cm (radius about 1 cm). A stack of 7 pennies is about 1 cm high. So 7 pennies form a cylinder of volume $\pi$ $cm^3$, or about 3.14 $cm^3$, so the volume of a single penny is about 0.45 $cm^3$. Or the volume of a strand of spaghetti with radius 1 mm and height 25 cm is 0.785 $cm^3$.

## Mixed Review

**Find the value of each expression.**

**18.** $4-(-3)$ 7

**19.** $10-(-4)$ 14

**20.** $13-(-10)$ 23

**21.** $-7-(-8)$ 1

**Rewrite in the form $a^b$.**

**22.** $6^9 \cdot 6$ $6^{10}$

**23.** $4^2 \cdot 4 \cdot 4^7$ $4^{10}$

**24.** $10^{11} \cdot 10^5$ $10^{16}$

**25.** $3^5 \cdot 3^5$ $3^{10}$

**Rewrite the expression as simply as possible. Use only positive exponents in your answers.**

**26.** $t \cdot t \cdot t^{-2}$ $t^0$, or 1

**27.** $x^7 \cdot x^{-2} \cdot x^{-8}$ $\frac{1}{x^3}$

**28.** $(a^{-3}b^2)^{-5}$ $\frac{a^{15}}{b^{10}}$

**29.** $\left(\left(\frac{1}{n}\right)^{-4}\right)^{-3}$ $\left(\frac{1}{n}\right)^{12}$

**Write each number in standard notation.**

**30.** $6 \times 10^4$ 60,000

**31.** $4.8 \times 10^{-3}$ 0.0048

**Evaluate without using your calculator. Write your answer in scientific notation.**

**32.** $3.2 \times 10^{-6} + 0.2 \times 10^{-7}$ $3.22 \times 10^{-6}$

**33.** $1.4 \times 10^{-3} + 0.9 \times 10^{-4}$ $1.49 \times 10^{-3}$

**34. Social Studies** In 2000, about 105,400,000 votes were cast in the United States presidential election.

**a.** Write this number of votes using scientific notation. $1.054 \times 10^8$

**b.** George W. Bush received about 48% of these votes. Approximately how many votes did he receive? About 50,592,000

On Your Own Exercises

## Quick Check

**Informal Assessment** Students should be able to:

✔ find the volume of any prism or cylinder as area of base times height

✔ understand that for a given volume, the cube is the rectangular prism with the minimum surface area

✔ articulate some applications of surface area and volume

## Quick Quiz

**1.** A block prism has a volume of 36 cubic units.

a. What is the least surface area it could have? 66 square units $(3 \cdot 3 \cdot 4)$

b. What is the greatest surface area it could have? 146 square units $(1 \cdot 1 \cdot 36)$

**2.** Find a cylinder and a rectangular prism that have the same volume. Describe the dimensions of each object. (Hint: It may be easier to start with the cylinder.) Possible answer: Cylinder has radius 4 units and height 5 units. Volume $= 16\pi \cdot 5 = 80\pi$ cubic units. Prism has dimensions of $5 \cdot 4 \cdot 4\pi$.

LESSON

5.2

# Nets and Solids

### Objectives

- To decide if a given net will fold into a closed three-dimensional solid
- To create nets that will fold into given shapes
- To use information about the nets of an object to find surface area and volume

## *Overview*

In this lesson, students extend several major themes of the chapter. First, they learn another two-dimensional description of a three-dimensional object, a net that will fold into a solid. Second, students use these nets to expand their abilities to find surface areas and volumes.

## *Advance Preparation*

Collect beverage cans for Investigation 3. About ten cans should be plenty. Rinse the cans and completely remove tabs. Most students will need to actually cut out the shapes and fold them to decide whether they are nets or not. Prepare at least one copy of each of the following Masters for each student, enlarging the nets if necessary: Lesson 5.2 Masters 1, 2, and 3.

| | Summary | Materials | On Your Own Exercises (pp. 235–239) | Assessment Opportunities |
|---|---|---|---|---|
| **Investigation 1** (p. 229) Pacing: 2 days | Students use nets to learn more about three-dimensional figures. They decide which measurements on a net must match up for the net to fold. | Lesson 5.2 Masters 1–7, scissors, graph paper | Practice & Apply: 1–4<br>Connect & Extend: 13–16<br>Mixed Review: 25–34 | • Share & Summarize (p. 230)<br>• Troubleshooting (p. 229) |
| **Investigation 2** (p. 230) Pacing: 1 day | Students use nets to find surface areas and to estimate volumes of solid objects. | Lesson 5.2 Masters 1, 2, 3, 8, 9, scissors, metric ruler | Practice & Apply: 5–11<br>Connect & Extend: 17, 18<br>Mixed Review: 25–34 | • On the Spot Assessment (p. 231)<br>• Share & Summarize (p. 233)<br>• Troubleshooting (p. 230) |
| **Investigation 3** (p. 233) Pacing: 1 day | Students explore whether the surface area of a beverage can is the best (least) possible for the volume it holds. They try to find the can with the required volume but with minimal surface area. | 12-oz. beverage can, metric ruler | Practice & Apply: 12<br>Connect & Extend: 19, 21<br>Mixed Review: 25–34 | • Share & Summarize (p. 234)<br>• Troubleshooting (p. 233) |

# Leveled Lesson Resources

CRM *Available in:* **Chapter 5 Resource Masters**

Also on TeacherWorks™ Lesson 5.2

## Study Guide and Intervention (p. 8) AL

**Lesson 5.2 Study Guide and Intervention**
***Nets and Solids***

A net is a flat figure that represents all the sides of a solid figure.
The surface area of a solid can be calculated by finding the area of its net.

**Example 1** **Decide whether the figure is a net. If it is a net, describe what shape it creates. If it is not a net, give an explanation.**

**a.**

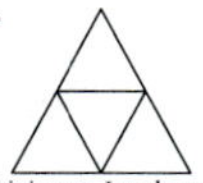

**b.**

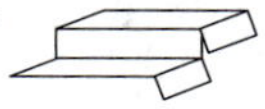

This is a net. It makes a solid with four triangular faces, which is called a tetrahedron.

This is not a net. There are two overlapping sides and one side that does not have an end.

**Example 2** **Use the net's measurements to find the surface area of the solid.**

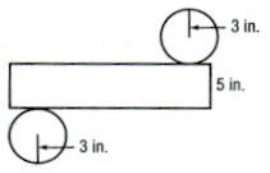


This is the net of a cylinder. To find its surface area, add the areas of the circles and the area of the rectangle. The circumference of the circle ($2\pi r$) is equal to the length of the rectangle.

$(\pi \times 3^2) + (\pi \times 3^2) + (2 \times \pi \times 3 \times 5) = 18\pi + 30\pi = 48\pi$

The surface area is $48\pi \approx 150.8$ in.$^2$

**Exercises**

**If the figure is a net, describe what shape it creates. If it is not a net, give an explanation.**

**1.**

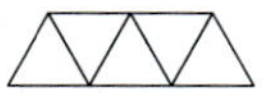

**2.**

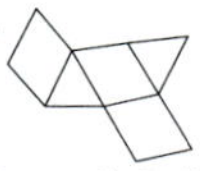

**Use the net's measurements to find the surface area of each solid.**

**3.**

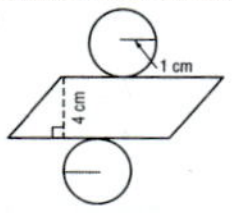


**4.**

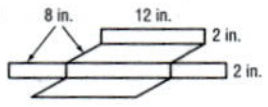


## Skills Practice (p. 9) AL OL

**Lesson 5.2 Skills Practice**
***Nets and Solids***

**Decide whether the figure is a net. If it is a net, describe what shape it creates. If it is not a net, give an explanation.**

**1.**

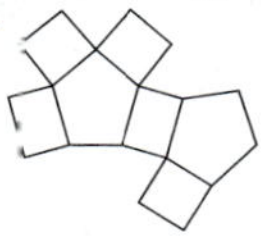

**2.**

**Find the surface area of the solid that can be created from the net.**

**3.** Each equilateral triangle in the net below has a side length of 3 centimeters. The squares also have side lengths of 3 centimeters.

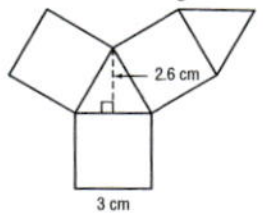


**4.** Each circle in the net below has a radius measure of 4 inches. The width of the rectangle is 6 inches.

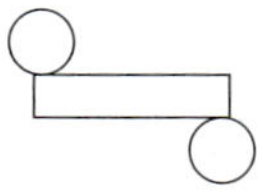

**5.** Each triangle in the net below is isosceles with a base of 8 feet and a height of 4 feet. The figure in the center is a square.

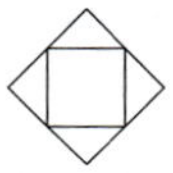

## Problem-Solving Practice (p. 10) AL OL

**Lesson 5.2 Problem-Solving Practice**
***Nets and Solids***

**Solve.**

**1. Packaging** To the right is a pattern that a packaging company is using to create boxes.

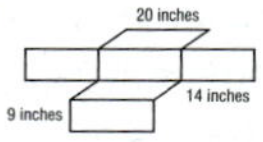


**a.** How much cardboard will be needed for each box?

**b.** What is the volume, in cubic inches, that the box can hold?

**2. Toys** A toy manufacturer fills plastic blocks for toddlers with different colored liquids. To the right is one pattern used to create these blocks. The side length of each square is 5 centimeters. The length of the rectangle is 7.1 centimeters and its width is 5 centimeters.

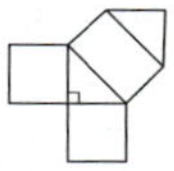

**a.** How much liquid is used to fill each block?

**b.** How much plastic, in square centimeters, is used to create this block?

**3. Containers** Consider the pattern for a container of oatmeal shown to the right.

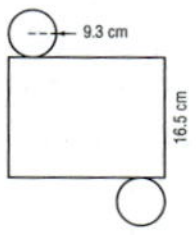


**a.** Plastic is used for the top of the container. How much plastic is used?

**b.** Cardboard is used to create the rest of the container. How much cardboard is used?

**4. Containers** Refer to Exercise 3.

**a.** Suppose a label is created for the oatmeal container that covers $\frac{3}{4}$ of the rectangular cardboard section of the container. What is the surface area that this label would cover?

**b.** How much oatmeal, in cubic centimeters, would fit in this container?

## Enrichment (p. 11) BL

**Lesson 5.2 Enrichment**
***Nets and solids***

**How Changes in Volume Affect Dimensions**

When the volume of a solid changes, so do its dimensions. However, all the dimensions do not change by the same factor as the volume.

A prism has a volume of 36 cubic units. A prism half its size has a volume of 18 cubic units.

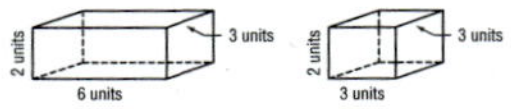


Look at the measures of the sides. To change the volume of a solid, you need to change only one of its measures. For example, if you want a solid to have twice its current volume, double one of its measures.

**1.** A toy company has asked you to create a box for its newest figurine. The new box should have $\frac{1}{4}$ the volume of its standard box. The standard box has a length of 8 inches, width of 5 inches, and a height of 7 inches.

**a.** What is the volume of the standard box?
**b.** Create a net as the pattern for the new box.
**c.** What is the volume of the new box?

**2.** A company that packages salt would like to create a smaller size salt container. The new container would hold half as much salt as the current container. The current cylindrical container has a height of 13 centimeters and a radius of 4 centimeters.

**a.** What is the volume of the original container of salt?
**b.** Create a net to show the new salt container.
**c.** What is the volume of the new container?

## Lesson Quick Quiz (p. 12) AL OL BL

**Lesson 5.2 Quick Quiz**

**1** Draw a net for a cube that has a volume of 8 cubic centimeters.

**2.** What is the surface area of a cube with a volume of 8 cubic centimeters?

## Lesson Masters (pp. 13–23)

**Lesson 5.2 Master I**

**Cube Nets, I**

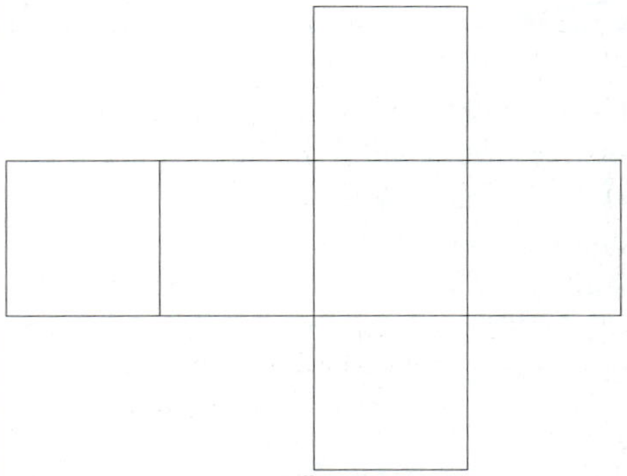

Net

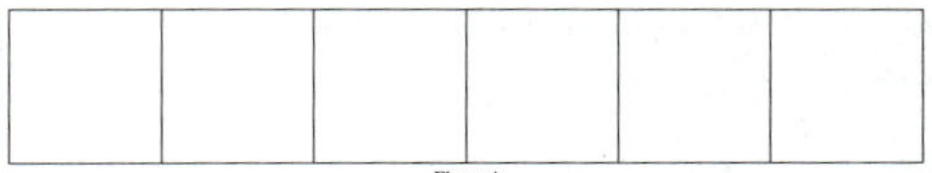

Figure A

# Additional Lesson Resources

### Teacher Tech Tools
- TeacherWorks
- ExamView Assessment Suite
- Classroom Presentation Toolkit
- Advance Tracker

### Student Tech Tools
- StudentWorks Plus
- Math Online eGlossary • Concepts in Motion

### Other Print Products
- Investigation Notebook and Reflection Journal
- Quick Review Math Handbook

## LESSON 5.2 Nets and Solids

### Introduce

**Nets** Hold up a cube prepared from the net on Lesson 5.2 Master 1. Have the sides loosely taped. Take the cube and unfold it for the class, and explain to them that this flat object is called a net. Nets are useful tools for calculating surface area since these flat objects represent the total surface area of the figure.

**Explore**

*Suggested Grouping: Pairs*

▶ **Prepare** You will need scissors and copies of Lesson 5.2 Masters 1–4.

▶ **Predict** Ask students to determine which of the shapes will fold up into a cube. Many students need to manipulate the shapes to answer this question. These are difficult to visualize without cutting.

After they have determined that Figure B and Figure D form nets, ask students to work in pairs to draw three other nets for a cube. Using Lesson 5.2 Master 4, Centimeter Graph Paper, will make it easier for students to draw their nets.

▶ **Report** As students are working, ask one pair of students to draw all the nets they have found so far on the board or to tape them to the board if the nets are big enough. Then ask another pair to add to that list. To tell if two nets are the same, students must check to see if they can rotate, flip, or move one net to lie exactly on top of the other.

There are 11 possibilities. The question about finding them all is not intended for in-depth class time, but you might offer it as an extra project. Tell students there are eleven and challenge them to find them all.

Students may notice without checking that some nets will definitely not form solids. For example, if four squares are around a single point, the shape will lie flat rather than fold up. If five or more squares are in a line, two faces will overlap and the figure will not close.

# LESSON 5.2 Nets and Solids



**Vocabulary**

**net**

**solid**

**Materials**

- scissors
- graph paper

① Answers will vary. There are 11 nets for a cube; the other 9 are shown here.

A **net** is a flat figure that can be folded to form a closed, three-dimensional object. This type of object is called a geometric **solid**.

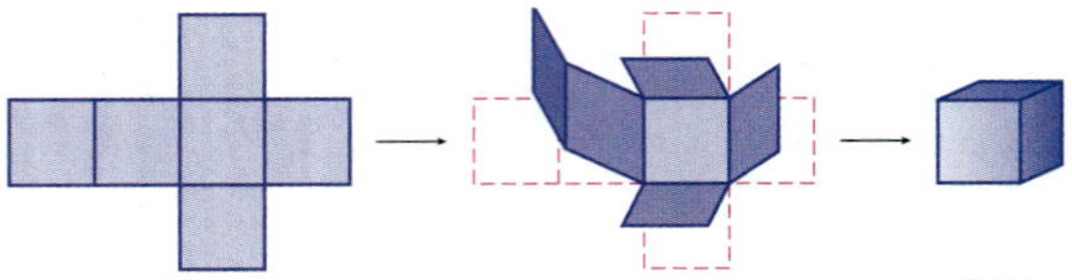


**Explore**

- Which of these figures are also nets for a cube? That is, which will fold into a cube? Cut out a copy of each figure. Try to fold it into a cube. B and D

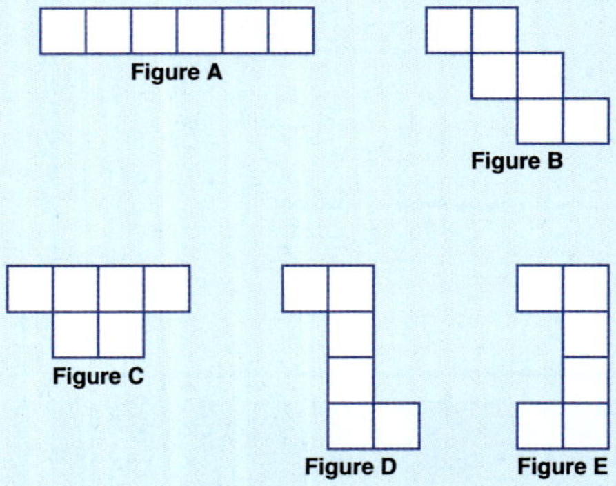


- Find and draw three other nets for a cube. See ①.

With your class, compile all the different nets for a cube that were found. How many nets are there? Do you think your class found all of them?



### *Reaching All Learners*

**BL Beyond Level** Have students try to find all eleven nets on their own and then explain why theirs is a complete list. Students may think about sorting the nets into categories of "main string" net length. For example, for a main string length of 4, 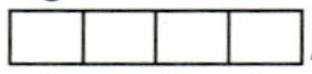, there are only 6 nets possible. They could look at cases of length 3, and so on.

## Investigation 1 Use a Net

**Materials**

- scissors

For a net to form a three-dimensional object, certain lengths have to match. For example, in the nets for cubes, the side lengths of all the squares must be the same. You will now investigate whether other nets will form closed solids. Pay close attention to the measurements that need to match.

### Develop & Understand: A

Decide whether each figure is a net, that is, whether it will fold into a solid. One way to decide is to cut out a copy of the figure and try to fold it. If the figure is a net, describe the shape it creates. If it is not a net, explain why not.

**1.**

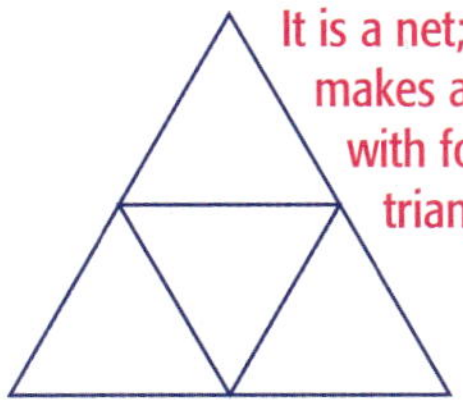

It is a net; it makes a shape with four triangular faces.

**2.**

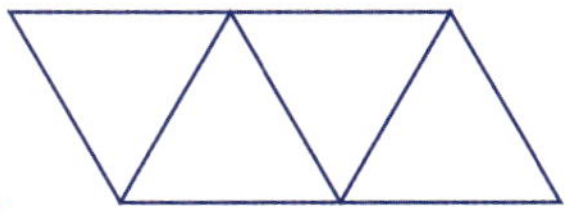

It is a net; it makes a shape with four triangular faces.

**3.**

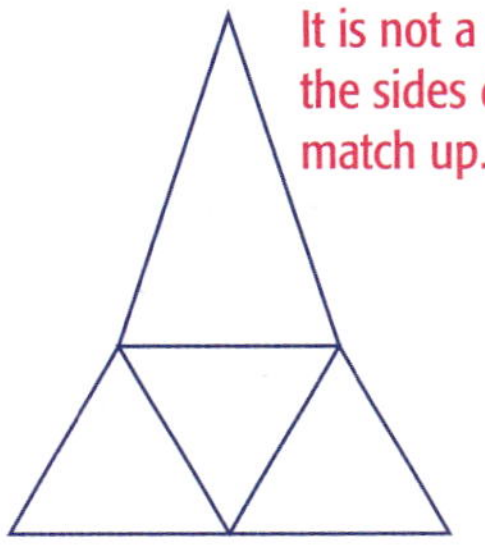

It is not a net; the sides do not match up.

**4.**

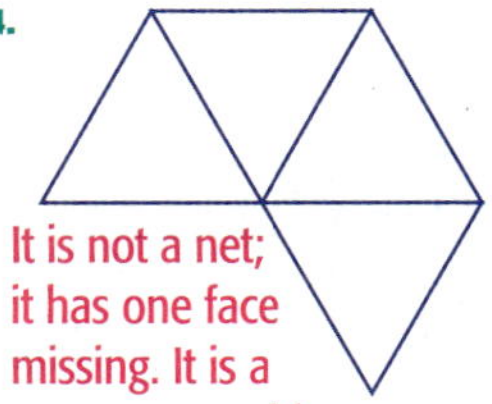

It is not a net; it has one face missing. It is a square pyramid without its base. Or, there is a hole and an extra face.

**5.**

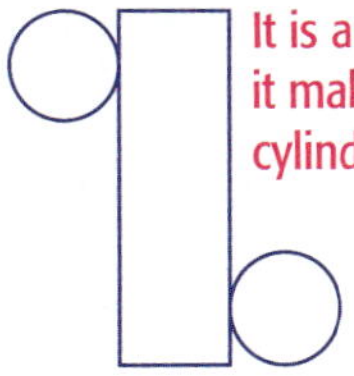

It is a net; it makes a cylinder.

**6.**

It is not a net; the sides of the rectangle are not long enough to wrap around the circles.



## Investigation 1

***On Your Own Exercises***
Pages 235–239
Exercises 1–4, 13–16

**Use a Net** In this investigation, students will decide whether or not certain nets will fold into a three-dimensional object. The nets pictured can be duplicated using Lesson 5.2 Masters 5, 6, and 7 so that students can cut each net out and try to fold it.

### Develop & Understand: A

*Suggested Grouping: Individuals*

In this exercise set, students are given several nets and are asked to determine whether the nets will form closed solids. If you do not use Lesson 5.2 Masters 5, 6, and 7, encourage students to trace the nets, cut them out, and try to fold the ones that might be difficult to determine visually. Some students may need to try folding all of them.

One important lesson is that sometimes "not possible" is an acceptable answer. In this exercise set, Exercises 3, 4, 6, 8, and 9 all fail to fold into a closed solid for various reasons.

### Troubleshooting

Students may have trouble determining if a figure represents a net. It may be helpful for these students to trace the figure and cut it out to assist them in making their decision. Remind students that the pieces of the net must stay connected; the lines are there to show us where to fold. Once the students get more practice working with nets, it will become easier for them to see.

### *Share & Summarize*

Students may have trouble articulating exactly what length they mean in Question 1. Acceptable answers would be, "The circumference needs to be the same length as the side where the circle is attached." or "It needs to be the same length as the side that wraps around it."

For Question 2, ask students what strategies they use to determine whether or not figures are actually nets. Here are some reasons that something that looks like a net won't form a solid.

- It is missing a face.
- Two faces are overlapping.
- The figure is impossible to fold. There is a vertex that won't fold out of the plane. This will happen with four squares, 6 triangles, or 3 hexagons around a central point, for example.

## Investigation 2

***On Your Own Exercises***
Pages 235–239
Exercises 5–11, 17, 18

**Explore Solids** In this investigation, students use nets with measurements given to determine both surface area and volume for various solids. This allows students to practice the concepts that they have learned in the previous lessons. In some cases, students will be able only to estimate the volume.

To find surface area, add the area of each face of the solid. If you have the net, you can compute the area rather than "count squares." For volume, the situation is a bit trickier. Given the net of a rectangular prism, you can find the volume from the three measurements. However, the net for a square pyramid, for example, doesn't give all the information you need. You can find the area of each face but not the height of the pyramid. However, you can use the net to estimate volume. In the example of a square pyramid, students may estimate the volume to be $\frac{1}{2}$ of the volume of a rectangular prism with the same base and with rectangles rather than triangles as sides. The ratio is $\frac{1}{3}$, and you can relate this back to the cones and cylinders; but in any case, you can get an idea for the volume.

7. 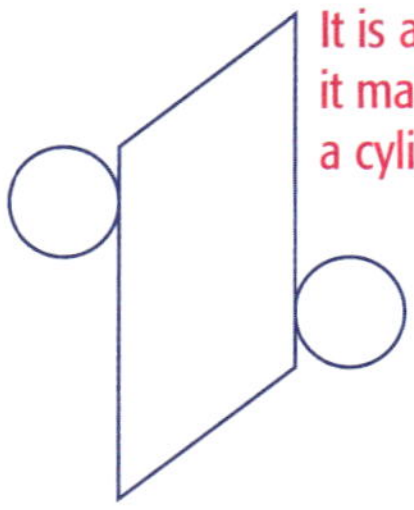

It is a net; it makes a cylinder.

8. 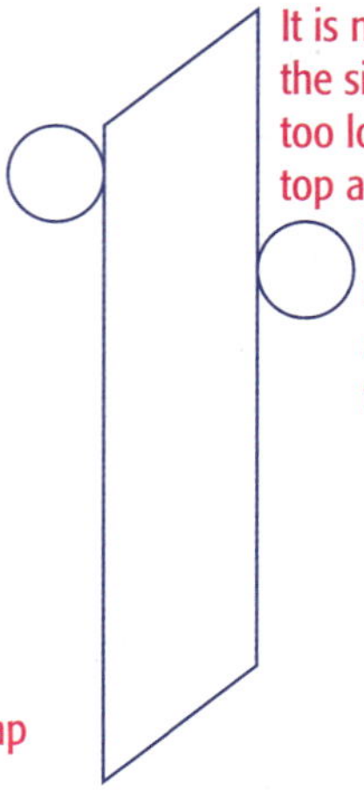

It is not a net; the sides are too long, so the top and bottom holes do not get closed by the circles.

9. 

It is not a net; the two circles overlap and the other end is uncovered.

### *Share & Summarize*

1. For a net to fold into a cylinder, the circumference of the circles must be the same as what other length?
   1. The sides of the parallelogram to which the circles are attached
2. Draw a net for a figure different from those in Exercises 1–9. Explain how you know your net will fold to form a solid.
   Answers will vary.

## Investigation 2 Use Nets to Investigate Solids

**Materials**
- scissors
- metric ruler

You have calculated surface area by counting the square units on the outside of a structure. If the faces of a solid are not squares, like the figures below, you can find the solid's surface area by adding the areas of all its faces.

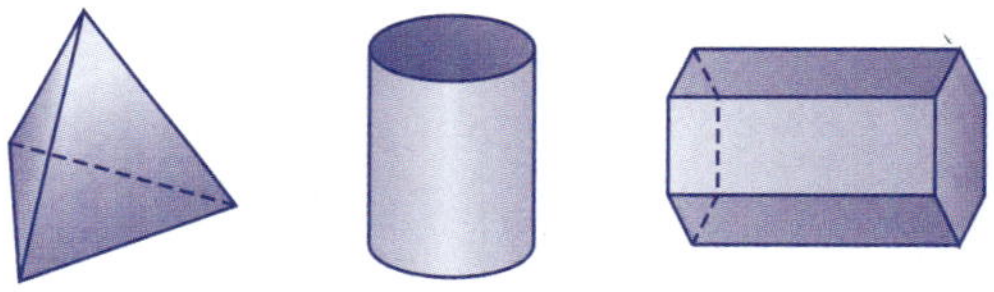



### *Troubleshooting*

For Question 1, if students are not sure that the circumference needs to be the same as any particular length, you may want to revisit the exercises that were not nets. Ask students to find their net from Exercise 6 and try to fold it up. What goes wrong? (The sides of the rectangle are not long enough to "wrap around" the circle.) Similarly for Exercise 8, ask students to fold the net. In this case, students may simply overlap the sides of the parallelogram to make everything fit. If so, explain that in a net, all the edges must meet exactly.

### Example

This net folds to form a cylinder.

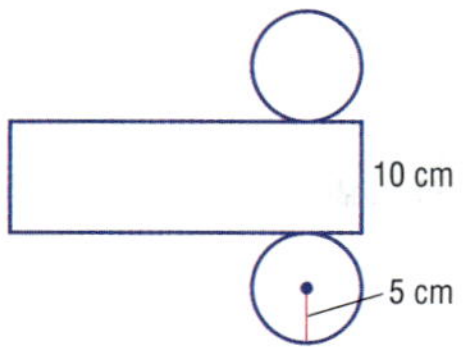


Because the net folds into a cylinder, the circles must be the same size. The area of each circle is $\pi r^2$ cm$^2$, or $25\pi$ cm$^2$. This is about 78.5 cm$^2$.

The length of the rectangle must be equal to the circumference of each circle, which is $10\pi$ cm, or about 31.4 cm. So, the area of the rectangle is about 314 cm$^2$.

To find the cylinder's surface area, add the three areas.

$$78.5 \text{ cm}^2 + 78.5 \text{ cm}^2 + 314 \text{ cm}^2 = 471 \text{ cm}^2$$

## Develop & Understand: A

Each net shown will fold to form a closed solid. Use the net's measurements to find the *surface area* and *volume* of the solid. If you cannot find the exact volume, approximate it. It may be helpful to cut out and fold a copy of the net.

**1.**

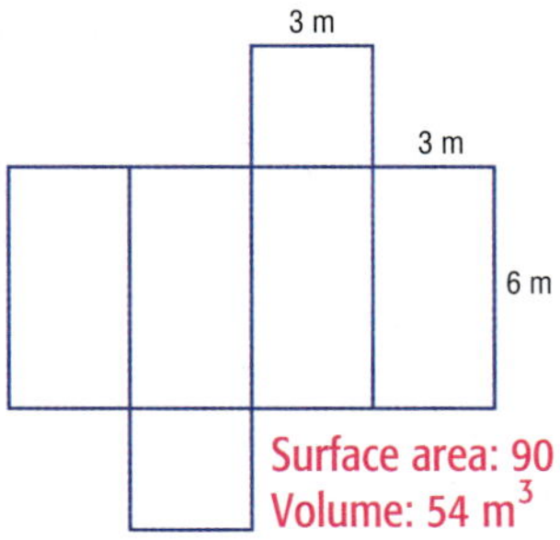


Surface area: 90 m$^2$; Volume: 54 m$^3$

**2.**

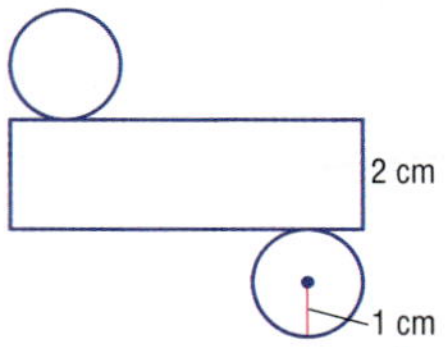


Surface area: $6\pi$ cm$^2$, or about 18.8 cm$^2$; Volume: $2\pi$ cm$^3$, or about 6.3 cm$^3$

**Math Link**

The formula for the circumference of a circle is $2\pi r$, where $r$ is the radius; or $\pi d$, where $d$ is the diameter.

The formula for the area of a circle is $\pi r^2$.



## On the Spot Assessment

What is the volume and surface area of a cylinder where the height is 14 millimeters, and the radius of the base is 3 millimeters (you may wish to draw and label the net for the solid instead of giving the measurements)?
Volume = $126\pi$ mm$^3 \approx 395.64$ mm$^3$; surface area = $102\pi$ mm$^2 \approx 320.44$ mm$^2$

You may know that there is a standard formula for surface area of prisms: $2 \cdot$ (area of the base) + (perimeter of the base $\cdot$ height). We do not develop this formula, but it may come up naturally as students work on finding surface areas. We are more concerned with the concept of surface area as "adding up the areas of the faces," whether the solid is a prism or some other object.

### Example

Start the lesson by discussing the Example. Give students another, similar example to work out. For example, use the same shape but change the radius to 1 cm. How does that affect the length of the rectangle? How does it affect the surface area of the cylinder? You can give another example where the length labeled 10 cm is very small, maybe $\frac{1}{2}$ cm. Ask if that affects whether or not the cylinder will fold up. Have them compute the surface area changing only the value of the radius to 1 cm (69.08 cm$^2$). Then have them compute the surface area changing only the value of the height to $\frac{1}{2}$ cm (172.7 cm$^2$).

You can also ask students to find the volume of the cylinder shown. What is the area of the circular base? ($25\pi$ cm$^2$) What is the height? (10 cm, the other side of the rectangle) If students have difficulty seeing that the length shown as 10 cm is really the height of the cylinder, you may want to have them trace the net, cut it out, and fold it up. When it is folded, students should place one of the circular faces on their desks and note that the segment marked 10 cm does, in fact, go from one base to the other. Since this appears to be a right cylinder, that segment is the height. Then have students calculate the volume. ($25\pi \cdot 10 = 250\pi$ cm$^3$, or about 785 cm$^3$)

## Develop & Understand: A

*Suggested Grouping: Pairs*

Students should be able to determine the surface areas and the volumes of all of the prisms. To identify the heights for the various nets, students may need to trace the net, cut it out, and fold it up. Or you can use Lesson 5.2 Masters 8 and 9, which duplicates the figures in this exercise set.

▶ **Exercise 5** Students may need help identifying the height of the prism, since the lateral face is shown as a parallelogram rather than as a rectangle. Cutting and folding should convince students that the height of the parallelogram is also the height of the cylinder. In fact, the parallelogram could be "dissected" into a rectangle while still part of the net, and the same cylinder would result:

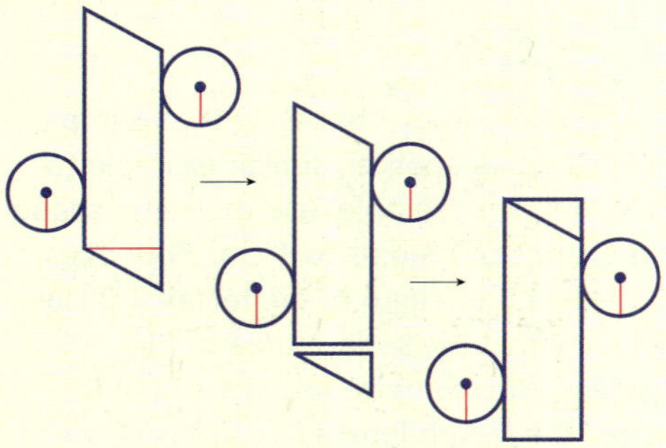

**Math Link**

The formula for the area $A$ of a triangle is $A = \frac{1}{2}bh$, where $b$ is the base and $h$ is the height.

3.

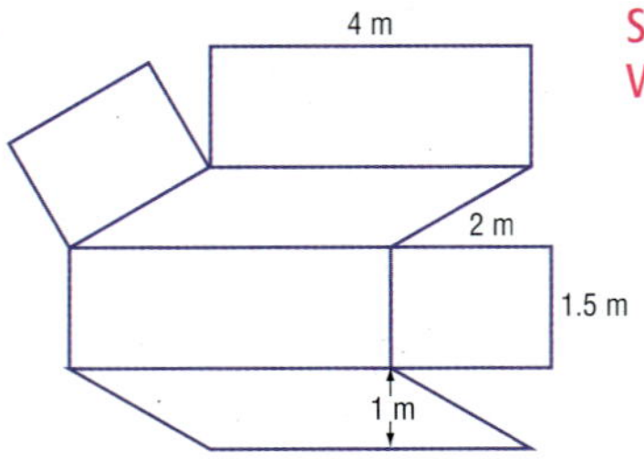


Surface area 26 m$^2$; Volume 6 m$^3$

4. Surface area: 48 m$^2$; Volume: 18 m$^3$ (area of base triangle is 6 m$^2$, height is 3 m)

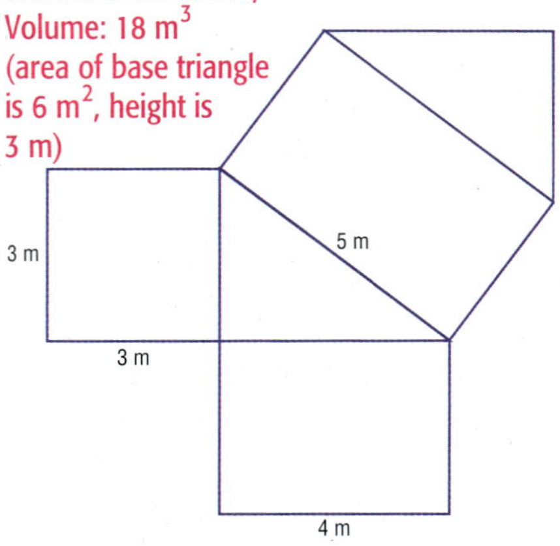


5.

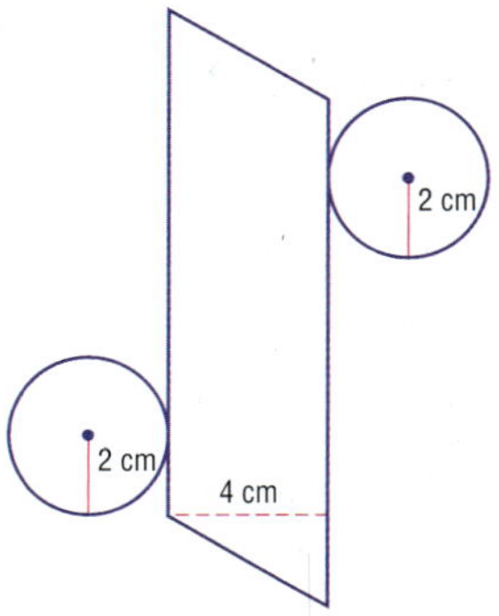


Surface area: $24\pi$ cm$^2$, or about 75.4 cm$^2$; Volume: $16\pi$ cm$^3$, or about 50.3 cm$^3$



## *Reaching All Learners*

**BL** **Beyond Level** Have the students work in small groups to construct an object, such as a castle, that incorporates at least one rectangular prism, one triangular prism, and one cylinder. The students should then construct a net of the object, determine the object's surface area and volume.

1. The solid's surface area is the same as the net's area, so just add the areas of the two-dimensional figures that make up the net.
2. To find the volume, measure length and width of a small rectangle, and length (long side) of one of the larger rectangles. Multiply those three numbers: 2 cm • 1 cm • 5 cm = 10 $cm^3$. To find the surface area, add the areas of all six rectangles: 5 $cm^2$ + 5 $cm^2$ + 10 $cm^2$ + 10 $cm^2$ + 2 $cm^2$ + 2 $cm^2$ = 34 $cm^2$.

### Share & Summarize

1. Explain how to find the surface area of a solid from the net for that solid.
2. Here is a net for a rectangular solid. Take whatever measurements you think are necessary to find the solid's volume and surface area. Explain what measurements you took and how you used them.

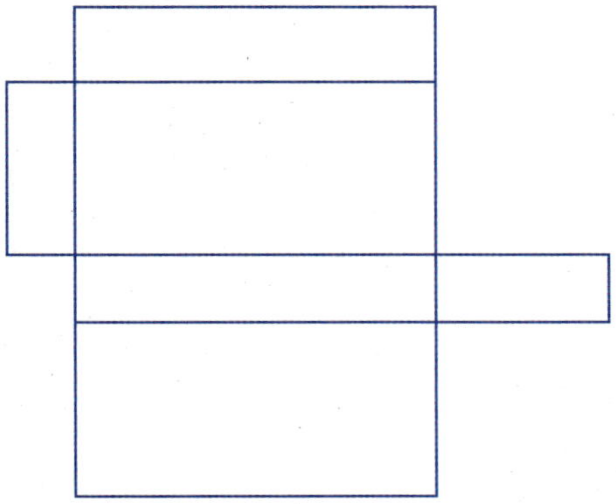

## Investigation 3 Is Today's Beverage Can the Best Shape?

**Materials**

- 12-oz beverage can
- metric ruler

The Bursting Bubbles company is trying to reduce its manufacturing costs in order to increase its profits. The president of the company wonders if there is a way to use less material to make a beverage can.

In this investigation, you will help Bursting Bubbles design a can that has the minimum surface area for the volume of beverage it contains.

### Develop & Understand: A

To get started, inspect a 12-ounce beverage can. Get an idea of its dimensions, volume, and surface area.

1. Find the area in square centimeters of the base of the can. If the can you are using is indented at the bottom, assume that it is not.
2. Measure the can's height in centimeters. About 12.4 cm

1. The diameter of the wider part is about 6.4 cm, so the area is about 32.2 $cm^2$.



## Troubleshooting

If students have difficulty measuring, they may need help using and reading a ruler. Some quick direct instruction on these skills should solve the problem.

If students misapply the formula for volume of a prism, you may need to revisit the idea of using blocks. Relate the question of volume to "How many 1 $cm^3$ blocks will fill this box?" Students should mark along the base in square cm and then stack the blocks to the right height. The total number of blocks is the number in that base layer (or length times width) times the total number of layers (the height in cm).

### Share & Summarize

The point of the first question is that the net is, exactly, the surface of a solid. So the area of the net is, exactly, the surface area of that solid. Since students have good ways for finding areas, they also have some good ways for finding surface areas.

## Investigation 3

**On Your Own Exercises**
Pages 235–239
Exercises 12, 19, 21

**Design a Can** Ask students whether they think beverage cans have the shape they do for a special reason. Why aren't the cans shaped like cereal boxes? And why aren't the cans short and stubby?

Ask students what factors they think companies consider when they design containers.

### Develop & Understand: A

*Suggested Grouping: Small Groups*

You will want a beverage can and a ruler per group for this exploration. Have students get into groups of 4. Ask each group to find the area of the base of the beverage can in square centimeters. Ask them to measure the height in centimeters. Beverage cans are not perfectly cylindrical, so students will have to approximate the measurements. If they do so carefully, students should come out with a volume close to the one shown on the can. If students' volumes are quite far off, they should redo their measurements with greater accuracy.

▶ **Exercise 1** If students have difficulty finding the diameter of the can, suggest that they trace the can on paper, cut out the circle, and fold to find the diameter. Then students can measure the length of their folds.

It is important to connect these ideas to things directly in students' experiences. Ask students this question: Which will take longer to melt? A big tub of ice cream or the same amount of ice cream dished up into lots of single bowls? The tub takes longer because it has much less exposed surface area.

**Lesson 5.2** Nets and Solids 233

Students will also need to calculate the surface area of the can. You may want to ask them to sketch the net for the can. Where is the radius of the circle in that net? Where is the height of the can? If students can correctly label the pieces of the net, they will see that they do have enough information to find the surface area.

**Wrap-Up** Before moving on to the next problem set, you may want to bring the whole class together and compare results. How close did each group come to the volume shown on the can? What were the individual measurements they took? Who thinks this shape gives the least surface area?

## Develop & Understand: B

*Suggested Grouping: Groups of 4*

As students work and find cans with the appropriate volume, each group should send a recorder to the board and add the measurements of their can to a table. The table should have three columns: height, radius, and surface area. Students may wish to record their data using a spreadsheet.

Encourage students to try cans that are close in shape to the original (maybe 1 cm shorter or taller) and cans that are quite different from the original (maybe 5 cm shorter or taller).

Finding cans of a given volume is not easy. If students have completed the Inquiry Investigation from Lesson 5.1, they will have some good strategies and they may even have all the data they need.

**Wrap-Up** Ask one student from each group to report on what the group decided for Exercise 8. An important point is that this is just a conjecture based on evidence and not a definite answer to the question. You may want to share with students the real answer: the can with minimal surface area is the one where the height is the same as the diameter.

### Share & Summarize

Students will realize that the shape generally used for beverage cans does not minimize the surface area for the volume. In thinking about why companies do not choose this "best" shape, (least surface area) you might consider issues like: How easy would it be to hold a can of the best shape? How easily could the companies display their logos?

4. About 313.7 $cm^2$; The area of each circular end is about 32.2 $cm^2$. The area of the surface that wraps around the can is about $12.4 \cdot 6.4\pi$ $cm^2$, or about 249.3 $cm^2$.

The volume printed on the can is given in milliliters (abbreviated mL). A milliliter has the same volume as a cubic centimeter, so 1 mL = 1 $cm^3$.

3. Does multiplying the area of the base by the height give the volume that is printed on the can? If not, why might the measures differ? See margin.
4. What is the surface area of the can in square centimeters? How did you find it? (Hint: Imagine what a net for the can would look like.)

## Develop & Understand: B

Now consider how the can design might be changed. For these exercises, use the volume that you *calculated* in Exercises 1–4, rather than the volume printed on the can. 5–7. See margin.

5. Design and describe five other cans that have approximately the same volume as your can. Sketch a net for each can. Record the radius of the base and the height. Include cans that are both shorter and taller than a regular beverage can. (Hint: First choose the height of the can and then find the radius.)
6. Calculate the surface area of each can you designed. Record your group's data on the board for the class to see.
7. Compare the surface areas of the cans that you and your classmates found. Which can has the greatest surface area? Which has the least surface area?

### Real-World Link

As water bubbles up through the earth from natural springs, it collects minerals and carbon dioxide. In the 1700s, chemists perfected a method of adding carbonation and minerals to plain water and bottling the result.

Bursting Bubbles wants to make a can using the least amount of aluminum possible. The company cannot do it by evaluating every possible can, like the five you found, and choosing the best. There are too many, an infinite number, and Bursting Bubbles could never be sure it had found the one using the *least* material.

One strategy that mathematicians use is to gather data, as you did in Exercise 5, and look for patterns in the data. For an exercise like this one, they would also try to show that a particular solution is the best in a way that does not involve testing every case.

8. Use what you know about volume and any patterns that you found in Exercises 5 and 6 to recommend a can with the least possible surface area to the president of Bursting Bubbles. Describe your can completely. Explain why you believe it has the least surface area.

8. Possible answer: The can with the least surface area will be the one whose diameter and height are closest to being equal. The surface areas in the class table decrease until the radius is about half the height, and then they increase again.

### Share & Summarize

Does the shape of standard beverage cans use the minimum surface area for the volume they contain? If not, what might be some reasons companies use the shape they do? No; the standard shape does not use the minimum surface area for the volume, but it is not far from the minimum. It is probably a more comfortable can to hold and more attractive.



### Additional Answers

3. Possible answer: Not quite. The formula gives about 399 mL, while the can claims 355 mL. Part of the difference may be that the can is not completely filled with liquid (carbonation takes up some of the space) and the fact that the can is not a true cylinder (its top and bottom aren't flat).
7. Answers will vary. Cans with slightly less height than the standard can will have less surface area. Cans with much less height or with greater height will have more surface area.

5–6. Possible answer:

| Radius (cm) | Height (cm) | Surface Area ($cm^2$) |
|---|---|---|
| 11.27 | 1 | 869 |
| 5.041 | 5 | 318 |
| 3.565 | 10 | 304 |
| 2.911 | 15 | 328 |
| 1.594 | 50 | 517 |

## Practice & Apply

Decide whether each figure is a net, that is, whether it will fold into a closed solid. One way to decide is to cut out a copy of the figure and try to fold it. If the figure is a net, describe the shape it creates. If it is not a net, explain why not.

**1.**

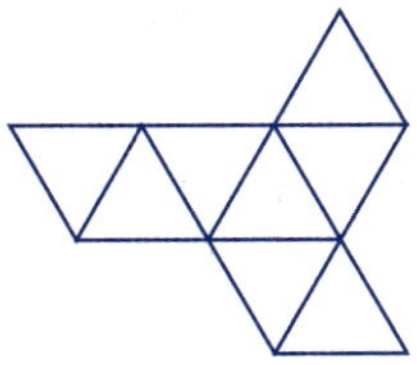

1. It is a net; it forms a solid with 8 triangular sides (an octahedron).

**2.**

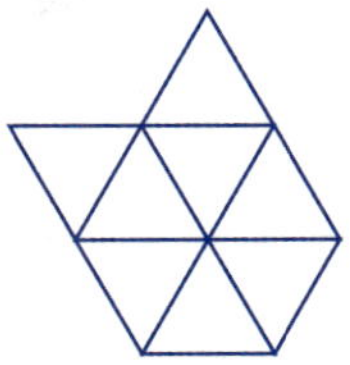

2. It is not a net; no matter how you try to fold the 6 triangles that meet at a point, you cannot get a closed solid.

**3.**

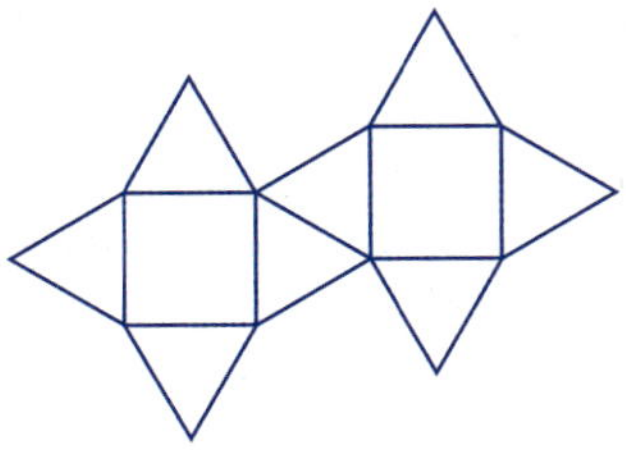

It is a net; it forms a solid with 2 parallel square faces connected by triangular faces (a square antiprism).

**4.** A *square pyramid* has a square base and triangular faces that meet at a vertex. Draw at least three nets for a square pyramid.

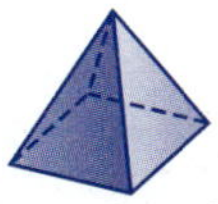

Square Pyramid

4. Possible answer:

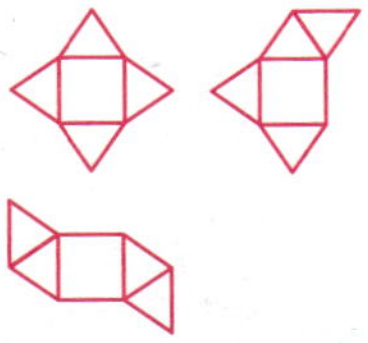

In Exercises 5–8, find the surface area of the solid that can be created from the net. Show how you found the surface area.

**5.** Each triangle is equilateral with sides 5 centimeters and height 4.3 centimeters.
Area of one triangle: 10.75 $cm^2$;
Total surface area: 86 $cm^2$

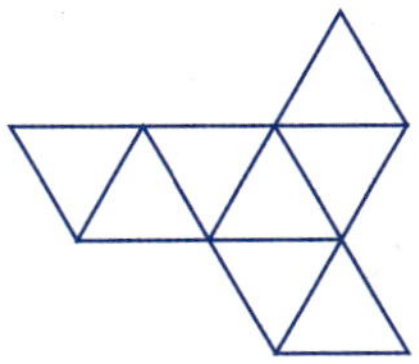

**6.** The radius of each circle is 2 centimeters. The height of the parallelogram is 2 centimeters.
Total area of circles: $8\pi$ $cm^2$;
Area of parallelogram: $8\pi$ $cm^2$;
Total surface area: $16\pi$ $cm^2$, or about 50.3 $cm^2$

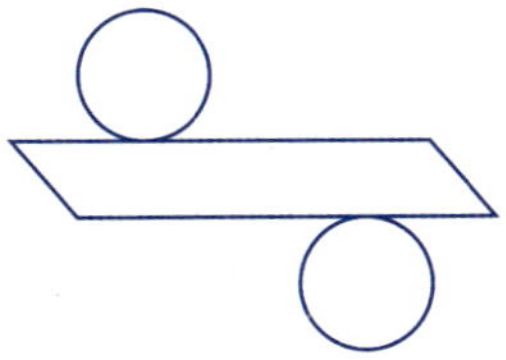



**On Your Own Exercises**
**Lesson 5.2**

**Investigation 1**
Pages 229–230
Practice & Apply: 1–4
Connect & Extend 13–16

**Investigation 2**
Pages 230–233
Practice & Apply: 5–11
Connect & Extend: 17–18

**Investigation 3**
Pages 233–234
Practice & Apply: 12
Connect & Extend: 19, 21

**Assign Anytime**
Mixed Review: 25–34

▶ **Exercises 1–3 and 5–8** These nets can be duplicated using Lesson 5.2 Masters 10 and 11.

▶ **Exercise 7** Students may need to be reminded that the area of a parallelogram is found the same way you would find the area of a rectangle; $A = bh$.

▶ **Exercise 8** If the students are struggling with computing the area of the pentagon, the problem tells them that the pentagon is broken up into 5 isosceles triangles. They should determine the area of one triangle and multiply that value by 5 to determine the area of the pentagon.

▶ **Exercise 9** Ask students what type of solid a tissue box would be classified as. This may help alleviate any confusion about where to start solving this problem.

▶ **Exercise 10** Students may answer in $cm^3$ or in mL or L. You might point out that milliliters and liters are more commonly used for liquids.

▶ **Exercise 10a** Remind students that when determining how much of something an object will hold, they are really looking to find the volume of the object.

On Your Own Exercises

**7.** The pentagons have side lengths of 3 centimeters. If you divide each pentagon into five isosceles triangles, the height of each triangle is 2 centimeters. The other shapes are squares.

Total area of pentagons: 30 $cm^2$; Total area of squares: 45 $cm^2$; Total surface area: 75 $cm^2$

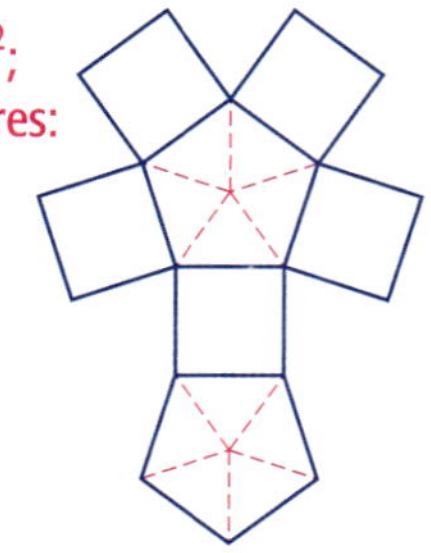

**8.** Each triangle is equilateral with sides 8 centimeters and height 7 centimeters. The other shapes are squares.

Total area of triangles: 224 $cm^2$; Total area of squares: 128 $cm^2$; Total surface area: 352 $cm^2$

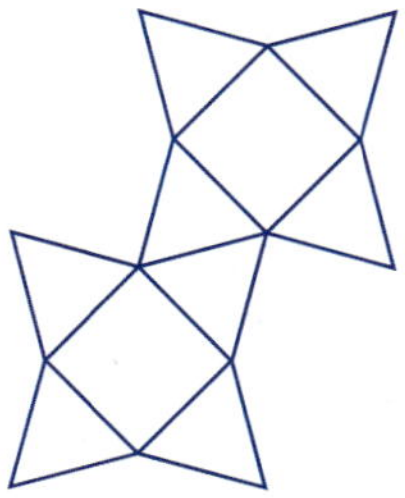

**9.** A box of tissues has length 24 centimeters, width 12 centimeters, and height 10.5 centimeters.

9a. 3,024 $cm^3$

**a.** What is the volume of the box?

**b.** What is the surface area of the box? 1,332 $cm^2$

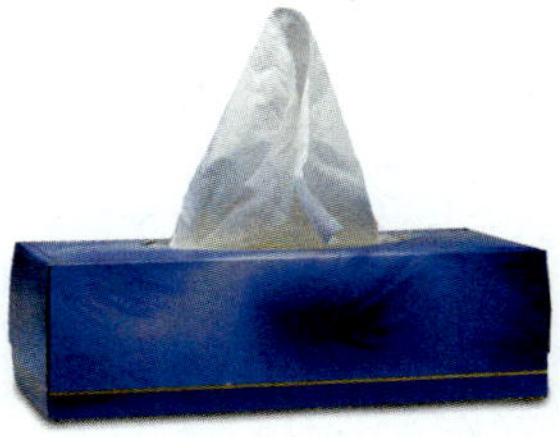

**10.** Alana has a juice pitcher that is shaped like a cylinder. It is 30 centimeters high and has a base with radius 6 centimeters. It has a flat lid.

**a.** How much juice will her pitcher hold? $1{,}080\pi$ $cm^3$, or about 3,393 $cm^3$ (about 3.4 L)

**b.** What is the surface area of her pitcher and its lid? $432\pi$ $cm^2$, or about 1,357 $cm^2$



236 **CHAPTER 5** Geometry in Three Dimensions

12c. Nets and surface areas will vary.

12d. Answers will vary. If the object is a prism, a cylinder will work. The cylinder with the same diameter as height will have less surface area than any other cylinder or prism.

14. Possible net:

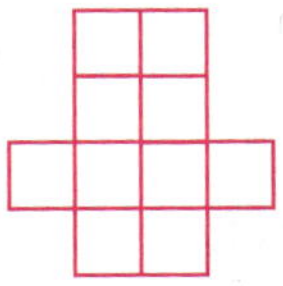

**Connect & Extend**

15. Possible net:

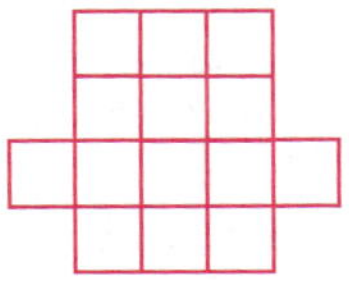

16. Possible net:

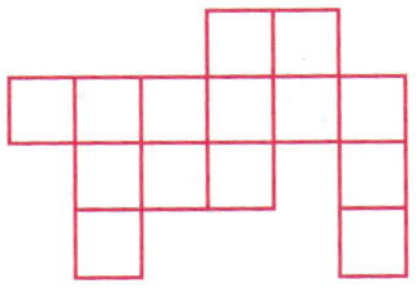

**11. Challenge** This net will fold into a *triangular pyramid.* Find the surface area of the pyramid. Estimate its volume. You may want to fold a copy of the net into the pyramid. Surface area: 15.6 $cm^2$; Volume: about 3 $cm^3$

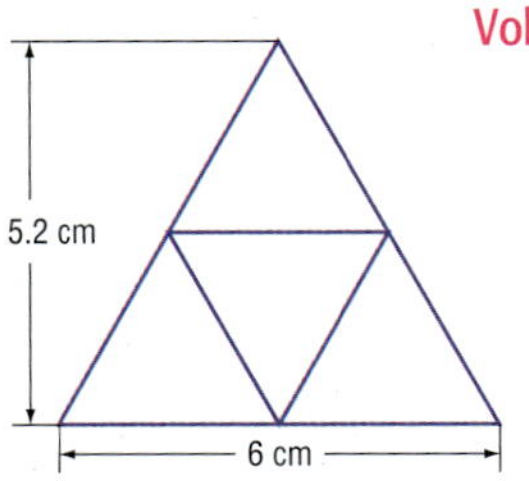


**12.** Choose a container in your house. You might choose a rectangular box, a can other than a beverage can, or some other object.

**a.** Draw a net for the object. Nets will vary.

**b.** Find the surface area and volume of the object by measuring its dimensions. Answers will vary.

**c.** Draw nets for three other objects with the same volume as your container. Find the surface area of each. The new objects do not have to be real containers from your home.

**d.** Is there a prism or cylinder with less surface area but the same volume as your container? If so, draw a net for it.

**13.** Imagine removing a label from a soup can.

**a.** What is the shape of the label? A rectangle

**b.** If the radius of the soup can is $r$ and the height is $h$, what are the dimensions of the label? $2\pi r$ and $h$

**Create a net for each block structure.**

**14.** 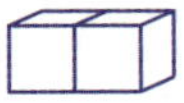

**15.** 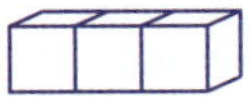

**16.** 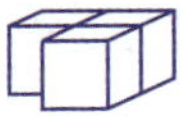





▶ **Exercise 11** Students can find the surface area of the pyramid by finding the area of the large triangular net or by finding the area of each face and adding these areas. The dimensions of the whole triangle are given, so the surface area is $\frac{1}{2}(bh)$, which is $\frac{1}{2}(6 \cdot 5.2)$, or 15.6 square cm. If students notice that the points on each side are midpoints (or appear to be), then they can find that each triangle has a base of 3 cm and height of 2.6 cm, so each small triangle has an area of $\frac{1}{2}(3 \cdot 2.6)$ or 3.9 square cm. Since there are four triangles in the larger one, the answer comes out the same (as it should!): 15.6 square cm.

▶ **Exercise 13** Students may note, rightly, that the label on the can actually overlaps itself a bit, so the length of the label will be a little bit more than $2\pi r$.

▶ **Exercises 14–16** Students may find it challenging to visualize the nets for a block structure rather than for other solids they have worked with. Partly, there are other squares to confuse the picture, squares that lie in the same plane rather than folding up. Encourage students to cut out their nets and fold them to test whether they work. They may also want to distinguish the lines between blocks from the lines along which you fold by using dashed lines or heavier lines for one of them. Lesson 5.2 Master 4, Centimeter Graph Paper, might help with this somewhat. If students create the nets on graph paper, then the lines of the graph paper can show the lines between blocks, and the lines students draw will be the lines of the net.

▶ **Exercises 17 and 18** If students are struggling with these exercises, ask them to create the solids out of paper and to use the solid to help them construct a net.

On Your Own Exercises

**17. Challenge** A cone has a circular base and a vertex some height away from that base. Make a net for a cone.
See margin.

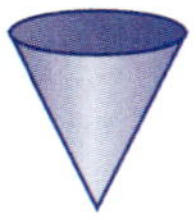

**18. Challenge** A *tetrahedron* is a solid with four triangular faces. You have made tetrahedrons from nets in this lesson. Nets for a tetrahedron contain only triangles. Can you make a net for another figure using only triangles? (Hint: You might try taping paper triangles together to form a new solid.)

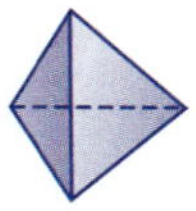

Tetrahedron

18. Possible answer: You can make a net for a solid with 8 triangular faces (an octahedron, as pictured in Exercise 1) and for a solid with 20 triangular faces (an icosahedron).

19a. $3{,}000\pi$ cm$^3$, or about 9,420 cm$^3$

19e. Surface area of single scoop: $32\pi$ cm$^2$, or about 100 cm$^2$; total surface area: about 12,600 cm$^2$

19f. The scooped frozen yogurt has more surface area and would therefore melt faster.

20. Answers will vary. Possible answer: Nets are templates for cutting out fabric and material and for forming the three-dimensional object.

**19. Food** Kinu's Frozen Yogurt store packs its product into cylindrical tubs that are 20 cm in diameter and 30 cm tall.

**a.** How much frozen yogurt does a tub hold?

**b.** Kinu's sells frozen yogurt in cylindrical scoops. If each scoop has base radius 2 cm and height 6 cm, what is the volume of a single scoop? $24\pi$ cm$^3$, or about 75.4 cm$^3$

**c.** How many scoops of frozen yogurt are in a tub? Show how you found your answer. 9,420 cm$^3$ ÷ 75.4 cm$^3$ = about 125 scoops

**d.** What is the surface area of a tub? $800\pi$ cm$^2$, or about 2,512 cm$^2$

**e.** What is the total surface area of the frozen yogurt from one tub *after* it has all been scooped?

**f.** Which has more surface area, the frozen yogurt in the tub or the scooped frozen yogurt? Which would melt faster?

**20. In Your Own Words** Explain why nets might be useful in sewing, manufacturing, or some other profession.

238 CHAPTER 5 Geometry in Three Dimensions

**Additional Answers**

17. Possible net

Note: The net is a quarter circle with a smaller circle tangent to the curve. The radius of the quarter circle is 4 times the radius of the smaller circle. Students may not get the proportions correct.

21. A circular pond is 100 feet in diameter. In the middle of winter, the ice on the pond is 6 inches thick.

a. Think of the ice on the pond as a cylinder. What is the volume of ice? About 3,927 $ft^3$

b. What is the surface area of the floating cylinder of ice?

21b. $5{,}050\pi$ $ft^2$, or about 15,900 $ft^2$

c. What would be the edge length of a cube of ice that had the same volume? About 15.8 ft

d. What would be the surface area of a cube of ice that had the same volume? About 1,493 $ft^2$

e. Which has greater surface area, the cylinder of ice or the cube of ice? How much more? The cylinder of ice; about 14,400 $ft^2$

**Preview** Match the following items with the most appropriate unit of weight.

22. an elephant C
23. a cup of yogurt A
24. a human being B

A. ounces
B. pounds
C. tons

## *Mixed Review*

**Find each product or quotient.**

25. $6(-12)$ $-72$

26. $-\frac{1}{5}\left(-\frac{2}{3}\right)$ $\frac{2}{15}$

27. $15 \div (-2)$ $-7.5$

28. $-\frac{4}{9} \div \left(-\frac{2}{3}\right)$ $\frac{2}{3}$

29. Copy and complete the chart.

| **Fraction** | $\frac{1}{2}$ | $\frac{3}{5}$ | $\frac{13}{20}$ | $\frac{21}{100}$ |
|---|---|---|---|---|
| **Decimal** | 0.5 | 0.6 | 0.65 | 0.21 |
| **Percent** | 50% | 60% | 65% | 21% |

**Rewrite each number in standard notation.**

30. $8 \times 10^2$ 800

31. $1.42 \times 10^6$ 1,420,000

32. $3.12 \times 10^{-4}$ 0.000312

33. $6.13 \times 10^{-2}$ 0.0613

34. Suppose you use a photocopying machine to reduce a photograph.

a. Your photograph is 10 cm wide, and you reduce it to 85% of its original size. What is the width of the reduced image? 8.5 cm

b. You use the same setting to reduce the copy. What is the width of the image after the second reduction? About 7.2 cm



On Your Own Exercises

## *Quick Check*

**Informal Assessment** Students should be able to:

✔ decide if a given net will fold into a closed three-dimensional solid

✔ create nets that will fold into given shapes

✔ use the nets of an object to find surface area and volume

## *Quick Quiz*

1. Draw a net for a cube that has a volume of 8 cubic centimeters. Possible answer:

2. What is the surface area of a cube with a volume of 8 cubic centimeters? 24 $cm^2$

LESSON 5.3

# Mass and Weight

### Objectives

- To identify the difference between weight and mass
- To measure the mass of an item
- To determine the volume of mass an object can hold
- To identify and use appropriate units for measuring mass and weight
- To convert between different customary units of mass and weight and between different metric units of mass and weight
- To use an object's mass or weight as a benchmark for discussing the mass and weight of other items

## *Overview*

This lesson reviews and extends what students know about measurements to include measuring weight and mass of items in both the metric and customary systems. Students will also learn how to use a benchmark as a starting point to describe the weight and mass of other items. Students will also gain skills in taking measurements of various items, and determining what units are appropriate for measuring various items based on their size.

## *Advance Preparation*

You may want to find some unique ideas of various mass and weight to put in your classroom for students to use in the lesson.

| | Summary | Materials | On Your Own Exercises (pp. 251–255) | Assessment Opportunities |
|---|---|---|---|---|
| **Investigation 1** (p. 241) Pacing: 2 days | Students will determine the mass of various objects in the metric system of measure. | kitchen or mail scale in grams, cup measure, flour, water | Practice & Apply: 1–2<br>Connect & Extend: 21<br>Mixed Review: 28–47 | • On the Spot Assessment (p. 241)<br>• Share & Summarize (p. 244)<br>• Troubleshooting (p. 242) |
| **Investigation 2** (p. 244) Pacing: 1 day | Students will estimate the mass of objects based on measures they already know or extend the measures of known mass to determine the mass of a new item. | kitchen, mail, or bathroom scale, ream of $8\frac{1}{2} \times 11$ paper, ruler, scissors | Practice & Apply: 3–13<br>Connect & Extend: 22<br>Mixed Review: 28–47 | • On the Spot Assessment (pp. 244, 245, 246)<br>• Share & Summarize (p. 247)<br>• Troubleshooting (p. 245) |
| **Investigation 3** (p. 247) Pacing: 1 day | Students will determine the weight of items in the customary scale of measurement. | kitchen or postal scale in ounces, bathroom scale in pounds | Practice & Apply: 14–20<br>Connect & Extend: 23–25<br>Mixed Review: 28–47 | • On the Spot Assessment (p. 248)<br>• Share & Summarize (p. 250)<br>• Troubleshooting (p. 250) |

# Leveled Lesson Resources

CRM *Available in:* **Chapter 5 Resource Masters**

Also on TeacherWorks™ Lesson 5.3

## Study Guide and Intervention (p. 24) AL

**Lesson 5.3 Study Guide and Intervention**
***Mass and Weight***

In the metric system, the most commonly used units of mass are the milligram (mg), gram (g), and kilogram (kg). One milligram is 0.001 gram and 1 kilogram is 1,000 grams.

**Metric Units of Mass**

| Unit | Model | Benchmark |
|---|---|---|
| 1 milligram (mg) | grain of salt | 1 mg ≈ 0.00004 oz |
| 1 gram (g) | small paper clip | 1 g ≈ 0.04 oz |
| 1 kilogram (kg) | six medium apples | 1 kg ≈ 2 lb |

Other small units of mass include the centigram, which is 0.01 gram, and the decigram, which is 0.1 gram. Larger units include the decagram, which is 10 grams, and the hectogram, which is 100 grams.

***Example 1*** **Which metric unit would be most appropriate to measure the mass of a portable radio?**

A portable radio has a mass greater than six apples. So, the kilogram is the appropriate unit.

***Example 2*** **A box of cereal contains 450 grams. How many kilograms is this?**

450 g = __?__ kg   THINK 1,000 grams = 1 kilogram
450 ÷ 1,000 = 0.45   Divide to change grams to kilograms.
So, 450 grams = 0.45 kilograms.

***Exercises***

**Write the metric unit that would be most appropriate to measure the mass of each of the following. Then estimate the mass.**

1. peanut
2. eyelash
3. house cat
4. pencil

**Convert each quantity to grams. Write your answers in scientific notation.**

5. 35,000 centigrams
6. 7.2 milligrams
7. 1,672 hectograms

## Skills Practice (p. 25) AL OL

**Lesson 5.3 Skills Practice**
***Mass and Weight***

**Convert each quantity to grams. Write your answers in scientific notation.**

1. 26,000 centigrams
2. 10 milligrams
3. 1,672 kilograms
4. 39,720 milligrams
5. 0.5 decigrams
6. 25 hectograms

**Write the metric unit that you would use to measure the mass of each of the following. Then estimate the mass.**

7. leaf
8. feather
9. crayon
10. mosquito
11. penny
12. bowling ball
13. rectangular eraser
14. banana

**Fill in the blanks to make each equation true.**

15. 2 lb = ___ oz
16. 40 oz = ___ lb ___oz
17. $1\frac{1}{2}$ T = ___ lb
18. 10,000 lb = ___ T
19. 2 T = ___ oz
20. 96 oz = ___ lb
21. 32,000 oz = ___ T
22. 2 lb 5 oz = ___ oz

**Choose the better estimate for each measure.**

23. the weight of a bag of potatoes: 5 tons or 5 pounds
24. the weight of an apple: $\frac{1}{2}$ pound or 32 ounces

## Problem-Solving Practice (p. 26) AL OL

**Lesson 5.3 Problem-Solving Practice**
***Mass and Weight***

**Solve.**

1. **Ants** Earl has an ant farm. What metric unit of mass would Earl use to measure one of his ants?
2. **Fishing** Which is the most likely unit of measure Jacob finds on his fishing weights: milligram, gram, or kilogram?
3. **Dogs** Toni's Shih Tzu puppy weighed 0.896 kilograms at 2 months. Her weight increased by 2,688 grams over the next 7 months. What was the puppy's weight, in kilograms, at 9 months old?
4. **Pets** Carla's dog eats 321 grams of beef chow and 410 grams of chicken chow each day. Meda's dog eats 1 kilogram of mixed chow each day. Whose dog eats more chow each day? Explain your reasoning.
5. **Weightlifting** At the gym, each 1-pound weight is marked by 0.454 kg. Amy reduces the weight on her barbell from $2.2 \times 10^4$ grams to $4.5 \times 10^3$ grams. By how many kilograms did she reduce the weight? Write your answer in scientific notation.
6. **Candy** Wade works at the candy shop. He wrapped 56 pieces of fudge to sell. How many total pounds of fudge did he wrap if each piece weighed 1 ounce? Give your answer in pounds and ounces.
7. **Trucks** Shauna's truck can handle up to 2 tons of weight. She wants to haul 3,500 pounds of wood. How many tons of wood is that? Can she haul all of it at once? Explain.
8. **Pets** Pam has a 4-pound bag of dry cat food. Every day she puts out 4 ounces of dry cat food for her cat. For how many days will the bag of cat food be enough to feed her cat? Explain.

## Enrichment (p. 27) BL

**Lesson 5.3 Enrichment**
***Mass and Weight***

**Relating Customary and Metric Units**

Both customary and metric measurements are used in the United States. Therefore, it is a good idea to develop some sense of the relationships between the two systems. Here is a *rule of thumb* that is commonly used.

A kilogram is a little more than 2 pounds.

**Use the relationship above. Tell whether each statement is true or false.**

1. A weight of 10 pounds is more than 5 kilograms.
2. A pound is a little more than half a kilogram.

**Estimate the mass of each animal using the relationship between a kilogram and a pound. Write your answers in scientific notation.**

3. Tiger: 500 pounds = ____________ kilograms
4. Hummingbird: 3.1 gram = ____________ pounds
5. Elephant: 15,400 pounds = ____________ grams
6. Monarch butterfly: 0.5 gram = ____________ pounds

**Solve.**

7. The elevator in a mall has a weight limit of 2,500 pounds. A construction crew needs to bring in some equipment that weighs 1,300 kilograms. Can the crew use the elevator safely for moving this equipment? Explain.
8. A newborn baby weighed 3.41 kilograms. At age one year, the baby weighed 20 pounds. How many pounds did the baby gain in her first year of life? If the value is a decimal, write your answer in pounds and ounces.
9. The posted load limit for a bridge is 5 tons. The mass of Darryl's truck is 1,500 kilograms, and it is holding cargo that weighs one-half metric ton. Can Darryl drive his truck across the bridge?
10. Some scientists believe that Giganotosaurus may have been the largest carnivore to roam Earth and weighed 8 tons. The largest carnivore on Earth today is the Southern Elephant Seal, which has a weight of 5,000 kilograms. Which carnivore was bigger? Explain.

## Lesson Quick Quiz (p. 28) AL OL BL

**Lesson 5.3 Quick Quiz**

1. How many hectograms are there in $1.45 \times 10^4$ milligrams?
2. Name an item that would have a mass of about 2.5 kilograms.
3. If 10 sheets of construction paper has a mass of about 80 grams, how many sheet of paper are there in 2.5 kilograms?
4. A ream of construction paper contains 500 sheets, what is the mass of the ream of paper in kilograms?
5. A loaf of bread requires 5 pounds of flour, about how many cups of flour will you use?
6. What is the most appropriate unit to use to record the weight of a case of oranges?

# Additional Lesson Resources

### Teacher Tech Tools

- TeacherWorks
- ExamView Assessment Suite
- Classroom Presentation Toolkit
- Advance Tracker

### Student Tech Tools

- StudentWorks Plus
- Math Online eGlossary
- Concepts in Motion

### Other Print Products

- Investigation Notebook and Reflection Journal
- Quick Review Math Handbook

## Introduce

**How Much Does an Item Weigh?** Ask students how much a box full of items weighs. Bring in a scale or borrow one from the nurse's office or athletic department to weigh a box full of items. Ask the students what the number means. This is a great way to start a discussion about mass and weight. It also ties in to the Think & Discuss.

### Think & Discuss

*Suggested Grouping: Individuals*

If students are having difficulty determining how a scale works, bring in a scale and allow students to weigh objects in the classroom.

### Real-World Link

It may be helpful to talk with a science teacher to get some specific examples of when it matters whether you are discussing mass versus weight. If possible, try to tie in some of the things students may learn in science related to mass and weight.

LESSON 5.3

# Mass and Weight



### Vocabulary

**mass**

**weight**

### Real-World Link

Although we typically talk about weight in everyday speech, the distinction between mass and weight is important in sciences such as physics, chemistry, and astronomy.

You are familiar with weight, or how heavy things are. So, what is mass, and what does it have to do with weight?

**Mass** is a measurement of the amount of matter in an object. **Weight** is the pull of gravity on that amount of matter. Gravity pulls everything down toward the center of Earth. The more matter that is in an object, the more gravity pulls it down, and the heavier it is. When you pick up a rock and a piece of paper, the rock feels heavier because there is more matter in the rock.

What about the weight of objects on the moon, where the pull of gravity is less? What about the weight of objects in outer space, where there is so little gravity that everything floats?

The same rock feels much heavier on Earth than it does on the moon, but the amount of matter has not changed. In other words, the weight of the rock is different on the moon than it was on Earth, but its mass is the same regardless of where it is.

On Earth, mass and weight are the same if the object is at sea level. Above sea level, the object's weight will be less than its mass. The difference is quite small, however, even on the highest mountains. So, as long as you are talking about objects that are on Earth, you can treat weight and mass as being equivalent.

### Think & Discuss

Suppose you weigh 120 pounds on Earth. How much do you think you would weigh on the moon? Estimates will vary. Answer should be 20 pounds.

In fact, the gravitational pull of the moon is only $\frac{1}{6}$ that of Earth. How close was your Think & Discuss estimate? Approximate your weight on the moon.



## *Reaching* All Learners

**ELL English Language Learners** Students may have difficulty with understanding the difference between mass and weight. Ask students to make a list of words, in their first language that have similar meanings to mass and weight. Work with students to find words that match the definitions of mass and weight as closely as possible.

# Investigation 1 Measure Mass

**Vocabulary**

**gram**

**metric system**

**Materials**

- kitchen or mail scale marked in 100-gram or 10-gram divisions that can weigh at least 2 kg
- scale, cup measure, flour, and water

In this investigation, you will measure and calculate mass using metric units since the **metric system** measures mass. Remember that because scales rely on gravity, you can use them to measure only weight and not mass. However, on Earth, weight and mass are approximately the same.

The metric system is compatible with our decimal number system. Whether you are measuring length, mass, or volume, the relationship between the units is the same. Ten of one unit equals one of the next larger unit.

The metric system uses a prefix to indicate the size of the unit. You are probably familiar with some of these prefixes from the metric units for length and volume.

| Prefix | Meaning |
|---|---|
| Milli- | Base unit ÷ 1,000 |
| Centi- | Base unit ÷ 100 |
| Deci- | Base unit ÷ 10 |
| No prefix | Base unit • 1 |
| Deca- | Base unit • 10 |
| Hecto- | Base unit • 100 |
| Kilo- | Base unit • 1,000 |

## Think & Discuss

The basic unit of mass in the metric system is the **gram**. What is a situation in which you have seen grams or kilograms used as a unit of measure? See ①.

What is a situation in which you have seen milligrams used as a unit of measure? Possible answer: Dosages of medicine

① Possible answer: Packages of cereal, rice, or other groceries. Heavy objects are measured in kilograms.

## Develop & Understand: A

1. Copy and complete this table that shows conversions among various metric units of mass. Use decimals when necessary.

| | | | | | | | |
|---|---|---|---|---|---|---|---|
| **Milligrams** | 1,000 | 55,000 | 7,000,000 | 830,000 | 1,950 | 4 | 3,589 |
| **Centigrams** | 100 | 5,500 | 700,000 | 83,000 | 195 | 0.4 | 358.9 |
| **Decigrams** | 10 | 550 | 70,000 | 8,300 | 19.5 | 0.04 | 35.89 |
| **Grams** | 1 | 55 | 7,000 | 830 | 1.95 | 0.004 | 3.589 |
| **Decagrams** | 0.1 | 5.5 | 700 | 83.0 | 0.195 | 0.0004 | 0.3589 |
| **Hectograms** | 0.01 | 0.55 | 70 | 8.30 | 0.0195 | 0.00004 | 0.03589 |
| **Kilograms** | 0.001 | 0.055 | 7 | 0.830 | 0.00195 | 0.000004 | 0.003589 |



## On the Spot Assessment

Give the students a list of 5 measurements: 125 centigrams, 1.3 kilograms, 1250 milligrams, 0.13 hectograms, and 130 grams and ask the students to list the measurements from least to greatest.

# Investigation 1

***On Your Own Exercises***
Pages 251–255
Exercises 1–2, 21

**Metric Prefixes** Have students write down as many metric units as they can remember. Start by asking the students to separate the units that are used for mass (grams) from those that are not (liter, meter, etc.). Now pick two examples that refer to grams and ask the students to tell you how they are related.

**Analyze the Table** Students may have experience with metric units, so this table may not look new to them. Ask students what they know about the metric system and tie that in to the units as expressed by the prefix in the table. There are more prefixes for even larger and smaller units, but the units of mass you are likely to come across in everyday contexts are grams, kilograms, and milligrams.

## Think & Discuss

Another unit you may see used is the *metric ton*, or *tonne*. One tonne equals 1,000 kilograms. Another name for a tonne is a *megagram*.

## Develop & Understand: A

*Suggested Grouping: Pairs*

▶ **Exercise 1** This exercise directly relates to the understanding of how units are related according to the table. Direct students to use the table to assist with conversions if they are struggling.

**Lesson 5.3** Mass and Weight **241**

▶ **Exercise 2** Students should have scientific notation fresh in their heads since it was just covered in Chapter 4. If they are having difficulty, remind the students to count the zeros and whether or not they are making the number larger (moving decimal to the right) or smaller (moving the decimal to the left).

▶ **Exercise 3** A common mistake that students will make with this exercise is to add the numbers before they convert all of the measurements to the same unit.

## Develop & Understand: B

*Suggested Grouping: Pairs*

If a kitchen or mail scale is unavailable, check with the science or home economics department to see if they have scales you can borrow. If you still have difficulty acquiring scales to use, offer an incentive to students who can bring in a scale for the class to use.

▶ **Exercises 5–7** Depending on the type of scale, the answers for these exercises can vary. It may be interesting if different types of scales are used to discuss whether the results should be different and why or why not. A kitchen scale with a flat surface to accommodate a bowl may work better than a balance scale for many of the measurements.

**Math Link**
The kilogram was originally defined as the mass of a liter of water at 4° Celsius. Because the ratio of water's mass to volume changes at different temperatures, a specific temperature had to be designated.

5a. A pencil is so light that the needle on the scale does not move.

5d. I cannot fit the backpack onto the scale, but it is probably so heavy that its reading would be off the end of the scale's numbers.

5e. I cannot fit the desk onto the scale, but it is probably so heavy that its reading would be off the end of the scale's numbers.

6a. A book, two shoes

6c. A stapler, a set of keys

Scientific notation is often used to express the magnitude of quantities that are very large or very small.

**2.** Use scientific notation to express the following conversions.

**a.** 6 grams = ______ milligrams $6 \times 10^3$

**b.** 5.3 hectograms = ________ grams $5.3 \times 10^2$

**c.** 702 grams = ________ centigrams $7.02 \times 10^4$

**d.** 45 grams = ______ kilograms $4.5 \times 10^{-2}$

**e.** 89.3 milligrams = ______ kilograms $8.9 \times 10^{-5}$

**3.** Theo bought the following food items.

1,300 milligrams of saffron — 68.5 grams of ground pepper

737 grams of salt — 5 kilograms of rice

What was the total mass of Theo's items? Express your answer in terms of one unit only. 5,806.8 grams

**4.** The mass of one biology textbook is 1,525 grams. Suppose 300 textbooks are loaded into a truck. What is the mass of all the textbooks in the truck? Express your answer in kilograms. 457.5 kilograms

## Develop & Understand: B

Use a small scale marked in metric units to investigate mass. Before you begin, make sure your scale reads 0 when there is nothing on it. If it does not, you will need to adjust it.

**5.** Record the mass of each object or explain why you cannot find its mass with your scale. Answers will vary depending on the scale and the exact mass of the objects.

**a.** a pencil

**b.** a textbook 1.75 kilograms

**c.** a paperback novel 250 grams

**d.** a full backpack

**e.** a desk

**f.** a calculator 210 grams

**6.** Find an object in your classroom whose mass is approximately the following. Answers will vary.

**a.** 1 kilogram

**b.** 2 kilograms A textbook

**c.** 200 grams

**d.** 500 grams A sneaker

**e.** 25 grams Scissors

**f.** 5 grams A pencil



## Troubleshooting

Students often forget that they cannot just add numbers together. They must look at the units and make sure that all of the numbers represent the same unit in order to be added together. It is a lot like adding fractions or combining like terms. Try to use similar scenarios to help students understand this concept.

① The box filled with books would be heavier because books are heavier for their size than tissues.

**Real-World Link**

When you zero out a scientific instrument, such as a scale, you are *calibrating it*. This ensures the instruments will measure readings accurately. *Taring* refers to adjusting a scale so that a number other than 0 shows when there is nothing on the scale. This is useful if you want to weigh something inside a container.

11. Possible answer: Approximately 125 grams; Subtract the mass of the cup from the mass of the weighed cup of flour. The remaining amount is the mass of just the flour.

12. Possible answer: Approximately 225 grams; Subtract the mass of the cup from the mass of the weighed cup of water. The remaining amount is the mass of just the water.

**7.** Find the mass of a collection of similar pens.

**a.** How many pens do you need to put on the scale to get a mass of approximately 100 grams? 17

**b.** Use your answer from Part a to estimate the mass of 1 pen. About 5.9 grams

**c.** About how many pens would you need to make a mass of 1 kilogram? About 170

**d.** One metric ton equals one thousand kilograms. About how many pens would you need to make a mass of 1 metric ton? About 170,000

### Think & Discuss

Suppose you have two cardboard boxes with dimensions 0.5 meters by 0.5 meters by 0.5 meters. You fill one box with pocket-sized packages of tissues and one with books. Which is heavier, or are their masses the same? Explain your reasoning. See ①.

Two objects can be the same size and yet have different masses. The saying "rock is heavier than butter" means that a given volume of rock is heavier than the same volume of butter. Put another way, a large amount of butter has the same mass as a small amount of rock.

## Develop & Understand: C

8–10. Answer depends on cup used.

**8.** What is the mass of the measuring cup your teacher provided?

**9.** Put 250 milliliters of flour in the measuring cup. What is the mass?

**10.** Empty the cup and put in 250 milliliters of water. What is the mass?

**11.** What is the mass of 250 milliliters of flour? Explain how you found your answer.

**12.** What is the mass of 250 milliliters of water?

**13.** Compare the masses of 250 milliliters of flour and 250 milliliters of water.

**a.** Which mass is greater? How much greater? See below.

**b.** Which has greater volume, 1 kilogram of water or 1 kilogram of flour? 1 kilogram of flour

**14.** Based on your measurements, what would be the mass of 1 liter of water? Approximately 1 kilogram but students' measurements may vary.

**15.** Based on your measurements, what volume of flour would have a mass of 1 gram? Possible answer: 2 milliliters

13a. Answer depends on students' answers to 11 and 12. Possible answer: The water's mass is 100 grams more than the flour's mass.



**Wrap-Up** In small groups, have the students discuss what new knowledge they have attained as a result of this investigation. Have the groups share their findings.

### Think & Discuss

*Suggested Grouping: Pairs*

If possible, bring to class objects that are far lighter or heavier than they appear, such as paperweights, an empty but opaque juice bottle, or a juice bottle full of sand.

## Develop & Understand: C

*Suggested Grouping: Pairs*

Depending on class size, classroom size, and other logistics, you may want to demonstrate the measuring yourself or supervise one or two student volunteers, rather than have all students take measurements themselves.

▶ **Exercises 9 and 10** When the students are working on these exercises explain that 1 cup is approximately 250mL. It is truly an estimation when filling a measuring cup with something and determining its mass. That is why bakers will measure their ingredients with a scale instead of measuring cups.

▶ **Exercises 14 and 15** Students may struggle with these exercises because they require a conversion in addition to unit changes. Refer students to the conversion table for assistance.

▶ **Exercise 16** Discuss units of temperature with students. Some students may not realize that we measure temperature in Fahrenheit in the United States, but the metric unit of temperature is Celsius. If time permits, convert 4°C to 39.2°F.

**Wrap-Up** In small groups have the students compare their results. Have the small groups write their solutions on the board or on an overhead sheet to share with the class. As a class compare the findings. Ask why the answers are not all the same, but also not incorrect.

**Share & Summarize**

Students may have varying ideas of what units are better. Remind students that some units are more appropriate than others because of the size of the item. Would you measure the mass of an elephant in milligrams? The number would be extremely large, so a larger unit would be more appropriate. Ask students to give other examples of items that could be measured with inappropriate units.

## Investigation 2

***On Your Own Exercises***
Pages 251–255
Exercises 3–13, 22

**Scale Check-up** Before beginning this investigation, it will be helpful to check the scales you will be using to ensure that the ream of paper's weight, or the book's weight registers. Mechanical scales are more likely to register lighter weights than electronic ones. The scale should be marked in 10-gram or 100-gram divisions and be able to weigh at least 2 kg.

### Develop & Understand: A

*Suggested Grouping: Pairs*

▶ **Exercises 1–3** For these exercises, encourage students to use the same procedures for each step. This method will help their measurements be consistent.

▶ **Exercises 4 and 5** Students will need to use their results from Exercises 1–3 to answer these questions.

16a. Answers may vary. Students will likely not have measured the mass of 250 mL of water as exactly 250 g.

**16.** By definition, the mass of 1 liter of water at 4°C is 1 kilogram.

**a.** How does your approximation of the mass of a liter of water compare to the theoretical mass?

**b.** What might account for any difference between your approximation and the theoretical mass? See margin.

**17.** If you used a scale that was marked in milligrams for this activity, how do you think it would affect your results? See margin.

**Share & Summarize**

Which metric units would be most appropriate as benchmarks to measure the mass of each item below?

book hectograms or kilograms

pencil grams

penny grams

person kilograms or something larger, though metric tons are too large

## Investigation 2 Estimate Mass

**Materials**

- kitchen or mail scale
- single sheets of $8\frac{1}{2}$-in. × 11-in. paper
- an unopened ream of $8\frac{1}{2}$-in. × 11-in. paper
- ruler
- scissors

In this investigation, you will use your knowledge to estimate measures of mass. To begin, how big is a gram?

### Develop & Understand: A

**1.** Weigh a piece of paper on a small scale. You may need to fold the paper to fit it on the scale. Does the paper's mass register on the scale? No, unless students are using a scale that measures extremely small masses

**2.** About how many pieces of paper do you need to put on the scale for the scale to show a number larger than 0? Answers will vary depending on scale. Possible answer: About 4

**3.** About how many pieces of paper have a mass of 100 grams? Possible answer: About 20

**4.** Based on your answer to Exercise 3, what is the approximate mass of one piece of paper? Possible answer: About 5 grams

**5.** Based on your answer to Exercise 3, compare the mass of one gram to a piece of paper. Sample answer: About $\frac{1}{5}$ of a piece of paper has a mass of 1 gram.

In the next exercise set, you will consider the mass of a kilogram.

**Math Link**
1 kilogram = 1,000 grams



**On the Spot Assessment**

Which unit would be most appropriate to measure the mass of a dog? Kilogram

Using a mass of 125 grams of flour being approximately 250mL, what volume of flour would yield a mass of 1 kilogram? 2000 mL or 2 liters

**Additional Answers**

16b. Possible answers: My temperature may not have been 4° C.; I might not have measured exactly 250 milliliters. The scale was difficult to read, so my mass reading was an approximation.

17. Possible answer: I would be able to measure the masses more exactly. I would probably get about the same numbers, but I would be able to more accurately find the water's mass.

7c. Possible answer: The estimate was close but not exact. It was hard to determine exactly how many pieces of paper had a mass of 100 grams.

## Develop & Understand: B

6. Based on your answer to Exercise 3, about how many pieces of paper have a mass of 1 kilogram? Sample answer: About 200
7. Examine a ream, or package, of paper.
   a. How many pieces of paper are in the ream? Answers depend on the ream, but 500 sheets is standard.
   b. Based on your answer to Exercise 4, estimate the mass of the ream of paper. Answer based upon a 500-sheet ream: About 2500 grams, or 2.5 kilograms.
   c. Was your estimate close to the mass you measured? If not, what might account for the difference?
8. Without using a scale, estimate the mass of your *IMPACT Mathematics* textbook.
   a. How many pages are in the book? How might you use this information to estimate the book's mass? See margin.
   b. Compare the book to the ream of paper whose mass you have already found. Does it look bigger or smaller? Does it feel heavier or lighter? See margin.
   c. Estimate the book's mass. Explain how you decided on your estimate. Possible answer: About 2 kilograms; Its mass is less than the mass of the ream of paper but maybe not by much.
9. Weigh the book on the scale. What is the book's mass? Answers will vary. Possible answer: 1.7 kg
10. Was your estimate close? Explain what you think might account for any difference between your estimate of the book's mass and the measured mass. See margin.
11. Based on your answer to Exercise 8, about how big is 1 kilogram compared to the mass of your Math book? See margin.

In Exercises 12–16, you will consider the mass of 100 kilograms.

### Real-World Link

About ninety billion kilograms of paper are used in the United States each year. According to the American Forest and Paper Association, about 50% of the used paper is recycled.

## Develop & Understand: C

12. Based on your answer to Exercise 9, about how many Math books would have a mass of 10 kilograms? Possible answer: Between 5 and 6
13. About how many Math books would have a mass of 30 kilograms? Possible answer: Between 17 and 18
14. About how many Math books would have a mass of 100 kilograms? Possible answer: About 60



## Develop & Understand: B

*Suggested Grouping: Pairs*

▶ **Exercise 6** This exercise is going to give the students the ability to make a prediction based on a smaller weight and measurement that they have taken.

▶ **Exercise 7** The answers to this exercise will depend on the answers the students found in Exercises 1–5 as well as the scale that they are using. It may be beneficial for the groups to record all of their answers in a table form on the board or overhead for comparison.

▶ **Exercise 8** To assist students in answering this question, have a full ream of paper out that the students can handle. In addition, it may be necessary to remind students that they already have the measurements of a sheet of paper and a ream of paper.

### Real-World Link

Refer to the Real-World Link and ask students: About how many sheets of paper is this? About 18 trillion sheets

## Develop & Understand: C

*Suggested Grouping: Pairs*

▶ **Exercises 12–14** The answers to these exercises depend on the measurements that the students made in Exercise 9. It may be helpful to the students to discuss the previous exercise set before answering these questions.

**See Additional Answers on p. 259A for Exercises 8, 10, and 11.**

## Troubleshooting

Students may become concerned if their answers are not exactly the same as everyone else's. Explain that measuring in this manner is not very exact and there should be a margin of error. Discuss what other factors can cause answers to be different.

## On the Spot Assessment

If 10 sheets of construction paper weighs 80 g, how many sheets would there be in 1 kg? 125 sheets

▶ **Exercise 16** This exercise can be done in pairs to save time. It may also be useful to provide items around the classroom that are of varying sizes and weights for the students to use.

**Wrap-Up** A class discussion is a great way to share information and to tie any loose ends of this investigation. It may be helpful for students to share their results on the board or on an overhead before proceeding.

## Develop & Understand: D

*Suggested Grouping: Pairs*

▶ **Exercises 17 and 18** If students are having difficulty placing items in the appropriate place in the table, it may be helpful to have a grain of rice, a paper clip (that has a mass of 0.5–1.5 g), a sugar packet (that has a mass of 1–3 grams), a penny, a nickel, and a paperback book (that has a mass of 1–2 kg) available for the students to handle for a point of reference.

▶ **Exercise 19** Make sure that you have items in your room that are not in the list for the students to add to the table.

**Think & Discuss**

*Suggested Grouping: Individuals*

Before proceeding to the Think & Discuss, provide students with a completed table of mass values. This will allow students the best opportunity to think about their work.

17. Answers are approximate masses. Students' answers will vary.; Push pin 500 milligrams

17a. Newborn human baby; Between a liter of water and a cat

17b. Nickel; Between penny and pencil

17c. Refrigerator (full size); Between human and cow

17d. Sugar packet; Between paper clip and penny

17e. Paperback book; Either between pencil and liter of water or between liter of water and cat

**15.** Suppose you stack all of the *IMPACT Mathematics* books belonging to you and your classmates. 15a–b. See margin.

**a.** Approximately what is the mass of the stack?

**b.** What is the height of the stack in meters?

**16.** Find three objects of different sizes. Estimate the mass of each one, using what you already know about the size of grams and kilograms. Record your estimates. Then weigh the objects on the scale. Record each object's actual mass. Answers will vary.

## Develop & Understand: D

**17.** Compare the following objects to those listed in the table. Put each object in its appropriate order in the list. A plastic-headed push pin, for example, would have a mass between a grain of a rice and a paper clip.

**a.** Newborn human baby

**b.** Nickel

**c.** Full-size refrigerator

**d.** Individual sugar packet

**e.** Paperback book

| Object | Approximate Mass |
|---|---|
| Grain of sand | $3.5 \cdot 10^{-4}$ milligrams |
| Grain of rice | 20–30 milligrams |
| Paper clip | 0.5–1.5 grams |
| Penny | 2.5 grams |
| Wooden pencil (unsharpened) | 7 grams |
| 1 liter of water | 1 kilogram |
| Cat | 5–7 kilograms |
| Dog | 5–70 kilograms |
| Adult human | 45–90 kilograms |
| Cow | 700 kilograms |
| Car | 800–1600 kilograms |
| Largest known dinosaur | 80–100 metric tons |
| Blue whale | 108 metric tons |
| Earth | $6.0 \times 10^{24}$ kilograms |
| Sun | $2 \times 10^{30}$ kilograms |

**18.** Estimate the mass of each object from Exercise 17, using the objects whose mass is given as benchmarks to help. Choose two objects from the list. Explain how you made your estimate. See margin.

**19.** Think of three objects whose masses you do not know. Use the benchmarks to help you estimate the mass of each object. Answers will vary.

**Think & Discuss**

Compare your estimates from Exercise 17 to the actual (approximate) masses of the objects.

Which of your estimates were close? Which were not close? Answers will vary.

Are there any masses that surprise you? For example, was there an object that you thought was heavier or lighter than it turned out to be? See ① in margin.



**On the Spot Assessment**

After Exercise 15, ask: What is the approximate mass of a stack of textbooks as tall as you? Possible answer: I am about 160 centimeters tall. The book is about 3 centimeters thick. So, 53 books would be almost as tall as me. Their mass would be 90.1 kilograms.

**Additional Answers**

15a. Answers depend on number of students in class. Possible answer: The mass of 1 book is about 1.7 kilograms, so the mass of 24 books would be about 40.8 kilograms.

15b. Possible answer: 1 book is about 3 cm thick, so 24 books would be 72 cm high, which is less than a meter.

**See Additional Answers on p. 259A for Exercise 18 and ①.**

② $0.001 = 1.00 \times 10^{-3}$
③ $0.000625 = 6.25 \times 10^{-4}$

***Share & Summarize***

How would you estimate the mass of an object if you did not have a scale to use? See ① in margin.

# Investigation 3 Measure Weight

**Vocabulary**

- **customary system**
- **ounce**
- **pound**
- **ton**

**Materials**

- kitchen or postal scale marked in ounces
- bathroom scale marked in pounds

7. $p = 2{,}000t$, $t = \frac{p}{2{,}000}$, $n = 32{,}000t$, $t = \frac{n}{32{,}000}$

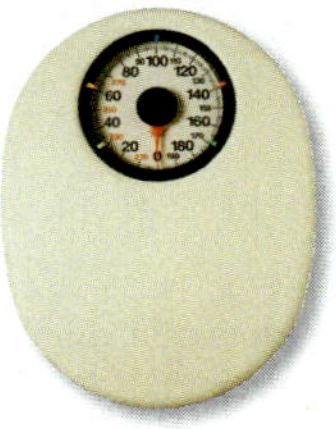

**Math Link**

The *ounce* is also a unit of capacity. There are eight ounces in one cup, or sixteen ounces in one pint. For clarity, *fluid ounces* describe capacity, and just *ounces* are used to describe weight.

As you saw in Investigations 1 and 2, metric units for mass, such as the kilogram, are often used as though they measure weight. Mass is a more scientific and precise property of objects than weight. However, we can perceive weight directly and measure it easily. In science and engineering, it is important to distinguish between mass and weight. For most other situations, it usually does not make a difference.

The **customary system** of measurement is used in the United States.

The most commonly used units of weight in the customary system are **ounces**, **pounds**, and **tons**. A decimal or a fraction can be used to express a fractional portion of a pound, 0.75 or $\frac{3}{4}$ pound.

## Develop & Understand: A

1. Copy and complete this table for converting customary units of weight.

| | | | | | | |
|---|---|---|---|---|---|---|
| **Ounces** | 32 | 256000 | 20 | 32,000 | 16 | 1 |
| **Pounds** | 2 | 16,000 | 1.25 | 2,000 | 1 | $0.0625 = 6.25 \times 10^{-2}$ |
| **Tons** | See ②. | 8 | See ③. | 1 | $0.0005 = 5.00 \times 10^{-4}$ | $0.00003125 = 3.125 \times 10^{-5}$ |

2. What fraction of 1 pound is 1 ounce? $\frac{1}{16}$
3. What fraction of 1 ton is 1 pound? $\frac{1}{2000}$
4. Write an equation that gives you weight in pounds $p$ if you know the weight in ounces $n$. $\frac{n}{16} = p$
5. Write a formula to convert weight in pounds to weight in ounces. $n = 16p$
6. How are these two formulas related? See below.
7. Write formulas to convert tons to pounds, pounds to tons, tons to ounces, and ounces to tons. Be sure to state what your variables represent.

6. Possible answer: They describe the same relationship. Going from pounds to ounces, you do the opposite of what you do to go from ounces to pounds. To convert from ounces to pounds, you divide by 16. To convert from pounds to ounces, you multiply by 16.

**Lesson 5.3** Mass and Weight **247**

## *Reaching All Learners*

**AL Approaching Level** Students may not feel comfortable approximating or estimating an object's mass. Encourage students by practicing estimation and approximation of money and making change. If you gave a cashier \$4 for a bill that was \$3.47, how much change should you receive? Use rounding to get the bill to \$3.50 which results in \$0.50 change. Several of these types of problems will get the students in the practice of estimating and approximating.

***Share & Summarize***

A classroom discussion will tie all of the parts of this investigation together as well as giving students a very useful means of approximation and estimation that can be extended to many other areas aside from weight and mass.

## Investigation 3

***On Your Own Exercises***
Pages 251–255
Exercises 14–20, 23–25

**Customary Units** This investigation uses customary units to measure weight. Explain that between engineering and mathematics there is a discrepancy about whether the pound is a measure of weight, mass, or both.

Have a class discussion regarding other units in the customary system that the students are familiar with such as inches and feet. The customary units that correspond to metric grams are ounces. One ounce is approximately 28.35 grams. There are 16 ounces in a pound and 2,000 pounds in a ton.

## Develop & Understand: A

*Suggested Grouping: Pairs*

▶ **Exercise 1** Students will take the given information and use it to complete the table. This may be frustrating for students because they do not have the first value in the table. Suggest students start in column 2 where 32 ounces is the same as 2 pounds. Ask: How would you determine the number of ounces in 1 pound? Divide by 2. This is how the students will complete the table as well as answer other questions to follow.

▶ **Exercise 4** If students are struggling with this question, ask them how they solved Exercise 1.

**Additional Answer**

① Possible answer: Think about an object for which you know the mass and think about whether the object is about the same size, bigger or smaller.

▶ **Exercise 8** The key to this question is to understand that if you are converting from a large unit to a smaller unit, you multiply. If you are converting from a small unit to a larger unit, you will divide the quantity.

**Wrap-Up** To tie the lesson together, ask for student volunteers to share how they arrived at the answer to each of the exercises.

### Think & Discuss

*Suggested Grouping: Individual*

There is not an absolute correct answer here. What is important is to see how a student thinks through a problem.

### Additional Answers

① Possible answers: For pounds: Butter, flour, people, meat, weights at the gym, animals; For ounces: Cereal and other dry packaged groceries, mail (for postage). Sometimes things are measured in pounds and ounces, like a baby's weight; For tons: Large animals like elephants and whales, cars and trucks, large amounts of products like grain

② Possible answer: the needle on the scale does not move or does not move enough to see. The numbers on an electronic scale do not change.

While fractions, decimals, and mixed numbers can be used to express a quantity like $1\frac{1}{2}$ pounds, or 1.5 pounds, you can also express some of these amounts in terms of a whole number of pounds and a whole number of ounces.

For example, 1.5 pounds is equivalent to 1 pound 8 ounces.

**8.** Fill in the blanks to make each equation true. Write your answer to Part c as a fraction and your answer to Part d as a decimal. Write your answer to Parts e–g as a fraction and as a decimal.

**a.** 2.5 pounds = __2__ pounds __8__ ounces

**b.** $\frac{3}{4}$ pounds = __12__ ounces

**c.** 38 ounces = ____ pounds   $2\frac{3}{8}$

**d.** 10 ounces = __0.625__ pound

**e.** 5 pounds 5 ounces = __See ①__ pounds or __5.3125__ pounds

**f.** 3 pounds 4 ounces = __See ②__ pounds or __3.25__ pounds

**g.** 2 tons 1,000 pounds = __See ③__ tons or __2.5__ tons

① $5\frac{5}{16}$

② $3\frac{1}{4}$

③ $2\frac{1}{2}$

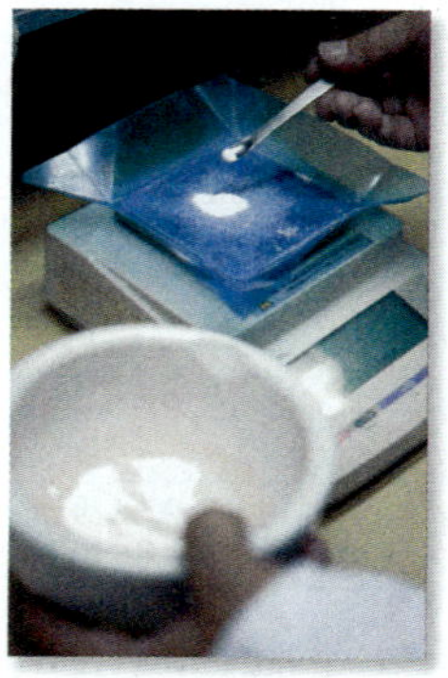

### Real-World Link

Pharmacists and jewelers measure very small quantities of material in the metric unit of milligrams or in the customary unit of grains. The grain is a very small unit. There are 7,000 grains in one pound. The grain as a unit of weight was originally based on the weight of 1 grain of barley.

### Think & Discuss

What things are commonly measured in pounds? In ounces? In tons? See ① in margin.

Not all scales are suitable for weighing every object.

How can you tell if an object is too small to weigh on the scale you are using? See ② in margin.

How can you tell if an object is too large to weigh on the scale you are using? Possible answers: The needle goes past the greatest number, or stops right at the greatest. The needle wraps around past zero. An electronic scale might give an error message.



### On the Spot Assessment

If an elephant weighs 5.5 tons, how many pounds does it weigh? How many ounces? $5.5 \cdot 2{,}000 = 11{,}000$ pounds; $11{,}000 \cdot 16 = 176{,}000$ ounces

### Reaching All Learners

**BL Beyond Level** Have students research other unique measurement units like the *grain*. Each student should find a unique unit, describe what it is used to measure and the historical purpose of the unit. Ask the students to present their finding to the class in the form of a poster that can be displayed for all students to view.

9f. Possible answer: Desk may be too large to put on a scale; a sweater may be too large and floppy for the small scale but not weigh enough for the large scale

## Develop & Understand: B

**9.** Find one object in the classroom that meets each of the following conditions. Possible answers given.

**a.** It can be weighed on the large scale but not on the small scale. Person

**b.** It can be weighed on the small scale but not on the large scale. Box of paper clips

**c.** It can be weighed on either scale. Textbook

**d.** It is too light to be weighed on either scale. Penny, paper clip, rubber band

**e.** It is too heavy to be weighed on either scale. Desk

**f.** It cannot be weighed on one of the scales for some reason other than inappropriate weight.

**10.** Weigh these sample objects. Copy and complete the table below. If you do not have the specified object available, substitute a similar object. Answers will vary depending on actual objects used.

| Object | Which scale did you use to weigh it? | Weight |
|---|---|---|
| Shoe | Small | Possible answer: 1 pound, 2 ounces |
| Textbook | Small or large | Possible answer: About 4 lbs |
| Stapler | Small | Possible answer: 8 ounces = 0.5 pounds |
| Paperback book | Small | Possible answer: 7 ounces = $\frac{7}{16}$ pounds ≈ 0.44 pounds |
| Overhead projector | Large | Possible answer: 15 pounds |
| Full box of paper clips | Small | sample answer: 2 ounces |

**11.** About how many of the following would make one pound?

**a.** staplers 2

**b.** paperback books 2

**c.** full boxes of paper clips 8

### Math Link

Why don't we have a unit somewhere between pounds and tons, when the difference in size is so big? *Hundredweight* is a customary unit equal to 100 pounds, but it is hardly ever used any more.



## Develop & Understand: B

*Suggested Grouping: Pairs*

When weighing objects that are small, it may be useful to weigh yourself holding a small object and not holding a small object. The weight of the object is the difference. You may wish to use yourself as a model and not students due to body-image concerns among middle school-aged students.

Make sure all students have a turn measuring objects and recording the measurements.

▶ **Exercise 10** Remind students to check that the scale is at zero before they begin to weigh an item. Movement can cause a mechanical scale to readjust itself. It is important to "tare" a scale or reset it to zero prior to any measurements.

▶ **Exercise 12** This exercise is asking students to make a comparison based on the information that they just evaluated. It is a base of information that is being used to estimate a measurement. This is an excellent skill to learn and use for the rest of their life.

▶ **Exercises 13–15** These exercises rely on the students having a benchmark for an ounce and then reversing the process to determine how heavy a small item is. If students go back through their exercises, they will have a place to start with their units.

**Wrap-Up** Ask students how many paperclips there would be in $\frac{1}{2}$ an ounce. Walk through the process with students. Show students how having a benchmark for a unit of measure can help them when they are shopping at a store on a budget or when they are baking to see if they have enough of an ingredient.

### Think & Discuss

*Suggested Grouping: Individuals*

Have students work individually to determine their answers. Then ask the students to meet in pairs and enlarge their list. Now have the pairs meet with another pair and enlarge their list. Ask one member from each small group to put their items on a class list either on the board or an overhead. Note the similarities and differences. Are there any disagreements about items placed in the lists? Discuss them.

### Share & Summarize

These questions will let you know if the students truly understand the way the customary system of measurement for weight works.

**Additional Answers**

② Possible answer: If the object has a number of identical parts, such as a stack of paper, or if you can take a piece that you know what fraction of the whole it is, then you could weigh the piece and multiply to find the weight of the whole thing. But that would not work for things like a car because you can not easily take a known fraction of a car, for example

12. Possible answer: A pound is about as heavy as a sneaker or two paperback books.

**Math Link**

You will often see these abbreviations used for units of mass.

g (grams)

mg (milligrams)

kg (kilograms)

13. Possible answer: About half as heavy as a box of paper clips; about an eighth of the weight of a stapler or a paperback book.

14. The full box weighs 2 ounces and the box says it has 100 paper clips in it. Assuming the box contains one hundred paper clips, one paper clip weighs a little less than $\frac{1}{50}$ of an ounce if you take into account the weight of the cardboard box.

**12.** Based on the results of Exercise 10, what could you say if someone asked you, "How heavy is a pound?"

**13.** What could you say if someone asked you, "How heavy is an ounce?"

**14.** Approximately how heavy is one paper clip? Explain your reasoning.

**15.** About how many Math books would weigh the following amounts?

**a.** 10 pounds About $2\frac{1}{2}$ **b.** 50 pounds About $12\frac{1}{2}$

**c.** 100 pounds About 25 **d.** 1 ton About 500

### Think & Discuss

How could you use a scale meant for heavy objects to estimate the weight of a light object? See ① below.

How could you use a scale meant for light objects to estimate the weight of a heavy object? See ② in margin.

Name some objects you could weigh on a bathroom scale. See ③ below.

Name some objects you could not weigh on a bathroom scale. See ④ below.

### Share & Summarize

How are mass and weight different? See ⑤ in margin.

What are appropriate customary units to measure the weight of each of the following?

apple Ounces bag of apples Pounds

truck Tons dog Pounds

① Possible answer: If you had a lot of objects all the same (like pennies or pieces of paper), you could put enough of them on the scale to measure the weight, and then divide that weight by the number of objects to estimate how much 1 of them weighs.

③ Possible answers: People, textbooks, gallon of milk, box full of books

④ Possible answers: Pencil, penny, car, refrigerator, elephant, piece of popcorn



⑤ Possible answer: Mass is the amount of substance you have and is measured in grams. Weight is is the pull of gravity on the amount of substance and is measured in ounces, pounds, and tons. However, on Earth, mass and weight are approximately the same.

### Troubleshooting

With all of the various types of conversions for units, students will sometimes have difficulty remembering if they should multiply or divide to convert units. If you remind students that multiplication makes numbers large, so when converting from a large unit to a smaller one, you multiply.

**Practice & Apply**

1a. $2.5 \times 10^4$ grams

1c. $3.4683 \times 10^{-1}$ grams

1e. $4.532 \times 10^6$ grams

2c. $5.4 \times 10^3$ milligrams
2d. $4 \times 10^5$ hectograms
3a. Tons, or something between kilograms and tons

6. Possible answers: books, clothing, shoes, small pets; liter or gallon of liquid

8. Possible answer: If we say the person's mass is 80 kilograms, then a car is 10 to 20 times heavier.
9. The grain of rice is about $7 \times 10^4$, or 70,000 times heavier than the grain of sand.

11. Possible answer: If we say a grain of rice is 25 milligrams, then there are 200,000 grains in a 5-kilogram bag.

**1.** Convert each quantity to grams. Write your answers in scientific notation.

**a.** 25 kilograms
**b.** 29,000 centigrams $2.9 \times 10^2$ grams
**c.** 34,683 milligrams
**d.** 4.2 milligrams $4.2 \times 10^{-3}$ grams
**e.** 4,532 kilograms
**f.** 0.5 kilograms $5 \times 10^2$ grams

**2.** Which of the following metric units is heavier?

**a.** 350 milligrams or 200 grams? 200 grams
**b.** 21 grams or 2 kilograms? 2 kilograms
**c.** $5.4 \times 10^3$ milligrams or $5.03 \times 10^{-3}$ kilograms?
**d.** $4 \times 10^5$ centigrams or $4 \times 10^5$ hectograms?

**3.** Which metric units would be most appropriate to measure the mass of each of the following?

**a.** a car
**b.** a china plate Grams or kilograms
**c.** a cat Kilograms
**d.** a pinch of salt Milligrams or centigrams

**4.** Which metric unit is most appropriate to measure the mass of each of the following items?

**a.** a person Kilograms
**b.** an apple Grams
**c.** a bulldozer Kilograms
**d.** a blade of grass Milligrams

**5.** Do you think you could lift 100 grams? 10 kilograms? 100 kilograms? 1,000 kilograms? Yes; yes; maybe not; no

**6.** Name an object whose mass might be between 1 and 10 kilograms.

Refer to the table on page 246 to answer Exercises 7–13.

**7.** Which of these are plausible masses for an adult human? a, b, c, d

**a.** 74 kilograms
**b.** 89 kilograms
**c.** $6.9 \times 10^4$ grams
**d.** $5.4 \times 10^{-2}$ tons

**8.** How does the mass of an adult compare to the mass of a car?

**9.** How does the mass of a grain of rice compare to the mass of a grain of sand?

**10.** About how many cows have the same mass as a blue whale? About 154 cows

**11.** About how many grains of rice are in a 5-kilogram bag?

**12.** How many pennies have the same mass as 6 liters of water? 2,400

**13.** A mouse has about the same mass as 3 pencils. What is the approximate mass of a mouse? 21 grams



On Your Own Exercises
Lesson 5.3

**Investigation 1**
Pages 241–244
Practice & Apply: 1–2
Connect & Extend: 21

**Investigation 2**
Pages 244–247
Practice & Apply: 3–13
Connect & Extend: 22

**Investigation 3**
Pages 247–250
Practice & Apply: 14–20
Connect & Extend: 23–25

**Assign Anytime**
Mixed Review: 28–47

▶ **Exercise 1** Remind students to look at their table of metric prefixes if they are having difficulty deciding whether to multiply or divide to convert.

▶ **Exercises 3 and 4** When choosing an appropriate unit of measure there is some cross over between what is and is not acceptable. If students have other answers, discuss them. In many cases, they may have a logical argument for their choice.

▶ **Exercises 8–13** This is a continuation of questions the students saw when they were completing Investigation 2. Remind students of the chart they used.

▶ **Exercises 14–18** The students are completing conversions in the customary system. If students are struggling, you may want to go over an example using 16 ounces = 1 pound, 2,000 pounds = 1 ton, and so on.

▶ **Exercise 19** This problem is a conversion problem. Remind students about their benchmarks when completing this exercise.

▶ **Exercise 20** Lead students to see that they need to compute the volume of the mattress.



21d. About 20–40 people (20 if they all weigh 90 kg, 40 if they all weigh 45 kg).

21e. Possible answer: they are not going to stand on each other's shoulders. The floor space they can fill is 1.5 m • 2.8 m people rectangles. So, 12 people can stand in the elevator. If they could stack on top of each other, at least another 12 could fit, which is unreasonable.

**Fill in the blanks to make each equation true.**

**14.** $\frac{3}{16}$ pounds = __3__ ounces

**15.** 9 pounds 6 ounces = __150__ ounces

**16.** 2.6 tons = __5,200__ pounds

**17.** 4.25 pounds = __4__ pounds __4__ ounces

**18.** 6,400 ounces = __0.2__ ton

**19.** Jasmine needed to send a report to a co-worker in another state. She knew that she needed to put one 41-cent stamp on a letter that weighed one ounce or less. For each additional ounce of weight, she needed to add an extra 17-cent stamp. (So, a 1.5-ounce letter would cost 58 cents to mail.) She does not have a scale, but the label on her printer paper said that 500 sheets of paper weighs 5 pounds.

**a.** If she only used one stamp, how many pages could she send? 6

**b.** If the report was 20 pages long, how much will it cost to mail? 92 cents

**c.** If Jasmine spends 75 cents on postage, what is the maximum number of pages she can send? 18

**20.** A queen-sized waterbed mattress is 5 feet wide, $6\frac{1}{3}$ feet long, and 8.3 inches tall. A cube of water 1 inch on each side weighs about 0.36 pounds. If the mattress is entirely filled with water, how much does it weigh? Volume = 37,848 cubic inches; weight = 13,625.28 pounds

## Connect & Extend

21f. Possible answer: Yes. Even if the 12 people all weigh 90 kilograms, their total mass is only 1080 kilograms, which is smaller than the elevator's capacity. If you could fill up the whole volume of the elevator with people, you would have to start worrying about exactly how much each person weighed because they might be too heavy.

**21.** The elevator in the Grand Hotel can safely carry a maximum of 1,820 kilograms. The elevator is 1.5 meters wide, 2.8 meters long, and 4 meters high.

**a.** What is the volume of the elevator? $16.8\ m^3$

**b.** If the elevator were filled with water, what would be the mass of the water? 16,800 kilograms = 16.8 tons

**c.** Could the elevator safely carry that much mass? No.

**d.** An adult human typically has a mass between 45 and 90 kilograms. How many people can the elevator safely carry?

**e.** Assume each person is 1.65 meters tall and needs an area of about 0.5 by 0.7 meters. How many people can fit into the elevator?

**f.** Can the elevator safely carry as many people as can fit into it? Explain your reasoning.

22c. 1,280 grams, 1.28 kilograms

22j. Possible answer: She would have to eat several whole boxes to consume even half of the daily value of sodium, so it does not seem like she has to worry about the sodium in the candy. She does need to worry about saturated fat. Just 6 pieces of candy contain almost her entire daily maximum of fat; if she had 6 chocolates, she could not eat anything else with saturated fat in it all day.

**22.** The United States Department of Agriculture (USDA) recommends the following Daily Values for various food ingredients.

| | |
|---|---|
| Total Fat | Less than 65 grams |
| Saturated Fat | Less than 20 grams |
| Cholesterol | Less than 300 milligrams |
| Sodium | Less than 2,400 milligrams |
| Potassium | 3,500 milligrams |

Packages of processed food list how much of each ingredient is in one serving. Ramona bought a box of chocolates with this nutritional information on the back.

**Nutrition Facts**

Serving size 4 pieces (32 grams)
Servings per container About 6

| **Amont per serving** | % Daily value |
|---|---|
| Total Fat 15g | 23% |
| Saturated Fat 12g | 60% |
| *Trans* Fat 0g | |
| Cholesterol 0 mg | 0% |
| Sodium 25 mg | 1% |
| Total Carbohydrate 13g | 4% |
| Dietary Fiber 1g | 6% |
| Sugars 12g | |
| Protein 2g | |

**a.** How many milligrams of dietary fiber are in one piece of chocolate? 250 milligrams

**b.** How many chocolates contain 1 gram of sodium? 160 pieces

**c.** How many grams of chocolate is that? How many kilograms?

**d.** Is 1 gram of sodium more or less than the maximum recommended daily value? Less

**e.** What is the mass of the whole box of chocolates? About 192 grams

**f.** How much saturated fat is in the amount of chocolate in Part b? 480 grams

**g.** What percent of the maximum recommended daily value is the amount of saturated fat in Part f? 2,400%

**h.** How many grams of chocolate contain the maximum recommended daily value of saturated fat? $53\frac{1}{3}$ grams

**i.** How many pieces of chocolate is that? $6\frac{2}{3}$ pieces

**j.** Ramona wants to follow the USDA dietary guidelines. Should she be worried about eating too much sodium if she eats some chocolate today? Should she be worried about eating too much saturated fat? Explain your reasoning.



On Your Own Exercises

▶ **Exercise 22** Instruct students to read each part of the question carefully. It is important to know if the question is asking for information about one serving of chocolate or one piece. The nutritional information is very different depending on the wording.

Some students may need a review of percent in order to complete this exercise.

▶ **Exercises 22h and 22i** Students may need clarification that one serving is 4 pieces of chocolate. This means that the information on the label is true if only 4 pieces are eaten at one time. To determine the amount of something in one piece of chocolate, the information from the label must be divided by 4.

▶ **Exercise 23** If students are not sure where to start, ask the students to find a row in the table where they have the mass in both metric units and customary units. The students have 2 choices where the information is given as distinct values; wooden pencil and blue whale. Have the students create a rule here and use it to check other values.

▶ **Exercise 24** Students will need to look at the table for specific information like a liter of water to best answer this question. They can then use their formula to verify other rows of information in the table.

▶ **Exercise 26** If students are not sure where to start, help them by asking them to list all of the units that they can think of that describe mass in the metric system and also the units in the customary system that represent weight. Once the students see their lists, help them to see how they can add descriptive words to turn the lists into a paragraph.

On Your Own Exercises

**23.** This table shows the approximate weights for some familiar objects in both metric and customary units. Use the data in the table to find a rule that will let you complete the table.

| Object | Approximate Mass (Metric) | Approximate Weight (U.S. Customary) |
|---|---|---|
| Penny | 2.5 grams | 0.088 ounces |
| Nickel | 5 grams | 0.176 ounces |
| Piece of paper (8.5 in. x 11. in.) | 5 grams | 0.176 ounces |
| Wooden pencil (unsharpened) | 7 grams | 0.25 ounces |
| Apple | 0.23–0.45 kilograms | 0.5–1 pounds |
| Ceramic coffee mug | 0.34 kilograms = 340 grams | 12 ounces |
| 1 liter of water | 1 kilogram | 2.2 pounds |
| Newborn human baby | 2.27–4.55 kilograms | 5–10 pounds |
| Cat | 5–7 kilograms | 11–15.4 |
| Adult human | 45–90 kilograms | 99-198 pounds |
| Refrigerator (full size) | 91–109 kilograms | 200–240 pounds |
| Car | 773–1,591 kilograms | 1,700–3,500 pounds |
| Largest known dinosaur | 80–100 tons | 88 tons–110 tons |
| Blue whale | 180 tons | 198 tons |

**24.** Use the data from Exercise 23 to create two rules, one for converting pounds to kilograms and one rule for converting kilograms to pounds. Since the weights in the table are approximate, your rules will also be approximate. Write a formula for each rule.

24. Divide the weight in pounds by 2.2 to get kilograms; $\frac{p}{2.2} = k$. Multiply the weight in kilograms by 2.2 to get pounds; $2.2k = p$.

**25.** Create two rules, one rule for converting ounces to grams and one rule for converting grams to ounces. Write a formula that expresses each rule.

25. Divide ounces by 16 to get pounds, divide that by 2.2 to get kilograms, multiply that by 1,000 to get grams; so, divide by 35.2 and multiply by 1,000; $\frac{1{,}000n}{35.2} = g$. To change grams to ounces, do the reverse: $\frac{35.2g}{1{,}000} = n$.

**26. In Your Own Words** Write a paragraph that describes the units of measure for mass and weight. Possible answer: Mass is measured in the metric unit of grams. Ten of one unit equals one of the next largest unit, and prefixes are used to indicate the size of the unit. The customary units of ounces, pounds, and tons are used to measure weight in the United States. Sixteen ounces equal one pound. Two thousand pounds equal one ton.

27. **Preview** In Chapter 6, you will further your understanding of probability. Consider the possibility of tossing a coin twice.

a. List all the possible outcomes. HH, HT, TH, TT

b. What is the probability of the toss being heads both times? $\frac{1}{4}$

## Mixed Review

**Expand each expression.**

28. $4(3m + 1)$ $12m + 4$

29. $10(6x + 5)$ $60x + 50$

30. $8(2v - 11)$ $16v - 88$

31. $7(9k - 4)$ $63k - 28$

32. $-2(6y + 13)$ $-12y - 26$

33. $-5(3t - 8)$ $-15t + 40$

34. $0.5(4g + 15)$ $2g + 7.5$

35. $0.25(9x - 12)$ $2.25x - 3$

36. $\frac{1}{2}\left(8w + \frac{3}{4}\right)$ $4w + \frac{3}{8}$

37. $\frac{3}{4}\left(\frac{1}{5}m - \frac{5}{7}\right)$ $\frac{3}{20}m - \frac{15}{28}$

**Use the distributive property to help you do each calculation mentally. Write the grouping that shows the method you used.**

38. $5 \cdot 14$ 70; $5(10 + 4)$

39. $6 \cdot 42$ 252; $6(40 + 2)$

40. $7 \cdot 19$ 133; $7(20 - 1)$

41. $9 \cdot 45$ 405; $9(40 + 5)$ or $9(50 - 5)$

**Combine like terms to simplify each expression.**

42. $5m + 12m$ $17m$

43. $10p - 7p$ $3p$

44. $40x + 16 + 12x + 3$ $52x + 19$

45. $23t + 1 - 11t - 7$ $12t - 6$

46. $5g + 2(8 + 7g)$ $19g + 16$

47. $5(2a + 6) - 2(3a - 1)$ $4a + 32$



On Your Own Exercises

## Quick Check

**Informal Assessment** Students should be able to:

- ✔ determine the mass of an item
- ✔ convert values of mass between units in the metric system
- ✔ use benchmark values of mass to approximate the mass of items
- ✔ determine appropriate units of weight or mass for an item
- ✔ convert values of weight between units of the customary system

## Quick Quiz

1. How many hectograms are there in $1.45 \times 10^4$ milligrams? 0.145 hectograms
2. Name an item that would have a mass of about 2.5 kilograms? Answers will vary; Sample answer: A bag of potatoes.
3. If 10 sheets of construction paper has a mass of about 80 grams, how many sheet of paper are there in 2.5 kilograms? About 313 sheets
4. A ream of construction paper contains 500 sheets, what is the mass of the ream of paper? About 4 kilograms
5. A loaf of bread requires 5 pounds of flour, about how many cups of flour will you use? 10 cups
6. What is the most appropriate unit to use to record the weight of a case of oranges? Pounds

CHAPTER 5

# Review & Self-Assessment

## Chapter Summary
This summary helps students recall the major topics of the chapter.

## Vocabulary
Students should be able to explain each of the terms listed in the vocabulary section.

▶ **Exercise 1** As students work on this exercise, encourage them to sketch a drawing of the figure described in each part of the exercise. Having a visual will allow the students to see what is changing in each part and will assist them in using the correct formula.

CHAPTER 5

# Review & Self-Assessment

## Chapter Summary

In this chapter, you worked with prisms and cylinders. You found a formula for the volume of prisms. You used cubic units to measure volume and square units to measure area and surface area.

You learned that nets are flat figures that can be folded to form a closed three-dimensional object. You also found a method for finding surface area by using nets.

You learned that mass is the measurement of the amount of matter in an object and weight is the pull of gravity on that amount of matter. You also learned that mass and weight are approximately the same on Earth. You used metric units to measure mass and customary units to measure weight. In addition, you used benchmarks to estimate the mass of objects and you used scientific notation to express extremely small masses.

### Vocabulary

- base
- customary system
- cylinder
- gram
- mass
- metric system
- net
- ounce
- pound
- prism
- solid
- surface area
- ton
- volume
- weight

## Strategies and Applications

The questions in this section will help you review and apply the important ideas and strategies developed in this chapter.

### Finding the volume and surface area of a geometric solid

**1.** A rectangular prism has a base 4 cm long and 3 cm wide. The prism is 5 cm tall.

**a.** What is the prism's volume? $60 \text{ cm}^3$

**b.** Suppose a different rectangular prism has the same height and volume as the original prism. What are the dimensions of its base?

**c.** Suppose a cylinder with height 5 cm has the same volume as the original prism. What is the area of its base? Estimate its radius.

**2.** Find all the rectangular prisms you can make with 24 blocks. Try to do this without building all of them.

**a.** Give the dimensions of each prism.

**b.** Which of your prisms has the greatest surface area? What is its surface area? $24 \times 1 \times 1$, 98 square units

**c.** Which of your prisms has the least surface area? What is its surface area? $4 \times 3 \times 2$, 52 square units

1b. Possible answers: $1 \text{ cm} \times 12 \text{ cm} \times 5 \text{ cm}$, $2 \text{ cm} \times 6 \text{ cm} \times 5 \text{ cm}$

1c. $12 \text{ cm}^2$, about 1.95 cm

2a. $24 \times 1 \times 1$, $12 \times 2 \times 1$, $8 \times 3 \times 1$, $6 \times 4 \times 1$, $6 \times 2 \times 2$, $4 \times 3 \times 2$

Review & Self-Assessment
Chapter 5

4. $52.5\pi$ cm$^2$, or about 165 cm$^2$; $50\pi$ cm$^3$, or about 157 cm$^3$
5. Yes; since the triangles are all isosceles and the same size, the sides will fit together.

**Find the surface area and volume of each figure.**

**3.**

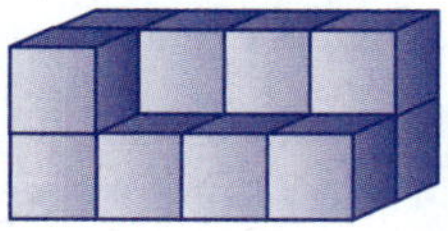

40 square units; 13 cubic units

**4.**

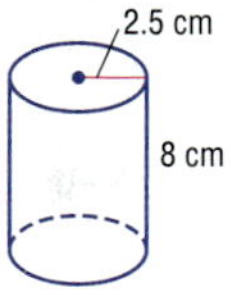


### Using nets to represent geometric solids

**5.** The square in the figure below has sides 3 centimeters long. The triangles are isosceles, and the height of each triangle is 4 centimeters. Is the figure a net? In other words, does it fold up to form a closed solid? Explain how you know.

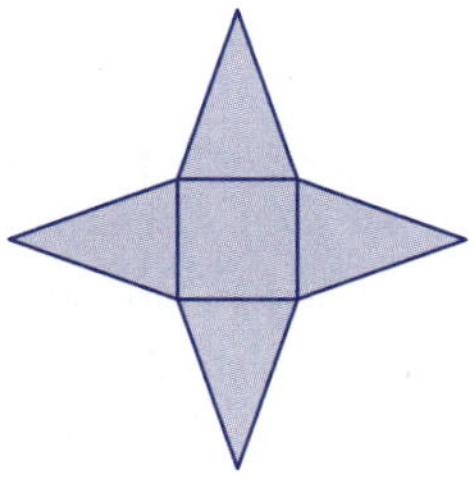

### Using scientific notation and benchmarks

**Use scientific notation to express the following conversions.**

**6.** 213 milligrams $2.13 \times 10^{-4}$ kilograms

**7.** 12 grams $1.2 \times 10^{3}$ centigrams

**8.** 50 grams $5.0 \times 10^{4}$ milligrams

**9.** 234 grams $2.34 \times 10^{-1}$ kilograms

**10.** 5.6 hectograms $5.6 \times 10^{2}$ grams

**Determine which benchmark would be closer to the given object.**

**11.** pencil Paper clip

**12.** a box of magazines 2-liter

**13.** your Math book 2-liter

**14.** an eraser Paper clip

Chapter 5 Review & Self-Assessment 257

▶ **Exercise 22** Students will be tempted to answer that the cube on the right has the greatest surface area because it looks the biggest. This is incorrect. Make sure you instruct the students to compute the surface area for each of the three figures. This exercise is a great place to discuss why what the students see is not necessarily correct.

16. $122.5\pi$ cm$^3$, or about 385 cm$^3$; $94.5\pi$ cm$^2$, or about 297 cm$^2$
17. $250\pi$ cm$^3$, or about 785 cm$^3$; $150\pi$ cm$^2$, or about 471 cm$^2$
18. 22.5 cm$^3$; 54 cm$^2$
19. $300\pi$ ft$^3$, or about 942 ft$^3$; $170\pi$ ft$^2$, or about 534 ft$^2$
20. About 258 cm$^3$; about 232 cm$^2$

22. Greatest: the 3 × 5 × 9 prism; least: the cylinder

Review & Self-Assessment
Chapter 5

## Demonstrating Skills

In Exercises 15–21, find the volume and surface area of the figure.

**15.**

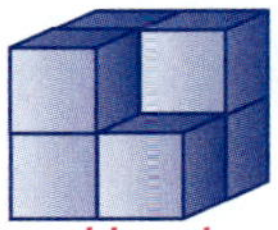

7 cubic units; 24 square units

**16.**

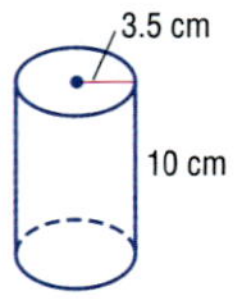


**17.**

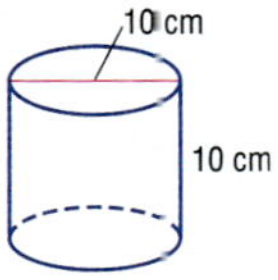


**18.**

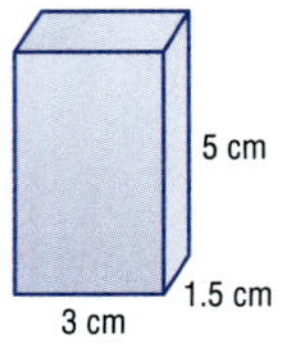


**19.** a cylindrical storage tank with radius 5 feet and height 12 feet

**20.** a can with height 10 centimeters and circumference 18 centimeters

**21.** a cube with side length 1.5 meters  3.375 m$^3$; 13.5 m$^2$

**22.** Which of these three solids has the greatest surface area? Which has the least surface area?

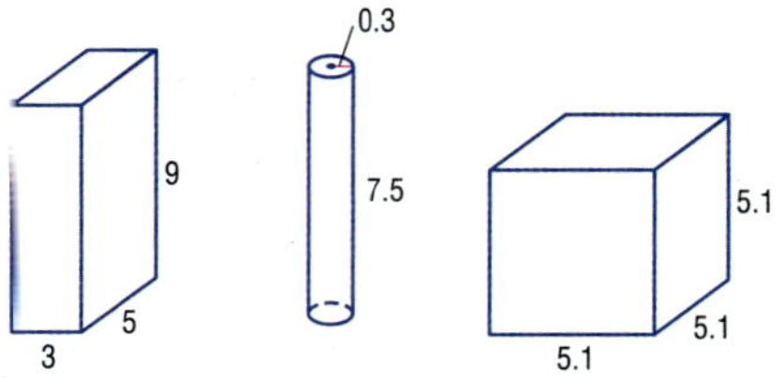


**Fill in the blanks to make each equation true.**

**23.** 3.75 pounds = __3__ pounds __12__ ounces

**24.** $\frac{1}{2}$ pounds = __8__ ounces

**25.** 12 ounces = __$\frac{3}{4}$, or 0.75__ pound

**26.** 20 ounces = __1__ pounds __4__ ounces

**27.** 49 ounces = __3__ pounds __1__ ounce

28. Milligrams or centigrams

30. Grams or kilograms

**Which metric unit would be most appropriate to measure the mass of each of the following?**

**28.** a teaspoon of sugar

**29.** a small dog Kilograms

**30.** a pottery bowl

**31.** a shoe Grams

## Test-Taking Practice

***SHORT RESPONSE***

**1** Meshack is building a dog house 3 feet long, 2 feet wide, and 2.5 feet high. The dog house will have a flat roof and a floor. How many square feet of wood will he need for the walls, roof, and floor of the dog house?

***Show your work.***

***Answer*** ____________________

*Show your work:* $SA = 2wl + 2lh + 2wh = 2(2)(3) + 2(3)(2.5) + 2(2)(2.5) = 12 + 15 + 10 = 37$; Meshack needs 37 $ft^2$ of wood

*Answer:* 37 $ft^2$

***MULTIPLE CHOICE***

**2** A water tank measures 110 feet in diameter and is 40 feet high. How many cubic feet of water can it hold, to the nearest cubic foot?

**A** 13,816
**B** 189,970
**C** 379,940 (circled)
**D** 1,519,760

**3** How many pounds are equal to 64 ounces?

**F** 3
**G** 4 (circled)
**H** 6.4
**J** 8

**4** Which metric measure indicates the least amount of mass?

**A** 20 g (circled)
**B** 2 kg
**C** 200,000 mg
**D** 200 g

**5** Which of the following measures is the best estimate for the mass of a thumb tack?

**F** 150 g
**G** 1.5 g (circled)
**H** 15 kg
**J** 1 lb

**6** The mass of an object is 325 mg. What is its mass in grams?

**A** 0.0325 g
**B** 0.325 g (circled)
**C** 3.25 g
**D** 32.5 g

**7** At birth, Stephen weighed 7.5 pounds. A bag of fruit weighs 70 ounces. Which weighs less?

**F** The fruit weighs less. (circled)
**G** Stephen weighs less.
**H** They both weigh the same.
**J** The answer cannot be determined from this information.





▶ **Exercise 7** In this exercise, the students may not notice that there are two different units to compare. Remind the students that they should convert to one unit, either all to pounds or all to ounces before they answer the question.

**Lesson 5.1, Develop & Understand: B** (p. 214)

6. $600 = 2 \cdot 2 \cdot 2 \cdot 3 \cdot 5 \cdot 5$; For example, by multiplying two factors together you could have a box with dimensions of 10 by 10 by 6 or 4 by 6 by 25.

6a.

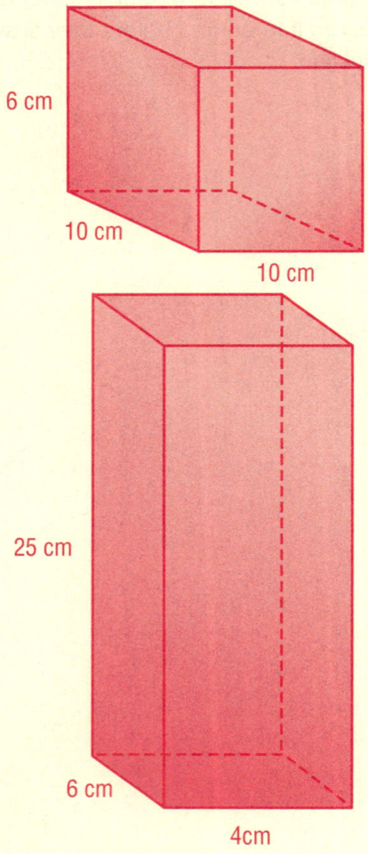


**Lesson 5.1, Share & Summarize** (p. 215)

1. Multiply length times width times depth (or height). Volume is also the area of the base multiplied by the height.
2. Possible answers: Calculate the area of each face and add the six areas. Calculate the area of a face and double for the parallel face, repeat for two other pairs of faces, and then add three results. $2(lw) + 2(l\,h) + 2(hw) = SA$
3. No, boxes with a given volume can have different surface areas.
4. If you find the prime factorization of the volume, you can use the prime factors to create three factors for possible values for length, width, and height of the box.

**Lesson 5.3, Develop & Understand: C** (p. 245)

8a. Possible answer: My book has about 600 pages, which is about 300 pieces of paper, plus covers. The mass of 600 pages should be about $600 \cdot 5$ grams, which is 3,000 grams, or 3.0 kilograms. I can also estimate the covers' mass. I can add the two mass estimates to approximate the book's mass.

8b. Possible answer: The book has the same area, but it is not as thick as the ream. It feels lighter, too, even though it has more pages than the ream and the ream has no covers.

10. Answers will vary. Possible answers: Perhaps the paper used in the book is a different stock of paper than the ream paper. Perhaps the cover's mass makes a difference.

11. Possible answer: 1 kilogram is about $\frac{2}{3}$ the mass of the book.

**Lesson 5.3, Develop & Understand: C and Think & Discuss** (p. 246)

18. See table for approximate masses. Possible answer: A nickel is bigger and thicker than a penny. It probably does not weigh as much as a pencil. So, I estimated a mass that was close to, but a little less than, the pencil's mass.

① Students are likely to have misestimated relative sizes since estimating mass is difficult, especially when the objects are not in front of you. The purpose of this discussion is to make them aware of how difficult it is and to help them start forming some instincts about benchmark masses.

Notes

CHAPTER 6

# Data and Probability

## Chapter Overview

In this chapter, students determine the probability of independent and dependent events, using theoretical and experimental probability. They use probability to decide if a game is fair.

Students predict the contents of a bag by taking a sample. They see that the sample does not always show the exact contents of the bag, and that there may be more than one reasonable prediction given the same sample. Then they look at some characteristics of a good sample, namely the size of the sample and how a representative sample population can be chosen.

The chapter concludes by having students choose appropriate graphs to display given sets of data. Students learn how graphs can be misleading.

## The Big Picture

| Links to the Past | Chapter 6 | Links to the Future |
|---|---|---|
| **Course 1, Chapter 2** (pp. 56–107) Fractions and Decimals<br>**Course 1, Chapter 10** (pp. 576–657) Data and Probability | **Lesson 6.1** (p. 262) Dependence | **Course 3, Chapter 11** (pp. 576–625) Data and Probability |
| **Course 1, Chapter 10** (pp. 576–657) Data and Probability | **Lesson 6.2** (p. 278) Make Predictions | **Course 3, Chapter 11** (pp. 576–625) Data and Probability |
| **Course 1, Chapter 8** (pp. 466–531) Coordinate Plane<br>**Course 1, Chapter 10** (pp. 576–657) Data and Probability | **Lesson 6.3** (p. 294) Data Graphs | **Course 3, Chapter 11** (pp. 576–625) Data and Probability |

# Mathematical Background

Chapter 6 begins with an informal review of elementary probability using a random drawing model. If a bag contains 2 white marbles and 8 purple marbles, then the probability of randomly drawing a purple marble is $\frac{8}{10}$ because there are 8 purple marbles that can be drawn out of the set of 10 marbles in the bag.

The random drawing model for probability extends to sequential events, like repeatedly tossing coins or rolling number cubes, provided that these can be described in terms of equally likely outcomes. For example, when two number cubes with sides 1 to 6 are rolled, and the top faces are added, the only possible sums are the eleven integers from 2 to 12. Each of these sums, however, are not equally likely: a 2 can be rolled in one way while a 7 can be rolled in six ways. When the number of ways each integer can be rolled is determined, the random drawing model for probability applies. For example, when you roll the two number cubes, there are 36 possible outcomes. Of these outcomes, there are six ways to roll a 7. Therefore the probability of rolling a 7 is $\frac{6}{36}$ or $\frac{1}{6}$.

**Counting Events** Techniques of counting—stem-and-leaf plots or simple trees—facilitate enumerating the number of possible ways an event can occur. Students use these to calculate theoretical probabilities.

Not all describable events are equally likely, and therefore the issue of fairness is important in applying probability theory to actual events. Students learn a number of games and determine the probability of various outcomes both theoretically and by experiment.

**Sampling** The issue of sampling is crucial in analyzing probabilities in the real world. For example: How many trials does it take to determine the makeup of a bag of marbles by repeated sampling? How many words must you measure to determine the average word length in a document? What sort of sample do you need to determine the characteristics of a school or town?

The chapter closes by reviewing the basic graphical methods of presenting statistical data such as line graphs, circle graphs, and bar graphs.

## *Additional Reading*

According to Shaughnessy and Bergman in "Thinking about Uncertainty: Probability and Statistics," it is important to give students opportunities to investigate probability problems by using a problem-solving approach. Each lesson in Chapter 6 contains real-world application problems involving probability.

CHAPTER 6

# Planning Guide

## *Lesson Resources*

| | Lesson 6.1 (Pacing: 5 days) | Lesson 6.2 (Pacing: 4 days) | Lesson 6.3 (Pacing: 5 days) |
|---|---|---|---|
| **Lesson Title** | **Dependence** (p. 262) | **Make Predictions** (p. 278) | **Data Graphs** (p. 294) |
| **Lesson Objectives** | • To answer questions about a single random drawing<br>• To extend the random drawing model to sequential drawings, with and without replacement<br>• To determine experimental probability<br>• To determine from the probabilities of the outcomes and the scoring system whether or not a game is fair | • To predict the characteristics of an entire population from a representative sample<br>• To appreciate some of the limitations inherent in using small or restricted samples<br>• To analyze a representative sample for flaws in its selection<br>• To choose a sample representative population for a survey | • To identify when to use a bar graph, line graph, or circle graph<br>• To construct stem-and-leaf plots, double-bar graphs and double-line graphs when appropriate<br>• To collect data, compute fractions and angle measures to use in constructing circle graphs<br>• To look at data and determine if the presentation is misleading |
| **Materials** | coin, Lesson 6.1 Masters 1 and 2 | protractor, Lesson 6.2 Master 1 | lines or grid paper, colored pencils, Lesson 6.3 Masters 1 and 2, protractor, 1-meter strip of heavy paper, scissors |
| ***Quick Review Math Handbook*** | **Lesson 6.3** Symmetry and Transformations | **Lesson 6.3** Symmetry and Transformations | **Lesson 6.3** Symmetry and Transformations |
| **Print Resources** | CRM Study Guide and Intervention (p. 3)<br>CRM Skills Practice (p. 4)<br>CRM Problem-Solving Practice (p. 5)<br>CRM Enrichment (p. 6)<br>• Investigation Notebook and Reflection Journal<br>• Differentiation Handbook | CRM Study Guide and Intervention (p. 10)<br>CRM Skills Practice (p. 11)<br>CRM Problem-Solving Practice (p. 12)<br>CRM Enrichment (p. 13)<br>• Investigation Notebook and Reflection Journal<br>• Differentiation Handbook | CRM Study Guide and Intervention (p. 16)<br>CRM Skills Practice (p. 17)<br>CRM Problem-Solving Practice (p. 18)<br>CRM Enrichment (p. 19)<br>• Investigation Notebook and Reflection Journal<br>• Differentiation Handbook |
| **Technology Resources** | TeacherWorks Plus<br>Classroom Presentation Toolkit<br>ExamView Assessment Suite<br>StudentWorks Plus<br>Math Online Brain Pops • Concepts in Motion | TeacherWorks Plus<br>Classroom Presentation Toolkit<br>ExamView Assessment Suite<br>StudentWorks Plus<br>Math Online Brain Pops • Concepts in Motion | TeacherWorks Plus<br>Classroom Presentation Toolkit<br>ExamView Assessment Suite<br>StudentWorks Plus<br>Math Online Brain Pops • Concepts in Motion |

*Included in the Impact Mathematics Manipulative Kit

# Assessment Resources

## MARS Assessment: Teaching with Purpose

### Meals

In *Meals,* students interpret a circle graph and solve a number problem in context. Students figure out how many people chose to eat either steak, burgers, or pizza, and match the totals with a circle graph showing the numbers of people who chose each of the meals.

### Targeting the Task

- **Diagnostic**—Use Exercises 1–2 in the *Meals* assessment to determine students' understanding of how to interpret a circle graph and how to solve a number problem in context. For those students who do not have this understanding, completing this unit is needed.
- **Formative**—Exercises 1–2 can be administered individually according to the lessons.
- **Summative**—Administer the complete *Meals* performance-based assessment.

CRM **Chapter 6 MARS Assessment** (pp. 39–40)

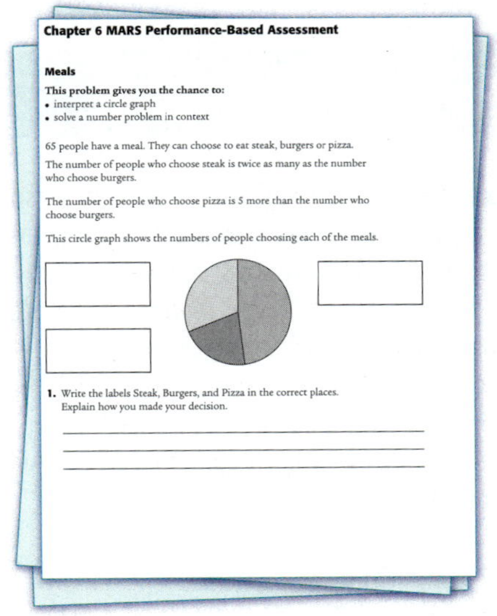
Chapter 6 MARS Performance-Based Assessment

**Meals**

**This problem gives you the chance to:**
- interpret a circle graph
- solve a number problem in context

65 people have a meal. They can choose to eat steak, burgers or pizza.

The number of people who choose steak is twice as many as the number who choose burgers.

The number of people who choose pizza is 5 more than the number who choose burgers.

This circle graph shows the numbers of people choosing each of the meals.

1. Write the labels Steak, Burgers, and Pizza in the correct places. Explain how you made your decision.

## Assessment Planning Guide

Assessments are available for investigations, lessons, and chapters.

ExamView Assessment Suite — Customize and create multiple versions of tests and quizzes.

| | Student Edition | Teacher Edition | Other Resources |
|---|---|---|---|
| **Diagnostic** | | | CRM Chapter 6 Pretest (p. 23–26)<br>Math Online Online Chapter Quiz |
| **Formative** | Share & Summarize (pp. 264, 267, 269, 280, 282, 285, 298, 301, 305, 308) | Troubleshooting (pp. 269, 279, 280, 285, 299, 300, 304, 305, 306)<br>On the Spot Assessment (pp. 281, 284, 296, 299)<br>Quick Check (pp. 277, 292, 313)<br>Quick Quiz (pp. 277, 293, 313) | CRM Quick Quiz (pp. 7, 14, 20) |
| **Summative** | Review & Self-Assessment (pp. 314–317) | | CRM Chapter 6 Test: Forms A and B (pp. 27–36)<br>CRM Standardized Test Practice (p. 41–42) |
| **Performance-Based** | In Your Own Words (p. 291) | | CRM Chapter Performance Assessment (pp. 37–38)<br>CRM MARS Performance-Based Assessment (pp. 39–40) |

# Differentiated Instruction

## *Reaching* All Learners

Below are suggestions on differentiating the materials presented in this chapter. Additional modifications should be considered.

### Approaching Level AL

**Experiment** To break up the work in Lesson 6.1, have students perform an experiment to practice computing probability. Place the students in small groups giving each group a different experiment to perform using a bag of marbles, a die, a spinner, a stack of cards numbered 1 to 15. Have each person in the group take on a role, such as recording the results, performing the experiment, calculator, and presenter. Have each group perform 50 trials and compute the probability for all possible results. Finally, have each group present their results to the class.

### Beyond Level BL

**Misleading Data** To close Lesson 6.3, have students work in small groups and collect data on a topic that is applicable to their classmates. Once the data are collected, have the students record the information in an appropriate graph. The students should presents at least 2 graphs, one that accurately shows the information collected and another that misleads the reader to make an inaccurate decision. Have the groups present both graphs to the class and ask them to determine which one is misleading.

### On Level OL

**Data Collection** To reinforce the concepts learned in Lesson 6.3, have students work in small groups and collect data on a topic that is relevant to their peers. Once the group has collected the data, have them create a graphic display for their results. Each group should share their graphs with the class making sure to justify why they chose the type of graph that they used.

### English Language Learners ELL

**Vocabulary Review** This chapter has a lot of unusual vocabulary that may be extremely challenging to students. Have students work in pairs or small groups. Give each student a sheet of paper, have the student fold the paper once horizontally, and once vertically creating four spaces. In the first space, have the student write a word that they are confused about. Have the students pass their paper to the left. Have the next student define the word, or if they are unsure they can ask for help from someone else in the group or use a resource book such as a dictionary. Then have the student write a word they are unsure about in the second space. Continue passing papers until all squares are complete.

**KEY**
AL Approaching Level OL On Level BL Beyond Level ELL English Language Learners

# Intervention Planning Guide

CRM Assess students' prerequisite skills and knowledge using the **Chapter Pretest** found in the Chapter 6 Resource Masters, pp. 23–26.

| **Intensive Intervention**<br>two or more years below grade level | **Strategic Intervention**<br>below grade level | **On Level** | **Beyond Level** |
|---|---|---|---|
| **If** students miss 75% of the exercises:<br>**Then** use *Math Triumphs,* an intensive intervention | **If** students miss 50% of the exercises:<br>**Then** choose a resource: | **If** students miss 25% of the exercises:<br>**Then** choose a resource: | **If** students miss 0%–10% of the exercises:<br>**Then** choose a resource: |
| *Math Triumphs,* Grade 7<br>• Chapter 3: Percents | CRM Study Guide and Intervention (pp. 3, 10, 16)<br>• Investigation Notebook and Reflection Journal<br>• Differentiation Handbook<br>Math Online Brain Pops • Concepts in Motion | CRM Skills Practice (pp. 4, 11, 17)<br>CRM Problem-Solving Practice (pp. 5, 12, 18)<br>• Investigation Notebook and Reflection Journal | CRM Enrichment (pp. 6, 13, 19)<br>• Differentiation Handbook |

## Literature Connections

### Recommended Outside Reading for Students

**Nonfiction**

Peterson, Ivars and Henderson, Nancy. *Math Trek: Adventures in Math Zone.* John Wiley and Sons, 1999.

This book shows students the math of an amusement park. Games and activities are included. "Trek 13: Luck on the Boredwalk" will be of special interest to students after competing their study of probability.

**Fiction**

Bruce, Colin. *Conned Again, Watson! Cautionary Tales of Logic, Math, and Probability.* Perseus Publishing, 2002.

Using the stories of Sherlock Holmes, the author creates mysteries that require mathematical skill to be solved. This book provides interesting insight as probability and statistics are used by Sherlock Holmes to outwit con men.

## Professional Development

Targeted professional development has been articulated throughout the *IMPACT Mathematics* series. The **McGraw-Hill Professional Development Video Library** provides short videos that support the mathematics standards. Log on to www.glencoe.com.

Model Lessons

Instructional Strategies

CHAPTER 6

# Data and Probability

## Introduce

**What Do Most Americans Think?** Ask students if they have ever participated in a survey. Encourage those who have to share the purpose of the survey and what it was about.

Have students read the paragraph "What Do Most Americans Think?" Discuss how the Gallop Organization conducts surveys. Students may be familiar with Gallop polls and want to share the topics in some recent polls.

Tell students that they will learn later in the chapter how to determine what makes a good survey and how survey results can be used to make predictions.

**Think About It** Discuss students' predictions, which will vary.

CHAPTER 6

# Data and Probability

### *Contents in Brief*



## Real-Life Math

**What Do Most Americans Think?** "Most Americans are optimistic about their futures." Have you ever wondered where statements like this orginate? After all, how would anyone know what "most Americans" think?

To uncover the American public's opinions, a group called the Gallup Organization conducts surveys on a variety of topics. This group, which has been conducting surveys for more than 60 years, polls a small sample of the American public and draws conclusions about the entire American population based on the responses. The Gallup Organization claims the margin of error in its survey results is plus or minus three percentage points.

**Think About It** Suppose you were to conduct a survey to determine students' favorite types of music in your class. If you were to conduct the same survey of all students in your school, do you think the results would be the same?

**Math Online** Take the **Chapter Readiness Quiz** at glencoe.com.

### Chapter Resources

- CRM Chapter 6 Resource Masters
- CRM English/Spanish Family Letter (pp. 1–2)
- CRM Lesson Masters (pp. 8, 9, 15, 21, 22)
- CRM Chapter 6 Pretest (pp. 23–26)
- CRM Chapter 6 Test (pp. 27–36)
- **Math Online** Online Readiness Quiz • eGlossary

# Dear Family,

Many games played at home rely on chance or probability. In the next chapter, the class will study the basics of probability. The chapter will begin by considering marbles drawn from a bag. For example, if there are six green and four yellow marbles in a bag, questions like these can be answered.

- If one marble is drawn at random, which color is it most likely to be?
- What are the chances that the marble drawn will be green?
- Suppose a yellow marble is drawn, put in a pocket, and then another marble is drawn. What are the chances of drawing a green marble?

The class will use probability to test whether games of chance are fair. A game that uses probability to develop a winning strategy will also be played.

### Key Concept–Statistical Sampling

Statistical sampling is another common use of probability. In statistical sampling, a small group is chosen at random and used to draw conclusions about the entire population. Can you think of surveys or statistics which may have been based on statistical sampling? Is this a fair and accurate way to draw conclusions about a large population?

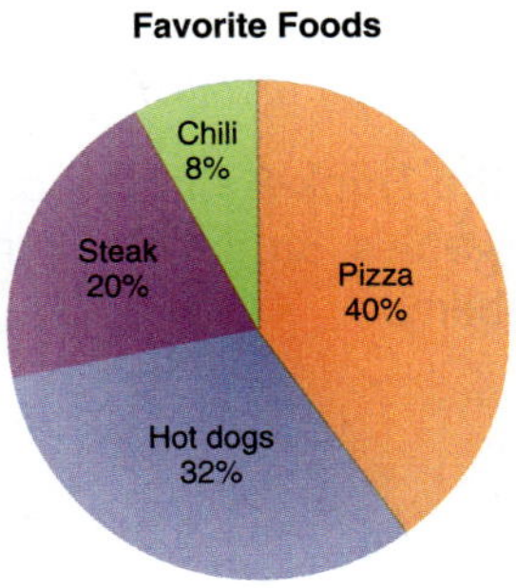


However used, finding probabilities depends on having data. The class will review and study many ways to display data, including circle graphs, and will discuss when it is most appropriate to use those displays.

### Chapter Vocabulary

double-bar graph
double-line graph
population
representative sample
sample

### Home Activities

- You can play different games of chance together. Your student can teach you the games that are played at school. Other games may include card games where it helps to know what cards you are likely or very unlikely to draw next.
- You can also talk about probabilities in our daily lives, such as the chance of rain.

261

## Family Letter

Another version of the Family Letter, available in English and Spanish, is found in the Chapter 6 Resource Masters. You may want to send a copy of this letter home with your students.

**Key Concept–Sampling** In this chapter, students will be studying statistical sampling and various methods of data analysis. If students do not seem familiar with the concept, take out a newspaper or a business magazine that will have graphical representations to show students. This will be a great place to start a conversation about how common data analysis is and also how real the data are.

### Home Activities

- Have students work with their families to determine how statistics are used in their favorite family game.
- Have the students ask their families what is the probability of flipping a coin and getting a tail. Then have the students and their families make a list of as many types of probability that they can think of that they hear or see in their daily lives. For example, there is a 40% chance of snow today.

## Key Vocabulary

**English (Spanish)** *Introduce the most important terms from Chapter 6.*

**population (población)** A larger group from which a sample is taken. (p. 279)

**representative sample (muestra representativa)** A part of a population that has approximately the same proportions as the whole population with respect to the characteristic being studied. (p. 284)

**double-bar graph (gráfica de barras dobles)** A bar graph with two bars for each category on the same graph. (p. 261)

**double-line graph (gráfica de líneas dobles)** Two sets of data displayed visually to compare how quantities of different groups change over the same time frame. (p. 261)

**sample (muestra)** A smaller group taken from a population that is used to represent the larger group. (p. 279)

LESSON 6.1

# Dependence

## Objectives

- To answer questions about a single random drawing
- To extend the random drawing model to sequential drawings, with and without replacement
- To determine experimental probability
- To determine from the probabilities of the outcomes and the scoring system whether or not a game is fair

## Overview

The lesson introduces probability using a random drawing model—marbles and cubes drawn from a bag. Students answer simple and compound questions about these models and find probabilities for sequential events. Then they toss coins to find experimental probabilities. Students use elementary probability theory to determine the fairness of a variety of games.

## Advance Preparation

If you choose to model the Think & Discuss question, you will need a bag, 6 blue marbles, and 4 purple marbles. Students will need coins or two-sided counters to find experimental probability.

| | Summary | Materials | On Your Own Exercises (pp. 272–277) | Assessment Opportunities |
|---|---|---|---|---|
| **Investigation 1** (p. 262) Pacing: 2 days | The investigation introduces the fundamental concepts of probability using a random drawing of objects from a bag as the basic model. | | Practice & Apply: 4–6<br>Connect & Extend: 9<br>Mixed Review: 14–20 | • Share & Summarize (p. 264) |
| **Investigation 2** (p. 264) Pacing: 1 day | Probability concepts are extended to include the probability of possible outcomes of multiple coin tosses. | Lesson 6.1 Masters 1 and 2 | Practice & Apply: 7–8<br>Connect & Extend: 10–11<br>Mixed Review: 14–20 | • Share & Summarize (p. 267) |
| **Investigation 3** (p. 268) Pacing: 1 day | Students analyze several games to see whether or not they are fair. | | Practice & Apply: 1–3<br>Connect & Extend: 12–13<br>Mixed Review: 14–20 | • Share & Summarize (p. 269)<br>• Troubleshooting (p. 269) |
| **Inquiry Investigation 4** (p. 270) Pacing: 1 day | Students investigate the best strategy for success in the *Hidden Prize* game show problem. | | | |

# Leveled Lesson Resources

CRM *Available in:* **Chapter 6 Resource Masters**

Also on TeacherWorks™
Lesson 6.1

## Study Guide and Intervention (p. 3) AL

**Lesson 6.1 Study Guide and Intervention**
***Dependence***

An organized list can help you find the probability of a combination of events.

***Example 1*** **A bag contains five cards labeled A, B, C, D, and E.**

**a. You draw a card, record its letter, and return it to the bag. Then you draw again. Find the probability that both cards are vowels.**

Make a list of all the possible ways you could draw the two cards.

A-A, A-B, A-C, A-D, A-E, B-A, B-B, B-C, B-D, B-E, C-A, C-B, C-C, C-D, C-E, D-A, D-B, D-C, D-D, D-E, E-A, E-B, E-C, E-D, E-E

There are 4 possible ways to draw two vowels. There are 25 possible ways to draw two cards. The probability that both cards are vowels is $\frac{4}{25}$.

**b. You draw a card, put it aside, and then draw again. Find the probability that both cards are vowels.**

Make a list of all the possible ways you could draw the two cards.

A-B, A-C, A-D, A-E, B-A, B-C, B-D, B-E, C-A, C-B, C-D, C-E, D-A, D-B, D-C, D-E, E-A, E-B, E-C, E-D

There are 2 possible ways to draw two vowels. There are 20 possible ways to draw two cards. The probability that both cards are vowels is $\frac{2}{20}$ or $\frac{1}{10}$.

***Example 2*** **You and a friend have a dime and a number cube that is numbered 1, 2, 3, 4, 5, and 6. If you toss heads and roll an even number, you score one point. If you toss tails and roll an odd number, your friend scores one point. Is this a fair game?**

Make a list of all the possible combinations.

H-1, H-2, H-3, H-4, H-5, H-6, T-1, T-2, T-3, T-4, T-5, T-6

There are 12 possiblities. The probability that you will get a point is $\frac{3}{12}$, or $\frac{1}{4}$.

The probability that your friend will get a point is $\frac{3}{12}$, or $\frac{1}{4}$. Since $\frac{1}{4} = \frac{1}{4}$, the game is fair.

***Exercises***

**A bag contains six cards numbered 1, 2, 3, 4, 5, and 6.**

**1.** You draw a card, replace it, and draw again. Find the probability that the second card is even.

**2.** You draw a card, put it aside, and draw again. Find the probability that the second card is less than 4.

## Skills Practice (p. 4) AL OL

**Lesson 6.1 Skills Practice**
***Dependence***

**1.** You toss a coin and roll a number cube labeled 1, 2, 3, 4, 5, and 6. Find the probability of getting each outcome.

**a.** rolling an even number and tossing heads

**b.** rolling a multiple of 3

**2.** There are 2 yellow marbles, 1 purple marble, 1 green marble, and 2 red marbles in a bag. You draw one marble, record its color, and put it back in the bag. Then you draw a second marble. Find the probability of getting each outcome.

**a.** a purple, then a red marble

**b.** two yellow marbles

**3.** Using the bag of marbles in Exercise 2, you draw one marble, put it in your pocket, and then draw a second marble. Find the probability of getting each outcome.

**a.** two red marbles

**b.** a yellow marble on the second draw

**4. Lunch** Tom is making a sandwich. He can have ham, turkey, or roast beef; Swiss or provolone cheese; and, mustard or mayonnaise.

**a.** Make a tree diagram to show all the possible sandwiches he can make with one meat, one cheese, and one condiment.

**b.** If he chooses his sandwich fixings randomly, what is the probability that he makes a sandwich with ham and Swiss cheese?

**5. Game** Derek and Latanya are playing a game with 4 chips numbered 1, 2, 3, and 4. Derek chooses two chips randomly. If the sum less than 6, he gets 1 point. If the sum is 6 or greater, Latanya gets 1 point.

**a.** List all the possible combinations that Derek could choose.

**b.** Is this a fair game? Explain.

## Problem-Solving Practice (p. 5) AL OL

**Lesson 6.1 Problem-Solving Practice**
***Dependence***

**1. Shopping** John is trying to decide which bag of dog food to buy. The brand he wants comes in liver, beef, lamb, and chicken. The package sizes are small, medium, and large.

**a.** Make a tree diagram to find all the possible combinations of dog food bags John could buy.

**b.** Find the probability that John buys a small bag of dog food.

**2. Vehicles** The rental car company has cars available in compact, midsize, and luxury. The colors are black, white, red, or gold. If Jailin is assigned a car randomly, what is the probability that she gets a red midsize or luxury car?

**3. Money** Mr. Santiago pulls two bills at random from the four $1 bills, three $5 bills, and one $20 bill in his pocket. What is the probability that the total amount pulled is $6? Hint: Use $1a, $1b, $1c, $1d, $5a, $5b, and $5c to list each bill separately. (Note: Drawing $1a and $5a is the same as drawing $5a and $1a)

**4. Game** Samantha and Karl have a number cube labeled 1, 2, 3, 4, 5, and 7. Samantha tosses the cube. If she tosses an even number, she gets 2 points. If she tosses a multiple of 5, she loses 2 points. Is this a fair game? Explain.

**5. Movies** Tina has 6 widescreen DVDs, 2 full-screen DVDs, and 1 special-edition DVD. Tina chooses one DVD at random, puts it back, and then chooses another. Hint: Use W1, W2, W3, W4, W5, W6, F1, and F2 to list each DVD separately.

**a.** Find the probability that Tina chooses 2 full-screen DVDs.

**b.** Find the probability that Tina chooses a special-edition DVD and then a widescreen DVD.

**c.** Would the probability of choosing 2 full-screen DVDs be different if she did not put the first one back before choosing the second? Explain.

## Enrichment (p. 6) BL

**Lesson 6.1 Enrichment**
***Dependence***

**Coin-Tossing Experiments**

If a coin is tossed 3 times, there are 8 possible outcomes. They are listed in the table below.

| Number of Heads | 0 | 1 | 2 | 3 |
|---|---|---|---|---|
| Outcomes | TTT | HTT | HHT | HHH |
| | | THT | THH | |
| | | TTH | HTH | |

Once all the outcomes are known, the probability of any event can be found. For example, the probability of getting 2 heads is $\frac{3}{8}$. Notice that this is the same as getting 1 tail.

**1.** A coin is tossed 4 times. Complete this chart to show the possible outcomes.

| Number of Heads | 0 | 1 | 2 | 3 | 4 |
|---|---|---|---|---|---|
| Outcomes | TTTT | | | | |
| | | | | | |
| | | | | | |
| | | | | | |
| | | | | | |
| | | | | | |

**2.** What is the probability of getting all tails?

**3.** Now complete this table. Make charts like the one in Exercise 1 to help find the answers. Look for patterns in the numbers.

| Number of Coin Tosses | 2 | 3 | 4 | 5 | 6 | 7 | 8 |
|---|---|---|---|---|---|---|---|
| Total Outcomes | | | | | | | |
| Probability of Getting All Tails | | | | | | | |

**4.** What happens to the number of outcomes? the probability of all tails?

## Lesson Quick Quiz (p. 7) AL OL BL

**Lesson 6.1 Quick Quiz**
***Dependence***

**1.** A bag contains 7 blocks labeled with the numbers 1 to 7. One block is drawn at random from the bag. What is the probability that

**a.** it is 5?

**b.** it is a number less than 11?

**c.** it is 11?

**d.** it is odd or even?

**e.** it is evenly divisible by 2 or 3?

**f.** it is evenly divisible by 2 and 3?

**2.** Shaunda has tossed a coin four times and obtained four heads.

**a.** If the coin is fair, is the probability that it will come up heads on the fifth toss greater, less, or the same as the probability that it will come up tails?

**b.** What is the probability that Shaunda will toss a coin four times and have it come up four heads in a row?

## Lesson Master (pp. 8–9)

**Lesson 6.1 Master 1**
***Dependence***

**Investigation 2: Develop & Understand: A**

T T T T H H T H H H T H H H H T H T H T H H T H T
H T T T H T H T T H T H T T H H T H T H T H H T T
T H T T T H H H T H T T T H H T T T T T T H H H T
T T T H T H H H H T T T T H T T T T H H T H T T H
H T T H T T H T T H H T H H H H T H T H T H H T H
T H H H T H T H T H T H T H T T T T T T H T H H T
T T H H H H H H H T T H T T H T H T H H H T T T T
H T T H H H T T H H T H H T H H T H H T T T H H H

# Additional Lesson Resources

### Teacher Tech Tools

- TeacherWorks
- ExamView Assessment Suite
- Classroom Presentation Toolkit
- Advance Tracker

### Student Tech Tools

- StudentWorks Plus
- Math Online eGlossary • Concepts in Motion

### Other Print Products

- Investigation Notebook and Reflection Journal
- Quick Review Math Handbook

LESSON 6.1

# Dependence

## Introduce

**Chance or Probability** This lesson focuses on finding the probability of different events taking place. Students may need to be reminded of the meanings of probability and chance. It is important that students understand that the probability of winning a game or of an event occurring is based on the specific event divided by the total possible outcomes.

### Think & Discuss

*Suggested Grouping: Whole Class*

Introduce the first investigation by presenting the Think & Discuss exercise. It is effective to start the class by drawing from a bag containing 6 blue and 4 purple marbles, asking the questions in the context of a real event.

### Investigation 1

**On Your Own Exercises**
Pages 272–277
Exercises 4–6, 9

**Find the Probability** In this investigation, students find the probability of a single random event. They list the outcomes for sequential events, with and without replacement, and find the probability for each outcome.

You might also point out that sometimes probability is written in simplest form. For example, 4 in 10 can also be written as 2 in 5.

### Develop & Understand: A

*Suggested Grouping: Individuals*

Students give the probability of drawing one block that will meet specific conditions from a bag of 6 blocks. While many students will be familiar with the basic concepts of probability, some may not be. This exercise set is a good opportunity to assess students' understanding of probability so that you can appropriately pace the lesson and chapter.

LESSON 6.1

# Dependence

Many board and card games rely on *chance* or *probability* to make them fun. With some games, whether you win depends on nothing more than the cards you choose or the dice rolls you make. In this lesson, you will explore situations and games involving probability.



### Think & Discuss

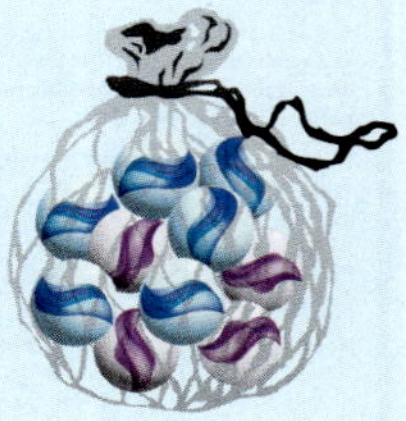

There are 10 marbles in a bag, 6 blue and 4 purple. If you draw out one marble at random, which color is it most likely to be? Blue

The chances that the marble you draw will be purple are 4 out of 10. What are the chances that the marble will be blue? 6 out of 10

Suppose you draw a blue marble and put it in your pocket. Then you draw another marble. What are the chances it will also be blue? 5 out of 9

## Investigation 1 Combinations and Probability

You have probably heard people talk about probabilities in many ways. In the above Think & Discuss, for example, it states that the chances of the marble being purple are 4 out of 10. You might also say that the chances of choosing purple are 4 in 10, 4:10, $\frac{4}{10}$, 0.4, or 40%.

### Develop & Understand: A

A bag holds six blocks, numbered 1 to 6. Imagine drawing one block from the bag.

1. What are the chances of drawing the number 2? Explain how you found your answer.
2. What are the chances of drawing an odd number? Explain.
3. What are the chances of drawing 2, 3, or 5?
4. What are the chances of drawing an odd number that is 3 or 5?

1. $\frac{1}{6}$; only 1 of the 6 blocks is numbered 2.
2. $\frac{3}{6}$, or $\frac{1}{2}$; 3 of the 6 blocks have odd numbers.
3. $\frac{3}{6}$, or $\frac{1}{2}$
4. $\frac{2}{6}$, or $\frac{1}{3}$



### *Reaching* All Learners

**ELL English Language Learners** Some students may be confused by the conjunction *or* in Exercise 3. This may be a good time to distinguish between the logical *or* (in Exercise 3, either 2 or 3 or 5 meet the conditions) and the logical *and* that is implicit in Exercise 4 (a number that is odd and a number that meets the conditions of Exercise 3) where *and* indicates that both conditions must apply at the same time.

6. $\frac{1}{6}$; they are the same.

7. $\frac{3}{6}$, or $\frac{1}{2}$; they are the same.

8a. 1-1, 1-2, 1-3, 1-4, 1-5, 1-6, 2-1, 2-2, 2-3, 2-4, 2-5, 2-6, 3-1, 3-2, 3-3, 3-4, 3-5, 3-6, 4-1, 4-2, 4-3, 4-4, 4-5, 4-6, 5-1, 5-2, 5-3, 5-4, 5-5, 5-6, 6-1, 6-2, 6-3, 6-4, 6-5, 6-6; There are 36 ways.

10a. 1-2, 1-3, 1-4, 1-5, 1-6, 2-1, 2-3, 2-4, 2-5, 2-6, 3-1, 3-2, 3-4, 3-5, 3-6, 4-1, 4-2, 4-3, 4-5, 4-6, 5-1, 5-2, 5-3, 5-4, 5-6, 6-1, 6-2, 6-3, 6-4, 6-5; There are 30 ways.

**Real-World Link**
Many people, such as meteorologists, engineers, insurance specialists, and geneticists, use the concepts of probability everyday.

**5.** Suppose a friend tells you that she drew 2, 3, or 5. What is the probability that she drew an odd number? $\frac{2}{3}$

## Develop & Understand: B

Suppose you take a block from the bag of six blocks and record its number. Then you return the block to the bag, mix the blocks, and draw another.

**6.** What is the probability that the number on the second block is 2? Compare your answer to Exercise 1.

**7.** What is the probability that the second number is odd? Compare your answer to Exercise 2.

**8.** Suppose the first block you drew was 3. You might have drawn 1, 2, 3, 4, 5, or 6 for the second block. That gives six ways that you could have drawn two blocks, 3-1, 3-2, 3-3, 3-4, 3-5, or 3-6.

**a.** List *all* the possible ways that you could have drawn two blocks. How many are there?

**b.** In how many of these ways are both numbers odd? What is the probability that you will draw two odd numbers? 9; $\frac{9}{36}$, or $\frac{1}{4}$

**c.** What is the probability that you will draw the same number twice? $\frac{6}{36}$, or $\frac{1}{6}$

Now imagine taking a block from the bag, putting it in your pocket, and then drawing a second block.

**9.** What is the probability that the first number is odd? $\frac{3}{6}$, or $\frac{1}{2}$

**10.** Now you will find the probability that the second number is odd.

**a.** List all the possible ways that you could have drawn the two blocks. How many ways are there?

**b.** In how many of these ways is the second number odd? What is the probability that you will draw an odd number the second time? 15; $\frac{15}{30}$, or $\frac{1}{2}$

**c.** Compare the probability that you found in Part b to the one you found in Exercise 9. What do you notice? (Hint: Write both probabilities as ratios to compare them.) They are equivalent.

**11.** What is the probability that both numbers will be odd? $\frac{6}{30}$, or $\frac{1}{5}$

**12.** Now suppose that, before you choose a second block, you look at the number on the first block.

**a.** If the first number is odd, what is the probability that the second number will also be odd? You might want to look at your list from Exercise 10 to help you answer this. $\frac{6}{15}$, or $\frac{2}{5}$

**b.** If the first number is even, what is the probability that the second number will be odd? $\frac{9}{15}$, or $\frac{3}{5}$



▶ **Exercise 5** This exercise changes the conditions of the drawing by restricting the possible outcomes to three. Because each outcome is equally likely, the probability of any one outcome is $\frac{1}{3}$ and the probability of two of the three is $\frac{2}{3}$. If the outcomes are not equally likely, the simple random drawing model does not apply. Con artists often take advantage of the fact that events that seem to be equally likely are in fact not.

## Develop & Understand: B

*Suggested Grouping: Pairs or Individuals*

This exercise set introduces outcomes that are actually composed of two or more sequential events. Students will need to list the possible sequences in an orderly way to find probabilities of sequential events.

▶ **Exercises 6–8** The two sequential events are independent because the probability of a particular event occurring on the second draw does not depend on the outcome of the first draw since you replace the first marble you draw from the bag before you draw the second marble.

▶ **Exercise 10c** The probability of drawing an odd number on the second block is the same as the probability of drawing an odd number on the first. In each case, there are 15 favorable outcomes out of the 30 possible outcomes. However, in Exercise 12a, the probability of picking an odd number on the second block is changed if you know you have picked an odd number on the first. This means that the possible outcomes are restricted to 15 of the 30 pairs. Of these, only 6 consist of pairs of odd numbers. Therefore the probability of a second odd number is $\frac{6}{15}$ or $\frac{2}{5}$. The probability of drawing a second odd number is changed if you have information about the number you drew first. Notice that this contrasts with the probability calculated in Exercise 11 that both will be odd: $\frac{6}{30}$.

**Wrap-Up** Take some time to discuss student answers to these questions in class. Encourage students to go back to listing all possible outcomes if they get confused. It is usually possible to deal with dependent events by interpreting them in terms of a subset of a set of all possible outcomes.

## Share & Summarize

For Question 1, it is important to point out that the probability of an impossible event is 0. This makes sense in reference to the "marbles in a bag model": if there are 5 purple marbles in a bag, then the probability of drawing a white marble is the number of white marbles (0) over the total number of marbles (5) for a probability of $\frac{0}{5}$ or 0. You may want to remind students that if an event is certain to occur, the probability for that event is 1. For example, given a bag of 5 purple marbles, the probability of drawing a purple marble is $\frac{5}{5}$ or 1.

In Questions 2 and 3, students compare the probabilities of two seemingly similar events, such as drawing two blocks from a bag. However, one time they replace the block before drawing again, and the other time they do not replace the block. They explain why the probabilities are not the same.

The most likely exercises in finding the probabilities in the exercise sets will relate to interpreting the *and* and *or* conjunctions. You may find it helpful to use Venn diagrams for sets to explain the interpretation of each conjunction.

## Investigation 2

**On Your Own Exercises**
Pages 272–277
Exercises 7–8, 10–11

**Experimental Probability** In this investigation, students find experimental probability and draw tree diagrams to record data. In this investigation, students work with possible outcomes of more than 200 and see the need for an orderly way of finding the number of possible outcomes. Tree diagrams are one such method.

Have the students read the cartoon in the text and discuss their opinions in pairs.

## Think & Discuss

*Suggested Grouping: Whole Class*

Have a class discussion about the results. It is important to assume that the coin is really fair. If it is a two-headed coin, then the next toss is certain to be a head.



1. The probability is 0. Possible explanation: In Exercise 8, we put the block back, so we could pull it out again. This time, the only block with that number had been removed, so there was no chance of drawing it again.

## Share & Summarize

1. Suppose you draw one block from the bag of 6 blocks and then, without putting it back, draw another. What is the probability of drawing the same number twice? Compare your answer to Part c of Exercise 8. Explain the reasons for any differences.
2. Compare the probabilities that you calculated for Part b of Exercise 8 and for Exercise 11. Explain any differences.
3. Look again at Exercises 10 and 12.
   a. Compare your answers to Parts a and b of Exercise 12. Try to explain any differences. See below.
   b. Now compare your answers for Part b of Exercise 10 with those for Exercise 12. Try to explain any differences.
   Problem 10b: $\frac{1}{2}$. Possible explanation: In Exercise 10, I did not know which block had been removed, so I had more possibilities to consider.

## Investigation 2 Heads or Tails?

**Materials**
- coin

Shaunda just tossed a coin twice and got heads both times.

2. Exercise 8b: $\frac{9}{36}$, or $\frac{1}{4}$; Exercise 11: $\frac{6}{30}$, or $\frac{1}{5}$. Possible explanation: In Exercise 11, there are 6 fewer possibilities, which represent drawing the same number twice. In 3 of these 6, the number is odd.

## Think & Discuss

With whom do you agree, Shaunda or Zach? Explain.
Answers will vary, but should show how students are understanding probability.

3a. Part b: $\frac{3}{5}$; Part a: $\frac{2}{5}$. Possible explanation: In Part a, one of the odd blocks was already removed, so the probability is lower than for Part b, when all the odd blocks were still in the bag.



## Reaching All Learners

**AL Approaching Level** It may help students to look at non-mathematical examples. The truth of a compound statement follows the same pattern. The sentence "It is raining and the sun is shining." is true only if both events occur at the same time. The sentence "It is raining or the sun is shining." is true if either event is occurring or *if both events are occurring.*

Shaunda and Zach decided to conduct an experiment to test their ideas.

Shaunda suggested, "We can toss a coin until we get two heads in a row. Then we can see what the next toss is."

Zach says, "If we only do it once, it won't prove anything. We need to do the experiment lots of times."

**Math Link**

One way to simulate tossing a coin is to have a computer or calculator give a random number between 0 and 1. If the number is less than 0.5, the result is heads. If the number is 0.5 or greater, the result is tails.

## Develop & Understand: A

**1.** Follow Zach's suggestion and try the experiment at least 10 times. Keep a tally of how many times you get tails after two heads and how many times you get heads after two heads. Answers will vary.

**2.** Do your results support Shaunda's argument that tails are more likely or Zach's argument that heads are just as likely as tails? Why? Answers will vary.

Shaunda and Zach thought they needed more than 10 results, but they were tired of tossing coins. They created a computer program to simulate tossing a coin many times. Here are the results of 200 tosses.

T T T T H H T H H H T H H H H T H T H T H H T H T
H T T T H T H T T H T H T T H H T H T H T H H T T
T H T T T H H H T H T T T H H T T T T T T H H H T
T T T H T H H H H T T T T H T T T T H H T H T T H
H T T H T T H T T H H T H H H H T H T H T H H T H
T H H H T H T H T H T H T H T T T T T T H T H H T
T T H H H H H H H T T H T T H T H T H H H T T T T
H T T H H H T T H H T H H T H H T H H T T T H H H

**3.** Starting from the first toss, reading left to right, find the first instance of two heads in a row. Tally the result of the next toss. Continue the process, looking for the next instance of two heads in a row. 14 T, 12 H

**4.** Do another experiment using the 200 tosses, this time looking for two tails in a row and tallying the results of the next toss. 15 T, 10 H

**5.** Comment on whose reasoning your results support, Shaunda's or Zach's. They support Zach's.

**6.** Shaunda and Zach ran another 500 tosses on their computer. For two heads in a row, the next toss was heads 38 times and tails 31 times. For two tails in a row, the next toss was heads 30 times and tails 38 times. Do these results support Shaunda or Zach? Zach



Tell students about Zach and Shaunda's experiment.

You might ask students why it's necessary to do the experiment lots of times.

## Develop & Understand: A

*Suggested Grouping: Pairs*

This exercise set introduces experimental probability. Allow plenty of time for pairs to conduct their experiments (10 times is a minimum!) and record results. It is difficult to accurately count these outcomes. If a pair's results are very different from the given answer, you may need to suggest that they count again.

Make sure students understand that the experiment in Exercise 1 consists of tossing two heads in a row, then recording the outcome of the third toss. It is likely that they will have some data, such as tossing a head first, then a tail, that is not relevant to the experiment.

Lesson 6.1 Master 1 reproduces the results of 200 tosses shown for Exercises 3–6. You may wish to provide students with copies of this master so they can keep track of the appropriate tosses.

**Wrap-Up** Discuss students' answers to Exercises 2, 5, and 6 to see if their results support Zach's or Shaunda's reasoning. A few students may find that their experimental results support Shaunda's reasoning, then change their opinion as they are given more data.

## Reaching All Learners

**AL Approaching Level** It is easy to get confused and think that since tossing the coin once doesn't affect the outcome of the second toss, the events are independent. This may be an overgeneralization from the marbles-in-a-bag model where drawing a marble and holding it more obviously affects the probability of the second draw. Be sure students understand that when finding two heads in a row in Exercise 3, they are actually working with four possible outcomes: HH, HT, TH, TT.

Discuss how the tree diagram is used to list outcomes. Be sure students understand what each branch represents and why Shaunda thinks that you can expect to toss 4 heads once in every 16 tosses. Students will use the tree diagram to find probabilities in Exercise 9.

## Develop & Understand: B

*Suggested Grouping: Pairs*

You may wish to provide students with copies of Lesson 6.1 Master 2, to help organize their work.

Zach remembered that he had once tossed four heads in a row. "That surprised me. How often do you think that would happen?" Shaunda suggested drawing a tree diagram to find a solution.

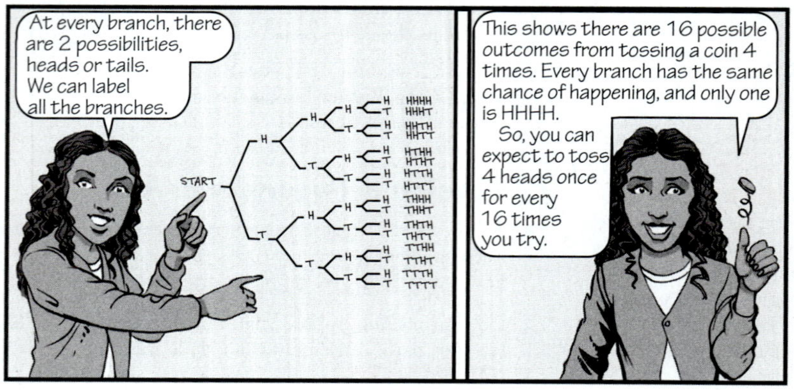


## Develop & Understand: B

Trying 16 times to get four heads is not enough to test Shaunda's conclusion. More data are needed, but tossing coins is tedious. Shaunda and Zach used their computer program to generate another 500 coin tosses.

H H H T H T T H H H T H H H H T H T T H H H H H T

T T T H T H H H T T T T H H T T T T T T T H H T T

T T T H T H T H H H H H H T T H T H T H H T T H H

T T T H H H T T H H H T H H H H T H H H T T H T H

T H T T T T H H T T H T T T H T T H T H T T H H T

H T T H T T T H H T T T T T H H H T T H H T T T T

T T H T T H H T H T T T T H T H T T H H H H H H T

T H H T H T T H H T T T H H T H H T H T T H H T T

T T T T T T H T H T H H H T H H T H T H H H H T T

H T H T H H H H H T T T H H T H T H H T T H H H H

T H T T T T T T H T T T T H H T T H T T H T T H T

T H H T T H T T H T H H H T T T H H H H H T H H H

T H T H H T H H H H H T T H H T T H H H H T T T H

T T T T T H T H H H H T T T H H H T T T T H H T H

T T T T T H T H H H H T T T H T H T H H T T H H T

H T T T T H T T H T H H H H H H H T H H T H T H H

H H H H T H T H H H H T H T T T T T T T H H H T T

H T H H T H T H T T H T H T H H H H H H H H H H T

T H T H T H T T H H T T H T H H H T T T T H T H T

T T T H H T H H H H T H H T T T H H H T T T T H T



### Reaching All Learners

**AL Approaching Level** Students may have difficulty understanding why people are interested in the probability of an event occurring. Put the students into pairs or small groups and have each group flip a coin 200 times. Assign each person in the group a job: recorder, coin flipper, presenter, or calculator. Once the groups have completed their coin flips have them determine the actual number of heads and tails and compute the probability. Have each group share their results. Discuss how close the results are to the actual probability of flipping a head or tail. Discuss other areas where determining the probability of an event occurring would be helpful.

Choose a starting point anywhere in this set of tosses. Look at the next four tosses. If they are all heads, make a note.

Then look at the four tosses after those four. Note whether they are all heads.

Examine at least 48 sets of four tosses. If you reach the end of the set, start over at the beginning.

7. How many times were all four tosses heads? Does your result support Shaunda's conclusion?

7. Results will vary; most will support Shaunda's conclusion.

8. In Shaunda's tree diagram, how many times does the combination of two heads and two tails, in any order, occur? This is a prediction of how many times out of 16 you could expect to get two heads and two tails. 6

9. Use the tree diagram to work out the chances of all of the combinations of heads and tails from four tosses. Enter the results in a table.

| Combination | 4H | 3H 1T | 2H 2T | 1H 3T | 4T |
|---|---|---|---|---|---|
| Probability | 1/16 | 4/16 | 6/16 | 4/16 | 1/16 |

10. Choose one of the predictions from your table. Then obtain some evidence by using the chart of 500 coin tosses. Comment on whether your evidence supports the prediction. Answers will vary, but the evidence should support the prediction.

### Math Link

When you are considering only final outcomes and not their order, tossing a coin five times in a row is the same mathematical situation as tossing five coins at once.

### Share & Summarize

1. If you are trying to estimate how likely something is, would it be better to run an experiment one time or 100 times? Explain your reasoning.

2. Jonah made a tree diagram for tossing a coin five times. From his diagram, he estimated he would get four heads and one tail five times out of every 32 tries. He then tossed five coins 64 times.

   a. What is the most likely number of times Jonah will toss four heads and one tail? 10

   b. Jonah actually got four heads and one tail eight times. Does this contradict your answer to Part a? Explain.

1. 100 times; if you run it only once, you could get the less likely result and not know it. If you do it 100 times, there is an opportunity for more of the possible results to happen.

2b. No; 8 times is close to 10; although 10 times is most likely, Jonah will not necessarily get that exact number.



You might want to tell students that the sum of the probabilities for all possible outcomes is 1. This can give them a way to check if their answers to Exercise 9 are reasonable.

▶ **Exercise 10** You can make sure that all combinations of heads and tails are researched by assigning pairs of students specific combinations to explore.

**Wrap-Up** Have students share their answers to Exercise 4, making sure that all combinations have been researched.

### Math Link

If order isn't important, tossing 5 coins at once is equivalent to tossing one coin 5 times. Not all students may be comfortable with this. The events are equivalent because the total number of outcomes for each are equivalent. It may help to construct a tree for tossing one coin 5 times in a row and then construct a tree for tossing 5 coins tossed at once and ordering the results according to denomination (for example, listing in the order penny, nickel, dime, quarter, half-dollar means that HHTHT records a head on a penny, a head on a nickel, and so on). The trees are, of course, identical. Often finding equivalent models is an excellent strategy for solving probability exercises. If students understand one model better than another, then they can use it for equivalent situations.

### Share & Summarize

It is important that students realize that theoretical probability predictions are extremely unlikely to match experimental results exactly. However, as the number of experiments increase, the actual results should increasingly come close to the theoretical expectations.

## Reaching All Learners

**OL On Level** Students will find that many people understand theoretical probability arguments but don't really believe them. For example, if a coin is tossed 5 times and all the results are heads, a lot of people will continue to believe that a tail is more likely on the sixth throw. You may want to discuss this in class, posing the following argument: if five heads are tossed in a row, the coin is probably a two-headed coin, and therefore the likelihood is that the sixth toss will be a head. The assumption of fairness is crucial in calculating probabilities.

## Investigation 3

***On Your Own Exercises***
Pages 272–277
Exercises 1–3, 12–13

**Fair Games** Tell students that they will use probabilities to test whether or not games are fair.

**Explore**

While the text calls for coins, using 2-color counters is, of course, perfectly fine. After students play the game, have the class combine their results and see if they think the game is fair. At this point, students will likely understand that the game is not fair, but they may not be able to explain why or what could be done to make the game fair.

### Develop & Understand: A

*Suggested Grouping: Pairs*

You might have single-color counters or other disks and some of the two-color counters available for students who want to experiment with the game. Using these counters is also an effective way for students to test their ideas about the theoretical probabilities.

Some students will probably comment that the two all-yellow disks are a distraction—one might just as well toss the red/blue disk. If students object that the distraction is irrelevant, you might observe that such distractions are often used by con artists.

**Wrap-Up** Students may have found different ways to alter the scoring system and make the game fair in Exercise 2. Discuss their ideas as a class, allowing them to decide whether an alternate scoring system does indeed make the game fair.

### Develop & Understand: B

*Suggested Grouping: Groups of Four*

The point here is to first determine the results of the game experimentally, and then calculate the theoretical results. Allow plenty of time for groups to play the game, and emphasize that groups must record their results.

## Investigation 3 Is It Fair?

In the following exercises, you will test whether games are fair by determining probabilities for them.

**Explore**

Suppose you and your friend play a game in which you toss two coins. If the coins show the same faces, you score 1 point. If they show different faces, your friend scores 2 points.

Is this a fair game? Play 10 rounds of the game to see what happens. See ①.

① The possible outcomes are HH, HT, TH, and TT. For half of the results, one player gets 1 point. For the other half, the other player gets 2 points. The game is unfair.

### Develop & Understand: A

Taylor and Manuel have three disks. Two are yellow on both sides. One is yellow on one side and red on the other.

The friends take turns tossing all three disks. Taylor scores one point if they all turn up yellow, and Manuel scores two points if they are not all yellow.

**1.** Is this a fair game? Why or why not?

**2.** If the game is not fair, assign points in a different way to make it fair.

1. No; half of the time the disks will all be yellow, so Taylor scores; and half of the time one will be red, so Manuel scores. They are both just as likely to score. Since they do not get the same number of points when they score, the game is not fair.
2. Taylor should score the same number of points if they all turn up yellow as Manuel scores if they are not all yellow.

### Develop & Understand: B

Three people are playing the game *1, 2, 3, Show*. On the count of three, each player shows 1, 2, or 3 fingers. Points are scored according to these rules.

- Player A receives one point if *exactly two* players show the same number of fingers.
- Player B receives one point if all three players show a *different* number of fingers.
- Player C receives one point if all three players show the *same* number of fingers.

The winner is the person with the most points after nine rounds.

**3.** Predict which player will win. Predictions will vary.

**4.** Play *1, 2, 3, Show* in groups of four. Three people are Players A, B, and C. The fourth should record the results to estimate the probabilities of winning. Play an entire game, which is nine rounds.



### *Reaching All Learners*

**AL Approaching Level** Watch for students who are having trouble deciding whether or not the game in Exercise 1 is fair. Work with these students to list all the possible outcomes and then count the ways in which Taylor scores points and the ways in which Manuel scores points.

5. Answers will vary. (Note: Player A has the greatest probability of winning.)
6. Answers will vary. Player A will likely have the greatest percentage and Player C the least.
7. 111, 112, 113, 121, 122, 123, 131, 132, 133, 211, 212, 213, 221, 222, 223, 231, 232, 233, 311, 312, 313, 321, 322, 323, 331, 332, 333
8. Player A: $\frac{18}{27}$, or $\frac{2}{3}$; Player B: $\frac{6}{27}$, or $\frac{2}{9}$; Player C: $\frac{3}{27}$, or $\frac{1}{9}$
9. No; the probabilities of winning a round are different for each player, and each player scores only 1 point for winning a round.
10. Answers will vary, but the ratio of points for Players A:B:C should be 1:3:6. Possible explanation: Player A is 6 times as likely as Player C to win and 3 times as likely as Player B. If Player A scores 1 point, B should score 3 and C should score 6.

Complete a table like the following for your game. Answers will vary.

| Player | Tally of Points Scored | Estimated Probability |
|---|---|---|
| A | | |
| B | | |
| C | | |

5. Which player was the winner? Was your prediction correct?
6. Now collect the data for the entire class. What percent of the time did each player win?
7. Using a tree diagram or a chart, list all the possible outcomes for a round of *1, 2, 3, Show*. For example, 122 is the outcome of Player A showing one finger and Players B and C each showing two fingers.
8. Given the outcomes you listed in Exercise 7, what is the probability of each player winning a round?
9. Is this a fair game? Explain.
10. How would you assign points to make the game fair? Explain why you think your system is fair.

## Share & Summarize

A certain game has four outcomes.

Outcome A has probability $\frac{1}{10}$.

Outcome B has probability $\frac{1}{5}$.

Outcome C has probability $\frac{3}{10}$.

Outcome D has probability $\frac{2}{5}$.

Four players choose outcomes and score a certain number of points when their outcomes arise. How should points be assigned to each outcome to make the game fair? Answers will vary. The ratio of points for A:B:C:D should be 12:6:4:3.



You may want to use a table like the one below to record the class data from Exercise 6 on the board or the overhead. Students can make the class table by recording points for each player in their group.

| Group | Player | | |
|---|---|---|---|
| | A | B | C |
| 1 | | | |
| 2 | | | |
| 3 | | | |
| 4 | | | |

▶ **Exercise 10** Students assign points so that the payoff for each player is the same. Have several groups present their proposed revision of the rules to the class.

**Wrap-Up** Discuss Exercises 5 and 6, focusing on whether students would revise their opinion of the game once they are given more data. As a preview to Lesson 6.2, you might point out that the probabilities derived using the class data usually come closer to the theoretical probability than do the probabilities derived using smaller sets of data. This will give students a chance to think about the ideas of sample size and prediction. Although this isn't the time to actually teach the ideas, you can point out instances where larger amounts of data do give experimental probabilities closer to the theoretical probabilities than do smaller amounts.

## Share & Summarize

This short question will tell you if students have the idea of assigning points to make a game fair. Pose it as a quick question to be answered individually, and then have students share their ways to make the game fair.

## Troubleshooting

Watch for students who have trouble listing all the possible outcomes in Exercise 7. This is an important part of calculating probabilities, and a part that is frequently poorly understood. If some groups are having trouble, you might stop the class and ask others to share their diagrams or charts and explain their reasoning.

Inquiry

## Investigation 4

*Suggested Grouping: Pairs*

### Materials and Preparation

You may want to review the steps of the experiment before having students conduct it.

This classic problem is a good one to discuss with the entire class. Poll students by having a show of hands for the three responses—change, don't change, or unsure. Let students volunteer their reasoning. Tell them that this problem has generated a lot of argument over the years.

### Try It Out

You can substitute three playing cards for the three papers, noting which is the prize or actually use three boxes or paper cups to hide a block or other prize.





Inquiry

## Investigation 4 The Hidden Prize

In the *Hidden Prize* game show, a prize is hidden under one of three boxes. Only the game show host knows where the prize is located.

Camila has won the right to try for a prize. The host asks her to name the box that she thinks has the prize: A, B, or C.

Once Camila has named a box, the host will show her that one of the unchosen boxes is empty. The host will then ask her, "Would you like to change your mind?"

The challenge in this situation is to advise Camila whether to change her mind once the host has revealed one of the empty boxes. What is your initial reaction? Would you advise Camila to change her mind or to stay with her first guess? See ①.

To solve, you will now run an experiment and collect data.

**Real-World Link**

Television game shows have been around since the first experimental TVs were made in the late 1920s. Commercial networks began operating in 1941, and color TV was introduced in the 1950s.

① Answers will vary. Most people initially believe it does not matter whether she changes her mind or not; the chances of winning seem to be the same either way.

### Try It Out

Work in pairs to set up and run the following experiment.

Write the word *Prize* on one of three identical sheets of paper. Then either fold all three sheets, being careful that you cannot tell them apart, or just place them on a desk with the "prize" face down.

**Step 1.** One person pretends to be the quiz show host, and the other pretends to be the contestant. While the contestant looks away, the host rearranges the papers, being careful to note where the prize is.

**Step 2.** The contestant indicates the paper that he or she thinks is the prize.

**Step 3.** The host turns over one of the unchosen sheets of paper. If the contestant did not choose the prize, the host must be careful to turn over the unchosen paper that is *not* the prize.

**Step 4.** The contestant decides whether to change his or her mind.

1. Answers will vary. Most students should find that the contestant wins about $\frac{1}{3}$ of the time.

**1.** First, see what happens when the contestant decides *not* to change his or her mind. Play the game ten times, always staying with the first choice. Record the number of wins in the middle column of a table like the one shown below. (Your table should have one row for each game.)

**Win or Lose?**

| Games | Do Not Change Your Mind | Change Your Mind |
|---|---|---|
| 1 | | |
| 2 | | |

**2.** Now see what happens when the contestant *always* changes his or her mind. Play another 10 times, always changing to the unchosen paper in Step 4. Record the results in the last column of your table. See margin.

**3.** Based on your results, do you think the contestant should or should not change his or her mind? See margin.

**4.** Does your initial guess agree with the result found through your experiment? Answers will vary.

**5.** Explain why the advice that you would now give Camila is correct. See margin.

## What Did You Learn

**6.** When deciding which strategy to use when playing a game, why is it useful to conduct an experiment? To collect data and look for patterns

**7.** Will an experiment always give you the best strategy? Explain. No, but if you do it enough times, it should give you a very good idea.

You might want to create a table of class data showing the results from Exercises 1 and 2.

▶ **Exercise 5** The challenge here is in describing the possible outcomes. When an empty box is revealed, you know that there are two possible situations: either you picked the prize box or one of the two non-prize boxes. The probability you picked the prize box is $\frac{1}{3}$ and if you stick with this, the probability of winning is $\frac{1}{3}$. The probability you picked a non-prize box is $\frac{2}{3}$ and switching in this case will win. Therefore, switching is the best strategy, and the probability of winning by switching is $\frac{2}{3}$.

## What Did You Learn?

If students have trouble making a formal analysis of the hidden prize exercise, don't worry. As noted earlier, it has generated a lot of arguments over the years. They should, however, believe the results of the experimental trials.

### Additional Answers

2. Answers will vary. Most students should find that the contestant wins about $\frac{2}{3}$ of the time.

3. Answers will vary. Most students should find that the contestant should change his or her mind.

5. If she sticks with her original choice, she has a 2 in 3 chance of not winning the prize. If she changes her mind, she has a 2 in 3 chance of not winning the prize initially, but if her initial guess is incorrect she will be correct when she switches; therefore she has a 2 in 3 chance of winning.

## On Your Own Exercises
**Lesson 6.1**

**Investigation 1**
Pages 262–264
Practice & Apply: 4–6
Connect & Extend: 9

**Investigation 2**
Pages 264–267
Practice & Apply: 7–8
Connect & Extend: 10–11

**Investigation 3**
Pages 268–269
Practice & Apply: 1–3
Connect & Extend: 12–13

**Assign Anytime**
Mixed Review: 14–20

▶ **Exercise 2** Students who are having difficulty can make a list of all possible outcomes in order to answer the question.

▶ **Exercise 2 Extension** Have students find ways to make the game fair.

▶ **Exercise 3** The exercise of indistinguishable checkers may confuse some students. It may help to say that although you can't distinguish one red checker from another, they really are different and therefore picking one or another represents a different outcome.

## On Your Own Exercises
**Lesson 6.1**

### Practice & Apply

1a. Yes; the possible outcomes are RR and RB. Each boy scores 1 point half the time.

1b. Possible answer: Alejandro scores 1 point if there is exactly one blue; Oliver scores 1 point if there are no blues or two blues.

2. No; there are four ways to get a sum of 5 (1-4, 4-1, 2-3, and 3-2) and only two ways to get a sum of 3 (1-2 and 2-1). For this to be a fair game, my friend should get twice as many points as I do for each score.

3b. R1, R2; R1, R3; R1, B1; R1, B2; R2, R3; R2, B1; R2, B2; R3, B1; R3, B2; B1, B2

**1.** Alejandro and Oliver have two chips. One is red on both sides. The other is red on one side and blue on the other. Each boy tosses a chip. Oliver scores one point if the chips match, and Alejandro scores one point if they do not match.

**a.** Is the game fair? Explain how you know.

**b.** The boys get a third chip, red on one side and blue on the other. Make up a fair game that involves tossing all three chips.

**2.** Suppose you turn the spinner below and then toss a cube that is numbered 1, 2, 3, 4, 5, and 6. You and another player add the two results. You score two points if the sum is 5, and your friend scores three points if the sum is 3. Is this a fair game? Why or why not?

**3.** Rashard and Kellie are getting ready to play checkers. They devise a competition to decide who will make the first move. They will put three red and two black checkers in a bag and then each draw one. If the two checkers are the same color, Rashard wins. If they are different colors, Kellie wins.

**a.** Design an experiment that could help you decide whether the competition is fair. Run the experiment 20 times. Describe your experiment and your results. See margin.

**b.** List all the possible pairs of checkers that could be chosen. (Hint: There are ten possible pairs, all equally likely.) Use R1, R2, and R3 to represent the red checkers and B1 and B2 for the black checkers. For example, one possible pair is R1, B2.

**c.** In how many of the ten possible pairs are the two colors the same? Does this agree with your experimental results? 4; Answers will vary.

**d.** Is the game fair? Explain. If it is not fair, who has the advantage? No; there are four ways for Rashard to win and six ways for Kellie to win, so Kellie has the advantage.



**Additional Answer**

3a. Possible answer: Put 5 pieces of paper with color labels in a bag to represent the checkers. Draw out two at a time. The results should be close to the theoretical probabilities of 4 chances out of 10 that they are the same color and 6 chances out of 10 that they are different colors.

4a. 1-2, 1-3, 1-4, 1-5, 1-6, 1-7, 1-8, 2-3, 2-4, 2-5, 2-6, 2-7, 2-8, 3-4, 3-5, 3-6, 3-7, 3-8, 4-5, 4-6, 4-7, 4-8, 5-6, 5-7, 5-8, 6-7, 6-8, 7-8

4e. $\frac{12}{28}$, or $\frac{3}{7}$

5a. YY, YP, YO, YG, GY, GP, GO, GG, RY, RP, RO, and RG. The first letter gives the color of the shirt; the second gives the color of the pants.

5c. $\frac{6}{12}$, or $\frac{1}{2}$

5d. $\frac{3}{12}$, or $\frac{1}{4}$

**4.** Arturo and Jill play a game with eight marbles numbered 1 to 8. They mix the marbles in a cup and then draw two.

**a.** List all the pairs of numbers that are possible to draw from the cup. (Note: Drawing 1 and 2 is the same as drawing 2 and 1.)

**b.** What are the chances that the two numbers are 4 and 7? $\frac{1}{28}$

**c.** What are the chances that the two numbers have a sum of 11? $\frac{3}{28}$

**d.** What are the chances that the two numbers include an even number? $\frac{22}{28}$, or $\frac{11}{14}$

**e.** What are the chances that the two numbers have an even sum?

**5.** Mr. Richards, a math teacher, works as a circus clown in the summer. His clown shirts come in three colors, which are yellow, green, and red. He also has four pairs of clown pants, which are yellow, purple, orange, and green.

**a.** List all 12 possible combinations of Mr. Richards' shirt and pants.

**b.** Mr. Richards chooses his clothes at random so that each outfit has the same chances of being selected. What is the probability that he will select a yellow shirt and orange pants? $\frac{1}{12}$

**c.** What is the probability that at least one item will be yellow?

**d.** What is the probability that he will choose purple pants?

**e.** What is the probability that his pants and shirt will be different colors? $\frac{10}{12}$, or $\frac{5}{6}$

On Your Own Exercises

▶ **Exercise 4** Students consider the issue of order. Some students may list too many outcomes without realizing that order doesn't count. However, in this case, the probability of each outcome is equivalent whether 56 outcomes or 28 outcomes are considered.

▶ **Exercise 5** If students are confused about order, point out that GY and YG are different because a green shirt and yellow pants is significantly different from a yellow shirt and green pants.

▶ **Exercise 6e** The most straightforward way to answer this exercise is to count the number of cards less than 8 (there are 6) and divide it by the total number of cards not counting her own (8). Some students may count possible outcomes using the list they made in Exercise 6c. They will find that there are eight pairs having a first number of 8 and in six of these, the first number is less than the second. Point out that listing all outcomes is often not necessary in answering questions like this.

▶ **Exercise 7d** Some students may have trouble with language like *at least*. You may want to take some time to cover expressions like *at least* and *at most*.

On Your Own Exercises

6a. $\frac{6}{9}$, or $\frac{2}{3}$

7a.

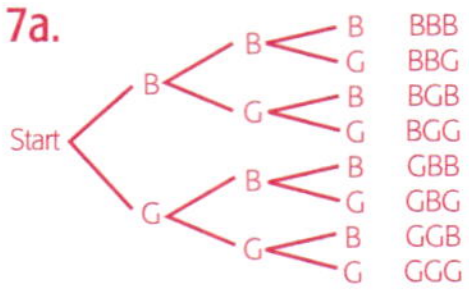


7c. $\frac{3}{8}$

8a. Answers will vary, but it should be approximately $\frac{1}{6}$ of the time.

**6.** Jerry has pulled all the numbered spades from a deck of cards. He now has nine cards: 2, 3, 4, 5, 6, 7, 8, 9, and 10 of spades. He shuffles them and then holds them out for Alanah to choose one. After Alanah chooses her card, Jerry holds them out for Marquez to choose one.

**a.** What is the probability that Alanah chose a number less than 8?

**b.** What is the probability that Alanah chose an even number? $\frac{5}{9}$

**c.** List all the possible ways Alanah and Marquez could have chosen their cards. For example, if Alanah chose 5 and Marquez chose 3, the combination is (5, 3). See margin.

**d.** What is the probability that Alanah chose a higher card than Marquez? $\frac{36}{72}$, or $\frac{1}{2}$

**e.** If Alanah drew the 8, what is the probability that she chose a higher card than Marquez? $\frac{6}{8}$, or $\frac{3}{4}$

**7.** Mrs. Cooper has three children. Assume she is just as likely to have a boy as a girl.

**a.** Make a tree diagram to find probabilities in this situation, such as how likely it is that all three of her children are boys.

**b.** What is the probability that all three children are boys? $\frac{1}{8}$

**c.** What is the probability that Mrs. Cooper has two girls and one boy?

**d.** Suppose you know that Mrs. Cooper has at least one girl. Now what is the probability that she has two girls and one boy? $\frac{3}{7}$

**8.** A bookshelf contains three books, *After the Bell Rings, Beware of the Frog,* and *Cornered.* When Diego accidentally knocked the books onto the floor, he put them back on the shelf without paying attention to their order.

**a.** Label three identical pieces of paper A for *After the Bell Rings,* B for *Beware of the Frog,* and C for *Cornered.* Fold each piece so you cannot see the labels. Shuffle them and then drop them on the floor. Pick them up one by one. How often do you pick them up in alphabetical order?

Run this experiment at least 12 times.

**b.** List all the ways the books could be put on the shelf.
ABC, ACB, BAC, BCA, CAB, CBA

**c.** In how many of these ways would the books be in alphabetical order? Does this agree with your experimental results from Part a?
1; Answers will vary.



**Additional Answer**

6c. (2, 3) (2, 4) (2, 5) (2, 6) (2, 7) (2, 8) (2, 9) (2, 10) (3, 2) (3, 4) (3, 5) (3, 6) (3, 7) (3, 8) (3, 9) (3, 10) (4, 2) (4, 3) (4, 5) (4, 6) (4, 7) (4, 8) (4, 9) (4, 10) (5, 2) (5, 3) (5, 4) (5, 6) (5, 7) (5, 8) (5, 9) (5, 10) (6, 2) (6, 3) (6, 4) (6, 5) (6, 7) (6, 8) (6, 9) (6, 10) (7, 2) (7, 3) (7, 4) (7, 5) (7, 6) (7, 8) (7, 9) (7, 10) (8, 2) (8, 3) (8, 4) (8, 5) (8, 6) (8, 7) (8, 9) (8, 10) (9, 2) (9, 3) (9, 4) (9, 5) (9, 6) (9, 7) (9, 8) (9, 10) (10, 2) (10, 3) (10, 4) (10, 5) (10, 6) (10, 7) (10, 8) (10, 9).

274 **CHAPTER 6** Data and Probability

## Connect & Extend

9a. Three: 0 and 11, 4 and 7, or 3 and 8

9b. Since 4 occurred 4 times out of 10, it is probably on the cube twice. So, the most likely result is 4 and 7.

**9.** Tess has a cube with numbered faces.

- Each face has a whole number.
- Two faces have the same number.
- The sum of all six numbers is 41.

Tess rolls the cube ten times with these results.

3 11 12 4 11 12 3 4 4 4

**a.** Obviously 3, 4, 11, and 12 are on four of the faces. How many possibilities are there for the other two faces? What are they?

**b.** Which of these possibilities do you think is most likely?

**10. Preview** A fairground entices customers with this game.

**a.** Draw a tree diagram to work out the chances of winning this game. See margin.

**b.** What is the probability that a player will win? What is the probability that a player will lose? $\frac{12}{32}$, or $\frac{3}{8}$; $\frac{20}{32}$, or $\frac{5}{8}$

**c.** The prizes for the winners cost the fairground $2 each. If 500 people play, how much money would the fair expect to make? Explain. For every 32 customers, the game pays out $24 and earns $8. For 500 customers, this works out to $125.



**See Answer Appendix p. 317A for Exercise 10a.**

On Your Own Exercises

▶ **Exercise 9** Students may not realize that the whole numbers include 0, which allows 0 and 11 as possible faces. Expect students to take some time just identifying the restrictions for this exercise.

▶ **Exercise 9a** Some students may use this strategy to find the faces: Since the sum of 3, 4, 11, and 12 is 30, the two remaining numbers must have a sum of 11 (41–30). Since one number must appear twice, the possible answers are 3 and 8, 4 and 7, and 0 and 11.

▶ **Exercise 10c** Be sure students understand that the $2 cost is for each plush toy prize awarded to a winner.

▶ **Exercise 11b** Students may be confused by the application of the word *further*. Remind them that desired outcomes (the top number of the probabilities) can be further apart but because probability is a ratio of desired to total outcomes, the probabilities can be closer together because the total number of outcomes (the bottom number) is getting larger too. This is a good chance to review the behavior of fractions!

▶ **Exercise 12** Students can use formulas to determine the area of each section. Some students may copy the figure, cut out each section, then physically compare the areas.

On Your Own Exercises

**11.** Cary ran an experiment. Using a computer program, he examined the number of heads in various numbers of coin tosses. For example, he simulated tossing a coin 10 times and got 4 heads. For 100 tosses, he got 46 heads. He made a table of his results.

| Number of Tosses | Actual Number of Heads | Expected Number of Heads | Difference \|Expected − Actual\| |
|---|---|---|---|
| 10 | 4 | 5 | 1 |
| 100 | 46 | 50 | 4 |
| 1,000 | 513 | 500 | 13 |
| 10,000 | 5,087 | 5,000 | 87 |

**Math Link**
The absolute value of a number is its distance from 0 on a number line.

$|3| = 3$

$|-3| = 3$

**a.** Complete the last two columns of Cary's table.

**b.** Cary noticed that the numbers in the "Difference" column were increasing. He claimed that this shows that as the number of trials grows, the results get further from the actual probabilities of the situation. Explain why his reasoning is incorrect. See below.

**12.** Kai, Steven, and Andrés are playing a dart game with this target.

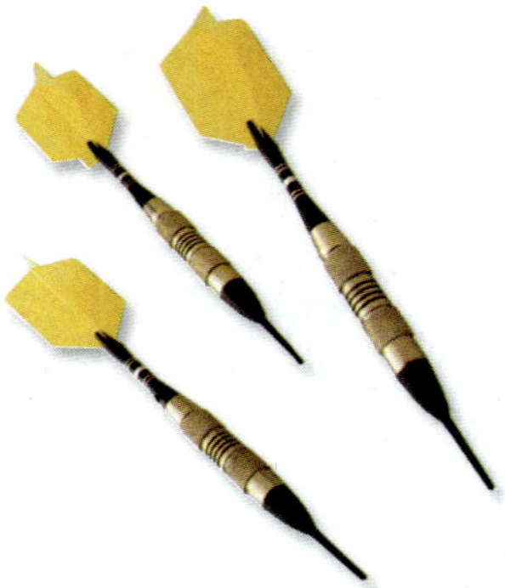

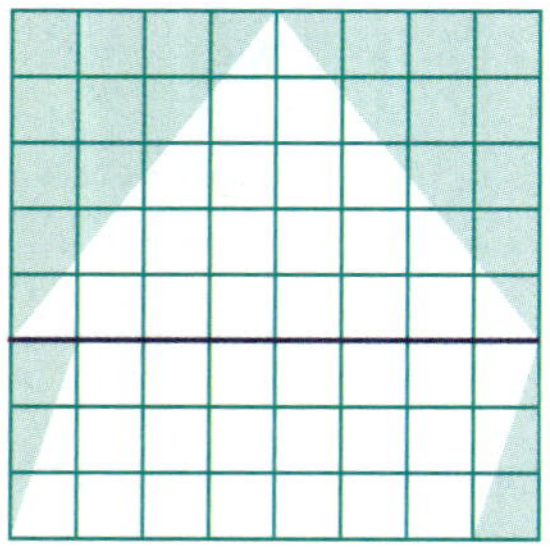

Kai scores one point if she hits the white triangle above the blue line. Steven scores one point if he hits the parallelogram below the blue line. Andrés must hit a blue region to score a point. Is this game fair? Why or why not? See margin.

13. No; 10 heads is the average, but for any 20 tosses it can vary.

**13.** Erika and Lani tossed a coin 20 times. Lani scored one point if it landed heads, and Erika scored one point if it landed tails. At the end of 20 tosses, there were 14 heads and 6 tails. Erika said that was impossible, since if you toss a coin 20 times, it should come out 10 heads and 10 tails. Is Erika correct? Why or why not?

11b. Possible answer: Cary should be looking at percents. The 4 heads for 10 tosses is 40% of the tosses, 10% away from the expected 50%. The 5,087 heads for 10,000 tosses is 50.87% of the tosses, only 0.87% away from the expected 50%.



**Additional Answer**

12. No; the area of the triangle is 20, the area of the parallelogram is 21, and the area of the shaded region is 23. If the three players have the same skill at throwing darts, Andrés has the largest target and Kai has the smallest. Some students might argue that since Andrés' area is split up, he has to aim at one of four small areas, so he actually has the smallest chance.

**276** **CHAPTER 6** Data and Probability

## Mixed Review

14a. $72\pi$ in$^3$, or about 226.2 in$^3$

**14. Geometry** Consider this cylinder.

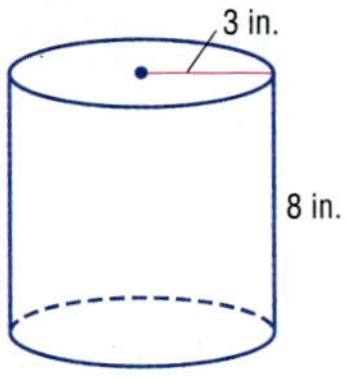


a. Find the volume of this cylinder.

b. Find the volume of a cylinder with the same height as this cylinder and twice the radius. $288\pi$ in$^3$, or about 904.8 in$^3$

c. Find the volume of a cylinder with the same radius as this cylinder and twice the height. $144\pi$ in$^3$, or about 452.4 in$^3$

**15.** A block structure and its top engineering view are shown. What are the volume and surface area of this structure?
8 cubic units, 34 square units

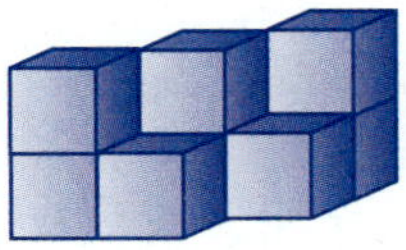

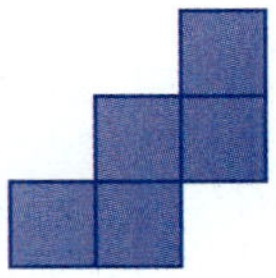

Top

**16.** Here is the top-count view of a block structure. What are the structure's volume and surface area? 16 cubic units, 48 square unit

| | | | |
|---|---|---|---|
| 2 | 2 | 2 | 2 |
| 2 | 1 | 1 | 2 |
| | 1 | 1 | |

**Rewrite each expression as addition, and then calculate the sum.**

**17.** $-10 - (-9)$ $-10 + 9 = -1$

**18.** $1.5 - (-0.14)$ $1.5 + 0.14 = 1.64$

**19.** $-3.33 - (-1.68)$ $-3.33 + 1.68 = -1.65$

**20.** How long will the gummy worm be when it exits this connection? Give your answer in meters. 900 m

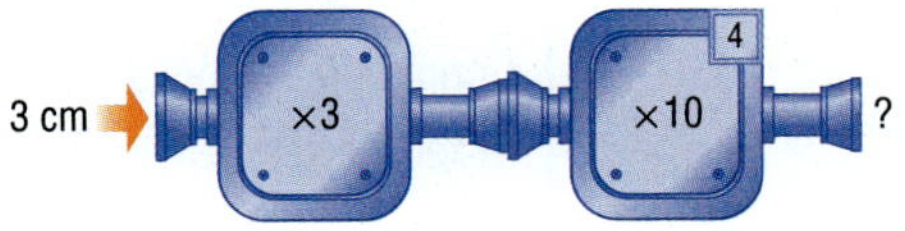




On Your Own Exercises

## Quick Check

**Informal Assessment** Students should be able to:

✔ answer questions about a single random drawing

✔ determine experimental probability

✔ understand that a fair game is one in which all participants have the same chance of winning

## Quick Quiz

**1.** A bag contains 7 blocks labeled with the numbers 1 to 7. One block is drawn at random from the bag. What is the probability that

a. it is 5? $\frac{1}{7}$

b. it is a number less than 11? $\frac{7}{7}$, or 1.

c. it is 11? 0

d. it is odd or even? $\frac{7}{7}$, or 1

e. it is evenly divisible by 2 or 3? $\frac{4}{7}$: the numbers 2, 3, 4, 6

f. it is evenly divisible by 2 and 3? $\frac{1}{7}$: the number 6

**2.** Shaunda has tossed a coin four times and obtained four heads.

a. If the coin is fair, is the probability that it will come up heads on the fifth toss greater, less, or the same as the probability that it will come up tails? Same; the fifth toss is independent of the first four tosses, so the probability is equal that it will come up heads or tails.

b. What is the probability that Shaunda will toss a coin four times and have it come up four heads in a row? $\frac{1}{16}$

LESSON

6.2

# Make Predictions

## Objectives

- To predict the characteristics of an entire population from a representative sample
- To appreciate some of the limitations inherent in using small or restricted samples
- To analyze a representative sample for flaws in its selection
- To choose a sample representative population for a survey

## *Overview*

This lesson deals with the problem of characterizing a population by sampling a subset of that population. One way to describe a population that, for some reason, you cannot see, count, or measure in some way, is to take a sample and assume that it is proportional to the whole population. Students consider how the size of a sample might change the accuracy.

## *Advance Preparation*

Each group of students will need 20 colored tiles and a paper bag. You may also wish to provide students with copies of Lesson 6.2 Master 1, since the poem and some of the related problems are on different pages in the text. Some students may want to use a protractor when working on Investigation 3.

| | Summary | Materials | On Your Own Exercises (pp. 286–293) | Assessment Opportunities |
|---|---|---|---|---|
| **Investigation 1** (p. 279) Pacing: 2 days | In this investigation, students predict the makeup of blocks in a bag by drawing blocks and replacing them. | | Practice & Apply: 1–5<br>Connect & Extend: 11–12<br>Mixed Review: 20–26 | • Share & Summarize (p. 280)<br>• Troubleshooting (p. 279) |
| **Investigation 2** (p. 280) Pacing: 1 day | Students determine word characteristics of a poem by examining selections of different sizes. | Lesson 6.2 Master 1 | Practice & Apply: 6–7<br>Connect & Extend: 13–14<br>Mixed Review: 20–26 | • On the Spot Assessment (p. 281)<br>• Share & Summarize (p. 282)<br>• Troubleshooting (p. 280) |
| **Investigation 3** (p. 283) Pacing: 1 day | This investigation deals with strategies for picking a representative sample of a population for a school survey. | calculator | Practice & Apply: 8–10<br>Connect & Extend: 15–19<br>Mixed Review: 20–26 | • Share & Summarize (p. 285)<br>• Troubleshooting (p. 285)<br>• On the Spot Assessment (p. 284) |

# Leveled Lesson Resources

CRM *Available in:* **Chapter 6 Resource Masters**

Also on TeacherWorks™ Lesson 6.2

## Study Guide and Intervention (p. 10) AL

**Lesson 6.2 Study Guide and Intervention**
***Make Predictions***

A **sample** is a small group that is selected from a larger group, or **population**. Any ratios studied within a **representative sample** should be approximately proportional to the ratios within the population.

**Example 1** **Marla and Stephan played a game called *What's in the Bag* with red, green, blue, and purple disks. They had a bag with 15 disks. They took three samples of 6 disks at a time. How many blue disks do you predict were in the group of 15?**

- Sample 1: R G B R B P
- Sample 2: G B P B B R
- Sample 3: B P G R R R

**Step 1** Check the ratios within each sample, and predict an equivalent ratio within the population.

Sample 1: There are 2 blues out of 6 disks, so there might be 5 blues out of 15 disks.

Sample 2: There are 3 blues out of 6, so there might be about 7.5 blues out of 15 disks.

Sample 3: There is 1 blue out of 6, so there might be about 2.5 blues out of 15 disks.

**Step 2** Average the results.
$(5 + 7.5 + 2.5) \div 3 = 5$, so there are probably 5 blue disks in the bag.

**Example 2** **Jimmy wants to find out what the children in his town like to play on the most at the playground. He thought he would either send questionnaires to every household with children or survey every tenth student who enters a local elementary school. Which strategy do you think is better?**

Sending the questionnaires would result in the largest representative sample, but it is the least practical method. Surveying every tenth student would result in a good representative sample and is a practical method. Therefore, this strategy is better.

**Exercises**

1. **Shopping** Which strategy for a survey is better to determine whether people would like to have a fountain built inside a mall? Explain.
   a. Poll every 15th shopper who enters the mall one day.
   b. Poll every household within a 10-mile radius of the mall.

## Skills Practice (p. 11) AL OL

**Lesson 6.2 Skills Practice**
***Make Predictions***

1. **Game** Becky and Kevin were playing *What's in the Bag* From 15 hidden tiles, they took four samples of 4. The tiles were red, yellow, green, and blue.

   Sample 1: Y G B B
   Sample 2: G B R B
   Sample 3: B B B Y
   Sample 4: B G Y B

   How many of each color do you predict were in the group of 15 tiles?

2. **Game** Louisa and Wyndel were playing *What's in the Bag* From 20 hidden chips, they took four samples of 6. The chips were red, yellow, green, and blue.

   Sample 1: R Y G B G Y
   Sample 2: B G Y G G Y
   Sample 3: R Y G Y G G
   Sample 4: G B G Y Y R

   How many of each color do you predict were in the group of 20 chips?

3. **Typing** Mr. Jacobson decided to survey students at Westview Junior High School to determine the skill levels at which students were typing. He is considering the following suggested strategies for conducting the survey. For each strategy, respond to these three questions.

   Is the sample large enough?
   Is the sample representative?
   Is the survey method practical?

   *Strategy 1* Hand out a survey to all students.

   *Strategy 2* Hand out a survey to all students who use the computer lab one Friday.

   *Strategy 3* Publish a questionnaire in the school newspaper that students can fill out and turn in to a teacher.

   *Strategy 4* Choose every 10th student on an alphabetical list of all the students in the school to fill out a questionnaire.

## Problem-Solving Practice (p. 12) AL OL

**Lesson 6.2 Problem-Solving Practice**
***Make Predictions***

1. **Cell Phones** A survey of students at Bethel Middle School was done to determine cell phone usage. The results are shown in the table.

   The population at Bethel Middle School is about five times the sample size used for the survey. How many students at the middle school would you predict use a cell phone more than twice a day?

| Student Cell Phone Usage | |
|---|---|
| **Frequency of Use** | **Number of Students** |
| More than twice a day | 30 |
| Once or twice a day | 19 |
| Less than once a week | 15 |
| Never used one | 12 |

2. **Movies** McAlister Movie Theaters recorded the following sales in one weekend.

   - Action: 275 tickets
   - Thriller: 310 tickets
   - Romantic Comedy: 420 tickets
   - Documentary: 150 tickets

   a. McAlister is one of four theaters in the city. If the other theaters have similar sales, predict the number of action tickets sold per weekend in the city.
   b. Do you think these data are enough to predict weekend sales for all four theaters for six months? Explain.

3. **Studying** Kenneth and Mary wanted to predict the average number of hours that students in a school study. Which sample is the most representative? Explain.

   Sample 1: every student whose last name begins with S
   Sample 2: members of the National Honor Society
   Sample 3: every 5th student in an alphabetical listing of the student body
   Sample 4: every 5th student in a homeroom class

4. **Fluids** The corner convenience store had the following sales in one week:

   - Milk: 350 containers
   - Juice: 320 bottles
   - Water: 480 bottles

   Assuming this store is representative of the six stores in the area, how many bottles of juice would you expect all the stores to sell in one week?

5. **Literature** Carmela is typing a book report. There are 210, 188, and 226 words on each of the first three pages of the report.
   a. What is the mean of this data set?
   b. Assuming these counts are typical for Carmela, predict the total number of words if she types eight pages.

## Enrichment (p. 13) BL

**Lesson 6.2 Enrichment**
***Make Predictions***

**Curious Cubes**

If a six-sided number cube is rolled any number of times, the theoretical probability of the number cube landing on any given side is $\frac{1}{6}$.

Each number cube below has six sides and has been rolled 100 times. The outcomes have been recorded in a table. Based on the data in each table, what can you say are probably on the unseen sides of each cube?

1. 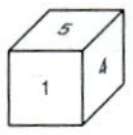


| Outcome | Number of Rolls |
|---|---|
| 1 | 15 |
| 2 | 14 |
| 3 | 18 |
| 4 | 16 |
| 5 | 19 |
| 6 | 18 |

2. 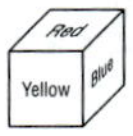


| Outcome | Number of Rolls |
|---|---|
| blue | 17 |
| red | 30 |
| yellow | 53 |

3. 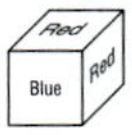


| Outcome | Number of Rolls |
|---|---|
| red | 30 |
| blue | 16 |
| blank | 54 |

4. 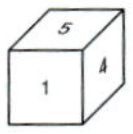


| Outcome | Number of Rolls |
|---|---|
| 1 | 34 |
| 4 | 32 |
| 5 | 34 |

5. 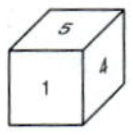


| Outcome | Number of Rolls |
|---|---|
| 1 | 14 |
| 5 | 13 |
| 4 | 18 |
| 2 | 16 |
| blank | 39 |

## Lesson Quick Quiz (p. 14) AL OL BL

**Lesson 6.2 Quick Quiz**
***Make Predictions***

Use this situation to answer Questions 1and 2: Kevin randomly draws one block from a bag of colored blocks. He replaces the block and shakes the bag after each draw. The results of five successive draws are RGGRR.

1. What colors do you predict are in the group of blocks if there are only
   a. two blocks in the bag?
   b. three blocks in the bag?
   c. four blocks in the bag?
   d. five blocks in the bag?
   e. three hundred blocks in the bag?

2. Look at your predictions in Question 1.
   a. Which, if any, prediction has a probability of zero of being correct? Explain.
   b. Which, if any, prediction has a probability of one of being correct? Explain.
   c. Which, if any, prediction has the least chance of being correct? Explain.

3. In taking a survey of students about classes at a school, the editors of the newspaper published the questions in the paper. They asked students to fill out the questionnaire and hand it in after school. They received 60 submissions in a school of 300.

   Is their choice of representative sample a good one? Describe any potential drawbacks with it.

## Lesson Master (p. 15)

**Lesson 6.2 Master 1**
***Make Predictions***

**Investigation 2: Develop & Understand: A**

**Love Lesson**
*by Kristen Pitts*
8th grade, Ohio

He is a four-year-old with blonde hair and blue eyes
He loves music about cheeseburgers and paradise

He lives each day to the fullest while he's awake
Always wanting a chocolate milkshake

He learns thorough his videos and hand-held games
He loves to play and play
He is a mastermind at puzzles

He reads his favorite books quite a bit
Reading them over and over before calling it quits

And when it's time for him to sleep
His blanket and warm thoughts he's sure to keep
Always such a sweet, innocent boy

He is one of the greatest boys I know
Because he taught me how his autism goes

# Additional Lesson Resources

### Teacher Tech Tools

- TeacherWorks
- ExamView Assessment Suite
- Classroom Presentation Toolkit
- Advance Tracker

### Student Tech Tools

- StudentWorks Plus
- Math Online eGlossary • Concepts in Motion

### Other Print Products

- Investigation Notebook and Reflection Journal
- Quick Review Math Handbook

LESSON 6.2

# Make Predictions

## Introduce

**Think About Samples** Have the students read the introductory paragraphs to the lesson.

### Explore

*Suggested Grouping: Groups of 2 or 3*

▶ **Prepare** Each group will need a paper bag and about 20 colored tiles.

▶ **Play** Make sure that in constructing the contents of the bag, each group keeps a record of what is actually in the bag that they trade with another group. An alternate way to conduct the Explore is to place the tiles under a sheet of paper rather than in a bag or other opaque container.

▶ **Report** As groups talk about the game, circulate and try to draw out their strategies by asking question such as:

- How close were your initial predictions?
- Were the second ones closer?
- Was the information from the second sample helpful?
- How did you use that information?

▶ **Score** You may want to give a prize for the most accurate prediction.

LESSON 6.2

# Make Predictions



Suppose you ask ten people in your class to name the all-time greatest professional basketball player, and seven say Michael Jordan. If your school had 1,000 students, you might predict that close to 700 of them would also name Michael Jordan. What if you were trying to predict for a group of 1,000 people in another area of the country? The seventh graders in Chicago, where Michael Jordan played for the Bulls, might not represent the opinions of people in Boston, where the Celtics play.

Understanding how to evaluate groups, and how to use that information to make predictions about larger groups, is the focus of this lesson.

### Materials

- colored tiles
- paper bag

### Explore

Work in groups of two or three to play *What's in the Bag*. Each group will need about 20 colored tiles. From these 20 tiles, your group should select a total of 10 tiles. Put the 10 tiles into a paper bag. Then, without revealing your colors, exchange bags with another group.

Someone in your group should draw 4 tiles from the bag you are given. Discuss how to predict, based on those 4 tiles, the number of tiles of each color in the bag. For example, if the tiles chosen are RBBY, 1 red, 2 blue, and 1 yellow, someone might say, "I think there are likely to be more blues than the others, so my guess is 5B, 2R, 2Y, 1G."

Return the tiles to the bag, shake the bag, and draw 4 tiles again. Record the tile colors in a table like the one below, adding a second prediction about the contents of the bag. As you make your new prediction, keep in mind the first group of tiles.

| Attempt | Tiles Drawn | Prediction |
|---|---|---|
| 1 | RBBY | 4B, 3R, 3Y, 0G |
| 2 | BBBG | 6B, 2R, 1Y, 1G |

Draw a third group of 4 tiles. Make another prediction. Finally, look at all the tiles in the bag. How close were your predictions?
Answers will vary.



## Reaching All Learners

**ELL** **English Language Learners** Predictions can take many forms and for students whose first language is not English, it will be useful to do several examples of events that can be represented using predictions. In small groups ask the students a question and record their responses. Have each person in the group think up a question and take turns asking these questions in English and recording their responses. Have each group share their most interesting question and response. Discuss where predictions are useful.

# Investigation 1 Samples and Predictions

**Vocabulary**
- population
- sample

Medical researchers often need to predict how well a new drug will work by testing it on part of the population. Advertisers test the effectiveness of a TV commercial on part of the viewing population before they spend large amounts of money airing it.

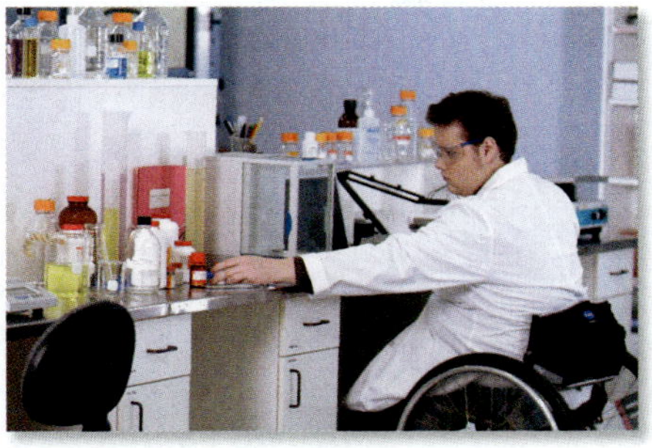

These people are all using a technique called *sampling*. The smaller group is called a **sample**. The larger group from which the sample is taken is called the **population**. In Explore, the population was the ten tiles in the bag, and you took samples of four tiles.

## Develop & Understand: A

Each of the following are actual *What's in the Bag* experiments conducted by students. Look at their samples. Make your own prediction about the contents of the bags. Then check your prediction against the actual contents of the bag, which your teacher will reveal.

**1.** In this game, there were 20 blocks in a bag. The blocks come in yellow, blue, red, and green. Dawn and Sabina drew three samples of 5 blocks. After drawing each sample, they replaced the blocks.

- Sample 1: YBRGG
- Sample 2: GYYBR
- Sample 3: RGRBY

**a.** Predict the colors of the 20 blocks. Answers will vary.

**b.** Dawn and Sabina have seen three samples of 5, or 15 data items in all. Since there are 20 tiles in the bag, they may have seen some tiles twice, and some tiles were not drawn at all. Should Dawn and Sabina be fairly confident about their prediction? Explain.

1b. They should be somewhat confident. They have much data compared to the population, but they still cannot be certain.

**c.** Check your predictions against the actual contents of the bag as given by your teacher. The actual contents were 7R, 5G, 5Y, 3B.



# Investigation 1

***On Your Own Exercises***
Pages 286–293
Exercises 1–5, 11–12

**Samples** In this investigation, students predict the population based on data from a series of samples.

Discuss the introductory paragraphs with students, making sure they understand the terms population and sample. Encourage them to make the connections to the *What's in the Bag?* game from the Explore.

## Develop & Understand: A

*Suggested Grouping: Individuals or Pairs*

This exercise set has students think about the size of a population, the size of the sample relative to the population, and their level of confidence that their predictions about the population from the sample are accurate. Obviously, the larger the sample the more confident one can be about a prediction, but students can ask themselves "How big is big enough?"

## Troubleshooting

Students may be uncomfortable with these tasks because there is not a correct answer. Making a prediction is not an exact procedure like solving an equation. If students are struggling with thinking about predictions, encourage them to conduct an experiment that mimics the question.

**Wrap-Up** A discussion of Exercise 3 is a good wrap-up for the exercise set. At this point in the lesson, it is enough to hear students' ideas and reasoning; the rest of the lesson leads them to think more carefully and deeply about sample size and confidence.

***Share & Summarize***

What's important here is that students apply some method of averaging the two samples to make a prediction. Students should be extending the ratios in their samples to predict the makeup of the population of 100 blocks.

## Investigation 2

***On Your Own Exercises***

Pages 286–293

Exercises 6–7, 13–14

**Sample Sizes** In this investigation, students look at how the size of the sample can affect the prediction of the characteristics of the population. They explore this relationship by using various sample sizes to predict mean word length.

2a. Answers will vary. The actual contents were 5R, 2G, 2B, 1Y.

3. In Exercise 1, 3 samples of 5 allow a look at 15 colors while there were 20 colors in the bag. In Exercise 2, with only 10 colors in the bag, 5 samples of 4 is 20 pieces of data. Although it is not guaranteed to be exact, we would expect the prediction in Exercise 2 to be more accurate.

**2.** Andrea and Tyson played a game with red, green, blue, and yellow disks. They had a bag with ten colored disks. They took five samples of four disks at a time.

- Sample 1: RRGG
- Sample 2: GYRR
- Sample 3: RBRG
- Sample 4: RYRR
- Sample 5: BRRR

**a.** What colors do you predict were in the group of ten?

**b.** Check your prediction against the actual contents of the bag.

**3.** Did you make a more accurate prediction in Exercise 1 or 2? In which would you *expect* to make a more accurate prediction? Why?

***Share & Summarize***

Kali and Kevin are playing *What's in the Bag* with 100 colored blocks. They took sample 1, returned the blocks to the bag, and then took sample 2.

- Sample 1: RRGYGBRRGR
- Sample 2: RGGRBRBGBY

Explain how you would use their sample data to make a prediction about the colors of the 100 blocks in the bag. See ① below.

## Investigation 2 Sample Sizes

People often use a sample to get a sense of the characteristics of a population, particularly when it would be time-consuming and costly to test the whole population. If you have a good sample, the proportion of the sample with a certain characteristic or holding a certain belief can be used to make a prediction about the population.

In a poem, for example, one characteristic you may consider is word length. The following poem has long words, such as *cheeseburgers*, which has 13 letters. It also has words with only two letters. The population in this situation is the 112 words of the poem.

① Possible answer: Predict the proportions to be the same. For example, in sample 1, there are 5 reds out of 10, so the prediction might be 50 reds out of 100. But sample 2 has only 3 reds, which would predict 30 out of 100. Averaging these two gives a prediction of 40 reds.



### *Troubleshooting*

Some students may have trouble applying ratios. Because they are making predictions using ratios, it's okay to relax requirements for precise calculations.

### *Real-World Link*

Although the poetry of American Emily Dickinson (1830–1886) is now known all over the world, only a couple of her almost 2,000 poems were published in her lifetime.

**Love Lesson**

*By Kristen Pitts, 8th grade, Ohio*

He is a four-year-old with blonde hair and blue eyes
He loves music about cheeseburgers and paradise

He lives each day to the fullest while he's awake
Always wanting a chocolate milkshake

He learns through his videos and hand-held games
He loves to play and play
He is a mastermind at puzzles

He reads his favorite books quite a bit
Reading them over and over before calling it quits

And when it's time for him to sleep
His blanket and warm thoughts he's sure to keep
Always such a sweet, innocent boy

He is one of the greatest boys I know
Because he taught me how his autism goes

## Develop & Understand: A

**1.** Before continuing, estimate or guess the mean word length in the poem. Answers will vary.

The *certain* way to find the mean word length is to count all the letters in the poem and divide by the number of words. However, your task here is to see how well you can *predict* the answer by using a sample.

**2.** The poem has 14 lines.

**a.** For each line, count the numbers of letters and words. Record your totals in a table like the one shown here.

| Line | 1 | 2 | 3 | 4 | 5 | 6 | 7 | 8 | 9 | 10 | 11 | 12 | 13 | 14 |
|---|---|---|---|---|---|---|---|---|---|---|---|---|---|---|
| Letters | 41 | 41 | 39 | 32 | 40 | 20 | 24 | 32 | 42 | 27 | 38 | 27 | 29 | 33 |
| Words | 12 | 7 | 10 | 5 | 9 | 6 | 6 | 8 | 9 | 8 | 9 | 6 | 9 | 8 |

**b.** Find the mean word length for Line 6. About 3.33

**c.** Find the mean word length for Line 10. About 3.38

**d.** Do you think you can estimate the mean word length for the poem from a one-line sample? Explain. No; Each line has very different counts. Your data would not be accurate if you used only one line as a sample.



Have someone read the poem aloud. You may want to discuss some of the characteristics of word choice that set the mood before moving on to the problem of counting word lengths. You may wish to use Lesson 6.2 Master 1 to help students record their answers.

## Develop & Understand: A

*Suggested Grouping: Pairs*

Students estimate, then find, the mean word length in a poem. You can provide students with copies of Lesson 6.2 Master 1.

### On the Spot Assessment

Have students think for a few seconds about the Pledge of Allegiance or a school song they all know. Then have them predict the mean word length.

**Lesson 6.2** Make Predictions **281**

▶ **Exercise 3** It is important that students select lines from the poem at random.

**Teacher Tips** After assigning numbers to each of the 14 lines, they can select lines randomly in one of these ways:

- using random number generators on a calculator
- using a random number table
- making simple spinners with paper and paper clips divided into 14 sections
- drawing slips of paper numbered 1–14 from a bag without looking

Be sure to point out that selecting lines by looking at them may be influenced by such things as where a person normally looks first on any piece of paper, the length (short or long) of the line, or other factors, so this method doesn't guarantee that the lines are selected randomly.

**Wrap-Up** Use Exercise 7 as the basis for a class discussion summarizing the investigation.

### Share & Summarize

Have students present their responses to these questions and discuss the answers in class.

Deciding the most appropriate sample size is a complex matter. Don't be concerned if students seem tentative with their ideas or if the class has different ideas. What is important is that students see that the larger the sample, the more accurate the prediction. Time or effort required to gather a large sample and the degree to which you need the prediction to be accurate are other intervening factors.

### Additional Answers

4. Possible answer: No, the largest sample should give the most accurate prediction.

7a. Answers will vary.

7b. The 10-line sample should be most reliable, though in the answers to Exercise 3, the 8-line sample is the most accurate.

---

3. Possible answers, using the following samples: 2 lines: 10, 14; 4 lines: 7, 9, 11, 14; 6 lines: 3, 5, 6, 8, 10, 14; 8 lines: 1, 2, 3, 4, 5, 7, 9, 11; 10 lines: 1, 2, 3, 6, 7, 8, 9, 12, 13, 14

**3.** Make a table for recording the results from different sample sizes.

| Lines | Letters | Words | Mean Word Length |
|---|---|---|---|
| 2 | 60 | 16 | 3.75 |
| 4 | 137 | 32 | 4.28 |
| 6 | 191 | 49 | 3.90 |
| 8 | 297 | 67 | 4.43 |
| 10 | 328 | 81 | 4.05 |

Randomly choose two lines from the poem. Add the numbers of letters for the two lines. Add the numbers of words. Calculate the mean word length. Write your results in the first row of your table.

Next, choose a sample of any four lines. Record the results. Then choose a sample of any six lines, then any eight lines, and then any ten lines. Enter the data you collect into your table.

**4.** Do all samples give the same mean word length? Discuss with your partner which sample you think gives the most accurate prediction. See margin.

**5.** Find the mean word length in the poem by dividing the total number of letters in the poem by the total number of words. How close was your prediction? 4.15; Possible answer: my prediction was off by about 0.15 letter per word.

**6.** If you wanted to choose a one-line sample to bias the prediction toward longer words, which line would you choose? Explain. I would choose Line 2. It has a lot of letters and few words.

**Real-World Link**
One way teachers check the "readability" of a piece of writing for their students is by using a similar sampling technique. They count the number of sentences and syllables in three randomly chosen 100-word passages and plot their results on a chart that gives them the approximate grade level of the reading material.

Your results may be different from those of other students in your class, depending on which lines you chose.

**7.** Create a class data set of the number of lines in the samples that gave the closest prediction. Each student should report how many lines he or she used for the sample that gave the best prediction.

**a.** Count the number of times each sample size was reported.

**b.** Which sample size seems to be most reliable for predicting the mean word length in the poem? See margin.

### Share & Summarize

**1.** Count the numbers of letters in the first names of the six students sitting nearest to you. What is the mean word length for these data? Answers will vary.

**2.** Do you think your group of six students is a reasonable sample for predicting the mean number of letters in the first names of everyone in your class? See margin.

**3.** Describe a situation for which six students is a good sample size and one for which six students is not a good sample size. See ①.

① Possible answer: It would be good for a survey of the school newspaper staff if it has only 10 members; it would be bad for a survey of the entire school.



### Additional Answer
### Share & Summarize

2. Answers will vary. Reasonableness depends on class size and how accurate you want the prediction to be. If there were 7 students in the class, a sample of 6 would be accurate; if there were 45, a sample of 6 might not be very accurate. Some students might also say the sample might not be a good one if all the students in it have unusually long or short names.

# Investigation 3 Representative Samples

**Vocabulary**

representative sample

**Materials**

- protractor

For a statistics project, Alison's group wanted to predict which of the following after-school activities were the favorites of seventh graders in the four schools in their district.

- playing sports
- playing music
- listening to music
- watching TV
- going to the mall
- playing video games
- reading
- drawing or painting

**Think & Discuss**

How would you recommend that Alison's group collect a sample that would help them make an accurate prediction? Make a list of suggestions. Answers will vary.

# Investigation 3

***On Your Own Exercises***
Pages 286–293
Exercises 8–10, 15–19

**Representative Samples** In this investigation, students look at factors other than size that are needed to make a good sample.

**Think & Discuss**

Set up the situation for Alison's statistics project. Have students present suggestions on how the sample could be collected. Write their suggestions on the board. Keep this list available for students to refer to throughout the class. Students can use that criteria to evaluate the suggestions.

## *Reaching All Learners*

**ELL English Language Learners**
This activity is a great way for students to practice their English language in a conversational manner. Have students begin by writing some ideas down in their first language, and then in small groups have them discuss their ideas in English.

Read together and discuss the paragraphs in the text about representative samples. Most students will understand the concept readily. You might ask for suggestions of other samples that would not necessarily represent a whole group.

## Develop & Understand: A

*Suggested Grouping: Small Groups*

Students compare five strategies for conducting a specific survey. You might want to tell them to be prepared to explain all of their answers. While Strategies 1 and 5 seem to be the best in some ways, they are also the worst in other ways. A balanced approach is needed to conduct the best survey.

**Wrap-Up** Discuss the answers to these questions, especially Exercise 4, with the class.

As you have learned, a good sample must be large enough to give accurate results. In addition, it must be *representative* of the population.

A **representative sample** has approximately the same proportions as the population with respect to the characteristic being studied. For example, Alison's group will want its sample to have about the same proportion as the district population of males and females. Boys might be more likely, or less likely, than girls to engage in a particular activity.

Finally, anyone conducting a survey using a sample will want a method that is practical to perform.

That gives three important questions to ask when examining whether a particular survey method is a good one.

- Is the sample *large enough* to give accurate results?
- Is the sample *representative* of the population?
- Is the survey method *practical*?

## Develop & Understand: A

Alison's group proposed five strategies for conducting its survey.

**Strategy 1.** Ask all 600 seventh graders in the four schools.

**Strategy 2.** Distribute questionnaires to the 130 seventh graders at the district band competition next week.

**Strategy 3.** Get a list of all the seventh graders in the district. Call 5% at random from each school.

**Strategy 4.** Survey every third seventh grader out of the 125 in our school as they enter their homerooms.

**Strategy 5.** Survey the 12 seventh graders on one student's bus.

1. Which strategy or strategies do you think would give the least representative data? The most representative data?
   Strategies 2 and 5; strategy 1
2. Which strategy would give the smallest sample size? The largest sample size? Strategy 5; strategy 1
3. Which strategy seems the least practical? The most practical?
   Strategy 1; strategy 5
4. Which strategy do you think is the best? Explain your reasoning.
   Answers will vary, but students should not choose strategies 1, 2, or 5.



## On the Spot Assessment

Tell the students that a survey was taken of 500 people who borrow books from the library. These people were asked whether or not they found the checkout procedure efficient. The survey concluded that the library does not need to change their checkout procedure. Ask students if the survey is a good one based on the three important questions in the text. Discuss possibilities for change.

## Develop & Understand: B

Alison's group decided to survey every fourth student to enter each seventh grade homeroom in the school. The six homerooms have 28 students each. The survey results are displayed below in a bar graph.

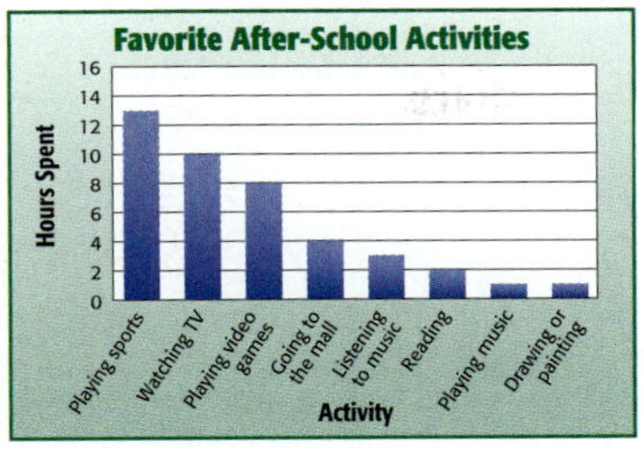


5. How large is the sample of students surveyed? 42

6. How many students in the sample prefer playing sports after school? 13

7. Based on the sample, predict how many in a district of 600 seventh graders would prefer reading. About 29

8. Suppose you could choose one seventh grader from the 600 in Alison's school district at random. What is the probability that he or she prefers playing video games? Explain how you found your answer.

9. If Alison was predicting the favorite leisure activities of all students in the district, from kindergarten to twelfth grade, would sampling only seventh graders give an accurate picture of the population? Explain. No; the activities that seventh graders enjoy will probably differ from those liked by kindergartners or seniors.

8. 19%, or $\frac{19}{100}$. If 8 out of 42 seventh graders like video games, then about 114 out of 600 seventh graders would like video games. $\frac{114}{600} = \frac{19}{100}$.

### Share & Summarize

1. Name some situations in which you are more likely to predict from a sample rather than measure an entire population.

2. Look back over your class' suggestions for the Think & Discuss on page 283. For each suggestion, respond to these three questions.
   - Is the sample large enough?
   - Is the sample representative?
   - Is the survey method practical? Answers will vary.

1. Possible answer: election polls; preferences for food or clothing; typical features of groups; or any situation where the population is very large or difficult or impossible to measure directly



## Develop & Understand: B

*Suggested Grouping: Individuals*

Students use the results of a survey to make predictions. They extract data from a bar graph. Some students may need a brief review of how such a graph is constructed.

**Wrap-Up** Exercises 8 and 9 are good discussion questions. You can use the discussion to assess students' ability to read the graph as well as their understanding of what makes up a good sample.

### Share & Summarize

Have students answer these questions individually. Then discuss their answers in class.

## Troubleshooting

Some students may look for absolute rules for sampling. Make it clear that the only absolutely representative sample is the whole population; various subsets represent the population to a greater or lesser extent. However, the methods you use to choose a representative subset can radically affect how valid a representation it is.

## On Your Own Exercises
**Lesson 6.2**

**Investigation 1**
Pages 279–280
Practice & Apply: 1–5
Connect & Extend: 11–12

**Investigation 2**
Pages 280–282
Practice & Apply: 6–7
Connect & Extend: 13–14

**Investigation 3**
Pages 283–285
Practice & Apply: 8–10
Connect & Extend: 15–19

**Assign Anytime**
Mixed Review: 20–26

▶ **Exercises 1–4** Students should know that each abbreviation stands for only one color. For example, B can stand for black or blue, but not both colors in the same exercise.

▶ **Exercise 3a** Point out that the answer should be given as a percentage, not as a quantity.

## On Your Own Exercises
**Lesson 6.2**

### Practice & Apply

**1.** Tobias and Kareem were playing *What's in the Bag*. From 12 hidden tiles, they took five samples of 3.

- Sample 1: BYG
- Sample 2: YBG
- Sample 3: BGB
- Sample 4: GBB
- Sample 5: RBG

What colors do you predict were in the group of 12 tiles?
Answers will vary. The actual contents were 1R, 5G, 4B, 2Y.

**2.** Jemma and Sarita were playing *What's in the Bag*. There were 20 hidden colors. They drew four samples of 5.

- Sample 1: RYRGR
- Sample 2: YBGYB
- Sample 3: BYGYB
- Sample 4: RYGRY

What colors do you predict were in the group of 20?
Answers will vary. The actual contents were 5R, 3G, 6B, 6Y.

**3.** Rico and Abby were playing a computer simulation of *What's in the Bag*. The software creates a group of 200 tiles in a bag with a combination of four colors. Users enter the sample size and the number of samples.

Rico and Abby selected four samples of 10.

- Sample 1: RBBGGGGYYY
- Sample 2: RRBGGGGGYY
- Sample 3: RRRGGGGYYY
- Sample 4: RRBBGGGGGY

**a.** From this sample, what do you think the software chose for the percentage of each color?

3a. Possible answer: R, 20%; B, 12.5%; G, 45%; Y, 22.5%

**b.** Is the sample large enough for you to feel confident about your prediction? Somewhat confident, but not certain

4. Akiko and Tankia are playing *What's in the Bag*. The bag has 15 marbles with a mixture of red, blue, yellow, and green. The girls decide to take five samples of four.

- Sample 1: GBGR
- Sample 2: BRGG
- Sample 3: RBGG
- Sample 4: BGRR
- Sample 5: RYGG

a. Predict what colors make up the group of 15 marbles.
Possible answer: G7, B3, R4, Y1

b. Describe a method for making a prediction.

4b. Calculate the percentages of the colors in the sample of 20, and find the same percentages of 15.

5. The local smoothie shop, Four Flavors, had the following sales in one week.

- Peach: 300 servings
- Strawberry: 350 servings
- Kiwi: 180 servings
- Banana: 70 servings

a. Four Flavors is one of a chain of four similar shops throughout the county. Assuming the other shops have similar sales, predict how many strawberry smoothies would be sold per week in the county.
1400

b. Do you think these data are enough to predict for all four shops for the year? Explain.

5b. No, one week's data are not enough. This week might be odd; for example, it might have included a nice spring weekend when an unusual number of people were out.

On Your Own Exercises

▶ **Exercise 4** Students will have many different answers. Discuss why this is acceptable.

▶ **Exercise 7 Extension** Some students will be interested in using a word processing application to analyze a sample of prose. You can often get a word count directly. Otherwise you can select text and replace spaces with a symbol (like $): the word processor will give you the number of replacements and hence a rough count of the number of words. The number of characters can often be obtained directly; dividing the number of characters by the number of words provides an average word length. The number of letters can also be obtained by adding up successive replacements of letters by symbols. A sentence rough count can be made by replacing end punctuation marks.

These calculations make a nice project for a computer lab. Suggest that students engaged in this enterprise always try to make replacements that can be reversed.



On Your Own Exercises

**6.** Read the poem below. Complete Parts a–c.

Canvas and elastic
Split sole and fit with ease
Theatrical and pretty
She asked me sweetly, "Please?"

I took her to the dance class
Sweet girl of five years old
So lovely and so graceful
My pride for her is told

For now that she is growing
Her love of dance remains
My joyful, beautiful dreamer
She continues to entertain

—*Carrie Mollette*

**a.** This poem has 12 lines. How many lines do you think you should use as a sample to predict the mean word length in the poem? Possible answer: 6

**b.** Choose a sample of lines at random. Predict the mean word length. Indicate which lines that you used.

6b. Using lines 1, 4, 5, 6, 9, and 12, the mean word length is 4.19.

**c.** Now find the actual mean word length in the poem. How close was your prediction? 4.28 (257 ÷ 60); somewhat close

**7.** Choose a page from a novel, a story you are reading for Language Arts class, or a book for a Social Studies class.

**a.** Look at the first full paragraph on a typical page. If the first line on the page is a continuation from the previous page, skip to the next paragraph. Count the number of words in the paragraph. Divide that by the number of sentences in the paragraph. What is the mean sentence length? Answers will vary.

**b.** Do you think you can now accurately predict the mean sentence length for the entire book? Explain.

7b. No; a sample size of one paragraph probably is not enough.

**c.** Find the mean sentence length for at least ten paragraphs chosen at random from ten different pages. Answers will vary.

**d.** Would you now have more confidence making a prediction for the mean sentence length in the book? Do you think your prediction would be accurate? Explain. Possible answer: I would be more confident than before, but my answer from just 10 paragraphs may still not be very accurate.

288 **CHAPTER 6** Data and Probability

8. Janna and Carmelita were trying to predict the outcome of an election for student president in which 350 students were eligible to vote. Janna sampled 50 students at a party given for the football team. Carmelita sampled the first 30 people entering the school after 8.00 A.M.

Whose sample is more likely to be representative? Why? See margin.

9. Ten students surveyed from a class of 100 seventh graders were asked this question, "What is the first fruit that comes to mind?"

   a. Of the ten students surveyed, six said oranges, two said apples, one said grapefruit, and one said lemons. Use the results of this sample to predict the results for the whole class.

   b. Comment on the accuracy of your prediction. See margin.

   c. The school these students attend is in Florida. Suppose the school had been in Hawaii. Do you think the students would be likely to name the same fruits? Explain.

10. Members of the drama club at Marilyn Middle School are planning to host a movie night to raise money for costumes and props. They want to know what type of movie would draw the most interest. The choices are comedy, romance, or action/adventure. The club members decide to conduct a survey. They have three suggestions for whom to ask.

    - all seventh graders
    - all students in one homeroom from each grade
    - the drama club

    a. For each suggestion, comment on the three issues of representativeness, sample size, and practicality. See margin.

    b. Which suggestion do you think is best?

9a. Assuming these students are representative of the class, 60 would say oranges, 20 apples, and 10 each grapefruit and lemons.

9c. No; students in Hawaii might be more likely to mention, say, pineapples or papayas than oranges.

10b. Answer will vary. Most students will probably choose one homeroom from each grade.

11c. Possible answer: Not very; four games is not much to predict from.

## Connect & Extend

11. Grace records her points in each basketball game that she plays. For the first four games, her results are 3, 3, 5, and 7.

    a. What is the mean of this set of points? 4.5

    b. Assuming these scores are typical for Grace, predict the total number of points she will score in the next ten games. 45

    c. How accurate do you think your prediction is? Explain.

**Math Link**
The *mean* is the sum of all the numbers divided by how many numbers there are.



On Your Own Exercises

▶ **Exercise 11c** Point out that although a prediction of 45 would be typical, it is based on the status quo. The actual number of points can be affected by changing conditions, such as Grace getting injured, becoming a better player with more practice, or becoming a more aggressive player and fouling out in later games.

### Additional Answers

8. Possible answer: Although neither sample is necessarily representative, Janna's 50 students at a party are more likely to share common characteristics, such as their circle of friends, so her results might be misleading. Even though Carmelita's sample of 30 is smaller, it might be more representative.

9b. Possible answer: Because the sample size is quite small, there are likely to be significant differences from the prediction to the whole population. Other fruits might be mentioned by a larger group. It's also possible that the sample is not representative of the population.

10a. All seventh graders would not necessarily be representative, although the sample size is large. If there are a lot of seventh graders, it wouldn't be very practical.

All students in one homeroom for each grade is probably representative. The sample size is probably large enough, unless it's a very big school with a lot of homerooms. This would be a practical way to do it.

The drama club is almost certainly not representative, and it's probably too small a sample. However, it would be easy to do.

**Lesson 6.2** Make Predictions 289

▶ **Exercise 12a** If students are having difficulty computing the mean, remind them that it is the number of runs scored divided by the number of games.

▶ **Exercise 13** Since there is the possibility of many different correct answers, it may be useful to have students share their answers with the class or for students to meet in small groups and discuss their answers.

**Additional Answers**

13b. The population is all the people who will eventually receive the vaccination. There is a greater need for accuracy in medical testing than in other situations, so they may need a relatively large sample (unless they notice many or severe side effects right away; then they might stop the testing early). They may not be able to pick people at random to give the vaccination to; they may need to ask for volunteers. To make a prediction for the population, they would look at how effective the vaccination is for the people in the sample and at what kinds and how many side effects it has.

13c. The population is all the toys the company would produce in a year (10,000, if they make their quota). The sample size needs to be large enough that the toy makers are confident of the 30-hour estimate, but not so large that a lot of money is wasted with unnecessary testing. In this situation, the toys are still salable after the testing. They should choose toys at random from those coming off the production line. To make a prediction for the population, they would look at how long the toys run, on average, before the batteries fail.

On Your Own Exercises

12c. Possible answer: Fairly accurate; I had quite a few games from which to make a prediction.

13a. The population is all the light bulbs the company would produce in a year: 1,000,000 plus the bulbs they test. Since bulbs are tested until they fail, they cannot then be sold. The sample size needs to be large enough for the company to be confident of its promise but not so large that money is wasted with unnecessary testing. They should choose bulbs at random from those coming off the production line. To make a prediction for the population, they would look at the average time it takes for the bulbs in the sample to fail.

**12.** Tyler keeps a record of the runs he makes in each baseball game he plays. His results for the first 16 games of the season are as follows.

2 1 1 1 0 2 3 2 3 4 3 2 2 4 0 5

**a.** What is the mean of Tyler's runs? About 2.19

**b.** Use Tyler's first 16 games to predict the total number of runs he is likely to score in the season, which lasts for 40 games. About 88

**c.** How accurate do you think your prediction is? Explain.

**13.** In the following situations, a sample must be taken to estimate information about the whole population. Analyze each situation by doing the following. Answers will vary. Given here are some observations students might make.

- Identify the population.
- Discuss what factors might be considered when deciding how large a sample to choose.
- Discuss how a sample might be chosen.
- Discuss how the sample data would be used to make a prediction for the population.

**a.** Clear Light Company wants to develop a new light bulb. It hopes to sell 1,000,000 a year and to guarantee customers that the bulbs will last an average of 6,000 hours before failing. To test a light bulb, it must be illuminated until it fails.

**b.** Authorities in a country of 25 million people need to test a new vaccination for effectiveness and side effects. The sample size of volunteers must be large enough for the authorities to be confident of the results before they let the vaccine be used. See margin.

**c.** ACME toy makers have a new electronic game that runs on batteries. They want to be confident the game will last 30 hours before it needs new batteries. They hope to sell 10,000 a year. See margin.

290 **CHAPTER 6** Data and Probability

**14.** On a sheet of paper, write the letters of the alphabet, one letter per line. Then choose some reading material, such as a book, magazine, or newspaper.

Randomly select a line of text from your chosen reading material. Carefully go through the line one letter at a time. For each letter, make a tally mark on your alphabet list next to that letter. For example, for the word *would*, you would make a tally mark next to *W, O, U, L,* and *D*.

**a.** From that one line of text, what are the three most common consonants? What is the most common vowel?
Answers will vary.

**b.** Choose another line at random. Add the letter counts for that line to the count for the first line. Now what are the three most common consonants and the most common vowel?
Answers will vary.

**c.** Continue choosing single lines at random until the most common letters are the same for three lines in a row. What are the letters? Possible answer: R, S, T, and E

**d.** How many lines did you have to test?

14d. Answers will vary but could be as low as three. Five will probably be enough for most students.

**e.** Do you think your sample is large enough to predict the most common letters in your reading material? Answers will vary.

**f.** Do you think your letters will be the most common letters in the language in which your reading material is written?
Answers will vary.

**15.** Suppose you want to find out the favorite food of all the students in your school.

**a.** Devise a strategy for finding a sample. Answers will vary.

**b.** What is the minimum size needed to get a reasonably accurate prediction? Answers will vary.

**16. In Your Own Words** Describe the characteristics of a good sample.

16. Sample answer: A good sample would be large enough to give accurate results, be representative of the population, and be practical enough to carry out the sampling method.



On Your Own Exercises

▶ **Exercise 14e** Since students are likely to get the same results each time they added a line for the first three lines, some students may feel that a three-line sample is sufficient, and they are probably correct. Others may feel that a different letter may emerge as the most frequent if the sample was larger.

Students' results will probably be most common for their language, unless the literature they used was devoted to a specific topic. For example, an article about armadillos in Texas might have more As, Ls, and Xs than usual.

▶ **Exercise 17** Students use different types of graphs to display data. This prepares students for Lesson 6.3, where they review these representations and learn about misleading graphs.

▶ **Exercise 18** A survey is only the context, not the focus, of this exercise. The skills used to solve this multiple-step exercise include critical thinking and logical reasoning.

## Quick Check

**Informal Assessment** Students should be able to:

✔ predict the characteristics of an entire population from a representative sample

✔ appreciate some of the limitations inherent in using small or restricted samples

✔ analyze a representative sample for flaws in its selection

✔ choose a sample representative population for a survey

On Your Own Exercises

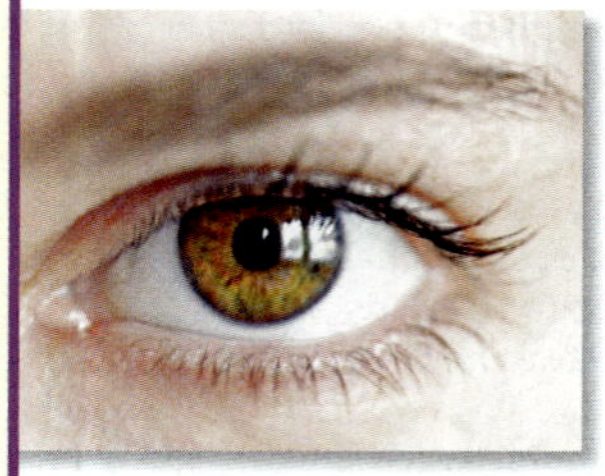

### Real-World Link

The color of the iris in the human eye is determined entirely by genetics.

**17.** Zara conducted a survey of eye color for the 25 students in her homeroom and put the results in a circle graph.

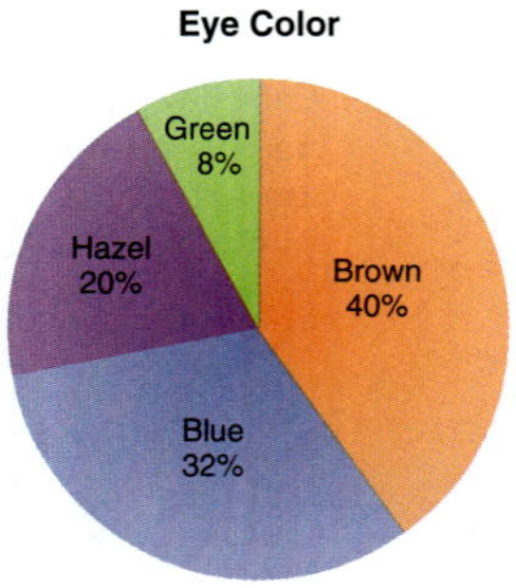


**a.** Brown eyes were reported by 40% of the students. How many students is this in the class of 25? 10

**b.** How many students had the other eye colors? 15

**c.** Draw a pictograph to present the data in another form. Remember, there are 25 students in the class. See margin.

**d.** Draw a line graph of the data.

**e.** Which type of data display do you feel is best for conveying the data?

**f.** Which type of data display do you feel conveys the data least well? Explain. The line graph is inappropriate because there is no meaning to the line connecting the data points.

17d.

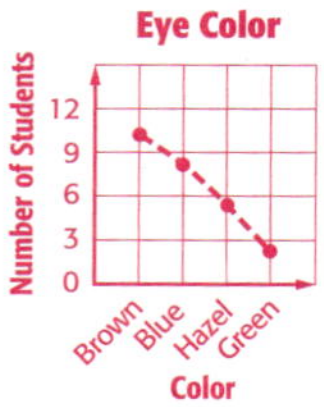


17e. The pictograph and the circle graph are more appropriate.

18b. Answers will vary but must be above 35.

**18.** A school wishing to run a road-safety campaign surveyed a group of 200 seventh graders in an urban area. The survey found that the students traveled to school in five ways. Bus and car travel were the two most common methods. The survey also found that 35 students take the subway, 30 walk, and 25 ride a bicycle.

**a.** How many students altogether travel to school in a bus or a car? 110

**b.** What is one possible result the survey would find for the number of students who travel by car?

**c.** **Challenge** Find all the possible solutions for the number of students who travel by car and the number who travel by bus.

| Bus | 36 | 37 | 38 | . . . | 73 | 74 |
|---|---|---|---|---|---|---|
| Car | 74 | 73 | 72 | . . . | 37 | 36 |

There are 39 possibilities.



**Additional Answer**

17c. Possible pictograph:

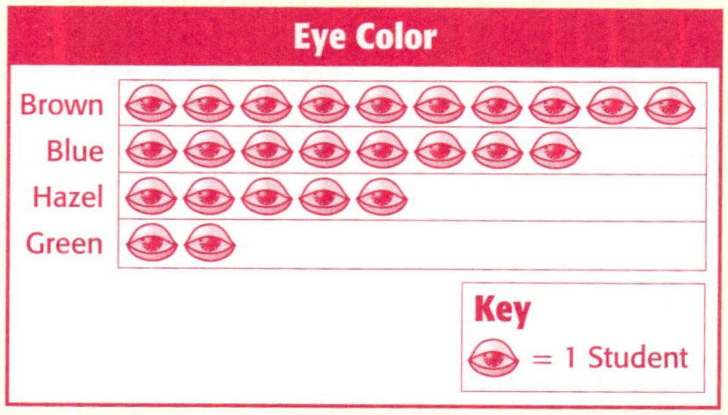

### Real-World Link

Gallup polls are named after George Horace Gallup (1901–1984). Born in Iowa, he is best known for his method of surveying public opinion on politics.

19a. To try to ensure that the 1,000 people are typical, or representative, of the population

**19. Social Studies** Gallup polls use a type of sampling to predict the outcome of elections. There is a way to determine how accurate these predictions are, based on the population and the sample size.

Suppose 1,000 people are chosen at random from a voting population of 1,000,000 and asked for which of two candidates they intend to vote. The *margin of error* for the poll is 4%. That means it is very likely that the percentage of votes for each candidate predicted by the poll will be within four percentage points of the real figure.

**a.** Why would a Gallup poll choose people at random?

**b.** If a sample of 1,000 people shows that 47% intend to vote for candidate A, what would you expect the range of percentage of votes for candidate A to be on the actual election day? Between 43% and 51%

**c.** It is unlikely that 47% is exactly correct. What are the least and greatest numbers of votes you would expect candidate A to receive? Is it possible the candidate would get more than 50% of the votes, therefore winning the election? Explain.

### Mixed Review

19c. Least: 430,000; greatest: 510,000; The candidate could get more than 50% since 510,000 > 500,000.

20a. 36 $in^3$

20b. 72 $in^3$

**20. Geometry** Consider this rectangular prism.

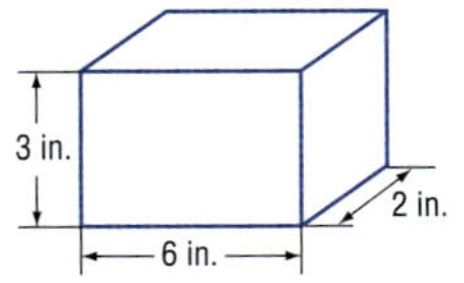


**a.** Find the volume of the rectangular prism.

**b.** Find the volume of a rectangular prism that is twice as high as this rectangular prism.

**Rewrite each expression in exponential notation.**

**21.** $c \cdot c \cdot c \cdot c$ $c^4$

**22.** $4 \cdot 4 \cdot 4$ $4^3$

**Rewrite each number in standard notation.**

**23.** $6 \times 10^2$ 600

**24.** $9 \times 10^5$ 900,000

**Rewrite each number in scientific notation.**

**25.** 654,000 $6.54 \times 10^5$

**26.** 9,500,000,000 $9.5 \times 10^9$



On Your Own Exercises

### Quick Quiz

Use this situation to answer Questions 1and 2: Kevin randomly draws one block from a bag of colored blocks. He replaces the block and shakes the bag after each draw. The results of five successive draws are RGGRR.

**1.** What colors do you predict are in the group of blocks if there are only

a. two blocks in the bag? They must be red and green.

b. three blocks in the bag? Answers may vary.

c. four blocks in the bag? Answers may vary.

d. five blocks in the bag? Answers may vary.

e. three hundred blocks in the bag? Possible answer: Ratio is 2:3, so there may be 120G and 180R.

**2.** Look at your predictions in Question 1.

a. Which, if any, prediction has a probability of zero of being correct? Explain. None; any reasonable prediction could be correct.

b. Which, if any, prediction has a probability of one of being correct? Explain. The prediction in Exercise 1a: There are two blocks in the bag and both colors were drawn.

c. Which, if any, prediction has the least chance of being correct? Explain. The prediction in Exercise 1e: The sample size is too small, there could be a different ratio or even other colors of blocks.

**3.** In taking a survey of students about classes at a school, the editors of the newspaper published the questions in the paper. They asked students to fill out the questionnaire and hand it in after school. They received 60 submissions in a school of 300.

Is their choice of representative sample a good one? Describe any potential exercises with it.

The sample might be acceptable if everyone reads the paper. However, not only is readership a drawback, but it is likely that those students who are willing to volunteer to fill out a sample form are not representative of the student body as a whole.

LESSON 6.3

# Data Graphs

## Objectives

- To identify when to use a bar graph, line graph, or circle graph
- To construct stem-and-leaf plots, double-bar graphs, and double-line graphs when appropriate
- To collect data, compute fractions and angle measures to use in constructing circle graphs
- To look at data and determine if the presentation misleads the reader about the actual information represented

## Overview

This lesson reviews and extends what students know about data displays. The students will look at data that has previously been displayed on separate graphs and combine the graphs. The students will collect data and construct circle graphs to represent data that is part of a whole. Data will also be presented to students in ways which may be misleading. Students will need to evaluate whether the graph shows the real picture of what the data expresses.

## Advance Preparation

You may want to begin working on the 1-meter strips for Investigation 2 as soon as possible. All students will need several copies of Lesson 6.3 Master 2 for Investigation 2.

| | Summary | Materials | On Your Own Exercises (pp. 309–313) | Assessment Opportunities |
|---|---|---|---|---|
| **Investigation 1** (p. 295) Pacing: 2 days | Students use data to create double-bar and double-line graphs. The students then use the graph to interpret the data. | lined or grid paper, colored pencils | Practice & Apply: 1–3<br>Mixed Review: 9–12 | • On the Spot Assessment (p. 296)<br>• Share & Summarize (p. 298) |
| **Investigation 2** (p. 299) Pacing: 1 day | Students use data to create circle graphs. | Lesson 6.3 Masters 1 & 2, protractor, 1-meter strip of heavy paper, scissors | Practice & Apply: 4<br>Connect & Extend: 6<br>Mixed Review: 9–12 | • On the Spot Assessment (p. 299)<br>• Share & Summarize (p. 301)<br>• Troubleshooting (pp. 299, 300) |
| **Investigation 3** (p. 302) Pacing: 1 day | Students create and interpret stem-and-leaf plots. | | Practice & Apply: 5<br>Connect & Extend: 8<br>Mixed Review: 9–12 | • Share & Summarize (p. 305)<br>• Troubleshooting (pp. 304, 305) |
| **Investigation 4** (p. 306) Pacing: 1 day | Students use their knowledge about graphs to determine if the information presented is misleading. | | Connect & Extend: 7<br>Mixed Review: 9–12 | • Share & Summarize (p. 308)<br>• Troubleshooting (p. 306) |

# Leveled Lesson Resources

CRM *Available in:* **Chapter 6 Resource Masters**

Also on TeacherWorks™ Lesson 6.3

## Study Guide and Intervention (p. 16) AL

**Lesson 6.3 Study Guide and Intervention**
***Data Graphs***

***Example 1*** Make a circle graph for the male data set in the table.

Step 1 Find the fraction of total males surveyed who prefer each material. Multiply each fraction by 360 to find the angle measure of the corresponding part of the circle graph.

Chips: $\frac{60}{400} = \frac{3}{20} \times 360 = 54°$

Mulch: $\frac{140}{400} = \frac{7}{20} \times 360 = 126°$

Rocks: $\frac{120}{400} = \frac{3}{10} \times 360 = 108°$

Straw: $\frac{80}{400} = \frac{1}{5} \times 360 = 72°$

| Preferred Landscaping Material | | |
|---|---|---|
| Material | Males | Females |
| Chips | 60 | 125 |
| Mulch | 140 | 110 |
| Rocks | 120 | 90 |
| Straw | 80 | 75 |

Preferred Landscaping Material, Males

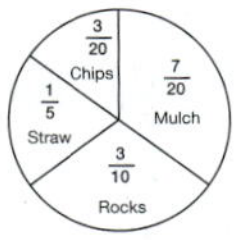


Step 2 Draw a circle and a radius. Then use a protractor to draw a 54° angle to represent the fraction of males who prefer chips.

Step 3 From the new radius, draw a 126° angle for Mulch. Repeat for the other two sections. Label each section and give the graph a title.

***Example 2*** Make a double-bar graph for both data sets given in the table in Example 1.

Step 1 Draw a set of vertical and horizontal axes. Mark every 20 homeowners on the vertical axis. Label each material on the horizontal axis.

Step 2 Using two shades of gray, create two adjacent bars in each category to represent the values from the table.

Step 3 Create a key to the side of the graph, and label the axes.

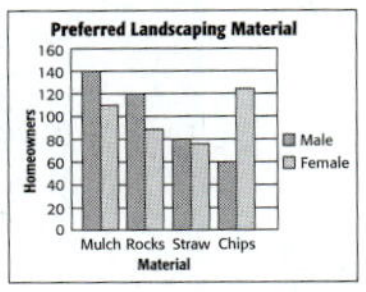


***Exercises***

1. According to the circle graph in Example 1, which two materials should a supply store order in large quantities?
2. Cher says the bar graph in Example 2 shows that about twice as many females as males prefer chips. Is this true? Explain.

## Skills Practice (p. 17) AL OL

**Lesson 6.3 Skills Practice**
***Data Graphs***

1. Make a double-bar graph of the data in the table.

| Points Earned | | |
|---|---|---|
| Game | Lois | Marsha |
| 1 | 8 | 12 |
| 2 | 5 | 8 |
| 3 | 10 | 6 |
| 4 | 8 | 7 |

2. Make a circle graph of the data in the table.

| Preferred Car Color | |
|---|---|
| Color | Automobile Owners |
| White | 12 |
| Silver | 50 |
| Gold | 10 |
| Black | 22 |
| Red | 6 |

3. Make a double-bar graph of the data in the table.

| Number of Sweaters Sold | | |
|---|---|---|
| Color | Fall | Spring |
| Red | 24 | 20 |
| White | 10 | 22 |
| Blue | 18 | 35 |
| Brown | 42 | 12 |

4. Make a circle graph of the data in the table.

| Enrollment | |
|---|---|
| Subject | Students |
| Math | 112 |
| English | 140 |
| Social Studies | 70 |
| Science | 98 |

## Problem-Solving Practice (p. 18) AL OL

**Lesson 6.3 Problem-Solving Practice**
***Data Graphs***

1. **Investments** Mr. Broussard owns a financial investment business. The table below shows how many clients he has for each type of investment.

| Investments | |
|---|---|
| Type | Clients |
| Savings | 60 |
| Money Market | 100 |
| Mutual Funds | 140 |
| Stocks | 500 |
| Bonds | 200 |

Which circle graph accurately displays the data in the table? Explain. Hint: Check angle measures.

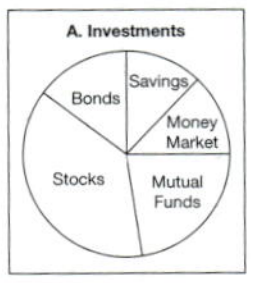


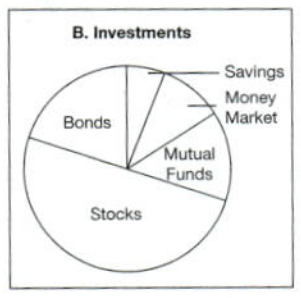


2. **Movies** A movie store records its total sales each month for two months. Make a double-bar graph of the data in the table.

| Number of DVDs Sold | | |
|---|---|---|
| Genre | June | July |
| Romance | 150 | 271 |
| Comedy | 312 | 280 |
| TV Series | 184 | 110 |
| Drama | 194 | 85 |

a. How many more Comedy DVDs were sold in June than July?
b. On the vertical axis, Justin wants to mark every 150 DVDs up to 900 DVDs. How would this change the appearance of the graph?
c. Draw a circle graph to represent the data for June.

## Enrichment (p. 19) BL

**Lesson 6.3 Enrichment**
***Data Graphs***

**Changing the Intervals**

1. Use the data in this chart to complete the four bar graphs below. Hint: the bars will be horizontal.

| Number of Countries Extending the Vote to Women | |
|---|---|
| Years | Number |
| 1893, 1902, 1906, 1913, 1915, 1917, 1920, 1930, 1931, 1933, 1937, 1944, 1948, 1955, 1963, 1971, 1973 | 1 |
| 1926, 1932, 1947 | 2 |
| 1945 | 3 |
| 1918 | 4 |
| 1919 | 5 |

2. Which graph supports each statement? Is each statement accurate or misleading?

a. There has been a steady decrease in the number of countries since 1893.
b. About half the countries gave women the vote since the beginning of the Great Depression in 1929.
c. There were three main periods in which women were granted the vote.

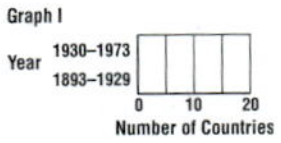


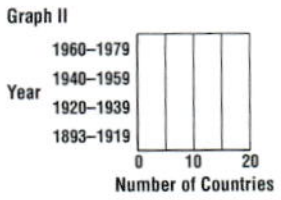


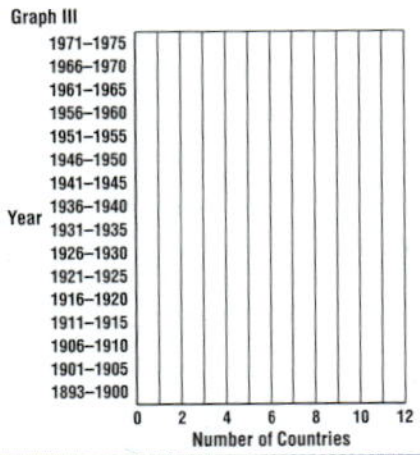


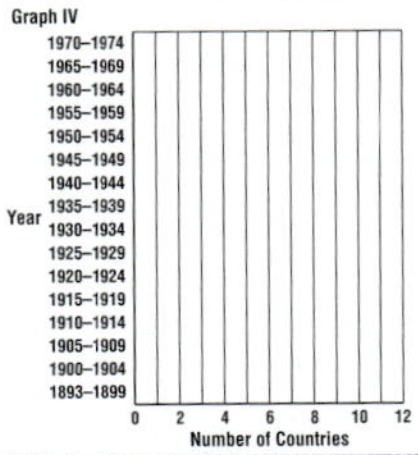


## Lesson Quick Quiz (p. 20) AL OL BL

**Lesson 6.3 Quick Quiz**
***Data Graphs***

1. The table shows the number of times Maurice and Raphael visited various places in their free time.

| Place Visited | Maurice | Raphael |
|---|---|---|
| Library | 4 | 10 |
| Gym | 12 | 7 |
| Recreation Center | 5 | 12 |
| Park | 9 | 1 |

a. If these data were placed in a double-bar graph, what would the horizontal and vertical axes represent?

b. How would you distinguish between Maurice and Raphael's information on the graph?

2. Gabriella is making a circle graph of the types of pets that students in the seventh grade have. 43 students of the 150 surveyed have a dog. What is the angle measure of the dog section of the circle graph?

3. When interpreting a graph that could be misleading, what are two things you should consider?

## Lesson Master (pp. 21–22)

**Lesson 6.3 Master 1**
***Data Graphs***

**Investigation 2: Think & Discuss**

| Sport | Number of Votes | Fraction of Total Votes | Angle Measure |
|---|---|---|---|
| Football | | | |
| Soccer | | | |
| Basketball | | | |
| Baseball | | | |
| Ice hockey | | | |
| Other | | | |
| None | | | |

**Investigation 2: Think & Discuss**

| Sport | Number of Votes | Fraction of Total Votes | Angle Measure |
|---|---|---|---|
| Football | | | |
| Soccer | | | |
| Basketball | | | |
| Baseball | | | |
| Ice hockey | | | |
| Other | | | |
| None | | | |

# Additional Lesson Resources

### Teacher Tech Tools

- TeacherWorks
- ExamView Assessment Suite
- Classroom Presentation Toolkit
- Advance Tracker

### Student Tech Tools

- StudentWorks Plus
- Math Online eGlossary
- Concepts in Motion

### Other Print Products

- Investigation Notebook and Reflection Journal
- Quick Review Math Handbook

# LESSON 6.3 Data Graphs

## Introduce

**Bar Graphs and Line Graphs** This lesson looks first at how to display and compare data using double-bar graphs and double-line graphs. Students may not remember what these data displays look like or how they are used. Start a class discussion and have volunteers describe or create a bar graph and a line graph. Discuss their uses and the reason to choose each type of display.

### Think & Discuss

*Suggested Grouping: Pairs*

There are many different types of graphs that you can use to display data but each type has a specific use. It is important for students to understand how to use each type of graph. It may be helpful for each pair to create a chart to list the characteristics of each type of data display. Have the pairs share their charts with the class and as a group determine the most concise form of the chart.

# LESSON 6.3 Data Graphs

In previous grades, you learned how to represent data using graphs. You also discovered that you cannot use just any graph for data, but that there are certain types of graphs that are appropriate for certain types of data.



Previously, you have used a graph to represent one set of data at a time. You used bar graphs and line graphs to look at the pattern and trends in that set of data. In this lesson, you will learn to compare two sets of data and find ways to show both on one graph.

① This is categorical data. A bar graph would show the relationship between the categories. You could discuss the item preferred most or least.

### Think & Discuss

Discuss the data Zach and Maya have. What type of data is it? What type of graph would best show the data? Which statistics can we discuss about this set of data? See ①.

For each type of graph, describe the type of data or situation that it could be used to display. Give an example for each.

**a.** bar graph
**b.** line graph
**c.** histogram
**d.** Venn diagram

Answers will vary.



### Troubleshooting

This lesson relies on students' prior knowledge. If you find that students do not remember how to use each type of data display, it may be beneficial to do the Think & Discuss as a whole class sharing session with a lot of teacher input to move the discussion in the correct direction. This will give the students the proper information and hopefully wake up their memory of data displays.

# Investigation 1 Double-Bar and Double-Line Graphs

**Vocabulary**

- double-bar graph
- double-line graph

**Material**

- lined or grid paper
- colored pencils or markers

***Real-World Link***
Many newspapers and Internet sites present data in charts and graphs. Knowing how to read and interpret them can help you understand the article or Web site you are reading.

① Mike's brother spends 3 hours on running and dirt biking compared to Mike's 2 hours on basketball. Mike spends 4 hours playing video games while his brother plays for 1 hour. Mike spends 2 hours less doing homework over the weekend.

## *Think & Discuss*

Mike and his twin brother each made a graph to show how they spend their weekend days. Mike wants to compare how he spends his free time to how his brother spends his free time.

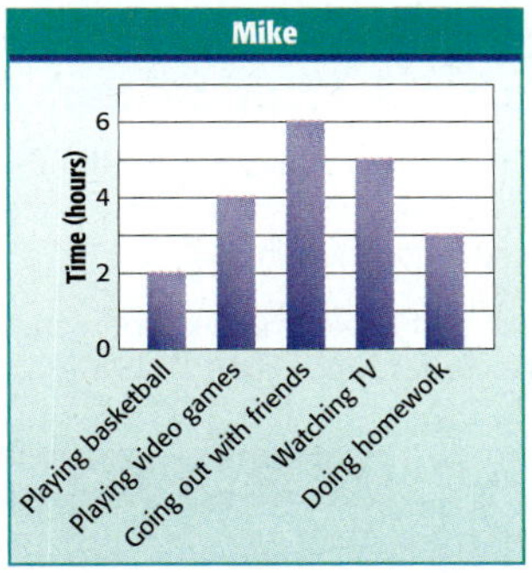


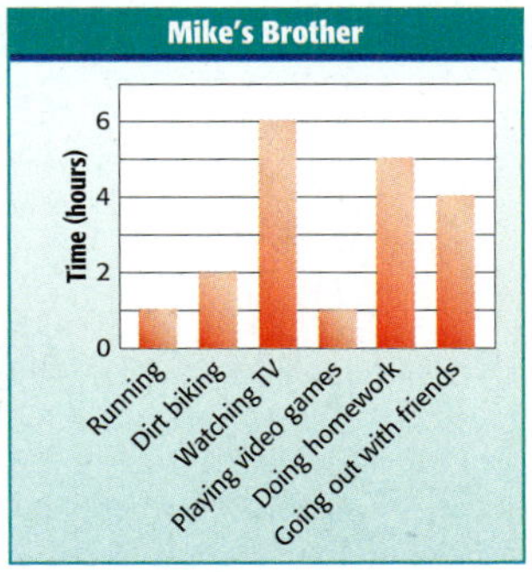


List three things you can tell about the similarities and differences in how Mike and his brother spend their days. See ①.

What would make it easier to compare the data? It would be easier to compare the data on the same graph and if they used same categories.

## *Develop & Understand: A*

1. Create one graph that shows the way both Mike and his brother spend their weekend time. Use the following guidelines to create the graph. 1a–e. See margin.
   a. Include a title at the top of a the graph.
   b. Draw a set of vertical and horizontal axes like the one that both boys used for their original bar graphs. Label the vertical axis "Time (hours)." Mark off each hour up to 7 hours.
   c. Label categories along the horizontal axis. Create a single category that can include basketball, running, and dirt biking. You should have five categories.
   d. Using blue for Mike and red for his brother, create two adjacent bars above each category name, one bar for each boy. The bars for one category will touch, but there will be space between each category.
   e. Create a key to the side of the graph to indicate that the blue bars show data for Mike and the red bars show data for Mike's brother.



# Investigation 1

***On Your Own Exercises***
Pages 309–313
Exercises 1–3

**Double Graphs** The purpose of a double graph is to compare the information from two different sources. Everything about the data must be measured and recorded in the same way or you cannot use a double graph as the means of display.

## *Think & Discuss*

*Suggested Grouping: Individuals or Pairs*

Students need to understand that in this case when choosing to display the data on the same graph they will need to modify the categories so that each graph displays the exact same information. The only time that it is appropriate for a category to not have both data represented is if the category truly does not contain data for one member.

## *Develop & Understand: A*

*Suggested Grouping: Pairs*

▶ **Exercise 1** The steps given here specifically address each point that the students need to consider when properly constructing a double-bar graph for the data. It is a great step-by-step introduction to creating a double-bar graph.

**Additional Answer**

1a–e.

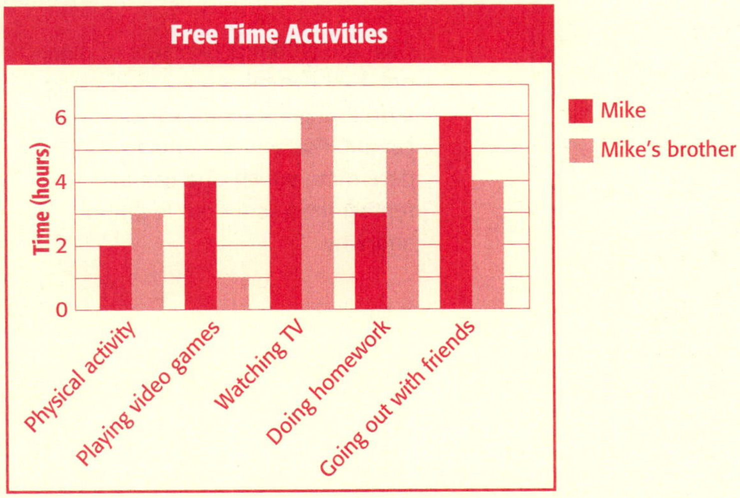

▶ **Exercises 2 and 3** These questions are very straight forward and will allow the students to use the graph that they just created to answer questions. It will show the students how much easier it is to read the data off a double-bar graph versus reading two individual bar graphs and then comparing the data.

## Develop & Understand: B

*Suggested Grouping: Individuals or Pairs*

▶ **Exercises 5a and 5b** The answers can be found without creating the double-bar graph. Make sure that the students create their data displays before answering the questions.

▶ **Exercise 5c** If students are having difficulty determining the answer, remind the students what each bar represents. Gradually ask questions to assist the students in understanding that they need to total the values of all of the bars.

3. No. He spends four times as much time playing video games which is shown by the bar being four times as tall.
4. Answers will vary: quicker than looking at two graphs, did not have to get two numbers to subtract, just counted how much taller or shorter one bar was than another

2. Which boy spends more time watching TV? How much more? Mike's brother spends one hour more watching TV.
3. Explain if this is an accurate statement. "Mike spends twice as much time playing video games as his brother."
4. How did the double-bar graph make comparing the brothers easier?

A bar graph with two bars for each category on the same graph is called a **double-bar graph**. A double-bar graph is used to compare two sets of data based on the same categories. For example, you could compare boys versus girls using the types of sports they play, such as football, softball/baseball, basketball, volleyball, or track.

## Develop & Understand: B

5. Jennifer and Selena have collected information about students in their class. They want to compare preferences of winter activities between the girls and boys.

   Create a double-bar graph to compare the data and answer the following questions. See margin.

| Activity | Girls | Boys |
|---|---|---|
| Skiing | 6 | 8 |
| Sledding | 2 | 2 |
| Building snowmen | 5 | 4 |
| Snow boarding | 1 | 7 |
| Snow shoeing | 10 | 2 |

   a. Which activity is preferred most by girls? By boys? Girls: Snow shoeing; Boys: Skiing.
   b. Which activity is preferred least by both boys and girls? Sledding
   c. If each student could pick only one activity, how many students did Jennifer and Selena interview? 47 students



### Additional Answer

5.

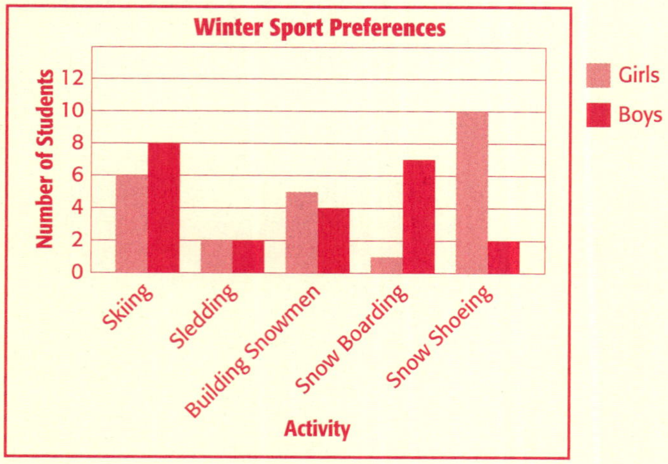


### On the Spot Assessment

Give the students two sets of data, one that can be represented using a double graph and one that cannot. Ask the students to determine which one can be represented as a double graph and why.

## Think & Discuss

In another situation, you have the following data about the use of cell phones and home Internet service in Cell Region IV. The second two columns show the number of users of each type of service throughout the day.

What graph type should we use to quickly compare how many people are using each service throughout the day? This data would be best shown on a line graph. A line graph shows you data over time, or as one variable changes.

| Use in the hour Ending at | Cell Phone Service | Home Internet Service |
|---|---|---|
| 9:00 A.M. | 2250 | 1000 |
| 10:00 A.M. | 2600 | 900 |
| 11:00 A.M. | 3000 | 750 |
| 12:00 P.M. | 2400 | 700 |
| 1:00 P.M. | 2100 | 800 |
| 2:00 P.M. | 2500 | 700 |
| 3:00 P.M. | 2600 | 700 |
| 4:00 P.M. | 1800 | 1100 |
| 5:00 P.M. | 1500 | 2500 |
| 6:00 P.M. | 2900 | 2750 |
| 7:00 P.M. | 3200 | 3300 |
| 8:00 P.M. | 2500 | 3300 |
| 9:00 P.M. | 2250 | 3200 |
| 10:00 P.M. | 2000 | 2400 |

## Develop & Understand: C

6. Use the same idea as the double-bar graph and put two line graphs on the same axis. Place the times of day along the horizontal axis and the number of users of each service along the vertical axis. See margin.
7. During which hour of the day is cell phone use the highest? Did you refer to the table or the graph to answer this question? Why?
8. During which hour of the day is home Internet use the highest? Did you refer to the table or the graph to answer this question? Why?
9. During what hour of the day does use of cell phone service increase the most? During what hour of the day does use of home Internet service increase the most? What factors might influence this?
10. Describe how use of cell service changes throughout the day. What factors influence use of cell service?
11. Describe how use of home Internet service changes throughout the day. What factors influence use of home Internet service? Use of home Internet is low in the morning and early afternoon but goes up in the evenings when people are home. It is still high late at night. Daytime use is probably people who work from home.

7. The hour ending at 7:00 PM; possible answer: table because there were two high places on the graph
8. Two hours ending at 7:00 and 8:00 PM; possible answer: graph because there was a clear highest point.
9. Cell phone use increases most in hour from 5:00–6:00 PM; home Internet increases most from 4:00–5:00 P.M.; students get out of school, adults get off work
10. Use of cell service is fairly high and steady all day, dipping right at the end of the work day. People get busy trying to finish tasks before getting off work. In the evenings, the number of users may go up because of calling friends and family and school-age people using the phones. Calls during the day could be a mix of personal and business calls.



## Think & Discuss

If students are not sure what type of display to use, ask the students if the data represents information about categories. They should respond no and this will show them that a bar graph is not an appropriate display. Continue asking probing questions regarding what the data represents getting the students toward a line graph.

## Develop & Understand: C

*Suggested Grouping: Pairs*

▶ **Exercise 6** This exercise specifically instructs the students how to create a double-line graph as long as they remember what a line graph looks like. If students need help remembering, remind students that it is data represented by plotting points and connecting them to show change over time.

▶ **Exercises 7–9** These questions are asking students to read the data from the graph that they created in Exercise 6. It may be useful to have the graph presented and discussed prior to students answering this question so that the correct answers will be seen.

▶ **Exercises 10 and 11** These questions refer to each line separately and will show students one of the benefits of a double-line graph.

### Additional Answer

6.

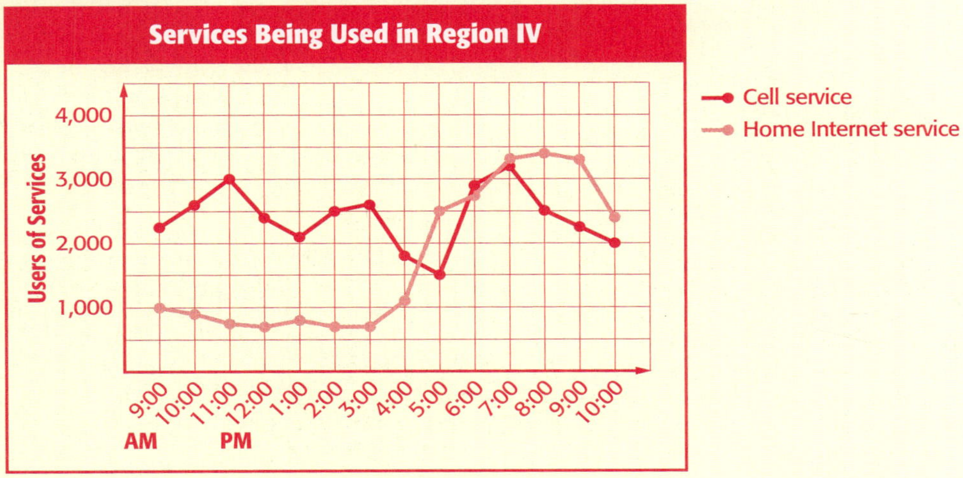

## Develop & Understand: D

*Suggested Grouping: Pairs*

▶ **Exercise 12** If students are having difficulty determining where to begin, have them refer to the Exercise 6 as a point of reference.

▶ **Exercise 13** Instead of asking specific questions about the data shown in the graph, this question is asking students to describe what they see. Tell students to be as specific as possible in comparing without telling individual facts about every point of the display.

**Wrap-Up** In small groups have the students make a list of what they find helpful about double graphs. Ask the students to give a situation where a double graph would not make the information easier to read. These questions tie up the investigation and also lead to the Share & Summarize.

### Share & Summarize

If students are struggling with ideas ask them what each type of display shows. This should give them assistance in thinking up ideas. Ask for several volunteers to share their thoughts.

**Additional Answers**

① One situation could be comparing the different balls that students play with during gym. You could compare the girls and boys that play with tennis balls, basketballs, dodge balls, footballs, etc.

② If you want to compare the changes in temperature over a 24-hour period in two different cities, a double-line graph could be used. The double-line graph would allow you to see how the temperatures were related to each other throughout the day.

In the last set of exercises, you created a *double-line graph*. A **double-line graph** can be used to compare how quantities of different groups change over the same time frame.

## Develop & Understand: D

Use the data in the table below for the Exercises 12–14.

**Sales in Hundreds of Dollars**

| Month | JAN | FEB | MAR | APR | MAY | JUN | JUL | AUG | SEP | OCT | NOV | DEC |
|---|---|---|---|---|---|---|---|---|---|---|---|---|
| Cold Beverages | 6 | 6.2 | 8 | 5.5 | 7 | 7.2 | 10 | 10 | 9 | 8 | 7.5 | 6 |
| Hot Beverages | 5.5 | 7.2 | 4.5 | 3 | 2.5 | 2.2 | 1.5 | 1 | 1.5 | 2.2 | 2 | 4.5 |

**Real-World Link**
Water is the most popular beverage consumed worldwide. Tea is second.

**12.** Create a double-line graph that shows the sales of hot beverages (coffee and hot chocolate) and cold beverages (sodas and water) at the school concession stand throughout the year. See margin.

a. What variable will you put along the horizontal axis? The vertical axis? Sales in hundreds of dollars; months

b. How will you indicate the cold beverages and the hot beverages?

12b. I could use different shapes as the data point, or different colors for each set.

**13.** Write a paragraph to describe the information that is presented by the graph and table in Exercise 12. Include information about when sales of each type of beverage were highest and lowest, when one kind of beverage outsold the other, and when overall sales of beverages seemed highest. Speculate about factors that might influence beverage sales. See below.

**14.** If you were to extend this graph by four more months after December, what might it look like?

14. The horizontal axis would be extended to include January, February, March, and April again. The lines would extend based on the sales of each month.

### Share & Summarize Answers will vary.

1. Give a description of a situation in which you would want to create a double-bar graph to compare two things. Explain why a double-bar graph would be the best choice. See margin.

2. Give a description of a situation in which you would want to create a double-line graph to compare two things. Explain why a double-line graph would be the best choice. See margin.

13. Possible answer: Cold beverages outsell hot beverages in every month except February. Hot beverages probably do best in February because it is the coldest month. Hot beverage sales were also high in January–March and in December. Cold beverage sales were pretty steady, but were really high in July and August, the hottest months of the year. Some people were still buying hot beverages in the summer months, but they were probably coffee drinkers. By looking at the table you can see that total beverage sales were highest in January, February, and March. This might be because there are a lot of basketball tournaments during that time, so there are a couple of games several nights per week.



12.

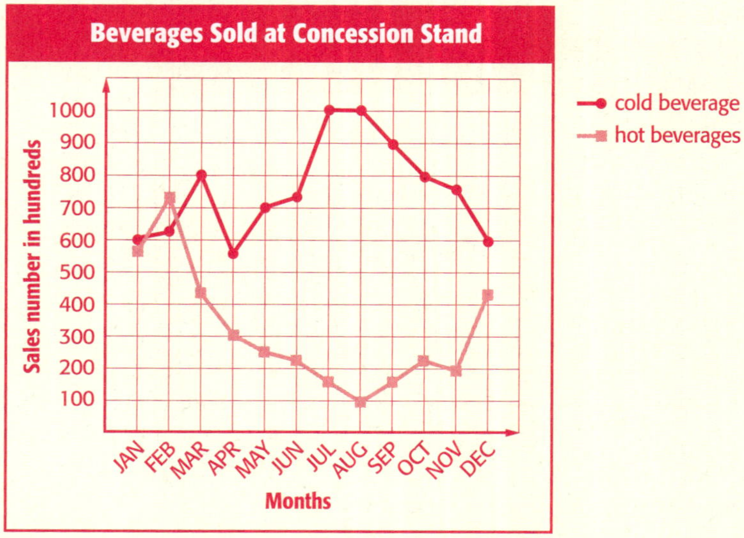

# Investigation 2 Make a Circle Graph

### Materials
- protractor
- 1-meter strip of heavy paper
- 4 copies of the quarter-circle template
- scissors
- tape
- colored pencils
- straightedge

### Real-World Link
Soccer's World Cup is the most-watched sporting event in the world. In 2006, an estimated 829 million North American and 26.3 billion worldwide television viewers watched World Cup broadcasts.

Data that represent parts of a whole are sometimes displayed in a circle graph, or pie chart. In this investigation, you will gather data from your class and use a circle graph to summarize your results.

### Think & Discuss Answers will vary.

Work as a class to gather student responses to this question.

*Which is your favorite sport to watch? Choose one.*

- ❑ *football*
- ❑ *soccer*
- ❑ *basketball*
- ❑ *baseball*
- ❑ *ice hockey*
- ❑ *other*

Copy this table. In the second column, record the number of students who voted for each choice. In the third column, record the fraction of the total votes each choice received. You will fill in the last column later.

| Sport | Number of Votes | Fraction of Total Votes | Angle Measure |
|---|---|---|---|
| Football | | | |
| Soccer | | | |
| Basketball | | | |
| Baseball | | | |
| Ice hockey | | | |
| Other | | | |

In the next set of exercises, you will create a circle graph to display the results of your survey.

### Develop & Understand: A Circle graphs will vary.

Your teacher will give you a strip of heavy paper exactly one meter long. The strip has been divided into equal-sized rectangles, one for each member of your class. The entire strip represents your whole class, or 100% of the votes.

**1.** On your strip, color groups of rectangles according to the number of votes each choice received. Use a different color for each choice. For example, if five students voted for football, color the first five rectangles orange. If seven chose soccer, color the next seven rectangles green. When you are finished, all the rectangles should be colored.

### On the Spot Assessment

If 10 students out of 30 responded that their favorite sport was baseball, what angle measure would represent this on a circle graph? 120°

### Troubleshooting

When constructing a circle graph students may have trouble using the protractor. They may only want to lay the edge on the radius in a straight manner as though they were measuring length. Instruct students that the protractor should go about the circle, as though it were a spinner. One slice of the graph is measured off the previous piece until the protractor has spun all the way around the circle.

## Investigation 2

**On Your Own Exercises**
Pages 309–313
Exercises 4, 6

**Make a Circle Graph** In this investigation, students gather data on the favorite spectator sports of their classmates. They analyze the data and use percents to describe the results. Finally, they make a circle graph that displays their findings.

You may want to introduce the investigation by reading the paragraph.

### Think & Discuss
*Suggested Grouping: Whole Class*

Have students suggest ways to collect the necessary information. Some may prefer a show of hands while others may want a "secret ballot."

For the sake of the circle graph, the total number of votes should equal the total number of students on your class list. If there are students absent on the day of this activity, you might assign students to cast proxy votes for those not present or add an "absent" category to their table.

Be sure students make copies of the table; they will need it in the rest of the investigation. Lesson 6.3 Master 1 reproduces the table, so you may want to give each student a copy of the table from that master. You may want to create one on the board or overhead and complete it with the class's help. Leave the table available while students continue their work.

### Develop & Understand: A
*Suggested Grouping: Small Groups*

In this problem set, students use 1-meter strips of paper to make circle graphs. Students will color sections corresponding to the number of students voting for each sport. Since the strips are 100 centimeters long, the length (in centimeters) of each colored section is equal to the percent of the class voting for that sport.

▶ **Exercise 1** It will be helpful for students to write the name of each sport on the corresponding colored section of the 1-meter strip.

▶ **Exercises 2–8** Hand out the materials. Posterboard would work well for the 1-meter strips; otherwise you may need to tape or staple strips together to total 1 meter. If you have students work in groups, each group will need only one of these strips.

Each strip should be divided into equal-sized rectangles. There should be as many rectangles on each strip as there are students in the class. To find out how long each rectangle should be, divide 100 cm by the number of students in the class. To speed up the work, you can make marks along the long edge of a sheet of paper to show the lengths of five or so of the rectangles. Then use that "ruler" to mark off the rectangles along the strips themselves. Alternatively, you can provide copies of the ruler to the groups and supervise their work as they mark the rectangles on their strips.

In addition, each group or student will need four copies of Lesson 6.3 Master 2, Quarter-Circle Template. Other materials needed are scissors, tape, colored pencils, and a straightedge.

▶ **Exercises 2–6** You may want to walk around the room and be sure no group has gotten too far off track. However, try to give students themselves the responsibility to follow the directions as they work through the sequence of steps.

▶ **Exercise 6** Students need to understand that their circle graphs will have at most six sections, but that if there were any 0s in Column 2 of the table, the circle graph will have fewer than six sections.

**Wrap-Up** After students have completed their circle graphs, you might allow groups to compare their graphs. Their graphs should have the same number of sections, and sections for the same sports should be the same size. However, the sections may be located in different positions relative to one another.

Have groups resolve any substantive differences in their graphs, that is, any differences other than positioning.

Now you are ready to create a circle graph.

**2.** Tape the ends of your strip together, with no overlap, to form a loop with the colored rectangles inside.

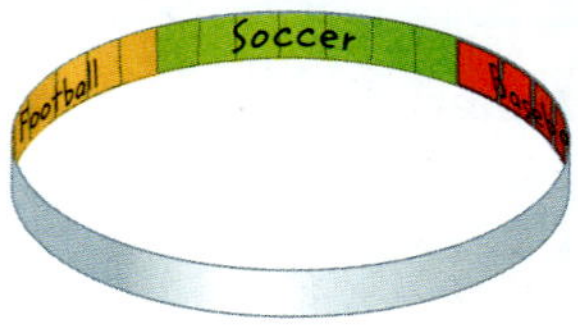


**3.** Next, tape four copies of the quarter-circle template together to form a circle. Find the center of the circle and mark it.

**4.** Place your loop around the circle. On the edge of the circle, mark where each color begins and ends.

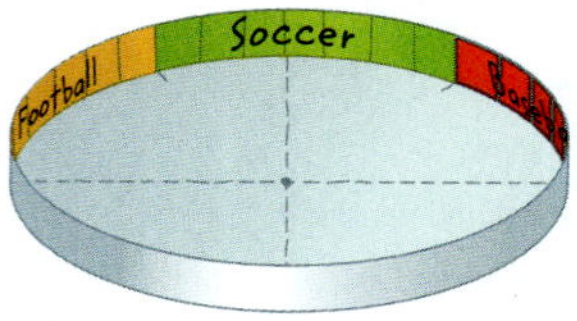


**5.** Remove the loop, and use a straightedge to draw a radius from the center of the circle to each mark where there is a color change. Repeat until you have drawn six radii, one for each change in color.

**6.** Measure each section with your protractor. Choose one of the six radii previously drawn and line up the zero on the straight edge of the protractor with one of the sides of the angle. Find the point where the second side of the angle intersects the curved edge of the protractor. Read the number written on the protractor at the point of intersection. This is the measure of the angle in degrees.

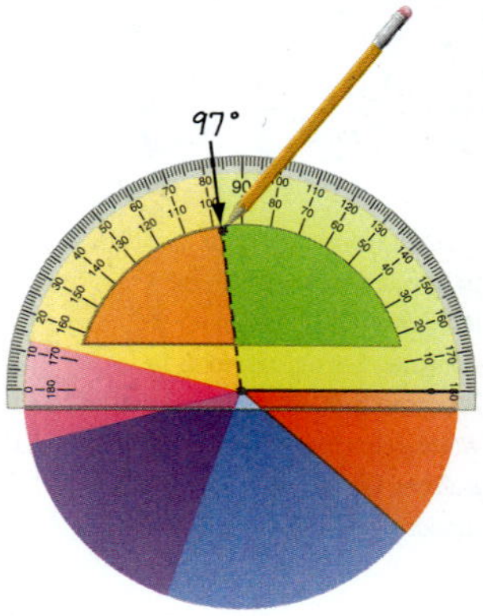


**7.** Fill in the *Angle Measure* column of the chart on page 299 with the angle measurements. There are 360 degrees in a circle, so your angles should have the sum of 360 degrees.

**Real-World Link**
Professional football is the most-watched sport in the United States, followed by figure skating.

**8.** Color the sections of your graph. Label each section with the sport name and the fraction of votes that sport received. For example, your circle graph might look like this.

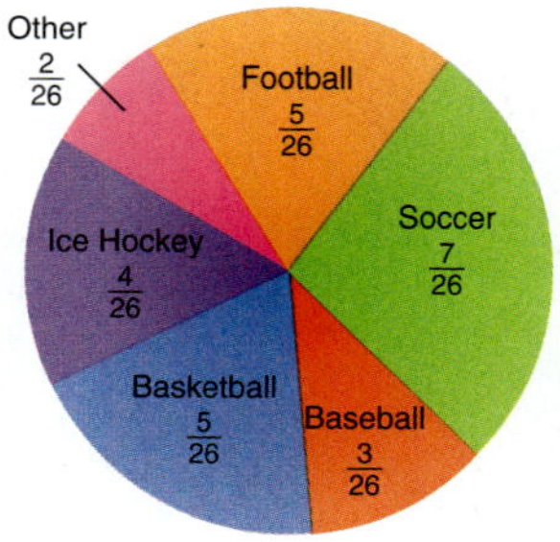


Check students' work.



## Troubleshooting

Students may be looking around the room and seeing that other circle graphs do not look the same. Assure students that as long as their sections of the graph for each sport are the same size, the order in which they are around the circle does not make their graph incorrect.

## Develop & Understand: B

In Exercises 1–8, you learned to make a circle graph using a strip of paper. You will now make a circle graph using a protractor.

9–13. Check students' work.

**9.** Work as a class to gather student responses to this question.

*What is your favorite season of the year? Choose one.*

- ❑ *Winter*
- ❑ *Spring*
- ❑ *Summer*
- ❑ *Fall*

**10.** Construct a table to record your data. You can set up a table like the one on page 299.

**11.** Calculate the fraction of the class in each category. A circle is 360 degrees. If you multiply the fraction representing the part of the circle times 360°, you will then have the angle measure of the respective part.

**12.** Construct a circle using the quarter-circle template and mark the center.

**13.** From the center point, draw a radius. Use this radius as a starting point to measure and draw the first angle with your protractor. Draw the remaining radii on the circle graph. You can check your calculations by making sure that the sum of all of your angles is 360°.

### Share & Summarize

Give a description of a situation in which you would want to create a circle graph. Explain why a circle graph would be the best choice. If you wanted to display data that represents parts of a whole you would use a circle graph. For example, if you asked the entire seventh grade to name their favorite color, you could display the results in a circle graph.



## Develop & Understand: B

*Suggested Grouping: Pairs or Small Groups*

▶ **Exercises 9–13** Each exercise provides the precise steps that the students need to complete a circle graph. It may be helpful to monitor the students' progress just to make sure that their work is progressing appropriately. It may also be beneficial to the students if a class discussion takes place when all pairs/groups complete Exercise 11, so that all students have the same information.

**Wrap-Up** Have each pair or small group share their circle graphs. As a class discuss the similarities and differences. If the tables in Exercise 10 are all the same, the graphs should all have the same wedge-shaped pieces.

### Share & Summarize

If students are having trouble coming up with ideas, remind them that circle graphs show data that is a part of a whole.

# Investigation 3

***On Your Own Exercises***
Pages 309–313
Exercises 5, 8

**Representing Distributed Data** Students will now be introduced to stem-and-leaf plots. They begin by reading and interpreting stem plots showing the time various students spent on homework. Then they use the homework data from the Think & Discuss to make a stem plot for their class data.

Students interpret the data and compare the two data sets. They reinforce these skills as they expand their knowledge to create stem-and-leaf plots with two-digit numbers in the stems.

### Think & Discuss

*Suggested Grouping: Pairs*

Have pairs of students think about how a circle graph of the data in the table would look and whether it would be a good way to display the data. Then have students share their ideas.

Once students understand that there are some disadvantages to displaying the data set as a circle graph, introduce stem-and-leaf plots.

# Investigation 3 Stem-and-Leaf Plots

## Vocabulary

- stem-and-leaf plot

## Materials

- homework—time data for your class

You have seen that line graphs, bar graphs, and circle graphs are useful for showing the distribution of numerical data. However, for some data sets, creating a line graph, bar graph, or circle graph may not be practical.

### Think & Discuss

Have each student in your class estimate how many minutes he or she spent doing homework yesterday. Your teacher should record the data on the board.

The students in Ms. Washington's class kept track of how many minutes they spent doing homework one evening. Their results are listed below.

| Student's Initials | Time Spent Doing Homework (minutes) |
|---|---|
| AF | 42 |
| JB | 5 |
| RC | 60 |
| HE | 30 |
| JL | 45 |
| MM | 47 |
| DL | 0 |
| SK | 25 |
| FR | 67 |
| CO | 51 |
| DW | 56 |
| PG | 20 |

| Student's Initials | Time Spent Doing Homework (minutes) |
|---|---|
| RL | 90 |
| DD | 39 |
| AG | 30 |
| RT | 49 |
| CB | 58 |
| MC | 55 |
| FB | 75 |
| JM | 45 |
| TK | 44 |
| MG | 37 |
| LK | 62 |
| EL | 65 |

Think about what a circle graph of these data would look like. Do you think a circle graph is a good way to display these data? Why or why not? See ①.

① No; Each student's minutes would have to be converted into a fraction over the total number of minutes. Then the graph would have to have a separate section for each student. This would be tedious, and difficult to draw.

When a data set contains many different values, or when the values are spread out, a **stem-and-leaf plot** (also called a *stem plot*) may give the best representation of the data's distribution.

302 CHAPTER 6 Data and Probability

## Example

To make a stem-and-leaf plot of the homework-time data, think of each data value as being made up of two parts: a tens digit and a ones digit.

Write the tens digits, from least to greatest, in a column. Draw a vertical line to the right of the digits. The values in this column are the *stems.*

| Stem | Leaf |
|---|---|
| 0 | |
| 1 | |
| 2 | |
| 3 | |
| 4 | |
| 5 | |
| 6 | |
| 7 | |
| 8 | |
| 9 | |

To add the *leaves*, write the ones digit for each data value to the right of the appropriate tens digit. For example, to plot the first time of 42 minutes, write a 2 next to the stem value 4. The first five data values have been plotted here. Those values are 42, 5, 60, 30, and 45.

| Stem | Leaf |
|---|---|
| 0 | 5 |
| 1 | |
| 2 | |
| 3 | 0 |
| 4 | 2 5 |
| 5 | |
| 6 | 0 |
| 7 | |
| 8 | |
| 9 | |

After you have plotted all the data values, redraw the plot, listing the ones digits for each stem in order from least to greatest.

| Stem | Leaf |
|---|---|
| 0 | 0 5 |
| 1 | |
| 2 | 0 5 |
| 3 | 0 0 7 9 |
| 4 | 2 4 5 5 7 9 |
| 5 | 1 5 6 8 |
| 6 | 0 2 5 7 |
| 7 | 5 |
| 8 | |
| 9 | 0 |

**Key:** 4|2 = 42

Stem plots and histograms both group data into intervals. However, unlike a histogram, a stem plot allows you to read individual values.

For example, if you made a histogram that grouped the data above into the intervals 0–9, 10–19, and so on, it would show that there are four values between 50 and 59, but it would not show that these values are 51, 55, 56, and 58.



### Example

As you discuss the example, you might model how to make the stem-and-leaf plot on the board or on a transparency. You can have students follow along at their desks. Students may initially resist the idea that these numerals must be separated into tens and ones before plotting the values, but most will understand the concept after entering a few data values.

For the first step, writing the stems, ask students why 0 is included as a stem. If no one mentions that 0 is needed to record values less than 10, point this out.

After discussing the leaves in the second step, have students look at the completed stem-and-leaf plot. Ask them such questions as these:

- How are the leaves for each stem similar? They are in numerical order from least to greatest.
- Why are there two 0s as leaves for stem 3? To show that two students, HE and AG, spent 30 minutes working on homework.
- How do you know that all the data values have been recorded? The number of leaves and the number of values in the table are the same.

Discuss the similarities and differences between stem plots and histograms, noting that both displays show numerical data in intervals, but the stem plot also shows individual values.

## Develop & Understand: A

*Suggested Grouping: Pairs*

▶ **Exercise 1c** It may take students some time to think through how to find the median. Not only are they becoming familiar with the stem plot, but the data set has an even number of values. You may want to point out that students will need to use the stem plot and some mathematical calculations to find the median of this data set.

▶ **Exercise 2** Data sets with more than two-digit values are used in Exercises 6-7. If your class has data values greater than or equal to 100, you can have pairs use all the data, model that aspect of the stem-and-leaf plot for the class, or eliminate those data pieces until students are more comfortable making stem plots.

Students may use one of the strategies below to make their stem-and-leaf plots:

- Order the values in the data set. Then use the ordered values to make the stem plot.
- Plot all the values as they appear in the table. Then revise the stem plot to put each set of leaves in numerical order.
- Plot the values as they appear in the table, but leave space between the leaves to insert other leaves. This may result in unevenly spaced leaves.

**Wrap-Up** Have volunteers explain how to use a stem plot to find the median and mode of a data set.

## Develop & Understand: B

*Suggested Grouping: Pairs*

Students make stem-and-leaf plots for data values in the thousandths and for data values in the tens and hundreds. They analyze the data in each data set.

### Additional Answers

1b. 30 min and 45 min; I looked for the digit that appears the most times in one stem. The digit 0 appears twice in the 3 stem, and the digit 5 appears twice in the 4 stem. No other digit appears more than once in the same stem.

1c. 46 min; Possible explanation: I put one finger on the first value and one on the last value and moved my fingers in, one value at a time, until they met in the middle. They met with one finger on 45 and the other on 47, so the median is 46 min.

1a. The minimum time is the first number in the first row (in this case, 0). The maximum time is the last number in the last row (in this case, 9). To find the range, subtract the minimum from the maximum. The range is 90 min.

## Develop & Understand: A

1. Look at the completed stem-and-leaf plot in the example on page 303.
   a. Explain how you can use this graph to find the range of the homework times.
   b. Use the stem plot to find the mode homework time. How did you find it? See margin.
   c. Use the stem plot to find the median homework time. Explain how you found it. See margin.
   d. Describe the shape of the graph. Explain what the shape tells you about how the data are distributed. See margin.
2. In the Think & Discuss at the beginning of this lesson, you collected homework times for your class. Make a stem plot of these data. If your data include values of 100 minutes or more, your plot will need to include two-digit stem values. For example, a value of 112 would have a stem of 11 and a leaf of 2. Plots will vary.
3. Find the range, median, and mode of your class data.
4. Describe the distribution of your class data. Answers will vary.
5. Write a few sentences comparing your class data to the data from Ms. Washington's class. Answers will vary.

In the plots in Exercises 1–5, the tens digits are used as stem values and the ones digits are used as leaves. The stem and leaf values you choose for a given situation depend on the minimum and maximum values in the data set.

**Real-World Link**
A player's batting average is the number of hits divided by the number of times the player is officially at bat.

## Develop & Understand: B

6. This table shows the batting averages for the 2007 Cleveland Indians baseball team.

**2007 Cleveland Indians**

| Batter | Average | Batter | Average |
|---|---|---|---|
| Barfield | .243 | Gomez | .283 |
| Blake | .270 | Gutierrez | .266 |
| Cabrera | .283 | Hafner | .266 |
| Choo | .294 | Lofton | .283 |
| Dellucci | .230 | Marte | .193 |
| Francisco | .274 | Michaels | .270 |
| Garko | .289 | Sizemore | .277 |



1d. Possible answer: There are two values in the 0 stem, indicating that two students spent less than 10 min on their homework. The number of values in each stem increases until the 4 stem and then decreases until the 7 stem. The 4 stem has the most values, indicating that more homework times were in the 40–49 interval than in any other 10-minute interval. There are no values in the 8 stem, indicating that no one spent from 80 to 89 min on homework. One student spent 90 min on homework.

### Troubleshooting

Watch for students who look only at the leaves when finding the mode in Exercises 1b and 3. For example, they may think that 4 is the mode in Exercise 1b because the greatest number of leaves have a value of 4. Remind them that each value is composed of a stem *and* a leaf.

**Real-World Link**
*Runs batted in,* or RBI, is the number of people who score a run as a result of a player's hitting the ball.

6a.

| Stem | Leaf |
|---|---|
| .19 | 3 |
| .20 | |
| .21 | |
| .22 | |
| .23 | 0 |
| .24 | 3 |
| .25 | |
| .26 | 6 6 |
| .27 | 0 0 4 7 |
| .28 | 3 3 3 9 |
| .29 | 4 |

6b. There are four values in the .270s and .280s. There are two values in the .260s. The .190s, .230s, .240s, and .290s have only one value.

7a.

| Stem | Leaf |
|---|---|
| 7 | 8 |
| 8 | |
| 9 | |
| 10 | |
| 11 | 2 9 |
| 12 | 1 2 3 4 4 6 6 9 |
| 13 | 2 3 3 4 7 9 9 |
| 14 | 1 2 5 5 5 7 8 8 |
| 15 | 0 6 7 |
| 16 | 5 |

**Key:** 11|2 = 112

7b. Possible answer: There is one data value in the 70s and then no data until the 110s. Most of the values clump around the 120s through 140s.

**a.** The batting averages range from .193 to .294. In this case, you can use the tenths and hundredths digits as stem values and the thousandths digits as leaves.

Make a stem-and-leaf plot using the stem values shown at right.

**b.** Describe the distribution of data values.

**c.** Find the mode and median batting average. Mode: .283; Median: .272

**2007 Cleveland Indians Batting Averages**

| Stem | Leaf |
|---|---|
| .19 | |
| .20 | |
| .21 | |
| .22 | |
| .23 | |
| .24 | |
| .25 | |
| .26 | |
| .27 | |
| .28 | |
| .29 | |

**Key:** .27|5 = .275

**7.** This table shows the American League RBI leaders for each season from 1978 to 2007:

**American League RBI Leaders**

| Year | Player | RBI | Year | Player | RBI |
|---|---|---|---|---|---|
| 1978 | Jim Rice | 139 | 1993 | Albert Belle | 129 |
| 1979 | Don Baylor | 139 | 1994 | Kirby Puckett | 112 |
| 1980 | Cecil Cooper | 122 | 1995 | A. Belle / M. Vaughn | 126 |
| 1981 | Eddie Murray | 78 | 1996 | Albert Belle | 148 |
| 1982 | Hal McRae | 133 | 1997 | Ken Griffey, Jr. | 147 |
| 1983 | C. Cooper / J. Rice | 126 | 1998 | Juan Gonzalez | 157 |
| 1984 | Tony Armas | 123 | 1999 | Manny Ramirez | 165 |
| 1985 | Don Mattingly | 145 | 2000 | Edgar Martinez | 145 |
| 1986 | Joe Carter | 121 | 2001 | Brett Boone | 141 |
| 1987 | George Bell | 134 | 2002 | Alex Rodriguez | 142 |
| 1988 | Jose Canseco | 124 | 2003 | Carlos Delgado | 145 |
| 1989 | Ruben Sierra | 119 | 2004 | Miguel Tejada | 150 |
| 1990 | Cecil Fielder | 132 | 2005 | David Ortiz | 148 |
| 1991 | Cecil Fielder | 133 | 2006 | David Ortiz | 137 |
| 1992 | Cecil Fielder | 124 | 2007 | Alex Rodriguez | 156 |

**Source:** *World Almanac and Book of Facts 2003.* Copyright © 2003 Primedia Reference Inc.

**a.** Make a stem-and-leaf plot of the RBI data.

**b.** Describe the distribution of data values.

**c.** Find the minimum, maximum, mode, and median of the RBI data. Minimum: 78; Maximum: 165; Mode: 145; Median: 135.5

**Share & Summarize**

**1.** In what types of situations would you use a stem-and-leaf plot, rather than a line plot, to display a set of data? See margin.

**2.** What information can you get from a stem plot that you cannot get from a histogram? Individual data values



**Wrap-Up** Have students describe the distributions of values from Exercises 6b and 7b.

You might extend the discussion by quickly sketching a line graph of the data in Exercise 7, and helping students compare the information shown in the line plot to that shown in the stem plot that students made. Students may realize that the line graph shows the values in a time continuum, making it easier to discover patterns, but the stem plot shows all the data values and can make it easier to find the median and mode of the data.

**Share & Summarize**

Have students work in pairs to answer these questions about when to use a stem-and-leaf plot and how stem plots and histograms differ.

Encourage students having difficulty making stem-and-leaf plots to write the values of the data set vertically, in order from least to greatest, aligning all place values. Have them then draw a vertical line so that one place value is to the right of the line. The numbers to the left of the line will be the stems in the stem plot. Then have students consolidate the leaves for each stem as they make the stem-and- leaf plot.

**Additional Answer**

1. Possible answer: when there are many different data values or when the data values are very spread out

## Troubleshooting

Watch for students who do not use hundreds and tens in the stems of their stem-and-leaf plots for Exercise 7. Remind them that a leaf can only have one digit, but a stem can have as many digits as needed to show the data values.

# Investigation 4

***On Your Own Exercises***
Pages 309–313
Exercise 7

**Misleading Statistics and Graphs** Students may not understand that a graph can be misleading if it is made from real data. Discuss with students how numbers can be misleading based on how they are used. For example, have students look at the increments between units, the starting points of the axes of the graphs, or whether the data are actual numbers or numbers that are the result of a calculation. All of these factors can change the way a person interprets what the graph is showing.

### Think & Discuss

*Suggested Grouping: Pairs or Small Groups*

In pairs, students will have a format in which they can discuss their ideas and share what they see. This is going to be crucial for students to hear different opinions of what the data show.

# Investigation 4 Misleading Statistics and Graphs

Many times, people do not trust statistics and data because they have been misled by people using statistics. If you know how data can be distorted, you know what to look for in charts and graphs to accurately interpret the data.

People can be misled by graphs or by statistics such as "average," or mean and median. This investigation will help you become aware of how the same data can be shown differently and determine what representation may be most appropriate.

### Think & Discuss

The world record for the men's 100-meter sprint has been broken six times since 1991. Below are two bar graphs that represent the times for the 100-meter sprint.

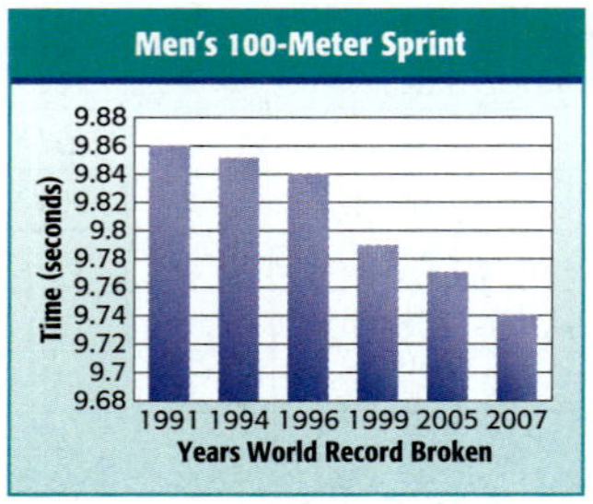


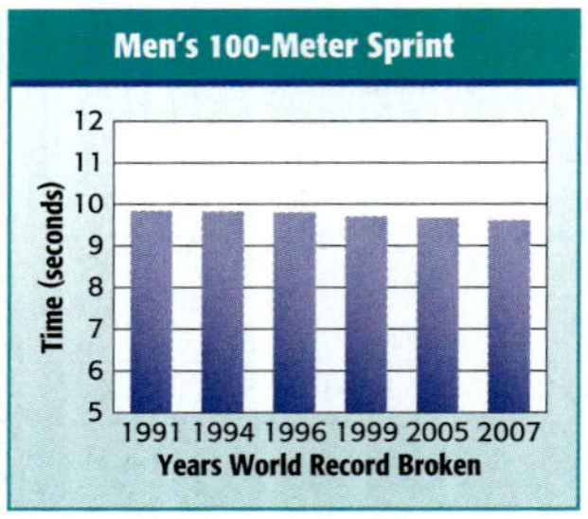


① Yes, the graphs do show the same data. The graphs look different because they have different scales. The graph with a scale of .02 changes allows you to see the change more easily.

Zoe, Darnell, and Maya discussed the graphs.

Do these graphs represent the same data? Why do they look different? See ① above.



### Troubleshooting

Many students may not see anything wrong with the data. Instruct students to look carefully at the information presented, especially the labels and increments on the axes. This is where many of the misleading interpretations are found.

306 CHAPTER 6 Data and Probability

**Real-World Link**
On September 9, 2007, Asafa Powell set the world record when he ran the 100-meter dash in 9.74 seconds.

## Develop & Understand: A

1. Using the graph from Think & Discuss, which headline could be paired with each graph? Explain.
   a. "100-meter sprint times stalled out for last two decades"
   b. "World record broken in amazing way in 2007"
2. Which graph do you think track athletes would argue is the best representation of the progress in the world record? Explain.

The mayor of Sunnybrook is planning to run for re-election. His campaign team brings him the graph at the right and proposes to use the phrase "consistently popular mayor" to describe him in his advertising campaign.

3. The mayor is concerned about missing information on the graph. What do you think concerns the mayor?
4. What labels would need to be on the vertical axis to make the claim "popular" true? What labels might be there that would make the claim untrue? Explain. See margin.
5. The mayor asks his staff to put the labels on the vertical axis. They produce these two different graphs.

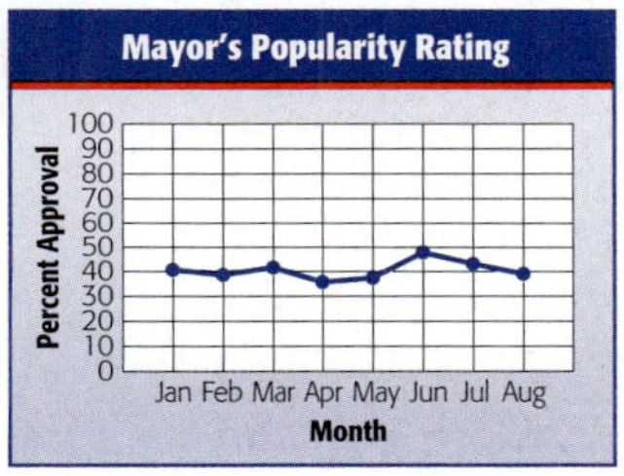


What do you think the mayor should do with this information? If he chooses to use a graph, which one appears more positive? See margin.

In your previous study of data and statistics, you learned about mean, median, and mode. We will now explore how each can be used to present data in different light.

1a. Goes with second graph; bars do not look like they change much over time
1b. Goes with first graph; scale is small so the drop from 1996 to 1999 looks huge
2. Athletes might say the first graph best represents the changes in the record time. If it was easy to run the sprint in 2 hundredths of a second less then it would not take 5 or 6 years before an athlete breaks the record. These tiny difference in time are actually major in the track world.
3. There are no numbers on the *y*-scale, so his popularity rating is actually unknown.



## Develop & Understand: A

*Suggested Grouping: Individuals and then discussion in pairs or small groups*

**Exercises 1 and 2** It will be important for students to form their own opinions of what they see. It will also be beneficial for students to hear how others see the data. This will show students that misleading graphs cause proper data to express false ideas for those who do not look carefully at all aspects of what the data display is showing.

**Exercise 3** Students may not see any problem with how the data are displayed. For a hint, tell the students to look for numbers on the graph to quantify the data. Students will see that there are no values given.

**Exercise 4** It may require additional explanation for students to understand how to make the graph mean something that is not necessarily true. Students will find this exercise challenging if they do not look carefully at the data with the idea of swaying the opinion of the reader.

### Additional Answers

4. If the lines are labeled 20%, 40%, 60%, 80%, and 100% at the top, then his popularity is 75% or higher all the time so the claim could be true.; If the lines are labeled 10%, 20%, 30%, 40%, and 50% at the top, then his popularity is in the 30s and 40s and the claim would not be true.
5. He could use the phrase and the first graph with the axis labeled and still probably mislead people. Some people will assume since the line is at the top of the chart that the information is positive.

## Develop & Understand: B

*Suggested Grouping: Individuals*

Students may need assistance in remembering how to determine the mean, median, and mode. In addition, the students may need to be reminded what each measure of central tendency is best used to interpret.

▶ **Exercise 6** In order to answer this question, students should compute the mean, median, and mode for both students.

▶ **Exercises 7 and 8** These questions will really make students think about how the mean, median, and mode can sway the readers' views of the actual information.

## Develop & Understand: C

*Suggested Grouping: Pairs*

▶ **Exercise 9** Students may not know where to begin constructing misleading graphs. Give students hints, such as compute the mean, median, and mode, use different increments on the *y*-axis to make Henry's argument convincing.

**Wrap-Up** Have each pair share their graphs with the class. Talk about similarities and differences. Also, discuss whether all of the representations meet the goal of the question.

### Share & Summarize

Use student examples from the lesson to lead discussions for these points. It will bring the students into the discussion because the work is their own.

### Additional Answers

9. Students will have varying scales to make it look like Henry makes about the same in tips all the time. The scales would have to go very high, so it will appear that Henry makes few tips. Students could use either a bar or line graph. On the bar graph they could show that Henry makes four times as much on Friday, Saturday, or Sunday than he does on Monday, Tuesday, or Thursday.

10. Henry used the median, which is $19.75, but the mean is $25.76, so his mother should consider that or the total tips as well.

**Real-World Link**
Some car insurance companies give "good student discounts" for teenage drivers with a B average or higher.

6. Mara is using the median (80); Santos could be using either the median (82) or the mean (83) of his grades

8. Possible answer: The mean is most appropriate because the purpose of the requirement is to ensure discounts are given to students with good performance. You could argue that for the median to be a B grade because then the student is making a B or better in more than half of their classes so the median could be appropriate.

## Develop & Understand: B

Partners' Insurance allows students with a B average to apply for a discount on car insurance.

| Subject | Mara's Grades | Santos' Grades |
|---|---|---|
| Science | 85 | 85 |
| Algebra | 37 | 82 |
| History | 80 | 70 |
| English | 32 | 77 |
| Band | 93 | 95 |
| Accounting | 80 | 80 |
| Health | 68 | 90 |

**6.** Mara and Santos both claim to have a B average in their classes, and neither student is untruthful. How can this be possible? What information is each student using to make the claim?

**7.** Mara says she used the median of her grades as the average, but she is not qualified for the discount. Santos says, "I used the median also, and they approved me for the discount." Why was Santos approved? His median and mean were both B.

**8.** Using different measures of the average, both students could meet the requirement of having a B. Make an argument for each student to receive the discount using their data.

## Develop & Understand: C

Henry is a waiter at a local steakhouse where he works for a few hours each night. He made the following amounts in tips over the past 7 days.

| Sun | Mon | Tues | Wed | Thurs | Fri | Sat |
|---|---|---|---|---|---|---|
| $40.50 | $10 | $9.60 | $19.75 | $11 | $45.95 | $43.50 |

**9.** Graph this data to convince someone that Henry earns about the same amount each night. Make another graph to convince someone that Henry earns much more on Friday, Saturday, and Sunday than the other nights. See margin.

**10.** Henry tried to convince his mother that he earns less than $20 a night on average so she would give him more allowance each week. What information allows him to use that argument? What should his mother also consider? See margin.

**11.** Could Henry use a histogram with two bars to support his claim? See margin.

### Share & Summarize

What parts of a graph should you pay close attention to in order to correctly interpret the graph? See ① in margin.

How can changing the scale on a histogram change the representation of the data? See ② in margin.



11. Yes. Henry could create a histogram with two bars. The first bar would have the range of $0 to $20 and the second bar would have the range of $21 and above. The scale on the left hand side could be 1 through 7 and titled Number of Days. The bar showing $0 to $20 would be taller because he makes less than $20 more days a week.

① Sample answer: The scale on each axis needs to be studied to know the range of the data. You should also look at the categories used because some data may be combined to alter the look of the graph. If you are looking at a histogram, knowing the range of each bar is important.

② Sample answer: If you change the range of each bar, this can change the height and how the graph may be interpreted.

## Practice & Apply

1. The Bears and the Panthers are football teams for two high schools that are about the same size. The double-line graph shows the attendance in the stadium each week when each team played.

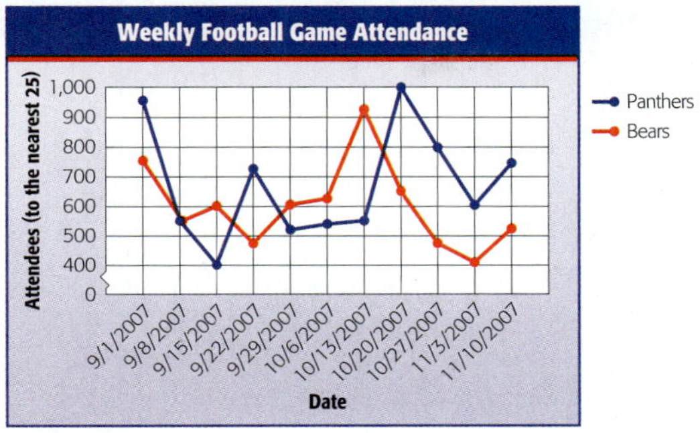


a. What is the minimum and maximum attendance for each team? What is the range of the data? Bears 400 to 925; Panthers 400 to 1,000; Range: 525 and 600

b. What date did the teams play each other? How do you know? September 8 because the attendance was the same number

c. What nights do you think each team played its homecoming game? Why? Bears October 13; Panthers October 20; their highest attendance of the season occurred then

d. Do the two teams have the same average season attendance? Explain.

1d. Both teams have the same median attendance (600), so they can make the claim. Based on the mean average, the Bears attendance is closest to 600 and the Panthers attendance is closer to 675.

2. Amado owns two restaurant locations (A and B). He asks each customer to rate the restaurant in five categories on a scale from 1–10, with 10 being "excellent" and 1 being "extremely poor." The table shows the average rating for each restaurant in each category for the month of October.

| Category | Location A | Location B |
|---|---|---|
| Helpful staff | 9.5 | 7.5 |
| Cleanliness | 9 | 9.5 |
| Taste of food | 9.5 | 7 |
| Speed of service | 7.5 | 8.5 |
| Quality for the price | 9 | 7 |

a. Create a double-bar graph for the data in the table. Be sure to include a title and labels. See margin.

b. In what areas should Amado work with his employees to improve? Why?

c. The category "Quality for the Price" means "Was what you got worth what you paid?" Which category do you think influences people's overall opinion more, *Speed of Service* or *Taste of Food*? Explain.

2b. Location A, speed; Location B, taste of food and quality for the price. These were the areas where the survey scores were the lowest.

2c. Taste of Food because the restaurant that was low in that area and high in Speed of Service still had a lower overall rating than the restaurant that was lower in Speed of Service but high in Taste of Food.



On Your Own Exercises
Lesson 6.3

**Investigation 1**
Pages 295–298
Practice & Apply: 1–3

**Investigation 2**
Pages 299–301
Practice & Apply: 4
Connect & Extend: 6

**Investigation 3**
Pages 302–305
Practice & Apply: 5
Connect & Extend: 8

**Investigation 4**
Pages 306–308
Connect & Extend: 7

**Assign Anytime**
Mixed Review: 9–12

▶ **Exercise 1** The exercise asks the students to interpret the information in the double-line graph. Students may need clarification about the horizontal axis. The horizontal axis represents the date of the game, it is written on a diagonal and may confuse some students.

▶ **Exercise 2** It may be helpful for students to be able to check if their double-bar graph is correct before they answer all of the parts. This way, students will know that they have the correct information.

### Additional Answer

2a.

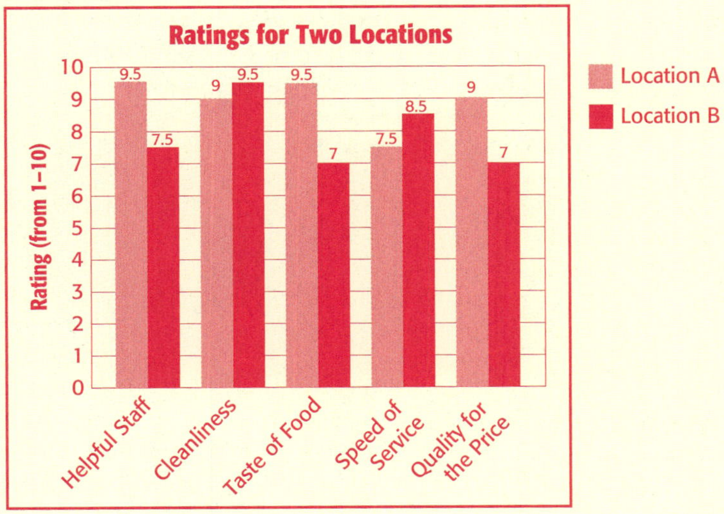

▶ **Exercise 3a** Students need to refer back to the graph in Exercise 1 to answer this question. Remind students to look closely at the axes of the graphs to decide how the graphs have been altered. This is the most common way to alter graphs and make their information misleading.

▶ **Exercise 4a** Remind students that in order to determine the angle measure, they need to determine what part of the whole each cartoon represents.

## Additional Answers

3a. The scale on Altered Graph #1 has been changed to go from 400 to 1000. I know this because the lowest attendance of 400 is now on the bottom of the graph and the highest attendance of 1000 is at the top of the graph. The scale on Altered Graph #2 has been changed to go up to a really high number, probably about 5000.

3b. Altered Graph #1 makes it look like there were two games that nobody attended, some games with very few people attending, and huge differences in the lowest to highest attendance.

3c. Altered Graph #2 makes it look like attendance was close to the same over time and between the two schools and that attendance for both teams was very low every week.

On Your Own Exercises

**3.** Examine two other versions of the graph from Exercise 1.
3a–c. See margin.

Altered Graph #1

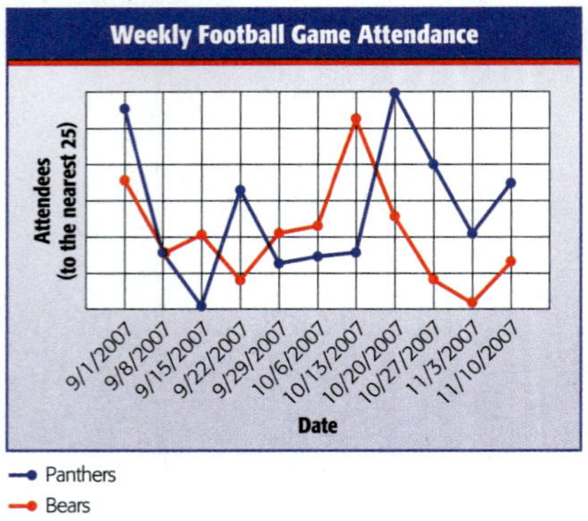


Altered Graph #2

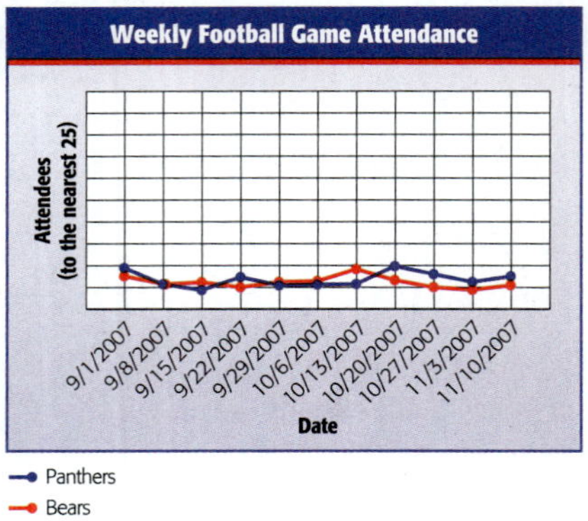


**a.** What change was made to the original graph to produce each of the altered graphs? How do you know?

**b.** Describe how Altered Graph #1 could be used to mislead people.

**c.** Describe how Altered Graph #2 could be misleading.

**4.** Dominique asked all the teachers in her school what their favorite cartoon was when they were kids. The results are displayed in the table to the right.

| Cartoon | Number of Teachers |
|---|---|
| *Scooby Doo* | 4 |
| *Bugs Bunny & Friends* | 15 |
| *Tom and Jerry* | 7 |
| *The Jetsons* | 9 |
| *The Flintstones* | 15 |

**a.** Which circle graph accurately displays the data in the table? Use angles measure to support your choice.

**I.** Favorite Cartoons

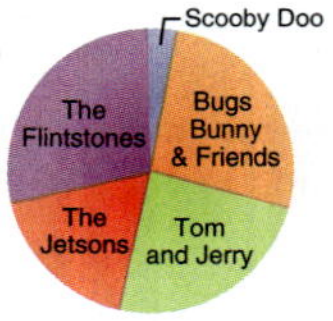


**II.** Favorite Cartoons

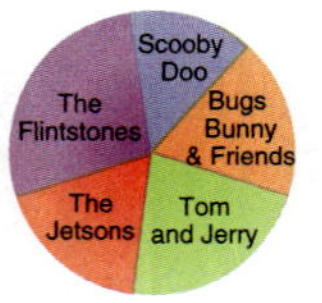


**III.** Favorite Cartoons

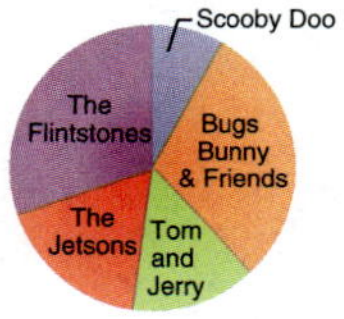


**b.** Give two accurate statements that compare the popularity of these cartoons.

4a. Choice III. Student answers should refer to the angle measures or the relative size of the parts. For example, the sections for *Bugs Bunny* and *The Flintstones* should be the same size and be twice as big as the section for *Tom and Jerry*.

4b. Possible answer: *The Flintstones* and *Bugs Bunny* were equally popular. A third as many people liked *Scooby Doo* as liked *Bugs Bunny*. Twice as many people liked *The Flintstones* as *Tom and Jerry*.

On Your Own Exercises

5a. Ms. Cho's Class

| Stem | Leaf |
|---|---|
| 9 | 9 |
| 10 | 7 |
| 11 | 4 4 4 7 7 9 9 |
| 12 | 0 2 2 5 7 7 7 |
| 13 | 7 |

Key: 11|4 = 114

Mr. Diaz's Class

| Stem | Leaf |
|---|---|
| 11 | 9 |
| 12 | 0 5 |
| 13 | 0 2 5 5 5 5 7 7 |
| 14 | 0 2 2 2 2 7 |

Key: 12|0 = 120

5b. Ms. Cho's class: range: 38; modes: 114 and 127; median: 119
Mr. Diaz's class: range 28; modes: 135 and 142; median: 135

**5. Measurement** Two classes of elementary school students measured their heights in centimeters. Here are the results.

Ms. Cho's class: 117, 117, 119, 122, 127, 127, 114, 137, 99, 107, 114, 127, 122, 114, 120, 125, 119

Mr. Diaz's class: 130, 147, 137, 142, 140, 135, 135, 142, 142, 137, 135, 132, 135, 120, 119, 125, 142

**a.** For each class, make a stem-and-leaf plot of the height data.

**b.** Find the range, mode, and median for each class.

**c.** The two classes are at two different grade levels. Which class do you think is the higher grade? Mr. Diaz's class

**d.** What percent of the students in Mr. Diaz's class are as tall or taller than the median height of the students in Ms. Cho's class? 100%

**6.** The two circle graphs below show two college roommates' budgets for how they spend their money each month.

| Rafael's Budget | Amount of Money |
|---|---|
| Rent and bills | 50% |
| School expenses | 10% |
| Food | 15% |
| Entertainment | 10% |
| Savings | 15% |

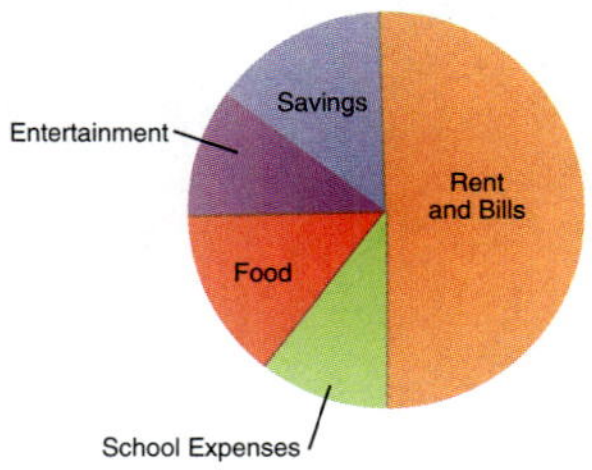


| George's Budget | Amount of Money |
|---|---|
| Rent and bills | 50% |
| School expenses | 10% |
| Food | 20% |
| Entertainment | 15% |
| Savings | 5% |

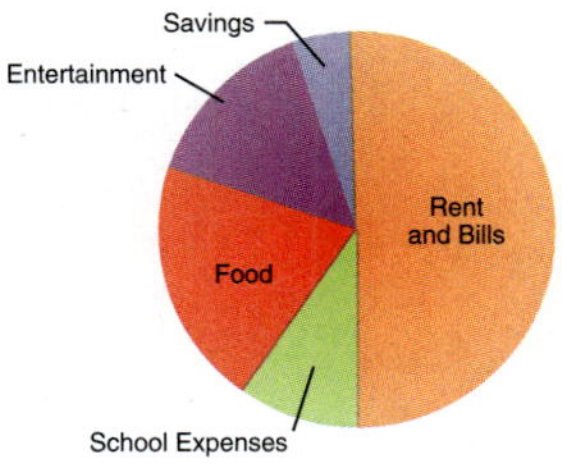


**a.** Create a double-bar graph to display the data from these two circle graphs. See margin.

**b.** Who is more responsible with his money? Explain.

6b. Rafael, because he saves more and spends less on food and entertainment



6a.

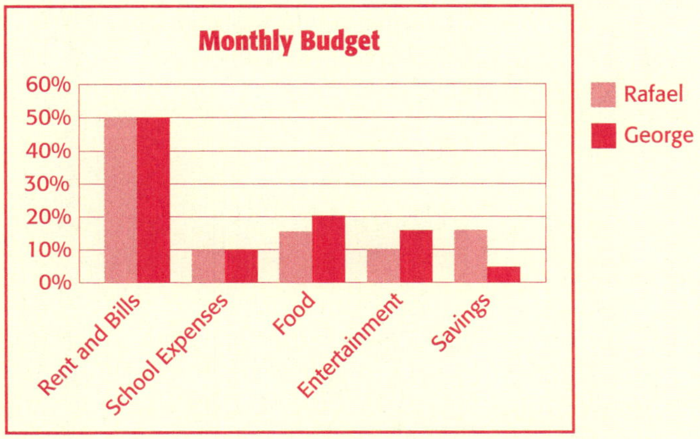


**Lesson 6.3** Data Graphs **311**

▶ **Exercise 7** This question has students create a misleading graph. Remind students that the data is accurate; the graphs just look different because of the values on the axes.

## Additional Answers

7a.

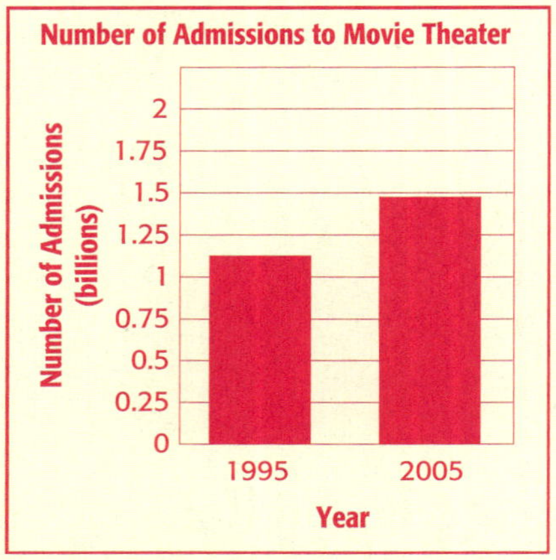


7b.

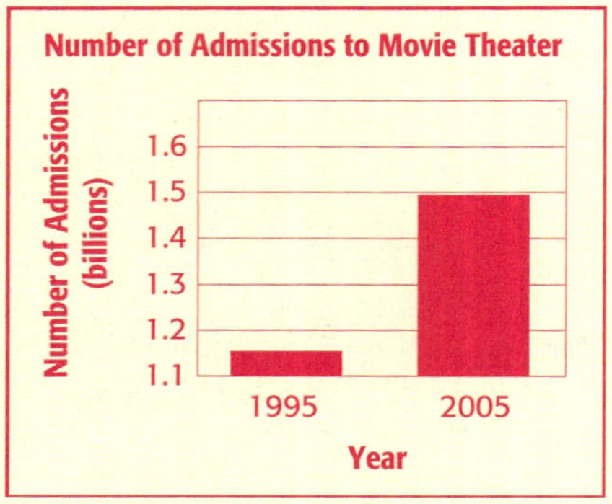


On Your Own Exercises

**7.** The number of admissions to movie theaters went from 1.14 billion in 1995 to 1.49 billion in 2005. 7a–b. See margin.

**a.** Make a graph that shows a small change in admission.

**b.** Make a graph that shows a large change in admission.

**c.** What is the difference between your two graphs? The intervals of the scales on the left hand side are different.

**8. Sports** You can create a *back-to-back stem plot* to display and compare two data sets. This plot shows the batting averages for the 2007 New York Yankees and the 2007 New York Mets.

Leaf values for the Yankees are given to the left of the stem, and leaf values for the Mets are given to the right of the stem. For example, the leaves 2 and 5 in the tenth row indicate a Yankee batting average of .322 and a Met batting average of .325.

**Yankees and Mets 2007**
**Batting Averages**

| Yankees | Stem | Mets |
|---|---|---|
| 6 | .23 | |
| | .24 | |
| | .25 | 8 |
| | .26 | |
| 7 3 0 | .27 | 2 2 6 |
| 5 3 | .28 | 0 0 |
| 2 | .29 | 1 5 6 |
| 6 | .30 | |
| 4 | .31 | |
| 2 | .32 | 5 |
| 8 | .33 | |
| | .34 | 1 |

**Key:** .21|5 = .215

**a.** Write a few sentences comparing the two teams' batting averages. Be sure to discuss the distribution of values and the mean and mode. The Mets have two modes. The Yankees have no mode. The Yankees mean batting average is 0.2905 versus the Mets mean batting average of 0.2896.

b. These data give the total number of home runs hit by American League and National League teams in 2002. Make a back-to-back stem plot comparing the number of home runs for the two leagues. See margin.

**National League**

| Team | Home Runs |
|---|---|
| Arizona | 165 |
| Atlanta | 164 |
| Chicago | 200 |
| Cincinnati | 169 |
| Colorado | 152 |
| Florida | 146 |
| Houston | 167 |
| Los Angeles | 155 |
| Milwaukee | 139 |
| Montreal | 162 |
| New York | 160 |
| Philadelphia | 165 |
| Pittsburgh | 142 |
| San Diego | 136 |
| San Francisco | 198 |
| St. Louis | 175 |

**American League**

| Team | Home Runs |
|---|---|
| Anaheim | 152 |
| Baltimore | 165 |
| Boston | 177 |
| Chicago | 217 |
| Cleveland | 192 |
| Detroit | 124 |
| Kansas City | 140 |
| Minnesota | 167 |
| New York | 223 |
| Oakland | 205 |
| Seattle | 152 |
| Tampa Bay | 133 |
| Texas | 230 |
| Toronto | 187 |

## Mixed Review

**Find the area of each trapezoid.**

**9.**

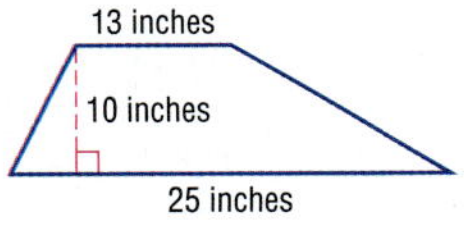


A = 190 in$^2$

**10.**

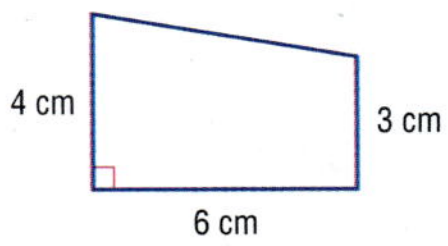


A = 21 cm$^2$

**Solve.**

**11.** $\frac{x}{12} = \frac{18}{24}$ 9

**12.** $\frac{3}{4} = \frac{x}{16}$ 12

**13.** $\frac{2}{6} = \frac{x}{36}$ 12



On Your Own Exercises

## Quick Check

**Informal Assessment** Students should be able to:

✔ construct a double-bar graph, a double-line graph, or a stem-and-leaf plot from a given set of data

✔ interpret data and answer questions comparing data represented in a double-line and a double-bar graph

✔ construct a circle graph using a protractor

✔ interpret data represented by a circle graph or a stem-and-leaf plot

✔ create and interpret misleading graphs

## Quick Quiz

**1.** The table shows the number of times Maurice and Raphael visited various places in their free time.

| Place Visited | Maurice | Raphael |
|---|---|---|
| Library | 4 | 10 |
| Gym | 12 | 7 |
| Recreation Center | 5 | 12 |
| Park | 9 | 1 |

a. If these data were placed in a double-bar graph, what would the horizontal and vertical axes represent? Places visited, number of visits

b. How would you distinguish between Maurice and Raphael's information on the graph? Use different colored bars for each person.

**2.** Gabriella is making a circle graph of the types of pets that students in the seventh grade have. 43 students of the 150 surveyed have a dog. What is the angle measure of the dog section of the circle graph? 103°

**3.** When interpreting a graph that could be misleading, what are two things you should consider? Answers will vary. Sample answer: The spacing of the units along the vertical axis, the combination of categories along the horizontal axis.

## Additional Answer

8b.

| National | | American |
|---|---|---|
| | 10 | |
| | 11 | |
| | 12 | 4 |
| 96 | 13 | 3 |
| 62 | 14 | 0 |
| 52 | 15 | 22 |
| 9755420 | 16 | 57 |
| 5 | 17 | 7 |
| | 18 | 7 |
| 8 | 19 | 2 |
| 0 | 20 | 5 |
| | 21 | 7 |
| | 22 | 3 |
| | 23 | 0 |

CHAPTER 6

# Review & Self-Assessment

## Chapter Summary

This summary helps students recall the major topics of the chapter.

## Vocabulary

Students should be able to explain each of the terms listed in the vocabulary section.

▶ **Exercise 1** If students are having difficulty determining the probability of an event, remind them to create a fraction in which the numerator represents the specific situation and the denominator represents the total possible number of coins. Instruct students to read carefully and look for words like replacement or return when moving past the first time a coin is pulled from the bag.

### Additional Answers

1b. Leaving it out; Possible explanation: If he leaves it out, there are fewer coins in the pack, so the probability of selecting a quarter will increase from $\frac{2}{7}$ to $\frac{2}{6}$. If he puts it back, the probability will remain $\frac{2}{7}$.

1c. No; Possible explanation: He still has more pennies than anything else in his pack, so he is most likely to choose a penny. The fact that he has done so three times already does not affect that.

2. There are 16 possible outcomes: HH HH, HH HT, HH TH, HH TT, HT HH, HT HT, HT TH, HT TT, TH HH, TH HT, TH TH, TH TT, TT HH, TT HT, TT TH, TT TT. The corresponding points for Ben are 2, 1, 1, 1, 1, 0, 0, 0, 1, 0, 0, 0, 1, 0, 0, 0. For these 16 outcomes, Ben scores 8 points and Gabriela scores 9. Gabriela has a slight advantage, so the game is unfair.

CHAPTER 6

# Review & Self-Assessment

## Vocabulary

double-bar graph
double-line graph
population
representative sample
sample

## Chapter Summary

In this chapter, you learned more about probability. You studied situations in which outcomes were influenced by previous outcomes and situations in which each outcome was independent of the others. You also determined the fairness of several games of chance and devised strategies, based on probabilities, to increase your chances of winning.

The basics of sampling a population and how to make predictions from samples were introduced in this chapter. You learned that the size of a sample and whether it is *representative* are important factors in sampling.

Finally, you encountered graphs that help you make comparisons, such as double-bar graphs and double-line graphs. You learned that circle graphs are useful for representing parts of a whole, or summarizing results.

## Strategies and Applications

The questions in this section will help you review and apply the important ideas and strategies developed in this chapter.

### Recognizing when previous outcomes influence later ones

**1.** Yago has two quarters, one dime, and four pennies in a pouch of his backpack. He needs a quarter for a vending machine. Suppose he reaches into his pack without looking and pulls out the first coin he touches.

**a.** What is the probability Yago will select a quarter? $\frac{2}{7}$

**b.** The first coin Yago pulled out was a penny, so he will reach in again and pull out the first coin he touches. Which would give him a better chance of choosing a quarter, putting the penny back into the pack first or leaving it out? Explain your reasoning. See margin.

**c.** Yago put the penny back before pulling out a second coin. He pulled out another penny. He put it back, then pulled out yet another penny. He put it back and tried once more, muttering, "This time, I will get something other than a penny!"

Is this true? Is Yago more likely to get a quarter or dime? Explain. See margin.

### Identifying whether a game is fair

**2.** Ben and Gabriela are playing a game with two dimes and two nickels. They toss the four coins. If one of the pairs of coins lands heads up, Ben scores 1 point. If both pairs land heads up, Ben scores 2 points. On every toss for which Ben does not score, Gabriela is awarded 1 point. They play to 5 points.

Determine whether this game is fair. Identify who has the advantage. Explain. See margin.

3a. C; There are two ways to get each number on Board C; for example, 2 can be 1 and 2 or 2 and 1. There is only one way each to get 1, 4, and 9.

3b. Neither is better. Each has 5 numbers with a $\frac{1}{9}$ chance of being the product and 4 numbers with a $\frac{2}{9}$ chance of being the product.

**Using probability to make decisions and create strategies**

**3.** Three boards and two spinners are used to play the game *Cover Up*.

To play the game, each of two players chooses a board. They take turns. On each turn, a player spins both spinners, computes the product of the two numbers, and then covers a space on the board with that product, if there is one. The winner is the first player to cover all the spaces.

**Board A**

| | | |
|---|---|---|
| 1 | 4 | 2 |
| 2 | 9 | 2 |
| 9 | 2 | 1 |

**Board B**

| | | |
|---|---|---|
| 3 | 9 | 4 |
| 1 | 3 | 9 |
| 3 | 4 | 3 |

**Board C**

| | | |
|---|---|---|
| 2 | 2 | 3 |
| 3 | 6 | 2 |
| 2 | 3 | 6 |

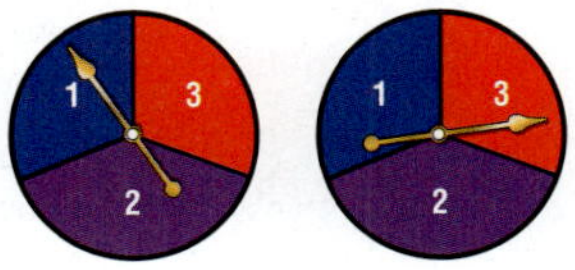


**a.** Which board gives the best chance of winning *Cover Up*? Explain your choice.

**b.** Of the remaining two boards, which is better? Explain.

**Analyzing the appropriateness of a sample or a sampling process**

**4.** A home-decorating magazine wanted to determine whether Americans think a living room should be painted or wallpapered. The people in charge of the survey considered different ways to gather this information. See margin for 4a–d.

For each suggestion, comment on whether the sample would be a good one and whether the process seems practical. Explain your answers.

**a.** Run a poll in the magazine with two toll-free numbers. If you prefer wallpaper, you call one number. If you prefer paint, you call the other number.

**b.** Get a listing of home purchases over the past month in 100 cities across the country, chosen at random. The surveyors would call 20% of the new homeowners and ask them what they prefer.

**c.** Call a random sample of 100 telephone numbers from across the country and ask the people who answer.

**d.** Call a random sample of 10,000 people across the country for their opinions.



Review & Self-Assessment
Chapter 6

▶ **Exercise 4** Students may need reminding how to determine if a sampling is good. Remind students that the sample must represent a variety of people and not just people who are directly involved in decorating.

**Additional Answers**

4a. This is practical since it would probably take only a small amount of time and money. But the sample would not likely be representative since the only people who would know about the poll are those who read this magazine. As a group, their tastes and the amount of money available to them is probably different from Americans in general. And if the magazine has a low circulation, they might not get a large enough sample.

4b. Assuming that getting a listing of home purchases is fairly easy, this seems like a practical method. The size of the sample is questionable, but it might be large enough. However, it is probably not representative. Although new homeowners will include other than first-time buyers, people who prefer staying in one place for a long time, and people who rent, a substantial portion of U.S. residents are not represented well or at all. Renters and long-term residents may have different preferences because of costs and ease of care.

4c. This seems practical and will produce a fairly representative sample because most people have phones. This may be too small to give good results, especially if a significant number of people refuse to answer the question.

4d. This seems like a practical method, although calling 10,000 people will take quite a while and could be costly. The method probably will produce a representative sample of a good size.

**Chapter 6** Review & Self-Assessment 315

▶ **Exercise 5** Remind students that when they are creating a double bar graph, the scale for the *y*-axis needs to allow all of the data to be viewed in a similar manner. For this case since the least data value is 2 and the greatest is 20, increments of 2 or 5 would work best.

Review & Self-Assessment
Chapter 6

15b. mode: 114; median: 111

15c. Possible answer: Although there is one low score of 52 and one high score of 185, most of the scores are in the 70s through the 130s. And, with the exception of the 11 stem (the 110s), the scores are fairly evenly distributed within this range. The 11 stem has the most values.

## Demonstrating Skills

Eddie conducted a survey to determine the favorite school lunch. His results are shown in the table to the right.

| Lunch | Boys | Girls |
|---|---|---|
| Hamburger | 12 | 10 |
| Salad | 2 | 5 |
| Grilled cheese | 10 | 20 |
| Hot dog | 13 | 13 |
| Pizza | 20 | 18 |

**5.** Create a double bar graph of the information given. See margin.

**6.** Which lunch is preferred most by boys? By girls? Pizza; grilled cheese

**7.** Which lunch do the same number of boys and girls prefer? Hot dog

**8.** If each student could only choose one lunch, how many students did Eddie survey about school lunches? 123

The table shows the results of a survey run by the student council.

| Color for School Shirts | Number |
|---|---|
| White | 20 |
| Grey | 40 |
| Black | 10 |
| Green | 20 |
| Pink | 5 |
| Yellow | 5 |

**9.** Create a circle graph using the data. See margin.

**10.** How many students were surveyed? 100

**11.** Which color received the most votes? Grey

**Use the circle graph to answer Questions 12–14.**

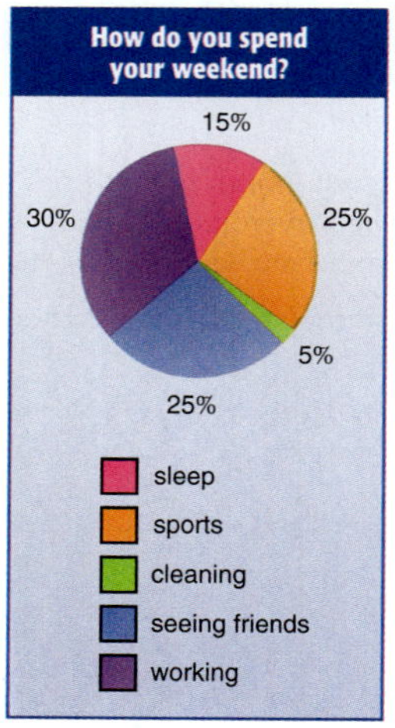


**12.** If 200 students were surveyed, how many spent the weekend cleaning? 10

**13.** How did most of the students spend the weekend? Working

**14.** If 300 students were surveyed, how many spent the weekend working? 90

**15. Sports** Caroline had a bowling party for her birthday. Each person at the party bowled three games. The stem-and-leaf plot shows their scores.

**a.** What is the lowest score? What is the highest score? 52, 185

**b.** Find the mode and median scores.

**c.** Describe the distribution of scores.

**Bowling Party Scores**

| Stem | Leaf |
|---|---|
| 5 | 2 |
| 6 | |
| 7 | 3 7 |
| 8 | 1 6 |
| 9 | 2 9 |
| 10 | 0 3 |
| 11 | 0 1 4 4 4 9 |
| 12 | 3 3 |
| 13 | 2 6 6 |
| 14 | |
| 15 | |
| 16 | |
| 17 | |
| 18 | 5 |

**Key:** 9|2 = 92



## Additional Answers

5.

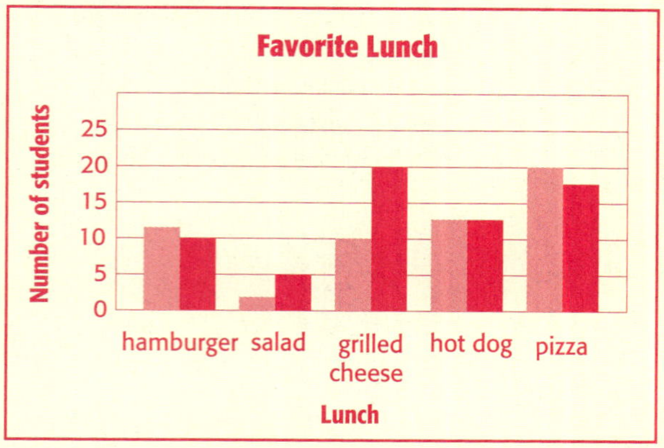


9.

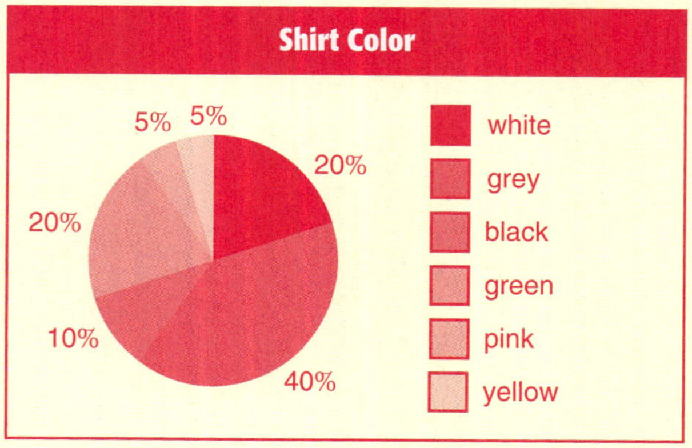


316 CHAPTER 6 Data and Probability

## Test-Taking Practice

*SHORT RESPONSE*

**1** For a class project, Elise questioned five families about how many basketball or football tickets were bought in the past four months. She wrote the information in the table below. Create a double-bar graph to represent the data in the table.

| Family | Basketball | Football |
|---|---|---|
| A | 5 | 3 |
| B | 8 | 6 |
| C | 4 | 11 |
| D | 10 | 5 |
| E | 6 | 7 |

*Show your work:*
*See margin.*

***Show your work.***

*MULTIPLE CHOICE*

**2** There are 10 tiles, numbered 1 through 10, turned face down. If the first tile turned over is 3, what is the probability that an odd numbered tile will be turned over as the second tile?

**A** $\frac{1}{2}$  **(C)** $\frac{4}{9}$

**B** $\frac{5}{9}$  **D** $\frac{2}{5}$

**3** Julia wants to predict the outcome of the sheriff election. Which of the following methods could she use to collect the best data for a prediction?

**F** Ask the parents of her friends for whom they plan to vote.

**G** Ask the students in her class who they prefer.

**(H)** Ask adults at the grocery store which candidate will receive their support.

**J** Ask her adult neighbors which candidate they support.

**4** Chris has 2 dimes and 3 nickels in his pocket. He pulls out two coins. What is the probability that both coins will be dimes?

**A** $\frac{1}{7}$  **C** $\frac{1}{3}$

**(B)** $\frac{1}{10}$  **D** $\frac{2}{3}$

**5** The table below shows the number of students with different pets.

| | |
|---|---|
| Dog | 5 |
| Cat | 6 |
| Fish | 4 |
| None | 8 |

Which category would take up about $\frac{1}{3}$ of the circle of a circle graph?

**F** Dog
**G** Cat
**H** Fish
**(J)** None





▶ **Exercise 2** In this question, one tile has been removed and it is odd. This causes the numerator of the fraction to decrease by one as well as the denominator of the fraction, since there is one fewer tile in the set.

## Additional Answer

1.

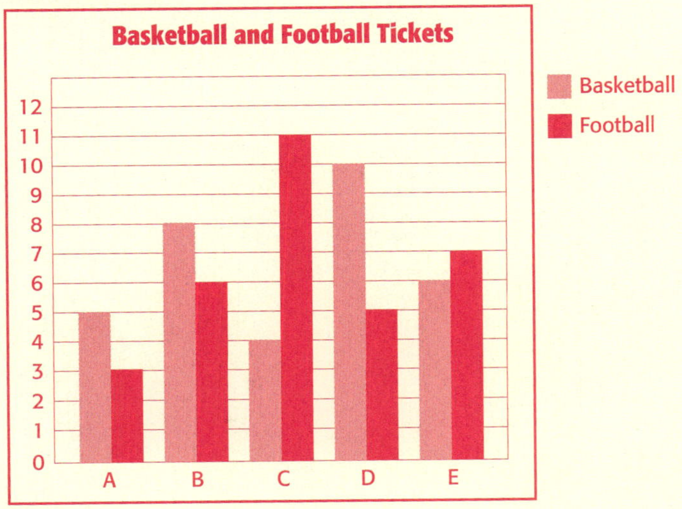

**Lesson 6.1, Preview** (p. 275)

10a.

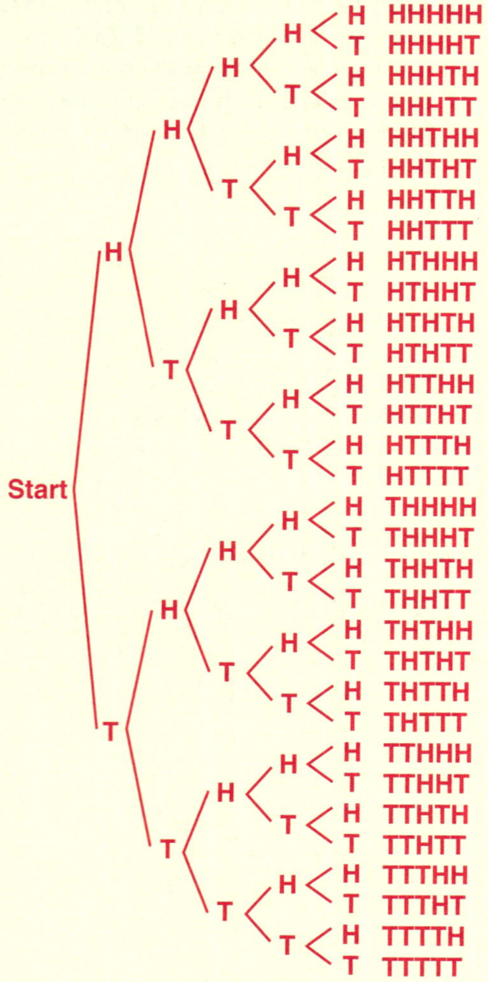

Notes

CHAPTER 7

# Real Numbers

## Chapter Overview

This chapter begins with students learning how number sets are related. Then they are introduced to the concept of comparing and ordering rational numbers using a number line. In the next lesson, the students are introduced to irrational numbers using squares and square roots and asked to identify numbers that are rational versus irrational.

This chapter concludes by tying these concepts together with the Pythagorean Theorem. Students use a graphical approach to see the pattern of the Pythagorean Theorem and then are shown the formula. Students finish the chapter by working on real world problems that need the Pythagorean Theorem to determine the solution.

## The Big Picture

| Links to the Past | Chapter 7 | Links to the Future |
|---|---|---|
| **Course 1, Chapter 2** (pp. 56–107) Fractions and Decimals | **Lesson 7.1** (p. 320) Rational Numbers | **Course 3, Chapter 7** (pp. 310–371) Inequalities and Linear Systems |
| **Course 1, Chapter 2** (pp. 56–107) Fractions and Decimals<br>**Course 1, Chapter 7** (pp. 396–465) Area, Volume, and Capacity | **Lesson 7.2** (p. 331) Irrational Numbers | **Course 3, Chapter 4** (pp. 144–203) Exponents and Exponential Variation<br>**Course 3, Chapter 9** (pp. 464–521) Solve Quadratic Equations |
| **Course 1, Chapter 1** (pp. 2–55) Polygons, Angles, and Circles<br>**Course 1, Chapter 7** (pp. 396–465) Area, Volume, and Capacity | **Lesson 7.3** (p. 343) The Pythagorean Theorem | **Course 3, Chapter 4** (pp. 144–203) Exponents and Exponential Variation<br>**Course 3, Chapter 9** (pp. 464–521) Solve Quadratic Equations |

# Mathematical Background

**Squaring and Square Roots** The operations of squaring a number and finding the square root of a number have natural geometric interpretations. The area of a square is equal to the square of a length of a side. The square root of the area of a square is equal to the length of a side of the square. The squaring and square root operations are used in the final lesson of the chapter, where students study the Pythagorean Theorem.

**The Pythagorean Theorem** If a right triangle *ABC* has legs of length $a$ and $b$, and a hypotenuse of length $c$, then $c^2 = a^2 + b^2$.

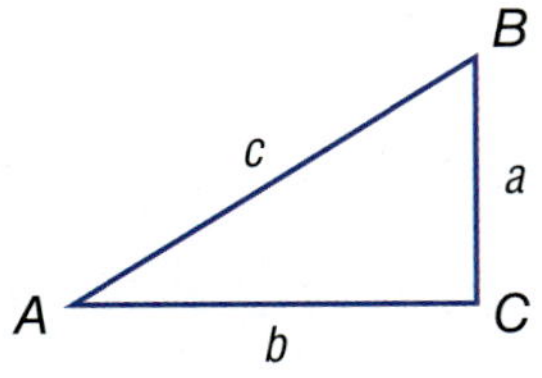


Another way of saying that is that the distance between points *A* and *B* is $\sqrt{a^2 + b^2}$.

The Pythagorean relationship also tells where the circumference points of circles are, in relationship to the center. Imagine all the points that are one specific distance, say 5, from the origin of a graph. They form a circle around the origin, with a radius of 5. Here's a picture.

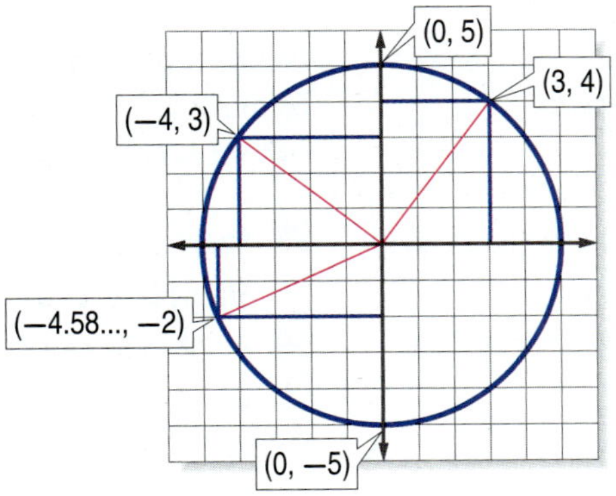


It appears that the point (3, 4) is on the circle. How could we know that it is exactly (3, 4), and not, say, (3.0000001, 4.0000237)?

The point (3, 4) is exactly 4 units from the *horizontal* axis, and exactly 3 units from the *vertical* axis. We see a right triangle. If its hypotenuse is 5, then the point (3, 4) would be 5 units from the origin, which would put it on the circle. $3^2 + 4^2 = 9 + 16 = 25 = 5^2$, so (3, 4) is on the circle. This is the Pythagorean relationship again:

$c^2 = a^2 + b^2$ where $c = 5$, $a = 3$, and $b = 4$ gives $5^2 = 3^2 + 4^2$

So (0, 5), (0, −5), (−4, 3), and infinitely many other points like (−4.58257569. . ., −2), whose coordinates, when squared and added, produce $5^2$.

The distance formula is derived from the Pythagorean Theorem. It will take on added meaning for your students when they take geometry and still more meaning in trigonometry.

## *Additional Reading*

According to Marzano, Pickering, and Pollock in *Classroom Instruction that Works: Research Based Strategies for Increasing Student Achievement,* the mental operations for comparing and classifying are central to thinking. In Lesson 7.1, students compare and classify numbers as in number sets. In Lesson 7.2, students classify real numbers as rational or irrational.

CHAPTER 7

# Planning Guide

## *Lesson Resources*

| | Lesson 7.1 (Pacing: 3 days) | Lesson 7.2 (Pacing: 3 days) | Lesson 7.3 (Pacing: 4 days) |
|---|---|---|---|
| **Lesson Title** | **Rational Numbers** (p. 320) | **Irrational Numbers** (p. 331) | **The Pythagorean Theorem** (p. 343) |
| **Lesson Objectives** | • To explore the relationship between number sets<br>• To use Venn diagrams to represent number sets<br>• To compare and order rational numbers<br>• To place rational numbers on a number line | • To relate square roots to the side length of a square<br>• To find the square root of a perfect square<br>• To approximate the square root of a number<br>• To place square roots and irrational numbers on a number line<br>• To classify a number as rational or irrational | • To determine a graphical understanding of the Pythagorean theorem<br>• To develop an understanding of how a right triangle and squares are related through the Pythagorean theorem<br>• To use the Pythagorean theorem to determine the missing side length or hypotenuse length of a right triangle<br>• To determine and use the distance formula |
| **Materials** | Chapter Master 1 | large number line | Lesson 7.3 Masters 1, 2, grid paper, ruler |
| ***Quick Review Math Handbook*** | **Lesson 2.9** Fraction, Decimal, and Percent Relationships | **Lesson 3.1** Powers and Exponents<br>**Lesson 3.2** Square Roots | **Lesson 5.3** Evaluating Expressions and Formulas<br>**Lesson 6.9** Pythagorean Theorem |
| **Print Resources** | CRM Study Guide and Intervention (p. 4)<br>CRM Skills Practice (p. 5)<br>CRM Problem-Solving Practice (p. 6)<br>CRM Enrichment (p. 7)<br>• Investigation Notebook and Reflection Journal<br>• Differentiation Handbook | CRM Study Guide and Intervention (p. 9)<br>CRM Skills Practice (p. 10)<br>CRM Problem-Solving Practice (p. 11)<br>CRM Enrichment (p. 12)<br>• Investigation Notebook and Reflection Journal<br>• Differentiation Handbook | CRM Study Guide and Intervention (p. 14)<br>CRM Skills Practice (p. 15)<br>CRM Problem-Solving Practice (p. 16)<br>CRM Enrichment (p. 17)<br>• Investigation Notebook and Reflection Journal<br>• Differentiation Handbook |
| **Technology Resources** | TeacherWorks Plus<br>Classroom Presentation Toolkit<br>ExamView Assessment Suite<br>StudentWorks Plus<br>Math Online Brain Pops • Concepts in Motion | TeacherWorks Plus<br>Classroom Presentation Toolkit<br>ExamView Assessment Suite<br>StudentWorks Plus<br>Math Online Brain Pops • Concepts in Motion | TeacherWorks Plus<br>Classroom Presentation Toolkit<br>ExamView Assessment Suite<br>StudentWorks Plus<br>Math Online Brain Pops • Concepts in Motion |

*Included in the Impact Mathematics Manipulative Kit

# Assessment Resources

## MARS Assessment: Teaching with Purpose

**Glass**

In *Glass,* students use geometry in a practical situation to calculate whether a glass window will fit through a doorway.

**Targeting the Task**

- **Diagnostic**—Use the Exercise in the *Glass* assessment to determine students' understanding of how to change dimensions to inches and how to use geometry to calculate the diagonal distance of the doorway. For those students who do not have this understanding, completing this unit is needed.
- **Formative**—The Exercise can be administered individually according to the lesson.
- **Summative**—Administer the complete *Glass* performance-based assessment.

CRM **Chapter 7 MARS Assessment** (pp. 37–40)

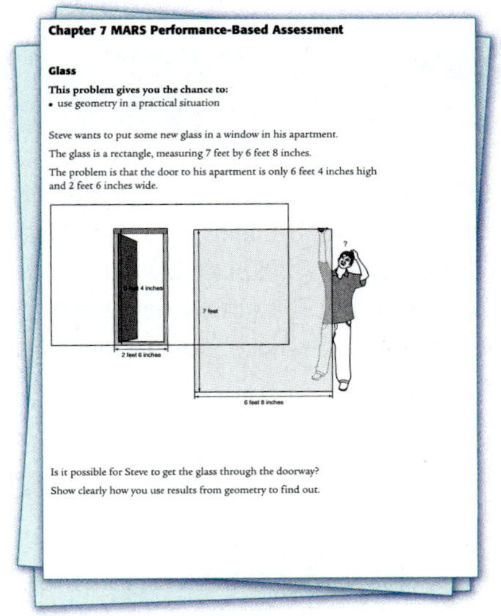
**Chapter 7 MARS Performance-Based Assessment**

**Glass**

**This problem gives you the chance to:**
- use geometry in a practical situation

Steve wants to put some new glass in a window in his apartment.

The glass is a rectangle, measuring 7 feet by 6 feet 8 inches.

The problem is that the door to his apartment is only 6 feet 4 inches high and 2 feet 6 inches wide.



Is it possible for Steve to get the glass through the doorway?

Show clearly how you use results from geometry to find out.

## Assessment Planning Guide

Assessments are available for investigations, lessons, and chapters.

ExamView Assessment Suite — Customize and create multiple versions of tests and quizzes.

| | Student Edition | Teacher Edition | Other Resources |
|---|---|---|---|
| **Diagnostic** | | | CRM Chapter 7 Pretest (pp. 21–24)<br>Math Online Online Chapter Quiz |
| **Formative** | Share & Summarize (pp. 323, 327, 335, 338, 347, 350) | Troubleshooting (pp. 322, 323, 325, 326, 333, 338, 344, 346, 347, 350)<br>On the Spot Assessment (pp. 325, 335, 343, 348)<br>Quick Check (pp. 330, 342, 360)<br>Quick Quiz (pp. 330, 342, 360) | CRM Quick Quiz (pp. 8, 13, 18) |
| **Summative** | Review & Self-Assessment (pp. 361–365) | | CRM Chapter 7 Test: Forms A and B (pp. 25–34)<br>CRM Standardized Test Practice (p. 41–42) |
| **Performance-Based** | In Your Own Words (pp. 330, 341, 360) | | CRM Chapter Performance Assessment (pp. 35–36)<br>CRM MARS Performance-Based Assessment (pp. 37–40) |

# Differentiated Instruction

## *Reaching* All Learners

Below are suggestions on differentiating the materials presented in this chapter. Additional modifications should be considered.

### Approaching Level AL

**Number Lines** In Lesson 7.1, have students write 6 numbers on a sheet of paper. Ask students to exchange papers. Their task is to order the numbers and place the numbers in their proper locations on a number line. This activity can be repeated with Lesson 7.2 by having the students make sure that at least 2 of their 6 numbers are irrational.

### Beyond Level BL

**Irrational Numbers** In Lesson 7.2 have students work in teams of two to determine a place in the real world where irrational numbers are used. Ask the pairs to identify the industry where the numbers are found as well as the specific task that the irrational numbers take their place. Ask the pairs to present their findings to the class in a visual manner, this could be a computer presentation, a video, a poster, anything that can be viewed by others.

### On Level OL

**Triangles** In Lesson 7.3 have students create a situation that mimics a real world scenario where the Pythagorean Theorem would be needed to complete the calculation. An example would be to find the number of tiles needed to fill tile a floor if the only measurement given were the length and the diagonal. Ask students to create the scenario and then to work out the solution. Include detailed notes about how they performed each step of the calculation.

### English Language Learners ELL

**Definitions** As a review of Lesson 7.1 and 7.2 have students work in teams to identify numbers that are rational and irrational. Now ask the students to define a rational number and an irrational number. It may be easier for the students to write their responses in their first language and then to translate their work into English. Ask the students to share their definitions. Discuss the similarities and differences. Are these differences acceptable?

**KEY**

AL Approaching Level OL On Level BL Beyond Level ELL English Language Learners

## Intervention Planning Guide

CRM Assess students' prerequisite skills and knowledge using the **Chapter Pretest** found in the Chapter 7 Resource Masters, p. 21.

| **Intensive Intervention** two or more years below grade level | **Strategic Intervention** below grade level | **On Level** | **Beyond Level** |
|---|---|---|---|
| **If** students miss 75% of the exercises: | **If** students miss 50% of the exercises: | **If** students miss 25% of the exercises: | **If** students miss 0%–10% of the exercises: |
| **Then** use *Math Triumphs,* an intensive intervention | **Then** choose a resource: | **Then** choose a resource: | **Then** choose a resource: |
| *Math Triumphs,* Grade 7<br>• Chapter 5: Two-Dimensional Figures<br>• Chapter 9: Variables and Expressions | CRM Study Guide and Intervention (pp. 4, 9, 14)<br>• Investigation Notebook and Reflection Journal<br>• Differentiation Handbook<br>Math Online Brain Pops • Concepts in Motion | CRM Skills Practice (pp. 5, 10, 15)<br>CRM Problem-Solving Practice (pp. 6, 11, 16)<br>• Investigation Notebook and Reflection Journal | CRM Enrichment (pp. 7, 12, 17)<br>• Differentiation Handbook |

### Literature Connections

**Recommended Outside Reading for Students**

**Nonfiction**

Vancleave, Janice Pratt. *Janice Vancleave's Geometry for Every Kid: Easy Activities That Make Learning Geometry Fun.* John Wiley & Sons, 1994.

This book from the Science for Every Kid series presents geometry concepts through fun activities. Students can use the activities to reinforce what they learn in this chapter about areas of parallelograms, triangles, trapezoids, and circles.

**Fiction**

Neuschwander, Cindy. *Sir Cumference and the Great Knight of Angleland: A Math Adventure.* Charlesbridge Publishing, 2001.

In this story, Sir Cumference's son, Radius, must complete a quest. Students will enjoy reading this fanciful tale about the geometric figures they study in this chapter.

### McGraw-Hill Professional Development

Targeted professional development has been articulated throughout the *IMPACT Mathematics* series. The **McGraw-Hill Professional Development Video Library** provides short videos that support the mathematics standards. Log on to www.glencoe.com.

Model Lessons

Instructional Strategies

CHAPTER 7

# Real Numbers

## Introduce

**Real-Life Math** Have students read the paragraph about Malina and her commute to school. Ask students if the situation is something that they can relate to, if not, ask the students to describe a similar situation that results in the formation of a right triangle. It may be useful to record what the students share to use in class discussions or on future forms of assessment.

**Think About It** Use probing questions, such as what needs to be added to the picture to show Malina's route straight to school, what shape is now formed, and how would they determine the distance represented by the hypotenuse to get students to think about the details that they need in order to answer the question.

CHAPTER 7

# Real Numbers

### Contents in Brief



## Real-Life Math

**Follow the Bike Path** Malina lives three miles from her school. On Saturdays, she bikes to school to participate in track practices and meets. She travels two miles east along McKinley Avenue and one mile north along Roosevelt. Because there is an abandoned factory on the land between McKinley and Roosevelt, Malina cannot bike directly from her house to the school.

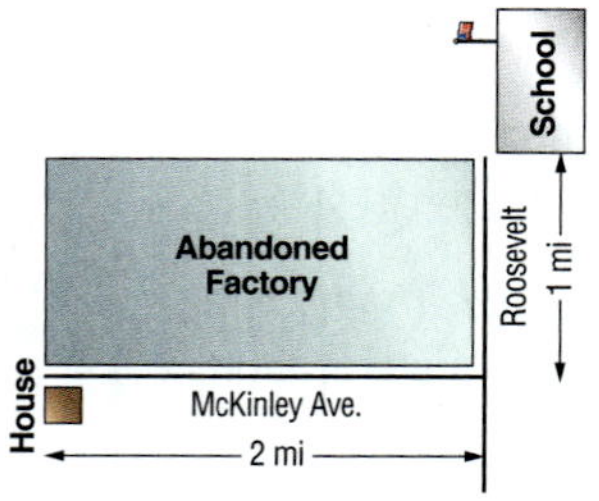

**Think About It** The mayor has proposed tearing down the factory and developing a park with bike paths in its place. Suppose a bike path runs from Malina's house to the school. How would this bike path affect her commute? Malina's commute would be about 0.76 mile shorter each way.

**Math Online** Take the **Chapter Readiness Quiz** at glencoe.com.



### Chapter Resources

- CRM Chapter 7 Resource Masters
- CRM English/Spanish Family Letter (pp. 1–2)
- CRM Lesson Masters (pp. 19–20)
- CRM Chapter 7 Pretest (pp. 21–24)
- CRM Chapter 7 Test (pp. 25–34)
- Math Online Online Readiness Quiz • eGlossary

# Dear Family,

In the elementary grades, students study the set of whole numbers, {0, 1, 2, 3, ...}. They also start working with fractions and decimals. In the middle grades, students expand their knowledge of numbers to include integers, {−3, −2, −1, 0, 1, 2, 3, ...}, and other signed numbers, such as $-2\frac{1}{2}$ and −0.75.

Any number that can be written as the ratio of two integers is called a **rational number**. In this chapter, your student will compare and order rational numbers.

### Key Concept–Ordering Rational Numbers

When ordering numbers, your student may find it helpful to first write numbers as whole numbers or decimals.

$$\{\sqrt{4}, -2\tfrac{1}{2}, 1^3, -0.75\} = \{2, -2.5, 1, -0.75\}$$

The number located furthest to the left on the number line has the least value. The number located furthest to right has the greatest value. The set {−2.5, −0.75, 1, 2} lists the numbers from least to greatest.

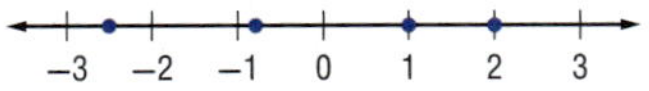


The class will also study **irrational numbers**, such as $\sqrt{5}$. Finally, your student will use rational and irrational numbers when applying the Pythagorean Theorem.

### Chapter Vocabulary

| | |
|---|---|
| **irrational number** | **rational number** |
| **Pythagorean Theorem** | **real number** |

### Home Connections

- Order numbers that you encounter in daily situations. Consider using grocery store or department store circulars to compare and order prices.
- Working with a map, determine the horizontal and vertical distances between two towns. Then, determine the diagonal distance between the same two towns. Use the Pythagorean Theorem to verify your measurements.

## Family Letter

Another version of the Family Letter, available in English and Spanish, is found in the Chapter 7 Resource Masters. You may want to send a copy of this letter home with your students.

**Key Concept–Ordering Rational Numbers** It is essential for students to find a method that is comfortable for them to determine the order of numbers. Suggest turning all numbers into decimals, start from least to greatest because that is how we read a number line. These suggestions will help students internalize the concept of ordering numbers.

### Home Activities

- Ask students to ask their families how they use the concept of ordering items in their daily lives. This does not necessarily have to be ordering numbers.
- Have the students draw a map for their family members. Instruct the students to have 2 or 3 locations that are connected by at least 2 vertical and 2 horizontal distances. Next, have the students ask their family members how they could get from one location to the next faster? Guide the students to guide their families into creating a triangle. Finally have the students ask their families how they would determine the distance of this line. Encourage students to measure and use the Pythagorean Theorem to find the correct distance.

## Key Vocabulary

**English (Spanish)** *Introduce the most important terms from Chapter 7.*

**real numbers (numeros reales)** The set of rational and irrational numbers. All the numbers that can be located on the number line. (p. 336)

**irrational numbers (números irracionales)** Numbers that cannot be written as ratios of two integers. In decimal form, irrational numbers are non-terminating and non-repeating. Examples of irrational numbers include $\pi$, $\sqrt{17}$, and $3\sqrt{2}$. (p. 336)

**Pythagorean Theorem (teorema de Pitágoras)** If $a$ and $b$ are the measures of the legs of a right triangle and $c$ is the measure of the hypotenuse, then $c^2 = a^2 + b^2$. (p. 345)

**rational numbers (números racionales)** Numbers that can be written as ratios of two integers. In decimal form, rational numbers are terminating or repeating. For example, 5, 20.274, and 0.3 are rational numbers. (p. 320)

LESSON

# 7.1 Rational Numbers

### Objectives

- ▶ To explore the relationship between number sets
- ▶ To use Venn diagrams to represent number sets
- ▶ To compare and order rational numbers
- ▶ To place rational numbers on a number line

## *Overview*

This lesson reviews and extends what students know about rational numbers. Students will explore the relationship between number sets and represent the number sets with Venn diagrams. They will use number lines to compare and order rational numbers, including negative rational numbers, and explore how to subdivide intervals on the number line so that rational numbers can be placed on a number line accurately.

## *Advance Preparation*

You may want to provide Chapter Master 1 so students can place rational numbers on number lines accurately.

| | Summary | Materials | On Your Own Exercises (pp. 328–330) | Assessment Opportunities |
|---|---|---|---|---|
| **Investigation 1** (p. 320)<br>Pacing: 2 days | Students explore the relationship between number sets. | | Practice & Apply: 1–13<br>Connect & Extend: 23<br>Mixed Review: 25–36 | • Share & Summarize (p. 323)<br>• Troubleshooting (pp. 322, 323) |
| **Investigation 2** (p. 324)<br>Pacing: 1 day | Students place rational numbers on a number line. | Chapter Master 1 | Practice & Apply: 14–22<br>Connect & Extend: 24<br>Mixed Review: 25–36 | • On the Spot Assessment (p. 325)<br>• Share & Summarize (p. 327)<br>• Troubleshooting (pp. 325, 326) |

# Leveled Lesson Resources

CRM *Available in:* **Chapter 7 Resource Masters**

Also on TeacherWorks™ Lesson 7.1

## Study Guide and Intervention (p. 4) AL

**Lesson 7.1 Study Guide and Intervention**
***Rational Numbers***

To compare fractions, write them in decimal form or locate them on a number line. A rational number is a number that can be written as a ratio of two integers. Integers include positive counting numbers, their opposites, and zero. Natural numbers are counting numbers. Whole numbers are counting numbers plus zero.

**Example 1** Consider the numbers below. Identify to which set(s) the numbers belong.

**1.** −8

**Answer:** −8 belongs to the integers and rational numbers, since it is a negative number that can be written as a ratio of $-\frac{8}{1}$.

**2.** $\frac{6}{7}$

**Answer:** $\frac{6}{7}$ belongs to the rational numbers since it is a ratio of two integers.

**Example 2** Which fraction is greater, $\frac{3}{4}$ or $\frac{4}{5}$?

Method 1 Write each fraction as a decimal. Then compare decimals.

$\frac{3}{4} = 0.75$

$\frac{4}{5} = 0.8$

Since 0.8 > 0.75, then $\frac{4}{5} > \frac{3}{4}$.

Method 2 Graph the numbers on a number line.

Since 0.8 is farther to the right on the number line, it is the greater number.

**Exercises**

**Consider the numbers below. They are natural numbers, whole numbers, integers, and rational numbers. Identify to which set(s) the numbers belong.**

**1.** 102
**2.** $-\frac{4}{9}$
**3.** 6.057
**4.** $3^2$
**5.** 0
**6.** −5

**Identify which number is greater. Explain how you found your answer.**

**7.** $\frac{1}{2}$ or 0.75
**8.** −2.4 or $-\frac{9}{4}$
**9.** $-3^{-2}$ or $-\frac{1}{6}$
**10.** 0.64 or $\frac{1}{8}$
**11.** $\frac{4}{3}$ or 1.25
**12.** −0.7 or $-\frac{7}{8}$

## Skills Practice (p. 5) AL OL

**Lesson 7.1 Skills Practice**
***Rational Numbers***

**Write a number that fits the conditions given. If no such number exists, write "impossible."**

**1.** a natural number between 5 and 7
**2.** an integer that is less than −2
**3.** a rational number that is a whole number
**4.** an integer between −7.45 and −8.16
**5.** a rational number between $\frac{1}{2}$ and $\frac{3}{4}$
**6.** a counting number between 12.68 and 13.24

**Graph the numbers on the number line. Then write the numbers in order from least to greatest.**

**7.** $\frac{3}{2}$, −0.25, 0.8
**8.** 5.7, $5\frac{1}{3}$, 5.01

**Use a number line to graph the numbers. Label the number line to indicate its scale.**

**9.** 0.8, −2, $1\frac{1}{2}$, $-\frac{9}{10}$

**10.** 6.3, $6\frac{5}{8}$, 6.02, $\frac{37}{6}$, 7

## Problem-Solving Practice (p. 6) AL OL

**Lesson 7.1 Problem-Solving Practice**
***Rational Numbers***

Solve.

**1. Rain** The amount of rainfall was measured after a recent storm. The north side of town received 0.87 inch of rain, and the south side received $\frac{13}{15}$-inch of rain. Which side of town received more rain from the storm?

**2. Secret Number** Tanisha is thinking of a number that when it is squared it is smaller than itself. When it is multiplied by 4 it is an integer. When it is added to itself it is a whole number. What is Tanisha's number?

**3. Secret Number** Roshad is thinking of an even number. When it is divided by 4 it is an odd number. His number squared is greater than 100, but less than 200. What is his number?

**4. Science** A sample in an experiment should be kept as close to 0°C as possible. A lab technician tests the temperature of the sample every hour. One morning the temperatures were 0.4°C, −1.5°C, 0.08°C, and −0.62°C. Which temperature was closest to 0°C? Which was furthest from it?

**5. Transportation** My-Lien has enough room in her truck to move 3.385 tons of gravel. Her father has asked her to move $3\frac{5}{16}$ tons. Will My-Lien be able to move all of the gravel in only one trip? Explain.

**6. Wood Working** Kishi has a bolt that is $\frac{5}{8}$-inch wide, and she drilled a hole 0.6 inch wide. Is the hole large enough to fit the bolt? Explain.

**7. Quality Control** Three auto parts failed a quality control check. The first part was $\frac{1}{12}$ mm more than the acceptable mark. The second was 0.05 mm more than the mark. The third was 0.18 mm less than the mark. List the measures of the parts' variation from the acceptable mark from least to greatest.

**8. Studying** For a recent algebra exam, Pat studied $1\frac{8}{15}$ hours, Toni studied 1.55 hours, and Morgan studied $1\frac{9}{16}$ hours. List the students in order, starting with the student who studied the most.

## Enrichment (p. 7) BL

**Lesson 7.1 Enrichment**
***Rational Numbers***

**Intersection and Union of Sets**

The darker shaded areas in the Venn diagrams show the *intersection* and *union* of sets *A* and *B*.

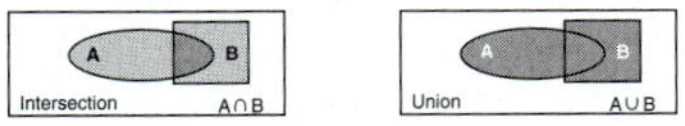


For example, if *A* = {1, 2, 3, 4} and *B* = {3, 4, 5, 6}, then their intersection and union are written as:

Intersection: $A \cap B = \{3, 4\}$ Union: $A \cup B = \{1, 2, 3, 4, 5, 6\}$

**Draw a Venn diagram that shows the relationship between each pair of sets. Then list the numbers included in A ∩ B and A ∪ B. In Exercises 2 and 4, record the numbers as decimals.**

**1.** *A* = {integers between 0 and 13}
*B* = {whole number factors of 12}

**2.** *A* = {rational numbers rounded to the tenths place between 0 and 0.6}
*B* = {fractions with 1, 2, 3, or 4 as numerator and 5 as a denominator}

**3.** *A* = {perfect squares between 0 and 30}
*B* = {odd whole numbers less than 10}

**4.** $A = \left\{\frac{1}{2}, \frac{1}{3}, \frac{1}{4}, \frac{1}{5}\right\}$
$B = \{0.\overline{1}, 0.\overline{2}, 0.\overline{3}, 0.\overline{4}, 0.\overline{5}, 0.\overline{6}, 0.\overline{7}, 0.\overline{8}, 0.\overline{9}\}$

## Lesson Quick Quiz (p. 8) AL OL BL

**Lesson 7.1 Quick Quiz**

**For Exercises 1–3, identify to which set(s) each of the following numbers belongs: the natural numbers, whole numbers, integers, or rational numbers.**

**1.** 3.241

**2.** $4^2$

**3.** $-\frac{3}{8}$

**For Exercises 4–6, use the following numbers.**

$-1.03, -\frac{5}{4}, -\frac{21}{8}, -\frac{112}{110}, -2.194, -\frac{1{,}087}{1{,}000}$

**4.** Which numbers are less than −1 and greater than −1.5?

**5.** Which numbers are less than −1 and greater than −1.1?

**6.** Which numbers are less than −1 and greater than −1.01?

**7.** Graph and label each of the numbers below on a number line.

$\frac{38}{100}, \frac{3}{8}, 0.365, \frac{4}{9}, \frac{5}{11}, \frac{325}{1{,}000}$

# Additional Lesson Resources

### Teacher Tech Tools

- TeacherWorks
- ExamView Assessment Suite
- Classroom Presentation Toolkit
- Advance Tracker

### Student Tech Tools

- StudentWorks Plus
- Math Online eGlossary • Concepts in Motion

### Other Print Products

- Investigation Notebook and Reflection Journal
- Quick Review Math Handbook

## LESSON 7.1 Rational Numbers

### Introduce

**Rational Numbers** Introduce this lesson by reminding students about the benchmark fractions like $\frac{1}{2}, \frac{1}{3}, \frac{1}{4}$ that are familiar. Define *rational number* as a number that can be written as the ratio of two integers, and point out that each of the benchmark fractions is a rational number. It might be helpful to give nonexamples of rational numbers like $\frac{\pi}{2}$, which is a quotient but not a rational number.

**Think & Discuss**

As students answer these questions, remind them of the last part of the definition of a rational number, " … or quotient, of two integers." When analyzing questions regarding rational numbers, it is always helpful to write the number in quotient, or fractional form. When dealing with zero, it is important to show students how zero is rational. It is also important to show students that any number divided by zero is NOT rational. Use an example such as $\frac{17}{0}$ and show that this is undefined through the definition of division. Ask students how you would take 17 items and break them up into groups of zero, which is impossible.

**Investigation 1**

***On Your Own Exercises***
Pages 328–330
Exercises 1–13, 23

**Number Sets** In this investigation, students explore the relationship between number sets. Point out that there is much overlap in these sets.

### Develop & Understand: A

*Suggested Grouping: Pairs*

▶ **Exercises 1–4** Point out that each of the numbers in these exercises is a rational number and that students are looking for other sets to which these numbers belong. For Exercise 4, emphasize that $8^2$ should be simplified before identifying the number set.



# LESSON 7.1 Rational Numbers



**Vocabulary**

- natural numbers
- rational numbers
- whole numbers

Integers and fractions such as $\frac{1}{2}$ and $\frac{7}{10}$ are rational numbers. The word *rational* comes from the word *ratio*, which should help you remember the definition of a rational number. A **rational number** is a number that can be written as the ratio, or quotient, of two integers.

**Think & Discuss**

Is 0.5 a rational number? Why or why not? See ①.

Is $0.\overline{3}$ a rational number? Why or why not? See ②.

Is 0 a rational number? Why or why not? Yes; It can be written as the quotient of zero and any nonzero number, such as $\frac{0}{1}$.

① Yes; It can be written as $\frac{5}{10}$ or $\frac{1}{2}$.
② Yes; It can be written as $\frac{1}{3}$.

You have already worked with special sets of numbers, such as odd and even numbers, prime numbers, and negative numbers. In Investigation 1, you will explore the relationship between number sets.

**Natural numbers** are counting numbers and can be represented as {1, 2, 3, ...}. **Whole numbers** are the counting numbers plus zero and can be represented as {0, 1, 2, 3, ...}. Integers are the counting numbers, their opposites, and zero, {..., −3, −2, −1, 0, 1, 2, 3, ...}.

## Investigation 1 Number Sets

In this investigation, you will explore the relationship among four number sets.

### Develop & Understand: A

Consider the four sets of numbers: natural, whole, integers, and rational. To which set(s) does each of the following numbers belong? For example, 0 belongs to the wholes, integers, and rationals.

1. −50 Integers, rationals
2. $2.\overline{6}$ Rationals
3. $-\frac{3}{4}$ Rationals
4. $8^2$ Naturals, wholes, integers, rationals



### Reaching All Learners

**ELL** **English Language Learners** Students learning English may have difficulty with the terminology on this page. Have them write a note card for each term that includes a description of the term and many examples of the term. Encourage them to look for the definitions of the terms in their native language, and then use the note cards to study for tests.

## Math Link

The number 6 is a rational number because it can be written as the ratio of 6 and 1, $\frac{6}{1}$. The decimal −1.8 is a rational number because it can be written as the ratio of −18 and 10, $-\frac{18}{10}$, or $-\frac{9}{5}$.

11. Possible answers: If you multiply two numbers in this set together, the product might not be an integer. If you divide one number in this set by another number in this set, the quotient must also be in this set.

For Exercises 5–11, indicate all the number sets (natural, whole, integers, and rational) for which the statement is always true. To be true for a set, the statement must be true for *all* the numbers in the set.

5. If you add two numbers in this set together, the sum must be greater than either of the numbers with which you started. Naturals, wholes
6. If you add two numbers in this set together, the sum must be greater than or equal to 0. Wholes, naturals
7. If you multiply three numbers in this set together, the product will be the same no matter the order in which you multiply them. Naturals, wholes, integers, rationals
8. If you multiply three numbers in this set together, the product might be a negative number. Integers, rationals
9. If you add two numbers in this set, you get a number in the same set. Naturals, wholes, integers, rationals
10. If you subtract two numbers in this set, you get a number in the same set. Integers, rationals
11. Write a statement that is true for the rational numbers but not for any of the other sets.

### Think & Discuss

Is Lucita's claim correct? See ①.

Would the same claim be true for integers? For whole numbers? For natural numbers? Yes, it would be true for all of them, though the claim, "I can always think of a *smaller* number in the set" would only be true for rational numbers and integers.

① Yes; You can always add 1 to a rational number and get a rational number. Whatever the denominator of a fraction is, you can write 1 as $\frac{n}{n}$, then add the two fractions to get a fraction whose denominator is $n$.



▶ **Exercises 5–10** Ask students to use examples to test the statements in these exercises. If they think Exercise 5, for example, is true for all integers, ask them to look for counterexamples of integers that do not fit the statement. Point out that it only takes one counterexample to say the statement is false.

▶ **Exercise 11** Ask students to check each other's statements and try to give a counterexample of their partner's statement.

### Think & Discuss

Make sure students understand that if you add any rational number like one to another rational number, you get a rational number. Discuss the kinds of problems that might arise if you tried to subtract any natural number from a natural number. One minus one is zero, and zero is not a natural number.

## Mathematical Background

Another property of the set of rational numbers is the property of *closure*. The set of rational numbers is said to be "closed under addition" because if you add two rational numbers, the sum is a rational number, or another number in the same set. The set of rational numbers is also closed under subtraction, multiplication, and division. For example, if you find $\frac{2}{3} + \frac{4}{5}$, $\frac{2}{3} \cdot \frac{4}{5}$, or $\frac{2}{3} \div \frac{4}{5}$, each answer is also a rational number.

**Teacher Tips** In these exercises, students explore how to use Venn diagrams to represent sets. You may want to show some examples on the overhead before assigning the exercises. Try to include an example that is non-mathematical, such as *Pets of Students* that would have non-intersecting circles for dogs, cats, mice, snakes, and so on.

## Develop & Understand: B

*Suggested Grouping: Pairs*

▶ **Exercise 12** Remind students that any numbers in the area that is shaded twice must be numbers in both sets. For this exercise, the numbers 3 and 5 are natural numbers that are also odd.

▶ **Exercise 13** If students are unfamiliar with Venn diagrams, they may not realize that −3 in this diagram is a number that is not in either of the circles, or sets. Point out that since −3 is an integer, they cannot answer "Integer" as one of the two sets the Venn diagram represents.

▶ **Exercise 15** If students are unfamiliar with drawing concentric circles, you may want to demonstrate how to do that for the class before asking students to work in pairs. Show them how the natural numbers are a subset of the whole numbers and how the set of whole numbers are a subset of the set of integers, and so on. Be sure to include examples of numbers for each set.

**Wrap-Up** Have students share their answers to Exercises 14 and 15. Ask volunteers to put their answers on the board and have other students add example numbers to their circles.

### Math Link

Ask students if they can think of examples of a Venn diagram that includes two circles that do not intersect. Possible answer: The set of even numbers and the set of odd numbers

### Math Link

Remember that in a Venn diagram, you need to be able to represent the intersection between each combination of sets, such as pairs, trios, or quartets of circles, as well as the part of each set that does not intersect the other.

## Develop & Understand: B

**12.** The following Venn diagram shows the relationship between the set of odd numbers and the set of natural numbers. Copy the diagram. In each section of the diagram, fill in at least three more numbers.

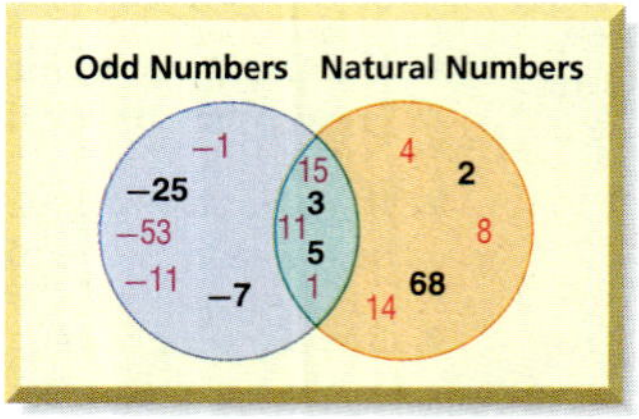


12. Many answers are possible. The intersection holds positive odd numbers, the rightmost area holds positive even numbers, the leftmost area holds negative odd numbers.

**13.** Which two sets could this Venn Diagram represent? Naturals and wholes

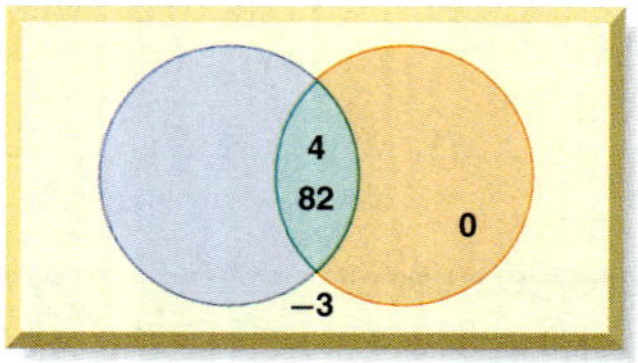


**14.** Draw a Venn diagram that shows the relationship between the integers and the whole numbers. Include at least three numbers in each section of the diagram.

**15.** Work with a partner to create a diagram with four concentric circles (circles having a common center) representing the natural numbers, whole numbers, integers, and rational numbers. Include sample numbers in each area of your diagram.

14.

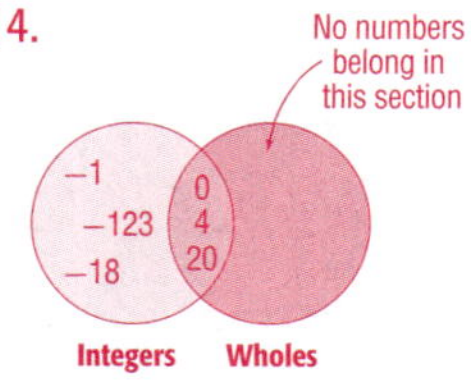


or

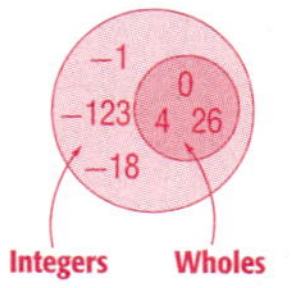


15.

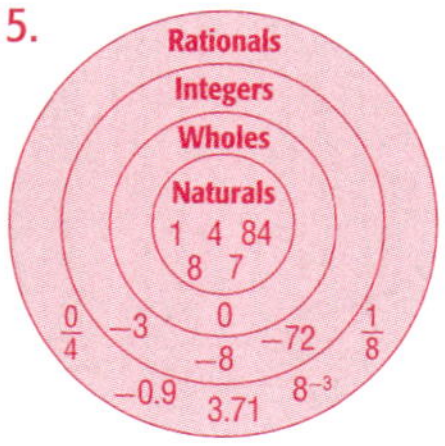


Anika, Haley, Antonio, and Kirk created number puzzles. Each student thought of a number and then gave clues so that the others could guess the secret number. Use your understanding of number sets to solve their number puzzles.

## Develop & Understand: C

For Exercises 16–18, the secret number lies between −10 and 10.

**16.** Anika's Puzzle  −1 or −3

- My number is not a natural number.
- My number is odd.
- If you add 5 to my number, the sum is a natural number.
- My number squared is more than my number doubled.



### Troubleshooting

Watch for students who do not draw their Venn diagrams correctly. Point out that data placed in the diagram has to have the specific attributes that are specified.

### Reaching All Learners

**BL Beyond Level** Challenge students to redo Exercise 15 to include numbers that are not rational numbers. That is, ask them to draw a box around the concentric circles representing the rational numbers and then think of the box as being the set of all real numbers. What are some examples of numbers that would not be in the circles but in the box? Possible answer: $\pi$

**17.** Haley's Puzzle $\frac{3}{4}$

- My number squared is smaller than my number itself.
- My number multiplied by 4 is an integer.
- My number multiplied by 10 is larger than 7.

**18.** Antonio's Puzzle 6

- My number is a whole number.
- My number is a multiple of 3.
- My number divided by 2 is an integer.

19. Many answers are possible. Possible answer: My number is bigger than 3 and smaller than 3.5

**19.** Kirk started to write a puzzle, but he was not sure how to finish it. His secret number is 3.25. Write another clue that would allow Anika and Haley to find out Kirk's secret number.

- My number is a rational number.
- My number is not an integer.
- My number is evenly divisible by $\frac{1}{4}$.

### Share & Summarize

Find a whole number that is not a natural number. 0

Find a rational number that is not a whole number. See ①.

Find an integer that is not a natural number. See ②.

Find an integer that is not a rational number. See ③.

If a number belongs to the set of whole numbers, to which other sets must it also belong? Integers and rationals. Unless the whole number happens to be 0, it also belongs to the naturals.

① Possible answers: $\frac{3}{4}$, $-1.2$

② Possible answers: $-2$, $-45$

③ There is no such number. All integers are rational numbers.



## Develop & Understand: C

*Suggested Grouping: Groups of 3*

▶ **Exercises 16–19** Have students share their puzzles in groups of four by doing this cooperative exercise: Have each student do one exercise and then pass his or her solution to the next student. The next student then checks the answer and provides another solution, if possible. Play continues by passing the puzzles again and repeating the instructions. After all students have done all four puzzles, have them discuss how they knew their answer for Exercise 19 is correct.

▶ **Exercise 19** You may need to give examples of numbers that are "evenly divisible by $\frac{1}{4}$" before you assign this exercise.

**Wrap-Up** Ask volunteers to discuss their solutions to the puzzles with the entire class. Ask them to explain why they know there are many answers possible for Exercise 19.

### Share & Summarize

Draw a Venn diagram on the board as you discuss these exercises and refer to it for each number chosen. Make sure students understand the context of each sentence that is stated, "Find a number that is not...." For the first question, point out that there is only one whole number that is not a natural number, the number zero.

## Troubleshooting

Watch for students who cannot answer the questions in the Share & Summarize because they cannot find numbers that fit more than one description. It may be easier for these students to find examples of numbers that are in the "not category" first, then fit them to the other description. For example, if students are trying to think of a number that is an integer but not a natural number, have them first think of a number that is not a natural number (like $-3$) and then ask if their choice is an integer.

## Investigation 2

***On Your Own Exercises***
Pages 328–330
Exercises 14–22, 24

**Compare and Order Rational Numbers**
Introduce this investigation by having a large number line displayed on the overhead or board and asking student volunteers to graph various rational numbers. Give them five or more numbers between zero and one to graph and ask them how they know there are more numbers there that are not yet shown on the graph. Then continue with the Think & Discuss exercise.

**Think & Discuss**
Make sure students understand that an infinite set is one with an endless number of members. Students may initially not grasp that just between the numbers 0 and 1 are an infinite number of other values.

**Teacher Notes** Here are two strategies to help students understand that there are always numbers between two others on a number line.

- Ask groups of students to each work with sections of the number line to subdivide the section in half several times. For example, if one group has the section between 2 and 3, ask those students to subdivide it in half until they show and label all the sixteenths in that interval. Then put together the sections to show the larger number line.
- Ask groups of students to each work with different sections of the number line and do a "round robin" activity. The first student in the group draws the section on paper and then places a number between the two points on that number line. Then he or she passes it to the next student and that student draws only one section of that number line and then places another number between the two points indicating that section. This continues until the time allotted ends or until all students have placed a number between two others on the number line.

# Investigation 2 Compare and Order Rational Numbers

**Think & Discuss**

How many rational numbers are there between 0 and 1? How do you know? See ①.

① There are an infinite number of rational numbers between 0 and 1. As the cartoon shows, you can always pick a number that is between 0 and whatever number you picked last. They never run out and just keep getting smaller.

Imagine a number line representing the set of integers. It goes on forever in both directions. Now imagine a new number line that is divided into smaller intervals. You can keep dividing the number line into smaller increments, finding numbers that are closer and closer together. No matter what two numbers you select, you can always find a number halfway between them.

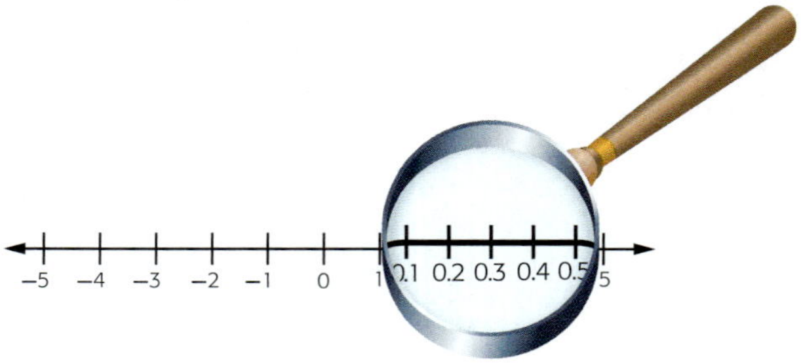


Number lines can help you compare rational numbers and arrange them in order of relative size. When you draw a number line, you have to select a scale. What are the least and greatest numbers you want to show on the line? What intervals will you mark along the line?

These answers depend on the range of numbers you need to graph and how easily you want to identify the location of the numbers. Whichever scale you use, there are always numbers between the ones you graph on the number line.



## *Reaching* All Learners

**AL Approaching Level** Students may have difficulty understanding how you can keep finding another rational number in between two others. Have them think of the rational numbers as decimals where they can always "tack on a 5" at the end of the decimal to get a smaller one. For example, to find a number between 3.1 and 3.2, "tack on a 5" to 3.1 to get 3.15. Point out that $3.1 < 3.15 < 3.2$. Convert these numbers to fractions to show they are rational numbers.

324 CHAPTER 7 Real Numbers

## Develop & Understand: A

**1.** Copy the number lines shown below. On each number line, graph the following numbers.

$\frac{1}{3}$ 0.338 $\frac{31}{100}$

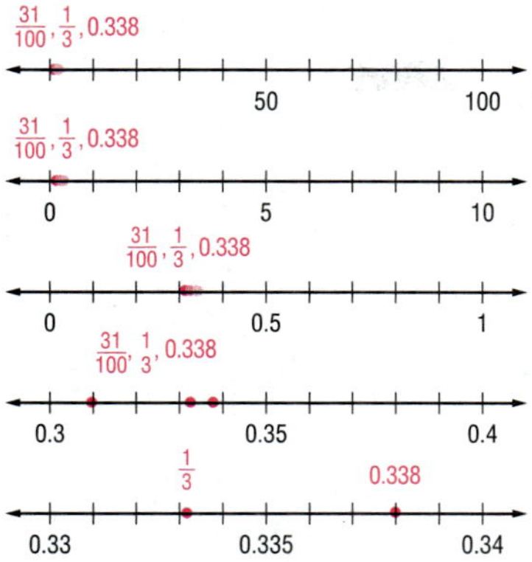


**2.** On which number lines can you graph all three numbers?

**3.** On which number line(s) can you graph the numbers most accurately?

**4.** How would you label a number line in order to graph $\frac{1}{3}$ exactly?

For Exercises 5–7, use the following numbers.

$-1.09$ $-\frac{6}{5}$ $-1\frac{1}{4}$ $-0.973$

$-\frac{113}{100}$ $-\frac{8}{9}$ $-1.902$ $-\frac{1{,}107}{1{,}000}$

**5.** Which numbers are less than $-1$ and greater than $-2$?

**6.** Which numbers are less than $-1.1$ and greater than $-1.2$?

**7.** Which number is less than $-1.11$ and greater than $-1.12$? None

**8.** Draw a number line to graph the numbers shown below. Label the number line to indicate its scale.

$10^{-2}$ $2^{-3}$ $10^{-1}$ $\frac{4}{25}$ $\frac{1}{5}$

$\frac{2}{20}$ $\frac{3}{100}$ 0.18 0.09

Check students' work. Possible number line shown.

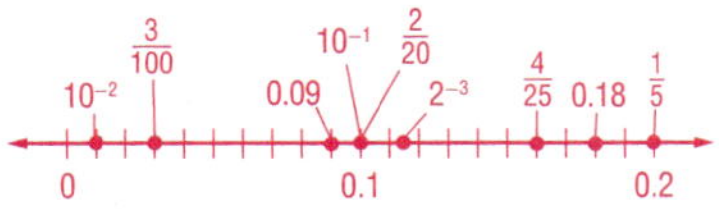


2. The first four; $\frac{31}{100}$ does not fit in the interval shown in the last one.

3. The fourth line showed $\frac{31}{100}$ exactly; the fifth line showed 0.338 exactly. If the fifth number line was extended, it would show $\frac{31}{100}$ exactly.

4. It would have to be labeled in thirds, instead of any power of 10. One-third as a decimal repeats forever. No matter how many decimal places you use to label the number line, $\frac{1}{3}$ will never be exactly on one of the marks.

5. $-1.09, -\frac{6}{5}, -1\frac{1}{4}, -\frac{113}{100}, -1.902, -\frac{1107}{1000}$

6. $-\frac{113}{100}, -\frac{1107}{1000}$



**Teacher Tips** Provide copies of Chapter Master 1 to help students make more accurate graphs. When working on Exercises 5–7, students may need a refresher in how to convert fractions to terminating decimals and the use of negative exponents. When answering Exercises 9–13, students may benefit from a quick review of how to compare fractions by finding the common denominator.

## Develop & Understand: A

*Suggested Grouping: Pairs*

▶ **Exercise 1** Have students compare and order these numbers before trying to graph them. Have them try to draw their own graph of the numbers before looking at the graphs in the exercise. Provide copies of Chapter Master 1 to increase their accuracy.

▶ **Exercise 2** Point out that the last graph in Exercise 1 does not show the graph of $\frac{31}{100}$. Ask students to describe the interval in this graph.

▶ **Exercises 5–7** Point out that students may need to convert the numbers to decimals before they can answer these questions.

▶ **Exercise 8** You may need to review how to evaluate a number raised to a negative power. For example, point out that $10^{-2}$ equals $\frac{1}{10^2}$, not $-10^2$.

**Wrap-Up** To wrap up Exercises 1 and 5–7, discuss how to subdivide intervals on a number line further and further until you can place a decimal or fraction accurately.

## Troubleshooting

Watch for students who confuse negative exponents with negative numbers in Exercise 8.

## On the Spot Assessment

Watch for students who have difficulty with the graphs in Exercise 1. The three given numbers are very close to each other in value, and you may need to have students express all three numbers as decimals to verify this. Have them brainstorm which number line they should use to represent these numbers clearly.

## Think & Discuss

*Suggested Grouping: Pairs*

Have students work with a partner to answer these questions. Have them discuss why finding a lowest common denominator is important when ordering fractions, and have them share their rule for finding a fraction halfway between two other fractions with the class.

**Teacher Tips** You may want to discuss the different strategies for estimating the value of a rational number shown in the cartoon. Ask students to think of other strategies and share them with a partner.

① Write each fraction using a common denominator. Find the mean, or average, of the numerators. Write the numerator over the common denominator. When necessary, multiply by 10 to obtain an integer value in the numerator. When necessary, simplify to lowest terms.

## Think & Discuss

What fraction, written in simplest form, is located halfway between $\frac{3}{4}$ and $\frac{5}{6}$? $\frac{19}{24}$

Can you find a general rule for finding a fraction that is halfway between two other fractions? See ①.

Can you find two more fractions between $\frac{3}{4}$ and $\frac{5}{6}$? See ②.

How many fractions are there between $\frac{3}{4}$ and $\frac{5}{6}$? See ③.

Ana, Marcus, and Simon use different strategies for estimating the value of a rational number and comparing two rational numbers. Consider their strategies, which are shown below.

② Yes; Possible answers: $\frac{7}{9}$, $\frac{29}{36}$

③ There are an infinite number of fractions between $\frac{3}{4}$ and $\frac{5}{6}$.

Which strategy appeals to you? What other strategies might you use?

In the exercises on page 327, you will graph rational numbers on a number line.



## Troubleshooting

Watch for students who think $\frac{4}{5}$ is a fraction between $\frac{3}{4}$ and $\frac{5}{6}$ in the Think & Discuss. Have them change the fractions to equivalent fractions with a common denominator before answering these questions.

## Develop & Understand: B

For these exercises, draw a number line that shows $-1$ and 0, like the one below. Graph $-\frac{1}{3}$ and $-\frac{2}{3}$.

Without folding or measuring, use your number line for Exercises 9–13.

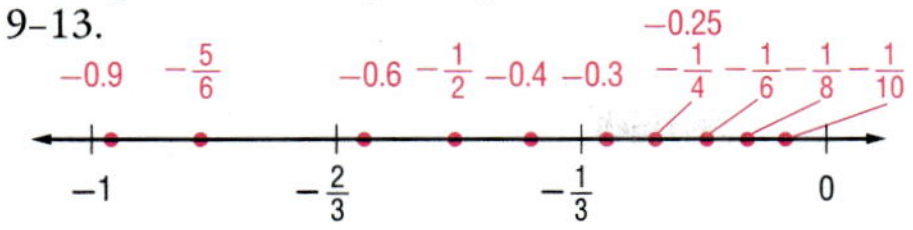


**9.** Graph $-\frac{1}{2}$.

**a.** How did you estimate the location of $-\frac{1}{2}$?

**b.** Is $-\frac{1}{2}$ closer to $-\frac{1}{3}$ or to $-\frac{2}{3}$? Explain your reasoning.

**10.** Mark the approximate location of $-\frac{1}{6}$ and $-\frac{5}{6}$ on the number line. Explain how you estimated the location of these numbers.

**11.** Mark the approximate location of $-\frac{1}{4}$ on the number line.

**a.** Explain how you estimated the location of $-\frac{1}{4}$. See margin.

**b.** Do you think your approximation of $-\frac{1}{4}$ is as accurate as your approximation of $-\frac{1}{6}$? See margin.

**12.** Consider the locations of $-\frac{1}{10}$ and $-\frac{1}{8}$.

**a.** Mark the approximate location of $-\frac{1}{10}$ on the number line. Check students' work.

**b.** Mark the approximate location of $-\frac{1}{8}$ on the number line. Check students' work.

**c.** When you tried to approximate $-\frac{1}{8}$, did that change your idea of where $-\frac{1}{10}$ ought to be? See margin.

**13.** Mark the approximate location of $-0.3$ and $-0.4$ on the number line. Explain your reasoning. See margin.

### Share & Summarize

Consider the following numbers.

$-1.3 \qquad \frac{17}{20} \qquad -\frac{7}{8} \qquad 5^{-2} \qquad \frac{123}{100} \qquad 1.92$

If you were going to put them on a number line, what range of points could you choose so that you could show all of the numbers? Possible answer: $-1.5$, 2

What scale would you need to use for the number line if you wanted to place each of the numbers exactly? You would need to divide the line into thousandths.

If you graphed these numbers on a number line divided into tenths, which ones would you have to approximate? Would it be easy to show the order of the numbers? See ①.

**Math Link**

To locate $-\frac{1}{3}$ and $-\frac{2}{3}$ precisely, you can measure with a ruler or you can fold the number line into three equal parts and mark where the folds are.

9a. Possible answer: I tried to graph the point halfway between $-1$ and 0.

9b. It is the same distance from both because $-\frac{1}{2}$ is exactly between $-1$ and 0, and $-\frac{1}{3}$ is the same distance from 0 as $-\frac{2}{3}$ is from $-1$. So, $-\frac{1}{3}$ and $-\frac{2}{3}$ must be equally close to the midpoint of $-\frac{1}{2}$.

10. Possible answer: $-\frac{1}{6}$ is exactly halfway between 0 and $-\frac{1}{3}$; $-\frac{5}{6}$ is exactly halfway between $-1$ and $-\frac{2}{3}$.

① All of the numbers except $-1.3$ would be approximate. It would still be easy to show the numbers in order, because no two would fall between the same two tenth-marks. In decimal form, each of these numbers has a different tenths digit.



## Develop & Understand: B

*Suggested Grouping: Pairs*

▶ **Exercises 9–13** You may want to review how to compare the negative integers before you assign these exercises. Point out that $-2 < -1$ because $-2$ is to the left of $-1$ on the number line.

▶ **Exercise 9** Help students make the connection that since $-\frac{2}{3}$ and $-\frac{1}{3}$ are negative, $-\frac{2}{3} < -\frac{1}{3}$, or $-\frac{2}{3}$ is to the left of $-\frac{1}{3}$ on the number line. Then help them compare $-\frac{1}{2}$ to $-\frac{2}{3}$ so they can place $-\frac{1}{2}$ on the number line. Ask them if they need to change the fractions to ones with common denominators before they compare them.

▶ **Exercise 11** Students may have difficulty placing or estimating $-\frac{1}{4}$ on the number line. Use common denominators, if necessary, to compare fourths and sixths, or place $\frac{1}{4}$ and $\frac{1}{6}$ on the positive side of the number line to give a visual of where the fractions should be. Then "flip" the fractions to the other side of the number line.

**Wrap-Up** Display a large number line showing halves, thirds, and fourths between $-1$ and 0 as you discuss Exercises 9–13 with the class. Then use it to help place the other fractions in these exercises.

### Share & Summarize

Students will have a tendency to draw a number line with integers as labels for tick marks. Point out that this model does not work for these exercises because tenths, hundreds, and thousandths are needed to represent the numbers accurately.

**Math Link**

Point out that a similar folding strategy can be used to find a number halfway between two others on the number line.

### Additional Answers

11a. Possible answer: $-\frac{1}{4}$ is farther from 0 than $-\frac{1}{6}$ because fourths are bigger than sixths; $-\frac{1}{4}$ is closer to 0 than $-\frac{1}{3}$ because fourths are smaller than thirds. If students convert everything to twelfths, they will see that $-\frac{1}{4}$, or $-\frac{3}{12}$, is exactly halfway between $-\frac{1}{6}$ and $-\frac{1}{3}$.

11b. Answers will vary. If students changed all denominators to twelfths, they may say yes. If not, they should say no, because they do not know exactly where in the interval between $-\frac{1}{6}$ and $-\frac{1}{3}$ the point should be.

12c. Answers will vary. Students may, for instance, decide that they put $-\frac{1}{8}$ too close to 0, if there does not seem to be enough room to fit $-\frac{1}{10}$ in between them.

13. Check students' work. Possible reasoning: $-0.3$ is less than $-\frac{1}{4}$ (0.25) and greater than $-\frac{1}{3}$ ($-0.3\overline{3}$). $-0.4$ $\left(-\frac{4}{10}\right)$ is less than $-\frac{1}{3}$ ($-0.3\overline{3}$) and greater than $-\frac{1}{2}$ ($-\frac{5}{10}$ or $-0.5$).

**Investigation 1**
Pages 320–323
Practice & Apply: 1–13
Connect & Extend: 23

**Investigation 2**
Pages 324–327
Practice & Apply: 14–22
Connect & Extend: 24

**Assign Anytime**
Mixed Review: 25–36

- **Exercises 2–5** Suggest that students find the example that fits the "not" category first before trying to fit the other condition. For example, in Exercise 2, have them find a number that is not an integer like $\frac{1}{4}$. Then ask, "is this a rational number?"
- **Exercises 12 and 13** You may want to review how to represent the rational numbers, the integers, the whole numbers, and the natural numbers in a Venn diagram before you assign these exercises.



## Practice & Apply

**1.** Consider the numbers listed below.

$$-10^2 \quad -21.3 \quad -\frac{1}{2} \quad -4 \quad 0 \quad \frac{1}{3}$$

$$12.6 \quad \frac{7}{4} \quad 5 \quad 6^{-3} \quad 17^4 \quad 0.004$$

Copy the table shown below. Write each number in all number set columns that apply.

| Natural Numbers | Whole Numbers | Integers | Rational Numbers |
|---|---|---|---|
| 5, $17^4$ | 0, 5, $17^4$ | $-10^2$, −4, 0, 5, $17^4$ | $-10^2$, −21.3, $-\frac{1}{2}$, −4, 0, $\frac{1}{3}$, 2.6, $\frac{7}{4}$, 5, $6^{-3}$, $17^4$, 0.004 |

For Exercises 2–11, write a number that fits the conditions given. If no such number exists, write "impossible."

**2.** a rational number that is not an integer Possible answer: $\frac{4}{5}$

**3.** a natural number that is not a rational number Impossible

**4.** an integer that is not a rational number Impossible

**5.** an integer that is not a natural number Possible answer: −8

**6.** a rational number that is also a natural number Possible answer: 5

**7.** a rational number less than the least whole number Possible answer: −0.1

**8.** a natural number between −3 and 0 Impossible

**9.** a rational number between 3 and 4 Possible answer: 3.84

**10.** a whole number between 6 and 7 Impossible

**11.** an integer between −10 and −12 −11

**12.** Draw a Venn diagram that shows the relationship between the prime numbers and the natural numbers.

**13.** Draw a Venn diagram that shows the relationship between integers and negative numbers. Write at least three numbers in each section of your diagram.

**a.** Stephanie thought of a whole number. Without knowing her number, can you tell where it belongs in your diagram? Explain.

**b.** Boris wrote a rational number on a piece of paper. Without knowing his number, can you tell where it belongs in your diagram? Explain your reasoning.

12.
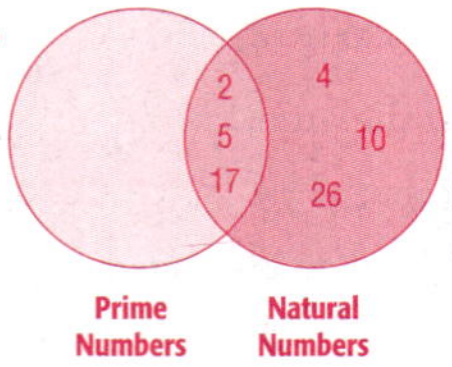


13.
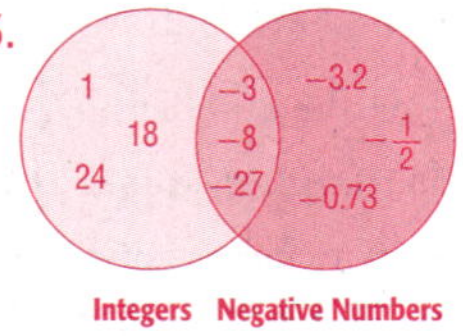


13a. Yes. If it is a whole number, it is an integer but not a negative number. It belongs in the integers circle but not in the section that overlaps the negative-numbers ring.

13b. No. It could be positive or negative, an integer or not an integer. There is no way of knowing where it belongs.

14. $\frac{1}{6}$. Possible explanation: $\frac{1}{6}$ is half of $\frac{1}{3}$. Half of $\frac{1}{3}$ is a little more than 0.16, which is more than 0.11.
15. $-\frac{6}{5}$. Possible explanation: $-\frac{6}{5}$ equals $-1.2$, which is greater than $-1.3$.
16. $-0.426$. Possible explanation: $-0.426$ is greater than $-\frac{1}{2}$; $-\frac{17}{30}$ is less than $-\frac{1}{2}$ because $-\frac{15}{30} = -\frac{1}{2}$.
17. 0.143. Possible explanation: $4^{-2}$ is $\frac{1}{16}$, which is half of $\frac{1}{8}$. $\frac{1}{8}$ is 0.125, which is already less than 0.143; $4^{-2}$ must be even smaller.
18. Check students' work. Shown points and intervals may vary, and students may choose an interval that indicates thousandths.

22a. Possible answers: $-\frac{6}{5}, -\frac{7}{5}, -\frac{8}{5}, -\frac{9}{5}$
22b. See margin.

For Exercises 14–17, identify which number is greater. Explain how you found your answer.

**14.** $\frac{1}{6}$ or 0.11

**15.** $-\frac{6}{5}$ or $-1.3$

**16.** $-0.426$ or $-\frac{17}{30}$

**17.** $4^{-2}$ or 0.143

**18.** Graph the following numbers on a number line. Label intervals to indicate your scale.

$\frac{43}{100}$ $\quad \frac{3}{8}$ $\quad 0.39$ $\quad \frac{2}{5}$ $\quad \frac{7}{16}$ $\quad \frac{365}{1000}$

**19.** Copy the number line shown below. Determine the scale that was used to create the line. Label the plotted points. Scale is tenths.

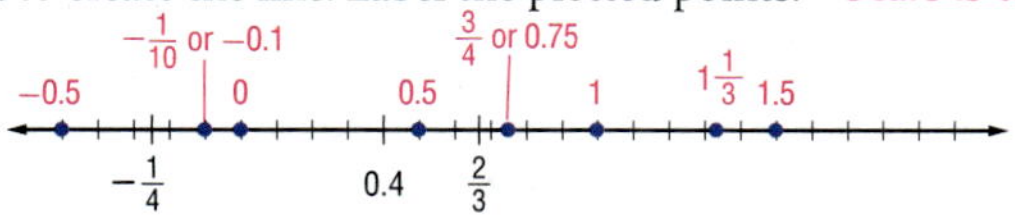


For Exercises 20–22, use the puzzle clues to determine the secret number. There is more than one secret number for the puzzle in Exercise 22.

**20. Puzzle A** 4
Clue A: The number is a whole number.
Clue B: The number doubled is less than 10.
Clue C: The number is evenly divisible by 4.
Clue D: The square root of the number is a whole number.

**21. Puzzle B** $-2$
Clue A: The number is an integer but not a whole number.
Clue B: The number squared is less than 10.
Clue C: The number is evenly divisible by 2 but not by 4.
Clue D: The sum of the number and 5 is a natural number.

**22. Puzzle C**
Clue A: The number is a rational number but not an integer.
Clue B: The product of the number and 5 is an integer.
Clue C: The number is less than $-1$ and greater than $-2$.

**a.** List all possible secret numbers.

**b.** Explain how you know there are no other possible answers.

**c.** Write one or more additional clues that would eliminate all but one of the possible answers. Write the answer that your clues indicate. Answers will vary. Check students' work. Possible answer for $-\frac{8}{5}$: When the number is multiplied by 5, the product is evenly divisible by 4.



On Your Own Exercises

▶ **Exercises 14, 15, and 16** You may need to review how to convert a fraction to a decimal before assigning these exercises.

▶ **Exercise 17** Remind students that a negative power does not mean a negative number. The value of $4^{-2}$ is $\frac{1}{16}$.

▶ **Exercises 20–22** Ask students to check their answers in pairs. Have them compare number line points and intervals and determine if their partner's puzzles are correct.

**Additional Answer**

22b. The number is a rational number, and the product of the number and 5 is an integer. Written in simplest form, the denominator must be 5. The number lies between $-2$ and $-1$; these are all the fractions with denominators of 5 in that range.

**Lesson 7.1** Rational Numbers 329

▶ **Exercises 24** If students are struggling to answer this question encourage them to create a set of numbers to use as an example.

## Quick Check

**Informal Assessment** Students should be able to:

- ✔ explore the relationship between number sets
- ✔ use Venn diagrams to represent number sets
- ✔ compare and order rational numbers
- ✔ place rational numbers on a number line

## Quick Quiz

For Exercises 1–3, identify to which set(s) each of the following numbers belongs: the natural numbers, whole numbers, integers, and the rational numbers.

**1.** 3.241 Rationals

**2.** $4^2$ Naturals, wholes, integers, rationals.

**3.** $-\frac{3}{8}$ Rationals

For Exercises 4–6, use the following numbers.

$-1.03 \quad -\frac{5}{4} \quad -2\frac{1}{8} \quad -\frac{112}{110} \quad -2.194 \quad -\frac{1087}{1000}$

**4.** Which numbers are less than −1 and greater than −1.5? $-1.03, -\frac{5}{4}, -\frac{112}{110}, -\frac{1087}{1000}$

**5.** Which numbers are less than −1 and greater than −1.1? $-1.03, -\frac{112}{110}, \frac{1087}{1000}$

**6.** Which numbers are less than −1 and greater than −1.01? None

**7.** Graph and label each of the numbers below on a number line.

$\frac{38}{100} \quad \frac{3}{8} \quad 0.365 \quad \frac{4}{9} \quad \frac{5}{11} \quad \frac{325}{1000}$

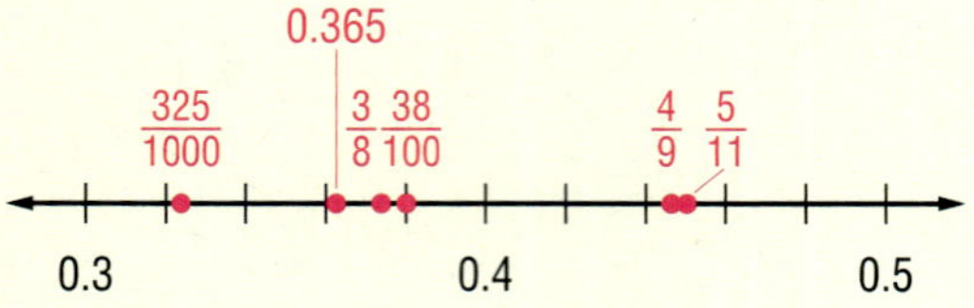




On Your Own Exercises

**23. Number Games** Maurk and Larisa played a number game. Maurk drew a Venn diagram and kept the labels secret. Larisa chose one number at a time, and Maurk put each number in the area of the diagram where it belonged. This is what the diagram looked like after Larisa had chosen three numbers.

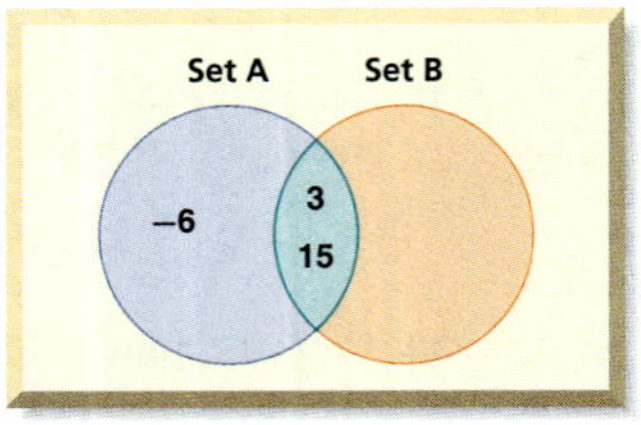


**For Parts a and b, choose from the number sets listed below.**

| | | |
|---|---|---|
| integers | natural numbers | whole numbers |
| rational numbers | odd numbers | even numbers |
| multiples of 3 | prime numbers | |

**a.** Which of the following number sets could set A represent? Integers, rational numbers, multiples of 3

**b.** Which of the number sets could set B represent? Natural numbers, whole numbers, odd numbers

**c.** Assume that the number sets you listed in Parts a and b are the only possible labels for set A and set B. Suggest three numbers that Larisa could choose next. For each number you suggest, explain how it will help her rule out the labels that are incorrect.

23c. Many answers are possible. Possible answers: For 6: If it belongs in set B, then set B cannot be odd numbers. If it belongs in set B but not set A, then set A cannot be multiples of 3. For $\frac{3}{4}$: If it belongs in set A, then set A is the rational numbers. For 0: If it belongs in set B, then set B cannot be the natural numbers or the odd numbers.

**24. In Your Own Words** Explain a strategy for ordering a set of rational numbers from least to greatest.

## Mixed Review

24. Possible answer: Write all numbers as integers or decimals, graph on a number line, and list numbers in the order they appear on the number line going from left to right.

**Write each expression using a single base and a single exponent.**

**25.** $x^3 \cdot x^2$ $x^5$

**26.** $(x^3)^2$ $x^6$

**27.** $y^6 \div y^2$ $y^4$

**28.** $\frac{(t^5)^2}{(t)(t^6)}$ $t^3$

**Find each sum or difference.**

**29.** $-2 + (-3)$ −5

**30.** $8 + (-10)$ −2

**31.** $7 - (-5)$ 12

**32.** $-8 - (-3)$ −5

**Find each product or quotient.**

**33.** $5 \cdot (-2)$ −10

**34.** $-6 \cdot \frac{1}{2}$ −3

**35.** $-10 \div (-5)$ 2

**36.** $12 \div (-\frac{1}{4})$ −48

LESSON

7.2

# Irrational Numbers

## Objectives

- To relate square roots to the side length of a square
- To find the square root of a perfect square
- To approximate the square root of a number
- To place square roots and irrational numbers on a number line
- To classify a number as rational or irrational

## *Overview*

In this lesson, students relate square roots to the side length of a square and then explore squares whose side lengths are not whole numbers. They learn how to express the square root of a number using a radical sign and then learn how to place square roots on a number line. Students are asked to estimate square roots to the nearest hundredth and then find square roots using calculators. They analyze irrational numbers and then classify numbers as rational or irrational.

## *Advance Preparation*

You may want to use a large number line to facilitate class discussion while presenting new topics, including locating square roots and placing rational and irrational numbers on the number line.

| | Summary | Materials | On Your Own Exercises (pp. 339–342) | Assessment Opportunities |
|---|---|---|---|---|
| **Investigation 1** (p. 331) Pacing: 2 days | Students relate the area of a square to its side length, the square root of a number. | large number line (optional) | Practice & Apply: 1–14<br>Connect & Extend: 28, 30–33<br>Mixed Review: 36–39 | • On the Spot Assessment (p. 335)<br>• Share & Summarize (p. 335)<br>• Troubleshooting (p. 333) |
| **Investigation 2** (p. 336) Pacing: 1 day | Students analyze irrational numbers and classify numbers as rational or irrational. | large number line (optional) | Practice & Apply: 15–21<br>Connect & Extend: 22–27, 29, 34, 35<br>Mixed Review: 36–39 | • Share & Summarize (p. 338)<br>• Troubleshooting (p. 338) |

# Leveled Lesson Resources

CRM *Available in:* **Chapter 7 Resource Masters**

Also on TeacherWorks™ Lesson 7.2

## Study Guide and Intervention (p. 9) AL

**Lesson 7.2 Study Guide and Intervention**
***Irrational Numbers***

The product of a number and itself is the **square** of the number. Numbers like 4, 25, and 2.25 are called **perfect squares** because they are squares of rational numbers. The factors multiplied to form perfect squares are called **square roots**. Both $5 \cdot 5$ and $(-5)(-5)$ equal 25. So, 25 has two square roots, 5 and −5.
A **radical sign**, $\sqrt{\ }$, is the symbol used to indicate the positive square root of a number. So, $\sqrt{25} = 5$.

**Example 1**

1. Find the square of 5.
$5 \cdot 5 = 25$
2. Find the square of 16.
16 $x^2$ 256
3. Find $\sqrt{49}$.
$7 \cdot 7 = 49$, so $\sqrt{49} = 7$.
4. Find the two whole numbers between which $\sqrt{17}$ is located. Do not use your calculator.
$\sqrt{16} = 4$ and $\sqrt{25} = 5$,
so $\sqrt{17}$ is between 4 and 5.

**Example 2** If a number is rational, it can be written as the ratio of two integers. Write $\sqrt{144}$ as the ratio of two integers.
$\sqrt{144} = 12 = \frac{12}{1}$

**Exercises**

Find the square of each number.
1. 2 2. 9 3. 14

Find the two whole numbers that each square root lies between without using your calculator.
4. $\sqrt{115}$ 5. $\sqrt{52}$ 6. $\sqrt{37}$

Write each number as the ratio of two integers.
7. −1.25 8. $\sqrt{\frac{1}{4}}$ 9. 2.5

## Skills Practice (p. 10) AL OL

**Lesson 7.2 Skills Practice**
***Irrational Numbers***

Find the square of each number.
1. 3 2. 22
3. 0.04 4. $\frac{3}{8}$

Find each square root.
5. $\sqrt{25}$ 6. $\sqrt{100}$
7. $\sqrt{\frac{81}{169}}$ 8. $\sqrt{64}$

Find the two whole numbers that each square root lies between without using your calculator.
9. $\sqrt{28}$ 10. $\sqrt{59}$
11. $\sqrt{200}$ 12. $\sqrt{72}$

Determine whether each number is rational or irrational. If it is rational, write it as a ratio of two integers. If it is irrational, explain how you know.
13. $\sqrt{\frac{2}{5}}$ 14. −5.36
15. $\sqrt{81}$ 16. 0.07

## Problem-Solving Practice (p. 11) AL OL

**Lesson 7.2 Problem-Solving Practice**
***Irrational Numbers***

Solve.
1. **Fertilizer** John bought a bag of lawn fertilizer that will cover 400 square feet. What are the dimensions of the largest square plot of lawn that the bag of fertilizer will cover?
2. **Algebra** Johann squared a number and the result was 15 times the original number. What was the original number?
3. **Track** A circular walking track has a circumference of 50 feet. Express the radius and area of the track in terms of π.
4. **Painting** A quart of paint covers an area of 64 square feet. What is the length of the square that this quart of paint will cover in one coat?
5. **Geography** Refer to the squares below. They represent the approximate areas of California, Alabama, and Nebraska. Find the area of Alabama.

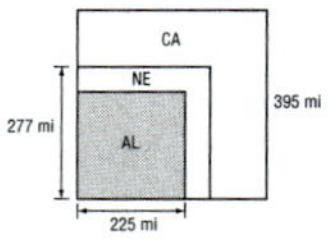


6. Use the figure in Exercise 5. How much larger is California than Nebraska?

## Enrichment (p. 12) BL

**Lesson 7.2 Enrichment**
***Irrational Numbers***

**The Geometric Mean**

The square root of the product of two numbers is called their geometric mean. The geometric mean of 12 and 48 is $\sqrt{12 \cdot 48} = \sqrt{576}$ or 24.

**Find the geometric mean for each pair of numbers.**
1. 2 and 8 2. 4 and 9 3. 9 and 16
4. 16 and 4 5. 16 and 36 6. 12 and 3
7. 18 and 8 8. 2 and 18 9. 27 and 12

Each term in a **geometric sequence** is found by multiplying the previous term by the same number. A missing term in a geometric sequence equals the geometric mean of the two terms on either side.

**Find the missing term in each geometric sequence.**
10. 4, 12, ?, 108, 324 11. 10, ?, 62.5, 156.25, 390.625
12. 1, 0.4, ?, 0.064, 0.0256 13. 700, 70, 7, 0.7, ?, 0.007
14. 6, ?, 24 15. 2, ?, 4

16. Fill in the blank using *always, sometimes,* or *never.*
The geometric mean used to find the missing term in a geometric sequence is ______ rational.

## Lesson Quick Quiz (p. 13) AL OL BL

**Lesson 7.2 Quick Quiz**

For Exercises 1–3, find the two whole numbers each given square root is between. Do not use a calculator.
1. $\sqrt{83}$
2. $\sqrt{8}$
3. $\sqrt{39}$

Find the square of each number.
4. 12.4
5. $\frac{6}{7}$
6. Draw a number line that extends from 5 to 10. Mark the approximate location of each square root below.
$\sqrt{40}$ $\sqrt{63}$ $\sqrt{92}$

For Exercises 7–10, determine whether each number is rational or irrational. Explain.
7. $\sqrt{64}$
8. $\sqrt{1.44}$
9. $\sqrt{84}$
10. $\sqrt{\frac{50}{150}}$

# Additional Lesson Resources

### Teacher Tech Tools
- TeacherWorks
- ExamView Assessment Suite
- Classroom Presentation Toolkit
- Advance Tracker

### Student Tech Tools
- StudentWorks Plus
- Math Online eGlossary • Concepts in Motion

### Other Print Products
- Investigation Notebook and Reflection Journal
- Quick Review Math Handbook

# LESSON 7.2

# Irrational Numbers

In Lesson 7.1, you worked with rational numbers. In this lesson, you will explore a new number set, the irrational numbers.



### *Think & Discuss*

Think of a number you can multiply times itself to get a product of 25. Is there more than one such number? Yes, 5 and −5

Next, think of two numbers you can multiply times themselves to get a product of $\frac{16}{25}$. How are these numbers different from your previous answers? $\frac{4}{5}$ and $-\frac{4}{5}$; $\frac{16}{25}$ is not an integer.

Now, what is a number you can multiply times itself to get a product of 5? $\sqrt{5}$ or $-\sqrt{5}$

In this lesson, you will work with numbers like $\sqrt{5}$.

## Investigation 1 Squares and Square Roots

**Vocabulary**

**square root**

***Math Link***

Remember that multiplying a number by itself is called *squaring* the number. The expression $7^2$ can be read "7 squared."

As you remember from previous lessons, area is found by multiplying the length and width of a two-dimensional figure. Area is measured in square units.

The exponent 2 is often used to represent square units of measurement. For example, square centimeter and square inch can be represented as $cm^2$ and $in^2$, respectively.

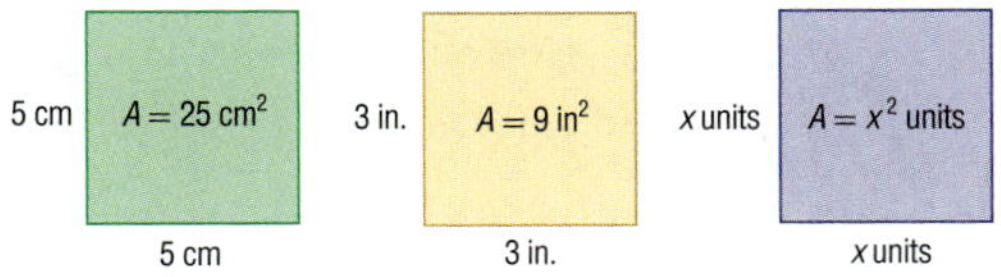




## Reaching All Learners

**ELL English Language Learners**
English Language learners should be familiar with square root notation since it is universal, but you may want to review it with them carefully so they understand how it is related to the square of a number and to the area of a square.

## Irrational Numbers — LESSON 7.2

### *Introduce*

**Irrational Numbers** Introduce this lesson by asking students if they can give examples of numbers that are terminating decimals and numbers that are repeating decimals. Ask them if they think a decimal may not repeat, and ask them if they can think of an example of one. (π) Remind them of the Venn diagrams they did in Lesson 7.1 that represented the set of rational numbers, and ask them to give any numbers they can think of that would not fit into the circles.

***Think & Discuss***

These exercises are designed to help students think about squares and square roots. Ask students to discuss how the numbers are different in each answer, and have them verify that $\sqrt{5}$ squared and $-\sqrt{5}$ squared both equal 5.

### Investigation 1

***On Your Own Exercises***
Pages 339–342
Exercises 1–14, 28, 30–33

**Squares and Square Roots** In this investigation, students will find the squares of numbers and the square roots of numbers. Begin the lesson by looking at squares in the geometric sense and use the side lengths of the squares to represent the area in square units of measurement. Remind students how to find the area of a square.

***Math Link***

Help students make the connection between "squaring" a number and the area of a square as its side length multiplied by itself.

## Develop & Understand: A

*Suggested Grouping: Small Groups*

▶ **Exercise 1** Make sure students do not confuse area with perimeter by trying to add up the sides. The numerator is the same (16), but the denominator should be 49.

▶ **Exercises 3–5** Remind students to use their knowledge about the relationship between the side length of a square and its area from Lesson 7.1.

▶ **Exercise 6** Emphasize that the sides cannot be whole numbers because there is no whole number that when squared will be 10 or $\frac{3}{7}$.

**Wrap-Up** Summarize Exercises 1–6 by saying that the side length of a square cannot be a whole number unless its area is a perfect square. Likewise, the side length of a square cannot be a rational number unless the area of the square is the square of a rational number.

### Think & Discuss

Students will need to review the concept of "perfect square" to answer this exercise. When you discuss this exercise, point out that the geometric model makes it possible to picture the perfect square as a square. Point out that the area formula, however, can be used even when the side lengths are not whole numbers.

**Teacher Tips** You may need to review how to use the square key on the calculator.

### Additional Answer

③ Yes; If you convert the area to a fraction, then you should always be able to tell by trying to find integers for the numerator and denominator of the side. Square integers until either you get the numerator and denominator of the area or until you have tested all the integers and found values less than or greater than the numerator and denominator.

## Develop & Understand: A

1. What is the area of the square shown below? $\frac{16}{49}$ cm$^2$

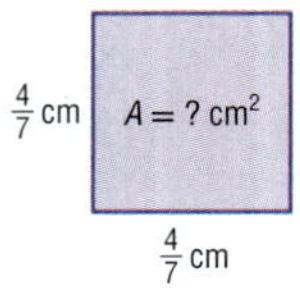


2. How long is each side of the square shown below? 0.5 in.

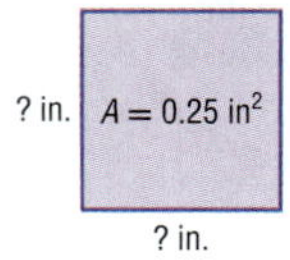


**Consider the following squares with the given areas.**

a.
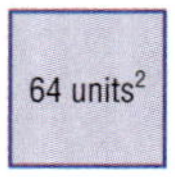


$S =$ 8 units

b.
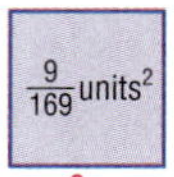


$S = \frac{3}{13}$ units

c.
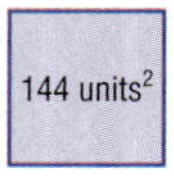


$S =$ 12 units

d.
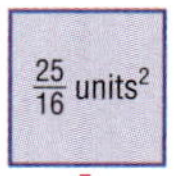


$S = \frac{5}{4}$ units

3. For each square, find the length of its sides. See squares.
4. Which of the squares have side measures that are whole numbers? a, c
5. Which of the squares have side measures that are rational numbers but not whole numbers? b, d
6. What can you say about the sides of a square with an area of 10 units$^2$? An area of $\frac{3}{7}$ units$^2$?

### Think & Discuss

If you know the area of a square, how can you tell if its sides are whole numbers? See ①.

How can you tell if side lengths are rational numbers? See ②.

Can you always tell? See ③ in margin.

A number is a *perfect square* if it is equal to a whole number multiplied by itself. Geometrically, a perfect square is the area of a square with whole-number side lengths.

For example, 64, 9, and 169 are perfect squares.

6. The sides cannot be whole numbers. It is not possible to think of a fraction that can be squared to produce either area.

① The set of perfect squares is {1, 4, 9, 16, 25, ...}. Squares with areas of perfect square units, {1, 4, 9, 16, 25, ...}, have whole number side lengths.

② A fraction whose numerator and denominator are perfect squares is the square of a rational number. If you cannot find an integer that squares to the numerator and the denominator of the area, then the side length cannot be a ratio of two integers, and the side length is not rational.



## Mathematical Background

The perfect squares are so named because they represent the area of a square with a whole number as a side. Students can easily see the square pattern in the numbers 1, 4, 9, 16, 25, and so on because they have previously seen the pattern. Use this opportunity to point out that there are also squares whose area falls in between the numbers above, and that these squares have irrational numbers as side lengths. To represent the side length of a square whose area is 3, for example, the square root notation $\sqrt{3}$ is used to show the side length.

Two operations that "undo" each other are called inverse operations. Addition and subtraction are *inverse operations.*

**Add 12 to 15 to get 27. To undo the addition, subtract 12 from 27 to get 15.**

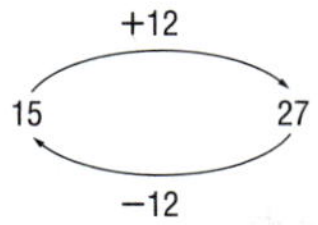


**Subtract 12 from 27 to get 15. To undo the subtraction, add 12 to 15 to get 27.**

Similarly, multiplication and division are inverse operations.

You will now work with the operation that undoes squaring.

## Think & Discuss

Luke squared some numbers on his calculator. His results are shown below. In each case, find the number with which he started.

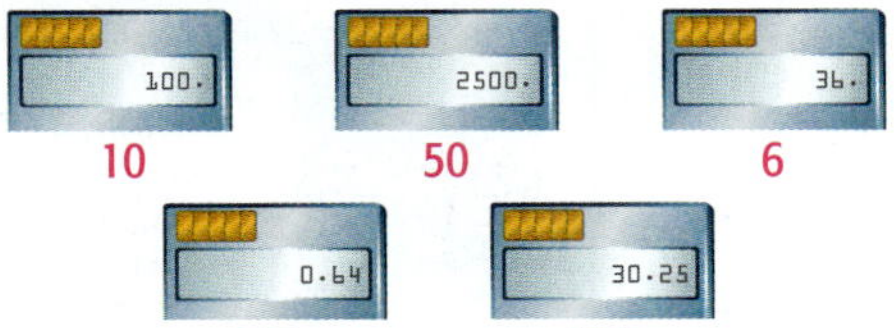


10 50 6 0.8 5.5

In each part of Think & Discuss, you found the number you need to square to get a given number. The number you found is the **square root** of the original number. For example, the square root of 36 is 6.

### Math Link

Every positive number has both a positive and a negative square root. For example, the square roots of 36 are 6 and −6. In this lesson, you will focus on positive square roots, also known as *principal roots.*

The square root is shown using a *radical sign,* $\sqrt{\phantom{x}}$. You can think of $\sqrt{36}$ in any of the following ways.

- the number you multiply by itself to get 36 $6 \cdot 6 = 36$
- the number you square to get 36 $6^2 = 36$
- the side length of a square with area 36

Squaring and taking the square root are inverse operations.

**Square 6 to get 36. To undo the squaring, take the square root of 36 to get 6.**

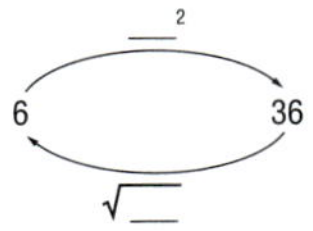


**Take the square root of 36 to get 6. To undo taking the square root, square 6 to get 36.**



## Think & Discuss

Review that addition and subtraction are inverse operations, as are multiplication and division. Go over the examples in the text and do some additional examples so that students are very familiar with the concept of "inverse operation" before finding the square root of a number in this exercise.

### Math Link

Have students note that a calculator only gives the principal square root of a number.

## Troubleshooting

Watch for students who do not understand the connection between a radical and the three ways you can interpret it shown at the bottom of the page. Ask them to do these additional examples using the statements shown at the bottom of the page.

Give three ways to interpret each of the following square roots.

1. $\sqrt{25}$ 2. $\sqrt{64}$

3. $\sqrt{16}$ 4. $\sqrt{9}$

## Example

When students work to estimate the value of square roots, encourage them to make a list of all of the perfect squares they know. They can use this list to give them a starting point for their estimation. Next they need to decide which number it is closer to and then make a guess as to the decimal between 0 and 9.

## Develop & Understand: B

*Suggested Grouping: Individuals*

- **Exercise 7** You may want students to do this exercise as an organized list or as a table with headings "Integer" and "Square" so they can use the table for reference later.
- **Exercises 9 and 10** You may want to use a number line to help you explain these exercises to students.
- **Exercise 13** Answers will vary for this exercise, but use the opportunity to make good connections to squaring numbers. Have students check their answers with a calculator.

**Wrap-Up** You might have groups put their results from Exercises 8, 12, and 13 on the board. The class can have an interesting discussion about how to represent the square roots on a number line.

### Math Link

Irrational numbers are defined in this segment. Emphasize that there are infinitely many irrational numbers, including square roots of numbers that are not perfect squares.

Not all whole numbers have whole-number square roots. In fact, whole numbers that are not perfect squares have square roots that are decimals that never end or repeat. So, you can only estimate the decimal equivalents of numbers such as $\sqrt{10}$ and $\sqrt{41}$.

### Math Link

Decimal numbers that never end or repeat are called **irrational numbers**. You have previously learned about the irrational number $\pi$.

$\pi = 3.14159265 \ldots$

### Example

Luke estimated the decimal equivalent of $\sqrt{10}$.

## Develop & Understand: B

7. Find the square of each integer from 0 to 15.
   0, 1, 4, 9, 16, 25, 36, 49, 64, 81, 100, 121, 144, 169, 196, 225
8. Draw a number line that extends from 0 to 10 with increments of 1.
   See margin.
9. What integers lie between 2 and 3? There are none.
10. What integers lie between $2^2$ and $3^2$? 5, 6, 7, 8
11. On your number line from Exercise 8, mark the location of $\sqrt{4}$ and $\sqrt{9}$. Then mark the approximate location of $\sqrt{7}$. Explain how you decided where to put it.
12. On your number line from Exercise 8, mark the approximate location of $\sqrt{5}$. Is it greater than or less than $\sqrt{7}$?
13. Give two examples of numbers whose squares must be between 144 and 169.

11. See number line from Exercise 8. The square root of 7 must be greater than 2 since $2^2 = 4$ and less than 3 since $3^2 = 9$.
12. See number line from Exercise 8. The square root of 5 is less than the square root of 7.
13. Any numbers between 12 and 13, such as 12.1 or $12\frac{3}{4}$, are correct answers.



### Additional Answer

8.

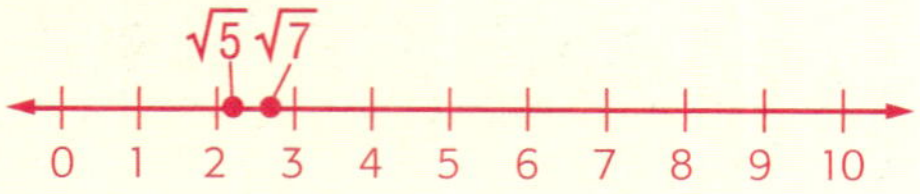


### Reaching All Learners

**BL Beyond Level** Challenge students to draw a number line with at least one square root placed between each integer on the number line. Ask them to explain how they know they placed the square roots properly.

## Develop & Understand: C

Find the two whole numbers each given square root is between. Do not use your calculator.

**14.** $\sqrt{2}$ 1 and 2

**15.** $\sqrt{75}$ 8 and 9

**16.** $\sqrt{20}$ 4 and 5

**17.** $\sqrt{26}$ 5 and 6

**18.** To the nearest tenth, between which two numbers is $\sqrt{26}$? Do not use your calculator. 5.0 and 5.1

**19.** In the example, Luke estimated $\sqrt{10}$ to one decimal place. Use Luke's method to estimate $\sqrt{10}$ to two decimal places. Explain each step in your work.

Your calculator has a command for finding square roots accessed by pressing [2nd] [$\sqrt{\ }$]. For example, to find $\sqrt{4}$, press [2nd] [$\sqrt{\ }$] 4 [ENTER].

## Develop & Understand: D

Use your calculator to approximate each square root to the nearest hundredth. Compare your results with your answers in Exercises 14–17.

**20.** $\sqrt{2}$ 1.41

**21.** $\sqrt{75}$ 8.66

**22.** $\sqrt{20}$ 4.47

**23.** $\sqrt{26}$ 5.10

**24.** Althea entered a number into her calculator. She then pressed [$x^2$] [ENTER] repeatedly until the calculator showed 43,046,721. What could have been her original number? List all the possibilities. 3; 9; 81; or 6,561

**25.** Suppose you enter a positive number less than 10 into your calculator and press [$x^2$] [ENTER] 5 times. Then you start with the final result and take the square root 5 times. What will happen? Explain why.

### Share & Summarize

1. Describe the relationship between squaring a number and taking its square root. See below.
2. Describe a method for approximating a square root *without* using a calculator. Possible answer: First, find the two whole numbers that the square root is between. Then find the two tenths it is between, and so on, until your estimate is as close as you want it to be.

19. Possible answer: $\sqrt{10}$ is between 3.1 and 3.2. It is closer to 3.2, so I will try 3.17; $3.17^2 = 10.0489$, which is too large. I will try 3.15: $3.15^2 = 9.9225$, which is too small. I will try 3.16: $3.16^2 = 9.9856$, which is also too small but closer than 3.15. So, $\sqrt{10}$ is between 3.16 and 3.17. Since 9.9856 is closer to 10 than 9.9225 is, $\sqrt{10}$ must be closer to 3.16.

25. You will get the original number. Each time you take the square root, you undo one of the squares.

1. The operations undo each other. To find the number that was squared to make another number, take the square root.



### On the Spot Assessment

Watch for students who cannot use their calculators correctly for Exercises 20–25. Monitor each student for entering the numbers correctly by using the correct order of operations, especially if they use their own individual calculator. Suggest that they estimate the answer first by thinking of the square root of the nearest perfect square so that it will be more obvious if they pressed an incorrect key. For example, in Exercise 23, they should be looking for a number slightly higher than $\sqrt{25}$, or 5.

## Develop & Understand: C

*Suggested Grouping: Individuals*

▶ **Exercises 14–17** You may want to use a number line to help students see how the square root is placed between two whole numbers.

▶ **Exercise 18** It is important for students to be able to recognize that if $5^2 = 25$ and $5.1^2 = 26.01$, $\sqrt{5^2} < \sqrt{26} < \sqrt{5.1^2}$.

**Wrap-Up** Use the results of Exercise 19 to discuss how to use estimation to get closer and closer to the square root. Emphasize that unless the square root is of a perfect square, the result will always be an estimate.

## Develop & Understand: D

*Suggested Grouping: Pairs*

▶ **Exercises 20–23** Students should see as many as ten digits in the calculator display for each of these square roots. You may need to review how to round a decimal to the nearest hundredth for these exercises.

▶ **Exercise 23** Ask students to estimate the answer before doing this exercise. Point out that they are looking for a number greater than 5, since $5^2 = 25$, and $26 > 25$.

▶ **Exercises 24 and 25** You may want to monitor students using their own calculators for these exercises to make sure key strokes are done correctly.

**Wrap-Up** Wrap up by having a volunteer describe how to find a square root using a calculator. Have the volunteer use an overhead calculator, if possible.

### Share & Summarize

For **Exercise 1**, it is very important students understand that squaring a number and taking its square root are inverse operations. Summarize the responses of several students.

Use **Exercise 2** to suggest that students always try to estimate the square root before finding it.

## Investigation 2

***On Your Own Exercises***
Pages 339–342
Exercises 15–21, 22–27, 29, 34, 35

**Analyze Irrational Numbers** Introduce this investigation by listing the square roots of the first sixteen whole numbers as $\sqrt{1}$, $\sqrt{2}$, $\sqrt{3}$, and so on. Then find the square roots of the perfect squares. Tell them that the numbers in between the perfect squares are called *irrational numbers*. Then define *irrational numbers* as numbers that cannot be written as the ratio of two integers, or non-repeating, non-terminating decimals.

### Think & Discuss

*Suggested Grouping: Pairs*

You may want to first review how to convert a decimal to a fraction before having students discuss these questions in pairs. Point out that the place value of the right-most digit gives the denominator of the fraction.

**Teacher Tips** Discuss the paragraphs below the Think & Discuss. Point out that no matter how many digits are to the right of the decimal point, if the decimal terminates, it is a rational number because a fraction *could* be found to represent it.

### Develop & Understand: A

*Suggested Grouping: Whole Class*

▶ **Exercise 2** As students work on this exercise show them how to use the store function on their calculator. Explain to the class that this feature allows them to use the entire value, not just the digits that are shown, which makes the answer more accurate.

▶ **Exercise 3** Remind students that the question is asking only for the digit that is on the right edge. If they have a different calculator from their neighbor, their answer may be different, and that is normal.



## Investigation 2 Approximate Irrational Numbers

**Vocabulary**
- **irrational numbers**
- **real numbers**

Remember that a rational number is a number that can be written as the ratio, or quotient, of two integers. For example, the numbers 3, 0.5, and $-1.8$ are all rational numbers because they can be written as $\frac{3}{1}$, $\frac{5}{10}$ or $\frac{1}{2}$, and $-\frac{18}{10}$ or $-\frac{9}{5}$, respectively.

Numbers that *cannot* be written as the ratio of two integers are called **irrational numbers**. The rational numbers and irrational numbers together form the set of **real numbers**. All real numbers can be located on the number line.

### Think & Discuss

Try to decide whether each of the six numbers below is rational by looking for a ratio of integers that is equal to the number. See ①.

$3 \quad 0.7 \quad -2.55 \quad \sqrt{20} \quad 4.5678 \quad \sqrt{25} \quad 7.\overline{4}$

① Only $\sqrt{20}$ is irrational; the others are rational, for example: $\frac{3}{1}$, $\frac{7}{10}$, $-\frac{255}{100}$, $\frac{45{,}678}{10{,}000}$, $\frac{5}{1}$, and $\frac{67}{9}$.

Think about numbers with one nonzero digit to the right of the decimal point, such as 0.7. Are all such numbers rational? Yes

Think about numbers that have two nonzero digits to the right of the decimal point, such as 2.55. Are all such numbers rational? Yes

Are numbers with *n* nonzero digits to the right of the decimal point rational? Yes

Can numbers whose nonzero digits to the right of the decimal point go on forever be rational? Explain. Yes; $1.\overline{3}$ is such a number because it is equal to $\frac{4}{3}$.

In the Think & Discuss above, you may not have been sure whether $\sqrt{20}$ is rational or irrational. You will now explore this number.

### Develop & Understand: A

1. Using your calculator, evaluate $\sqrt{20}$. What does the calculator display for the decimal form of $\sqrt{20}$? Most will display 4.472135955.
2. Multiply your answer to Exercise 1 by itself, using your calculator. What do you get? Answers will vary. Most students will answer 20.
3. Now imagine multiplying your answer for Exercise 1 by itself *without* using a calculator. What would be the rightmost digit of the product?
4. Could the number your calculator displayed in Exercise 1 really be equal to $\sqrt{20}$? How might your findings be explained? No; Possible explanations: The calculator rounded. Or, there are more digits in the number than can fit on the screen.

3. Answers will vary. If the rightmost digit of the original number is 5, the rightmost digit of the squared number will also be 5.

**Math Link**
The rightmost digit of 4.36 is 6 and the rightmost digit of 121.798 is 8.



## Reaching All Learners

**AL Approaching Level** Students may have difficulty understanding irrational numbers because, by their very nature, there is no pattern to them. Provide extra assistance to these students by having them work with partners that seem to understand the concepts. Have them volunteer their own examples of irrational numbers and then describe why they think they are irrational.

336 **CHAPTER 7** Real Numbers

### Math Link

A bar written over one or more numerals means those numerals repeat. For example,

$2.1\overline{5} = 2.1555 \ldots$

$9.\overline{32} = 9.323232 \ldots$

5a.

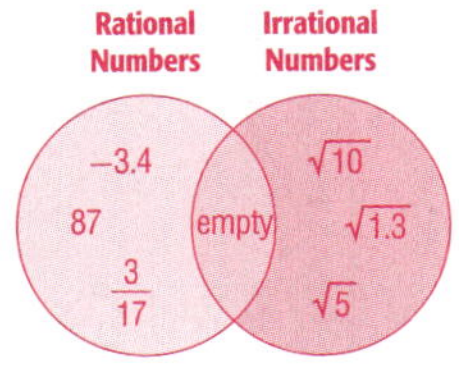


5b.

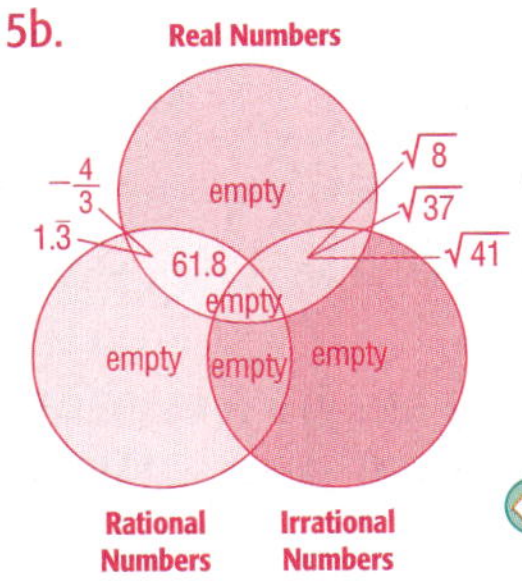


6. No; All integers are rational numbers. Irrational numbers are decimals that are not rational. So, no integer can also be irrational.

Calculators can be deceptive because they can only show a certain number of digits. If a number has more digits than a calculator can handle, some of the digits at the end simply do not appear on the screen.

So, what about a number like $\sqrt{20}$? Use your calculator to find the value of $\sqrt{20}$. You will discover that it has more digits than a calculator will display. That means it could be one of three types of numbers.

- It could have a set number of nonzero digits to the right of the decimal point.

  Such numbers are called *terminating decimals* because the digits eventually stop, or terminate. Since you can find a ratio of integers equal to a terminating decimal, these numbers are rational.
- It could have nonzero digits to the right of the decimal point that continue forever in a repeating pattern; $0.3\overline{24}$ is an example of such a number.

  Such numbers are called *nonterminating, repeating decimals.* They are also rational, although this fact will not be shown here. For example, $0.\overline{3}$ is equal to $\frac{1}{3}$.
- It could have nonzero digits to the right of the decimal point that continue forever without ever repeating.

  Such numbers are called *nonterminating, nonrepeating decimals.* As it turns out, *any* such number is irrational.

The number $\sqrt{20}$ is a nonterminating, nonrepeating decimal, so it is irrational.

In fact, any whole number that is not a perfect square has an irrational square root.

## Develop & Understand: B

**5.** Draw a Venn diagram that shows each relationship. Write three numbers in each area of the diagram. If no numbers belong in an area, label the area "empty."

**a.** The relationship between rational and irrational numbers

**b.** The relationship among rational numbers, irrational numbers, and real numbers

**6.** Could there be a number that is both an integer and an irrational number? Explain your answer.



**Teacher Tips** Have students read the discussion in the text about the square root of 20, then discuss the three types of numbers that $\sqrt{20}$ might be using an overhead calculator display, if possible.

An alternate way to approximate the value of a square root is to use unit cubes or blocks to create a model. To determine the square root of 11, start by creating a square of blocks for the closest perfect square to 11, which is 9. This tells you that the whole number part of the approximation is the square root of 9 which is 3. Once you have the $3 \times 3$ square, add enough blocks to create the next perfect square. In this case, add 7 blocks to create a $4 \times 4$ square. Now ask the students, how many of these new blocks were needed to have a total of 11 blocks? The answer is 2 which can be expressed as the fraction $\frac{2}{7}$.

## Develop & Understand: B

*Suggested Grouping: Small Groups*

▶ **Exercise 5** Have volunteers display their Venn diagrams. Then discuss their answers as a class.

### Math Link

Students should be familiar with repeating decimal notation. Point out that if a decimal repeats, it is *not* irrational.

## Mathematical Background

Some students may be curious about finding the square root of a negative number. Ask them, "What is the square root of −1?" Emphasize that the product of any real number with itself is positive, even if the number is negative. There is no real number that is the square root of −1. The square root of negative numbers belong to a different set of numbers called the *imaginary numbers.* These numbers have applications in advanced science and engineering.

▶ **Exercise 7** This exercise may be confusing for students, especially if they try to find the square root of the negative integer, which is not a real number.

▶ **Exercise 8** You may want to discuss this exercise as a class. Point out that this expression gives a negative number because it asks you to find the opposite of a number. Since there are two numbers whose square is a positive number, this expression represents how you find the second of the two numbers (the "non-principal" square root).

**Wrap-Up** Summarize the results of Exercise 7 by giving more examples. Make sure students understand the notation in Exercise 8 so they do not confuse it with finding the square root of a negative number.

## Develop & Understand: C

*Suggested Grouping: Individuals*

▶ **Exercise 11** These square roots are all between 11 and 12. Encourage students to estimate these whole numbers first and then draw the number line with one-tenth as the interval between tick marks.

▶ **Exercise 12** Extend Exercise 11 by saying that if you want to estimate a square root that is in an interval of one-tenths, then you have to show hundredths on your number line.

▶ **Exercise 13** Because pi is irrational, it does not have an exact numerical value. It is the ratio of the circumference of a circle to its diameter. This ratio is represented by the symbol $\pi$. For example, the circumference of a circle with a radius of 1 equals $2\pi$.

If you wish to calculate a numerical value for the circumference, you could approximate the value of $\pi$. The approximatation often used by engineers is 3.14159, and the approximation of 3.14 is used in many daily applications.

**Wrap-Up** Point out that while a calculator gives a quick answer to finding the square root of a number, these exercises show the relative placement of square roots between two other numbers.

### Share & Summarize

Ask students to give examples for each of these groups. Discuss the answers as a class and provide more examples.



7. All but irrational. The square of a negative integer must be a positive integer, which makes it also a whole number, a natural number, and a rational number.

**Real-World Link**

Mathematicians have been approximating $\pi$ for a very long time. In the 19th century B.C., the Babylonians approximated $\pi$ as $\frac{25}{8}$, or 3.125. An Egyptian document from before 1500 B.C. approximates $\pi$ as $\frac{256}{81}$, which is a little greater than 3.16. Today, mathematicians use computers to calculate $\pi$ to over a trillion decimal places.

8. By order of operations, it means take the square root of 25 and then multiply it by $-1$. So, $-\sqrt{25} = -5$.

12. Answers will vary. $\sqrt{142}$ and $\sqrt{143}$ are reasonable guesses given the placement of $\sqrt{140}$. All are indeed between 11.9 and 12.

**7.** To which of the following sets does the square of a negative integer belong? Explain your reasoning.

| | | |
|---|---|---|
| rational numbers | irrational numbers | integers |
| natural numbers | whole numbers | real numbers |

**8.** What is meant by the expression $-\sqrt{25}$?

**9.** What is the value of $(-\sqrt{25})^2$? 25

In the next exercise set, you can use a number line to approximate the value of irrational square roots.

## Develop & Understand: C

For Exercise 10, consider the following numbers.

$$\sqrt{35},\ \sqrt{50},\ \sqrt{60},\ \sqrt{90},\ \sqrt{115},\ \sqrt{125},\ \sqrt{150},\ \sqrt{200}$$

**10.** Draw a number line that extends from 5 to 15. Mark the approximate location of each square root. See margin.

For Exercises 11 and 12, consider these numbers.

$$\sqrt{125},\ \sqrt{126},\ \sqrt{130},\ \sqrt{137},\ \sqrt{140}$$

**11.** Use a number line to mark the approximate location of each square root to the nearest tenth. See margin.

**12.** Without using your calculator, find a square root that you estimate to be between 11.9 and 12. Then calculate to check your estimate. Were you correct?

**13. Challenge** Not all irrational numbers are roots. One famous irrational number with which you are already familiar is $\pi$.

**a.** What is $\pi$ to five decimal places? 3.14159

**b.** You may recall that $\pi$ is the ratio of the circumference to the diameter of a circle and is an irrational number. Can both the circumference and the diameter be rational? Why or why not? See margin.

### Share & Summarize

Tell whether the members of each group are *always rational, sometimes rational,* or *never rational.* Explain your reasoning or give examples.

**a.** integers Always rational

**b.** square roots See margin.

**c.** decimals See margin.

**d.** expressions that use a radical sign in their simplified form Never rational. Examples: $\sqrt{7}$, $\sqrt{11}$



## Troubleshooting

Watch for students who think that the negative integers are not rational numbers. Point out that a negative integer can also be expressed as the ratio of two integers (using 1 as the denominator), and therefore it is rational.

See p. 365A for answers to 10, 11, 13b, Share & Summarize b, c.

## Practice & Apply

**Find the square of each number.**

**1.** 5 25
**2.** 13 169
**3.** 20 400
**4.** 24.5 600.25
**5.** $\frac{5}{6}$ $\frac{25}{36}$
**6.** 0.7 0.49

**7.** List five perfect squares between 100 and 500. Possible answers: 121, 144, 169, 196, 225.

**8.** The area of a square garden is 324 $ft^2$. How long is each side of the garden? 18 ft

For Exercises 9–14, determine whether each number is rational or irrational. If a number is rational, write it as a ratio of two integers. If it is irrational, explain how you know.

**9.** $\sqrt{36}$ Rational; $\frac{6}{1}$
**10.** $\sqrt{\frac{25}{144}}$ Rational; $\frac{5}{12}$
**11.** $-3.125$ Rational; $-\frac{25}{8}$
**12.** $\sqrt{170}$
**13.** $-\sqrt{4}$
**14.** $\pi\sqrt{4}$

12. Irrational; Since $13^2 = 169$, $14^2 = 196$, 170 is not a perfect square. The square root of a whole number that is not a perfect square is irrational.
13. Rational; $-\frac{2}{1}$
14. Irrational. $\pi$ is irrational and cannot be expressed as the quotient of two integers.

For Exercises 15–20, find the two whole numbers that each square root lies between without using your calculator.

**15.** $\sqrt{66}$ 8 and 9
**16.** $\sqrt{80}$ 8 and 9
**17.** $\sqrt{150}$ 12 and 13
**18.** $\sqrt{17}$ 4 and 5
**19.** $\sqrt{71}$ 8 and 9
**20.** $\sqrt{4.3}$ 2 and 3

**21.** Refer back to Exercises 15–20 to find three square roots that lie between the same two whole numbers. Without using your calculator, draw a number line to mark the approximate locations of these square roots. See below.

## Connect & Extend

**22.** Ajay squared a number, and the result was the same as the number with which he started. What number might he have squared? Give all the possibilities. 0 or 1

**23.** Hector squared a number, and the result was 10 times the number with which he started. What was his starting number? 10

**24.** Marjorie squared a number, and the result was less than the number with which she started. Give two possible starting numbers for Marjorie. Possible answer: 0.3, 0.99

**25.** Beng squared a number and got 390,625. Without using your calculator, find the possible ones digit of his original number. Explain. See margin.

21.
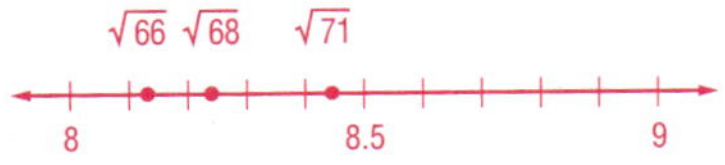




**Additional Answer**

25. 5; The product of 5 and 5 is 25.



**Investigation 1**
Pages 331–335
Practice & Apply: 1–14
Connect & Extend: 28, 30–33

**Investigation 2**
Pages 336–338
Practice & Apply: 15–21
Connect & Extend: 22–27, 29, 34, 35

**Assign Anytime**
Mixed Review: 36–39

▶ **Exercises 9–14** Tell students they can double-check their answers by asking if the number underneath the radical sign is a perfect square. If so, they can say "rational" immediately.

▶ **Exercise 14** Point out that if any part of an expression is irrational, then the entire expression is irrational. Since this product has a factor of $\pi$, the expression is irrational (even if the other factor is a perfect square).

▶ **Exercises 15–20** If students are having difficulty with these exercises, suggest they make a table listing the first 20 integers and their squares. Then, each square root has to be between two of these integer square roots.

▶ **Exercises 27 and 28** You may want students to use the solve a simpler problem problem-solving strategy for this exercise. Have them make a table of values for smaller squared numbers and then decide how to answer the question without a calculator.

▶ **Exercise 28** You may want students to order these prices from least to greatest as if on a number line. Then have them estimate the square root and give one-half the number for each number before they answer the question.

## Additional Answers

26. 4 or 6; Both numbers square to give a number that ends in 6.

29b. $\sqrt{9.87}$: Possible explanation: use a calculator to approximate $3\frac{10}{71}$ as 3.141 and $3\frac{1}{7}$ as 3.143. Then square these two decimals to get about 9.877 and about 9.878. Find a square root between $\sqrt{9.866}$ and $\sqrt{9.878}$.

28f. When the price is more than \$4.00; When the price is less than \$4.00

29a. Answers will vary. Check students' work. Possible answers: 3.1409, 3.141, 3.1411, 3.1412, 3.1413; Possible strategy: Use a calculator to approximate $3\frac{10}{71}$ as 3.1408 and $3\frac{1}{7}$ as 3.1429. Then locate terminating or repeating decimals less than $3\frac{1}{7}$ and greater than $3\frac{10}{71}$.

On Your Own Exercises

**26.** Marcela squared a number and got 15,376. Without using your calculator, find the possible ones digit of her original number. Explain. See margin.

**27.** Joseph squared a number and got 284,089. Without using your calculator, find the possible ones digit of his original number. Explain. 3 or 7; Both numbers square to give a number that ends in 9.

**28.** **Economics** The school store is having a two-day sale. If you shop Thursday, the sale price of any item is the square root of the original price. If you shop Friday, the sale price of any item is half of the original price.

In Parts a–e, tell which day you should shop to get the item at the lowest price.

**a.** 

Thursday

**b.** 

Friday

**c.** 

Friday

**d.** 

Friday

**e.** 

Thursday

**f.** In general, for what prices do you save more by taking the square root? For what prices do you save more by taking half?

**29.** In the third century B.C., a Greek mathematician named Archimedes used a geometric proof to show that $3\frac{10}{71} < \pi < 3\frac{1}{7}$.

**a.** Find five rational numbers that lie between $3\frac{10}{71}$ and $3\frac{1}{7}$. Explain how you know they are within the range.

**b.** Find an irrational number that lies between $3\frac{10}{71}$ and $3\frac{1}{7}$. Explain how you found it. See margin.



340 CHAPTER 7 Real Numbers

Refer to the circle for Exercises 30–33. The circumference of the circle is 18 units. For Exercises 30 and 31, express answers in terms of $\pi$.

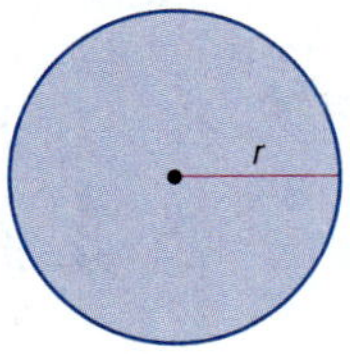


32.

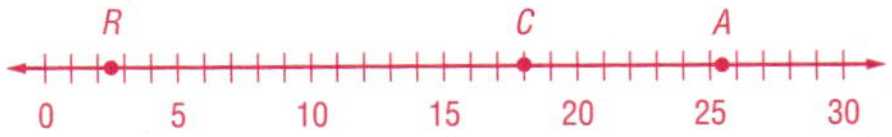


**30.** Find the radius of the circle. $\frac{9}{\pi}$ units

**31.** Find the area of the circle. $\frac{81}{\pi}$ units$^2$

**32.** Use a number line to graph the approximate location of the values of the circumference, radius, and area. Use *C*, *R*, and *A* to label the points.

**33.** Which, if any, of the three were you able to locate exactly? Circumference

**34.** The Venn diagram below shows the relationship between the negative numbers and the rational numbers.

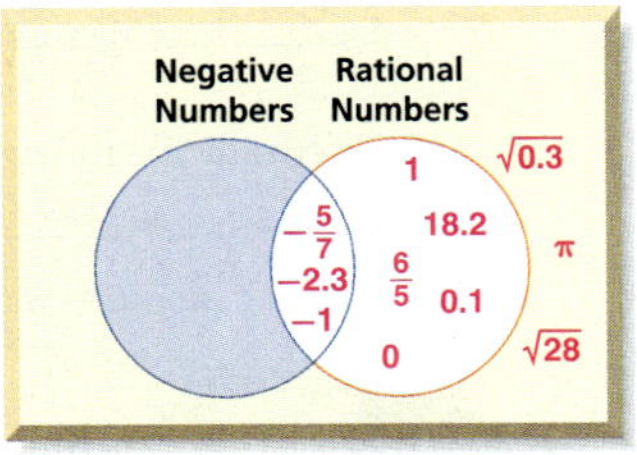


**a.** In each *unshaded* area, including the area outside the circles, write three numbers that represent the indicated relationship.

**b.** Describe the set of numbers that belong in the shaded area. Give three examples.

**c.** Where does $\sqrt{140}$ belong in this diagram? Outside all the rings; It is irrational but positive.

**35.** **In Your Own Words** Write a paragraph about rational, irrational, and real numbers. How are rational and irrational numbers different? How are they alike? What is their relationship to the real numbers? See margin.

34a. See diagram above. Possible answers given.

34b. Irrational numbers that are negative. Possible examples: $-\sqrt{7}$, $-\sqrt{3.5}$, $-\sqrt{101}$.



**On Your Own Exercises**

▶ **Exercises 30–32** Discuss with the class the meaning of "locate exactly." Point out that if an approximation is not given for $\pi$ or for a square root, then they are giving exact answers. In other words, if $\pi$ appears in the answer, they are giving an exact answer.

▶ **Exercise 34** Ask pairs of students to check their answers. Ask them to list any numbers they think do not fit in their partner's Venn diagram and explain their reasoning.

▶ **Exercise 35** Encourage students to use a Venn diagram in their explanation.

## Additional Answer

35. Possible answer: Rational numbers can be written as the quotient of two integers. They include natural numbers, whole numbers, integers, fractions, mixed numbers, repeating and terminating decimals. Irrational numbers cannot be written as the quotient of two integers. Examples include $\pi$ and the square roots of non-perfect squares, such as $\sqrt{7}$. Rational and irrational numbers are real numbers.

## Quick Check

**Informal Assessment** Students should be able to:

- ✔ relate square roots to the side length of a square
- ✔ find the square root of a perfect square
- ✔ approximate the square root of a number
- ✔ place square roots and irrational numbers on a number line
- ✔ classify a number as rational or irrational

## Quick Quiz

For Exercises 1–3, find the two whole numbers each given square root is between. Do not use a calculator.

1. $\sqrt{83}$ 9 and 10
2. $\sqrt{8}$ 2 and 3
3. $\sqrt{39}$ 6 and 7

Find the square of each number.

4. 12.4 153.76
5. $\frac{6}{7}$ $\frac{36}{49}$
6. Draw a number line that extends from 5 to 10. Mark the approximate location of each square root below.

$\sqrt{40}$ $\sqrt{63}$ $\sqrt{92}$

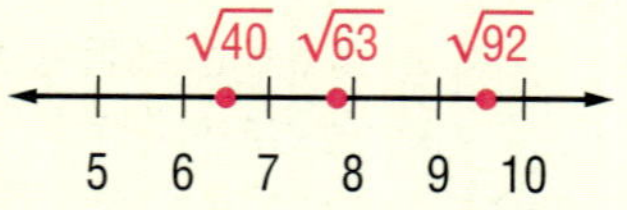


For Exercises 7–10, determine whether each number is rational or irrational. Explain.

7. $\sqrt{64}$ Rational; it is an integer
8. $\sqrt{1.44}$ Rational; it can be written as a ratio of two integers
9. $\sqrt{84}$ Irrational; it is a non-terminating, non-repeating decimal
10. $\sqrt{\frac{50}{150}}$ Irrational; it is a non-terminating, non-repeating decimal



### Mixed Review

36a. Yes, the game is fair; each girl has a one in four chance of winning each time the two chips are tossed.

36b. No, the game is not fair, since the new chip has no blue sides, it is impossible for Sue to score any points.

**36.** Sue and Evelyn have two chips. Both are red on one side and blue on the other. Each girl tosses a chip. Sue scores one point if the chips are blue. Evelyn scores one point if the chips are red. Neither girl receives a point if the chips are not the same color.

**a.** Is the game fair? Explain how you know.

**b.** Suppose a chip that is red on both sides is added. Is the game fair now? Explain.

**37.** Ms. Martino wants to ship several smaller boxes in one larger box to save on postage. Each small box measures 6 inches by 12 inches by 18 inches. The larger box measures 2 feet by $1\frac{1}{2}$ feet by 1 foot.

**a.** How many smaller boxes can Ms. Martino fit into one larger box? 4

**b.** Find the surface area of the boxes used by Mr. Martino. Small: 792 square inches; large: 13 square feet

**38.** Determine the following metric measurement conversions.

**a.** 5 grams = 5,000 milligrams

**b.** 63 grams = 0.063 kilograms

**c.** 702 grams = 70,200 centigrams

**d.** 1.8 hectograms = 180 grams

**39.** Determine the following customary measurement conversions.

**a.** 2 pounds = 32 ounces **b.** 3 tons = 6,000 pounds

**c.** 0.5 pound = 8 ounces **d.** 1.5 pounds = 24 ounces

LESSON

# 7.3 The Pythagorean Theorem

## Objectives

- ▶ To determine a graphical understanding of the Pythagorean theorem
- ▶ To develop an understanding of how a right triangle and squares are related through the Pythagorean theorem
- ▶ To use the Pythagorean theorem to determine the missing side length or hypotenuse length of a right triangle
- ▶ To determine and use the distance formula

## Overview

This lesson reviews and extends what students know about right triangles and distances. In addition, students will use their skills of graphing coordinates to assist in their development of the distance formula.

## Advance Preparation

You may want to have several copies of dot paper available for students to use in making sketches and answering their assigned questions.

| | Summary | Materials | On Your Own Exercises (pp. 355–360) | Assessment Opportunities |
|---|---|---|---|---|
| **Investigation 1** (p. 343) Pacing: 2 days | Students will use a graphical approach to understand how the Pythagorean theorem works. | Lesson 7.3 Masters 1, 2, scissors, copies of the figures | Practice & Apply: 1–5<br>Connect & Extend: 11<br>Mixed Review: 16–39 | • On the Spot Assessment (p. 343)<br>• Share & Summarize (p. 347)<br>• Troubleshooting (pp. 344, 346) |
| **Investigation 2** (p. 347) Pacing: 1 day | Students use their knowledge of the Pythagorean Theorem to find missing lengths of right triangles. | | Practice & Apply: 6–10<br>Connect & Extend: 12–13<br>Mixed Review: 16–39 | • On the Spot Assessment (p. 348)<br>• Share & Summarize (p. 350)<br>• Troubleshooting (pp. 347, 350) |
| **Inquiry Investigation** (p. 351) Pacing: 1 day | Students use their knowledge of graphing coordinates and the Pythagorean theorem to determine distances and ultimately determine the distance formula. | copy of grid, ruler | | |

# Leveled Lesson Resources

CRM *Available in:* **Chapter 7 Resource Masters**

Also on TeacherWorks™ Lesson 7.3

## Study Guide and Intervention (p. 14) AL

**Lesson 7.3 Study Guide and Intervention**
***The Pythagorean Theorem***

The sides of a right triangle have special names. The sides adjacent to the right angle are the **legs.** The side opposite the right angle is the **hypotenuse.**

The **Pythagorean Theorem** describes the relationship between the length of the hypotenuse and the lengths of the legs. In a right triangle, the square of the length of the hypotenuse equals the sum of the squares of the lengths of the legs.

$c^2 = a^2 + b^2$

**Example** Find the missing measure of a right triangle if $a$ = 4 inches and $b$ = 3 inches.

| | |
|---|---|
| $c^2 = a^2 + b^2$ | Pythagorean Theorem |
| $c^2 = 4^2 + 3^2$ | Replace $a$ with 4 and $b$ with 3. |
| $c^2 = 16 + 9$ | Evaluate $4^2$ and $3^2$. |
| $c^2 = 25$ | Add. |
| $\sqrt{c^2} = \sqrt{25}$ | Take the square root of each side. |
| $c = 5$ | Simplify. |

The length of the hypotenuse is 5 inches.

**Exercises**

**Find the missing measure of each right triangle. Round to the nearest tenth if necessary.**

1. 9 in., 4 in., c in.
2. 5 m, c m, 7.5 m
3. a cm, 13 cm, 16 cm

## Skills Practice (p. 15) AL OL

**Lesson 7.3 Skills Practice**
***The Pythagorean Theorem***

Find each missing area.

1. ? in², 576 in², 100 in²
2. 81 in², 225 in², ? in²

Find each missing side length.

3. 20 m, 25 m, b m
4. c in., 5 in., 5 in.
5. 15 ft, c ft, 8 ft
6. c in., 20.3 in., 32 in.
7. a yd, 2.7 yd, 3 yd
8. 6.7 mm, c mm, 14 mm

Use the distance formula or the Pythagorean Theorem to find the distance between the given points.

9. (5, 6) and (0, –6)
10. (–1, 9) and (2, 5)
11. (10, –14) and (3, 10)
12. (0, 0) and (–4, –4)

## Problem-Solving Practice (p. 16) AL OL

**Lesson 7.3 Problem-Solving Practice**
***The Pythagorean Theorem***

Solve.

1. **Origami** Chee has a piece of paper measuring 8.5 inches by 8.5 inches. If she folds the paper diagonally in half, how long is the folded side? Round to the nearest tenth.
2. **Computers** In a computer catalog, a computer monitor is listed as 19 inches. This distance is the diagonal distance across the screen. If the screen is 10 inches high, what is the width of the screen? Round to the nearest tenth.
3. **Antennas** A wire 10 meters long is supporting a utility pole. The wire is anchored to the ground and is attached to the pole 9 meters above the ground. What is the distance from the bottom of the pole to the point where the wire is attached to the ground? Round to the nearest tenth.

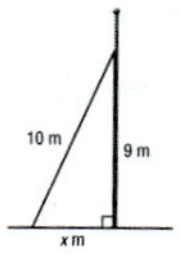


4. **Maps** A map of the local mall shows the location of each store with respect to the entrance (0, 0). How far did Francisco walk to go from the music store to the clothing store? Round your answer to the nearest tenth of a meter.

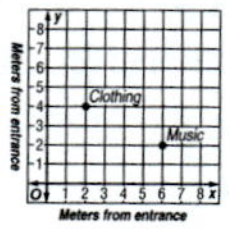


5. **Construction** A zoo is building a triangular deck between two square buildings. The buildings meet at a right angle. The side length of one building is 25 feet, and the side length of the other building is 30 feet. What will be the measurement of the third side of the deck, the hypotenuse?
6. **Ramps** Crystal wants to build a ramp that will rise 4 feet over a horizontal distance of 20 feet. How long will the ramp be? Round to the nearest tenth.

## Enrichment (p. 17) BL

**Lesson 7.3 Enrichment**
***The Pythagorean Theorem***

**Pythagoras in the Air**

In the diagram at the right, an airplane heads north at 180 mi/h. But, the wind is blowing towards the east at 30 mi/h. So, the airplane is really traveling east of north. The middle arrow in the diagram shows the actual direction of the airplane.

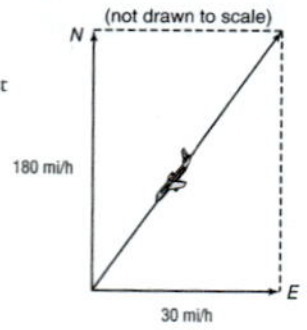


The actual speed of the plane can be found using the Pythagorean Theorem.

$$\sqrt{30^2 + 180^2} = \sqrt{900 + 32{,}400}$$
$$= \sqrt{33{,}300}$$
$$\approx 182.5$$

The plane's actual speed is about 182.5 mi/h.

**Find the actual speed of each airplane. Round answers to the nearest tenth. (You might wish to draw a diagram to help you solve the problem.)**

1. An airplane travels at 240 mi/h east. A wind is blowing at 20 mi/h toward the south.
2. An airplane travels at 620 mi/h west. A wind is blowing at 35 mi/h toward the south.
3. An airplane travels at 450 mi/h south. A wind is blowing at 40 mi/h toward the east.
4. An airplane travels at 1,200 mi/h east. A wind is blowing at 30 mi/h toward the north.

## Lesson Quick Quiz (p. 18) AL OL BL

**Lesson 7.3 Quick Quiz**

1. Draw a right triangle and label the sides as legs or hypotenuse.
2. If a right triangle with squares attached has areas of 9 square units for the smallest square and 25 square units for the largest square, what is the area for the third square? What are the side lengths for the triangle?
3. A right triangle has legs that measure 1 cm and 12 cm, what is the measure of the hypotenuse?
4. Hsin Lee wants to purchase a television that will fit into an entertainment center that has an opening of 30 inches by 40 inches. The size of a television is given in inches, and that number represents the diagonal of the screen. What is the largest television Hsin Lee can purchase?

## Lesson Masters 1–2 (pp. 19–20)

**Lesson 7.3 Master 1**
***The Pythagorean Theorem***

**Investigation 1: Develop & Understand: A**

| Problem | Area of Square on Side $a$ (units²) | Area of Square on Side $b$ (units²) | Area of Square on Side $c$ (units²) |
|---|---|---|---|
| 1 | | | |
| 2 | | | |
| 3 | | | |
| 4 | | | |

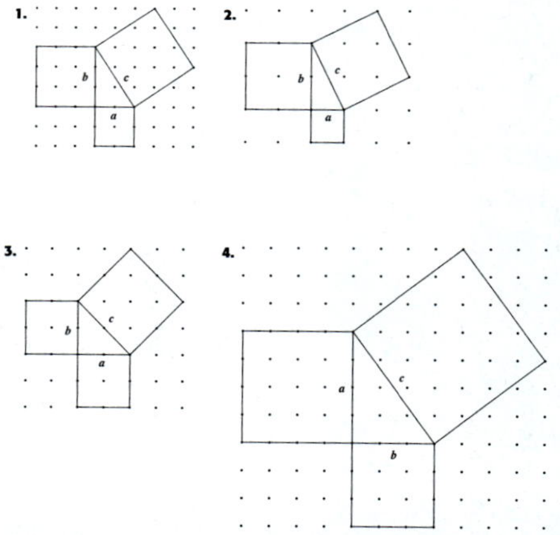


# Additional Lesson Resources

### Teacher Tech Tools
- TeacherWorks
- ExamView Assessment Suite
- Classroom Presentation Toolkit
- Advance Tracker

### Student Tech Tools
- StudentWorks Plus
- Math Online eGlossary • Concepts in Motion

### Other Print Products
- Investigation Notebook and Reflection Journal
- Quick Review Math Handbook

LESSON 7.3

# The Pythagorean Theorem

In this lesson, you will learn about a famous mathematical concept known as the *Pythagorean Theorem*. The Pythagorean Theorem expresses a remarkable relationship between **right triangles**, which are triangles that have one 90° angle, and squares.



Before you investigate the theorem, you will find the area of a square drawn on dot paper.

### Vocabulary

- right triangle

### Materials

- copy of the square

### Explore

Find the exact area of this square. Describe the method you use.

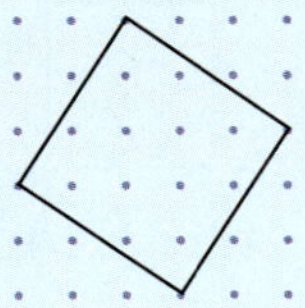

13 sq units; See the teaching notes for possible strategies.

## Investigation 1 Right Triangles and Squares

### Vocabulary

- hypotenuse
- leg
- Pythagorean Theorem

### Materials

- copies of the figures
- dot paper
- scissors

Every right triangle has one right angle. The side opposite the right angle is called the **hypotenuse**. The other two sides are called the **legs**.

The relationship expressed in the Pythagorean Theorem involves the areas of squares built on the sides of a right triangle. You will discover that relationship in Exercises 1–6.

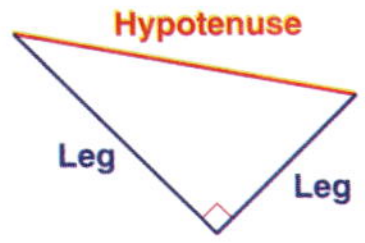




### On the Spot Assessment

How do you identify the hypotenuse in a right triangle? It is the side opposite the right angle and it is also the longest side of a right triangle.



## Introduce

**Background** Tell students that the Pythagorean Theorem was discovered many centuries ago. It is one of the most famous facts in mathematics, and it has many uses in mathematics and real life. Discuss the meaning of the term *right triangle*, and sketch some right triangles on the board.

### Explore

Students will be using right triangles and squares drawn on dot paper in the problems leading up to the Pythagorean Theorem. This Explore will serve as a warm-up. You may want to allow students to work in pairs. Each pair will need one copy of Lesson 7.3 Master 1.

One way to find the area of the square is to enclose the given square in a larger square, as shown below. To find the area of the original square, find the area of the larger square and subtract the areas of the four right triangles that surround the smaller square.

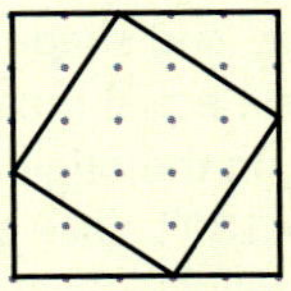

## Investigation 1

***On Your Own Exercises***
Pages 355–360
Exercises 1–5, 11

**New Terms** In this investigation, students learn the terms *hypotenuse* and *legs*. They examine several figures on dot paper that illustrate the Pythagorean Theorem. They learn what the theorem says and examine a proof.

Discuss the new vocabulary with the class. Emphasize that the term *hypotenuse* is used only in connection with right triangles. In a right triangle, the hypotenuse is always the side opposite the right angle. It is always the longest side of the right triangle.

## Develop & Understand: A

*Suggested Grouping: Pairs*

In this problem set, students use Lesson 7.3 Master 2 to examine right triangles and squares drawn on their sides. Studying the relationship between the areas of the squares leads students to the Pythagorean Theorem.

Students have probably overlooked one subtle but important detail: how do we know that the quadrilateral drawn on each hypotenuse really is perfectly square? They certainly look square, but how can we be sure the interior angles are exactly 90°? A look at the figure for Exercise 1 can resolve this question.

The diagram below shows the figure for Exercise 1. Notice that another right triangle has been included on the right side.

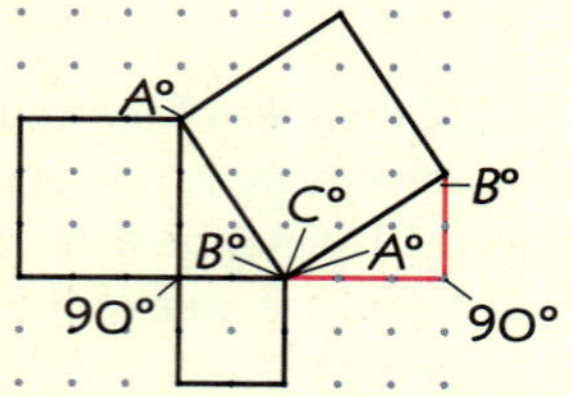


Notice the labels indicating angle measures in the right triangles. The two right triangles are the same size and shape, so the two acute angles have equal measures $A^\circ$ and $B^\circ$, as indicated. In the original right triangle, $A^\circ + B^\circ + 90^\circ = 180^\circ$, since the measures of the angles of a triangle have a sum of 180°. From this equation, it follows that $A^\circ + B^\circ = 90^\circ$. At the point where the two right triangles touch, the sum of the three angles composing the 180° straight angle can be written as $A^\circ + C^\circ + B^\circ = 180^\circ$. Regrouping the addends gives $(A^\circ + B^\circ) + C^\circ = 180^\circ$. Since $A^\circ + B^\circ = 90^\circ$, then $C^\circ = 90^\circ$. In a similar manner, all the other angles of the quadrilateral drawn on the hypotenuse are 90° angles. The side lengths of the quadrilateral are all the same, so the quadrilateral is indeed a square.

## Develop & Understand: A

Exercises 1–4 show right triangles with squares drawn on their sides. Find the exact area of each square. Record your results in a copy of the table.

| Exercise Number | Area of Square on Side *a* (units$^2$) | Area of Square on Side *b* (units$^2$) | Area of Square on Side *c* (units$^2$) |
|---|---|---|---|
| 1 | 4 | 9 | 13 |
| 2 | 1 | 4 | 5 |
| 3 | 4 | 4 | 8 |
| 4 | 16 | 9 | 25 |

### Real-World Link

The Pythagorean Theorem is named for Greek mathematician Pythagoras, who lived from approximately 580 to 500 B.C. Records show that the Babylonians understood the Pythagorean Theorem more than 900 years before Pythagoras was born.

**1.**

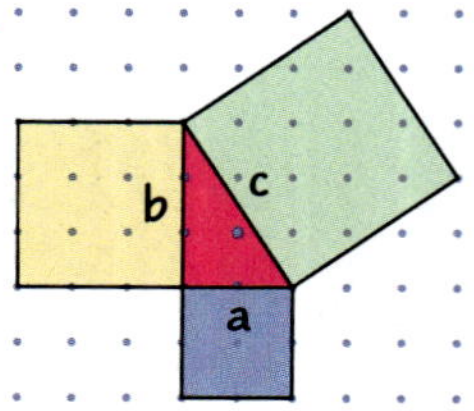


**2.**

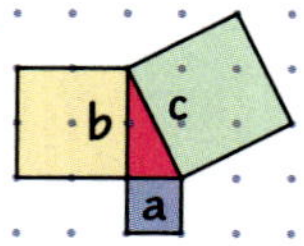


**3.**

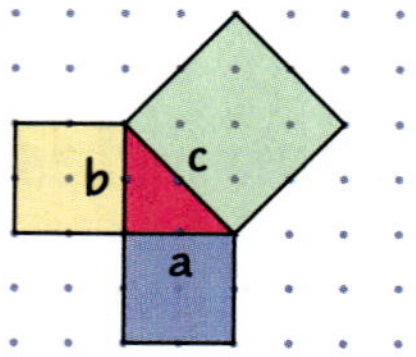


**4.**

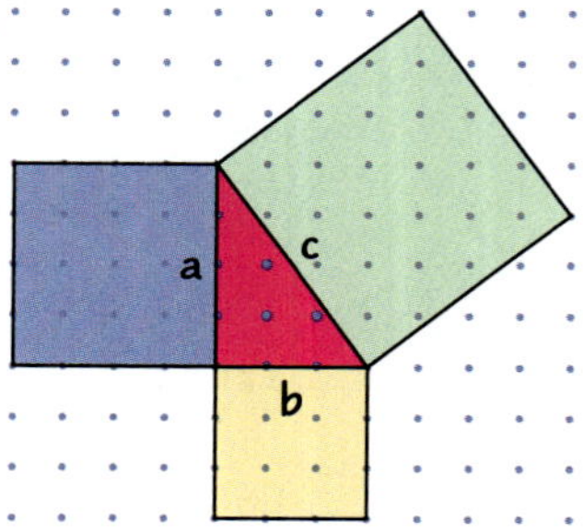




### Troubleshooting

If students are having difficulty answering Exercise 5, give them a hint that there is a relationship between the legs of the triangle and the hypotenuse of the triangle.

5. The area of the square on side *a* plus the area of the square on side *b* equals the area of the square on side *c*.

**5.** Look for a pattern in your table. For the cases you considered, what is the relationship among the areas of the three squares?

**6.** Draw your own right triangle on dot paper. Does the relationship you described in Exercise 5 hold for your triangle as well? Yes

Exercises 1–6 illustrate the **Pythagorean Theorem**, which states the following.

**The Pythagorean Theorem**

In a right triangle, the area of the square built on the hypotenuse of the triangle is equal to the sum of the areas of the squares built on the legs.

The Pythagorean Theorem is often stated this way: If $c$ is the length of the hypotenuse of a right triangle and $a$ and $b$ are the lengths of the legs, then $a^2 + b^2 = c^2$.

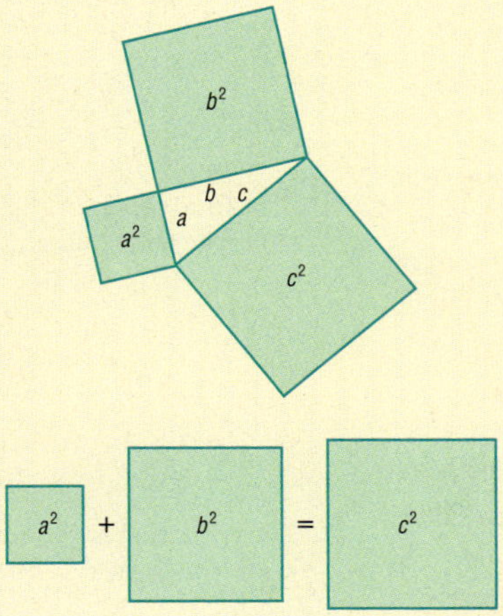

An Ionic column in Olympia, Greece

Throughout history, people have found new ways to prove the Pythagorean Theorem; that is, to show that it is always true. In Exercises 7–10, you will explore one such proof.



▶ **Exercise 6** Students should have a copy of Lesson 7.3 Master 3 (1-centimeter dot paper). You will need to take a careful look at the diagrams students draw. They must be sure that the quadrilaterals they draw on the sides of the right triangle really are squares.

**Wrap-Up** Be sure to discuss the answer for Exercise 5, because the pattern students discover points the way to the Pythagorean Theorem.

When you talk about the Pythagorean Theorem, be sure to discuss both versions stated in the box. Be sure students understand that although the words are different, the two versions state the same fact. Use the diagram to help students understand this.

## *Mathematical Background*

The relationship stated in the Pythagorean Theorem is remarkable for the fact that it is true for all right triangles. There is good historical evidence that its truth for particular right triangles was known in ancient times in Egypt, Babylonia, India, and China. Greek mathematicians were able to prove that it is true for *all* right triangles.

Many historians of mathematics think that Pythagoras himself was not aware of a general proof of the theorem that bears his name. Whether he was or not, it is clear that his successors were. This theorem has deep connections with many parts of mathematics, both elementary and advanced.

## Develop & Understand: B

*Suggested Grouping: Pairs*

In this exercise set, students examine an actual proof of the Pythagorean Theorem.

The main idea used in the proof can be described as follows: Start with eight copies of the right triangle and the square drawn on its sides. Using these pieces, build two squares that you are sure have the same area. Remove identical pieces from each construction. The areas that remain from the two constructions will be equal.

**Wrap-Up** Conduct a thorough discussion of the activity with the class. You may want to run through all the exercises using a transparency on the overhead projector.

Some students may understand the activities in the problems and have a full appreciation of why proof is desirable. Other students may arrive at that stage later down the road. What is important is to give all students an opportunity to get there.

## Develop & Understand: B

In these exercises, you will use paper triangles and squares to construct a proof of the Pythagorean Theorem.

- Start with a right triangle with squares drawn on its sides.
- Carefully cut out eight copies of the triangle and one copy of each square.

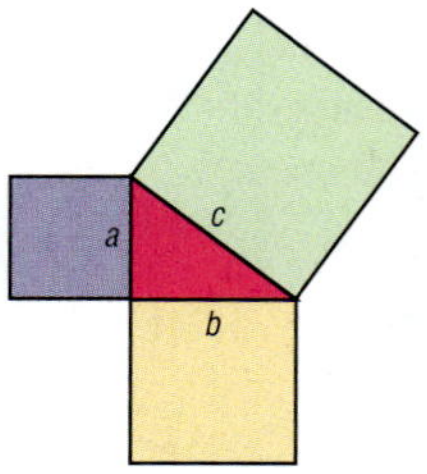


- Use four copies of the triangle and the square from side $c$ to make this square.

- Use four copies of the triangle and the squares from sides $a$ and $b$ to make this square.

**7.** The two squares you made have the same area. Explain how you know this is true.

Now take the four triangles away from each square you constructed.

**8.** Describe what is left of each square.

**9.** Explain why the area of what is left must be the same for both squares.

**10.** Explain how your work in Exercises 7–9 shows that $a^2 + b^2 = c^2$.
The area that is left in the first square is $c^2$. The area that is left in the second square is $a^2 + b^2$. Since the areas are equal, $a^2 + b^2 = c^2$.

7. In both squares, the length of each side is $a + b$, the sum of the lengths of the legs of the right triangle. If two squares have the same side length, they must have the same area.
8. In the first square, the square from side $c$ remains. In the second, the squares from sides $a$ and $b$ remain.
9. I started with two squares with the same area and took away the same four pieces from each square. So, the area of what is left must be the same.



## Troubleshooting

Be on the lookout for common misstatements of the Pythagorean Theorem. Students often come up with the statement, "The square of the length of the longest side of a triangle is equal to the sum of the squares of the other two sides." It would be nice to speak of the squares of the lengths of the other two sides, but not doing so is a minor slip. The defect is that the statement does not say that the triangle is a right triangle. The Pythagorean Theorem is true only for right triangles.

Other students may say, "In a right triangle, $a^2$ plus $b^2$ equals $c^2$." The trouble here is that if the statement were being made to someone who was hearing it for the first time, that person would have no way of knowing that c is the length of the hypotenuse and that a and b are the lengths of the legs of the right triangle. This information should have been included.

## Share & Summarize

State the Pythagorean Theorem in your own words. You might want to draw a picture to illustrate what you mean.

Possible answer: For any right triangle, the sum of the squares of the legs equals the square of the hypotenuse.

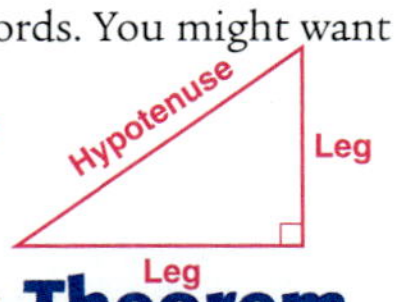


# Investigation 2 Use the Pythagorean Theorem

In this investigation, you will have a chance to use the Pythagorean Theorem.

### Develop & Understand: A

**Find each missing area. Then use the areas of the squares to find the side lengths of the triangle.**

**1.**

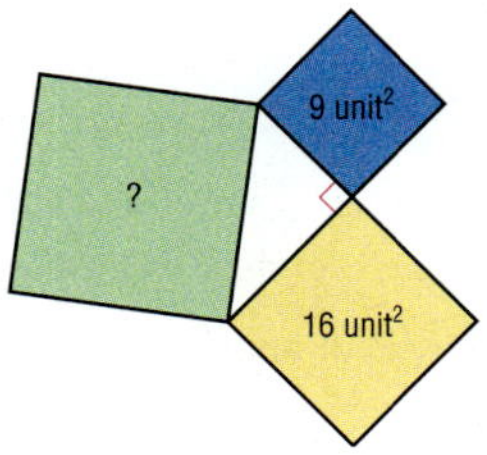


**2.**

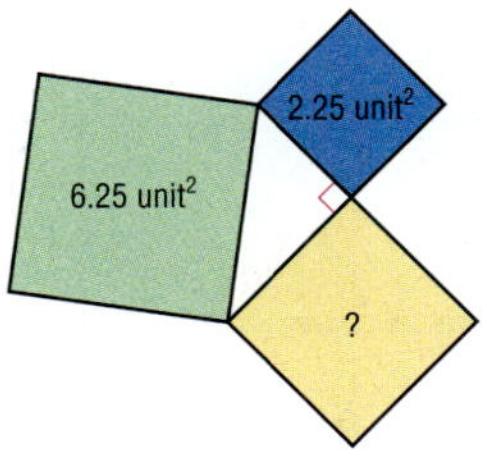


**3.**

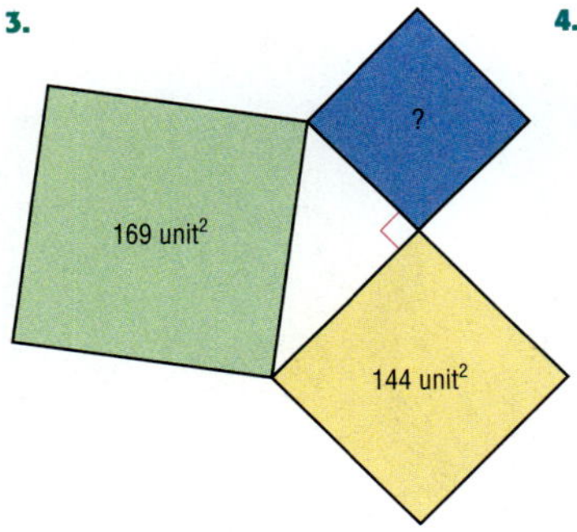


**4.**

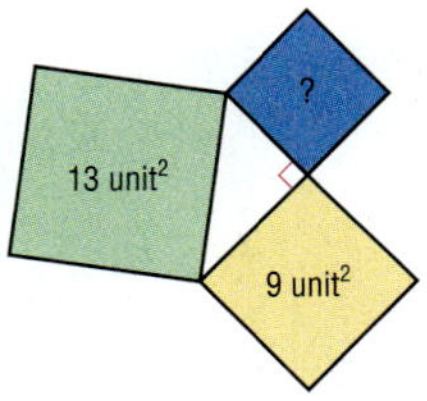


1. 25 unit$^2$; 3 units, 4 units, 5 units
2. 4 unit$^2$; 1.5 units, 2 units, 2.5 units
3. 25 unit$^2$; 5 units, 12 units, 13 units
4. 4 unit$^2$; 2 units, 3 units, $\sqrt{13}$ units (about 3.6 units)



## Troubleshooting

For students having difficulty answering the Exercises, you may want to remind them of the formula for the Pythagorean Theorem. In addition, you may need to remind them that once they find the missing area, they need to take the square root of each area to find the side lengths.

## Share & Summarize

You may want to call on volunteers to read their answers to the class. Discuss their answers to be sure the key points are clearly included.

## Investigation 2

**On Your Own Exercises**
Pages 355–360
Exercises 6–10, 12–13

**Find Missing Measures** In this investigation, students will apply the Pythagorean Theorem to find missing lengths and areas.

### Develop & Understand: A

*Suggested Grouping: Individuals*

In this exercise set, students use the Pythagorean Theorem to find missing areas of squares drawn on sides of right triangles. They then use the square root operation to find the lengths of the sides.

▶ **Exercise 1** Students should note that the unknown area is the area of the square drawn on the hypotenuse. By the Pythagorean Theorem, this area is equal to 9 unit$^2$ + 16 unit$^2$, or 25 unit$^2$. The length of each side of the squares is found by taking the square root of the area values.

▶ **Exercise 2** The missing area, call it $A$, is the area of a square drawn on a leg of the right triangle. By the Pythagorean Theorem, $A + 2.25 = 6.25$. So $A = 4$ unit$^2$. To find the side lengths, take the square root of the area values.

▶ **Exercises 3 and 4** Note that the exact length of the hypotenuse is written as $\sqrt{13}$. If students give the length of this side as a decimal, the decimal should be preceded by the word *about*, since the decimal is an approximate value of $\sqrt{13}$.

## Example

Students may get hung up on the way the triangle is oriented. As you are working on examples in class, try to mix up the orientation of the triangles. Students will need to locate the legs of the triangle. Remind them that they are the sides that form the right angle. This should assist them in determining which values to use in the formula.

The triangle in this example has a hypotenuse measure that is irrational. It may be beneficial to the students if you do an additional example where the triangle has a rational side measure. A simple example could involve a Pythagorean Triple, such as 3, 4, 5 or 5, 12, 13. The use of these measures guarantees not only a rational answer, but a whole number answer.

If you know the lengths of any two sides of a right triangle, you can use the Pythagorean Theorem to find the length of the third side.

### Real-World Link

They may not have known the Pythagorean Theorem, but the Egyptians who built the pyramids knew that a triangle with side lengths of 3, 4, and 5 units must be a right triangle.

They used a rope device, like the one pictured here, to check that they made perfect right angles at the corners of the pyramids.

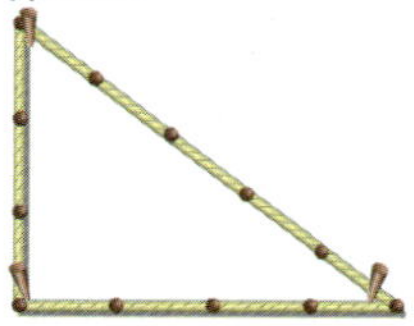

### Example

A right triangle has legs of length 1 inch and 2 inches. How long is the hypotenuse?

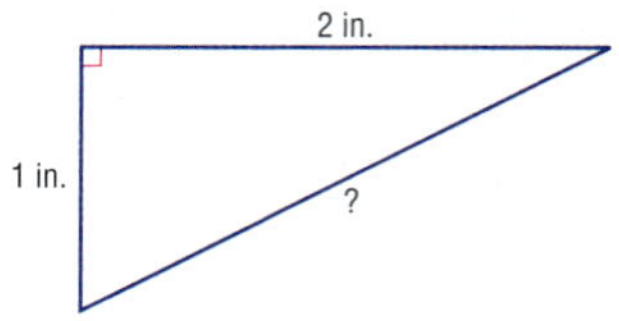


If $a$ and $b$ represent the lengths of the legs and $c$ represents the length of the hypotenuse, the Pythagorean Theorem states that $a^2 + b^2 = c^2$.

In the triangle above, $a = 1$, $b = 2$, and $c$ is the length of the hypotenuse.

$$1^2 + 2^2 = c^2$$
$$1 + 4 = c^2$$
$$5 = c^2$$

Therefore, $c = \sqrt{5}$, or approximately 2.24 inches.

The Great Sphinx in Giza, Egypt

348 CHAPTER 7 Real Numbers

## On the Spot Assessment

Ask the students to write down the formula for the Pythagorean Theorem. Then ask the students to draw a right triangle and label the legs and hypotenuse.

## Develop & Understand: B

**Find each missing side length. Then find the area of the triangle.**

**5.**

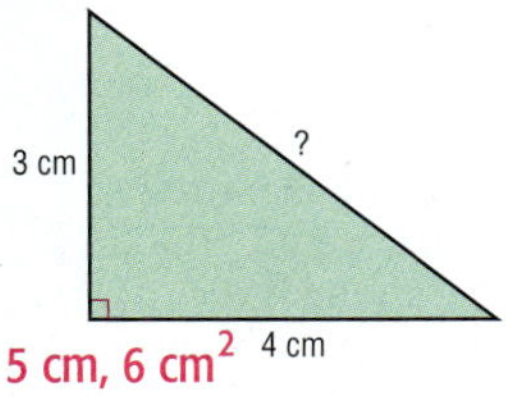


5 cm, 6 cm$^2$

**6.**

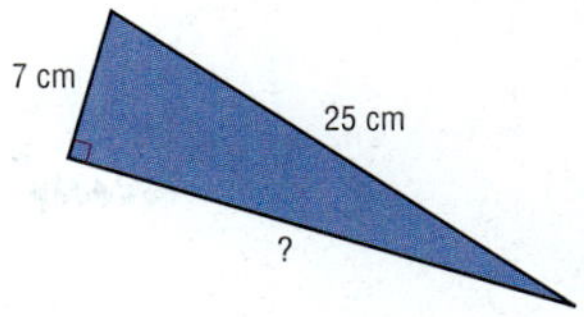


24 cm, 84 cm$^2$

**7.** A rectangular lawn measures 9 meters by 12 meters. Suppose you want to walk from point *A* to point *B*.

**a.** If you obey the sign and walk around the lawn, how far will you walk? 21 m

**b.** If you ignore the sign and walk directly across the lawn, how far will you walk? 15 m

**8.** A baseball diamond is a square measuring 90 feet on each side. What is the distance from home plate to second base? About 127 ft

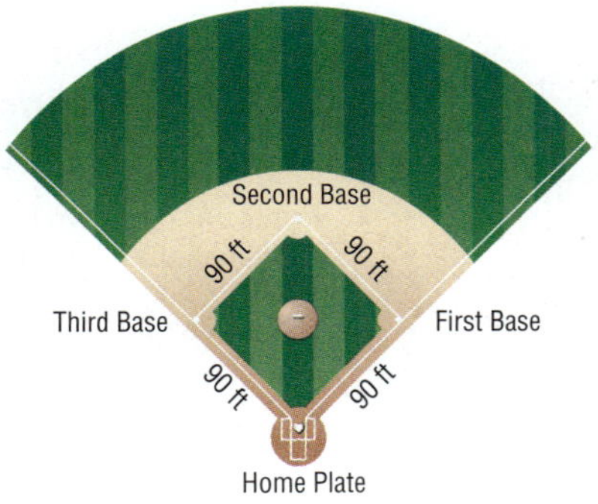




## Develop & Understand: B

*Suggested Grouping: Individuals*

In this exercise set, students look at more applications of the Pythagorean Theorem, including some real-life applications.

▶ **Exercise 7** The diagonal from Point *A* to Point *B* can be thought of as the hypotenuse of a right triangle whose legs have lengths 9 m and 12 m.

### Reaching All Learners

**BL Beyond Level** Ask the students to create a real world problem where they would need to use the Pythagorean theorem to solve the problem. Once the students complete the activity, use their work as a class activity or as part of their assessment.

▶ **Exercise 9** Students will probably find it helpful to sketch a diagram like the one shown below.

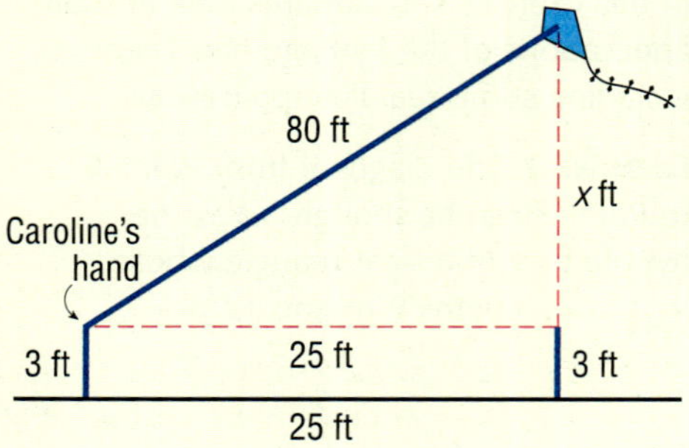


Students can use the Pythagorean Theorem to find the length $x$ and then add 3 ft to find the height of the kite.

▶ **Exercise 10** In part a, students must multiply 11.5 by 2.5. In part b, ask students to sketch the right triangle they will use. Ask them to include the lengths of the legs in the diagram.

▶ **Exercise 11** This exercise takes a touch of insight. It uses the idea that the area of a triangle is the same no matter which side is chosen as a base.

### Share & Summarize

Have volunteers present their exercises to the class. Check that each exercise is clearly stated and solvable. Then ask the class for ideas about how to solve the exercise.

### Additional Answer

9. 79 ft; Possible explanation: The height of the kite is 3 feet plus the length of one leg of this right triangle:

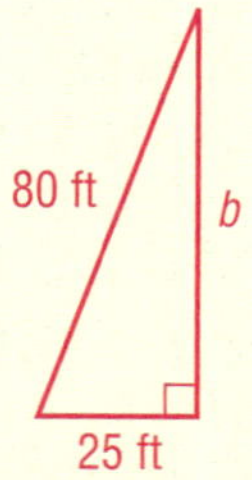


I can use the Pythagorean Theorem to find the missing length:

$25^2 + b^2 = 80^2$

$625 + b^2 = 6{,}400$

$b^2 = 6{,}400 - 625 = 5{,}775$

$b = \sqrt{5{,}775} \approx 76$

Adding 3 ft, the total height above the ground is about 79 ft.

**Real-World Link**

In Thailand, *kite fighting* is a popular sport. A kite-fighting match involves a minimum of two heavy, star-shaped kites called *chulas* and at least four light, diamond-shaped kites called *pakpaos*. Although pakpaos are usually manipulated by a single person, it can take up to 20 people to handle a chula.

11. $c = 13$ cm, $h \approx 4.6$ cm; To find $c$, I used the Pythagorean Theorem: $c^2 = 5^2 + 12^2 = 169$, so $c = 13$. To find $h$, I used the fact that the area of the triangle is $\frac{1}{2} \cdot 12 \cdot 5$, or 30. If the hypotenuse is the base, then $h$ is the height, so $\frac{1}{2} \cdot 13 \cdot h = 30$. So, $h = 30 \div 6.5$, or about 4.6 cm.

1. When you have a right triangle and want to find a missing side length.

**9.** Caroline and Trevor are flying a kite. Caroline is holding the kite and has let out 80 feet of kite string. Trevor is standing 25 feet from Caroline and is directly under the kite.

Caroline is holding the string 3 feet above the ground. How far above the ground is the kite? Explain how you found your answer. See margin.

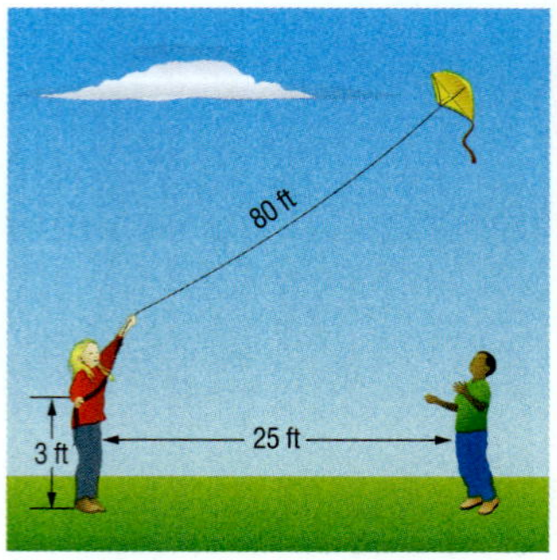


**10.** Safety regulations state that wheelchair ramps cannot be too steep. Suppose that, for every one foot a wheelchair ramp rises, it must cover a horizontal distance of at least 11.5 feet.

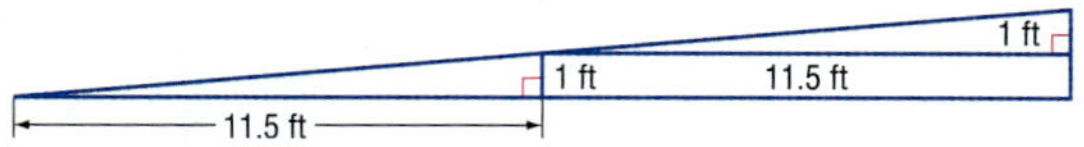


A ramp is being built to a restaurant entrance that is 2.5 feet above the ground.

**a.** How much horizontal distance does the ramp require? At least 28.75 ft

**b.** How long must the ramp be? At least 28.9 ft

**11. Challenge** Find the values of $c$ and $h$. Explain the method you used.

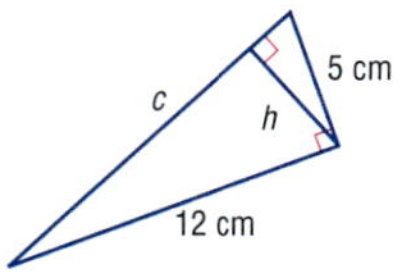


### Share & Summarize

**1.** When do you use the Pythagorean Theorem?

**2.** Write your own exercise that can be solved by using the Pythagorean Theorem. Then show how to solve your equation. Answers will vary. Possible answer: The cross section of a camping tent is shown. Find the side of the tent.

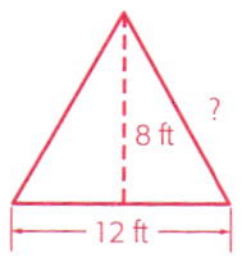


$a^2 + b^2 = c^2$

$8^2 + 6^2 = c^2$

$c^2 = 100$

$c = 10$



### Troubleshooting

When students use the Pythagorean Theorem to find missing lengths, they may correctly find the square of the missing length but forget to take the square root. Students can usually catch the error if you ask whether the answer seems reasonable.

Inquiry

# Investigation 3 The Distance Formula

**Vocabulary**

distance formula

When archaeologists set up a dig, they create a grid on the ground with a string so they can record the locations of the objects they find. In this investigation, you will learn how to find distances between points on a coordinate grid.

## The Situation

Dr. Davis is working on an archaeological dig. He has used string to lay out a grid on the ground. The lines of the grid are one foot apart.

So far, Dr. Davis has unearthed sections of two walls and an object he thinks might have been a toy. He drew this diagram to show the location of these objects on the grid. He labeled the corner of the walls (0, 0).

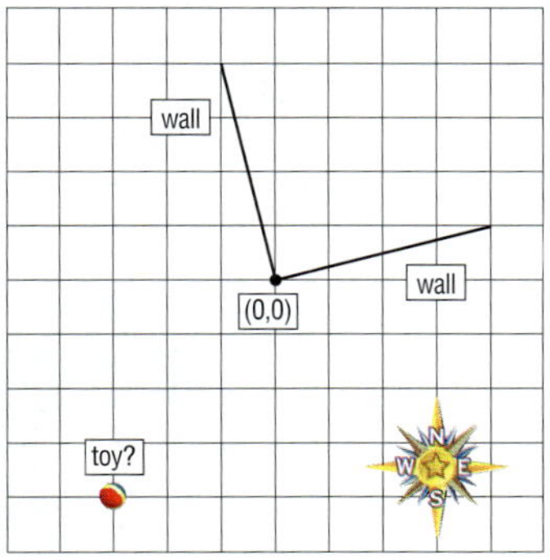


Dr. Davis wants to find the distance from the toy to the corner where the walls meet.

## Try It Out

1. Estimate the distance from the toy to the corner where the walls meet. Estimates will vary.

   Dr. Davis notices that the point (0, 0) and the toy form two vertices of a triangle. He decides to use the Pythagorean Theorem to find the distance from the toy to the corner where the walls meet.

2. Determine the coordinates of the toy and use the Pythagorean Theorem to find the actual distance. How close was your estimate? $(-3, -4)$; 5 ft

Go on



Inquiry

Inquiry

# Investigation 3

*Suggested Grouping: Pairs*

## Materials and Preparation

Supply each student with a copy of the grid with the problem drawn on it and a ruler. This will help students to perform the requested measurements and computations in a more effective manner.

## The Situation

Ask students what they picture when they hear about an archaeological site or dig. Depending on your students' language ability, you may need to describe it as a place where scientists uncover very old objects that have been buried in the ground for many years. Explain that archaeologists frequently make a map of the area they are digging up by creating a grid on the ground with string. This gives them a way to describe the location of different objects that they find.

## Try It Out

Make sure students understand what is shown by the grid. Then give them time to estimate the length of each section of wall and the distance from the toy to the corner of the building. The triangle that is drawn that relates the toy to the origin (corner of the building) will assist the students in visualizing how to find the distance using the Pythagorean Theorem. Some students may choose to use a ruler and then use a scale factor to convert their answer to feet or inches. Other students may just estimate the distance based on the information in the problem.

Students need to save their estimates for use later in the lesson.

As a class, discuss students' estimates and have them explain how they arrived at their estimates. Explain that in this lesson, they will learn some ways to make more accurate measurements of these distances.

**Question 3** If students are struggling to determine which student performed the correct steps, suggest that the students work through the question on their own and then compare their work to each of the students given. This should show them that Len made the mistake.

Inquiry

**3.** Len and Ava calculated the distance from the toy to the corner where the walls meet differently.

| Len's Steps | | Ava's Steps | |
|---|---|---|---|
| Step 1 | How far left or right do I go? Find this length. | Step 1 | How far left or right do I go? Find this length. |
| Step 2 | How far up or down do I go? Find this length. | Step 2 | How far up or down do I go? Find this length. |
| Step 3 | Add the two lengths. | Step 3 | Square both lengths. |
| Step 4 | Square the sum from Step 3. | Step 4 | Add the two squared lengths from Step 3. |
| Step 5 | Find the square root of the answer from Step 4. | Step 5 | Find the square root of the sum from Step 4. |

3a. Ava's steps are correct. For Len's Steps 3 and 4, he got the order backward: lengths must be squared, then added.

**a.** Which student wrote the correct set of steps? Identify the mistakes the other student made.

**b.** How does your method for finding the distance in Question 2 compare with the correct series of steps in the table? Do you have all the same steps? Are your steps in the same order?
Answers will vary.

352 CHAPTER 7 Real Numbers

4. The steps for finding the distance between two points can be written in symbols as well as with words. Use $(x_1, y_1)$ to represent one point and $(x_2, y_2)$ to represent the other.

Refer to the correct set of steps from Question 3. Parts a–e each show one of the steps from that set in symbols. Tell which step the symbols represent.

**a.** $y_2 - y_1$ Ava's Step 2

**b.** $(x_2 - x_1)^2$ and $(y_2 - y_1)^2$ Ava's Step 3

**c.** $x_2 - x_1$ Ava's Step 1

**d.** $\sqrt{(x_2 - x_1)^2 + (y_2 - y_1)^2}$ Ava's Step 5

**e.** $(x_2 - x_1)^2 + (y_2 - y_1)^2$ Ava's Step 4

**Math Link**

The variables $x_1$, $y_1$, $x_2$, and $y_2$ are called *subscripted* variables. They are like any other variables, just with lowered numbers called subscripts.

The symbol ≈ means "approximately equals."

The **distance formula** gives the symbolic rule for calculating the distance between any two points in the coordinate plane.

## Try It Again

**Distance Formula**

If $(x_1, y_1)$ and $(x_2, y_2)$ represent the points, then

$$\text{distance} = \sqrt{(x_2 - x_1)^2 + (y_2 - y_1)^2}.$$

To find the distance between two given points, first decide which point will be $(x_1, y_1)$ and which will be $(x_2, y_2)$.

In the following example, the distance formula is used to find the distance between (1, −3) and (−4, 5).

Let (1, −3) be $(x_1, y_1)$. Let (−4, 5) be $(x_2, y_2)$. Substitute the coordinates into the distance formula.

$$\begin{aligned} \text{distance} &= \sqrt{(x_2 - x_1)^2 + (y_2 - y_1)^2} \\ &= \sqrt{((-4) - 1)^2 + (5 - (-3))^2} \\ &= \sqrt{(-5)^2 + 8^2} \\ &= \sqrt{25 + 64} \\ &= \sqrt{89} \\ &\approx 9.43 \text{ units} \end{aligned}$$



Inquiry

**Question 4** Discuss this question as a whole class. This leads into the example using the distance formula.

## Try It Again

Introduce the distance formula to students. Then discuss the example.

Show students how to use this formula to find the length of a line segment by walking them through the example. If students question how you know which point is $(x_1, y_1)$ and which is $(x_2, y_2)$, you may want to rework the example interchanging the points to show that the answer is the same whether a point is $(x_1, y_1)$ or $(x_2, y_2)$. Have students try to explain why they are the same.

**Lesson 7.3** The Pythagorean Theorem 353

## What Have You Learned?

Help students see that the distance formula and the Pythagorean Theorem involve most of the same steps. Some students may point out that when using the Pythagorean Theorem, you are given the length of the sides, whereas in the distance formula, you have to subtract to find the lengths.

**Questions 6–9** Watch for students who substitute the coordinates of one point as the value $(x_2 - x_1)$ in the distance formula. Remind them to use the *x*-coordinates from each point in the first expression of the formula and the *y*-coordinates in the second expression.





**5.** Use the distance formula to find the distance between the toy and the corner where the walls meet. Let the origin be $(x_1, y_1)$. Let the toy's coordinates be $(x_2, y_2)$.

Use the distance formula or the Pythagorean Theorem to find the distance between the given points. If needed, round answers to the nearest hundredth.

**6.** (3, 1) and (6, −3) 5

**7.** (1, 15) and (6, 3) 13

**8.** (−3, −5) and (7, −1) ≈10.77

**9.** (6, 4) and (2, −3) ≈ 8.06

### What Have You Learned?

**10.** Explain how the distance formula and the Pythagorean Theorem are related. Use drawings or examples if they help you explain.

5. $$\begin{aligned}\text{distance} &= \sqrt{(x_2 - x_1)^2 + (y_2 - y_1)^2} \\ &= \sqrt{(-3 - 0)^2 + (-4 - 0)^2} \\ &= \sqrt{(-3)^2 + (-4)^2} \\ &= \sqrt{9 + 16} \\ &= \sqrt{25} \\ &= 5\end{aligned}$$

10. In the distance formula, you subtract *x*-coordinates and *y*-coordinates to find the horizontal and vertical distances between two points. This gives the same information as knowing the lengths of the legs in a right triangle. The remaining steps are the same in both methods.

354 **CHAPTER 7** Real Numbers

## Practice & Apply

Find the exact area of each figure. Figures are drawn on one-centimeter dot grids.

**1.** 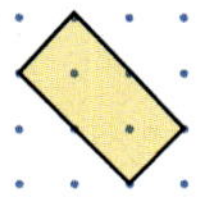 4 $cm^2$

**2.** 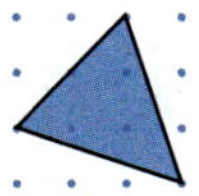 4 $cm^2$

**3.** In this exercise, you will look at the relationship among the areas of semicircles drawn on the sides of a right triangle.

**a.** Find the area, in square units, of each semicircle.

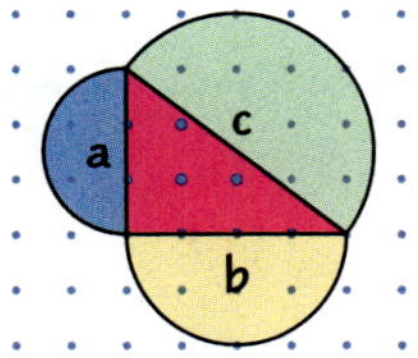


**b.** Find the area of each semicircle.

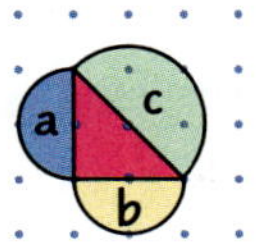


**c.** Find the area of each semicircle.

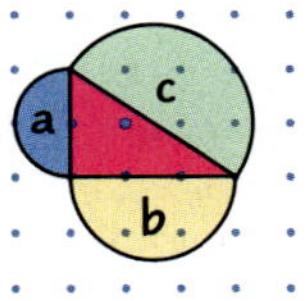


**d.** In the cases you have seen, is there a relationship among the areas of the three semicircles? If so, describe it. The area of the semicircle on the hypotenuse is equal to the sum of the areas of the semicircles on the two legs.

3a. Area of semicircle on side *a*: about 3.5 $unit^2$; area of semicircle on side *b*: about 6.3 $unit^2$; area of semicircle on side *c*: about 9.8 $unit^2$

3b. Area of semicircles on sides *a* and *b*: about 1.6 $unit^2$; area of semicircle on side *c*: about 3.1 $unit^2$

3c. Area of semicircle on side *a*: about 1.6 $unit^2$; area of semicircle on side *b*: about 3.5 $unit^2$; area of semicircle on side *c*: about 5.1 $unit^2$



On Your Own Exercises
Lesson 7.3

**Investigation 1**
Pages 343–346
Practice & Apply: 1–5
Connect & Extend: 11

**Investigation 2**
Pages 347–350
Practice & Apply: 6–10
Connect & Extend: 12–13

**Assign Anytime**
Mixed Review: 16–39

▶ **Exercises 1 and 2** Watch for students who mistake the dimensions. In Exercise 1 the rectangle is not a 2 × 1 rectangle. The upper-left side of the triangle in Exercise 2 does not have a length of 2 units.

▶ **Exercise 3** When you discuss this exercise, you may want to check if any students can see how the Pythagorean Theorem might help explain the relationship in Part d.

▶ **Exercise 8** If $x$ is the length (in centimeters) of each leg, then $x^2 + x^2 = 10^2$. So $2x^2 = 100$, which means that $x^2 = 50$. Taking the square root gives $x = \sqrt{50}$ cm.

▶ **Exercise 9c** Students may need help getting started. If $x$ ft is the highest distance above ground the ladder can reach, then the base of the ladder will be $\frac{x}{4}$ ft from the wall. So $x^2 + \left(\frac{x}{4}\right)^2 = 10^2$.



**Find each missing area.**

**4.** $\frac{5}{4}$ cm$^2$, or $1\frac{1}{4}$ cm$^2$

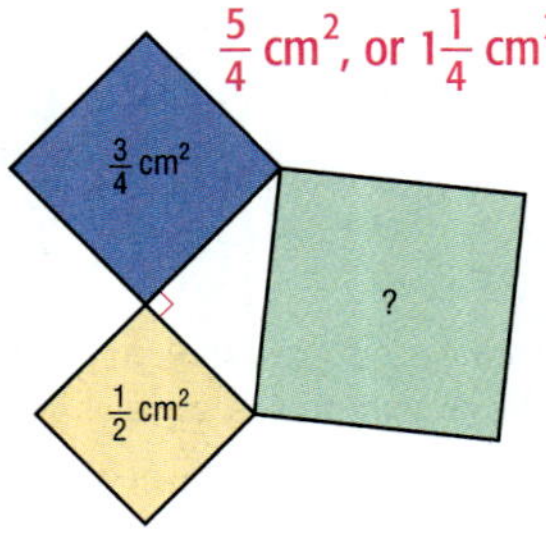


**5.** 10.25 cm$^2$

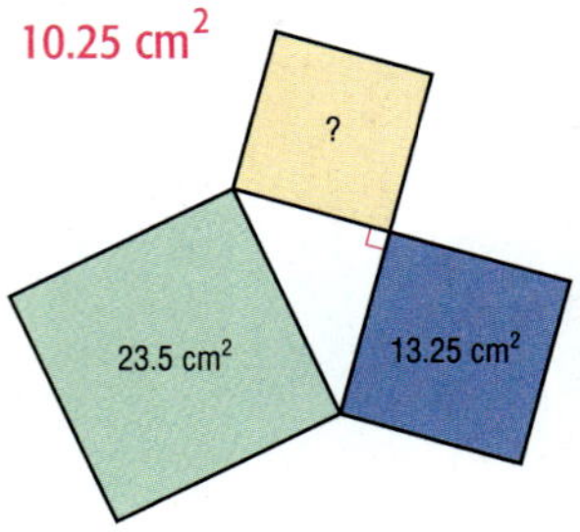


**Find each missing side length.**

**6.** 15 cm

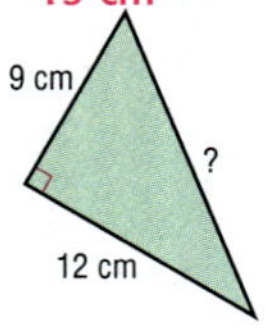


**7.** $\sqrt{500}$ cm, or about 22.4 cm

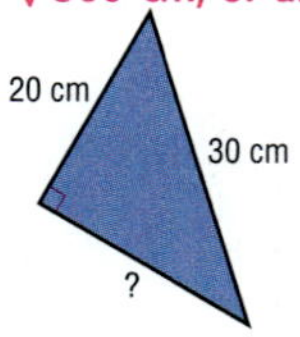


**8.** The legs of this right triangle are the same length. How long are they?

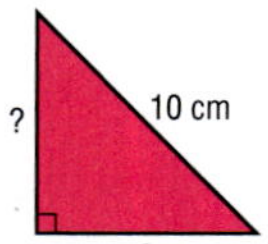


$\sqrt{50}$ cm, or about 7.1 cm

**9.** To ensure the safety of his workers, Walter requires that the base of a ladder be one foot from a wall for every four feet it reaches up the wall.

**a.** If a ladder reaches eight feet up a wall, how far should its base be from the wall? 2 ft

**b.** How long must the ladder be to reach a height of eight feet?

**c.** **Challenge** Using the given safety requirements above, what is the highest a ten-foot ladder can reach? About 9.7 ft

9b. $\sqrt{68}$ ft, or about 8.25 ft

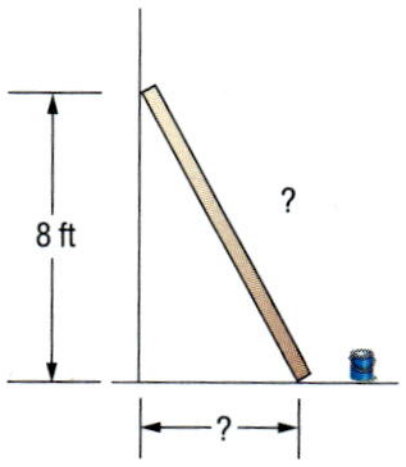

**10. Physical Science** During its initial climb, an airplane flew 14.4 miles, reaching an altitude of 5 miles. After the initial climb, how far was the airplane from its starting point, as measured along the ground?

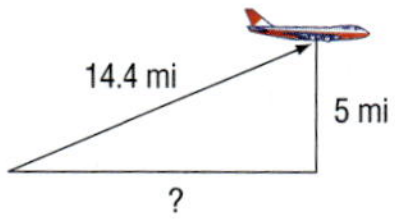


About 13.5 mi

## Connect & Extend

**11.** You know that a *right triangle* has one angle that measures 90°. In an *acute triangle,* all three angles have measures less than 90°. In an *obtuse triangle,* one angle has a measure greater than 90°.

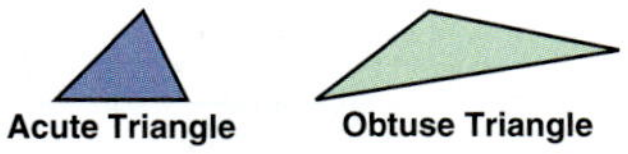


**a.** Three acute triangles are drawn on the centimeter dot grid below. Squares are drawn on their sides. Find the area of each square. Record your results in a table like this one.

**Acute Triangles**

| Triangle | Area of Square on Side *a* | Area of Square on Side *b* | Area of Square on Side *c* |
|---|---|---|---|
| I | 10 $cm^2$ | 16 $cm^2$ | 18 $cm^2$ |
| II | 5 $cm^2$ | 8 $cm^2$ | 9 $cm^2$ |
| III | 4 $cm^2$ | 5 $cm^2$ | 5 $cm^2$ |

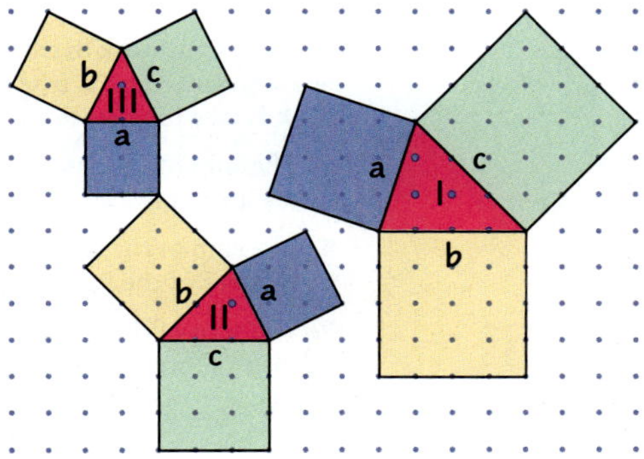


### Real-World Link

The word *acute* has many meanings. Here are just a few.

- having a sharp point
- shrewd
- sensitive
- severe or intense
- of great importance



On Your Own Exercises

▶ **Exercise 11a** To find the areas of the squares drawn on the sides of the triangle that are not horizontal or vertical, students can use a combination of counting squares and using the Pythagorean Theorem. For example, they can count the number of squares for the area of the square on side *b* in Triangle I. Then, they would need to use the Pythagorean Theorem for the other two sides (*a* and *c*). To do this, students can drop a perpendicular line from the vertex to side *b*, forming two right triangles. For the left triangle, the base is 1 cm and the height is 3 cm. Thus, $1^2 + 3^2 = a^2$; $a^2 = 10\ cm^2$. For the right triangle, the base is 3 cm and the height is 3 cm. Thus, $3^2 + 3^2 = c^2$; $c^2 = 18\ cm^2$.

**Lesson 7.3** The Pythagorean Theorem **357**

▶ **Exercise 11c** It is important for students to know that the Pythagorean Theorem only works for right triangles, but there are relationships that will always be true for acute and obtuse triangles.



**b.** Three obtuse triangles are drawn on the centimeter dot grid below. Squares are drawn on their sides. Find the area of each square. Record your results in a table like this one.

**Obtuse Triangles**

| Triangle | Area of Square on Side *a* | Area of Square on Side *b* | Area of Square on Side *c* |
|---|---|---|---|
| I | 2 cm$^2$ | 10 cm$^2$ | 16 cm$^2$ |
| II | 5 cm$^2$ | 5 cm$^2$ | 16 cm$^2$ |
| III | 2 cm$^2$ | 16 cm$^2$ | 26 cm$^2$ |

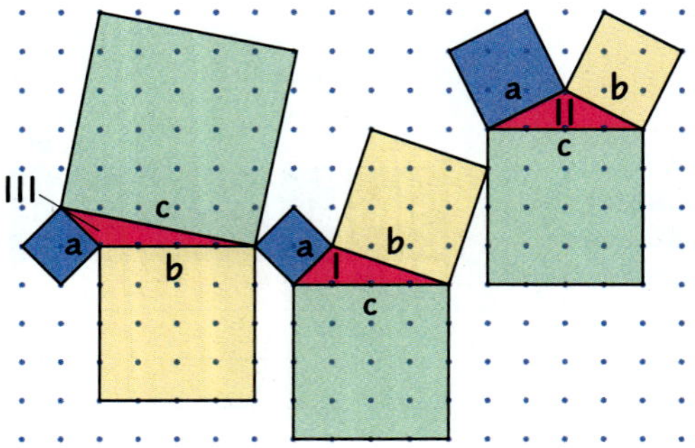


**Math Link**
The word *obtuse* has several other meanings.

- blunt or dull
- slow to understand
- hard to comprehend

**c.** Based on your work in this exercise, which of the statements below do you think is true for acute triangles? Which do you think is true for obtuse triangles? Statement iii, statement i

**i.** The sum of the areas of the two smaller squares is less than the area of the largest square. That is, $a^2 + b^2 < c^2$.

**ii.** The sum of the areas of the two smaller squares is equal to the area of the largest square. That is, $a^2 + b^2 = c^2$.

**iii.** The sum of the areas of the two smaller squares is greater than the area of the largest square. That is, $a^2 + b^2 > c^2$.

**12.** Rey and Lydia have found the perfect couch for their living room, but they are not sure whether it will fit through the doorway. The doorway measures 37 inches wide and 79 inches high.

They know they can take the legs off the couch. Figure 1 is a side view of the couch with the legs removed.

The couch is too wide to fit if they carry it upright, but Rey thinks it might fit if they tilt it as shown in Figure 2.

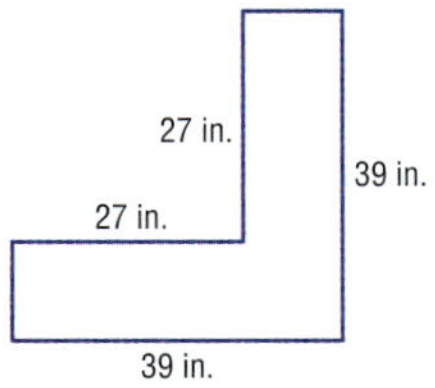

Figure 1

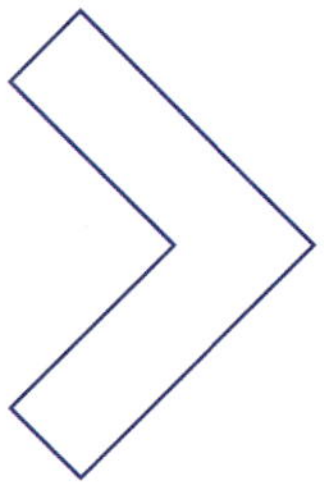
Figure 2

In this exercise, you will use the Pythagorean Theorem to figure out whether the couch will fit through the doorway.

**a.** For Figure 3, explain why the dashed segments shown here each have length 12 inches. Then find the length of segment *c*. Explain how you found it. Round your answer up to the nearest tenth of an inch.

12a. The outside lengths are both 39 in. and the inside lengths are both 27 in. The difference between them is shown by the dashed segments, so they must be 12 in. long. Using the Pythagorean Theorem, $c^2 = 12^2 + 12^2 = 288$, so $c = \sqrt{288}$, or about 17.0 in.

**b.** For Figure 4, find the length of segment *d* to the nearest tenth of an inch. 38.2 in.

**c.** In Figure 5, segment *b* divides segment *d* in half. Find the length of segment *b* to the nearest tenth. 19.1 in.

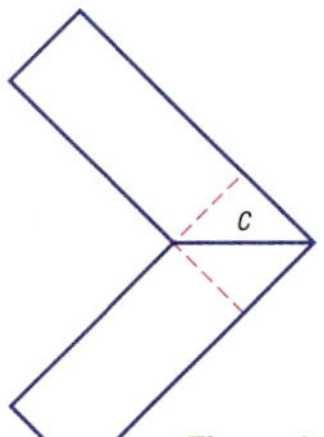

Figure 3

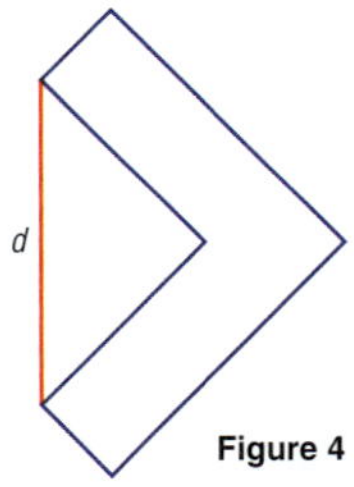

Figure 4

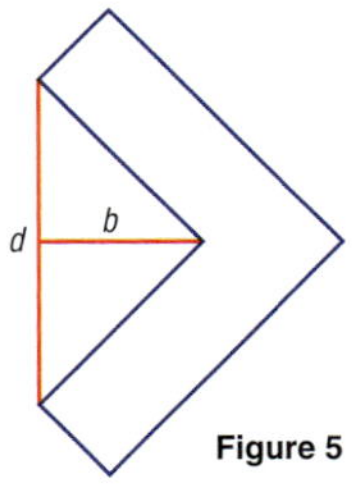

Figure 5

**d.** Will the couch fit through the doorway? Explain how you know.

12d. Yes; if the couch is tilted, its width will be $b + c$, which is about 36.1 in. This is less than the width of the doorway.





▶ **Exercise 12a** If students are having difficulty seeing what this question is asking, give the students dot paper and have them make a scale model of the couch. Allow them to cut out the model if necessary to determine the needed measurements.

▶ **Exercise 13** Logic and the Pythagorean Theorem can often tell you when a triangle is not a right triangle. However, the Pythagorean Theorem cannot tell you that a triangle is a right triangle. For that, you need the *Converse of the Pythagorean Theorem*: If the sum of the squares of the lengths of two sides of a triangle is equal to the square of the length of the third side, then the triangle is a right triangle and the third side is the hypotenuse.

▶ **Exercise 15** This exercise is a preview of work to come in Chapter 8 involving linear relationships. The data in the table represent the linear relationship $y = 5x$. When discussing this with students, it may help them to see the connection to Chapter 8 if you plot the coordinates from the table and then show how the $x$- and $y$-values change.

## Quick Check

**Informal Assessment** Students should be able to:

- ✔ identify the legs and hypotenuse of a right triangle
- ✔ use squares attached to the right triangle to determine the areas of the legs and hypotenuse
- ✔ use the Pythagorean theorem to find a missing leg or hypotenuse of a right triangle
- ✔ apply the Pythagorean theorem to solve real world problems



13. No; if it were a rectangle, the sides would make right angles, and the length of the diagonal squared would equal $45^2 + 60^2$, or 5,625 in. But $73.5^2 = 5{,}402.25$, so the table is not a rectangle.

**13.** Mr. Mackenzie built a table. He had intended for the table to be rectangular, but he is not sure it turned out that way. He carefully measured the tabletop and found that the side lengths are 60 inches and 45 inches, and the diagonal is 73.5 inches. Is the table a rectangle? Explain how you know.

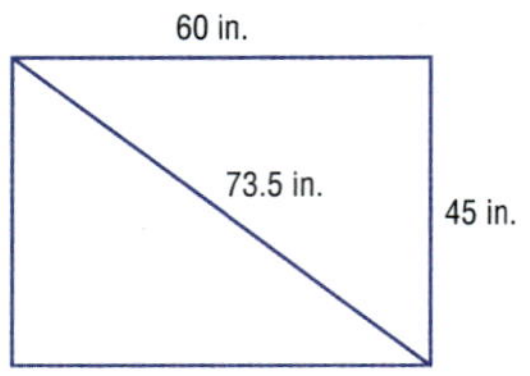


**14. In Your Own Words** Explain what the Pythagorean Theorem is and how it is useful for finding lengths.

**15. Preview** Consider the following table of values. What pattern do you see in the $x$-values? In the $y$-values?

| $x$ | 1 | 2 | 3 | 4 |
|---|---|---|---|---|
| $y$ | 5 | 10 | 15 | 20 |

Possible answer: The $x$-values increase by 1, the $y$-values by 5.

### Mixed Review

14. Possible answer: The Pythagorean Theorem is used to find any missing side of any right triangle. It can be used to find the length of an object when a right triangle is created and two sides are known.

20. $25a^8$
21. $(ab)^{100}$
25. $a^0$, or 1

**If possible, rewrite each expression using the laws of exponents.**

**16.** $y^2 \cdot y^6$ $y^8$ **17.** $a^n \cdot a^n$ $a^{2n}$ **18.** $2b \cdot 3b^2$ $6b^3$ **19.** $4^5 \cdot 9^5$ $36^5$

**20.** $5a^4 \cdot 5a^4$ **21.** $a^{100} \cdot b^{100}$ **22.** $(1.1^2)^4$ $1.1^8$ **23.** $(0.9^4)^3$ $0.9^{12}$

**24.** $(a^3)^4$ $a^{12}$ **25.** $(a^4)^0$ **26.** $(x^2)^3$ $x^6$ **27.** $(3^n)^m$ $3^{nm}$

**Simplify each expression as much as possible.**

**28.** $x^2 + x^2$ $2x^2$ **29.** $(x^2)^4$ $x^8$ **30.** $x^3 \div x^2$ $x$

**31.** $\frac{2x^2}{x^2} - 1$ $1$ **32.** $2x^2 - x^2$ $x^2$ **33.** $\frac{(x^2)^3}{x^2}$ $x^4$

**Find each indicated sum, difference, product, or quotient. Give answers in lowest terms.**

**34.** $-\frac{3}{7} + \frac{1}{7}$ $-\frac{2}{7}$ **35.** $-\frac{2}{3} + \frac{5}{8}$ $-\frac{1}{24}$

**36.** $\frac{4}{9} - \frac{2}{3}$ $-\frac{2}{9}$ **37.** $\frac{3}{8} - \left(-\frac{2}{5}\right)$ $\frac{31}{40}$

**38.** $\left(\frac{1}{5}\right)\left(-\frac{10}{14}\right)$ $-\frac{1}{7}$ **39.** $-\frac{3}{5} \div \left(-\frac{9}{7}\right)$ $\frac{7}{15}$



## Quick Quiz

1. Draw a right triangle and label the sides as legs or hypotenuse. Check students' answers
2. If a right triangle with squares attached has areas of 9 square units for the smallest square and 25 square units for the largest square, what is the missing area? What are the side lengths for the triangle? 16 square units; 3 units, 4 units, and 5 units
3. A right triangle has legs that measure 1 cm and 12 cm, what is the measure of the hypotenuse? $\sqrt{145} \approx 12.04$ cm.
4. Hsin Lee wants to purchase a television that will fit into an entertainment center that has an opening of 30 inches by 40 inches. The size of a television is given in inches, and that number represents the diagonal of the screen. What is the largest television Hsin Lee can purchase? 50 in.

# CHAPTER 7

# Review & Self-Assessment

## Chapter Summary

In Lesson 7-1, you were asked to take your previous understanding of types of numbers and apply it one step further to rational numbers. You used Venn diagrams to group numbers into sets including natural numbers, whole numbers, integers, and rational numbers to show your understanding of how different number sets are related. To further solidify your understanding of the relationship of these number sets, you solved number puzzles. Next, you compared pairs of rational numbers and ordered sets of rational numbers, giving justifications for your reasoning.

You were introduced to the set of irrational numbers in Lesson 7-2. You used area models to explore the inverse relationship between squares and square roots. You used Venn diagrams to explore the relationship between rational and irrational numbers. Additionally, you used calculators and number lines to show the approximate value of irrational numbers.

In the last lesson, you investigated the Pythagorean Theorem and used the theorem to find the lengths of missing triangle sides. Finally, you used the distance formula to calculate the lengths of line segments on a coordinate grid.

### Vocabulary

- distance formula
- hypotenuse
- irrational number
- leg
- natural number
- Pythagorean Theorem
- rational number
- real number
- right triangle
- square root
- whole number

## Strategies and Applications

The questions in this section will help you review and apply the important ideas and strategies developed in this chapter.

### Identifying rational and irrational numbers

**Identify all the number sets (natural, whole, integers, and rational) to which the following numbers belong.**

**1.** $-5$ Integers, rationals

**2.** $2.\overline{6}$

**3.** 4.72 Rationals

**4.** $\frac{3}{4}$ Rationals

**5.** $5^3$

**6.** $\sqrt{49}$

**7.** 2

**8.** 0 Whole, integers, rationals

**9.** Is it always possible to think of a smaller whole number? Explain your reasoning.

**10.** Is the following statement true or false? Explain your reasoning.

*All integers are rational numbers,*
*but not all rational numbers are integers.*

Possible answer: The statement is true; every integer is a rational number but there are rational numbers that are not integers such as 4.75 and $\frac{3}{4}$.

2. Rationals

5. Naturals, wholes, integers, rationals

6. Naturals, wholes, integers, rationals

7. Naturals, wholes, integers, rationals

9. No, it is not possible because the smallest whole number is 0 so it is impossible to think of a smaller whole number than 0.



# Review & Self-Assessment

CHAPTER 7

## Chapter Summary

This summary helps students recall the major topics of the chapter.

## Vocabulary

Students should be able to explain each of the terms listed in the vocabulary section.

▶ **Exercises 1–7** If students are having difficulties working on these exercises, it may be helpful for the students to look back in their notes for the Venn diagram that relates the numbers.

▶ **Exercise 12** Encourage students to recreate the drawing or to trace the drawing onto their work space and to draw triangles to help them visualize the distances that the question is asking for. The triangles will also allow the students to see that the most accurate way to solve the problem is by using the Pythagorean Theorem.



11.
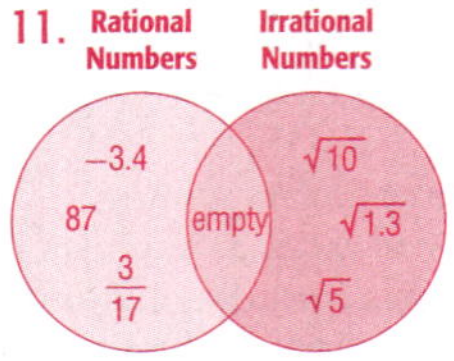


**Using Venn diagrams to show number relationships**

**11.** Copy the following Venn diagram. In each area, write three numbers. If no numbers belong in an area, label the area "empty."

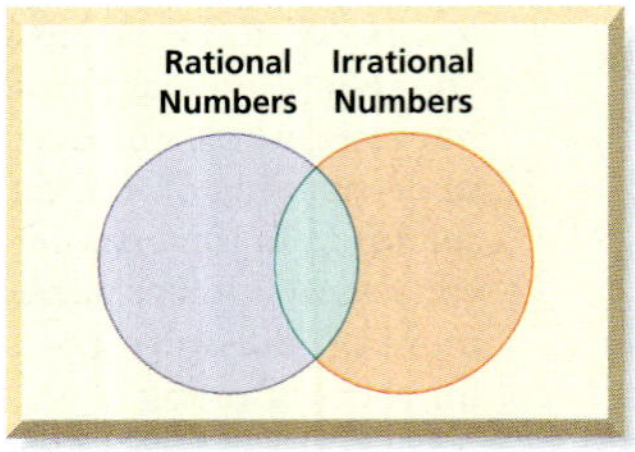


**Calculating lengths using the Pythagorean Theorem**

**12.** Before moving into her new house, Katrina is trying out furniture arrangements on graph paper. She wants to make sure there is enough room to walk around the furniture. She decides she needs at least 3 feet between pieces of furniture, except for the coffee table, which can be directly in front of the couch, and the lamp. Each square on her grid represents 1 square foot.

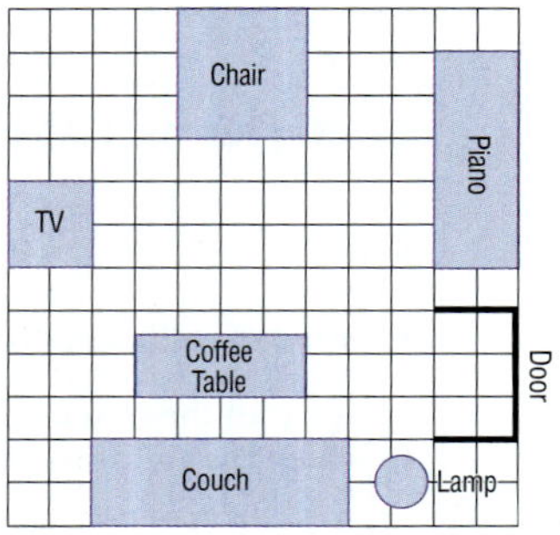


**a.** How many feet are there between the closest corners of the TV and the chair? $\sqrt{5}$ ft ≈ 2.24 ft

**b.** How many feet are there between the closest corners of the coffee table and the piano? $\sqrt{11.25}$ ft ≈ 3.35 ft

**c.** Are any pieces of furniture too close together? The TV is too close to the chair and to the coffee table.

14. 27 in.; the length and width of the TV screen are the legs of a right triangle and the diagonal is the hypotenuse. Using the Pythagorean Theorem, $21.75^2 + 16.25^2 = \text{diagonal}^2$, and $21.75^2 + 16.25^2 = 737.125$. So the length of the diagonal is $\sqrt{737.125}$, or about 27.15 in.

17. 0.58. Possible explanation: $\frac{1}{2}$ equals 0.5 or 0.50, which is less than 0.58

18. 0.67. Possible explanation: $\frac{2}{3}$ equals $0.\overline{6}$, which is less than 0.67

19. $-\frac{3}{4}$. Possible explanation: $-\frac{3}{4}$ is $-0.75$ which is greater than $-0.8$

20. $-1\frac{2}{5}$. Possible explanation: $-1\frac{2}{5}$ is $-1.4$ which is slightly greater than $-1.45$.

21. $-0.745$. Possible explanation: $-0.745$ is slightly greater than $-\frac{3}{4}$; $-\frac{19}{25}$ is slightly less than $-\frac{3}{4}$ because $-\frac{19}{25}$ is $-0.76$.

**13.** Use the Pythagorean Theorem to find the missing side length.
About 11.8

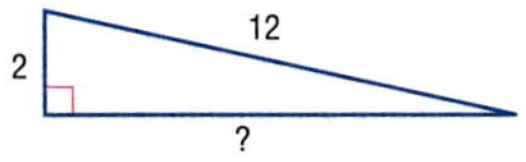


## Demonstrating Skills

**14.** The size of a television is given in terms of the length of the diagonal of its screen. For example, a 19-inch television has a screen with diagonal length 19 inches.

Mr. Franco's television screen has a length of 21.75 inches and a width of 16.25 inches. What is the size of his television? Give your answer to the nearest inch. Explain how you found it.

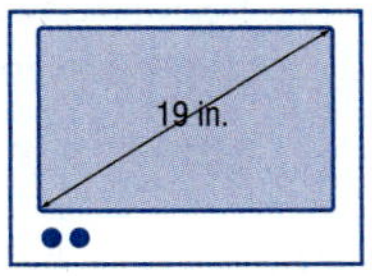


**15.** Order the following numbers from least to greatest.

$-1.275 \quad -1.2 \quad -\frac{7}{5} \quad -1.027 \quad -1\frac{1}{4}$

$-\frac{7}{5}, -1.275, -1\frac{1}{4}, -1.2, -1.027$

**16.** Which of the following numbers are less than $-0.4$? $-0.48, -\frac{9}{20}, -\frac{1}{2}$

$-0.48 \quad -0.39 \quad -\frac{9}{20} \quad -\frac{2}{5} \quad -\frac{1}{2}$

**For Exercises 17–22, identify which number is greater. Explain how you found your answer.**

**17.** $\frac{1}{2}$ or 0.58

**18.** 0.67 or $\frac{2}{3}$

**19.** $-\frac{3}{4}$ or $-0.8$

**20.** $-1.45$ or $-1\frac{2}{5}$

**21.** $-0.745$ or $-\frac{19}{25}$

**22.** $-0.875$ or $-0.578$ $-0.578$. Possible explanation: $-0.578$ is further to the right on a number line than $-0.875$.



Review & Self-Assessment
Chapter 7

▶ **Exercise 14** Tell students to draw a picture of a television and include a line for the diagonal as described in the problem. The students should label the side lengths with the values that are given and then use the Pythagorean Theorem to find the measure of the diagonal which represents the size of the television.

▶ **Exercises 17–22** When students complete these exercises, remind them to convert the fractions to decimals if they are not sure of the size of the number.

▶ **Exercise 37** This exercise mixes rational and irrational numbers. Tell students that they can use any method they wish to approximate the irrational numbers. A number line may also be useful in assisting the students to see how the positive and negative values relate to each other.



25. 19 in. Possible explanation: Since the area of a square is the square of one of its sides, to find the length of a square when given the area, one must find the square root.

27. Answers will vary. See students' work. Possible answers: 8.65, 8.8, $8\frac{3}{4}$, $8\frac{7}{10}$, 8.802

**23.** To the nearest tenth, between which two numbers is $\sqrt{40}$? Do not use your calculator. 6.3 and 6.4

**24.** Explain why it is impossible to have a number that is both rational and irrational. See students' work.

**25.** Judith wants to paint a square that has an area of 361 $in^2$. How long must each side of her square be? Explain your reasoning.

**26.** Explain in your own words what an imaginary number is and why the word "imaginary" is a good explanation of these types of numbers. See students' work.

**27.** Find five rational numbers that lie between $8\frac{11}{17}$ and $8\frac{17}{21}$.

**28.** Randall squared a number and the result was double the number with which he started. What was his starting number? 2

**For Exercises 29–36, find the two whole numbers that each square root lies between without using your calculator.**

**29.** $\sqrt{32}$ 5 and 6

**30.** $\sqrt{7}$ 2 and 3

**31.** $\sqrt{19}$ 4 and 5

**32.** $\sqrt{83}$ 9 and 10

**33.** $\sqrt{127}$ 11 and 12

**34.** $\sqrt{99}$ 9 and 10

**35.** $\sqrt{150}$ 12 and 13

**36.** $\sqrt{200}$ 14 and 15

**37.** Order the following numbers from least to greatest.

$\sqrt{16}$ $\quad -4.1 \quad -\sqrt{21} \quad \sqrt{21} \quad 4.1$

$-\sqrt{21}, -4.1, \sqrt{16}, 4.1, \sqrt{21}$

**38.** Order the following numbers from greatest to least.

$\sqrt{31} \quad \frac{36}{7} \quad -\frac{36}{7} \quad -\sqrt{31} \quad -5.2$

$\sqrt{31}, \frac{36}{7}, -\frac{36}{7}, -5.2, -\sqrt{31}$

## Test-Taking Practice

**SHORT RESPONSE**

**1** Find the length of the diagonal of the quadrilateral shown below.

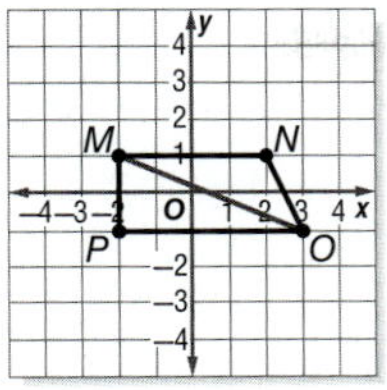


***Show your work.***

***Answer*** See below. units

**MULTIPLE CHOICE**

**2** Which number set does not include the number −37?
- **A** integers
- **B** rational numbers
- **C** real numbers
- **D** whole numbers

**3** Which of the following numbers is an irrational number?
- **F** $\sqrt{49}$
- **G** 0.728
- **H** $\sqrt{34}$
- **J** $\frac{1}{9}$

**4** Which list has the numbers ordered from least to greatest?
- **A** $3.\overline{3}, \frac{17}{5}, 2\frac{2}{5}, 3.34$
- **B** $2\frac{2}{5}, 3.\overline{3}, 3.34, \frac{17}{5}$
- **C** $2\frac{2}{5}, \frac{17}{5}, 3.\overline{3}, 3.34$
- **D** $3.\overline{3}, 3.34, 2\frac{2}{5}, \frac{17}{5}$

**5** Between what two consecutive whole numbers is $\sqrt{47}$?
- **F** 5, 6
- **G** 7, 8
- **H** 6, 7
- **J** 3, 4

*Show your work:*
Use the distance formula to find the length of the diagonal:

$$d = \sqrt{(x_2 - x_1)^2 + (y_2 - y_1)^2} = \sqrt{(3 - (-2))^2 + (-1 - 1)^2} = \sqrt{5^2 + (-2)^2} = \sqrt{25 + 4} = \sqrt{29} \approx 5.4$$

*Answer:* 5.4



Review & Self-Assessment
Chapter 7

▶ **Exercise 1** Students should see that there are multiple ways to solve this problem using techniques such as the Pythagorean Theorem or the Distance Formula. Instruct the students that they should choose a method that is accurate and not an approximation.

**Lesson 7.2, Develop & Understand: C** (p. 338)

10.

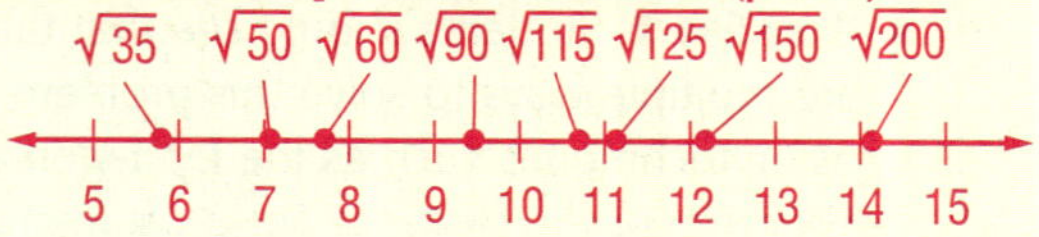


11.

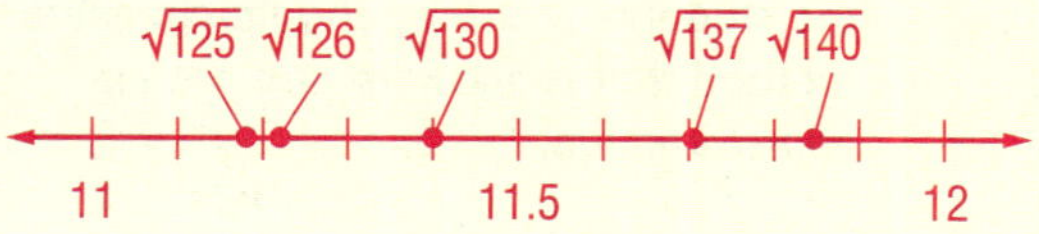


13b. The circumference equals $\pi d$. If the diameter is rational, the product $\pi d$ is irrational.

---

**Lesson 7.2, Share & Summarize** (p. 338)

b. Sometimes rational. The square root of a perfect square is an integer and therefore rational. The square root of a fraction, such as $\frac{4}{9}$, would be rational, but not an integer. The square root of a postive integer that is not a perfect square is irrational, such as $\sqrt{5}$.

c. Sometimes rational. Terminating or repeating decimals, such as 3.578 or 0.333 ..., are rational; Non-terminating, non-repeating decimals, such as the one that represents $\pi$, are irrational.

Notes

CHAPTER 8

# Linear Relationships

## Chapter Overview

In this chapter, students will begin learning about rates and how to represent them in words, tables, symbolic rules, and graphs. Then they relate speed (a special rate) to the slope, both positive and negative, of a graph of distance over time.

Students learn how to use change to see if a pattern is linear or not. After graphing the relationships in the patterns, they learn how to determine the symbolic rule from the graph and how to predict the graph from the symbolic rule.

After being introduced to $y = ax + b$, the standard form for the symbolic rule for linear relationships, students are introduced to techniques for determining $a$ and $b$ in the rule. Inequalities are also informally introduced.

## The Big Picture

| Links to the Past | Chapter 8 | Links to the Future |
|---|---|---|
| **Course 1, Chapter 5** (pp. 288–345) Rate, Ratio, and Proportion | **Lesson 8.1** (p. 368) Rates | **Course 3, Chapter 3** (pp. 110–143) Percents and Proportions |
| **Course 1, Chapter 2** (pp. 56–107) Fractions and Decimals<br>**Course 1, Chapter 8** (pp. 466–531) Coordinate Plane | **Lesson 8.2** (p. 389) Speed and Slope | **Course 3, Chapter 1** (pp. 2–63) Linear Relationships |
| **Course 1, Chapter 8** (pp. 466–531) Coordinate Plane | **Lesson 8.3** (p. 410) Recognize Linear Relationships | **Course 3, Chapter 1** (pp. 2–63) Linear Relationships<br>**Course 3, Chapter 2** (pp. 64–109) Lines and Angles |

# Mathematical Background

The idea that runs throughout the chapter is looking at tables, graphs, or equations that show how two variable quantities are related to each other and then analyzing how a change in one of them is related to a change in the other. The focus is on how the variables change from one moment to the next, more than on what the variables are at any particular time.

**Proportional Linear Relationships** In the algebraic rule $y = ax + b$, where the input is represented by $x$ and the output by $y$, the rate of change of $y$ is represented by $a$. In the graph of $y = ax + b$, $a$ is called the slope of the line, with steeper lines representing greater rates of change. If there is nothing else to the relationship (if $b$ is 0), then we say that $y$ is proportional to $x$.

That is not the case in *any* relationship that is not linear. It is also not true with *all* linear relationships. Here is an example.

**Nonproportional Linear Relationships** For an increase of 1°C, there is an increase of 1.8°F, no matter what the starting temperature. The two ways of reporting temperature are linearly related. A table that shows evenly spaced values in °C will have evenly spaced corresponding values of °F. The change in the output is proportional to the change in the input. But the ratio of input to output is not constant (for example 0°C/32°F is not the same as 100°C/212°F), so the output and input themselves are not proportional. This is a nonproportional linear relationship.

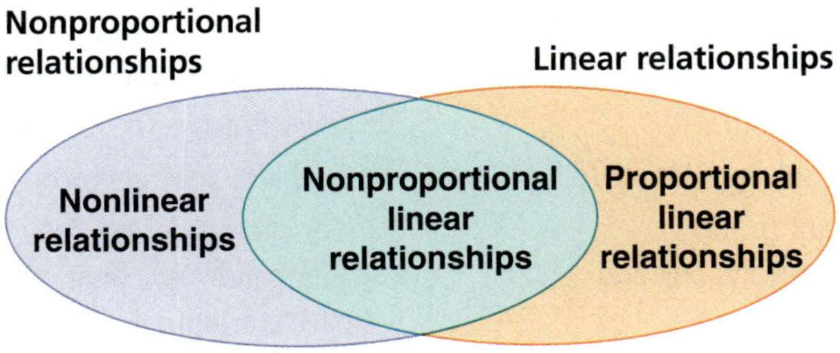


In this chapter, and in many mathematics curricula, students are asked to extend sequences of numbers on the basis of patterns they find in the numbers. One of the subtleties of making predictions on the basis of data alone is that this simply cannot be done with any certainty at all. Only a mechanism—a rule, a physical principle, or the like—can tell one whether the pattern that presents itself so far actually continues.

So, for example, the obvious pattern suggested by the sequence 1, 2, 3, 4, 5, 6, 7, 8, 9, 10, ... , even despite the very long string of data, is followed by 11 and 12 but is not followed by 13 if the numbers represent hours on a clock.

The chapter gives a few examples of patterns that seem to suggest one pattern and then do not continue as expected. One begins 1, 2, 4 and then continues with 7 instead of 8. Another goes a step further 1, 2, 4, 8 and then continues with 15 instead of 16.

## Additional Reading

According to Miller and Mercer in "Educational Aspects of Mathematical Disabilities," students with learning disabilities benefit from activities-based, hands-on learning, as well as reasoning and problem-solving experiences. Lesson 8.1 contains an Inquiry Investigation that has students collect data and then graph the results.

CHAPTER 8

# Planning Guide

## *Lesson Resources*

| | Lesson 8.1<br>Pacing: 5 days | Lesson 8.2<br>Pacing: 5 days | Lesson 8.3<br>Pacing: 5 days |
|---|---|---|---|
| **Lesson Title** | **Rates**<br>(p. 368) | **Speed and Slope**<br>(p. 389) | **Recognize Linear Relationships**<br>(p. 410) |
| **Lesson Objectives** | • To develop strategies for describing rates<br>• To recognize rates presented in symbolic and graphic forms<br>• To develop strategies for comparing proportional and nonproportional relationships<br>• To represent proportional and nonproportional relationships in words, tables, symbols, and graphs<br>• To get hands-on experience with collecting data<br>• To determine the nature of the relationship between two variables | • To relate speed to the slope of a graph of distance over time<br>• To develop an understanding of negative slope and a negative constant term<br>• To gain skill in recognizing proportional and nonproportional relationships between distance and time<br>• To recognize linear relationships from different forms: symbolic rules, graphs, patterns, and tables<br>• To easily convert one form of representation into another | • To recognize linear relationships in a variety of representations: symbolic rules, graphs, visual patterns, and tables<br>• To translate from one representation to another<br>• To recognize the symbolic representation of a linear relationship in more than one form.<br>• To explain the connection between the constant difference, the slope of the graph, and the symbolic representation of the relationship<br>• To determine $b$ in the rule $y = ax + b$ from a graph |
| **Materials** | Chapter 8 Master 1, 1 box, 3 cans, cylindrical pens, books, lined paper | Chapter 8 Master 1 | Chapter 8 Master 1 |
| ***Quick Review Math Handbook*** | **Lesson 5.5** Ratio and Proportion | **Lesson 5.8** Slope and Intercept | **Lesson 4.2** Displaying Data |
| **Print Resources** | CRM Study Guide and Intervention (p. 4)<br>CRM Skills Practice (p. 5)<br>CRM Problem-Solving Practice (p. 6)<br>CRM Enrichment (p. 7)<br>• Investigation Notebook and Reflection Journal<br>• Differentiation Handbook | CRM Study Guide and Intervention (p. 9)<br>CRM Skills Practice (p. 10)<br>CRM Problem-Solving Practice (p. 11)<br>CRM Enrichment (p. 12)<br>• Investigation Notebook and Reflection Journal<br>• Differentiation Handbook | CRM Study Guide and Intervention (p. 14)<br>CRM Skills Practice (p. 15)<br>CRM Problem-Solving Practice (p. 16)<br>CRM Enrichment (p. 17)<br>• Investigation Notebook and Reflection Journal<br>• Differentiation Handbook |
| **Technology Resources** | TeacherWorks Plus<br>Classroom Presentation Toolkit<br>ExamView Assessment Suite<br>StudentWorks Plus<br>Math Online Brain Pops • Concepts in Motion | TeacherWorks Plus<br>Classroom Presentation Toolkit<br>ExamView Assessment Suite<br>StudentWorks Plus<br>Math Online Brain Pops • Concepts in Motion | TeacherWorks Plus<br>Classroom Presentation Toolkit<br>ExamView Assessment Suite<br>StudentWorks Plus<br>Math Online Brain Pops • Concepts in Motion |

*Included in the Impact Mathematics Manipulative Kit

# Assessment Resources

## MARS Assessment: Teaching with Purpose

### Party

In *Party,* students choose and use number operations in context; find and use an algebraic formula; and relate formulas and graphs. Students calculate the cost of people attending a party and identify the graph that shows the connection between the number of people at the party (P), and the cost ($C).

### Targeting the Task

- **Diagnostic**—Use Exercises 1–5 in the *Party* assessment to determine students' understanding of how to choose and work with number operations, algebraic formulas, and relate formulas and graphs. For those students who do not have this understanding, completing this unit is needed.
- **Formative**—Exercises 1–5 can be administered individually according to the lessons.
- **Summative**—Administer the complete *Party* performance-based assessment.

CRM **Chapter 8 MARS Assessment** (pp. 35–36)

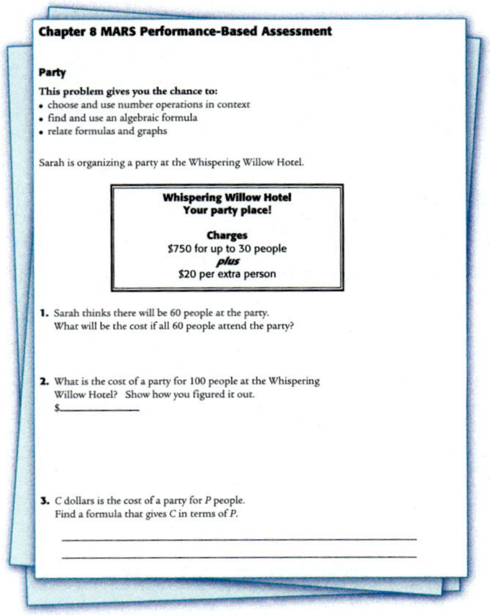

**Chapter 8 MARS Performance-Based Assessment**

**Party**

**This problem gives you the chance to:**
- choose and use number operations in context
- find and use an algebraic formula
- relate formulas and graphs

Sarah is organizing a party at the Whispering Willow Hotel.

**Whispering Willow Hotel**
**Your party place!**
**Charges**
$750 for up to 30 people
***plus***
$20 per extra person

1. Sarah thinks there will be 60 people at the party. What will be the cost if all 60 people attend the party?

2. What is the cost of a party for 100 people at the Whispering Willow Hotel? Show how you figured it out.
$\_\_\_\_\_\_\_\_\_\_$

3. C dollars is the cost of a party for *P* people. Find a formula that gives C in terms of *P*.

## Assessment Planning Guide

Assessments are available for investigations, lessons, and chapters.

ExamView® Assessment Suite — Customize and create multiple versions of tests and quizzes.

| | Student Edition | Teacher Edition | Other Resources |
|---|---|---|---|
| **Diagnostic** | | | CRM Chapter 8 Pretest (pp. 19–22)<br>Math Online Online Chapter Quiz |
| **Formative** | Share & Summarize (pp. 373, 376, 378, 393, 396, 397, 401, 413, 416, 419, 422) | Troubleshooting (pp. 373, 374, 376, 390, 394, 395, 398, 410, 413, 416)<br>On the Spot Assessment (p. 379)<br>Quick Check (pp. 388, 408, 429)<br>Quick Quiz (pp. 388, 409, 430) | CRM Quick Quiz (pp. 8, 13, 18) |
| **Summative** | Review & Self-Assessment (pp. 431–433) | | CRM Chapter 8 Test: Forms A and B (pp. 23–30)<br>CRM Standardized Test Practice (pp. 37–38) |
| **Performance-Based** | In Your Own Words (pp. 385, 406) | | CRM MARS Performance-Based Assessment (pp. 33–36)<br>CRM Chapter Performance Assessment (pp. 31–32) |

# Differentiated Instruction

## *Reaching* All Learners

Below are suggestions on differentiating the materials presented in this chapter. Additional modifications should be considered.

### Approaching Level AL

**Connections** During Lesson 8.1, have students work in pairs for this activity. Each student should describe an event that they participate in on a regular basis. For instance a student may babysit for a family twice a week, every week. Have the students assist each other in creating a graph to represent the event. For students who are having a difficult time determining what values go on the $x$- and $y$-axes, ask for a volunteer to describe an event. Use this event to assist the students in seeing the difference between dependent and independent variables.

### Beyond Level BL

**Teaching** Have students create a problem to share with a student who is having difficulty understanding linear relationships. Pair up with a student and assist them in understanding the concept. Make sure to answer any questions that occur. This activity works well with Lesson 8.1.

### On Level OL

**Models** Have students work in pairs. One student creates a linear relationship and the other student must determine if the rate is reasonable. Switch roles, until each student has created 3 graphs. This activity can be used as a review for Lesson 8.1 or an introduction to Lesson 8.2.

### English Language Learners ELL

**Rate Words** Have students work in pairs to write out as many phrases or words in English and the translated phrase/word in their first language that refer to rates of change, i.e. . . rate, miles per hour, cost per sandwich. Some students may feel more comfortable working in their first language and then translating into English. Then have the students share their lists with the class. This activity will assist the students in understanding of Chapter 8 with a major point of understanding for Lesson 8.1.

**KEY**

AL Approaching Level OL On Level BL Beyond Level ELL English Language Learners

## *Intervention Planning Guide*

CRM Assess students' prerequisite skills and knowledge using the **Chapter Pretest** found in the Chapter 8 Resource Masters, p. 19.

| **Intensive Intervention** two or more years below grade level | **Strategic Intervention** below grade level | **On Level** | **Beyond Level** |
|---|---|---|---|
| **If** students miss 75% of the exercises:<br>**Then** use *Math Triumphs,* an intensive intervention | **If** students miss 50% of the exercises:<br>**Then** choose a resource: | **If** students miss 25% of the exercises:<br>**Then** choose a resource: | **If** students miss 0%–10% of the exercises:<br>**Then** choose a resource: |
| *Math Triumphs,* Grade 7<br>• Chapter 2: Ratios, Rates, and Proportional Relationships | CRM Study Guide and Intervention (pp. 4, 9, 14)<br>• Investigation Notebook and Reflection Journal<br>• Differentiation Handbook<br>Math Online Brain Pops • Concepts in Motion | CRM Skills Practice (pp. 5, 10, 15)<br>CRM Problem-Solving Practice (pp. 6, 11, 16)<br>• Investigation Notebook and Reflection Journal | CRM Enrichment (pp. 7, 12, 17)<br>• Differentiation Handbook |

## *Literature Connections*

### Recommended Outside Reading for Students

**Nonfiction**

Gillings, Richard. *Mathematics in the Time of the Pharaohs.* Dover, 1992.

This book examines the development of Egyptian mathematics from its origins in practical and commercial computations to its applications involving proportions and linear equations. Students will learn to write, solve, and graph linear equations.

**Fiction**

Merrill, Jean. *The Toothpaste Millionaire.* Houghton Mifflin, 1974.

*The Toothpaste Millionaire* is a funny story of how two friends solve real-world mathematics problems involved in starting a toothpaste business and making a profit.

### Mc Graw Hill Professional Development

Targeted professional development has been articulated throughout the *IMPACT Mathematics* series. The **McGraw-Hill Professional Development Video Library** provides short videos that support the mathematics standards. Log on to www.glencoe.com.

Model Lessons

Instructional Strategies

CHAPTER 8

# Linear Relationships

## Introduce

**At Any Rate** After a student reads aloud the first paragraph in "At Any Rate," ask the class whether they can think of examples of rates involving speed. Then ask whether they can think of any examples of rates that do not involve speed, such as price per pound.

Then ask a student to read aloud the second paragraph and compare the actual speeds of the trains. Some students may volunteer to do further research on trains and their speeds over the years. Other volunteers may want to research the speeds of other means of transportation: people walking, horses and buggies, cars, planes, and rockets. Have the volunteers make a time-line chart to show the differences in speeds to the entire class.

**Think About It** Assume the Eurostar travels 80 mph. If it travels 80 miles in 1 hour, it will travel 160 miles in 2 hours.

CHAPTER 8

# Linear Relationships

### Contents in Brief



## Real-Life Math

**At Any Rate** Linear relationships always involve a constant rate. One of the most common types of rates is *speed.* The speed of an object, like a train, is a relationship between time and distance.

Imagine yourself behind the controls of the British Eurostar, the fastest train in Europe. What makes this train unique is that it runs through the Channel Tunnel, or Chunnel, an expansive tunnel drilled under the English Channel connecting Britain to France. The Eurostar, which first traveled through the Chunnel on June 30, 1993, can reach speeds of 186 mph on land and 80 mph in the Chunnel. That is more than twice the rate of an average train. People can now travel from Paris to London in just 3 hours, a journey that used to take days.

**Think About It** How long would it take to go 160 miles on the Eurostar through the Chunnel?

**Math Online** Take the **Chapter Readiness Quiz** at glencoe.com.

366

### Chapter Resources

- CRM Chapter 8 Resource Masters
- CRM English/Spanish Family Letter (pp. 1–2)
- CRM Chapter 8 Test (pp. 23–30)
- Math Online Online Readiness Quiz • eGlossary

# Dear Family,

Chapter 8 introduces linear relationships, where a change in one variable results in a fixed change in another variable. In class, students will describe situations, make tables of data about the situations, graph the data, and write linear equations that describe the relationships.

### Key Concept–Tables or Algebraic Rules

Here is an example of one kind of exercise with which the class will be working.

Three telephone companies have long-distance rates.

| Company | Rate |
|---|---|
| Easy Access Company | \$1.00 for the first minute; 25 cents per minute thereafter |
| Call Home | 20 cents per minute |
| Metro Communication | \$3.00 for the first minute; 15 cents per minute thereafter |

Here is a question to consider.

- For each company, calculate the amount due for calls lasting 5 minutes, lasting 15 minutes, and for two other lengths of time. Show your results in a table.

Students will also learn to predict which equations have graphs that are straight lines by looking at ta bles or algebraic rules. Then, the class will be able to determine the slope and $y$-intercept.

### Chapter Vocabulary

**linear relationship**
**proportional**
**rate**
**slope**
**speed**
**velocity**
**$y$-intercept**

### Home Activities

- Discuss with your student linear relationships and different ways linear equations appear in the world outside of school.
- Use linear equations to calculate payments for jobs using different hourly rates.

367

## Family Letter

Another version of the Family Letter, available in English and Spanish, is found in the Chapter 8 Resource Masters. You may want to send a copy of this letter home with your students.

### Key Concept–Tables or Algebraic Rules

Students may have difficulty determining if a verbal situation represents a linear relationship or not. It is helpful for students to graph the relationship and then determine if the data is linear or not.

### Home Activities

- Daily Activities—For a week, ask students to record at least two events daily. At the end of the week have the students take at least one activity and represent it in a graphical form. Discuss in small groups whether or not the data represents a linear relationship. If not, how can the data be changed to have a linear relationship.
- Analysis—Have the students create a graph of any linear relationship. Ask the students to take the graph home and discuss with their families what the graph could represent. Have the students share their families interpretations with the class.

## Key Vocabulary

**English (Spanish)** *Introduce the most important terms from Chapter 8.*

**linear relationship (relación lineal)** A relationship whose graph is a straight line. Linear relationships have a constant rate of change. As one variable changes by 1 unit, the other variable changes by a set amount. (p. 375)

**proportional (proporcional)** An equation that states that two ratios are equal. (p. 381)

**rate (tasa)** Describes how two unlike quantities are related or how they can be compared. (p. 372)

**slope (pendiente)** The steepness of a line. (p. 396)

**speed (rapidez)** How fast an object is going (always positive). (p. 401)

**velocity (velocidad)** The rate at which an object is moving from or toward a designated point (can be positive or negative). (p. 401)

***y*-intercept (intersección *y*)** The point at which a graph intersects the $y$-axis. (p. 404)

LESSON

# 8.1 Rates

## Objectives

- To develop strategies for describing rates
- To recognize rates presented in symbolic and graphic forms
- To represent proportional and nonproportional relationships in words, tables, and graphs
- To get experience collecting data
- To determine the nature of the relationship between two variables

## *Overview*

This lesson focuses on describing rates. Students learn about two types of linear relationships: those where the two variables are proportional and those where the two variables are not proportional. They also learn to represent these two types of relationships in words, tables, symbolic rules, and graphs. Students use graphs and symbolic rules to distinguish these two types of linear relationships: graphically by finding the starting point of the graph and symbolically by finding the constant term in a rule.

## *Advance Preparation*

You may want to use an overhead transparency of Chapter 8 Master 1, quarter-inch graph paper for class discussion. You may also want to make copies for students to do their work.

| | Summary | Materials | On Your Own Exercises (pp. 382–388) | Assessment Opportunities |
|---|---|---|---|---|
| **Investigation 1** (p. 369) Pacing: 2 days | Students gain experience in describing rates using words, tables, symbolic rules and graphs. | Chapter 8 Master 1 or quarter-inch graph paper | Practice & Apply: 1–2<br>Connect & Extend: 7–10<br>Mixed Review: 14–27 | • Share & Summarize (p. 373)<br>• Troubleshooting (pp. 373, 374, 376) |
| **Investigation 2** (p. 373) Pacing: 1 day | Students compare different ways of describing rates. | Chapter 8 Master 1 or quarter-inch graph paper | Practice & Apply: 3–5<br>Connect & Extend: 11<br>Mixed Review: 14–27 | • Share & Summarize (p. 376) |
| **Investigation 3** (p. 377) Pacing: 1 day | Students are introduced to proportional and nonproportional relationships. | Chapter 8 Master 1 or quarter-inch graph paper | Practice & Apply: 6<br>Connect & Extend: 12–13<br>Mixed Review: 14–27 | • On the Spot Assessment (p. 379)<br>• Share & Summarize (p. 379) |
| **Inquiry Investigation 4** (p. 380) Pacing: 1 day | Students collect data to determine whether or not a relationship is proportional. | Chapter 8 Master 1 or quarter-inch graph paper, 1 box, 3 cans, For each group: 2 sets of cylindrical pens, 1 book, 1 piece of lined paper | | |

# Leveled Lesson Resources

CRM *Available in:* **Chapter 8 Resource Masters**

Also on TeacherWorks™ Lesson 8.1

## Study Guide and Intervention (p. 4) AL

**Lesson 8.1 Study Guide and Intervention**
***Rates***

Rate describes how two unlike quantities are related or how they can be compared.

***Example*** **a. Alita's car can travel 26 miles on one gallon of gasoline. What is the car's gas mileage in miles per gallon?**

The car's gas mileage is 26 miles per gallon.

**b. Using *m* for the number of miles, write a rule that tells how many miles Alita can travel on *g* gallons of gasoline.**

$m = 26g$

**c. Copy and complete the table without using the rule. Then use your table to check that your rule is correct.**

To find the number of miles traveled, multiply the number of gallons by 26.

| Gallons | 1 | 2 | 3 | 4 | 5 |
|---|---|---|---|---|---|
| Miles | 26 | $2 \cdot 26 = 52$ | $3 \cdot 26 = 78$ | $4 \cdot 26 = 104$ | $5 \cdot 26 = 130$ |

The table says the car travels 104 miles on 4 gallons of gas. Does that match the result if you use $g = 4$ in $m = 26g$?

$m = 26g$
$m = 26 \cdot 4$
$m = 104$

The results match. Your rule is correct.

***Exercises***

1. a. One liter is equivalent to 1,000 cubic centimeters. Rewrite this fact using the word *per*.
   b. Write an algebraic rule to represent this relationship.
2. a. Each minute Oscar walks he burns 4.7 calories. Rewrite this fact using the word *per*.
   b. Write an algebraic rule to find the total number of calories Oscar burns.
3. a. Lydia earns 23 points every time she plays basketball. Rewrite this fact using the word *per*.
   b. Write an algebraic rule to represent this relationship.
   c. Copy and complete the table without using the rule. Then use your table to check that your rule is correct.

| Game, *g* | 1 | 2 | 3 | 4 | 5 |
|---|---|---|---|---|---|
| Points, *p* | 23 | 46 | 69 | | |

## Skills Practice (p. 5) AL OL

**Lesson 8.1 Skills Practice**
***Rates***

**Write a rule describing the relationship in words using the word *per*. Then write a rule using variables.**

1. Each week Alawahi jogs 20 miles. $m$ = miles and $w$ = weeks
2. Sunil earns $12 in one hour. $d$ = dollars and $h$ = hours
3. An elephant's trunk holds 2 gallons of water. $g$ = gallons and $t$ = trunks
4. Gloria worked 60 problems in one hour. $p$ = problems and $h$ = hours

**Solve.**

5. Dr. Santiago sees 120 patients every 4 weeks.
   a. Use $p = 30w$ to complete the table.

| Week, *w* | 1 | 2 | 3 | 4 | 5 |
|---|---|---|---|---|---|
| Patients, *p* | | | | 120 | |

   b. Use the table to graph $p = 30w$.

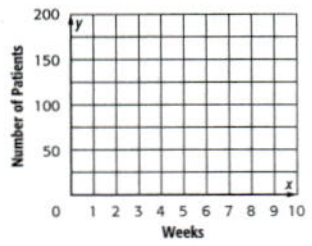


   c. Should the points of this graph be connected? Explain.

6. George purchased 12 CDs for $99.
   a. Use $d = 8.25c$ to complete the table.

| CDs, *c* | 2 | 4 | 6 | 8 | 10 |
|---|---|---|---|---|---|
| Dollars, *d* | | | | | |

   b. Use the table to graph $d = 8.25c$.

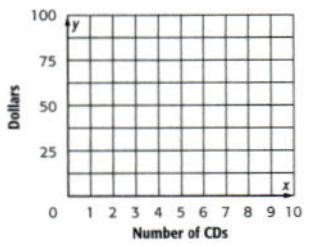


   c. Use your graph to estimate the cost of 5 CDs.

## Problem-Solving Practice (p. 6) AL OL

**Lesson 8.1 Problem-Solving Practice**
***Rates***

**Solve.**

1. **Music** Randall recorded 8 songs on his most recent CD. The total length of the CD is 49 minutes. Write a rule to represent the average length, *l*, per song, *s*, on the CD.
2. **Budget** Steve was offered $5,025 per year for a weekend lifeguarding job at a local pool. He wants to know how much his monthly income will be at this salary level. Write a rule that relates dollars, *d*, and months, *m*.
3. **Travel** During Sonia's trip across the country, she traveled 2,884 miles. Her trip took 7 days. Write a rule using words that describes the relationship between the number of days she travels and the miles traveled. How many miles does Sonia travel in one day?
4. **Carpeting** Each square foot of Hana's new carpeting cost $4.78. Write a rule using variables that relates the two measures. Then complete the table. Use your table to check that your rule is correct.

| Sq. ft, *f* | 15 | 30.25 | 45.5 | 60.75 | 76 |
|---|---|---|---|---|---|
| Dollars, *d* | | | | | |

5. **Travel** Charmaine's plane traveled 212 miles per hour. Write a rule using variables to describe the relationship between miles, *m*, and hours, *h*. Use the rule to draw a graph that shows the relationship between the variables. If you think it makes sense to do so, join the points with a line and extend the line.
6. **Pets** Each day last month, Hao's dog ate 1.5 cans of dog food. Write a rule using variables to describe the relationship between cans, *c*, and days, *d*. Use the rule to draw a graph that shows the relationship between the variables. If you think it makes sense to do so, join the points with a line and extend the line.

## Enrichment (p. 7) BL

**Lesson 8.1 Enrichment**
***Rates***

**An Educated Consumer**

Choosing a checking account is something that most people do at some point in their lives. Because checking accounts vary from institution to institution, and from one type of account to another, you will need to consider the options associated with each account before choosing one of them.

Suppose a bank offers two kinds of checking accounts.

**Account A:** a $0.20 charge for writing each check and no service charge

**Account B:** a $0.10 charge for writing each check and a monthly service charge of $1.50

1. Write a rule to represent the monthly charges, *m*, of each account for writing a certain number of checks, *c*.
2. Complete the table to show the monthly charges for writing checks for Account A.

| Checks, *c* | 5 | 10 | 15 | 20 | 25 |
|---|---|---|---|---|---|
| Monthly Charges, *m* | | | | | |

3. Complete the table to show the monthly charges for writing checks for Account B.

| Checks, *c* | 5 | 10 | 15 | 20 | 25 |
|---|---|---|---|---|---|
| Monthly Charges, *m* | | | | | |

4. Use the data in the table to help you draw a graph of both accounts to show the relationship between the variables. If you think it makes sense to do so, join the points with a line and extend the line.

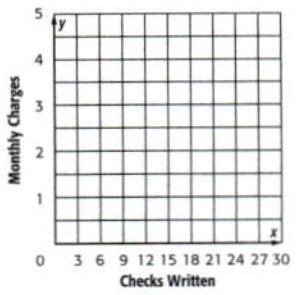


5. Using the information from your graph, explain why someone may choose Account B instead of Account A.

## Lesson Quick Quiz (p. 8) AL OL BL

**Lesson 8.1 Quick Quiz**
***Rates***

1. For the following relationships, determine the rate.
   a. $y = 53x$
   b. $y = 15 + 0.1x$
2. State an equation that describes a proportional relationship.
3. State an equation that describes a nonproportional relationship.
4. On the same axes draw two graphs: one for a proportional relationship and one for a nonproportional relationship. Label which graph is proportional and which is nonproportional.
5. Caitlin works for a fresh-fish supplier. They offered a special price to restaurants for shrimp at $7 per pound. A local restaurant wanted a quote for the cost of enough shrimp for 40 shrimp cocktails. Each cocktail needs six shrimp.

   Clearly, Caitlin would not want to waste time counting all of the shrimp. Work out an easy way to estimate the weight of shrimp the restaurant should order and the cost. What might Caitlin do to estimate the cost?

# Additional Lesson Resources

### Teacher Tech Tools

- TeacherWorks
- ExamView Assessment Suite
- Classroom Presentation Toolkit
- Advance Tracker

### Student Tech Tools

- StudentWorks Plus
- **Math Online** eGlossary • Concepts in Motion

### Other Print Products

- Investigation Notebook and Reflection Journal
- Quick Review Math Handbook

**LESSON 8.1** **Rates**

## *Introduce*

**Understanding Rates** Most students have heard and used the term rate-informally. However, they will vary widely in their understanding of what a rate is, and many will have only an informal sense of its meaning. This lesson helps students refine their notion of a rate by adding a mathematical meaning to the term. Students learn to represent simple rate relationships symbolically and graphically. You might introduce this lesson by inviting students to give examples of rates that they've heard of, looking for applications in and out of mathematics.

### *Think & Discuss*

*Suggested Grouping: Small Groups*

Have students read the four statements involving rates on page 300. You might ask students what each of these rates (pulse, exchange, pay, unit cost) means or in what sense each is a rate. Introduce the language of *per* and *for each*.

Students may work with a partner or group to think about three more rates. Give them about 5 minutes to write three statements involving rates. Then have a whole-class discussion to draw out their ideas. Ask students to describe the rates using the expression *for each*.

You may want to ask students whether they think the rates they listed fluctuate rapidly or remain relatively stable over time. Students should see a wide variety of rates that are in everyday use, and should understand the sense of *per* or *for each* that they all have in common.

# LESSON 8.1 Rates



**Vocabulary**

**rate**

In the statement "Carlos types 30 words per minute," the rate *30 words per minute* describes the relationship between the number of words Carlos types and time in minutes. The speed of light, 186,000 miles per second, is a rate that describes the relationship between the distance light travels and time in seconds. In general, a **rate** describes how two unlike quantities are related or how they can be compared.

Here are some other statements involving rates.

*When she babysits, Yoshi earns $3.50 per hour.*

*At the Better Batter donut shop, donuts cost $3.79 per dozen.*

*Franklin's resting heart rate is 65 beats per minute.*

*On June 24, 2003, the exchange rate from U.S. to British currency was 0.602031 pound per dollar.*

### Think & Discuss

Each rate above involves the Latin word *per*, which means "for each." Try using the phrase "for each" to explain the meaning of each rate. For example, the exchange rate is the number of pounds you receive for each dollar you exchange.
See ① in margin.

Work with a partner to write three more statements involving rates. Explain what your rates mean using the phrase "for each."
Answers will vary.

You can use rates to write algebraic rules relating variables. For example, the equation $d = 186{,}000t$ uses the speed of light to describe the distance $d$ in miles that light travels during a particular number of seconds $t$.

In this lesson, you will explore many situations involving rates. You will also look at tables, graphs, and algebraic rules for these situations.



**Additional Answer**
**Think & Discuss**

1. 65 beats per minute describes the number of times Franklin's heart beats for each minute that passes. 0.60203 pound per dollar tells the number of pounds you get for each dollar exchanged. $3.50 per hour describes the number of dollars Yoshi earns for each hour she works. $3.79 per dozen tells the price for each dozen donuts.

# Investigation 1 Understand Rates

**Vocabulary**

linear relationship

**Materials**

- graph paper

You have probably used rates often, right in your own kitchen. Working with cooking measures will help you understand different ways of thinking about and describing rates.

**Real-World Link**

One type of spider spins an entire web in just 20 minutes. It weaves at the rate of 1,000 operations per minute.

## Develop & Understand: A

Here is a rate expressed in words.

*A teaspoon contains 5 milliliters.*

This rate could also be stated this way.

*There are 5 milliliters per teaspoon.*

1. Suppose you double the number of teaspoons of some ingredient in a recipe. Does that double the number of milliliters? If you triple the number of teaspoons, do you triple the number of milliliters? Yes; yes
2. Using $m$ for the number of milliliters, write a rule that tells how many milliliters are in $t$ teaspoons. $m = 5t$
3. A table of values can help you check that you have written a rule correctly. Copy this table. Without using your rule, complete the table to show the number of milliliters in $t$ teaspoons. Use the table to check that your rule for $t$ and $m$ is correct.

**Converting Teaspoons to Milliliters**

| Teaspoons, $t$ | 0 | 1 | 2 | 3 | 4 | 5 | 10 |
|---|---|---|---|---|---|---|---|
| Milliliters, $m$ | 0 | 5 | 10 | 15 | 20 | 25 | 50 |



# Investigation 1

***On Your Own Exercises***
Pages 382–388
Exercises 1–2, 7–10

**Exploring Rates** In this investigation, students use rules, tables, and graphs to explore rates. They first see how rates and rules can be used in a cooking situation. Then they draw a graph to show the linear relationship. They also look at situations where it is not reasonable to connect the points on a graph. Students will need graph paper or Chapter 8 Master 1, Quarter-Inch Graph Paper, for this investigation.

## Develop & Understand: A

*Suggested Grouping: Pairs or Small Groups*

In this exercise set, students encounter rates used in the kitchen. In the first three exercises, students look at rates and rules. In the last three exercises, they explore graphing rates.

▶ **Exercise 2** Watch for students who write $t = 5m$ as the rule for the statement "1 teaspoonful is 5 mL." You may want to ask these students which is bigger: the number of teaspoons in a certain amount ($t$) or the number of milliliters in the same amount ($m$).

▶ **Exercise 3** The table gives students a way to use substitution to check whether their rule is correct.

## Reaching All Learners

**AL Approaching Level** Students who have difficulty seeing the relationship between the number of teaspoons and the number of milliliters may find it helpful to draw a number line and shade the part representing each teaspoon a different color. For example, they can shade 0–5 red, 5–10 blue, and so on and count the number of colors to find the number of teaspoons. They can find the number of milliliters by looking at the number line.

**Wrap-Up** Discuss Exercises 5 and 6 with the class. These exercises raise the issues of when it makes sense to connect the points on a graph and when the graph can be extended. Students look at the domain and restrictions on the values of the variable, although they use a different vocabulary. They think about whether the values can be fractions as well as whole numbers. Students should realize that because they can have fractions of teaspoons, they can connect the points. Because the graph shows only Quadrant I, you may want to ask students whether the graph could be extended below (0, 0). Students should recognize that this extension makes no sense since there is no definition of a negative teaspoon. They should also see that they can extend the points for all values of *t* greater than or equal to 0 and that the points seem to lie on a line.

### Think & Discuss

*Suggested Grouping: Whole Class*

Discuss the cartoon and the rule relating pints and quarts. Some students may find it helpful to think about whether you need more pints or more quarts to fill a given container, such as the one below.

You may want to draw the measuring cup on the chalkboard and then ask students these questions:

How many pints of liquid are in the measuring cup? 3

How many quarts of liquid are in the measuring cup? $1\frac{1}{2}$

Which number is larger—the number of pints or the number of quarts? number of pints, 3 is greater than $1\frac{1}{2}$

Relate their answers to the rule. Remind students that they can make a table to check their rules.

**Real-World Link**
A woodpecker has a tough head. It can pound its beak against wood at a rate of 20 times per second.

**4.** On axes like those below, plot the data from your table.

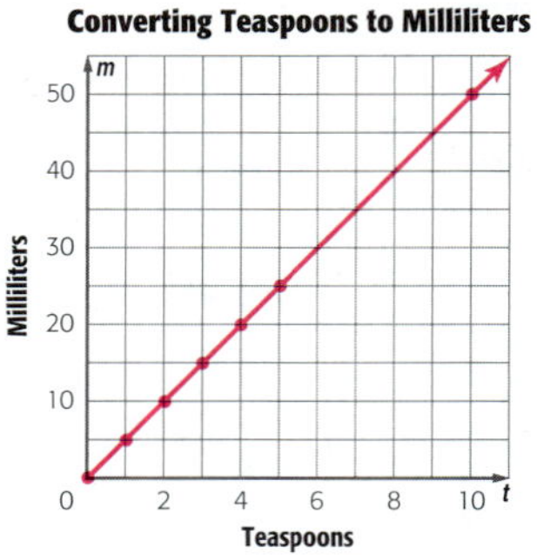


**5.** Does it make sense to connect the points on your graph with a line? Explain. If it does make sense, do it. See margin.

**6.** Does it make sense to extend your graph beyond the points? Explain. If it does make sense, do it.
Yes; it is possible to have more than 10 teaspoons of something.

### Think & Discuss

Darnell and Maya wrote rules relating pints and quarts.

Whose rule is correct? Explain your answer. Maya's rule is correct. Darnell is multiplying the number of pints by 2, which gives, for example, 2 pints is 4 quarts, which is not true. Maya's rule multiplies the number of quarts by 2 to get the number of pints, which is correct.



**Additional Answer**

5. Yes; you can have fractions of teaspoons. The points between the plotted points represent actual quantities, and the relationship is true for those quantities. For example, 2.5 tsp = 12.5 mL.

The relationship between teaspoons and milliliters is called a **linear relationship** because the points on its graph lie on a straight line. In a linear relationship, as one variable changes by 1 unit, the other variable changes by a set amount. The amount of change per unit is the *rate*. In the rule $m = 5t$, the 5 shows that $m$ changes 5 units per 1-unit change in $t$.

Because you can have 1.5 teaspoons, 2.25 teaspoons, and so on, it is sensible to connect the points you plotted in Exercise 4 using a straight line. It is also sensible to extend the line beyond the points from the table since you can have 11, 16, 27, or even more teaspoons of an ingredient.

There are situations for which it is not sensible to connect the points on a graph. For example, this graph shows the relationship between the number of skateboards and the total number of wheels.

**Relationship Between Skateboards and Wheels**

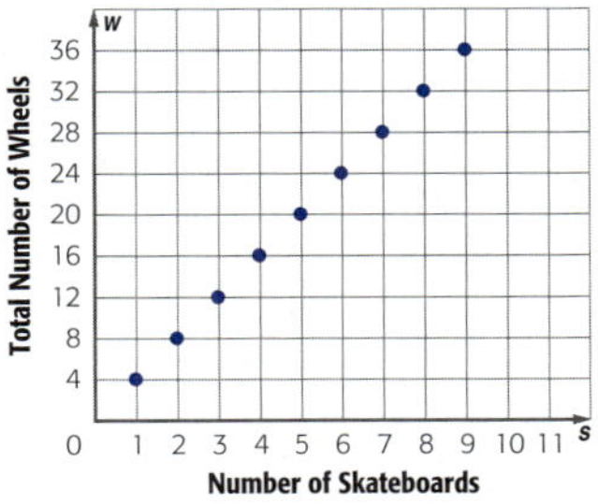


Connecting the points does not make as much sense in this case because the points in between would represent partial skateboards. For example, you would not connect the points for 5 skateboards and 6 skateboards because you could not have 5.5 skateboards or 5.976 skateboards.

Even when it does not make sense to connect the points on a graph, sometimes you may want to do so anyway to help you see a relationship. In this case, it is best to use a dashed line. You will learn more about this later.



**Teacher Tips** Have students look at their graph from Exercise 4. Tell students that the graph shows a linear relationship. Then explain what constitutes a linear relationship and discuss how the graph meets these criteria.

Point out the line students drew to connect the points on the graph. If necessary, have students reiterate why they could draw the line to show the relationship. Tell them that this is not true for all situations.

Direct students' attention to the graph showing the relationship between the number of wheels and the number of skateboards on page 371. Discuss why it is not sensible to connect the points on this graph.

**Lesson 8.1** Rates **371**

## Develop & Understand: B

*Suggested Grouping: Pairs*

It is important for students to realize that they can use a variety of representations to obtain information about the relationship between *c* and *p*.

▶ **Exercise 9** Students will need to use graph paper or Chapter 8 Master 1, Quarter-Inch Graph Paper, to complete Exercise 9.

▶ **Exercise 10** This exercise opens up the domain of the relationship to nonintegers.

▶ **Exercise 11** Students use a graph to find the value of *p*, given $c = 7$.

▶ **Exercise 13** Students compare working with the graph and working with the rule. It is important to mention here that the graph may not give exact information regarding the value of the points. You may want to ask students to compare graph-based answers with rule-based ones.

## Develop & Understand: B

Some recipes give quantities in *weight.* However, in the United States, most recipes specify quantities by *volume,* using such measures as teaspoons, tablespoons, and cups. If you know how much a cup of a particular ingredient weighs, you can write a rate statement to calculate the number of cups for a given weight. For example, it is a fact that one cup of sugar contains about a half pound of sugar.

**7.** Rewrite the fact above using the word *per.*

**8.** Write an algebraic rule relating the number of cups of sugar *c* and weight in pounds *p*. Check your rule by completing the table.

7. There is 1 cup of sugar per $\frac{1}{2}$ pound, or $\frac{1}{2}$ pound of sugar per cup.

8. $p = \frac{1}{2}c$ or $2p = c$

**Relationship Between Cups and Pounds**

| Cups, *c* | 0 | 1 | 2 | 3 | 4 | 5 | 10 |
|---|---|---|---|---|---|---|---|
| Pounds, *p* | 0 | 0.5 | 1 | 1.5 | 2 | 2.5 | 5 |

**9.** Use the data in your table to help you draw a graph to show the relationship between the number of cups of sugar and the number of pounds. Use a set of axes like the one shown.

**Relationship Between Cups and Pounds**

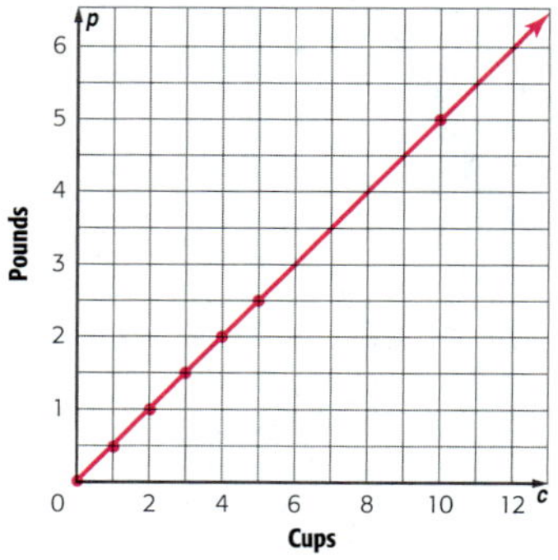


**10.** Does it make sense to connect the points or to extend the graph beyond the points? If so, do these things. Explain your reasoning.

**11.** From your graph, find the value of *p* when *c* is 7. Is that value what you would expect from your rule?

**12.** From the graph, find how many cups of sugar you would need if a recipe calls for 1.4 pounds. Is your answer what you would expect from your rule? About 2.8 c; yes

**13.** Do you find it easier to work from the graph or the rule? Explain. Answers will vary.

10. Yes; connect the points to show the number of pounds for fractional numbers of cups, and extend the graph to show the number of pounds for more than 10 cups.

11. When *c* is 7, *p* is 3.5, which is what I would expect from my rule, $p = \frac{1}{2}c$.



### Reaching All Learners

**BL Beyond Level** Have students write and answer exercises that can be solved using either the rule or the graph. You may wish to have students present their exercises to the class or to use the exercises to provide additional practice for students having difficulty solving Exercises 11 and 12.

### Share & Summarize

1. You may have noticed that on many visits to the doctor, someone measures your pulse, or heart rate, to determine how fast your heart is beating. Measure your pulse by putting your fingers to the side of your neck and counting the number of beats you feel. Record the number of beats in one minute. Explain what makes the number of beats per minute a *rate*.

1. Heart rates will vary. This is a rate because we are comparing the number of beats to the amount of time; for example, "80 beats per minute."

2. Use your heart rate to write an equation relating the number of beats $b$ to any number of minutes timed $t$. Explain what your equation means. Equations should look like $b = rt$ or $\frac{b}{t} = r$, where $r$ is the rate from Exercise 1. An equation with a rate of 80 means the heart is beating 80 times per minute.

## Investigation 2 Describe Rates

**Materials**

- graph paper

Rate relationships can be described in many ways.

### Think & Discuss

Are these three students thinking of the same or different relationships? Why do you think so? The same; all three describe the same rate of typing, which is 30 words per minute. The relationships look different because the same rate is represented in different ways.



### Troubleshooting

If students still have trouble writing a correct equation for Exercise 2, you might ask them what is bigger: the number of pulses or the number of minutes. In this way they can check their formula.

### Share & Summarize

These questions provide students with hands-on experience in finding a pulse, or heart rate, describing it, and using it in relating the number of pulses to the number of minutes. Be sure students can explain how they found their rates and what their equations mean.

## Investigation 2

***On Your Own Exercises***
Pages 382–388
Exercises 3–5, 11

**Describe Rates** This investigation starts by giving three representations—words, symbols, and graphs—to describe a rate. The exercises on pages 374–376 provide students with describing proportional and then nonproportional types of relationships. Students do not use the term *proportional.* All three representations are used to describe two types of relationships within a context of a pay rate.

### Think & Discuss

Ask students to read the cartoon. Ask them whether these three students are thinking of the same or different relationships, and to explain their thinking.

Make sure students understand that each representation describes the same relationship. However, sometimes it is more convenient to talk about the relationship in words, at other times symbols are helpful, and at still other times graphs are a better way to show the relationship. You may want to ask whether any of these give more information than the others. The goal is to be able to move easily among the various ways of expressing the relationship.

## Develop & Understand: A

*Suggested Grouping: Individuals*

In this exercise set, students learn how a rate can be represented in a symbolic rule. They use words and rules to represent the total pay for two boys. Students should begin to realize that the rate of pay is the number that multiplies the number of hours, *h*.

Students should understand that if they double the number of hours, the pay should also be doubled, as asked in Exercises 1 and 7. Exercises like this call attention to strict proportionality and are repeated throughout the lesson.

▶ **Exercise 6** Students may use one of these methods:

- Some students may use mental math and think 10 times what number equals 300.
- Other students may backtrack, possibly using a flowchart or following the steps to solve an equation.
- Still other students may continue the table until the pay is $300.

▶ **Exercise 8** Students should understand that the number multiplied by *h* to find Alec's total pay is different from the number used to calculate Mario's pay.

**Wrap-Up** You may ask students to share their answers to Exercises 4, 10, and 12. Students should recognize that the rates in the rules are different.

## Develop & Understand: A

Mario works in a market. His rate of pay is $10 per hour.

1. If Mario works twice as many hours one week than he does another week, will he earn twice as much? If he works three times as many hours, will he earn three times as much? Yes; yes

2. Copy and complete the table to show what pay Mario should receive for different numbers of hours worked.

**Mario's Rate of Pay**

| Hours Worked, *h* | 0 | 1 | 2 | 3 | 4 | 5 | 10 | 15 |
|---|---|---|---|---|---|---|---|---|
| Pay (dollars), *p* | 0 | 10 | 20 | 30 | 40 | 50 | 100 | 150 |

3. Write a rule in words that relates Mario's pay in dollars to the number of hours worked. Begin your rule, "The number of dollars earned is equal to ... ." Then rewrite the rule using the variables *p* for pay and *h* for hours.

   3. The number of dollars earned is equal to 10 times the number of hours worked; $p = 10h$.

4. What part of your rule shows Mario's rate of pay? The 10

5. Mario usually works a 35-hour week. How much does he earn in a typical week? $350

6. One week, Mario earned $300. How many hours did he work that week? 30

Alec works in a local take-out restaurant. His rate of pay is $7 per hour.

7. If Alec works twice as many hours one week than he does another week, will he earn twice as much? If he works three times as many hours, will he earn three times as much? Yes; yes

8. Complete the table to show what Alec would be paid for different numbers of hours worked.

**Alec's Rate of Pay**

| Hours Worked, *h* | 0 | 1 | 2 | 3 | 4 | 5 | 10 | 15 |
|---|---|---|---|---|---|---|---|---|
| Pay (dollars), *p* | 0 | 7 | 14 | 21 | 28 | 35 | 70 | 105 |

9. Write a rule for Alec's pay in words and in variables.

   9. The number of dollars earned is equal to 7 times the number of hours worked; $p = 7h$.

10. What part of your rule shows Alec's rate of pay? The 7

11. One week, Alec worked 30 hours. How much did he earn that week? $210

12. Compare your symbolic rules for Mario and Alec. How are they the same? How are they different? Mario: $p = 10h$; Alec: $p = 7h$; Both rules have $p$ equal to a number multiplied by $h$, but the numbers are different to match the rates.



### Troubleshooting

Watch for students who mistake rate of pay with total pay. Show with examples that rate is the number that multiplies the number of hours.

## Develop & Understand: B

In addition to variables, tables, and words, graphs are useful for comparing rates of pay.

**13.** Draw a graph of the data for Mario's pay. Use a set of axes like the one below.

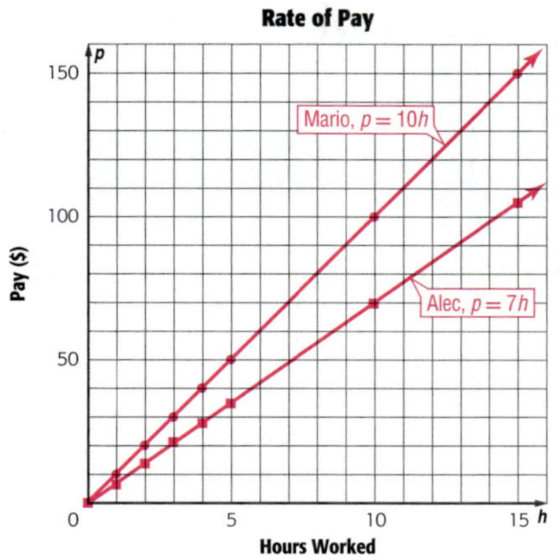


14. Yes; connect the points to show what he earns for fractions of hours, and extend the graph to show what he earns for longer times worked.

**14.** Does it make sense to connect the points on your graph? Does it make sense to extend the graph beyond the points? If so, do these things. Explain your reasoning.

**15.** On the same grid, draw a graph to show how much Alec earns. Label your graphs so you know which is for Mario and which is for Alec. Write each symbolic rule from Exercises 3 and 9 next to the appropriate graph. See the graph.

16. The graphs both start at 0 and are straight lines. Mario's graph is above Alec's. Mario's is steeper; because of a higher rate of pay

**16.** Compare the graphs for Mario and Alec. In what ways are they the same? In what ways are they different? Which is steeper? Why?

**17.** Joelle earns $15 per hour. If you added a line to your graph to show Joelle's pay, how would it compare to Mario's and Alec's graphs? The line would be steeper than and above both Mario's and Alec's lines.



## Develop & Understand: B

*Suggested Grouping: Individuals*

In this exercise set, students learn informally to associate the value of the rate with the steepness of the line. At this stage, the relationships are confined to non-negative values. Students will use graphs produced in this exercise set again in the On Your Own Exercises where they will graph another rate of pay and then compare the three graphs. Make sure that students save these graphs to use later.

▶ **Exercise 13** Students will need graph paper or a copy of Chapter 8 Master 1, Quarter-Inch Graph Paper to complete the exercise.

▶ **Exercise 14** Students look at the domain and determine whether there are any restrictions on the value of *p*.

▶ **Exercise 17** Students visualize how the graph of the pay of a person with a pay rate of $15 per hour would compare to the two graphs they have drawn. If students have difficulty visualizing the graph, have them draw the graph on the grid and then compare the three graphs.

**Wrap-Up** Invite students to present their answers to Exercise 16. Encourage them to use their own words in describing the steepness. For example, they might use a skiing analogy: which lines would be faster to ski down?

## Develop & Understand: C

*Suggested Grouping: Individuals*

This exercise set is different because it intends to help students distinguish rate situations that involve an additional constant amount from the situations that do not involve an additional constant amount. Students use all three representations to describe a relationship between hourly rates and total pay.

Students will need graph paper, or Chapter 8 Master 1, Quarter-Inch Graph Paper, to graph the data in this exercise set.

▶ **Exercise 21** Students are asked to think about what the different numbers and symbols in their rules represent. The fixed amount paid for being "on call" is 40, the number added on, and the rate of pay is 10, the number that multiplies the number of hours worked.

**Wrap-Up** Ask several students to share their answers to Exercises 19 and 21. In Exercise 19, it is important for students to realize that if Tamsin works two times as many hours this weekend as she did last weekend, she will *not* earn two times as much money. In the next investigation, the term *proportional* is introduced and the link is made with fixed rates and the associated graphs.

### Share & Summarize

Students should notice that the graphs showing Mario's and Alec's earnings pass through the origin and that Tamsin's graph does not. They should associate this characteristic with the symbolic representation of the rule: Tamsin's rule has a constant amount added on.

## Develop & Understand: C

Tamsin works for an automobile association. Every second weekend, she is "on call." This means she must be available all weekend in case a car breaks down in her area. She is paid a fixed amount of $40 for the weekend, even if she does not have to work. If she is called, she earns an additional $10 per hour worked.

**18.** Complete the table to show what Tamsin would be paid for different numbers of hours worked during a single weekend.

**Tamsin's Pay**

| Hours Worked, $h$ | 0 | 1 | 2 | 3 | 4 | 5 | 10 | 15 |
|---|---|---|---|---|---|---|---|---|
| Pay (dollars), $p$ | 40 | 50 | 60 | 70 | 80 | 90 | 140 | 190 |

**19.** If Tamsin works twice as many hours one weekend as she does another weekend, will she earn twice as much? Explain. No; the constant amount of $40 is added to an hourly rate.

**20.** Write the rule for Tamsin's pay for a single weekend in words and in variables. Tamsin's pay is $40, plus $10 multiplied by the number of hours worked; $p = 40 + 10h$.

**21.** What part of your rule shows the amount Tamsin earns for being on call? What part shows her hourly rate? The 40; the 10

**22.** Use the data in your table to draw a graph showing how much Tamsin earns for various numbers of hours worked. Use the same grid you used for Exercise 13 or a similar one.

22.
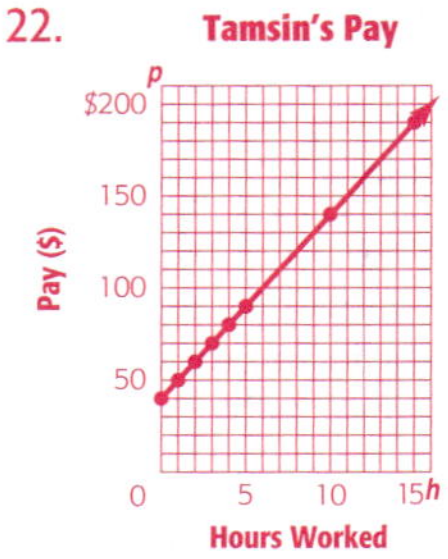


### Share & Summarize

1. Look again at the graphs that show how much Alec, Mario, and Tamsin earn. How do the graphs show differences in pay? How is a higher rate shown in a graph?

2. How do the symbolic rules show the differences in the rates at which the three people are paid? How is a higher rate shown in a symbolic rule?

1. Tamsin's graph starts at (0, 40) because she earns money even for working zero hours. The graphs have different degrees of steepness, which shows that the people are paid at different rates. A steeper graph indicates a higher rate.
2. The numbers multiplying the variables are the pay rates. A greater number indicates a higher rate.



## Troubleshooting

In comparing Tamsin's graph with those for Alec and Mario, students may tend to focus only on the steepness of the line. If necessary, draw their attention to where the graph begins, that is, the point where it intersects the vertical axis.

Don't worry if the students did not make the connections between the rules and the graph for the two types of relationships. The next investigation will explore the differences between simple fixed rate and a rate plus a constant in greater detail.

# Investigation 3 Proportional Relationships

**Vocabulary**

proportional

**Materials**

- graph paper

Alec and Mario, from Investigation 2, are paid at a simple hourly rate. If they work double the number of hours, they receive double the pay. If they work triple the hours, they receive triple the pay, and so on.

The word **proportional** is sometimes used to describe this kind of relationship between two variables. We can say that for Alec and Mario, the number of dollars earned is proportional to the number of hours worked. The graphs for Alec's pay and Mario's pay are shown below. They are each a straight line that begins at the point (0, 0).

**Alec's Graph**

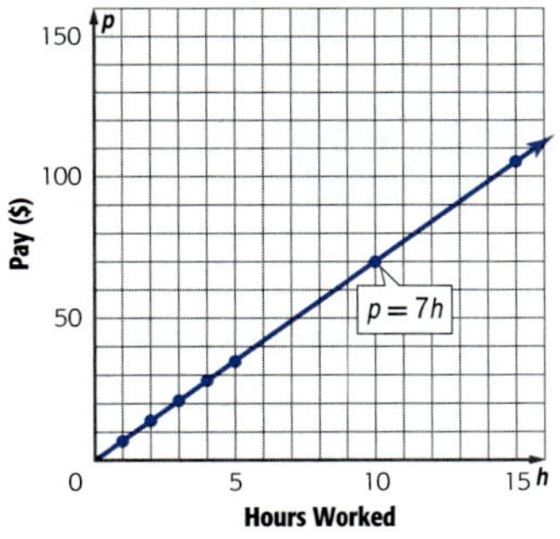


**Mario's Graph**

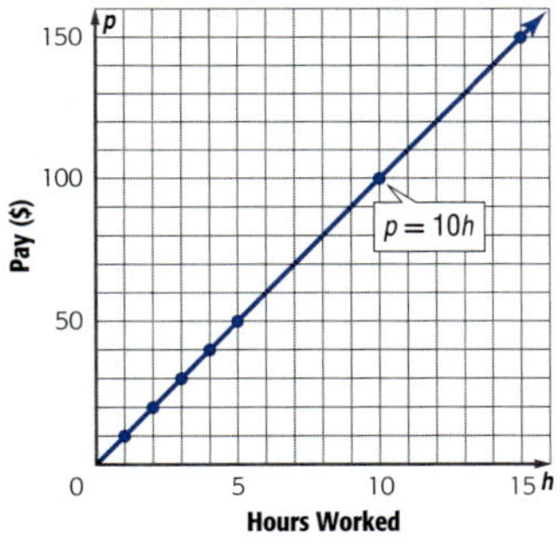


Tamsin is not paid at a simple hourly rate. She receives a fixed amount plus an hourly rate. For Tamsin, doubling the number of hours worked does not double the total pay received. The number of dollars earned is not proportional to the number of hours worked. The graph for Tamsin's pay is also a straight line, but it does not begin at the point (0, 0).

**Tamsin's Graph**

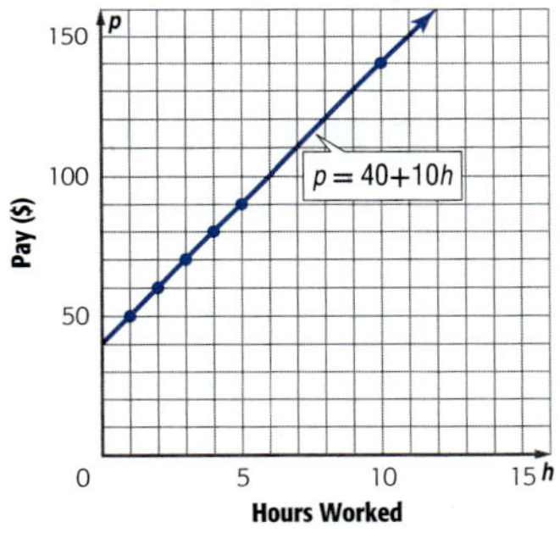


Although the relationships for Alec and Mario are proportional and the relationship for Tamsin is not, all three relationships are *linear relationships* because their graphs are straight lines.



# Investigation 3

***On Your Own Exercises***

Pages 382–388
Exercises 6, 12–13

**Proportional Relationships** Investigation 3 further develops the notion of proportional versus nonproportional relationships. Although both exercise sets deal with proportional relationships only, the Think & Discuss and homework exercises deal with both types of relationships.

Use the Share & Summarize questions in Investigation 2 to launch this investigation. Explain to students that we sometimes use the word *proportional* to describe the kind of relationship that exists between the two variables in Mario's and Alec's situations: if they work double the number of hours, they get double the pay. If they work triple the hours, they get triple the pay, and so on.

Relate this rule to the two graphs of the boys' wages. You may wish to make a transparency of the two graphs, or direct students' attention to the graphs on page 377 labeled *Alec's Graph* and *Mario's Graph*. Make it clear that the graph of a proportional relationship is a straight line that passes through (0, 0).

Compare the rules and graphs for Mario and Alec respectively with the rule and graph for Tamsin, and help students see why the relationship between the number of hours that Tamsin works and her total pay is not proportional. Emphasize that despite the differences, all of these types of relationships are linear and are represented by a straight line.

## Think & Discuss

*Suggested Grouping: Whole Class*

Ask students to explain why some of the relationships between the rate and time on the calling cards are proportional and others are not. Access, Budget, and Cheap cards have rates proportional to the number of minutes of long distance calls while Dollar, Easy, and Fantastic cards are not proportional since there is a standard fee regardless of usage.

At the end of the discussion mention that if a rate, *x*, is proportional to a total, *y*, then the total, *y*, is also proportional to the rate, *x*. You don't have to dwell on that concept, because students will have experience with these inverse relationships later in Lesson 8.2.

## Develop & Understand: A

*Suggested Grouping: Individuals or Pairs*

This exercise set provides practice describing a variety of rate situations with symbolic rules. All of these relationships are proportional.

**Wrap-Up** You can wrap up this exercise set by asking several students to state their symbolic rules and tell whether the relationships are proportional.

## Develop & Understand: B

*Suggested Grouping: Individuals or Pairs*

This exercise set provides an additional practice for representing proportional rates in table and graphs, while also reviewing percents.

Students will need graph paper or Chapter 8 Master 1, Quarter-Inch Graph Paper, to draw the graph in this exercise set.

▶ **Exercises 6–9** Students look at how the number of correct answers and the percentage are related.

① Access, Budget, and Cheap are proportional; Dollar, Easy, and Fantastic are not. Since the first three do not have a charge other than the rate, they are proportional. Talking twice as long will cost twice as much, and the graphs of charge versus time will go through (0, 0).

5. Possible answer: Since none has a constant term, they are all proportional relationships. They differ in that they have different rates.

## Think & Discuss

Many companies issue cards for charging telephone calls. For which cards below are the charges proportional to the number of minutes? For which are they not proportional? Explain. See ①.

## Develop & Understand: A

In Exercises 1–4, the rule describes two variables that are proportional to each other. Rewrite each rule in symbols.

1. The circumference of a circle *c* is 3.14 times the diameter *d*. $c = 3.14d$
2. The perimeter of a square *p* is 4 multiplied by the length of a side *L*. $p = 4L$
3. At a certain time of day, the length of a shadow *s* cast by an object is twice the length of the object *L*. $s = 2L$
4. Each length *h* in a copy is $\frac{1}{100}$ the length *k* in the original. $h = \frac{1}{100}k$
5. Compare the four rules you developed in Exercises 1–4. In what ways are they similar? In what ways are they different?

## Develop & Understand: B

Ms. Cruz gave her class a test with 40 questions.

6. Latisha got 100% correct; Kate got only 50% correct. How many of the 40 questions did each answer correctly? 40, 20
7. Lupe got fewer than 20 questions correct. If she could retake the test and double the number right, would that double her percentage? Yes
8. Does halving the number of correct answers out of 40 halve the percentage? Yes
9. Is the number of correct answers out of 40 proportional to the percentage? Yes



## Reaching All Learners

**OL On Level** For Exercise 7, have students explain why the exercise is restricted to Lupe's answering 20 or fewer questions correctly. Students should realize that although the relationship is proportional, it doesn't make sense that Lupe would answer more questions than were on the test.

**10.** One evening, Ms. Cruz had to convert her class' test results into percentages. She had left her calculator at school and decided to use a graph to help her.

**a.** She first calculated a few values and put them in a table. Copy and complete her table.

**Class Test Results**

| Number Correct (out of 40), *n* | 0 | 10 | 20 | 30 | 40 |
|---|---|---|---|---|---|
| Percentage Correct, *p* | 0 | 25 | 50 | 75 | 100 |

**b.** Ms. Cruz then drew a graph on graph paper by plotting the points from her table and drawing a line through them. She made the horizontal axis the number of correct questions out of 40 with one grid unit on the axis equal to 2 questions correct. She put percentage points on the vertical axis with one grid unit on the axis equal to 5 percentage points. She could then quickly read percentages from the graph for the various scores out of 40.

Draw Ms. Cruz's graph. Does it make sense to extend the line beyond the point (40, 100)? Explain your thinking. See margin.

**11.** Use your graph to convert each score out of 40 into a percentage.

**a.** 38 95% **b.** 36 90%

**c.** 33 82.5% **d.** 29 72.5%

**e.** 25 62.5% **f.** 23 57.5%

Note: Answers will vary, depending on the accuracy of the graphs.

**12.** Lucas, Opa, and Raheem scored 65%, 75%, and 85%, respectively, on the test. How many questions out of 40 did each get correct?
26, 30, 34

## Share & Summarize

**1.** Without graphing, do you think the graphs of the relationships described in Exercises 1–4 would pass through the origin? Explain your reasoning. Yes; all the relationships are proportional.

**2.** A graph of a linear relationship goes through the point (0, 4). Is this a proportional relationship? Explain your reasoning.

**3.** Is $y = 5x + 7$ a proportional relationship? Explain your thinking.

2. No; the graph of a proportional relationship must pass through (0, 0).

3. No; it has a constant term added, so the graph would go through (0, 7), not (0, 0).

**Math Link**

The point (0, 0) is called the origin.



## On the Spot Assessment

If students are not able to solve the exercises correctly, give them this additional example and ask them where the graph begins and whether or not the relationship is proportional.

Mark started a new baseball card collection. At the beginning his father bought him 30 cards, and then he bought 5 additional cards every week. Graph starts at (0, 30). Relationship is not proportional.

▶ **Exercise 10** Students graph the relationship. They should understand that it does not make sense to extend the graph beyond the point (40,100) because no one answered more than 40 questions.

▶ **Exercise 11** You might want to ask students to find the pattern in the percentages and explain that this pattern will help Ms. Cruz read the graph and find the correct percentages. Students may see that each answer is worth 2.5 points, so all scores will end in 0.0, 2.5, 5.0, or 7.5. Although students may have inaccurate graphs and not have exact answers, you might want to reassure them that the teacher has ways to correctly score the tests.

▶ **Exercises 11 and 12** Make sure that students can easily convert between scores and percents.

**Wrap-Up** Discuss Exercises 7 and 10 with the class. In answering Exercise 7, students need to understand that if multiplying a score by a certain number multiplies the percent by the same number, it means that the relationship is proportional.

## Share & Summarize

By this time students should be able to distinguish between proportional and nonproportional relationships in a graphical representation. These exercises assess their understanding.

### Additional Answers

10b. No; no one could have answered more than 40 questions.

**Class Test Results**

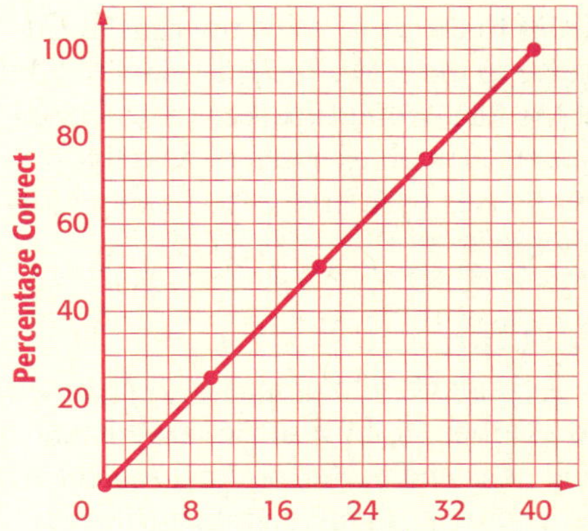

## Inquiry Investigation 4

*Suggested Grouping: Small Groups*

### Materials and Preparation

You will need a box and three cans for the demonstrations to begin the investigation. Students will need two different-sized sets of cylindrical pens or other tubes, with all cylinders in each set having the same diameter. They will also need lined paper, a hardcover book, and Chapter 8 Master 1, Quarter-Inch Graph Paper, or graph paper. Other materials can be used to conduct the experiment, such as straws or wooden dowels instead of pens. Be aware that pencils are usually not smooth on the surface and may not roll properly. You may wish to use a paper pad in place of a book.

Introduce the Investigation by telling students that our knowledge about the nature of the relationships usually comes from collecting data. Let them know that they will be collecting measurements to determine whether or not the relationship between two variables is proportional.

### Work with Your Class

Begin with a demonstration of a heavy box rolling over three aluminum drink cans. The box will move on the cans while the cans will be coming out from behind the box. This happens because the box moves relative to the cans, while the cans move relative to the table. You may want to point out the Real-World Link feature to provide students with an example of how this method was used in real life. Then discuss Exercises 1–3.

### Try It Out

Divide students into groups of 2–4 students and ask them to try a similar experiment using pens and books, or other materials of your choice. It is important that students use lined paper for their experiments so they can reliably measure the distance. Remind them to count carefully.





## Inquiry Investigation 4 Rolling Along

### Materials

- 2 cylindrical pens or pencils (without edges) with different diameters
- lined paper
- hardcover book
- graph paper

**Real-World Link**
Historians believe that this method of rollers was used to move very heavy stones used to build the Egyptian pyramids.

In this investigation, you will conduct an experiment to understand the relationship between two variables.

### Work with Your Class

Watch how a heavy box rolls on three drink cans. The rollers will keep coming out from behind the box.

1. Do the rollers go backward? No
2. Does the box go faster than the rollers? Yes
3. Why do the rollers keep coming out the back? The box moves faster than the rollers, so it eventually rolls off them.

### Try It Out

With your group, conduct an experiment that involves rolling one object on top of another. Use a perfectly round cylindrical pen or pencil, a book, and a sheet of lined paper with wide lines. Set up the paper, pencil, and book as shown.

4. Roll the book on the pen until the pen has moved two line spaces. How far has the book moved? 4 line spaces
5. Continue to roll the book to complete the table. When you collect your data, count and measure accurately. Otherwise, you might not see the patterns that show the relationship between the variables.

**Number of Line Spaces Moved**

| | | | | | | |
|---|---|---|---|---|---|---|
| Distance Moved by Pen, $p$ | 0 | 2 | 4 | 6 | 8 | 10 |
| Distance Moved by Book, $b$ | 0 | 4 | 8 | 12 | 16 | 20 |

6. The book moves twice as far as the pen; $b = 2p$.

7. Number of Line Spaces Moved

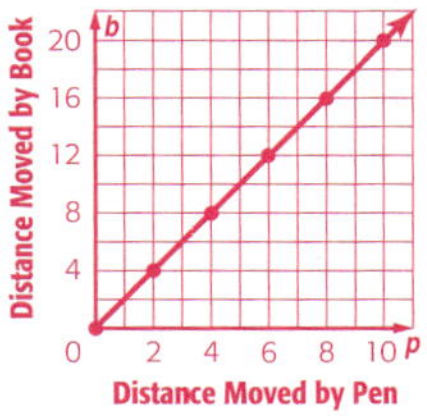


## Analyze Your Data

**6.** Describe how the distance the book moves is related to the distance the pen moves. Write the relationship using the symbols $p$ and $b$.

**7.** Draw a graph with the distance moved by the pen on the horizontal axis and the distance moved by the book on the vertical axis. Plot the values you found in Exercise 5. If you think it makes sense to do so, join the points with a line, and extend the line.

## Apply Your Results

**8.** Using your rule, predict how far the book will move when the pen moves 16 line spaces. Check by doing it. 32 line spaces

**9.** How many line spaces does the book move if the number of line spaces moved by the pen is 0.5? 1.5? 7.5? 1,350? 1; 3; 15; 2,700

**10.** If the book moves 9 line spaces, how far does the pen move? Test it with your equipment. 4.5 line spaces

**11.** Describe in words how the distance the pen moves is related to the distance the book moves. Write this rule in symbols. The pen moves half as far as the book; $p = \frac{1}{2}b$.

## Try It Again

Replace the pen with a different-sized pen or some other cylinder, and repeat the experiment.

**12.** Complete a new table. Are your results the same? Yes

**Number of Line Spaces Moved**

| Distance Moved by Pen, $p$ | 0 | 2 | 4 | 6 | 8 | 10 |
|---|---|---|---|---|---|---|
| Distance Moved by Book, $b$ | 0 | 4 | 8 | 12 | 16 | 20 |

**13.** Is this a proportional relationship? How can you tell? Yes; the relation is linear and includes the point (0, 0).

## What Did You Learn?

**14.** Write a short report describing your experiments and the results. Reports will vary.

Inquiry

▶ **Exercises 4–7** Students look at the relationship between the number of spaces the pen has moved and the number of spaces the book has moved, then organize their data in a table.

▶ **Exercise 6** Students are asked to come up with a rule that describes the relationship. It is important for students to express the rule in words as well as in symbols. The rule $b = 2p$ may look abstract to many students until they can read it as the book goes twice as far as the pen.

▶ **Exercise 7** Students determine domain and restrictions on the values of the variables when they graph their data.

## Apply Your Results

Students use their rules to make a prediction in Exercise 8. If their prediction was reasonable, they may want to use the same strategy to answer Exercise 9.

▶ **Exercises 10 and 11** These exercises introduce the inverse relationship between the distance moved by the book and the distance moved by the pen. Point this out to students. These exercises emphasize the ability to work backward from the answer to the question. They also provide an informal introduction to the concept of inverse functions.

## Try It Again

Students repeat the experiment using a different-sized pen. You may want them to predict how the rule will change. They may be surprised to find that the results are the same as in the previous experiment.

## What Did You Learn?

Students' reports should discuss the factors that define the rule. It is important that students understand that the book is moving twice as far as the pen regardless of the size of the diameter of the pen or the size of the evenly spaced lines on the paper.

Students may also mention that because the relationship is proportional, the graph will begin at (0, 0).

**Investigation 1**
Pages 369–373
Practice & Apply: 1–2
Connect & Extend: 7–10

**Investigation 2**
Pages 373–376
Practice & Apply: 3–5
Connect & Extend: 11

**Investigation 3**
Pages 377–379
Practice & Apply: 6
Connect & Extend: 12–13

**Assign Anytime**
Mixed Review: 14–27

▶ **Exercises 1–2 and 8–11** These exercises not only review the concepts taught in the first investigation, but, in many cases, they also provide practice converting between metric and English measures of weight and volume.

***Math Link***
To assist students in understanding whether or not it is necessary to connect the data points or to extend a line when plotting data, have a class discussion about when it is not appropriate. One thing to bring up in the discussion is plotting birthdays. It is not appropriate to connect these data points because they are not related to each other. In terms of extending lines, discuss a problem about spending money. Ask the class how far they would extend the line for a graph modeling starting with $50 and spending $7.50 a week. How do you know when to stop plotting points?

On Your Own Exercises
Lesson 8.1

***Practice & Apply***

1. **Measurement** A kilogram is equivalent to 1,000 grams.
   a. Describe this relationship in words using the word *per*.
   There are 1,000 grams per kilogram.
   b. Write a rule in symbols that relates the two measures. Use $k$ to represent the number of kilograms and $g$ the number of grams.
   $g = 1{,}000k$
   c. Copy and complete the table without using the rule. Then use your table to check that your rule is correct.

**Converting Kilograms to Grams**

| Kilograms, $k$ | 1 | 2 | 3 | 4 | 5 |
|---|---|---|---|---|---|
| Grams, $g$ | 1,000 | 2,000 | 3,000 | 4,000 | 5,000 |

   d. Use the data in the table to help you draw a graph to show the relationship between the measures. If it makes sense to connect the points, do so. If it makes sense to extend the line beyond the points, do so.

1d.
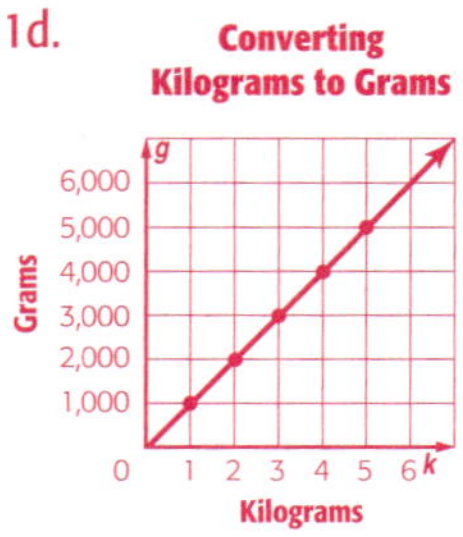


   e. Use your table, formula, or graph to find the number of grams in 1.5 kg, 3.2 kg, 0.7 kg, and 0.034 kg. 1,500; 3,200; 700; 34

2. **Measurement** A pound is equivalent to 0.454 kilogram.
   a. Describe the relationship in words using the word *per*.
   There is 0.454 kg per pound.
   b. Write a rule in symbols that relates the two measures. Use $p$ for the number of pounds and $k$ for the number of kilograms.
   $k = 0.454p$
   c. Complete the table without using your rule. Then use your table to check that your rule is correct.

**Converting Pounds to Kilograms**

| Pounds, $p$ | 1 | 2 | 3 | 4 | 5 |
|---|---|---|---|---|---|
| Kilograms, $k$ | 0.454 | 0.908 | 1.362 | 1.816 | 2.27 |

   d. Use the data in the table to help you draw a graph to show the relationship between the measures.

2d.
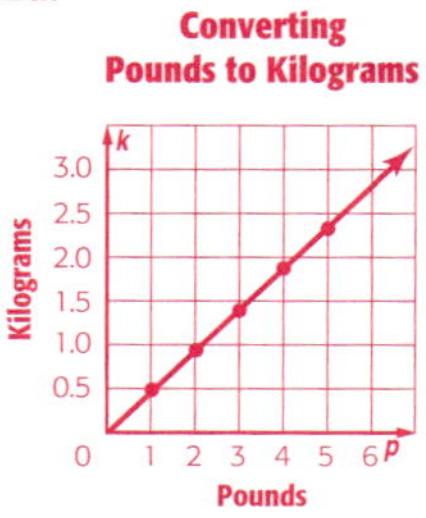


   e. Use your table, formula, or graph to find the number of kilograms in 7 lb, 40 lb, 100 lb, and 0.5 lb. 3.178; 18.16; 45.4; 0.227

***Math Link***
When you plot points from a table of data, connect the points and extend the line beyond the points, if it makes sense to do so.

On Your Own Exercises

**3.** These three phone cards have different charge plans for their customers.

3a. Dollar: $d = 3 + \underline{0.10}m$; Easy: $d = 4 + \underline{0.10}m$; Fantastic: $d = 5 + \underline{0.10}m$

**a.** Write the rule for each card's charge plan for 1 month, using $d$ for charge in dollars and $m$ for minutes of calls. Underline the part of each rule that shows the rate of charge.

**b.** Copy the table. For each card, fill in the table to show the monthly bill for different numbers of minutes of calls.

**Phone Card Charges**

| Minutes, *m* | 0 | 10 | 20 | 30 | 40 | 50 | 100 | 150 | 200 |
|---|---|---|---|---|---|---|---|---|---|
| Dollar Bill, $ | 3 | 4 | 5 | 6 | 7 | 8 | 13 | 18 | 23 |
| Easy Bill, $ | 4 | 5 | 6 | 7 | 8 | 9 | 14 | 19 | 24 |
| Fantasic Bill, $ | 5 | 6 | 7 | 8 | 9 | 10 | 15 | 20 | 25 |

**c.** On one set of axes, draw a graph for each card's charge plan. Put minutes on the horizontal axis and dollars on the vertical axis. Label the graphs to identify which card goes with which graph. See margin.

**d.** Does it make sense to connect the points? Does it make sense to extend the graphs beyond the points? If so, do it.

3d. It makes sense to connect the points because a person can talk any number of minutes. It makes sense to extend the graphs because a person can talk more than 200 min in a month.

**e.** How are the graphs similar? How are they different? The graphs have the same steepness, but they start at different points.

**f.** How much would the monthly bill for 85 minutes be with the Dollar card? $11.50

**g.** For $12, how many minutes of calls could you make in one month with the Dollar card? With the Easy card? With the Fantastic card? If your answers are more than 59 minutes, convert them to hours and minutes. Dollar: 1 h 30 min; Easy: 1 h 20 min; Fantastic: 1 h 10 min



▶ **Exercise 3d** Students should assume that customers can be billed for fractional minutes.

▶ **Exercise 3f** Be sure students understand that the 85 minutes occurred in the same month.

**Additional Answer**

3c.

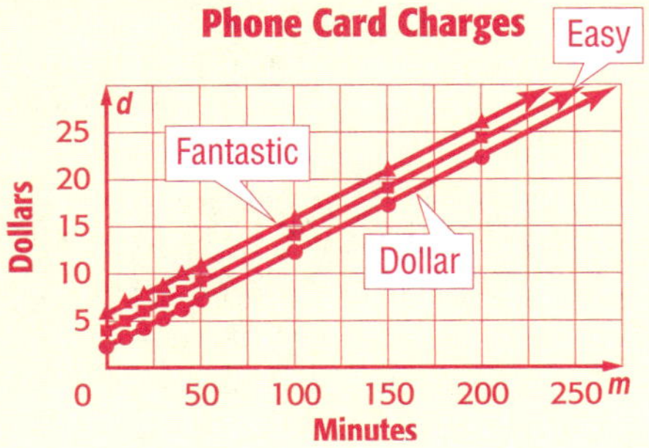

▶ **Exercises 4b and 4d** Have students refer to and use their graphs from Investigation 2 to answer these problems.

▶ **Exercise 5e** Students work backward to find the number of minutes given the total number of revolutions.

On Your Own Exercises

**4.** In Exercises 1–17 in Investigation 2, you solved exercises about Alec's and Mario's rates of pay. Suppose that Alec receives a raise to $8 per hour.

**a.** Write a rule in symbols relating the number of dollars $p$ that Alec earns to the number of hours $h$ that he works. $p = 8h$

**b.** What would the graph that shows his new pay rate look like? How would it compare to the two graphs you have already drawn for Mario's pay and Alec's pay at the old rate? It would be a straight line between the two lines already drawn.

**c.** Make a table to show what Alec would now earn for 0, 1, 2, 3, 4, 5, and 10 hours of work. See below.

**d.** On your grid from Exercise 13, draw a graph to show how much Alec is paid at the new rate. Does the graph look as you predicted in Part b? If not, try to figure out where your thinking went wrong. See margin.

**5.** Before compact discs became popular, people listened to music and other sound recordings on record players. A record player that runs at 45 rpm turns a record 45 times per minute. The unit rpm is an abbreviation for *revolutions per minute.*

**a.** Complete the table to show the number of times a record turns in a given number of minutes.

**Playing Records**

| **Minutes, $t$** | 1 | 2 | 3 | 4 | 5 | 6 |
|---|---|---|---|---|---|---|
| **Revolutions, $r$** | 45 | 90 | 135 | 180 | 225 | 270 |

**b.** Write in words a rule that gives the number of times a record turns in a given number of minutes. Then write the same rule in symbols. Underline the part of your rule that shows the constant rate of turning. The number of revolutions is equal to 45 times the number of minutes; $r = \underline{45}t$

**c.** Using your rule, predict the number of revolutions in 12 seconds, or 0.2 minute. $r = 45 \cdot 0.2 = 9$

**d.** Draw a graph to show how the number of revolutions is related to time. Put time on the horizontal axis.

**e.** Use your graph to estimate how long it would take for a record to revolve 100 times and 300 times. About 2.2 min, about 6.7 min

5d.

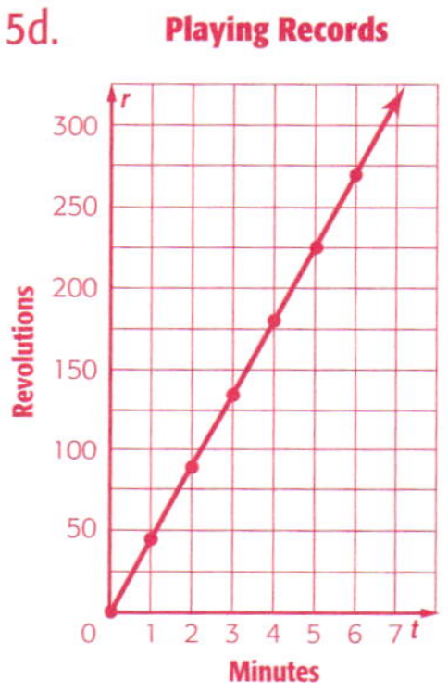


4c. **Alec's Pay**

| **Hours Worked, $h$** | 0 | 1 | 2 | 3 | 4 | 5 | 10 |
|---|---|---|---|---|---|---|---|
| **Pay (dollars), $p$** | 0 | 8 | 16 | 24 | 32 | 40 | 80 |



**Additional Answer**

4d.

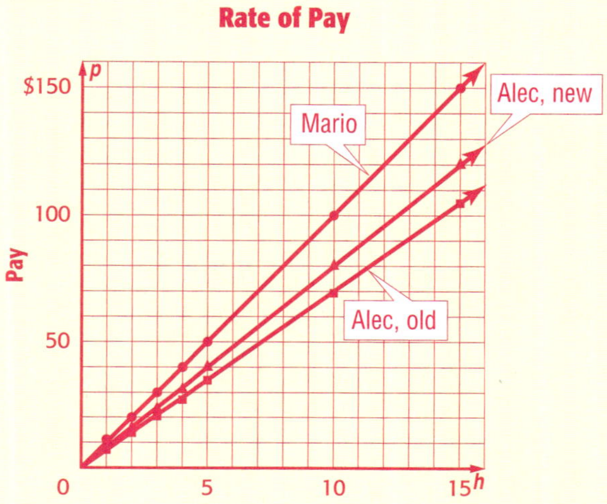

6e. **Painting Walls**

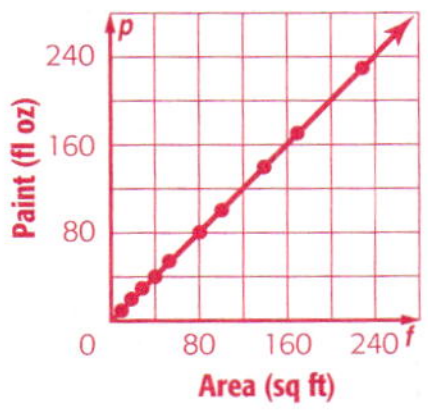


7. For a graph, you can look at the points for the relationship and the differences between each consecutive point to find the rate. Using a symbolic rule, you can look at the rate for which one variable changes based on the relationship. For a table, you can find the difference between two consecutive pairs to find the rate.

**Connect & Extend**

8c. **Converting Ounces to Grams**

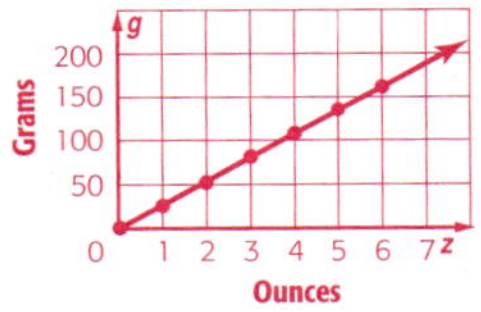


**Real-World Link**

The metric system was first proposed in 1670 and is now used in most countries around the world.

**6.** A painter needs about 1 fluid ounce of paint for each square foot of wall she paints.

**a.** Write a rule in symbols for this situation, using $p$ for fluid ounces of paint and $f$ for square feet. Underline the part of your rule that shows the constant rate of paint use. $p = \underline{1}f$

**b.** Complete the table.

**Painting Walls**

| Paint (fluid oz), $p$ | 0 | 10 | 20 | 30 | 40 | 50 | 80 | 100 | 140 | 170 | 220 |
|---|---|---|---|---|---|---|---|---|---|---|---|
| Area (sq ft), $f$ | 0 | 10 | 20 | 30 | 40 | 50 | 80 | 100 | 140 | 170 | 220 |

**c.** How many fluid ounces of paint are needed to paint a wall with area 120 sq ft? 120

**d.** How many gallons of paint are needed to cover 450 sq ft? There are 128 fluid ounces in 1 gallon. 3.52

**e.** Draw a graph to show how the amount of paint depends on the area to be painted. Put area on the horizontal axis.

**f.** Use your graph to estimate the area covered with 1 gallon of paint, 2 gallons of paint, and 3 gallons of paint. 128 sq ft, 256 sq ft, 3844 sq ft

**g.** If a painter uses twice as much paint, can she cover twice as much area? If she uses three times as much paint, can she cover three times as much area? Is the relationship between area and amount of paint proportional? Yes; yes; yes

**7. In Your Own Words** How can you find the rate of a linear relationship using a graph? Using a symbolic rule? Using a table? Which do you prefer for this task? Why?

**8. Measurement** 24 ounces is equivalent to 680 grams.

**a.** Describe the relationship in words using the word *per.* There are 680 g per 24 oz, or 28.33 g per oz.

**b.** Complete the table. Write a rule in symbols that relates the two measures. Use your table to check that your rule is correct. $g = 28.33z$

**Converting Ounces to Grams**

| Ounces, $z$ | 0 | 1 | 2 | 3 | 4 | 5 | 6 |
|---|---|---|---|---|---|---|---|
| Grams, $g$ | 0 | 28.33 | 56.66 | 84.99 | 113.32 | 141.65 | 169.98 |

**c.** Use the data in the table to help you draw a graph to show the relationship between the measures. If you think it makes sense to do so, join the points with a line, and extend the line.



On Your Own Exercises

▶ **Exercise 6** Watch for students who have trouble recognizing the rate in $p = f$. Some may say there is no rate; others may say the rate is $f$. Remind them that when there is no number in front of a variable, the variable is multiplied by 1; therefore, the rate is 1.

▶ **Exercise 6d** Tell students to round their answers to the nearest hundredth.

▶ **Exercises 11d and 11e** In order to make the conversions, students may need to be reminded that 1,000 mL = 1 L and that 16 c = 1 gal.



**Measurement** A kilogram, kg, is equivalent to 1,000 grams, g. A pound, lb, is equivalent to 0.454 kilogram.

**9.** Find the number of grams in 1 lb, 2 lb, 0.6 lb, and 0.1 lb. 454, 908, 272.4, 45.4

**10.** Find the number of pounds in 3 kg, 17 kg, 0.5 kg, 900 g, 300 g, and 56 g. Round to the nearest hundredth. 6.61, 37.44, 1.10, 1.98, 0.66, 0.12

| |
|---|
| 1 fl oz = 29.573 mL |
| 1 oz = 28.350 g |
| 1 gal = 3.785 L |

**11. Challenge** Darnell bought a gallon of spring water. The label indicated that a serving size is 1 cup, or 236 mL. Use the conversions at the left to answer the questions. Round to the nearest hundredth.

**a.** What is the volume of the 1-cup serving size in fluid ounces? 7.98

**b.** The mass of 1 mL of water is 1 g. What is the mass of 1 cup of water in grams? 236

**c.** What is the weight of 1 cup of water in ounces? 8.32

**d.** What is the volume of 1 cup of water in liters? 0.24

**e.** What is the volume of 1 cup of water in gallons? 0.06

**f.** There are 16 ounces in a pound. What is the weight of 1 cup of water in pounds? 0.52

**g.** How many cups are in 1 gallon? 16

**Real-World Link**
The very first movie theaters were built in the late 1890s. By the 1920s and 1930s, grand "picture palaces" were springing up everywhere. The first drive-in movie opened in 1933.

**12. Challenge** An architect is designing a building with two movie theaters. The Green Theater will be rectangular in shape with each row holding 16 seats. The Blue Theater will be wider at the back. The first row will have 8 seats, the second row will have 16 seats, and all other rows will have 20 seats. The architect will decide how many rows to put in each theater on the basis of the number of people it is meant to hold. 12a–12c. See margin.

**a.** Make a table showing how the number of seats for each theater relates to the number of rows. Assume each theater will have at least 3 rows.

**b.** On one set of axes, draw graphs to show how the number of seats in each theater depends on the number of rows.

**c.** Does it make sense to connect the points on the graphs? Explain.

**d.** For each theater, write a rule in symbols that tells how the number of seats depends on the number of rows. Green: $g = 16r$; Blue: $b = 24 + 20(r - 2)$

**e.** How many rows should be in each theater to give the theaters an equal number of seats? 4



## Additional Answers

12a. Possible table.

**Theater Seating**

| Rows, $r$ | 3 | 4 | 5 | 6 | 7 | 10 | 20 |
|---|---|---|---|---|---|---|---|
| Seats in Green Theater, $g$ | 48 | 64 | 80 | 96 | 112 | 160 | 320 |
| Seats in Blue Theater, $b$ | 44 | 64 | 84 | 104 | 124 | 184 | 384 |

12b. See Additional Answers on page 433.

12c. No; there can be only whole numbers of rows in the theater. However, dashed lines might be drawn to help show the relationship between the variables.

**f.** Which theater will have more seats if both have 11 rows? Blue

**g.** Is the number of seats in each theater proportional to the number of rows? Why do you think so? See margin.

**13.** Carmen started to read a book at 10:20 A.M. She usually reads a page in 2 minutes. Half an hour later, her friend Yolanda started to read. She reads 15 pages per hour.

**a.** How many pages did Carmen read before Yolanda started to read? 15

**b.** Create a table showing how many pages Carmen and Yolanda read by 10:50, 11:00, 11:10, 11:20, 11:30, 11:40, 11:50, and 12:00. See margin.

**c.** Based on your table, draw graphs on the same axes showing how many pages Carmen and Yolanda read between 10:50 A.M. and noon. Does it make sense to connect the points on the graphs? Does it make sense to continue the lines beyond the 12 o'clock mark? Explain your answers. See margin.

**d.** Write a rule in symbols for the number of pages Carmen read since 10:50. Write a rule in symbols for the number of pages Yolanda read since 10:50. Use $m$ for number of minutes passed after 10:50. Underline the parts of the rules that show the constant rates of reading. Carmen: $C = 15 + \underline{0.5}m$; Yolanda: $Y = \underline{0.25}m$

**e.** Is the relationship for Carmen proportional? Is the relationship for Yolanda proportional? No; yes

**f.** How many pages would each girl read in 5 minutes? In 16 minutes? In 48 minutes? Carmen: 2.5, 8, 24; Yolanda: 1.25, 4, 12

**g.** At what time will Carmen finish 40 pages of her book? At what time will Yolanda finish 40 pages of her book? Carmen: 11:40; Yolanda: 1:30

**h.** At what time will the number of pages Carmen has read be three times the number of pages Yolanda has read? 11:50

▶ **Exercise 13** Watch for students who are having trouble writing the rule. Although the table shows the change every 10 minutes, the rule has to show the change every minute.

**Additional Answers**

12g. Green: yes, Blue: no; The Green Theater's graph is a series of points that fall on a line that goes through (0, 0). The Blue Theater's graph is a series of points that fall on a line that does not go through (0, 0). (Note: Students may need to draw lines through the points to see these relationships.)

**Additional Answers**

13b. Possible table:

**Reading Books**

| Time | 10:50 | 11:00 | 11:10 | 11:20 | 11:30 | 11:40 | 11:50 | 12:00 |
|---|---|---|---|---|---|---|---|---|
| Pages Carmen Read, $C$ | 15 | 20 | 25 | 30 | 35 | 40 | 45 | 50 |
| Pages Yolanda Read, $Y$ | 0 | 2.5 | 5 | 7.5 | 10 | 12.5 | 15 | 17.5 |

13c. See Additional Answers on page 433A.

## Quick Check

**Informal Assessment** Students should be able to:

- ✔ develop strategies for describing rates
- ✔ recognize rates presented in symbolic and graphic forms
- ✔ compare proportional and nonproportional relationships
- ✔ represent proportional and nonproportional relationships in words, tables, symbols, and graphs
- ✔ get hands-on-experience with collecting data
- ✔ determine the nature of the relationship between two variables

## Quick Quiz

**1.** For the following relationships, determine the rate.
a. $y = 53x$ 53
b. $y = 15 + 0.1x$ 0.1

**2.** State an equation that describes a proportional relationship. Answers will vary. Possible answer: $y = 2x$

**3.** State an equation that describes a nonproportional relationship. Answers will vary. Possible answer: $y = 2x + 3$

**4.** On the same axes draw two graphs: one for a proportional relationship and one for a nonproportional relationship. Label which graph is proportional and which is nonproportional. Check students' graphs. The graph of the proportional relationship will be linear with a point at (0, 0). The nonproportional graph will have none or only one of these characteristics, not both.

**5.** Caitlin works for a fresh-fish supplier. They offered a special price to restaurants for shrimp at \$7 per pound. A local restaurant wanted a quote for the cost of enough shrimp for 40 shrimp cocktails. Each cocktail needs six shrimp.

Clearly, Caitlin would not want to waste time counting all of the shrimp. Work out an easy way to estimate the weight of shrimp the restaurant should order and the cost. What might Caitlin do to estimate the cost?



## Mixed Review

**14.** To simulate drawing one of three marbles from a bag, Neeraj rolled a die several times. The marbles were blue, white, and purple. Rolling 1 or 2 represented drawing the blue marble. Rolling 3 or 4 represented drawing the white marble. Rolling 5 or 6 represented drawing the purple marble.

Does this simulation represent drawing a marble and putting it back before drawing the next? Or does it represent keeping the drawn marble out of the bag before drawing the next one? How do you know?

14. Putting it back; Possible explanation: The probabilities do not change each time, which they would if you kept the drawn marble. Also, Neeraj keeps rolling the same die, so the simulation cannot represent keeping them out; if it did, it would end after the first roll.

**Geometry** Find the volume and the surface area of each solid.

**15.**

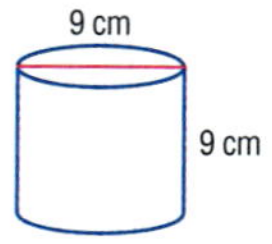


**16.**

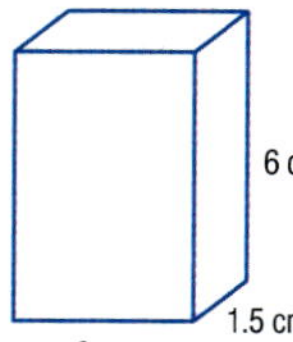


15. $182.25\,\pi\text{ cm}^3 \approx 572.6\text{ cm}^3$; $121.5\,\pi\text{ cm}^2 \approx 381.7\text{ cm}^2$

16. $27\text{ cm}^3$; $63\text{ cm}^2$

**17.** Calculate the area and circumference of a circle with radius 2 cm. $12.57\text{ cm}^2$, 12.57 cm

**18.** **Challenge** Calculate the area of a square with a side length of $s$ cm and a diagonal of 1.5 cm. Show how you found your answer.

18. $s^2 + s^2 = 1.5^2$
$2s^2 = 2.25$
$s^2 = 1.125$
area $= 1.125\text{ cm}^2$

**Evaluate.**

**19.** $3^{-2}$ $\frac{1}{9}$

**20.** $2^2 \cdot 2^3$ 32

**21.** $2^2 \div 2^{-2}$ 16

**22.** $0.005 \cdot 0.1$ 0.0005

**23.** $10^2 \cdot 0.1$ 10

**24.** $100^2 \cdot 0.3$ 3,000

**25.** $0.2^2$ 0.04

**26.** $0.2^{-2}$ 25

**27.** $\sqrt{169}$ 13



**Quick Quiz (continued)**

5. Caitlin can weigh 6 shrimp and multiply by 40 to get the total weight. To find the cost, she would multiply the total weight by \$7. Or, she can weigh 1 pound of shrimp to find the number of shrimp per pound, and then divide 240 by the number per pound to find the number of pounds needed. To find the cost, she will multiply the total number of pounds needed by \$7. She will try to be reasonably close but will overestimate a little so there is enough shrimp to make all 40 shrimp cocktails.

LESSON 8.2

# Speed and Slope

## Objectives

- ▶ To relate speed to the slope of a graph of distance over time
- ▶ To develop an understanding of negative slope and a negative constant term
- ▶ To recognize proportional and nonproportional relationships between distance and time
- ▶ To recognize linear relationships from symbolic rules, graphs, patterns, and tables and to convert one form into another

## Overview

This lesson focuses on one particularly common and important rate, *speed*, and develops students' understanding of proportional and nonproportional linear relationships in the context of speed. They learn to relate speed to the slope of the line by investigating the relationship between distance and time. They learn about negative slope by looking at situations in which distance decreases over time.

## Advance Preparation

You may want to provide copies of Chapter 8 Master 1 for the students or quarter-inch praph paper for their work.

| | Summary | Materials | On Your Own Exercises (pp. 402–409) | Assessment Opportunities |
|---|---|---|---|---|
| **Investigation 1** (p. 390) Pacing: 2 dayS | Students learn about speed as a special rate and make connections between speed and the slope of the graph relating distance and time. | Chapter 8 Master 1 or quarter-inch graph paper | Practice & Apply: 1–3<br>Connect & Extend: 26<br>Mixed Review: 35–37 | • Share & Summarize (p. 393)<br>• Troubleshooting (p. 390) |
| **Investigation 2** (p. 394) Pacing: 1 day | Students learn to interpret graphs. Negative slope is introduced through distance decreasing with time. | Chapter 8 Master 1 or quarter-inch graph paper | Practice & Apply: 4–5<br>Connect & Extend: 21–25<br>Mixed Review: 35–37 | • Share & Summarize (p. 396)<br>• Troubleshooting (pp. 394, 395) |
| **Investigation 3** (p. 396) Pacing: 1 day | Students learn to extract the essential information about the movement of the objects such as speed, direction, and relative location from graphs. | | Practice & Apply: 6<br>Connect & Extend: 13–19, 27–33<br>Mixed Review: 35–37 | • Share & Summarize (p. 397) |
| **Investigation 4** (p. 398) Pacing: 1 day | Students practice distinguishing between proportional and nonproportional relationships. | Chapter 8 Master 1 or quarter-inch graph paper | Practice & Apply: 7–12<br>Connect & Extend: 20, 34<br>Mixed Review: 35–37 | • Share & Summarize (p. 401)<br>• Troubleshooting (p. 398) |

# Leveled Lesson Resources

CRM *Available in:* **Chapter 8 Resource Masters**

Also on TeacherWorks™ Lesson 8.2

## Study Guide and Intervention (p. 9) AL

**Lesson 8.2 Study Guide and Intervention**
***Speed and Slope***

Speed relates distance traveled to the time it took to travel that distance. Speed is measured in units of length per unit of time.
Slope describes the steepness of a line. The slope of a line tells how much the $y$ variable changes per unit change in the $x$ variable.

***Example***

**Daniel plans to run the next marathon at a speed of 8.5 minutes per mile.**

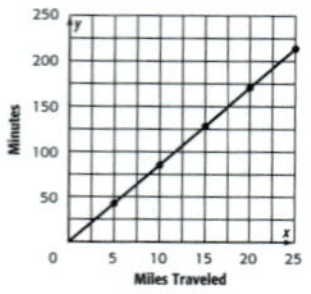


**a. Choose two points on the graph to find the slope of the line that passes through the points.**

(10, 85) and (20, 170) $\frac{\text{rise}}{\text{run}} = \frac{\text{changes in } y}{\text{changes in } x} = \frac{(170 - 85)}{20 - 10} = \frac{85}{10} = 8.5$

The slope of this line, 8.5, represents Daniel's speed of 8.5 minutes per mile.

**b. What is the value of the $y$-intercept?**

The $y$-intercept is the point where the line crosses the $y$-axis. In this situation it is (0, 0). After 0 minutes Daniel has run 0 miles.

**Use the graph to solve the problems.**

Mario walks every morning at a rate of 3 miles per hour. Antonio walks 2 miles every morning. Then he runs at a pace of 2.5 miles per hour.

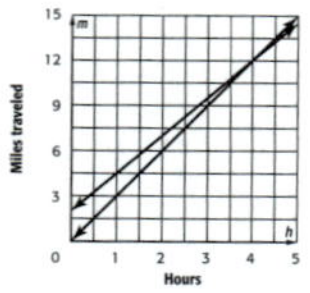


1. Choose two points on each line to find the slope of the lines.
2. What do the slopes represent in this situation?
3. What are the $y$-intercepts of these lines? What do they represent?

## Skills Practice (p. 10) AL OL

**Lesson 8.2 Skills Practice**
***Speed and Slope***

**Draw a graph of the data. Write a rule for the relationship between hours and miles.**

1. The average turtle's speed is about 4 miles per hour.

| Hours, $h$ | 1 | 2 | 3 | 4 |
|---|---|---|---|---|
| Miles, $m$ | 4 | 8 | 12 | 16 |

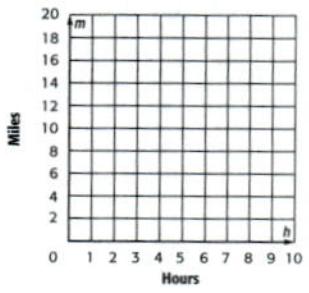


2. The average hare's speed is about 40 miles per hour.

| Hours $h$ | 1 | 2 | 3 | 4 |
|---|---|---|---|---|
| Miles, $m$ | 40 | 80 | 120 | 160 |

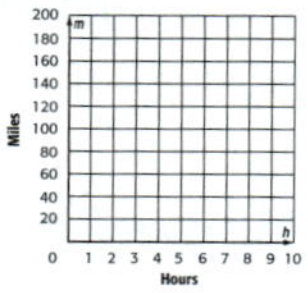


**Graph the line and identify its slope.**

3. $y = \frac{1}{3}x + \frac{2}{3}$

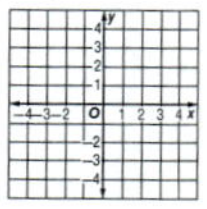

4. $y = \frac{3}{2}x - 2$

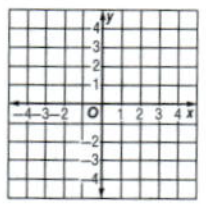

**For each equation, give the $y$-intercept.**

5. $y = 4x + 1$
6. $y = -\frac{4}{5}x - 3$
7. $y = 3x$
8. $y = -4x + \frac{1}{2}$

## Problem-Solving Practice (p. 11) AL OL

**Lesson 8.2 Problem-Solving Practice**
***Speed and Slope***

Solve.

1. **Travel** Write a rule for each of the relationships in the table. Use $h$ for hours traveled and $d$ for distance.

| Hours Traveled | Distance (mi) | |
|---|---|---|
| | Scott | Amparo |
| 1 | 55 | 60 |
| 2 | 110 | 120 |
| 3 | 165 | 180 |
| 4 | 220 | 240 |

2. **Travel** Draw a graph of the data in Exercise 1.

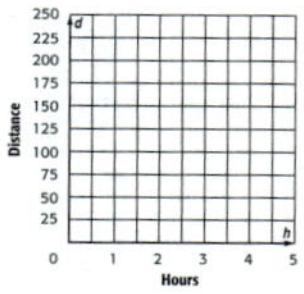


3. **Travel** What is the slope of each line that you graphed in Exercise 2? Who traveled faster?

4. **National Parks** Which two years represent the least increase in recreational visits? Describe the slope of this part of the graph.

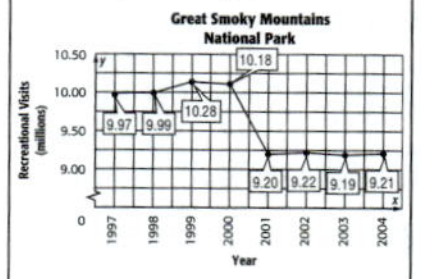


5. **National Parks** Use the graph in Exercise 4. What happened to the recreational visits between 2000 and 2001? Describe the slope of this part of the graph.

6. **National Parks** Use the graph in Exercise 4. Does this graph have a $y$-intercept? Can you write a rule for the data in the graph? Explain your answers.

## Enrichment (p. 12) BL

**Lesson 8.2 Enrichment**
***Speed and Slope***

**Distance and Time**

A linear relationship between two variables can be shown by the equation $y = mx + b$, where the slope is represented by the variable $m$ and the $y$-intercept is represented by the variable $b$. The linear relationship between distance $d$ and time $t$ can be similarly expressed as $d = mt + b$.

Ingrid's family spends one week of their summer vacation on a cruise ship. The top speed of a cruise ship is 20 knots per hour or about 22 miles per hour.

1. Write an equation that can be used to show the relationship between the distance $d$, in miles, Ingrid's cruise ship travels in $t$ hours if it travels at 20 miles per hour. What is the $y$-intercept of the equation?
2. There are many cruise ships leaving the same port as Ingrid's ship. Ship A begins her trip 2 hours ahead of Ingrid's ship and travels at a rate of 18 miles per hour. Ship B begins her trip 2 hours after Ingrid's ship and travels at a rate of 22 miles per hour.
   a. Find the point that represents the distance ship A has traveled one hour after Ingrid's ship leaves the port.
   b. Find the point that represents the distance ship B has traveled four hours after Ingrid's ship leaves the port.
3. Write rules that can be used to show the relationship between the distance $d$, in miles, ships A and B travel in $t$ hours.
4. Use the rules to graph the distance $d$ the cruise ships travel in $t$ hours. Use different colors to represent each ship.

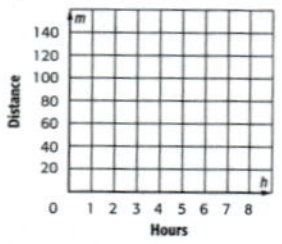


5. Will these lines ever intersect? Explain.

## Lesson Quick Quiz (p. 13) AL OL BL

**Lesson 8.2 Quick Quiz**
***Speed and Slope***

1. Below are five graphs and their rules. Match the graphs to the rules.

$p = q + 2$ $p = 5 - q$
$p = 2q$ $p = 2$
$p = 2q + 1$

a.
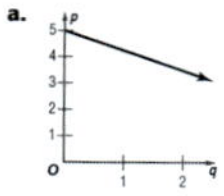

b.
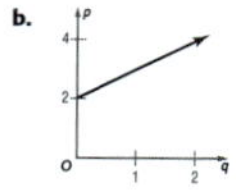

c.
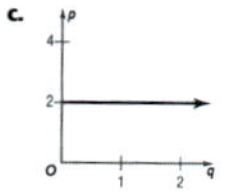

d.
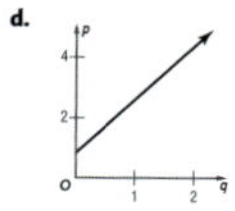

e.
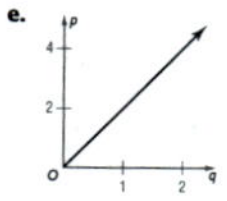

2. A strip of cloth 12 yards long is cut into two smaller pieces. If $A$ stands for the number of yards in one piece and $B$ stands for the number of yards in the other piece, they are related by the rule $A + B = 12$.
   a. Draw a graph for this rule. Completing a table of values first may help you.
   b. Find another way to write the rule that relates the two lengths.

# Additional Lesson Resources

**Teacher Tech Tools**
- TeacherWorks
- ExamView Assessment Suite
- Classroom Presentation Toolkit
- Advance Tracker

**Student Tech Tools**
- StudentWorks Plus
- Math Online eGlossary • Concepts in Motion

**Other Print Products**
- Investigation Notebook and Reflection Journal
- Quick Review Math Handbook

LESSON 8.2

# Speed and Slope

Speed is a very common rate. It tells how the distance something travels depends on the time traveled. Speed can be measured in many ways. Here are a few common units of speed.

- miles per hour (mph)
- kilometers per hour (km/h or kph)
- feet per second (ft/s)
- meters per second (m/s)
- millimeters per second (mm/s)



## Materials

- stopwatch
- yardstick

## Explore

Guess an average student's normal walking speed and record your guess. Then one person in the class should walk at a "normal" speed from the back of the classroom to the front while another person accurately times him or her. Record that time and the distance the student walked, in feet.

Now here is a challenge. Several students should try to cross the classroom at a steady pace taking the amounts of time specified by the teacher, some greater and some less than it takes to cross at a "normal" speed.

You or a classmate should time how long it actually takes each student to cross the room. Then everyone in the class can compute the students' true speeds. To find the speeds, divide the distance walked by the time it took.

After you have an idea about how fast or slow the various speeds are, answer these questions.

- If a person travels 1.5 feet per second, is this a fast walk, a slow walk, or a run? Slow walk
- If a second person moves with a speed of 9 feet per second, is this a fast walk, a slow walk, or a run? Run
- How much faster is the second person in comparison with the first? 6 times faster



## Speed and Slope

LESSON 8.2

## *Introduce*

**Understanding Speed** Many students are familiar with at least one rate of speed. Ask them to use their familiarity to explain why speed is a rate and to give some examples of how speed can be measured.

### *Explore*

*Suggested Groups: Whole Class*

▶ **Prepare** For this activity, students will need a stopwatch or a watch with a second hand and a way to measure the length of the room.

▶ **Guess** Begin the lesson by asking students to guess their normal walking speed and to record their guesses. Ask several students to share their guesses and record their responses on the chalkboard. It is fine if the answers are in different units of measurement. You can use them later to discuss how the same speed may be expressed in different ways.

▶ **Measure** Have one or two students measure the length in feet of the room with a yardstick or measuring tape. Put this measure on the board. Then choose several students to walk, one at a time, from the back wall of the classroom to the front wall.

Tell the first student: *Think hard before you start walking. Your job is to try to cover this distance, walking at a steady pace, in exactly 15 seconds. We'll time you to see how long it really takes. Ready? Go.*

Ask the rest of the class to measure the time with their stopwatches. Be sure that the walkers understand that no speeding or slowing down should occur once they have started. Ask students to calculate the speed of the walker in feet per second and record it on the chalkboard.

Now, ask a second student to walk at a steady pace and cover the same distance in exactly 10 seconds. Again, the rest of the class records the time. Ask other students to complete their walk in longer or shorter amounts of time. Write all these speeds on the chalkboard. Have students compare the actual speeds with their estimated speeds.

## Investigation 1

***On Your Own Exercises***
Pages 402–409
Exercises 1–3, 26

**Varying Rates** Ask students whether they ever have to change their walking rate when walking with someone else. You may want to discuss how the rates may vary.

### Develop & Understand: A

*Suggested Grouping: Pairs*

Students represent various speeds with symbolic rules and graphs as they did with rates in Lesson 1.

Students will need graph paper or copies of Chapter 8 Master 1, Quarter-Inch Graph Paper, to complete the exercise set.

▶ **Exercise 4** Remind students to use values from their table to test that the rule they wrote is correct.

## Investigation 1 Walk and Jog

**Vocabulary**
- slope

**Materials**
- graph paper

Some people walk quickly, taking several steps in a few seconds. Others walk more slowly, taking more than a second for each step. Some people naturally take longer strides than others. When you are walking with a friend, one or both of you probably changes something about the way you walk so you can stay side by side.

### Develop & Understand: A

Zach's stride is 0.5 meters long. Imagine that he is walking across a room, taking one step each second.

1. At what speed is Zach walking? 0.5 m/s
2. Copy and complete the table to show Zach's distance from the left wall at each time. See below.

| **Time (seconds), $t$** | 0 | 1 | 2 | 3 | 4 | 5 | 6 |
|---|---|---|---|---|---|---|---|
| **Distance from Left Wall (meters), $d$** | 0 | 0.5 | 1 | 1.5 | 2 | 2.5 | 3 |

3. At this constant speed, is the distance traveled proportional to the time? How do you know? Yes; if you multiply the time by any number, the distance is multiplied by the same amount.
4. Write a rule that shows how to compute $d$ if you know $t$. $d = 0.5t$
5. What would Zach's speed be if he lengthened his stride to 1 meter but still took 1 second for each step? Make a table of values, and write a rule for this speed. 1 m/s; $d = t$; Possible table:

2.

| **Time (s), $t$** | 0 | 1 | 2 | 3 | 4 | 5 | 6 |
|---|---|---|---|---|---|---|---|
| **Distance from Left Wall (m), $d$** | 0 | 1 | 2 | 3 | 4 | 5 | 6 |



### Troubleshooting

Watch for students who say that the relationship in Exercise 3 is proportional because one solution could be graphed at (0, 0). Remind them that this is only one characteristic of a proportional relationship. Students must also know that the relationship is linear.

7.

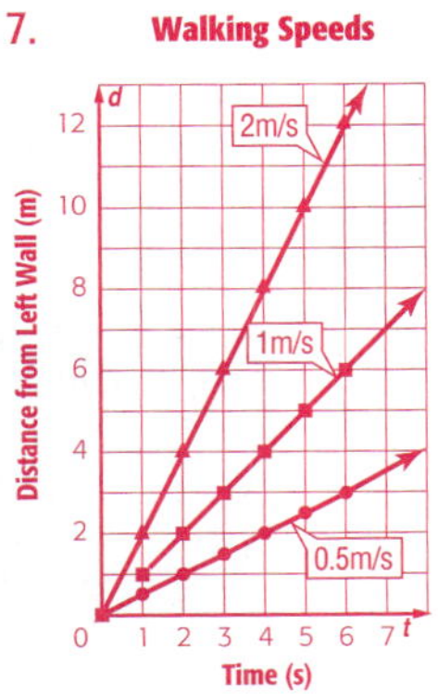


① They are all straight lines that go through (0, 0). They are all proportional but with different degrees of steepness.

**6.** Imagine that Maya is also crossing the room, but she is taking two steps each second. Her steps are 1 meter long. What is her speed? Make a table of values, and write a rule for her speed. See margin.

**7.** For all three tables, plot each set of points in the table and then draw a line through them. Put all three graphs on one grid with time on the horizontal axis. Label each graph with its speed.

### Think & Discuss

Compare the three graphs you drew in Exercise 7. See ①.

- In what ways are they the same? In what ways are they different?
- What does the steepness in these distance-time graphs show? The steeper the graph, the faster the walking speed.

## Develop & Understand: B

Many joggers try to jog at a steady pace throughout most of their runs. This is particularly important for long-distance running.

- Terry tries to jog at a steady pace of 4 meters per second.
- Maria tries to jog at a steady pace of 3 meters per second.
- Bronwyn does not know how fast she jogs, but she tries to keep a steady pace.

**8.** Make tables for Terry and Maria to show the distances they travel, $d$ meters, in various times, $t$ seconds. See margin.

**9.** Write rules that show how distance $d$ changes with time $t$ for Terry and for Maria. Terry: $d = 4t$; Maria: $d = 3t$

**Real-World Link**
The maximum speed a human being has ever run is about 27 miles per hour. The fastest animal on Earth, the cheetah, has been clocked at about 60 miles per hour.

▶ **Exercise 7** Students should draw three graphs on the same axes and, prior to a whole-class discussion of the Think & Discuss, talk with their partners about what their graphs show.

### Think & Discuss

The questions in the Think & Discuss call for an understanding of speed as a rate. The steepness of the distance-time graphs indicates the relative speed of each person. Later students will be able to determine speed by looking at the graph.

Draw a parallel with the questions about rate from Lesson 1, such as

- How do the graphs show differences in speed?
- How is faster speed shown on the graph?

## Develop & Understand: B

*Suggested Grouping: Individuals*

▶ **Exercises 8–12** are similar to Exercises 1–7. Students should be able to complete this exercise set independently. Students will need graph paper or copies of Chapter 8 Master 1, Quarter-Inch Graph Paper, to complete this exercise set.

### Additional Answers

6. 2 $m/s$; $d = 2t$; Possible table:

| **Time (s), t** | 0 | 1 | 2 | 3 | 4 | 5 | 6 |
|---|---|---|---|---|---|---|---|
| **Distance from Left Wall (m), d** | 0 | 2 | 4 | 6 | 8 | 10 | 12 |

8. Possible table:

| **Time (s), t** | 0 | 5 | 10 | 15 | 20 |
|---|---|---|---|---|---|
| **Terry's Distance (m), d** | 0 | 20 | 40 | 60 | 80 |
| **Maria's Distance (m), d** | 0 | 15 | 30 | 45 | 60 |

▶ **Exercise 11** Students will need to save their graphs to use later in this investigation.

***Math Link***

You may want to point out the general rule, $d = rt$, in the Math Link feature. Some students may find that knowing the general rule helps them write and check the rules they write.

**Wrap-Up** Have students share the rules they wrote for Exercises 9 and 10.

Ask students what the steepness of the lines on their distance graphs indicate. Most students will realize that it indicates relative speed: a steeper line shows a faster speed. Then relate the steepness to how much the distance changes over a given amount of time. Tell students that another way to describe steepness is slope.

Discuss the definition of *slope.* You might want to prepare an overhead or direct students' attention to the graph showing rise and run, the changes in *x*- and *y*-values, on page 380. It is essential that they be familiar with the term slope before moving on.

12. The graph of the fastest jogger is the steepest, and the graph of the slowest jogger is the least steep.

***Math Link***

The general rule connecting distance, rate, and time is $d = rt$, where $d$ is the distance, $r$ is the rate or speed, and $t$ is the time.

**10.** A timekeeper measured times and distances traveled for Bronwyn and put the results in a table.

| **Time (seconds), *t*** | 0 | 5 | 10 | 15 | 20 |
|---|---|---|---|---|---|
| **Distance (meters), *d*** | 0 | 17.5 | 35 | 52.5 | 70 |

How fast does Bronwyn jog? Write a rule that relates Bronwyn's distance to time.
3.5 m/s, $d = 3.5t$

**11.** On one grid, draw graphs for Terry, Maria, and Bronwyn. Put time on the horizontal axis. Label each graph with the name of the person and the speed. See margin.

**12.** Explain how you can tell from looking at the graph who jogs most quickly and who jogs most slowly.

All the points on each graph you drew are on a line through the point (0, 0). The steepest line is the one for which distance changes the most in a given amount of time, that is, when the speed is the fastest. The line that is the least steep is the one for which distance changes the least in a given amount of time, that is, when the speed is the slowest.

*Slope* describes the steepness of a line. In this case, the slope tells how much the distance changes per unit of time. More generally, the **slope** of a line tells how much the $y$ variable changes per unit change in the $x$ variable.

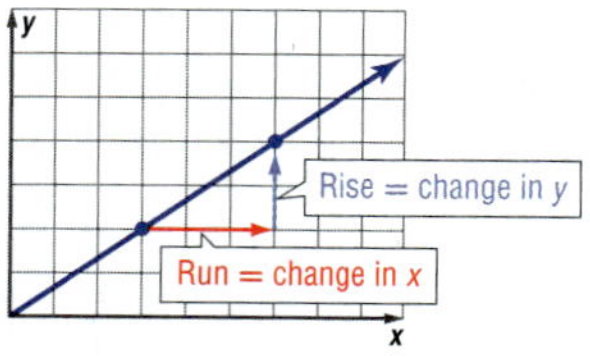


Sometimes slope is described as *rise* divided by *run*. This makes sense because $y$ changes in the vertical direction, or "rises," and $x$ changes in the horizontal direction, or "runs."



**Additional Answer**

11. **Jogging Speeds**

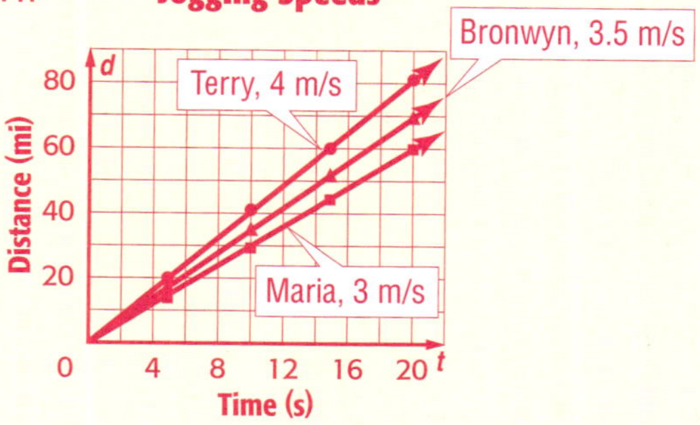

## Example

This graph shows how Terry's distance changed over time. To find the slope, choose two points, such as (10, 40) and (20, 80). From the left point to the right point, the $y$ value changes from 40 to 80. The *rise* between these points is 80 − 40, or 40. The $x$ value changes from 10 to 20, so the *run* between these points is 20 − 10, or 10. The slope, the rise divided by the run, is $\frac{40}{10}$, or 4.

**Terry's Jogging Speed**

## Think & Discuss

Look at your graphs for Maria and Bronwyn. What are the slopes of Maria's and Bronwyn's lines? What does the slope mean in Terry's, Maria's, and Bronwyn's graphs? See ①.

① 3, 3.5; The slope is the same as the speed. A slope of 4 means distance changes 4 m for each 1 s increase in time; a slope of 3 means distance changes 3 m in 1 s; and a slope of 3.5 means distance changes 3.5 m in 1 s.

## Share & Summarize

1. Javier walks at a speed of 5 feet per second. If you graphed the distance he walks over time, with time in seconds on the horizontal axis and distance in feet on the vertical axis, what would be the slope of the line? 5

2. Dulce walks at a speed of 7 feet per second. Suppose you graphed the distance she walks over time on the same grid as Javier's line. How would the steepness of her line compare to the steepness of Javier's line? Explain. Dulce's line would be steeper because her speed is greater.

### Example

Walk students through the Example showing how to find the slope of a line. Some students may need verification that the slope for a given line remains the same regardless of the two points chosen. You may wish to let students choose two other points to show that this is true.

Remind students that the terms *rise* and *run* describe the movement along the axes. Be sure that students understand that the term *run* has nothing to do with the fact that distance is being graphed.

### Think & Discuss

Students refer to their graphs from Exercises 8–12. Give them time to think about and solve these exercises before discussing them. Have students describe how they found the slope and what points they used to make their calculations. Students who have a solid understanding at this point will see the relation of slope to speed. They may use this reasoning to explain the relationship: If Maria's graph has a slope of 3, this means that her distance changes 3 meters every second. That is her speed.

### Share & Summarize

These questions take students' understanding of the relation of slope to speed to another level. Students determine slope from speed without looking at a graph.

### Reaching All Learners

ELL **English Language Learners** Help students remember the terms *rise* and *run* by associating the terms with the actions they take on the axes. When something rises, it comes up, so the term rise describes movement on the vertical axis. Likewise when animals run, they move forward, so this term describes movement on the horizontal axis.

# Investigation 2

***On Your Own Exercises***
Pages 402–409
Exercises 4–5, 21–25

**Distance and Time** This investigation introduces situations in which distance decreases with time. The graphs for these situations consequently have negative slope.

### Think & Discuss

Present the example of distance decreasing with time from the student book. Then ask students to think of other situations when the distance decreases instead of increases with time. Some situations students suggest might include an approaching car; one person running after another and getting close; something falling to the ground.

### Develop & Understand: A

*Suggested Grouping: Pairs*

In this exercise set, students work out a situation in which the distance between the person and the wall is decreasing over time. They make a table, draw a graph, and write a symbolic rule to describe the distance. Be sure students have graph paper or copies of Chapter 8 Master 1, Quarter-Inch Graph Paper, before beginning Exercise Set C.

▶ **Exercise 2** Make sure students understand that the distance is decreasing as time passes.

▶ **Exercise 4** Students find a negative slope for the first time in exercise sets. You may want to emphasize that when calculating slope, the *x*-coordinates must be subtracted in the same order as the *y*-coordinates.

**Wrap-Up** Discuss Exercises 4 and 7. Students should realize that even though a slope can be positive or negative, the calculation is the same. They should also see how the negative slope, −1.5, is shown in the symbolic rule.

# Investigation 2 Distance and Time

**Materials**
- graph paper

An airplane flies from New York to Los Angeles. There are two distances that are changing, the distance between the airplane and the New York airport and the distance between the airplane and the Los Angeles airport.

### Think & Discuss

Which of the two distances described above is decreasing over time? See ①.

Think of other situations in which distance decreases over time. See ②.

① Distance between the airplane and the L.A. airport

② Possible answer: Driving to school, walking toward a friend, dropping a book onto a table; distance between book and table decreases

### Develop & Understand: A

On pages 390 and 391, Zach and Maya were walking from the left wall of a room to the right wall. You figured out how far each person was from the left wall at different points in time. Suppose instead you want to know how far the person is from the *right* wall at each point in time.

1. Is the person closest to the right wall at the beginning of the walk or at the end of the walk? The end

2. Suppose Maya walks at 1.5 meters per second across a room that is 10 meters wide. Copy and complete this table.

**Maya's Walk**

| Time (seconds), $t$ | 0 | 1 | 2 | 3 | 4 |
|---|---|---|---|---|---|
| Distance from Right Wall (meters), $d$ | 10 | 8.5 | 7 | 5.5 | 4 |

3. Use the data in Exercise 2 to draw a graph that shows the relationship between Maya's distance from the right wall and time. See margin.

4. What is the slope of the line that you drew? −1.5

5. Use your graph to estimate when Maya would reach the right wall. Just before 7 s

6. Explain how you can find the distance from the right wall if you know the time.

7. Write a symbolic rule that relates $d$ to $t$. $d = 10 - 1.5t$

6. The distance walked can be found by multiplying the time by Maya's speed, 1.5 m/s. Since the wall is 10 m away to begin, and the distance decreases over time by the distance walked, subtract the distance walked from 10.



## Troubleshooting

Watch for students who add 1.5*t* instead of subtracting it in Exercise 7. Have these students substitute values from their table in their rules to see that it doesn't make sense that the distance becomes greater as the person nears the wall. In the following class discussion, make sure that all students understand where the negative sign comes from.

**Additional Answer**

3.

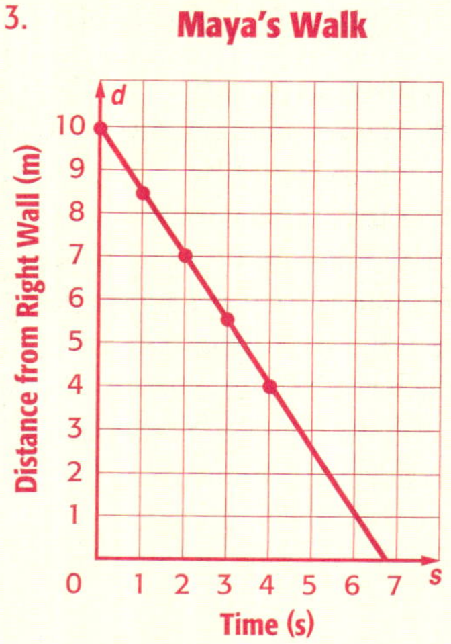

## Think & Discuss

Bianca and Lorenzo solved an equation on a quiz. Bianca wrote the rule $d = -2t + 20$. Lorenzo wrote the rule $d = 20 - 2t$. Can they both be right? Explain your thinking. See ①.

① Yes; order does not affect sums, so $-2t + 20 = 20 + -2t$. Adding the opposite of $2t$ is the same as subtracting, so $-2t + 20 = 20 - 2t$.

Create a problem that can be described by one or both of these rules. Possible answer: A turtle is moving at a speed of 2 ft/min toward a creek 20 ft away. How far is the turtle from the creek after $t$ minutes?

## Develop & Understand: B

Ruben and Kristen started walking away from a fence at the same time. Ruben walked at a brisk pace, and Kristen walked at a slow pace. They each measured the distance they had walked in 10 seconds. From this, they estimated how far from the fence they would have been at various times if they had continued walking. They drew distance-time graphs from their data.

**Ruben's and Kristen's Walks**

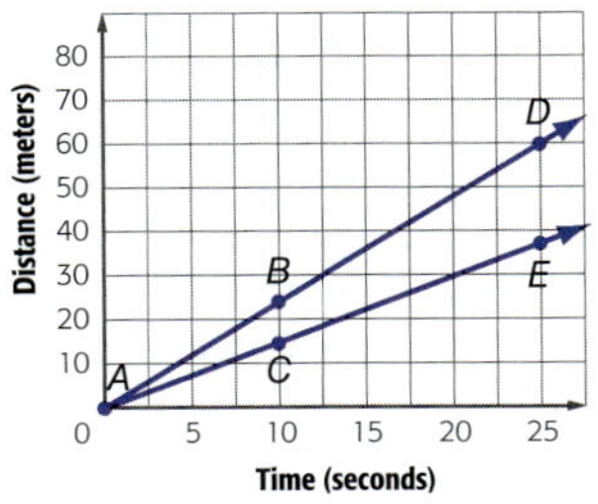


8. Which graph represents Ruben's walk, and which represents Kristen's? Explain how you know.
9. What events in the story above match points $A$, $B$, and $C$?
10. What do points $D$ and $E$ tell you about the positions of Ruben and Kristen?
11. Use the graphs to estimate each person's walking speed in meters per second. Give your answers to the nearest tenth. Ruben: 2.4 m/s; Kristen: 1.5 m/s
12. Which line has the greater slope, Ruben's or Kristen's? Explain why. Ruben's; his speed is greater.
13. What are the slopes of the two lines? How are they related to Ruben's and Kristen's speeds? Ruben: 2.4; Kristen: 1.5; The slopes are the speeds.

8. Graph $AB$ is Ruben's because it has a steeper slope, which means he walked faster. Graph $AC$ is Kristen's.
9. Point $A$ is the starting point at the fence. Points $B$ and $C$ represent Ruben's and Kristen's distance after 10 s.
10. They tell how far Ruben and Kristen would have traveled after 25 s and show that Ruben would have traveled farther.



## Think & Discuss

*Suggested Grouping: Pairs*

This section presents two correct rules for the same situation. Both rules have a negative sign before $2t$ which shows that the distance is decreasing. Remind students that subtracting $2t$ has the same result as adding $-2t$. If they think of the rule $20 - 2t$ as $20 + -2t$, they can apply the commutative property of addition to verify that both $d = 20 - 2t$ and $d = -2t + 20$ are correct rules.

## Develop & Understand: B

*Suggested Grouping: Individuals*

In this exercise set, students estimate the speed, distance, and time from a graph and further develop their understanding of slope.

## Troubleshooting

Watch for students who calculate incorrect speeds in Exercise 11 and incorrect slopes in Exercise 13. Check that they have made reasonable estimates of the values in the graphs, made the proper calculations, and rounded correctly.

### *Share & Summarize*

After students think about these questions for a few minutes, discuss the questions as a class. Students should notice that the graph in Exercises 1–7 decreases while the graphs in Exercises 8–13 grow over time. They may note that the increasing graph goes through the origin while the decreasing graphs do not.

They should also notice that the rates for the increasing graphs are positive, while the rate for a decreasing graph is negative. They should see that the signs for these rates are shown in the rule and that the rule for the decreasing graph has a constant number.

Finally students should note that the signs of the rates in the rule indicate the direction of the graph.

## Investigation 3

**On Your Own Exercises**
Pages 402–409
Exercises 6, 13–19, 27–33

**Describe Graphs** In this investigation, students learn to extract the essential information about the movement of different objects from the graph. Students build on their experience in the prior investigations as they encounter positive slopes which characterize the graphs of people or objects moving away from the point of reference, and negative slopes which characterize the people or objects approaching the point of reference.

Ask students to name some of the rates they have studied in this chapter. They may mention speed, wage, measurement conversions, and heart rate, among others. Then ask them how long they would expect each of these rates to stay the same. Students should note that heart rates change frequently, speed rates often change, wages change occasionally, and measurement conversions can be considered fixed rates because they are likely to never change. Tell students that the changes in these rates can be shown by a graph.

### *Share & Summarize*

1. How are the graphs in Exercises 8–13 different from the graphs in Exercises 1–7?
2. How is the rule in Exercises 1–7 different from the rules in Exercises 8–13? How are they the same?
3. Explain how the differences in the rules relate to the differences in the graphs. The negative sign means the line is going down; the slope is negative; the constant term means the line does not start at (0, 0).

1. In Exercises 1–7 the line goes down from left to right, and in Exercises 8–13 the lines go up.

2. The rule in Exercises 1–7 has a negative sign in front of the rate; the rules in Exercises 8–13 have positive signs. The rule in Exercises 1–7 has a constant term; the rules in Exercises 8–13 do not. They all represent straight lines.

## Investigation 3 Describe Graphs

**Vocabulary**
speed
velocity

Some rates vary. For example, if you count your pulse for one minute and then count it for another minute, you will probably get different results. It is normal for pulse rates to fluctuate, or change.

At least for a while, you would expect other rates to be fixed, or stay the same. For example, if your employer said your pay rate was $7 per hour, you would expect to earn that for each hour you work.

In this investigation, you will inspect the graphs below to find the directions, speeds, and relative locations of a group of cars along a particular highway.

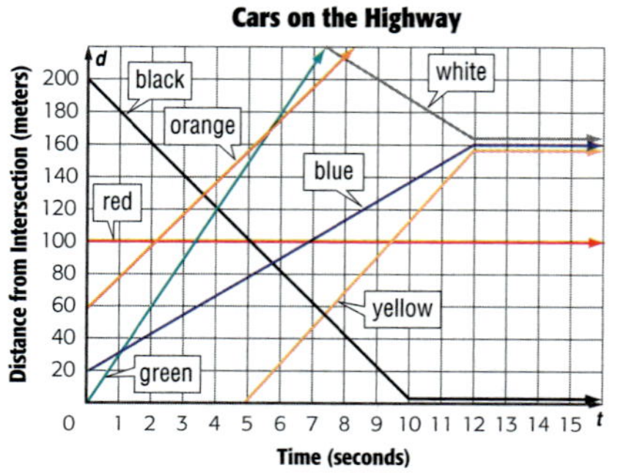




### *Reaching All Learners*

**AL Approaching Level** Students may be confused about how to interpret the difference between slope and speed on graphs with a negative slope. To help students understand the negative slope, make clear what is being measured. Speed is positive and, in these examples, neither increases nor decreases. Time increases. Distance decreases. It is the *difference between distances* in consecutive times, or the *change in distance per unit time,* that is shown by the slope, and that change is negative.

## Develop & Understand: A

Seven cars are all near an intersection. The graphs on page 396 show the distances between the cars and the intersection as time passes.

In your group, study the graphs carefully. Then discuss the following questions. Record your group's decisions, and be prepared to talk about them in class.

1. In what direction is each car moving in relation to the intersection? See margin.
2. Compare the cars' speeds.
3. Do any of the cars stop during their trips? If so, which cars? Yes; yellow, blue, white, and black
4. Prepare a group report for one of the cars. Imagine you are in that car, and give the highlights of your trip for these 15 seconds. Include such observations as where and when you started the trip and what you saw going on around you in front of the car, to the sides, and through the rearview mirror. Answers will vary.

2. Answers will vary. From slowest to fastest, during the time when the blue, yellow, white, and black cars are moving, the cars are: red, blue, white, orange and black (tie), yellow, and green.

People often use one of two words when they describe how fast something is moving: *speed* or *velocity*. In fact, these two words mean different things mathematically.

**Speed** is always positive. It shows how fast an object is moving, but it does not reveal anything about the object's direction.

**Velocity** can be either positive or negative, as can slope. The sign of the velocity shows whether an object is moving from or toward a designated point. The absolute value of the velocity is the same as the speed. While the black car is moving, for example, it has a positive speed of 20 meters per second. However, its distance to the intersection is decreasing, so its velocity is −20 meters per second.

### Share & Summarize

1. How can you determine from the graph whether a car is moving toward or away from the intersection? See ①.
2. How can you determine the speed of a car from the graph? By the absolute value of the slope
3. How can you determine from the graph whether a car is moving? When a car is not moving, the graph of the distance in relation to time is a horizontal line.

① By the slope; if the graph moves down from left to right (negative slope), the car is moving toward the intersection.



### Additional Answer

1. The orange, green, yellow, and blue cars are moving away from the intersection, but the yellow and blue cars stop moving at 12 s. The black and white cars are moving toward the intersection, although they also stop moving at 10 s and 12 s, respectively. The red car isn't moving at all.

## Develop & Understand: A

*Suggested Grouping: Small Groups*

▶ **Exercises 1–4** asks students to create a story on the basis of the information they can extract from the graph. Divide students into groups of 3–5. Tell them to take 5–10 minutes to talk about what they can see in the graph. Then ask them to answer the questions in their groups.

▶ **Exercise 4** There is more than one way to interpret the data. Some students may assume two cars that are the same distance from the intersection are side-by-side. Other students may assume that the two cars are on a straight line with the intersection forming the midpoint of the line. For example, after 6 seconds, both the orange car and the green car are 180 m from the intersection. They could either be next to one another or 360 m apart.

**Teacher Tips** The text after Exercises 1–4 explains that the concept of velocity directly corresponds to positive and negative slopes. That is, velocity can accept both positive and negative values depending on the direction the object is moving. In contrast, speed can only accept positive values and is the absolute value of velocity. The distinction between these two concepts deserves a good discussion because it previews the concepts of a vector and of an absolute value.

### Share & Summarize

Students have to realize that features of the graphs such as the value of the slope and the sign of the slope give us information about the speed and direction of the car. Exercise 3 calls for an interpretation of a horizontal line as a change in time with no change in space.

**Teacher Tips** If students are not sure how to figure out that the car is not moving, ask them what the speed is and then what the slope of the graph for such a car is. Ask them what the line with slope 0 would look like.

## Investigation 4

**On Your Own Exercises**
Pages 402–409
Exercises 7–12, 20, 34

**Change the Starting Point** Investigation 4 brings up the comparison between proportional and nonproportional relationships in the context of speed. It also introduces a negative constant term in a linear relationship, using an example of five brothers starting a race at staggered starting points.

### Develop & Understand: A

*Suggested Grouping: Individuals or Pairs*

This exercise set compares proportional and non-proportional relationships between distance and time. Although Lesson 1 addressed the same idea, this context will be relatively new for students. Students will need graph paper or copies of Chapter 8 Master 1, Quarter-Inch Graph Paper, to complete Exercises 1–4.

**Math Link**
Encourage students to find the similarities as well as the differences for the graphs in Exercise 2. Some similarities that students might mention are that both graphs are linear and have positive slopes. They both contain the point (4, 12). Some differences are the endpoint on the $y$-axis and the slope of the line.

**Wrap-Up** You may want to check the answers for Exercise 4 before moving on. Look for correct rules: $d = 3t$ for the older sister and $d = 2t + 4$ for the younger sister. Students should note that the proportional relationship does not have a constant, while the nonproportional relationship does. Also make sure students understand that the graph of the proportional relationship starts at the origin and the graph of the non-proportional relationship starts at point (0, 4).

## Investigation 4 Change the Starting Point

**Vocabulary**
*y*-intercept

**Materials**
- graph paper

You will now explore a situation in which runners start a race at different points. You will see how rules and graphs show these differences.

### Develop & Understand: A

Alita ran a race with her younger sister, Olivia. Alita let Olivia start 4 meters ahead of the starting line. Alita ran at a steady rate of 3 meters per second while Olivia ran at a steady rate of 2 meters per second.

1. Make a table to show how many meters each sister was from the starting line at various times. See margin.
2. On the same grid, draw a graph for each sister showing the relationship between distance from the starting line and time. Compare the graphs. See margin.
3. Is Alita's distance from the starting line proportional to time? Is Olivia's distance proportional to time? Yes; no
4. For each sister, write a rule in symbols to relate distance $d$ and time $t$. How are the numbers in the rules reflected in the graphs? See margin.

**Math Link**
When you compare two things, look at both similarities and differences.

### Troubleshooting

Watch for students who start the graph for Olivia in Exercise 2 at (4, 0) instead of (0, 4). Remind them which variable is represented by the horizontal coordinate (time) and which is represented by the vertical coordinate (distance).

**Additional Answers for Exercises 1, 2, and 4 continued on page 433A.**

① Possible answer: Locations of numbers on a number line, where negative means to the left of 0; distance from the top of mercury in a thermometer to the 0° mark, where negative means below the 0° mark

## Think & Discuss

In Chapter 3, you learned about elevations below sea level. For example, suppose Candace ended a hike at an elevation of −150 feet. The number −150 shows two things. First, the 150 tells Candace's distance from sea level. What does the negative sign show? That this distance is *below* sea level

Describe some other situations in which you might use a negative sign along with a distance. Explain the meaning of the negative sign in each situation. See ①.

## Develop & Understand: B

Five brothers ran a race. The twins began at the starting line. Their older brother began behind the starting line, and their two younger brothers began at different distances ahead of the starting line. Each boy ran at a fairly uniform speed. Here are rules for the relationship between distance $d$ meters from the starting line and time $t$ seconds for each boy.

| | |
|---|---|
| Adam: | $d = 6t$ |
| Brett: | $d = 4t + 7$ |
| Caleb: | $d = 5t + 4$ |
| David: | $d = 5t$ |
| Eric: | $d = 7t - 5$ |

5. Adam and David are the twins because when $t = 0$, $d = 0$. Eric is the oldest because when $t = 0$, $d = -5$.

**5.** Which brothers are the twins? How do you know? Which brother is the oldest? How do you know?

**6.** For each brother, describe how far from the starting line he began the race and how fast he ran.
Adam: At the starting line, 6 m/s; Brett: 7 m in front, 4 m/s; Caleb: 4 m in front, 5 m/s; David: at the starting line, 5 m/s; Eric: 5 m behind, 7 m/s

## Think & Discuss

*Suggested Grouping: Whole Class*

This discussion introduces the idea of the sign associated with distance to indicate the direction from a given starting point.

Ask students to come up with more examples of the same kind. Students might think of going opposite directions from one point, or suggest an elevator coming down from the ground level to basement levels 1, 2, and so on. Help them notice the connection between the direction of a distance as it relates to a given point, such as sea level, and the sign (positive or negative) attached to it. For example, a distance below or behind a given point may be shown as a negative number.

## Develop & Understand: B

*Suggested Grouping: Pairs*

In this exercise set, students use rules to find rate information. Then they interpret information from graphs and match the graphs to symbolic rules. Suggest that students work in pairs and take turns asking each other questions from the exercise set.

▶ **Exercises 5, 6** Students are asked to interpret the meaning behind the terms in a rule. Students should realize that Adam and David began at the starting line because their respective rules do not contain any constants. They should realize that Eric started behind the starting line because the constant in this rule is a negative number—subtracting 5 has the same result as adding −5.

▶ **Exercise 6** Students use coefficients to determine speed and constants to determine starting place.

▶ **Exercise 7** The graph shows negative values of *d* to represent a runner starting behind the starting line. Encourage students to verbalize how this information helps them know which graph represents Eric.

▶ **Exercise 9** Students need to focus on the vertical line going through $t = 2$ and through $t = 3$ and order the points of intersection from top to bottom. This orders the runners from first to last.

▶ **Exercise 10** Help students realize that since Caleb and David run at the same rate, the lines representing them on the graph are parallel. Therefore the vertical distance between the lines is constant.

▶ **Exercise 11** Students should draw or imagine a horizontal line going through $d = 30$ and find the intersecting line that has the smallest value for *t*.

**Wrap-Up** Discuss how to represent the negative values of distance on a graph. Then discuss students' answers to Exercises 9–11.

**7.** Which graph below represents which brother?

7. Adam: iii; Brett: i; Caleb: ii; David: iv; Eric: v

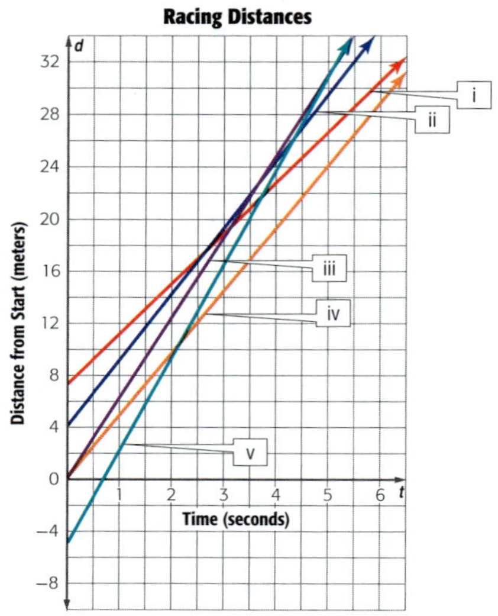


**8.** What events match the intersection points of the graphs?

8. These are times when two brothers are side by side. Except for the intersection of the twins' lines at the origin, these are also times when one boy passes another.

**9.** Use the graphs to help you find the order of the brothers at the given times.

**a.** 2 seconds after the race began Brett (in the lead), Caleb, Adam, David, Eric

**b.** 3 seconds after the race began Caleb and Brett (tied for the lead), Adam, Eric, David

**10.** Which two brothers stay the same distance apart throughout the race? How do you know?

10. Caleb and David; they travel at the same speed, and their graphs, ii and iv, are the same distance apart at all points.

**11.** If the finish line was 30 meters from the starting line, who won? It was a tie between Adam and Eric.

**12.** Which brothers' rules are proportional? Which are not? Adam's and David's are proportional; the others are not.



## ***Reaching** All Learners*

**OL** **On Level** Some students may confuse the five graphs on the grid. These students may benefit by placing a piece of tracing paper over the grid and writing the brothers' names beside their respective graphs.

The rules for Exercises 5–12 have the form $d = rt + p$, with numbers in place of $r$ and $p$. The value of $r$ is the velocity, it gives the rate at which distance changes as time passes. The value of $p$ tells the starting point. For example, Brett's rule is $d = 4t + 7$. His velocity is 4 meters per second. He began 7 meters ahead of the starting line.

If you graph $d = rt + p$, with $t$ on the horizontal axis, or $x$-axis, and $d$ on the vertical axis, or $y$-axis, the coordinates of the starting point on the graph are $(0, p)$. When $t = 0$, $d = p$. Therefore, $p$ is the value of $d$ at which the graph intersects the $y$-axis. That is why $p$ is also called the ***y*-intercept**. For Brett's rule, the $y$-intercept is 7.

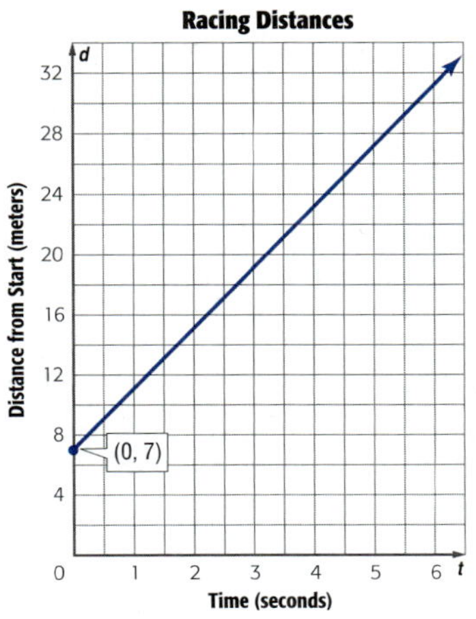


## Share & Summarize

1. In Exercises 5–12, who began behind the starting line? Which part of the graph shows this? Which part of the rule shows this?
2. The brothers' dog, King, ran the race with them. His rule was $d = -15 - 2t$. What does the rule reveal about King's speed and starting position?
3. In what direction is King running? Away from the finish line

1. Eric; his graph starts below the $x$-axis. His rule has a negative constant term.
2. His speed was 2 m/s, and he began 15 m behind the starting line.



**Teacher Tips** Tell students that the rules in the prior exercise set have the form $d = rt + p$. Discuss what each term represents.

Have students think about how they might graph Brett's rule, $d = 4t + 7$, if they graph the $t$ values on the horizontal axis, or $x$-axis, and $d$ values on the vertical axis, or $y$-axis. Help students see that since the starting point of the race is at 0 seconds, the starting point of the runner will be plotted on that line, the vertical or $y$-axis.

Introduce the term $y$-intercept and relate it to Brett's starting point (0, 7) and what would be the starting point in the general rule, $(0, p)$.

Be sure that students understand that horizontal and vertical axes are often referred to as the $x$-axis and $y$-axis, respectively, even when the variables being graphed are not $x$ and $y$. You may want to use the graph as an example, pointing out that the axis labeled $t$, for Time, is also known as the $x$-axis and the axis labeled $d$, for Distance from Start, is also known as the $y$-axis. This terminology is used in some homework exercises.

## Share & Summarize

By this time students should be able to recognize the roles of the rate and constant term in the symbolic rules and graphs of linear relationships. They should be able to interpret the positive or negative sign for both the rate and the constant term.

## On Your Own Exercises
**Lesson 8.2**

**Investigation 1**
Pages 390–393
Practice & Apply: 1–3
Connect & Extend: 26

**Investigation 2**
Pages 394–396
Practice & Apply: 4–5
Connect & Extend: 21–25

**Investigation 3**
Pages 396–397
Practice & Apply: 6
Connect & Extend: 13–19, 27–33

**Investigation 4**
Pages 398–401
Practice & Apply: 7–12
Connect & Extend: 20, 34

**Assign Anytime**
Mixed Review: 35–37

▶ **Exercise 1d** Students use dimensional analysis as they convert their answers from ft/s to mi/h. Watch for students who give their answers in feet. Remind them to divide the number of feet by 5,280.

▶ **Exercise 2b** If students write the rule as $t = 0.58L$, have them substitute the data from the table into their rule to see that their rule will not work.

## On Your Own Exercises
**Lesson 8.2**

### Practice & Apply

1. **Sports** Suppose you are riding a bicycle at a steady rate of 16 feet per second.

   a. Imagine that you rode at this pace for various lengths of time. Copy and complete the table.

| Time (s) | 0 | 10 | 20 | 30 | 35 | 40 | 50 | 55 | 60 | 70 |
|---|---|---|---|---|---|---|---|---|---|---|
| Distance (ft) | 0 | 160 | 320 | 480 | 560 | 640 | 800 | 880 | 960 | 1,120 |

**Math Link**
1 mile = 5,280 feet

   b. Write a rule relating the number of feet you travel $d$ to the time in seconds $t$. Use your rule to find how long it would take you to travel 900 feet. $d = 16t$; $900 = 16t$ so $t = 56.25$ and time = 56.25 s

   c. From your table, find how many feet you ride in 1 minute. About how many miles is this? 960 ft, about 0.18 mi

   d. Use the distance in feet that you travel in 1 minute to find how far you could ride in 1 hour if you kept up your pace. What is your traveling speed in miles per hour? 57,600 ft or 10.9 mi in an hour; 10.9 mph

   e. Write a second rule that relates the number of miles you travel $d$ to the time in hours $t$. $d = 10.9t$

   f. Draw a graph for the distance in feet traveled in relation to time in seconds. Draw another graph for the distance in miles traveled in relation to time in hours. See margin.

   g. What is the slope of each line you graphed? ft/s: 16; mph: 10.9

   h. Compare the two slopes. How can they be different if the speeds are the same?

1h. The ft/s slope is greater than the mph slope. Since the units are not the same for the variables, it makes sense that the graphs could have different slopes.

2. A 90-minute cassette tape plays for 45 minutes per side. The tape is about 26 meters long and moves at a steady rate.

   a. Complete the table to show how many meters of tape play in given numbers of minutes.

| Time (min), $t$ | 0 | 1 | 10 | 20 | 30 | 40 | 45 |
|---|---|---|---|---|---|---|---|
| Length Played (m), $L$ | 0 | 0.58 | 5.8 | 11.6 | 17.4 | 23.2 | 26 |

   b. Write a rule relating length of tape played to time. $L = 0.58t$

   c. What is the speed of the tape through the recorder in meters per minute? If you graphed the length of tape played in relation to time, what would be the slope of the line? 0.58 m/min, 0.58

   d. Find the length of a 120-minute cassette tape, which has 60 minutes per side. Assume that tapes of different lengths run at the same speed. 34.8 m



Additional Answer for Exercise 1 on page 433A.

3d. $N = 5.2t$, $M = 3.8t$, $d = 1.4t$

3e. The rate is the difference between Nadia's speed and Mark's speed.

**Real-World Link**

The word *marathon* comes from the name of a famous plain in Greece. In 490 B.C., a runner was sent from this plain to Athens, which was about 25 miles away, to report the Athenians' victory in a battle against the Persians.

**3. Sports** A marathon is a race of 26.2 miles. Nadia and Mark are running a marathon. Nadia's speed is 5.2 miles per hour, and Mark's is 3.8 miles per hour. Assume their speeds are steady throughout the race.

**a.** Complete the table for Nadia and Mark. Distances are in miles.

| Time (hours), $t$ | 0 | 1 | 2 | 3 | 4 |
|---|---|---|---|---|---|
| Nadia's Distance from Start, $N$ | 0 | 5.2 | 10.4 | 15.6 | 20.8 |
| Mark's Distance from Start, $M$ | 0 | 3.8 | 7.6 | 11.4 | 15.2 |
| Distance between Nadia and Mark, $d$ | 0 | 1.4 | 2.8 | 4.2 | 5.6 |

**b.** On a single grid, draw graphs that show these three relationships.

- time and Nadia's distance from start  3b–3c. See margin.
- time and Mark's distance from start
- time and the distance between Nadia and Mark

**c.** What is the slope of each line? Which line is the steepest? Which line is the least steep? Why?

**d.** Write a rule for each of these three relationships.

**e.** Think about the distance between Nadia and Mark. How is the rate this distance changes related to Nadia's speed and Mark's speed?

**4. Sports** Nadia, Helena, Bryson, and Mark start their marathon run, which is 26.2 miles long. Nadia's speed is 5.2 miles per hour, Helena's is 4.1 miles per hour, Bryson's is 4.85 miles per hour, and Mark's is 3.8 miles per hour. Assume their speeds are steady throughout the run.

**a.** Complete the table. Distances are in miles.

**Marathon Results**

| Time (hours), $t$ | 0 | 1 | 2 | 3 | 4 |
|---|---|---|---|---|---|
| Nadia's Distance from Finish, $N$ | 26.2 | 21 | 15.8 | 10.6 | 5.4 |
| Helena's Distance from Finish, $H$ | 26.2 | 22.1 | 18 | 13.9 | 9.8 |
| Bryson's Distance from Finish, $B$ | 26.2 | 21.35 | 16.5 | 11.65 | 6.8 |
| Mark's Distance from Finish, $M$ | 26.2 | 22.4 | 18.6 | 14.8 | 11 |



On Your Own Exercises

**Additional Answers**

3b. Possible Graph:

**Nadia's and Mark's Marathon**

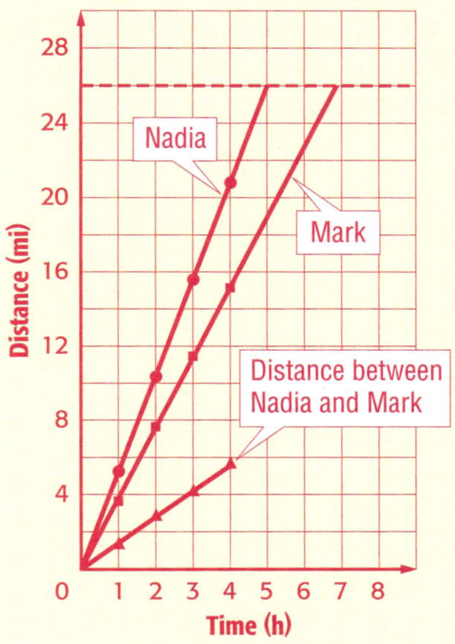


3c. Nadia: 5.2; Mark: 3.8; between: 1.4; Nadia's line is the steepest because it has the greatest slope. The line representing the distance between the runners is the least steep because it has the least slope.

**Lesson 8.2** Speed and Slope 403

▶ **Exercise 4e** Students will need to refer to Exercises 8–12 in Investigation 1 to answer this question.

▶ **Exercise 5a** Some students may forget to add 200 when calculating distance. Remind them to find 14*t* and then add 200 to find the total distance.

On Your Own Exercises

4b.

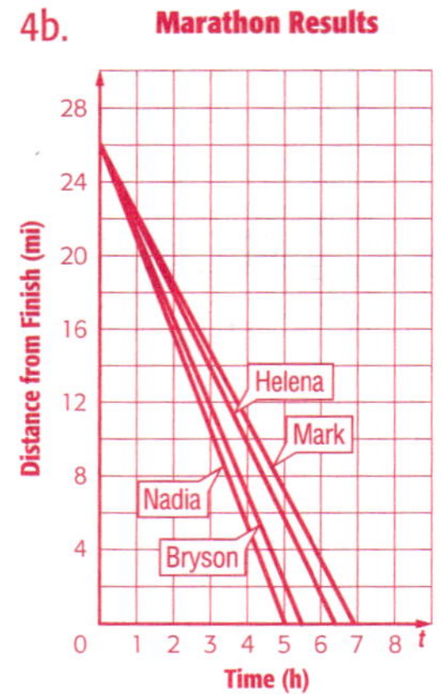


4c. All show distance decreasing with time, so their slopes are negative and the lines slant down from left to right. They all have different slopes (steepness): Nadia: −5.2; Helena: −4.1; Bryson: −4.85; Mark: −3.8. (Note: Slopes may be estimates.)

4d. Nadia: about 5.0 h; Helena: about 6.4 h; Bryson: about 5.4 h; Mark: about 6.9 h

4e. $N = 26.2 - 5.2t$, $H = 26.2 - 4.1t$, $B = 26.2 - 4.85t$, $M = 26.2 - 3.8t$; These rules are similar in two ways: they all have a constant term, and the rates are negative.

**b.** On a single grid, draw graphs that show the relationships between time and distance from the finish for all four runners.

**c.** Compare the four graphs. In what ways are they similar, and in what ways are they different? What is the slope of each graph?

**d.** How much time will it take for each of the four runners to finish the marathon? You may want to extend your graph or table.

**e.** For each runner, write a rule in symbols that relates that runner's distance from finish (*N, H, B,* or *M*) to *t*.

**5. Geography** Soon after Trina's trans-Australia flight left Adelaide for Darwin, the pilot announced they were 200 kilometers from Adelaide and cruising at a speed of 840 kilometers per hour. The plane was flying north from Adelaide, toward the South Australia border. To pass the time, Trina decided to calculate her distance from Adelaide at various times after the pilot's message.

**a.** Complete the table to show the distance in kilometers from Adelaide at various times in minutes after the pilot spoke.

**Trans-Australia Flight**

| Time after Pilot's Message (min), *t* | 0 | 1 | 15 | 30 | 60 | 90 | 120 |
|---|---|---|---|---|---|---|---|
| Distance from Adelaide (km), *d* | 200 | 214 | 410 | 620 | 1,040 | 1,460 | 1,880 |

**b.** Draw a graph of the data. See margin.

**c.** The South Australia border is 1,100 km from Adelaide. Use your graph to determine about how long after the pilot's message the plane crossed the border. About 64 min

**d.** Alice Springs is 1,400 km from Adelaide. How long after the message would Trina expect to pass over it? About 86 min



**Additional Answer**

5b.

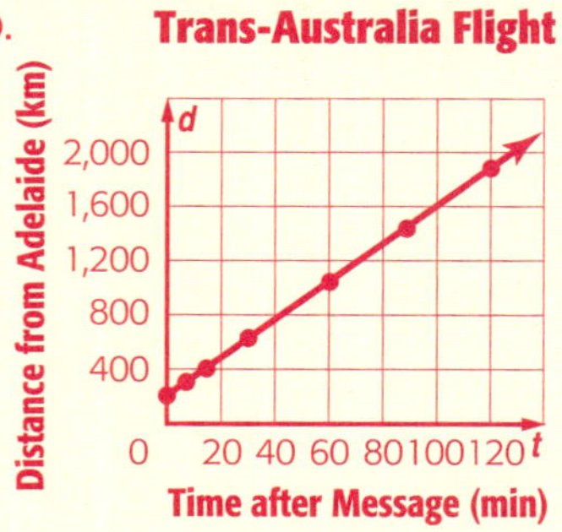

5e. Multiply by 14 and add 200; $d = 14t + 200$; 200 is the intercept on the $d$-axis, and 14 is the slope.

**e.** Explain in words how to find the distance from Adelaide if you know the time after the pilot's message. Write the rule in symbols. Explain how each number in your rule is shown in the graph.

**6.** One Sunday, Benito, Julie, Sook Leng, Edan, and Tia visited a park at different times. They rented bikes of different colors and rode them along the park's bike route. The bike route goes from the rental shop to a cafe. It also goes in the opposite direction, from the rental shop to a lake.

The graphs show the friends' locations from noon until 2 P.M.

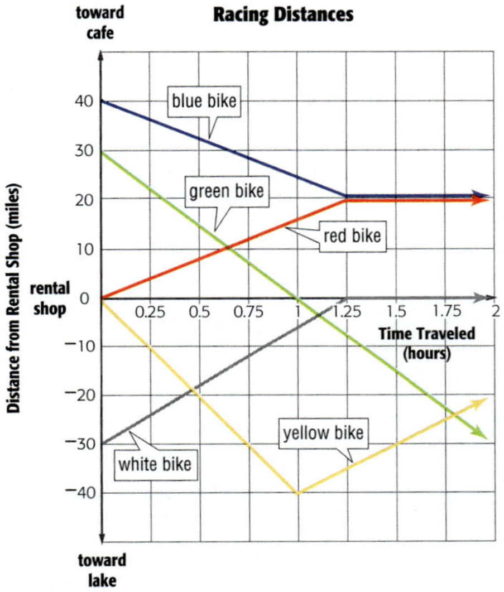


**a.** Describe the route taken by each bike. For example, the blue bike moves from the direction of the cafe toward the rental shop, and then stops.

**b.** Determine the speed of each bike. If a bike's speed changes, list all of its speeds.

6a. Red: from the rental shop toward the cafe, then stops; Green: from the direction of the cafe toward the lake; Yellow: from the rental shop toward the lake and back; White: from the direction of the lake toward the rental shop, then stops

6b. Blue: 16 mph, 0 mph; Red: 16 mph, 0 mph; Green: 30 mph; Yellow: 40 mph, 20 mph; White: 24 mph, 0 mph



On Your Own Exercises

▶ **Exercise 6** Be sure students understand that a line on this graph reflects distance traveled on the vertical axis and time traveled on the horizontal axis.

**Lesson 8.2** Speed and Slope 405

▶ **Exercise 20 Extension** You may wish to suggest to students that they try out this rule the next time a thunderstorm is in the area.



6f. No; the speeds are always positive, but the slopes can be positive or negative. The slopes are positive if the bikes are moving toward the cafe, negative if they are moving toward the lake.

9. (0, 2.4)

11. (0, −35)

12. $(0, \frac{-3}{5})$

**Connect & Extend**

19. You can determine the speed by the absolute value of the slope.

**c.** Tia and Julie met about 20 miles from the rental shop and talked for an hour. Julie had come directly from the rental shop, and Tia had already visited the cafe and was returning her bike. What were the colors of their bikes? Julie: red; Tia: blue

**d.** From noon to 1 P.M., Benito had the highest speed. Sook Leng had the second highest, and Edan had the lowest. What color bikes were Benito, Sook Leng, and Edan riding? Benito: yellow; Sook Leng: green; Edan: white

**e.** Determine the slope of the line for each bike. If the slope changes, list all of them. Blue: −16, 0; Red: 16, 0; Green: −30; Yellow: −40, 20; White: 24, 0

**f.** Are the bikes' speeds and the slopes of their lines always equal to each other? Why or why not?

**For each equation, give the coordinates of the graph's intersection with the $y$-axis. In other words, give the $y$-intercept.**

**7.** $y = 3x - 5$ (0, −5) **8.** $y = -7x + 14$ (0, 14) **9.** $y = 1.5x + 2.4$

**10.** $y = 27 - 9x$ (0, 27) **11.** $y = -35 + 3.1x$ **12.** $y = \frac{-3}{5} + \frac{3}{5}x$

**Determine the slope of each line.**

**13.** $y = 7x - 12$ 7 **14.** $y = 31 - 4.6x$ −4.6 **15.** $y = 8 + 3x$ 3

**16.** $y = -x - 1$ −1 **17.** $y = -0.21x + 98$ −0.21 **18.** $y = \frac{1}{4}x - \frac{7}{2}$ $\frac{1}{4}$

**19. In Your Own Words** Explain how the speed in a distance-time situation is related to the slope of the graph for the situation.

**20. Physical Science** When you see lightning and then hear the clap of thunder, you are hearing what you have just seen. The thunder takes longer to reach you because sound travels much more slowly than light. Sound takes about 5 seconds to travel 1 mile, but light travels that distance almost instantly.

**a.** Complete the table to show the relationship between $d$ distance in miles from a thunderstorm and $t$ time in seconds between seeing the lightning and hearing the thunder.

| Seconds between Lightning and Thunder, $t$ | 0 | 5 | 10 | 15 | 20 | 25 |
|---|---|---|---|---|---|---|
| Distance from Storm (mi), $d$ | 0 | 1 | 2 | 3 | 4 | 5 |

**b.** If thunder and lightning happen at the same time, where is the storm? Very close to the observer

**c.** How could you calculate how far away a storm is? Write a rule that relates distance $d$ from a storm to the time $t$ between seeing it and hearing it. $d = t \div 5$

**Graph a line with the indicated slope.** 21–25. Possible graphs:

**21.** 1

**22.** 12

**23.** −3

**24.** 0.37

**25.** −270

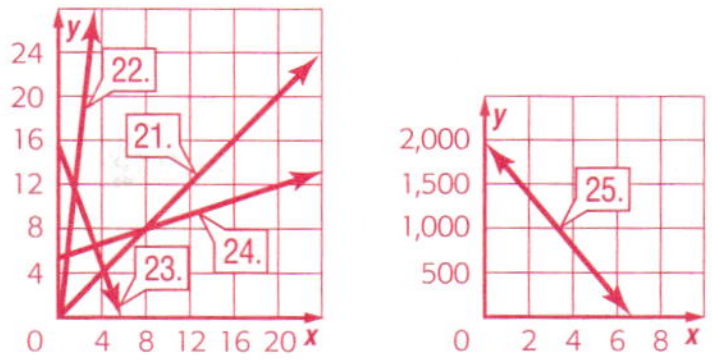


**26. Astronomy** *Pioneer 10* was launched on March 3, 1972. Designed to last at least 21 months, the spacecraft outlived and outperformed the fondest dreams of its creators. On April 25, 1983, *Pioneer 10* sent radio signals to Earth from Pluto, $4.58 \cdot 10^9$ km away.

**a.** Radio signals travel at the speed of light, about $3.00 \cdot 10^5$ km/s. How long did it take signals to reach Earth from Pluto? About 15,267 s, or 4.24 h

★**b. Challenge** What was *Pioneer 10*'s average speed, in kilometers per hour, kph, between March 3, 1972, and April 25, 1983?

In Exercises 27–31, do Parts a, b, and c for the given speed.

**a.** Express the speed in feet per minute.

**b.** Graph the distance moved over time, with time in minutes on the horizontal axis and distance in feet on the vertical axis.

**c.** Determine the slope of the graph.

**Math Link**

1 mile = 5,280 feet

**27.** 3 meters per minute; 1 foot is approximately 0.3 meter.

**28.** 15 meters per second

**29.** 60 kilometers per hour

**30.** 45 feet per second

**31.** 75 miles per hour

**32.** Write the speeds given in Exercises 27–31 from slowest to fastest. 3 m/min, 45 ft/s, 15 m/s, 60 kph, 75 mph

**33.** Redraw the two graphs for Exercises 29 and 31 on a single grid.

**a.** What do you notice about the slopes of the two graphs? (Hint: Look at the angle each line makes with the horizontal axis.) The slope for 75 mph is about twice the slope for 60 kph.

**b.** Explain your result in Part a. When both speeds are expressed in ft/min, the second slope is about twice the first (6,600 versus 3,300).

26b. About $4.69 \cdot 10^4$ km/h; ($4.58 \cdot 10^9$ km) ÷ 97,600 h gives the average speed.)

27–31. See margin.





▶ **Exercises 27–32** Caution students that the speed must be expressed in feet per minute so they can order the speeds in Exercise 32. Tell students to save their answers and their work for Exercises 29 and 31 to use when working Exercise 33.

**Additional Answers**

27a. about 10 ft/min

27b.

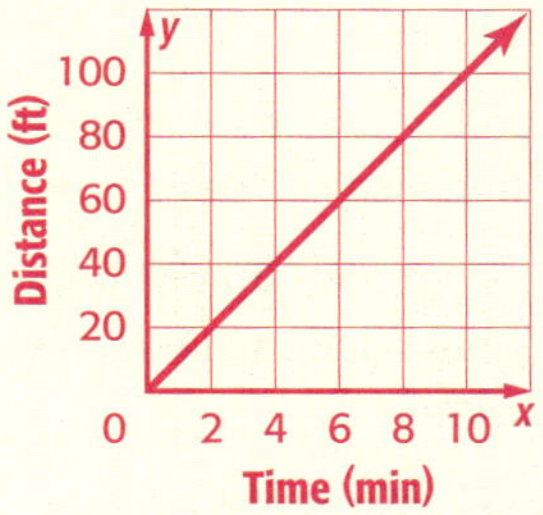


27c. about 10

28a. about 3,000 ft/min

28b.

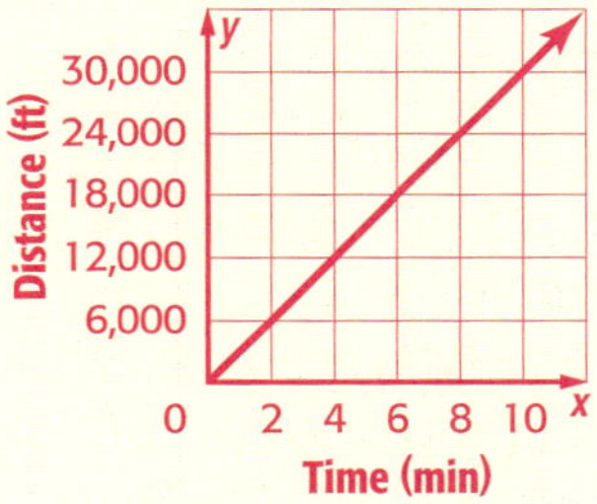


28c. about 3,000

29a. about 3,300 ft/min

29b.

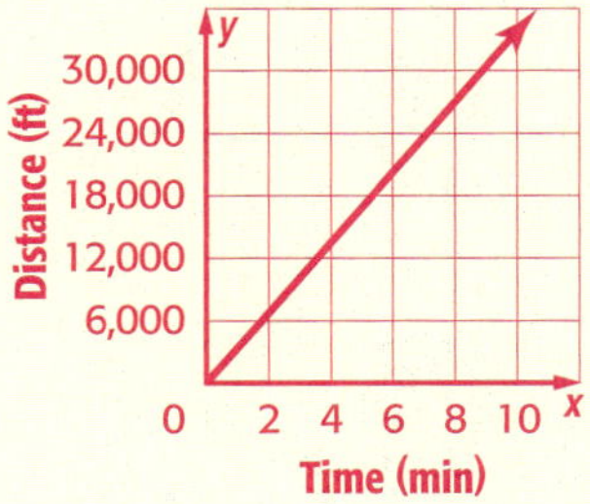


29c. about 3,300

**Additional Answers**

30a. 2,700 ft/min

30b.

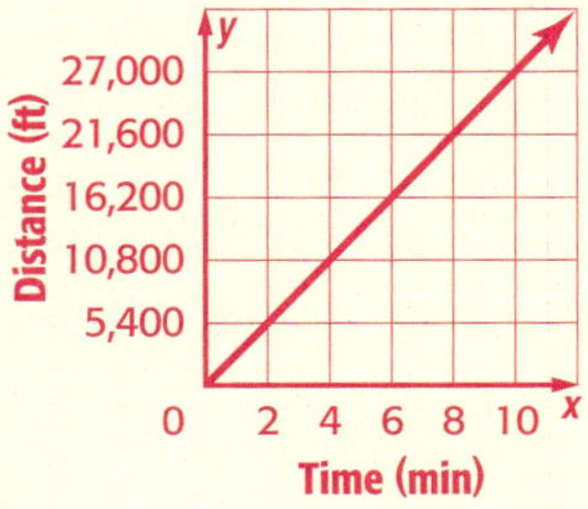


30c. 2,700

**Additional Answers for Exercise 31 continued on page 433B.**

**Exercise 34 Extension** Ask students to write a short report stating which animal the lion pursued and why the lion would have chosen this animal to pursue.

## Quick Check

**Informal Assessment** Students should be able to:

- ✔ relate speed to the slope of a graph of distance over time
- ✔ develop an understanding of negative slope and a negative constant term
- ✔ gain skill in recognizing proportional and non-proportional relationships between distance and time
- ✔ recognize linear relationships from different forms: symbolic rules, graphs, patterns, and tables
- ✔ easily convert one form of representation into another



34b–d. See margin.
34e. The points of intersection indicate when the lion would catch the horse and the giraffe.

34g. Lion: 22.2; horse: 20; giraffe: 14.3; lion-horse distance: −2.2; lion-giraffe distance: −7.9; Slopes for lion, horse, and giraffe are positive because distance increases with time; slopes for lion-horse and lion-giraffe distances are negative because distance decreases with time.

34h. Lion: $d = 22.2t$; horse: $d = 20t + 500$; giraffe: $d = 14.3t + 1{,}000$; lion-horse distance: $d = 500 - 2.2t$; lion-giraffe distance: $d = 1{,}000 - 7.9t$

**34.** A lion surveying his surroundings from a tall tree saw a horse half a kilometer to the south. He also spotted a giraffe 1 kilometer to the west. The lion jumped from the tree to chase one of these animals, and both the horse and the giraffe ran away from the lion with the maximum speed.

A lion can run 200 meters in 9 seconds, a horse can run 200 meters in 10 seconds, and a giraffe can run 200 meters in 14 seconds. The lion went after the animal that would take him less time to catch. After you solve this problem, you will know which animal he pursued.

**a.** Complete the table. For the distance between the lion and each of the other animals, assume the lion is running toward the animal. Distances are in meters.

| Time (seconds) | 0 | 50 | 100 | 150 | 200 |
|---|---|---|---|---|---|
| Lion's Distance From Tree | 0 | 1,111 | 2,222 | 3,333 | 4,444 |
| Horse's Distance From Tree | 500 | 1,500 | 2,500 | 3,500 | 4,500 |
| Giraffe's Distance from Tree | 1,000 | 1,714 | 2,429 | 3,143 | 3,857 |
| Distance between Lion and Horse | 500 | 389 | 278 | 167 | 56 |
| Distance between Lion and Giraffe | 1,000 | 603 | 207 | −190 | −587 |

**b.** On a single set of axes, with time on the horizontal axis and distance on the vertical, draw these three graphs.

- the lion's distance from the tree
- the horse's distance from the tree
- the giraffe's distance from the tree

**c.** On another set of axes, draw these two graphs.

- the distance between the lion and the horse
- the distance between the lion and the giraffe

**d.** How are the five graphs similar, and how are they different?

**e.** What events match the points of intersection of the graphs for Part b?

**f.** Use the graphs to help you find how much time it would take the lion to catch the horse and how much time it would take the lion to catch the giraffe. About 230 s, about 130 s

**g.** What are the slopes of the five lines? How are they different and why?

**h.** Write a rule in symbols for each line you graphed.



**Additional Answers for Exercise 34 continued on page 433B.**

## Mixed Review

**35. Geometry** Match each solid to its name. (Hint: For those of which you are unsure, think about what the term might mean.)

**a.** square pyramid N
**b.** cone K
**c.** cylinder P
**d.** triangular prism T
**e.** oblique prism R
**f.** hexagonal prism M
**g.** octahedron Q
**h.** tetrahedron S
**i.** hemisphere L

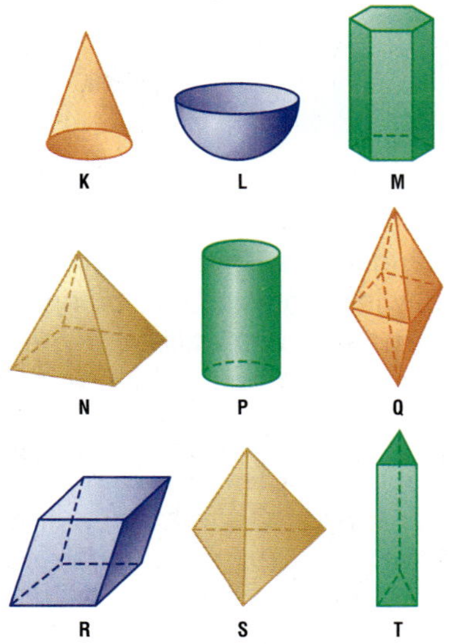


**36.** Mr. Ritter was curious about the copy machine in his office. He wanted to know if pressing the 200% button meant that the area of a picture would be doubled. What would you tell him? No; if the dimensions of the picture are doubled, the area is multiplied by 4.

**37. Geometry** A rectangular prism has a base 5 inches long and 2 inches wide. The prism is 6 inches tall.

**a.** What are the prism's volume and surface area? $60\text{ in}^3$, $104\text{ in}^2$

**b.** Another block prism is four times the height of the original prism. What are its volume and surface area? $240\text{ in}^3$, $356\text{ in}^2$

**c.** If a cylinder has the same volume as the original prism and the area of its base is 10 square inches, what is the cylinder's height? 6 in.



**2.** A strip of cloth 12 yards long is cut into two smaller pieces. If $A$ stands for the number of yards in one piece and $B$ stands for the number of yards in the other piece, they are related by the rule $A + B = 12$.

a. Draw a graph for this rule. Completing a table of values first may help you.

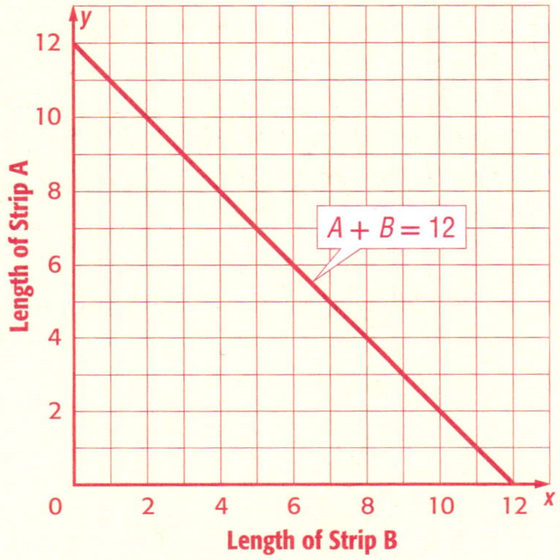


b. Find another way to write the rule that relates the two lengths.
Possible answers: $A = 12 - B$, $B = 12 - A$

On Your Own Exercises

## Quick Quiz

**1.** Below are five graphs and their rules. Match the graphs to the rules.
$p = q + 2$, graph b; $p = 5 - q$, graph a; $p = 2q$, graph e; $p = 2$, graph c; $p = 2q + 1$, graph d

$p = q + 2$ $\quad p = 5 - q$
$p = 2q$ $\quad p = 2$
$p = 2q + 1$

a.
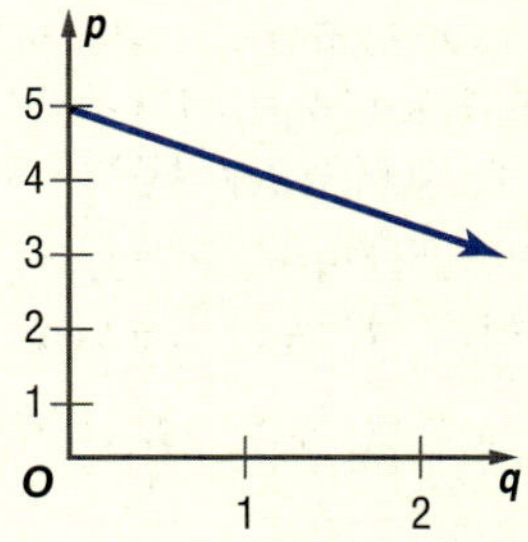


b.
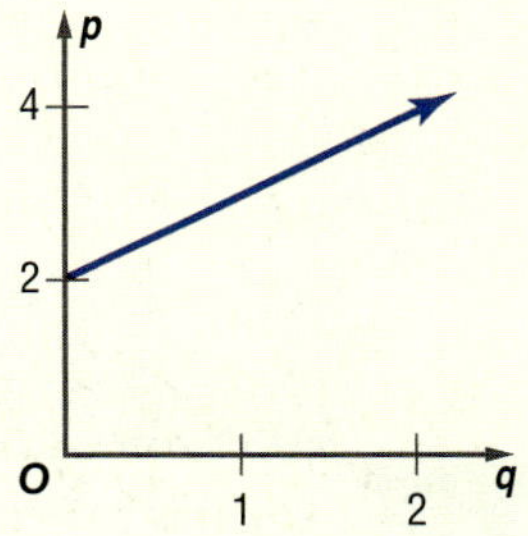


c.
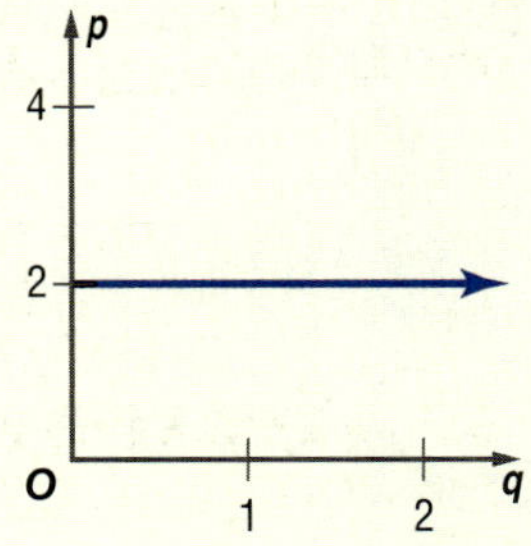


d.
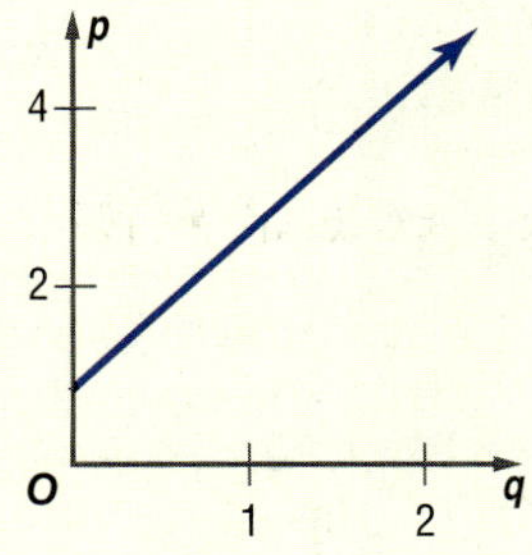


e.
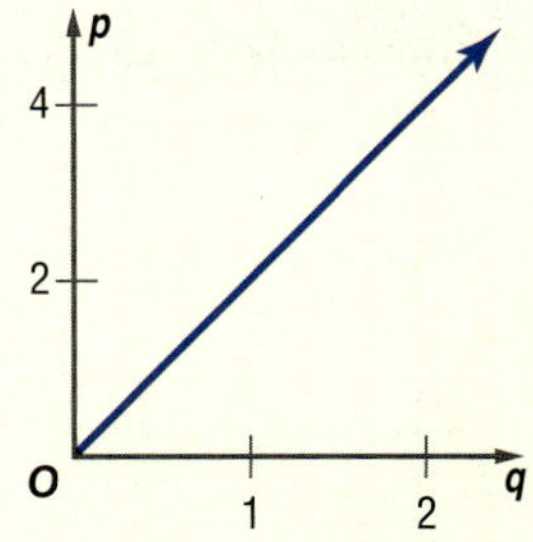

LESSON
# 8.3 Recognize Linear Relationships

### Objectives

- To recognize linear relationships in a variety of representations
- To translate from one representation to another
- To explain the connection between the constant difference, the slope of the graph, and the symbolic representation of the relationship (the $a$ in $y = ax + b$)
- To determine $b$ in the rule $y = ax + b$ from a graph

## Overview

Students learn to recognize linear relationships represented as symbolic rules, graphs, visual patterns, and tables. They start by extending patterns and describing them symbolically. They learn how to use change – the difference between one stage and the next in patterns – to determine whether the pattern is linear or not, and they learn how the rate of growth is reflected in the symbolic rule.

Students graph the relationships in the patterns and learn to make links between the rules and the graphs; they learn how to determine the symbolic rule from the graph and how to predict the graph from the symbolic rule. The symbolic rule for linear relationships is generally given in standard form, $y = ax + b$. Students will also learn how to put relationships in this form.

## Advance Preparation

You may want to use an overhead of transparency Chapter 8 Master 1 or quarter-inch graph paper as you discuss the problems. Students will need copies of this to complete their work.

| | Summary | Materials | On Your Own Exercises (pp. 423–430) | Assessment Opportunities |
|---|---|---|---|---|
| **Investigation 1** (p. 411) Pacing: 2 days | Students investigate patterns and write rules to describe them. | Chapter 8 Master 1 or quarter-inch graph paper | Practice & Apply: 4, 5<br>Connect & Extend: 14, 15, 17<br>Mixed Review: 22–34 | • Share & Summarize (p. 413)<br>• Troubleshooting (pp. 410, 413) |
| **Investigation 2** (p. 414) Pacing: 1 day | Students describe patterns with graphs and practice to match graphs to their rules. | Chapter 8 Master 1 or quarter-inch graph paper | Practice & Apply: 6–11<br>Connect & Extend: 18–20<br>Mixed Review: 22–34 | • Share & Summarize (p. 416)<br>• Troubleshooting (p. 416) |
| **Investigation 3** (p. 417) Pacing: 1 day | Students learn to recognize multiple forms of symbolic representations of linear relationships. | Chapter 8 Master 1 or quarter-inch graph paper | Practice & Apply: 12–13<br>Connect & Extend: 21<br>Mixed Review: 22–34 | • Share & Summarize (p. 419) |
| **Investigation 4** (p. 420) Pacing: 1 day | Students try to develop an effective strategy to discover the symbolic rule from the data. | Chapter 8 Master 1 or quarter-inch graph paper | Practice & Apply: 1–3<br>Connect & Extend: 16<br>Mixed Review: 22–34 | • Share & Summarize (p. 422) |

# Leveled Lesson Resources

CRM *Available in:* **Chapter 8 Resource Masters**

Also on TeacherWorks™ Lesson 8.3

## Study Guide and Intervention (p. 14) AL

**Lesson 8.3 Study Guide and Intervention**
***Recognize Linear Relationships***

For every pattern, there is an input value that generates an output value. We can show patterns by using rules or graphs.

*Example 1* **Complete the table. Then write a rule that relates the number of line segments to the number of triangles.**

| Number of triangles, *n* (*input values*) | 1 | 2 | 3 | 4 | 5 |
|---|---|---|---|---|---|
| Number of line segments, *s* (*output values*) | 3 | 5 | 7 | 9 | 11 |

Notice that the output values increase by 2. That will be part of your rule.

$2 \cdot 1 + 1 = 3$ or $2 \cdot n + 1 = s$

Try the rule with other input values to make sure it works. It does, so you have found your rule.

*Example 2* **Create a graph to help you write a rule. Choose letters to represent each variable.**

(1, 3), (2, 7), (3, 11), (4, 15)

Try to link $x$ and $y$.

$(1 \times 4) - 1 = 3$

Try the rule $y = 4x - 1$. It works for the rest of the points, so it must be the rule.

*Exercises* **Complete the table. Then describe a general rule that relates the input value to the output value.**

1.

| Input, *x* | 2 | 3 | 4 | 5 | 6 | 7 | 8 |
|---|---|---|---|---|---|---|---|
| Output, *y* | 0 | 3 | 6 | | | | |

2.

| Input, *x* | 1 | 2 | 3 | 4 | 5 | 6 | 7 |
|---|---|---|---|---|---|---|---|
| Output, *y* | $1\frac{1}{2}$ | 2 | $2\frac{1}{2}$ | | | | |

**Draw a graph using the points. Describe the rule for the graph in symbols.**

3. (1, −1), (2, 3), (3, 7), (4, 11)
4. (0, 2), (1, 4), (2, 6), (3, 8)

## Skills Practice (p. 15) AL OL

**Lesson 8.3 Skills Practice**
***Recognize Linear Relationships***

**Complete the table. Then write a rule for the input/output pairs.**

1.

| Figure number, *f* | 1 | 2 | 3 | 4 | 5 |
|---|---|---|---|---|---|
| Perimeter of figure, *p* | 4 | 12 | | | |

2.

| Number of squares, *s* | 4 | 6 | 8 | 10 | 12 |
|---|---|---|---|---|---|
| Number of shaded squares, *h* | 1 | 2 | | | |

**For each equation, draw a graph with *x* on the horizontal axis and *y* on the vertical axis. Include negative values for *x* and *y*.**

3. $0.2y = -0.5x + 1$
4. $4(x - 1) - y = 0$

**Plot the input/output pairs. Decide whether the rule could be linear. If you think the rule could be linear, find the rule that fits the numbers and write it in symbols.**

5. (−2, 6), (0, 2), (1, 3), (2, 6)
6. (−2, 8), (1, −1), (1.5, −2.5), (3, −7)

## Problem-Solving Practice (p. 16) AL OL

**Lesson 8.3 Problem-Solving Practice**
***Recognize Linear Relationships***

**Solve.**

1. **Savings** Kiah has been working to save up for a trip with her friends.

| Number of hours, *h* | 4 | 5 | 6 | 7 | 8 |
|---|---|---|---|---|---|
| Salary, *s* | 56 | 65 | 74 | 83 | 92 |

Kiah's trip will cost $500. How many hours will she have to work to go on her trip?

2. **Construction** The rule for the area of a deck is $d = 8p + 16$, where $d$ is the area of the deck in square feet and $p$ is the length of a square swimming pool. A deck has an area of 256 square feet. What is the length of the pool?

3. **Florist** Abigail creates birthday bouquets for her customers. Complete the table to answer the question.

| Number of red flowers, *r* | 1 | 3 | 5 | | |
|---|---|---|---|---|---|
| Total flowers, *t* | 6 | 12 | 18 | 24 | 30 |

How many red flowers will be in a bouquet of 36 flowers?

4. **Florist** In Exercise 3, does the relationship between the number of total flowers *t* and the number of red flowers *r* appear to be linear? Find a rule to link the number of total flowers *t* and the number of red flowers *r*.

5. **Botany** A certain type of bamboo can grow 10 feet in one year. A 3-foot plant's growth can be demonstrated by the equation $y = \frac{5}{6}x + 3$. Draw a graph of this equation to show the growth of this bamboo plant. How tall will it be in 12 months?

6. **Construction** Nicholas is going to build a dog run. He creates a graph and plots the points (5, 25), (6, 36), (7, 49), and (8, 64). The first number represents the length of the dog run in *f* feet. The second number represents its area in a square feet.

Nicholas draws a straight line through the points. Has he correctly displayed his input/output pairs? Explain.

## Enrichment (p. 17) BL

**Lesson 8.3 Enrichment**
***Recognize Linear Relationships***

**Graphing Inequalities**

The possible solutions to $y < 2x + 1$ lie only in the shaded region. They cannot lie on the line since the line is dashed. The possible solutions to $y \geq 2x + 1$ lie in the shaded region and on the line because the line is solid. Inequalities with $\leq$ or $\geq$ are graphed with a solid line. Inequalities with $<$ or $>$ are graphed with a dashed line.

1. Patton makes trail mix to take on his hiking trips. He uses dried fruit and nuts. He has made at least 12 cups of trail mix.

a. Complete the table.

| Cups of dried fruit, *f* | 0 | 2 | 4 | 6 | 8 |
|---|---|---|---|---|---|
| Cups of nuts, *n* | 12 | 10 | | | |

b. Patton made at least 12 cups of trail mix. Write a rule using an inequality to show the relationship between the amount of nuts, *n*, and the amount of dried fruit, *f*.

c. Graph the inequality in Exercise 1b. Shade all the possible answers. Pick a point in the shaded region and check it against your rule.

2. The dried fruit costs $1.25 per cup and the nuts cost $1.75 per cup. The last trail mix Patton created cost him less than $17.

a. Write an inequality to show the relationship between the cost per *n* cups of nuts and the cost per *f* cups of fruit.

b. Use another color and graph the inequality in Exercise 2b on the graph from Exercise 1. Shade all the possible answers. Pick a point in the shaded region and check it against your rule.

## Lesson Quick Quiz (p. 18) AL OL BL

**Lesson 8.3 Quick Quiz**
***Recognize Linear Relationships***

1. Here are five tables. For each:
- determine whether it is a linear relationship,
- explain briefly how you decided, and
- write its symbolic rule (if it is linear).

a.

| Input | 6 | 8 | 10 | 12 | 14 |
|---|---|---|---|---|---|
| Output | 4 | 3 | 2 | 1 | 0 |

b.

| Input | 6 | 5 | 4 | 3 | 2 |
|---|---|---|---|---|---|
| Output | 0 | 1 | 4 | 9 | 16 |

c.

| Input | −1 | 0 | 1 | 2 | 3 |
|---|---|---|---|---|---|
| Output | 8 | 16 | 24 | 32 | 40 |

d.

| Input | 1 | 2 | 3 | 4 | 5 |
|---|---|---|---|---|---|
| Output | 4 | 8 | 16 | 32 | 64 |

e.

| Input | 0.2 | 0.3 | 0.4 | 0.5 | 0.6 |
|---|---|---|---|---|---|
| Output | 3.5 | 3.4 | 3.3 | 3.2 | 3.1 |

2. Explain in your own words how $a$ and $b$ affect the graph of $y = -ax + b$.

# Additional Lesson Resources

### Teacher Tech Tools
- TeacherWorks
- ExamView Assessment Suite
- Classroom Presentation Toolkit
- Advance Tracker

### Student Tech Tools
- StudentWorks Plus
- Math Online eGlossary • Concepts in Motion

### Other Print Products
- Investigation Notebook and Reflection Journal
- Quick Review Math Handbook

LESSON **8.3** **Recognize Linear Relationships**

## *Introduce*

**Patterns** In this lesson students learn to recognize linear relationships in various contexts and from various types of information.

You might begin this lesson by reminding students of the various patterns they've seen. They may recall 3-dimensional cube patterns or hexagon and tile patterns from last year. You might provide examples of patterns or ask other students to do this.

### *Explore*

*Suggested Groups: Pairs*

▶ **Study** Ask students to look at the two patterns in the Explore section and find the rules for different sizes of these patterns. The patterns for perimeter present a linear relationship, and the patterns for area present a quadratic relationship. This activity prepares students to be attentive to the features that characterize linear relationships in comparison to other relationships.

▶ **Write Rules** Students may remember the formulas for area and perimeter, count individual tiles, or use other methods to find these rules.

LESSON
# 8.3 Recognize Linear Relationships

You have learned about linear relationships between variables such as pay earned and time worked. In this lesson, you will look at both linear and nonlinear relationships, but it will not always be obvious which is which.

***Real-World Link***

Tiles are typically made from clay that has been hardened by *firing*, or *baking*, at very high temperatures in a special oven called a *kiln*. A glaze might then be applied to the tiles.

① $b = 2s + 2(s - 2)$, or $b = 4s - 4$; $c = (s - 2)^2$, where $s$ is the side length of the patio, $b$ is the number of border tiles, and $c$ is the number of center (nonborder) tiles

### *Explore*

Pat and Tillie are patio tilers who specialize in two-color rectangular patios. All of their patios are constructed from tiles measuring 1 foot by 1 foot. The border is one color, and the center is another color. The patio shown here is 9 feet by 6 feet.

Their Totally Square line of patios contains a variety of square patio designs. Below is a Totally Square patio measuring 6 feet by 6 feet.

Find a rule that tells how many border tiles will be used on a Totally Square patio of a specified size. Then find a rule that tells how many nonborder tiles there will be. Tell what each variable in your rules represents. See ①.

Pat and Tillie call their patio designs that are not square their ColorQuad line. Find a rule that expresses the number of border tiles in a ColorQuad patio with width $w$ and length $l$. Then write a rule that expresses the number of nonborder tiles in a ColorQuad patio. $b = 2w + 2l - 4$, $c = (w - 2)(l - 2)$



### *Troubleshooting*

Watch for students who forget to subtract 2 from both dimensions when using the formula for area for the nonborder tiles. Remind them that they are looking for the area of an interior section that is not as large as the entire tiled area.

# Investigation 1 Explore and Describe Patterns

In the next set of exercises, you will review and extend your ability to find patterns and to write rules in symbols.

## Develop & Understand: A

**1.** This hexagon pattern can continue in either direction.

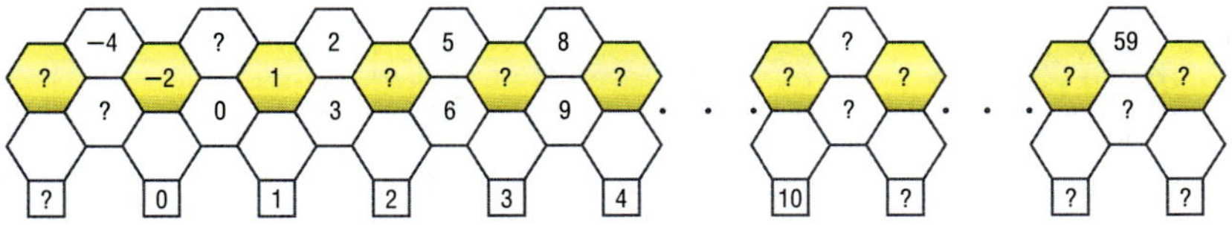


**a.** Find the missing numbers in the hexagon pattern. Then copy and complete the table. Discuss with your partner how you found the numbers. Explanations will vary.

| Number in Square, *s* | −1 | 0 | 1 | 2 | 3 | 4 | 10 | 11 | 20 | 21 |
|---|---|---|---|---|---|---|---|---|---|---|
| Number in Shaded Hexagon, *h* | −5 | −2 | 1 | 4 | 7 | 10 | 28 | 31 | 58 | 61 |

**b.** Write a rule in symbols for computing *h* if you know *s*.
$h = 3s - 2$

**2.** This sequence of squares is made from small tiles.

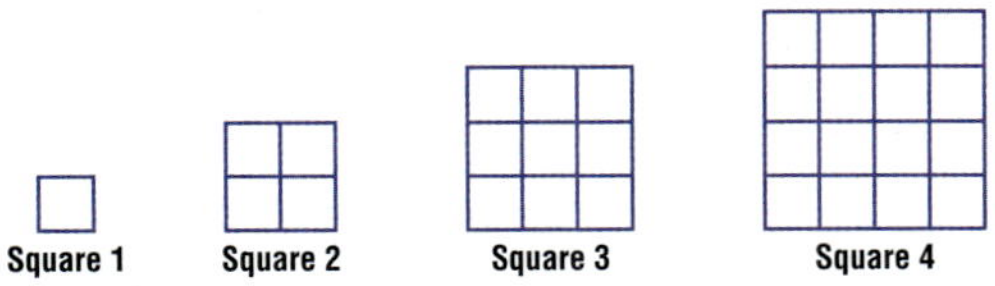


2a. $A = n^2$, where $A$ is the area and $n$ is the square number

**a.** Find a relationship between the number of the square and its area. The area is equal to the number of tiles in the square.

**b.** Complete the table to show the area of each square.

| Square Number | 1 | 2 | 3 | 4 |
|---|---|---|---|---|
| Area of Square | 1 | 4 | 9 | 16 |



# Investigation 1

***On Your Own Exercises***
Pages 423–430
Exercises 4–5, 14, 15, 17

**Extend Patterns** The exercises in this investigation require that students extend and/or describe the pattern symbolically. Students will refer back to these tables and rules in subsequent investigations. You may want to suggest that they save their work and bring it to class with them each day.

## Develop & Understand: A

*Suggested Grouping: Pairs*

▶ **Exercise 1** Students have to find what numbers fit into the shaded and white hexagons above 10, and which numbers fit into the hexagons around number 59. Students also must find what numbers belong in four of the squares.

If students are confused by all the different numbers in the pattern, draw their attention to the numbers in the squares. These numbers are orderly enough to be a kind of index to the pattern of numbered hexagons.

▶ **Exercise 1a** Students may notice that each number in the shaded hexagons is 3 more than the previous one. This, however, can be a risky strategy since two numbers do not form a pattern.

Some may notice the multiples of 3 in the lower row of white hexagons, and some may see that 0, 1, and 2 lie on an oblique line; 3, 4, and 5 lie on the parallel oblique line to the right; and then 6, 7, and 8 lie on the next line to the right, and so on.

▶ **Exercise 1b** Students may come up with a rule that will help them connect the stage number with a matching number in the hexagon. Other students will work the problem by matching the numbers in the hexagons to certain stages.

## Develop & Understand: B

*Suggested Grouping: Pairs*

Exercises 3–15 help develop students' ability to translate from the features of a visual geometric pattern to the numbers that describe these features. They ask students not merely to follow the pattern but to come up with the rule that describes the pattern. Students must justify their rule, or generalization, first by checking special cases and then by relating the rule to the structure of the pattern, convincing themselves and their partner not only that the rule works for the cases tested, but also that the rule is always true.

▶ **Exercise 5** Watch for students who multiply the stage number and a rate but neglect to add the constant term. For example in Exercise 5, students may forget to add 3 to 2*n* when writing the rule. It can help to ask these students to identify the part in the shapes that remains constant in all stages and also the part that changes.

**Wrap-Up** If students have difficulties coming up with the rules for patterns, you may draw these patterns on the board and use different colors for the constant and the changing parts of each pattern so students can better visualize them. If you do it with several patterns, this will give a firm base for students' understanding of where the rule comes from.

## Develop & Understand: C

*Suggested Grouping: Pairs*

This exercise set practices translating the structure of the pattern into the rule that describes this pattern.

5. The number of squares is equal to 2 multiplied by the stage number, plus 3; $s = 2n + 3$.

## Develop & Understand: B

This pattern of Z-shapes is made from small squares.

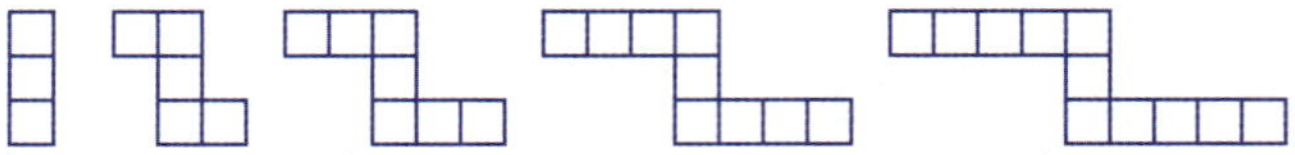


**3.** Complete the table.

| **Stage Number, *n*** | 0 | 1 | 2 | 3 | 4 | 5 | 9 | 10 |
|---|---|---|---|---|---|---|---|---|
| **Squares, *s*** | 3 | 5 | 7 | 9 | 11 | 13 | 21 | 23 |

**4.** Zach found that it took 21 squares to make stage 9. How many will it take for stage 10? Add two columns to your table for stages 9 and 10. See the table.

**5.** Explain how the number of squares in a stage is related to the stage number. Be sure your explanation will work for all stages. Write a symbolic rule for finding *s* if you know *n*.

**6.** Use your rule to predict how many squares are needed for stages 11 and 12. Draw the stages to test your rule. See below.

**7.** Explain how the two numbers in your rule relate to the pattern of Z-shapes.

## Develop & Understand: C

Now you will investigate this pattern of T-shapes.

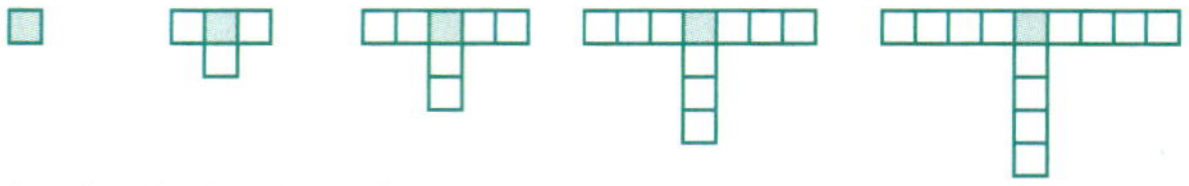


7. The 2 is how many squares are added at each stage; the 3 represents the 3 squares in the center column.

**8.** Complete the table.

| **Arm Length, *L*** | 0 | 1 | 2 | 3 | 4 | 5 | 100 | 1,000 |
|---|---|---|---|---|---|---|---|---|
| **Squares, *s*** | 1 | 4 | 7 | 10 | 13 | 16 | 301 | 3,001 |

6. Stage 11: 25 squares; Stage 12: 27 squares

9. Each arm has 100 squares, so three arms have 300 squares plus 1 in the center is 301. Each arm has 1,000 squares, so three arms have 3,000 plus 1 is 3,001.

**9.** How did you decide how many squares were needed to make a T-shape with arm length 100? With arm length 1,000?

**10.** Write a general formula or rule in words and then in symbols to relate the total number of squares to the arm length. Multiply the arm length by 3 and add 1; $s = 3L + 1$.

**11.** Use your formula to predict the number of squares for other arm lengths. Draw the shapes to check that your formula works. Possible answer: arm length 6: 19; arm length 10: 31

**12.** Explain how the two numbers in your formula relate to the T-shapes. The 3 is the number of squares added each time; the 1 is the teal square in the center.

**13.** Simon made a T-shape with 160 squares. Write and solve an equation to find its arm length. $160 = 3L + 1$, so $3L = 159$ and $L = 53$. The arm length is 53.

**14.** Could Simon make a T-shape with 100 squares? Explain your reasoning. Yes; $33 \cdot 3 + 1 = 100$, so the arm length would be 33.

**15.** Could Simon make a T-shape with 200 squares? Explain your reasoning. No; there is no whole number $L$ so that $3L + 1 = 200$.

### Share & Summarize

Look at the tables you made for the Z-shapes and the T-shapes. The numbers in the second row show how each pattern grows.

1. How much does each pattern grow from stage to stage?
2. For each table, compare the amount of growth with the rule you wrote. How is the growth reflected in the rule?
3. How does this growth relate to the rate of change?

1. Z-shapes grow by 2; T-shapes grow by 3.
2. The amount of growth is the number that is multiplied by the variable.
3. The amount of growth is the rate of change.



▶ **Exercise 10** The term *rule* is used with the term *formula* as students are asked to write the formula in words and in symbols.

▶ **Exercise 13** Students work backward from the total number of squares to find the arm length in the T-shape. This prepares them to solve the last two exercises.

▶ **Exercise 15** This exercise prepares students for the discussion of discrete sets of numbers. Simon cannot make a shape with 200 squares because there is no stage that uses this number of squares.

**Wrap-Up** Discuss Exercises 12–15 as a whole class. Students can tell how the numbers in the formula relate and share their strategies for solving the last three exercises.

### Share & Summarize

The purpose of these questions is to make students aware that the amount of growth from stage to stage in these patterns remains constant and that this amount of growth relates to the rate in the rule.

## Troubleshooting

If students have difficulties relating the amount of growth to the rate, use the table in Lesson 8.1, Exercise 18, that shows the amount Tamsin gets paid. Draw an analogy between the number of hours Tamsin worked (0, 1, 2, 3, ...) and the stage number in the pattern. Similarly, draw an analogy between the number of dollars she was paid and the number of tiles or squares in the pattern. Ask students the ways they figured out the rate of Tamsin's pay, and tell them to use the same strategy for figuring out the rule for the patterns.

# Investigation 2

***On Your Own Exercises***
Pages 423–430
Exercises 6–11, 18–20

**Draw Graphs** Students revisit patterns from Investigation 1 and draw graphs of the pairs of values generated by the patterns. Students will need graph paper or copies of Chapter 8 Master 1, Quarter-Inch Graph Paper, to complete exercises in Investigation 2.

### Think & Discuss

*Suggested Grouping: Pairs*

Ask students to draw a graph for the T-shape pattern. Students should be able to relate the rate in the rule to the slope of the graph and relate the constant term to the *y*-intercept of the graph.

Students already encountered the question about connecting the dots in the graph. This time there are no stages between stages 1 and 2 or 2 and 3, so there is no sense in connecting the points in this graph. These points are said to be discrete.

# Investigation 2 Graphs and Rules from Patterns

**Materials**

- graph paper

In the last investigation, you wrote rules to describe visual patterns. As you know, graphs can help you find rules for patterns.

### Think & Discuss

Look again at the T-shapes you studied on page 412.

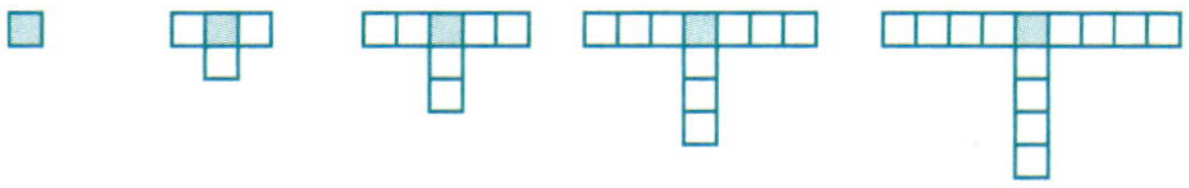


- Draw a graph of the table data shown below. Put the arm length on the horizontal axis. What is the shape of the graph? See ①.

| **Arm Length, *L*** | 0 | 1 | 2 | 3 | 4 | 5 |
|---|---|---|---|---|---|---|
| **Squares, *s*** | 1 | 4 | 7 | 10 | 13 | 16 |

- What is the rule for this pattern? $s = 3L + 1$
- Where do the two numbers in the rule appear in your graph? See ②.
- Does it make sense to connect the points in this graph? Why or why not? No; you cannot have a fraction of an arm length.

① The graph is a series of points that would lie on a line if they were connected.

**Pattern of T-Shapes**

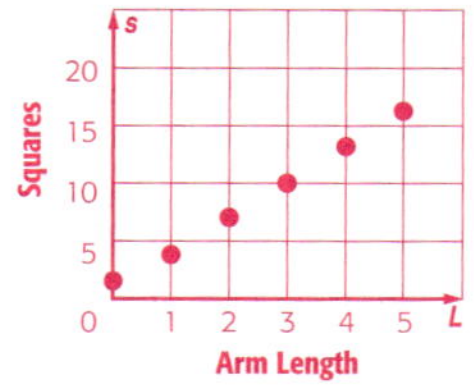


② The slope of the graph is 3, and the graph crosses the *s*-axis at 1.

As you have seen before, when you graph data for some situations, it can be helpful to sketch a line through the points even though you know not all of the points on the line make sense for the situation. The line can help you find other points that do make sense. It can also help you show the relationship between the variables.

If all the points on a line do not really make sense, draw a dashed line instead of a solid one. This will show that the line is not really part of the graph.



## Mathematical Background

Some mathematicians feel entirely comfortable sketching a solid line here to express the relationship of discrete points, as long as it is well understood that the picture does not represent all aspects of the relationship. A solid line can be a sketch—an approximation of sorts—rather than an explicit statement that all the points on it are really part of the table. What is important for your students is that they attend seriously to the domain of a relationship—what numbers can and cannot be inputs. It is then up to you and your students how explicit you want to make that understanding as you draw your graphs. However, the text frequently refers to drawing dashed lines to show this relationship.

## Develop & Understand: A

Look again at the Z-shape patterns from page 412.

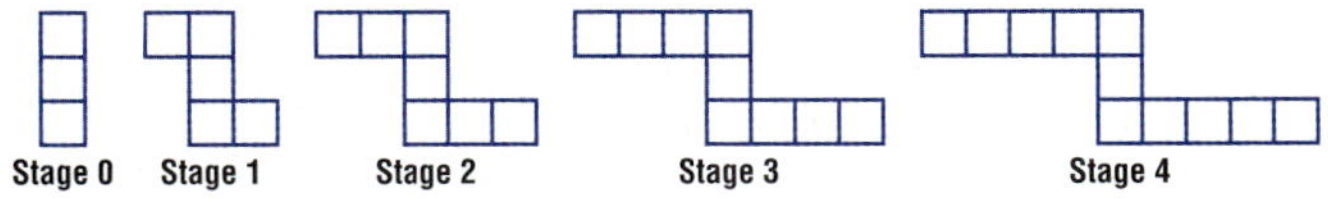


| Stage Number, $n$ | 0 | 1 | 2 | 3 | 9 |
|---|---|---|---|---|---|
| Squares, $s$ | 3 | 5 | 7 | 9 | 21 |

1. Would it make sense to connect points on a graph of these data? Explain. No; you cannot have a fraction of a stage number or of a square.
2. Draw a graph of the table data. Try to draw a line through the points. Use a dashed line or a solid line, whichever makes more sense.
3. What kind of pattern do the points make? Linear
4. Use your graph to predict the value of $s$ if $n$ is 8. Check with your table and your rule from Exercise 3 on page 412 to see if you are correct. 19
5. Use your graph to predict the value of $n$ if $s$ is 17. Check with your table and your rule to see if you are correct. 7
6. Does a point fall on the $s$-axis? What part of the pattern of Z-shapes does this show? It crosses the $s$-axis at 3, which is the number of squares for stage 0.
7. How does the slope of your line relate to the pattern of Z-shapes?
8. The rule for this pattern is $s = 2n + 3$. Explain where each number in the rule appears in your graph. The graph crosses the $s$-axis at 3; 2 is the slope of the line.

2. Pattern of Z-Shapes

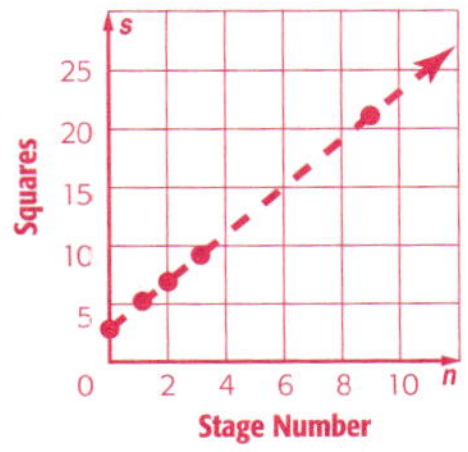


7. The slope is 2, which is the number of squares added at each stage.

## Develop & Understand: B

You investigated this pattern on page 411.

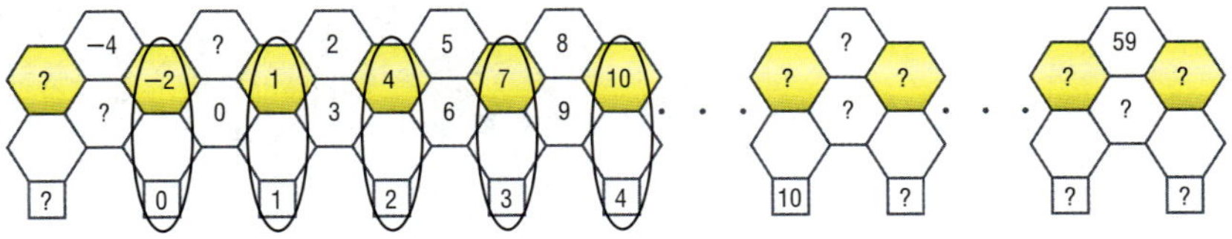


9. Five pairs of numbers have been circled, (0, −2), (1, 1), (2, 4), (3, 7), and (4, 10). What is the next pair of numbers in this sequence? (Note: This part of the pattern is not visible.) (5, 13)



## Develop & Understand: A

*Suggested Grouping: Pairs*

Students graph pairs of values generated from the pattern discussed in Exercises 1–5 of Investigation 1. From the graphs, they derive rules for the patterns. They will need graph paper or copies of Chapter 8 Master 1, Quarter-Inch Graph Paper, to solve these exercises.

▶ **Exercises 4, 5** You may want to remind students that their predictions may not exactly match the values in the table or the value they calculated using the rule. Unless the scale to graph the data is extremely large, predictions should fall within about two numbers of the value in the table.

**Wrap-Up** Discuss Exercises 2–4 together. Remind students that, though it does not make sense to connect the points because the values between the points do not exist, a dashed line helps one see the relationship and predict values for points not found in the table.

Then discuss Exercises 6–8 to revisit the concepts of slope and $y$-intercept on this graph and relate them to the structure of the pattern. The shape at Stage 0 has 3 squares; the $y$-intercept is 3. The slope of the line reflects the number of squares added on from stage to stage.

## Develop & Understand: B

*Suggested Grouping: Individuals or Pairs*

Students revisit the hexagon pattern they worked with in Exercise 1 of Investigation 1. In these exercises, the information about the pattern is given not in table form but as a set of coordinate pairs. Students practice the sequence **coordinates → graph → rule**.

### *Share & Summarize*

Exercise 1 assesses students' grasp of one of the major points developed in this investigation—the distinction between continuous and discrete graphs.

Exercise 2 assesses students' understanding of the second major emphasis of this investigation—the relations between the numbers in a rule and the features of its graph.

**10.** Plot the points from Exercise 9 on a copy of the grid shown below. If the points lie on a straight line, draw the line using a dashed or a solid line, whichever makes more sense.

**Hexagon Pattern**

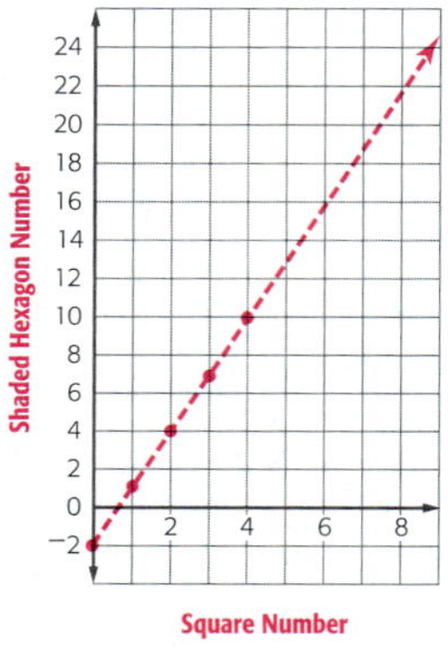


**11.** If you continue the sequence and graph the points, what would be the coordinates of the ninth point on the graph? Continue the pattern of hexagons. Check that your prediction is correct. (8, 22)

**12.** Use your graph to help you write a rule to link the two numbers in each pair. Choose letters to represent each variable. Check your rule with the pairs of values you already have. If the first number is $f$ and the second number is $s$, then $s = 3f - 2$.

**13.** Fill in the missing numbers in this part of the pattern. Use your rule to check your work.

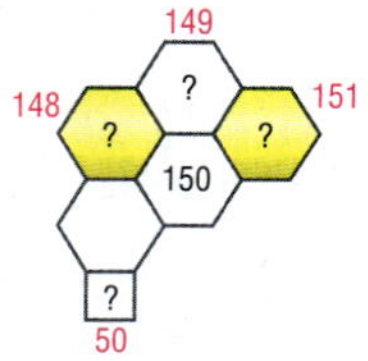


① Possible answer: It makes sense to connect points when one variable is the side length of a square and the other is the square's area. Length and area can be any positive number. It does not make sense when one variable is number of people and the other is total number of eyes. You cannot have a partial person.

### *Share & Summarize*

**1.** Describe a situation in which it makes sense to connect the points on a graph. Then describe a situation in which it does not make sense to connect the points on a graph. Explain your thinking. See ①.

**2.** What is the slope of the line described by the rule $y = -0.5x + 8$? What is the $y$-intercept of the line? −0.5; 8



## *Troubleshooting*

If students have trouble relating slope and $y$-intercept to numbers in the rule, review some of the graphs in this investigation again, and call students' attention to the $y$-intercept. Using examples, show them that this number is the constant term in the rule. Similarly, on all of these graphs, draw right triangles with a horizontal change of one unit, and draw students' attention to the fact that the vertical change in these triangles shows the rate in the rule.

# Investigation 3 From Rules to Graphs

**Materials**

- graph paper

In Investigation 2, you probably found that whenever a rule looked like

$y = ax + b$ (with numbers instead of $a$ and $b$)

the graph of the points formed part of a straight line. Whenever a rule looks like this, you can be sure that all the points in its graph will be on a straight line. This is why these relationships are called *linear*.

The table summarizes the relationships among the numbers in the rule $y = ax + b$, the features of the pattern described by this rule, and the features of the graph of this rule.

| In Patterns | On Graphs |
|---|---|
| As the quantity $x$ changes by 1 unit, the quantity $y$ changes by $a$ units. | The number $a$ is the slope of the line. It shows the rate at which $y$ changes as $x$ changes. |
| $b$ is the constant, or fixed, part of the pattern. | $b$ is the constant. It shows where the line crosses the $y$-axis. $b$ is called the $y$-intercept. |

You can tell a lot about how a graph will look just by inspecting its rule.

## Think & Discuss

Whose equation is correct? How could you explain to the other two students why they are incorrect? Simon's ($y = x + 2$); Possible explanation: Jin Lee: Point out that if $x$ is 0, $y$ would be $-2$ in her equation; Zoe: Point out that the slope must be 1, not 2.



# Investigation 3

***On Your Own Exercises***
Pages 423–430
Exercises 12, 13, 21

**Standard Form** Students link the symbolic and graphical representations of linear relationships. Students learn to rewrite the relationship in standard form.

In the beginning of the investigation, students can read a table that summarizes the relations between the structure of the pattern, the numbers in the corresponding rule, and the features of the corresponding graph. Remind them that these connections are appropriate only for linear relationships and are not appropriate for any other kind of relationships (quadratic, cubic, exponential, etc.).

Any relationship that can be expressed in the form $y = ax + b$ is linear; all linear relationships can be expressed in that form, but they can also be expressed in other forms.

Students might use a graphing calculator or one of the computer graphing packages. Be sure students have a supply of graph paper or copies of Chapter 8 Master 1, Quarter-Inch Graph Paper, to complete exercises in this Investigation.

## Think & Discuss

*Suggested Grouping: Whole Class*

Ask students to read the cartoon and decide who has a correct rule for the graph. Ask several students in your class to provide these explanations for the whole class. Discuss their reasoning with the rest of the class.

## Develop & Understand: A

*Suggested Grouping: Pairs*

This exercise set provides practice matching rules with their graphs through a two-person game. Allow about 15 minutes for this exercise set. Students will need graph paper or copies of Chapter 8 Master 1, Quarter-Inch Graph Paper, to complete the exercise set.

▶ **Exercise 1** The rules are specially designed so that pairs of them are similar in all but one feature. For example, $c = 2d + 3$ and $c = d + 3$ differ only by the value of the slope. This should help students to pay closer attention to the individual features of the rules and how they relate to the features of the graphs. Students don't have to graph all nine rules if they seem to be clear about the connections after graphing only a few equations.

▶ **Exercise 3** This exercise introduces the rules in a nonstandard form, which may be a challenge for some students. Although students have had no formal experience with strategies for transforming a rule into a standard form in order to graph it, the rules are made simple enough so students can intuitively find ways to calculate $y$ for each $x$. Students are not expected to master graphing linear relationships in a nonstandard form. The purpose of this exercise is to make them aware that other forms of rules can produce lines.

**Wrap-Up** Discuss the text after this exercise set that defines a standard form of a linear relationship and provides examples of rules in standard and nonstandard forms.

**Additional Answers for Exercises 1 and 3 on pages 433B and 433C.**

## Develop & Understand: A

You and a partner are going to play a detective game. One of you will draw a graph for one of the rules below. The other will be the detective, looking for clues in the graph to decide which rule was used.

| | |
|---|---|
| $c = 2d + 3$ | $c = 10 + d$ |
| $c = d + 3$ | $c = d + 4$ |
| $c = -2d + 3$ | $c = 10 - 2d$ |
| $c = 2d - 1$ | $c = 10 + 2d$ |
| $c = 10 - d$ | |

1. Take turns drawing and being the detective until each of you has drawn four graphs. Use $d$ for the horizontal axis and $c$ for the vertical axis. See margin.
2. Explain in a few sentences how you matched each graph with an equation.

Here is another set of equations that can be graphed. These equations are not quite like the others, so you may need to look harder for clues.

| | |
|---|---|
| $x = 7 + y$ | $2x = 2(6 - y)$ |
| $x = 7 - y$ | $3x = 3y - 9$ |
| $2x = 2(6 + y)$ | $3x = 3y + 9$ |

3. Take turns drawing and being the detective until you and your partner have each drawn two graphs. Use $x$ for the horizontal axis and $y$ for the vertical axis. See margin.
4. Explain how you matched each graph with an equation.

Most of the equations you have encountered in this chapter describe linear relationships in the form $y = ax + b$, for example, $y = 2x + 7$. Linear relationships can also be described by other forms of equations.

A graph is a good way to figure out whether a relationship written in a form other than $y = ax + b$ is linear. A graph will also help you to find the answers to Exercises 5–7.

2. Possible answer: I looked at where the line intersected the vertical axis, which gave me the constant term for the rule. If the graph went down from left to right, the slope was negative, so I could narrow my choices further. Then if I needed to, I looked closer to see if the slope was 1 or 2 (or −1 or −2).
4. Possible answer: The slopes and intercepts were harder to see in these rules, so I rewrote them first. Then I used the same strategy as before.



### Reaching All Learners

**AL Approaching Level** Watch for students who have no strategy for determining how to draw the graphs and match them to the equations in Exercise 3. You might suggest the problem-solving strategy *make a table or chart.* Suggest that students make a table of $x$ and $y$ values in order to make the graphs and then have their partners independently make their own tables in order to check the match between the graph and the rule.

## Develop & Understand: B

A fitness test has two parts, skipping and running in place. For each part of the test, you can earn a whole-number score from 0 to 10. Your total score is given by the rule

$$\text{total score} = s + r$$

where $s$ is the skipping score and $r$ is the running score.

**5.** To be classified as "fit," you need a total score of at least 15. Use a grid like this one to represent all the ways a person doing this test could earn *just enough* points to be judged "fit." See the dots and the dashed line.

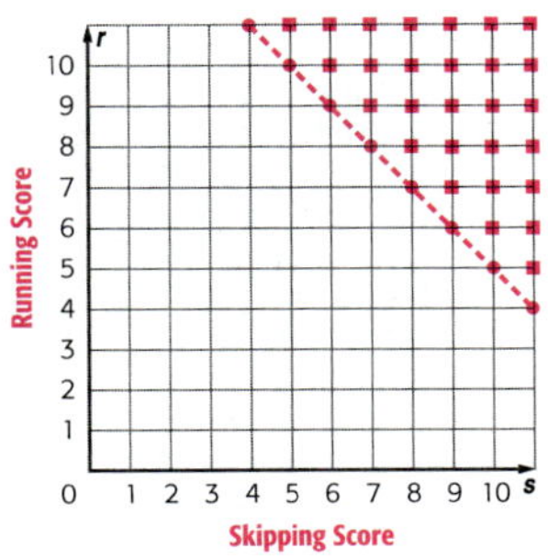


**Math Link**

If some of the points on a line do not make sense, draw a dashed line instead of a solid one.

**6.** Use the same grid to represent *all* the ways a person could be judged fit. Use a different color from Exercise 5. See the squares on the graph.

**7.** Which of the following describe the possible scores for fit people? Explain your reasoning.

$s + r = 15$ $\qquad$ $s + r \leq 15$ $\qquad$ $s + r \geq 15$

7. $s + r \geq 15$ because $s + r$ must be at least 15 in order for a person to be judged fit.

### Share & Summarize

**Consider these four equations.**

$$10 - 2d = 2c \qquad 2c = 2(5 - d)$$
$$2(c + d) = 10 \qquad d = 5 - c$$

**1.** Draw graphs of the equations, and discuss what you notice. Put $c$ on the horizontal axis.

**2.** Explain *why* what you noticed is happening. See below.

**3.** Find some other equations that fit the pattern. Possible answer: $10 = 2c + 2d$, $5 = c + d$, $c = 5 - d$

1. All four graphs coincide.

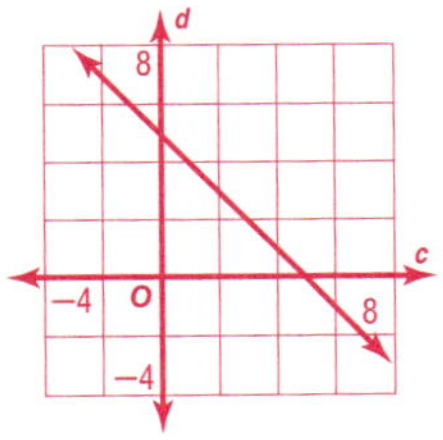


2. Possible explanation: For each $c$, all four equations produce the same $d$.



## Develop & Understand: B

*Suggested Grouping: Whole Class*

▶ **Exercise 5** Students essentially graph the rule $s + r = 15$ taking into account the constraints $s < 11$ and $r < 11$.

▶ **Exercise 6** You might write all three constraints on the chalkboard. Ask students to write all pairs of numbers $(s, r)$ they can come up with that satisfy these constraints and then plot them on their grids. Then ask students how these points relate to the constraints on the board. Finally ask students to graph the constraints. This may be an unfamiliar way to graph data for some students. You may want to have a completed graph against which students can check their answers.

▶ **Exercise 7** Ask students which of the following rules describe the scores for fit people. Then have them explain their answers. Depending on your class, you may want to have students notice that the correct rule $s + r \geq 15$ does not consider the constraints on $s$ and $r$ since it includes points such as (100, 100).

### Share & Summarize

In Exercise 1, students should notice that all four rules represent the same graph.

They may explain this situation differently in Exercise 2. For example, they can say that each rule produces the same $d$ for each $c$. Or they can say that these rules are different forms of the same rule. Or they can say that you can get one rule from another by some manipulations.

**Wrap-Up** Don't worry too much if some students remain puzzled that different formulas can describe the same relationship and be represented by the same graph. They will return to this idea later in the year.

# Investigation 4

***On Your Own Exercises***
Pages 423–430
Exercises 1–3, 16

**Find a Rule** The exercises in this investigation require that students describe a pattern symbolically. You will need to have copies of Chapter 8 Master 1, Quarter-Inch Graph Paper, or graph paper available for students as they complete the exercises in this investigation.

You may wish to briefly review how to play *What's My Rule?* before students start working on the exercises in the first exercise set.

## Develop & Understand: A

*Suggested Grouping: Pairs*

Students use input and output pairs from given *What's My Rule?* games to find relationships. They do not actually play the games themselves.

▶ **Exercises 1, 2** Students use data from the cartoons to make graphs and write symbolic rules for the number pairs. Be sure that they understand the importance of telling what each variable in their rule stands for.

▶ **Exercise 2** Watch for students who sometimes graph an input value as the $x$-coordinate and sometimes as a $y$-coordinate in the same graph. Review the problem-solving strategy *Make a table or chart.* Students may need to list the input/output values in a T-chart, table, or other list to organize their data before plotting the points.

# Investigation 4 Secret Rules

**Materials**
- graph paper

You can use some of the things you have learned about relationships to help you discover the secret rules in games of *What's My Rule?*

## Develop & Understand: A

Several students are playing *What's My Rule?*

**1.** In this game, Shaunda is the Rule Keeper, and Luis is the Guesser.

**a.** On a graph, plot the pairs of inputs and outputs. Decide whether the relationship could be linear. See margin.

**b.** Find a symbolic rule that fits the number pairs. Choose letters for the inputs and outputs. Be careful to make it clear which is which. Possible rule: $b = 2a + 3$, where $a$ is the input and $b$ is the output

**2.** In this game, Darnell is the Rule Keeper and Kate is the Guesser.

**a.** On a graph, plot the pairs of inputs and outputs. Decide whether the relationship could be linear. See margin.

**b.** Find a symbolic rule that fits the numbers. Choose letters for the inputs and outputs. Make it clear which is which. Possible rule: $q = 3p - 4$, where $p$ is the input and $q$ is the output

**Math Link**
One Rule Keeper and any number of Guessers can play *What's My Rule?* The Rule Keeper makes up a secret rule that takes inputs and produces outputs. Guessers give inputs to the Rule Keeper, who gives outputs until someone guesses the rule.



**Additional Answers**

1a. The points lie on a line, so it could be linear.

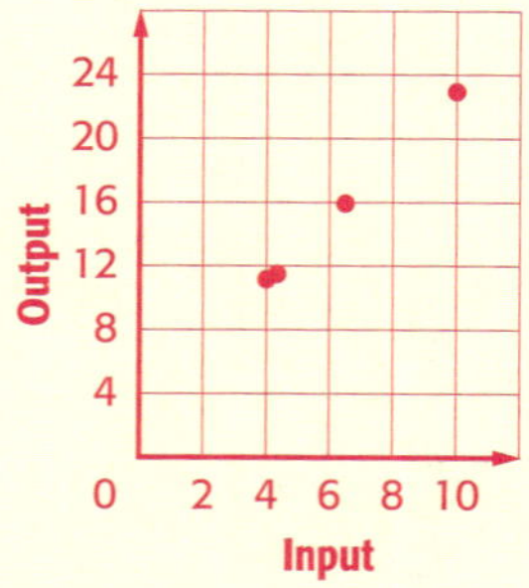


2a. The points lie on a line, so it could be linear.

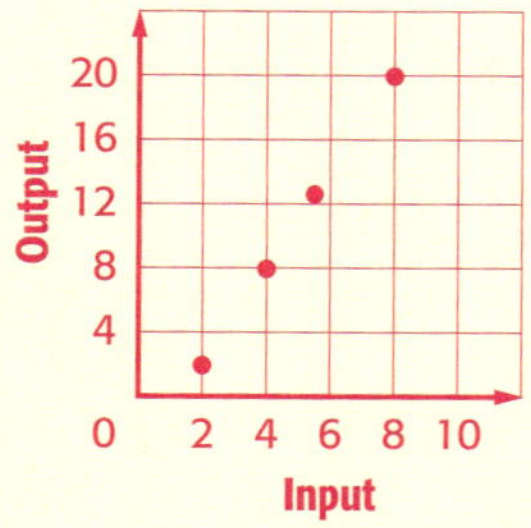

3. The points do not lie on a line, so it is not linear. The rule could be $y = x^2$.
4. The points lie on a line, so it could be linear. The rule could be $y = 10 - x$.

**For each set of input/output pairs, tell whether the relationship could be linear. Then find a rule that fits the pairs.**

3. (4, 16), (1, 1), $\left(\frac{1}{2}, \frac{1}{4}\right)$, (3, 9)
4. (10, 0), (2, 8), (4.5, 5.5), (5, 5)
5. Jin Lee is the class *What's My Rule?* champion. Her secret is to plot points to see whether they lie along a line. If the rule describes a linear relationship, she can look at the graph and guess a rule that fits the points.

   Explain how Jin Lee might derive a rule from the graph. Use illustrations, if you like. See margin.

## Develop & Understand: B

Jin Lee developed a quick strategy for finding rules in the game. She found that if she chooses consecutive integers as inputs, she can tell whether the relationship could be linear *just by looking at how the outputs change*. Look at the numbers she collected for four games she played.

**Game 1**

| Input | 1 | 2 | 3 | 4 | 5 |
|---|---|---|---|---|---|
| Output | 4 | 7 | 10 | 13 | 16 |

**Game 2**

| Input | 0 | 1 | 2 | 3 | 4 |
|---|---|---|---|---|---|
| Output | 1 | 6 | 11 | 16 | 21 |

**Game 3**

| Input | 0 | 1 | 2 | 3 | 4 |
|---|---|---|---|---|---|
| Output | 29 | 27 | 25 | 23 | 21 |

**Game 4**

| Input | 2 | 3 | 4 | 5 | 6 |
|---|---|---|---|---|---|
| Output | 10 | 15 | 21 | 28 | 36 |

**Additional Answer**

5. Possible answer: She could find the slope using the rise and run from one point to another. Then she could multiply the slope by one input and subtract the result from the output. The rule is the slope times an input plus the result from the subtraction.

▶ **Exercises 3 and 4** Students will probably need to graph the points to determine whether the relationship is linear, even though this is not specified in their textbooks.

**Wrap-Up** Discuss Exercise 5 as a class. Have students share any illustrations they made. This trick allows students to use what they have learned about slope and about what the terms in a rule signify.

## Develop & Understand: B

*Suggested Grouping: Pairs*

Students deduce the strategy of looking for constant differences that Jin Lee uses for finding out the rule. The strategy relies on her choice of consecutive numbers as input numbers. This is important because by choosing consecutive whole numbers, the difference in the outputs (if it is constant) is the slope of the graph, or $a$ in the rule $y = ax + b$.

Students find the value of $b$ by finding the output when the input is 0. This can be done in *What's My Rule?* games just by giving the input of 0. In the case of the tables, some of which do not contain 0 as input, students must extend the table backward.

Some of the students may try to guess the rule without graphing the points by simply calculating the differences between input and output numbers. This works quite well as long as the input numbers differ by 1. However this method is incomplete if the input numbers differ by more or less than 1, even if they are equally spaced. Encourage students to check their guess with a graph.

**Wrap-Up** Have the students explain their strategies for finding the rule. Their wording may vary, but if their ideas do not at least paraphrase the key techniques—using consecutive whole numbers, attending to constant differences, and finding output value when input is 0—you might refer back to an exercise.

**Share & Summarize**

Ask students: *What kinds of input/output pairs can you not expect to figure out from a graph?* Any that would require too large a graph, too much precision in reading the graph, etc. For these, the rule allows one to calculate new entries more easily.

A class discussion of these questions, possibly livened up with a game of *What's My Rule?* can help students articulate the strategies sought in the Wrap-Up.

6. Jin Lee concluded that Games 1, 2, and 3 could be linear, but Game 4 could not be. Inspect her tables of input/output pairs. What pattern might have led Jin Lee to her decision? If the output increases or decreases by equal amounts, the relationship could be linear.

7. For each game that Jin Lee thinks could be linear, write a symbolic rule that fits all the input/output pairs. Choose letters for the inputs and outputs. Be careful to say which is which.

7. Game 1. input $m$, output $n$: $n = 3m + 1$ Game 2. input $d$, output $c$: $c = 5d + 1$ Game 3. input $v$, output $z$: $z = 29 - 2v$

8. Make a graph for each of the four games. Extend your graphs. Use them to estimate the output each game's rule would give for an input of $-3$. Which estimates are you confident are most accurate? Explain. See margin.

**Share & Summarize**

1. Using just a graph, you can tell whether a rule could describe a linear relationship. How? If the points lie on a line, the relationship could be linear.

2. Using just a table with consecutive integers for inputs, you can tell whether a rule could describe a linear relationship. How?

2. If the differences between consecutive outputs are constant, the relationship could be linear.

3. Suppose a table shows some input/output pairs in a linear relationship. How can you use a graph of the table values to find other input/output pairs? Draw a line through the plotted points, and then find coordinates for other points on the line.



**Additional Answer**

8. Estimates will vary, but those for Games 1–3 should be close; actual outputs: Game 1: –8; Game 2: –14; Game 3: 35; Game 4: 0. Possible explanation: The estimates for Games 1–3 are probably accurate, because you can draw a line through the points and read the output for an input of –3. Game 4 isn't linear, so you can't be sure how the graph curves beyond the data points.

## Practice & Apply

**In Exercises 1–3, do Parts a and b.**

**a.** Plot the input/output pairs. Decide whether the rule could be linear.

**b.** If you think the rule could be linear, find a rule that fits the numbers and write it in symbols.

1a. Could be linear.

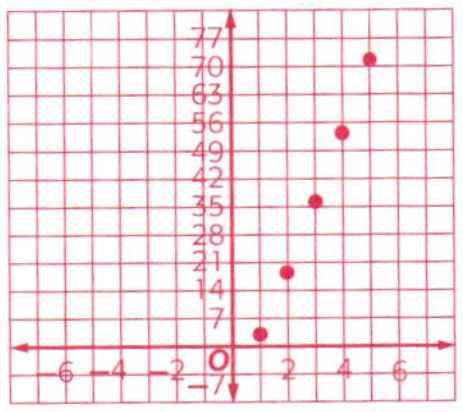


1b. $y = 17x - 14$

**1.**

| Input | 1 | 2 | 3 | 4 | 5 |
|---|---|---|---|---|---|
| Output | 3 | 20 | 37 | 54 | 71 |

2a. Could be linear.

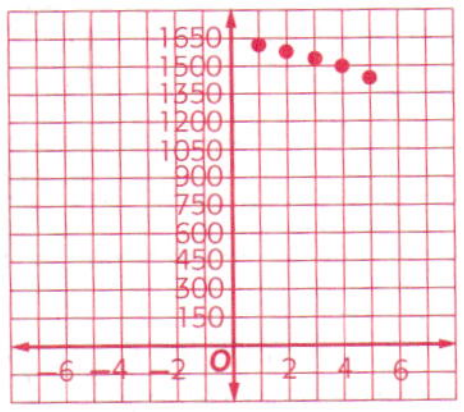


2b. $y = -38x + 1{,}637$

**2.**

| Input | 1 | 2 | 3 | 4 | 5 |
|---|---|---|---|---|---|
| Output | 1,599 | 1,561 | 1,523 | 1,485 | 1,447 |

3a. Could not be linear.

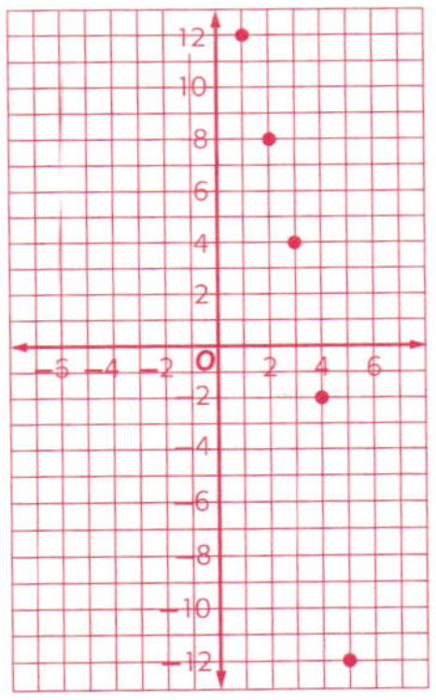


**3.**

| Input | 1 | 2 | 3 | 4 | 5 |
|---|---|---|---|---|---|
| Output | 12 | 8 | 4 | −2 | −12 |

**4.** Shaunda made this pattern from toothpicks.

**a.** How many toothpicks are needed for stage 4? For stage 5? 21, 26

**b.** Shaunda used 56 toothpicks to make stage 11. How many would it take to make stage 12? 61

**c.** Copy and complete the table.

| Stage, $n$ | 0 | 1 | 2 | 3 | 4 | 5 | 11 | 12 |
|---|---|---|---|---|---|---|---|---|
| Toothpicks, $t$ | 1 | 6 | 11 | 16 | 21 | 26 | 56 | 61 |

**d.** Describe a general rule that shows how you can find the number of toothpicks from the stage number. Write the rule in symbols. Check that your rule works on all pairs of numbers in the table.
Multiply the stage number by 5 and add 1; $t = 5n + 1$.

**e.** Use your rule to predict the number of toothpicks for two other stages. Test your prediction by building or drawing the stages.
Possible answer: Stage 6, 31; Stage 7, 36

**f.** Use the way the pattern grows from stage to stage to explain why your rule always works. Stage 0 starts with 1 toothpick, and each stage adds 5 toothpicks. So for $n$ stages, $5n$ toothpicks are added to the original 1.



**On Your Own Exercises**
**Lesson 8.3**

**Investigation 1**
Pages 411–413
Practice & Apply: 4, 5
Connect & Extend: 14, 15, 17

**Investigation 2**
Pages 414–416
Practice & Apply: 6–11
Connect & Extend: 18–20

**Investigation 3**
Pages 417–419
Practice & Apply: 12–13
Connect & Extend: 21

**Investigation 4**
Pages 420–422
Practice & Apply: 1–3
Connect & Extend: 16

**Assign Anytime**
Mixed Review: 23–34

▶ **Exercise 5** Some students may have difficulty identifying the pattern. If they need a hint, tell them that no matter what the length, the end tiles are the same. Any change affects only the sets of four tiles in the middle.

▶ **Exercises 6 and 7** Watch for students who try to graph on a grid with four quadrants. While the end result may not be incorrect, it is more common to make a graph with only one quadrant when there are no negative numbers.

**Additional Answers**

6b. Possible answer: The number of white tiles is 2 side lengths taken 4 times, added to 4 tiles at each of the 4 corners; $b = 4(2s) + 4(4) = 8s + 16$.

6c.

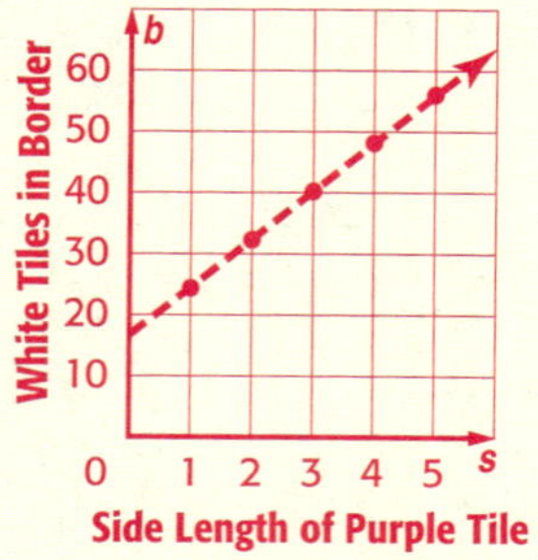


6d. Yes; this is expected because the numbers increase by 8 each time.



**5.** The patio tilers, Pat and Tillie, designed a tile pattern that can be adapted for floors of various sizes. The strip of tiles can be any length, as long as it begins and ends with a column of white tiles.

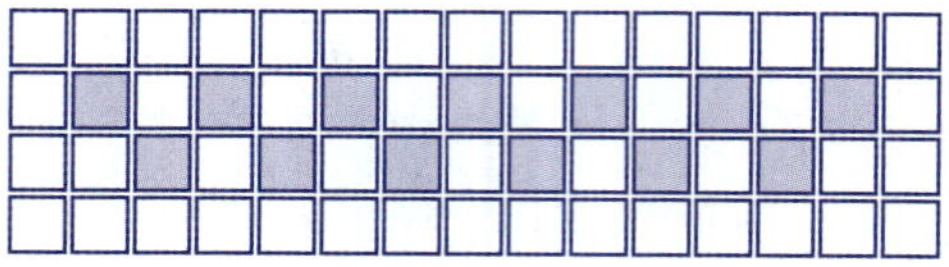

Write a rule for the pattern, giving the relation between the number of white tiles and the number of purple tiles for various lengths of the strip. $w = 3p + 8$

6b–d. See margin.

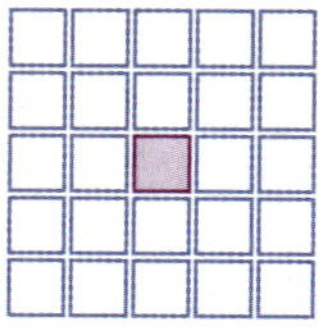

Side length 1

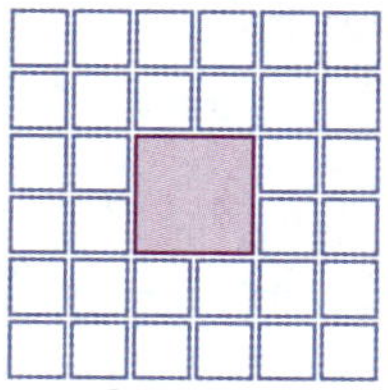

Side length 2

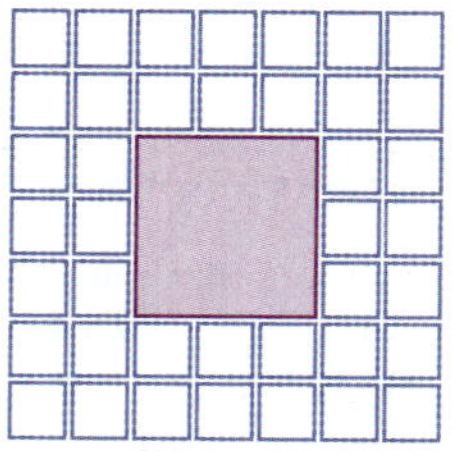

Side length 3

**6.** Sabrina and Rosalinda made a sequence of tile designs from square white tiles surrounding one square purple tile. The purple tiles come in many sizes. Three of the designs are shown at left.

**a.** Copy and complete the table.

| Side Length of Purple Tile, $s$ | 1 | 2 | 3 | 4 | 5 | 10 | 100 |
|---|---|---|---|---|---|---|---|
| White Tiles in Border, $b$ | 24 | 32 | 40 | 48 | 56 | 96 | 816 |

**b.** Find a rule to link the number of white tiles in the border to the side length of the purple tile. Describe the rule in words and symbols.

**c.** Draw a graph using the first five pairs of numbers in your table. When graphing an ordered pair, refer to the horizontal axis for the first number and to the vertical axis for the second number.

**d.** Do the points lie on a line? Is this what you expected? Tell why or why not.

**7.** Rick and Cheri, who are also patio tilers, created a different type of patio.

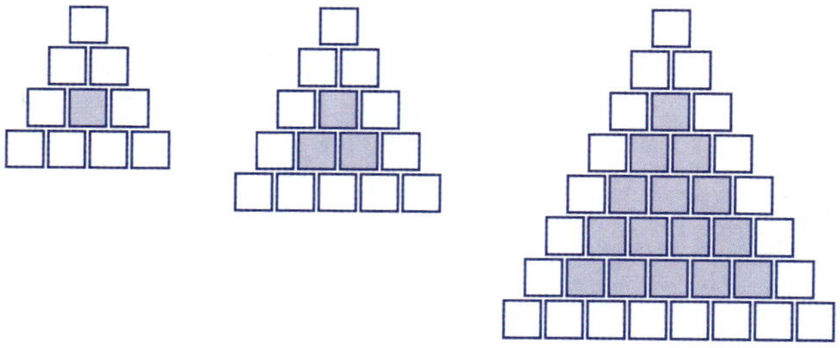

a. Complete the table.

| Rows, $r$ | 4 | 5 | 8 |
|---|---|---|---|
| White Tiles, $w$ | 9 | 12 | 21 |
| Purple Tiles, $p$ | 1 | 3 | 15 |

7b.

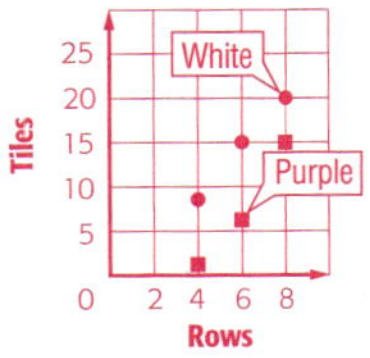


b. Make a graph that shows how the number of rows relates to the number of white tiles. Make another graph that shows how the number of rows relates to the number of purple tiles. Put the number of rows on the horizontal axis.

c. Which graph is linear, the graph for the white tiles or the graph for the purple tiles? Write a rule for the linear graph. Check it with the numbers in the table. White; $w = 3r - 3$

**For each equation, draw a graph with $x$ on the horizontal axis and $y$ on the vertical axis. Draw four-quadrant graphs. Include negative values for both $x$ and $y$.** 8–11. See margin.

8. $0.4y = 3x - 7$

9. $y = 5(x + 5)$

10. $y - 3x = 6$

11. $2.5(y + x) = 9$

12. Match each equation with one of the graphs below.

a. $y = 2x$ iv

b. $y = 0.5x$ i

c. $3y + 1.5x = 11$ iii

d. $x = 0.3(y - 4)$ ii

i.

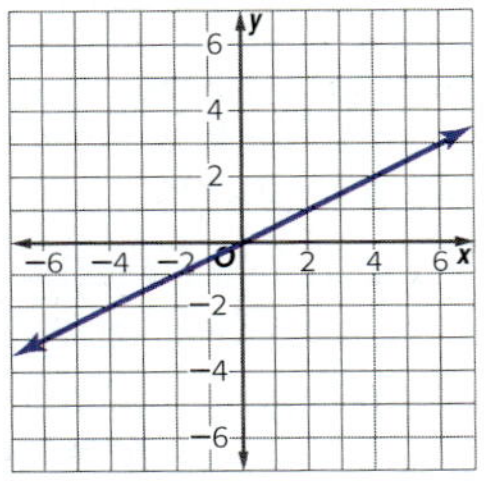

ii.

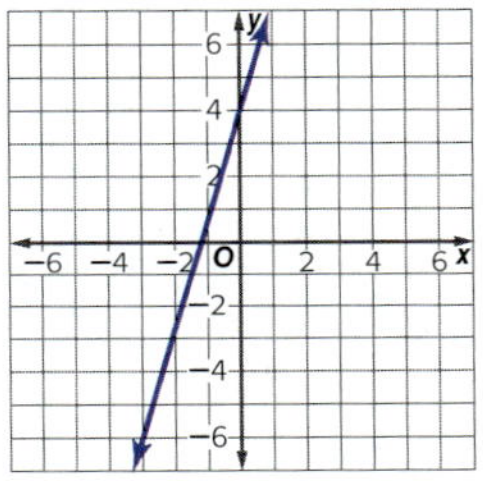

iii.

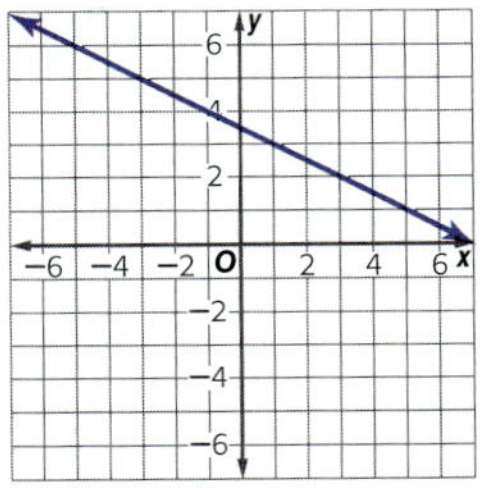

iv.

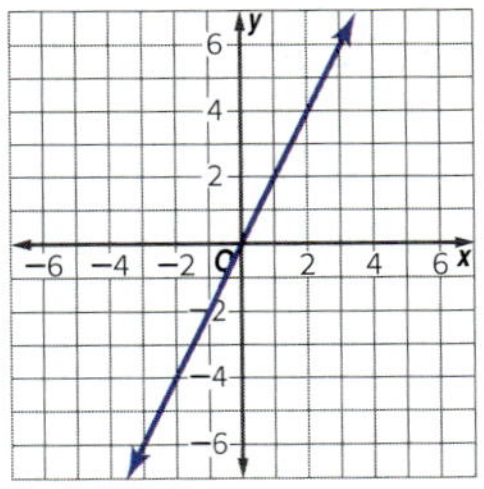



On Your Own Exercises

**Additional Answers**

8–11.

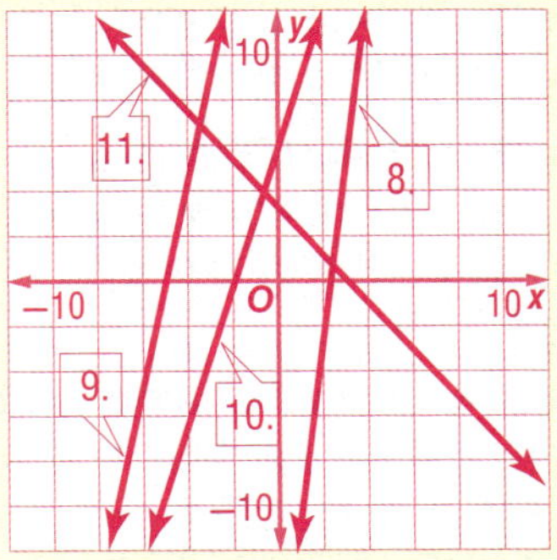


Lesson 8.3 Recognize Linear Relationships 425

▶ **Exercise 13a** Be sure students understand they are to use the entire rope, or 20 meters, to mark the entire border.

▶ **Exercise 13e** Students consider a shorter portion of the 20-meter rope for this exercise. They plot points showing an inequality.

▶ **Exercise 13f** You might want to suggest that students check a part outside the shaded area they are testing. This may make them feel more confident about their answers, but it does not ensure that their answer is correct.

**Additional Answers**

13b. **Dimensions of Rectangles**

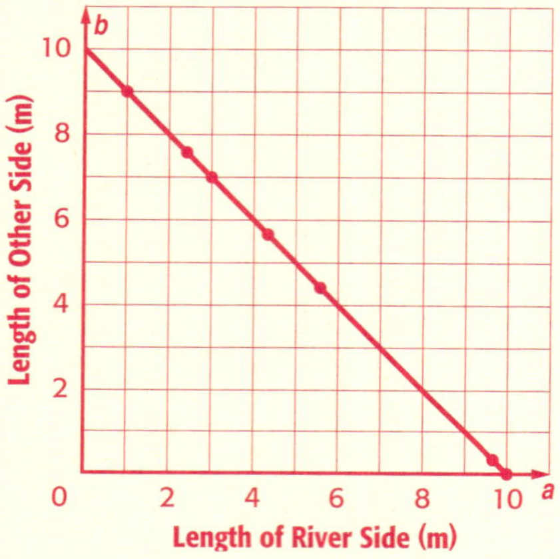


13e. Possible answer: 1 × 6, 2 × 4, 2 × 3, 4 × 5, 7.5 × 1

**Dimensions of Rectangles**

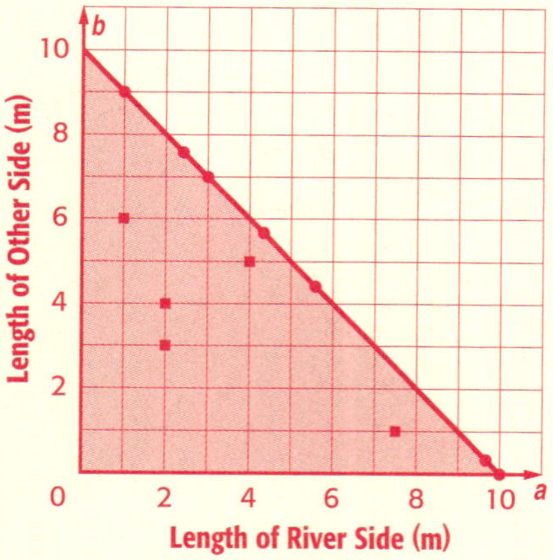


On Your Own Exercises

**13.** When Zoe's family checked into a campground, the manager gave them a 20-meter piece of rope. He said they could mark out any campsite they liked, as long as its border was no longer than the rope.

**a.** Zoe suggested they use all the rope to make a rectangular shape. She chose some values for the side of the rectangle they wanted to place facing the river. Then she calculated the other side of the rectangle. Copy and complete her table.

| Length of River Side (meters), *a* | 0 | 1 | 2.5 | 3 | 4.2 | 5.5 | 9.9 | 10 |
|---|---|---|---|---|---|---|---|---|
| Length of Other Side (meters), *b* | 10 | 9 | 7.5 | 7 | 5.8 | 4.5 | 0.1 | 0 |

**b.** Draw a graph to show all possible side lengths for a rectangle with a 20-meter perimeter. Put the length of the river side on the horizontal axis. See margin.

**c.** Does it make sense to connect the points? Why or why not? Yes; sides can have fractional lengths, not just whole-number lengths.

**d.** Use your graph to write a rule relating *a* and *b*. Possible rule: $b = 10 - a$

**e.** The length of rope was the *maximum* border Zoe's family could use. They could also have used less rope. List the dimensions of five other rectangles that would be acceptable but that use less rope. Plot points on your graph to represent these rectangles. See margin.

**f.** What do you notice about the location of the points you chose, in relation to the line? On your grid, shade the region that includes these points. The points are all on the same side of the line; see graph in answer to Part e.

**g.** Which equation or inequality below describes the shaded region of your graph? Explain in words what it means.

$2(a + b) = 20 \qquad 2(a + b) \leq 20 \qquad 2(a + b) \geq 20$

13g. $2(a + b) \leq 20$; The lengths of all four sides add to 20 or less than 20.

**h.** Choose some points in the shaded region, other than the points in Part e. Test these points in the equation or inequality you chose for Part g. What do you notice? Possible answers: (2, 6); (1, 4); (3, 3); all make the inequality true.

*On Your Own Exercises*

## Connect & Extend

**14.** This tiling pattern can be any length as long as the pattern is complete. The first two columns and last two columns must look as shown here. Write a rule for the pattern, giving the relation between the number of white tiles and the number of purple tiles for various strip lengths. $p = w + 5$; $w$ must be 2, 5, 8, 11, ... .

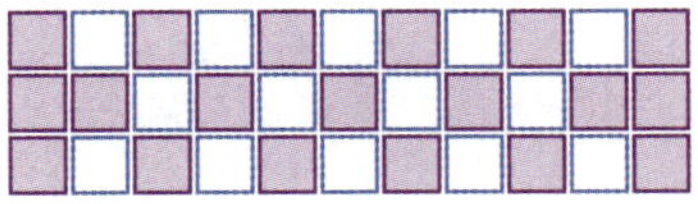

▶ **Exercise 14** Some students may not see the restriction on $w$ in this exercise.

**15.** Invent a tiling pattern that shows a *linear* relationship between the number of purple tiles and the number of white tiles.

**a.** Draw a few examples of your pattern.

15a. Possible pattern:

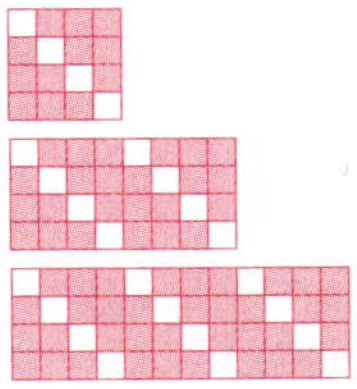

**b.** Create a table that shows the number of purple tiles and the number of white tiles for your examples. See margin.

**c.** Write a symbolic rule for that relationship. Possible answer: $p = 3w$

**16.** This set of squares is made from toothpicks.

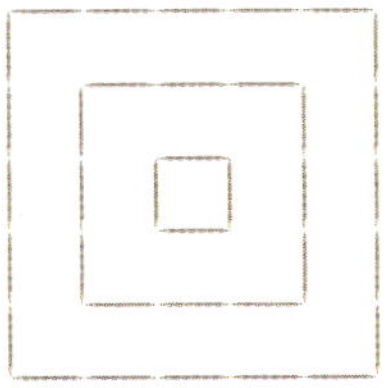

**a.** How many toothpicks are needed for each square shown? Outer: 20; Middle: 12; Inner: 4

**b.** Copy and complete the table.

| **Toothpicks along side of square** | 1 | 3 | 5 | 7 | 9 | 11 | 15 | 19 |
|---|---|---|---|---|---|---|---|---|
| **Toothpicks to make square** | 4 | 12 | 20 | 28 | 36 | 44 | 60 | 76 |

**c.** The relationship shown in the table is linear. How could you prove this with a graph?

16c. If you graph the pairs of values, they will lie on a line.

**d.** How could you prove the relationship is linear by inspecting the table?

16d. The differences between consecutive inputs (toothpicks along side of square) and their outputs (toothpicks to make square) are both constant.

**e.** Write a rule to calculate the number of toothpicks needed to make a square for a given number of toothpicks along the side of the square. $p = 4s$, where $p$ is the number of toothpicks needed to make the square and $s$ is the number of toothpicks along each side.



**Additional Answer**

15b. Possible answer:

| **White Tiles, *w*** | 4 | 8 | 12 |
|---|---|---|---|
| **Purple Tiles, *p*** | 12 | 24 | 36 |

▶ **Exercise 17a and 17c** You may wish to have a discussion allowing students to share their patterns from 17a and their answers for 17c.

**Additional Answers**

17b. Possible answer:

| Yellow Tiles, $y$ | 1 | 2 | 3 | 4 |
|---|---|---|---|---|
| Green Tiles, $g$ | 0 | 2 | 6 | 12 |

19a.

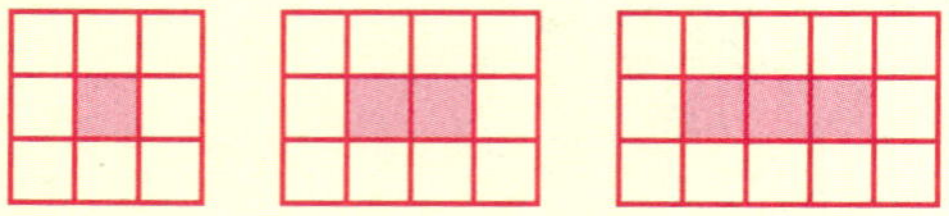

19c. Possible table:

| Purple Tiles, $p$ | 2 | 4 | 6 | 8 | 10 |
|---|---|---|---|---|---|
| White Tiles, $w$ | 10 | 14 | 18 | 22 | 26 |

19d. **Tile Walkway**

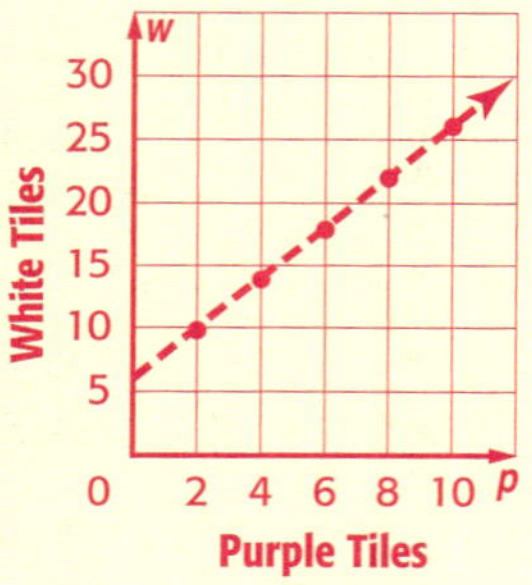


On Your Own Exercises

17a. Possible pattern:

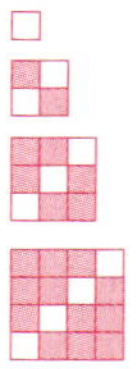

17c. Possible answer: If you graph the table values, the points do not lie on a straight line.

18.

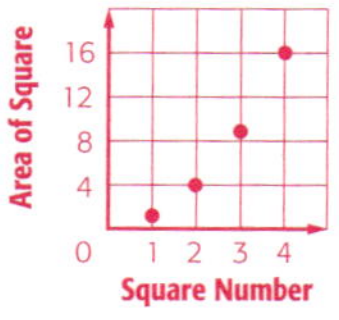


17. **Challenge** Invent a tiling pattern with green tiles and yellow tiles in which the relationship between the numbers of green tiles and yellow tiles is *nonlinear*.

   a. Illustrate your pattern with a few examples.

   b. Make a table for your pattern. See margin.

   c. Write a clear explanation of how you know the relationship is nonlinear.

   d. If possible, write a rule describing the relationship between the number of yellow tiles and the number of green tiles in your pattern. Possible answer: $g = y^2 - y$

18. Look back at your table for Exercise 2 on page 411. The pattern in that table is different from most of the patterns you worked with in this investigation. Draw a graph for the pairs of numbers in that table.

19. Pat and Tillie often tile walkways by surrounding a single strip of purple tiles with white tiles. Here is one walkway that they made with 9 purple tiles. 19a, 19c, 19d. See margin.

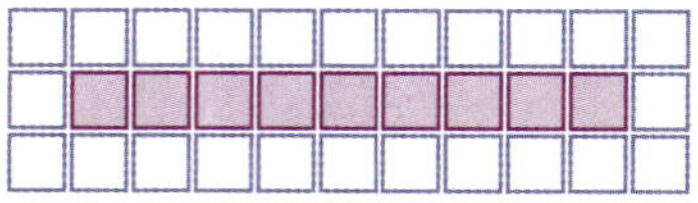

   a. Draw this pattern for 1, 2, and 3 purple tiles.

   b. Write a rule that relates the number of white tiles $w$ to the number of purple tiles $p$. $w = 2p + 6$

   c. Use your rule to make a table of values for the tiles needed for walkways of different lengths.

   d. Draw a graph from your table. Put the number of purple tiles on the horizontal axis. Connect the points using a dashed line or a solid line, whichever makes more sense.

   e. How are the two numbers in your rule shown in your graph? The line crosses the $w$-axis at 6 and has a slope of 2.

   f. How do these two numbers relate to the pattern of tiles in the walkway? The 2 is multiplied by $p$ because there are 2 rows of white tiles, 1 on each side of and equal in length to the row of purple tiles. The 6 shows that there are 3 + 3 white tiles on the ends of these 3 rows.

20b.

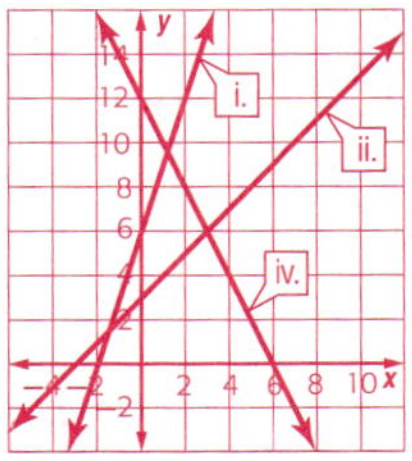


20c.

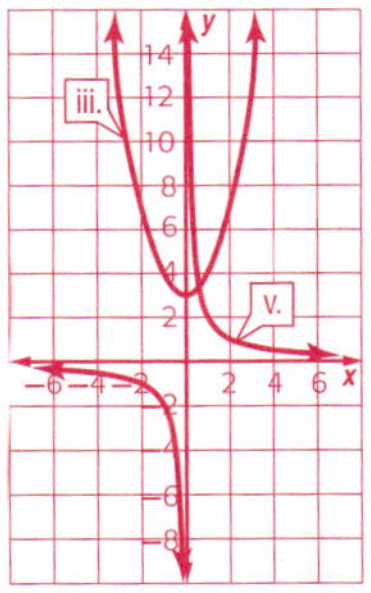


21f. **Lengths of Licorice**

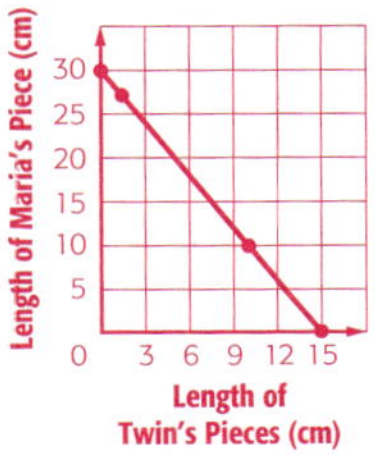


**20.** If you mark two points, only one straight line can be drawn through them. This means that when you have the rule for a linear relationship, you need to plot only two points to draw the line. Of course, even if you use this handy "two point" rule, it is not a bad idea to check a couple of more points to make sure you have not made a mistake.

Here are five rules.

**i.** $y = 3x + 6$

**ii.** $y = x + 3$

**iii.** $y = x^2 + 3$

**iv.** $y = 12 - 2x$

**v.** $y = \frac{2}{x}$

**a.** Decide whether each of the rules is linear. i: Yes; ii: Yes; iii: No; iv: Yes; v: No

**b.** For each relationship that you think is linear, find two points that will be on the graph, and use them to draw the graph. Then find a third point and check that it is on your line.

**c.** For each relationship you think is *not* linear, find several points and use them to draw the graph.

**21.** The three Pauli children love licorice. Their mother often buys them a 30-centimeter strand of licorice. After the twins, Carmelo and Biagio, have had some, the rest goes to Maria, the youngest child. The twins have the same amount each.

**a.** What is the least amount the twins could have? How much would Maria then get? 0 cm, 30 cm

**b.** What is the greatest amount each twin could have? How much would Maria then get? 15 cm each, 0 cm

**c.** Choose some values for the length each twin has and then calculate how long Maria's piece will be. See below.

**d.** Write a rule in symbols for finding the length of Maria's piece if you know the length of each twin's piece. $M = 30 - 2T$

**e.** Use your rule to find how long Maria's piece will be if Carmelo and Biagio have 5.5 cm each. 19 cm

**f.** Draw a graph of your data. Do not forget to label the axes. Draw a line through your points if it makes sense to do so.

**g.** Use your graph to predict the length of the twin's pieces if Maria's piece is 9 cm long. Check your prediction with your rule. 10.5 cm

21c. Possible answer:

| Length of Twin's Pieces (cm), *T* | 0 | 1 | 10 | 15 |
|---|---|---|---|---|
| Length of Maria's Piece (cm), *M* | 30 | 28 | 10 | 0 |





▶ **Exercise 20** Students practice using the two-point rule to graph linear equations.

▶ **Exercise 21b** Watch for students who answer 30 cm. Remind them that 30 cm must be divided by 2 if each twin receives an equal part.

## Quick Check

**Informal Assessment** Students should be able to:

✔ recognize linear relationships in a variety of representations: symbolic rules, graphs, visual patterns, and tables

✔ translate from one representation to another

✔ recognize the symbolic representation of a linear relationship in more than one form

✔ explain the connection between the constant difference, the slope of the graph, and the symbolic representation of the relationship (the $a$ in $y = ax + b$)

✔ determine $b$ in the rule $y = ax + b$ from a graph (the $y$-intercept, the intersection with the vertical axis)

✔ students try to develop an effective strategy to discover the symbolic rule from the data

## Quick Quiz

**1.** Here are five tables. For each:
- determine whether it is a linear relationship,
- explain briefly how you decided, and
- write its symbolic rule (if it is linear).

a.

| Input | 6 | 8 | 10 | 12 | 14 |
|---|---|---|---|---|---|
| Output | 4 | 3 | 2 | 1 | 0 |

Linear; Possible explanation and rule: rate of change is constant, $y = -\frac{1}{2}x + 7$.

b.

| Input | 6 | 5 | 4 | 3 | 2 |
|---|---|---|---|---|---|
| Output | 0 | 1 | 4 | 9 | 16 |

Nonlinear; Possible explanation: rate of change is not constant.

c.

| Input | −1 | 0 | 1 | 2 | 3 |
|---|---|---|---|---|---|
| Output | 8 | 16 | 24 | 32 | 40 |

Linear; Possible explanation and rule: rate of change is constant, $y = 8x + 16$.

d.

| Input | 1 | 2 | 3 | 4 | 5 |
|---|---|---|---|---|---|
| Output | 4 | 8 | 16 | 32 | 64 |

Nonlinear; Possible explanation: rate of change is not constant.

e.

| Input | 0.2 | 0.3 | 0.4 | 0.5 | 0.6 |
|---|---|---|---|---|---|
| Output | 3.5 | 3.4 | 3.3 | 3.2 | 3.1 |

Linear; Possible explanation and rule: rate of change is constant, $y = -x + 3.7$.

**2.** Explain in your own words how $a$ and $b$ affect the graph of $y = -ax + b$. Possible answer: Increasing $a$ makes the graph steeper and negative $a$ makes the graph go downward from left to right. The variable $b$ is the point where the graph crosses the vertical or $y$-axis.



On Your Own Exercises

## Mixed Review

**22.** Which of these figures are nets for a cube? That is, which of them will fold into a cube? B, C, and E

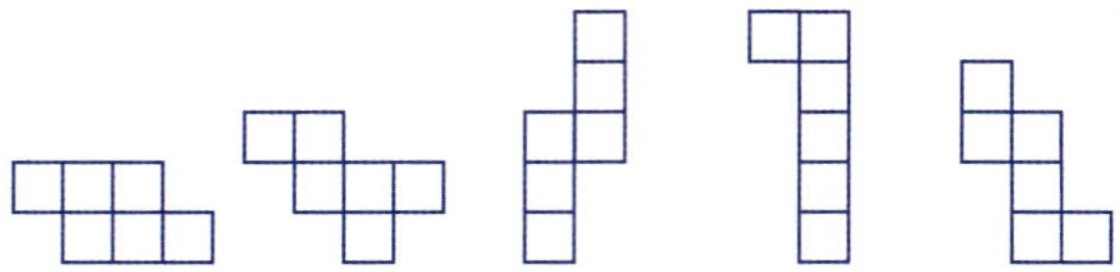

Figure A Figure B Figure C Figure D Figure E

**23.** Two cylinders have the same radius. The height of one cylinder is three times the height of the other cylinder. How do the volumes of the cylinders compare? The volume of one is three times the volume of the other.

**Evaluate each expression. Write your answers in standard notation.**

**24.** $(4.5 \cdot 10^{-3}) - (2.5 \cdot 10^{-5})$ 0.004475

**25.** $(1.7 \cdot 10^{-4}) + (9.2 \cdot 10^{-5})$ 0.000262

**Rewrite each expression as a fraction.**

**26.** $(-10^{-5})$

**27.** $(-4^{-2}) \cdot (-4^{-2})$

**28.** $3^{-6} \div 3^{-2}$

26. $\frac{1}{-10^5}$, or $-\frac{1}{100{,}000}$

27 $\frac{1}{(-4^4)}$, or $\frac{1}{256}$

28. $\frac{1}{3^4}$, or $\frac{1}{81}$

**Evaluate each expression.**

**29.** $-3 \cdot 20$ −60

**30.** $-4 \cdot -5.5$ 22

**31.** $-2 \cdot -5 \cdot -8$ −80

**Without using a calculator, predict whether each product is less than 0, equal to 0, or greater than 0.**

**32.** $-45 \cdot -2^6$ Greater than 0

**33.** $-n^2$ Less than or equal to 0

**34.** $(-3)^7 \cdot 3^7$ Less than 0

# Review & Self-Assessment

CHAPTER 8

## Chapter Summary

In this chapter, you looked at linear relationships. The relationship between two variables is *linear* if all possible points, when graphed, are on a straight line. You began looking at linear relationships defined by a *rate,* which describes how two quantities change in relation to each other.

You may be able to guess whether a linear relationship will describe a situation just by looking at the equation. You can find an equation for a line from a graph or a table of values. From a graph, you can determine the slope $a$ and the $y$-intercept $b$. From a table, you may be able to use the method of constant differences to find the slope. If you cannot get the $y$-intercept directly from the table, you can use the slope and one data pair to calculate it.

### Vocabulary

- linear relationship
- proportional
- rate
- slope
- speed
- velocity
- $y$-intercept

## Strategies and Applications

The questions in this section will help you review and apply the important ideas and strategies developed in this chapter.

### Understanding and representing rates and proportional relationships

**1.** After her last haircut, Angelina's hair was 8 inches long. In three months, it grew another inch. Assume that the hair growth was steady over the three months and that it continues at the same rate.

**a.** Write the rate that shows Angelina's hair growth per month.

**b.** If you drew a graph showing the relationship between Angelina's hair length and time, where would the graph start? At (0, 8)

**c.** Is Angelina's hair length proportional to the time it is allowed to grow since the haircut? Explain. No; it starts at 8 in., not at 0 in.

**d.** Write the rule for this relationship. Be sure to define your variables.

1a. 0.3 in., or $\frac{1}{3}$ in., per month

1d. $h = \frac{1}{3}m + 8$, where $h$ is hair length in inches and $m$ is months since the haircut

### Recognizing linear relationships from tables and graphs

**2.** The thickness of a book depends on several things, including the number of sheets of paper it has and how thick the paper is. For one type of paper, a stack of sheets one-inch thick contains 250 sheets.

**a.** Complete the table for this relationship.

| Number of Sheets | 0 | 250 | 500 | 750 | 1,000 | 1,250 |
|---|---|---|---|---|---|---|
| Thickness of Stack (in.) | 0 | 1 | 2 | 3 | 4 | 5 |



# Review & Self-Assessment

CHAPTER 8

## Chapter Summary

This summary helps students recall the major topics of the chapter

## Vocabulary

Students should be able to explain each of the terms listed in the vocabulary section.

▶ **Exercise 1** Students may need a lot of guidance with each part of this exercise. In part a, encourage students to write the rate in words and then substitute the numbers. For part b, ask the students how long Angelina's hair is when she starts measuring. The students already have the slope (part a) and the y-intercept (part b), now all they need to do is put it all together and they have the solution to part d.

▶ **Exercise 3** If students are having difficulty identifying the slope or rate in this exercise, encourage the students to read the question out loud. When they get to 45 mph, make sure they use the words for *miles per hour*. Stress to students that miles per hour is a rate and therefore the slope.

▶ **Exercise 4** Remind students that lines with positive slope go up from left to right and lines with negative slopes go down from left to right. Also, ask the students to identify the slope and y-intercept from each equation. This should reinforce the main points that are needed when graphing lines.

▶ **Exercises 6–8** Remind students to identify the slope and the *y*-intercept before they begin graphing. This will give them all of the information they need to complete the graph.

### Additional Answer

5. $y = -2x - 2$; Possible answer: I found the slope, the coefficient, by looking at how many units y changes when $x$ changes 1 unit. I found the $y$-intercept by looking at where the graph hit the $y$-axis, the constant term.





2c.
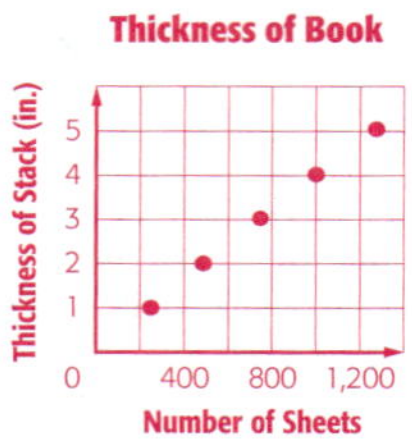


3a. $d = 45t + 3$, for distance $d$ in miles and time $t$ in hours, or $d = 0.75t + 3$ for distance $d$ in miles and time $t$ in minutes

3b.
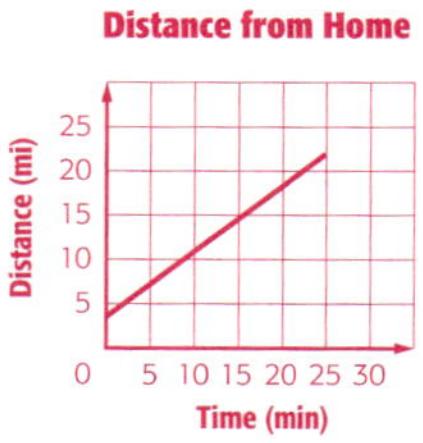


4a. i: up, intersects at 1; ii. down, intersects at 2; iii. up, intersects at −1; iv. down, intersects at −2

4b.
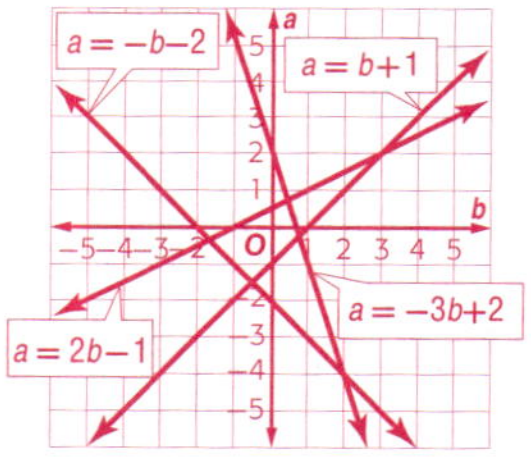


**b.** From the table, do you think this is a linear relationship? Explain. Yes; as the inputs change at a constant rate, so do the outputs.

**c.** Plot the data points in your table. Put the number of sheets on the horizontal axis and the thickness of the stack on the vertical axis.

**d.** From your graph, do you think this is a linear relationship? Explain. Yes; the points lie on a line.

**e.** Is this relationship proportional? Explain. Yes; the line goes through (0, 0).

### Understanding slope and *y*-intercept in graphs

**3.** Dion left home in his car and drove three miles to the gas station. At a speed of 45 mph, he continued in the same direction to work. The drive from the gas station to work took 25 minutes.

**a.** Write a rule that represents Dion's distance from home at any time since he left the gas station until he arrived at work.

**b.** Graph this relationship.

**c.** What is the slope of the line? What does this number represent? 45 (mph) or 0.75 (mi/min). Dion's speed

**d.** What are the coordinates of the point where the line intersects the vertical axis? What does this tell you about Dion's distance from home? (0, 3); Dion is 3 mi from home when he leaves the gas station, at $t = 0$.

**e.** Is the relationship between Dion's distance from home and the time proportional? No

### Understanding the connection between a linear equation and its graph

**4.** Consider these rules for lines.

**i.** $a = b + 1$ **ii.** $a = -3b + 2$ **iii.** $a = 2b - 1$ **iv.** $a = -b - 2$

**a.** Predict what the graph of each rule will look like before you draw it. Will the line go up or down as you look from left to right? Where will it intersect the vertical axis?

**b.** On one grid, draw the graph for each rule. Test your predictions on a new rule and its graph.

**5.** The graph shows a linear relationship. Write an equation for the line. Explain how you found your equation.
See margin.

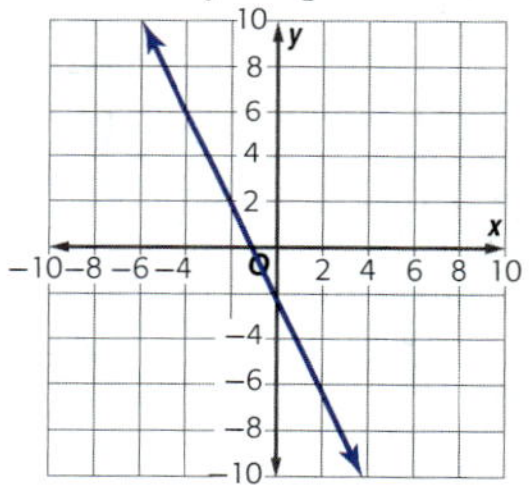


## Demonstrating Skills

**Graph each linear relationship.**

**6.** $y = 3x + 19$ **7.** $y = -1.7x + 7$ **8.** $y = -5x - 1$

Review & Self-Assessment
Chapter 8

6–8.

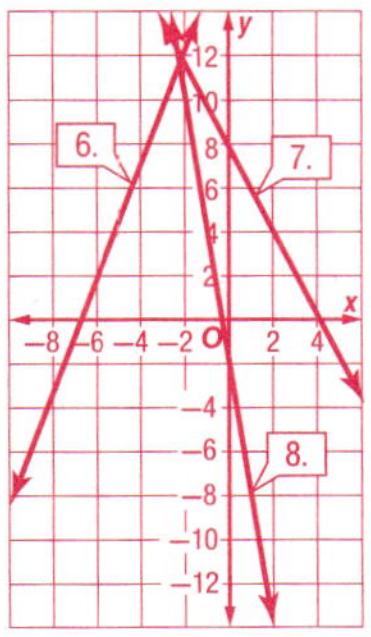


Decide whether each set of number pairs could describe a linear relationship.

**9.** (0, 20); (2, 0); (1, 10); (3, −10); (−1 , 30) Yes

**10.** (−1, 21); (1, 25); (3, 29); (−3, 17); (0, 23) Yes

Determine the slope and give the coordinates of the *y*-intercept for each relationship.

**11.** $y = 3x + 9$ 3; (0, 9)

**12.** $y = -15x + 39$ −15; (0, 39)

**13.** $y = x - 17$ 1; (0, −17)

Find a rule for each graph.

**14.**

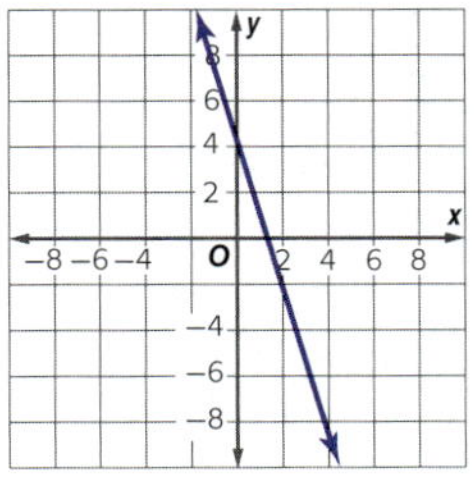


$y = -3x + 4$

**15.**

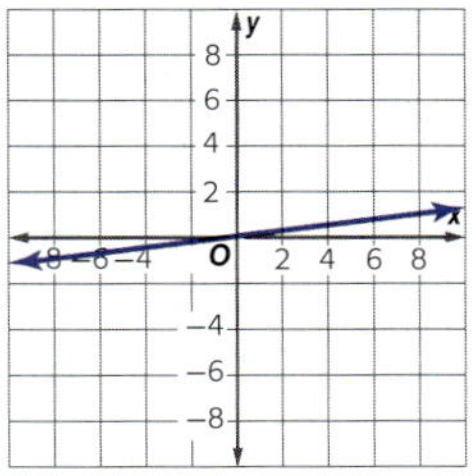


$y = 0.125x$ or $y = \frac{1}{8}x$

## Test-Taking Practice

***SHORT RESPONSE***

**1** Write a rule for the following pattern.

***Show your work.***

| x | 1 | 2 | 3 | 4 | 5 |
|---|---|---|---|---|---|
| y | 1 | 3 | 5 | 7 | 9 |

***Answer*** ______________

1. *Show your work:* To get the *y* value, multiply the *x* value by 2 and subtract 1, so the rule is $y = 2x - 1$

*Answer:* $y = 2x - 1$

***MULTIPLE CHOICE***

**2** Determine the slope and give the coordinates of the *y*-intercept for $y = -5x - 12$.

**A** −5; (−12, 0)

**(B)** −5; (0, −12)

**C** 5; (0, 12)

**D** 12; (0, −5)

**3** Which of the following is *not* proportional to $\frac{36}{45}$?

**F** $\frac{4}{5}$

**G** $\frac{12}{15}$

**(H)** $\frac{3}{12}$

**J** $\frac{32}{40}$



▶ **Exercises 9 and 10** Students can go about answering these exercises in a number of ways. If students are struggling, encourage them to plot the points on a graph. Other students may wish to find the rate of change between the *x*- and *y*-coordinates for each pair.

▶ **Exercises 14 and 15** When determining the slope between points, make sure that students remember lines going down from left to right have a negative slope and lines going up from left to right have a positive slope.

**Lesson 8.1, On Your Own Exercises** (p. 386)

12.

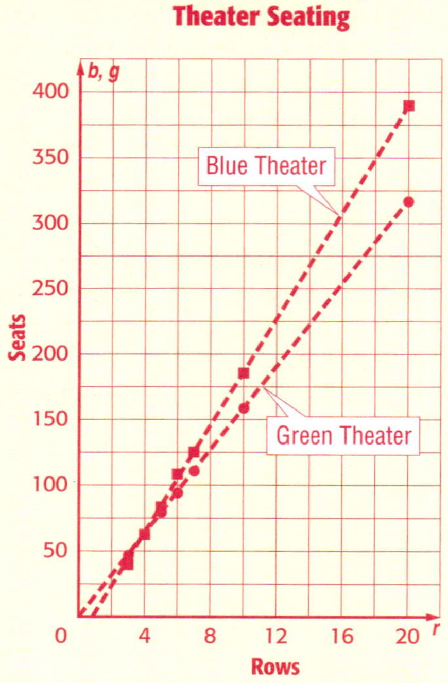


**Lesson 8.1, On Your Own Exercises** (p. 387)

13c.

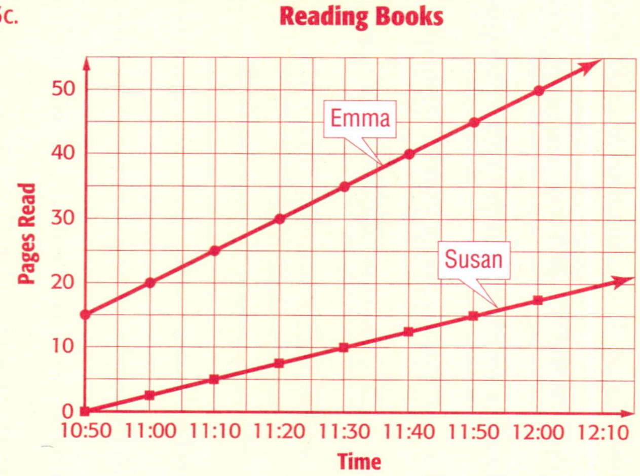


It makes sense to connect the points since each girl is reading at other times, like 10:52 and 11:23. It makes sense to continue the line beyond 12:00 if the girls are still reading.

**Lesson 8.2, On Your Own Exercises** (p. 398)

1. Possible table:

| Time (s) | 0 | 1 | 2 | 3 | 4 | 5 |
|---|---|---|---|---|---|---|
| Alita's Distance from Start (m) | 0 | 3 | 6 | 9 | 12 | 15 |
| Olivia's Distance from Start (m) | 4 | 6 | 8 | 10 | 12 | 14 |

2. Alita's graph is steeper and starts at (0, 0).

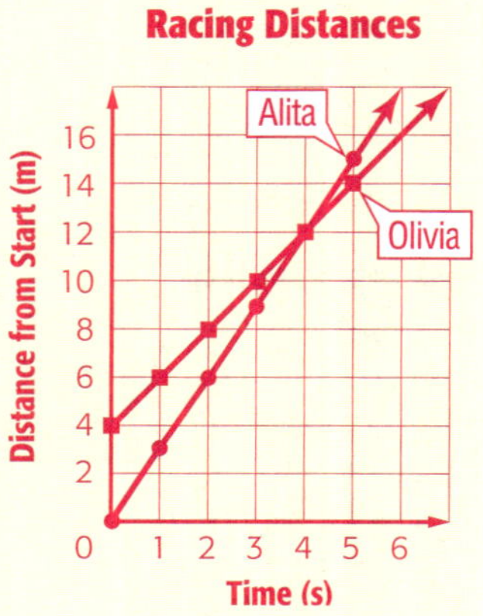


4. Alita: $d = 3t$; Olivia: $d = 4 + 2t$; The number multiplied by $t$ gives the slope of the graph. The 4 in Olivia's rule shows that her graph starts at (0, 4) instead of (0, 0).

**Lesson 8.2, On Your Own Exercises** (p. 402)

1f.

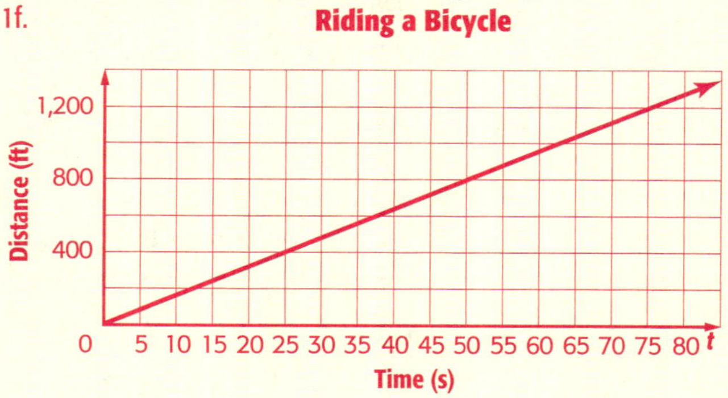


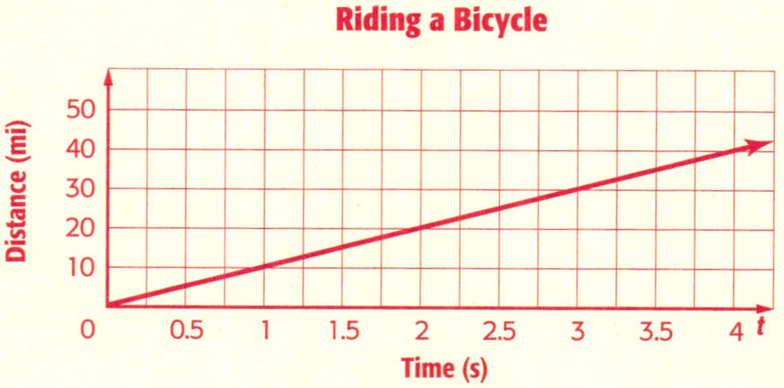

**Lesson 8.2, On Your Own Exercises** (p. 407)

31a. 6,600 ft/min

31b.

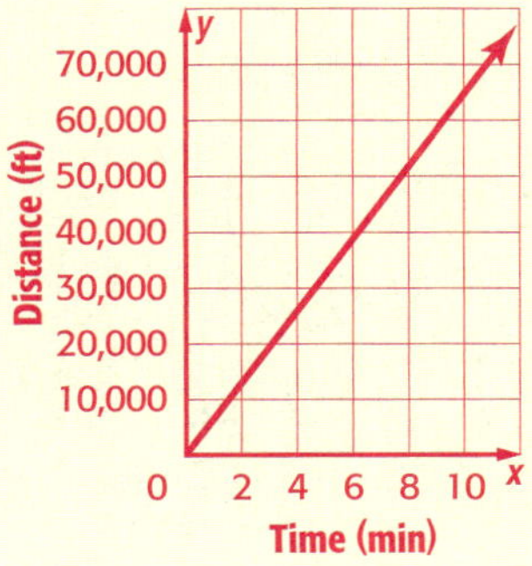


31c. 6,600

**Lesson 8.2, On Your Own Exercises** (p. 408)

34b. **Animals' Distances from Tree**

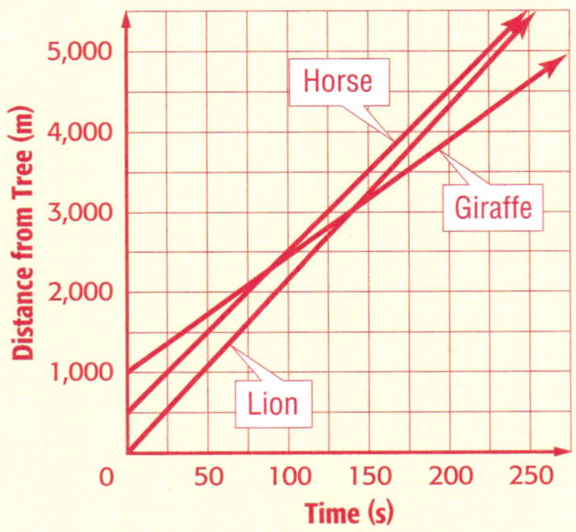


34c. **Distance Between Animals**

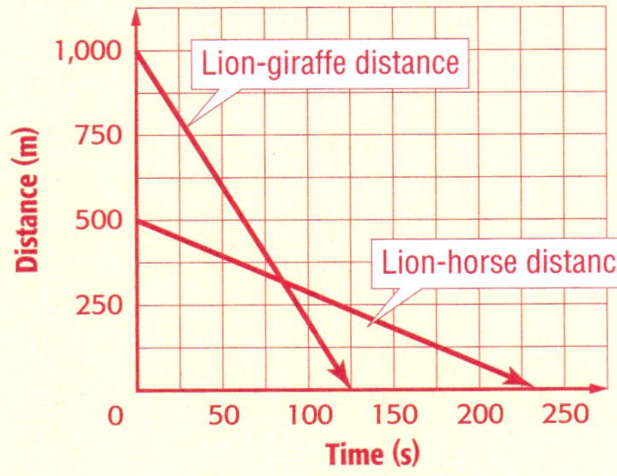


34d. All the graphs are straight lines. The graphs in Part b increase from left to right; the graphs in Part c decrease from left to right. The graph of the lion's distance from the tree is different from the others because it starts at (0, 0).

**Lesson 8.3, Investigation 3** (p. 418)

1.

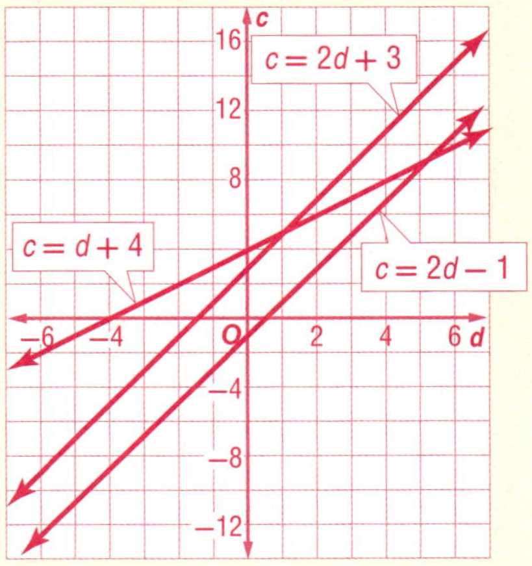


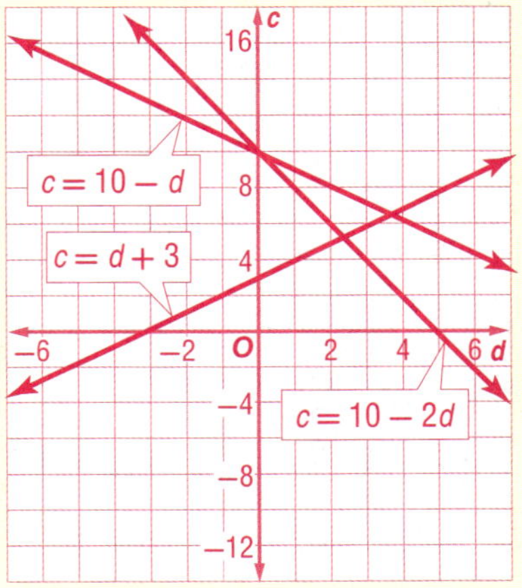


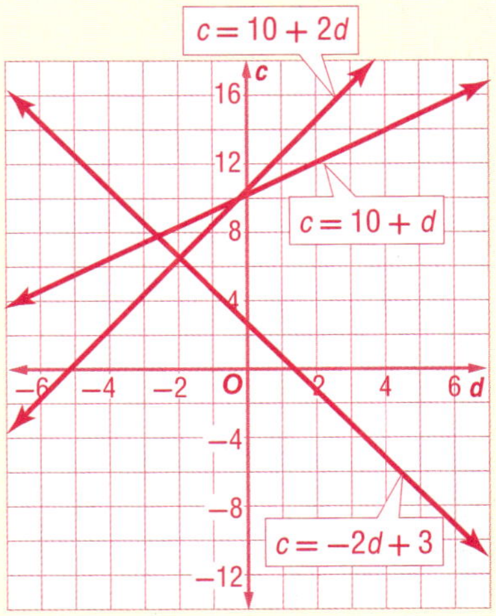

**Lesson 8.3, Investigation 3** (p. 418)

3.

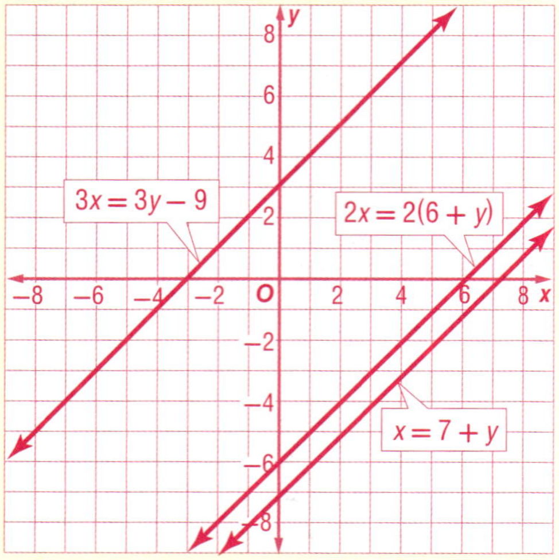


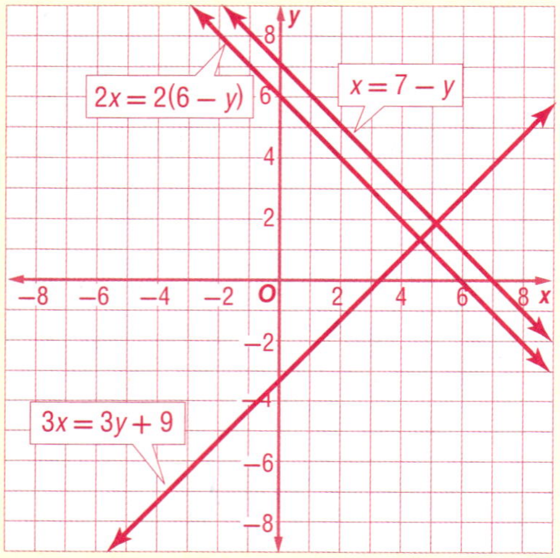

Notes

CHAPTER

9

# Equations

## Chapter Overview

In this chapter, students will learn more ways to write, simplify, and solve equations. They first review the guess-check-and-improve and backtracking methods of solving equations that were introduced earlier. Students also revisit the use of bags and blocks as they use balance models to solve basic equations.

Before solving equations symbolically, students are asked to visualize the balance model as they solve equations by doing the same thing to both sides of the equations.

Students use these methods to solve word exercises and to play and construct number games.

## The Big Picture

| Links to the Past | Chapter 9 | Links to the Future |
|---|---|---|
| **Course 1, Chapter 9** (pp. 532–575) Equations | **Lesson 9.1** (p. 436) Find a Solution Method | **Course 3, Chapter 7** (pp. 310–371) Inequalities and Linear Systems |
| **Course 1, Chapter 9** (pp. 532–575) Equations | **Lesson 9.2** (p. 446) A Model for Solving Equations | **Course 3, Chapter 7** (pp. 310–371) Inequalities and Linear Systems |
| **Course 1, Chapter 9** (pp. 532–575) Equations | **Lesson 9.3** (p. 460) Solve Equations | **Course 3, Chapter 7** (pp. 310–371) Inequalities and Linear Systems |
| **Course 1, Chapter 9** (pp. 532–575) Equations | **Lesson 9.4** (p. 474) Solve Equations with Parentheses | **Course 3, Chapter 7** (pp. 310–371) Inequalities and Linear Systems |

# Mathematical Background

Many students will come to the chapter thinking of an equation as an exercise about a process. One example might be a number puzzle such as this: I have a number, multiply it by 3 and add 5. The result is 11. What is the number? This interpretation reflects an important concept in modern mathematics, that of function.

A fundamental goal of any first course in algebra is to introduce students to several standard, formal strategies used to solve linear equations. They will meet the traditional "do the same thing to both sides" equation-solving strategy in this chapter.

Students already know how to solve linear equations using the two fundamental techniques of guess-check-and-improve and backtracking.

**Guess-Check-and-Improve** Although the process of guess-check-and-improve pervades mathematics at every level, the iterative calculations required can be tedious and often seem haphazard and non-mathematical to students. The lab investigation introduces the spreadsheet as a tool for solving equations by this technique. A spreadsheet can quickly compare many guesses to a desired outcome, thus demonstrating the power of the technique while eliminating the need for lots of paper-and-pencil calculations.

**Backtracking** The process of backtracking to solve an equation may still seem informal to students. However, the student who describes the equation $3n + 5 = 11$ using a flow chart and then reasons backwards is, in fact, inverting the composition of the functions multiply by 3 and add 5 by undoing them in reverse order.

Inverting the composition of functions is an important concept that will be made explicit in later courses.

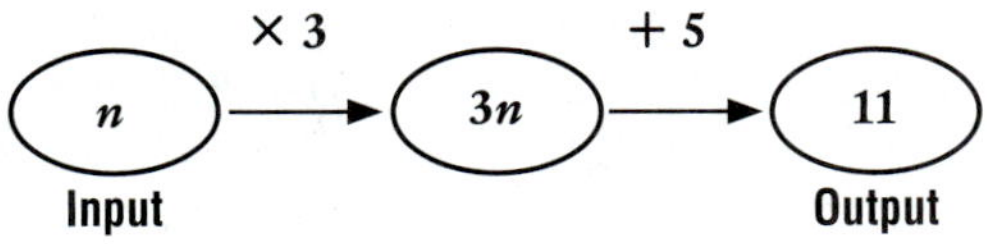


Solving Equations Using a Balance Model The traditional method of solving a linear equation by doing the same thing to both sides of an equation depends on a more static interpretation of an equation. A student must see an expression, let's say $3n + 5$, as a single number, that is equal to another number, 11. Students often have difficulty interpreting an expression as an object rather than a process.

The balance model helps the student think of algebraic expressions as objects. For example, the expression $3n + 5$ refers to a scale containing three bags and five blocks in balance with 11 blocks.

Students receive a lot of practice in interpreting algebraic sentences as balance problems and translating balance problems into equations to help them make this objective shift.

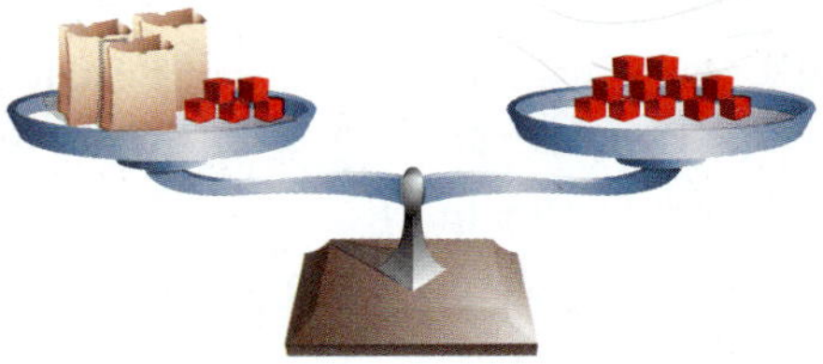

## Additional Reading

According to Kinzel in *Understanding Algebraic Notation from the Students' Perspective,* using symbols and interpreting symbols should receive explicit attention in algebra instruction. In Lesson 9.1, students use variables to write algebraic expressions. In Lessons 9.3 and 9.4, students work with symbols as they solve equations.

CHAPTER 9

# Planning Guide

## Lesson Resources

| | Lesson 9.1 (Pacing: 3 days) | Lesson 9.2 (Pacing: 4 days) | Lesson 9.3 (Pacing: 5 days) | Lesson 9.4 (Pacing: 4 days) |
|---|---|---|---|---|
| **Lesson Title** | **Find a Solution Method** (p. 436) | **A Model for Solving Equations** (p. 446) | **Solve Equations** (p. 460) | **Solve Equations with Parentheses** (p. 474) |
| **Lesson Objectives** | • To solve linear equations using guess-check-and-improve or backtracking strategies<br>• To use variables to write algebraic expressions for a variety of situations and numerical relationships | • To develop strategies for solving equations through operations with the balance model<br>• To provide experience in assigning variables and translating exercises into algebraic sentences | • To solve equations without using the balance puzzle model<br>• To solve simple word exercises by writing and solving equations<br>• To solve simple inequalities and graph the solution set on a number line | • To add and subtract parenthetical expressions<br>• To solve equations by adding, multiplying, or dividing both sides by the same quantity<br>• To describe variable quantities that appear in typical word exercises, including those that refer to signed numbers |
| **Materials** | Lesson 9.1 Master 1 | Chapter 9 Masters 1–3 | Chapter 9 Masters 1–3 | Lesson 9.4 Master 1 |
| ***Quick Review Math Handbook*** | **Lesson 5.4** Solving Linear Equations | **Lesson 5.4** Solving Linear Equations | **Lesson 5.4** Solving Linear Equations | **Lesson 5.4** Solving Linear Equations |
| **Print Resources** | CRM Study Guide and Intervention (p. 6)<br>CRM Skills Practice (p. 7)<br>CRM Problem-Solving Practice (p. 8)<br>CRM Enrichment (p. 9)<br>• Investigation Notebook and Reflection Journal<br>• Differentiation Handbook | CRM Study Guide and Intervention (p. 12)<br>CRM Skills Practice (p. 13)<br>CRM Problem-Solving Practice (p. 14)<br>CRM Enrichment (p. 15)<br>• Investigation Notebook and Reflection Journal<br>• Differentiation Handbook | CRM Study Guide and Intervention (p. 17)<br>CRM Skills Practice (p. 18)<br>CRM Problem-Solving Practice (p. 19)<br>CRM Enrichment (p. 20)<br>• Investigation Notebook and Reflection Journal<br>• Differentiation Handbook | CRM Study Guide and Intervention (p. 23)<br>CRM Skills Practice (p. 24)<br>CRM Problem-Solving Practice (p. 25)<br>CRM Enrichment (p. 26)<br>• Investigation Notebook and Reflection Journal<br>• Differentiation Handbook |
| **Technology Resources** | TeacherWorks Plus<br>Classroom Presentation Toolkit<br>ExamView Assessment Suite<br>StudentWorks Plus<br>Math Online Brain Pops • Concepts in Motion | TeacherWorks Plus<br>Classroom Presentation Toolkit<br>ExamView Assessment Suite<br>StudentWorks Plus<br>Math Online Brain Pops • Concepts in Motion | TeacherWorks Plus<br>Classroom Presentation Toolkit<br>ExamView Assessment Suite<br>StudentWorks Plus<br>Math Online Brain Pops • Concepts in Motion | TeacherWorks Plus<br>Classroom Presentation Toolkit<br>ExamView Assessment Suite<br>StudentWorks Plus<br>Math Online Brain Pops • Concepts in Motion |

*Included in the Impact Mathematics Manipulative Kit

# Assessment Resources

## MARS Assessment: Teaching with Purpose

**Correcting Errors**

In *Correcting Errors,* students solve linear equations. In the exercise, students first identify and then correct five incorrect solutions to ten equations.

**Targeting the Task**

- **Diagnostic**—Use Exercises 1–2 in the *Correcting Errors* assessment to determine students' understanding of how to solve linear equations. For those students who do not have this understanding, completing this unit is needed.
- **Formative**—Exercises 1–2 can be administered individually according to the lessons.
- **Summative**—Administer the complete *Correcting Errors* performance-based assessment.

CRM **Chapter 9 MARS Assessment** (pp. 42–43)

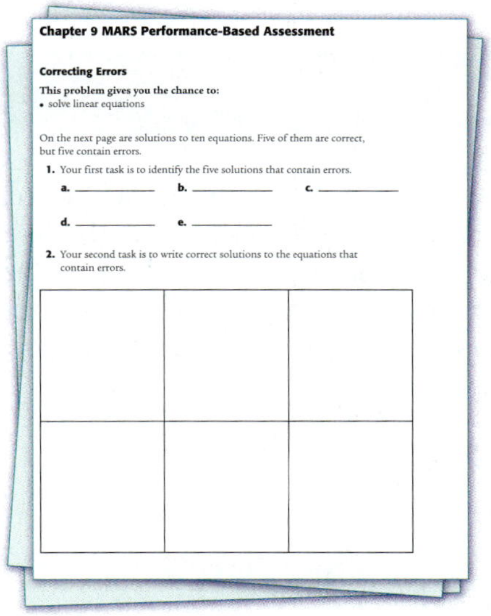

Chapter 9 MARS Performance-Based Assessment

Correcting Errors

This problem gives you the chance to:
• solve linear equations

On the next page are solutions to ten equations. Five of them are correct, but five contain errors.

1. Your first task is to identify the five solutions that contain errors.
a. ______ b. ______ c. ______
d. ______ e. ______

2. Your second task is to write correct solutions to the equations that contain errors.

## Assessment Planning Guide

Assessments are available for investigations, lessons, and chapters.

ExamView Assessment Suite — Customize and create multiple versions of tests and quizzes.

| | Student Edition | Teacher Edition | Other Resources |
|---|---|---|---|
| **Diagnostic** | | | CRM Chapter 9 Pretest (pp. 29–32)<br>Math Online Online Chapter Quiz |
| **Formative** | Share & Summarize (pp. 439, 448, 452, 454, 461, 463, 465, 468, 476, 480, 483) | Troubleshooting (pp. 437, 448, 454, 464, 466, 468, 476, 482)<br>On the Spot Assessment (pp. 466, 467, 476, 478)<br>Quick Check (pp. 445, 459, 473, 488)<br>Quick Quiz (pp. 445, 459, 473, 488) | CRM Quick Quiz (pp. 10, 16, 21, 27) |
| **Summative** | Review & Self-Assessment (pp. 489–491) | | CRM Chapter 9 Test: Forms A and B (pp. 33–40)<br>CRM Standardized Test Practice (pp. 44–45) |
| **Performance-Based** | In Your Own Words (pp. 445, 458, 473, 488) | | CRM Chapter Performance Assessment (p. 41)<br>CRM MARS Performance-Based Assessment (pp. 42–43) |

# Differentiated Instruction

## *Reaching* All Learners

Below are suggestions on differentiating the materials presented in this chapter. Additional modifications should be considered.

### Approaching Level (AL)

**Balancing Act** For Lesson 9.2, have students work with a pan balance and bags and blocks to practice balancing. Gradually give the students more problems to solve and then take the pan balance away, leaving them just the bags and blocks. This hands on practice will help the students make the jump to using just paper and pencil.

### Beyond Level (BL)

**Inequality Applications** Ask students to create a real-world problem that would have $x > 15$ as the solution. Have the students share their problems. As part of their solution, ask students to write down steps on how they would assist a student who does not grasp the concept of inequalities. Tell them to be specific and direct. Discuss similarities and differences in the topics chosen. This activity can be assigned after Investigation 4 in Lesson 9.3 is completed.

### On Level (OL)

**Solving Stations Review** Set up 8–10 stations in your classroom. Give each student a piece of paper that has space allocated to solve each problem; include graph paper in the spot where graphing will be done to ease understanding and accuracy. At each station have a different type of problem from Chapter 9 for the student to solve. Once the stations are complete, have the students meet in pairs or small groups to compare their answers. Assign each group a station to be responsible for and ask the group to present the solution to their problem to the class.

### English Language Learners (ELL)

**Solving Equations** Use this as a time to praise English Language Learners for their math abilities and allow and encourage these students to act as mentors for students who are having difficulty solving equations. Set up "Study Buddies" in class with an English Language Learner and another student who needs help in solving equations. This will give the English Language Learner an opportunity to practice speaking English about a topic they know which will benefit everyone involved.

**KEY**

AL Approaching Level OL On Level BL Beyond Level ELL English Language Learners

## Intervention Planning Guide

CRM Assess students' prerequisite skills and knowledge using the **Chapter Pretest** found in the Chapter 9 Resource Masters, pp. 29–32

| Intensive Intervention<br>two or more years below grade level | Strategic Intervention<br>below grade level | On Level | Beyond Level |
|---|---|---|---|
| **If** students miss 75% of the exercises:<br>**Then** use *Math Triumphs,* an intensive intervention | **If** students miss 50% of the exercises:<br>**Then** choose a resource: | **If** students miss 25% of the exercises:<br>**Then** choose a resource: | **If** students miss 0%–10% of the exercises:<br>**Then** choose a resource: |
| *Math Triumphs,* Grade 7<br>• Chapter 9: Variables and Expressions<br>• Chapter 10: Equations | CRM Study Guide and Intervention (pp. 6, 12, 17, 23)<br>• Investigation Notebook and Reflection Journal<br>• Differentiation Handbook<br>Math Online Brain Pops • Concepts in Motion | CRM Skills Practice (pp. 7, 13, 18, 24)<br>CRM Problem-Solving Practice (pp. 8, 14, 19, 25)<br>• Investigation Notebook and Reflection Journal | CRM Enrichment (pp. 9, 15, 20, 26)<br>• Differentiation Handbook |

## Literature Connections

### Recommended Outside Reading for Students

**Nonfiction**

Guillen, Michael. *Five Equations That Changed the World.* Fine Communications, 2000.

These five equations are pulled from the history of science and equated by the author to a great discovery. Each scientist is studied in a biographical sketch. How they came to their discovery and a few of the subsequent effects also are included.

**Fiction**

Farlow, Jerry. *The Girl Who Ate Equations for Breakfast.* Aardvark Press 1997.

*The Girl Who Ate Equations for Breakfast* is a collection of short stories with a mathematics theme. Students will enjoy the humor as well as learn some math through them. The title story involves an eighth grade Math Bee. Students will enjoy solving problems along with the contestants while they relate to the reactions of the characters involved.

## Professional Development

Targeted professional development has been articulated throughout the *IMPACT Mathematics* series. The **McGraw-Hill Professional Development Video Library** provides short videos that support the mathematics standards. Log on to www.glencoe.com.

Model Lessons

Instructional Strategies

CHAPTER 9

# Equations

## Introduce

**For Your Amusement** Have students share some of their experiences at amusement parks or fairs. Ask them how much money they spent and what they bought. Then tell them that they could use equations to help them decide how to spend their money.

**Think About It** To give the students additional practice, ask them how much they would spend if they bought four sandwiches, a small and a large lemonade. \$27 Then ask the students how the equation changes. $2(9.00) + 3.50 + 5.50 = T$

CHAPTER 9

# Equations

## Real-Life Math

**For Your Amusement** Imagine that you and your friends are going to an amusement park. It has the most gravity-defying rides in the country.

Did you know that engineers use equations to design and build park rides? Equations are also used by park vendors to determine the cost of souvenirs and concessions.

**Think About It** Sandwiches cost \$5.00 for one or two for \$9.00. Lemonade costs \$3.50 for a small or \$5.50 for a large. How much would you spend to buy three sandwiches and one large lemonade? Write an equation that represents this total cost. \$19.50; $9.00 + 5.00 + 5.50 = T$

### *Contents in Brief*



**Math Online** Take the **Chapter Readiness Quiz** at glencoe.com.

434

### Chapter Resources

- CRM Chapter 9 Resource Masters
- CRM English/Spanish Family Letter (pp. 1–2)
- CRM Lesson Masters (pp. 11, 22, 28)
- CRM Chapter 9 Pretest (pp. 29–32)
- CRM Chapter 9 Tests (pp. 33–40)

**Math Online** Online Readiness Quiz • eGlossary

# Dear Family,

The next chapter is about solving equations. The class will start by reviewing the backtracking and guess-check-and-improve methods of solving equations. Then a third, more efficient, solution method that involves doing the same thing to both sides of an equation will be learned. Combined with previously learned skills, your student will be able to solve a variety of equations, including equations with parentheses.

### Key Concept–Solving Equations

| | |
|---|---|
| $x + 5(x + 2) = 100$ | |
| $x + 5x + 10 = 100$ | Apply the Distributive Property. |
| $6x + 10 = 100$ | Combine like terms. |
| $6x = 90$ | Subtract 10 from both sides of the equation. |
| $x = 15$ | Divide both sides of the equation by 6. |

Finally, the class will use equations to solve real-world situations. For example, the equation $x + 5(x + 2) = 100$ could be used to model the following example.

Marla and her brothers, Pete and Max, collect souvenir postcards. Marla has two more postcards than Pete. Max has five times as many postcards as Marla. Pete and Max have a total of 100 postcards. How many postcards does Pete have? Pete has 15 postcards.

### Chapter Vocabulary

conjecture    model

### Home Activities

- Review the backtracking and guess-check-and-improve methods of equation solving.
- Write equations to represent daily situations, such as the cost of a family dining out for the evening.
- Look for examples of linear equations in your workplace. Work together to solve them.

435

## Family Letter

Another version of the Family Letter, available in English and Spanish, is found in the Chapter 9 Resource Masters. You may want to send a copy of this letter home with your students.

**Key Concept–Solving Equations** To enable students to have a better grasp of the concepts of solving equations, it may be helpful to have the students discuss with their families the various methods they have learned. This will include backtracking and guess-check-and-improve methods that were covered in Chapter 8, plus a new method of balancing. Have the students interview family members asking them which method they use to solve problems at home or at work.

**Home Activities**

- Have students create a problem to take home that uses backtracking or guess-check-and improve method to have family members solve as review of these concepts.
- Have students keep a problem solving journal at home where they can record the problems that they solve with their families. Near the end of the chapter these journals can be turned in and a collection made for the class.

## Key Vocabulary

**English (Spanish)** *Introduce the most important terms from Chapter 9.*

**conjecture (conjetura)** A statement that is believed to be true but has not yet been proven. (p. 435)

**model (modelo)** Something that has the key characteristics of something else. For example, in mathematics you could use a balance to model an equation. (p. 435)

LESSON 9.1

# Find a Solution Method

### Objectives

- ▶ To solve linear equations using guess-check-and-improve or backtracking strategies
- ▶ To use variables to write algebraic expressions for a variety of situations and numerical relationships

## *Overview*

In this lesson, students solve a variety of equations using either the guess-check-and-improve strategy or backtracking. Some equations will lend themselves to one method, some to another. Students are asked to think about the method that is most appropriate. In the course of the lesson, they acquire practice in using the language of algebra to describe a problem. The process of guess-check-and-improve becomes more efficient by using a spreadsheet, and the process of constructing spreadsheets provides practice in applying variables to problems.

## *Advance Preparation*

If you intend to conduct the spreadsheet activities in a computer laboratory, you will need to make sure that all the computers have the same spreadsheet. You may also need to reintroduce students to working with a spreadsheet.

| | Summary | Materials | On Your Own Exercises (pp. 444–445) | Assessment Opportunities |
|---|---|---|---|---|
| **Investigation 1** (p. 437) Pacing: 2 days | Students work together to select the best method for solving a series of equations: either guess-check-and-improve or backtracking. | Lesson 9.1 Master 1 | Practice & Apply: 1–13<br>Connect & Extend: 14–18<br>Mixed Review: 19–24 | • Share & Summarize (p. 439)<br>• Troubleshooting (p. 437) |
| **Inquiry Investigation 2** (p. 440) Pacing: 1 day | Students learn to set up spreadsheets to facilitate the guess-check-and-improve method of solving equations. | computers | | |

# Leveled Lesson Resources

Also on TeacherWorks™ Lesson 9.1

CRM *Available in:* **Chapter 9 Resource Masters**

## Study Guide and Intervention (p. 6) AL

**Lesson 9.1 Study Guide and Intervention**
***Find a Solution Method***

***Example 1*** **Use backtracking to solve $7v - 3 = 25$.**

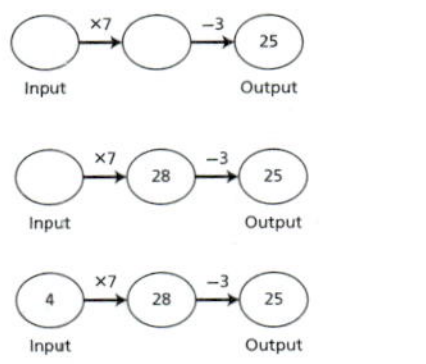


Create a flowchart for the equation $7v - 3 = 25$. The input is $v$, or the value you want to find. The output is 25.

Since you need to subtract 3 to get 25, the value in the second oval must be 28.

Since you need to multiply by 7 to get 28, the value in the first oval must be 4.

The solution is 4. Check with substitution: $(4)7 - 3 = 28 - 3 = 25$.

***Example 2*** **Use guess-check-and-improve to solve $12 + x = 6 + 3x$.**

| Guess | $12 + x$ | $6 + 3x$ | Difference |
|---|---|---|---|
| 1 | 13 | 9 | $13 - 9 = 4$ |

Begin with 1 as a guess for the solution. Substituting 1 for $x$ gives 13 for the left side of the equation and 9 for the right side. The difference between 13 and 9 is 4, so you might try 2 or 3 as your second guess.

| Guess | $12 + x$ | $6 + 3x$ | Difference |
|---|---|---|---|
| 3 | 15 | 15 | $15 - 15 = 0$ |

Substituting 3 for $x$ gives 15 on both sides.

The solution is 3.

***Exercises***

**Use backtracking to solve each equation.**

**1.** $4y + 1 = 13$ **2.** $2(2x + 6) = 26$ **3.** $7 = \frac{-3c + 2}{-1}$

**Use guess-check-and-improve to solve each equation.**

**4.** $11 + 7n = 4$ **5.** $\frac{(15 + 2p)}{3} = 9$ **6.** $5(z + 2) = 6(2z - 3)$

## Skills Practice (p. 7) AL OL

**Lesson 9.1 Skills Practice**
***Find a Solution Method***

**Use backtracking to solve each equation.**

**1.** $2x + 1 = 9$
**2.** $7k - 3 = 32$
**3.** $\frac{3w + 5}{7} = 23$
**4.** $5(n - 8) = 25$
**5.** $2(2t - 1) = 14$
**6.** $\frac{7b + 1}{4} = 2$
**7.** $8x - 1 = 63$
**8.** $2x - 5 = 15$
**9.** $54 = 6\left(\frac{4 - 7v}{2}\right)$
**10.** $8\left(\frac{5b + 12}{3} - 1\right) = 64$
**11.** $4\left(20 - \frac{4n + 27}{3}\right) = 40$
**12.** $\frac{10r - 2}{5} + 8 = 11$
**13.** $3 = \frac{2 - 4p}{9}$
**14.** $2 = 6 - \left(\frac{7 - 15z}{10}\right)$

**Use guess-check-and-improve to solve each equation.**

**15.** $2(p + 7) = 5p + 2$
**16.** $3y + 10 = y + 2$
**17.** $4g - 8 = 5g - 11$
**18.** $24 - 8g = 2 - 30g$
**19.** $18 - 3w = w - 6$
**20.** $9(2d + 5) = 3d$
**21.** $\frac{7x + 2}{4} = \frac{13x - 2}{6}$
**22.** $\frac{4m - 8}{3} = 2m - 6$

## Problem-Solving Practice (p. 8) AL OL

**Lesson 9.1 Problem-Solving Practice**
***Find a Solution Method***

**Solve.**

**1. Golf** Mike has three packs of golf balls and 12 individual balls. Sam has two packs of golf balls and 15 individual balls.

**a.** Write an expression to represent the number of golf balls Mike has.
**b.** Write an expression to represent the number of golf balls Sam has.
**c.** Write an equation that represents Mike and Sam having the same number of golf balls.
**d.** Solve your equation. How many golf balls are in each pack?

**2. Office** Caitlin has 34 pens. She rubber bands ten groups of $p$ pens and then puts them in a drawer. Janet has 28 pens. She rubber bands eight groups of $p$ pens and then puts them in a drawer.

**a.** Write an expression to represent the number of pens Caitlin has left over.
**b.** Write an expression to represent the number of pens Janet has left over.
**c.** Write an equation that represents Caitlin and Janet having the same number of pens left over.
**d.** Solve your equation. How many pens does each person group together?

**3. Geometry** Two angles in a triangle each measure 26° more than a given number. The third angle is 14° times the given number. The sum of all the angles in a triangle is 180°.

**a.** Write an equation that relates the angle measures. Use $n$ to represent the given number.
**b.** Solve the equation using whatever method you like.
**c.** Find the measures of all three angles.

**4. Homework** Constantina creates this spreadsheet while doing her homework.

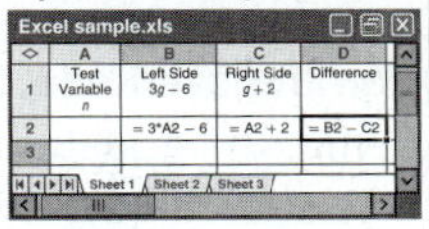


**a.** What equation is Constantina trying to solve?
**b.** What results will Constantina get in Cells B2, C2, and D2 if she enters 1 in Cell A2?
**c.** What value should Constantina enter in Cell A2 if she wants the resulting value in Cell D2 to be 0?

## Enrichment (p. 9) BL

**Lesson 9.1 Enrichment**
***Find a Solution Method***

Some equations contain like terms that can be combined. For example, in the equation $3a + 2a + 4 = 14$, the expressions $3a$ and $2a$ can be combined first before solving the equation. To solve $3a + 2a + 4 = 14$, proceed as follows.

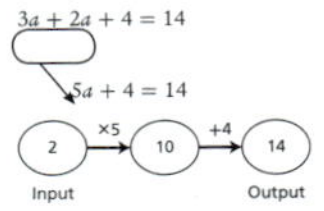


Combine like terms. Then solve the equation using any method you like.

You can use backtracking to find that the solution is 2.

**Solve each equation. Then locate the solution on the number line below. Place the letter corresponding to the answer on the line at the right of the exercise.**

**1.** $3x + 4x + 3 = -39$ ______
**2.** $-3x + 2 + 5x = 4(x - 3)$ ______
**3.** $-5 - 4x + 7x = 1$ ______
**4.** $2x - 6 + 7x = 5(x + 2)$ ______
**5.** $\frac{3x + 8 - 4x}{22} = \frac{-x}{6}$ ______
**6.** $\frac{6 - x}{3} = -1$ ______
**7.** $7x + (-2x) + x = -36$ ______
**8.** $x + 9 = \frac{-x + 3x}{4} + 5$ ______
**9.** $9(5 - x) + 10 = -20x$ ______

## Lesson Quick Quiz (p. 10) AL OL BL

**Lesson 9.1 Quick Quiz**

**1.** Use backtracking to solve the equation $3n - 2 = 49$.

**2.** Which is a better technique, guess-check-and-improve or backtracking, for solving the equation $3n - 2 = 2(n + 3)$? Solve the equation using this technique.

**3.** A DVD store charges a customer a \$5 fine if a DVD is late and \$2 a day for each day it is overdue.

**a.** Jamar returns a DVD that is $x$ days overdue. Write an expression for the total amount he must pay.

**b.** Write an equation showing that Jamar owes the store \$75.

**c.** Solve the equation in Part b to find the number of overdue days Jamar has kept the DVD.

**4.** To ship a package, one shipping company charges \$3 plus \$2 per pound. Another company charges \$7 plus \$1 per pound. It would cost Ally the same amount to ship her package by either company. What is the weight of Ally's package?

**a.** Write an equation that describes the situation.

**b.** Solve the equation in Part a to determine the weight for which the two shipping charges are equal.

## Lesson Master (p. 11)

**Lesson 9.1 Master 1**
***Find a Solution Method***

**Investigation 1: Introduction**

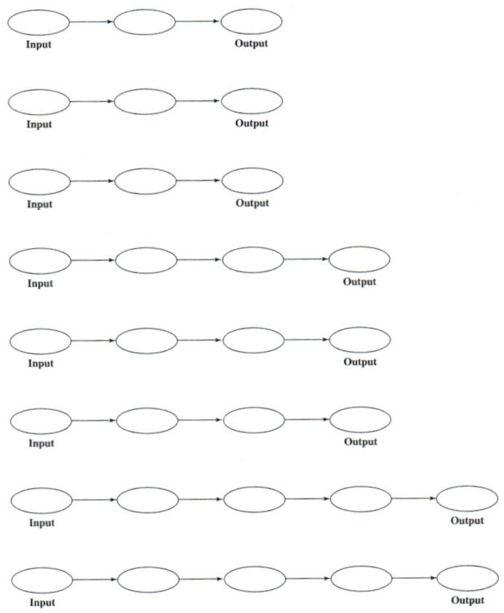


# Additional Lesson Resources

### Teacher Tech Tools

- TeacherWorks
- ExamView Assessment Suite
- Classroom Presentation Toolkit
- Advance Tracker

### Student Tech Tools

- StudentWorks Plus
- Math Online eGlossary •
  Concepts in Motion

### Other Print Products

- Investigation Notebook and Reflection Journal
- Quick Review Math Handbook

# LESSON 9.1 Find a Solution Method

## Introduce

**Find a Method** Tell the class that they will be extending their equation-solving skills in this chapter. Ask them what strategies they have learned to solve equations. Students should mention backtracking and guess-check-and-improve.

Have volunteers present an example of each strategy.

### Think & Discuss

*Suggested Grouping: Pairs*

Write the equation $\frac{5b+3}{3} = 6$ on the board or on the overhead, and work with students to write the equation in the form of a flowchart. Using the text as needed, review how to use backtracking to solve an equation, and have students find the solution. Then ask a volunteer to explain the steps.

At this time, it is worth pointing out that, if students have trouble backtracking, they can always try a value (as if starting a guess-check-and-improve process) to establish the sequence of steps in the flow chart.

# LESSON 9.1 Find a Solution Method



You already know the methods of solving equations: backtracking and guess-check-and-improve. *Backtracking,* which you used in Chapter 1, can help you solve many equations. For example, consider this equation.

$$\frac{5b+3}{3} = 6$$

To find the solution, first set up a flowchart for the expression $\frac{5b+3}{3}$. The flowchart shows the steps for calculating the value of the expression, the *output,* for any *input b.*

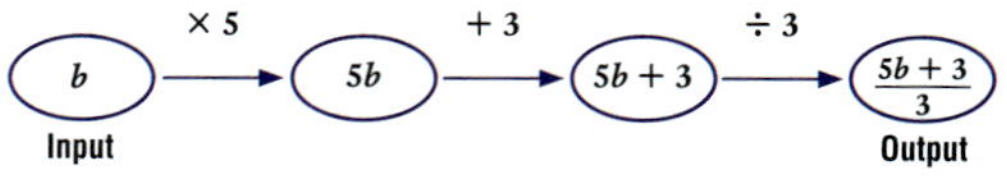


To solve $\frac{5b+3}{3} = 6$, you need to find the input that gives an output of 6. Draw the flowchart again, this time entering 6 as the output and leaving the other ovals blank.

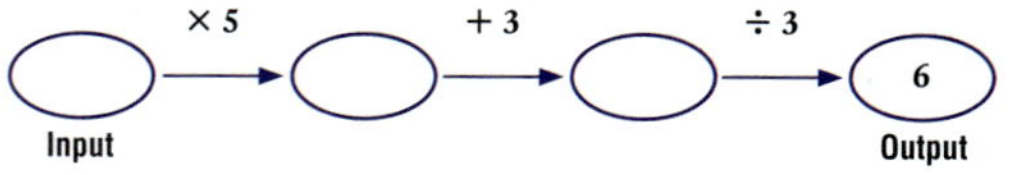


Now you can work backward, step by step, from the output to find the input. First, ask yourself, "What number divided by 3 gives 6?" Write that number in the oval to the left of the 6.

### Real-World Link

Flowcharts are used in many professions. Builders use them to specify the steps in a home's construction, engineers to diagram how a part travels through the manufacturing process, and electricians to show how current flows in a circuit.

### Think & Discuss

Continue backtracking from right to left to find the values for each oval in the flowchart. The number in leftmost oval is the solution of the equation. See ① in margin.

What is the solution? Check your answer by substituting it into the equation. 3; Check: $\frac{5 \cdot 3 + 3}{3} = \frac{15+3}{3} = \frac{18}{3} = 6$

You can use the *guess-check-and-improve* method to solve any equation, even equations that are difficult to solve by backtracking. To use this method, *guess* what the solution might be and then *check* your guess by substituting it into the equation. If your guess is incorrect, guess again. By comparing the results of each substitution, you can *improve* your guesses and get closer and closer to a solution.



### Additional Answer

①

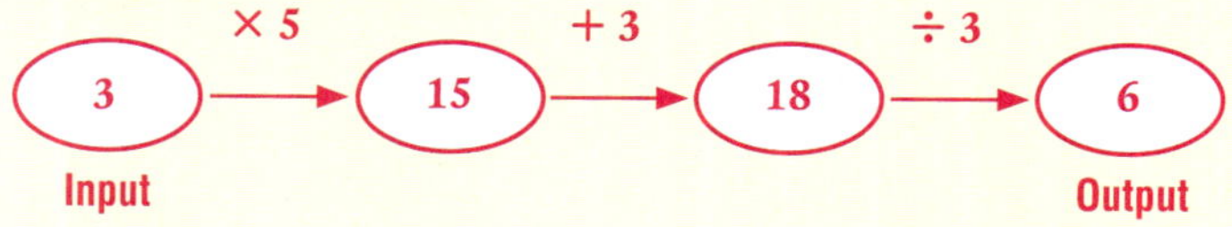

### Think & Discuss

Consider the equation $3b + 5 = b + 17$.

Suppose you begin with 1 as a guess for the solution. Substituting 1 for $b$ gives 8 for the left side of the equation and 18 for the right side. You might enter these results in a table.

| Guess | $3b + 5$ | $b + 17$ |
|---|---|---|
| 1 | 8 | 18 |
| 4 | 17 | 21 |
| | | |

Try 4 as your second guess. Substitute 4 for $b$ in both sides of the equation. Record your answers in a copy of the table.

For a guess of 1, the difference between the two sides of the equation is 10. Are the two sides closer together or further apart when you substitute 4? Closer together

If 4 is not the solution, continue to adjust your guess until the two sides of the equation have the same value. What is the solution? Explain. 6; When $b$ is 6, both sides have a value of 23.

## Investigation 1 Choose a Solution Method

Backtracking is sometimes much easier or more efficient than guess-check-and-improve. You will now practice using these two methods to solve equations. As you work on the exercises, think about how you could decide which method is easier for a particular equation.

### Develop & Understand: A

**Use backtracking to solve each equation. Check your solutions by substituting them into the original equations.**

1. $3f - 2 = 13$ 5
2. $3(2g + 12) = 51$ 2.5
3. $\frac{2a + 1}{3} = 5$ 7
4. $2(\frac{3n + 4}{5} - 1) = 6$ $\frac{16}{3}$, or $5\frac{1}{3}$

**Use guess-check-and-improve to solve each equation.**

5. $u + 4 = 4u - 8$ 4
6. $2q - 2 = 4q - 7$ 2.5
7. $m(m - 6) = 91$ (There are two solutions. Try to find both.) −7 and 13



### Troubleshooting

Watch for students having difficulty making the flowchart for the equation in Exercise 4. These students may find it helpful to try a number and keep track of what they do to evaluate the left side of the equation. For example, if the guess is 2, then a student might write the stages in evaluation like this:

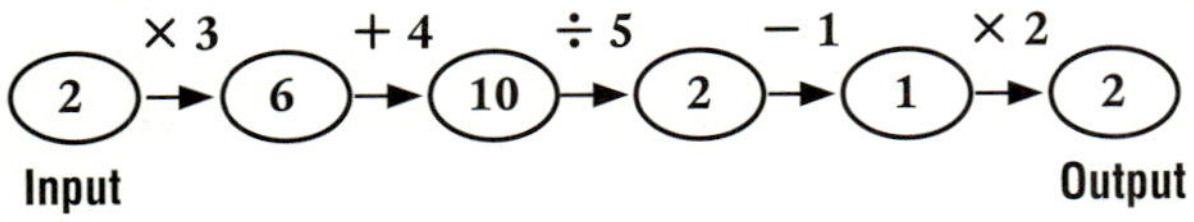


Some students may want to copy the equation and then draw circles around the parentheses in the equation and around the related operations in the flowchart, to emphasize the grouping.

### Think & Discuss

*Suggested Grouping: Whole Class*

After you are satisfied that students understand the backtracking method, present $3b + 5 = b + 17$, an equation that doesn't lend itself to backtracking. As a class, work through solving this equation using guess-check-and-improve. If students have trouble accepting guess-check-and-improve as a valid equation-solving method, emphasize that the technique is always useful for any equation and that it is an "if all else fails" technique that has been used by mathematicians for centuries.

## Investigation 1

**On Your Own Exercises**
Pages 444–445
Exercises 1–13, 14–18

**Choose a Method** Students use backtracking and guess-check-and-improve strategies to solve equations. You may wish to have students use Lesson 9.1 Master 1, Flowcharts, to record their thinking.

You may want to present the following model as a guide for students working together in pairs on a guess-check-and-improve equation: A pair agrees on a guess. Then each person in the pair evaluates a different side of the equation for that guess. After calculating how far apart these values are, they decide together on an improved guess and repeat the process until they find the solution.

### Develop & Understand: A

*Suggested Grouping: Pairs*

In this exercise set, students are asked to consider whether backtracking or guess-check-and-improve is the more efficient solution strategy as they solve equations. You can provide them with Lesson 9.1 Master 1 to record their answers.

▶ **Exercise 7** This exercise offers a challenge in adjusting guesses in a nonlinear context.

▶ **Exercises 8–12** The discussion among partners is important. Remind pairs to focus on the choice of strategies before discussing answers.

**Wrap-Up** Discuss Exercises 7 and 12. For Exercise 7, ask students if they should look for more than one solution in exercises of this type, and have them explain their reasoning. Many will see that there may be two solutions since the exercise requires multiplying *m* by itself.

Exercise 12 is intended to emphasize that guess-check-and-improve is always a valid strategy, although there is a need for additional strategies that are easier and faster to use. Algorithmic strategies such as backtracking meet these needs.

Have groups share their results. Some students may find interesting ways to use backtracking that aren't at first obvious.

Tell students that the exercises in the next exercise set will help them to develop their algebraic skills.

## Develop & Understand: B

*Suggested Grouping: Pairs*

In this exercise set, students practice translating numerical information from word exercises into the language of algebra as they write and solve equations for a variety of exercises.

▶ **Exercise 17** This exercise guides students through writing an equation with a variable on both sides of the equals sign. Students can use the questions in this exercise as a guide when writing similar equations later in this exercise set.



For each equation in Exercises 8–11, discuss with your partner which solution method, backtracking or guess-check-and-improve, would be easier or more efficient. Then solve the equations.

**8.** $\frac{5k-4}{3} = 7$ Backtracking; 5

**9.** $\frac{3n+5}{2} = \frac{5n+3}{3}$

**10.** $5B + 2(B + 1) = 16$ Guess-check-and-improve; 2

**11.** $4j + 74 = 478$ Backtracking; 101

**12.** Look at the equations in Exercises 8–11. Are any of them difficult to solve by backtracking? If so, explain why backtracking is difficult to use for these equations.

9. Guess-check-and-improve; 9

12. Answers will vary. All the equations can be solved by backtracking, but since the variable appears twice in Exercises 9 and 10, these equations must be rewritten first.

**Solve each equation using any method you like. Check your solutions.**

**13.** $4(5g - 1) = 56$ 3

**14.** $\frac{3d+1}{3} = 6d - 3$ $\frac{2}{3}$

**15.** $35 - 2s = 11$ 12

**16.** $4x + 3 = -3x - 4$ $-1$

Algebra is a powerful tool for solving real and important situations. The exercises that follow are generally much easier to solve than real situations, but they will help you develop needed algebraic skills.

## Develop & Understand: B

**17.** Kaylee has $20 now and saves $6 per week. Noah has $150 now and spends $4 per week.

**a.** How much money will Kaylee have *n* weeks from now? $20 + 6n$ dollars

**b.** How much money will Noah have *n* weeks from now? $150 - 4n$ dollars

**c.** Write an equation that represents Kaylee and Noah having the same amount of money after *n* weeks. $20 + 6n = 150 - 4n$

**d.** Solve your equation for *n*. What does the solution tell you about this situation?

**e.** How can you check your solution? Substitute 13 into both sides of the equation. If the sides are equal, the solution is correct.

17d. 13; In 13 weeks, Kaylee and Noah will have the same amount of money.

**18.** Inez's family is purchasing a new stereo system from Sharon's Sound Shop. The salesperson offers a choice of payment plans.

**Plan A:** Make a \$100 down payment and then pay \$35 per month for 24 months.

**Plan B:** Make no down payment and pay \$40 per month for 24 months.

**a.** Which plan is more expensive? Explain. Plan B is more expensive: Plan B, $24 \cdot 40 = \$960$; Plan A, $100 + 24 \cdot 35 = \$940$.

**b.** For each plan, write an expression for the amount Inez's family will have paid after $n$ months. Plan A: $100 + 35n$; Plan B: $40n$

**c.** After how many months will the family have paid the same amount no matter which payment plan is selected? 20

In Exercises 19–23, write an equation that fits the situation. Solve the equation using whatever method you like. Check your solution.

### Math Link

The sum of the measures of the angles in any triangle is 180°.

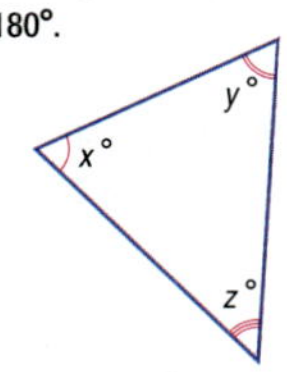


$x° + y° + z° = 180°$

**19.** Finding 5 more than a given number gives the same result as 3 times the sum of that number and 1. What is the number? $5 + n = 3(n + 1)$; 1

**20.** One angle of a triangle measures $f$ degrees. One of the other angles of the triangle is twice this size, and the third angle is three times this size. Find the measures of all three angles. $f + 2f + 3f = 180$, so $f = 30$; The angles measure 30°, 60°, and 90°.

**21.** A rectangular field is three times as long as it is wide. The fence around the perimeter of the field is 800 meters long. How wide is the field? $3w + w + 3w + w = 800$, or $8w = 800$; 100 m

**22.** An apartment building has a TV antenna on its roof. The top of the antenna is 66 meters above the ground. The building is ten times as tall as the antenna. How tall is the antenna? $a + 10a = 66$, or $11a = 66$; 6 m

**23.** In a class of 25 students, there are seven more girls than boys. How many boys are in the class? $b + (b + 7) = 25$; 9 boys

### Share & Summarize

**1.** Write an equation that *cannot* be solved easily by backtracking. Explain why backtracking would be difficult.

**2.** Together, Hally and Trey have \$14. If Hally had \$1 more, she would have twice as much money as Trey.

**a.** Write and solve an equation to find how much money Hally and Trey each have. See margin.

**b.** Explain how you wrote your equation and how you decided which method to use to solve it. See margin.

1. Possible answer: $6n + 5 = 42 + 4n$; The variable appears twice, so we need two input ovals; you cannot put a number in the output oval from which to backtrack.



### Share & Summarize

In **Question 1**, students are asked to provide examples of equations that cannot be solved by backtracking. These explanations provide a good evaluation of the student's understanding.

It is often hard for students to explain how they accomplished complicated tasks, as they are asked to do in **Question 2b**. It may be helpful to go over the suggested answers as a model.

### Additional Answers

2a. If $t$ is the amount Trey has, $t + (2t - 1) = 14$. Or, if $h$ is the amount Hally has, $h = 14 - \frac{h+1}{2}$. Trey has \$5; Hally has \$9.

2b. Possible answer: If Trey has $t$ dollars, then since Hally has \$1 less than twice as much as Trey, she has $2t - 1$ dollars. Since they have a total of \$14, $t + (2t - 1) = 14$. Guess-check-and-improve is easier because the variable appears twice.

## Reaching All Learners

**AL Approaching Level** In Exercise 21, students who do not understand the phrase *as long as* may think that $3l = w$ rather than $3w = l$, with $l$ representing the length and $w$ the width.

It may be helpful for these students to rephrase *is three times as long as it is wide* to *its length is three times its width.* Ask students to pause before writing the sentence and then check that their expressions for the length and width are in the proper size relationship.

Students can choose simpler numbers and use the context of their sentences to check that their answers work.

Inquiry

Inquiry

## Investigation 2

*Suggested Grouping: Small Groups*

### Materials and Preparation

This lab investigation requires a spreadsheet program that runs either over a network or on each individual computer. If the network is slow, a single-server version of the spreadsheet may not be satisfactory since the purpose of the lab is to make the guess-check-and-improve process fast and easy, not slower and more cumbersome.

If possible, the machines should be up and the spreadsheet program running when the students sit down. Ideally, you will have a sufficient number of computers so that there are two or three students at each. If you have four or five students at each computer, consider giving students specific roles so that each is engaged. If you have one machine for the class and a projector, it is possible to have the entire class interact to solve a single exercise. This makes the lab, however, much more of a demonstration than a lab.

This lab can be more complicated than it first seems. Many students who understand how to write the formulas may have forgotten how to refer one cell to another. Other technical mistakes, such as failing to hit the Return key after entering a formula, can reduce the speed, which is the primary benefit of using a spreadsheet for this strategy. If you aren't familiar with spreadsheets, you'll get a good preview of some of the mistakes that may show up in class if you complete a trial spreadsheet before committing any class periods to this lab.

**Setting Up the Spreadsheet** If you can project your computer screen, you can begin this lab with the entire class, entering the first example yourself. You can then pose Exercise 1 as a full class activity that parallels the explanation in the text.



Inquiry

Inquiry

## Investigation 2 Use a Spreadsheet to Guess-Check-and-Improve

### Materials

- computer with spreadsheet software (1 per group)

Guess-check-and-improve is a great method for solving simple equations, but it can be tedious when the equations are more complicated. The process is more efficient when you have a computer do the calculations while you do the thinking.

Sonia decided to use a spreadsheet to help her solve the following equation using guess-check-and-improve.

$$\frac{3n + 5}{2} = \frac{5n + 3}{3}$$

### Setting Up the Spreadsheet

First, Sonia entered headings and formulas in the top two rows of the first four columns of her spreadsheet.

Guess-Check-and-Improve.xls

| ◇ | A | B | C | D |
|---|---|---|---|---|
| 1 | Test Variable $n$ | Left Side $(3n + 5)/2$ | Right Side $(5n + 3)/3$ | Difference |
| 2 | | = (3 * A2 + 5)/2 | = (5 * A2 + 3)/3 | = B2 − C2 |
| 3 | | | | |

Sheet 1 | Sheet 2 | Sheet 3

As Sonia entered guesses for $n$ into her spreadsheet, she observed how the results changed so she could make a good choice for her next guess. When her guess is correct, the two sides of the equation will have the same value.

**1.** The formula in Cell D2 calculates the difference between the values in Cells B2 and C2. How do you think Sonia will use the difference to help make her next guess? Possible answer: She will check to see if the difference is 0 or is getting closer to 0.

Sonia started guessing the solution by entering 0 in Cell A2. The following are her results.

**Guess-Check-and-Improve.xls**

| | A | B | C | D |
|---|---|---|---|---|
| 1 | Test Variable $n$ | Left Side $(3n + 5)/2$ | Right Side $(5n + 3)/3$ | Difference |
| 2 | 0 | 2.500 | 1.000 | 1.500 |

Sheet 1 Sheet 2 Sheet 3

Sonia formatted the numbers in Cells B2, C2, and D2 to show three decimal places.

She decided to try 1 for her next guess. So, she entered 1 in Cell A2.

**Guess-Check-and-Improve.xls**

| | A | B | C | D |
|---|---|---|---|---|
| 1 | Test Variable $n$ | Left Side $(3n + 5)/2$ | Right Side $(5n + 3)/3$ | Difference |
| 2 | 1 | 4.000 | 2.667 | 1.333 |
| 3 | | | | |

Sheet 1 Sheet 2 Sheet 3

## Try It Out

2. Set up a spreadsheet like Sonia's on your computer. Enter Sonia's first two guesses to make sure your spreadsheet works. See students' work.
3. Use your spreadsheet to solve Sonia's equation. How do you know when you have found the solution? 9; The values in Cells B2 and C2 are the same, and the value in Cell D2 is 0.
4. Use your spreadsheet to solve each equation below. You will have to change the formulas in Cells B2 and C2 for each equation. Pay attention to the strategies you use to improve your guesses. You will be asked about them later.

   **a.** $4S - 70 = 18S$ $-5$   **b.** $4n + 1 = \frac{3n + 8}{2}$ 1.2

5. What strategies did you use to help you improve your guesses? Answers will vary. See teaching notes for possible strategies.

**Math Link**
Answers may be positive or negative, and they may be whole numbers or decimals.

Go on



Inquiry

## Try It Out

If you can project a spreadsheet, you may want to model the setup while students set up their own spreadsheets at their computers. Otherwise, it will be necessary for you to move from group to group, making sure that each group has made the correct entries in the spreadsheet.

▶ **Exercise 2** Make sure students recognize that a slash "/" is used in a spreadsheet instead of a division sign.

▶ **Exercise 3** Discuss this as a class to be sure that students understand how to interpret the data in the spreadsheet and recognize when they have solved the equation.

▶ **Exercise 4** As students work, make sure that each group is successfully working with the program. Encourage them to record their guesses and values in a table or list.

▶ **Exercise 5** Before discussing Exercise 5, tell groups to examine their tables or spreadsheets carefully. Then discuss the strategies that students use to improve their guesses.

Lesson 9.1 Find a Solution Method 441

## Try It Again

Discuss the "fill down" command before students begin this section. Students may take more time than you expect to become comfortable using this option.

## Use Your Spreadsheet

Remind the students that the formulas can be incremented by *any* fixed amount, positive or negative. They may need detailed technical, rather than conceptual, directions on how to accomplish this. If necessary, remind students that in the Try It Again section they used an incremental change of 1 when they copied the formula for the test variable in Column A. If they want a negative increment, they can change +1 to −1 in the formula. If they change the numerical value in the formula, they will change the size of the increment. For example, copying the formula A2 − 2 will result in a negative increment of 2.

▶ **Exercise 7** This exercise prompts students to see that they need to use negative numbers and decimals as guesses. Students may use these techniques to answer Exercises 8–10.

Inquiry

6. She will look for a value in Column A that produces a difference of 0 in Column D. The value 9, in Cell A11, gives a difference of 0 in Cell D11.

7a. Possible answer: Try a negative series of test values, starting from 0 and decreasing by some amount.

### Real-World Link

Spreadsheets range from quite simple to extremely complex. A family might use a spreadsheet to plan its monthly budget and a corporation might use one to help with financial planning.

## Try It Again

Sonia's friend Teresa solved the equation by making a spreadsheet to try a series of 20 guesses at once. She started by setting up a spreadsheet like Sonia's. Teresa then used the spreadsheet's "fill down" command to copy the formulas in Cells B2, C2, and D2 into Rows 3–21 of Columns B, C, and D.

To make a series of guesses, Teresa modified Column A. She entered 0 in Cell A2 and the formula A2 + 1 in Cell A3. Then she copied this formula into Cells A4 to A21. The program created a column of numbers that increased by 1, from 0 in Cell A2, to 19 in Cell A21.

**Guess-Check-and-Improve.xls**

| ◇ | A | B | C | D |
|---|---|---|---|---|
| 1 | Test Variable *n* | Left Side (3*n* + 5)/2 | Right Side (5*n* + 3)/3 | Difference |
| 2 | 0 | = (3 * A2 + 5)/2 | = (5 * A2 + 3)/3 | = B2 − C2 |
| 3 | = A2 + 1 | = (3 * A3 + 5)/2 | = (5 * A3 + 3)/3 | = B3 − C3 |
| 4 | = A3 + 1 | = (3 * A4 + 5)/2 | = (5 * A4 + 3)/3 | = B4 − C4 |

Sheet 1 / Sheet 2 / Sheet 3

**6.** Try this on your spreadsheet. How will Teresa know which value of $n$ gives a correct answer? Where is the solution on Teresa's spreadsheet?

## Use Your Spreadsheet

Not every equation has a solution that is an integer between 0 and 19.

**7.** Try to solve the equation $\frac{8x + 3}{3} = x - 3$ using Teresa's method. Make your first series of guesses the set of integers from 0 to 19.

**a.** Notice that the differences in Column D increase as the values in Column A increase. These guesses do not get closer to a solution. How could you modify Teresa's strategy to get closer?

**b.** Modify the formula in Column A to match your new strategy. Does 0 ever appear in Column D? If not, where does it look like the solution to this equation should be? Answers will vary; the solution is between −2 and −3.

**c.** Refine your guesses, if needed, and solve the equation. −2.4

Use a spreadsheet to solve the equations on page 443. Some solutions may not be positive and may not be integers. If you use Teresa's method, you may need to try more than one series of test values. Pay attention to the strategies you use to improve your guesses.



442 CHAPTER 9 Equations

12b. B2 and C2 correspond to the expressions on the left and right sides of the equation. D2 gives the difference between the values on the left and right sides.

**8.** $15x + 32 = 3x - 16$ $-4$

**9.** $\frac{7P + 34}{3} = \frac{13P - 4}{2}$ 3.2

**10.** Choose one of Exercises 8–11 on page 438. Use a spreadsheet to solve the equation. See answers to Exercises 8–11 on page 438.

## What Did You Learn?

**11.** When you solve equations with a spreadsheet, what strategies can you use to improve your guesses? Be sure to consider how to find negative and decimal solutions as well as positive integers.
Answers will vary.

**12.** Analyze this spreadsheet.

Guess-Check-and-Improve.xls

| | A | B | C | D |
|---|---|---|---|---|
| 1 | Test Variable $n$ | Left Side $4n + 2$ | Right Side $7n + 12$ | Difference |
| 2 | | =4 * A2 + 2 | =7 * A2 + 12 | = B2 − C2 |

Sheet 1 / Sheet 2 / Sheet 3

**a.** What equation was this spreadsheet set up to help solve?
$4n + 2 = 7n + 12$

**b.** What do the formulas in Cells B2, C2, and D2 mean?

**c.** What results will you get if you enter 1 in Cell A2?
B2: 6; C2: 19; D2: −13

Inquiry

## What Did You Learn?

You can use Exercises 11–12 for informal assessment during a class discussion or as a formal assessment to be done in class.

**Investigation 1**
Pages 437–439
Practice & Apply: 1–13
Connect & Extend: 14–18

**Assign Anytime**
Mixed Review: 19–24

▶ **Exercises 1–4, 7–9** You may wish to have students use Lesson 9.1 Master 1, Flowcharts, when they backtrack to solve the exercises.

▶ **Exercise 4** This equation is more complicated than many of those that students have solved. Some students may have trouble making a correct flowchart. Encourage them to choose a number and write the steps they would use to evaluate the expression substituting that number for the variable.

▶ **Exercise 12** Some students may translate this exercise by interpreting *16 more blue whistles than red* as $16 + b = r$. In such cases, have them look carefully at the quantities they have written and ask the Exercise "Which is larger?" Then have them compare this relation to that of the exercise.

▶ **Exercise 13 Extension** You may want to present this cubic equation as a challenge: $m(m(m + 3) - 1) = 3$. The solutions are $-1$, 1, and $-3$.

▶ **Exercise 14** Although students use the guess-check-and-improve strategy to solve this exercise, they look at the equality of the two sides of the equation. This will prepare them to use the balance model to solve equations in Lesson 2.

▶ **Exercise 14 Extension** It is worthwhile to have students redo this exercise using a spreadsheet after they have completed the lab investigation. You may want to give some students another quadratic equation to solve as well. For example, students could solve $x^2 = 2x + n$ with you assigning $n$ a different value for each group of students. If students use the "fill down" command to change the increment by tenths, they can find the change of signs and approximate both solutions.



On Your Own Exercises
Lesson 9.1

## Practice & Apply

**Use backtracking to solve each equation.**

1. $4d + 7 = -15$ $-5.5$
2. $4(2w + 1) = 52$ 6
3. $\frac{4x + 7}{5} = 3$ 2
4. $3(\frac{2c + 1}{5} + 1) = 6$ 2

**Use guess-check-and-improve to solve each equation.**

5. $b + 5 = 3b - 9$ 7
6. $4t - 3 = 3t + 7$ 10

**Which would be a better way to solve each equation, backtracking or guess-check-and-improve? Use the method you think is best to find each solution.**

7. $\frac{6y - 7}{3} = 5$ Backtracking; $3\frac{2}{3}$
8. $4u + 7 = 5 + 3u$ Guess-check-and-improve; $-2$
9. $5t + 34 = 17$ Backtracking; $-3.4$
10. Marcus has 20 comic books and gives 3 to his cousin Lelia every week. Mike has 10 comic books and buys 2 new ones each week.
    a. How many comic books will Marcus have after $w$ weeks? $20 - 3w$
    b. How many comic books will Mike have after $w$ weeks? $10 + 2w$
    c. Write an equation that represents Marcus and Mike having the same number of comic books after $w$ weeks. $20 - 3w = 10 + 2w$
    d. Solve your equation to find after how many weeks the two boys will have the same number of comic books. Check your solution. 2
11. Kiran said, "Eleven more than my number is the same as 18 more than twice my number." What is Kiran's number? $-7$
12. In a box of 64 red and blue whistles, there are 16 more blue whistles than red whistles. Write and solve an equation to determine how many are red. If $r$ = number of red whistles, $r + (r + 16) = 64$; $r = 24$ red whistles.
13. Solve this equation by guess-check-and-improve. There are two solutions. Find both. 12 and $-14$

$$m(m + 2) = 168$$

## Connect & Extend

14. **Preview** Charles was thinking about how to solve the equation $d(d - 2) = 46$. He said, "This seems simple. I want to know two numbers that multiply to give 46. One of the numbers is 2 less than the other. I'll use 8 as my first guess. Since 6 is two less than 8, that's $8 \cdot 6 = 48$. So, 8 is not the solution."
    a. What should Charles choose as his next guess? Answers will vary but should be less than 8.
    b. Use guess-check-and-improve to find a solution for $d$ to the nearest hundredth that gives a result within 0.1 of 46. Possible answers: 7.85, 7.86, $-5.85$, $-5.86$

## Real-World Link

The first drive-in theater opened June 6, 1933, in Camden, New Jersey. The idea was a success with close to 5,000 drive-ins operating by 1958. As the car became a part of daily life, the thrill of sitting in one to watch a movie declined. In 2007, a little more than 500 drive-ins remained in the United States.

**15.** At a drive-in theater, admission is \$4.00 per vehicle plus \$1.50 per person in the car.

**a.** Write an equation. Use $a$ to represent the total admission, $v$ for the number of vehicles, and $p$ for the number of people. $a = 4v + 1.50p$

**b.** Use your equation to determine how much money the theater will collect if 43 cars carrying a total of 93 people see a movie. $a = 4(43) + (93 \cdot 1.50) = 311.5$; \$311.50

**c.** Find the admission price for a car holding three people. $a = 4(1) + (3 \cdot 1.50) = 8.5$; \$8.50

**d.** The admission for one van was \$16. Use your equation to find how many people were in the van. $16 = 4(1) + 1.50p$; $p = 8$; 8 people

**16.** **Preview** Try to solve this equation using any method you choose. What do you discover? No positive or negative number is a solution of this equation.

$$n^2 + 3 = 2$$

**17.** Jim and Lillian were playing *Think of a Number.* Jim said, "Think of a number. Triple it. Add 5. Multiply your result by 10." Lillian said that her answer was 320.

**a.** What equation could Jim solve to find Lillian's number? $(3n + 5)10 = 320$

**b.** Use backtracking to solve the equation. 9

**18.** **In Your Own Words** Describe the types of equations that are better solved by backtracking, and the types that are better solved by guess-check-and-improve. Explain your reasoning. See margin.

## Mixed Review

**Determine the slope for each relationship.**

**19.** $y = 2x + 1.7$ 2 **20.** $y = -x - 1.2$ $-1$ **21.** $2y = 6x + 9$ 3

**Geometry** Find the value of the variable in each drawing.

**22.** $a = 3$

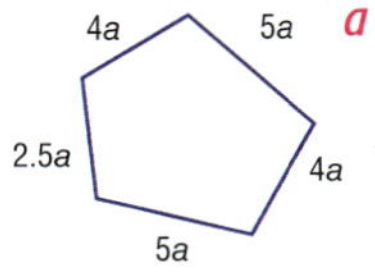


Perimeter = 61.5

**23.** $k = 2.5$

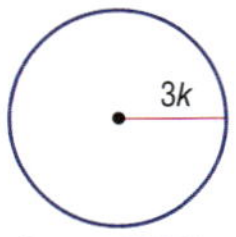


Area = $56.25\pi$

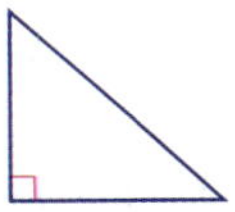


**24.** **Geometry** Consider the triangle at left.

**a.** What is the area of the triangle? 6 $cm^2$

**b.** Suppose you use this triangle as the base of a prism 1 cm high. What would be the prism's volume? 6 $cm^3$

**c.** Suppose you use the triangle to make a prism $h$ cm high. What would be the prism's volume? $6h$ $cm^3$



18. Answers will vary. Students may find backtracking more useful for equations with fraction or decimal solutions and guess-check-and-improve more useful for equations with variables on both sides.

On Your Own Exercises

## Quick Check

**Informal Assessment** Students should be able to:

- ✔ solve linear equations using guess-check-and-improve or backtracking strategies
- ✔ use variables to write algebraic expressions for a variety of situations and numerical relationships

## Quick Quiz

**1.** Use backtracking to solve the equation $3n - 2 = 49$. $n = 17$

**2.** Which is a better technique, guess-check-and-improve or backtracking, for solving the equation $3n - 2 = 2(n + 3)$? Solve the equation using this technique. Guess-check-and-improve; $n = 8$

**3.** A DVD store charges a customer a \$5 fine if a DVD is late and \$2 a day for each day it is overdue.

a. Jamar returns a DVD that is $x$ days overdue. Write an expression for the total amount he must pay. $5 + 2x$

b. Write an equation showing that Jamar owes the store \$75. $5 + 2x = 75$

c. Solve the equation in Part b to find the number of overdue days Jamar has kept the DVD. $x = 35$; 35 days

**4.** To ship a package, one shipping company charges \$3 plus \$2 per pound. Another company charges \$7 plus \$1 per pound. It would cost Ally the same amount to ship her package by either company. What is the weight of Ally's package?

a. Write an equation that describes the situation. $3 + 2x = 7 + x$

b. Solve the equation in Part a to determine the weight for which the two shipping charges are equal. $x = 4$; 4 pounds

LESSON 9.2

# A Model for Solving Equations

## Objectives

- To develop strategies for solving equations through operations with the balance model
- To extend the techniques of solving balance puzzles to equation-solving techniques that are independent of the model
- To provide experience in assigning variables and translating problems into algebraic sentences

## *Overview*

Students use a balance model to solve equations. Students previously used the bags and blocks part of this model when they wrote expressions in Chapter 1. Adding the balance pan to the model helps students see how to use equivalencies by doing the same thing to both sides of the model. It also helps them to think of an equation as a statement about the equality of two numbers rather than as a statement about the output of a series of operations on a number.

## *Advance Preparation*

You may find it helpful to create a variety of balance problems on sheets that can be handed out. You can also use Chapter 9 Masters 1–3, to create transparences of empty scales with bags and blocks.

| | Summary | Materials | On Your Own Exercises (pp. 455–459) | Assessment Opportunities |
|---|---|---|---|---|
| **Investigation 1** (p. 447) Pacing: 2 days | Students create and solve a number of balance puzzles. They reflect on the strategies they need to solve the balance puzzles. | Chapter 9 Masters 1–3, pan balance, bags and blocks | Practice & Apply: 1–4<br>Connect & Extend: 10<br>Mixed Review: 17–27 | • Share & Summarize (p. 448)<br>• Troubleshooting (p. 448) |
| **Investigation 2** (p. 449) Pacing: 1 day | Students write equations to describe balance puzzles, solve them by keeping things in balance, and create balance puzzles for their partners. | Chapter 9 Masters 1–3, pan balance, bags and blocks | Practice & Apply: 5–7<br>Connect & Extend: 11–12<br>Mixed Review: 17–27 | • Share & Summarize (p. 452) |
| **Investigation 3** (p. 453) Pacing: 1 day | Students solve equations by modeling them with balance problems. | | Practice & Apply: 8–9<br>Connect & Extend: 13–16<br>Mixed Review: 17–27 | • Share & Summarize (p. 454)<br>• Troubleshooting (p. 454) |

# Leveled Lesson Resources

CRM *Available in:* **Chapter 9 Resource Masters**

Also on TeacherWorks™ Lesson 9.2

## Study Guide and Intervention (p. 12) AL

**Lesson 9.2 Study Guide and Intervention**
***A Model for Solving Equations***

Balance puzzles help you visualize the steps involved in solving equations.
- In any puzzle, each bag must hold the same number of blocks.
- The total number of blocks on each side must be the same.

**Example 1** **Write an equation to fit the balance puzzle. Let $x$ represent the number of blocks in each bag. Use the puzzle to find the value of $x$.**

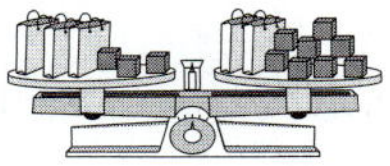

**Step 1** Use $3x$ to represent 3 bags and $2x$ to represent 2 bags.

3 bags and 3 blocks is $3x + 3$.
2 bags and 8 blocks is $2x + 8$.
The equation is $3x + 3 = 2x + 8$.

**Step 2** Remove 2 bags from each side and 3 blocks from each side.

Each bag has 5 blocks in it, so $x$ is 5.

**Example 2** **Draw a balance puzzle for $4x + 3 = 2x + 5$. Use your puzzle to solve the equation.**

**Step 1** Let $x$ represent the number of blocks in each bag.

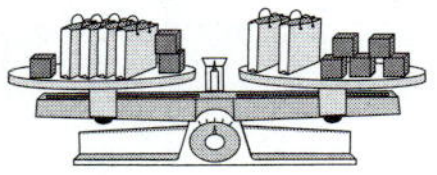

**Step 2** If you eliminate 2 bags and 3 blocks from each side, you will have 2 bags on the left side and 2 blocks on the right side. So, each bag holds 1 block.

The solution is 1. Check your solution: $4(1) + 3 = 7$; $2(1) + 5 = 7$.

**Exercises**

**Solve.**

1. Write an equation to fit a balance puzzle that has 5 bags and 6 blocks on its left side and 4 bags and 10 blocks on its right side.
2. Draw a balance puzzle for $2x + 9 = 6x + 1$. Use your puzzle to solve the equation.

## Skills Practice (p. 13) AL OL

**Lesson 9.2 Skills Practice**
***A Model for Solving Equations***

**Write an equation to fit the balance puzzle. Let $x$ represent the number of blocks in each bag. Then use the puzzle to find the value of $x$.**

1. 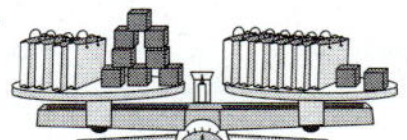
2. 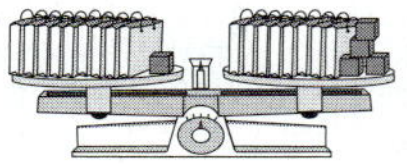
3. 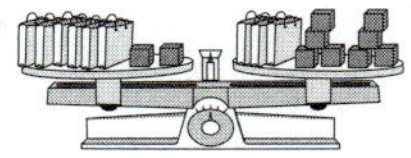
4. 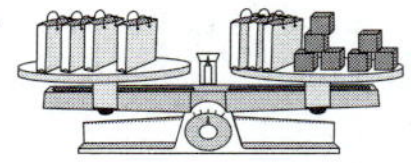

**Draw a balance puzzle to represent the equation. Use your puzzle to solve the equation. Check your solution by substituting it into the equation. (Hint: In these puzzles, the bags might hold fractions of blocks.)**

5. $2x + 7 = 4x + 3$
6. $3x + 6 = 5x + 1$
7. $2n + 6 = 8n + 3$
8. $6n + 9 = 9n + 6$

## Problem-Solving Practice (p. 14) AL OL

**Lesson 9.2 Problem-Solving Practice**
***A Model for Solving Equations***

1. **Balance Puzzle** Dalila created a balance puzzle.

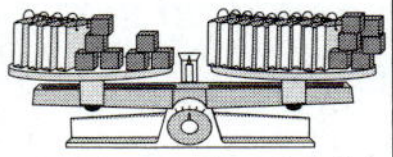

   a. Write an equation to fit Dalila's puzzle. Let $n$ represent the number of blocks in each bag.
   b. Dalila used her puzzle and found that the value of $n$ is 6. Is she correct? If not, give the correct answer, and explain Dalilia's mistake.

2. **Snack Packs** A wholesale center sells boxes of snack packs. There are a certain number of snack packs in each box. Jingdan purchases 4 boxes and 14 individual packs of trail mix. Akira purchases 2 boxes and 30 individual packs of trail mix. They each buy the same number of snack packs.
   a. Let $p$ represent the number of snack packs in a box. Write an equation you could use to find the value of $p$.
   b. Solve your equation by imagining a balance puzzle. Check your solution.
   c. How many snack packs did Jingdan buy?

3. **Number Game** Veronica said, "I'm thinking of a number. If I multiply my number by 11 and add 9, I get the same result as when I multiply it by 12 and add 3."
   a. Use $v$ to represent Veronica's number. Write an equation you could use to find the value of $v$.
   b. Solve your equation by imagining a balance puzzle. Check your solution.

4. **Flowers** Avita has picked 5 bundles of flowers so far this weekend and plans to pick an additional 64 flowers. Odina has picked 13 bundles of flowers this weekend. By the end of this weekend they will have picked the same number of flowers.
   a. Use $f$ to represent the number of flowers in each bundle. Write an equation you could use to find the value of $f$.
   b. Solve your equation by imagining a balance puzzle. Check your solution.
   c. How many flowers will each of the girls have picked by the end of this weekend?

## Enrichment (p. 15) BL

**Lesson 9.2 Enrichment**
***A Model for Solving Equations***

You have used balance puzzles to represent equations with positive numbers. You can also represent equations with *algebra tiles*. Algebra tiles allow you to work with both positive and negative numbers.

In a balance puzzle, you used a bag to represent a variable. With algebra tiles, you use an $x$-tile to represent a variable.

In a balance puzzle, you used blocks to represent positive numbers. With algebra tiles, you use 1-tiles to represent positive numbers and −1-tiles to represent negative numbers.

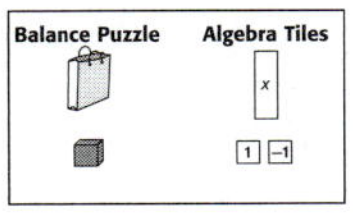


Consider the equation $3x + 6 = 7x - 10$. Use three $x$-tiles and six 1-tiles to represent the left side. Use seven $x$-tiles and ten −1-tiles to represent the right side.

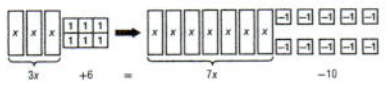

First, remove three $x$-tiles on each side.

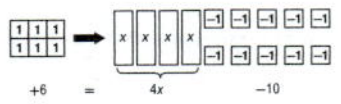

Next, you will eliminate all the −1-tiles on the side with $x$-tiles. Recall that $-1 + 1 = 0$. To eliminate ten −1-tiles, add ten 1-tiles to the right side. To keep the sides balanced, add ten 1-tiles to the left side.

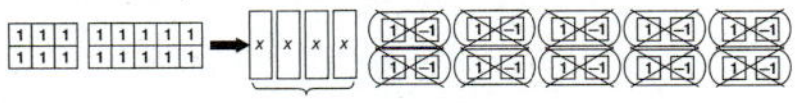

You are left with sixteen 1-tiles on the left and four $x$-tiles on the right. Each $x$ tile "contains" four 1-tiles. So, the value of $x$ is 4. Check the solution: $3(4) + 6 = 18$; $7(4) - 10 = 18$.

**Draw algebra tiles to represent each equation. Solve and check your solution with substitution.**

1. $4x + 8 = 7x - 7$
2. $6x - 1 = 5x + 2$
3. $2x + 8 = 4x - 4$
4. $8x - 5 = 3x + 5$

## Lesson Quick Quiz (p. 16) AL OL BL

**Lesson 9.2 Quick Quiz**

1. Three bags and 7 blocks are in balance with one bag and 12 blocks.
   a. Write an equation for this exercise.
   b. Solve the equation by using balance operations. Write an equation that matches each step and describe each step of the solution in terms of the balance.
2. Consider the equation $2n + 8 = 5n + 2$.
   a. Draw a picture of a balance puzzle that it might describe.
   b. Solve the equation matching each step with a balance operation.
3. **Challenge** Complete the equation $2x + 3 = ?$ so that it describes a balance puzzle that has an answer of 5.5 blocks.

# Additional Lesson Resources

### Teacher Tech Tools
- TeacherWorks
- ExamView Assessment Suite
- Classroom Presentation Toolkit
- Advance Tracker

### Student Tech Tools
- StudentWorks Plus
- Math Online eGlossary
- Concepts in Motion

### Other Print Products
- Investigation Notebook and Reflection Journal
- Quick Review Math Handbook

LESSON 9.2

# A Model for Solving Equations

## Introduce

**Using Models** This is a good time to talk about the usefulness of models. Give the class an example of a simple model that you have used. For example, you might say: *I often use my fingers to count up the successive days of the week to find the weekday five days from today.*

Then have students come up with their own examples of solving a exercise by manipulating something quite different. A few may remember using some identifying mark, perhaps a freckle or scar, on one hand to identify which is right and which is left. As soon as the point is made, introduce the pan balance with bags and blocks as a model of an equation.

## Explore

*Suggested Grouping: Individuals*

Give students an opportunity to work on this exercise individually. Then have them share with the class how they did the exercise. Some students may use guess-check-and-improve. If any students mentally move bags and blocks to keep the scale in balance, explicitly note that they seem to be applying some useful principles.



LESSON 9.2

# A Model for Solving Equations



**Vocabulary**

**model**

In this lesson and the next, you will learn an equation-solving method that is more efficient than guess-check-and-improve. This new method can often be used when backtracking will not work.

First, you will learn to use a model to help you think about solving equations. The word *model* has several meanings. A model can be something that *looks* like something else. For example, you have probably built or seen model cars or airplanes that look just like the real vehicles with all the parts of the model proportional to the actual parts.

In mathematics, a **model** is something that has some of the *key characteristics* of something else. In Chapter 1, you used bags and blocks as a model for algebraic expressions. Just as you can put any number of blocks into a bag, you can substitute any value for the variable in an expression.

Mathematical and scientific models help people understand complex ideas by simplifying them or making them easier to visualize. In this lesson, bags and blocks are again useful as models for algebraic expressions. By adding a balance, you can model algebraic *equations* and find more efficient ways to solve them.

## Explore

On this balance, each bag contains the same number of blocks. The bags weigh almost nothing compared to the blocks.

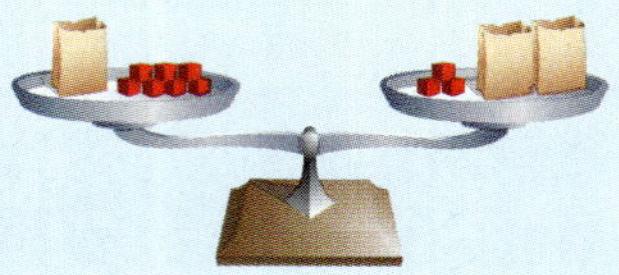

How many blocks are in each bag? Explain how you found your answer. See ①.

Check to make sure your answer is a solution to the puzzle.
1 bag of 4 blocks + 7 blocks = 11 blocks; 2 bags of 4 blocks + 3 blocks = 11 blocks

① 4; Possible explanation: I imagined removing 3 blocks from each side to get 1 bag and 4 blocks on the left balancing 2 bags on the right. Then I could see that 1 bag must contain 4 blocks. See teaching notes for other possibilities.

## Investigation 1 Balance Puzzles

Now it is your turn to draw some balance puzzles to try with your classmates. Here are the rules for creating balance puzzles.

- In any puzzle, all bags must hold the same number of blocks.
- The two sides of the balance must have the same total number of blocks with different combinations of bags and blocks on each side.

### Develop & Understand: A

1. Work by yourself to draw a puzzle with no more than 10 blocks on each side of the balance, including the blocks hidden in the bags. Exchange puzzles with your partner. Solve your partner's puzzle. Puzzles will vary.

2. Now draw a more difficult puzzle, using a total of 12 or more blocks on each side. Exchange puzzles with your partner. Solve your partner's puzzle. Puzzles will vary.

As you work with the balance puzzles in Exercises 3–7, try to think of more than one strategy for solving each puzzle.

### Develop & Understand: B

3. Melina and Sancho challenged their classmates to solve this balance puzzle.

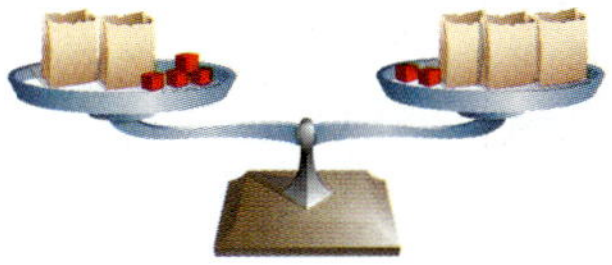

a. How many blocks are in each bag? Check your solution.
2; Check: $2 \cdot 2 + 4 = 8$, $3 \cdot 2 + 2 = 8$

b. What strategy did you use to solve the puzzle? Possible answer: I took 2 bags from each side. That left 4 blocks balancing 1 bag and 2 blocks, so there had to be 2 blocks in each bag.



## Investigation 1

***On Your Own Exercises***
Pages 455–459
Exercises 1–4, 10

**Balance Puzzles** All the exercises in this investigation, as well as Exercises 1–2 in Investigation 2, have positive whole numbers as the domain. The domain extends to fractions in Investigation 2 and to negative numbers in Lesson 3.

Review the rules for creating balance puzzles before having students work on the exercise sets. You may wish to provide students with copies of Chapter 9 Masters 1–3 to solve and record their puzzles.

### Develop & Understand: A

*Suggested Grouping: Pairs*

▶ **Exercises 1 and 2** This is a good activity in that students may present exercises to each other that are more difficult than you would assign at this point. If you want to present a student-generated exercise to the whole class, choose an interesting exercise and have the authors write their puzzle on an overhead.

**Wrap-Up** Discuss some of the strategies that students used to solve the balance puzzles. This will help prepare them for the puzzles in Exercises 3–7.

Point out that students should try to think of more than one strategy for solving the balance puzzles in the next exercise set.

### Develop & Understand: B

*Suggested Grouping: Pairs*

▶ **Exercises 3–7** Students solve balance puzzles. Some students may use the guess-check-and-improve strategy to find the number of blocks. Others may mentally move the bags and blocks to create a simpler exercise. Some students may start to use algebraic notation to symbolize these puzzles because it is simpler than mentally keeping track of the bags and blocks. These strategies are discussed in the Share & Summarize.

**▶ Exercise 6** Some students may neglect to count the block between the two bags on the left-hand pan.

### *Share & Summarize*

Allow students some time to work individually, with each selecting an exercise from Exercises 3–7 and reviewing how he or she solved it. Then have a volunteer describe to the class his or her method of solving one of the puzzles. When the presentation is concluded, ask if anyone else who selected that exercise used a different method to solve it, and have them share their method. Try to discuss all the exercises in the exercise set. If no student selected one of the puzzles, you may want to describe it as a class.

**Teacher Tips** Students may use one of these strategies to solve balance puzzles:

- Some students may use the guess-check-and-improve strategy, by either randomly selecting numbers or by systematically trying 1 block, 2 blocks, and so on.
- Other students may mentally remove bags and blocks to create a simpler puzzle.
- Some students may use algebraic symbols to solve the exercise.

Make sure that the concept of changing the balance puzzle to a simpler one, that is mentally removing bags and blocks, is clearly emphasized as a useful technique.

Melina and Sancho's classmates created similar puzzles. Solve each puzzle by finding how many blocks are in each bag.

**4.** Tanya and Craig's puzzle 2

**5.** Margaret and Aida's puzzle 6

**6.** Uma and Ted's puzzle 3

**7.** Will and Trent's puzzle 5

### *Share & Summarize*

Select one of the balance puzzles from Exercises 4–7. Explain your solution method so that someone in another class could understand it. Be sure to justify your reasoning. Answers will vary.



## *Troubleshooting*

Students having difficulty drawing balance puzzles may find using concrete materials helps to clarify the concepts. They can use blocks and bags to model each exercise, physically trying different quantities of blocks until the sides are equal.

Some students may insist on using algebraic symbols to describe a balance puzzle. This is fine, since they are asked to do this in the next investigation. However, when you talk about balance operations, refer to operations using bags and blocks.

## Investigation 2 Keep Things Balanced

By now, you have probably seen and used a variety of strategies to solve exercises about balance. In this investigation, you will focus on solving puzzles by "keeping things balanced." Soon, you will see how the thinking involved in this strategy can help you solve equations.

### *Example*

Here is how Malik solved Exercise 7 on page 448.

Malik kept things balanced by taking the same number of bags or blocks from each side until he had only 1 bag on the right and 5 blocks on the left.

### Develop & Understand: A

Solve each puzzle by keeping things balanced. For each step, record what you do and what is left on each side of the balance. You may draw each step if you prefer. Be sure to check your solutions.

**1.**

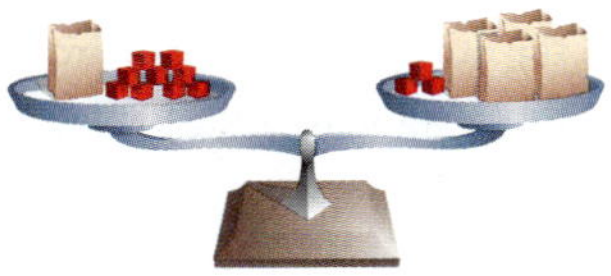

**2.**

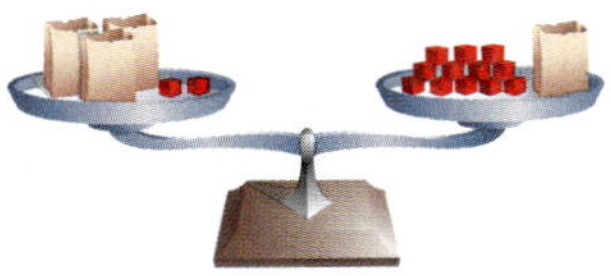



1. Possible answer: Remove 1 bag from each side, leaving 9 blocks on the left, 3 bags and 3 blocks on the right. Then remove 3 blocks from each side, leaving 6 blocks on the left, 3 bags on the right. Each bag must hold 2 blocks.
2. Possible answer: Remove 2 blocks from each side, leaving 3 bags on the left, 1 bag and 10 blocks on the right. Then remove 1 bag from each side, leaving 2 bags on the left, 10 blocks on the right. Each bag must hold 5 blocks.

## Investigation 2

***On Your Own Exercises***
Pages 455–459
Exercises 5–7, 11–12

**Balance** Investigation 2 introduces the idea of making changes to each side of the pan balance in such a way as to keep the sides in balance, which sets the stage for doing the same thing to both sides of an equation.

### *Example*

Have students read the example on page 449. You might make transparencies of Chapter 9 Masters 1–3 to demonstrate Malik's thinking.

Be sure students understand the illustration in the third frame of the Example.

### Develop & Understand: A

*Suggested Grouping: Individuals*

In this exercise set, students record what they are doing at each step as they solve balance exercises. This establishes a structure for solving equations using the balance model in Exercises 3–4.

**Wrap-Up** Have students share their answers to Exercises 1–2. Be sure students explain the steps they used to solve each exercise.

### *Reaching All Learners*

**ELL English Language Learners**
If students find it difficult to describe in words the steps they use to solve the puzzles, encourage them to use drawings or even symbols. As an alternative, a student who speaks English as a second language might find it easier to write answers in the native language and then translate the answers at a later time.

**Lesson 9.2** A Model for Solving Equations **449**

## Example

Tell students that the techniques they used to write expressions in Chapter 1 can also be used to write algebraic equations describing balance puzzles. Then read and discuss the Example. Call on students to use Meg's method to write equations for Exercises 1–2.

1. $n + 9 = 4n + 3$
2. $3n + 2 = n + 12$

If you find that students have difficulty writing the equations, consider doing Exercises 3–4 as a whole-class activity.

## Develop & Understand: B

*Suggested Grouping: Individuals*

This exercise set extends the Example and provides students with practice using algebraic symbolism to describe balance problems.

Students solve the equations by referring to operations on the balance. Encourage students to refer to the model.

All students should be able to express operations in the model with algebraic symbolism. However, some students don't need the model and consider it busywork. Don't insist that these students continue to use it.



In Chapter 1, you wrote algebraic *expressions* to represent situations involving bags and blocks. In the same way, you can write algebraic *equations* to describe balance puzzles.

### Example

Here is how Meg made a balance puzzle.

On this side, Meg put 2 bags of blocks and 5 single blocks. If $n$ stands for the number of blocks in each bag, then the number of blocks in "two bags and five blocks" is $2n + 5$.

On this side, Meg put 3 bags of blocks and 2 single blocks. The number of blocks in "three bags and two blocks" is $3n + 2$.

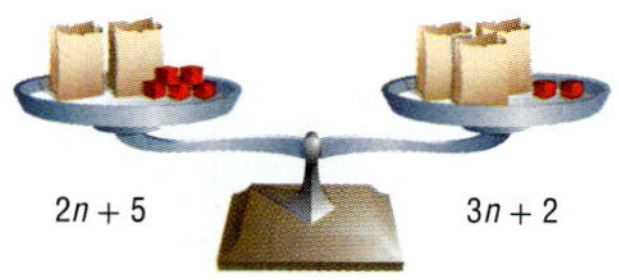


Since the sides balance, the number of blocks on the left, $2n + 5$, is equal to the number of blocks on the right, $3n + 2$. This can be expressed with the following equation.

$$2n + 5 = 3n + 2$$

When you find the number of blocks in each bag, you have found the value of $n$.

## Develop & Understand: B

**3.** Look at Meg's balance.

**a.** Find the number of blocks in each bag. 3

**b.** Check that your answer is a solution of the equation $2n + 5 = 3n + 2$. $2 \cdot 3 + 5 = 11, 3 \cdot 3 + 2 = 11$

**4.** Nguyen created this balance puzzle.

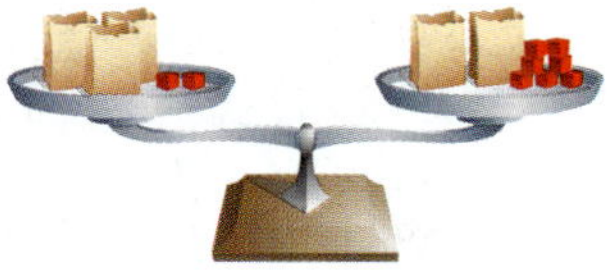

**a.** Let $b$ stand for the number of blocks in each bag. Write an equation that fits Nguyen's balance puzzle. $3b + 2 = 2b + 7$

**b.** Use the drawing to help you find the value of $b$. 5

**c.** Check that your answer to Part b is a solution of your equation.
$3 \cdot 5 + 2 = 17, 2 \cdot 5 + 7 = 17$

### Think & Discuss

Shada created this balance puzzle.

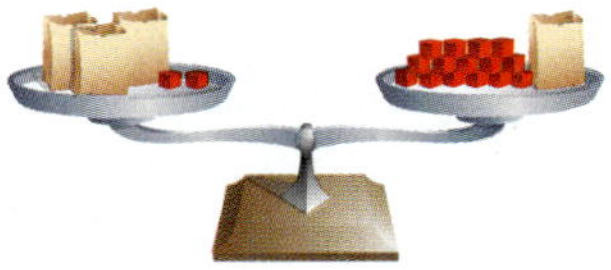

- Write an equation to represent Shada's puzzle.
  $3n + 2 = n + 15$
- How many blocks are in each bag? $6\frac{1}{2}$
- Check that your answer is a solution of your equation.
  $3 \cdot 6\frac{1}{2} + 2 = 21\frac{1}{2}, 6\frac{1}{2} + 15 = 21\frac{1}{2}$

Joel said that Shada would not be able to create her puzzle with real blocks because each bag would have to include a half of a block. Shada said she was thinking of a slightly different model, one with blocks made of clay so they could be easily divided. That way, her balance puzzles can include fractions of blocks.

### Think & Discuss

This activity expands the domain of the variable to include fractions. Read and discuss the Exercises in this section. Some students may question how the model can be used to show fractional amounts. It is likely that other students will provide explanations. If not, have them read Shada's response in the paragraph following this section.

Before moving on to Exercises 5–6, be sure that students understand that the solutions to the balance puzzles can use fractions of blocks.

**Lesson 9.2** A Model for Solving Equations **451**

## Develop & Understand: C

*Suggested Grouping: Individuals*

These exercises involve balance puzzles that have fractions of blocks in the bags, and hence in the solutions.

**Wrap-Up** Discuss the solutions for both equations. You may want to point out that either fractions or decimals can be used to write and solve the equation in Exercise 6.

### Share & Summarize

The activity of exchanging puzzles gives lots of practice in an informal environment. As you circulate, note some of the best puzzles and have them presented to the class as a whole.

Some students may write puzzles that are too difficult. You may need to restrict the complexity of the fractions or the quantities on the scales.

## Develop & Understand: C

In these puzzles, the bags might hold fractions of blocks.

**5.** Karena made this puzzle.

**a.** Write an equation that fits Karena's puzzle. $5h + 1 = 2h + 5$

**b.** How many blocks are in each bag? Explain how you found your solution.

**c.** Check that your answer to Part b is a solution of your equation.
$5\left(\frac{4}{3}\right) + 1 = \frac{23}{3}, 2\left(\frac{4}{3}\right) + 5 = \frac{23}{3}$

5b. $\frac{4}{3}$, or $1\frac{1}{3}$; Remove 2 bags and 1 block from each side, leaving 3 bags balancing 4 blocks.

**6.** Toby made this puzzle.

**a.** Write an equation that fits Toby's puzzle. $4t + 1 = 2t + 8$

**b.** How many blocks are in each bag? Explain how you found your solution.

**c.** Check that your answer to Part b is a solution of your equation.
$4 \cdot 3.5 + 1 = 15, 2 \cdot 3.5 + 8 = 15$

6b. 3.5; Remove 2 bags and 1 block from each side, leaving 2 bags balancing 7 blocks.

### Share & Summarize

**1.** Create a balance puzzle for which the solution is not a whole number of blocks. Exchange puzzles and solve your partner's puzzle. Puzzles will vary.

**2.** Write an equation that describes your puzzle. Explain how the equation fits the puzzle. Answers will vary.

**3.** Check that the solution to your puzzle is also a solution of the equation. Answers will vary.



## Reaching All Learners

**AL Approaching Level** In Exercise 5, watch for students who think that they can only use whole or half-blocks to solve equations. They will write their answers using halves instead of thirds. You may want to provide these students with copies of Chapter 9 Masters 1–3, so that they can physically remove bags and blocks until they have three bags on one side and four blocks on the other. They may want to cut one of the blocks into equal-sized pieces and then distribute all the pieces, placing an equal number in each bag to check their answers.

# Investigation 3 Solve Problems with Balance Puzzles

You have seen that the solution of a balance puzzle is the same as the solution of an equation that represents the puzzle. Now you will solve equations by creating and solving balance puzzles. In some cases, the solutions may not be whole numbers.

## Develop & Understand: A

**1.** Consider the equation $3n + 8 = 5n + 2$.

**a.** Draw a balance puzzle to represent the equation. Explain how you know your puzzle matches the equation. See margin.

**b.** Use your puzzle to solve the equation. Check your solution by substituting it into the equation. 3

**2.** Consider the equation $4t + 6 = 13 + 2t$.

**a.** Draw a balance puzzle to represent the equation. Explain how you know your puzzle matches the equation. See margin.

**b.** Use your puzzle to solve the equation. Check your solution by substituting it into the equation. 3.5

Try to solve these equations by imagining a balance puzzle, rather than actually drawing one. Check each solution by substituting it into the equation.

**3.** $2h + 3 = h + 10$ 7

**4.** $4t + 6 = 13 + 3t$ 7

# Investigation 3

***On Your Own Exercises***
Pages 455–459
Exercises 8–9, 13–16

**Solve Equations** In previous work, students have been creating equations to describe balance puzzles. This investigation asks students to use balance puzzles to solve given equations. Students should apply the methods of solving balance puzzles to the solution of equations. Eventually, of course, these methods will be described in terms of operations performed on both sides of the equations themselves rather than in reference to the balance model.

## Develop & Understand: A

*Suggested Grouping: Pairs*

▶ **Exercises 1 and 2** Students' explanations will differ greatly. We suggest that you interpret students' responses flexibly, keeping in mind that the important objective is to have students associate elements of the equation with the balance exercise.

▶ **Exercises 3 and 4** Students should try to solve the equation by imagining the model without actually drawing it. Too often the process of recording information interferes with the process of thinking about it.

**Wrap-Up** Have students share their explanations for Exercises 1–2 to reinforce their understanding. You may want to point out that the order of the bags and blocks in each pan doesn't matter. It is the number of each that determines the expression on that side of the equation.

**Additional Answers**

1a. $n$ stands for the number of blocks in a bag, so the balance has 3 bags ($3n$ blocks) plus 8 blocks on one side, and 5 bags ($5n$ blocks) plus 2 blocks on the other.

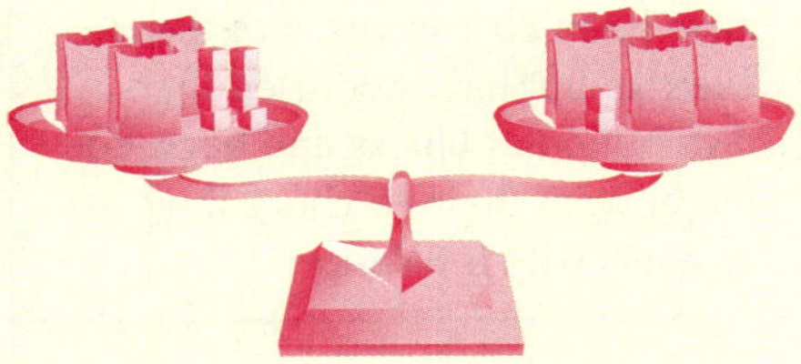

2a. $4t$ and $2t$ stand for the number of blocks in 4 bags and 2 bags, so I drew 4 bags on one side and 2 on the other. Then I added the loose blocks, 6 on the side with 4 bags and 13 on the side with 2 bags.

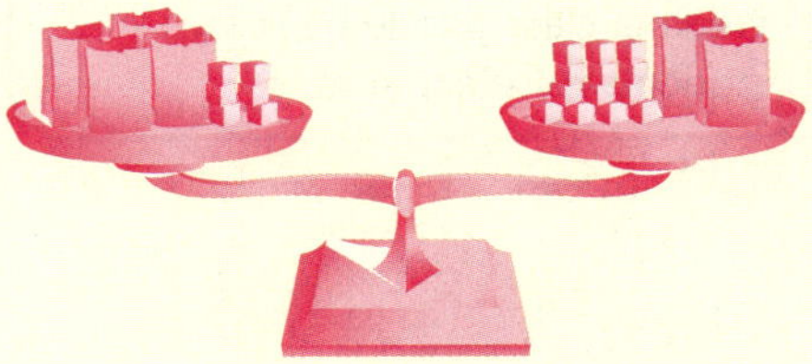

## Develop & Understand: B

*Suggested Grouping: Individuals*

This exercise set introduces two variations on the balance puzzle: a continuously variable quantity (liquid) and a number puzzle. Some students may find it intriguing that a balance puzzle can be used to solve a number puzzle.

**Wrap-Up** Have students describe the imaginary balances that they used to solve Exercises 5–6.

### Share & Summarize

You may want to select a few students to present their responses to the whole class.

Students who have difficulty explaining how to use the balance puzzle may benefit from working in pairs. One student can describe what they are doing to solve the equation while the other student writes the steps. As students describe the model, encourage them to explain which number on the left side of an equation represents the number of bags and which number represents the number of blocks. Repeat for the right side of the equation.

Some students will be thinking of an equation quite independently of a balance. Others will still depend on modeling an equation with a balance exercise. Either way of thinking is reasonable as long as students are able to model an equation with a balance exercise and represent a balance exercise with an equation.

If you can represent a problem situation with an equation, you can sometimes draw or imagine a balance puzzle to find the solution.

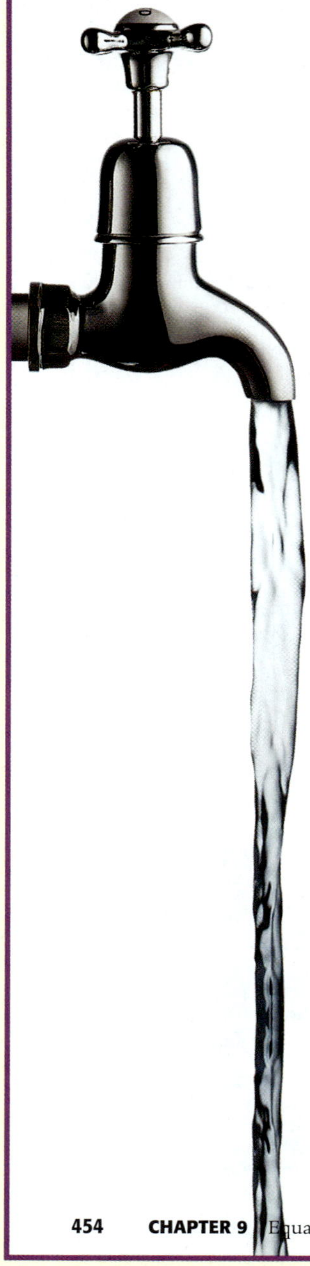

## Develop & Understand: B

**5.** Jenny was filling bottles from a tank of water. When she had filled two bottles, 7 liters of water remained in the tank. When she had filled four bottles, 2 liters of water were left in the tank.

**a.** Let $v$ represent the amount of water each bottle holds. Write an equation you could solve to find the value of $v$. $2v + 7 = 4v + 2$

**b.** Solve your equation by imagining a balance puzzle. Check your solution. 2.5

**6.** Miriam said, "I am thinking of a number. If I multiply my number by 6 and add 5, I get the same result as when I multiply it by 3 and add 17."

**a.** Use $M$ to represent Miriam's number. Write an equation you could solve to find the value of $M$. $6M + 5 = 3M + 17$

**b.** Solve your equation by imagining a balance puzzle. Check your solution. 4

**7.** Marvin said, "I am thinking of a number. If I add 3 to my number, I get the same result as when I multiply it by 4 and add 21."

**a.** Use $m$ to represent Marvin's number. Write an equation you could solve to find the value of $m$. $m + 3 = 4m + 21$

**b.** Solve your equation by imagining a balance puzzle. Check your solution. $-6$

### Share & Summarize

Explain how you can use a balance puzzle to solve an equation. Your explanation should be clear enough that someone from another class could understand it. Answers will vary.



### Reaching All Learners

**BL Beyond Level** Challenge students to create number puzzles like Miriam's in Exercise 6 that can be modeled by balance puzzles. You might use workable puzzles to create a class puzzle bank for students to select from.

### Troubleshooting

Watch for students who confuse the numerator and the denominator in Exercise 5 and answer $\frac{2}{5}$ instead of $\frac{5}{2}$ or 2.5. These students may have been able to visualize the exercise but have confused the distribution of blocks and bags. You might want them to check their answers with a balance.

**Practice & Apply**

The students in Ms. Avila's class made some balance puzzles. In Exercises 1–4, tell how many blocks are in each bag. Remember, in a balance puzzle, every bag holds the same number of blocks.

**1.** Carla and Toshiro's puzzle 1

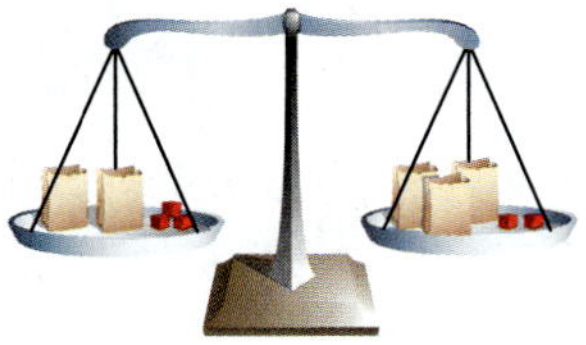

**2.** Alberto and Elena's puzzle 2

**3.** Benita and Ayana's puzzle 4

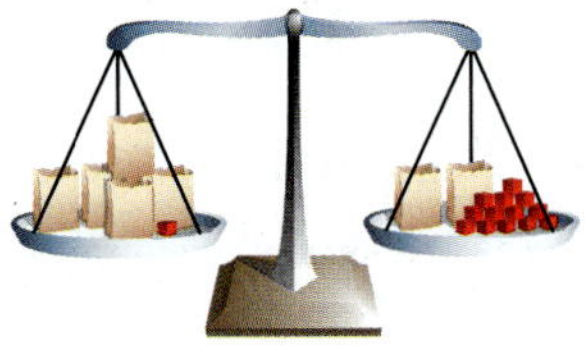

**4.** Maggie and Jonas' puzzle 2

**5.** Make up three balance puzzles with 11 blocks total on each side. Write an equation for each puzzle, and solve each equation.
Possible answer: $2x + 1 = x + 6, x = 5$; $2x + 5 = 3x + 2, x = 3$; $5x + 1 = x + 9, x = 2$

**6.** Raphael and Gary made this balance puzzle. How many blocks are in each bag? Write down each step you take to solve this puzzle.

6. 5; Possible steps: Remove 4 bags from each side, leaving 8 blocks on the left, 1 bag and 3 blocks on the right; remove 3 blocks from each side, leaving 5 blocks balancing 1 bag.



On Your Own Exercises
Lesson 9.2

**Investigation 1**
Pages 447–448
Practice & Apply: 1–4
Connect & Extend: 10

**Investigation 2**
Pages 449–452
Practice & Apply: 5–7
Connect & Extend: 11–12

**Investigation 3**
Pages 453–454
Practice & Apply: 8–9
Connect & Extend: 13–16

**Assign Anytime**
Mixed Review: 17–27

▶ **Exercise 5 Extension** As a follow-up discussion, collect all the student-created puzzles and note the number of different puzzles. Challenge the group to find six possible answers not already found.

**▶ Exercise 10** This exercise can be a challenge, and students may spend more time on it than you would first think. Encourage a discussion of solution strategies.

On Your Own Exercises

10a. Possible answer: From the right balance, 6 marbles are 60 g, so 4 jacks are 60 g and 1 jack is 15 g. From the left balance, remove 1 jack and 1 marble from each side, leaving 2 blocks on the left; 2 jacks plus 3 marbles on the right. Two jacks and 3 marbles are $30 + 30 = 60$ g. Therefore, 2 blocks are 60 g, and 1 block is 30 g.

**7.** Consider this balance puzzle.

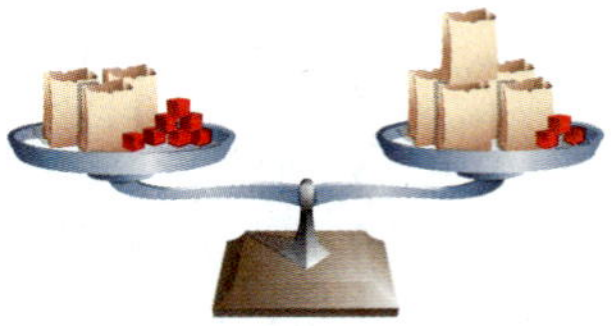

**a.** Write an equation to fit this puzzle. Let $n$ represent the number of blocks in each bag. $3n + 7 = 5n + 3$

**b.** Use the drawing to find the value of $n$. 2

**c.** Check that your answer to Part b is a solution of your equation. $3 \cdot 2 + 7 = 13, 5 \cdot 2 + 3 = 13$

**8.** Consider the equation $3p + 10 = 5p + 3$.

**a.** Draw a balance puzzle to represent the equation. Explain how you know your puzzle matches the equation. See margin.

**b.** Use your drawing to solve the equation. Check your solution by substituting it into the equation. 3.5

**9.** Nicky said, "The sum of my number and 21 is the same as 4 times my number. What is my number?"

**a.** Use $N$ to represent Nicky's number. Write an equation you could solve to find the value of $N$. $N + 21 = 4N$

**b.** Solve your equation by imagining a balance puzzle. Check your solution. 7

## Connect & Extend

**10. Mass** The balances below each hold different sets of blocks, jacks, and marbles. Each marble has a mass of ten grams.

**a.** Find the mass of each jack and the mass of each block. Describe the steps you take.

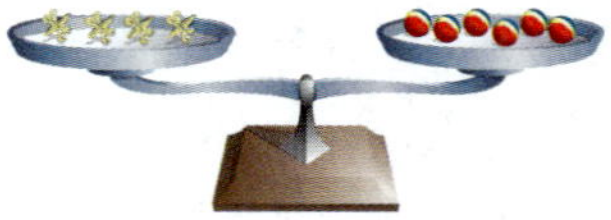

**b.** This balance has blocks, marbles, and jacks from Part a, plus some toothpicks. Find the mass of each toothpick. 10 g

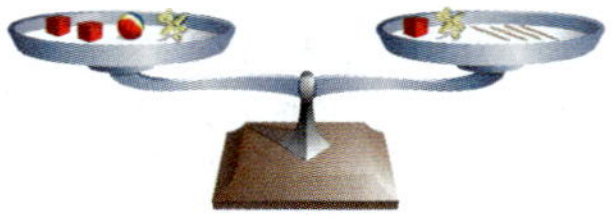



**Additional Answer**

8a. The 3 bags on the left and the 5 bags on the right represent $3p$ and $5p$; the 10 individual blocks on the left and the 3 on the right represent 10 and 3.

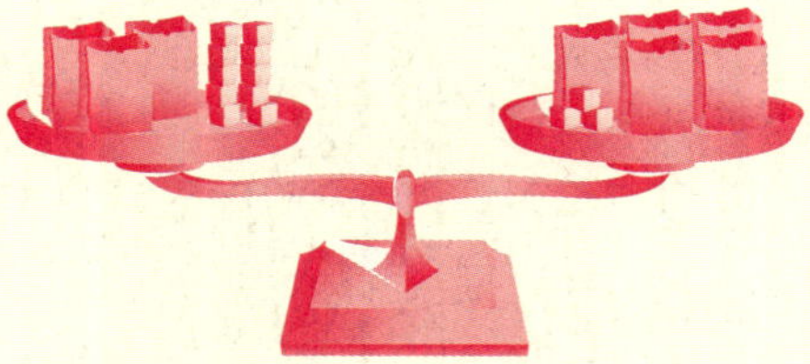

**11.** Sareeta and her brother Rashid put stickers in bags to give away at Sareeta's birthday party. They started with an equal number of stickers and put the same number in each bag. Sareeta filled five bags and had one sticker left. Rashid filled four bags and had seven stickers left.

**a.** Let $n$ represent the number of stickers in a bag. Write an expression that describes the way Sareeta distributed her stickers. $5n + 1$

**b.** Write an expression that describes Rashid's four bags and seven extra stickers. $4n + 7$

**c.** Because Sareeta and Rashid started with the same number of stickers, it is possible to balance their distributions of stickers. Draw a balance puzzle to show this. See margin.

**d.** Write an equation that matches your balance puzzle. $5n + 1 = 4n + 7$

**e.** Use your balance puzzle to find how many stickers are in each bag. 6

**f.** Show that your answer to Part e is a solution of the equation. $5 \cdot 6 + 1 = 31, 4 \cdot 6 + 7 = 31$

**12.** Read the story about Sareeta and Rashid in Exercise 11.

**a.** Create a similar story that can be represented by the equation $3n + 2 = 2n + 9$. Stories will vary.

**b.** Draw a balance puzzle for this equation, and find the value of $n$. See margin.

**c.** Show that your answer to Part b is a solution of the equation. $3 \cdot 7 + 2 = 23, 2 \cdot 7 + 9 = 23$

**13.** Consider the equation $2v + 50 = 7v + 30$.

**a.** Describe a situation that matches this equation. Answers will vary.

**b.** Find the value of $v$. Check your solution. 4

**c.** Explain what your solution means in terms of the situation you described in Part a. Answers will vary.



On Your Own Exercises

▶ **Exercises 11 and 12** These exercises are a preview of the next investigations where students are asked to draw a balance puzzle to represent equations. Students who understand the concepts in Investigations 1 and 2 should have sufficient skills to complete these exercises.

## Additional Answers

11c.

12b. $n = 7$

**Lesson 9.2** A Model for Solving Equations **457**

▶ **Exercise 14** Students write expressions to describe geometric patterns and then use their expressions to find the number of squares in a particular stage in the sequence. You may need to tell students that Shape 0, not Shape 1, contains the first number of squares.

▶ **Exercise 15** The exercise asks for the length of the streamers. However, students may choose to let the variable denote the length of the crepe paper. In either case, there are several ways to write correct equations, such as $S + 3 + 1 = 2S$ or $\frac{1}{2}(S + 3 + 1) = S$. You may want to have students present their solutions.





**14. Patterns** Study the pattern of shapes.

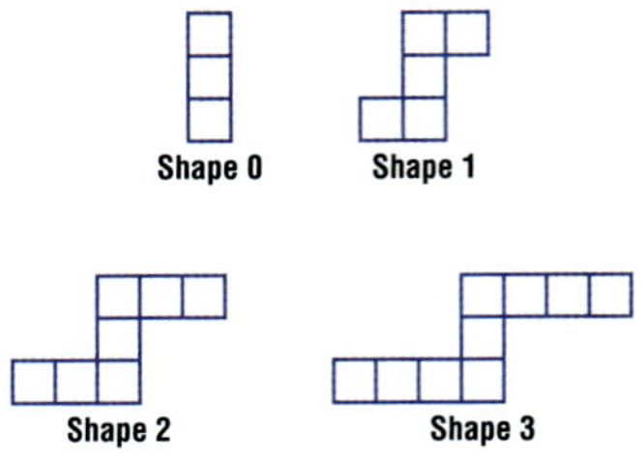


**a.** How many squares will be in shape 4? In shape 5? 11, 13

**b.** Write an expression for the number of squares in shape $n$. $2n + 3$

**c.** How many squares will be in shape 20? 43

**d.** Write an equation to find which shape will have 25 squares. Solve your equation. $2n + 3 = 25$; $n = 11$ (shape 11)

15a. If $S$ = streamer length, crepe paper length = $S + 3$; 1 ft longer is $S + 4$, which is equal to $2S$; so, $2S = S + 4$, and the streamer length is 4 ft.

16. Answers will vary. Possible answer: Doing the same thing to both sides of an equation maintains a balance since both sides remain balanced or equal.

**15. Challenge** Sergei and Hilary were cutting streamers of a particular length for a party. Sergei held up a strip of crepe paper and said he could cut one streamer from it and have three feet left. Hilary said that if the strip of crepe paper was one foot longer, she could cut exactly two streamers from it.

**a.** Find the length of the streamers cut by Sergei and Hilary. Show how you found your answer.

**b.** Find the length of Sergei's strip of crepe paper. $S + 3 = 7$ ft

**16. In Your Own Words** Susan said, "When I think about solving equations using a balance puzzle, I think about doing the same thing on each side." What do you think she means?

## Mixed Review

**17. Probability** Kayla fills a jar with 100 chips, some blue and some orange. She asks Ignacio to guess how many of each color are in the jar.

**a.** Ignacio reaches in without looking and removes ten chips, four blue and six orange. What reasonable guess might he make for the number of chips of each color in the jar? Possible answer: 40 blue, 60 orange

**b.** Ignacio takes out five more chips, and all are orange. What reasonable guess might he now make for the number of chips of each color in the jar? Possible answer: 27 blue, 73 orange

**c.** Kayla tells Ignacio there are actually three times as many orange chips as blue chips in the jar. How many of each are there? 25 blue, 75 orange

**18.** You are traveling by train and bus. The train averages 70 mph, and the bus averages 50 mph.

**a.** Let $t$ and $b$ represent how many hours you ride on the train and the bus, respectively. Write an expression for the total miles you travel on your trip. $70t + 50b$

**b.** Suppose the total distance you travel is 600 miles. Use your answer from Part a to express this as an equation. $70t + 50b = 600$

**c.** If you travel 600 miles and spend five hours on the train, how many hours is the bus ride? 5 hours

**Find each sum or difference.**

**19.** $\frac{1}{5} + \frac{2}{5}$ $\frac{3}{5}$

**20.** $\frac{1}{4} + \frac{3}{4}$ $\frac{4}{4}$ or 1

**21.** $\frac{7}{8} - \frac{6}{8}$ $\frac{1}{8}$

**22.** $\frac{3}{7} + \frac{1}{6}$ $\frac{25}{42}$

**23.** $\frac{2}{3} + \frac{5}{8}$ $\frac{31}{24}$ or $1\frac{7}{24}$

**24.** $\frac{3}{4} - \frac{2}{3}$ $\frac{1}{12}$

**25.** $\frac{1}{2} + \left(-\frac{1}{4}\right)$ $\frac{1}{4}$

**26.** $\frac{3}{7} + \left(-\frac{4}{9}\right)$ $-\frac{1}{63}$

**27.** $\frac{6}{11} - \left(-\frac{2}{5}\right)$ $\frac{52}{55}$



On Your Own Exercises

## Quick Check

**Informal Assessment** Students should be able to:

- ✔ develop strategies for solving equations through operations with the balance model
- ✔ extend the techniques of solving balance puzzles to equation-solving techniques that are independent of the model
- ✔ assign variables and translate exercises into algebraic sentences

## Quick Quiz

**1.** Three bags and 7 blocks are in balance with one bag and 12 blocks.

a. Write an equation for this exercise.
$3b + 7 = b + 12$

b. Solve the equation by using balance operations. Write an equation that matches each step and describe each step of the solution in terms of the balance.

$3b + 7 = 1b + 12$
$3b = 1b + 5$ Subtract 7 blocks from each side.
$2b = 5$ Subtract 1 bag from each side.
$b = 2.5$ Divide by 2.

**2.** Consider the equation $2n + 8 = 5n + 2$.

a. Draw a picture of a balance puzzle that it might describe. Students may use either type of scale:

b. Solve the equation matching each step with a balance operation.

$2n + 8 = 5n + 2$
$2n + 6 = 5n$ Subtract 2 blocks from each side.
$6 = 3n$ Subtract 2 bags from each side.
$2 = n$ Divide each side by 3.

**3. Challenge** Complete the equation $2x + 3 = ?$ so that it describes a balance puzzle that has an answer of 5.5 blocks.
$2x + 3 = 14$

LESSON 9.3

# Solve Equations

## Objectives

- To solve equations without using the balance puzzle model
- To express a balance puzzle as an algebraic equation
- To represent an equation as a balance puzzle
- To solve simple word problems by writing and solving equations

## *Overview*

This lesson reviews and extends what students know about using balance puzzles with operations to solve equations and has them apply this technique to solve equations without reference to the model. The primary purpose of this lesson is to make this transition.

## *Advance Preparation*

None

| | Summary | Materials | On Your Own Exercises (pp. 469–473) | Assessment Opportunities |
|---|---|---|---|---|
| **Investigation 1** (p. 461) Pacing: 2 days | Students solve equations by imagining a balance puzzle. They focus on changes made to equations they have solved using a balance model. | Chapter 9 Masters 1–3 | Practice & Apply: 1–6<br>Connect & Extend: 32–33<br>Mixed Review: 44–51 | • Share & Summarize (p. 461) |
| **Investigation 2** (p. 462) Pacing: 1 day | Students solve equations by doing the same thing to each side rather than thinking about operating with a balance model. | | Practice & Apply: 7–17<br>Connect & Extend: 34–36<br>Mixed Review: 44–51 | • Share & Summarize (p. 463) |
| **Investigation 3** (p. 464) Pacing: 1 day | This investigation provides more practice in solving equations by doing the same thing to both sides. | | Practice & Apply: 18–23<br>Connect & Extend: 37–39<br>Mixed Review: 44–51 | • Share & Summarize (p. 465)<br>• Troubleshooting (p. 464) |
| **Investigation 4** (p. 466) Pacing: 1 day | Students solve inequalities. | pan balance, bags and blocks | Practice & Apply: 24–31<br>Connect & Extend: 40–42<br>Mixed Review: 44–51 | • Share & Summarize (p. 468)<br>• Troubleshooting (pp. 466, 468)<br>• On the Spot Assessment (pp. 466, 467) |

# Leveled Lesson Resources

CRM *Available in:* **Chapter 9 Resource Masters**

Also on TeacherWorks™
Lesson 9.3

## Study Guide and Intervention (p. 17) AL

**Lesson 9.3 Study Guide and Intervention**
***Solve Equations***

When solving an equation, make sure you perform the same **mathematical operation** on both sides. Solving an **inequality** means finding values for the variable that make the inequality true.

**Example 1** Solve $3x + 9 = 6x$.

| | |
|---|---|
| $3x + 9 = 6x$ | Write the equation. |
| $3x + 9 - 3x = 6x - 3x$ | Subtract 3x from each side. |
| $9 = 3x$ | Combine like terms. |
| $9 \div 3 = 3x \div 3$ | Divide each side by 3. |
| $3 = x$ | |

The solution is 3.

**Example 2** Solve and graph $2x \geq 4x + 6$.

| | |
|---|---|
| $2x \geq 4x + 6$ | Write the inequality. |
| $2x - 4x \geq 4x + 6 - 4x$ | Subtract 4x from each side. |
| $-2x \geq 6$ | Combine like terms. |
| $-2x \div -2 \leq 6 \div -2$ | Divide each side by −2. Reverse the direction of the inequality symbol when dividing by a negative number. |
| $x \leq -3$ | Simplify. |

−6 −5 −4 −3 −2 −1 0 1 2 3

Since the symbol in the inequality is ≤, place a closed circle on −3 and point the arrow to the left.

**Exercises**

Solve each equation.

1. $6t + 8 = 14t$
2. $k + 20 = 9k + 4$
3. $11m + 4 = 3m + 36$

Solve and graph each inequality.

4. $s + 8 < 10$ (0 1 2 3 4 5 6 7 8)
5. $d - 3 \geq -11$ (−10 −9 −8 −7 −6 −5 −4 −3 −2)
6. $4x > 10x - 18$ (0 1 2 3 4 5 6 7 8)

## Skills Practice (p. 18) AL OL

**Lesson 9.3 Skills Practice**
***Solve Equations***

**Solve each equation by doing the same thing to both sides.**

1. $8z + 6 = 7z + 4$
2. $12k + 5 = 8k + 25$
3. $2d + 10 = 6d + 2$
4. $3a - 9 = 6a + 15$
5. $8 - 3k = 3k + 2$
6. $7t = 10t + 18$
7. $3y - 5.2 = 10.8 - 5y$
8. $\frac{3}{5}w + 1 = -2$

**Solve and graph each inequality.**

9. $v + 9 > 23$ (10 11 12 13 14 15 16 17 18)
10. $w + 4 \geq -3$ (11 12 13 14 15 16 17 18 19)
11. $z + 5 < 1$ (−6 −5 −4 −3 −2 −1 0 1 2)
12. $s - 7 \geq -6$ (−4 −3 −2 −1 0 1 2 3 4)
13. $3b - 3 \leq 27$ (6 7 8 9 10 11 12 13 14)
14. $\frac{z}{8} - 5 > -3$ (11 12 13 14 15 16 17 18 19)
15. $3a + 2 < 2a$ (−4 −3 −2 −1 0 1 2 3 4)
16. $v - 6 \leq 5v - 2$ (−4 −3 −2 −1 0 1 2 3 4)

## Problem-Solving Practice (p. 19) AL OL

**Lesson 9.3 Problem-Solving Practice**
***Solve Equations***

1. **College** Jeff is a part-time student at Horizon Community College. He currently has 22 credits, and he plans to take 6 credits per semester until he is finished. Jeff's friend Kila is also a student at the college. She has 4 credits and plans to take 12 credits per semester.
   Write an equation to find out how many semesters it will take for Jeff and Kila to have the same number of credits. Solve your equation.
2. **Cousins** Julia said, "If I multiply the number of cousins I have by 9 and then subtract 4, I get the same number as when I double the number of cousins I have and add 38."
   Write an equation to find how many cousins Juila has. Solve your equation.
3. **Age** Abigail said, "If you multiply $\frac{3}{4}$ by my age and add 9, it is the same as adding my age to 6."
   Write an equation to find Abigail's age. Solve your equation.
4. **Driving** Michael is driving from Lakeview to Dodge City, a distance of more than 250 miles. After driving 60 miles, Michael stops for gas.
   Write and solve an inequality to find how many miles Michael has to drive to reach Dodge City.
5. **Files** Jamie and Keisha have flash disks with the same number of files. Jaime has more files on 8 disks than Keisha has on 6 disks plus 24 extra files.
   Write and solve an inequality to find the number of files on each flash disk.
6. **Cooking** Len wants to make several batches of cookies. He is starting with fewer than 2 cups of raisins, and each batch takes $\frac{1}{3}$ cup. Let $b$ stand for batches of cookies. The inequality $\frac{1}{3}b < 2$ can be used to find how many batches of cookies Len can make.
   a. Solve the inequality.
   b. Graph the solution.
   1 2 3 4 5 6 7 8 9 10
   c. Do all the numbers in the solution set make sense as answers in the context of this situation? Explain.

## Enrichment (p. 20) BL

**Lesson 9.3 Enrichment**
***Solve Equations***

**Al-Khwarizmi**

In the ninth century A.D., the Arabian mathematician Muhammed ibn-Musa al-Khwarizmi wrote a book called *Hisab al-jabr w' al muqabalah*. In this book, he explained about the process of solving equations. Although some of the methods he described had been used in the Middle East for nearly 2,500 years, it was through his book that the methods came to Europe. The book became known simply as *Al-jabr*, and it is from this phrase that we get the word "algebra."

One method described in al-Khwarizmi's writings is called the *rule of false position*. To solve an equation by this method, first choose any number as a trial value of the variable. Substitute this number for the variable in the equation, and then make a correction based on the result. At the right, there are two examples of how this method can be used.

$c + 9 = 47$
trial value: 31
If $c = 31$,
then $c + 9 = 40$.
40 $\boxed{+7}$ = 47
So, $c = 31$ $\boxed{+7}$ or 38.

$3y = 84$
trial value: 7
If $y = 7$,
then $3y = 21$.
21 $\boxed{\times 4}$ = 84
So, $y = 7$ $\boxed{\times 4}$ or 28

**Solve each equation by the rule of false position, using the given trial value for the variable.**

1. $m + 58 = 125$ trial value: 42
2. $4k = 60$ trial value: 5
3. $r - 34 = 79$ trial value: 100
4. $a \div 5 = 32$ trial value: 20

**Solve each equation by the rule of false position. This time, make your own choice for the trial value of the variable.**

5. $y + 16 = 51$
6. $3t = 48$
7. $d - 42 = 88$
8. $z \div 4 = 18$
9. Write a short statement relating this method to inequalities.

## Lesson Quick Quiz (p. 21) AL OL BL

**Lesson 9.3 Quick Quiz**

1. In a balance puzzle, 4 bags and 2 blocks balance 4 bags and 10 blocks.
   a. Write an equation describing the balance.
   b. What can you say about the number of blocks in each bag?
2. Solve the inequality $3s - 2 > 19$ by doing the same thing to both sides.
3. Amelia is selecting a new printer for the school newspaper staff. Printer A costs \$500. It costs \$0.07 for each page printed. Printer B costs \$800. It costs \$0.05 for each page printed.
   a. Write an equation you could solve to find the number of pages at which the total cost for each printer is the same. The total cost of the printer is the purchase cost and the cost to print each page.
   b. Solve the equation in 3a by doing the same thing to both sides.
   c. Solve the equation $x + 3 = \frac{9x + 6}{3}$ by doing the same thing to both sides.

## Lesson Master (p. 22)

**Lesson 9.3 Master 1**
***Solve Equations***

**Investigation 4: Develop & Understand: C, On Your Own Exercises**

−9 −8 −7 −6 −5 −4 −3 −2 −1 0 1 2 3 4 5 6 7 8 9

−9 −8 −7 −6 −5 −4 −3 −2 −1 0 1 2 3 4 5 6 7 8 9

−9 −8 −7 −6 −5 −4 −3 −2 −1 0 1 2 3 4 5 6 7 8 9

−9 −8 −7 −6 −5 −4 −3 −2 −1 0 1 2 3 4 5 6 7 8 9

−9 −8 −7 −6 −5 −4 −3 −2 −1 0 1 2 3 4 5 6 7 8 9

−9 −8 −7 −6 −5 −4 −3 −2 −1 0 1 2 3 4 5 6 7 8 9

# Additional Lesson Resources

## Teacher Tech Tools

- TeacherWorks
- ExamView Assessment Suite
- Classroom Presentation Toolkit
- Advance Tracker

## Student Tech Tools

- StudentWorks Plus
- Math Online eGlossary • Concepts in Motion

## Other Print Products

- Investigation Notebook and Reflection Journal
- Quick Review Math Handbook

LESSON 9.3 Solve Equations

## Introduce

**Model Equations** Remind the class that balance puzzles are models for equations and that the techniques they used to solve them apply to equations as well. Use the cartoon puzzle in the book as an example. Point out how Kate used symbols to summarize her solutions and how she kept the equals signs aligned in the summary. Tell students that keeping the symbols aligned helps to organize the solution and keep track of which numbers and variables are on each side of the equation. Then move on to the Explore activity in the text.

### Explore

Have students work individually at their desks. Then have a student write the equation at the board while another draws a picture of the balance next to it. Have another student draw the first balance step and record it using an equation. Most students will simply erase to indicate the movement of blocks and bags, which will be fine. Call on volunteers for each new step, keeping in mind that students may solve the equation in different ways. Most students will follow Kate's model, subtracting the terms with variables (the bags) first. However, some students may start by subtracting the constant terms (the blocks) first.

# LESSON 9.3 Solve Equations



Kate solved the equation $2k + 11 = 4k + 3$ by using a balance puzzle.

Kate summarized her solution in symbols.

| | | |
|---|---|---|
| $2k + 11$ | $= 4k + 3$ | |
| $-2k$ | $-2k$ | *removing 2 bags from each side* |
| $11$ | $= 2k + 3$ | |
| $-3$ | $-3$ | *removing 3 blocks from each side* |
| $8$ | $= 2k$ | |
| $8 \div 2$ | $2k \div 2$ | *dividing what's left on each side into two equal groups* |
| $4$ | $= k$ | |

### Explore

Think about how you would solve the following equation by using a balance puzzle.

$$14 + 3a = 7a + 2$$

For each step in your solution, use an equation to express what is left on the balance. Then summarize your solution using symbols like Kate did. If it is helpful, draw what is left on the balance after each step. **Possible answer:**

$14 + 3a = 7a + 2$ left: 14 blocks, 3 bags; right: 7 bags, 2 blocks
$14 = 4a + 2$ after taking 3 bags from each side
$12 = 4a$ after taking 2 bags from each side
$3 = a$ after dividing both sides by 4

# Investigation 1 Symbolic Solutions

You have solved equations by drawing and imagining balance puzzles. Now you will practice using symbols to record your solution steps.

## Develop & Understand: A

**Solve each equation by drawing or imagining a balance puzzle. Summarize your solution in symbols as Kate did.** 1, 2. See margin.

**1.** $2x + 7 = 5x + 4$

**2.** $4r + 20 = 10r + 5$

For the balance at the beginning of this lesson, Kate labeled her solution to describe how the sides of the *balance* changed at each step.

Here is Kate's solution with labels describing *mathematical operations.* They show how the *equation* changed at each step.

### Example

| | |
|---|---|
| $2k + 11 = 4k + 3$ | |
| $2k + 11 - 2k = 4k + 3 - 2k$ | Subtract $2k$ from each side. |
| $11 = 2k + 3$ | |
| $11 - 3 = 2k + 3 - 3$ | Subtract 3 from each side. |
| $8 = 2k$ | |
| $8 \div 2 = 2k \div 2$ | Divide each side by 2. |
| $4 = k$ | |

## Develop & Understand: B

**3.** Copy your symbolic solutions for Exercises 1–2. Next to each step, explain how the *equation* changed from the previous step. See margin.

Try to solve each equation below by working with just the symbols and doing the same operations on both sides. Try to make the equation simpler each time. Next to each step in your solution, explain how the equation changed from the previous step. If you have trouble, draw or imagine a balance puzzle. 4, 5. See margin.

**4.** $3y + 17 = 4y + 6$

**5.** $3x + 4 = x + 14$

### Share & Summarize

Explain how doing the same mathematical operation to both sides of an equation is like doing the same thing to both sides of a balance puzzle. See ①.

① Possible answer: Doing the same thing to both sides of an equation ensures that the sides remain equal (have the same value). Doing the same thing to both sides of a balance puzzle ensures that the sides remain balanced.



**Additional Answers**

1. Possible answer:

| | |
|---|---|
| $2x + 7 = 5x + 4$ | |
| $7 = 3x + 4$ | after taking 2 bags from each side |
| $3 = 3x$ | after taking 4 blocks from each side |
| $x = 1$ | after dividing both sides by 3 |

2. Possible answer:

| | |
|---|---|
| $4r + 20 = 10r + 5$ | |
| $20 = 6r + 5$ | after taking 4 bags from each side |
| $15 = 6r$ | after taking 5 blocks from each side |
| $r = 2.5$ | after dividing both sides by 6 |

**See page 491A for additional answers to Exercises 3–5.**

# Investigation 1

***On Your Own Exercises***
Pages 469–473
Exercises 1–6, 32–33

**Use Symbols** In this investigation, students first use symbols to record the operations they perform on the balance model to solve balance puzzles. They then use the same methods to solve equations without considering the balance model.

## Develop & Understand: A

*Suggested Grouping: Individuals*

▶ **Exercises 1 and 2** Discuss the steps and symbols used to solve Exercises 1–2. Make sure that all students have the correct equations in their solutions. They will use these symbolic solutions in Exercises 3–5.

**Wrap-Up** If students are having difficulty with balance puzzles such as these, the next exercise sets will be difficult for them. You might provide additional work with concrete representations of the balance model—a pan balance, bags, and blocks if you have them or transparencies made from Chapter 9 Masters 1–3.

### Example

Discuss the labels describing the steps Kate takes in this version of her solution, comparing them to those used in the version on the previous page. Students should intuitively see the relationship between the labels: *taking → subtracting* and *taking half → dividing.*

## Develop & Understand: B

*Suggested Grouping: Individuals*

▶ **Exercises 4 and 5** Watch for students who describe how the balance changes rather than how the equation changes. Remind them that each label should contain a mathematical operation.

### Share & Summarize

Students' explanations will show how well they understand the relationship between actions on a balance and changes in equations. It will also show how prepared students are to solve equations symbolically.

# Investigation 2

***On Your Own Exercises***
Pages 469–473
Exercises 7–17, 34–36

**Solve without Modeling** Students continue to use mathematical operations to solve equations. They are introduced to equations that are not easily solved using the balance puzzle.

You may want to introduce the names of some of the mathematical properties that students are using to solve their equations: the inverse property of addition and the inverse property of multiplication.

For example, in Exercise 1, students use the inverse property of addition when they subtract *x* from both sides. They use the inverse property of multiplication when they multiply the result by $\frac{1}{4}$ to isolate *x*.

## Develop & Understand: A

*Suggested Grouping: Individuals*

In this exercise set, students are asked to solve equations without thinking of the balance model. Emphasize that their reasons should relate to operations on equations, not to the model.

▶ **Exercise 5** This exercise looks back at equations produced by number puzzles. These reflect a series of operations to be performed on an unspecified number, rather than a statement about numbers as objects. It is important that students be able to switch from one point of view to the other. The operational point of view led to backtracking. The exercise also has the objective of separating the equation from the balance model.

**Wrap-Up** Before moving on, read together the discussion of when the balance is not a helpful model for equation-solving. Students may enjoy thinking of other kinds of equations when considering the balance model is more complicated than helpful.

**Additional Answers**
See page 491A for answers to Exercises 1–5.

# Investigation 2 Do the Same Thing to Both Sides

Balance puzzles and equations can be solved by doing the same thing to both sides. Each step simplifies the problem until the solution is clear.

## Develop & Understand: A

Try to solve each equation in Exercises 1–4 by doing the same mathematical operation to both sides without thinking about a balance puzzle. Next to each step in your solutions, explain how the equation changed from the previous step. 1–5. See margin.

**1.** $5x = x + 4$

**2.** $r + 12 = 3r + 4$

**3.** $2P + 20 = 5P + 6$

**4.** $5y + 3 = 3y + 15$

**5.** Kenneth made up a number puzzle.

Write an equation you can solve to find Kenneth's number. Solve your equation by doing the same thing to both sides. Next to each step in your solution, explain how the equation changed from the previous step. Be sure to check your solution.

Kenneth's number puzzle is an example of when thinking about a balance puzzle would not be helpful. This is because it is difficult to show subtracting 9 blocks from 5 bags using a balance puzzle. Try it and see.



## Mathematical Background

Although the phrase do the same thing to both sides is a useful one in respect to solving balance puzzles and equations, we should be careful about using it in any formal sense. Solving an equation generally involves writing a succession of easier-to-solve equivalent equations—that is, equations that have the same solution set. Any principle of operating on both sides depends on whether or not the operation always produces an equivalent equation.

If an equation is true for some values of the variable, adding or subtracting the same quantity to both sides produces an equation that is true for the same values of the variable. Multiplication and division, however, are reversible "both sides" operations only for nonzero numbers.

12a. $5r - 16 = r$
$-16 = -4r$
$4 = r$
12b. $5r - 16 = r$
$5r = r + 16$
$4r = 16$
$r = 4$
12c. Possible answer:
$5r - 16 = r$
$r - \frac{16}{5} = \frac{r}{5}$
$\frac{4}{5}r - \frac{16}{5} = 0$
$\frac{4}{5}r = \frac{16}{5}$
$r = 4$
12d. Possible answer: Shane's and Nestor's methods are both easier than Chantal's. Her first step made the equation more complicated. Nestor's method seems easiest. It does not require arithmetic with negative numbers, although it has more steps than Shane's.

Doing the same thing to both sides works for a great many equations. From now on, you can use this method to solve any equation, whether or not the equation fits the model of a balance puzzle.

## Develop & Understand: B

Solve each equation in Exercises 6–11 by doing the same thing to both sides. If it helps, explain how the equation changed at each step. Check your solutions.

**6.** $2p + 7 = 4p + 10$ $-\frac{3}{2}$

**7.** $3r - 2 = r$ 1

**8.** $2a - 6 = 0$ 3

**9.** $y - 3 = 2y - 6$ 3

**10.** $1.5x + 3.5 = 8 + x$ 9

**11.** $\frac{4}{5}x = 12$ 15

**12.** Shane, Nestor, and Chantal found the correct solution to this equation.

$$5r - 16 = r$$

Shane started by subtracting $5r$ from both sides. Nestor started by adding 16 to both sides. Chantal started by dividing both sides by 5.

**a.** Solve the equation by starting with Shane's first step.

**b.** Solve the equation by starting with Nestor's first step.

**c.** Solve the equation by starting with Chantal's first step.

**d.** Whose method seems easiest? Explain why.

1a. Possible answer: It is hard to think of taking 1 block from 2 bags, or of half a bag of blocks.
1b. Possible answer: With this method, it is just as easy to work with subtraction as addition.

## Share & Summarize

**1.** Consider the equation $2x - 1 = \frac{1}{2}x + \frac{7}{2}$.

**a.** Explain why the equation is difficult to solve by thinking about a balance puzzle.

**b.** Explain why the equation can be solved by doing the same thing to both sides.

**2.** Solve $2x - 1 = \frac{1}{2}x + \frac{7}{2}$ by doing the same thing to both sides. Explain how the equation changed at each step. Possible answer:

$2x - 1 = \frac{1}{2}x + \frac{7}{2}$
$4x - 2 = x + 7$ after multiplying both sides by 2
$3x - 2 = 7$ after subtracting $x$ from both sides
$3x = 9$ after adding 2 to both sides
$x = 3$ after dividing both sides by 3



## Develop & Understand: B

*Suggested Grouping: Individuals*

As students solve equations, they are no longer required to give reasons for each step. However, some students may still need to give these reasons in order to solve the equations. You may want these students to provide explanations.

▶ **Exercise 10** This exercise involves decimals, including decimal coefficients. Point out that students can multiply both sides of an equation containing decimals by a power of 10 to change the decimals to integers, if they find integers easier to work with.

▶ **Exercise 12** This exercise focuses on the process of selecting strategies in the context of doing the same thing to both sides.

**Wrap-Up** Discuss Exercise 12 as a class. Focus on students' answers to Part d, which asks about the option that seems easiest.

## Share & Summarize

You can use these Exercises as a class assessment in the form of a discussion or as an individual assessment. If you don't want the students thinking about the balance model, ask them to solve the equation.

## Reaching All Learners

**AL Approaching Level**
Encourage students who depend on the balance model to solve equations by imagining the model instead of drawing it. Their dependence should fade as they do more complicated exercises.

# Investigation 3

**On Your Own Exercises**
Pages 469–473
Exercises 18–23, 37–39

**More Complicated Equations** Investigation 3 presents more complicated linear equations for students to solve by doing the same thing to each side.

## Develop & Understand: A

*Suggested Grouping: Individuals*

▶ **Exercises 1–3** These equations are efficiently solved by operations that leave the variable on the right. Reassure students that it is correct to have the variable on either side of the equals sign; there is no need to add steps to the solution solely to move the variable to the left side of the equation.

▶ **Exercise 9** Students may approach this in one of these ways:

- Some students may let x stand for the total number of hamsters and write the equation $\frac{3}{4}x = x - 3$. Then they subtract 3 from the value of $x$ to find the number of hamsters remaining.
- Other students may find the total number of hamsters, then multiply that total by $\frac{3}{4}$.
- Other students may use number sense to deduce that $\frac{1}{4}$ of the litter is three hamsters. Since $\frac{3}{4}$ is three times $\frac{1}{4}$, the number of hamsters remaining is three times the number of hamsters given away, or $3 \times 3 = 9$. Although this strategy does not use equations, it is a valid way to solve the exercise.

**Wrap-Up** Have students share the steps they used to solve Exercises 5–8. If there are different approaches, encourage students to point out the benefits of solving by each method.

**Example**

Tell students that they can also do the same thing to both sides of an equation to make an equation more complicated. Some students may be curious about why anyone would want to do this. One reason is to create number puzzles. Then discuss the steps in the Example.

★ indicates multi-step problem

# Investigation 3 Solve More Equations

You have seen that by doing the same thing to both sides, you can solve equations that are difficult to solve with balance puzzles. Now you will practice solving some more equations.

## Develop & Understand: A

1. Solve the equation $5 - 2x = 3x$ by first adding the same amount to both sides. Check your solution.
2. Solve the equation $10 + 4z = 2z - 2$. Check your solution. $-6$
3. Solve the equation $\frac{1}{2}B = B - 4$ by first multiplying both sides by the same amount. Check your solution.
4. Solve the equation $\frac{k}{3} = 8 - k$. 6

1. Possible answer:
$5 - 2x = 3x$
$5 = 5x$
$1 = x$

3. Possible answer:
$\frac{1}{2}B = B - 4$
$B = 2B - 8$
$0 = B - 8$
$8 = B$

**Solve each equation by doing the same thing to both sides.**

5. $4b - 2 = 6b - 4$ 1
6. $2c + 1 = 9 + 3c$ $-8$
7. $2d + 1 = 14 - d$ $\frac{13}{3}$, or $4\frac{1}{3}$
8. $5e + 2.5 = 2.5 - 7.5e$ 0

★9. Toya's hamster had a litter of babies. After Toya gave away three of the babies, $\frac{3}{4}$ of the litter remained. How many baby hamsters did Toya have *left?* 9

**Real-World Link**
A litter of hamsters averages 6 to 8 babies per litter. They occasionally have 15 or more. Babies are born furless, and their eyes do not open for one to two weeks.

When you solve an equation by doing the same thing to both sides, you usually try to make the equation simpler at each step. What if you made an equation *more complicated* at each step?

**Example**

| | |
|---|---|
| Start by writing the solution. | $x = 7$ |
| Multiply both sides by 3. | $3x = 21$ |
| Add $2x$ to both sides. | $5x = 21 + 2x$ |
| Subtract 2 from both sides. | $5x - 2 = 19 + 2x$ |
| Divide both sides by 2. | $2.5x - 1 = 9.5 + x$ |



## Troubleshooting

In Exercises 3 and 4, watch for students who do not use the distributive property correctly. These students may have $B = 4$ as the solution to Exercise 3 and $K = 12$ as the solution to Exercise 4. Ask them to solve the equation again as you watch so that you can correct any misunderstandings.

In Exercises 10–13, you will create complicated algebra equations. You will start with a simple equation and do the same thing to both sides to make it more complex. When you are satisfied that your equation is sufficiently difficult, challenge a partner to solve it.

## Develop & Understand: B

**10.** Check to make sure the solution of the final equation in the example on the previous page is 7.
$2.5 \cdot 7 - 1 = 16.5$, $9.5 + 7 = 16.5$

**11.** Explain why 7 is the solution of *each* equation in the example.

11. To derive each equation, the same thing was done to both sides of the previous equation. Since 7 was the solution of the original equation, 7 is the solution after each change.

**12.** Create your own "complicated" equation. Start by choosing a number. Write the equation $x =$ *your number.* Then make the equation more complicated by doing the same thing to both sides three or four times. Verify that the number you first chose is the solution of your final equation. If it is not, retrace your steps to correct the error. Equations will vary.

**13.** Exchange equations, and solve your partner's equation.

**14.** Erina's partner created the following "complicated" equation.

| | |
|---|---|
| Start by writing the solution. | $x = 7$ |
| Multiply both sides by 5. | $5x = 35$ |
| Add $2x$ to both sides. | $7x = 2x + 35$ |
| Subtract 40 from both sides. | $7x - 40 = 2x + 75$ |

What did Erina's partner do incorrectly in creating the equation?
In the last step, Erina's partner added 40 to the right side instead of subtracting 40.

## Share & Summarize

Explain why the solution of an equation does not change when you alter the equation by doing the same thing to both sides.
Possible answer: The expressions on the two sides of an equation have the same value. When you do a mathematical operation on both sides, the sides remain equal. This is true no matter how many operations you do.



## Develop & Understand: B

*Suggested Grouping: Pairs*

▶ **Exercise 12** Students generate equations. If the competitive spirit takes over, the equations may tend to get too hard. If this seems to be happening, you can set some restrictions on the number of operations or the character of the numbers they can use.

**Wrap-Up** Have pairs select one of their equations to present to other pairs. This exercise set is flexible enough so that you can help some students while the others are working.

## Share & Summarize

Pose the question, and have students work on it individually for several minutes. Then discuss the answers with the whole class. Make sure to use the term *equivalent equations* to describe two equations that have the same solution set.

# Investigation 4

***On Your Own Exercises***
Pages 469–473
Exercises 24–31, 40–42

**Inequalities** Tell the students that in the past they have been able to determine what value makes an equation true. Here, the students will be deciding how solutions relate to each other – a comparison of size. Ask the students what words they would use to make comparisons. Number lines may be helpful for showing students relationships between values.

## Develop & Understand: A

*Suggested Grouping: Individuals*

This set of exercises will lead students to discover what happens when you add, subtract, multiply, or divide both sides of an inequality by the same number.

▶ **Exercise 3** Students may have a difficult time determining a conjecture for their work. Remind students that a conjecture is just a guess at what is happening. It may be helpful to point out what is happening in parts c and d.

**Wrap-Up** Have students share one of their test problems. As a class compare the results. What do the students notice? It may be helpful to demonstrate one problem with the pan balance or the bags and blocks.

***Math Link***
Show the students how the symbols relate to numbers on a number line. This will help their interpretation and understanding.

# Investigation 4 Inequalities

**Vocabulary**
**inequality**
**solution set**

As you know, an *equation* is a mathematical sentence stating that two quantities have the same value. An **inequality** is a mathematical sentence stating that two quantities have different values.

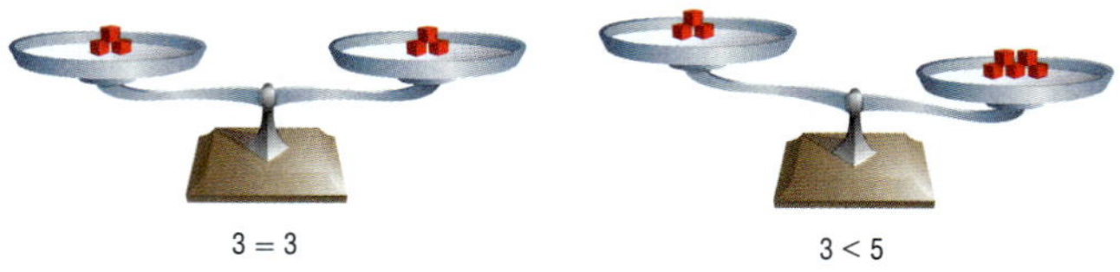


***Math Link***
Inequalities use the following symbols.

$>$ greater than
$<$ less than
$\geq$ greater than or equal to
$\leq$ less than or equal to

## Develop & Understand: A

1. Which of the following statements are true? $25 \geq 25, \frac{5}{9} < \frac{4}{7}$

| | | |
|---|---|---|
| $25 \geq 25$ | $3.2 < 3.14$ | $\frac{4}{5} > \frac{5}{6}$ |
| $\frac{5}{9} < \frac{4}{7}$ | $-5 \geq 0$ | $-100 < -101$ |

In the last investigation, you solved equations by doing the same thing to both sides. If you do the same thing to both sides of an inequality, does the relationship between the two sides always stay the same?

2. Copy and complete the table below by performing the indicated operations to each side of the inequality $2 < 6$.

| Original Inequality | Operation Performed | New Inequality | True/False |
|---|---|---|---|
| $2 < 6$ | Add 2 | $4 < 8$ | True |
| $2 < 6$ | Add $-2$ | $0 < 4$ | True |
| $2 < 6$ | Subtract 2 | $0 < 4$ | True |
| $2 < 6$ | Subtract $-2$ | $4 < 8$ | True |
| $2 < 6$ | Multiply by 2 | $4 < 12$ | True |
| $2 < 6$ | Multiply by $-2$ | $-4 < -12$ | False |
| $2 < 6$ | Divide by 2 | $1 < 3$ | True |
| $2 < 6$ | Divide by $-2$ | $-1 < -3$ | False |

3. Use your results from Exercise 2 to write a conjecture about what happens to an inequality when you do each of the following.
   a. add the same number to both sides
   b. subtract the same number from both sides
   c. multiply both sides by the same number
   d. divide both sides by the same number See margin.

3a. Possible answer: When you add the same number to both sides of a true inequality, the new inequality is true.
3b. When you subtract the same number from both sides of a true inequality, the new inequality is true.
3c. When you multiply each side by the same positive number, the inequality stays true. When you multiply each side by the same negative number, the new inequality is false.



## On the Spot Assessment

Use the pan balance and construct an inequality. Ask students to determine what symbol represents the relation between the pans.

## Troubleshooting

Students may have difficulty determining which symbol to use, especially when multiplying or dividing by negative values. This is normal. Additional examples and the use of a number line will help to clarify this with the students.

**Additional Answer**

3d. When you divide each side by the same positive number, the inequality stays true. When you divide each side by the same negative number, the new inequality is false.

4. Test your conjectures. Write two different inequalities that are true. Test each of your rules on each of the inequalities. Do you end with similar results? Check student's work. Answers will vary. The possible answers in Exercise 3 work for all inequalities.

### Think & Discuss

Share your conjectures from Exercise 3 and your test results from Exercise 4. Explain why you think your rules work for all inequalities. See ① in margin.

5. We do not know how many blocks are in the bag, but the number has to be more than 10. Ten blocks would make the scale balance. Fewer than 10 blocks would tip it the other way.
6. $x$ can be any number less than 10, including negative numbers, fractions, and decimals. We do not know for sure what it equals.

5. How many blocks are in the bag shown to the right?

6. In the inequality $x < 10$, what does $x$ equal?

The **solution set** to an inequality is the set of all possible values of a variable that make the inequality true. For the inequality $x \geq 10$, the solution set is 10 and all numbers greater than 10.

You can solve inequalities by *doing the same thing to both sides.* But, there is one important difference. If you multiply or divide each side of an inequality by a negative number, the direction of the inequality sign reverses.

To understand why this happens, consider the numbers $-1$ and 3. Multiply each number by $-1$. The new numbers 1 and $-3$ are the same distance from zero as $-1$ and 3. However, each new number lies on the opposite side of the number line. Figure 1 shows that $-1$ is less than 3. In Figure 2, the red circles represent the new numbers, 1 and $-3$.

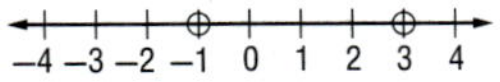


Figure 1

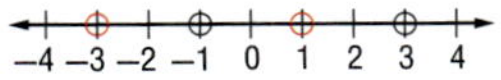


Figure 2

The inequality $1 > -3$ represents this new relationship. When you multiply or divide each side of an inequality by a negative number, switch the direction of the inequality sign in order to produce a true statement.



### Think & Discuss

*Suggested Grouping: Pairs*

Make sure students are not just answering the question but are using statements to justify their answers.

Explain that after you have reversed the direction of the inequality sign, the side that had the greater value will now be the side with the lesser value. Show students on a number line that whichever number was further to the right will end up further to the left.

#### Additional Answer

① Adding or subtracting the same number to each side is like moving both numbers the same amount in the same direction along a number line. The distance apart does not change. Multiplying or dividing by a positive number is repeated addition or subtraction of a positive number. Multiplying or dividing by a negative number flips both numbers to the mirror-image positions on the number line. The number that used to be farther to the left is now farther to the right. This means that the number that used to be lesser is now greater.

### Reaching All Learners

**ELL English Language Learners**

Have students make a list of all words in their first language that are used for comparison. Assist the students in connecting these words with English words that will help them understand the concept of an inequality.

### On the Spot Assessment

Give students the inequality $x \geq -2$ and ask them to write an inequality that has this solution. There will be many correct answers; tell students that this is natural for an inequality.

## Develop & Understand: B

*Suggested Grouping: Individuals*

- **Exercises 7–12** If students are having trouble testing their solutions, instruct them to use a number line to help determine where the solution set lies.
- **Exercise 13** Students may not be sure where to start creating a problem. Have them refer to the number line and work in reverse, just like they do to solve the inequality.

**Wrap-Up** Have students meet in small groups or pairs to share their work. Ask students to look at the values that were used to test their results. Have the group or pair make a conjecture about what they see and share their results with the class.

**Example**

Reinforce that graphing is a visual way to look at a problem. Students may wonder why solutions are graphed on a number line and not using a coordinate plane. In this case, a number line is used because only one variable is present.

## Develop & Understand: C

*Suggested Grouping: Individuals*

- **Exercises 14-17** Students may need help in remembering when to use a closed circle or an open circle when they graph inequalities. Stress what it means to be equal versus just greater than or less than.

**Wrap-Up** Ask students to create a number line and then an inequality problem that has the number line as its solution.

### Share & Summarize

It may be helpful for students to discuss their results in pairs, then small groups, and finally as a whole class. In this manner, students will have more opportunities to use the vocabulary associated with inequalities.

**Additional Answer**

② Sample answer: You can solve equations and inequalities by doing the same thing to both sides. But, in an inequality, you must switch the direction of the inequality sign when multiplying or dividing by a negative number. Also, the solution to an equation such as $3x = 24$ is a number, but the solution to an inequality such as $3x < 24$ is a set of numbers.

---

7. $x < 1$; $0 + 2 < 3$
8. $z > 9$; $3 \cdot 10 > 27$
9. $-8 > y$ or $y < -8$; $-10 - 3 > 2(-10) + 5$; $-13 > -15$
10. $n \geq -3$; $\frac{1}{3}(0) + 5 \geq 4$; $5 \geq 4$
11. $x < -25$; $\frac{3}{5}(-30) + 7 > \frac{4}{5}(-30) + 12$; $-11 > -12$
12. $q < 1.2$; $5(1) - 0.8 < 3(1) + 1.6$; $4.2 < 4.6$

① Possible answer: An inequality shows the relationship between two quantities on either side of the inequality sign, like an equation shows the relationship between two quantities on either side of the equals sign. But, in an equation, the two quantities have the same value. In an inequality, the quantities do not have the same value. One quantity is greater than the other.

## Develop & Understand: B

Solve each inequality by doing the same thing to both sides. Test each solution by choosing a number from the solution set and substituting it into the original inequality.

**7.** $x + 2 < 3$ **8.** $3z > 27$ **9.** $y - 3 > 2y + 5$

**10.** $\frac{1}{3}n + 5 \geq 4$ **11.** $\frac{3}{5}x + 7 > \frac{4}{5}x + 12$ **12.** $5q - 0.8 < 3q + 1.6$

**13.** Create an inequality whose solution is $x < 17$. Answers will vary. Possible answers: $3x < 51$ or $-x + 4 > -13$

**Example**

You can graph the solution set of an equation or an inequality on a number line.

$x = 3$

$x > 3$

$x \geq 3$

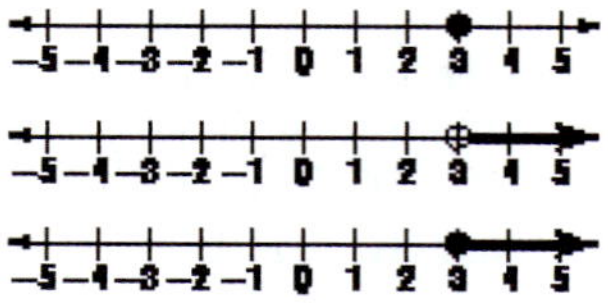


The open circle in the graph of $x > 3$ indicates that the number 3 itself is not part of the solution set. The closed circle in the graph of $x \geq 3$ indicates that 3 is included in the solution set. The arrow indicates that the solution set also includes all the numbers greater than 3.

## Develop & Understand: C

**14.** Write the inequality whose solution is shown by the number line below. $x < 3$

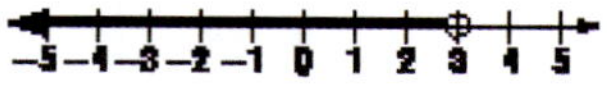


For Exercises 13–15, solve and graph each inequality.

**15.** $3y < -15$ $y < -5$

**16.** $-4x + 5 < 8$ $x > -\frac{3}{4}$

**17.** $5m + 1 \geq 7m + 10$ $m \leq -4.5$

### Share & Summarize

In what ways is an inequality similar to an equation? In what ways is it different? See ①.

How is solving an inequality similar to solving an equation? How is it different? See ② in margin.

468 CHAPTER 9 Equations

### Reaching All Learners

**AL Approaching Level**
Challenge students who are competent with inequalities to write a inequality that has the solution of $t < -4.7$. Ask the students to provide the inequality and all of the steps needed to arrive at the solution.

### Troubleshooting

Students may need additional help working with constructing an inequality to match a number line. Remind them that they are working in reverse. As long as they balance their steps, they are going to have a correct statement.

## Practice & Apply

1. Possible answer:
$2x + 9 = 6x + 1$
$9 = 4x + 1$
$8 = 4x$
$2 = x$

2. Possible answer:
$6z + 28 = 12z + 10$
$28 = 6z + 10$
$18 = 6z$
$3 = z$

3. Possible answer:
$29 + 6w = 11w + 4$
$29 = 5w + 4$
$25 = 5w$
$5 = w$

4. Possible answer:
$9 + 5v = 2v + 12$
$9 + 3v = 12$
$3v = 3$
$v = 1$

16a. $\frac{a}{4} - 2 = \frac{a}{8}$

**Solve each equation by drawing or imagining a balance puzzle. Use symbols to record your solution steps. Check your solutions.**

1. $2x + 9 = 6x + 1$
2. $6z + 28 = 12z + 10$
3. $29 + 6w = 11w + 4$
4. $9 + 5v = 2v + 12$

**Solve each equation by working with the symbols. Next to each step in your solution, explain how the equation changed from the previous step. Check your solutions.** 5, 6. See margin.

5. $2a + 10 = 6a + 2$
6. $9b + 28 = 12b + 7$

**Solve each equation by doing the same thing to both sides. Check your solutions.**

7. $3 + 9c = 12c$ 1
8. $18 + d = 7d + 6$ 2
9. $2k - 6 = 4k + 5$ $-\frac{11}{2}$
10. $\frac{1}{4}m - 3 = 0$ 12
11. $9.25n + 3.3 = 1.3 - 0.75n$ $-0.2$
12. $0.1p + 6 = 7$ 10
13. $17r + 4 = 34r + 2$ $\frac{2}{17}$, or about 0.118
14. $2s + 7 = 10s - 7$ $\frac{14}{8}$, or $\frac{7}{4}$, or 1.75

15. Curtis said, "If you multiply the number of dogs that I have by 8 and then subtract 10, you get the same number as when you triple the number of dogs that I have and add 5."
   a. Write an equation to find how many dogs Curtis has. $8d - 10 = 3d + 5$
   b. Solve your equation by doing the same thing to both sides. Check your solution. 3

16. Karl said, "If I divide my dog's age by 4 and subtract 2, I get the same result as when I divide my dog's age by 8."
   a. Write an equation you can solve to find the dog's age.
   b. Solve your equation by doing the same thing to both sides. Check your solution. 16

17. Consider the equation $27q - 100 = 2q$. 17a–c. See margin.
   a. Solve the equation by first adding 100 to both sides.
   b. Solve the equation by first subtracting $2q$ from both sides.
   c. Solve the equation by first subtracting $27q$ from both sides.
   d. Which of your solution methods was easiest? Answers will vary.



On Your Own Exercises
Lesson 9.3

**Investigation 1**
Pages 461
Practice & Apply: 1–6
Connect & Extend: 32–33

**Investigation 2**
Pages 462–463
Practice & Apply: 7–17
Connect & Extend: 34–36

**Investigation 3**
Pages 464–465
Practice & Apply: 18–23
Connect & Extend: 37–39

**Investigation 4**
Pages 466–468
Practice & Apply: 24–31
Connect & Extend: 40–42

**Assign Anytime**
Mixed Review: 44–51

▶ **Exercise 9** Some students may prefer to write their solutions using decimals.

▶ **Exercises 15–16** Students write and solve equations in a situational context for the first time in this lesson. They use skills from prior lessons to write the equation. Then they solve it by doing the same thing to both sides.

### Additional Answers

5.
$2a + 10 = 6a + 2$
$10 = 4a + 2$ after subtracting 2a from both sides
$8 = 4a$ after subtracting 2 from both sides
$2 = a$ after dividing both sides by 4

6.
$9b + 28 = 12b + 7$
$28 = 3b + 7$ after subtracting 9b from both sides
$21 = 3b$ after subtracting 7 from both sides
$7 = b$ after dividing both sides by 3

17a.
$27q - 100 = 2q$
$27q = 2q + 100$
$25q = 100$
$q = 4$

17b.
$27q - 100 = 2q$
$25q - 100 = 0$
$25q = 100$
$q = 4$

17c.
$27q - 100 = 2q$
$-100 = -25q$
$4 = q$

▶ **Exercise 21** This exercise may be challenging for some students since it has both a fractional coefficient and a fractional constant. Watch for students who first focus on the fractions, subtracting $\frac{2}{7}$ from each side, and ignore the fact that one fraction is a coefficient and the other is a constant.

▶ **Exercise 22** Students may see that Keri used 10 bottles to fill four 10-oz glasses, so each bottle must hold 4 ounces. However, the directions specifically ask them to write an equation and solve it. You may need to tell students that communication is an important part of mathematics and writing equations not only helps them to solve exercises but also to communicate their solutions. This exercise provides students with the opportunity to check their equations by seeing if they give the same solution as their reasoning.

▶ **Exercise 23 Extension** Encourage students to use squared numbers, fractions, and decimals when writing their equations.

## Additional Answers

27. $x > 11$

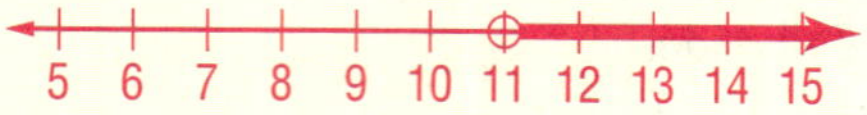

28. $12 < y$ or $y > 12$

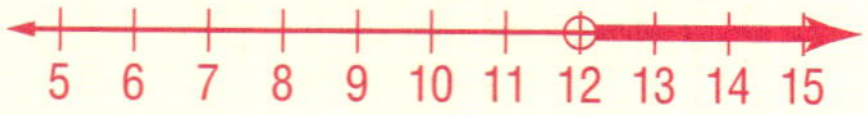

29. $n \le -30$

30. $z \le -0.9$

**Solve each equation by doing the same thing to both sides.**

**18.** $\frac{1}{2}q + 3 = 10.5 + q$ $-15$

**19.** $\frac{1}{3}c = 3c - 9$ $\frac{27}{8}$, or $3\frac{3}{8}$

**20.** $\frac{d}{7} = 12 + d$ $-14$

**21.** $\frac{2}{7}d - 2 = 3d - 4\frac{5}{7}$ $1$

**22.** Keri is making lunch for her three best friends, but the only juice she has is in the little bottles her sister likes. She has 16 small bottles of apple juice. She fills a 10-ounce glass for each friend and one for herself, and she still has 6 bottles of juice left. Write an equation to find how many ounces of juice a bottle holds. Solve your equation.

22. $16j = 40 + 6j$
$10j = 40$
$j = 4$

**23.** Write three equations with a solution of $-5$.

23. Possible answer: $3x + 14 = -1$; $-x + \frac{1}{2}(4x + 5) = 3x + 12\frac{1}{2}$; $x - 1 = -6$

**24.** For which of the following inequalities is 7 a member of the solution set? $x \ge 7, x \le 10, x > 5, x \le 7\frac{1}{3}$

| | | |
|---|---|---|
| $x \ge 7$ | $x < 0$ | $x \le 10$ |
| $x > 5$ | $x < 6.9$ | $x \le 7\frac{1}{3}$ |

For Exercises 25–26, write the inequality whose solution set is shown by each graph.

**25.**  $x < 1$

**26.** 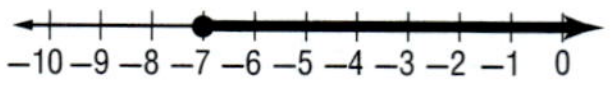 $x \ge -7$

For Exercises 27–30, solve and graph each inequality.
27–30. See margin.

**27.** $2x - 2 > 20$

**28.** $3y + 22 < 4y + 10$

**29.** $\frac{1}{6}n + 5 \le 0$

**30.** $-2z + 0.6 \ge 2.4$

**31.** Write three different inequalities each with a solution of $x > 3$.
Possible answers: $x + 2 > 5$, $4x > 12$, $x - 18 > -2x - 9$

## Connect & Extend

**32.** Yago tried to solve this equation using a balance puzzle.

$$5r + 7 = 13 + 2r + 3r$$

What solution do you think Yago found? There is no solution since $5r + 7$ cannot equal $13 + 5r$.

★ indicates multi-step problem

33. Odell should have applied the distributive property first. Then he would have seen that he had to subtract 42, not 7.

34. $x = 3^2$
$x = 9$

35. $\sqrt{v} = 3$
$v = 9$

36. $5x - 9 = 16$
$5x = 25$
$x = 5$

**33. Find the Error** Odell tried to solve the equation $6(x + 7) = 4x - 3$. He recorded the following steps.

$6(x + 7) = 4x - 3$

| | |
|---|---|
| $6x = 4x - 10$ | after subtracting 7 from both sides |
| $2x = -10$ | after subtracting $4x$ from both sides |
| $x = -5$ | after dividing both sides by 2 |

When Odell checked his solution, it did not work. What was his mistake?

**Challenge** Solve each equation by doing the same thing to both sides.

**34.** $\sqrt{x} = 3$ **35.** $\sqrt{v} - 2 = 1$ **36.** $\sqrt{5x - 9} = 4$

**37.** You can solve many equations by drawing two graphs and finding the point where they intersect. Consider the equation $2x + 3 = 1 + 3x$. 37a, d, e. See margin.

**a.** On the same set of axes, graph $y = 2x + 3$ and $y = 1 + 3x$.

**b.** Give the coordinates of the point where the graphs intersect. (2, 7)

**c.** Now solve $2x + 3 = 1 + 3x$ by doing the same thing to both sides. 2

**d.** How does the $x$-coordinate of the intersection point of the equations $y = 2x + 3$ and $y = 1 + 3x$ compare to the solution of $2x + 3 = 1 + 3x$? Explain why this makes sense.

**e.** Solve $3x - 4 = -2x + 6$ by drawing two graphs.

**38.** Kate has four packages of balloons and eight single balloons. Her brother gave her 20 more balloons and three more packages. She now has twice the number of balloons than she initially had.

★ **a.** Write and solve an equation to find how many balloons are in a package. See below.

**b.** With how many balloons did Kate start? 56

38a. $4b + 8 + 20 + 3b = 2(4b + 8)$
$7b + 28 = 8b + 16$
$28 = b + 16$
$12 = b$



On Your Own Exercises

## Additional Answers

37a.

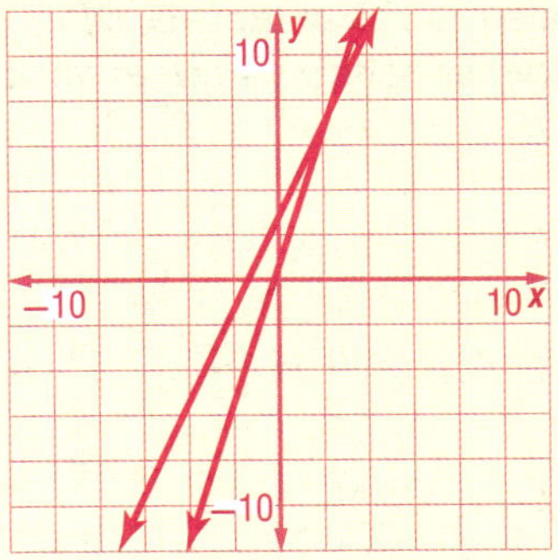


37d. The intersection of the two lines is the point they have in common. That is, the $x$-coordinate is the value of $x$ that makes the $y$ values equal. Since the expressions for $y$ are the expressions in the equation, when the $y$ values are equal, the expressions are equal.

37e. The lines meet at the point where $x = 2$ and $y = 2$, so the solution is 2.

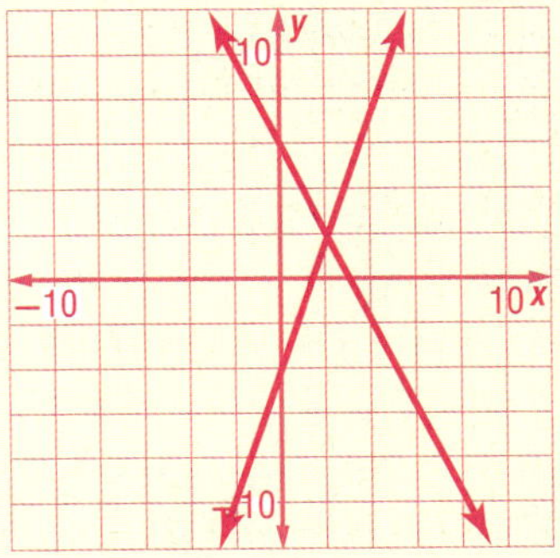


**Lesson 9.3** Solve Equations **471**

▶ **Exercise 39** Watch for students who use the diameter instead of the radius for cylinder B when setting up the equation.

On Your Own Exercises

39a. The volume of cylinder A is $\pi \cdot 4^2 \cdot 6 = 96\pi$; the volume of cylinder B is $\pi \cdot 3^2 \cdot h = 9\pi h$; since the volumes are equal, $9\pi h = 96\pi$.

**39. Geometry** The volume of a cylinder is given by the formula $V = \pi r^2 h$, where $r$ is the radius and $h$ is the height.

**a.** Cylinders A and B have the same volume. Write an equation to find the height of cylinder B. Explain how you wrote your equation.

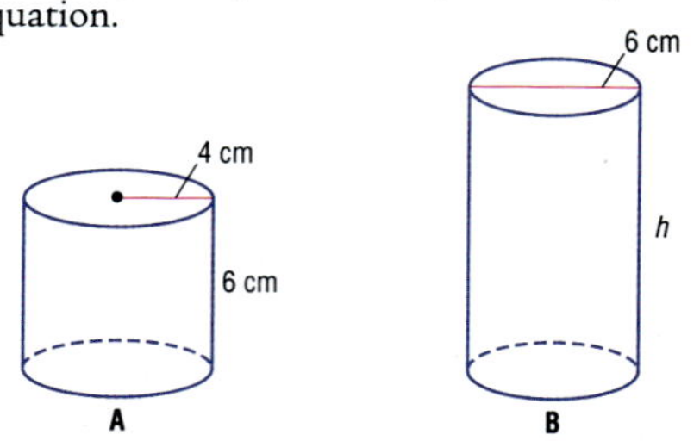


**b.** Solve your equation to find the height of cylinder B to the nearest tenth of a centimeter. 10.7 cm

**40.** Tasha filled several bags each with the same number of marbles. She said, "There are more marbles in four bags than there are in two bags plus four extra marbles."

**a.** Write and solve an inequality to find the number of marbles in each bag. $4m > 2m + 4$; $m > 2$

**b.** Write a sentence describing the number of marbles in each bag. Possible answer: There are more than 2 marbles in each bag.

41b. Each shelf holds more than 4 books.

41c. Possible answer: No. Mathematically, any number bigger than 4 satisfies the equation, but the bookstore probably does not have shelves big enough to hold a thousand books on one shelf.

**41.** Derrick works in a bookstore. On Monday, he received a shipment of books. When he put all of the books on shelves, he filled 5 shelves and had 13 books left over. On Tuesday, a bigger shipment arrived. This shipment filled 9 shelves, and almost filled a tenth shelf. There was room for 7 more books on the tenth shelf.

**a.** Write and solve an inequality to find the number of books on a shelf. $5b + 13 < 10b - 7$, $4 < b$ or $b > 4$

**b.** Write a sentence describing the number of books a shelf can hold.

**c.** Do all the numbers in the solution set make sense as answers in the context of this situation?

42c. Answers will vary. Possible answer: Fahrenheit temperature readings during a winter month.

**42.** It is sometimes convenient to combine two inequalities into one. Consider the statement $5 < x < 35$.

**a.** Write a sentence that describes the meaning of the combined inequality. All the values of $x$ that are greater than 5 and less than 35.

**b.** Graph the combined inequality.

**c.** Describe a real-world situation that $5 < x < 35$ would represent.

**43. In Your Own Words** Describe two or more types of equations that are difficult to model with balance puzzles. Do you think those equations can be solved easily by doing the same thing to both sides? Explain.

## Mixed Review

43. Answers will vary. Students may respond that equations involving parentheses or proportions are difficult to model with balance puzzles. Check students' work for explanations.

45a. $48\text{ in}^3$, $124\text{ in}^2$

45b. $144\text{ in}^3$, $340\text{ in}^2$

45c. $4\text{ in}^2$

**44. Geometry** Recall that a two-dimensional figure that can be folded into a closed three-dimensional figure is called a net. For example, this is a *net* for a cube.

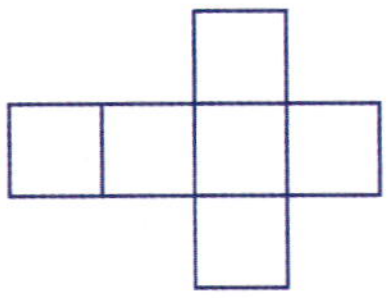

Draw another net for a cube. Possible answer:

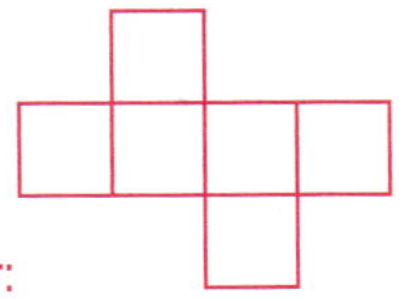

**45. Geometry** A block prism has length 8 in., width 1 in., and height 6 in.

**a.** What is the prism's volume? What is its surface area?

**b.** Another block prism is three times as tall as the first prism. What is the volume of this prism? What is its surface area?

**c.** A cylinder has the same volume as the original prism and a height of 12 in. What is the area of the cylinder's base?

**Find each product or quotient.**

**46.** $\frac{3}{5} \cdot \frac{2}{7}$ $\quad \frac{6}{35}$

**47.** $\frac{1}{9} \cdot \frac{6}{11}$ $\quad \frac{2}{33}$

**48.** $\frac{5}{8} \div \frac{10}{3}$ $\quad \frac{3}{16}$

**49.** $-\frac{1}{3} \cdot \frac{4}{9}$ $\quad -\frac{4}{27}$

**50.** $-\frac{3}{10} \cdot \left(-\frac{7}{8}\right)$ $\quad \frac{21}{80}$

**51.** $\frac{12}{5} \div \left(-\frac{13}{6}\right)$ $\quad -\frac{72}{65}$ or $-1\frac{7}{65}$





## Quick Check

**Informal Assessment** Students should be able to:

- ✔ solve equations without using the balance puzzle model
- ✔ express a balance puzzle as an algebraic equation
- ✔ represent an equation as a balance puzzle
- ✔ solve simple word exercises by writing and solving equations
- ✔ solve simple inequalities and graph the solution set on a number line

## Quick Quiz

**1.** In a balance puzzle, 4 bags and 2 blocks balance 4 bags and 10 blocks.

a. Write an equation describing the balance. $4b + 2 = 4b + 10$

b. What can you say about the number of blocks in each bag? No number makes the exercise possible.

**2.** Solve the inequality $3s - 2 > 19$ by doing the same thing to both sides. $s > 7$

**3.** Amelia is selecting a new printer for the school newspaper staff. Printer A costs \$500. It costs \$0.07 for each page printed. Printer B costs \$800. It costs \$0.05 for each page printed.

a. Write an equation you could solve to find the number of pages at which the total cost for each printer is the same. The total cost of the printer is the purchase cost and the cost to print each page.

$500 + 0.07x = 800 + 0.05x$

b. Solve the equation in 3a by doing the same thing to both sides.

$500 + 0.07x = 800 + 0.05x$

$0.02x = 300$

$2x = 30{,}000$

$x = 15{,}000$

The total cost is the same when 15,000 pages are printed.

c. Solve the equation $x + 3 = \frac{9x + 6}{3}$ by doing the same thing to both sides. $\frac{1}{2}$

LESSON

# 9.4

# Solve Equations with Parentheses

### Objectives

- To add and subtract parenthetical expressions
- To solve equations by adding, multiplying, or dividing both sides by the same quantity
- To describe variable quantities that appear in typical word problems, including those that refer to signed numbers

## *Overview*

This lesson provides practice in simplifying expressions, solving equations, and translating word problems into the language of algebra. Students test conjectures and remove parentheses when they rewrite equations in which they learn rules for adding and subtracting with parentheses.

## *Advance Preparation*

You may want to make copies of Lesson 9.4 Master 1 or quarter-inch graph paper for students to use.

| | Summary | Materials | On Your Own Exercises (pp. 484–488) | Assessment Opportunities |
|---|---|---|---|---|
| **Investigation 1** (p. 474) Pacing: 2 days | Students are asked to assign variables and write equations to describe word problems. They focus on writing equations and then simplifying expressions that occur within them. | | Practice & Apply: 1–5<br>Connect & Extend: 44–46<br>Mixed Review: 55–59 | • On the Spot Assessment (p. 476)<br>• Share & Summarize (p. 476)<br>• Troubleshooting (p. 476) |
| **Investigation 2** (p. 477) Pacing: 1 day | Students learn to simplify expressions containing parentheses. The text pays particular attention to the problem of subtraction. | | Practice & Apply: 6–22<br>Connect & Extend: 47–51<br>Mixed Review: 55–59 | • On the Spot Assessment (p. 478)<br>• Share & Summarize (p. 480) |
| **Investigation 3** (p. 481) Pacing: 1 day | The problem sets in this investigation provide more practice in solving equations and simplifying complex algebraic expressions. | Lesson 9.4 Master 1 or quarter-inch graph paper | Practice & Apply: 23–43<br>Connect & Extend: 52–54<br>Mixed Review: 55–59 | • Share & Summarize (p. 483)<br>• Troubleshooting (p. 482) |

# Leveled Lesson Resources

CRM *Available in:* **Chapter 9 Resource Masters**

Also on TeacherWorks™ Lesson 9.4

## Study Guide and Intervention (p. 23) AL

**Lesson 9.4 Study Guide and Intervention**
***Solve Equations with Parentheses***

**Example 1** Simplify and solve the equation $2(6m - 1) = 8m$.

| | |
|---|---|
| $2(6m - 1) = 8m$ | Write the equation. |
| $12m - 2 = 8m$ | Apply the distributive property. |
| $12m - 12m - 2 = 8m - 12m$ | Subtract 12*m* from each side. |
| $-2 = -4m$ | Simplify. |
| $\frac{-2}{4} = \frac{-4m}{-4}$ | Divide each side by –4. |
| $\frac{1}{2} = m$ | Simplify. |

**Example 2** Evaluate $7.8 - (1.3 + 9.6)$.

**Method 1**

| | |
|---|---|
| $7.8 - (1.3 + 9.6)$ | Write the expression. |
| $7.8 - 10.9$ | Add 1.3 and 9.6. |
| $-3.1$ | Simplify. |

**Method 2**

| | |
|---|---|
| $7.8 - (1.3 + 9.6)$ | Write the expression. |
| $7.8 - 1.3 - 9.6$ | Apply the distributive property. |
| $6.5 - 9.6$ | Subtract 1.3 from 7.8. |
| $-3.1$ | Simplify. |

**Example 3** Rewrite each expression without parentheses. Simplify.

**a.** $3 - (6x - 6)$

| | |
|---|---|
| $3 - 6x + 6$ | Rewrite the expression. |
| $9 - 6x$ | Simplify. |

**b.** $7g - (4h + 9g)$

| | |
|---|---|
| $7g - 4h - 9g$ | Rewrite the expression. |
| $-2g - 4h$ | Combine like terms. |

**Exercises**

Solve each equation. Check your solution.

**1.** $2(s + 11) = 5(s + 2)$ **2.** $7y - 1 = 2(y + 3) - 2$ **3.** $1 + 2(b + 6) = 5(b - 1)$

Evaluate each expression.

**4.** $48 - (21 - 37)$ **5.** $1.9 - (3 + 1.1)$ **6.** $41 - (107 - 77)$

Rewrite each expression without parentheses. Simplify.

**7.** $40 - (10f - 19)$ **8.** $16x - (6 + 9x)$ **9.** $9n - (15n - m)$

## Skills Practice (p. 24) AL OL

**Lesson 9.4 Skills Practice**
***Solve Equations with Parentheses***

Solve each equation. Check your solution.

**1.** $2(g - 7) = 16$ **2.** $5(x + 2) = 30$

**3.** $3(2d + 7) = 39$ **4.** $4(a - 2) = 3(a + 4)$

**5.** $3(f + 2) + 9 = 13 + 5f$ **6.** $2(x - 4) = 3(1 + x)$

**7.** $2n + 2.5 = 4(n + 2) - n$ **8.** $4(x + 3) = x$

**9.** $2(6x + 1) = 4(x - 5) - 2$ **10.** $3(4k + 14) = 10k - 2(k - 7)$

Evaluate each expression.

**11.** $1.7 - (1.6 - 20.2)$ **12.** $4 - (28 + 3)$

**13.** $25 - (17 - 15)$ **14.** $14 - (6 + 28)$

Rewrite each expression without parentheses. Simplify.

**15.** $22 - (60x - 41)$ **16.** $56f - (23 + 5f)$

**17.** $3 - (x - 34) + x$ **18.** $7s + 6(3s + 1)$

**19.** $y + 5(y + 5x)$ **20.** $13p - \frac{1}{4}(4p - 16m)$

## Problem-Solving Practice (p. 25) AL OL

**Lesson 9.4 Problem-Solving Practice**
***Solve Equations with Parentheses***

**1. Hiking** A group of friends went on a 3-day hike. During day 2, the group hiked three times as far as they did on day 1. On day 3, they hiked twelve miles fewer than four times the miles hiked on day 1. They hiked the same distance on day 2 as they hiked on days 1 and 3 combined. Write and solve an equation to find the number of miles the group hiked each day.

**2. Photography** Barasa and three friends took pictures at the school dance. Two of his friends each took six more pictures than Barasa took. The other friend took four times the number of pictures Barasa took. They have a total of 376 pictures. Write and solve an equation to find how many pictures each friend took.

**3. Phones** A local cell phone company offers four different calling plans. Plan A offers twice as many minutes as Plan B. The number of minutes in Plan B plus 225 equals the number of minutes offered by Plan C. Plan D offers 2,025 minutes. This is the same number of minutes as the first three plans combined. Write and solve an equation to find how many minutes each plan offers.

**4. Health** Al uses 6 slices of kiwi, 12 slices of banana, and 10 strawberries in a fruit smoothie. The smoothie contains 646 milligrams of vitamin C. A kiwi slice has 3 milligrams fewer than seven times the amount of vitamin C in a banana slice. A strawberry has 4 milligrams fewer than the amount of vitamin C in a banana slice. Write and solve an equation to find the amount of vitamin C each fruit contains.

**5. Gardening** Taru purchased 5 packages of tulip bulbs to plant in her garden. She also bought a bag of mulch for \$7.50. The sales tax for her purchase was 8%. She spent a total of \$51.30 including tax. Write and solve an equation to find the cost of each package of tulip bulbs.

## Enrichment (p. 26) BL

**Lesson 9.4 Enrichment**
***Solve Equations with Parentheses***

***Sonya Vasilievna Kovalevsky***

Sonya Vasilievna Kovalevsky (1850–1891), a Russian mathematician, achieved a good education and a successful career despite the disadvantage at that time of being female. Discover her accomplishments by working the problems at the bottom of the page. If you find your answer in the chart, circle the fact in that square. Each circled fact is a true statement about Kovalevsky's life.

**SONYA VASILIEVNA KOVALEVSKY (1850–1891)**

| | | |
|---|---|---|
| She was denied an education in Russia. $\frac{1}{4}$ | She was married just so the European universities would allow her to attend higher education classes. 3 | Upon receiving her doctorate, she was offered several professional appointments all over Europe. 156 |
| Sonya was a Russian mathematician and physicist. 33 | She wrote a play that was produced in Moscow. 10 | Sonya was born in Poland and became a well-known mathematician and novelist. −5 |
| She became a Lecturer and later Professor of Higher Mathematics in Stockholm. $-1\frac{1}{2}$ | She began her formal study at the Naval Academy in St. Petersburg. 6 | She was taught privately by renowned mathematician Karl Weierstrass in Berlin. $\frac{1}{2}$ |

**1.** $2(z - 4) = 12$ **2.** $2(x + 1) = \frac{8}{3}x$

**3.** $5n = n - 6(11 - n)$ **4.** $31 - 9x = 1 - 3(4x - 17)$

**5.** $4(6 + 8s) - (2s + 1) = 60s + 8$ **6.** $\frac{x}{9} - (1 + 2x) = 19 - 2x$

**7.** $9 - (2a + 6) = -9$ **8.** $28x - 8(4x + 3) = 3(2x - 3)$

**9.** $2x - 4(2x + 1) = x - 3(2x - 1)$

## Lesson Quick Quiz (p. 27) AL OL BL

**Lesson 9.4 Quick Quiz**

**1.** An airplane climbs at a rate of $n$ feet per minute. The same airplane glides down to Earth without power at a rate of $q$ feet per minute.

**a.** Write an expression describing the change in altitude if it first climbs for 5 minutes and then glides for 2 minutes.

**b.** The same airplane starts at 5,000 feet above sea level. It climbs for 10 minutes and then glides to earth for 8 minutes. Write an expression that describes the glider's altitude above sea level at that point.

**2.** Rewrite each expression without parentheses. Then evaluate both versions to check your work.

**a.** $2 - 3(4 - 6)$

**b.** $-7 + (-2 + 3)$

**3.** Simplify $5n - 3(2 - 6n)$. Show each step in your solution.

**4.** Solve the equation

$3g + 2(6 - g) = 4 + 5(g + 1)$. Show each step and check your solution.

## Lesson Master (p. 28)

**Lesson 9.4 Master 1**
***Solve Equations with Parentheses***

**On Your Own Exercise 52**

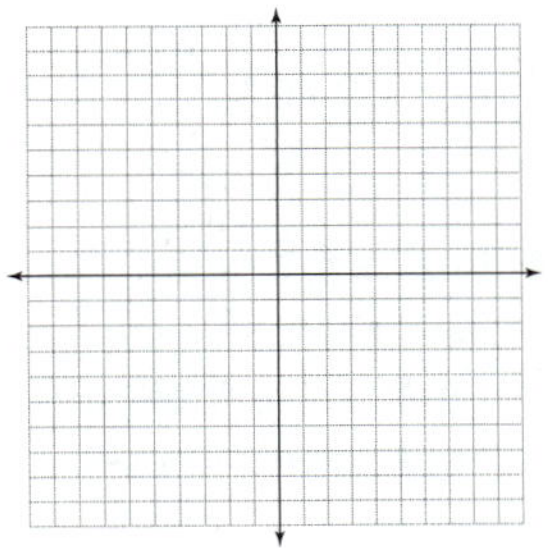

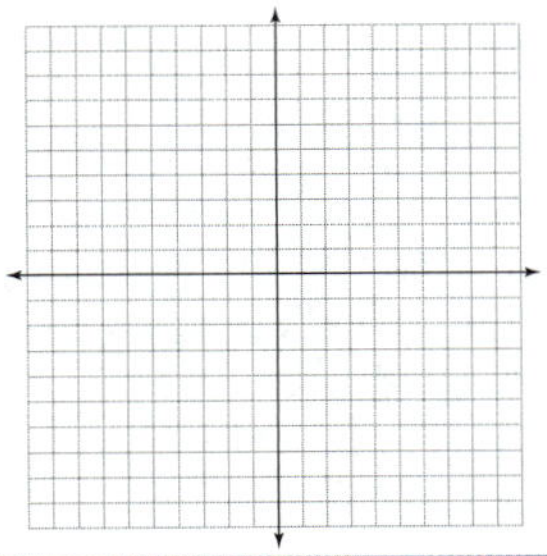

# Additional Lesson Resources

### Teacher Tech Tools

- TeacherWorks
- ExamView Assessment Suite
- Classroom Presentation Toolkit
- Advance Tracker

### Student Tech Tools

- StudentWorks Plus

Math Online eGlossary • Concepts in Motion

### Other Print Products

- Investigation Notebook and Reflection Journal
- Quick Review Math Handbook

LESSON 9.4 Solve Equations with Parentheses

## Introduce

**Work with Parentheses** You can introduce this lesson by telling the class that they will learn how to simplify equations to make them easier to solve. They will learn different ways to work with parentheses.

They will also learn how to apply algebra to the solution of exercises. Often exercises come in many parts that are related in confusing ways. Translating them into the precise language of algebra lets you see how the components are related, and hence often lets you write an equation that describes the exercise. If you can do this, then the rest is relatively mechanical; just solve the equation and interpret the answer in terms of the exercise.

**Think & Discuss**
Solve the equation as a class. Make sure that students understand the steps required to simplify it.

## Investigation 1

***On Your Own Exercises***
Pages 484–488
Exercises 1–5, 44–46

**Construct** In this investigation, students construct an equation to fit a particular situation. Then they solve the equation and use that answer to solve the exercise.

**Example**

As a class read the situation in the Example. An alternative way to solve this exercise is shown in Exercise 1 on the following page. You can include that exercise as part of a whole-class discussion.

LESSON 9.4

# Solve Equations with Parentheses



Many situations that people encounter every day can be tackled by using mathematical techniques such as writing and solving algebraic equations. Sometimes, an equation that is written to solve a problem looks quite complicated. However, equations can often be simplified to make them easier to solve.

**Think & Discuss**

Rewrite this equation to make it easier to solve. Provide an explanation for each step. Possible answer: Use the distributive property: $2n + 3n + 3 = 43$. Then combine $2n$ and $3n$: $5n + 3 = 43$.

$$2n + 3(n + 1) = 43$$

Solve your simplified equation. Check that your solution is a solution of the original equation.
8; Check: $2(8) + 3(8 + 1) = 16 + 27 = 43$

## Investigation 1 Build and Solve Equations

You have solved many exercises by writing and solving equations. Sometimes, after you write an equation for a situation, you can rewrite it before you solve. You already know some techniques for rewriting expressions to make them simpler.

**Example**

Jenna and Don collect autographs of baseball players. Jenna has five more autographs than Don. If they have 19 autographs altogether, how many does each friend have?

Here is Maya's solution.

Let $n$ be the number of autographs Don has. Then Jenna has $n + 5$.

| | |
|---|---|
| $n + (n + 5) = 19$ | Combine Don's and Jenna's autographs. |
| $n + n + 5 = 19$ | Remove the parentheses. |
| $2n + 5 = 19$ | Add $n$ and $n$. |
| $2n = 14$ | Subtract 5 from both sides. |
| $n = 7$ | Divide both sides by 2. |

So, Don has 7 autographs and Jenna has 12. This adds to 19, so it checks.

★ indicates multi-step problem

## Develop & Understand: A

1b. Possible answer: Yes; their equations will have different solutions because Maya's variable stands for the number of autographs Don has and Zoe's stands for the number Jenna has, but they will get the same answers for the number each friend has.

**1.** Zoe thought about the situation in the example differently.

"I'll let $J$ stand for the number of autographs Jenna has. Don has 5 fewer than Jenna, so he must have $J - 5$ autographs."

**a.** Write the equation Zoe had to solve. $J + J - 5 = 19$, or $2J - 5 = 19$

**b.** Do you think Zoe will get the same numbers of autographs for Jenna and Don as Maya did? Why or why not?

**c.** Solve Zoe's equation. Check your solution. $J = 12$, so Jenna has 12 and Don has 7. The total is 19, so it checks.

**2.** Jorge and Talia have 48 model planes altogether. Jorge has three times as many model planes as Talia. Write and solve an equation to find how many model planes each student has. See margin.

**3.** Melissa has one more than twice the number of beanbag animals Rachel has. Latanya has a third as many beanbag animals as Melissa has. Together, the three friends have 38 beanbag animals. Write and solve an equation to find how many beanbag animals each friend has. See margin.

In Exercises 4–14, you will practice rewriting expressions to make them simpler and easier to handle.

**Real-World Link**
The first baseball cards were printed in the late 1800s. In 1933, they began to be packaged with a stick of bubble gum and one card for a penny.

## Develop & Understand: B

Veronica is sorting groups of baseball cards by brand. They are Players, Best, and Atlantic. In Exercises 4–7, write and solve an equation to find the number of baseball cards in each pile. Check that your solutions make sense. 4–6. See margin.

★**4.** Veronica begins with 103 baseball cards, all Players and Best. There are 11 more Best cards than Players cards.

★**5.** The next group Veronica sorts has a total of 98 Players and Atlantic cards. It has 36 fewer Atlantic cards than Players cards.

★**6.** The third group has 112 cards, which Veronica divides into two piles. The Atlantic pile has three times as many cards as the Best pile.

★**7.** The last pile, a mix of all three brands, contains 136 cards. Once Veronica sorts it into three piles, the Players pile has seven more than twice the number in the Best pile. The Atlantic pile has three times as many as the Players pile. $b + (2b + 7) + 3(2b + 7) = 136$; Best: 12, Players: 31, Atlantic: 93



## Develop & Understand: A

*Suggested Grouping: Individuals*

Students write and solve equations for various contexts.

▶ **Exercise 1** Students solve the exercise posed in the Example by constructing the equation in terms of the number of autographs that Jenna has. The alternative solution emphasizes the importance of paying attention to what the variable stands for.

▶ **Exercises 2 and 3** Watch for students confusing the phrases *three times as many and a third as many.* Have students begin by substituting some numbers that make sense. In Exercise 3, for example, if Melissa has 30 beanbag animals, then Latanya has 10. It is fairly easy to translate the number pairs into appropriate algebraic expressions.

**Wrap-Up** Have students share their equations and exercise-solving methods for Exercises 2–3. Be sure students realize that they can write different equations to solve an exercise and still arrive at the correct solution.

## Develop & Understand: B

*Suggested Grouping: Individuals*

▶ **Exercises 4–6** Students write equations with two or three terms.

▶ **Exercises 7–10** These equations are more complex. In Exercise 7, some students may not read the exercise carefully and write an expression for the Atlantic pile that reflects three times as many cards as in the Best pile, instead of in the Players pile.

### Additional Answers

2. If $T$ is the number Talia has, $T + 3T = 48$, so $T = 12$; Talia has 12, and Jorge has 36.
3. If $R$ is the number Rachel has, $R + (2R + 1) + \frac{1}{3}(2R + 1) = 38$, so $R = 10$; Rachel has 10, Melissa has 21, and Latanya has 7.
4. $p + (p + 11) = 103$; Players: 46, Best: 57
5. $p + (p - 36) = 98$; Players: 67, Atlantic: 31
6. $b + 3b = 112$; Best: 28, Atlantic: 84

▶ **Exercise 10** Watch for students who do not write a subtraction equation. This is the first exercise in which students subtract expressions to solve a exercise. Encourage them to reread the exercise and look for key words describing the operation needed to find the solution as well as the kinds of books involved.

## Develop & Understand: C

*Suggested Grouping: Individuals*

▶ **Exercise 14** Students work with fractions, both in the equation and in the solution.

**Wrap-Up** Have volunteers explain how to solve each equation. You can have them demonstrate the solution steps on the board.

### Share & Summarize

Have students solve these individually. Call on two students to present their solutions at the board. Discuss the reasons recorded for each step, making sure there is general agreement before going on.

### Additional Answers

8. $f + (f - 5) + (f + 15) = 31$; fiction: 7, nonfiction: 2, children's: 22

9. $c + 3c + (c - 2) = 78$; children's: 16, fiction: 48, nonfiction: 14

★ indicates multi-step problem

A bookstore clerk is sorting boxes of books to be shelved. From each box, he makes three stacks of books. They are fiction, nonfiction, and children's. In Exercises 8–10, write and solve an equation to find the number of books in each stack. 8, 9. See margin.

★**8.** The first box has 31 books. The nonfiction stack has 5 fewer books than the fiction, and the children's has 15 more than the fiction.

★**9.** From the next box, the fiction stack has three times as many as the children's, and the nonfiction has two fewer than the children's. There are 78 books altogether.

★**10.** From a third box, the nonfiction stack has one more than double the number in the fiction stack, and the children's stack has double the number in the nonfiction stack. The difference between the numbers of books in the children's stack and the fiction stack is 47. $2(2f + 1) - f = 47$; fiction: 15, nonfiction: 31; children's: 62

## Develop & Understand: C

**Solve each equation.**

**11.** $3n + 2 = n$ $-1$

**12.** $5(s - 2) - 22 = -32$ $0$

**13.** $7(t - 3) + 1 = 3(t + 4)$ $8$

**14.** $3(2x + 1) + 2(x - 3) = \frac{1}{2}(x - 10)$ $-\frac{4}{15}$

### Share & Summarize

**1.** Simplify and solve the equation $3(n + 4) + 2(n - 12) = 2n$. Explain each step in your solution.

**2.** Solve the equation $3x + x + 5(x + 4) = 56$. Check your solution.

1. $3(n + 4) + 2(n - 12) = 2n$
$3n + 12 + 2n - 24 = 2n$
$5n - 12 = 2n$
$-12 = -3n$
$4 = n$
$n = 4$
Apply distributive property.
Add $3n$ and $2n$. Combine 12 and $-24$.
Subtract $5n$ from both sides.
Divide by $-3$.

2. 4; $3(4) + 4 + 5(4 + 4) = 56$
$3(4) + 4 + 5(8) = 56$
$12 + 4 + 40 = 56$
$56 = 56$

## On the Spot Assessment

Exercises 11–14 are four equations that increase in complexity. You can use these equations to assess students' skills in simplifying algebraic expressions and solving linear equations.

## Troubleshooting

If students are still failing to multiply the second term in a distributive property example, try drawing a closed loop around the parenthesized expression. This has the effect of making it clear that the product applies to both terms.

# Investigation 2 Subtract with Parentheses

**Vocabulary**

conjecture

At the beginning of Investigation 1, Maya wrote an equation to show how two collections of baseball players' autographs were added. She used parentheses around the sum $n + 5$, because that sum represents Jenna's number of autographs.

$$n + (n + 5) = 19$$

To add such an expression, you can simply remove the parentheses. For example, the equation above can be rewritten.

$$n + n + 5 = 19$$

In this investigation, you will explore what happens when you *subtract* expressions in parentheses.

**Real-World Link**

Some of the rarest and most valuable baseball cards can actually be worth less if they are signed by the player than if they are not.

### Think & Discuss

How would you find the value of the expression $63 - (10 + 3)$? See ①.

Simon and Jin Lee evaluated $63 - (10 + 3)$ in different ways.

- Simon added 10 and 3 and then subtracted the sum from 63.
- Jin Lee subtracted one number at a time from 63. First, she subtracted 10, and then she subtracted 3.

Which method do you prefer? Are both approaches correct? Explain. See ②.

Simon wondered whether *any* sum could be subtracted by subtracting the numbers one at a time. After testing several cases, Simon said he thinks $a - (b + c)$ and $a - b - c$ are *equivalent expressions*. Remember that two expressions are *equivalent* if they have the same value for any values of the variables. Is he correct? Explain. See ③.

① Possible answer: Add within the parentheses to get 13, and then subtract to get 50.

② Preferences will vary. Both approaches are correct because $63 - (10 + 3) = 63 - 10 - 3$.

③ He is correct, though students may not be sure about this at this point.

Simon's statement is a **conjecture**, a statement which he believes to be true based on some cases he has considered. If Simon's conjecture is true, the two expressions, $a - (b + c)$ and $a - b - c$, will give identical results no matter what numbers are substituted for the variables. If you can find even *one* case for which the two expressions give different results, you can conclude that they are *not* equivalent and that Simon's conjecture is false.



## Investigation 2

**On Your Own Exercises**
Pages 484–488
Exercises 6–22, 47–51

**Subtract with Parentheses** In this investigation, students are introduced to subtracting expressions that are enclosed in parentheses, for example $15 - (a + 6)$ or $25 - (10 - a)$. Students often have more difficulty with this concept than they do with adding expressions in parentheses.

### Think & Discuss

*Suggested Grouping: Whole Class*

Have the class read the expression and how both Simon and Jin Lee evaluated it. Then discuss students' preferred evaluation method. Discuss Simon's idea that $a - (b + c)$ is equivalent to $a - b - c$, but at this point neither confirm nor correct students' suggestions. Students will further explore and then prove this conjecture in Exercise 1 and the Think & Discuss section on the following page.

Emphasize the meaning of the word *conjecture.* Make sure that students understand its meaning before beginning Exercise 1.

## Develop & Understand: A

*Suggested Grouping: Individuals*

This exercise set establishes the basic method of using substitution to check the equivalence of two equations as well as testing the conjecture $a - (b + c) = a - b - c$. Make sure that students understand how to use substitution to evaluate expressions before they begin the exercise set. It is important that each student try values for each case rather than have a pair divide up the tasks. This will enable them to see that the conjecture is true for their values, and then verify that their partner's values produce the same results.

**Wrap-Up** Discuss students' tables and their ideas about whether Simon's conjecture is correct. Students will perform a similar test for another conjecture in Exercises 8–12.

Read together the discussion in the text describing how to determine if a conjecture is true.

### Think & Discuss

Present the exercise at the board or on an overhead. Encourage students to copy and record the reasons for each step as they discuss the proof as a class. They may want to refer to this proof when writing a similar proof in Exercises 8–12.

## Develop & Understand: A

**1.** Test Simon's conjecture by trying at least four sets of values for *a*, *b*, and *c*. Record your results in a table like the one shown, which displays the results for $a = 50$, $b = 3$, and $c = 12$. Test a variety of values for *a*, *b*, and *c*. Consider cases in which the following occurs.

- *a* is greater than $(b + c)$
- *a* is less than $(b + c)$
- *c* is a negative number
- *b* is a negative number

| a | b | c | b + c | a − (b + c) | a − b − c |
|---|---|---|---|---|---|
| 50 | 3 | 12 | 15 | 35 | 35 |
| | | | | | |
| | | | | | |
| | | | | | |
| | | | | | |

Based on your research, do you think Simon's conjecture is correct? Answers will vary.

You may already be convinced that Simon's conjecture is correct. To *prove* it is correct, you must show that it makes no difference what the values of the variables are. You cannot test every possible combination, but you can use algebra and what you know about operations with negative numbers to show that the conjecture is true for all sets of values.

You know that subtracting a number is the same as adding its opposite and that adding a number is the same as subtracting its opposite.

$$5 - (-2) = 5 + 2 \qquad 15 + (-8) = 15 - 8$$

You also know that the opposite of a number equals −1 times the number.

$$-3 = -1 \cdot 3 \qquad -(-11) = -1 \cdot (-11)$$

### Think & Discuss

The series of steps below *proves* that $a - (b + c) = a - b - c$. Provide a reason for each step. See ①.

**Step 1.** $a - (b + c) = a + -(b + c)$

**Step 2.** $= a + -1(b + c)$

**Step 3.** $= a + (-1) \cdot b + (-1) \cdot c$

**Step 4.** $= a - b - c$

So, $a - (b + c) = a - b - c$.

① Step 1: Subtracting a number is the same as adding the number's opposite. Step 2: The opposite of a number is −1 times the number. Step 3: Distributive property. Step 4: Adding −1 times a number is the same as subtracting the number.



### On the Spot Assessment

Consider having students keep a notebook of the proofs done in class and those that they have done themselves. It makes a good reference and study aid for them, and is a quick place for you to see how well the students comprehend the math.

## Develop & Understand: B

**Evaluate each expression.**

2. $40 - (10 + 6)$ 24
3. $35 - (5 + 8)$ 22
4. $17.5 - (6.4 + 0.7)$ 10.4

**Rewrite each expression without parentheses. Then rewrite the expression again, if possible, to make it as simple as you can.**

5. $7 - (7 + s)$ $7 - 7 - s = -s$
6. $12 - (r + 8)$ $12 - r - 8 = 4 - r$
7. $(t - 7) + 3$ $t - 7 + 3 = t - 4$

Shaunda has a strategy for quickly solving difficult subtraction expressions in her head.

### Example

To compute $63 - 19$, Shaunda estimates the answer by first subtracting 20 from 63 to get 43. Then she corrects her estimate. She knows that she subtracted one too many since 20 is one greater than 19, so she adds back one to get 44 as the result.

Here is Shaunda's strategy in symbols.

$$63 - 19 = 63 - 20 + 1 = 43 + 1 = 44$$

## Develop & Understand: C 8, 9. See margin.

8. Evaluate each expression by using Shaunda's method. First, approximate by subtracting 20 and then add back the amount needed to correct the result. Write the steps in symbols as done in the example.
   a. $63 - 18$ b. $63 - 17$ c. $63 - 15$

9. In these expressions, the number being subtracted is close to 200. Modify Shaunda's method and apply it to find each difference. Write the steps in symbols.
   a. $351 - 197$ b. $351 - 195$ c. $351 - 190$

Zach said that after looking at his answers for Exercises 8 and 9, he thinks $a - (b - c)$ is equivalent to $a - b + c$.

10. Look at the symbolic version of Shaunda's example, which is $63 - 19 = 63 - 20 + 1 = 43 + 1 = 44$. What do you think Zach would say are the values for $a$, $b$, and $c$? $a = 63, b = 20, c = 1$



### Additional Answers

8a. $63 - 18 = 63 - 20 + 2 = 43 + 2 = 45$

8b. $63 - 17 = 63 - 20 + 3 = 43 + 3 = 46$

8c. $63 - 15 = 63 - 20 + 5 = 43 + 5 = 48$

9a. $351 - 197 = 351 - 200 + 3 = 151 + 3 = 154$

9b. $351 - 195 = 351 - 200 + 5 = 151 + 5 = 156$

9c. $351 - 190 = 351 - 200 + 10 = 151 + 10 = 161$

## Develop & Understand: B

*Suggested Grouping: Pairs*

Have students first evaluate each expression by themselves and then compare answers with their partners. Pairs should work together until both partners agree on their answers.

▶ **Exercises 2–4** You may want to have students solve each exercise first using Simon's method and then using Jin Lee's method. Another option is to have one partner use one method and the other partner use the other method. However, solving with both methods can reinforce the idea that $a - (b + c) = a - b - c$.

### Example

Do this exercise as part of a whole-class discussion. Stress how Shaunda used one form of mental math, compensation, to find the answer more quickly. Point out that knowing how and when to apply mental math is a valuable skill, particularly when a calculator is not handy. Be sure that students can look at the strategy in symbols and explain what Shaunda did to solve the exercise. Although Shaunda's method is used in the following exercise set, you may want students to share other examples of how they use mental math tricks to solve problems.

## Develop & Understand: C

*Suggested Grouping: Pairs*

This exercise set gives practice in using Shaunda's method in increasingly more complicated settings. Working in pairs will be helpful, particularly for those students who are still uncertain about subtracting expressions in parentheses.

▶ **Exercise 10** Students try to see how the expression $a - (b - c)$ is shown in Shaunda's equation. Remind them that there is an equivalent expression, $a - b + c$, that they may find easier to use to solve the exercise.

▶ **Exercise 11** Students test values in the conjecture from Exercise 10. You might want to tell students that each student should evaluate all the expressions for their chosen values rather than split the tasks with their partners. This will enable them to see that the conjecture is true for their values, and then verify that their partner's values produce the same results.

**Wrap-Up** Have a student write his or her proof from Exercise 12 on the board. Use this proof as the basis of a class discussion.

## Develop & Understand: D

*Suggested Grouping: Individuals*

▶ **Exercises 13 and 17** Students subtract an addition expression in parentheses. The remaining exercises use subtraction expressions instead.

▶ **Exercises 16–19** Students simplify algebraic expressions.

### Share & Summarize

Students explain how they rewrote the expressions for Exercises 16–19. Have a few students present their answers for discussion.

**Teacher Tips** If students are still making random mistakes, suggest that they pick one method to evaluate expressions containing parentheses and use only that method until they feel comfortable and proficient with its use. They can then use the other way until they are proficient with it as well. For example, they could evaluate all expressions with parentheses by first evaluating the numbers in parentheses, then evaluating the entire expression. Once they are comfortable with that method, they can begin to evaluate the expressions by rewriting the expression without parentheses and then evaluating the new expression. Students' random errors will fade as students become more experienced.

11. Answers will vary. However, every example students tested should be evidence that it is correct.

**11.** Use the table to test the two expressions in Zach's conjecture with at least four sets of values for $a$, $b$, and $c$. One example is shown. Try cases in which the following occurs.

- $a$ is greater than $(b - c)$
- $a$ is less than $(b - c)$
- $c$ is greater than $b$
- $b$ is a negative number

| $a$ | $b$ | $c$ | $b - c$ | $a - (b - c)$ | $a - b + c$ |
|---|---|---|---|---|---|
| 50 | 12 | 3 | 9 | 41 | 41 |
| | | | | | |
| | | | | | |
| | | | | | |
| | | | | | |

Based on your results, do you think Zach's conjecture is correct?

**12.** Zach said the proof of his conjecture is very similar to the proof of Simon's conjecture in Think & Discuss on page 477. Here is the first step of Zach's proof.

$$a - (b - c) = a + -(b - c)$$

12a. Subtracting a number is the same as adding its opposite.

**a.** Explain how you know this first step is a true statement.

**b.** Finish the proof. If you need help, look back at the proof of Simon's conjecture. Be sure to provide a reason for each step in your proof. See margin.

## Develop & Understand: D

**Evaluate each expression.**

**13.** $50 - (10 + 6)$ 34 **14.** $50 - (10 - 6)$ 46 **15.** $50 - (6 - 10)$ 54

**Rewrite each expression without parentheses. Then rewrite the expressions again, if possible, to make them as simple as you can.**

**16.** $12 - (r - 8)$
$12 - r + 8 = 20 - r$

**17.** $5 - (5 + n)$
$5 - 5 - n = -n$

**18.** $3 - (7 - t)$
$3 - 7 + t = t - 4$

**19.** $15r - (3r - s)$
$15r - 3r + s = 12r + s$

### Share & Summarize

Select one of the expressions from Exercises 16–19 and explain how you thought about it. Write an explanation to convince someone that your simplified version is correct. Answers will vary.



**Additional Answer**

12b. Possible proof:

| | |
|---|---|
| $a - (b - c) = a + -(b - c) = a + -1(b - c)$ | The opposite of a number is $-1$ times the number. |
| $= a + (-b - (-c))$ | applying the distributive property |
| $= a + (-b + c)$ | Subtracting a number is the same as adding its opposite. |
| $= a + -b + c$ | removing parentheses |
| $= a - b + c$ | Adding the opposite of a number is the same as subtracting the number. |

So, $a - (b - c) = a - b + c$.

# Investigation 3 More Practice with Parentheses

As you saw in Investigation 2, the two expressions below will always be equal, no matter what the values of $x$ and $y$ are. But maybe you are still not sure it really makes sense that they are equal.

$$10 - (x + y) \qquad 10 - x - y$$

Think about the following. Imagine that you have \$10. You owe your parents $x$ dollars, and you owe your best friend $y$ dollars. How much money will you have left if you can pay both your debts?

You can add your debts together, $x + y$, and then subtract the total from \$10. The amount you have left is $10 - (x + y)$. Or, you can subtract your debts one at a time, and so the amount you have left is $10 - x - y$. In either case, you will have the same amount of money left, so these two expressions must be equal.

## Develop & Understand: A

1. Leon owed his little sister $x$ dollars. She wanted to buy a new book, so she asked Leon to pay back some of the money. He said he would give her $y$ dollars.
   a. After paying back $y$ dollars, how much did Leon still owe his sister? $x - y$ dollars
   b. Leon had \$15 after paying his sister the $y$ dollars that he promised. If he paid the rest of the money that he owed, how much would he have left? Find two expressions to represent this amount. $15 - (x - y)$ dollars, $15 - x + y$ dollars
2. Ron wanted to borrow money from two of his siblings. Neither wanted to make him a loan, so he struck a deal with them. If he took more than a week to repay them, he would pay them double the amount borrowed. His brother loaned him $x$ dollars, and his sister loaned him $y$ dollars. Ron was not able to get any money for two weeks, when a friend paid him \$25 that she had borrowed.

   Which expressions represent the amount of money Ron had left after paying his siblings double the amount he had borrowed from them? All three are correct.

   a. $25 - 2(x + y)$   b. $25 - (2x + 2y)$   c. $25 - 2x - 2y$



# Investigation 3

**On Your Own Exercises**
Pages 484–488
Exercises 23–43, 52–54

**Equations Containing Parentheses**
Students frequently have difficulty working with expressions in parentheses. In this investigation, students practice simplifying expressions and solving equations containing parentheses.

Discuss the three introductory paragraphs as a class.

## Develop & Understand: A

*Suggested Grouping: Individuals*

Students write expressions to represent situations in word exercises.

**Wrap-Up** Discuss why the three expressions in Exercise 2 represent the money Ron had left. For example, a volunteer might identify the steps taken to rewrite $25 - 2(x + y)$ as $25 - (2x + 2y)$ as the distributive property and use the rule $a - (b + c) = a - b - c$ to explain why $25 - (2x + 2y) = 25 - 2x - 2y$. The Example on the following page explores these ideas further.

**Example**

Discuss this alternative method of subtracting. Initially some students may want to follow the order of operations and find $3 - 8$ first. Reassure them that this is a correct solution method but that learning and understanding the alternative solution method can help them simplify algebraic expressions.

## Develop & Understand: B

*Suggested Grouping: Individuals*

Students simplify and write equivalent expressions. Suggest that they use the method that works best for them to solve the exercises.

▶ **Exercises 9–12** Students write equivalent expressions for four expressions that contain the same variables but different operations.

▶ **Exercise 13** Students may give a variety of justifications for Exercise 13, some of which may be true and not general or true and only peripherally related to the step. For example, a student might justify that $5 - 2(3 - 8) = 5 + -2(3 - 8)$, by saying the opposite of the product of two numbers is the same as the opposite of the first number times the second. Of course, the minus sign in the first expression represented subtraction, not the opposite of.

Jared says that when he has to multiply an expression in parentheses by a quantity, he first uses the distributive property to multiply each item inside the parentheses. Then he uses the rules for adding and subtracting expressions in parentheses.

**Example**

Here is how Jared simplified $5 - 2(3 - 8)$.

First, he distributed the 2. $5 - (6 - 16)$

Then he applied the rule for subtracting parentheses. $5 - 6 + 16$

Then he subtracted and added. $15$

Jared used the same approach to simplify $12k - 3(7 - 2k)$.

$$12k - 3(7 - 2k) = 12k - (21 - 6k)$$
$$= 12k - 21 + 6k$$
$$= 18k - 21$$

In order to become more skilled at simplifying expressions with parentheses, you will combine adding and subtracting with parentheses with some of the earlier skills that you developed.

## Develop & Understand: B

**Simplify each expression as much as possible.**

**3.** $5r - 2(r - 8)$ $3r + 16$

**4.** $32L - 3(L - 7)$ $29L + 21$

**5.** $12n - 2(n - 4)$ $10n + 8$

**6.** $4(3x - 2) - 3x$ $9x - 8$

**7.** $-5(g - 3)$ $-5g + 15$

**8.** $8t - \frac{1}{3}(12t - 30)$ $4t + 10$

**For each expression, write an equivalent expression without parentheses.**

**9.** $a + d(b + c)$ $a + db + dc$

**10.** $a - d(b + c)$ $a - db - dc$

**11.** $a + d(b - c)$ $a + db - dc$

**12.** $a - d(b - c)$ $a - db + dc$

**13.** In the example, you saw how Jared simplified $5 - 2(3 - 8)$. Here is another way to simplify $5 - 2(3 - 8)$. Provide a reason for each step.

**a.** $5 - 2(3 - 8) = 5 + -2(3 - 8)$

**b.** $= 5 + (-6 - (-16))$ Distributive property

**c.** $= 5 + (-6 + 16)$

**d.** $= 5 + -6 + 16$

**e.** $= 15$ Adding and subtracting

13a. Subtracting a number is the same as adding its opposite.

13c. Subtracting a number is the same as adding its opposite.

13d. Applying the rule for adding parentheses



### Troubleshooting

Watch for students who ignore the closing parenthesis in Exercise 6 and multiply all terms by 4. These students will first simplify the expression as $12x - 8 - 12x$, then further simplify it to $-8$. Remind them that only the terms within the parentheses should be multiplied.

★ indicates multi-step problem

**Choose any method to solve each equation. Check your answers.**

**14.** $2(2q + 4) - 2q = 24$ 8

**15.** $12 - \frac{1}{2}(2n - 6) = 7$ 8

**16.** $2x - (4 - x) = 5$ 3

**17.** $4r - 3(r + 1) = 0$ 3

**Real-World Link**

Until the 1980s, tennis rackets were made from wood. Wood tennis rackets, first made in the U.S. in the 1870s, are now collectors' items.

**18.** Sunny Sports Shop sells beginner's tennis rackets for $40 each. Most customers who buy one of these rackets also buy several cans of tennis balls, which cost $2.50 each. The customer's bill has three parts.

- the price of the racket
- the total price of the balls
- the sales tax, which is 7% of the combined price of the racket and the balls

**a.** A customer buys a racket and $x$ cans of balls. Write expressions for each of the three parts of the customer's bill.
Racket: 40; balls: $2.5x$; tax: $0.07(40 + 2.5x)$

**b.** Write an expression for the total bill, which includes the racket, $x$ cans of balls, and the sales tax.
$40 + 2.5x + 0.07(40 + 2.5x)$

★ **c.** Aurelia bought a racket and some cans of balls. Her total bill came to $53.50. Write and solve an equation to find how many cans of balls she bought.
$40 + 2.5x + 0.07(40 + 2.5x) = 53.50$; $x = 4$ cans

## Share & Summarize

**1.** Simplify and solve the following equation. Write an explanation of your work that would convince someone that your simplified equation is correct. See margin.

$$5n - \frac{1}{3}(3n - 6) = \frac{1}{4}(8n + 12)$$

**2.** Check your answer by substituting it into the original equation.
$5\left(\frac{1}{2}\right) - \frac{1}{3}\left(3 \cdot \frac{1}{2} - 6\right) = 5\left(\frac{1}{2}\right) - \left(\frac{1}{2} - 2\right) = \frac{5}{2} - \frac{1}{2} + 2 = 4$, and $\frac{1}{4}\left(8 \cdot \frac{1}{2} + 12\right) = 1 + 3 = 4$



▶ **Exercise 18** You may want to tell students that they do not need to simplify their expressions. If students elect to do so anyway, they should answer $42.8 + 2.675x$ for Part b.

## Share & Summarize

Students who can do this exercise are in good equation-solving shape. This is a good exercise to assign and then discuss using the overhead or board.

Some students may still be making mistakes with subtraction. As long as they recognize their mistakes, don't worry. However, students who cannot find and correct their errors or do not have a solution method that works may need additional practice.

**Additional Answer**

1. The simplified equation is $4n + 2 = 2n + 3$; the solution is $\frac{1}{2}$. Possible explanation:

| | |
|---|---|
| $5n - \frac{1}{3}(3n - 6) = \frac{1}{4}(8n + 12)$ | |
| $5n - (n - 2) = 2n + 3$ | applying the distributive property |
| $5n - n + 2 = 2n + 3$ | applying the rule for subtracting parentheses |
| $4n + 2 = 2n + 3$ | combining terms |

## On Your Own Exercises
**Lesson 9.4**

**Investigation 1**
Pages 474–476
Practice & Apply: 1–5
Connect & Extend: 44–46

**Investigation 2**
Pages 477–480
Practice & Apply: 6–22
Connect & Extend: 47–51

**Investigation 3**
Pages 481–483
Practice & Apply: 23–59
Connect & Extend: 52–54

**Assign Anytime**
Mixed Review: 55–59

▶ **Exercise 5** This is a new situation for students. They are not given the total number of coins. They must use the expressions for each stack and the relationship between the number of coins in the stacks to solve the exercise.

## On Your Own Exercises
**Lesson 9.4**

★ indicates multi-step problem

### Practice & Apply

3–5. See margin.

★**1.** Together, Lee and Joanna have 19 computer games. Joanna has 3 more games than Lee. Write and solve an equation to find the number of games each friend has. Check your answer. $c + (c + 3) = 19$, $c = 8$; Lee: 8, Joanna: 11

★**2.** Martin and five of his friends donated change to a school fundraiser to buy food for children in need. Together, they donated \$4.40. Three of the friends gave 20¢ less than Martin, and two gave 10¢ more. Write and solve an equation to find how much Martin donated. Check your answer. $M + 3(M - 20) + 2(M + 10) = 440$, $M = 80$; Martin donated 80¢.

★**3.** Peter had three piles of pickled peppers. He has a total of 52 pickled peppers. His second pile has seven more peppers than the first pile. His third pile has three fewer than the first pile. Write and solve an equation to find how many pickled peppers are in each pile. Check your answer.

★**4.** Mr. Álverez baked 60 fruit tarts for the school bake sale. He put them on four trays. The second tray had twice as many tarts as the first. The third tray had 1 more than the second. The fourth tray had five more than the first. Write and solve an equation to find how many tarts were on each tray. Check your answer.

★**5.** Gloria sorted her collection of Winged Liberty Head dimes into three stacks based on their quality. The second stack has twice as many coins as the first, the third stack has 36 more than the second, and the first stack has 43 fewer than the third. How many dimes are in each stack? Show how you found your answer.

**Real-World Link**
The Winged Liberty Head dime was minted from 1916 to 1945. The coin's designer put wings on Liberty's cap to represent freedom of thought. But the image is often mistaken for the Roman god Mercury, and thus the coin is commonly known as the Mercury dime.

**Solve each equation.**

**6.** $d + (2d - 3) = 13(d - 1)$ 1

**7.** $5(2x - 1) + 3x = 2(x + 5)$ $\frac{15}{11}$, or $1\frac{4}{11}$

**Evaluate each expression.**

**8.** $72 - (12 + 9)$ 51

**9.** $72 - (12 - 9)$ 69

**10.** $12.5 - (3.3 - 9.5)$ 18.7

**11.** $38 - (7 + 28)$ 3

**12.** $291 - (84 - 45)$ 252

**13.** $5 - (2.8 + 5.9)$ −3.7

**Rewrite each expression without parentheses. Then rewrite the expressions again, if possible, to make them as simple as you can.**

**14.** $8 - (x - 8)$

**15.** $15 - (8 + y)$

**16.** $x - (37 + x)$

**17.** $6 - (12 - n)$

**18.** $5s - (6r + s)$

**19.** $8x - (-2x - 3y)$

14. $8 - x + 8 = 16 - x$
15. $15 - 8 - y = 7 - y$
16. $x - 37 - x = -37$
17. $6 - 12 + n = n - 6$
18. $5s - 6r - s = 4s - 6r$
19. $8x + 2x + 3y = 10x + 3y$



### Additional Answers

3. $n + (n + 7) + (n - 3) + 52$, $n = 16$; first: 16, second: 23, third: 13

4. $n + 2n + (2n + 1) + (n + 5) + 60$, $n = 9$; first: 9, second: 18, third: 19, fourth: 14

5. Let the first pile $= n$, second pile $= 2n$, third pile $= 2n + 36$; then, $n = (2n + 36) - 43$. The stacks have 7, 14, and 50 coins.

20. $A + B - C$
21. $A - B + C$
22. $A - B - C$
23. $2a - 16 + 30 = 2a + 14$
24. $30 + 4t - 28 = 2 + 4t$
25. $5 + 3n + 15 = 20 + 3n$
26. $15r + 2r + 2s = 17r + 2s$
27. $3t + 30 - 3t = 30$
28. $7x + x - 2y = 8x - 2y$
29. $m + 4m + 20 = 5m + 20$
30. $4p + 14p + 14 = 18p + 14$
31. $4x + 8 + 15x + 10 = 19x + 18$

42a. $400 + 50g + 0.06(400 + 50g)$

42b. $400 + 50g + 0.06(400 + 50g) = 742$, $g = 6$; 6 games

**For each expression, write an equivalent expression without parentheses.**

**20.** $A + (B - C)$ **21.** $A - (B - C)$ **22.** $A - (B + C)$

**Rewrite each expression without parentheses. Then rewrite the expressions again, if possible, to make them as simple as you can.**

**23.** $2(a - 8) + 30$ **24.** $30 + 4(t - 7)$ **25.** $5 + 3(n + 5)$

**26.** $15r + 2(r + s)$ **27.** $3t + 3(10 - t)$ **28.** $7x + \frac{1}{2}(2x - 4y)$

**29.** $m + 4(m + 5)$ **30.** $4p + 7(2p + 2)$ **31.** $4(x + 2) + 5(3x + 2)$

**Solve each equation.**

**32.** $8 - (4 - n) = 18$ 14 **33.** $8 - (n - 4) = 18$ $-6$

**34.** $6x - 2(x + 1) = 10$ 3 **35.** $2x - 3(x - 1) = 17$ $-14$

**36.** $3y + 4(y + 2) = 78$ 10 **37.** $2(x + 3) + x = 63$ 19

**38.** $5(x + 2) = 6x$ 10 **39.** $6 - 2(8 - 2r) = 20$ 7.5

**40.** $3 - 2.5(m + 2) = \frac{m}{2} + 4$ $-2$ **41.** $r + 8 = 3(1 - r) + 2$ $-\frac{3}{4}$

**42.** GameWorld is selling SuperSpeed game systems for $400. Game cartridges are $50 each. Sales tax is 6% of the total price for all items.

**a.** Write an expression for the total, with tax, of one SuperSpeed system with $g$ game cartridges.

★ **b.** One customer bought several games and had a final bill of $742. Write and solve an equation to find how many games the customer bought.

**43.** Create an equation about two friends who collect postage stamps. Make sure your equation can be solved so that each friend has a different whole number of stamps. Include an explanation of how you created your equation and how it can be solved. Answers will vary.

**Connect & Extend**

★ **44.** In a town election, the three candidates receiving the most votes were Malone, Lawton, and Spiros. Malone received 60 more than twice as many votes as Lawton. Spiros received 362 votes more than Lawton. In all, 2,430 votes were cast. How many votes did each candidate receive? Who won the election? Show how you found your answer. Lawton's vote: 502; Malone's vote: 1,064; Spiros' vote: 864; Malone won. If $L$ = Lawton's votes, $L + 362$ = Spiros' votes and $2L + 60$ = Malone's votes; $L + (L + 362) + (2L + 60) = 2,430$.



On Your Own Exercises

▶ **Exercises 23–41** Check that students are using the distributive property accurately.

▶ **Exercise 43** Have students share their exercises in small groups. Students can discover and correct any errors that occur in the word exercises.

▶ **Exercise 47** This exercise presents another model for thinking about adding and subtracting expressions in parentheses.

On Your Own Exercises

★ indicates multi-step problem

45. If Lu-Chan got L votes, Mai got $2L$ votes and Evita got $2L + 1$ votes. $L + 2L + (2L + 1) + 1 = 27$, or $5L + 2 = 27$; Lu-Chan got 5 votes, Mai got 10, and Evita got 11.
46. $y + 30 = 3y$, $y = 15$; Nuna is 15.

**Real-World Link**
Monarch caterpillars eat milkweed leaves. These leaves contain a poison that makes the caterpillars taste bad to birds and other predators.

★**45.** This conversation occurred the day after the class election.

| | |
|---|---|
| Desiree: | I heard that Evita won our class election. |
| Reynoldo: | Yes, but it was really close! She received only one more vote than Mai. |
| Troy: | It sure wasn't very close for third place. Mai received twice as many votes as Lu-Chan. |
| Laura: | Everybody voted except James, who's home with chicken pox. |

Of the 27 students in the class, only Evita, Mai, and Lu-Chan received votes. How many votes did each of the three students receive? Show how you found your answer.

**46.** Nuna is $y$ years old. In 30 years, she will be three times as old as she is now. Write and solve an equation for this situation.

**47.** Two caterpillars are crawling in and out of a hole in a fence. The caterpillars take turns being in the lead. The length of the longer caterpillar is $L$, and the length of the shorter caterpillar is $S$. The hole is 9 cm above the ground.

Look at the caterpillars on the far left. The expression $9 + L - S$ represents the height reached by the head of the lead caterpillar.

i ii iii iv v vi vii viii

Match each of the 12 expressions with the drawings. Some positions match more than one expression, and some expressions match more than one position.

**a.** $9 + (S - L)$ ii, vi **b.** $9 + (S + L)$ iii, viii **c.** $9 - (S + L)$ iv, v

**d.** $9 - S - L$ iv, v **e.** $9 - L - S$ iv, v **f.** $9 - L + S$ ii, vi

**g.** $9 + (L + S)$ iii, viii **h.** $9 - (L + S)$ iv, v **i.** $9 - S + L$ vii

**j.** $9 + S - L$ ii, vi **k.** $9 - (S - L)$ vii **l.** $9 - (L - S)$ ii, vi



486 CHAPTER 9 Equations

**48.** Find all the sets of equivalent expressions in Parts a–l of Exercise 47.
a, f, j, and l; b and g; c, d, e, and h; i and k

**Replace each $\square$ with + or − to make the statement correct.**

**49.** $7 - (A + B) = 7 - A \boxed{-} B$

**50.** $14 + (A - B) = 14 + A \boxed{-} B$

**51.** $12 - (A - B) = 12 \boxed{-} A \boxed{+} B$

**Math Link**

Equivalent expressions give identical results when the same values are used for identical variables.

**52. Graphs** Graphing can often help you identify equivalent expressions. For example, $x - 5$ and $5 - x$ are not equivalent expressions because $y = x - 5$ and $y = 5 - x$ do not produce the same graph.

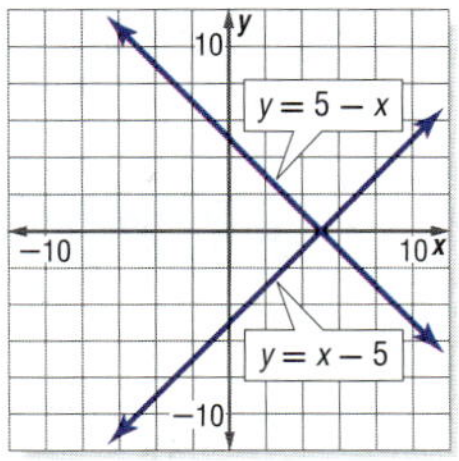


However, $8 - (x + 5)$ and $8 - x - 5$ *are* equivalent because $y = 8 - (x + 5)$ and $y = 8 - x - 5$ produce the same graph.

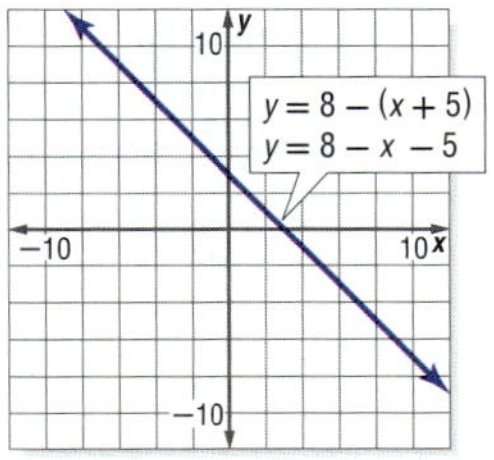


For each pair of equations, plot several points on a coordinate grid to draw the lines. Determine whether the related expressions are equivalent. See margin.

**a.** $y = 4 - (x + 5)$ and $y = 4 + (5 - x)$

**b.** $y = 7 - (3 - x)$ and $y = 7 + x - 3$



On Your Own Exercises

▶ **Exercise 52 Extension** In this exercise, students graph expressions to decide whether they are equivalent. As an extension, you might have students use their graphs to find the slope and $y$-intercept and then relate these values to the simplified expressions. You may want to provide students with graph paper or copies of Lesson 9.4 Master 1, to graph their equations.

**Additional Answers**

52a. not equivalent

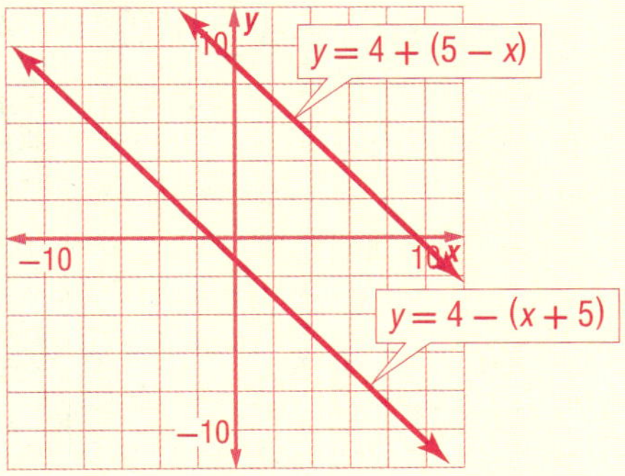


52b. equivalent

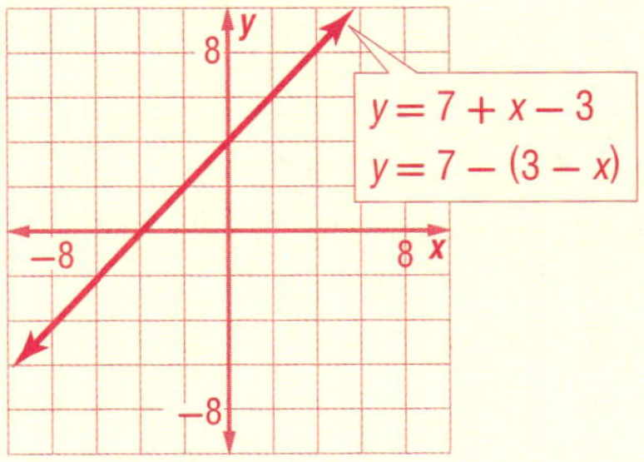

## Quick Check

**Informal Assessment** Students should be able to:

✔ add and subtract parenthetical expressions

✔ solve equations by adding, multiplying, or dividing both sides by the same quantity

✔ describe variable quantities that appear in typical word exercises, including those that refer to signed numbers

## Quick Quiz

**1.** An airplane climbs at a rate of $n$ feet per minute. The same airplane glides down to Earth without power at a rate of $q$ feet per minute.
   a. Write an expression describing the change in altitude if it first climbs for 5 minutes and then glides for 2 minutes. $5n - 2q$
   b. The same airplane starts at 5,000 feet above sea level. It climbs for 10 minutes and then glides to earth for 8 minutes. Write an expression that describes the glider's altitude above sea level at that point.
   $5{,}000 + 10n - 8q$

**2.** Rewrite each expression without parentheses. Then evaluate both versions to check your work.
   a. $2 - 3(4 - 6)$ $2 - 12 + 18 = 8$
   b. $-7 + (-2 + 3)$ $-7 - 2 + 3 = -6$

**3.** Simplify $5n - 3(2 - 6n)$. Show each step in your solution. Possible answer:
$5n + -3(2 + -6n)$
$5n + -6 + 18n$
$5n + 18n + -6$
$23n + -6$
$23n - 6$

**4.** Solve the equation
$3g + 2(6 - g) = 4 + 5(g + 1)$. Show each step and check your solution.
$3g + 12 - 2g = 4 + 5g + 5$
$g + 12 = 5g + 9$
$12 = 4g + 9$
$3 = 4g$
$\frac{3}{4} = g$

On Your Own Exercises

**53.** Albert and Mary were trying to simplify this expression, which looks a bit complicated.

$$4 - 2(-5x - 10)$$

Albert said the expression is equal to $2(-5x - 10)$. Mary said it is equal to $4 + 10x - 20$. Is Albert correct? Is Mary correct? If they are not correct, what mistakes did they make? See margin.

**54. In Your Own Words** Describe a situation that can be represented by both $a - (b - c)$ and $a - b + c$. Explain how both expressions apply to the situation.

**55.** Use the expression given to complete the table. Then write another expression that gives the same values. Check with the values in the table. Possible expression: $2n^2 + \frac{1}{2}$

| $n$ | 0 | 1 | 2 | 3 | 100 |
|---|---|---|---|---|---|
| $\frac{4n^2 + 1}{2}$ | $\frac{1}{2}$ | $2\frac{1}{2}$ | $8\frac{1}{2}$ | $18\frac{1}{2}$ | $20{,}000\frac{1}{2}$ |

**Write a symbolic rule that fits each input-output table.**

**56.**

| Input | 0 | 1 | 2 | 3 | 4 |
|---|---|---|---|---|---|
| Output | 1 | 4 | 7 | 10 | 13 |

$y = 3x + 1$

**57.**

| Input | 10 | 20 | 30 | 40 | 50 |
|---|---|---|---|---|---|
| Output | 15 | 20 | 25 | 30 | 35 |

$y = 0.5x + 10$

**Geometry** Find the area and perimeter of each figure.

**58.** This is a rectangle.

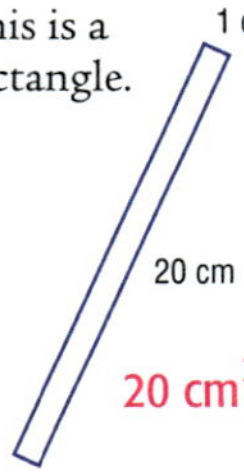


$20\text{ cm}^2$, 42 cm

**59.** This is a trapezoid.

About $67.5\text{ cm}^2$, 38 cm

### Mixed Review

54. Answers will vary. Possible situation: Let $a$ represent Alberto's amount of money, $b$ represent the amount Alberto spends at the store, and $c$ represent the amount his cousin pays. In $a - (b - c)$, $b - c$ represents the cost to Alberto and $a - (b - c)$ represents the amount of money he has left. In $a - b + c$, the amount Alberto spends is subtracted while the amount his cousin pays is added to Alberto's original amount.



### Additional Answer

53. Neither is correct. Albert subtracted 2 from 4, instead of subtracting everything following the first minus sign. Mary forgot to distribute the minus sign to the $-10$ in the parentheses. The expression is actually equal to $4 + 10x + 20$, or $10x + 24$.

CHAPTER 9

# Review & Self-Assessment

## Chapter Summary

In this chapter, you reviewed two methods of solving equations, backtracking and guess-check-and-improve. You also learned new ways to solve equations, beginning with a *balance puzzles* model. By using the model, you learned to do the same thing to both sides of an equation.

You learned some ways to simplify complicated equations, including rules for adding and subtracting expressions in parentheses.

Finally, you wrote expressions and equations for various situations and used your new skills to simplify and solve them. By using your knowledge of algebra to rewrite expressions, you also proved conjectures.

**Vocabulary**

conjecture

model

1a. $-\frac{4}{3}$; Possible explanation: Use backtracking; it is quicker.

1b. 17; Possible explanation: Use guess-check-and-improve because the variable appears twice.

## Strategies and Applications

The questions in this section will help you review and apply the important ideas and strategies developed in this chapter.

### Solving equations using different methods

**1.** Solve each equation using guess-check-and-improve or backtracking. Explain why you chose the method that you used.

**a.** $(3x + 32) \div 4 = 7$ **b.** $-2x + 3(x - 5) = 2$

**2.** Describe each method for solving equations. Give two examples of equations for which each method works well. See margin.

**a.** guess-check-and-improve

**b.** backtracking

**c.** using a balance puzzle

**d.** doing the same thing to both sides

### Writing equations to solve problems

**3.** Alisha's three cats are on special diets. Scout is the least active. Squeaky, the most active, is allowed twice as much cat food as Scout. The third cat, Picard, gets 90 grams of food each day. Alisha gives the cats a total of 240 grams of food each day. Write and solve an equation to find the amount of food each cat receives each day.

$f + 2f + 90 = 240$; $f = 50$; Scout: 50 grams; Squeaky: 100 grams; Picard: 90 grams



# Review & Self-Assessment

CHAPTER 9

## Chapter Summary

This summary helps students recall the major topics of the chapter

## Vocabulary

Students should be able to explain each of the terms listed in the vocabulary section.

**Exercises 1 and 2** Students use various methods to solve equations, then explain their methods.

### Additional Answers

2a. Guess a value for the solution and check by substitution. If the value isn't the solution, make a new guess, trying to get closer to the solution. Possible examples: $3x + 2(x - 1) = 4$, $x - 3(1 - 2x) = 3x + 5$

2b. Create a flowchart that shows how to calculate one side of the equation, and then use the other side as the output and move backward through the flowchart, determining the value for the previous oval. Possible examples: $-2(3x - 5) = 32$, $\frac{7 + x}{3} = 9$

2c. Make a puzzle using bags and blocks; remove pieces until you can see how many blocks must be in each bag. Keep the puzzle balanced by removing the same pieces from both sides of the balance. Possible examples: $3x + 7 = 5x + 3$, $2x + 1 = x + 2$

2d. Add, subtract, multiply, or divide both sides of the equation by the same amounts until you can see the solution. Try to get the variable on one side by itself. Possible examples: $3(x - 3) + 2 = 7(-2x + 1)$, $5x + 13 = 8(x - 1)$.

★ indicates multi-step problem

▶ **Exercises 3–5** Students assign a variable and write an equation expressing the relationships in a word exercise. Then they solve the equation and apply that solution to the original exercise.

▶ **Exercises 7–11** These exercises test students' ability to simplify expressions containing parentheses.

★ **4.** Francisco was copying some computer files. He had four CDs, but none of them were completely blank. The first CD had the least amount of free space on it. The second CD had 100 kilobytes (Kb) more free space than the first one. The third had 10 Kb more than three times as much free space as the second one. The fourth CD had 78 Kb less than six times as much free space as the first one.

**a.** Choose a variable. Use it to write expressions for the amount of free space on each CD.

**b.** The second and third CDs together had the same amount of free space than the fourth CD. Write and solve an equation to find the amount of free space on each CD. See margin.

4a. first: $r$;
second: $100 + r$;
third: $10 + 3(100 + r)$;
fourth: $6r - 78$

**5.** Camden divided his music downloads into three categories. They are rock, hip-hop, and movie soundtracks. He had 10 more hip-hop songs than soundtracks and 3 fewer than four times as many rock songs as hip-hop songs. Camden also had 33 more rock songs than hip-hop songs. Write and solve an equation to find how many songs he had in each category. See margin.

### Writing equivalent equations

**6.** Consider the relationship described by this equation.

$$2(x + y) - 3(5 - x) = 3$$

**a.** Rearrange this equation into the familiar form $y = ax + b$.

**b.** Graph the relationship. Choose at least two points on the graph. Substitute the coordinates into the original equation to check your work.

6a. $y = -\frac{5}{2}x + 9$

6b. Possible points to check: (0, 9), (2, 4), (4, −1)

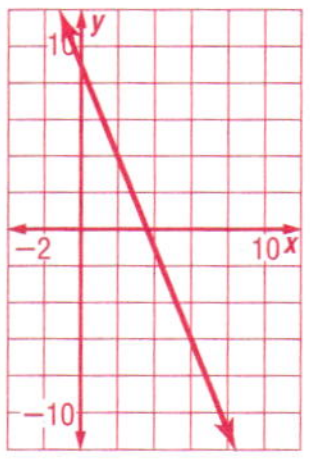


## Demonstrating Skills

**Simplify each expression as much as possible.**

**7.** $a + 2(a - 3)$ $3a - 6$

**8.** $2b - (3 + b)$ $b - 3$

**9.** $12 - (3r - 7)$ $19 - 3r$

**10.** $2d(1 + c) - (3 + d)$ $d + 2cd - 3$

**11.** $-4(3 - b) + 2(3b + 2) - 7(b + 2)$ $3b - 22$



### Additional Answers

4b. $(100 + r) + [10 + 3(100 + r)] = 6r - 78$; $r = 244$; first: 244 Kb; second: 344 Kb; third: 1,042 Kb; fourth: 1,386 Kb

5. $s$ = soundtracks, $10 + s$ = hip hop, $4(10 + s) - 3$ = rock; $4(10 + s) - 3 - (10 + s) = 33$; $s = 2$; 2 soundtracks, 12 hip hop, 45 rock

**Solve each equation.**

**12.** $7s - 12 = 3s - 4$ 2

**13.** $2(1 + c) - (2 + c) = 10$ 10

**14.** $\frac{2}{3}M = M + 4$ −12

**15.** $3t + 1.3 = 2.6 - 3.5t$ 0.2

**16.** $\frac{3x + 5}{3} = \frac{8x + 12}{6}$ −1

**17.** $4(5 - 2b) + 3(2b - 10) = -7(b + 2)$ $-\frac{4}{5}$

▶ **Exercises 12–17** Students solve complex equations using whichever method they prefer.

## Test-Taking Practice

***SHORT RESPONSE***

**1** Kira walks at a steady rate of 3 miles per hour. Liz leaves 10 minutes later to catch up, running steadily at 5 miles per hour. How long will it take Liz to catch up with Kira?

***Show your work.***

***Answer*** ____________________

*Show your work:*
Let *t* equal Liz's time, so Kira's time, expressing 10 minutes as $\frac{1}{6}$ hour, will be $t + \frac{1}{6}$. Liz will catch up when they have traveled equal distances, so write an equation with the distance each travels on the two sides of the equation. Using $d = rt$, Kira's distance $= 3(t + \frac{1}{6})$ and Liz's distance $= 5t$. $3(t + \frac{1}{6}) = 5t$; $3t + \frac{3}{6} = 5t$; $\frac{1}{2} = 2t$; $t = \frac{1}{4}$. $\frac{1}{4}$ of an hour = 15 minutes, so Liz will catch up in 15 minutes.

*Answer:* 15 minutes

***MULTIPLE CHOICE***

**2** Which of the following equations would be simplified the most if 32 were added to both sides?

**A** $32 = 4(x + 32)$
**B** $32 = 4x + 32$
**C** $32 = 4x - 32$ (circled)
**D** $32 = 4(x - 32)$

**3** In science class, there are 4 more girls than boys. If there are 24 people in the class, how many are girls?

**F** 10
**G** 14 (circled)
**H** 20
**J** 24

**4** Which is a solution to the equation $2 - 3x = x + 10$?

**A** −6
**B** −2 (circled)
**C** 2
**D** 4

**5** Solve the following equation.
$5.6m = 2(m - 5.4)$

**F** −3 (circled)
**G** −1.5
**H** 3
**J** 10

**6** A rectangle has the dimensions shown.

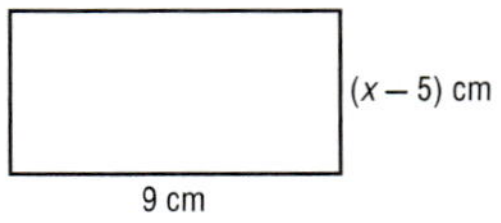


The area of the rectangle is 36 square centimeters. What is the value of *x*?

**A** 7
**B** 8
**C** 9 (circled)
**D** 10

**Additional answers from page 461**

3. Possible answer:
   a. $2x + 7 = 5x + 4$
      $7 = 3x + 4$ after subtracting $2x$ from both sides
      $3 = 3x$ after subtracting 4 from both sides
      $1 = x$ after dividing both sides by 3

   b. $4r + 20 = 10r + 5$
      $20 = 6r + 5$ after subtracting $4r$ from both sides
      $15 = 6r$ after subtracting 5 from both sides
      $2.5 = r$ after dividing both sides by 6

4. $3y + 17 = 4y + 6$
   $17 = y + 6$ after subtracting $3y$ from both sides
   $11 = y$ after subtracting 6 from both sides

5. $3x + 4 = x + 14$
   $2x + 4 = 14$ after subtracting $x$ from both sides
   $2x = 10$ after subtracting 4 from both sides
   $x = 5$ after dividing both sides by 2

**Additional answers from page 462**

1. $5x = x + 4$
   $4x = 4$ after subtracting $x$ from both sides
   $x = 1$ after dividing both sides by 4

2. $r + 12 = 3r + 4$
   $12 = 2r + 4$ after subtracting $r$ from both sides
   $8 = 2r$ after subtracting 4 from both sides
   $4 = r$ after dividing both sides by 2

3. $2P + 20 = 5P + 6$
   $20 = 3P + 6$ after subtracting $2P$ from both sides
   $14 = 3P$ after subtracting 6 from both sides
   $\frac{14}{3} = P$ after dividing both sides by 3

4. $5y + 3 = 3y + 15$
   $2y + 3 = 15$ after subtracting $3y$ from both sides
   $2y = 12$ after subtracting 3 from both sides
   $y = 6$ after dividing both sides by 2

5. $5d - 9 = 2d$
   $3d - 9 = 0$ after subtracting $2d$ from both sides
   $3d = 9$ after adding 9 to both sides
   $d = 3$ after dividing both sides by 3

Notes

CHAPTER 10

# Proportional Reasoning and Percents

## Chapter Overview

In this chapter, students look at ways to compare data using ratios, proportions, and percentages. Students find eqivalent ratios and they build on this knowledge when they write and solve proportions. In the Lab Investigation, students use proportions and similar triangles to estimate the height of tall objects.

Students discover that percentages are good ways to compare data since they have a common scale. Finally, students find unit rates and compare currencies.

## The Big Picture

| Links to the Past | Chapter 10 | Links to the Future |
|---|---|---|
| **Course 1, Chapter 2** (pp. 56–107) Fractions and Decimals<br>**Course 1, Chapter 5** (pp. 288–345) Rate, Ratio, and Proportion | **Lesson 10.1** (p. 494) Ratios | **Course 3, Chapter 3** (pp. 110–143) Percents and Proportions |
| **Course 1, Chapter 2** (pp. 56–107) Fractions and Decimals<br>**Course 1, Chapter 5** (pp. 288–345) Rate, Ratio, and Proportion | **Lesson 10.2** (p. 505) Proportions and Similarity | **Course 3, Chapter 3** (pp. 110–143) Percents and Proportions |
| **Course 1, Chapter 6** (pp. 346–395) Percents | **Lesson 10.3** (p. 530) Percents and Proportions | **Course 3, Chapter 3** (pp. 110–143) Percents and Proportions |
| **Course 1, Chapter 5** (pp. 288–345) Rate, Ratio, and Proportion | **Lesson 10.4** (p. 540) Rates | **Course 3, Chapter 1** (pp. 2–63) Linear Relationships |

# Mathematical Background

Ratio and proportion are two basic ideas that permeate all of mathematics and its applications. Basically, ratios are a way of comparing two quantities or magnitudes. Chapter 10 explores these ideas in a wide variety of contexts, starting with basic applications such as: "If 3 apples cost $1, how much do 12 apples cost?" It continues by looking at applications of ratio and proportion to change-of-units exercises, percentage exercises, the theory of similar figures in geometry, and currency conversions.

**Ratios and Equivalent Ratios** In practice, ratios are used in several different kinds of situations. Ratios can compare:

- *part* of a group to the *whole* group
  For example: the ratio of girls in a school to all the students in the school
- *part* of a group to another *part* of the same group
  For example: the ratio of students taking French to the students taking German
- two *different* groups
  For example: the ratio of teachers to students in the school

A special case of part-to-part ratios is when the two parts have no common members and together comprise the whole group; for example, the ratio of boys in a school to the girls in the school. In cases like this, we can think about all kinds of different ratios, including

boys to total students ($b : s$)
girls to total students ($g : s$)
boys to girls ($b : g$)
girls to boys ($g : b$)

where $s$ = total number of students; $b$ = number of boys; $g$ = number of girls.

Since $b + g = s$, if you know any *one* of the four ratios, you can calculate the other 3 without any further information.

For example, if $\frac{b}{g} = \frac{3}{4}$, then you know that

$$\frac{b}{s} = \frac{b}{b+g} = \frac{3}{7}$$
$$\frac{g}{s} = \frac{g}{b+g} = \frac{4}{7}$$
$$\frac{g}{b} = \frac{4}{3}$$

For ratios to be equivalent, you have to multiply the two parts of a ratio by the same number, not add the same number, just as you would do with fractions.

## Additional Reading

According to Lamon in "Ratio and Proportion: Connecting Content and Children's Thinking," which appeared in *Journal for Research in Mathematics Education*, the concept of unit rate is useful to students in solving problems involving proportions. Lesson 10.1 reinforces unit rate. This concept helps students solve problems involving proportions in Lesson 10.2.

CHAPTER 10

# Planning Guide

## *Lesson Resources*

| | Lesson 10.1 (Pacing: 3 days) | Lesson 10.2 (Pacing: 7 days) | Lesson 10.3 (Pacing: 3 days) | Lesson 10.4 (Pacing: 3 days) |
|---|---|---|---|---|
| **Lesson Title** | **Ratios** (p. 494) | **Proportions and Similarity** (p. 505) | **Percents and Proportions** (p. 530) | **Rates** (p. 540) |
| **Lesson Objectives** | • To recognize and express equivalent ratios in different situations | • To set up and use proportions to solve problems | • To compare ratios and solve percent problems using proportions | • To determine unit prices and unit rates<br>• To convert currencies |
| **Materials** | | Computers with Internet access, rulers, blank paper, Lesson 10.2 Master 1, protractor, string or thread, weight, paper clip or cube, tape measure, yard stick, tape (optional) | Lesson 10.3 Master 1, graph paper | Newspaper circulars with grocery store sale prices, retail catalog, calculator, current currency rate information from the Internet |
| ***Quick Review Math Handbook*** | **Lesson 5.5** Ratio and Proportion | **Lesson 5.5** Ratio and Proportion | **Lesson 2.8** Using and Finding Percents<br>**Lesson 5.5** Ratio and Proportion | **Lesson 5.5** Ratio and Proportion |
| **Print Resources** | CRM Study Guide and Intervention (p. 4)<br>CRM Skills Practice (p. 5)<br>CRM Problem-Solving Practice (p. 6)<br>CRM Enrichment (p. 7)<br>• Investigation Notebook and Reflection Journal<br>• Differentiation Handbook | CRM Study Guide and Intervention (p. 9)<br>CRM Skills Practice (p. 10)<br>CRM Problem-Solving Practice (p. 11)<br>CRM Enrichment (p. 12)<br>• Investigation Notebook and Reflection Journal<br>• Differentiation Handbook | CRM Study Guide and Intervention (p. 15)<br>CRM Skills Practice (p. 16)<br>CRM Problem-Solving Practice (p. 17)<br>CRM Enrichment (p. 18)<br>• Investigation Notebook and Reflection Journal<br>• Differentiation Handbook | CRM Study Guide and Intervention (p. 20)<br>CRM Skills Practice (p. 21)<br>CRM Problem-Solving Practice (p. 22)<br>CRM Enrichment (p. 23)<br>• Investigation Notebook and Reflection Journal<br>• Differentiation Handbook |
| **Technology Resources** | TeacherWorks Plus<br>Classroom Presentation Toolkit<br>ExamView Assessment Suite<br>StudentWorks Plus<br>Math Online Brain Pops • Concepts in Motion | TeacherWorks Plus<br>Classroom Presentation Toolkit<br>ExamView Assessment Suite<br>StudentWorks Plus<br>Math Online Brain Pops • Concepts in Motion | TeacherWorks Plus<br>Classroom Presentation Toolkit<br>ExamView Assessment Suite<br>StudentWorks Plus<br>Math Online Brain Pops • Concepts in Motion | TeacherWorks Plus<br>Classroom Presentation Toolkit<br>ExamView Assessment Suite<br>StudentWorks Plus<br>Math Online Brain Pops • Concepts in Motion |

*Included in the Impact Mathematics Manipulative Kit

# Assessment Resources

## MARS Assessment: Teaching with Purpose

### The Poster

In *The Poster*, students calculate sizes in an enlargement. Students enlarge a photograph to poster size.

### Targeting the Task

- **Diagnostic**–Use Exercises 1–2 in *The Poster* assessment to determine students' understanding of how to calculate sizes in an enlargement and the ability to explain their work. For those students who do not have this understanding, completing this unit is needed.
- **Formative**–Exercises 1–2 can be administered individually according to the lessons.
- **Summative**–Administer the complete *The Poster* performance-based assessment.

CRM **Chapter 10 MARS Assessment** (pp. 44–46)

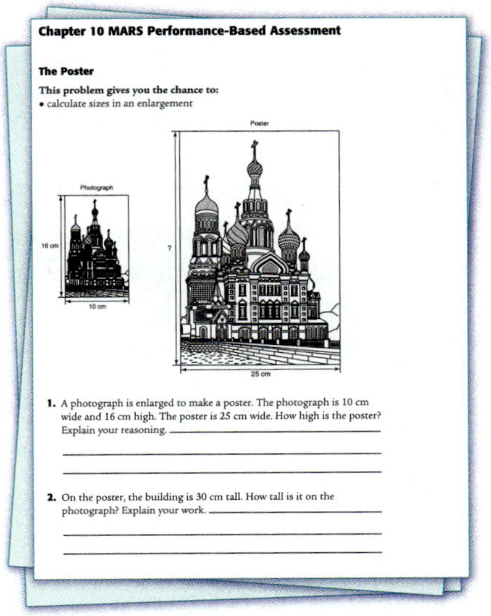
Chapter 10 MARS Performance-Based Assessment

The Poster

This problem gives you the chance to:
• calculate sizes in an enlargement



1. A photograph is enlarged to make a poster. The photograph is 10 cm wide and 16 cm high. The poster is 25 cm wide. How high is the poster? Explain your reasoning.

2. On the poster, the building is 30 cm tall. How tall is it on the photograph? Explain your work.

## Assessment Planning Guide

Assessments are available for investigations, lessons, and chapters.

ExamView Assessment Suite — Customize and create multiple versions of tests and quizzes.

| | Student Edition | Teacher Edition | Other Resources |
|---|---|---|---|
| Diagnostic | | | CRM Chapter 10 Pretest (pp. 25–28)<br>Math Online Online Chapter Quiz |
| Formative | Share & Summarize (pp. 497, 499, 507, 510, 513, 516, 518, 533, 536, 543, 546) | Troubleshooting (pp. 495, 497, 499, 507, 508, 510, 511, 515, 536, 541, 545)<br>On the Spot Assessment (pp. 496, 498, 509, 513, 514, 531, 540, 542, 544)<br>Quick Check (pp. 504, 529, 539, 550)<br>Quick Quiz (pp. 504, 529, 539, 550) | |
| Summative | Review & Self-Assessment (pp. 551–555) | | CRM Chapter 10 Test: Forms A and B (pp. 29–38)<br>CRM Standardized Test Practice (p. 42) |
| Performance-Based | In Your Own Words (pp. 527, 539, 550) | | CRM MARS Performance-Based Assessment (p. 44)<br>CRM Chapter Performance Assessment (pp. 39–41)<br>CRM Semester Performance Assessment (pp. 59–62) |

# Differentiated Instruction

## *Reaching* All Learners

Below are suggestions on differentiating the materials presented in this chapter. Additional modifications should be considered.

### Approaching Level AL

**Scale Map** After completing Lesson 10.2, have the students create a scale map of their neighborhood, or town. The map does not have to be complex, it can include main streets or locations. It would be helpful if you gave the students a list of possible sites, streets, and their distances from school. Stress to the students that they need to choose a scale and stick with it when they create their map.

### Beyond Level BL

**Currency Conversion** After students complete Lesson 10.4, have students work in small groups to plan a trip to a foreign country of their choice. The challenge will be that you will give them a budget in U.S. dollars that they cannot exceed. The groups must plan where they will stay, and allocate money for food and sightseeing. The groups may become exceedingly challenged by the conversion of U.S. dollars to the currency of their chosen country. In some cases, the money will go a long way, in others, it will be spent faster than they expect. The students can find helpful information on the internet or through travel guides that can be borrowed from the library. Once their planning is complete, have the groups present their trip, itinerary, and expense list to the class.

### On Level OL

**Similar Triangles** After completing Lesson 10.2, have students work in pairs or small groups and venture outdoors to use similar triangles to find the actual height of a tall object (tree, building, flagpole), Give the students a ruler and the use of the tool that they created in Inquiry Investigation 6. The object must be taller than the tallest person in class to qualify as a tall object. Instruct the students to sketch the object and describe its location. Then they detail all of the steps that they performed in order to determine the object's height. Offer bonus points for the group that measures the most creative object, the tallest object, or the most exact measurement. These will encourage students to think a bit more and take more ownership in what they are doing.

### English Language Learners ELL

**Terminology Trivia** After completing Lesson 10.4, have students work in small groups or pairs to develop a trivia type game to assist them in understanding the words in this chapter. The students can work in their first language or in English, but the game must be played in English. The object is for students to develop a way to understand the vocabulary in a fun and meaningful way. Assist students by giving examples, or even playing a trivia game in class to encourage their creative thinking.

**KEY**

AL Approaching Level  OL On Level  BL Beyond Level  ELL English Language Learners

# Intervention Planning Guide

CRM Assess students' prerequisite skills and knowledge using the **Chapter Pretest** found in the Chapter 10 Resource Masters, p. 25.

| Intensive Intervention<br>two or more years below grade level | Strategic Intervention<br>below grade level | On Level | Beyond Level |
|---|---|---|---|
| **If** students miss 75% of the exercises:<br>**Then** use *Math Triumphs,* an intensive intervention | **If** students miss 50% of the exercises:<br>**Then** choose a resource: | **If** students miss 25% of the exercises:<br>**Then** choose a resource: | **If** students miss 0%–10% of the exercises:<br>**Then** choose a resource: |
| *Math Triumphs,* Grade 7<br>• Chapter 2: Ratios, Rates, and Proportional Relationships | CRM Study Guide and Intervention (pp. 4, 9, 15, 20)<br>• Investigation Notebook and Reflection Journal<br>• Differentiation Handbook<br>Math Online Brain Pops • Concepts in Motion | CRM Skills Practice (pp. 5, 10, 16, 21)<br>CRM Problem-Solving Practice (pp. 6, 11, 17, 22)<br>• Investigation Notebook and Reflection Journal | CRM Enrichment (pp. 7, 12, 18, 23)<br>• Differentiation Handbook |

## Literature Connections

### Recommended Outside Reading for Students

**Nonfiction**

Wright, Joseph & Salvadori, Mario. *Math Games for Middle School: Challenges and Skill Builders for Students at Every Level.* Chicago Review Press, 1998.

This book uses activities and games to reinforce middle school mathematics concepts. Fractions and decimals are among the topics addressed in the book.

**Fiction**

Greenburg, Dan. *Funny and Fabulous Fraction Stories.* Scholastic, 1996.

This book is a series of stories written to reinforce skills with fractions, decimals, and ratios. The stories are appropriate for students in Grades 4–8.

## McGraw Hill Professional Development

Targeted professional development has been articulated throughout the *IMPACT Mathematics* series. The **McGraw-Hill Professional Development Video Library** provides short videos that support the mathematics standards. Log on to www.glencoe.com.

Model Lessons

Instructional Strategies

CHAPTER 10

# Proportional Reasoning and Percents

## *Introduce*

**Scale Models** Using scales to create a model or replica of an object is done all of the time. You may have seen model cars, trains, and buildings. Even movie sets can be made to scale so that when the camera takes the picture, people feel that they are seeing a real situation. All of this is with the help of scale models. Think of stretching and shrinking machines or enlargements of photographs, it is all the same concept. A fun activity for students would be to use a scale to create an enlargement of a comic strip or a photo.

**Think About It** Students have seen and worked with proportions. This chapter will expand on their knowledge. It may be helpful to review what a proportion is to assist the students in their understanding.

CHAPTER 10

# Proportional Reasoning and Percents

***Contents in Brief***



## Real-Life Math

**Scale Models** At 1,250 feet tall, the Empire State Building in New York City is one of the world's tallest buildings. Maya and Darnell made a replica of the Empire State Building as a class project. They decided to make their replica to scale. Their replica's height was 2 feet 1 inch.

**Think About It** What scale did Maya and Darnell use in making their model? 1 inch = 50 feet

The Space Needle in Seattle is 605 feet tall. Suppose Maya and Darnell used the same scale to make a replica of the Space Needle. Set up a proportion to determine the height of their replica. Then, solve the proportion. $\frac{1 \text{ in.}}{50 \text{ ft}} = \frac{x}{605 \text{ ft}}$; 12.1 in., or about 1 foot

**Math Online** Take the **Chapter Readiness Quiz** at glencoe.com.

492

### Chapter Resources

- CRM Chapter 10 Resource Masters
- CRM English/Spanish Family Letter (pp. 1–2)
- CRM Lesson Masters (p. 14)
- CRM Chapter 10 Pretest (pp. 25–28)
- CRM Chapter 10 Tests (pp. 29–38)
- **Math Online** Online Readiness Quiz • eGlossary

# Dear Family,

In this chapter, the class will explore the relationship between ratios and proportions. A ratio is a comparison of two numbers, such as 0.25 : 1. A **proportion** is an equation that states two ratios are equal.

$$\frac{0.25}{1} = \frac{10}{x}$$

Then, students will use ratios and proportions to explore **proportional relationships**, including similarity. For example, your student will use shadow lengths to find the height of a tree.

### Key Concept–Similarity

Proportionality and similarity can be used to find the tree's height. Similar figures have the same shape but not necessarily the same size.

A proportion comparing the heights of the ruler's shadow and ruler to the heights of the tree's shadow and the tree can be set up to find the tree's height. Students can then use strategies learned in the previous chapter to determine the tree's height is 40 feet.

$$\frac{\text{ruler's shadow height}}{\text{ruler height}} = \frac{\text{tree's shadow height}}{\text{tree height}}$$

$$\frac{0.25 \text{ ft}}{1 \text{ ft}} = \frac{10 \text{ ft}}{h}$$

### Chapter Vocabulary

**map scale** | **proportion**

### Home Activities

- Use a map to plan the route for a family road trip. Determine the total distance. Calculate the cost of gasoline.
- Calculate discounted prices for sale items using percents when shopping.
- Determine unit prices when grocery shopping.

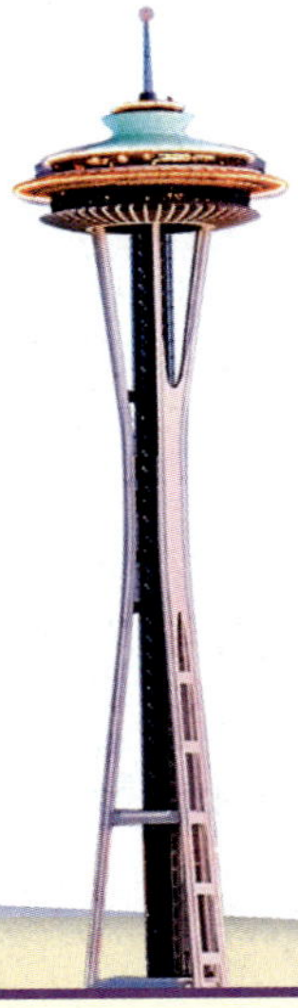



## Family Letter

Another version of the Family Letter, available in English and Spanish, is found in the Chapter 10 Resource Masters. You may want to send a copy of this letter home with your students.

**Key Concept–Similarity** There are many things in our daily lives that are similar in a mathematical sense. Socks for a child and a parent are similar if they are the same, just different sizes. Tiles in the kitchen or bathroom are mathematically similar. It will be important to show how the word similar means the same as the mathematical term with the exception that mathematically, we have very specific requirements for objects to be similar, not just that they have something in common.

### Home Activities

- Have students and their families go on a similarity scavenger hunt. The hunt can take place at home or somewhere else like the grocery store. Have the student explain the concept of similarity to their family members. Then have each person spend a short period of time looking around and noting all of the similar items they see. Now have a group meeting where all of the family members share what they found and discuss why the items are similar.
- Have students and their families plan their menu for a week using the grocery sales paper. Have the families determine all ingredients that are needed to be purchased. Using the sales flyers, determine the unit prices for each object and predict the amount of money that will be spent. Once the shopping is complete, discuss how the unit prices helped keep the prediction of money spent close.

## Key Vocabulary

**English (Spanish)** *Introduce the most important terms from Chapter 10.*

**map scale (escala de mapa)** A ratio of a single unit of distance on the map to the equivalent distance on the ground. (p. 514)

**proportion (proporción)** An equation that states that two ratios are equal. For example, 2:3 = 6:9. (p. 510)

**angle of elevation (El ángulo de elevación)** The angle made by (1) the imaginary horizontal segment extending from a person's eye to an object and (2) the imaginary segment from the same person's eye to the top of the object. (p. 519)

**proportional relationship (relación proporcional)** A relationship in which all pairs of corresponding values have the same ratio. (p. 505)

LESSON

10.1

# Ratios

### Objectives

- To recognize and express ratios in different situations
- To recognize equivalent ratios
- To use tables to compare ratios of mixtures

## Overview

This lesson reviews and extends what students know about ratios and rates. They will apply their knowledge to compare information that can be presented as a rate or ratio. In addition, students will work with data presented in a table that represents comparison of ratios. They will fill in the missing data pieces and use patterns to determine the scale used to create the table.

## Advance Preparation

You may want to see how much students remember. It may be prudent to review basic facts about rates and ratios prior to beginning the lesson.

| | Summary | Materials | On Your Own Exercises (pp. 500–504) | Assessment Opportunities |
|---|---|---|---|---|
| **Investigation 1** (p. 495) Pacing: 2 days | Students use their prior knowledge of ratios and rates to make comparisons. | | Practice & Apply: 1–3<br>Connect & Extend: 13, 16<br>Mixed Review: 19–27 | • On the Spot Assessment (p. 496)<br>• Share & Summarize (p. 497)<br>• Troubleshooting (p. 495) |
| **Investigation 2** (p. 497) Pacing: 1 day | Students use ratios to make comparisons and use ratio tables to compare data. | | Practice & Apply: 4–12<br>Connect & Extend: 14, 15, 17, 18<br>Mixed Review: 19–27 | • On the Spot Assessment (p. 498)<br>• Share & Summarize (p. 499)<br>• Troubleshooting (pp. 497, 499) |

# Leveled Lesson Resources

CRM *Available in:* **Chapter 10 Resource Masters**

Also on TeacherWorks™
Lesson 10.1

## Study Guide and Intervention (p. 4) AL

**Lesson 10.1 Study Guide and Intervention**
***Ratios***

**Example 1** **Lee Ann made the bracelet shown.**

**a.** Find the ratio of charms to beads.
There are 5 charms and 15 beads, so the ratio is $\frac{5}{15}$ or $\frac{1}{3}$.

**b.** Lee Ann wants to make a necklace with charms and beads in the same pattern. She plans to use 42 beads. How many charms will she need?
One-third of 42 is 14. She will need 14 charms for the necklace.

**Example 2** **Jack took a cross-country trip with his family. The graph shows the progress of the trip.**

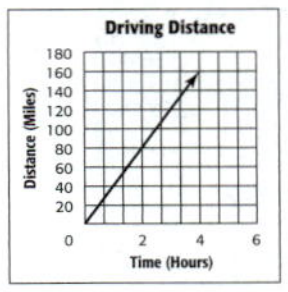


**a.** At what rate is Jack traveling?
He travels 160 miles in 4 hours, so his rate is $\frac{160 \text{ miles}}{4 \text{ hours}}$ or $\frac{40 \text{ miles}}{1 \text{ hour}}$.
He is traveling at a rate of 40 miles per hour.

**b.** How many miles would you expect Jack to travel in 6 hours?
Multiply 40 miles per hour by 6 hours.
Jack will probably travel 240 miles in 6 hours.

**Exercises**

1. Of 2,000 beads in a beaded rug, 350 are blue. What is the ratio of blue beads to all beads?

2. Kelsey bikes 16 miles in 2 hours. At what rate is she traveling?

## Skills Practice (p. 5) AL OL

**Lesson 10.1 Skills Practice**
***Ratios***

**A beaded rug has 500 beads. There are 150 black beads, 140 green beads, and 210 white beads in the rug. Find the ratio.**

1. black beads to white beads

2. green beads to total beads

**A group of students is traveling to Washington, DC. They graph their progress for two days. At what rate did the group travel each day?**

3.

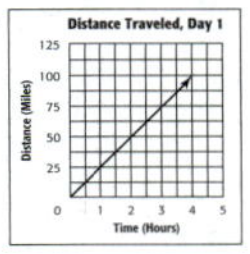


4.

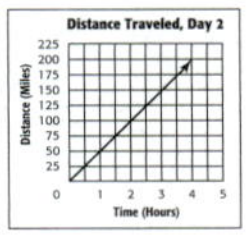


**Which mixture is a darker blue? Describe a larger batch that will match the darker mixture's shade.**

5. Mixture A / Mixture B

6. Mixture A

Mixture B

## Problem-Solving Practice (p. 6) AL OL

**Lesson 10.1 Problem-Solving Practice**
***Ratios***

Solve.

1. **E-mail** Mirna specializes in reducing the number of junk E-mails that are delivered to customer accounts. The table shows the weekly E-mail counts for four companies. According to Mirna, the company with the greatest ratio of junk E-mails to total E-mails has the greatest need. List the companies in order from greatest need to least need.

| Company | Junk E-mails | Total E-mails |
|---|---|---|
| A | 90 | 270 |
| B | 102 | 510 |
| C | 187 | 374 |
| D | 225 | 400 |

2. **Quilting** Maxine is using this pattern to make a quilt.

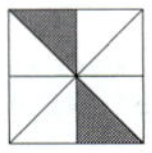

   **a.** What is the ratio of white triangles to total triangles?
   **b.** The entire quilt will have 240 total triangles. How many black triangles will it have?

3. **Baseball** In baseball, a player's batting average is the ratio of hits to the number of times at bat. David has 10 hits out of 14 times at bat. Adam has 15 hits out of 20 times at bat. Who has a higher batting average? Explain.

4. **Driving** Sarah can drive 198 miles on 11 gallons of gasoline.
   **a.** Complete the ratio table.
   **b.** If Sarah maintains the same miles per gallon rate, how many miles can she drive on $n$ gallons of gasoline.

| gallons | 1 | 5 | 11 | 33 | 77 |
|---|---|---|---|---|---|
| miles | | | | | |

5. **Cycling** Hope and Jennifer are cycling across Georgia. The graph shows their progress.
   **a.** At what rate did the girls cycle?
   **b.** How many miles would you expect the girls to cycle in 7 hours?

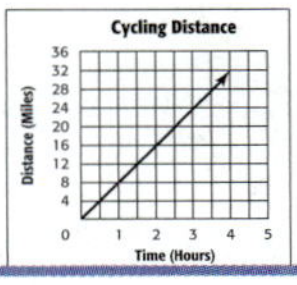


## Enrichment (p. 7) BL

**Lesson 10.1 Enrichment**
***Ratios***

**Chien-Shiung Wu**

American physicist Chien-Shiung Wu (1912–1997) was born in Shanghai, China. In 1936, she came to the United States to further her studies in science. She received her doctorate in physics in 1940 from the University of California. In 1975, she was awarded the National Medal of Science.

Wu is most famous for an experiment that she conducted in 1957. The outcome of the experiment was considered the most significant discovery in physics in more than seventy years. The exercise below will help you learn some facts about it.

**Choose the value that completes an equivalent ratio. The word or phrase following the solution will complete the statement correctly.**

1. $\frac{10}{6} = \frac{m}{15}$ At the time of the experiment, Wu was a professor at ___?___.
   $m = 25$: Columbia University
   $m = 9$: Stanford University

2. $\frac{8}{2} = \frac{t}{2.5}$ The site of the experiment was the ___?___ in Washington, D.C.
   $t = 10$: National Bureau of Standards
   $t = 6.4$: Smithsonian Institution

3. $\frac{5}{y} = \frac{12}{3}$ The experiment involved a substance called ___?___.
   $y = 20$: carbon 14
   $y = 1.25$: cobalt 60

4. $\frac{5}{4} = \frac{4}{n}$ In the experiment, the substance was cooled to ___?___.
   $n = 5$: −100°C
   $n = 3.2$: −273°C

5. $\frac{6}{c} = \frac{0.3}{9}$ The experiment proved that a physical reaction could ___?___.
   $c = 180$: have a "right side" and a "left side"
   $c = 0.2$: occur at a temperature called "absolute zero"

6. $\frac{24}{5.4} = \frac{6}{j}$ Before Wu's experiment, scientists had believed that all physical reactions ___?___.
   $j = 21.6$: occurred at temperatures greater than −250°C
   $j = 1.35$: were perfectly symmetric

## Lesson Quick Quiz (p. 8) AL OL BL

**Lesson 10.1 Quick Quiz**

1. Helio has traveled to 18 different states by car, another 5 states by train, and 7 more states by airplane. What is the ratio of states Helio traveled to by car versus the total number of states he has traveled to?

2. Mia has traveled to a total of 40 different states. If her ratio of states traveled to by car is the same as Helio's, how many states has Mia traveled to by car?

3. The school play is using a mixture of 7 containers of white paint and 3 containers of red paint to create the pink paint they are using for the walls of a scene. They need to make a batch of paint from 40 containers. How much red paint do they need to use?

4. Complete the ratio table.

| | | | | |
|---|---|---|---|---|
| Blue | 2 | 4 | | |
| Red | | 6 | 9 | 12 |

# Additional Lesson Resources

### Teacher Tech Tools
- TeacherWorks
- ExamView Assessment Suite
- Classroom Presentation Toolkit
- Advance Tracker

### Student Tech Tools
- StudentWorks Plus
- Math Online eGlossary • Concepts in Motion

### Other Print Products
- Investigation Notebook and Reflection Journal
- Quick Review Math Handbook

LESSON 10.1 Ratios

## Introduce

**Baseball Statistics** In baseball, statistics are kept of everything a player has the opportunity to do during a game. Make sure that students understand the meanings of all of the terms used on Salvador and Howie's cards. Also discuss with students how the rates, ratios, and percentages are found for each of the comparison statements.

### Explore

For students to make a case for Salvador or Howie to be the most valuable player means that the statistical data needs to make that player look better than the other. To do this, the students may wish to make several comparisons of their own using the data that is provided.

# LESSON 10.1 Ratios



Salvador and Howie are the best hitters on their baseball teams. The baseball cards show statistics from the last season.

Many comparison statements can be made from these statistics. Beneath the cards, you will find comparisons involving ratios, rates, and percents.

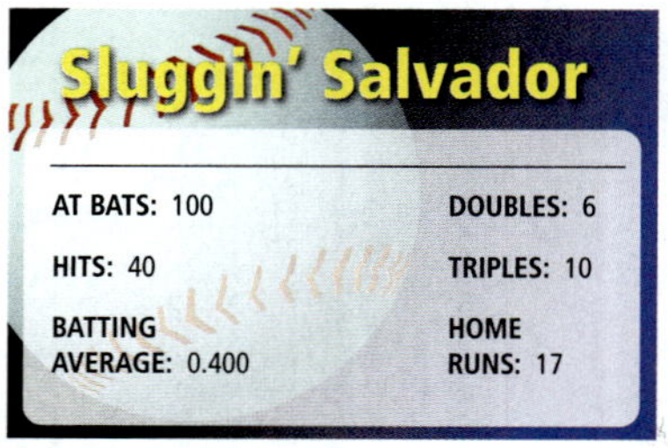

| | Ratios | Rates | Percents |
|---|---|---|---|
| | Home Runs to Hits | Hits per At Bats | Percent of Triples |
| Salvador | 17:40 | 400 per 1000 | 25 |
| Howie | 12:80, or 3:20 | 500 per 1000 | 5 |

### Explore

Work with a partner to write more comparison statements about the baseball data. Try to write a ratio comparison, a rate comparison, and a percent comparison. See ①.

The managers for the baseball league are selecting the most valuable player. Use statistics to convince the managers to select Salvador. Then, use statistics to convince the managers to select Howie instead. See ②.

① Howie has 8 fewer triples than Salvador. Salvador's ratio of singles to hits is 7:40. Howie hits three home runs in every twenty at bats. Fifteen percent of Salvador's hits are doubles.

② Possible answers: Salvador has a better ratio of homeruns to hits, 17:40 compared to 12:40. Howie has a better batting average, 0.500 compared to 0.400.



## Mathematical Background

Students learned how to work with rates in Chapter 8. A ratio is a rate that compares items of different units of measure. It is a slight difference, but a distinct one of which students need to be aware.

# Investigation 1 Ratios and Rate Comparisons

You already know about ratios and rates from work in earlier grades and from your own life. You will now use that knowledge to reason about ratio and rate comparisons.

## Develop & Understand: A

1. The triangular tiles on The Art Institute's wall are laid in this pattern.

a. What is the ratio of white tiles to blue tiles in this pattern? $\frac{3}{6}$, or $\frac{1}{2}$

b. The entire wall contains 900 blue tiles. How many white tiles does it have? 450

c. What is the ratio of white tiles to all tiles in this pattern? $\frac{3}{9}$, or $\frac{1}{3}$

d. If an area with this pattern has 2,880 tiles in all, how many white tiles does it have? 960

**Math Link**

Ratios may be written in several ways. Here are three ways to express the ratio "four to one."

4 to 1 4:1 $\frac{4}{1}$

2. Tehani made this flower necklace.

a. What is the ratio of white flowers to pink flowers? $\frac{10}{8}$, or $\frac{5}{4}$

b. Tehani wants to make a longer necklace with flowers in the same pattern. If she plans to use 20 pink flowers, how many white flowers will she need? 25

c. What is the ratio of pink flowers to all flowers in this necklace?

2c. $\frac{8}{18}$, or $\frac{4}{9}$

d. Tehani wants to make a long necklace for her older sister in the same pattern. If she uses 27 flowers in all, how many white flowers will she need? 15



### Troubleshooting

The most common mistake made by students when writing rates and ratios is that they do not write the information in the proper order. Stress to students that it is important to write the rate or ratio in the order in which the information is requested.

# Investigation 1

***On Your Own Exercises***
Pages 500–504
Exercises 1–3, 13, 16

**Rates and Ratios** Students are told that they will be using knowledge from previous grades to study this topic. It may be helpful to have a group discussion to see what students remember and fill in the gaps as needed.

## Develop & Understand: A

*Suggested Grouping: Pairs*

▶ **Exercise 1** It is important to remind students to read the questions carefully. Most mistakes are made because they do not write the information as the problem states.

▶ **Exercise 2b** Students may use one of these strategies:

- They may use the mathematical idea presented on the previous page and think $r = 5:4$; so for every 5 white flowers, there are 4 pink flowers. Since Tehani has 20 white flowers, that means that there are 4 groups of white flowers. So there must be 5 corresponding groups of 5 pink flowers. This means that there must be 25 pink flowers.
- Some may write the ratios in the form $\frac{5}{4}$, then find an equivalent ratio: $\frac{5}{4} \cdot \frac{5}{5} = \frac{25}{20}$.
- Others may look for a pattern and record their results in a table.
- Still others may draw a picture.

Discuss with the class strategies that students used to solve Exercise 2b.

**Math Link**

Discuss with students how they see ratios represented most often. Is one way of writing ratios better than another?

▶ **Exercise 3** When reading a graph, instruct students to pay close attention to the labels on the axes and the units. These small changes can change the interpretation of the data.

▶ **Exercises 4 and 5** These are more abstract and general than the preceding exercises. Some exercises involve non-integers. You may want to suggest that students look for a pattern when solving these exercises. In Exercise 4, the top number is always 5 times the bottom number. In Exercise 5, the bottom number on every card is 1.5 times the top number.

**Wrap-Up** In general, all of the information covered in the investigation is review from prior course work. Students who are having difficulties should seek extra assistance.

**3.** Carlita took a canoe trip with her family. The graph shows the progress of her trip.

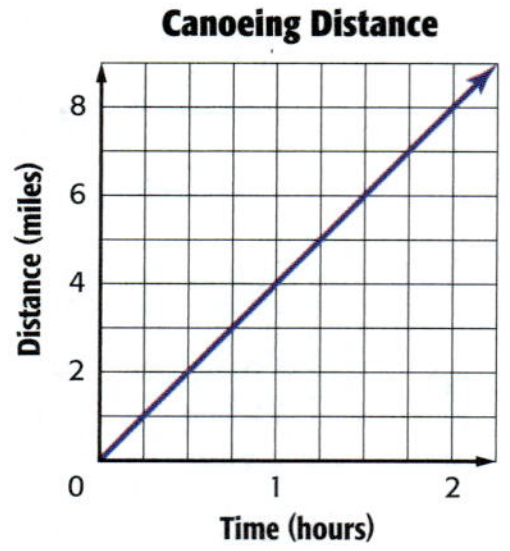


**a.** At what rate is Carlita traveling? 4 mph

**b.** How many miles would you expect Carlita to canoe in 3.5 hours? 14

**4.** The two numbers on each card in this set are in the same ratio.

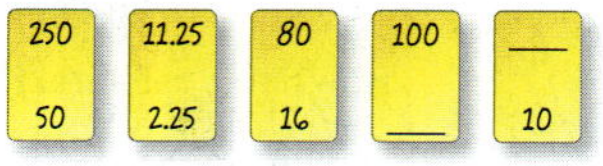


**a.** Find the missing numbers. 20, 50

**b.** Draw three more cards that belong in this set.

4b. Possible answer:

**5.** The two numbers on each card in this set are in the same ratio.

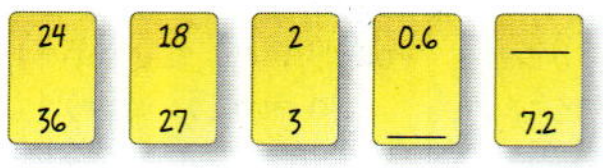


**a.** Find the missing numbers. Explain how you found your answers.

**b.** What ratio expresses the relationship between the top number and the bottom number on each card? $\frac{2}{3}$

**c.** Draw three more cards that belong in this set.

Possible answer:

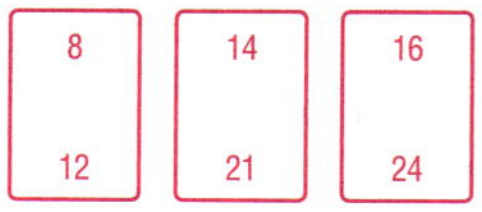


5a. 0.9, 4.8; Possible explanation: On each card the bottom number is 1.5 times the top number; $1.5 \cdot 0.6 = 0.9$ and $7.2 \div 1.5 = 4.8$.

**CHAPTER 10** Proportional Reasoning and Percents

**On the Spot *Assessment***

What are the missing values for the following equal ratios: $\frac{12}{96}, \frac{?}{8}, \frac{3}{24}, \frac{6}{?}$? 1; 48

## Share & Summarize

1. Consider this keyboard.

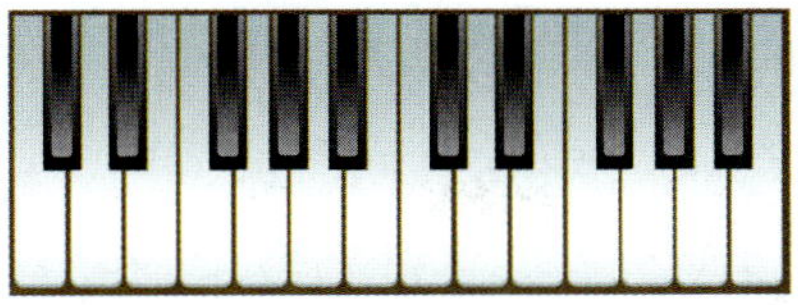

a. What is the ratio of white keys to black keys on the keyboard?

1a. $\frac{14}{10}$, or $\frac{7}{5}$

b. This pattern of keys is repeated on larger keyboards. How many black keys would you expect to find on a keyboard that has 42 white keys? 30

c. What is the ratio of black keys to *all* keys on this keyboard?

1c. $\frac{10}{24}$, or $\frac{5}{12}$

d. How many black keys would you expect to find on a keyboard with 72 keys in all? 30

# Investigation 2 Compare and Scale Ratios

You have practiced writing ratios to express comparisons between quantities. Reasoning about ratios will help you solve the exercises in this investigation.

### Develop & Understand: A

Researchers are developing a shade of orange paint. They are experimenting by mixing containers of red and yellow paints.

1. Below are two mixtures the researchers tested. Each red bottle represents a container of red paint. Each yellow bottle represents a container of yellow paint. All hold the same amount of paint. Which mixture is darker orange? Explain how you decided.
Mixture A; see teaching notes for possible strategies.

Mixture A Mixture B

2. Tell which mixture is darker orange. Mixture D

Mixture C Mixture D

## Troubleshooting

Watch for students who reverse the numbers in the ratio. For example, in Exercise 1a, these students will say the ratio of white keys to black ones is 5:7 rather than 7:5. If that happens, remind the students that the order of the numbers in the ratio matters. A quick memory aid is: "The numbers in the ratio must appear in the same order as the words." So, the ratio of white to black keys is 7:5, while the ratio of black to white keys is 5:7.

## Share & Summarize

In Exercise 1, students can count the 14 white and 10 black keys, so the ratio of white to black keys is 14:10. The same ratio can also be expressed as 7:5. Considering 7:5 the basis of a pattern, the third repetition of the pattern would result in the ratio: 21 (white) to 15 (black); and so on for successive repetitions. Although in principle it does not matter how you express a given ratio such as 7:5, 14:10, 21:15, you may want to discuss with your class the pros and cons of various ways of expressing the same ratio. One advantage of 7:5 over other representations is that it may be easier to work with because it involves smaller numbers. However, people don't always represent ratios in simplest terms. The most notable example is the use of percentages to represent ratios, such as writing 25% instead of $\frac{1}{4}$.

## Investigation 2

***On Your Own Exercises***

Pages 500–504

Exercises 4–12, 14, 15, 17, 18

### Develop & Understand: A

*Suggested Grouping: Pairs*

▶ **Exercise 1** There are many ways in which students can determine which color mixture is darker. One way is to look at the number of red bottles of paint to the total number of bottles of paint. A second way is to look at the number of red bottles of paint to yellow bottles of paint. Another way would be to look at the number of yellow bottles of paint to total bottles. This will show which mixture is the lighter and therefore the other color is the darker.

▶ **Exercise 3** Students can answer this question correctly without using ratios by creating a picture that is three times what is shown. Discuss this with students but stress that you are interested in their understanding of ratios.

▶ **Exercise 4** Students may find this question more challenging because it is open ended. The students will get a correct response as long as they use a ratio where the total number of containers is a multiple of 5 and the ratio of red is $\frac{2}{5}$ and the ratio of yellow is $\frac{3}{5}$.

### Think & Discuss

*Suggested Grouping: Pairs*

If the students are having difficulty determining what is happening with each of the three students, have the students recreate the color. Students may go to Simon's explanation first because he is the only student who used 10 containers. Show the students how the ratio is not the same with 10 containers. The students must stop at 9 containers to maintain the proper ratio.

The researchers have found some shades they like. Now they want to make larger batches of paint.

**3.** The researchers call this mixture Awesome Orange. Draw a picture to show how Awesome Orange can be created using 12 containers in all. See below.

**4.** This mixture is called Sunset. Draw a set of containers that could be used to create a larger batch of Sunset.

**5.** Compare the two mixtures above. Use ratios in your comparison.

4. Answers will vary; 2 out of every 5 containers should be red.

5. Possible explanation: Awesome Orange is $\frac{3}{4}$ red and Sunset is $\frac{2}{5}$ red; $\frac{3}{4} > \frac{2}{5}$.

### Think & Discuss

The mixture at the right is Tropical Paradise. Maya, Simon, and Zach tried to make a batch of Tropical Paradise using 9 containers.

Simon extended the pattern.

"I'll draw copies of the 3 containers until I have 9 in all. First, I draw the 3 containers that I know. Then I draw them again to get 6 containers. I draw them once more to get 9 containers.

Maya thought about ratios.

"In the original mixture, $\frac{2}{3}$ of the containers are red. If I use 9 containers, $\frac{2}{3}$ of them must be red. Two-thirds of 9 is 6, so 6 containers must be red and 3 must be yellow."

Zach used a ratio table to record several equivalent ratios.

| | | | |
|---|---|---|---|
| **Red Containers** | 2 | 4 | 6 |
| **Total Containers** | 3 | 6 | 9 |

Did the students reason correctly? Explain any mistakes they made. Yes

Did any of the students use reasoning similar to your own? Answers will vary.

3. 

498 CHAPTER 10 Proportional Reasoning and Percents

## On the Spot Assessment

Tell which mixture is darker orange.

**Mixture C**

**Mixture D**

Neither: They are the same shade.

1. Possible answer: Express the ratios of red containers to all containers as fractions and compare the fractions; the greater fraction corresponds to the darker mixture. The ratio of red containers to all containers for Mixture X is $\frac{4}{7}$ and for Mixture Y is $\frac{3}{5}$. Since $\frac{3}{5} > \frac{4}{7}$, Mixture Y is darker.

## Develop & Understand: B

**6.** Complete this ratio table to show the number of red containers and the total number of containers for various batches of this shade.

| Red | 2 | 4 | 6 | 8 | 10 | 60 | 200 |
|---|---|---|---|---|---|---|---|
| Total | 3 | 6 | 9 | 12 | 15 | 90 | 300 |

**7.** The ratio table in Exercise 6 compares the number of red containers to the total number of containers. Complete the next ratio table to compare the number of red containers to the number of yellow containers in this mixture.

| Red | 3.5 | 7 | 14 | 21 | 28 | 35 |
|---|---|---|---|---|---|---|
| Yellow | 1.5 | 3 | 6 | 9 | 12 | 15 |

**8.** Soup and Salad, Inc. is catering a winter luncheon. According to the company, 8 cans of soup can feed 20 people.

**a.** Complete this ratio table based on this information.

| People | 5 | 10 | 15 | 20 | 25 | 30 |
|---|---|---|---|---|---|---|
| Cans of Soup | 2 | 4 | 6 | 8 | 10 | 12 |

**b.** How many people will two cans of soup feed? 5

**c.** If Soup and Salad, Inc. is planning to feed 25 people, how many cans of soup will they need? 10

### Share & Summarize

**1.** Which mixture below is darker orange? Describe your strategy.

**2.** Make a ratio table to show the number of red containers and the total number of containers you would need to make five different-sized batches of Mixture X.

2. Possible table:

| | | | | | |
|---|---|---|---|---|---|
| 4 | 8 | 12 | 16 | 24 | 32 |
| 7 | 14 | 21 | 28 | 42 | 56 |



## Develop & Understand: B

*Suggested Grouping: Pairs*

▶ **Exercise 6** It may be helpful to show students that the beginning of the table can be completed by following the pattern. Use prior information to complete the last 2 columns of the table by taking 10 times the values in column 3, and 100 times the values in the first column. The most accurate way of determining the correct solutions would be to create ratios.

▶ **Exercise 8** This exercise can be completed by determining the pattern in the table. There are no places where the table jumps values—all values fit the pattern of people increasing by 5 and cans of soup increasing by 2.

**Wrap-Up** Students will use their prior knowledge of rates and ratios to compare values. They will then use that knowledge to construct and complete tables of values to show how the mixtures relate. Students can use patterns to work with tables, but stress to students that it is still desirable to use ratios to solve for missing data.

### Share & Summarize

Students will show how to compare mixtures using ratios as well as how to take a ratio and create a table of values to show how to make a larger mixture.

## Troubleshooting

When working with a table that illustrates a ratio, a pattern is usually able to be determined. Students may have difficulty when the values in a table jump. Show students that a ratio is still applicable and will be helpful when they are not sure how the numbers of the table will jump.

### Investigation 1
Pages 495–497
Practice & Apply: 1–3
Connect & Extend: 13, 16

### Investigation 2
Pages 497–499
Practice & Apply: 4–12
Connect & Extend: 14, 15, 17, 18

### Assign Anytime
Mixed Review: 19–27

▶ **Exercise 1** The interpretations of *i–iv* are what the students use to answer the questions in parts a and b. It is important for students to know whether they are correctly interpreting the statements, prior to completing parts a and b.

▶ **Exercise 2b** Students can pick any point on the graph to determine the rate. Remind students that they should simplify the fraction and that they need to attach units. The rate is always determined by taking the *y*-value over the *x*-value.

### Additional Answers

1a. i is true since $\frac{32{,}158}{3{,}565} \approx \frac{9}{1}$

ii is true since the ratio is consistent with the given data.

iii is true since $\frac{39{,}888}{32{,}158} \approx \frac{40{,}000}{32{,}000} = \frac{5}{4}$

iv is true since 10% of 39,888 is about 4,000 and 3,565 is close to that amount.

**On Your Own Exercises**
Lesson 10.1

## Practice & Apply

**Real-World Link**
Great Smoky Mountains National Park is the most visited national park in the United States. Almost 95% of the park is forested.
**source:** National Park Service: www.nps.gov

**1.** During September 2007, Great Smoky Mountains National Park had 39,888 overnight guests. There were 3,565 overnight backcountry campers in the park. An additional 32,158 visitors stayed overnight in the campgrounds. The four comparisons below are based on this information.

**i.** About nine times as many visitors used the campgrounds compared to those who were backcountry campers.

**ii.** The ratio of those who camped in the backcountry to those who stayed in the campgrounds is 3,565 to 32,158.

**iii.** The ratio of overnight visitors to the number of campground visitors is about 5 to 4.

**iv.** Almost 10% of the overnight visitors were backcountry campers.

**a.** Explain why each statement above is true. See margin.

**b.** Suppose that Great Guides arranges backcountry camping trips. Which statement do you think they should use in an advertising brochure? Explain. Answers will vary. Many students may think that Statement iv sounds the most positive.

**2.** Mitchell and Elias went hiking. The graph shows their progress.

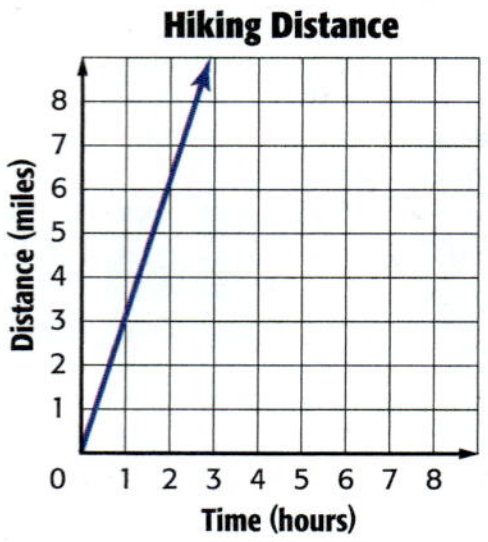


**a.** At what rate did the boys hike? 3 miles per hour

**b.** How many miles would you expect the boys to hike in 4 hours? 12 miles



500 **CHAPTER 10** Proportional Reasoning and Percents

3a. title to ads
3b. title to text
3c. photographs to text

**3.** Roberta is laying out the pages of a magazine. She divides one of the pages into 20 sections and decides which sections will be devoted to titles, to text, to photographs, and to advertisements.

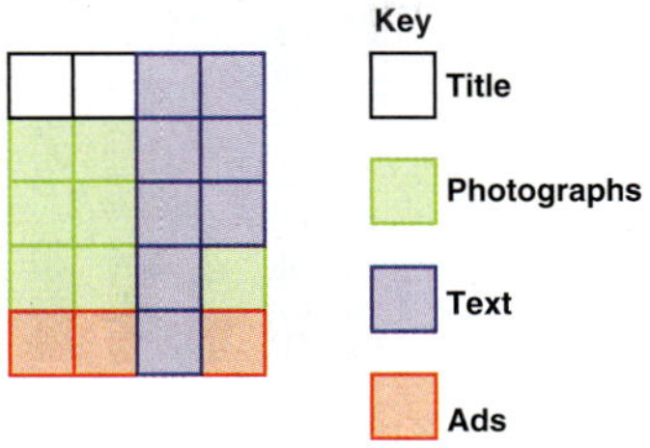


Describe something in the layout that has each given ratio.

**a.** 2 to 3

**b.** 1:4

**c.** $\frac{7}{8}$

**Math Link**

Remember that ratios can be expressed three ways.

1 to 3

1:3

$\frac{1}{3}$

**4.** Decide whether Mixture A or Mixture B is darker. Provide an explanation for your choice. Mixture A; $\frac{3}{5} > \frac{2}{4}$

**5.** Brigade Blue paint is shown below. How many containers of blue and white paints are needed for a batch of paint that has a total of 75 containers? 45 blue, 30 white

On Your Own Exercises

▶ **Exercise 3** It may be helpful to guide students to create all possible ratios for the given information. Students may get stuck if they try to write only the ratios with total sections as the denominator.

▶ **Exercise 5** Students can go about solving this problem in many different ways. The variety of possibilities can be overwhelming to students and can cause frustration for some students. It may be helpful to give students a starting point to help narrow their focus such as to start by finding the ratio of blue to total for the current mixture and then for the 75 container mixture.

**Lesson 10.1** Ratios **501**

▶ **Exercises 6–8** Students need to determine a ratio for the first mixture versus the second mixture. Once they determine which mixture is lighter they need to find out how to create a larger batch. There are many possible answers to this part of the question. Stress to students that this is a scale problem and that the larger batch must have a denominator that is a multiple of the original.

▶ **Exercises 10–12** The key to these tables is to determine the pattern. If students struggle with this, it is still acceptable for them to create and solve ratios. Stress to students that once they can find the pattern, it minimizes the work that they need to do.

On Your Own Exercises

For Exercises 6–8, tell which mixture is lighter green. Then draw or describe a larger batch that will make the lighter green mixture.

6. Mixture B; Answers will vary, but the blue:yellow ratio should be 2:5.
7. Mixture D; Answers will vary, but the blue:yellow ratio should be 3:2.
8. Mixture H; Answers will vary, but the blue:yellow ratio should be 4:3.

**6.**

**7.**

**8.**

**9.** Complete this ratio table to show the number of blue and yellow containers for various batches of this shade.

| **Yellow** | 1 | 2 | 6 | 10 | 50 | 100 | *n* |
|---|---|---|---|---|---|---|---|
| **Blue** | 2 | 4 | 12 | 20 | 100 | 200 | 2*n* |

In Exercises 10–12, is the given table a ratio table? If so, tell the ratio. If not, explain why not.

**10.**

| | | | | |
|---|---|---|---|---|
| 2 | 4 | 6 | 8 | 10 |
| 5 | 10 | 15 | 20 | 25 |

Yes, $\frac{2}{5}$

**11.**

| | | | | |
|---|---|---|---|---|
| 1 | 3 | 5 | 8 | 10 |
| 2 | 5 | 8 | 11 | 14 |

No; the ratios of each pair of numbers are not equivalent.

**12.**

| | | | | |
|---|---|---|---|---|
| 4 | 40 | 400 | 4,000 | 40,000 |
| 7 | 70 | 700 | 7,000 | 70,000 |

Yes, $\frac{4}{7}$

On Your Own Exercises

## Connect & Extend

13a.

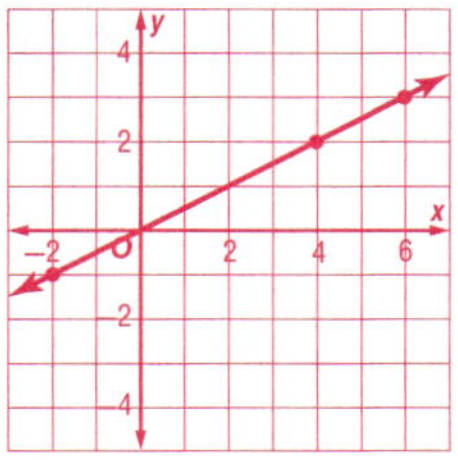


13e. Possible answer: They all go through the origin; they all have positive slope.

13f. Part a: $\frac{1}{2}$; Part c: $\frac{5}{1}$; Part d: $\frac{3}{2}$; The slopes are the reciprocals of the ratios.

**Real-World Link**
The Golden Ratio is thought to be a central theme in the design of the mosque of Uqba's prayer space and minaret.

**13. Preview** Explore the ratios of $x$- and $y$-coordinates for some lines.

a. Graph the line that goes through the points (4, 2), (6, 3), and (−2, −1).

b. What is the ratio of $x$ to $y$? 2:1

c. Choose some points with an $x$:$y$ ratio of $\frac{1}{5}$. Graph the points on the same axes as in Part a. Draw a line through your points. Graphs will vary.

d. Now choose some points with an $x$:$y$ ratio of $\frac{2}{3}$ and graph them. Draw a line through your points. Graphs will vary.

e. What do you notice about the three lines you graphed?

f. Calculate the slope of each line. How are the slopes related to the ratios?

**14.** Consider this mixture. See margin.

a. Draw a mixture that is darker than this one but uses fewer containers. Do not make *all* the containers blue.

b. Explain why you think your mixture is darker.

**15. Architecture** Architects have used a particular rectangular shape to design buildings. For rectangles of this shape, the ratio of the long side to the short side is roughly 1.6 : 1. This ratio is very close to what is known as the *Golden Ratio*. Rectangles of this shape look pleasing to the eye.

a. Try drawing three rectangles of different sizes that look "ideal" to you. For each rectangle, measure the side lengths and find the ratio of the long side to the short side. Rectangles and ratios will vary.

b. Which of your rectangles has the ratio closest to the Golden Ratio? Answers will vary.

**16. Measurement** Marsha always forgets how to convert miles to kilometers and back again. However, she remembers that her car's speedometer shows both miles and kilometers. She knows that traveling 25 miles per hour is the same as traveling 40 kilometers per hour. So, in one hour, she would travel 25 miles, or 40 kilometers.

a. From this information, find the ratio of miles to kilometers in simplest terms. 5:8

b. To cover 100 km in an hour, how fast would Marsha have to go in miles per hour? Explain how you found your answer. See margin.



▶ **Exercise 13** This exercise will be more accurately completed if the students use graph paper. This exercise is also an excellent example of how ratios tie into other areas of mathematics. The students have already studied slope, but have not looked at it as a ratio.

▶ **Exercise 14** This is an open ended question and may challenge some students because there is not one correct solution. When answering students' questions, try to show a number of correct solutions to this problem to reinforce that open-ended questions can have many different answers.

▶ **Exercise 15** Stress to students that they should not try to draw rectangles that fit the golden ratio. The goal here is to draw rectangles that the student sees as "pleasing to the eye" and then see how close each rectangle is to the golden ratio.

**Additional Answers**

14a. Check students' drawings. Possible mixture: 4 blue containers, 1 yellow container.

14b. Possible answer: the ratio of my blue containers to my yellow containers is greater than 4 : 2, or 2 : 1.

16b. 62.5; Possible explanation: 40 multiplied by 2.5 is 100. So, I multiplied 25 by 2.5 to get 62.5.

**Lesson 10.1** Ratios **503**

▶ **Exercise 18** Stress to students that they need to read the words of the question prior to beginning to complete their work. The given table is not a ratio table, it is merely a set of points that the students will use to create a ratio table.

## Quick Check

**Informal Assessment** Students should be able to:

✔ write ratios that coordinate with given situations

✔ recognize and determine equivalent ratios

✔ compare ratios

✔ use tables to compare ratios

✔ determine patterns from ratio tables

## Quick Quiz

1. Helio has traveled to 18 different states by car, another 5 states by train, and 7 more states by airplane. What is the ratio of states Helio traveled to by car versus the total number of states he has traveled to? $\frac{18}{30} = \frac{3}{5}$
2. Mia has traveled to a total of 40 different states. If her ratio of states traveled to by car is the same as Helio's, how many states has Mia traveled to by car? 24
3. The school play is using a mixture of 7 containers of white paint and 3 containers of red paint to create the pink paint they are using for the walls of a scene. They need to make a batch of paint from 40 containers, how much red paint do they need to use? 12
4. Complete the ratio table.

| | | | | |
|---|---|---|---|---|
| **Blue** | 2 | 4 | 6 | 8 |
| **Red** | 3 | 6 | 9 | 12 |

## Additional Answers

18b. Check students' tables. Possible table:

| | | | | |
|---|---|---|---|---|
| *x* | 20 | 30 | 40 | 50 |
| *y* | 3 | 4.5 | 6 | 7.5 |

17. Crafts Unlimited sells ribbon by the foot. Serena needs ribbon for an art project. The cost of the ribbon is 5 feet for $3.00.

| Feet of Ribbon | 1 | 5 | 10 | 15 | 20 |
|---|---|---|---|---|---|
| Cost (in dollars) | $0.60 | $3.00 | $6.00 | $9.00 | $12.00 |

a. Complete this ratio chart based on the information provided.

b. How many feet of ribbon can Serena buy for $12.00? 20 feet

c. If Serena needs 17 feet of ribbon, how much will she pay? How do you know?

17c. Serena will pay $10.20. Possible answer: You can add $9.00 that she will pay for 15 feet, $0.60 for the sixteenth foot, and $0.60 for seventeenth foot to find the total.

18. This table is not a ratio table.

| *x* | 10 | 20 | 30 | 40 |
|---|---|---|---|---|
| *y* | 1.5 | 2 | 2.5 | 3 |

a. Graph the values in the table. Draw a line or a smooth curve through the points. Describe the shape of the graph.

b. Make a table of ratios equivalent to 10 : 1.5. Include at least four entries. Call the values corresponding to the first quantity in the ratio *x* and the other values *y*. See margin.

c. Graph the values from Part b. Draw a line or a smooth curve through the points. See margin.

d. How are the two graphs alike? How are they different? See margin.

e. Make another ratio table of *x* and *y* values using a ratio close to 10 : 1.5, such as 8 : 1.5 or 12 : 1.5. Graph the values in your table. Draw a line or a smooth curve through the points. See margin.

f. **Challenge** What characteristic do the graphs in Parts c and e share but the graph in Part a does not? Explain why this is so. See margin.

## Mixed Review

18a. The graph is a line.

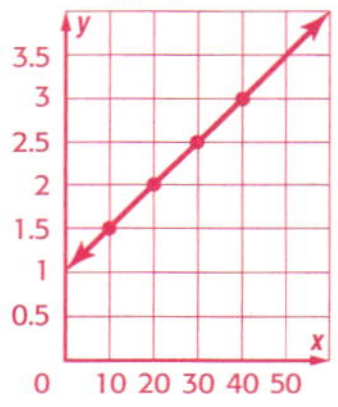


**Evaluate each expression.**

19. $23 \cdot 2 - 5(3.1)$ 30.5
20. $23 \cdot [2 - 5(3.1)]$ −310.5
21. $23 \cdot (2 - 5)(3.1)$ −213.9
22. $3^3 \cdot \frac{4}{3} - 2$ 34

**Solve each equation by doing the same thing to both sides.**

23. $5x + 7 = 3x + 3$ $x = -2$
24. $21a + 5 = 6a + 35$ $a = 2$
25. $3t + 4 = t - 8$ $t = -6$
26. $6.25x - 30 = 0.25x + 6$ $x = 6$
27. Elaine told her banker, "If I put my money in Account A, which will double it and add 24 dollars, I will have the same amount as if I put my money in Account B, which will triple it and add 4 dollars."

a. Write an equation to find how much money Elaine has. $2x + 24 = 3x + 4$

b. Solve your equation by doing the same thing to both sides. 20 dollars



18c. Possible graph:

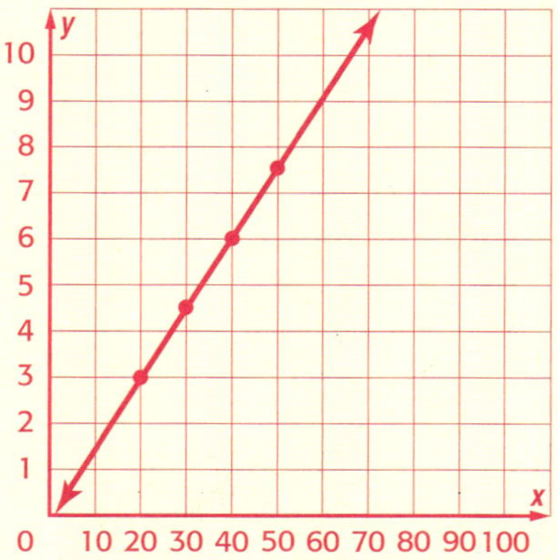


18d. They are both lines. Possible differences: The lines have different slopes; the line for Part c goes through the origin, but the line for Part a doesn't.

18e. Answers will vary, but the graph should be a line through the origin.

18f. Possible answer: The lines in parts c and e go through the origin. Since these graphs were created using ratios, any point on one of the lines can be found by multiplying both parts of the ratio by the same number. If you multiply both parts by 0, you get (0, 0).

LESSON

10.2

# Proportions and Similarity

### Objectives

- To recognize proportions as pairs of equivalent ratios
- To set up and solve proportions
- To use proportions and similar triangles to calculate distances

## Overview

In this lesson, students are formally introduced to proportions and to setting up proportions to solve real-world problems. The lesson begins by introducing the term *proportion* for sets of equivalent ratios, a concept that students began working with in Lesson 10.1. They use equivalent ratios to solve simple problems.

## Advance Preparation

You may want to make a transparency of Lesson 10.2 Master 1 to use with Investigation 5. Students can also use the master as a basis for their sketches.

| | Summary | Materials | On Your Own Exercises (pp. 522–529) | Assessment Opportunities |
|---|---|---|---|---|
| **Investigation 1** (p. 505) Pacing: 2 days | Students will analyze situations to determine if a proportional relationship applies. | | Practice & Apply: 1–3<br>Connect & Extend: 14–15<br>Mixed Review: 28–45 | • Share & Summarize (p. 507)<br>• Troubleshooting (p. 507) |
| **Investigation 2** (p. 508) Pacing: 1 day | Students will use equal ratios to solve problems. | | Practice & Apply: 4–6<br>Connect & Extend: 16–17<br>Mixed Review: 28–45 | • On the Spot Assessment (p. 509)<br>• Share & Summarize (p. 510)<br>• Troubleshooting (pp. 508, 510) |
| **Investigation 3** (p. 510) Pacing: 1 day | Students will set up proportions to solve problems. | | Practice & Apply: 7<br>Connect & Extend: 18, 19, 21–23<br>Mixed Review: 28–45 | • On the Spot Assessment (p. 513)<br>• Share & Summarize (p. 513)<br>• Troubleshooting (p. 511) |
| **Investigation 4** (p. 514) Pacing: 1 day | Students will use proportions to solve problems relating to scales used to construct maps. | computers with Internet access, rulers | Practice & Apply: 8–10<br>Connect & Extend: 20, 24, 25<br>Mixed Review: 28–45 | • On the Spot Assessment (p. 514)<br>• Share & Summarize (p. 516)<br>• Troubleshooting (p. 515) |
| **Investigation 5** (p. 517) Pacing: 1 day | Students will use proportions and similar triangles to find missing measurements. | rulers, blank paper, Lesson 10.2 Master 1 | Practice & Apply: 11–13<br>Connect & Extend: 26–27<br>Mixed Review: 28–45 | • Share & Summarize (p. 518) |
| **Inquiry Investigation 6** (p. 519) Pacing: 1 day | Students will estimate the height of objects using a measurement device they construct. | protractor, string or thread weight (paper clip or cube), tape measure, yard stick, tape (optional) | | |

# Leveled Lesson Resources

CRM *Available in:* **Chapter 10 Resource Masters**

Also on TeacherWorks™ Lesson 10.2

## Study Guide and Intervention (p. 9) AL

**Lesson 10.2 Study Guide and Intervention**
***Proportions and Similarity***

A **proportional relationship** is a relationship in which all pairs of corresponding values have the same ratio. You can use proportions to solve similarity problems.

***Example 1*** **Solve $\frac{a}{10} = \frac{28}{35}$.**

**Method 1** Solve the equation.

$\frac{a}{10} = \frac{28}{35}$ Write the proportion.

$\frac{a}{10} = 0.8$ Divide 28 by 35.

$10 \cdot \frac{a}{10} = 0.8 \cdot 10$ Multiply both sides by 10.

**Method 2** Multiply or divide.

Note that $35 \div 10 = 3.5$. Dividing both parts of $\frac{28}{35}$ by 3.5 gives $\frac{28 \div 3.5}{35 \div 3.5} = \frac{8}{10}$. So, $a = 8$.

***Example 2*** **A map shows a scale of 1 inch = 40 miles. The distance between two places on the map is 3.25 inches. What is the actual distance?**

Let $x$ represent the actual distance. Write and solve a proportion.

map → $\frac{1 \text{ inch}}{40 \text{ miles}}$ $\frac{3.25 \text{ inches}}{x \text{ miles}}$ ← map
actual → ← actual

Multiplying both parts of $\frac{1}{40}$ by 3.25 gives $\frac{1 \times 3.25}{40 \times 3.25} = \frac{3.25}{130}$.
The actual distance is 130 miles.

***Example 3*** **A statue casts a shadow 30 feet long. At the same time, a person who is 5 feet tall casts a shadow that is 6 feet long. How tall is the statue?**

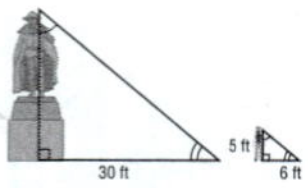


Let $x$ represent the actual distance. Write and solve a proportion.

person → $\frac{5 \text{ feet}}{6 \text{ feet}}$ $\frac{x \text{ feet}}{30 \text{ feet}}$ ← statue
person's shadow → ← statue's shadow

Multiplying both parts of $\frac{5}{6}$ by 5 gives $\frac{5 \times 5}{6 \times 5} = \frac{25}{30}$. The statue is 25 feet tall.

***Exercises***

1. A walking path is 18 feet long. Sam draws a map that includes this path. If he uses a scale of 2 inches = 3 feet, how long will the path be on the map?
2. Emily measures the shadow of a building to be 26 feet. Emily is 4.5 feet tall, and her shadow is 3 feet long. How tall is the building?

## Skills Practice (p. 10) AL OL

**Lesson 10.2 Skills Practice**
***Proportions and Similarity***

**A proportion is formed when two ratios are equal. Determine whether each pair of ratios forms a proportion. Write *yes* or *no*.**

1. $\frac{17}{10}, \frac{12}{5}$
2. $\frac{6}{9}, \frac{12}{18}$
3. $\frac{8}{12}, \frac{10}{15}$

**Solve each proportion.**

4. $\frac{5}{8} = \frac{s}{12}$
5. $\frac{a}{26} = \frac{24}{13}$
6. $\frac{2.8}{4} = \frac{7}{q}$
7. $\frac{8}{m} = \frac{120}{75}$
8. $\frac{4.2}{t} = \frac{8}{5}$
9. $\frac{b}{0.5} = \frac{3.6}{9}$

**On a map, the scale is 5 centimeters = 2 kilometers. Find the missing distances.**

10. Map Distance: 10 centimeters
Actual Distance: ________
11. Map Distance: ________
Actual Distance: 3.2 kilometers
12. Map Distance: ________
Actual Distance: 5.6 kilometers
13. Map Distance: 2.5 centimeters
Actual Distance: ________

**Estimate the height of the tall object.**

14. 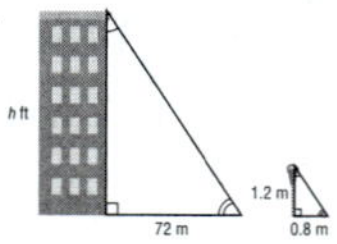


15. 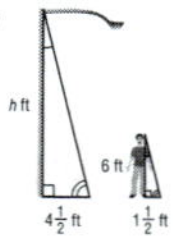


## Problem-Solving Practice (p. 11) AL OL

**Lesson 10.2 Problem-Solving Practice**
***Proportions and Similarity***

**Solve.**

1. **Cooking** A cookie recipe calls for 2 cups of sugar to make 36 cookies. Write and solve a proportion to find how much sugar Theo should use to make 24 cookies.
2. **Medicine** June's nurse counted 18 beats in her pulse in 15 seconds. Write and solve a proportion to find how many beats she would have in 60 seconds.
3. **Travel** Susan is driving to Mount Shasta. On her map, she is a distance of $7\frac{3}{4}$ inches away. The scale of the map is $\frac{1}{2}$ inch = 50 miles. How far must Susan travel to reach her destination?
4. **Maps** A map of Levi's property is being made with a scale of 2 centimeters = 3 meters. The distance across the back of his property is 19.2 meters. How many centimeters will represent this distance on the map?
5. **Flagpole** Beatrice stands $6\frac{1}{2}$ feet tall and casts a shadow that is 9 feet long. She measures the shadow of the school flagpole and finds it is $31\frac{1}{2}$ feet long. How tall is the flagpole?

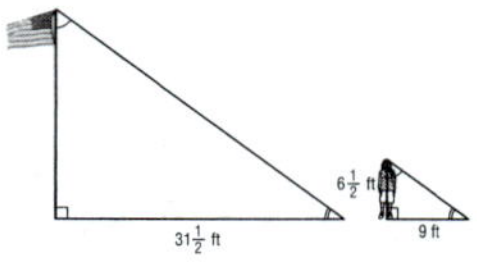


6. **Testing** The table shows Maura's results on several practice tests. Is there a proportional relationship between the problems answered correctly and total test problems? Explain.

| Answered Correctly | Total Problems |
|---|---|
| 4 | 10 |
| 6 | 15 |
| 10 | 25 |
| 12 | 30 |

## Enrichment (p. 12) BL

**Lesson 10.2 Enrichment**
***Proportions and Similarity***

**Indirect Measurement**

A proportion can be used to determine the height of tall structures if three variables of the proportion are known. The three known variables are usually the height $a$ of the observer, the length $b$ of the observer's shadow, and the length $d$ of the structure's shadow. However, a proportion can be solved given any three of the four variables.

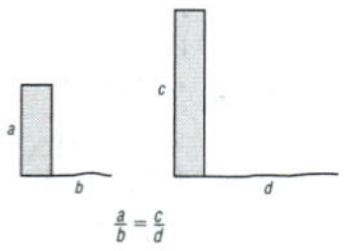


$\frac{a}{b} = \frac{c}{d}$

**This chart contains information about various observers and tall buildings. Use proportions and your calculator to complete the chart of tall buildings of the world.**

| | Height of Observer | Length of Shadow | Building Location | Height of Building | Length of Shadow |
|---|---|---|---|---|---|
| 1. | 5 ft | 8 in. | Natwest,London | | 80 ft |
| 2. | 4 ft 9 in. | | Columbia Seafirst Center, Seattle | 954 ft | 318 ft |
| 3. | 5 ft 10 in. | 14 in. | Wachovia Building, Winston-Salem | 410 ft | |
| 4. | | 15 in. | Waterfront Towers, Honolulu | 400 ft | 83 ft 4 in. |
| 5. | 6 ft | | CN Tower,Toronto | 1,821 ft | 303 ft 6 in. |
| 6. | 5 ft 9 in. | 1 ft 11 in. | Gateway Arch,St. Louis | 630 ft | |
| 7. | 5 ft 3 in. | 1 ft 9 in. | Eiffel Tower, Paris | | 328 ft |
| 8. | | 8 in. | Texas Commerce Tower, Houston | 1,002 ft | 167 ft |
| 9. | 5 ft 6 in. | 11 in. | John Hancock Tower, Boston | | 131 ft 8 in. |
| 10. | 5 ft 4 in. | 8 in. | Sears Tower, Chicago | | 181 ft 9 in. |
| 11. | 5 ft 6 in. | | Barnett Tower, Jacksonville | 631 ft | 105 ft 2 in. |

## Lesson Quick Quiz (p. 13) AL OL BL

**Lesson 10.2 Quick Quiz**

1. Mixture A is made up of 6 containers of paint, 4 yellow and 2 blue. Mixture B is made up of 9 containers of paint, 5 yellow and 4 blue. Are the numbers of yellow containers of paint proportional? How do you know?
2. Hobson School has a student-teacher ratio of 9:2 for their current school year. Next year the enrollment of the school is expected to be 178 students. What proportion would you use to determine how many teachers are needed to maintain this ratio? How many teachers will be employed next year?
3. A map has a scale of 3 centimeters equals 100 miles. If two cities are 12.5 centimeters apart, approximately how many miles separate the cities?
4. A 25 foot tall flag pole casts an 8 foot shadow on the ground. A nearby tree casts a 14 foot shadow. How tall is the tree?

## Lesson Master (p. 14)

**Lesson 10.2 Master 1**
***Proportions and Similarity***

**Investigation 5: Explore**

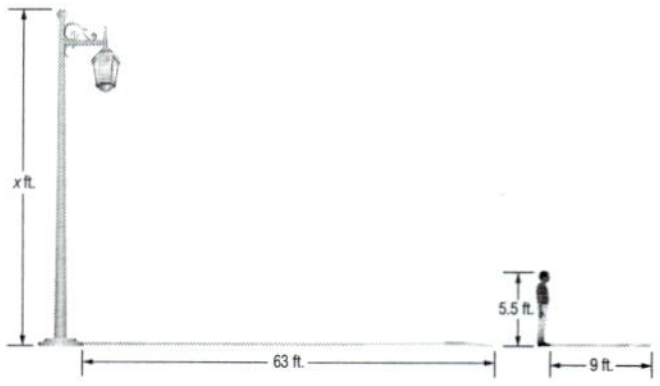


**Investigation 5: Develop & Understand A**

# Additional Lesson Resources

### Teacher Tech Tools

- TeacherWorks
- ExamView Assessment Suite
- Classroom Presentation Toolkit
- Advance Tracker

### Student Tech Tools

- StudentWorks Plus
- Math Online eGlossary •
  Concepts in Motion

### Other Print Products

- Investigation Notebook and Reflection Journal
- Quick Review Math Handbook

LESSON 10.2

# Proportions and Similarity



Theresa is making trail mix to sell for a seventh-grade fundraiser. The amount of peanuts in the recipe is proportional to the amount of raisins.

As with any proportional relationship, the graph of the relationship between peanuts and raisins is a line through the origin.

**Trail Mix Recipe**

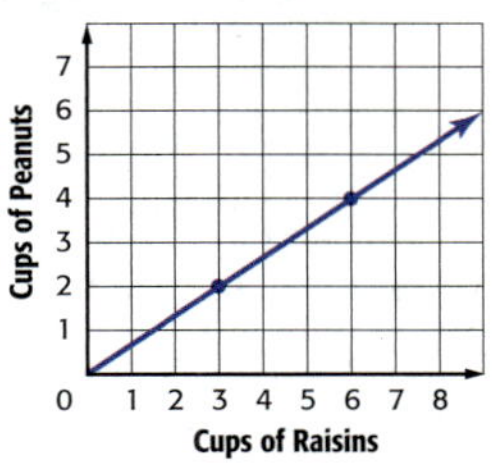


### Think & Discuss

The point (6, 4) is on the graph. What does this tell you about the trail mix? For every 6 cups of raisins, there are 4 cups of peanuts.

Identify two more points on the graph. Find the ratio of peanuts to raisins for all three points. How do the ratios compare? See ①.

Find the slope of the line. Remember that the slope of a line is rise divided by run. What does it tell you about the trail mix? How does it relate to the ratios you found? See ② below.

Give the coordinates of two other points that are on the line but that are beyond the boundaries of the graph. Explain how you found the points. Possible answer: (15, 10), (18, 12); Any point for which the ratio of peanuts to raisins is 2:3, or, 1:1.5 is on the graph. I chose 10 and 12 as possible cups of peanuts and multiplied them by 1.5.

① Possible answer: (6, 4), (3, 2), (9, 6); 6:4, 3:2, 9:6; The ratios are equivalent.

**Math Link**

*Proportional* means that as one variable doubles the other doubles, as one variable triples the other triples, and so on.

## Investigation 1 Proportional Relationships

**Vocabulary**

**proportional relationship**

A **proportional relationship** is a relationship in which all pairs of corresponding values have the same ratio. In Think & Discuss, you found that the ratio of peanuts to raisins is the same for any point on the graph. For example, (3, 2) and (6, 4) both lie on the same graph.

$$\text{So, } \frac{3}{2} = \frac{6}{4}.$$

② $\frac{2}{3}$; The slope indicates that for every 2 cups of peanuts, there are 3 cups of raisins. The slope is equal to the ratios.



### Mathematical Background

Students studied slope in Lesson 8.2, so the concept should be fresh. If students are struggling, give a quick refresher that slope is the ratio of the difference in *y*-coordinates over the difference in *x*-coordinates, or the rise over the run.

## Proportions and Similarity LESSON 10.2

### Introduce

**Proportionality** The lesson opener shows the following fact: If a quantity *y* is proportional to quantity *x*, then the graph of *y* as a function of *x* is a straight line through the origin. The converse is also true: if the graph of *y* as a function of *x* is a straight line through the origin, then quantity *y* is proportional to quantity *x*.

Read through the introductory paragraph, reviewing the term *proportional*. Then pose the questions raised in Think & Discuss.

**Think & Discuss**

If the variables *y* and *x* are proportional, then for any corresponding values of *x* and *y*, the ratio $\frac{y}{x}$ in simplest terms is a constant. This constant of proportionality is equal to the slope of the line. The term *constant of proportionality* is not used in the text, but it is a term you may want to use informally.

The last question asks students to find two points on the line that lie outside the shown boundaries of the graph. You may get answers that use negative values of *x* and *y*. Mathematically, answers with negative coordinates are perfectly correct. However, these values do not make sense in the context of the original situation. Point out that mathematical models may extend beyond the real life situations from which they originally came.

## Investigation 1

**On Your Own Exercises**
Pages 522–529
Exercises 1–3, 14–15

**Proportional Relationships** Read the introduction and introduce the term *proportional relationship*. Make connections with the study of direct linear relationships in Chapter 8.

It is possible to solve a proportion using cross-products. Cross-products were studied in Course 1 Chapter 5, and allow you to verify or solve proportional relationships by multiplying values along the diagonals.

## Develop & Understand: A

*Suggested Grouping: Pairs*

This exercise set places the mathematical ideas explored in Lesson 10.1 in different contexts. Students use ratios and proportional relationships to solve geometry, mixture, and other word problems.

▶ **Exercise 1** Students may use one of these strategies:

- Consider the numbers on each card as ratios and find equivalent ratios.
- Find patterns in the cards shown, then continue the pattern.
- Consider the numbers on the cards to be coordinates, then graph them on a coordinate grid. While it is unlikely that any student will approach the exercise in this manner, it is a possible way to solve the exercise.

▶ **Exercise 2** This relates proportionality to similarity, which students should recall from previous coursework.

You can test for proportionality by using cross-products or by writing fractions in lowest terms.

| **Cross-Products** | **Lowest Terms** |
|---|---|
| $\frac{3}{2} \times \frac{6}{4}$   $3 \cdot 4 = 12$, $6 \cdot 2 = 12$ | $\frac{6}{4} = \frac{3 \cdot 2}{2 \cdot 2} = \frac{3}{2} \cdot \frac{2}{2} = \frac{3}{2} \cdot 1 = \frac{3}{2}$ |

## Develop & Understand: A

**1.** On the cards below, the top numbers are proportional to the bottom numbers. Find another card that belongs in this set. Explain how you know your card belongs. Possible answer: 10:30; The ratio of the top number to the bottom number is 1:3.

**2.** Consider these triangles.

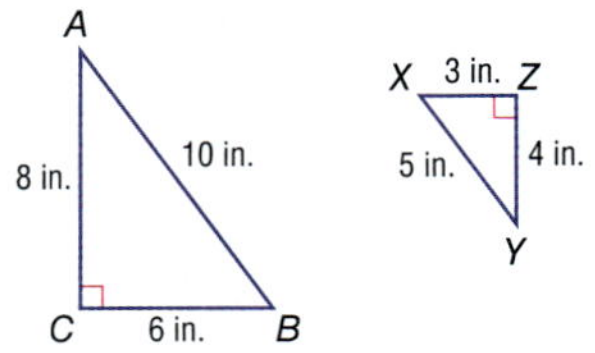


**a.** Are the side lengths of triangle *ABC* proportional to those of triangle *XYZ*? Explain how you know.

**b.** Remember that similar figures have the same shape but possibly different sizes. Are the triangles similar? Explain. Yes; ratios of corresponding side lengths are equal.

**3.** Bryan says, "I created Mixture B by adding one red container and one white container to Mixture A. Then I made Mixture C by adding one red container and one white container to Mixture B. Since I added the same amount of red and white each time, the number of red containers is proportional to the number of white containers."

Is Bryan correct? Explain.

2a. Yes; Possible explanation: $\frac{3}{6} = \frac{4}{8} = \frac{5}{10}$; All ratios of corresponding side lengths are equivalent.

3. No; Possible explanation: The ratios of red containers to white containers for the mixtures are 2:1, 3:2, and 4:3, which are not equal.



## Mathematical Background

The general mathematical principle underlying Exercises 3 and 4 is that, in order to preserve a ratio a:b, any additions must also be in the ratio of a:b. In Exercise 3, the initial ratio of red containers to white containers is 2:1. To preserve this ratio, any red containers and white containers added to the mixture must also be in the same ratio, 2:1. So, when Bryan starts adding 1 red container and 1 white container (a 1:1 ratio) to a 2:1 mixture, the initial red to white ratio will not stay the same. The same analysis works for Exercise 4. There, the Stage 1 ratio of green to yellow tiles is 1:8. Thereafter, at each successive stage, Kenyan added 1 green and 2 yellow tiles (a ratio of 1:2).

Since $1:2 \neq 1:8$, the initial ratio of tiles will not be preserved. The simplest way to preserve the initial ratio of 1:8 is to replicate the initial pattern over and over again.

**Math Link**
To be a pattern, the arrangement of tiles must change in a *predictable* way from stage to stage.

4a. Possible answer: 1 green tile is added to the center row, and 2 yellow tiles are added to the border.

4b. No; the ratios of green tiles to yellow tiles for the four stages are $\frac{1}{8}$, $\frac{2}{10}$, $\frac{3}{12}$, and $\frac{4}{14}$, which are not equal.

4c. Possible pattern:

1. Possible answer: Check that all pairs of values are in the same ratio. Or graph the values, and check that they fall on a line through the origin.
2. Possible answer: The number of hours I babysit and the number of dollars I earn
3. Possible answer: The number of books I read and the amount of food I eat

**4.** Kenyon created this tile pattern.

**a.** Describe how the pattern of green and yellow tiles changes from one stage to the next.

**b.** For the stages shown, is the number of green tiles proportional to the number of yellow tiles? Explain.

**c.** Starting with stage 1 above, draw the next two stages for a tile pattern in which the number of green tiles *is* proportional to the number of yellow tiles.

**5.** Stores are able to make a profit by buying in bulk. They are charged less per item because they agree to buy a large number of items.

For Parts a–c, compare the two situations. Determine if the two situations are proportional or not proportional.

**a.** A store may purchase 100 t-shirts for \$28 or 3,000 t-shirts for \$12,180. Not proportional

**b.** A store may purchase 5 digital cameras for \$150 or 45 digital cameras for \$1,350. Proportional

**c.** A store may purchase 36 packs of gum for \$7.20 or 800 packs of gum for \$96. Not proportional

## Share & Summarize

1. Describe at least two ways to determine whether a relationship is proportional.
2. Describe two quantities in your daily life that are proportional to each other.
3. Describe two quantities in your daily life that are not proportional to each other.
4. Use the word *proportional* to explain how you can tell whether two triangles are similar. If corresponding side lengths are proportional, the triangles are similar.



▶ **Exercise 5** Students are asked to determine if relationships are proportional or not. In order to do this, students will need to create ratios and determine if the ratios are equal. Watch to make sure that students are setting up their ratios in the same order, otherwise they will not find any of the relationships proportional.

**Wrap-Up** At the end of this investigation, students should be comfortable working with ratios and determining if relationships are proportional. This is really a continuation of what the students were working on in Lesson 10.1.

## Share & Summarize

In Exercises 2 and 3, students are asked to relate proportionality to their lives. Since not all things in the everyday world are precise, some of the students' examples may be correct only over a limited range. That does not mean such answers are wrong, but you may want to have a class discussion about the limitations inherent in some of the student answers. For example, for Exercise 2, the text provides the possible answer: "The number of hours I babysit and the amount of dollars I earn." Some things one might consider here include:

a. This babysitter charges the same, no matter how many children are involved.

b. This babysitter charges the same, no matter how late the hour.

c. This babysitter does not round off his/her charges, for example, to the nearest quarter hour. You might want to graph charges vs. time with rounding, and see how the graph compares to a straight line.

## Troubleshooting

If students are having difficulty understanding the meaning of proportional, you may want to review Exercise 4. This exercise requires students to describe a pattern and continue it to maintain a proportional relationship. Watch for students who use additive strategies for continuing a proportional pattern. You may want to have these students use tiles to construct the pattern. If necessary, have them make several models of the figure in Stage 1. Then have them attach two models, three models, and so on, counting the tiles in each and writing ratios to show the proportional relationships.

# Investigation 2

**On Your Own Exercises**
Pages 522–529
Exercises 4–6, 16–17

**Equal Ratios** Remind students about the proportional relationships they explored in the last investigation. Point out that in a proportional relationship, all corresponding values are in the same ratio. Tell students they will use proportional relationships to solve exercises.

## Develop & Understand: A

*Suggested Grouping: Pairs*

▶ **Exercise 1** One of the most common problems with solving proportions is not properly setting up the proportion using corresponding pieces. Remind students that when they write the proportion, make sure they are matching up the short side of the small rectangle with the short side of the large rectangle.

▶ **Exercise 2a** Remind students that the explanation of what the coordinates represents is given in the same order as the coordinates are.

▶ **Exercise 2d** Students are mathematically correct if they answer with negative values for the coordinates. In terms of the real world concept of the question, a negative value does not make sense. Remind students that there are mathematically correct responses and responses that fit the situation. Both need to be considered when correctly answering a problem.

# Investigation 2 Equal Ratios

You know that in a proportional relationship, all pairs of corresponding values are in the same ratio. You may find it helpful to think about this idea as you solve the following exercises.

## Develop & Understand: A

1. The rectangles below are similar. Find the value of $x$. 5.2 ft

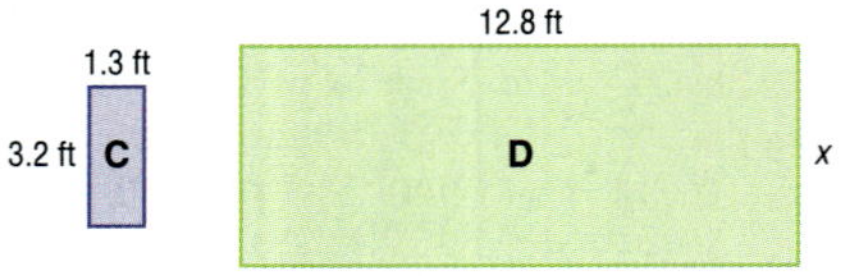


2. Ms. Palmer manages a craft shop. She uses this graph to quickly find the cost of different amounts of cotton fabric.

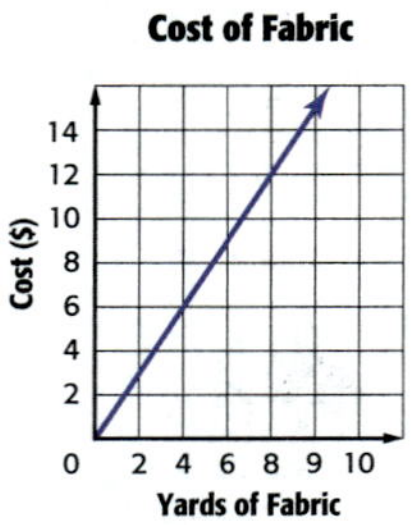


a. Give the coordinates of two points that lie on the graph. Explain what the ordered pairs mean with respect to this real-world context.

2a. Possible answers: (4, 6) and (8, 12); Four yards of cotton fabric cost \$6. Eight yards of cotton fabric cost \$12.

b. Show that your two points have the same ratio. $\frac{6}{4} = \frac{12}{8} = \frac{3}{2}$

c. A customer wants to buy 30 yards of fabric, but the graph does not extend that far. How much will the fabric cost? \$45.00

d. Give the coordinates of two other points that lie on the line but are beyond the boundaries of the graph. Show that the points have the same ratio.
Possible answers: (10, 15), (12, 18); $\frac{15}{10}, \frac{18}{12}; \frac{15}{10} = \frac{18}{12} = \frac{3}{2}$



## Troubleshooting

In Exercise 1, watch for students who consider the sides measuring 1.3 feet and 12.8 feet as corresponding sides and calculate the ratio accordingly. Encourage them to check their answers by comparing the measures of the sides of Rectangle D to make sure that the longer side actually has a greater measure.

## Think & Discuss

When the seventh grade trail mix sale began, Mr. Malone, a Math teacher, bought the first six packages. From his purchase alone, the class raised \$27.00.

By the end of the first day of the sale, the class had raised \$121.50. How many packages had been sold by the end of the first day? 27

There is more than one way to solve an exercise involving proportional relationships. Ramiro, Mali, and Jeremy each thought about the trail mix problem in a different way, but all three found the same answer.

Ramiro used unit rates. He said, "I found the cost of one package of trail mix by solving for *x*. Then I divided \$121.50 by that amount."

$$\frac{\$27}{6 \text{ packages}} = x$$

$$\frac{\$121.50}{x} = \text{sold packages}$$

Mali wrote and scaled a ratio. She said, "I multiplied both parts of the ratio by the same number to find an equal ratio in the form of *\$121.50 to something*."

$$\frac{\$27}{6 \text{ packages}} \cdot \frac{\$4.50}{\$4.50}$$

Jeremy wrote and solved an equation. He said, "I wrote an equation to find how many packages they must sell to raise \$121.50. Then I solved the equation to find the answer."

$$\frac{\$27}{6} = \frac{\$121.50}{n}$$

## Develop & Understand: B

3. Complete each student's method to find the number of trail mix packages sold the first day. You should find the same answer with each method. 27

4. The last time Ian rented a canoe at Budget Livery, he paid \$28.95 for 3 hours. Today, he used the canoe for 4 hours 45 minutes. If the rental cost is proportional to time, what will be his rental charge? \$28.95 ÷ 3 h = \$9.65 per hour. The rental cost for 4.75 h is \$9.65 per hour • 4.75 h ≈ \$45.84.



## Think & Discuss

*Suggested Grouping: Pairs*

As the students read through each person's method for solving the problem, have them work through and solve the proportion. Ask the pairs to discuss their findings. Write down similarities and differences in the methods used. The students should see that each approach yields the same result.

## Develop & Understand: B

*Suggested Grouping: Pairs or Individuals*

Students use proportions to solve exercises in various contexts. It is important to note that proportions can be set up in many equivalent ways: $\frac{b}{a} = \frac{x}{c}$ is equivalent to $\frac{a}{b} = \frac{c}{x}$ and $\frac{a}{c} = \frac{b}{x}$ to $\frac{b}{a} = \frac{x}{c}$, for example.

▶ **Exercise 3** In discussing answers, have students talk about the different methods and which they found easier or more comfortable.

## On the Spot Assessment

Last week, Kyong purchased 8 potted plants for \$10.80. Today, she spent \$20.25. If the cost per plant is proportional, what proportion could you use to determine the number of plants that Kyong purchased today? Solve the proportion.
*Possible proportion*: $\frac{8}{10.80} = \frac{p}{20.25}$; 15 plants

**▶ Exercise 5** Have students choose a country and look up the conversion rates for a U.S. dollar and that country's currency in the newspaper. You might even ask them to research why the "price" of foreign currencies might go up or down with respect to the dollar.

**▶ Exercise 6** To solve by scaling up, students must figure out what number to multiply 8 by to get 136. In general, scaling from the ratio $a : b$ to the ratio $x : c$ (where $x$ is unknown), leads to a missing factor exercise: $b$ multiplied by what number equals $c$. The missing factor is always $c \div b$. Once a student knows how to solve the exercise, the calculator makes doing it routine. Still, you may want to point out that sometimes it is not necessary to use a calculator. In the present case of 8 times what number = 136, a guess-check-and-improve strategy works quite nicely. For example, students could first try 10 for the missing factor, calculating $8 \cdot 10 = 80$ and $136 - 80 = 56$. Since $8 \cdot 7 = 56$, students could write $8 \cdot (10 + 7) = 8 \cdot 17 = 136$. Then students can multiply 17 by 3 to find the number of containers with blue paint.

***Share & Summarize***

Students may be reluctant to redo a exercise they have already done. Point out that some methods are easier to use on one kind of exercise than on another. Consider this example:

Ponytail holders have a sales price of 4 for $7. Melinda has $56 and wants to buy as many as she can to give as gifts. How many ponytail holders can she buy?

It is easy to solve this exercise by writing and scaling ratios, $\frac{4}{7} = \frac{x}{56}$, but is not so easy to find the unit rate or solve an equation.

## Investigation 3

***On Your Own Exercises***
Pages 522–529
Exercises 7, 18, 19, 21–23

**Proportions** Begin by introducing the vocabulary term *proportion*: a proportion is an equation stating that two ratios are equal.

5. $6.76; Possible explanation: If $n$ is the number of dollars equivalent to 10 euros, then $\frac{50}{74} = \frac{n}{10}$.
$\frac{50}{74} = \frac{n}{10}$
$\frac{500}{74} = n$
$6.76 \approx n$

6. 51; The ratio of blue containers to all containers is $\frac{3}{8}$, so we need to find an equivalent ratio in the form "something to 136." Multiplying both parts of the ratio by 17 gives $\frac{3 \cdot 17}{8 \cdot 17} = \frac{51}{136}$.

**5.** Justin and his parents went to Ireland during his winter break. Before they left, Justin exchanged some money for euros. In exchange for $50 U.S., he received 74 euros. He returned with 10 euros.

If the exchange rate is still the same, how many dollars will he receive for his euros?

**6.** First-Rate Paint wants to make a large batch of the shade below. The final batch must have 136 containers of blue and yellow paints. How many containers of blue paint will be needed?

***Share & Summarize***

Choose one exercise from Exercises 3–6. Solve it using a different method than the one you previously used. Explain each step clearly enough that someone from another class could understand what you did. Answers will vary.

## Investigation 3 Solve Proportions

**Vocabulary**

proportion

You have solved many exercises involving equal ratios. An equation that states that two ratios are equal is called a **proportion**.

$$2:3 = 10:15 \quad \text{or} \quad \frac{n}{25} = \frac{3}{15}$$

One of the solution methods you used in Exercises 3–6 on pages 509 and 510 involved writing and solving a proportion. This method is useful for solving many different situations.



### *Troubleshooting*

Students need to be comfortable with at least one way of solving rate exercises. If they are having difficulty using a particular method, encourage them to find an alternative way of solving the exercise. Since scaling up isn't always easy to do, given the numbers, you may want them to use unit rates to solve the On Your Own Exercises. Also, since they will be solving proportions using equations in the next investigation, it might be worthwhile for them to preview this method in at least one of these exercises so that they have some practice in working with equations.

## Example

Malik saw a photograph of Vincent van Gogh's famous painting *Starry Night* in a book about art history. The book stated that the actual painting is 73.7 centimeters high, but it did not give the width.

**Real-World Link**

The Dutch artist Vincent van Gogh (1853–1890) was a painter for only the last ten years of his life. Many of his famous works show motion through the use of swirling patterns of color.

73.7 cm

*x* cm

The Museum of Modern Art, New York/Art Resource, NY

Malik decided to measure the photograph and calculate the painting's length. The photograph measured 6.9 centimeters high and 8.6 centimeters wide.

Since the photograph is a scaled version of the painting, the dimensions of the painting are multiplied by the same number to get the dimensions of the photograph.

That means that the photograph's $\frac{\text{height}}{\text{length}}$ ratio is a scaled height-to-length ratio for the painting. Since the two ratios are equivalent, Malik set up this proposition.

**Actual dimensions** ⟶ $\frac{73.7}{x} = \frac{6.9}{8.6}$ ⟵ **Photo dimensions**

To find $x$, he solved his equation.

$\frac{73.7}{x} = \frac{6.9}{8.6}$

$\frac{73.7}{x} = 0.8$ Divide 6.9 by 8.6.

$73.7 = 0.8x$ Multiply both sides by $x$.

$92.1 \approx x$ Divide both sides by 0.8.

Malik concluded that the real painting's length must be about 92.1 centimeters.



## Example

This Example starts with a concrete situation, a photograph of van Gogh's painting Starry Night. It shows how to set up an appropriate proportion and then solve that proportion.

The solution to this example again illustrates the power and beauty of algebra. Once students have learned and understood a few rather simple rules such as "do the same thing to both sides," they can use the machinery of algebra to find the solution.

You may want to point out that, when solving the proportion $\frac{73.7}{x} = \frac{6.9}{8.6}$, the equals sign in the top row changes to an approximately equals sign in the fourth row since the solution has many decimal places. Generally speaking, at this stage, it is probably not a good idea to insist that students be very careful about the correct use of these two signs; you should make students aware of the different meanings of the two signs but give them considerable latitude in using them.

## Troubleshooting

When solving proportions, students often find it challenging that their proportion is not necessarily the one in the text or answer, yet they found the same solution. It is important to show the students that there are many ways to write an equivalent proportion. The key is to check that each ratio is set up in the same way.

## Develop & Understand: A

*Suggested Grouping: Individuals*

These exercises offer opportunities for students to practice setting up and solving proportions. Some students may prefer other methods; have them solve the exercises with their methods and by setting up proportions, showing the steps of their work in each case. This will help them become comfortable with proportions and help them see that certain methods can be more convenient in some situations than others. It may also help them see why each method works.

▶ **Exercise 2** You might want to point out that this is somewhat idealized. Banks typically charge service fees of various kinds for exchanging foreign currencies, and these fees may not be proportional to the amount being exchanged. Still, the calculation probably gives a reasonable approximation to what Nailah might have received for her Australian dollars.

**Wrap-Up** Have volunteers write the proportion they used to solve Exercises 2 and 3 on the board. Then have them show how they solved the proportion.

## Develop & Understand: B

*Suggested Grouping: Individuals*

The instructions say to use any method to solve these exercises, but you should encourage students to use a variety of methods as they go through these exercises. Ask them to write down which method they used for each exercise.

▶ **Exercise 4b** You may want to point out that while it might take only $9\frac{1}{3}$ cans of paint for 140 feet of fence, you will probably have to buy 10 cans.

1a. Possible answer: It doesn't matter whether the ratios are $\frac{\text{length}}{\text{height}}$ or $\frac{\text{height}}{\text{length}}$, as long as they are equivalent.

2a. Possible answers: $\frac{50}{56.61} = \frac{72}{x}$, $\frac{56.61}{50} = \frac{x}{72}$, $\frac{50}{72} = \frac{56.61}{x}$, $\frac{72}{50} = \frac{x}{56.61}$

3. Possible proportion: $\frac{1}{5} = \frac{x}{32.5}$; 6.5 h

## Develop & Understand: A

1. Maya suggested to Malik that he could have used a different proportion.

$$\frac{x}{73.7} = \frac{8.6}{6.9}$$

   a. Explain why Maya's proportion is also correct.

   b. Solve Maya's proportion. Do you think it is easier or more difficult to solve than Malik's proportion? See margin.

2. Consider this situation.

   In January 2008, Aaron went to the bank and exchanged 50 Australian dollars for 56.61 U.S. dollars. Later that day, Nailah went to the same bank to exchange 72 Australian dollars for U.S. dollars. How many U.S. dollars did she receive?

   a. Set up two proportions you could use to solve this situation.

   b. Solve one of your proportions. How much money in U.S. dollars did Nailah receive? About $81.52

3. Augustin earns $5 per hour mowing lawns. He wants to buy two DVDs that cost a total of $32.50. Set up and solve a proportion to determine how many hours he needs to work to earn enough money.

By now, you probably have several strategies for solving exercises involving proportional relationships and equal ratios. Now you will have a chance to practice these strategies.

## Develop & Understand: B

**Solve these exercises using any method you like.**

4. This ratio table shows the number of cans of paint needed to cover various lengths of fence.

| Cans of Paint | 2 | 4 | 6 | 8 | 10 | 12 |
|---|---|---|---|---|---|---|
| Feet of Fence | 30 | 60 | 90 | 120 | 150 | 180 |

   a. Find the number of cans needed to paint 75 feet of fence. 5

   b. Find the number of cans needed to paint 140 feet of fence. $9\frac{1}{3}$

5. The Holmes family has two adults and three children. The family uses an average of 1,400 gallons of water per week. Last month, two houseguests stayed for a week. Assuming that the water usage is proportional to the number of people in the house, about how much water did the household use during the guests' visit? 1,960 gal



### Reaching All Learners

**BL Beyond Level** Have students check their answers to Exercises 2 and 3 by writing and solving a different proportion.

**Additional Answer**

1b. $\frac{x}{73.7} = \frac{8.6}{6.9}$

$\frac{x}{73.7} = 1.25$ Simplify.

$x \approx 92.1$ Multiply both sides by 73.7.

Possible answer: Maya's proportion is easier because it requires fewer steps.

6. The week before Thanksgiving, turkeys are on sale for \$1.29 per pound at the EatMore grocery store. How much will a 14-pound turkey cost? \$18.06

7. Alvin is using a trail map to plan a hiking trip. The scale indicates that $\frac{1}{2}$ inch on the map represents $1\frac{1}{2}$ miles. Alvin chooses a trail that is about $5\frac{1}{2}$ inches long on the map. How long is the actual trail? 16.5 mi

8. Viviana loves mixed nuts. The local farmer's market sells a mix for \$2.79 per pound. How many pounds can she buy for \$10.85? About 3.9

9. Joe is making his popular waffles for Sunday brunch. He knows that five waffles usually feed two people. If he wants to serve 11 people, how many waffles should he make? 28

10. At Camp Maple Leaf, there are two counselors for every 15 campers. The camp directors expect 75 campers next summer. How many counselors will they need? 10

**Share & Summarize**

Did you use the same strategy for solving all of the exercises in this investigation? If so, explain it. If not, choose one of the strategies you used and explain it. Answers will vary.

▶ **Exercise 7** It may be helpful for students to see several different versions of the proper proportion. This will reaffirm to the students that there are many ways to solve the problem and it makes a great teaching moment to show why the different proportions all result in the same solution.

▶ **Exercise 9** The mathematical answer to this proportion is 27.5, and this may confuse students when they see that the correct answer is 28 waffles. Discuss with the students that 27.5 is not correct in the context of the problem because you cannot make half a waffle.

**Wrap-Up** It is important for students to see that the same situation can be represented by different proportions. For example, any situation that can be represented as $\frac{a}{b} = \frac{c}{d}$ can also be represented as $\frac{b}{a} = \frac{d}{c}$. Notice that in the second proportion both sides of the first proportion have been inverted. However, it is crucial that students invert both sides of the proportion.

**Share & Summarize**

The exercise asks students to explain their solutions. You cannot overemphasize the importance of such communication skills: it is often important, particularly in day-to-day situations, to be able to explain your solution to other people, and convince them you are right. Use this opportunity to compare and contrast the different methods that students used to solve the exercises.

**On the Spot Assessment**

Ask students to justify their answers to Exercise 9. It is possible to make one half of a waffle on some waffle irons, but students should question whether or not Joe would want to serve one different waffle.

**Lesson 10.2** Proportions and Similarity 513

# Investigation 4

***On Your Own Exercises***
Pages 522–529
Exercises 8–10, 20, 24, 25

**GPS** Global Positioning Systems have become very popular. They can be found in many new cars with features that include turn by turn directions, to locating a specific restaurant. They are also found in sports such as fishing to help find spots in lakes or rivers that have specific geographical markers. Airplanes also use GPS to plan their routes. All of these systems use a complex mathematical process of triangulation with the assistance of satellites for additional information.

### Think & Discuss

*Suggested Grouping: Pairs*

Students studied stretching and shrinking machines earlier, so it may be prudent to have a group brainstorming session prior to beginning the Think & Discuss to assist the students with recalling how stretching and shrinking occurs.

### Explore

When working on this task, it will be interesting to see if students choose to make their measurements in centimeters or inches. Either one will work, but make sure to ask why the pairs chose the units they did. Also, in terms of a point of reference for the computer responses, it will be helpful if you give the students some internet sites where they can look for reliable information about the distances.

# Investigation 4 Map Scales

**Vocabulary**

**map scale**

① You can shrink something by dividing by a number greater than 1 or by multiplying by a fraction less than 1.

② Answers will vary. Responses should include ratios of the length of the walls of the room to the length of the sides of a piece of paper.

③ Answers will vary depending on the chosen cities. More detailed maps are more likely to result in closer estimates.

④ Possible answer: The size of the map; a detailed map with a lesser map scale ratio will produce more accuracy than a larger map

A global positioning system, or GPS, is a device that can easily fit in your hand but provides a great deal of information about exactly where you are. You could also use a map to determine where you are in the world or in your own neighborhood.

### Think & Discuss

Maps are drawn accurately by taking the actual distances of features on Earth and shrinking them.

Thinking back to stretching and shrinking machines, what are two different ways you can shrink a number? See ①.

Suppose you wanted to make a map of your room, and it needed to fit on a regular sheet of paper. How much would you need to shrink your room's dimensions? See ②.

In this investigation, you will use several strategies for finding the distance between two locations. These strategies include using a **map scale** and equivalent ratios to estimate the distance between two cities.

### Explore

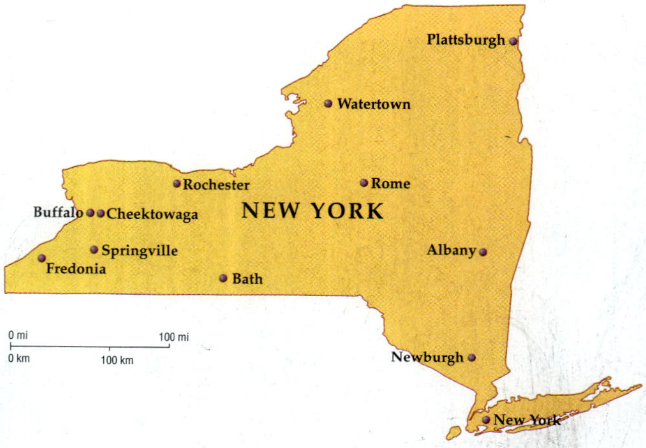

With a partner, measure the distance between three pairs of cities. Use the map scale to determine an estimate of the actual distance. Look up the actual distance between each pair of cities using the Internet. How close were your estimates? See ③.

What factors do you think might affect your estimate? See ④.



### On the Spot Assessment

A scale on a map is 0.5 inches = 150 kilometers. If the actual distance from Buffalo to White Plains is 638 kilometers, how many inches is that on a map? About $2\frac{1}{8}$ in.

Suppose a map scale shows that 1 inch is equal to 150 miles in real life.

**Map Key**

0 mi — 150 mi

You measure and find that the distance between two cities is about $3\frac{1}{4}$ inches. One way to determine actual miles is to use a ratio table.

| **Map Distance (in.)** | $\frac{1}{4}$ | $\frac{1}{2}$ | 1 | 2 | 3 | $3\frac{1}{4}$ |
|---|---|---|---|---|---|---|
| **Actual Distance (mi)** | 37.5 | 75 | 150 | 300 | 450 | 487.5 |

So, the estimated distance between the two cities in real life is about 488 miles.

In addition to ratio tables, proportions can also be used to estimate distances. Consider the following example.

### *Example*

The Chang family is planning the route for its annual vacation. The Changs are using a map with a scale of 1 inch equal to 50 miles. On the map, the roundtrip route measures 6.5 inches. Mrs. Chang sets up and solves a proportion to estimate the actual distance.

$$\frac{1\text{ in.}}{6.5\text{ in.}} = \frac{50\text{ mi}}{x\text{ mi}}$$ Set up a proportion.

$$\frac{1}{6.5} = \frac{50}{x}$$ Divide out common units.

$$\left(\frac{6.5x}{1}\right)\left(\frac{1}{6.5}\right) = \left(\frac{6.5x}{1}\right)\left(\frac{50}{x}\right)$$ Multiply each side by the common denominator, $6.5x$.

$$x = 325$$ Simplify.

The Chang family trip will be about 325 miles.

## Develop & Understand: A

**Use your knowledge of ratio and proportion to find the following distances.**

1. Douglas is helping his dad plan a trip from their house across town to his Uncle Warren's house. The city map scale shows that 0.5 inch is equal to 3 miles. After measuring streets and turns carefully, Douglas estimated the distance to be about 4.5 inches. How far does Douglas live from his Uncle Warren? About 27 miles



**Analyze the Table** Discuss with the students what the rows and columns of the table represent. It is important for students to see that the top row represents measurements for the distance on a map and the bottom row represents the actual distance between the cities. What does not always have to be the same is how the proportion is set up to solve for a distance. The key is that each ratio of the proportion must compare the information in exactly the same way. When the information is in table form, if a pattern can be found between the values, this can be used to assist in completing the table and will save time from writing and solving several proportions.

### Example

There are other ways to solve the proportion and students may see that. This is a great opportunity to let the students ask questions and show them alternatives, such as cross multiplication. Often times, students find that there is only one way to solve a math problem.

## Develop & Understand: A

*Suggested Grouping: Pairs*

▶ **Exercise 1** Discuss with students how they think the table should be completed. Guide students to see that the map distance needs to go from 0.5 inches to 4.5 inches, this can be done either by half inches or whole inches. Once they decide how to proceed, they can begin setting up their proportion.

## *Troubleshooting*

Watch for students who are trying to complete tables using the pattern without ever setting up a proportion. At times, students will make assumptions regarding data in table form and not ever use a proportion to solve. While this shows great use of mental math abilities, it can hurt them if they make assumptions without using the proportion to confirm their results. Stress that they should use a proportion once, and then they can use the pattern that they find.

**Lesson 10.2** Proportions and Similarity **515**

▶ **Exercise 2a** Encourage students to set up a proportion using the given column of information and find the actual distance that corresponds to 1 cm on the map. Now if the students see the pattern, they can complete the table. Otherwise, show them that the original ratio remains and they only need to change the value of the map distance and solve for the actual distance.

▶ **Exercise 2b** In order to answer this part of the question, the students will take the value from the last column of the table and multiply it by the rate. This is the use of the formula distance = rate × time. This is a formula that students will see very often in their mathematical careers.

▶ **Exercises 3 and 4** Students can set the proportion up in many different ways. Students who compare answers may become concerned if their work is not the same and yet they get the same solution.

**Wrap-Up** Once students complete the exercise set on their own, have the students pair up and share their results. Then have the pairs form small groups and share their results. Ask the students to share some of the things that they did differently from their classmates.

### Share & Summarize

These questions will get the students thinking about the reasons we use scales on maps. In addition, the students' responses will give insight into how well they truly understand what they have been working on.

**Use your knowledge of ratio and proportion to find the following distances.**

**2.** Jessica wants to know about how far she lives from her grandmother. She is using a map that has a scale of 2 cm = 70 km. Jessica found the distance from her house to her grandmother's house to be about 5 centimeters.

   **a.** How far does Jessica live from her grandmother? 175 km

   **b.** Jessica will be traveling by bus to her grandmother's house. Suppose the bus travels at an average speed of 30 kilometers per hour. How long will the trip take, not including scheduled stops for gasoline and food? About 6 hours

**3.** Marquell drew a map that shows the bus route from her house to her school. She used a scale of 2 centimeters equal to 1 mile. Marquell measured the bus route distance as 9 centimeters. What is the actual distance from Marquell's house to the school? 4.5 mi

**4.** The Johnsons planned their trip to the annual family reunion using a map with a scale of 1 inch equal to 25 miles. Measuring carefully, Mr. Johnson estimated the distance to be 12.5 inches. How far will the Johnsons travel on their trip? About 313 mi

**5.** To compete in a debate, the school debate team traveled 50 miles. Using a map, Joaquin measured the trip distance as 2.5 inches. On the map, how many miles did 1 inch represent? 20 mi

### Real-World Link

Travel on the ocean is measured in *nautical miles*. Travel on land is measured in *statute miles*. A statute mile is equal to 5,280 feet. A nautical mile is equal to 6,080 feet, or one minute of arc of a great circle of Earth.

① The map scale is the ratio of the distance on paper to the actual distance in real life. The distance has to be shrunk to fit on a piece of paper that is manageable to carry.

### Share & Summarize

Reading and interpreting maps are two important skills. Explain what the map scale represents to someone who has not used a map. See ①.

One map shows a distance of 1.5 inches between two cities. Another map shows a distance of 2 inches between the same two cities. Can both be correct? Explain. Yes, both can be correct. The scale is different between the two maps. The map with 2 inches between the cities may show a smaller area.



### Reaching All Learners

**BL Beyond Level** Ask students to think of other places where a scaled picture would be useful. Have the students research and find examples on the internet and share what they find with the class.

516 CHAPTER 10 Proportional Reasoning and Percents

# Investigation 5 Similarity

Did you ever wonder how people measure the width of the Grand Canyon or the height of a giant Sequoia tree? Clearly, measurements like these cannot be made with a ruler or yardstick. Measurements of very large or very small objects or distances are often made indirectly, by using proportions.

### Explore

Zach and Jin Lee are on the decorating committee for their town's Independence Day parade. They plan to hang balloons on the streetlights along the parade route. First, they want to determine how tall the streetlights are so they can find ladders of the right size.

It is late afternoon, and Zach notices that everything is casting long shadows. This gives him an idea.

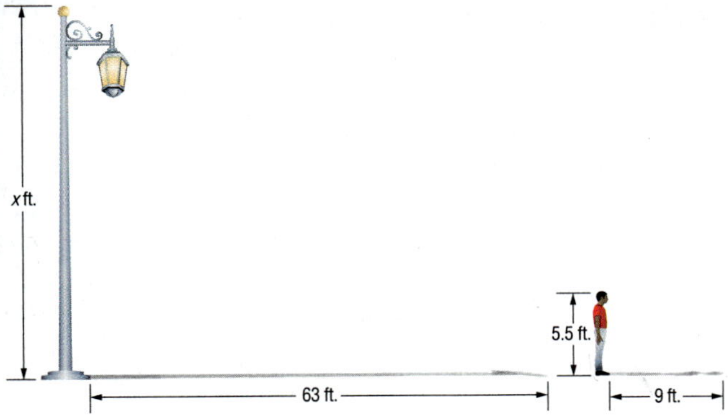


Zach asks Jin Lee to measure his shadow. She finds that it is about 9 feet long. Using a tape measure, Zach finds that the streetlight's shadow is about 63 feet long.

Zach says, "I know that my height is 5.5 feet. Since the sunlight is coming at me and the pole from the same angle, I have two similar triangles. I can figure out how tall the streetlight is!"

- What are Zach's similar triangles? Make a sketch if it helps you think about this. See ① in margin.
- How do you know Zach's triangles are similar? See ②.
- How can you use the triangles to find the height of the streetlight? See ③ in margin.
- How tall is the streetlight? About 39 ft

② These triangles are similar because they have two pairs of corresponding angles with the same measure: the right angle and the angles from the tip of the shadow to the sun.



### Additional Answers

1. The sides of one triangle are the streetlight, its shadow, and the segment from the top of the light to the tip of the shadow. The other triangle's sides are Zach, his shadow, and the segment from the top of Zach to the tip of his shadow.

3. Possible answer: I can set up and solve this proportion:

$$\frac{\text{light's height}}{\text{Zach's height}} = \frac{\text{length of light's shadow}}{\text{length of Zach's shadow}}$$

$$\frac{x}{5.5} = \frac{63}{9}$$

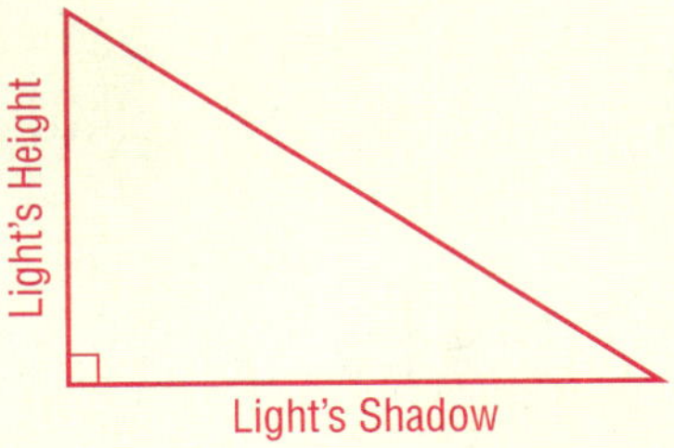


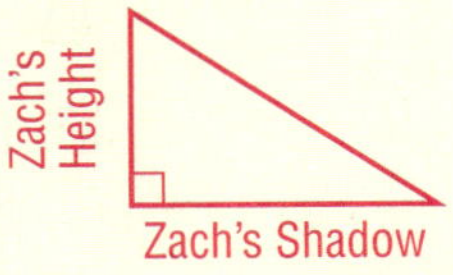


## Investigation 5

**On Your Own Exercises**
Pages 522–529
Exercises 11–13, 26–27

**Similarity** Introduce the investigation by asking students how they would measure the height of a tall tree. Point out that it is not always physically possible to make some measurements. Sometimes the measures must be made indirectly using proportions.

You may wish to make a transparency of Lesson 10.2 Master 1 to use while discussing the Explore and the exercises that follow. Students can use the master to make triangles and measure their sides to prove that the triangles are similar, but this is not essential to their solving the exercises.

### Explore

Make sure students understand that both the street lamp's and Zach's shadows are created by the sun, not by the streetlight.

Draw students' attention to Zach's remark: "Since the sunlight is coming at me and the pole from the same angle, I have two similar triangles." Make sure students appreciate that both objects are perpendicular to the ground.

Then have students work with a partner to answer the questions. Once they have completed the exercises, discuss their answers as a class.

As an extension, you may want to discuss the science behind the application. The shadows form sides of similar triangles because the sun is so far away. When its rays hit the earth, they are, for all practical purposes, parallel. That is why the angle the sun's rays make with the top of the streetlight and the top of the boy are equal, and that, in turn, is why the two triangles are similar. You might also note that, if the light source is close by, then the two triangles would not be similar. One way to see this is to have your students note that at a given time during the day their sun-shadows don't change in length as they move about. But at night, their shadows do change in length as they move closer to or further away from a light source, like a streetlight.

## Develop & Understand: A

*Suggested Grouping: Pairs*

▶ **Exercises 5 and 6** These exercises raise some issues pertaining to how the units related to the numbers in a proportion are connected. In these exercises, students use ratios that compare lengths to lengths to solve a proportion relating the height of the tree with the height of the ruler. One possible proportion that can be used to find the height of the tree is $\frac{n \text{ ft}}{12 \text{ in.}} = \frac{24.5 \text{ ft}}{4.75 \text{ in.}}$

But in many other cases, ratios compare amounts with very different units. For example, if 3 pounds of potatoes cost $1.00, to find the cost of 10 pounds of potatoes, we can set up the proportion $\frac{3 \text{ lb}}{\$1} = \frac{10 \text{ lb}}{\$n}$. In this example, both of the top numbers are in pounds and both of the bottom numbers are in dollars. However, as long as the units in a proportion are in comparable positions, the proportion is correct. The proportion $\frac{3 \text{ lb}}{10 \text{ lb}} = \frac{\$1}{\$n}$ is also an acceptable way to solve the exercise. In this proportion, the values relating to the small bag are the top numbers and the values relating to the large bag are the bottom numbers. However, $\frac{3 \text{ lb}}{\$1} = \frac{\$n}{10 \text{ lb}}$ is not correct because the units are not in comparable positions.

Students should also understand that related values in a proportion need to be expressed with the same units. So if one unit is in dollars, the related unit should also be in dollars, not in cents. For example, in the potato exercise above, it would not make sense to set up the proportion as $\frac{3 \text{ lb}}{\$1} = \frac{10 \text{ lb}}{n \text{ cents}}$ because the comparable bottom numbers are not expressed in the same unit.

## Share & Summarize

Students need to understand in Exercise 1 that corresponding sides are proportional if and only if the triangles are similar. In the shadow exercises, sometimes it is easy to see the correspondence between sides. In other situations, the correspondence may need to be stated. It is important for students to be able to verbalize the process for setting up the proportion in Exercise 2. Make sure that they are clear about how to match the corresponding sides.

## Develop & Understand: A

Jin Lee likes Zach's method of using shadows to find heights. She shows her grandfather how to find the height of the tree in his yard.

She measures the length of the tree's shadow and finds it is 24.5 feet long. Then she holds a 12-inch ruler perpendicular to the ground and finds that it casts a 4.75-inch shadow.

**1.** Draw and label a simple sketch of the situation. See margin.

**2.** Describe two similar triangles Jin Lee can use to find the tree's height. See margin.

**3.** Set up a proportion Jin Lee could solve to find the tree's height. See margin.

**4.** How tall is the tree? About 62 ft

**5.** When Jin Lee found the tree's height, she thought all the measurements should be in the same unit. So, she converted everything to inches.

Her grandfather asked her, "Could you have left inches as inches and feet as feet and still found the correct answer?" Explain why the answer to his question is yes. See margin.

**6.** Later, Jin Lee and Zach set up this proportion.

$$\frac{1 \text{ ft}}{n \text{ ft}} = \frac{4.75 \text{ in.}}{24.5 \text{ ft}}$$

They found that the tree was only about 5 feet tall. What did they do incorrectly?

6. They mixed up the units within the "ruler triangle," giving the ruler's height in feet but the length of the ruler's shadow in inches. So, one of the ratios in their proportion compares feet to feet and the other compares inches to feet.

### Share & Summarize

**1.** When setting up a proportion involving two triangles, why is it important for the triangles to be similar?

**2.** The rope on the flagpole at school has frayed and snapped, and a dog ran off with part of it. The principal wants to buy a new rope, but she does not know how tall the pole is.

Write a paragraph explaining to the principal the method of indirect measurement used in this investigation. Make your explanation as complete as you can so she could use it to find the height of the pole. See margin.

1. To set up a correct proportion, the ratios between the side lengths of the triangles must be equivalent. That means the triangles have to be similar.



**See page 555A for answers to Exercises 1, 2, 3, 5, Share & Summarize, Exercise 2.**

Inquiry

# Investigation 6 Estimate Heights of Tall Objects

### Vocabulary

angle of elevation

### Materials

- protractor
- string or thread
- weight (paper clip or cube)
- tape (optional)
- tape measure, yardstick, or meterstick

In this investigation, you will estimate the height of a tall object without actually measuring it. First, you will need to measure the angle of elevation.

The **angle of elevation** is the angle made by the imaginary horizontal segment extending from your eye to an object and the imaginary segment from your eye to the top of the object.

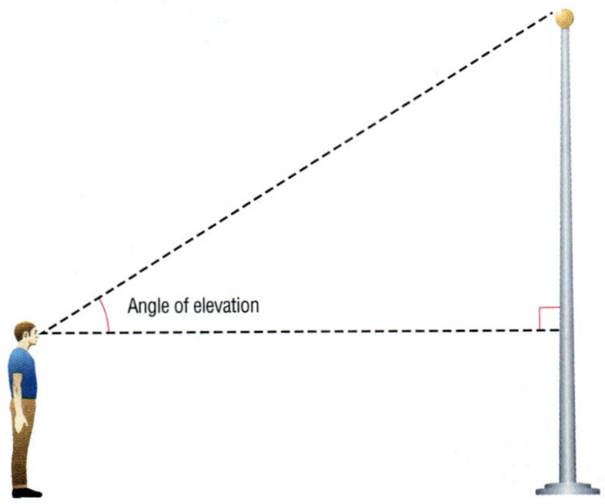


First, assemble your measurement instrument. Tie a piece of string to a protractor at the middle of the straight side. Attach a weight to the string. Now you are ready to measure the angle of elevation.

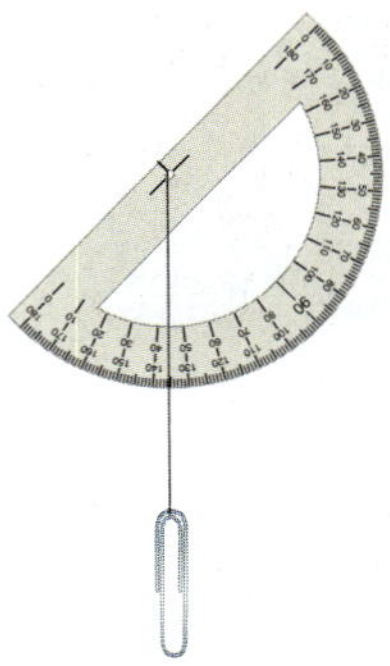

Go on



Inquiry

Inquiry

## Investigation 6

*Suggested Grouping: Pairs or Small Groups*

Students estimate the height of an object using the angle of elevation. They make a measurement tool and use it to collect data needed to make their estimates. You can decide what object students will measure before class or allow students to make suggestions and vote for what object they will measure. If you cannot take the students outside to estimate the height of a tree, flagpole, or other tall object, you can have them measure the height of a wall.

### Materials and Preparation

Have students work in pairs or small groups so they can help one another in making the instrument needed to measure the angle of elevation and in actually making the measurements. Provide one set of materials for each group if possible.

Each group should have the following materials:

- protractor
- string or thread
- weight, such as paper clip or cube
- tape measure, yardstick, or meter stick
- tape (optional)

In earlier investigations, students were given data and asked to use the data in their calculations. In this investigation, students actually work with real materials and tools to collect their own real data. In short, they will have to confront the exercises of gathering and interpreting real, rather than prepared, data.

The text defines the term *angle of elevation*, a useful and important term that may be more easily understood by just drawing some pictures and pointing to the appropriate angles.

The lab begins by having students construct a device for measuring angles of elevation, using a protractor, string, and a weight.

After students make their measurement instruments, you might want to tell them that the string with the weight attached is called a *plumb line*. Now note that the measure of the angle of elevation of any object is always exactly 90° less than the measure of the angle between the sight line and the *vertical* plumb line.

## Collect Your Data

Each student in the pair or group should make a sighting to get the angle of elevation, and the team should record the results. Students should be clear from the very outset that the purpose of making these measurements is to enable them to make a scale drawing of the situation.

## Sketch the Situation

To draw the scaled version of the right triangle in Exercise 5, all students need to know is the measure of one of the acute angles. That, along with the length of one of the legs, is precisely what the students have just measured.

Some students may record the angle incorrectly or not understand which angle they are measuring. You may need to review how to use a protractor with these students. If necessary, help them see how to use their measurements to draw a similar triangle. You can use the steps below to guide them through the process:

1. Draw a right angle.
2. Pick a point somewhere along the ray of the angle.
3. Measure the acute angle from the chosen point and draw a segment to form an angle with that measure.
4. Extend the segment until it crosses the other ray that is part of the right angle.

Students should discover that they can easily measure all the parts of the scaled triangle, including the vertical side that corresponds to the unknown (tree, tower, or whatever) in the "real world" triangle. They use the relationship to find the height in the next set of questions.

Inquiry

Select a position at some distance from the object your class will be measuring. Line up the straight side of your protractor with an imaginary line from your eye to the top of the object. On the drawing below, the top of the object from the person's point of view is labeled point *E*. Hold the protractor close to your eye.

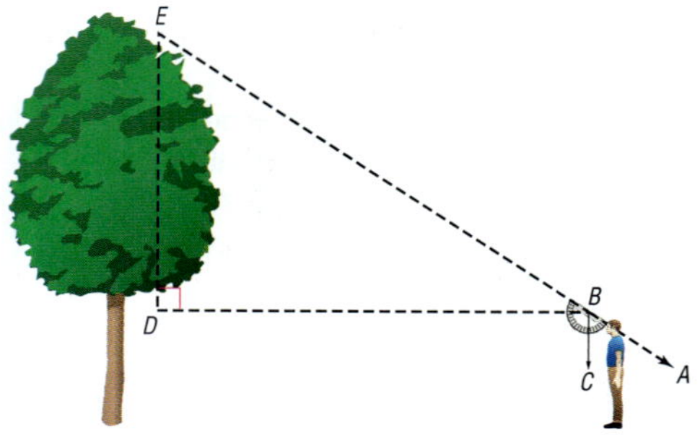


## Collect Your Data Answers will vary.

1. Look at angle *ABC* in the drawing. It is formed by the imaginary line through the top of the object and your eye and the line made by the string. Read the measure of this angle from your protractor. Record it.
2. Now measure the distance from the object to your position. This is side *DB* in the drawing above. You might need to mark where you are standing. Or, have a partner measure the distance while you remain standing where you are.

**Math Link**
In *similar triangles,* corresponding angles have the same measures.

## Sketch the Situation Answers will vary.

3. Make a sketch similar to the one on the previous page that represents your situation. Include the same labels for the important points. Label any lengths or angle measures you know.
4. You measured angle *ABC* with your device. Use that measurement to calculate the measure of angle *DBE,* which is the angle of elevation.
5. Use your protractor to draw a triangle similar to triangle *BDE.* Measure the sides of your triangle. Label your drawing with the side lengths.

## Calculate the Height

You can use the triangle you drew for Question 5 to find the object's height.

6. Answers will vary.
7. I need to add the distance from my eye to the ground. Heights will vary.

**6.** Set up and solve a proportion to calculate the length of side *DE*.

**7.** Notice in your diagram that the length of side *DE* is not the height of the object. What is the last thing you need to do to find the height of the object? What is the object's height?

**8.** Compare the height you found with the heights your classmates determined. How close are they? What might account for any differences? Answers will vary.

## What Did You Learn?

**9.** Describe in your own words how you can use the angle of elevation to find the height of a tall object. Be sure to explain how similar triangles help. See margin.

### Additional Answer

9. Possible answer: Using the angle of elevation and the right angle formed by the ground and the object, draw a triangle similar to the one that has these sides: from your eye to the top of the object; from your eye to the object, parallel to the ground; and from the object at the height of your eye to the top of the object. By measuring the distance from your eye to the object and the lengths in a similar triangle you draw, you can set up a proportion:

$$\frac{x}{\text{distance from object}} = \frac{\text{height of similar triangle}}{\text{base of similar triangle}}$$

Solve the proportion, and add the distance from your eye to the ground to the result.

Inquiry

## Calculate the Height

In Exercise 7, students are reminded that they still need to compensate for the height of their eye above the ground.

Exercise 8 provides an opportunity to do a statistical analysis of students' answers. If you choose to do this as a class activity, consider the following:

- Encourage the students not to compare answers with their partners or group members before submitting them to allow them to analyze the entire data set objectively. Calculation errors can be used to illustrate the concept of outliers, as discussed in the following bulleted section. Have volunteers prepare a list of all the calculated heights so that you can share them with everyone in the class.
- If there are any answers that are way off from the majority, you might define the term *outlier* and discuss how such outliers might occur, whether such data should be disregarded, or perhaps re-measured.

Presumably even those answers that are reasonably close to each other will differ somewhat. Try to get as complete a listing as possible of where and how errors might have crept into the data or the calculations. It will help if students have kept good records of all the various data they have collected or calculated, for example, their original angle measurements, the distance on the ground, and the various distances in the scale drawing.

Now raise the question of how to get the best *single* answer. Some students will probably suggest averaging. Opinions may differ about using the mean, the mode, or the median.

## What Did You Learn?

You might have groups prepare posters or brief presentations of their answers to Exercise 9 to share with other groups.

Finally, if the object you selected for study has a height that is actually known (e.g., some tower, the roof of the school, etc.) you might have students check the results of their investigation against the "true" figure.

## On Your Own Exercises
Lesson 10.2

**Investigation 1**
Pages 505–507
Practice & Apply: 1–3
Connect & Extend: 14–15

**Investigation 2**
Pages 508–510
Practice & Apply: 4–6
Connect & Extend: 16–17

**Investigation 3**
Pages 510–513
Practice & Apply: 7
Connect & Extend: 18, 19, 21–23

**Investigation 4**
Pages 514–516
Practice & Apply: 8–10
Connect & Extend: 20, 24, 25

**Investigation 5**
Pages 517–518
Practice & Apply: 11–13
Connect & Extend: 26–27

**Assign Anytime**
Mixed Review: 28–45

▶ **Exercises 1 and 2** These exercises are really straight forward proportions. Make sure to remind students to read the questions carefully, to make sure that they are using the proper information to set up their proportions.

▶ **Exercise 4** This question can easily be solved without using proportions. If students recognize this, they may not follow the directions. While this is not bad, stress to the students the importance of solving a problem according to the directions. Also praise them for recognizing that a proportion may not be necessary.

## On Your Own Exercises
Lesson 10.2

### Practice & Apply

1a. No; in the Itty Bitty Beads Package, it is $\frac{7}{20}$, or 0.35:1; in the Bead-U-T-ful Beads Package, it is $\frac{5}{15}$, or about 0.33:1.

1b. Yes; in the Itty Bitty Beads Package, it is $\frac{8}{20}$, or $\frac{2}{5}$; in the Bead-U-T-ful Beads Package, it is $\frac{6}{15}$, or $\frac{2}{5}$.

2. Yes; the ratio of red containers to all containers in Mixture A is $\frac{4}{6}$ and in Mixture B is $\frac{6}{9}$. These ratios are equivalent, so the number of red paint containers is proportional to the total number of containers.

3. Yes; the ratios of the entries in each column are the same. The number of miles is 40 times the number of gallons; the ratio of gallons to miles is 1:40.

**1.** The Huntsville Craft Shop sells two types of pre-packaged beads. Here are the contents.

| Itty Beady Beads | Bead-U-T-ful Beads |
|---|---|
| 8 oz red | 6 oz red |
| 7 oz white | 5 oz white |
| 5 oz blue | 4 oz blue |

**a.** Is the amount of white beads in each package proportional to the total ounces of beads? Why or why not?

**b.** Is the amount of red beads in each package proportional to the total ounces of beads? Why or why not?

**2.** Is the number of red paint containers in these two mixtures proportional to the total number of containers? Explain how you know.

**3.** **Ecology** A hybrid car will travel many miles on a gallon of gas by using a combination of electricity and gasoline for fuel. The table shows estimates of how far the car will travel on various amounts of gas.

| Gallons of Gas | 0.5 | 1 | 1.5 | 2 | 2.5 | 3 |
|---|---|---|---|---|---|---|
| Miles | 20 | 40 | 60 | 80 | 100 | 120 |

Are the miles traveled proportional to the gallons of gas? How do you know? If so, describe how they are related and write the ratio.

**4.** Set up a proportion for the following situation. Solve it using any method you choose.

Grant Middle School held a recycling drive to raise funds for the class trip to Washington, D.C. The recycling center will pay $1.20 per pound of aluminum. The school was paid $7.20 for the aluminum cans that were collected.

How many pounds of aluminum did the school recycle?

$\frac{1.20}{1} = \frac{7.20}{x}$

$1.20x = 7.20$

$x = 6$

They collected 6 pounds of aluminum.

On Your Own Exercises

**5.** Many schools have a recommended student : teacher ratio. At Quality Care Preschool, the ratio is 9 : 1. Next year, Quality Care expects enrollment to increase by 135 students. How many new teachers will need to be hired to maintain the student : teacher ratio? 15

6. $\frac{3}{4}$ C oats, $2\frac{1}{4}$ c flour, $\frac{1}{4}$ C cranberries, $\frac{3}{8}$ C butter, $\frac{15}{16}$ c water, 3 eggs, $\frac{3}{4}$ t salt, $\frac{3}{4}$ C sugar

7a. No; the ratio of girls to all students are $\frac{12}{20}$ and $\frac{14}{25}$, which are not equivalent.

**6.** Esperanza is following this recipe for cranberry oatmeal breakfast bars.

Just as Esperanza is preparing to mix the ingredients, she realizes she has only $\frac{1}{4}$ cup of cranberries, so she decides to make a smaller batch of breakfast bars. How much of each ingredient should she use?

**7.** One seventh-grade homeroom class has 20 students, 12 of which are girls. Another homeroom has 25 students, 14 of which are girls.

**a.** Do these two classes have the same proportion of girls? Explain how you know.

**b.** How many girls would have to be in a class of 25 students for it to have the same ratio of girls to students as the smaller class? 15

**8.** Using a map with a scale of 2 centimeters equal to 1 mile, Marcos measures the distance to his grandfather's house as 11 centimeters. Copy and complete the ratio table below to find the distance to Marcos' grandfather's house. See table.; 5.5 mi

| Map Distance (cm) | 2 | 3 | 4 | 5 | 6 | 7 | 8 | 9 | 10 | 11 |
|---|---|---|---|---|---|---|---|---|---|---|
| Actual Distance (mi) | 1 | 1.5 | 2 | 2.5 | 3 | 3.5 | 4 | 4.5 | 5 | 5.5 |

**9.** Confirm your answer to Exercise 8 by setting up and solving a proportion. $\frac{2 \text{ cm}}{11 \text{ cm}} = \frac{1 \text{ mi}}{x \text{ mi}}$; 5.5 mi

▶ **Exercise 5** Some students may think this exercise is impossible to solve, since they are only given the student: teacher ratio but not the actual number of students (or teachers) in the school. However, the important thing to note is that to preserve the 9 : 1 ratio, as you add more students, you have to add more teachers in the same 9 : 1 ratio.

▶ **Exercise 6** This exercise is straight forward proportions, but dealing with fractional values. What will cause the students difficulty is working with the fractions that cannot be used as a decimal. Students may understand the concept of proportions, but may struggle with the work involved with the fractions.

Remind students that dividing is the same as multiplying by the reciprocal. This adds an extra step to the work of solving a proportion, but it will make the numbers work easier for the students.

▶ **Exercise 10** Students may be confused as to what to write a proportion with, the cities or the locations on the map. If this happens, rephrase the question for the students and try to simplify the question.

▶ **Exercise 11** Encourage students who have difficulty organizing the data to first draw a picture of the situation.

On Your Own Exercises

**10.** Haylee has a map that measures $8\frac{1}{2}$ inches by 11 inches. Briartown is situated in the center of the map. Suppose the map scale is $\frac{3}{4}$ inches to 40 miles.

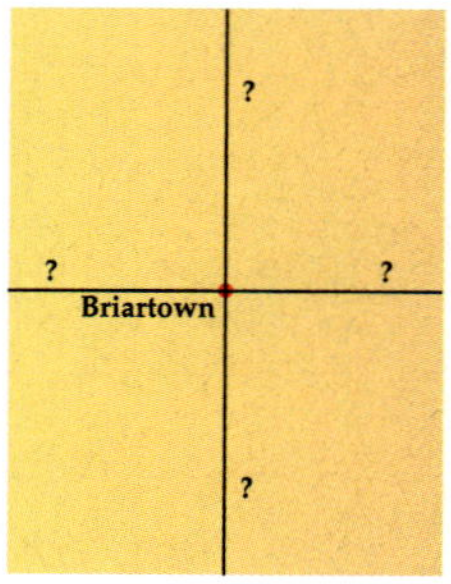


The following cities are the given distances from Briartown. Each city is situated due north, due south, due east, or due west.

**a.** Which cities could be on the same map as Briartown?

Riverside: 82 miles Yes

Morsetown: 287 miles Yes, just barely

Everton: 197 miles Yes

Greenwood: 177 miles Yes

Crestville: 431 miles No

Franklin: 299 miles No, it just misses.

**b.** Haylee wants to find a map with the same dimensions that will include Georgeville, which is 642 miles due south from Briartown. Is this possible? Explain your reasoning.

10a. Along the longer edge: maximum distance is $293\frac{1}{3}$ miles; Along the shorter edge: maximum distance is $226\frac{2}{3}$ miles

10b. Yes, she could find a map that also includes Georgeville. The scale would be greater, meaning the same distance on the map represents more miles.

**11.** A farmer wants to cut down three pine trees to use for a fence he is building. To decide which trees to cut, he wants to estimate their heights. He holds a 9-inch stick perpendicular to and touching the ground. He measures its shadow to be about 6 inches. If he wants to cut down trees that are about 40 feet tall, how long are the tree shadows? 26 ft to 27 ft

**12.** Booker is working on a layout for the school newspaper. He is using a unit of measure commonly used in publishing called a pica. The allotted space for a photograph is 10 picas by 15 picas. The photograph he wants to use is 8 inches by 10 inches. Are the allotted space and the photograph similar? Can Booker use the photograph for the layout?

12. Possible answer: No, the space and photograph are not proportional. 10:15 simplifies to 2:3, while 8:10 simplifies to 4:5. The only way Booker can use the photograph is to select a 2:3 section of the photograph that can be enlarged to fill the space.

524 CHAPTER 10 Proportional Reasoning and Percents

**13.** At 212 feet high, the tallest Ferris wheel in the United States is at Fair Park in Dallas, Texas. Suppose a man standing near the Ferris wheel casts a shadow of 3.5 feet. At the same time, the Ferris wheel's shadow is 110 feet long.

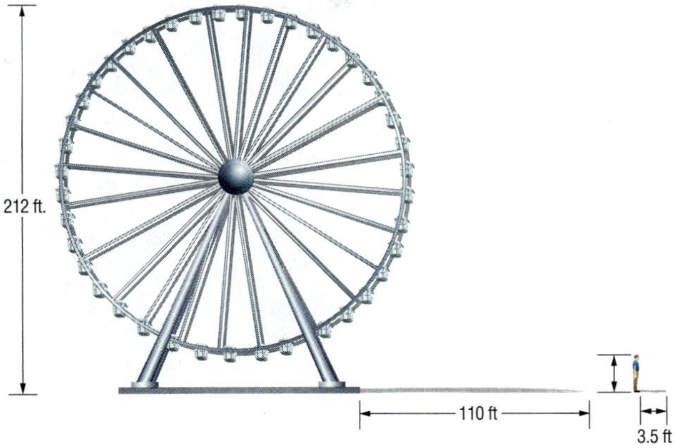


**a.** Set up a proportion to find the approximate height of the man.

$\frac{3.5}{110} = \frac{x}{212}$

**b.** Approximately how tall is the man?

About 6.7 feet or 6 feet, 9 inches

14. $\frac{3}{4}$ C grapes,
$\frac{3}{2}$ C strawberries,
$\frac{3}{4}$ C peaches,
$1\frac{1}{8}$ C apples,
$\frac{3}{8}$ C pineapple juice,
3 oranges,
$1\frac{1}{2}$ tsp. ginger,
$\frac{1}{2}$ tsp. salt

***Connect & Extend***

15. Possible answer: These numbers are not proportional because Mr. Mills' birthday is always the number of wedding anniversaries + 30, and proportional relationships are related by multiplication. Or, if you graph these numbers, the graph does not pass through the origin.

**14.** This recipe makes twelve servings. Write a new recipe that will serve eighteen people and has correctly proportioned ingredients.

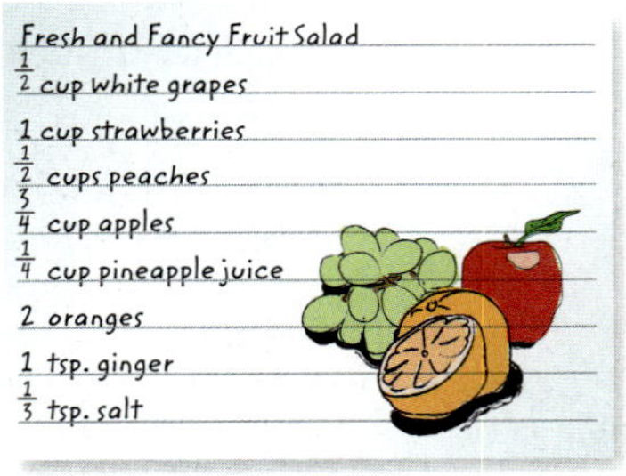
Fresh and Fancy Fruit Salad
$\frac{1}{2}$ cup white grapes
1 cup strawberries
$\frac{1}{2}$ cups peaches
$\frac{3}{4}$ cup apples
$\frac{1}{4}$ cup pineapple juice
2 oranges
1 tsp. ginger
$\frac{1}{3}$ tsp. salt

**15.** Mr. Mills turned 30 years old on the day of his wedding. Today, he and his wife will celebrate their 30th wedding anniversary and his 60th birthday. Mr. Mills has celebrated twice as many birthdays as wedding anniversaries. Does this mean that these numbers are proportional?



*On Your Own Exercises*

▶ **Exercise 13a** Make sure that students see all of the equivalent proportions or ask them to determine all of the equivalent proportions, so that they are aware of the different possibilities that still yield the same solution.

▶ **Exercise 14** This exercise does not require a proportion to find the solution. Take the opportunity to discuss how problems of this type are illustrations of proportionality, yet do not require a proportion to solve.

▶ **Exercise 15** Students may find this question challenging because there is not enough information to actually use a proportion. If the students are struggling, tell them to write out a few pieces of the data and use that to determine if the numbers are proportional.

**Lesson 10.2** Proportions and Similarity **525**

▶ **Exercises 16 and 17** The patterns need to be broken down into individual color components and students may not realize that. Additional explanations or examples may be needed to assist the students' understanding of these exercises since they are slightly different from similar problems that the students have already experienced.

▶ **Exercise 18** Remind students that it is always a good idea to check that the units correspond in a proportion; for example, the same unit is used in both top numbers and the same unit is used in both bottom numbers. You might also point out that, if they solve the proportion given, *G* would be 30,000 gallons, which is not reasonable.

▶ **Exercise 19** How the students answer this question will show how well the students have internalized and understood the concept of proportions.

▶ **Exercise 20** It may be helpful for students to be given a hint that they need to work with a triangle to answer this question. If students still seem perplexed, tell them that they should use the Pythagorean Theorem for help.

On Your Own Exercises

For each tile pattern, decide whether the numbers of tiles of any two colors are proportional to each other. That is, consider three ratios, white : blue, blue : red, and white : red, for each stage of the tile patterns. Explain your answers. 16, 17. See margin.

**16.**

**17.**

**18.** Renee is trying to set up a proportion to determine how much gas she will need for a 1,000-mile car trip. She averages 30 miles per gallon of gas. Here is what she wrote. See margin.

$$\frac{1{,}000 \text{ miles}}{G \text{ gallons}} = \frac{1 \text{ gallon}}{30 \text{ miles}}$$

**a.** Explain why Renee's "proportion" is not correct.

**b.** Set up a correct proportion. Solve it using any method you choose.

**c.** Find another proportion that Renee could use to solve this situation. Solve your proportion to check your answer to Part b.

**19.** Casey found a photograph of himself that was taken when he was three years old. In the photo, he is standing next to a bookcase that his parents still have. Explain how he could figure out how tall he was when the photo was taken. See margin.

**20. Challenge** Consider the map described in Exercise 10. Suppose cities can also be situated diagonally from Briartown. What is the maximum distance a city can be located from Briartown and still be on the map? Using the Pythagorean Theorem, a little more than 370 mi



**Additional Answers**

16. Yes; The pattern is made by adding stage 1 each time, so the tiles remain in proportion. At each stage, blue:red = 1:1.

17. Yes; The ratio blue:red is equivalent to 1:1 for each stage.

18a. Shedid not keep corresponding units in the numerator and denominator.

18b. Possibleanswer:

$$\frac{1{,}000 \text{ mi}}{G \text{ gal}} = \frac{30 \text{ mi}}{1 \text{ gal}}$$ The trip will take $33\frac{1}{3}$ gal.

18c. Possibleproportion:

$$\frac{1 \text{ gal}}{30 \text{ mi}} = \frac{G \text{ gal}}{1{,}000 \text{ mi}}$$

19. Possible answer: He could make the necessary measurements to set up this proportion:

$$\frac{\text{his height in photo}}{\text{bookcase's height in photo}} = \frac{\text{his actual height}}{\text{bookcase's actual height}}$$

526 **CHAPTER 10** Proportional Reasoning and Percents

22. In 2006, the family had £636.00 to spend. In 2007, the family had £588.00 pounds to spend. The difference between these amounts is £48.00. Using 2007's exchange rate, £48.00 is equal to $97.96.

**Real-World Link**

The dollar, equal to 100 cents, is part of a decimal currency system used in several countries, including Australia, New Zealand, Liberia, and the Bahamas.

**21. Economics** When traveling to another country, you often have to exchange U.S. dollars for the country's currency. Exchange rates for currency fluctuate every day, depending on world economies. For this exercise, use these exchange rates.

One U.S. dollar ($) equals:

- 0.5 English pound (£)
- 0.99 Canadian dollars ($)
- 0.67 Euro (€)
- 106.7 Japanese yen (¥).

**a.** How many Canadian dollars would you receive for $250 U.S.? $247.50

**b.** How many U.S. dollars would you receive for 375 yen? $3.51

**c.** Suppose you are returning to the United States from a trip to England, and you have £200 left. How many U.S. dollars will you receive for your pounds? $400

**d.** Suppose you are traveling from France to England and have 1,523 euros left. How many pounds will you receive for your remaining euros? £1,136.57

**22. Challenge** Alma's family took trips to England during two summer breaks. The exchange rates for both of the trips are shown below.

2006: 1 U.S. dollar equals 0.53 English pound
2007: 1 U.S. dollar equals 0.49 English pound

Alma's mother converted $1,200 into pounds for both trips. How many pounds did the family have to spend for each trip? What is the difference in the amount of money the family had for these trips in U.S. dollars, using 2007's exchange rate?

**23. In Your Own Words** An architect has agreed to visit a seventh grade class to talk about how architects use scale drawings in their work. She is not sure all the students will know what it means when she talks about shapes being "in proportion." Write some advice telling her how to explain what this means. Possible explanation: Shapes are in proportion when the ratios of their corresponding sides are equal.



On Your Own Exercises

▶ **Exercise 21** Students may be confused about the information needed to write a proportion. The one U.S. dollar equals gives them the first piece of a proportion. A total of 4 different proportions, one for each foreign currency can be written.

▶ **Exercise 24** Students will need a ruler to assist them in determining the proportion for the scale of the map.

▶ **Exercise 25** The students are making a scaled version of a map that is on the following page. Students do not necessarily need to see the map to answer the question, but it may make the students understand the difference in the 2 types of paper size choices available.

On Your Own Exercises

24c. Answers will vary. Possible answer: Proceed north on the 1.5 mile leg, turn right to point D, proceed from point D to point C, and then retrace the route to return to starting point; Length of 5.75 miles

25b. A 12" by 12" sheet of paper is not proportional to the original 8.5" by 11" size. Using the same scale and maintaining proportionality requires having blank space around the edges of the map.

**24.** Della's scout troop hikes in the Evergreen Recreational Area. The troop is planning a trip, and Della wants to provide recommendations for three different hiking distances. The options are for hikes of short, medium, and long distances. She also wants to provide different sightseeing choices.

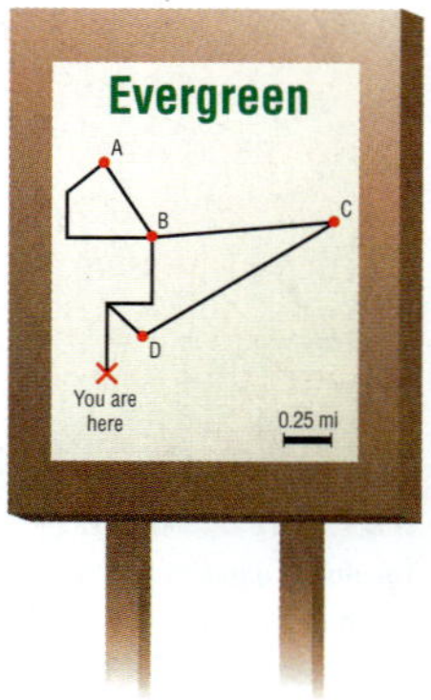


Help Della decide recommended routes by answering the following questions.

**a.** If Outlook Point is at point A, what is the shortest distance someone can hike to see it? 1.5 miles

**b.** What is the shortest possible route that allows a hiker to see all points of interest, points A–D and return to the original starting point? 4.875 miles

**c.** Assuming that hikers start and return to the "You Are Here" spot, describe a route that hikers could take that would be between five and six miles in length.

**25.** Nick and Maina are members of Della's troop. They have volunteered to make a map that is a smaller version of the wooden sign shown above.

**a.** If the map needs to fit on an 8.5″ by 11″ sheet of paper, what scale can they use and still make the map as large as possible? 17.2 in. to 2 mi

**b.** Suppose Nick and Maina try to put the map on a 12-by-12-inch sheet of paper. What difficulty would this present? How could they overcome the difficulty?

**26. Prove It!** One way to check whether rectangles are similar is to place them so that one of the corners overlaps, as shown below. Then look at the diagonals of each rectangle.

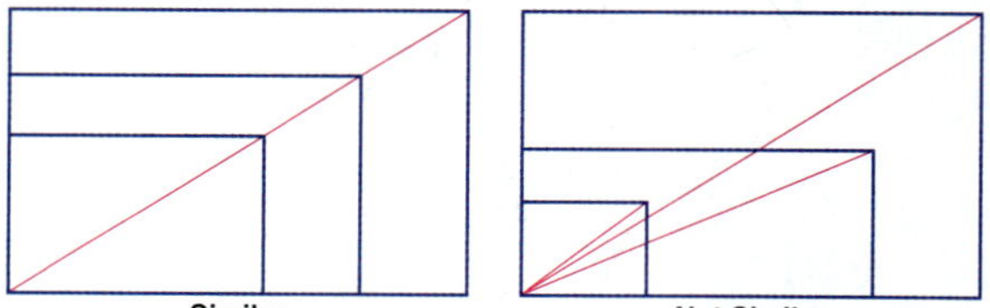

Similar    Not Similar

If the diagonals all align, as in the diagram on the left, the rectangles are similar. Prove that this is true. (Hint: Consider the triangles that are formed by the diagonals.) See margin.

528 **CHAPTER 10** Proportional Reasoning and Percents

## Additional Answer

26. The diagonal forms a right triangle within each rectangle.

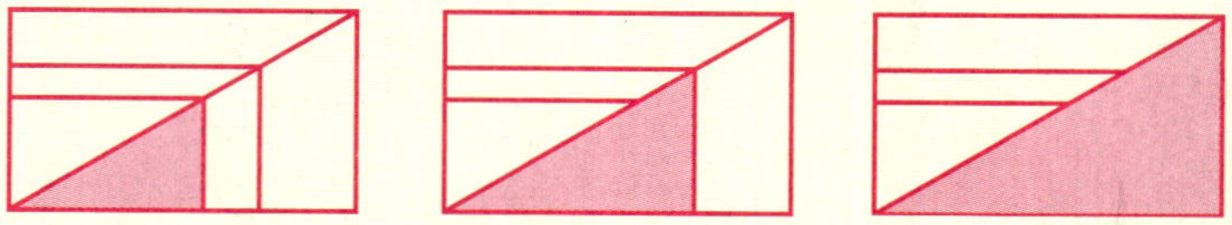

Within each of these right triangles, the lower left angles are congruent because they all overlap.

In addition, each triangle has a right angle.

If two angles within a triangle are congruent, the triangles must be similar. And if these triangles are similar, the rectangles must be similar because the ratios of their side lengths are in proportion.

**27. Challenge** These two right triangles are similar.

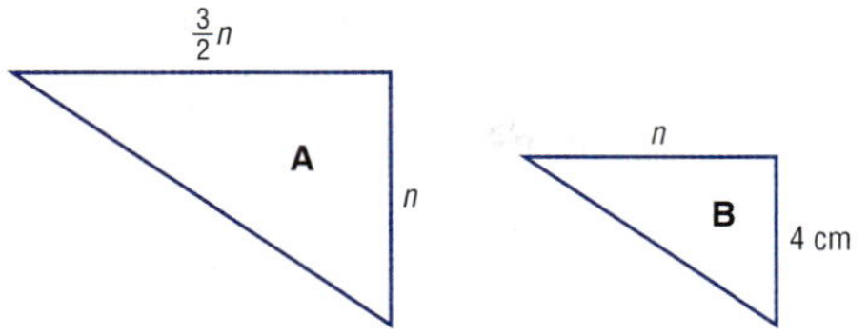


Find the lengths of the legs of both triangles. Show your work. See margin.

## Mixed Review

**Expand each expression.**

**28.** $5(m + 2)$ $5m + 10$

**29.** $6(2y + 9)$ $12y + 54$

**30.** $\frac{1}{2}(6k - 30)$ $3k - 15$

**31.** $1.2(5p - 1.2)$ $6p - 1.44$

**32.** $3a(2a + 5b)$ $6a^2 + 15ab$

**33.** $-7s(6r - 11s)$ $-42rs + 77s^2$

**Factor each expression completely.**

**34.** $7t + 14$ $7(t + 2)$

**35.** $33n - 44$ $11(3n - 4)$

**36.** $5c + 5d$ $5(c + d)$

**37.** $10a^2 - 20ab$ $10a(a - 2b)$

**38.** Eleven times a number increased by thirty is equal to 45 less than the same number.

**a.** Write an equation to solve for the missing number $n$. $11n + 30 = n - 45$

**b.** Solve the equation for $n$. $n = -7.5$

**39.** Write two equations with a solution of 6.

39. Check students' work. Answers may vary. Possible answers: $5x - 11 = 3x + 1$, $3x + 2 = 20$

For Exercises 40–45, identify to which sets each of the following numbers belong. Choose from natural numbers, whole numbers, integers, irrational numbers, and rational numbers.

**40.** $\frac{17}{2}$ Rational

**41.** $0$ Whole, integer, rational

**42.** $-45$ Integer, rational

**43.** $-6.373$ Rational

**44.** $\sqrt{16}$ Natural, whole, integer, rational

**45.** $\sqrt{7}$ Irrational



### Additional Answer

27. The legs of Triangle A are 9 cm and 6 cm, and the legs of Triangle B are 6 cm and 4 cm.

$$\frac{4}{n} = \frac{n}{\frac{3}{2}n}$$

$$\frac{4}{n} = \frac{1}{\frac{3}{2}}$$

$$4\left(\frac{3}{2}\right) = n$$

$$6 = n$$

On Your Own Exercises

## Quick Check

**Informal Assessment** Students should be able to:

✔ recognize proportions as pairs of equivalent ratios

✔ use equivalent ratios to find the missing part of a proportion

✔ set up and use proportions to solve problems

✔ use proportions and similar triangles to calculate distances

## Quick Quiz

**1.** Mixture A is made up of 6 containers of paint, 4 yellow and 2 blue. Mixture B is made up of 9 containers of paint, 5 yellow and 4 blue. Are the numbers of yellow containers of paint proportional? How do you know? No; Mixture A has a proportion of $\frac{4}{6}$ yellow to entire mix where as Mixture B has a proportion of $\frac{5}{9}$, these values are not the same, therefore the yellow is not proportional.

**2.** Hobson School has a student-teacher ratio of 9:2 for their current school year. Next year the enrollment of the school is expected to be 178 students. What proportion would you use to determine how many teachers are needed to maintain this ratio? How many teachers will be employed next year? $\frac{9}{2} = \frac{178}{t}$; 40 teachers

**3.** A map has a scale of 3 centimeters equals 100 miles. If two cities are 12.5 centimeters apart, approximately how many miles separate the cities? About 417 miles

**4.** A 25 foot tall flag pole casts an 8 foot shadow on the ground. A nearby tree casts a 14 foot shadow. How tall is the tree? 43.75 feet

**Lesson 10.2** Proportions and Similarity **529**

LESSON 10.3

# Percents and Proportions

### Objectives

- To recognize percents as ratios with a common scale of 100
- To recognize percents as a convenient way to compare ratios
- To solve percent exercises using proportions

## Overview

In this lesson, students work with percentages as proportions. Percentages allow you to use a common scale, 100, to compare two ratios. For example, suppose 7 out of 10 doctors recommend a certain type of exercise and 4 out of 5 recommend another type; 7 out of 10 doctors is 70%, while 4 out of 5 is 80%, so the advice of the second group might be better to follow. Students work with percentages to compare different ratios.

## Advance Preparation

If you decide to have students use graph paper to make percent diagrams, you may want to have sheets of graph paper available.

| | Summary | Materials | On Your Own Exercises (pp. 537–539) | Assessment Opportunities |
|---|---|---|---|---|
| **Investigation 1** (p. 530) Pacing: 2 days | Students will learn to use percents as a common scale to compare different ratios and will draw percent diagrams. | graph paper | Practice & Apply: 1–12<br>Connect & Extend: 22–23<br>Mixed Review: 27–36 | • On the Spot Assessment (p. 531)<br>• Share & Summarize (p. 533) |
| **Investigation 2** (p. 534) Pacing: 1 day | Students will solve percent exercises by setting up and solving a proportion. | graph paper | Practice & Apply: 13–21<br>Connect & Extend: 24–26<br>Mixed Review: 27–36 | • Share & Summarize (p. 536)<br>• Troubleshooting (p. 536) |

# Leveled Lesson Resources

CRM *Available in:* **Chapter 10 Resource Masters**

Also on TeacherWorks™ Lesson 10.3

## Study Guide and Intervention (p. 15) AL

**Lesson 10.3 Study Guide and Intervention**
***Percents and Proportions***

*Example 1* **Use the percent diagram to determine the greater number or percent.**

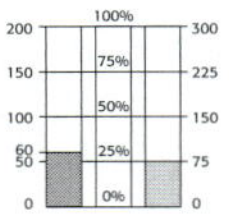


**a. 60 out of 200 or 75 out of 300**
According to the diagram, 75 out of 300 is 25%, and 60 out of the 200 is slightly over 25%. So, 60 out of 200 is a greater percentage.

**b. *P*% of 200 or *P*% of 300**
Choose any percent on the diagram. The percent is at the same level on the two scales, but the number on the 300 side is greater than the number on the 200 side. So, *P*% of 300 is a greater number.

**c. *t* out of 200 or *t* out of 300**
Suppose $t = 150$. This number is 75% on the 200 side and 50% on the 300 side. Notice that this would be true for any value of $t$. So, $t$ out of 200 is a greater percentage.

*Example 2* **Express each question as a proportion and solve it.**

**a. What is 15% of 200?**

$\frac{n}{200} = \frac{15}{100}$ Write a proportion.

$200 \cdot \frac{n}{200} = \frac{15}{100} \cdot 200$ Multiply.

$n = 30$

So, 30 is 15% of 200. Simplify.

**b. What percent of 25 is 3?**

$\frac{3}{25} = \frac{p}{100}$

$100 \cdot \frac{3}{25} = \frac{p}{100} \cdot 100$

$12 = p$

So, 3 is 12% of 25.

*Example 3* **Consider the ratios $\frac{12}{15}$ and $\frac{15}{18}$. Determine which ratio is greater by finding the percentages they represent.**

$\frac{12}{15} = 0.8$ Divide. $\frac{15}{18} \approx 0.833...$

$0.8 = 80\%$ Move the decimal 2 places to the right. $0.833... \approx 83.3\%$

Since $83.3\% > 80\%$, $\frac{15}{18}$ is the greater ratio.

*Exercises*

**Find each number. Round to the nearest tenth if necessary.**

**1.** What number is 25% of 20? **2.** What percent of 50 is 20?

**Determine which is greater.**

**3.** *P*% of 50 or *P*% of 45 **4.** $\frac{7}{9}$ or $\frac{11}{12}$

## Skills Practice (p. 16) AL OL

**Lesson 10.3 Skills Practice**
***Percents and Proportions***

**Find each number. Round to the nearest tenth if necessary.**

**1.** Fifty is 20% of what number? **2.** What percent of 20 is 4?

**3.** What number is 70% of 250? **4.** Ten is 5% of what number?

**5.** What number is 45% of 180? **6.** What percent of 90 is 36?`

**Use the percent diagram to determine the greater number or percent.**

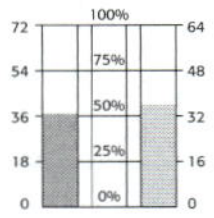


**7.** 50% of 72 or 50% of 64

**8.** *P*% of 72 or *P*% of 64

**9.** 48 out of 72 or 48 out of 64

**10.** *t* out of 72 or *t* out of 64

**For each pair of ratios, determine which is greater by finding the percentages they represent.**

**11.** $\frac{6}{18}$ and $\frac{9}{25}$ **12.** $\frac{14}{17}$ and $\frac{19}{35}$ **13.** $\frac{22}{36}$ and $\frac{32}{48}$

**14.** $\frac{42}{63}$ and $\frac{8}{15}$ **15.** $\frac{5}{9}$ and $\frac{14}{27}$ **16.** $\frac{24}{75}$ and $\frac{18}{50}$

## Problem-Solving Practice (p. 17) AL OL

**Lesson 10.3 Problem-Solving Practice**
***Percents and Proportions***

Solve.

**1. Driving** David, Josh, and Zachary are on a road trip. So far, Josh has driven 224 miles. David and Zachary have each driven 42% of the total miles traveled. Find the total miles traveled and the amounts driven by David and Zachary.

**2. Election** Going into a recent election, only about 62% of people old enough to vote were registered. In a community of about 55,200 eligible voters, how many people are registered?

**3. Election** Yolanda's club has 35 members. Its rules require that 60% of them must be present for any vote. At least how many members must be present to have a vote?

**4. Garbage** This month, Chun's office produced 690 pounds of garbage. Chun wants to reduce the weight of garbage produced to 85% of the weight produced this month. What is the target weight for the garbage produced next month?

**5. Salary** Alma just received a 6% raise in salary. Before the raise, she was making $52,000 per year. How much more will Alma earn next year?

**6. Soccer** Sally's soccer team played 25 games and won 17 of them. Morgan's soccer team played 32 games and won 20 of them. Whose team won a higher percentage of games? Explain.

## Enrichment (p. 18) BL

**Lesson 10.3 Enrichment**
***Percents and Proportions***

**Working Backward**

Working backward can be a helpful problem-solving tool, especially in problems where the answer is given and information you would expect to have is omitted.

A large corporation reports that [  ] % of its employees exercise on a regular basis. If 2,120 employees exercise regularly, how many employees does the corporation have? Answer: 2,650 employees

Use the percent proportion to solve for the missing percent.

$\frac{2,120}{2,650} = \frac{x}{100}$

$0.8 = \frac{x}{100}$

$80 = x$

So, 80% of the employees exercise on a regular basis.

**Write the missing information for each exercise.**

**1.** A progressive community states that 96% of its households recycle materials at least once monthly. If [ ? ] households recycle at least once monthly, how many households are in the community? Answer: 15,475 households

**2.** The purchase price of a digital music player is $139.00. The sales tax rate is [ ? ] %. Find the cost of the digital music player. Answer: $148.73

**3.** In a seventh grade class, 60% of the students participate in extra-curricular activities. The class has [ ? ] students. How many students participate in extra-curricular activities? Answer: 15 students

**4.** Claims by a manufacturer state that 3 out of 4 people prefer their product when compared to a similar product of another manufacturer. If [ ? ] people were surveyed, how many did not prefer the product? Answer: 35

**5.** Seventy percent of the students entering a certain high school complete their studies and graduate. If [ ? ] students did not complete their studies and graduate, how many students earned a diploma? Answer: 455

**6.** A middle school survey discovered that 15% of the student body watched two hours or less of television each week and 45% watched ten or more hours each week. If [ ? ] students were surveyed, how many students watched between 2 and 10 hours of television each week? Answer: 48

## Lesson Quick Quiz (p. 19) AL OL BL

**Lesson 10.3 Quick Quiz**

**1.** Manny finished 9 of the 15 homework exercises assigned. Janellen has finished 8 of the 12 exercises assigned in her class. Who is closer to being finished? Use percentages to tell how much closer.

**2.** Joanna collects stamps and recently increased her stamp collection by 10%. Before the increase, Joanna had 1,370 stamps, how many does she have now?

**3.** Jong wanted to purchase a new pair of rollerblades. Store A sold the pair he wanted for $79 and all rollerblades were currently on sale for a 20% discount. Store B sold the same rollerblades for $69, but the rollerblades were only on sale for a 10% discount. If Jong wants to get the rollerblades from the store with the lower price, where should he purchase his rollerblades? Why?

# Additional Lesson Resources

### Teacher Tech Tools
- TeacherWorks
- ExamView Assessment Suite
- Classroom Presentation Toolkit
- Advance Tracker

### Student Tech Tools
- StudentWorks Plus
- Math Online eGlossary • Concepts in Motion

### Other Print Products
- Investigation Notebook and Reflection Journal
- Quick Review Math Handbook

LESSON 10.3 **Percents and Proportions**

## Introduce

**Percents** Launch this lesson by moving right into the Think & Discuss.

### Think & Discuss

*Suggested Grouping: Whole Class*

Present the situation and pose the question to students before having them open their books. The solution is not immediately obvious by looking at ratios of tickets sold to goal, since the goals for the two grades are different. Although the seventh grade has sold fewer tickets, their goal is lower than that of the eighth grade. This sets the stage for using a common scale, which percentages provide.

### Investigation 1

***On Your Own Exercises***
Pages 537–539
Exercises 1–12, 22–23

**Common Scale** This investigation introduces one important use of percentage as a common scale. Often the actual amounts of two quantities are not as important as the percentage or fraction of two wholes each of these quantities represents. For example, in comparing school attendance figures in Illinois and Massachusetts, the percentage of absentees is probably more informative than the total number.

Introduce the percent diagram and the term percent scale. Be sure that students understand that the same line is labeled 100%, which is 300 tickets for the eighth grade goal and 250 tickets for the seventh grade goal. They should see that there are three scales given in the diagram. The common percent scale is given between the two bars; the absolute scales (on the extreme left and right) are different for the two bars.

LESSON 10.3

# Percents and Proportions



Meredith Middle School is putting on a production of *The Music Man.* The eighth grade had 300 tickets to sell, and the seventh grade had 250 tickets to sell. One hour before the show, the eighth grade had sold 225 tickets, and the seventh grade had sold 200 tickets.

### Think & Discuss

Which grade was closer to the goal of selling all its tickets? Explain your answer. See ①.

To figure out which grade was closer to its goal, you may have tried to compare the ratios 225 : 300 and 200 : 250. One way to compare ratios easily is to change them to percentages.

## Investigation 1 Find Percents

**Materials**

- graph paper (optional)

This diagram is called a *percent diagram.* It represents the seventh and eighth grade ticket sales. The heights of the left and right bars represent the goal for each grade. The bar in the middle is called the *percent scale.* It is a common scale for the two different ratios.

Notice that the three bars are the same height even though they represent different numbers. On the percent scale, the height always represents 100%.

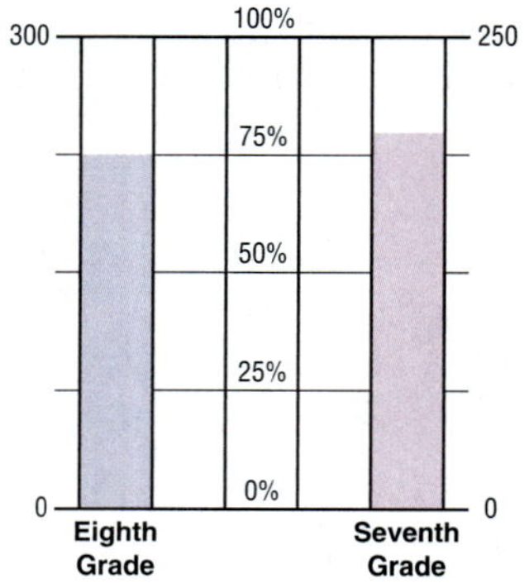


① Students will likely agree that the seventh grade was closer. Some may say that is because they sold $\frac{4}{5}$, or 80%, of its tickets, while the eighth grade sold only $\frac{3}{4}$, or 75%, of its tickets. Others may say the eighth grade needed to sell 75 more tickets and the seventh grade needed to sell only 50 more tickets.



### Reaching All Learners

OL **On Level** Students are familiar with percents from previous courses. Ask the students to keep a percent journal for a week. Every time they see or hear a reference to a percent, they should record it. The record could be anything from the newspaper, a picture from a store, or even just a short paragraph describing what they heard. After the week, have the students meet in small groups to discuss their findings.

Percents make it possible to represent both grades' ticket sales as some number out of 100. For the eighth grade, 100% represents 300 tickets. For the seventh grade, 100% represents 250 tickets.

### Think & Discuss

The eighth grade sold 225 tickets, and the seventh grade sold 200 tickets. Why is the bar for the seventh grade taller, when they sold fewer tickets? See ①.

① The bar height compares the number sold to the number they had to sell. Since the seventh grade sold a greater percentage of its tickets, its bar is taller.

## Develop & Understand: A

Jefferson Middle School has 600 students, and Memorial Middle School has 450 students. For Exercises 1–6, use this percent diagram to estimate an answer.

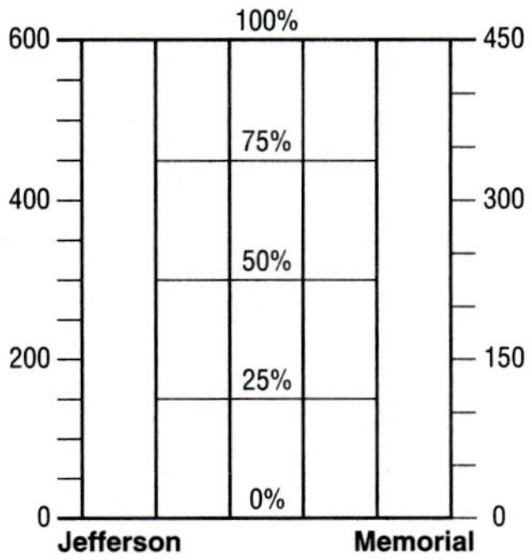


1. A survey of the two schools finds that 300 Jefferson students watch more than one hour of television every night, and 270 Memorial students watch more than one hour per night.
   a. What percentage of Jefferson students watch more than one hour of TV each night? 50%
   b. What percentage of Memorial students watch more than one hour of TV each night? 60%
   c. Comparing percentages, do more Jefferson students or more Memorial students watch more than one hour of TV each night? More Memorial students
2. Jefferson has 275 girls and Memorial has 250 girls. Which school has a greater percentage of girls? Explain. Memorial; Jefferson is about 46% girls, and Memorial is about 56% girls.
3. At each school, 75% of the students play a musical instrument.
   a. About how many students at Jefferson play an instrument? 450
   b. About how many students at Memorial play an instrument? 338

### Think & Discuss

*Suggested Grouping: Whole Class*

Answers to this question will likely reveal much about students' understanding of percentages as a common scale, although this may be a difficult concept for students to articulate clearly. If it seems that students really don't understand the basic idea, you might review the ticket sale example again or provide students the Additional Example below.

**Additional Example** Harold and Grady are each saving for a boom box, although each wants a different brand. Harold has saved $125 toward his goal of $150. Grady has saved $150 toward his goal of $175. Which boy is closer to his goal? Grady is closer with about 86% saved. Harold has about 83% saved.

### Develop & Understand: A

*Suggested Grouping: Pairs*

In these exercises, students are asked to use percent diagrams to estimate answers. They are not expected to do any calculations; the intent of the exercise set is to familiarize students with percent diagrams.

▶ **Exercises 2–4** Students need to move back and forth between the absolute number scale that shows quantities and the percent scale. They are given the percentage and asked to find the related number of students, and vice versa. Students should understand that these exercises can be solved because the actual number of students at both schools is known. Without that information, these exercises could not be done.

▶ **Exercise 3** Answers are estimates. Most students will answer that there are 450 students at Jefferson, while the number of students at Memorial is more likely to vary.

### On the Spot Assessment

On Friday, the library had 177 people check out materials. If 102 people checked out movies, what percent of people checked out movies? 58%

**Lesson 10.3** Percents and Proportions **531**

▶ **Exercise 5** Students are not given a numerical percentage. The exercise involves a generalization: No matter what *P* may be, *P*% of a larger number is bigger than *P*% of a smaller number. Implicit in this statement is a basic convention of algebra: In the context of a given exercise, when a single letter, say *P*, occurs more than once, it always stands for the same quantity. To indicate different quantities, different letters such as *P* and *Q* must be used. (However, *P* and *Q* could stand for the same value.) You might take the opportunity here to quickly review this convention.

▶ **Exercise 6** In Exercise 6, *t* out of 450 is a greater percentage than *t* out of 600, when $t \neq 0$. This principle holds for fractions and ratios in general: If two fractions have the same numerator, then the one with the larger denominator is the smaller fraction.

## Develop & Understand: B

*Suggested Grouping: Pairs or Individuals*

In this exercise set, students continue to compare percentages and absolute numbers. The first four exercises are in the context of two classes selling tickets to the school play, and the last three exercises are practice exercises. In most exercises, students are now expected to make calculations; they also make percent diagrams themselves, using their calculations.

▶ **Exercise 7c** The answer is an estimate.

**Additional Answers**

6. *t* out of 450; Possible explanation: A unit is a greater portion when the total is smaller, so a given number of those portions would be greater as well.

7a.

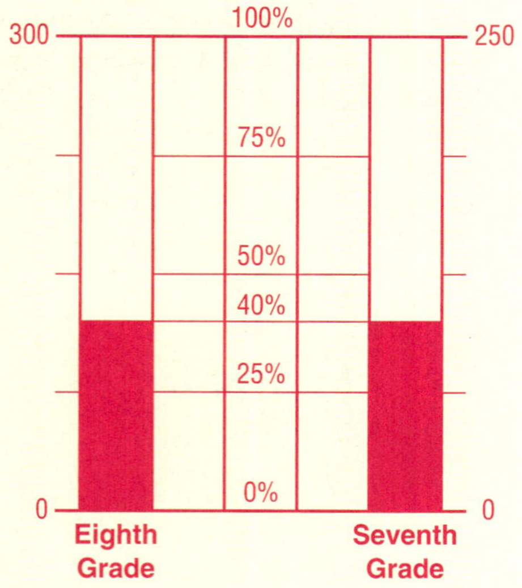


5. *P*% of 600; Possible explanation: The percentage is at the same level on the two scales, but the numbers on the 600 side would be greater than those on the 450 side.

7b. Visually compare the height of the shaded portion of the seventh grade bar with the total height of that bar; 100.

8. Possible answer (answer depends on the calculator): Divide 225 by 300 and move the decimal two places to the right to convert the answer to a percentage.

4. The Math teachers at each school selected 50 students to represent the school at a Math competition.
   a. About what percentage of Jefferson students attended the Math competition? 8%
   b. About what percentage of Memorial students attended the Math competition? 11%
5. Suppose you looked for *P*% of 450 and *P*% of 600 on a percent diagram. Which would be the greater number? Explain your answer in terms of the diagram.
6. Which represents a greater percentage, *t* out of 450 or *t* out of 600? Explain your answer. See margin.

## Develop & Understand: B

Look again at the ticket sales by the seventh and eighth grades at Meredith Middle School. The eighth grade had 300 tickets to sell, and the seventh grade had 250 tickets to sell.

7. At the end of the first week, each grade had sold 40% of its goal.
   a. Draw a percent diagram to represent this situation. See margin.
   b. Explain how you can use your diagram to estimate the number of tickets the seventh grade sold. Give your estimate.
   c. Use your diagram to estimate the number of tickets the eighth grade sold. 120
8. One hour before the show started, the seventh grade had sold 200 tickets and the eighth grade had sold 225. Melanie used her calculator to express the ratios of sold tickets to sales goal for both grades as percentages. How could you use your calculator to find $\frac{225}{300}$ as a percentage?
9. Suppose each grade was only 25 tickets short of meeting its goal.
   a. How many tickets would the eighth grade have sold? 275
   b. How many tickets would the seventh grade have sold? 225
   c. Calculate the percentages sold for each grade. Comparing percentages, which grade came closer to its goal? Eighth grade: 91.7%, seventh grade: 90%; Eighth grade came closer.

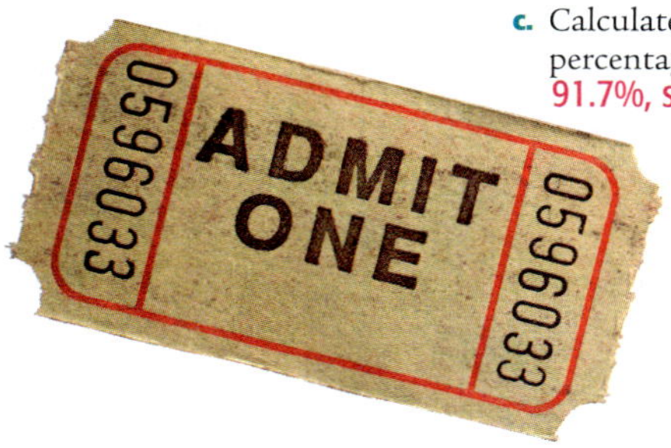




### Reaching All Learners

**AL Approaching Level**

Encourage students to substitute numbers for *P* in Exercise 5 and *t* in Exercise 6 if necessary. Then have them use the percent diagram to find the corresponding numerical values.

10. By the time the play began, each grade had sold exactly 270 tickets.

a. What percentage of its goal did the eighth grade sell? 90%

b. What percentage of its goal did the seventh grade sell? 108%

c. Draw a percent diagram to represent this situation. Since the seventh grade sold *more* than its goal, you will need to extend the bar for the seventh grade. See margin.

11. Determine which ratio in each pair is greater by finding the percentage each represents.

a. $\frac{56}{69}$ or $\frac{76}{89}$ $\frac{56}{69} \approx 81.2\%$, $\frac{76}{89} \approx 85.4\%$; $\frac{76}{89}$ is greater.

b. $\frac{106}{210}$ or $\frac{206}{310}$ $\frac{106}{210} \approx 50.5\%$, $\frac{206}{310} \approx 66.5\%$; $\frac{206}{310}$ is greater.

c. $\frac{50}{45}$ or $\frac{210}{205}$ $\frac{50}{45} \approx 111.1\%$, $\frac{210}{205} \approx 102.4\%$; $\frac{50}{45}$ is greater.

12. Find four ratios equivalent to 75%. Possible answer: $\frac{75}{100}, \frac{225}{300}, \frac{3}{4}, \frac{6}{8}$

13. Find four ratios equivalent to 115%. Possible answer: $\frac{115}{100}, \frac{23}{20}, \frac{46}{40}, \frac{69}{60}$

### *Share & Summarize*

Here are two statements about Jefferson and Memorial Middle Schools.

a. Jefferson has 275 girls and Memorial has 250 girls, so there are more girls at Jefferson.

b. Jefferson is almost 46% girls and Memorial is almost 56% girls, so there are more girls at Memorial.

1. Which statement uses a common scale to make a comparison? Statement b

2. Which statement do you think is a better answer to the question, "Which school has more girls?" Explain your thinking. Answers will vary. Some students may think statement a is better because 275 is clearly greater than 250. Others may think statement b is better because, for example, if you observed classes of 25 students at each school, there will probably be more girls in the classes at Memorial. The greater percentage means that it "feels like" there are more girls as you look around, though there are fewer total.



## *Reaching All Learners*

**OL On Level** The dual meanings (absolute and relative) of more in this investigation is likely to cause some confusion among students. At this stage, however, students should be comfortable with thinking about and describing situations using the common percent scale. Refer back to the Share & Summarize Exercise 1 if students seem confused. Ask them to construct the percent diagram to represent this situation if they need more practice.

Note the statement at the end of the answer provided for Exercise 2: "The greater percentage means that it 'feels like' there are more girls as you look around, though there are fewer total." This is an important observation. Share and discuss this way of looking at percentages with your class. Another way to say this is that the relative (percentage) point of view really gives you a kind of "density" measure, in this case the density of girls in the school population.

▶ **Exercise 10b** The answer is 108%. It is important that students become comfortable with percentages greater than 100%. Point out that this language is often used in real life: We made 108% of our goal! As an extension, you might also point out that people sometimes say that they are "110% certain" of something. You can then discuss whether this is really possible, and if not, why people still say things like that.

▶ **Exercise 11** This moves beyond a concrete situation by asking students to use percentages to compare ratios without using the percent diagram. The exercise is designed to show how percentages can be used to compare fractions. By converting fractions to percentages, students use a common scale to make a comparison. You might remind the students that they have compared unlike fractions by finding common denominators (which also provides a common scale). You might start a discussion about the pros and cons of using common denominators or percentages for comparing fractions.

▶ **Exercises 12 and 13** These are an inverse of the preceding exercises. Students start with a given percentage and are asked to find ratios equal to that percentage. It is possible to do these exercises without doing any serious arithmetic. For example, in Exercise 12, two easy solutions might be: $75\% = \frac{7.5}{10} = \frac{0.75}{1} = \frac{0.075}{0.01}$ and so on.

### *Share & Summarize*

Once again, the point is made that two quantities can be compared in two very different ways—absolutely or relatively. Exercise 2 asks students to explain which of the two ways is better. Discussing students' explanations is very worthwhile and strongly recommended. It is important that students understand that there is no simple yes or no answer to this question. In fact, as students mature mathematically, they should come to appreciate more that the way a exercise is answered depends crucially on the context of the exercise and how you intend to use your answer.

**See page 555A for answer to 10c.**

# Investigation 2

**On Your Own Exercises**
Pages 537–539
Exercises 13–21, 24–26

**Percent Problems** In this investigation, students solve a variety of percent exercises. They are also shown how proportions can be used to solve percent exercises.

The exercises in this investigation are examples of what used to be called the "three kinds" of percent exercises involving two quantities, $a$ and $b$, and a certain percentage, $n$%. In a classic percent exercise, you are given two of these, and asked to find the third. One way to solve all such exercises is to set up the equation $\frac{b}{a} = n\%$, which in turn leads to the proportion: $\frac{b}{a} = \frac{n}{100}$. Given any two of the three variables, $a$, $b$, and $n$, you can use algebra to get the third.

Tell students that they will use percentages to solve exercises.

## Develop & Understand: A

*Suggested Grouping: Small Groups*

Students work in groups to solve percent exercises. Some students may use multiplication to solve these exercises. Others may set up proportions. This set gives students the opportunity to try different ways before being formally introduced to a solving method.

▶ **Exercise 1** Make sure that all the students understand that the item is marked down to 30% of the original price, not off the original price. It is easy to confuse *of* and *off* in these contexts, if only because the two words look and sound so similar.

**Wrap-Up** Discuss answers as a class, focusing on how groups arrived at their answers. If any students set up proportions to solve these exercises, be sure to have them share their method. In any case, this method is explained in some detail in the paragraphs following the exercise set, and you and the class should go over this explanation with some care.

# Investigation 2 Proportions Using Percents

**Materials**

- graph paper (optional)

In Lesson 10.2, you used ratios to write proportions and represent real-world situations. In the last investigation, you saw that you can use percentages as a common scale to compare ratios. Percents can also be used to solve equations.

## Develop & Understand: A

Work with your group to solve these exercises. Be ready to explain your reasoning.

1. Two department stores, Gracie's and Thimbles, are having holiday sales. The stores sell the same brand of men's slacks. Gracie's usually sells them for \$50 but has marked them down to 30% of that price for the sale. At Thimbles, the slacks are marked down to 40% of the usual price of \$30. Which store has the better sale price? Explain.
   Thimbles; 30% of \$50 is \$15, and 40% of \$30 is \$12.
2. Steve and Anna went shopping during a sale at the KC Wheels bike store. Anna looked at her receipt and saw that the total before the discount was \$72, but she paid only \$40. Steve's total before the discount was \$38, but he paid only \$18. Who saved a greater percentage off the original price? Explain.
   2. Steve; Anna saved \$32, which is 44.4% of the original price. Steve saved \$20, which is 52.6% of the original price.
3. You are making punch for the class party. The punch will contain juice and soda with at least 70% juice. You have four gallons of juice. What is the greatest amount of punch you could make?
   About 5.7 gal

One way to solve a percent situation is to set up and solve a proportion. In most percent situations, you have values for two things and you want to know the value of the third. Your proportion might look like this.

$$\frac{b}{a} = \frac{n}{100}$$

For example, in Exercise 3 above, you knew the percent of juice that the punch should contain, 70%. You know how much juice you actually had, four gallons. You could have set up this proportion.

$$\frac{4}{a} = \frac{70}{100}$$

534 CHAPTER 10 Proportional Reasoning and Percents

① Possible answers: 80 is what percent of 200? Or, What percent of 200 is 80?

② $\frac{80}{200} = \frac{n}{100}$;

$n = \frac{8{,}000}{200} = 40$,

so 80 is 40% of 200. Possible explanation: The ratio of numbers on the left bar is equal to the corresponding ratio of numbers on the right bar.

6. 346; Possible explanation:

$\frac{45}{T} = \frac{13}{100}$

$45 = \frac{13}{100} \cdot T$

$\frac{100}{13} \cdot 45 = T$

$346 \approx T$

**Real-World Link**

The enormous blue whale's primary source of food is plankton, tiny animals and plants that float near the surface of the water.

## Think & Discuss

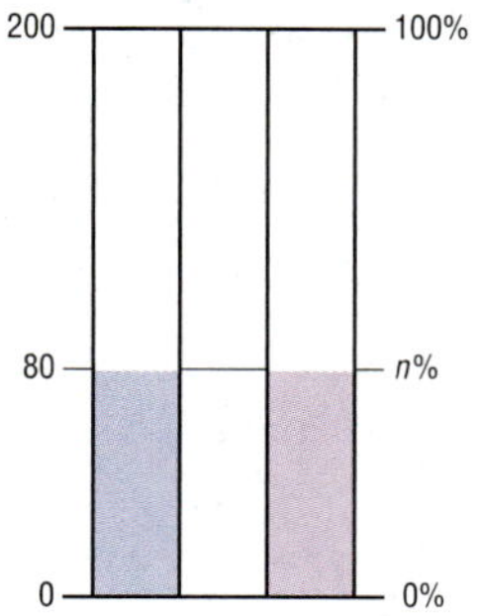


This type of percent diagram is used to help compare two numbers. State in words the situation represented by this percent diagram. See ①.

Write a proportion that is illustrated by the diagram and solve it. How did you think about setting up the proportion? See ②.

## Develop & Understand: B

**4.** Consider this question. *What percent of 150 is 6?*

**a.** Draw a percent diagram to represent the question. See margin.

**b.** Express the question as a proportion and solve it. $\frac{6}{150} = \frac{n}{100}$, $n = 4$

**5.** Now consider this question. *What is 185% of 20?*

**a.** Draw a percent diagram to represent the question. See margin.

**b.** Express the question as a proportion and solve it. $\frac{x}{20} = \frac{185}{100}$, $x = 37$

**6.** A gardener planted 13% of his tulip bulbs in the border of his garden and the rest in the garden bed. In spring, every one of the bulbs grew into a tulip. He counted 45 tulips in the border. How many bulbs had he planted altogether? Show how you found your answer.

**7.** Of 75 flights leaving from Hartsfield Airport in Atlanta, 33 went to the west coast. What percentage of the 75 flights went to the west coast? Show how you found your answer. See margin.

**8.** The largest land animal, the African bush elephant, may weigh as much as 8 tons. However, that is only about 3.9% of the weight of the largest animal of all, the blue whale. How heavy can a blue whale be? Show how you found your answer. About 205 tons; Possible explanation: $\frac{8}{b} = \frac{3.9}{100}$, $b = \frac{8(100)}{3.9}$



## Think & Discuss

The diagram is a visual representation of the basic percent proportion $\frac{b}{a} = \frac{n}{100}$ for particular values of the variable. From $a = 80$ and $b = 200$, students can conclude that $n = 40$. In this case, they can check the answer mentally since 80 out of 200 is equivalent to 40 out of 100.

Encourage students to use shortcuts in percent exercises whenever they can. A good example of a candidate for mental arithmetic might be: 12 is 50% of what? 24 Students should understand that they can always solve any basic percent exercise by setting up a proportion and then applying the basic rules of algebra.

## Develop & Understand: B

*Suggested Grouping: Pairs*

You may want to supply students with copies of Lesson 10.3 Master 1 or sheets of graph paper on which to draw their percent diagrams.

▶ **Exercises 4 and 5** Students set up and solve proportions after they have represented the data in a percent diagram. You might remind them of the general proportion on the previous page, and then point out that $a$ corresponds to 100%, while $b$ corresponds to $n$%. Students may find that referring to the percent diagram they drew in Part a of both exercises can help them keep track of what proportion they should be solving and check that their final answers make sense.

▶ **Exercise 8** This involves a noninteger percentage, 3.9%. You may need to review quickly what such percentages mean, reminding students that $3.9\% = \frac{3.9}{100} = \frac{39}{1000}$. They may note that 3.9% is just a little less than 4%.

7. 44%; Possible explanation:

$\frac{w}{100} = \frac{33}{75}$

$w = \frac{33(100)}{75}$

$w = \frac{3{,}300}{75 \cdot 100}$

$w = 44\%$

**Additional Answers**

4a.

5a.

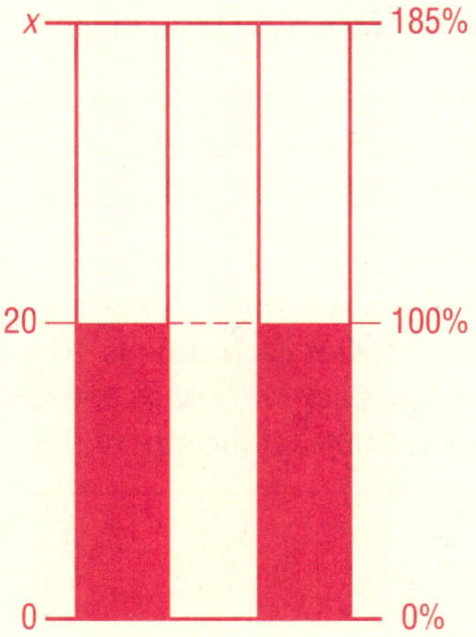


**Lesson 10.3** Percents and Proportions **535**

▶ **Exercise 10** These exercises 10a and 10b are inverses of each other, in the sense that students are asked to calculate both $\frac{a}{b}$ and $\frac{b}{a}$ as percentages. The following observations may be of interest:

- Unless $a = b$, one of the two percentages must be greater than 100, the other less than 100.
- A percentage that is less than 100 cannot fall below 0, but percentages over 100 can be made as large as you like.

### Share & Summarize

Exercise 2 is a generalization of the preceding work. Students use variables and the language of algebra to write a general proportion relating ratios and percentages.

The exercises in this investigation represent typical percent exercises that students will confront over and over again. Many students are hindered later on if they do not master the different forms that percent exercises can take. If students are having difficulty with those in this investigation, however, it would serve them well to solve additional exercises such as those in the Additional Examples before continuing. To help you pinpoint what students' difficulties may be, you may want to have them explain their reasoning as they work through an exercise.

#### Additional Examples

- Susanna's class meets for 45 minutes. They spent 25 minutes working in groups. About what percent of the class time was spent in groups? About 56%
- James's dad always tips waiters and waitresses 20% of the total bill if the service is good.
  a. After one meal, his dad left $20.00. How much did the meal cost? $100
  b. How much would James's dad leave as a tip for a meal costing $25? $5

9. According to the Bureau of Labor Statistics, in 2006, the average American spent about $2,376 on entertainment, including admission fees, pets, hobbies, and entertainment equipment. They spent 363% of that amount on housing. How much did the average American spend on housing in 2006? $8,624.88

10. According to the U.S. Census Bureau, in 1950, the estimated world population was 2.6 billion. In 2007, it was 6.6 billion.
    a. What percentage of the 2007 population is the 1950 population? About 39%
    b. What percentage of the 1950 population is the 2007 population? About 254%
    c. In 2007, about 303 million people lived in the United States. What percentage of the world's population lived in the United States in 2007? About 4.6%

### Share & Summarize

1. Write a proportion that expresses the statement 32% of 25 is $b$. Solve your proportion for $b$. $\frac{b}{25} = \frac{32}{100}$, $b = 8$
2. Write a proportion that expresses the statement $n$% of $a$ is $b$. Explain why your proportion is useful for solving percent situations. $\frac{n}{100} = \frac{b}{a}$; This proportion works for all kinds of percent situations, and you can solve for any of the three variables, depending on what is known and unknown.

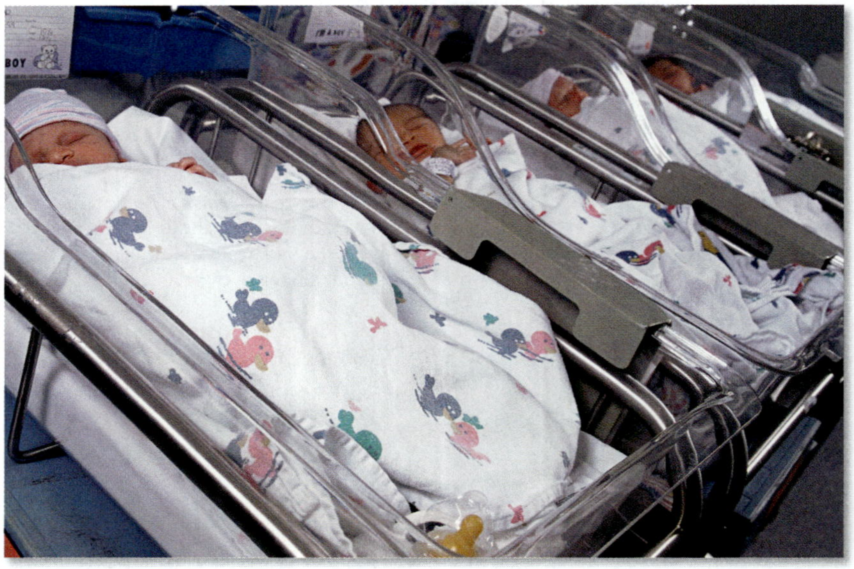



## Troubleshooting

Watch for students who give the same answer for Exercises 10a and 10b. Have them write the proportion for each part. Students who do not see how a percentage can be 200% or more may benefit from using a concrete model.

Have students compare four cubes to determine that they are the same size. Choose one cube to use as a benchmark and compare the other cubes to it. Point out that each cube is 100% of the size of the benchmark cube. Then have students stack two cubes and compare the stack to the benchmark cube. The stack is 200% of the size of the benchmark cube. Repeat with three cubes.

## Practice & Apply

1. Travel surveys show that 68% of people who travel for pleasure do so by car. Of 338 students from Brown Middle School who traveled for pleasure last year, 237 did so by car. The same year, 134 students from Mayville Middle School traveled for pleasure, and 88 did so by car.

   **a.** Draw a percent diagram to illustrate this situation. See margin.

   **b.** From which school did a higher percentage of those who traveled for pleasure do so by car? Brown

   **c.** How do the two schools compare to the survey results? See below.

For each pair of ratios, determine which is greater by finding the percentages they represent.

**2.** $\frac{13}{12}$ or $\frac{65}{60}$ **3.** $\frac{23}{28}$ or $\frac{44}{51}$ **4.** $\frac{328}{467}$ or $\frac{16}{23}$

**5.** Find four ratios equivalent to 30%. Possible answer: $\frac{3}{10}, \frac{12}{40}, \frac{39}{130}, \frac{150}{500}$

**6.** Find four ratios equivalent to 25%. Possible answer: $\frac{25}{100}, \frac{4}{16}, \frac{7}{28}, \frac{100}{400}$

In Exercises 7–9, decide which is a greater number.

**7.** $P$% of 13 or $P$% of 23 $P$% of 23

**8.** $P$% of 368 or $P$% of 712 $P$% of 712

**9.** $P$% of 3 or $P$% of 4.7 $P$% of 4.7

In Exercises 10–12, decide which represents a greater percentage.

**10.** $t$ out of 100 or $t$ out of 200 $t$ out of 100

**11.** $t$ out of 89 or $t$ out of 91 $t$ out of 89

**12.** $t$ out of 0.7 or $t$ out of 0.5 $t$ out of 0.5

**13.** Consider the question *5% of what number is 15?*

   **a.** Draw a percent diagram to represent the question.

   **b.** Express the statement as a proportion and solve it. $\frac{15}{n} = \frac{5}{100}$, $n = 300$

**14.** 98% of what number is 50? About 51.02

**15.** 117% of what number is 3.5? About 2.99

**16.** 7.5 is what percent of 9? $83\frac{1}{3}$%

**17.** 20 is what percent of 15? $133\frac{1}{3}$%

1c. About 70.1% of Brown students traveled by car, which is greater than average. About 65.7% of Mayville students traveled by car, which is below average.

2. $\frac{13}{12} \approx 108.3\%$, $\frac{65}{60} \approx 108.3\%$; They are the same.

3. $\frac{23}{28} \approx 82.1\%$, $\frac{44}{51} \approx 86.3\%$; $\frac{44}{51}$ is greater.

4. $\frac{328}{467} \approx 70.2\%$, $\frac{16}{23} \approx 69.6\%$; $\frac{328}{467}$ is greater.

13a.

### Additional Answer

1a.

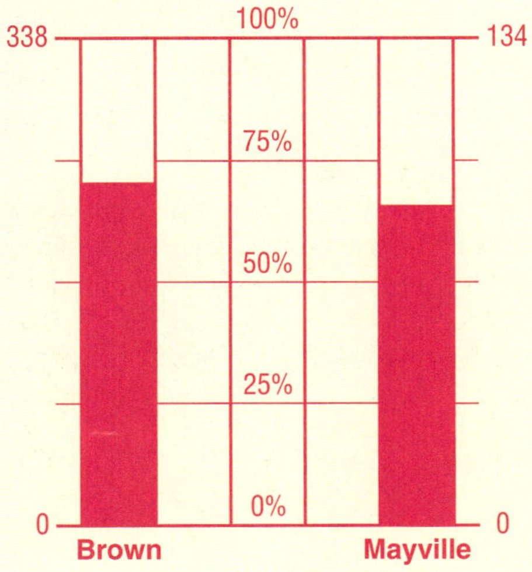




**Investigation 1**
Pages 530–533
Practice & Apply: 1–12
Connect & Extend: 22–23

**Investigation 2**
Pages 534–536
Practice & Apply: 13–21
Connect & Extend: 24–26

**Assign Anytime**
Mixed Review: 27–36

▶ **Exercise 1** Some students may be confused by the information given from the survey, which is irrelevant to Parts a and b of the exercise. Point out that this information is required to solve Part c of the exercise. You might also point out that the students in these two schools are remarkably close to the national averages in their travel habits.

▶ **Exercises 7–12** Students compare statements containing variables. It is interesting to note that all these exercises have a definite answer, even though one of the variables is not known. If necessary, remind students of the following basic convention of algebra: When a letter is used more than once in a exercise, it always stands for the same number.

▶ **Exercises 10–12** Some students may write each comparison as a ratio with t as the top number. Then they can use the size of the bottom number to order the ratios.

▶ **Exercise 18a** Many students may solve the exercise incorrectly by finding that 5% of \$115.92 is \$5.80; then they might subtract \$5.80 from \$115.92, leaving \$110.12. You might point out that since 5% of their answer of \$110.12 is \$5.51, adding this raise to the original salary gives a final salary of \$115.63. But this is not the final salary of \$115.92 given in the exercise.

Some students may think that this discrepancy is due to rounding errors, in which case you might have them redo the calculation carrying out all decimal places. The real trouble is that students have calculated the amount of the raise using the later, not the initial salary.

One way to do the exercise correctly is to use the following calculations. Use a calculator to carry out all decimal places.

$$\begin{aligned} \text{new} &= \text{old} + (5\% \cdot \text{old}) \\ &= 105\% \cdot \text{old} \\ &= \frac{105}{100} \cdot \text{old} \\ \text{old} &= \left(\frac{100}{105}\right) \cdot \text{new} \\ &= 0.952\ldots \cdot 115.92 \\ &= \$110.40 \end{aligned}$$

▶ **Exercise 18c** Point out that when the weekly pay goes up by 5%, so does the hourly pay.

**Additional Answer**

22. Possible answer: There are 120 seventh graders at Roosevelt Middle School. 65% are going on a field trip to Gettysburg. How many students are going? Solution: $\frac{x}{120} = \frac{65}{100}$; $x = 78$.





**18.** Seth works 12 hours a week. He recently received a 5% raise. His new weekly pay is \$115.92.

- **a.** What was Seth's weekly pay before the raise? \$110.40
- **b.** What was his hourly pay before the raise? \$9.20
- **c.** What is his new hourly rate? \$9.66

**19.** In Woodrow Wilson Middle School, three-fourths of the students study a foreign language.

- **a.** Suppose 540 students study a foreign language. How many students attend Woodrow Wilson Middle School? 720
- **b.** Of the students studying a foreign language, 60% study Spanish. How many students study Spanish? 324
- **c.** Of the students studying a foreign language, 15% study French. How many students study French? 81

20. Jeans Are Us; Price at Jeans Are Us: \$25.60; Price at Denim World: \$26.78

**20.** Nora and her mother went shopping for jeans. Two stores, Jeans Are Us and Denim World, carried Nora's favorite pair of jeans. At Jeans Are Us, the jeans were discounted 20% off the regular price of \$32. At Denim World, the jeans typically sold for \$35. However, the jeans had been discounted an additional 10% off a 15% sale price.

From which store should Nora have purchased the jeans? Explain your reasoning.

**21. Social Studies** In 2000, about 20,530,000 children between the ages of 10 and 14 lived in the United States. That was about 7.3% of the entire U.S. population. Find the 2000 U.S. population.

## Connect & Extend

21. About 281,232,877

**22.** Create a real-world word problem that requires finding 65% of 120. Show how to solve your situation. See margin.

**23.** The students at Graves Middle School held a fundraiser to help purchase new gym equipment. The school newspaper reported that the eighth grade raised the most, \$234. The sixth and seventh grades each raised 30% of the total amount collected. However, the paper did not report the total amount raised by the three grades.

Use the information given to find the total amount raised and the amounts raised by the sixth and seventh grades.
Total: \$585; sixth and seventh grades: \$175.50 each

**24. Challenge** Suppose $S > 0$ and $S = 2T$.

- **a.** Which is greater, 80% of $T$ or 40% of $S$? Explain your answer.
- **b.** Does your answer to Part a hold if $S < 0$? Explain. Yes; 40% of $S$ equals 40% of $2T$ or 80% of $T$. The sign of $S$ does not change anything in the equation.

24a. They are the same. Substituting $2T$ for $S$, 40% of $S$ is equal to 40% of $2T$, or 80% of $T$.

**25.** The table below shows data collected by a school district regarding its high school students.

| | Athletes, per 100 Students | Honor Roll Students, per 100 Students |
|---|---|---|
| Freshmen | 23 About 311 | 35 About 473 |
| Sophomores | 48 About 648 | 47 About 635 |
| Juniors | 41 About 554 | 54 About 729 |
| Seniors | 52 About 702 | 36 About 486 |

**a.** Suppose the district has about 1,350 students in each grade. About how many students at each grade level are athletes? About how many students are on the honor roll? See table.

**b.** The entries in both columns are "per 100 students." What would be the entry for freshmen athletes if the scale was per 10 students? What if the scale was per 1,000 students? 2.3; 230

**26. In Your Own Words** Describe several ways that percents are used to compare different quantities.

26. Answers will vary. Possible answers: Percents are used to compare performances, such as batting averages or test scores. Percents are also used to indicate sale prices.

***Mixed Review***

**Determine whether the following statements are *always, sometimes,* or *never* true.**

**27.** A rational number is also an integer. Sometimes

**28.** A natural number is also a whole number. Always

**29.** A smaller whole number can be given than the original whole number given. Sometimes

**30.** A number can be both rational and irrational. Never

For Exercises 31 and 32, identify which number is greater. Explain how you found your answer.

**31.** $\frac{5}{8}$ or $\frac{10}{22}$

**32.** $-9.275$ or $-9\frac{6}{20}$

31. $\frac{5}{8}$; Possible explanation: $\frac{5}{8}$ is a little bit more than $\frac{1}{2}$ and $\frac{10}{22}$ is a little bit less than $\frac{1}{2}$.

32. $-9.275$; Possible explanation: $-9\frac{6}{20}$ is $-9.3$ which is less than $-9.275$.

In Exercises 33–36, $\Delta ABC$ is a right triangle, and $c$ represents the hypotenuse. Use the Pythagorean Theorem to find each missing side. Round answers to the nearest hundredth, if necessary.

**33.** $a = 6$ inches, $b = 8$ inches, $c = ?$ 10 inches

**34.** $a = 5$ centimeters, $b = 7$ centimeters, $c = ?$ 8.60 centimeters

**35.** $a = 5$ feet, $b = ?$, $c = 13$ feet 12 feet

**36.** $a = ?$, $b = 4$ units, $c = 9$ units 8.06 units



On Your Own Exercises

▶ **Exercise 25** The table in this exercise may cause some confusion for students. The students may assume that the numbers in the table represent the number of students in each category, when they actually represent the number per 100 students in each category. Take this opportunity to discuss with students the importance of reading the headings of the tables and not just jumping into calculations.

## *Quick Check*

**Informal Assessment** Students should be able to:

- ✔ recognize percents as ratios with a common scale of 100
- ✔ recognize percents as a convenient way to compare ratios
- ✔ solve percent exercises using proportions

## *Quick Quiz*

**1.** Manny finished 9 of the 15 homework exercises assigned. Janellen has finished 8 of the 12 exercises assigned in her class. Who is closer to being finished? Use percentages to tell how much closer. Janellen is closer by $6\frac{2}{3}$%, Manny has finished 60% while Janellen has finished $66\frac{2}{3}$%.

**2.** Joanna collects stamps and recently increased her stamp collection by 10%. Before the increase, Joanna had 1,369 stamps, how many does she have now? 1,506 stamps

**3.** Jong wanted to purchase a new pair of rollerblades. Store A sold the pair he wanted for $79 and all rollerblades were currently on sale for a 20% discount. Store B sold the same rollerblades for $69, but the rollerblades were only on sale for a 10% discount. If Jong wants to get the rollerblades from the store with the lower price, where should he purchase his rollerblades? Why? Store B, the rollerblades will cost $62.10. If Jong bought them from Store A, they would cost $63.20.

LESSON

# 10.4 Rates

## Objectives

- ▶ To use rates to determine unit prices
- ▶ To determine a unit rate
- ▶ To use rates, proportions, or equations to convert currency rates

## Overview

This lesson reviews and extends what students know about ratios to include unit rates, In addition, students will use their knowledge to convert money into different countries currency. This can be done with rate, proportions, or equations.

## Advance Preparation

You may want to look through sales ads for current sales of food to assist with determining unit prices.

| | Summary | Materials | On Your Own Exercises (pp. 547–550) | Assessment Opportunities |
|---|---|---|---|---|
| **Investigation 1** (p. 540) Pacing: 2 days | Students will use their knowledge of rates to determine the unit price of items. | newspaper, circulars with grocery store sale prices | Practice & Apply: 1–5<br>Connect & Extend: 9–14<br>Mixed Review: 19–23 | • On the Spot Assessment (pp. 540, 542)<br>• Share & Summarize (p. 543)<br>• Troubleshooting (p. 541) |
| **Investigation 2** (p. 544) Pacing: 1 day | Students use their skills with proportions to determine currency exchange rates. | newspaper, circulars or retail catalog, calculator, current currency rate information from the Internet | Practice & Apply: 6–8<br>Connect & Extend: 15–18<br>Mixed Review: 19–23 | • On the Spot Assessment (p. 544)<br>• Share & Summarize (p. 546)<br>• Troubleshooting (p. 545) |

# Leveled Lesson Resources

CRM *Available in:* **Chapter 10 Resource Masters**

Also on TeacherWorks™
Lesson 10.4

## Study Guide and Intervention (p. 20) AL

**Lesson 10.4 Study Guide and Intervention**
***Rates***

A ratio that compares two quantities with different kinds of units is called a **rate**. When a rate is simplified so that it is given in terms of one unit, it is called a **unit rate**. You can use **exchange rates** to find equivalent **currencies**.

***Example 1*** **Alita drove her car 78 miles and used 3 gallons of gas. What is the car's gas mileage in miles per gallon?**

$\frac{78 \text{ miles}}{3 \text{ gallons}} = \frac{x \text{ miles}}{1 \text{ gallon}}$ Write a proportion.

$1 \text{ gallon} \cdot \frac{78 \text{ miles}}{3 \text{ gallons}} = \frac{x \text{ miles}}{1 \text{ gallon}} \cdot 1 \text{ gallon}$ Multiply each side by 1 gallon.

$26 = x$ Simplify, dividing out the common units.

So, the car's gas mileage is 26 miles per gallon.

***Example 2*** **Joe is shopping for cereal. The 12-ounce box costs $2.54, and the 18-ounce box costs $3.50. Which box costs less per ounce?**

Divide each price by the number of ounces.

12-ounce box $\$2.54 \div 12 \text{ ounces} \approx \$0.21$ per ounce
18-ounce box $\$3.50 \div 18 \text{ ounces} \approx \$0.19$ per ounce

So, the 18-ounce box costs less per ounce.

***Example 3*** **Via went shopping in Brazil. The exchange rate was 1 U.S. dollar equals 1.09984 Brazilian reals. She paid 142.50 reals for a necklace. What was the approximate cost of the necklace in U.S. dollars?**

$\frac{1 \text{ dollar}}{1.09984 \text{ reals}} = \frac{x \text{ dollar}}{142.5 \text{ reals}}$ Write a proportion.

$142.5 \text{ reals} \cdot \frac{1 \text{ dollar}}{1.09984 \text{ reals}} = \frac{x \text{ dollar}}{142.5 \text{ reals}} \cdot 142.5 \text{ reals}$ Multiply each side by 142.5 reals.

$129.56 = x$ Simplify, rounding to the nearest hundredth.

So, the necklace costs about $129.56.

***Exercises***

1. Juanita paid $156 for 3 books. Find the unit rate.
2. Which is the better buy: 3 pounds of nuts for $12.95 or 5 pounds of nuts for $21.45?
3. Jane paid 21 euros for dinner in France. The exchange rate was 1 U.S. dollar equals 0.66175 euros. What was the approximate cost in U.S. dollars?

## Skills Practice (p. 21) AL OL

**Lessons 10.4 Skills Practice**
***Rates***

Find each unit rate.

1. $118 in 8 hours
2. 150 miles in 6 gallons
3. 49 points in 7 games
4. 105 students in 3 classes
5. 112 patients in 4 weeks
6. $8.43 for 3 pounds

Choose the better unit price.

7. $4.99 for 6 cans or $7.99 for 10 cans
8. $21.50 for 4 pounds of lunch meat or $15.10 for 3 pounds of lunch meat
9. $99 for 12 DVDs or $58 for 7 DVDs
10. $0.89 for 0.65 pounds or $1.29 for 0.95 pounds
11. **Shopping** Robbie went shopping in Quebec, Canada. The exchange rate was 1 U.S. dollar equals 1.02969 Canadian dollars. Complete the table.

| Item | Cost in Canadian dollars | Cost in U.S. dollars |
|---|---|---|
| Book | 28.95 | |
| Taxi Fare | 45.60 | |
| Lunch | 15.82 | |
| Pants | 68.45 | |
| Coffeemaker | 125.10 | |
| Lamp | 96.54 | |

## Problem-Solving Practice (p. 22) AL OL

**Lesson 10.4 Problem-Solving Practice**
***Rates***

Solve.

1. **Budget** Steve was offered $5,025 per year for a weekend lifeguarding job at a local pool. He wants to know how much his monthly income will be at this salary level. What is his rate of pay in dollars per month?
2. **Carpeting** Hana paid $1,200 for the carpet in her living room. The room has an area of 251.2 square feet. What was her unit cost of carpeting in dollars per square foot? Round to the nearest cent.
3. **Tomatoes** An 8-ounce can of tomatoes costs $1.14. A 12-ounce can costs $1.75. Which can of tomatoes has the better unit price? Explain.
4. **Shopping** Colleen and Bill were shopping in London. The exchange rate was 1 U.S. dollar equals 0.47938 pounds. Colleen paid 18 pounds for a pair of shoes, and Bill paid 52 pounds for a guitar. What was the total amount spent in U.S. dollars?
5. **Restaurant** Melvena wants to purchase coconut oil for her restaurant. The 24-ounce jar sells regularly at $18 but is currently on sale at a 10% discount. The 48-ounce jar is on sale for three-fourths of the regular cost of a 60-ounce jar. The 60-ounce jar usually sells for $50 and is on sale for $42.50.
   a. Identify the cost of each jar.
   b. Find the difference in cost between the most expensive unit cost and the least expensive unit cost.
   c. Melvena is going to buy two jars. If she selects the best unit cost, what will be her total cost before tax?
6. **Travel** Quinn is traveling to Denmark this summer. He finds the following information on the Internet about the value of Danish currency.

   1 U.S. dollar = 4.93314 Danish krones (DKK)

   Quinn saved $5,680 in his bank account. He plans to convert three-fifths of his savings into Danish krones. How much money will he have to spend while in Denmark?

## Enrichment (p. 23) BL

**Lesson 10.4 Enrichment**
***Rates***

**What Am I?**

Find each unit rate. Then, starting at the box marked "Start here," draw an arrow to the adjacent box containing the unit rate with the least value. (You may move horizontally or vertically. You may use each box at most once.)

| | | | | |
|---|---|---|---|---|
| | 24-ounce **s**moothie for $4.88 | 6 **p**apayas for $7.27 | 3 pairs of **p**ants for $45.56 | 15 bags of **m**ulch for $130.22 |
| 20 **l**ight bulbs for $14.03 | 4 cans of **t**una for $4.81 | 5 bushels of **o**ats for $70.62 | 25 **n**otebooks for $27.74 | 4 baskets of **p**ineapples for $52.21 |
| **Start here.** 6 **a**pples for $2.84 | 8 **p**ears for $4.23 | 3 bags of **i**ce for $3.96 | 12 crates of **z**innias for $186.60 | 5 **u**mbrellas for $43.35 |
| 15 **o**ranges for $10.21 | 7-pound bag of **r**ice for $4.15 | 9 boxes of **t**issues for $28.25 | 2 **z**ip-up jackets for $33.91 | 4 **s**hirts for $70.05 |
| 5 **p**eaches for $2.57 | 3 cans of **o**lives for $3.85 | 8 boxes of **r**aisins for $19.25 | 3 packages of **l**emons for $10.02 | **Stop here.** 12 **e**ggs for $3.86 |
| 14 **n**otebooks for $18.08 | 6 jars of **p**ickles for $14.60 | 2 cans of **a**lmonds for $6.45 | 16 **m**angos for $14.25 | 9 **s**tickers for $1.05 |

Use the first letters of the products to fill in the table below in the order in which you found them. Now you can say what I am.

## Lesson Quick Quiz (p. 24) AL OL BL

**Lesson 10.4 Quick Quiz**

1. A store is selling a 3-pound bag of apples for $1.49. What is the cost per pound of apples?
2. Store A sells a 4-pack of AA size batteries for $3.79. Store B sells a 6-pack of AA size batteries for $4.19. Which store has the better price per battery?
3. Jaxon is going to Belgium for spring break. He wants to convert $250 to euros. If the conversion rate is 1 euro = $1.59, how many euros will Jaxon have?

# Additional Lesson Resources

### Teacher Tech Tools
- TeacherWorks
- ExamView Assessment Suite
- Classroom Presentation Toolkit
- Advance Tracker

### Student Tech Tools
- StudentWorks Plus
- Math Online eGlossary • Concepts in Motion

### Other Print Products
- Investigation Notebook and Reflection Journal
- Quick Review Math Handbook

## LESSON 10.4 Rates

### *Introduce*

**Rates versus Ratios** The lesson begins by giving a brief synopsis of what makes a rate different from a ratio. Students are aware of rates and ratios, but probably do not think much about the distinction. Take time to ask students for examples of rates and ratios and compare how they are alike and different. This leads right in to the Think & Discuss.

**Think & Discuss**

*Suggested Grouping: Small Groups*

Compare similarities and differences of rates and ratios. Have the students make a list of at least four rates that compare distance and time.

**Investigation 1**

***On Your Own Exercises***
Pages 547–550
Exercises 1–5, 9–14

**Unit Rate** This investigation focuses on unit prices. Express to students that this really is just the cost of one of something. It is a rate because it compares money to an item.

**Think & Discuss**

*Suggested Grouping: Pairs*

Not all students will be familiar with the intricacies of cell phone plans. It may be helpful to go on the internet and gather information about a variety of cell phone plans from a variety of companies for the students to use as background information.

# LESSON 10.4 Rates



Rates are special types of ratios. You might not realize that you read, write, and speak about rates in everyday situations. A rate, like a *ratio*, involves division. What is unique about rates is that they represent the comparison of two related, but different quantities.

When someone has a job, he or she thinks about how money and time are related. The more hours a person works, the more money he or she earns. You can say that time and money are *related*. You can write the rate as money compared to time or dollars per hour.

**Think & Discuss**

Can you think of more related quantities? See ①.

What about distance compared to time? Possible answers: Miles per hour, meters per second, feet per minute.

① Possible answers: Amount of homework per class, number of students per classroom, miles per gallon, words per minute

In this lesson, you will learn to read, write, and solve real-world problems involving rates.

## Investigation 1 Unit Prices

**Vocabulary**
unit rate

**Materials**
- newspaper circulars with grocery store sales prices

Going to the market or grocery store is a real-life situation loaded with mathematics. To be a wise consumer, you want to learn how to get the best buy for your money. There are different factors that determine how most people spend their money, but one of the most common factors is the lowest unit rate.

In this investigation, you will explore real-world situations related to shopping and the use of **unit rates**.

**Think & Discuss**

When have you heard prices stated "per unit"? Possible answer: Cars and miles per gallon

List three different situations that involve unit rates. See ②.

Think of a cell phone plan. Name some parts of the plan that are given in a unit rate. How much is each minute you use? How much is each text message? Possible answer: Cost per minute used, cost per text message

② Possible answer: Cost per movie ticket, dollars earned per hour, distance traveled per hour, cost per pound of grapes



**On the Spot Assessment**

Write down at least three rates. Do not use dollars per hour or miles per hour.

### Example

| These *are* unit rates. | These are *not* unit rates. |
|---|---|
| 2 lb oranges/$1.00 | 3/$15.00 to purchase t-shirts |
| $3.55/gallon for gas | 100/$5.00 for text messages |
| 0.25 miles/$1 for a taxi | $25/8 hours for parking |
| $10/hour to rent a bicycle | $200/5 days of work |

In Course 1, you learned that a unit rate is a term used when a quantity is compared to one unit of another quantity. In the example, each unit rate has a denominator equal to one.

**Math Link**

When you talk about a *unit* price, the unit must always be included so it is clear what quantities and relationships are being compared. If you say oranges are $2.25, others would not know if that is for one orange, one bag of oranges, or one box of oranges. The units make a difference.

### Explore

With a partner, prepare for a trip to the market or grocery store. You only have $25 to spend. You want to make sure to spend the money wisely, so you use newspaper advertisements to comparison shop.

Your task is to create a list of six similar items that are listed in at least two of the flyers. Then determine the unit rate of each item in order to determine which items are the best buys.

### Example

The cost of six cans of fruit juice is $3.20. How would you determine the cost of one can of the fruit juice?

To determine the cost of one can of fruit juice, set up the ratio $\frac{\$3.20}{6 \text{ cans}}$.

By dividing the quantities, you find the cost of one can is about $0.53. So, the unit price can be written as the ratio $0.53/1 can.

You can also find unit rates by setting up and solving proportions. If six cans cost $3.20, how much does one can cost?

$$\frac{\$3.20}{6 \text{ cans}} = \frac{x}{1 \text{ can}}$$

$$1 \text{ can} \cdot \left(\frac{\$3.20}{6 \text{ cans}}\right) = 1 \text{ can} \cdot \left(\frac{x}{1 \text{ can}}\right)$$ To solve, multiply each side by 1 can, the denominator of the right side.

$$\frac{\$3.20}{6} = x$$ Divide out the common units on both sides.

$$\$0.53 = x$$ Divide $3.20 by 6. Round to the nearest cent.

One can costs $0.53.



### Example

Ask the students to give rates for items. Make two columns like in the example and separate the unit rates from the non-unit rates. Discuss what makes the non-unit rates not unit rates.

### Explore

It will be helpful for you to go through the grocery sales flyers prior to this activity to make sure that there are six similar items listed in two different flyers. If not, modify the directions to fit the sales for the week.

### Example

Take the items from the lists you made in the previous example and discuss with the students how you would make these non-unit rates into unit rates. If using proportions does not come about on its own, encourage the use of proportions and tie it into what the students have been doing.

## Troubleshooting

If students are having difficulty distinguishing what qualifies as a unit rate, have the students ask, "How many items is this for?" If the answer is more than one, than the rate is not a unit rate. Writing the rate as a fraction can also help students see that if the denominator is not 1, the rate is not a unit rate.

## Develop & Understand: A

*Suggested Grouping: Pairs*

▶ **Exercise 2** Students need to determine the unit rate prior to being able to answer the question. If students are struggling with this concept, this exercise is an excellent place to show how to use proportions to determine the unit rate.

▶ **Exercise 4** The students are being asked to determine the unit rate for tickets purchased at a group rate. Next, the students need to determine how much the 16 tickets would have cost at the regular price and determine the difference between that value and $300, which is what the group tickets cost.

### Think & Discuss

*Suggested Grouping: Whole Class*

When discussing these questions as a large group, allow the students time to formulate a response before asking for volunteers. The concept of a per dollar rate is not something that students probably see or hear very often.

## Develop & Understand: B

*Suggested Grouping: Individuals*

▶ **Exercise 5** This is an excellent question to determine if the students are comprehending the concept of unit rates.

▶ **Exercise 6** If students are having trouble determining how to set up a proportion to solve for a unit rate, tell them to look for the word "per," as in miles per hour. This becomes the fraction bar and whatever comes before the word "per" goes in the numerator of the fraction and whatever word follows "per" goes in the denominator of the fraction. So miles per hour would become $\frac{\text{miles}}{\text{hour}}$.

## Develop & Understand: A

1. Edwin is shopping with his mom. He sees that oranges are on sale. A bag of 15 oranges cost $3.75. Calculate the unit rate of each orange. $0.25 per orange
2. Mandy and her twin brother Miles are looking at a sales flyer for a local discount store. They see that one of their favorite snacks is on sale at three snacks for $4.50. If the regular cost of one bag of the snacks is $1.95, how much will Mandy and Miles save on one bag of snacks at the sale price? $0.45
3. Mr. Hernandez is comparison-shopping for DVDs at two stores. Hi-Mart is selling three DVDs for $41.94. Super-Saver is selling four DVDs for $54.84. If Mr. Hernandez wants to purchase one dozen DVDs, which store is offering the better buy? Super-Saver
4. Parker is going to a professional baseball game with his scouting group. The regular cost of a ticket is $23.50 per person. His scout leader bought the tickets at a special group rate. The total cost was $300 for all 16 people to attend the game. What was the cost per ticket at the group rate? How much did the scouts save? $18.75 per person; They saved $76 as a group.

Unit rates can also be expressed using the opposite relationship. In Exercise 3, you found the unit rate of one DVD at Super-Saver to be $13.71. You can also express the relationship as how many DVDs you can buy for one dollar.

### Think & Discuss

How would you rewrite the unit rate for the DVDs in terms of a per dollar rate? See ①.

Why do you think that you do not typically see unit rates expressed this way? See ②.

Are there other situations where this might be useful? See ③.

① I would set up the proportion $\frac{1}{\$13.71} = \frac{x}{\$1.00}$. This comes to .073 DVD per dollar.

② You cannot have part of a DVD. While the answer is mathematically possible, it does not make sense in a real-life situation.

③ Yes. Possible answer: The amount of gasoline that can be purchased for a dollar.

## Develop & Understand: B

5. Destiny wants to go roller-skating with her friends. The skating rink offers a "Terrific Tuesday" rate of $15 for four hours of skating. How much are Destiny and her friends being charged per hour? $3.75/hour
6. If Nina drives from Spokane, Washington, to Portland, Oregon, in 6.5 hours, what is her speed in miles per hours? Approximately 56.2 MPH

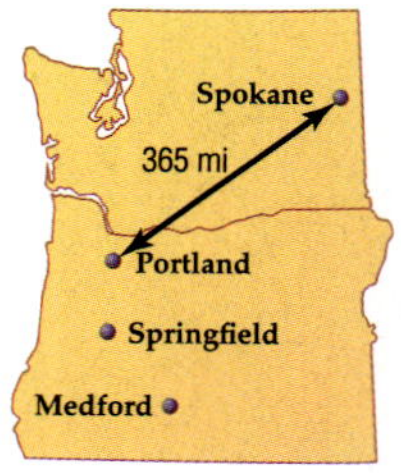




### On the Spot Assessment

Ursula is traveling 946 kilometers from Chicago, IL to Topeka, KS. She expects it to take her about 9 hours to make the trip. What is the approximate unit rate that Ursula would be traveling? ≈105 km/h

542 CHAPTER 10 Proportional Reasoning and Percents

**7.** Juan and Amelia are driving from school to a concert. The concert location is 18 miles from school. Suppose it takes Juan 33 minutes to drive from the school to the concert. It takes Amelia 25 minutes to drive the same route. How much greater is Amelia's speed?

## Develop & Understand: C

Knowledge of unit rates can help budget expenses for a project.

**8.** Mallory and her sister want to paint the four walls of their rectangular-shaped bedroom. The bedroom's length is 10 feet, the width is 8 feet and the height is 9 feet. One gallon of paint costs $25 and covers 300 square feet. Suppose Mallory and her sister want to apply two coats of paint. Will they be able to paint the bedroom for a cost of $50? Explain your reasoning.

**9.** The Fuentes family is comparison shopping for a fish aquarium. A local pet store sells two sizes of aquariums. The aquariums' dimensions and prices are listed below.

| | Width (in.) | Depth (in.) | Height (in.) | Price |
|---|---|---|---|---|
| **Aquarium 1** | 24 | 12 | 16 | $156.74 |
| **Aquarium 2** | 36 | 15 | 16 | $239.99 |

Which aquarium is the better buy? Explain your thinking.

### Share & Summarize

Compare these two advertisements.

Which is the better deal? Use rate, proportion, and unit rate in your explanation. See ①.

7. Juan's speed = 32.7 mph; Amelia's speed = 43.2 mph; Amelia's speed is 10.5 mph greater.

8. No. $50 is the cost for two gallons of paint. Two gallons of paint cover 600 square feet of surface area. The girls will be painting a total of 648 square feet when they apply two coats.

9. Aquarium 2 is the better deal. The volume of the first aquarium is 4,608 cubic inches for a cost of a little more than 3 cents per cubic inch. The volume of the second aquarium is 8,640 cubic inches for a cost of a little less than 3 cents per cubic inch.

① 5 pair for $18.99 is the better deal; The two rates are $\frac{\$18.99}{5}$ pair and $\frac{\$12.50}{3}$ pair. To compare the unit rate, or price for one pair of socks, I can set up the proportion *rate* = $\frac{\$X}{1}$ pair to see which deal is better. Or, I can set up the ratios $\frac{\$18.99}{5}$ and $\frac{\$12.50}{3}$ then divide to get a per pair rate to compare the two rates to each other.



## Develop & Understand: C

*Suggested Grouping: Pairs*

▶ **Exercise 8** Students may have difficulty with this exercise because they need to determine the surface area of each wall, not the area of the room or the volume of the room. Students may become discouraged when their computation is not correct.

▶ **Exercise 9** It may be helpful to students if you give them a hint that they need to do their calculation to the nearest tenth or hundredth of a cent. The unit rate is about 3 cents for this exercise, tank 1 slightly higher and tank 2 slightly lower. Students may not see a difference because money is always rounded to the hundredths position and therefore both tanks cost about the same amount per cubic inch.

**Wrap-Up** As the pairs complete the Develop & Understand, use these exercises as a way to verify that students understand the concept of unit rates. Have each pair meet with another pair to share their responses and to determine if they have any additional questions.

### Share & Summarize

The students should feel very comfortable once they successfully complete this activity. If questions remain, instruct the students to seek additional assistance. Take that time to walk through the process of constructing a unit rate at a slower pace with additional examples.

## Investigation 2

***On Your Own Exercises***
Pages 547–550
Exercises 6–8, 15–18

**Currency** Students are already experienced working with unit conversions of foreign currency to the dollar. Students may have asked questions referring to a constant value for the currency and that is never the case. The conversion changes hourly, and many institutions are there to assist in the process.

### Explore

When looking for exchange rates, many banks and financial institutions post their conversion rates on the internet. Encourage students to pick major foreign countries to travel to as it may be more difficult to find the conversion to smaller, not as widely traveled to, countries.

### Example

As students work through this example, try to have the current conversion available for the U.S. dollar to the yen. Discuss with students why they think that the rate changes so frequently.

***Real-World Link***
Have the students calculate the average amount spent per visitor. About $2,121

## Investigation 2 Converting Currencies

### Materials

- newspaper circulars or retail catalogs
- calculator
- current currency rate information from the Internet

As you discovered earlier, you will want to know the current exchange rate for the U.S. dollar if you travel to another country. *Currency* is the legal tender of a country. In the United States, it is the dollar. The exchange rate for the U.S. dollar with foreign currencies fluctuates, or changes, daily.

In this investigation, you will use your calculator to convert currencies of other countries to U.S. dollars. Comparing currencies involves ratios.

### Explore

Use your newspaper circular or catalog to find the retail prices of five different items. Then, select a country that you would like to visit. Convert the price of your five items from U.S. dollars to your selected country's currency.

***Real-World Link***
In 2005, 49.4 million foreign visitors spent a total of 104.8 billion dollars in the United States.

### Example

Mr. Marcel is in Japan. He wants to buy a watch for his daughter. The watch costs 7,696.58 Japanese yen. Mr. Marcel sees the current exchange rate posted in the store.

What is the cost of the watch in U.S. dollars? To find out, you can set up and solve a proportion.

- Set up your proportion.

$$\frac{1 \text{ Japanese yen}}{0.008835 \text{ U.S. dollars}} = \frac{7{,}696.58 \text{ Japanese yen}}{x \text{ U.S. dollars}}$$

- Multiply both sides by $x$ U.S. dollars.

$$\frac{1 \text{ Japanese yen} \cdot (x \text{ U.S. dollars})}{0.008835 \text{ U.S. dollars}} = \frac{7{,}696.58 \text{ Japanese yen} \cdot (x \text{ U.S. dollars})}{x \text{ U.S. dollars}}$$

- Simplify each side.

$$\frac{1 \text{ Japanese yen} \cdot (x)}{0.008835} = 7{,}696.58 \text{ Japanese yen}$$

- Divide both sides by 1 Japanese yen.

$$\frac{1 \text{ Japanese yen} \cdot (x)}{(1 \text{ Japanese yen}) \cdot 0.008835} = \frac{7{,}696.58 \text{ Japanese yen}}{1 \text{ Japanese yen}}$$

- Simplify each side.

$$\frac{x}{0.008835} = 7{,}696.58$$

- Multiply both sides by 0.008835.

$$x \approx 68$$

So, $x \approx 68$. The watch costs about $68.



### On the Spot Assessment

On Monday one Euro was equivalent to $1.58. If Conrad spent 235 Euro to purchase a gift for his grandmother, how much money did he spend in US dollars?
About $372

## Develop & Understand: A

**Real-World Link**
In 2007, global tourism reached a record level with 898 million people visiting a foreign land.

1. Kara went shopping with her sister Sarah in Ireland. The currency in Ireland is the euro. The exchange rate was 1 U.S. dollar equals 0.69638 euro. The girls paid 179.50 euros for a digital camera. What was the approximate cost of the digital camera in U.S. dollars? About \$258

2. Zhen lives in Mexico. For a summer vacation, she went to China to visit family members. While visiting, she bought a bracelet that cost 34.50 pesos. The bracelet would cost about 23.48796 Chinese yuan renminbi. What was the approximate exchange rate of pesos to yuan? 1 Mexican Peso ≈ 0.68081 Chinese Yuan Renminbi

3. Vincent traveled abroad with several of the school's foreign language club members. The students visited Switzerland, the United Kingdom, and Romania. Each student had to raise \$800 for travel money. How much would the \$800 be worth in each country?

   1 U.S. dollar = 0.69638 euro and 0.69638 euro (EUR) = 1.12326 Switzerland francs (CHF) \$800 U.S. dollar ≈ 557.104 euro, which is ≈ 898.608 Switzerland francs (CHF)
   1 U.S. dollar = 0.69638 euro and 0.69638 euro (EUR) = 0.51962 United Kingdom pounds (GBP) \$800 U.S. dollar ≈ 557.107 euro, which is ≈ 415.696 United Kingdom pounds (GBP)
   1 U.S. dollar = 0.69638 euro and 0.69638 euro (EUR) = 2.53557 Romania new leu (RON) \$800 U.S. dollar ≈ 557.107 euro, which is ≈ 2,028.456 Romania new leu (RON)

In addition to setting up a proportion to find an exchange rate, you can use your knowledge of equations and graphs to convert currencies from different countries.

### Think & Discuss

Suppose you know that the current exchange rate between U.S. dollars and Mexican pesos is \$1.00 to 10.75. How can you set up an equation that shows this relationship? See ①.

Graph your equation. Discuss what you can determine from the graph. See ②.

① Let $x$ be dollars and $y$ be pesos. Set up the equation $1x = 10.75y$ and solve for $y$.
$y = \left(\frac{1}{10.75}\right)x$
or $y = 0.093x$.

②
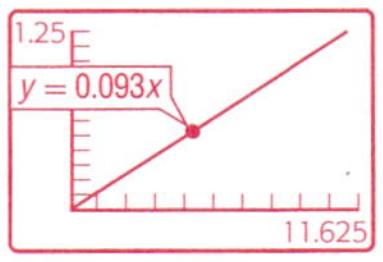


I can see what the number of U.S. dollars are for any given amount of pesos.



## Develop & Understand: A

*Suggested Grouping: Pairs*

▶ **Exercise 2** This exercise requires the students to convert between two different types of foreign currency. It is important to discuss with students that the process is not any different from when they were converting in dollars. Remind students to be consistent in setting up their proportions.

▶ **Exercise 3** This question is a good place to show students other ways, such as graphs or equations, that can be used to convert currencies.

### Think & Discuss

*Suggested Grouping: Pairs*

When students answer these questions, it may be easiest for them to use an example to make their case. Show students how to do this with one of the options not discussed. It may also be helpful to remind students that slope is a rate of change.

## Troubleshooting

The most common mistake that students make when using proportions to solve problems is that they do not keep their ratios and rates in the same order from one part of the proportion to the next. When using rates, stress the importance of using the words given to set up the rate and/or proportion. By using the words, you will always set the proportion up consistently.

**Lesson 10.4** Rates **545**

## Develop & Understand: B

*Suggested Grouping: Individuals*

▶ **Exercises 4 and 5** Remind students that when they set up an equation to solve a problem, the rate of change is the same as the slope of a line.

▶ **Exercise 6** This exercise is a great opportunity to talk about conversions in general, not just with currency. Rates, proportions, and equations can be used any time you are converting from one unit to the next.

**Wrap-Up** Show students that this investigation focused mainly on using unit rates, proportions, and equations as a means to determine the conversion of one unit of currency to the next. Take out currency, and you have a new tool to assist you in many daily tasks.

### Share & Summarize

These questions will assist the students in understanding the practical nature of currency rates and exchanges.

4. 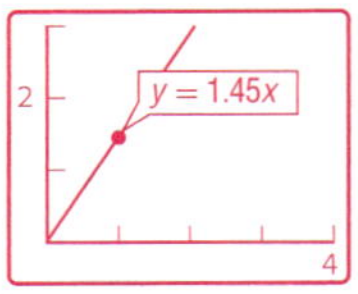

Let $x$ = the number of euros and $y$ = the number of U.S. dollars. $1x = 0.69y$; $1y = 1.45x$

5. 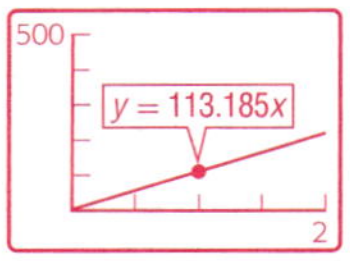

Let $x$ = the number of U.S. dollars and $y$ = the number of Japanese yen. $1y = 113.185x$

6. Answers will vary. Possible answer: Just as with currency conversions, there is a linear relationship between Fahrenheit and Celsius temperatures. A graph can be used to find equivalent temperature measures.

① You want to be a knowledgeable consumer and not get shortchanged, so it is important that you always know the correct currency exchange rate from day to day.

## Develop & Understand: B

In Exercises 4 and 5, a relationship is given between currencies. Describe each relationship with an equation. Graph the equation.

**4.** 1 euro equals 1.45 U.S. dollars.

**5.** 1 U.S. dollar equals 113.185 Japanese yen.

**6.** You have previously converted Fahrenheit and Celsius temperatures. What similarity is there between currency conversions and temperature conversions?

### Share & Summarize

Discuss with a partner why it is important to know the correct daily currency exchange rate when you are traveling abroad. See ①.

How could you use the daily rates if you are in traveling in another country? You can create a conversion chart that will help you keep track of how much money you have spent and will be able to spend.

## Practice & Apply

1. Taryn is shopping with her mother. Bananas are on sale at two different stores. The Best Cost Market advertised price is 4 pounds for $1.25, while the Super Saver Market is advertising their bananas 3 pounds for $0.75.

   Which store has the better price? If the other store agrees to match the sale price of the less expensive store, what will be that store's loss on its original price?

2. The Chang family is remodeling its kitchen and wants to tile the floor. A box of 18 slate tiles costs $54.86. A dozen granite tiles cost $42.36. Which is the better buy based on unit cost? Slate costs $3.05 per tile and granite costs $3.53 per tile. The slate is the better buy.

3. TaKeisha and Jeffery are tiling a mural. The cost of 142 blue tiles was $156.00. The cost of 81 white tiles was $74.00. What was the unit cost of each of the tiles?
   $1.10 for the blue tiles; $0.91 for the white tiles.

4. Belinda wants to buy several strings of miniature lights. One package contains 150 lights and costs $4.65. Another package contains 100 lights and costs $3.87. Belinda needs 600 lights. Which package of lights should she purchase? Explain your reasoning.

5. Mrs. Ramirez is shopping for marigolds to plant in her garden. She needs 48 total plants. A six-pack flat of marigolds costs $1.95. A 48-pack flat of marigolds costs $10.80.

   a. Which flat is the better buy? Explain your reasoning.

   b. Describe a situation in which Mrs. Ramirez may be willing to pay a higher unit cost for the marigolds of her choice. See margin.

6. Weston is planning a spring break trip to Venezuela. The exchange rate is 1.00 U.S. dollar for 2,148.80 Venezuelan bolivars. Weston plans on taking $850 with him on the trip. If Weston converts $\frac{3}{4}$ of his money to bolivars, how many bolivars will he receive in return?
   1,369,860 bolivars

7. Yogi is returning from India where he visited his grandmother this summer. He wants to convert 450 Indian rupees he has back into euros, but there are two ways to do this. Yogi could convert rupees to pounds and then pounds to euros.

   1 Indian rupee is equal to 0.01281 British pounds.

   1 British pound is equal to 1.37259 Euros.

   Or, Yogi could convert rupees directly into Euros?

   1 Indian rupee is equal to 0.01758 Euros.

   Which way do you recommend? Why? Yogi would have 7.912 euros using the first process of changing the rupees into pounds and then changing the pounds into euros. Using the second process, he would have 7.911. Both processes produce about the same result.

1. Super Saver Market has a unit cost of $0.25 per pound. Best Cost Market has a unit cost of $0.31 per pound. If Best Cost Market matches Super Saver Market, it will lose about $0.06 per pound.

4. Belinda should purchase 4 packages of 150 lights for $4.65, which would total $18.60. She would need 6 packages of the 100 lights, which would cost her $23.22.

5a. The 48-pack is a better buy because she would need eight 6 packs to total 48 marigolds, which would total $15.60, which is higher than the 48-pack flat at $10.80.



### Additional Answer

5b. The marigolds in the 48-pack flat may all be the same color. She may be willing to pay more to get a variety of colors by purchasing the smaller 6-pack flats of marigolds.

On Your Own Exercises
Lesson 10.4

**Investigation 1**
Pages 540–543
Practice & Apply: 1–5
Connect & Extend: 9–14

**Investigation 2**
Pages 544–546
Practice & Apply: 6–8
Connect & Extend: 15–18

**Assign Anytime**
Mixed Review: 19–23

▶ **Exercise 2** This exercise is comparing two different types of tiles. The question asks for the better buy based on unit cost. If students have knowledge about these materials, they may argue that the granite is a better buy because of the overall cost. Make sure to discuss that better buy typically means the best price for an item.

▶ **Exercise 4** The reasoning that students exhibit in this exercise will give you good insight into their overall knowledge regarding unit prices.

▶ **Exercise 7** This exercise requires multiple conversions between currency. Instruct students that this is a good place to use proportions.

▶ **Exercise 9** Remind students that when interpreting unit costs from a graph, they need to look at the slope of the line. Slope is a rate of change.

▶ **Exercise 10** This question is a great place to draw students in who like the culinary arts. Ask the students if there is an advantage to using one combination of meat over another.



8. Andrew will have 33,268.32 in Russia rubles, and Megan will have 29,109.78 in Russia rubles.
9. Brand A costs slightly less than Brand B, but much less than either Brand C or Brand D.

**Connect & Extend**

10a. $\frac{85}{15}$ — $0.92 per pound; $\frac{90}{10}$ — $1.19 per pound and $\frac{95}{5}$ — $1.24 per pound.

10b. Difference of $0.32 between the $\frac{85}{15}$ package and the $\frac{95}{5}$ package.

10c. $0.05 between the $\frac{90}{10}$ package and the $\frac{95}{5}$ package.

10d. Possible answer: The difference is that the $\frac{95}{5}$ has a higher percentage of meat and less fat whereas the $\frac{90}{10}$ and $\frac{85}{15}$ packages have more fat, therefore a lower percentage of meat.

**8.** Twins Andrew and Megan are in college. They are going to Russia as exchange students for the fall semester. They found the following information on the Internet about the value of Russian currency.

1 US dollar = 24.6432 Russia rubles (RUB)

Andrew has saved $1,350.00 to take on the trip, and Megan has saved $\frac{7}{8}$ that amount for the trip. If the twins convert all of their U.S. dollars into the Russian ruble, how much money will each have to spend while in Russia?

**9.** The graph below shows the approximate relationship between the costs of four popular brands of dog food. Write a sentence comparing the unit costs for each brand of dog food.

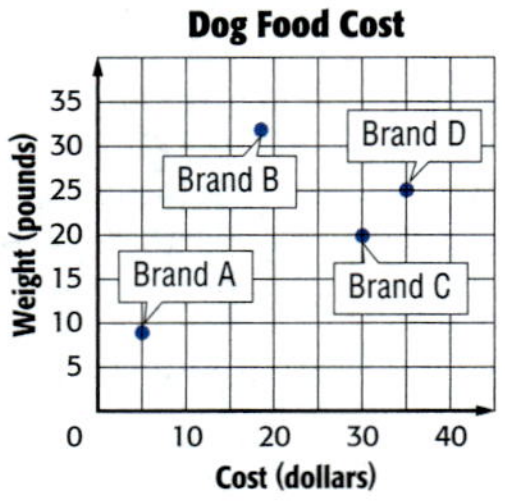


**10.** At Super Cost Market, ground beef has three different prices. Beef that is $\frac{85}{15}$, containing 15% fat, costs $13.85 for 15 pounds. The ground beef that is $\frac{90}{10}$ costs $14.85 for a 12.5 pound package. The ground beef that is $\frac{95}{5}$ costs $17.36 for a 14-pound package.

**a.** Identify the unit cost of each package of ground beef.

**b.** Find the difference in cost between the most expensive unit cost and the least expensive unit cost.

**c.** Find the difference between the most expensive unit cost and the middle unit cost.

**d.** Make a conjecture about why the $\frac{95}{5}$ ground beef costs more than the $\frac{90}{10}$ and the $\frac{85}{15}$ ground beef.

**11.** Peyton is pricing video games for his new game system. Game A has six game variations and costs $27.99. Game B has five game variations and costs $25.39. Peyton is also considering game C, which costs $31.49 and has a total of eight game variations.

If Peyton likes each of the games equally, which would be the best buy? Explain your reasoning. Game C would be the best buy based on the lowest unit cost of about $3.94. Game A has a unit cost of about $4.67 and game B has a unit cost of about $5.08.

12. Shannon would purchase the $114 tank because it has 12.5 $ft^3$ and costs $9.12 per cubic foot; however, the tank that costs $100 has only 10.5 $ft^3$ and costs $9.52 per cubic foot.

13a. The twelve-packs would have been a better buy. Convert 16 liters ≈ 541 ounces. Each 12 pack of 12-ounces equals 144 total ounces. The 541 ounces divided by 144 ounces per pack would be about 3.75 packs. Since we cannot split packs, Ruby would need to purchase four 12-packs. Four 12-packs of beverages would cost $11, which is less than Ruby paid for the eight 2-Liter bottles, $11.60. The better buy would have been four of the 12-packs.

**12.** Shannon is purchasing a new tank for her fish. She wants to buy the largest tank for the money. The tank shown below on the left costs $100. The tank shown below on the right costs $114. Which tank would be the better buy for Shannon? Explain your reasoning.

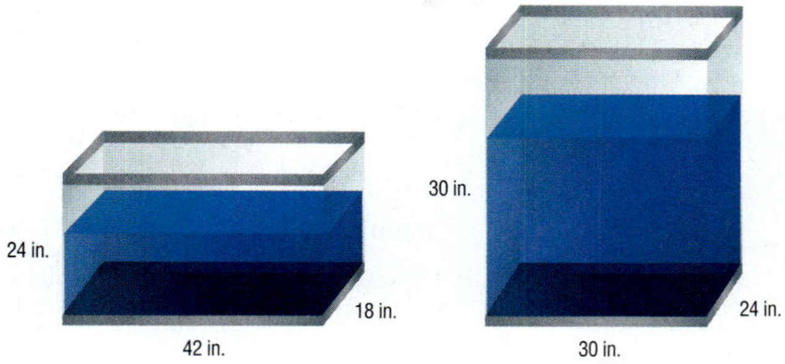


**13.** Ruby is getting ready for her Sweet Sixteen party. She paid $11.60 before tax for eight 2-liter bottles of beverages. Later that day, she saw an advertisement for 12-packs of beverages in 12-ounce cans. The twelve packs are on sale for $2.75 per pack.

**a.** If Ruby wants approximately the same amount of beverages, would the 12-packs have been a better buy? Explain your reasoning process.

**b.** Is there any reason Ruby might have decided that her original purchase was a better idea? Explain your reasoning. See margin.

**14.** Jamal wants to purchase perfume for his mother's birthday. A 3-ounce bottle of perfume is on sale for one-third the cost of a 5.4 ounce bottle. The 5.4 ounce bottle costs $36. Which bottle is the more economical purchase in terms of unit cost? How do you know? See margin.

**15.** Study the following relationships. See margin.

1 Canadian dollar = 1.01595 U.S. dollar

1 U.S. dollar (USD) = 0.98430 Canadian dollar (CAD)

Based on this information, would you make more profit selling a home that cost $260,000 in Canadian dollars or a $263,000 home in U.S. dollars? Explain your reasoning.



On Your Own Exercises

▶ **Exercise 13b** The way in which a student answers this question can give you great insight into the lifestyle choices the students have been exposed to. If students do not bring up the concept of recycling, it is a great opportunity to discuss how the ability to recycle an object can have an impact on their decision to buy.

## Additional Answers

13b. Possible answers: There might be less waste with 8 bottles versus 48 cans. She might purchase eight different flavors of beverages versus only four flavors with the twelve packs; It might be easier to cool eight bottles versus 48 cans.

14. The 5.4-ounce bottle cost about $6.67 per ounce, and the 3-ounce bottle cost about $4.00 per ounce. The 3-ounce bottle is the better buy when comparing unit costs.

15. You want to sell the $260,000 home in Canadian dollars because it equals $264,147.00 in U.S. dollars. You would have a $1,147.00 profit over the home in the U.S.

## Quick Check

**Informal Assessment** Students should be able to:

- ✔ use rates to determine unit prices
- ✔ determine a unit rate
- ✔ use rates, proportions, or equations to convert currency rates

## Quick Quiz

1. A store is selling a 3-pound bag of apples for $1.49. What is the cost per pound of apples? About $0.50 per pound
2. Store A sells a 4-pack of AA size batteries for $3.79. Store B sells a 6-pack of AA size batteries for $4.19. Which store has the better price per battery? Store B; about $0.70 per battery
3. Jaxon is going to Belgium for spring break. He wants to convert $250 to Euro. If the conversion rate is 1 Euro = $1.59, how many Euro will Jaxon have? 157.23 Euro





16. $1.508 \times 10^1$

17. 1 Belize dollar ≈ 17.31 Dominican pesos; 1 Dominican peso ≈ 0.058 Belize dollars.

**16.** Camille's class is studying scientific notation. Her teacher wrote the following on the board.

$$1 \text{ Mexican peso} = 6.417 \times 10^{-2} \text{ euro}$$

What is the value of 235 Mexican pesos in euros? Write the solution in scientific notation. Round to the thousandths place.

**17.** Mr. Sanchez was moving from Belize to the Dominican Republic. He learned that the currency exchange rates are as follows.

3,500 Belize dollar = 60,576.9 Dominican R. peso

3,500 Dominican R. peso (DOP) = 202.222 Belize dollar (BZD)

What is the unit rate for Belize dollars to Dominican pesos? What is the unit rate for Dominican pesos to Belize dollars based on this information? Explain your reasoning.

**18.** **In Your Own Words** Explain how you can use unit rates to choose the better buy between two food items when grocery shopping.

18. Possible answer: You can divide the item's cost by the amount in the package, such as number of ounces.

### Mixed Review

**19.** Suppose Laurie invests $200 on January 1, 2000, at 8% interest per year. Her original investment and the yearly interest are reinvested each year for ten years.

a. How much money is in Laurie's account at the end of 2000 (to be reinvested for 2001)? $216

b. Make a graph, on axes like those at right, showing the growth of the account's value for the ten years the money is invested. See graph.

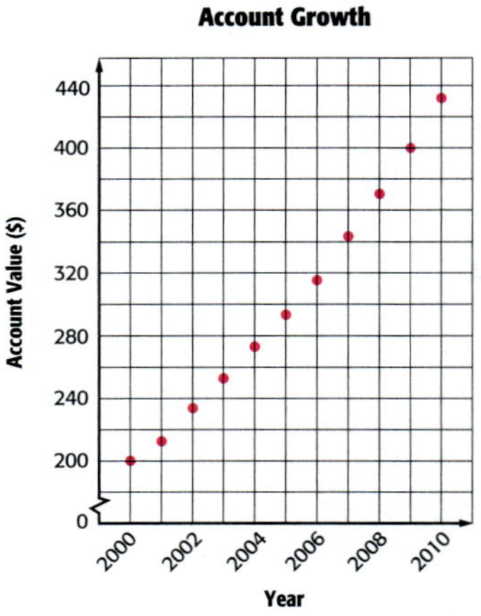


**Solve each equation or inequality.**

**20.** $5x + 3 = 2x + 10$ $\frac{7}{3}$ or $2\frac{1}{3}$

**21.** $\frac{1}{2}y + \frac{2}{5} = \frac{1}{4}y - \frac{3}{2}$ $-\frac{38}{5}$ or $-7\frac{3}{5}$

**22.** $12n - 9 > 4n + 1$ $n > \frac{5}{4}$

**23.** $\frac{5}{3}t + 7 \geq \frac{8}{3}t - 10$ $t \leq 17$

550 **CHAPTER 10** Proportional Reasoning and Percents

CHAPTER 10

# Review & Self-Assessment

## Chapter Summary

Comparisons can take many forms, including ratios, rates, and percents. In this chapter, you compared ratios using equivalent ratios, unit rates, and ratio tables.

You learned how to use proportions to solve real-world problems involving ratios and percents. You also used proportionality when working with similar figures and map scales.

Next, you used percent diagrams to show a common scale for two different ratios. In addition, you used percents to solve equations representing real-world situations.

Rates are special types of ratios. You used rates to find unit prices and calculate currency conversions.

**Vocabulary**

- angle of elevation
- map scale
- proportion
- proportional relationship

## Strategies and Applications

The questions in this section will help you review and apply the important ideas and strategies developed in this chapter.

### Comparing and scaling ratios and rates

**1.** The Quick Shop grocery store sells four brands of yogurt.

| Brand | Maddie's | Quick Shop | Rockyfarm | Shannon |
|---|---|---|---|---|
| Price | 2 for $1.50 | 3 for $2 | $0.75 each | $0.80 each |
| Size | 8 oz | 6 oz | 6 oz | 8 oz |

**a.** For each brand, find the ratio of price to ounces.

**b.** For each brand, find the unit price.

**c.** Use the unit rates to list the brands from least expensive to most expensive. Maddie's, Shannon, Quick Shop, Rockyfarm

**d.** Explain how you could use the ratios in Part a instead of the unit rates to list the brands by how expensive they are.

1a. Maddie's: 1.5:16; Quick Shop: 2:18; Rockyfarm: 0.75:6; Shannon: 0.8:8

1b. Maddie's: $0.094 per oz; Quick Shop: $0.111 per oz; Rockyfarm: $0.125 per oz; Shannon: $0.10 per oz

1d. Possible answer: Write each ratio as a decimal and compare them.



# Review & Self-Assessment

CHAPTER 10

## Chapter Summary

This summary helps students recall the major topics of the chapter.

## Vocabulary

Students should be able to explain each of the terms listed in the vocabulary section.

▶ **Exercise 1a** Remind students that when determining how to write a ratio the order in which the words are written determines what is represented in the top and bottom of the fraction. In this case, the word *to* is the separator—price to ounces tells us that the price goes in the numerator of the fraction and the number of ounces goes in the denominator of the fraction. The ratio is not complete until the numerical values are simplified.

▶ **Exercise 3a** Students may not get the correct proportion for solving this problem. Many students will write the proportion $\frac{3}{17} = \frac{20}{m}$. Students often write the proportions based on the numbers that they see, not what the words describe. Remind students that the words are just as important as the numbers and cannot be overlooked.



2d. 6 qt fruit juice, 1 qt ginger ale

2e. Possible answer: The ratio of fruit juice to drink is 3:3.5, which is equivalent to 6:7. That means it takes 6 quarts of fruit juice to make 7 quarts of drink; the remaining quart is ginger ale.

**2.** Erin is making punch for her friends. To make the drink, she mixes three quarts of fruit juice with $\frac{1}{2}$ quart of ginger ale.

**a.** Find the ratio of fruit juice to ginger ale in Erin's punch. 3:0.5

**b.** Find the ratio of fruit juice to punch, that is, to the final drink. 3:3.5

**c.** Suppose Erin has only two quarts of fruit juice. How much ginger ale should she add? $\frac{1}{3}$ qt

**d.** For a party, Erin wants to make seven quarts of punch. How much fruit juice and ginger ale does she need?

**e.** Explain how you found your answer for Part d.

### Writing and solving proportions

**3.** Mac found a box full of paperclips. He wanted to know about how many paperclips were in the box without counting them one by one. All the paperclips were silver, so Mac had an idea.

Mac added 20 colored paperclips, mixed all the paperclips in the box thoroughly, and then, without looking, drew out 20 paperclips. He had drawn 3 colored paperclips and 17 silver paperclips.

**a.** Write a proportion that Mac could use to estimate how many paperclips are in the box. $\frac{3}{20} = \frac{20}{m}$

**b.** Solve your proportion. $m = 133\frac{1}{3}$

**c.** How many paperclips should Mac guess are in the box? About 133

### Using proportions to explore similarity

**4.** Nicolas wanted to know the height of the flagpole in front of his school. He measured his friend's height and the lengths of the shadows cast by his friend and the flagpole's shadow. Nicolas' measurements are listed below.

Height of friend: 5 feet

Friend's shadow: 2 feet

Flagpole's shadow: 10 feet

**a.** Write a proportion Nicolas could use to calculate the height of the flagpole. $\frac{5}{2} = \frac{x}{10}$

**b.** Solve your proportion. 25

5c. Although Mississippi does not receive as much federal money as California, a greater percentage of Mississippi's money comes from the federal government than does the funding of any other of these states.

**Using percents to make comparisons**

5. **Social Studies** Public elementary and secondary schools in the United States receive money from different levels of government. The table shows National Education Association estimates for three states for the 2005–06 school year.

**School Funding Sources (Thousands of Dollars)**

| State | Total | Federal | State | Local and Intermediate |
|---|---|---|---|---|
| California | 69,054,472 | 7,256,396 | 39,302,232 | 17,495,944 |
| Maine | 2,309,974 | 221,601 | 941,399 | 1,146,974 |
| Mississippi | 3,768,462 | 571,554 | 2,038,039 | 1,158,869 |

a. Which of these states received the most federal money? California

b. Which of these states relies most on federal money? Mississippi

c. Explain why Part b is a different question from Part a.

6b. Possible answer: blue to purple: 9:24, or 3:8; blue to white: 9:16; blue to all: 9:49; white to all: 16:49; purple to all: 24:49

7. Possible table:

| Purple | 24 | 48 | 72 | 96 | 120 | 144 |
|---|---|---|---|---|---|---|
| White | 16 | 32 | 48 | 64 | 80 | 96 |

## Demonstrating Skills

6. Examine the tile pattern.

a. Write the ratio of white tiles to purple tiles. 16:24, or 2:3

b. Write at least five ratios for the tile pattern.

7. Paul wants to tile a large area using this pattern. Make a ratio table of possible numbers of purple and white tiles that he could use.

**Find the value of the variable in each proportion.**

8. $\frac{12}{5} = \frac{x}{9}$ 21.6

9. $\frac{3.2}{y} = \frac{4}{7}$ 5.6

10. $\frac{92}{36} = \frac{23}{w}$ 9

11. $\frac{a}{4.7} = \frac{13}{61.1}$ 1



▶ **Exercises 8–11** As students work on these exercises, encourage them to try to solve the proportions by using different methods. The students need to be exposed to a variety of ways to solve problems. It is also important for students to feel comfortable with their mathematical skills. Some students may only be comfortable solving a problem in one way, and while this is acceptable, remind students that not all problems have one path to their answer.

▶ **Exercises 14–16** These questions involve percentages. Students may need to be reminded of how to set up a proportion to find the missing information. A percent is always written as a fraction of the number given over 100. The rest of the information becomes the second fraction in the proportion and can be determined by remembering the phrase, *is over of*—the number preceding *is* goes in the numerator of the fraction and the number following *of* goes in the denominator of the fraction.

*Review & Self-Assessment*
**Chapter 10**

**Find the missing measures for these similar figures.**

**12.** 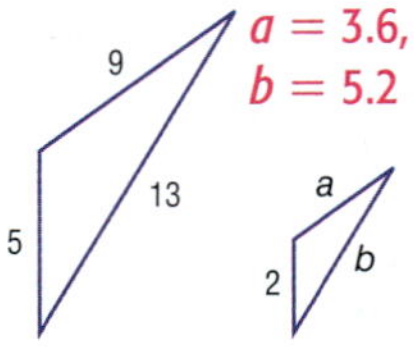

$a = 3.6$, $b = 5.2$

**13.** 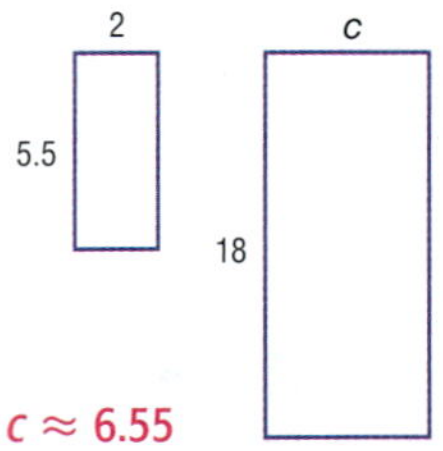

$c \approx 6.55$

**For Exercises 14–24, set up and solve a proportion to answer each question.**

**14.** 17 is 5% of what number? $\frac{17}{x} = \frac{5}{100}$, $x = 340$

**15.** What percent of 450 is 25? $\frac{25}{450} = \frac{n}{100}$, $n = 5\frac{5}{9}$

**16.** What is 32% of 85? $\frac{x}{85} = \frac{32}{100}$, $x = 27.2$

**17.** Jocelyn finds bouncy balls on sale. A box of 12 bouncy balls costs \$1.44. Calculate the unit rate of each ball. \$0.12

**18.** Jeremiah is looking for juggling balls for his school's juggling club. A Catch Above the Rest sells their juggling balls for 3 for \$4.50. Just Jugglers sells their juggling balls for 5 for \$10. Which store offers the better deal? A Catch Above the Rest

**19.** Jesse wants to go to the pool. The pool offers a special rate after 5 P.M. of four hours for \$10. How much will Jesse pay per hour of swimming? \$2.50

**20.** Susan and Alexis are going to a spa. The spa charges \$150 for four hours. How much will Susan and Alexis pay per hour at the spa? \$37.50

**21.** Bi-Rite grocery store has cans of chicken soup on sale for \$2.40 for six cans. The cans are normally priced \$0.60 a can. How much will you save per can with the sale? \$0.20

**22.** One U.S. dollar equals 0.99688 Canadian dollars. How many U.S. dollars equal one Canadian dollar? 1.00313

**23.** One British pound equals 208.817 Japanese yen. How many British pounds equal one Japanese yen? 0.00479

**24.** One U.S. dollar equals 0.69058 euros. How many U.S. dollars equal one euro? 1.44806

## Test-Taking Practice

***SHORT RESPONSE***

**1** A tall building casts a shadow of 15 meters. Stacie, who is 1.3 meters tall, casts a shadow of 15 centimeters. How tall is the building? Watch your units of measure.

***Show your work.***

*Show your work:* Solve using a proportion. Let $h$ = the height of the building. 15 cm = 0.15 $m$ • $\frac{1.3}{0.15} = \frac{h}{15}$; $1.3 \cdot 15 = 0.15h$; $19.5 = 0.15h$; $130 = h$

***Answer*** ____________________

*Answer:* The height of the building is 130 meters.

***MULTIPLE CHOICE***

**2** Which of the following shows the cross products of $\frac{7}{12} = \frac{x}{8}$?

**A** $7(12) = 8x$
**(B)** $12x = 7(8)$
**C** $7x = 12(8)$
**D** $x = 7(8)$

**3** A map shows the following scale. How many kilometers would be represented by 3.2 centimeters?

1 centimeter = 8 kilometers

**(F)** 25.6
**G** 32
**H** 256
**J** 320

**4** A candidate earned 100 out of the first 125 votes cast in an election. Suppose the candidate earned the same ratio of total votes cast. How many votes did the candidate receive if a total of 720 votes were cast?

**A** 695
**(B)** 576
**C** 100
**D** 80

**5** The cost for 3 pounds of apples is $4.95. At the same rate, which of the following would be true?

**F** 1 pound costs $1.60
**G** 2 pounds costs $3.40
**(H)** 4 pounds costs $6.60
**J** 5 pounds costs $7.95

**6** Samantha bought a new DVD player for $50 off its original price. The $50 was a 20% discount. Find the original cost of the DVD player.

**A** $40
**B** $100
**(C)** $250
**D** $300

**7** In a tile floor, there are 5 blue squares for every 2 green squares. Which of the following is *not* an equivalent ratio?

**F** 10:4
**(G)** 10:7
**H** 15:6
**J** 100:40



Review & Self-Assessment
Chapter 10

▶ **Exercise 1** The question warns the students to watch their units of measure because the measure of Stacie's shadow is given in centimeters while all the other measurements are given in meters. Encourage students to convert all of the measures to one unit before proceeding. The solution is given in meters, so offer that unit as a hint to the students as they solve the problem.

**Develop & Understand: A** (p. 518)

1.

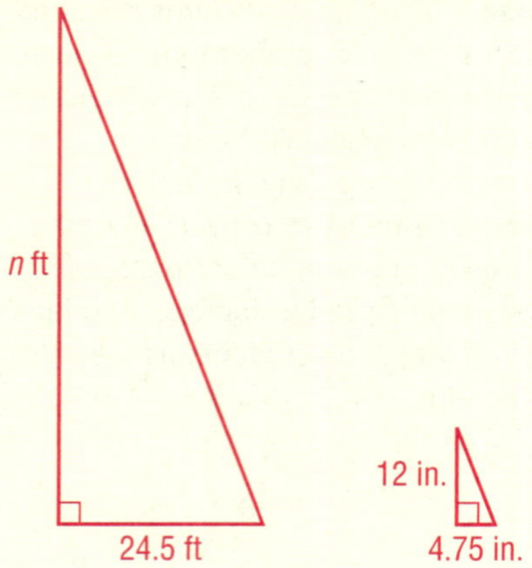


2. The sides of one triangle are the tree, the tree's shadow, and the segment from the top of the tree to the tip of its shadow. The sides of the other triangle are the ruler, the ruler's shadow, and the segment from the top of the ruler to the tip of its shadow.

3. Possible answer (Note: Students may convert all units to feet or to inches.):

$$\frac{\text{tree's height}}{\text{ruler's height}} = \frac{\text{length of tree's shadow}}{\text{length of ruler's shadow}}$$

$$\frac{n \text{ ft}}{12 \text{ in.}} = \frac{24.5 \text{ ft}}{4.75 \text{ in.}}$$

5. Possible answer: As long as corresponding parts of the proportion have the same units, the ratios will be equivalent because the quantities they compare have the same units. For example,

$\frac{\text{length of ruler's shadow}}{\text{length of tree's shadow}}$ is $\frac{\text{inches}}{\text{feet}}$, and $\frac{\text{ruler's length}}{\text{tree's height}}$ is $\frac{\text{inches}}{\text{feet}}$.

Both ratios compare inches to feet.

**Share and Summarize** (p. 518)

2. Possible answer: Because, at a given time of day, the sun hits everything from essentially the same angle, the triangle formed using the flagpole and its shadow as legs and the one formed using any other vertical object (such as a person) and its shadow will be similar. If you measure the shadows and you know the height of the other object, you can set up a proportion like this one:

$$\frac{\text{pole's height}}{\text{other object's height}} = \frac{\text{length of pole's shadow}}{\text{length of object's shadow}}$$

You can then solve the proportion to find the flagpole's height.

**Develop & Understand: B** (p. 533)

10c.

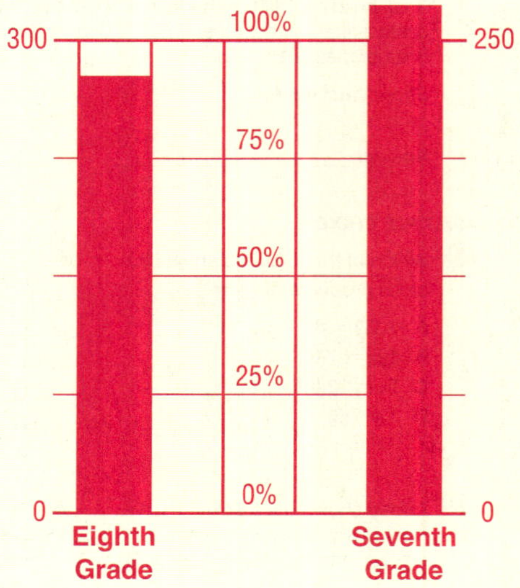

Notes

# Glossary/Glosario

**Math Online** A mathematics multilingual glossary is available at glencoe.com. The glossary includes the following languages.

| | | | | |
|---|---|---|---|---|
| Arabic | Cantonese | Hmong | Russian | Urdu |
| Bengali | English | Korean | Spanish | Vietnamese |
| Brazilian Portuguese | Haitian Creole | Portuguese | Tagalog | |

**Cómo usar el glosario en español:**

1. Bussca el término en inglés que desees encontrar.
2. El término en español, junto con la definición, se encuentran en la columna de la derecha.

## English / Español

### A

**absolute value** (p. 126) The absolute value of a number is its distance from 0 on the number line, and is indicated by drawing a bar on each side of the number. For example, $|-20|$ means "the absolute value of $-20$." Since $-20$ and 20 are each 20 units from 0 on the number line, $|20| = 20$ and $|-20| = 20$.

**valor absoluto** (pág. 126) El valor absoluto de un número es su distancia desde 0 en la recta numérica, lo cual se indica trazando una barra en cada lado del número. Por ejemplo, $|-20|$ significa "el valor absoluto de $-20$". Como $-20$ y 20 se encuentran a 20 unidades de 0 en la recta numérica, $|20| = 20$ y $|-20| = 20$.

**algebraic expression** (p. 10) A mathematical statement that contains at least one variable and may contain operations.

**expressión algebraica** (pág. 10) Enunciado matemático que contiene por lo menos una variable y puede contener operaciones.

**angle of elevation** (p. 519) The angle made by the imaginary horizontal segment extending from a person's eye and the imaginary segment from the same person's eye to the top of the object.

**ángulo de elevación** (pág. 519) Ángulo formado por el segmento horizontal imaginario que se extiende desde el ojo del observador hasta un objeto y el segmento imaginario a partir del ojo del mismo observador hasta la parte superior del objeto.

### B

**backtracking** (p. 19) A method of solving algebraic equations by working backwards from the known answer to figure out the value of the variable.

**expressión algebraica** (pág. 10) Enunciado matemático que contiene por lo menos una variable y puede contener operaciones.

**base** (p. 93) The number in an exponential expression that is multiplied by itself. For example, in $t^3$, $t$ is the base; in $10^4$, 10 is the base.

**base** (pág. 93) El número en una expresión exponencial que se multiplica por sí misma. Por ejemplo: en $t^3$, $t$ es la base; en $10^4$, 10 es la base.

**base** (p. 216) The parallel faces of a prism.

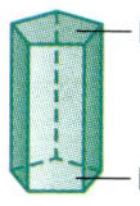


**base** (pág. 216) Las caras paralelas de un prisma.

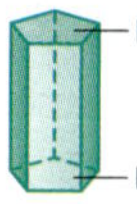






### C

**common factor** (p. 80) A common factor of two or more numbers is a number that is a factor of all the numbers. For example, 5 is a common factor of 15, 25, and 40.

**factor común** (pág. 80) Un factor común de dos o más números es un número que es un factor de todos los números. Por ejemplo, 5 es un factor común de 15, 25 y 40.

**common multiple** (p. 83) A common multiple of a set of numbers is a multiple of all the numbers. For example, 24 is a common multiple of 3, 8, and 12.

**múltiplo común** (pág. 83) Un múltiplo común de un conjunto de números es un múltiplo de todos los números. Por ejemplo, 24 es un múltiplo común de 3, 8 y 12.

**composite number** (p. 78) A whole number greater than 1 with more than two factors. For example, 12 is a composite number since it is greater than 1 and has more than two factors. In fact, it has six factors: 1, 2, 3, 4, 6, and 12.

**número compuesto** (pág. 78) Un número entero mayor que 1 con más de dos factores. Por ejemplo, 12 es un número compuesto dado que es mayor que 1 y tiene más de dos factores. De hecho, tiene seis factores: 1, 2, 3, 4, 6 y 12.

**conjecture** (p. 477) A statement that is believed to be true but has not yet been proven.

**conjetura** (pág. 477) Enunciado que se cree que es verdadero, pero el cual no se ha probado todavía.

**customary system** (p. 247) The system of measurement used in the United States to measure length in inches, feet, yards, and miles; capacity in cups, pints, quarts, and gallons; weight in ounces, pounds, and tons; and temperature in degrees Fahrenheit.

**sistema inglés** (pág. 247) Sistema de medidas que se usa en Estados Unidos para medir la longitud en pulgadas, pies, yardas y millas; la capacidad en tazas, pintas, cuartos de galón y galones; el peso en onzas, libras y toneladas; y la temperatura en grados Fahrenheit.

**cylinder** (p. 217) A figure that is like a prism, but its two bases are circles.

Cylinder

**cilindro** (pág. 217) Figura que parece un prisma, pero que tiene un par de bases circulares.

Cilindro

### D

**distance formula** (p. 353) The symbolic rule for calculating the distance between any two points, $(x_1, y_1)$ and $(x_2, y_2)$, in the coordinate plane: distance $= \sqrt{(x_2 - x_1)^2 + (y_2 - y_1)^2}$.

**fórmula de la distancia** (pág. 353) Regla simbólica para calcular la distancia entre cualquier par de puntos, $(x_1, y_1)$ y $(x_2, y_2)$, en el plano the coordenadas: distancia $= \sqrt{(x_2 - x_1)^2 + (y_2 - y_1)^2}$.

**distributive property** (p. 49) The distributive property of multiplication over addition states that for any numbers $n$, $a$, and $b$, $n(a + b) = na + nb$. The distributive property of multiplication over subtraction states that for any numbers $n$, $a$, and $b$, $n(a - b) = na - nb$.

**propiedad distributiva** (pág. 49) La propiedad distributiva de la multiplicación sobre la adición establece que para cualquier número $n$, $a$, y $b$, $n(a + b) = na + nb$. La propiedad distributiva de la multiplicación sobre la sustracción establece que para cualquier número $n$, $a$, y $b$, $n(a - b) = na - nb$.

**double-bar graph** **(p. 296)** A graphical display that uses paired horizontal or vertical bars to compare data.

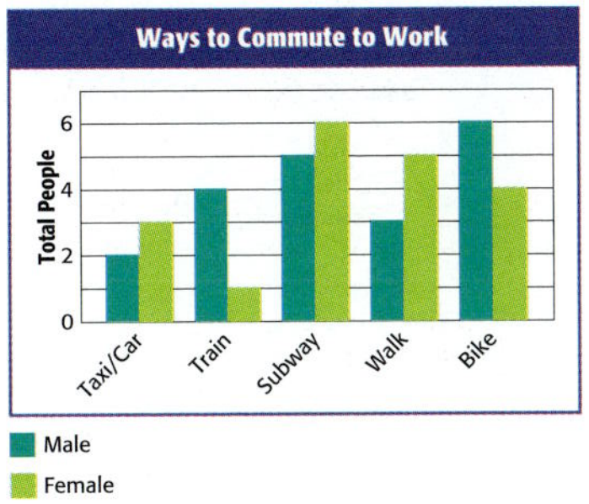


**double-line graph** **(p. 298)** A graphical display that uses paired lines to compare data.

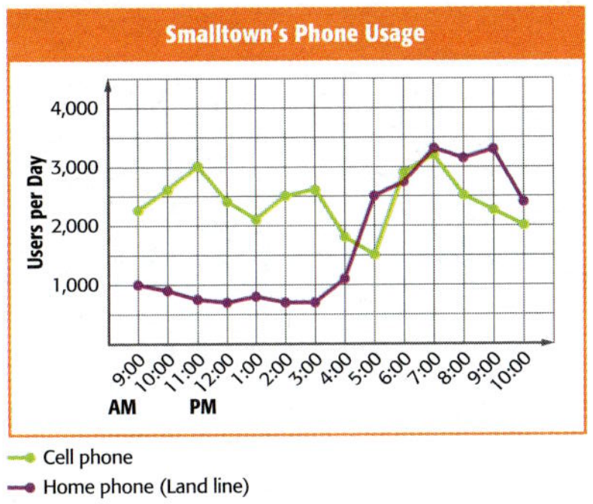


## E

**equivalent expressions** **(p. 54)** Expressions that always give the same result when the same values are substituted for the variables. For example, $2k + 6$ is equivalent to $2(k + 3)$.

**expand** **(p. 56)** To use the distributive property to remove parentheses.

**gráfico de barras dobles** **(pág. 296)** Representación gráfica que emplea pares de barras horizontales o verticales para comparar datos.

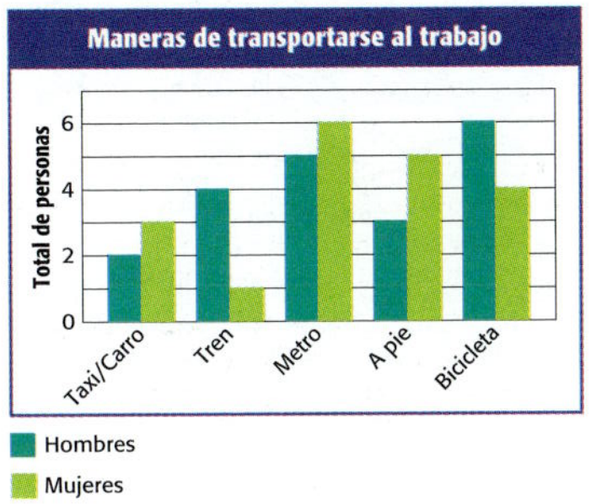


**gráfico de lineal dobles** **(pág. 298)** Representación gráfica que emplea pares de lineal para comprar datos.

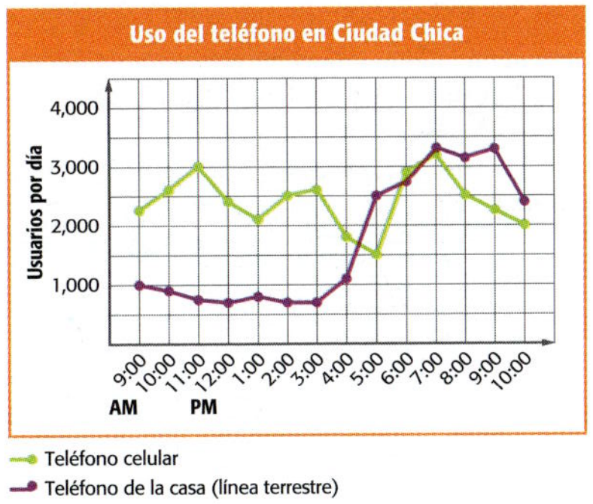


**expresiones equivalentes** **(pág. 54)** Expresiones que siempre dan el mismo resultado cuando los mismos valores se reemplazan con las variables. Por ejemplo: $2k + 6$ es equivalente a $2(k + 3)$.

**expandir** **(pág. 56)** Use la propiedad distributiva para eliminar los paréntesis.





**exponent** **(p. 12)** A symbol written above and to the right of a quantity that tells how many times the quantity is multiplied by itself. For example: $t \times t \times t$ is written $t^3$.

## F

**factor** **(p. 56)** To use the distributive property to insert parentheses.

**factor** **(p. 76)** A factor of a whole number is another whole number that divides into it without a remainder. For example, 1, 2, 3, 4, 6, 8, 12, and 24 are factors of 24.

**factor pair** **(p. 76)** A factor pair for a number is two factors whose product equals that number. For example, the factor pairs for 24 are 1 and 24, 2 and 12, 3 and 8, and 4 and 6.

**flowchart** **(p. 18)** A visual diagram that shows each step in evaluating an algebraic expression.

**formula** **(p. 35)** An algebraic "recipe" that shows how to calculate a particular quantity. For example, $F = \frac{9}{5}C + 32$ is the formula for converting Celsius temperatures to Fahrenheit temperatures.

## G

**gram** **(p. 241)** A unit of mass in the metric system. 1000 grams = 1 kilogram

**greater** **(p. 178)** A relationship showing that one term or expression has a value larger than a second term or expression.

**greatest common factor, GCF** **(p. 81)** The greatest common factor (often abbreviated GCF) of two or more numbers is the greatest of their common factors. For example, the greatest common factor (or GCF) of 24 and 36 is 12.

**exponente** **(pág. 12)** Símbolo que se escribe arriba y a la derecha de una cantidad y el cual indica cuántas veces la cantidad se multiplica por sí misma. Por ejemplo: $t \times t \times t$ se escribe $t^3$.

**factor** **(pág. 56)** El uso de la propiedad distributiva para agregar paréntesis.

**factor** **(pág. 76)** Un factor de un número entero es otro número entero que lo divide sin que quede un residuo. Por ejemplo, 1, 2, 3, 4, 6, 8, 12 y 24 son factores de 24.

**par de factores** **(pág. 76)** Un par de factores para un número consta de dos factores cuyo producto es igual al número. Por ejemplo, los pares de factores para 24 son 1 y 24; 2 y 12; 3 y 8; y 4 y 6.

**flujograma** **(pág. 18)** Diagrama visual que muestra cada paso en la evaluación de una expresión algebraica.

**fórmula** **(pág. 35)** Una "receta" algebraica que muestra cómo calcular una cantidad dada. Por ejemplo: $F = \frac{9}{5}C + 32$ es la fórmula para convertir temperaturas Celsius en temperaturas Fahrenheit.

**gramo** **(pág. 241)** Unidad de masa del sistema métrico. 1000 gramos = 1 kilogramo

**mayor que** **(pág. 178)** Relación que muestra que un término o expresión tiene un valor más grande que un segundo término o expresión.

**máximo común divisor, MCD** **(pág. 81)** El máximo común divisor (a menudo abreviado, MCD) de dos números es el mayor de sus factores comunes. Por ejemplo, el máximo común divisor (o MCD) de 24 y 36 es 12.

## Glossary/Glosario

### H

**hypotenuse** **(p. 343)** The side opposite the right angle in a right triangle. The hypotenuse is the longest side of a right triangle.

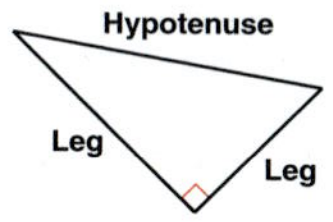


**hipotenusa** **(pág. 343)** El lado opuesto al ángulo recto en un triángulo rectángulo. La hipotenusa es el lado más largo de un triángulo rectángulo.

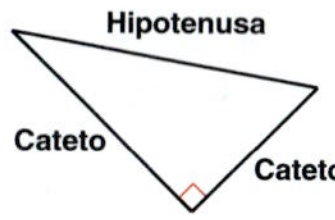


### I

**inequality** **(p. 466)** A mathematical sentence stating that two quantities have different values. For example, $5 + 9 > 12$ is an inequality. The symbols $\neq$, $<$, and $>$ are used in writing inequalities.

**desigualdad** **(pág. 466)** Enunciado matemático que establece que dos cantidades tienen distintos valores. Por ejemplo, $5 + 9 > 12$ es una desigualdad. Los símbolos $\neq$, $<$, y $>$ se usan para escribir desigualdades.

**irrational numbers** **(p. 336)** Numbers that cannot be written as ratios of two integers. In decimal form, irrational numbers are non-terminating and non-repeating. Examples of irrational numbers include $\pi$, $\sqrt{17}$, and $3\sqrt{2}$.

**números irracionales** **(pág. 336)** Números que no se pueden escribir como razones de dos enteros. En forma decimal, los números irracionales son decimales no terminales y no periódicos. Ejemplos de números irracionales incluyen $\pi$, $\sqrt{17}$, y $3\sqrt{2}$.

### L

**least common multiple, LCM** **(p. 83)** The least common multiple (often abbreviated LCM) of two or more numbers is the smallest of their common multiples. For example, the least common multiple (or LCM) of 6 and 15 is 30.

**mínimo común múltiplo, MCM** **(pág. 83)** El mínimo común múltiplo (a menudo abreviado MCM) de dos o más números es el menor de sus múltiplos comunes. Por ejemplo, el mínimo común múltiplo de 6 y 15 es 30.

**leg** **(p. 343)** One of the sides of a right triangle that is not the hypotenuse, or one of the shorter two sides of a right triangle. The figure below shows the two legs and hypotenuse of a right triangle.

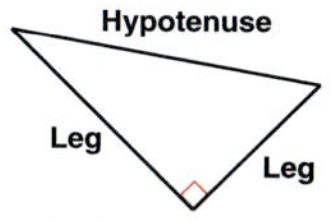


**cateto** **(pág. 343)** Uno de los lados de un triángulo rectángulo que no es la hipotenusa o uno de los dos lados más cortos de un triángulo rectángulo. La siguiente figura muestra los dos catetos y la hipotenusa de un triángulo rectángulo.

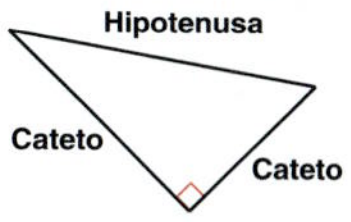


**lesser** **(p. 178)** A relationship showing that one term or expression has a value smaller than a second term or expression.

**menor que** **(pág. 178)** Relación que muestra que un término o expresión tiene un valor más pequeño que un segundo término o expresión.



## Glossary/Glosario

**like terms** **(p. 62)** In an algebraic expression, terms with the same variables raised to the same powers. For example, in the expression $x + 3 - 7x + 8x^2 - 2x^2 + 1$, $8x^2$ and $-2x^2$ are like terms, $x$ and $-7x$ are like terms, and 3 and 1 are like terms.

**términos semejantes** **(pág. 62)** En una expresión algebraica, los términos con las mismas variables elevadas a las mismas potencias. Por ejemplo: en la expresión $x + 3 - 7x + 8x^2 - 2x^2 + 1$, $8x^2$ y $-2x^2$ son términos semejantes, $x$ y $-7x$ son términos semejantes y 3 y 1 son términos semejantes.

**linear relationship** **(p. 371)** A relationship whose graph is a straight line. Linear relationships have a constant rate of change. As one variable changes by 1 unit, the other variable changes by a set amount. For example, $m = 5t$ shows that $m$ changes 5 units per 1-unit change in $t$.

**relación lineal** **(pág. 371)** Relación cuya gráfica es una recta. Las relaciones lineales muestran una tasa constante de cambio. A medida que una variable cambia en 1 unidad, la otra variable cambia en la misma cantidad. Por ejemplo: $m = 5t$ muestra que $m$ cambia 5 unidades por 1 unidad de cambio en $t$.

### M

**map scale** **(p. 514)** A ratio of a single unit of distance on the map to the equivalent distance on the ground.

**escala de mapa** **(pág. 514)** Razón de una sola unidad de distancia en el mapa a la distancia equivalente en la tierra.

**mass** **(p. 240)** A measurement of the amount of matter in an object.

**masa** **(pág. 240)** Medida de la cantidad de materia en un cuerpo.

**metric system** **(p. 241)** A base-ten system of measurement using the basic units: meter for length, gram for mass, and liter for capacity.

**sistema métrico** **(pág. 241)** Sistema de medición decimal que usa las siguientes unidades básicas: metro para longitud, gramo para masa y litro para capacidad.

**model** **(p. 446)** Something that has the key characteristics of something else. For example, in mathematics you could use a balance to model an equation.

**modelo** **(pág. 446)** Algo que tiene una característica clave de algo más. Por ejemplo: en matemáticas podrías usar una ba-lan-za para hacer un modelo de una ecuación.

**monomial** **(p. 61)** A number, a variable, or a product of a number and one or more variables. Examples: 3, $y$, $2x$, $5xy^2$

**monomio** **(pág. 61)** Número, variable o producto de un número y de una o más variables. Ejemplos: 3, $y$, $2x$, $5xy^2$

**multiple** **(p. 83)** A multiple of a whole number is the product of that number and another whole number. For example, 35 is a multiple of 7 since $35 = 7 \times 5$.

**múltiplo** **(pág. 83)** Un múltiplo de un número entero es el producto de ese número y otro número entero. Por ejemplo, 35 es un múltiplo de 7 dado que $35 = 7 \times 5$.

## Glossary/Glosario

### N

**natural numbers** **(p. 320)** The set {1, 2, 3, ... }.

**net** **(p. 228)** A flat figure that can be folded to form a closed, three-dimensional object called a solid.

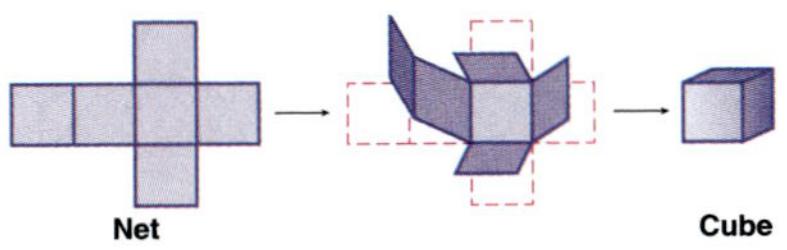


### O

**order of operations** **(p. 99)** A convention for reading and evaluating expressions. The order of operations says that expressions should be evaluated in this order:

- Evaluate any expressions inside parentheses and above and below fraction bars.
- Evaluate all exponents, including squares.
- Do multiplications and divisions from left to right.
- Do additions and subtractions from left to right.

For example, to evaluate $5 + 3 \times 7$, you multiply first and then add: $5 + 3 \cdot 7 = 5 + 21 = 26$. To evaluate $10^2 - 6 \div 3$, you evaluate the exponent first, then divide, then subtract: $10^2 - 6 \div 3 = 100 - 2 = 98$.

**ounce** **(p. 247)** A customary unit of weight. 16 ounces = 1 pound.

### P

**polynomial** **(p. 61)** A monomial or sum of monomials. Examples: $5x$, $3x^2 + 2$.

**population** **(p. 279)** A larger group from which a sample is taken.

**pound** **(p. 247)** A customary unit of weight. 1 pound = 16 ounces.

### N

**número naturales** **(pág. 320)** Conjunto {1, 2, 3, ... }.

**red** **(pág. 228)** Figura plana que al doblarse forma un cuerpo tridimensional cerrado llamado sólido.

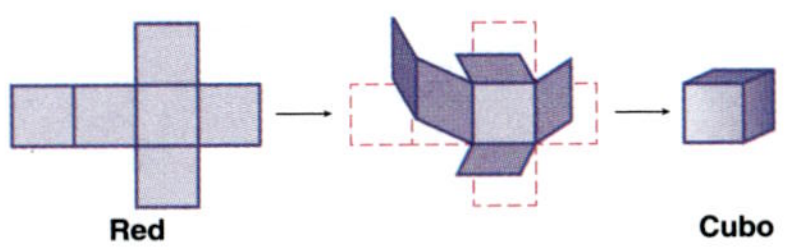


### O

**orden de las operaciones** **(pág. 99)** Una convención para leer y evaluar expresiones. El orden de las operaciones indica que las expresiones se deben evaluar en el siguiente orden:

- Evalúa cualquier expresión entre paréntesis y sobre y debajo de barras de fracciones.
- Evalúa todos los exponentes, incluyendo los cuadrados.
- Efectúa las multiplicaciones y las divisiones de izquierda a derecha.
- Efectúa las sumas y las restas de izquierda a derecha.

Por ejemplo, para evaluar $5 + 3 \times 7$, multiplica primero y luego suma. $5 + 3 \cdot 7 = 5 + 21 = 26$. Para evaluar $10^2 - 6 \div 3$, evalúa primero el exponente, luego divide y por último resta. $10^2 - 6 \div 3 = 100 - 2 = 98$.

**onza** **(pág. 247)** Unidad tradicional de peso. 16 onzas = 1 libra.

### P

**polinomio** **(pág. 61)** Monomio o suma de monomios. Ejemplos: $5x$, $3x^2 + 2$.

**población** **(pág. 279)** Grupo grande del cual se toma una muestra.

**libra** **(pág. 247)** Unidad tradicional de peso. 1 libra = 16 onzas.





**power** **(p. 93)** A number that is written using an exponent.

**prime factorization** **(p. 78)** The prime factorization of a composite number shows that number written as a product of prime numbers. For example, the prime factorization of 98 is $2 \cdot 7 \cdot 7$.

**prime number** **(p. 78)** A whole number greater than 1 with only two factors: itself and 1. For example, 13 is a prime number since it only has two factors, 13 and 1.

**prism** **(p. 212)** A figure that has two identical, parallel faces that are polygons, and other faces that are parallelograms.

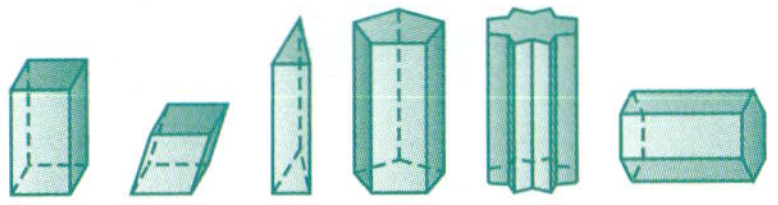

**product law of exponents** **(p. 98)** Law that states when the bases of two factors are the same, the power of their product is the sum of their exponents. Example: $x^a x^b = x^{a+b}$

**proportion** **(p. 510)** A statement that two ratios are equal. For example, 2:3 = 6:9.

**proportional** **(p. 377)** Used to describe the relationship between two variables in which the value of one variable is multiplied by a number, the value of the other variable is multiplied by the same number. For example, when someone is paid an hourly rate and works double the hours, that person gets double the pay. When someone works triple the hours, that person gets triple the pay. The hours worked and rate of pay per hour are proportional to each other.

**proportional relationship** **(p. 505)** A relationship in which all pairs of corresponding values have the same ratio.

**potencia** **(pág. 93)** Número que se escribe usando un exponente.

**factorización prima** **(pág. 78)** La factorización prima de un número compuesto muestra ese número escrito como un producto de números primos. Por ejemplo, la factorización prima de 98 es $2 \cdot 7 \cdot 7$.

**número primo** **(pág. 78)** Número entero mayor que 1 cuyos únicos factores son 1 y el número mismo. Por ejemplo, 13 es un número primo dado que sólo tiene dos factores: 13 y 1.

**prisma** **(pág. 212)** Figura con dos caras paralelas idénticas, las cuales son polígonos, y otras dos caras que son paralelogramos.

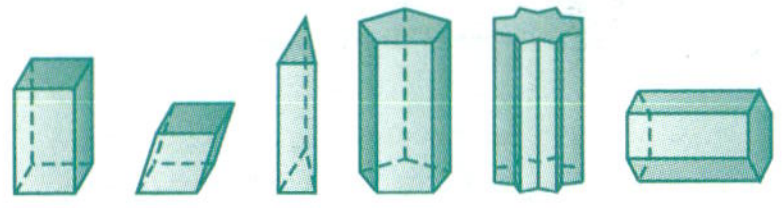

**ley del producto de exponentes** **(pág. 98)** Ley que establece que cuando las bases de dos factores son iguales, la potencia de su producto es la suma de sus exponentes. Ejemplo: $x^a x^b = x^{a+b}$

**proporción** **(pág. 510)** Ecuación que establece que dos razones son iguales. Por ejemplo: 2:3 = 6:9.

**proporcional** **(pág. 377)** Se usa para describir la relación entre dos variables en las cuales, cuando el valor de una variable se multiplica por un número, el valor de la otra variable se multiplica por el mismo número. Por ejemplo: cuando a alguien se le paga un sueldo a cierta tasa por hora y esa persona trabaja el doble del número de horas, dicha persona obtiene el doble del pago. Cuando alguien trabaja el triple de las horas, esa persona obtiene el triple del pago. Las horas trabajadas y la tasa de pago por hora son proporcionales entre sí.

**relación proporcional** **(pág. 505)** Relación en que todos los pares de valores correspondientes tienen la misma razón.

## Glossary/Glosario

**pythagorean theorem** **(p. 345)** If *a* and *b* are the measures of the legs of a right triangle and *c* is the measure of the hypotenuse, then $c^2 = a^2 + b^2$.

**teorema de pitágoras** **(pág. 345)** Si *a* y *b* son las longitudes de los catetos de un triángulo rectángulo y *c* es la longitud de la hipotenusa, entonces $c^2 = a^2 + b^2$.

### R

**rate** **(p. 368)** Describes how two unlike quantities are related or how they can be compared.

**rational numbers** **(p. 320)** Numbers that can be written as ratios of two integers. In decimal form, rational numbers are terminating or repeating. For example, 5, $-0.274$, and $0.\overline{3}$ are rational numbers.

**real numbers** **(p. 336)** The set of rational numbers and irrational numbers together.

**relative error** **(p. 185)** The ratio of the half-unit difference in precision to the entire measure, expressed as a percent.

**relatively prime** **(p. 81)** Two or more numbers are relatively prime if their only common factor is 1. For example, 7 and 9 are relatively prime.

**representative sample** **(p. 284)** A part of a population that has approximately the same proportions as the whole population with respect to the characteristic being studied.

**right triangle** **(p. 343)** A triangle that has one 90° angle.

**tasa** **(pág. 368)** Describe la relación entre dos cantidades diferentes o la manera de comparar dichas cantidades.

**números racionales** **(pág. 320)** Números que se pueden escribir como razones de dos enteros. En forma decimal, los números racionales son números terminales o periódicos. Por ejemplo: 5, $-0.274$ y $0.\overline{3}$ son números racionales.

**números reales** **(pág. 336)** Conjunto de números racionales y números irracionales.

**error relativo** **(pág. 185)** Relación entre la diferencia de media unidad en precisión y la medida entera, expresada en forma porcentual.

**relativamente primo** **(pág. 81)** Dos o más números son relativamente primos si su único factor común es 1. Por ejemplo, 7 y 9 son relativamente primos.

**muestra representativa** **(pág. 284)** Una parte de la población que tiene aproximadamente las mismas proporciones que la población entera con respecto a las características bajo estudio.

**triángulo rectángulo** **(pág. 343)** Triángulo que posee un ángulo de 90°.

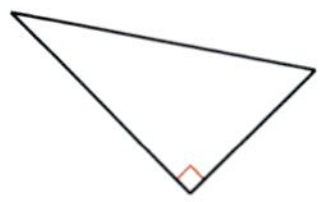



## Glossary/Glosario

### S

**sample** **(p. 279)** A smaller group taken from a population that is used to represent the larger group.

**scientific notation** **(p. 178)** A number that is expressed as the product of a number greater than or equal to 1 but less than 10, and a power of 10. For example, 5,000,000 written in scientific notation is $5 \times 10^6$.

**slope** **(p. 392)** The steepness of a line.

**solid** **(p. 228)** A three-dimensional figure formed by intersecting planes.

**solution set** **(p. 467)** The set of elements from the replacement set that make an open sentence true.

**speed** **(p. 397)** How fast an object is going (always positive).

**square root** **(p. 333)** The number you need to square to get a given number. For example, the square root of 36 is 6.

**surface area** **(p. 213)** The area of the exterior surface of an object, measured in square units.

**muestra** **(pág. 279)** Un grupo más pequeño que se toma de la población y el cual se usa para representar el grupo más grande.

**notación científica** **(pág. 178)** Número que se expresa como el producto de un número mayor que o igual a 1, pero menor que 10 y una potencia de 10. Por ejemplo: 5,000,000 escrito en notación científica es $5 \times 10^6$.

**pendiente** **(pág. 392)** El grado de inclinación de una recta.

**sólido geométrico** **(pág. 228)** Figura tridimensional formada por planos intersecantes.

**conjunto de soluciones** **(pág. 467)** Conjunto de elementos del conjunto de reemplazo que hace que un enunciado abierto sea verdadero.

**rapidez** **(pág. 397)** El grado de velocidad con que viaja un cuerpo (es siempre un número positivo).

**raíz cuadrada** **(pág. 333)** El número que debes elevar al cuadrado para obtener un número dado. Por ejemplo, la raíz cuadrada de 36 es 6.

**área de superficie** **(pág. 213)** El área de las superficies exteriores de un cuerpo, medida en unidades cuadradas.

### T

**ton** **(p. 247)** A customary unit of weight. 1 ton = 2000 pounds.

**tonelada** **(pág. 247)** Unidad tradicional de peso. 1 tonelada = 2000 libras.

### U

**unit rate** **(p. 541)** Term used when one of two quantities being compared is given in terms of one unit. Example: 65 miles per hour or $1.99 per pound.

**tasa unitaria** **(pág. 541)** Término que se usa cuando una de dos cantidades bajo comparación se da en términos de una unidad. Ejemplo: 65 millas por hora o $1.99 por libra.



Glossary/Glosario

# Glossary/Glosario

## V

**variable** **(p. 10)** A quantity that can change or vary, or an unknown quantity.

**variable** **(pág. 10)** Cantidad que puede cambiar o variar, o una cantidad desconocida.

**velocity** **(p. 397)** The rate at which an object is moving from or toward a designated point (can be positive or negative).

**velocidad** **(pág. 397)** Tasa a la cual se mueve un cuerpo desde un punto o hacia un punto designado (puede ser positiva o negativa).

**volume** **(p. 213)** The space inside a three-dimensional object, measured in cubic units.

**volumen** **(pág. 213)** El espacio dentro de un cuerpo tridimen-sio-nal, medido en unidades cúbicas.

## W

**weight** **(p. 240)** The pull of gravity on a amount of matter.

**peso** **(pág. 240)** Atracción de la gravedad sobre una cantidad de materia.

**whole numbers** **(p. 320)** The set {0, 1, 2, 3, ...}.

**números enteros** **(pág. 320)** Conjunto {0, 1, 2, 3, ... }.

## Y

***y*-intercept** **(p. 401)** The point at which a graph intersects the *y*-axis.

**intersección *y*** **(pág. 401)** El punto en que una gráfica interseca el eje *y*.

# Index

## A



## B



## C

## D



## E

# Index

## R

## S



## T

# Index

# Photo Credits

While every effort has been made to secure permission for reproduction of copyright material, there may have been cases where we are unable to trace the copyright holder. Upon written notification, the publisher will gladly correct this in future printings.

**Student Edition Photo Credits**

**viii** Gail Shumway; **ix** NASA/EPA/Corbis; **xi** Jupiter Images/Brand X/Alamy; **xii** Jose Luis Pelaez Inc; **xiii** Jack Hollingsworth; **xiv** John Kirkpatrick/Alamy; **xv** Peter Bowater/Alamy; **xvi** Lester Lefkowitz; **xvii** Hermann Erber/Getty Images; **1** Jerry Driendl; **2** Gail Shumway; **3** Redmond Durrell/Alamy; **5** PhotoSpin, Inc/ Alamy; **6** (l)D. Hurst/Alamy, (r)Ralph Wetmore; **7** Dave King; **8** Peter Gridley; **9** Redfx/Alamy; **10** Bon Appetit/Alamy; **11** Alan SCHEIN/Alamy; **22** Anna Peisl/ Zefa/Corbis; **23** Ilian Animal/Alamy; **24** Supapixx/Alamy; **28** Kuttig-People/ Alamy; **32** (t)Tony Cordoza/Alamy, (b)D. Hurst/Alamy; **34** Willie Sator/Alamy; **35** Randy Lincks/Alamy; **37** Tim Hill/Alamy; **39** Jerry Young; **42** Mazer Creative Services; **43** Comstock/Corbis; **44** Haruyoshi Yamaguchi/Corbis; **45** Image Source Pink/Alamy; **47** Don Tremain/Getty Images; **52** Sumos/Alamy; **60** Ros Drinkwater/Alamy; **65** Tom Grill/Corbis; **72** NASA/EPA/Corbis; **74** Wildlife GMBH/Alamy; **79** Kevin Britland/Alamy; **80** Mazer Creative Services; **85** Photodisc/Alamy; **86** Thomas Northcut; **89** Reuters/Corbis; **90** Visions of America/Joe Sohm; **95** Ladi Kirn/Alamy; **100** Ashley Cooper/Corbis; **108** UpperCut Images/Alamy; **111** Nordicphotos/Alamy; **124** Hermann Erber/ Getty Images; **125** Alaska Stock LLC/Alamy; **129** William Whitehurst/Corbis; **132** Stuart Westmorland/Corbis; **133** Mazer Creative Services; **134** Image Source Pink/Alamy; **139** Corbis; **154** Richard Broadwell/Alamy; **161** Ian Cartwright/Getty Images; **163** Design Pics Inc./Alamy; **166** Ingram Publishing/ AGE Fotostock; **172** Stocktrek Images/Alamy; **173** Jupiter Images/Brand X/ Alamy; **176** Mazer Creative Services; **180** Space Frontiers; **184** Andersen Ross; **186** Mazer Creative Services/Texas Instruments; **191** Michael Houghton/ StudiOhio; **212** Jose Luis Pelaez Inc; **213** Siede Preis/Getty Images; **214** Richard Drury; **215** Owaki-Kulla/Corbis; **217, 220** Pixtal/SuperStock; **222** Mazer Creative Services/Texas Instruments; **223** Photodisc/PunchStock; **226** Bruce Laurance; **227** Ken Cedeno/Corbis; **236** Stockbyte/PictureQuest; **240** Burke/Triolo/Brand X Pictures/Jupiter Images; **242** Westend61/Alamy; **243** Stephen Wisbauer; **245** David Seed Photography; **246** Renee Lynn/Corbis; **247** Getty Images; **248** Digital Archive Japan/Alamy; **257** (t)PhotoDisc/Getty Images, (b)The McGraw-Hill Companies, Inc/Ken Karp; **260** Jack Hollingsworth; **263** Stockbyte/ Alamy; **265, 267** United States Mint; **268** Mazer Creative Services; **270** Judith Collins/Alamy; **271** Mazer Creative Services; **273** LHB Photo/Alamy; **274** Zia Soleil; **278** Mazer Creative Services; **279** James Ingram/Alamy; **281** Dmitri Kessel; **283** Corbis Premium RF/Alamy; **284** Photodisc/Getty Images; **286** Mazer Creative Services; **287** D. Hurst/Alamy; **288** Mary Evans Picture Library/Alamy; **289** Image Source/PunchStock; **290** Burke/Triolo/Brand X Pictures/Jupiter Images; **292** K-PHOTOS/Alamy; **299** Brand X Pictures/PunchStock; **304** Image Source/ PunchStock; **307** Michael Steele; **308** Jupiter Images/Brand X/Alamy; **314** United States Mint; **318** John Kirkpatrick/Alamy; **319, 338** D. Hurst/Alamy; **342** C Squared Studios/Getty Images; **345** Nicholas Pitt/Alamy; **349** PhotoLink/ Getty Images; **350** Photo Japan/Alamy; **352** Mazer Creative Services; **354** Richard T. Nowitz/Corbis; **356** Ingram Publishing/Alamy; **362** Peter Bowater/Alamy; **363** Judith Collins/Alamy; **365** Gary Pearl; **366** Arthur Morris/ Corbis; **367** Ian Shaw/Alamy; **370** Andersen Ross; **372** ColorBlind Images; **374** PhotoAlto/Alix Minde; **376** John Elk III; **377** Mazer Creative Services; **380** Paul Springett/Alamy; **382** Archive Holdings Inc.; **383** Jose Luis Pelaez, Inc./ Blend Images/Corbis; **385** Guillermo Hung; **387** Martin Harvey; **388** Nick Dolding; **389** UK Stock Images Ltd/Alamy; **394** Kim Karpeles/Alamy; **397** Kate Kunath; **398** Jim Craigmyle/Corbis; **399** David Madison; **399** RubberBall Productions/Getty Images; **402** Gandee Vasan; **403** Stocktrek/Corbis; **406** Reuters/Corbis; **408** PhotoDisc/Getty Images; **414** Ralf Schultheiss/zefa/ Corbis; **417** Mark Gibson/Alamy; **422** Stockbyte; **432** Lester Lefkowitz; **433** Trolley Dodger/Corbis; **436** Sheer Photo, Inc.; **438** Tom Grill/Corbis; **441** Mazer Creative Services; **443** Sean Gallup; **445** image100/Corbis; **446** Jack Hollingsworth; **451** Stockbyte; **452** Still Images; **455** (l)Creatas/PunchStock, (r)D. Hurst/Alamy; **456** Peter Gridley; **457** Dominic Burke/Alamy; **462** vario images GmbH & Co.KG/Alamy; **468** Emilio Ereza/Alamy; **473** Douglas Pulsipher/Alamy; **474** Brand X Pictures/PunchStock; **479** Tetra Images/Corbis; **481** Patrick Steel/Alamy; **482** Jupiter Images/Comstock Images/Alamy; **483** Mario Tama; **484** The McGraw-Hill Companies, Inc./Ken Cavanagh Photographer; **487** DAJ/Getty Images; **492** Jerry Driendl; **493** Corbis; **499** Photodisc; **500** Dr. Parvinder Sethi; **503** Perry Mastrovito/Corbis; **504** Stockdisc/PunchStock; **509** S. Wanke/PhotoLink/Getty Images; **510** Paul Thompson/Corbis; **511** *Starry Night,* 1889. Vincent Van Gogh. Oil on canvas, 73 x 92 cm. Museum of Modern Art, New York City, New York; **512** B&Y Photography/Alamy; **513** Richard Hamilton Smith/CORBIS; **514** ScotStock/ Alamy; **515** Creatas/PunchStock; **517** Joseph Sohm; Visions of America/ CORBIS; **518** George Diebold; **520** A & L Sinibaldi; **521** Mazer Creative Services; **523** Stockbyte; **527** PhotoLink/Getty Images; **531** Gabe Palmer/CORBIS; **532** C Squared Studios/Getty Images; **534** Oleksiy Maksymenko/Alamy; **536** Photodisc Collection/Getty Images; **537** Digital Vision; **538** D. Hurst/ Alamy; **541** Digital Vision/Getty Images; **544** (l) Directphoto.org/Alamy; **546** (br) Brand X Pictures; **547** (tl) Burke Triolo Productions/Getty Images.

**Teacher Guide Photo Credits**

**T4** Mazer Creative Services; **T5** Mazer Creative Services; **viii** Gail Shumway; **ix** NASA/EPA/Corbis; **xi** Jupiter Images/Brand X/Alamy; **xii** Jose Luis Pelaez Inc; **xiii** Jack Hollingsworth; **xiv** John Kirkpatrick/Alamy; **xv** Peter Bowater/ Alamy; **xvi** Lester Lefkowitz; **xvii** Hermann Erber/Getty Images; **1** Jerry Driendl